NICHD—Mental Retardation Research Centers Series
Special Issue with the University-Affiliated Facilities

INTERVENTION STRATEGIES FOR HIGH RISK INFANTS AND YOUNG CHILDREN

Edited by
Theodore D. Tjossem, Ph.D.
Director, Mental Retardation and Developmental Disabilities Branch
National Institute of Child Health and Human Development
National Institutes of Health

University Park Press
Baltimore · London · Tokyo *1976*

UNIVERSITY PARK PRESS
International Publishers in Science and Medicine
233 East Redwood Street
Baltimore, Maryland 21202

Copyright © 1976 by University Park Press
Second printing, May 1978

Typeset by The Composing Room of Michigan, Inc.
Manufactured in the United States of America by Universal Lithographers, Inc.

Library of Congress Cataloging in Publication Data
Main entry under title:
Intervention strategies for high risk infants and
young children.
(NICHD-Mental retardation research centers series)
"Based on the conference "Early Intervention with
High Risk Infants and Young Children" held at the
University of North Carolina at Chapel Hill, May 5—8,
1974."
1. Handicapped children—Care and treatment—
Congresses. 2. Handicapped children—Education—
Congresses. 3. Child development—Research—Congresses.
4. Child development—Testing—Congresses. I. Tjossem,
Theodore D. II. Series: United States. National
Institute of Child Health and Human Development.
NICHD-Mental retardation research centers series.
RJ138.I56   362.7'8'3   76-41256
ISBN 0-8391-0760-9

Contents

Conference Contributors and Participants ix
Foreword
   Fred T. Krause and Alberta L. Meyer xxi
Preface
   Theodore D. Tjossem and Beth Stephens xxiii
Introduction to the Child Development Research Institute, University of North
   Carolina at Chapel Hill: Its Story
   James J. Gallagher xxix

Early Intervention

Early Intervention: Issues and Approaches
   Theodore D. Tjossem 3

Research

Recovery "?" from Early Brain Damage
   Robert L. Isaacson 37
Early Experience and Plasticity in the Central Nervous System
   Morris A. Lipton 63
Discussant's Comments
   Dominick P. Purpura 75
From Animal to Infant Research
   Victor H. Denenberg and Evelyn B. Thoman 85
Process Research: Its Use in Prevention and Intervention with High Risk
   Children
   Leonard E. Ross and Lewis A. Leavitt 107
Caregiver-Infant Interaction and the Development of the High Risk Infant
   Leila Beckwith 119
Discussant's Comments
   Harriet L. Rheingold 141
The Infant's Auditory Environment
   Earl C. Butterfield and George F. Cairns 143
Use of Longitudinal Research in the Study of Child Development
   James J. Gallagher, Craig T. Ramey, Ron Haskins, and
   Neal W. Finkelstein 161

Community-based Language Training
  Betty Hart and Todd R. Risley 187
Discussant's Comments: Language and Communication Aspects
  Lyle L. Lloyd 199
A Programmatic Test of Behavioral Technology: Can It Recover Deviant
  Children for Normal Public Schooling?
  Donald M. Baer, Trudilee Rowbury, Ann M. Baer, Emily Herbert,
  Hewitt B. Clark, and Annabelle Nelson 213
Some Comments on Trends in Behavioral Research with Children
  Sidney W. Bijou 235
Scope and Focus of Research Relevant to Intervention: A Socioecological
  Perspective
  Earl S. Schaefer 237

Case Finding, Screening, Diagnosis, and Tracking

Screening, Assessment, and Intervention for Young Children at Developmental
  Risk
  John H. Meier 251
Diagnosis of the Infant at High Risk for Mental, Motor, and Sensory Handicaps
  Arthur H. Parmelee, Marian Sigman, Claire B. Kopp, and
  Audrey Haber 289
Mental Health and the Medicaid Screening Program
  Stephen J. Rojcewicz and Mae Aaronson 299
Comprehensive Developmental Health Services: A Concept and a Plan
  Theodore D. Scurletis, Mary Headrick-Haynes, Craig D. Turnbull,
  and Richard Fallon 305
Discussant's Comments
  T. Berry Brazelton 325

Demonstration Projects

The Portage Project: A Model for Early Childhood Intervention
  David E. Shearer and Marsha S. Shearer 335
The Read Project: Teaching Manuals for Parents of Retarded Children
  Bruce L. Baker and Louis J. Heifetz 351
Early Intervention for Hearing-impaired Infants and Young Children
  Kathryn B. Horton 371
Parent Programs for Developmental Management
  Eric Denhoff and Irma Hyman 381
Programs Developed in a Rehabilitation Center to Educate and Study Young
  Multihandicapped Children: State-of-the-Art, 1976
  Ronnie Gordon and Barbara Schwartz 467
The National Collaborative Infant Project
  Una B. Haynes 509
Educational Intervention with High Risk Infants
  Ethel R. Kass, Marian Sigman, Rose F. Bromwich, and
  Arthur H. Parmelee 535
The Infant, Toddler, and Preschool Research and Intervention Project
  William A. Bricker and Diane D. Bricker 545

Early Intervention for High Risk Infants and Young Children: Programs for
Down's Syndrome Children
   Alice H. Hayden and Norris G. Haring 573
Early Intervention with Biologically Handicapped Infants and Young Children:
A Preliminary Study with Each Child as His Own Control
   *Maria E. C. Barrera, Donald K. Routh, Carol A. Parr, Nancy M.
   Johnson, Donna S. Arendshorst, Elaine L. Goolsby, and
   Stephen R. Schroeder* 609
The Carolina Abecedarian Project: A Longitudinal and Multidisciplinary
Approach to the Prevention of Developmental Retardation
   *Craig T. Ramey, Albert M. Collier, Joseph J. Sparling,
   Frank A. Loda, Frances A. Campbell, David L. Ingram, and
   Neal W. Finkelstein* 629

State-of-the-Art   HCEEP Prog

Delivery of Educational Services to Preschool Handicapped Children
   Paul R. Ackerman, Jr., and Melvin G. Moore 669
Pediatric Care and Training: A Paradox?
   Felix F. de la Cruz 689
Nursing: High Risk Infants
   Kathryn E. Barnard 703
Early Intervention with High Risk Infants and Young Children: Implications for
Education
   Godfrey D. Stevens 727

International Perspective

Canadian Perspective
   G. Allan Roeher 733
Latin American Perspective
   Eloisa Garcia Etchegoyhen de Lorenzo 737

Committee Reports

Report of the Education Committee
   Willard W. Hartup 747
Report of the Pediatrics Committee
   Paul H. Pearson 751
Report of the Nursing and Habilitation Committee
   Barbara E. Bishop 755
Report of the Research Committee
   Sidney W. Bijou 759
Report of the Community Development Committee
   Ronald Wiegerink 761
Report of the Parents' Committee: Families in Crises, Families at Risk
   H. Rutherford Turnbull, III 765

Conclusion

The Present and the Future
  George Tarjan 773

Index 779

Conference Contributors and Participants

*Mae R. Aaronson,
Program Specialist, Early Childhood Care
  Research Section,
Center for Studies of Child and Family
  Mental Health,
National Institute of Mental Health,
  Rockville, Md. 20852

*Paul R. Ackerman, Jr., Ph.D.
Chief, Program Development Branch,
Bureau of Education for the Handicapped,
  U.S. Office of Education,
Department of Health, Education, and
  Welfare, Washington, D.C. 20013

Anne H. Adams
Professor, Department of Education, Duke
  University, Durham, N.C. 27706

Mrs. Sharon Adler
Parent participant,
Durham, N.C.

Jeffrey Alexander
Assistant Professor of Pediatrics,
  Department of Pediatrics
Riley Child Development Center, Indiana
  University Medical Center,
  Indianapolis, Ind. 46202

Charles A. Anderson
Director, Developmental Disabilities
  Evaluation Center,
University of South Dakota,
  Vermillion, S.D. 57069

Mable B. Anderson
Professor of Education, and Director,
  Teachers Corps,
Albany State College, Albany, N.Y. 12210

Madeline Appell
Assistant Professor of Pediatrics, and
  Assistant Director,
Rubella Project, College of Physicians and
  Surgeons,
Columbia University, New York, N.Y.
  10027

*Donna S. Arendshorst, B.A.
Division for Disorders of Development and
  Learning,
University of North Carolina at Chapel
  Hill, Chapel Hill, N.C. 27514

*Donald M. Baer, Ph.D.
Professor, Department of
  Human Development
University of Kansas,
  Lawrence, Kan. 66044

*Ann M. Baer, M.A.
Department of Human Development,
University of Kansas, Lawrence, Kan.
  66044

Earladeen Badger
Instructor in Pediatrics (Early Childhood
  Education),
Newborn Division,
Children's Hospital Research Foundation,
  Cincinnati, Ohio 45229

---

*Denotes conference contributors.

*Bruce L. Baker, Ph.D.
Associate Professor, Department of
  Psychology,
University of California at Los Angeles,
  Los Angeles, Ca. 90024

Marcia G. Barbara
Principal, Fasanarm Fundacion de
  Assistencia Psicopedagógica a Los Niños
  y Adolesents Retardados Mentales,
Guayaquil, Ecuador

Allan Barclay
Director, Child Development Center,
Saint Louis University, St. Louis, Mo.
  63103

Ann S. Bardwell
Associate Professor and Chief, Home
  Economics Component,
Nisonger Center for Mental Retardation,
Ohio State University, Columbus, Ohio
  43210

*Kathryn E. Barnard, R.N., Ph.D.
Professor, School of Nursing,
Child Development and Mental Retarda-
  tion Center,
University of Washington, Seattle, Wash.
  98195

Ellis I. Barowsky
Coordinator, National Collaborative Infant
  Project,
United Cerebral Palsy Association, Inc.,
  New York, N.Y. 10016

*Maria E. C. Barrera, M.A.
Director, Early Intervention Program for
  Biologically Handicapped Young
  Children,
Division for Disorders in Development and
  Learning,
Child Development Institute,
University of North Carolina at Chapel
  Hill, Chapel Hill, N.C. 27514

Constance U. Battle
Medical Coordinator,
Hospital for Sick Children,
Washington, D.C. 20019

Norton L. Beach
Professor and Dean of Education,
School of Education,

University of North Carolina at Chapel
  Hill, Chapel Hill, N.C. 27514

*Leila Beckwith, Ph.D.
Psychologist, Infant Studies Project,
University of California at Los Angeles,
  Los Angeles, Ca. 90024

Harold A. Benson
State Program Consultant,
Washington Government Activities Office,
United Cerebral Palsy Association, Inc.,
  Washington, D.C. 20001

Dallas E. Beyer
Director of Special Education,
Special Education District of Macon
  County, Decatur, Ill. 62522

*Sidney W. Bijou, Ph.D.
Professor of Psychology,
Department of Psychology,
University of Illinois, Urbana, Ill. 61801

William Bird-Forteza
Parent participant,
Brentwood, N.Y.

*Barbara E. Bishop, R.N., M.N.
Program Coordinator, Division of Maternal
  and Child Health Nursing Practice,
American Nurses' Association,
  Kansas City, Mo. 64106

Elizabeth M. Boggs
Chairman, National Advisory Council on
  Developmental Disabilities,
Department of Health, Education, and
  Welfare, Washington, D.C. 20013

David L. Braddock
Director, Head Start Information Project,
Council for Exceptional Children,
Reston, Va. 22091

*T. Berry Brazelton, M.D.
Associate Professor of Pediatrics,
Child Development Unit, Children's
  Hospital Medical Center,
Harvard Medical School, Cambridge, Mass.
  02138

*Diane D. Bricker, Ph.D.
Mailman Center for Child Development,
University of Miami, Miami, Fla. 33124

*William A. Bricker
Mailman Center for Child Development,
University of Miami, Miami, Fla. 33124

*Rose F. Bromwich, Ed.D.
Infant Studies Project
University of California at Los Angeles,
  Los Angeles, Ca. 90024

A. D. Buchmueller
Program Specialist, President's Committee
  on Mental Retardation,
Washington, D.C. 20201

Honorable Clair W. Burgener
United States House of Representatives
Forty-third District, Ca.

Annie L. Butler
President, Association for Childhood
  Education International,
College of Education,
University of Indiana, Bloomington, Ill.
  47401

*Earl C. Butterfield, Ph.D.
Co-director, Ralph L. Smith Center for
  Research in Mental Retardation,
University of Kansas Medical Center,
  Kansas City, Kan. 66103

*George F. Cairns, Ph.D.
Research Associate, Bureau of Child
  Research, Ralph L. Smith Center for
  Research in Mental Retardation
University of Kansas Medical Center,
  Kansas City, Kan. 66103

*Frances A. Campbell, M.D.
Research Associate, Frank Porter Graham
  Child Development Center,
Child Development Institute,
University of North Carolina at Chapel
  Hill, Chapel Hill, N.C. 27514

Arnold J. Capute
Deputy Director, The John F. Kennedy
  Institute, The Johns Hopkins
  University, Baltimore, Md. 21205

Sara Carlton
Director, Infant Stimulation,
Hunterdon Medical Center,
  Flemington, N.J. 08822

*Harrie R. Chamberlin
Director, Division for Disorders of
  Development and Learning,
Child Development Institute,
University of North Carolina at Chapel
  Hill, Chapel Hill, N.C. 27514

*Hewitt B. Clark, Ph.D.
Acting Director,
Johnny Cake Child Study Center,
Mansfield, Ariz. 72944

James D. Clements
Director, Georgia Retardation Center,
Georgia Department of Human Resources,
  Atlanta, Ga. 30341

Dorothy H. Cohen
Bank Street College of Education,
  New York, N.Y. 10025

Herbert J. Cohen
Co-director, University-Affiliated Facility,
Rose F. Kennedy Center for Research in
  Mental Retardation and Human
  Development,
Albert Einstein College of Medicine,
  Bronx, N.Y. 10461

*Albert M. Collier, M.D.
Assistant Professor of Pediatrics,
  Department of Pediatrics,
School of Medicine, Frank Porter Graham
  Child Development Center, Child
  Development Institute,
University of North Carolina at Chapel
  Hill, Chapel Hill, N.C. 27514

Frances P. Connors
Chairman, Department of Special
  Education,
Teachers' College, Columbia University,
  New York, N.Y. 10027

Mr. and Mrs. William Coolidge
Parent participants,
Chapel Hill, N.C.

Louis Z. Cooper
Consultant, President's Committee on
  Mental Retardation, Washington, D.C.,
  and
Professor of Pediatrics, College of
  Medicine,

Columbia University, New York, N.Y.
10027

Pamela Coughlin
Director of Special Projects, Program
Development and Innovation Division,
Office of Child Development, Office of the
Assistant Secretary for Human
Development,
Department of Health, Education, and
Welfare, Washington, D.C. 20013

B. Patrick Cox
Director, Communications Disorders,
Department of Pediatrics, University-
Affiliated Program for Child
Development,
Georgetown University, Washington, D.C.
20007

Mrs. Henry Crais
Parent participant,
Murfeesboro, Tenn.

Marie Skodak Crissey
Consulting Psychologist,
Swartz Creek, Mich.

Allan C. Crocker
Director, Developmental Evaluation Clinic,
Children's Hospital Medical Center,
Boston, Mass. 02115

Robert W. Deisher
Professor of Pediatrics, Department of
Pediatrics,
Child Development and Mental
Retardation Center,
University of Washington, Seattle, Wash.
98195

*Felix F. de la Cruz, M.D. M.RH. F.A.A.P.
Special Assistant for Pediatrics, Mental
Retardation and Developmental
Disabilities Branch,
National Institute of Child Health and
Human Development,
National Institutes of Health,
Bethesda, Md. 20014

***Eloisa Garcia Etchegoyhen de Lorenzo,
M.A.**
Interamerican Children's Institute,
Montevideo, Uruguay

*Eric Denhoff, M.D.
Medical Director, Meeting Street School
Children's Rehabilitation Center,
Providence, Rhode Island, and
Clinical Professor of Pediatrics,
Brown University, Providence, R.I. 02912

*Victor H. Denenberg, Ph.D.
Professor, Biobehavioral Sciences,
University of Connecticut, Storrs, Conn.
06268

Valentine Dmitriev
Coordinator, Multidisciplinary Programs
for Down's Syndrome Children,
Model Preschool Center for Handicapped
Children, Experimental Education Unit,
Child Development and Mental
Retardation Center,
University of Washington, Seattle, Wash.
98195

Nancy J. Douglas
Associate Professor, Early Childhood
Education,
School of Education,
Florida State University, Tallahassee, Fla.
32306

James P. Doyle
Child Development Specialist,
Administrative Branch,
Specialists Unit, Child Development
Division,
Office of Human Development,
Office of the Assistant Secretary for
Human Development
Department of Health, Education, and
Welfare, Washington, D.C. 20013

Kenneth W. Dumars
Director, Division of Developmental
Disabilities and Clinical Genetics,
Department of Pediatrics, Orange County
Medical Center,
University of California at Irvine,
Irvine, Ca 92664

Irvin Emanuel
Director, Child Development and Mental
Retardation Center,
University of Washington, Seattle, Wash.
98195

Edmund N. Ervin
Chairman, Advisory Committee on Mental
    Retardation,
Waterville, Ma. 04901

*Richard Fallon, M.D.
North Carolina Department of
    Human Resources, Division of
    Health Statistics, Raleigh, N.C. 27602

Joseph Fenton
Chief, Special Centers,
Social and Rehabilitation Service,
Department of Health, Education, and
    Welfare, Washington, D.C. 20013

Marvin Fifield
Director, Exceptional Children Center,
Utah State University, Logan, Utah, 84321

*Neal W. Finkelstein, Ph.D.
Frank Porter Graham Child Development
    Center,
Child Development Institute,
University of North Carolina at Chapel
    Hill, Chapel Hill, N.C. 27514

Nelson M. Ford
Education Planning Specialist,
Education Planning Staff of the Assistant
    Secretary for Planning and Evaluation,
Department of Health, Education, and
    Welfare, Washington, D.C. 20013

Florence P. Foster
Regional Training Officer, Head Start,
Office of Child Development,
Rider College, Westfield, N.J. 07090

Joe L. Frost
Associate Professor of Curriculum and
    Instruction,
College of Education,
University of Texas at Austin,
    Austin, Texas 78712

Steven Friedman
Assistant Professor of Psychology,
John F. Kennedy Center for Research on
    Education and Human Development,
George Peabody College for Teachers,
    Nashville, Tenn. 37203

Joseph W. Gallagher
Director, Center for Developmental and
    Learning Disorders,

University of Alabama, University, Ala.
    35486

*James J. Gallagher, Ph.D.
Director, Frank Porter Graham Child
    Development Center,
Child Development Institute,
University of North Carolina at Chapel
    Hill, Chapel Hill, N.C. 27514

Margaret J. Giannini
Director, Mental Retardation Institute,
New York Medical College, Valhalla, N.Y.
    10595

William M. Gibson
Director, The Nisonger Center for Mental
    Retardation and Developmental
    Disabilities,
Ohio State University, Columbus, Ohio
    43210

*Elaine L. Goolsby, M.S.W.
Chief Social Worker and Assistant Director
    for Patient Services,
Division for Disorders of Development and
    Learning,
Child Development Institute,
University of North Carolina at Chapel
    Hill, Chapel Hill, N.C. 27514

*Ronnie Gordon, M.S.
Associate Professor of
    Clinical Rehabilitation Medicine, and
Director, Preschool and Infant
    Developmental Programs,
Institute of Rehabilitation Medicine,
New York University Medical Center,
    New York, N.Y. 10016

Ernest A. Gotts
Assistant Professor and Program Director,
Early Education for the Handicapped,
Department of Special Education,
University of Texas at Austin,
    Austin, Texas 78712

Mary Z. Gray
Writer-Editor,
President's Committee on Mental
    Retardation, Washington, D.C. 20201

Herbert J. Grossman
Director, Illinois State Pedatric Institute,
    Chicago, Ill. 60608

Beverly Gunst
Assistant Principal, Kaiser Elementary
  School, Denver Public Schools,
  Lakewood, Colo. 80227

*Audrey Haber, Ph.D.
Research Psychologist, Infant Studies
  Project,
University of California at Los Angeles,
  Los Angeles, Ca. 90024

Bertha J. Hall
Program Specialist, Career Development
  and Technical Assistant Division,
Office of Child Development, Project Head
  Start,
Department of Health, Education, and
  Welfare, Washington, D.C. 20013

Wylda Hammond
University-Affiliated Facility Training
  Program,
Children's Hospital of Los Angeles,
  Los Angeles, Ca. 90024

*Norris G. Haring, Ed.D.
Director of the Experimental Education
  Unit, and
Co-director of the Model Preschool Center
  for Handicapped Children,
Child Development and Mental
  Retardation Center,
University of Washington, Seattle, Wash.
  98195

Judith A. Harris
Director, Developmental Disability Center
  for Children,
Louisiana State University Medical Center,
  New Orleans, La. 70112

Mahala J. Harrison
Day Care Specialist, Athens Unit, Georgia
  Retardation Center,
University of Georgia, Athens, Ga. 30602

*Betty Hart, Ph.D.
Research Associate, Bureau of Child
  Research,
Department of Human Development and
  Family Life,
University of Kansas, Lawrence, Kan.
  66044

*Willard W. Hartup, Ed.D.
Professor and Director, Institute of Child
  Development, University of Minnesota,
  Minneapolis, Minn. 55455

*Ron Haskins, Ph.D.
Frank Porter Graham Child Development
  Institute,
University of North Carolina at Chapel
  Hill, Chapel Hill, N.C. 57514

*Alice H. Hayden, Ph.D.
Project Director, Multidisciplinary
  Programs for Down's Syndrome
  Children,
Model Preschool Center for Handicapped
  Children, Experimental Education Unit,
Child Development and Mental
  Retardation Center,
University of Washington, Seattle, Wash.
  98195

*Una H. Haynes, R.N., M.P.H.
Associate Director of Professional Services,
  and Director,
National Collaborative Infant Project,
United Cerebral Palsy Association, Inc.,
  New York, N.Y. 10016

*Mary Headrick-Haynes, Ph.D.
North Carolina Department of Human
  Resources,
Division of Health Statistics, Raleigh, N.C.
  27602

Alfred Healy
Associate Medical Director, University
  Hospital School, University of Iowa,
  Iowa City, Iowa 52242

*Louis J. Heifetz, Ph.D.
Asst. Professor, Department of Psychology
Yale University, New Haven, Conn. 06520

Elsie D. Helsel
Washington Representative for United
  Cerebral Palsy Association, Inc., New
  York, and
Member, National Advisory Child Health
  and Human Development Council,
National Institute of Child Health and
  Human Development,
National Institutes of Health,
  Bethesda, Md. 20014

*Emily Herbert, Ph.D.
Department of Human
  Development,
University of Kansas, Lawrence, Kan.
  66044

Rudolf P. Hormuth
Specialist in Services for Mentally Retarded
  Children,
Division of Clinical Services,
Bureau of Community Health Services,
  Rockville, Md. 20852

Mr. and Mrs. Heinz L. Horstmeier
Parent participants,
Worthington, Ohio

*Kathryn B. Horton
Chief, Language Development Programs
  and Associate Professor,
Bill Wilkerson Hearing and Speech Center,
  and Vanderbilt University,
  Nashville, Tenn. 37212

*Irma Hyman, M.S.W.
Social worker, Parent Program for
  Developmental Management,
Meeting Street School, Providence, R.I.
  02906

*David L. Ingram, M.D.
Assistant Professor of Pediatrics,
Department of Pediatrics, School of
  Medicine,
University of North Carolina at Chapel
  Hill, Chapel Hill, N.C. 27514

*Robert L. Isaacson, Ph.D.
Professor, Department of Psychology,
University of Florida, Gainesville, Fla.
  32601

Cecil Jacobson
Member, President's Committee on Mental
  Retardation,
Washington, D.C. 20201

Vernon L. James
Director, University Center for the
  Handicapped,
College of Medicine,
University of Kentucky, Lexington, Ky.
  40506

*Nancy M. Johnson, Ph.D.
Clinical Specialist, Division for Disorders of
  Development and Learning,
Child Development Institute,
University of North Carolina at Chapel
  Hill Chapel Hill, N.C. 27514

*Ethel R. Kass, M.A.
Education Specialist, Infant Studies
  Project,
University of California at Los Angeles,
  Los Angeles, Ca. 90024

Alice L. Kjer
Director of Training and Early Childhood
  Education,
Martin Luther King, Jr., Parent-Child
  Center,
The Johns Hopkins Hospital,
  Baltimore, Md. 21205

Dell C. Kjer
Professor and Chairman, Department of
  Early Childhood Education,
Towson State College, Towson, Md. 21204

*Claire B. Kopp, Ph.D.
Psychologist, Infant Studies Project,
University of California at Los Angeles,
  Los Angeles, Ca. 90024

*Fred J. Krause, M.S.
Executive Director, President's Committee
  on Mental Retardation,
Washington, D.C. 20201

Mr. and Mrs. Clifton E. Latta
Parent participants,
Hillsborough, N.C.

*Lewis A. Leavitt, M.D.
Assistant Professor, Department of
  Pediatrics,
Center for the Health Sciences,
University of Wisconsin, Madison, Wisc.
  53706

David L. Lillie
Developmental Disabilities Technical
  Assistance Program,
University of North Carolina at Chapel
  Hill, Chapel Hill, N.C. 27514

Mrs. Jay E. Linder
Parent participant,
Raleigh, N.C.

*Morris A. Lipton, M.D.
Director, Biological Sciences Research
  Center,
Child Development Institute,
University of North Carolina at Chapel
  Hill, Chapel Hill, N.C. 27514

*Lyle L. Lloyd, Ph.D.
Executive Secretary, Mental Retardation
  Research Committee,
National Institute of Child Health and
  Human Development,
National Institutes of Health,
  Bethesda, Md. 20014

*Frank A. Loda, M.D.
Associate Professor of Pedatrics,
Department of Pediatrics, School of
  Medicine,
University of North Carolina at Chapel
  Hill, Chapel Hill, N.C. 27514

Andrew E. Lorincz
Professor of Pediatrics and Director,
Center for Developmental and Learning
  Disorders,
University of Alabama in Birmingham,
  Birmingham, Ala. 35294

Francis X. Lynch
Director, Division of Developmental
  Disabilities,
Office of the Assistant Secretary for
  Human Development,
Office of the Secretary,
Department of Health, Education, and
  Welfare, Washington, D.C. 20013

Antoinette Marchand
Assistant Professor, Early Childhood
  Education,
Temple University, Philadelphia, Pa. 19122

Helen Martin
Maternal and Child Health Nurse
  Consultant,
Division of Maternal and Child Health,
Kansas State Department of Health,
  Topeka, Kan. 66603

James McLean
Associate Professor and
Chairman, Department of Special
  Education,

George Peabody College for Teachers,
  Nashville, Tenn. 37203

Robert P. McNeil
Executive Director,
Association of University-Affiliated
  Facilities, Washington, D.C. 20007

*John H. Meier, Ph.D.
Director, Office of Child Development, and
Chief, Children's Bureau,
Department of Health, Education, and
  Welfare, Washington, D.C. 20013

Victor D. Menashe
Director, University-Affiliated Facility and
  Crippled Children's Division,
University of Oregon Medical School,
  Portland, Ore. 97520

Ruth Metzer
Administrative Aide, President's
  Committee on Mental Retardation,
Washington, D.C. 20201

Sherwood A. Messner
Director, Professional Services Program
  Department,
United Cerebral Palsy Association, Inc.,
  New York, N.Y. 10016

*Alberta L. Meyer, M.A.
Executive Secretary,
Association for Childhood Education
  International, Washington, D.C. 20016

Martha Moersch
Program Director for Occupational
  Therapy,
Institute for Study of Mental Retardation
  and Related Disabilities,
The University of Michigan,
  Ann Arbor, Mich. 48104

Mary W. Moffitt
Professor of Education, Early Childhood
  Education,
Queens College of The City University of
  New York, Flushing, N.Y. 11367

Carol Molloy
Early Childhood Consultant,
Developmental Disabilities Evaluation
  Center,
University of South Dakota,
  Vermillion, S.D. 57069

*Melvin G. Moore, Ph.D.
Department of Special Education,
University of North Carolina at Chapel
Hill, Chapel Hill, N.C. 27514

A. Esther Morgan
Professor and Counselor of Undergraduate
Studies,
College of Education, University of
Florida, and
Intermediate Past President,
Association for Childhood Education
International, Gainesville, Fla. 32601

*Annabelle Nelson, Ph.D.
Center for the Study of Human
Development,
University of Kansas, Lawrence, Kan.
66044

Shirley A. Nelson
Director, Consortium on Early
Childbearing and Childrearing,
Child Welfare League of America,
Washington, D.C. 20036

Ronald Neman
Research Director, National Association
for Retarded Citizens,
Arlington, Texas 76011

David Nessenholtz
Director of Planning, Office of Early
Childhood Development,
Texas Department of Community Affairs,
Austin, Texas 78704

*Carol Ann Parr, M.S.
Head, Physical Therapy Section, Division
for Disorders of Development and
Learning;
Assistant Professor, Department of Allied
Health, Division of Physical Therapy,
School of Medicine,
University of North Carolina at Chapel
Hill, Chapel Hill, N.C. 27514

Mrs. Digby Palmer
Parent participant,
Shelbyville, Tenn.

*Arthur H. Parmelee, M.D.
Professor of Pediatrics and Head, Division
of Child Development,

Department of Pediatrics, School of
Medicine,
University of California at Los Angeles,
Los Angeles, Ca. 90024

Virle C. Payne
Assistant Professor in Child Development
and Family Life,
Radford College, Radford, Va. 24142

*Paul H. Pearson, M.D., M.P.H.
Meyer Professor of Child Health and
Director, Meyer Children's Rehabilitation
Institute,
University of Nebraska Medical Center,
Omaha, Nebr. 68131

Charlene Pehoski
Director, Occupational Therapy,
Eunice Kennedy Shriver Center,
Waltham, Mass. 02154

Mrs. David Pressly
Parent advisor,
Statesville, N.C.

*Dominick P. Purpura, M.D.
Professor and Chairman, Director of Rose
F. Kennedy Center for Research in
Mental Retardation,
Albert Einstein College of Medicine,
Bronx, N.Y. 10461

Robert Rabinowitz
Director, Developmental Disabilities,
Pennsylvania Hospital, Philadelphia, Pa.
19104

*Craig T. Ramey, Ph.D.
Senior Investigator and Associate Professor
of Psychology,
Frank Porter Graham Child Development
Center, Child Development Institute,
University of North Carolina at Chapel
Hill, Chapel Hill, N.C. 27514

Louise Ravenel
Member, President's Committee on Mental
Retardation,
Washington, D.C. 20201

Ronald E. Reed
Region IV Representative for
Developmental Disabilities,

Social and Rehabilitation Service,
Department of Health, Education, and
Welfare, Atlanta, Ga. 30323

Robert J. Reichler
Associate Professor of Child Psychiatry,
and
Co-director, Division TEACCH,
Department of Psychiatry and Basic
Sciences Research Center, School of
Medicine,
University of North Carolina at Chapel
Hill, Chapel Hill, N.C. 27514

*Harriet L. Rheingold, Ph.D.
Professor, Department of Psychology,
University of North Carolina at Chapel
Hill, Chapel Hill, N.C. 27514

Paul A. Ritmanick
Program Policy Advisor, Speech Pathology
and Audiology,
Clinical Services and Special Programs,
Illinois Department of Mental Health and
Developmental Disabilities, Dixon, Ill.

*Todd R. Risley, Ph.D.
Professor, Department of Human
Development,
University of Kansas, Lawrence, Kan.
66044

William B. Robertson
Member, President's Committee on Mental
Retardation,
Washington, D.C. 20201

*G. Allan Roeher, Ph.D.
Director, National Institute on Mental
Retardation,
York University Campus, Ontario, Canada
M3J 1P3

*Stephen J. Rojcewicz, M.D.
Center for Studies of Child and Family
Mental Health,
National Institute of Mental Health,
Rockville, Md. 20852

William A. Rose
Assistant to the Director, Division of
Developmental Disabilities,
Rehabilitation Services Administration,
SRS,
Department of Health, Education, and
Welfare, Washington, D.C. 20013

Susan Rosen
Child Development Specialist,
Sewall Rehabilitation Center,
Denver, Colo. 80222

*Leonard E. Ross, Ph.D.
Professor, Department of Psychology,
Waisman Center on Mental Retardation
and Human Development,
University of Wisconsin, Madison, Wisc.
53706

*Donald K. Routh, Ph.D.
Associate Professor of Psychiatry, Division
for Disorders of Development and
Learning,
Child Development Institute,
University of North Carolina at Chapel
Hill, Chapel Hill, N.C. 27514

*Trudilee Rowbury, M.A.
Center for the Study of Human
Development, University of Kansas,
Lawrence, Kan. 66044

Jack H. Rubinstein
Director,
University-Affiliated Cincinnati Center for
Developmental Disorders, Cincinnati, Ohio
45229

Mary Scahill
Chief Nursing Consultant,
Eunice Kennedy Shriver Center,
Waltham, Mass. 02154

*Earl S. Schaefer, Ph.D.
Professor of Maternal and Child Health and
Chief, Section on Family Research,
Frank Porter Graham Child Development
Center, Child Development Institute,
University of North Carolina at Chapel
Hill, Chapel Hill, N.C. 27514

Henry J. Schroeder
Director, Developmental Training Center,
University-Affiliated Facility,
Indiana University, Bloomington, Ind.
47401

*Stephen R. Schroeder, Ph.D.
Research Scientist, Biological Sciences
Research Center,
Child Development Research Institute,
University of North Carolina at Chapel
Hill, Chapel Hill, N.C. 27514

*Barbara Schwartz, M.S.
Research Associate, Preschool and
  Infant Developmental Programs,
Institute of Rehabilitation Medicine,
New York University Medical Center,
  New York, N.Y. 10016

Robert H. Schwarz
Director, Center on Human Development,
University of Oregon, Eugene, Ore. 97403

*Theodore D. Scurlesis, M.D.
Director, Maternal and Child Health,
Iowa State Department of Health,
Lucas Building, Des Moines, Iowa 50319

Marian Seifert
Associate Director, Research and Policy
  Development,
Human Services Institute for Children and
  Families, Inc., Washington, D.C. 20009

Eleanor Shaheen
Associate Chairman and Professor of
  Pediatrics;
Co-director of University-Affiliated
  Facility,
Columbia Medical Center, University of
  Missouri, Columbia, Mo. 65201

*David E. Shearer, M.A.
Project Director, Portage Project,
Cooperative Educational Service Agency
  No. 12, Portage, Wisc. 53901

*Marsha S. Shearer, M.A.
Training Coordinator, Portage Project,
Cooperative Educational Service Agency
  No. 12, Portage, Wisc. 53901

Cecil G. Sheps
Vice-Chancellor for Health Sciences,
University of North Carolina at Chapel
  Hill, Chapel Hill, N.C. 27514

*Marian Sigman, Ph.D.
Psychologist, Infant Studies Project,
University of California at Los Angeles,
  Los Angeles, Ca. 90024

James Q. Simmons, III
Associate Program Director of Mental
  Retardation and Child Psychiatry,
Center for Health Sciences, University-
  Affiliated Facility, Department of
  Psychiatry,

University of California at Los Angeles,
  Los Angeles, Ca. 90024

Sabin T. Snow
Clinical Psychologist, Community Mental
  Health Center,
Hunterdon Medical Center,
  Flemington, N.J. 08822

*Joseph L. Sparling, Ph.D.
Assistant Professor, Frank Porter Graham
  Child Development Center, Child
  Development Institute,
University of North Carolina at Chapel
  Hill, Chapel Hill, N.C. 27514

Pierette Spiegler
Staff, President's Committee on Mental
  Retardation,
Washington, D.C. 20201

Joyce Stancliffe
Chief, Physical Therapy, Physical Therapy
  and Wheelchair Modification,
Kansas Neurological Institute,
  Topeka, Kan. 66614

Donald J. Stedman
Professor of Education and Associate
  Director, Frank Porter Graham Child
  Development Center,
Child Development Institute,
University of North Carolina at Chapel
  Hill, Chapel Hill, N.C. 27514

Robert S. Stempfel, Jr.
Professor of Pediatrics and
Director, Mailman Center for Child
  Development, University of Miami,
  Coral Gables, Fla. 33124

*Beth Stephens
Member, President's Committee on Mental
  Retardation, Washington, D.C., and
  Head, Special Education Program,
University of Texas at Dallas,
  Richardson, Texas 75080

*Godfrey D. Stevens, Ed.D.
Professor of Education, Department of
  Special Education and Rehabilitation,
School of Education, University of
  Pittsburgh, Pittsburgh, Pa. 25123

Carlyle B. Storm
President, Maryland Association for
  Retarded Citizens,
Silver Spring, Md. 20902

Harold R. Strang
Associate Professor of Education,
Foundations of Education,
University of Virginia, Charlottesville, Va.
22903

Ruth C. Sullivan
Director, Information and Referral Service,
National Society for Autistic Children,
Huntington, W.V. 25702

Laurence T. Taft
Professor and Chairman, Department of
Pediatrics,
Rutgers University Medical School,
New Brunswick, N.J. 08903

*George Tarjan, M.D.
Professor of Psychiatry and
Director, Mental Retardation and Child
Psychiatry Program,
Neuropsychiatric Institute, University of
California at Los Angeles Center for the
Health Sciences, Los Angeles, Ca. 90024

Honorable Stanley B. Thomas, Jr.
Assistant Secretary for Human
Development,
Office of the Secretary,
Department of Health, Education, and
Welfare, Washington, D.C. 20013

*Evelyn B. Thoman, Ph.D.
Associate Professor, Department of
Biobehavioral Sciences,
University of Connecticut, Storrs, Conn.
06268

Robert S. Thurman
Professor, College of Education,
University of Tennessee, Knoxville, Tenn.
37916

*Theodore D. Tjossem, Ph.D.
Director, Mental Retardation and
Developmental Disabilities Branch,
National Institute of Child Health and
Human Development,
National Institutes of Health,
Bethesda, Md. 20014

***Mr. and Mrs. H. Rutherford Turnbull, III,
LL.M.**
Parent participants,

Institute of Government, University of
North Carolina at Chapel Hill,
Chapel Hill, N.C. 27514

*Craig D. Turnbull, Ph.D.
Department of Biostatistics,
University of North Carolina at Chapel
Hill, Chapel Hill, N.C. 27514

Gioconda Vallarino
Resource Room Teacher, Intermediate
Unit No. 1, Visually Handicapped
Children, California Public Schools,
California, Pa. 15419

Evadean M. Watts
Director, Mental Retardation Services,
Augustana Nursery, Lutheran Welfare
Services of Illinois, Chicago, Ill.
60657

Charlotte L. White
Department of Pediatrics, School of
Medicine, University of California
at San Diego, LaJolla, Ca. 92037

*Ronald Wiegerink, Ph.D.
Director, Developmental Disabilities
Technical Assistance Program,
University of North Carolina at Chapel
Hill, Chapel Hill, N.C. 27514

William H. Wilsnack
Staff, President's Committee on Mental
Retardation,
Washington, D.C. 20201

Miriam G. Wilson
Member, President's Committee on Mental
Retardation,
Washington, D.C. 20201

William C. Wilson
Council of Great City Schools,
Washington, D.C. 20006

Byrn T. Witt
Executive Director, National Association
for Down's Syndrome, Arlington
Heights, Ill. 60005

Donald Wood
Assistant Director, Child Development
Research Institute,
University of North Carolina at Chapel
Hill, Chapel Hill, N.C. 27514

Foreword

Educational programs leading to the optimal development of *all* children is a united concern of the President's Committee on Mental Retardation and the Association for Childhood Education International. As cosponsors of this conference, the PCMR and ACEI express this joint interest focused on early educational interventions for very young children at risk for developmental disorders.

Emergent events over the past decade have provided compelling reasons to hold the conference. A growing body of research has demonstrated the beneficial effects of early stimulation on human development and the infant's capacity for learning under responsive environmental conditions. Under the impetus of this research, early educational intervention began to be applied to infants and young children as a means for enhancing their development. Meanwhile, expanded educational opportunities were being opened to school age retarded and handicapped children as the barriers precluding them from school services crumbled under legal and social pressures. The convergence of these events point to new opportunities and responsibilities for education in providing educational services to developmentally disordered children from infancy through the elementary school years.

The development of successful early intervention programs requires the participation not only of education but of virtually every discipline and profession. The science that undergirds and guides early intervention is an interaction science involving many disciplines. Similarly, full implementation of this knowledge in interventions for risk children requires the contributions of many professions. Finally, the ultimate success of these efforts depends upon the understanding and participation of parents and families who, during infancy and the early years, are the primary mediators of intervention strategies.

The topics and organization of the conference reflect the broad scope and complexity of the diverse elements involved in the development of early intervention programs for risk children. Presented as a collective effort by conference organization, each independent part of the complex assumes new dimensions and significance. Viewed from this perspective, the interdependence and relatedness of each part to the whole emerge with greater clarity. Progress and innovation in one area impact on another to create new problems as well as opportunities; and lagging progress in key areas retards progress in related fields and the effort as a whole.

The organizational and functional separation of constituent program elements creates barriers to communication across the full range of program effort. The conference meets this communication problem by bringing together for interactive exchange all relevant program elements for the broad purpose of effecting a coherent program unity. It is the earnest hope of the PCMR and the ACEI that this conference effort is productive of new insights leading to more effective methods for serving risk children and their families. The PCMR and ACEI acknowledge with grateful appreciation the cooperation and support of the conference by the following agencies of the U.S. Department of Health, Education, and Welfare: National Institute of Child Health and Human Development, Bureau of Education for the Handicapped, Developmental Disabilities Office, National Institute of Mental Health, and the Office of Child Development.

As host sponsor for the conference, the University of North Carolina at Chapel Hill merits special recognition. Presented for participant study and observation, the programs of the University's Child Development Research Institute provided ongoing demonstration of the research and service activities under conference consideration. These demonstrations of research and service progress added immeasurably to the success of the conference, and warm appreciation is extended to the University staff who made this possible.

Fred J. Krause
PCMR Executive Director

Alberta L. Meyer
ACEI Executive Secretary

Preface

Infancy and the first 2 years of life provide the foundation upon which the cognitive, social, and biological performance of the school age child moving to adulthood is formed. The importance of this period for later development is evidenced by an emergent body of research and theory supported by intervention experience at later ages with children and their families. It assumes even greater importance for developmentally disordered and environmentally deprived infants whose early experiences so often disrupt the course of normal development. Recognition has been given to the importance of this period for these children by increased application of early intervention programs designed to enhance their development. Cognizant of the opportunities to effect beneficial changes during this period, education has moved vigorously to extend downward its educational offerings to risk infants and their families. In this effort, education has emerged as a significant, growing force in the constellation of community health, social, and developmental services provided during this period of development.

The downward extension of educational services to the first 2 years of life has far-reaching implications for the organization of community services. The principal site of intervention services has shifted from the clinic, preschool, and child development centers to the home. Here, in the risk child's natural surrounds, parents and families, not professionals, serve as the mediators of interventions through guided interactions with the infant. In the home, constructive interaction opportunities exist throughout the child's day; they are not limited to the therapeutic hour of the clinic or the few hours of preschool experience. Just as parents require educational support to guide their intervention efforts, so, too, they need the support of community health, social, and developmental services as required to assist them in providing a care and training program in the home. The confluence of education with health services, for so long the primary source of guidance for parents of risk infants, calls for reorientation of health care approaches. In particular, the prospects for beneficial gains through early education interventions brings with it new pressures for change in traditional health service approaches to diagnosis and referral. A redefinition of professional and parental roles and responsibilities is imminent as communities begin organizing for the delivery of early intervention services having unity, continuity, and direction.

This volume is the product of a conference organized to provide a comprehensive perspective of the new concepts and developments generated by and related to the early intervention movement. Formed of multiple components, the movement is broad and complex. New developments in each contributing component interact with those in other components to create new opportunities for advances; they also present new problems requiring adaptive changes among related components. The exchange of information and joint consideration of developments and issues between components are rare. For these reasons, the conference was structured to present developments for each contributing component within the interactive context of all components forming the whole of early intervention activities. Thus, each major component of the effort, from research development to consumer utilization, was presented for joint consideration. From this perspective, early intervention for risk infants and their families is made visible as a collective enterprise of considerable magnitude with direction and promise for the future.

RESEARCH

The topics and organization of the section on research reflect the wide scope and diversity of the research efforts undergirding early intervention programs. Progressing from fundamental laboratory studies to research applications at the age of school entry, the chapters of this section present a sampling of the research endeavor through the developmental continuum from infancy to school age.

The chapters by Isaacson, Lipton, and Purpura initiate the section by establishing the neural basis for early intervention in the plasticity of the developing central nervous system. Here, the effects of early stimulation are evidenced by alterations in the organization and function of neural cells and structures. Behavioral changes consequent to early experience are the objects of study in the chapter by Denenberg and Thoman who carry the research progression forward from the animal laboratory to the human infant. The importance of mother-infant interactions to the development of organized infant behaviors is demonstrated in this chapter. Beckwith extends still further understanding of this important dimension of early development in her chapter devoted to research on caregiver-infant interactions with high risk infants. At this point, the research foundations for early interventions focused on the mother-infant interaction system are revealed.

Research concerned with audition and speech and language development is highlighted for the period of infancy and the preschool years. The reasons for this are two-fold. First, the incidence of hearing impairment is high among the mentally retarded, for whom deficits in speech and language development are characteristic. Second, the intervention programs that appear most beneficial at this age level place stress on verbal interactions and language development.

In their studies of the infant's response to his auditory environment, Butterfield and Cairns convincingly demonstrate infant responsiveness to variations in the auditory environment. Not at all a passive listener, the infant attends auditory variations selectively and, given the opportunity, actively works to control his auditory environment. This work directs attention to the importance of early auditory experience in infancy as a determinant of later language development. The chapter by Hart and Risley traces the acquisition of language from infancy through the preschool years. Their presentation of the process for building the child's spontaneous, working language in the natural environment through "incidental teaching" points to the opportunities available to parents and teachers for early intervention through language training.

Early intervention for deaf and hearing-impaired infants is vital. This point is affirmed in the chapter by Lloyd who calls attention to the pressing need for assessment of the suspect infant's auditory acuity during early life. The benefits of early detection of auditory dysfunction are amply demonstrated in the chapter by Horton, concerned with early intervention for hearing-impaired infants, which follows in the section on demonstration projects.

Many risk children come to school age with behavior problems that lessen their suitability for normal public schooling. Acquired during the early developmental years, these deviant behaviors form barriers to the child's social acceptance and later learning, which act to further exclude the child from normal experiences. The chapter by Baer et al. addresses these problems by reporting on research aimed at the behavioral remediation of deviant behaviors necessary to ensure the child's success in school. The success of behavioral technology in recovering deviant children for normal public schooling points to the need for its wider application both at this age level and, more importantly, at earlier developmental periods when signs of deviant behaviors first emerge.

The research component is set in comprehensive perspective by the chapters authored by Ross and Leavitt, Gallagher et al., and Schaefer. In their presentation, Ross and Leavitt call for a closer integration of process-oriented research with applied early assessment and intervention activities. Poorly understood outside the scientific community, process-oriented research is aimed at gaining understanding of the mechanisms and processes underlying behavior. These authors argue persuasively for the development of fundamental knowledge leading to the formulation of a theory that can be applied to further our understanding and control of human development and behavior.

The processes guiding the unfolding of human development from infancy to school age are central to early intervention concerns. Longitudinal research which studies these processes over time is essential to our understanding. Time consuming, difficult, and expensive, longitudinal studies represent but a small fraction of the total research effort. Gallagher et al. speak to this issue with a strong advocacy for longitudinal research designs and their support.

Finally, the chapter by Schaefer directs attention to changing research directions that imply future change in our systems for the delivery of early intervention services. In his presentation, Schaefer points to the changing focus of research progressing from focus on the child, to the mother-child dyad, to the parent-professional-child triad, and on to the larger ecosystems that influence child care and development. With this change in focus, attention moves from direct care of the child by professionals to support for the family and community care of the child and to the organization of community services that make this possible.

CASE FINDING, SCREENING, DIAGNOSIS, AND TRACKING

This section is concerned with the early identification of risk infants which permits the timely initiation of early intervention. To this end, the chapter by Meier offers a comprehensive statement on the state of the art for early diagnosis of risk infants. The limitations of contemporary diagnostic and assessment methodologies for serving the requirements of early intervention are made evident in this presentation. But emerging new approaches offer the prospect of advances in assessment technology more congenial to the needs of early intervention. Among these, the determination of infant risk status described in the chapter authored by Parmelee et al. represents an emerging new approach to early assessment holding future promise. Linked to a program of early educational intervention for risk infants, described by Kass et al. in the section on demonstration projects, this approach to the establishment of risk status shows its potential utility as a mechanism for entering infants into early intervention service programs.

Still another promising approach is offered by Scurletis et al. In this approach, focus is on the prospective mother of the risk infant. The effort here is to identify the characteristics of mothers at risk for bearing a developmentally disordered child and, from this, to move them and their infant into a system for the delivery of comprehensive developmental health services. The section provides a presentation concerned with the integration of early screening and diagnosis with a broad social action program of health services. Here, Rojcewicz and Aaronson describe the Early and Periodic Screening, Diagnosis, and Treatment Program (EPSDT). With this presentation, the need for early screening and diagnosis is made apparent, as are the limitations of the art.

DEMONSTRATION PROJECTS

The demonstration projects presented in this section were selected from many models of early intervention having national recognition. Also, they were selected to offer a variety of approaches. Collectively, they represent our nation's best efforts to demonstrate early intervention services.

Home-based intervention programs with parents serving as mediators are presented in the chapters by Shearer and Shearer and by Baker and Heifetz. Kass et al. employ a similar approach focusing on supportive help for mothers in guiding their interactions with their risk infants. Aimed at helping parents to assist their risk children in the mastery of early developmental tasks, these projects demonstrate the effectiveness of parents as teachers.

Preschool-based programs providing for the active involvement and participation of parents are dominant among the models for early intervention. These programs represent a departure from traditional preschool programs in that the resources and skills available through the preschool are expanded by the instruction of parents for the conduct of home training programs. These programs serve infants with a variety of disorders and degrees of impairment.

The program for Down's syndrome children detailed by Hayden and Haring shows the benefits to these children of intervention initiated in infancy and sustained to school age. The adaptations of educational approaches and settings to meet the special problems of multiply handicapped and hearing-impaired children emerge clearly in the chapters by Gordon and Horton, respectively. Bricker and Bricker present a program serving children heterogenous for developmental disorders. The emphasis of this program is on parent training and noncategorical education. The National Collaborative Infant Project described by Haynes serves the intervention needs of cerebral palsied children and extends its aid to children with related handicapping conditions. The efforts to replicate these services give evidence for the growth of these intervention programs. The chapter by Denhoff and Hyman presents a medical model for early intervention. This multidisciplinary approach reflects the transition of early medical models for early intervention under the impact of emerging new concepts for the delivery of intervention services.

The University of North Carolina intervention projects described by Barrera et al. and Ramey et al. demonstrate intervention approaches to biologically vulnerable and environmentally deprived children, respectively. Implemented in the research and training setting of a university, these projects illustrate the efforts of higher education to provide the research knowledge and professional training necessary for the development of effective early intervention programs.

STATE-OF-THE-ART

The major professions with responsibilities and capabilities for the delivery of early intervention services are education, nursing, and medicine. How these professions are moving to discharge these responsibilities through the training of personnel and the actual delivery of intervention services is the subject of the chapters in this section.

Ackerman and Moore present the state of the early intervention art for education. Evidenced in this chapter is the impetus given to educational efforts by legislatively mandated activities. Added responsibilities have not always been matched by increased financial support. Accordingly, the preparation of trained personnel, especially advanced level trainees, lags behind requirements.

Barnard's chapter delineates the potential of nursing for the delivery of early intervention services. It reflects, too, the great need of parents for help in making their early adjustments to life with a risk child. Barnard shows the supply of trained nursing personnel to be far below requirements relative to the potential contributions from this profession. Again, as with education, the preparation and training of leadership personnel lag most.

No other professional has greater opportunity for early involvement and assistance with the risk infant and family than the physician. Pediatric contributions to early diagnosis and intervention are brought forward in the chapter by de la Cruz. This chapter also points to deficiencies in the training of physicians and pediatricians for meeting the broad needs of risk infants and their families. This is echoed by Pearson in the report of the Pediatrics Committee and by Turnbull reporting for the Parent's Committee.

The preparation of trained personnel in sufficient numbers to meet the expanding requirements of early intervention services is a concern common to all of these professions. In particular, leadership training which expands traditional professional roles and responsibilities to include training in early child development and the broad aspects of family and community life is advanced as a major need of all concerned professions. To this end, multidisciplinary training following the model employed in the University-Affiliated Facilities program is suggested as a desirable training approach.

INTERNATIONAL PERSPECTIVE

The development of early intervention programs is not unique to the United States. Interest and concern for these programs are shown in most nations of the world. The comments of Roeher and de Lorenzo in this section express this interest for our Canadian and Latin American neighbors. In his comments, Roeher expresses a pragmatic view of organizational and administrative considerations having great value for guiding the development of early intervention programs. The enthusiastic embrace of early intervention by Latin American countries is reflected in the comments by de Lorenzo. Here, the adaptation of the basic concepts of early intervention to the varied needs and resources of the different Latin American countries is remarkable. Parents and professionals in the United States will find the Latin American developments both helpful and encouraging.

PARENT PARTICIPATION

Parents of risk infants are parents at risk. They are at risk for the uncertainties posed for the future of their risk child, their lack of knowledge for meeting new and unusual problems in child rearing, and because of the stresses risk infancy so often imposes on family life. They are still further at risk because of limited community resources to guide and assist them and, often, they experience added risk from the attitudes and approaches to their problems taken by some professionals and agencies. Though they are at risk, the evidence from the conference shows that these parents, in large measure, hold the key to the success of early intervention.

Risk parents are essential to early intervention developments in two major ways. First, during infancy and the first 2 years of life, they are the primary mediators of intervention technology applied to their child. It is their sensitivity to early signs of developmental disorder that most often brings the risk child to the attention of services; and it is their guided interactions with their child through which the benefits of early intervention are most likely to be achieved. Second, it is parent leadership which, historically, has led to major advances in the establishment of programs and policies serving developmentally disordered children. And it is evident from their present activities that they will lead again in the development of programs for early intervention.

The essential nature of parent involvement and participation in all phases of early intervention activities dictated that they be represented as full partners in the conference.

To this end, parents of very young children were invited to participate in all aspects of the conference program. These parents were not the seasoned veterans of past efforts in behalf of mentally retarded and developmentally disordered children. They were parents who, at this time, were experiencing the problem of a risk infancy and risk parenting. With their active involvement and participation in the conference, the full voice of early intervention was heard.

The results of their participation are reflected in the report by Turnbull provided in the section devoted to committee reports. It is evident from this report that parents can, indeed, be significant contributors as well as eager learners if given the opportunity.

COMMITTEE REPORTS AND SUMMATION

Six committees were formed to review and to assess the implications of the conference for the development of early intervention strategies. These committees covered each major component of the early intervention movement, including education, pediatrics, nursing and habilitation, research, community development, and parents. The committees operated under conference instruction to bring forward the important issues, needs, problems, and opportunities found in each area. Their task did not include responsibility for producing firm recommendations. To the extent, then, that recommendations appear in the reports of the different committees given in this section, they should be regarded as suggestions giving general direction to future developments.

Tarjan, in his summation of the conference, concludes with an optimistic view for the future of early intervention. In doing so, he creates awareness of the problems, needs, and limitations attendant to its future development. He cautions against over optimism and false hopes. As a safeguard, he recommends continuous and rigorous evaluation of early intervention programs and activities. The future of early intervention, he concludes, is for continued progress involving the cooperative efforts of all program components. These efforts represent both an opportunity and an obligation to serve risk children and their families.

Theodore D. Tjossem
Beth Stephens

Conference cochairpersons

Introduction to the Child Development Research Institute, University of North Carolina at Chapel Hill: Its Story

The Child Development Research Institute, directed by Dr. Cecil Sheps, Vice Chancellor for Health Affairs at the University of North Carolina, is composed of two major units: the Biological Sciences Research Center (BSRC) and the Frank Porter Graham Child Development Center (FPG). These centers employ an impressive range of professionals from pediatricians to experimental psychologists, from geneticists to educators.

We have long recognized the complexity of human development. The human neurological, glandular, and psychological systems interact with one another in a yet unknown way to facilitate or inhibit development. We know that the physical state of the child can influence the psychological state, and this can lead to poor school performance, which can lead to depression, which can lead to a lowered physical state, etc. We also know that the child's psychological state can affect his physical health and his intellectual and social performance.

In mental retardation some physical, psychological, or social barriers prevent the relevant systems from developing properly. To understand this condition and what needs to be done about it, we need teams of specialists who can observe and interpret events and interactions between systems that would be beyond the understanding of any one profession. So these centers operate across traditional professional dividing lines in the medical school and the academic departments in order to give a wide range of understanding and insight necessary to grasp the complex issues in mental retardation.

This emphasis on multidisciplinary research at the University of North Carolina at Chapel Hill fits well into the National Institutes of Health tradition. The individual Institutes comprising the National Institutes of Health have augmented the ideas of Dr. James Shannon, its first director, by expanding the strict definitions of biology and medicine and encompassing the social, behavioral, and environmental sciences as well.

This has been especially true of the National Institute of Child Health and Human Development, which, in the development of the mental retardation centers, recognized the contributions of biology, medicine, and the behavioral sciences to the genesis of mental retardation research and related aspects of human development.

BIOLOGICAL SCIENCES RESEARCH CENTER

Fifteen senior researchers in the Biological Science Research Center (BSRC), directed by Dr. Morris Lipton, simultaneously hold faculty positions ranging from Assistant Professor to Professor in departments of the Medical School. They study the biological systems to seek answers which can lead to prevention and treatment that will maximize the development of already damaged persons. Several teams of investigators have taken different approaches to the general problem area.

The laboratory of genetics addresses itself to a variety of problems ranging from clinical genetic counseling to the detection of those inborn errors of metabolism which so often lead to mental retardation. Fortunately, it has been learned that genetic diseases can be prevented from expressing themselves, even though the genes themselves cannot yet be altered. As one example after several, it has been learned that the retardation associated with phenylketonuria can be prevented by keeping the child on a special diet, low in amino acid phenylalanine, during the early years while the brain is developing. When he is developed, the child is able to resume a normal diet without damaging consequences. However, a carrier of such a genetic defect offers a risk to his children and is therefore a subject for genetic counseling.

The treatment of genetic defects requires procedures for very early detection, before birth if possible, and certainly as quickly as possible thereafter. Sophisticated biochemical technology is required for such diagnosis. Thus, metabolic defects may be found by the analysis of fetal amniotic fluid directly or by the culture of fetal cells obtained by amniocentesis, a procedure for analyzing fluid withdrawn from the amniotic sac.

After birth, the detection of metabolic defects requires methods that can analyze the chemical constituents of a few drops of blood or urine. Ideally, such methods should be adaptable to mass screening. The development of such microtechnology is difficult and expensive, but less expensive, as a preventive method, than the psychological and social costs of the lifetime treatment of severely retarded persons. The BSRC has a laboratory devoted to the development of such microtechnology.

Still another area of research into primary prevention at the BSRC deals with the environment of the fetus and the conditions of the birth process. Drugs taken by the mother during pregnancy and environmental pollution to which she may be exposed cross the placenta and enter the body of the unborn child. Since drugs are administered frequently by prescription, or are taken independently by pregnant mothers, much remains to be learned about the effects of such agents upon the highly vulnerable nervous system of the unborn child. Similarly, the uterine conditions that determine prematurity demand study because prematurity is so frequently associated with mental retardation, and the prevention of prematurity would represent a major advance in the treatment of retardation.

Despite the best efforts of all concerned, a significant number of children will continue to be born with such defects. Some of these, like children with convulsive disorders or hyperkinesis, will need treatment with drugs for prolonged periods. The study of the inadvertent side effects of these drugs demands attention because it is possible that, while effectively treating the primary condition, they may do long-range harm to the developing nervous system. The study of appropriate dosage, and of the mode of action of drugs may lead to knowledge of the optimum conditions for treating children and even to the development of new drugs. BSRC has a laboratory of Developmental Neuropsychopharmacology and a laboratory of Neuroendocrinology that addresses these issues.

FRANK PORTER GRAHAM CHILD DEVELOPMENT CENTER

The Frank Porter Graham Child Development Center (FPG), directed by Dr. James Gallagher, is concerned with those sociocultural barriers that interfere with the proper development of children and lead to mental retardation. Accordingly, the FPG Center takes a special interest in children from socioeconomic backgrounds that previous experience would show to be a high risk environment for their normal development.

To study this problem, the Center has embarked on a major longitudinal investigation on children from poverty families and has drawn together researchers and practitioners in pediatrics, psychology, social work, day care, nutrition, maternal and child health, nursing, and education for that purpose. While psychologists organize the infant stimulation program, educators develop a set of curriculum items that parents or day care workers can use to help stimulate the child. Specialists in the family as a social institution study the impact of the program on the family, and they contribute to the generation of parent training programs. Pediatricians monitor each child's health status, while they conduct more fundamental research on the role of microbial interaction in the pathogenesis of respiratory diseases.

Therefore, while the psychologist has a rare opportunity to benefit from careful and systematic health status examinations, the pediatrician can extend his data with psychological and educational indicators. Each has the opportunity for a sustained look at specific children over a period of several years. This kind of collaborative research will be needed if we are to understand the interacting developmental systems of the young child, and especially the child at social risk.

FPG's staff includes 17 senior researchers who have joint appointments at FPG and with several of the academic departments on the Chapel Hill campus. These investigators study a variety of problems relating to health care, psycholinguistics, social development, and cognitive style.

In addition to research, this interdisciplinary approach is also followed in FPG's other major areas of activity: demonstration day care, curriculum development, research training, and technical assistance.

The need to conduct longitudinal research requires that a relatively stable population of children be available for several years. FPG conducts a demonstration day care program for children from 4 weeks of age through the first grade. After the children reach 5 years of age, they transfer to the adjacent kindergarten and elementary school. This makes it possible to follow their progress in our research activities throughout their elementary school years.

Other FPG staff members are developing model curricula for preschool youngsters. One curriculum project is aimed at children under 3 years of age. These tasks and games are intended to develop the earliest skills, so they are of critical importance to children who face a high risk of slow development. Another curriculum project has produced packages that aid in the development of primary reasoning abilities of preschool and kindergarten youngsters.

FPG is conducting a training program in mental retardation research that is intended to produce researchers in the field who are not only well versed in the latest designs and techniques, but also—more importantly—have a firsthand understanding of the problems of the mentally retarded and the significant problems that need research attention.

Finally, FPG houses two technical assistance programs that are designed to put new knowledge into practice. The systematic application of technical assistance is one way to form a bridge that allows research and development knowledge to be transported to those in-service roles for handicapped children. One program, the Technical Assistance Development System (TADS), aids 130 preschool programs for handicapped children throughout the United States. Another program, the Developmental Disabilities Technical Assistance System (DD/TAS), helps state planning councils on developmental disabilities that have been appointed by governors in 56 states and territories. These councils are charged with the design of comprehensive service plans for citizens who are handicapped by mental retardation, cerebral palsy, epilepsy, and related disorders.

This mixture of research, development, and technical assistance provides FPG with a spectrum of activities along the knowledge dimension, from discovery to refinement to delivery.

DIVISION FOR DISORDERS IN DEVELOPMENT AND LEARNING

While the two centers focus on research and related activities, there is additional need for specific professional training. Despite research on primary prevention and the development of better medical therapeutics, a significant number of children will remain with some degree of disability. These children will require more precise diagnosis of the nature of the disability, as well as specific educational and psychological management procedures aimed at utilizing their strengths. The Division for Disorders in Development and Learning (DDDL), directed by Dr. Harrie Chamberlin, is a component of BSRC, which is concerned with the training of professionals to work with these handicapped children and with developing new and better methods for teaching them.

The DDDL is one of the original 20 University-Affiliated Facilities for the Developmentally Disabled (originally "for the Mentally Retarded"). It had its beginnings in January 1962, as one of North Carolina's developmental evaluation clinics.

The DDDL's primary mandate is the interdisciplinary training of students and professionals in the evaluation and management of children who are chronically handicapped by mental retardation, learning disabilities, and related developmental problems. The focus on interdisciplinary training is based on the same premise as the research programs: no one discipline can understand the complex interacting systems of human development. Service to children and their families, limited only by the requirements of the training program, is the second major DDDL component. Clinical research, essential to any strong training program, is the third component.

Although the majority of DDDL's students come from this University, some are drawn from other universities, four-year colleges, and community colleges from across the state (and occasionally from other states). The emphasis is on interdisciplinary training for graduate students, but DDDL's trainees range from postdoctoral fellows (in communicative disorders, pedodontics, psychology, psychiatry, and pediatrics) to a few students from community colleges who will supervise and staff child day care centers or who are attendants in the nearby state residential center for the retarded.

The professional staff averages about 38 persons and is divided into 13 sections of one to six members each: the chaplaincy, child psychiatry, communicative disorders (speech pathology, language, and audiology), health administration, nursing, nutrition, occupational therapy, pediatrics and neurology, pedodontics, physical therapy, psychology, social work, and special education. The heads and many other staff members have academic appointments in the University that spread among seven graduate programs, one institute, and a dozen University departments.

A program of this sort has no excuse for being if it merely provides an extension of the activities of the departments and schools that represent the various disciplines existing within the DDDL. It must provide extensive interaction among them. Indeed, the most distinctive characteristic of a program of this sort is its strong interdisciplinary emphasis, which has succeeded in drawing together faculty and students from throughout the University to concentrate on the problems of the developmentally handicapped.

These three units, BSRC, FPG, and DDDL, provide a diverse approach to the multidisciplinary problems posed by mental retardation.

James J. Gallagher

This book is dedicated
to the parents of risk children
in recognition of their present and
future contributions to early intervention.

Intervention Strategies for High Risk Infants and Young Children

EARLY
INTERVENTION

Early Intervention: Issues and Approaches

Theodore D. Tjossem, Ph.D.

The prevention of mental retardation and related developmental disabilities is the ultimate goal of our national effort to combat these disorders. Significant progress toward this objective is evidenced by advances in research incorporated in improved and expanded service programs. Contributions to this progress have come from all concerned professions and related scientific disciplines. Still, attainment of this national goal is not in sight and, for the many children for whom prevention of their disorder is not possible, there remains the task of finding better means to ameliorate their condition. The confluence of efforts directed toward these goals has directed increased attention to infancy and the first years of life as the periods in which fresh, new advances toward both prevention and amelioration might be accomplished. The development of intervention strategies for high risk infants and young children is the result.

Motivation and support for the development of early approaches to intervention come from several sources. Fundamental to this development is a growing appreciation for the remarkable plasticity of the central nervous system during infancy and the early years, indicated in the chapters by Isaacson, Lipton, and Purpura (this volume). Additional support is found in the growing body of research pointing to the beneficial effects of early stimulation on developing animals and humans (Bronfenbrenner, 1968). Evaluations of experimental intervention programs offered during the first 3 years of life provide still further support. These intervention efforts, presented later in this chapter, point to the mother-child interaction system as the agent responsible for producing enduring developmental gains. This relationship and the conditions that support it are at the core of early intervention strategies.

Evaluations of intervention programs aimed at combating the destructive effects of poverty on human development provide most of the information on the effectiveness of early educational intervention. Primarily preschool based and offering intervention for disadvantaged preschool children, these programs' early hopes have not been fulfillled.

3

The early gains in cognitive skills produced by these programs have not been sustained when intervention is discontinued. Accordingly, the search for approaches to intervention productive of enduring benefits has turned toward study of the family and the earlier years of development for an answer.

Much less is known regarding the effects of early educational/developmental intervention for children with developmental disorders of constitutional origin. Support for these efforts comes primarily from research on animals and from fundamental research on developmental processes limited to study of discrete functions. Major intervention studies following sound principles of research design, initiated in infancy, and employing adequate samples drawn from a well defined population have only recently been initiated (Kass et al., this volume; Parmelee et al., this volume). The available evidence from fundamental research, studies of intervention effects on disadvantaged children, and clinical judgment prompts the development of early intervention programs for developmentally disordered infants and young children.

Clear evidence of developmental delay or disorder has, for years, been taken as the basis for initiating intervention. The resulting programs have, therefore, been largely compensatory. For the disadvantaged child, this has meant that the decline in cognitive development, appearing in the second year following normal development in the first year, continues without intervention. Similarly, the early deviancies appearing in developmentally disordered children have gone unattended pending later diagnosis.

The press to the early initiation of intervention for both disadvantaged and developmentally disordered children conflicts with the established patterns of diagnosis and identification. The indicators of prospective disorders for both populations exist in known factors, both medical and social, which contribute to risk for faulty development. New approaches to the identification of children for entry into intervention service programs are emerging. The determination of early risk status for these children, among these, appears most promising.

CONCEPTS OF RISK STATUS

Categories of Vulnerable Infants

Three types of vulnerable infants can be identified, which, for different reasons, can be regarded as in need of special early intervention to ensure their optimal cognitive development and life adjustment. These are: 1) infants manifesting early appearing aberrant development related to diagnosed medical disorders with *established risk* for delayed development; 2) infants at *environmental risk* consequent to depriving life experiences; and 3) infants at *biological risk* as determined by increased probability for delayed or aberrant development consequent to biological insult(s). Each group, as defined below, has its own distinctive requirements for diagnosis, identification, and intervention strategies.

Established Risk Established risk infants are those whose early appearing aberrant development is related to diagnosed medical disorders of known etiology bearing relatively well known expectancies for developmental outcome within specified ranges of developmental delay. The Down's syndrome infant is a classic example of established risk. The early medical, educational, and social interventions employed with these children are aimed at aiding them to develop and function at the higher end of the range for their limiting disorder.

Environmental Risk Environmental risk applies to biologically sound infants for whom early life experiences including maternal and family care, health care, opportunities for expression of adaptive behaviors, and patterns of physical and social stimulation are sufficiently limiting to the extent that, without corrective intervention, they impart high probability for delayed development.

Biological Risk Biological risk specifies infants presenting a history of prenatal, perinatal, neonatal, and early development events suggestive of biological insult(s) to the developing central nervous system and which, either singly or collectively, increase the probability of later appearing aberrant development. Early diagnosis of enduring developmental fault is often difficult and inconclusive in these biologically vulnerable infants who, most often, require close surveillance and modified care during the early developmental years.

These categories of risk are not mutually exclusive, and the determining elements of each can, and often do, occur in interaction to still further increase the degree of, or probability for, delayed or aberrant development for many children. Sources of such interactions are readily evident. They are found in the biologically vulnerable premature and low birth weight infants born to adolescent mothers themselves living in and victims of poverty. They occur in the placement, in infancy, of Down's syndrome infants in the impersonal care of some custodial institutions. They are manifest in the hearing impaired infant born into a poverty stricken home deficient in language stimulation, without systematic health care, and without knowledge of and motivation to seek corrective resources. They function subtly in affluent homes in which an infant's early problem is met by low parental involvement, nonacceptance, and withdrawal of relationship by the parents. In these and other conditions, the synergistic interaction of environmental with biological risk factors serves to further limit the infant's cognitive and noncognitive development, confounds early diagnosis, and poses unique and difficult problems for early corrective interventions.

The interactions of environmental with biological risk factors that act to limit the development of established and biological risk infants are pervasive. Precipitated by early developmental flaw, they are often joined sequentially in the life of a child to establish interaction patterns that systematically act to diminish his developmental potential and opportunities for normal life experiences. Thus, as can occur, a newborn infant made vulnerable by biological insult from a faulty pregnancy experiences separation from the mother for intensive newborn care. Returned to the mother with altered and deviant behavioral capabilities, the infant is unresponsive to the mother, who cannot interpret his altered behavior and, therefore, does not respond appropriately to his signals of need (Brazelton, this volume). There follows, then, a failure of mother and child to communicate effectively, and the synchrony of their behaviors necessary to optimal development is not established (see Denenberg and Thoman, this volume). Sensing mutual rejection, each withdraws from relationship, still further diminishing opportunities for their positive interactions to guide the child's development.

An active learner despite his insult (Siqueland, 1969), the infant seeks out opportunity to control his stimulus environment. The effective environments (Butterfield and Cairns, this volume), the ones the infant will work to explore, are not necessarily those followed by normally developing infants. They may be aspects of the infant's surrounding social and physical environment which provide opportunity for learning of deviant behaviors. Emerging during infancy and the early years, these deivant behaviors evoke a broad range of social responses that further guide and shape the child's behavior. Thus, by preschool age, the child may present any of an array of established behaviors that can isolate and estrange him from constructive interactions with family and peers and preclude preschool enrollment and experience.

Intervention strategies designed to prevent or ameliorate enduring developmental deficits in risk children involve manipulation of the infant's early experience with understanding of his needs and response capabilities. A stimulus environment adapted to the infant's immediate capacities for response, which consistently and systematically creates learning environments responsive to his gradually expanding response capabilities, will, it is believed, lead ultimately to improved functional levels of cognitive and adaptive behavior for many risk children.

Opportunities for effective intervention span the developmental continuum from birth to school age. They are found in the newborn nursery, the infant's home, the preschool, and the community child development resource centers. They also occur before birth in programs for prospective mothers, both medical and social, aimed at their improved care and preparation for motherhood. Here, as for risk children, early identification of prospective mothers with increased probability for bearing a risk infant is needed to assure appropriate intervention (Scurletis et al., this volume).

Past and contemporary approaches to intervention have taken diagnosis of developmental disorder as the point for initiation of intervention. Developmental disorders, by their nature, evolve with the gradual unfolding of development. As a result, diagnosis is often deferred until there is clear evidence to support it. Meanwhile, the child's treatment and management program is one of concerned neglect. The effects of intervention programs tied to diagnosis are, therefore, primarily compensatory and ameliorative, and most are not initiated until the child reaches preschool age.

Innovative new approaches are on the horizon. They involve the establishment of infant risk status as a valid means for identifying infants and families in need of intervention services (Heber et al., 1972; Parmelee et al., this volume; Scurletis et al., this volume). These approaches extend to children at risk as a result of both biomedical and environmental causes. Full development of these approaches, if realized, will permit the development and expansion of interventions aimed at prevention as well as amelioration.

EARLY IDENTIFICATION

Entry into systems for the delivery of intervention services is difficult for many children with denotable handicaps. It is even more difficult for infants and young children subject to risk for retarded cognitive development. Significant delay in the detection and confirmation of mental retardation among young children is evident in comtemporary systems for delivery of diagnostic services. If, as believed, *early* intervention is effective in promoting the development of risk children, provision must be made for their early identification and timely entry into their community's service delivery system.

Aldrich and Holliday (1971), in a study of the age at which children were first suspected and confirmed as mentally retarded, offer evidence indicating the problems encountered in the early identification of these children. As expected, they found that the first suspicion of retardation is earlier for the profoundly retarded at 7.8 months, as compared to the mildly retarded at 34.5 months. For all sample children, the average was 25 months. The elapsed time between first suspicion and confirmation of retardation was 12 months for mildly retarded children and 6.2 months for the profoundly retarded. Mental retardation seemed to be suspected and confirmed at considerably later ages in rural as compared to urban-suburban areas. Clearly, a delay to near school age for a diagnosis of mental retardation in those mildly afflicted and past 1 year for the profoundly retarded points to marked deficits in our diagnostic capabilities and the screening-diagnosis service delivery system. If early interventions designed to prevent and/or ameliorate mental retardation are to be effective, this degree of delay is untenable.

The basis for the problems encountered in effecting early diagnosis and referral to services for risk children is to be found in several sources. These include, among others, divided professional responsibilities in both the public and private sectors, in the technical limitations of screening and diagnostic methodologies, the criteria establishing eligibility for services, and the problems involved in linking screening and diagnosis to intervention services. Without this linkage, screening and diagnosis are of dubious worth and, at worst, can be a disservice to children and parents whose problems are crystallized by an anxiety-evoking diagnosis in the absence of appropriate intervention services. Examination of these issues indicates clear need for adaptive reorientation of the approaches to screening, diagnosis, and the provision of intervention services in the early years.

Professional Responsibilities

In the arena of professional services, responsibilities for case identification, screening, and diagnosis leading to referrals for service are divided primarily between medicine, nursing, education, and social work. Among these, the physician is positioned most advantageously to be first to identify the risk conditions suggestive of need for follow up and referral. At hand to the attending newborn's physician are the maternal history and family data; record of the pregnancy, natal, and perinatal events; the findings from the newborn examination; observations of the infant's early adaptation to extrauterine life; and the mother's adaptation to the child. In the private sector, where continuity of care is usually provided by the same physician, the child's developmental record is soon supplemented by findings and observations from early periodic examinations. Although continuity of care is less likely for the child whose early medical care depends upon public support, an adequate medical record that follows the child receiving early periodic medical care can soon provide the information necessary for determination of risk status. Because of their advantageous position, it comes as somewhat of a surprise that physicians, among other professionals, are relatively slow in effecting diagnosis and making referrals to community intervention resources (de la Cruz, this volume; Denhoff and Hyman, this volume; Haynes, this volume).

Several reasons can be offered to account for the diagnostic and referral practices of physicians. First among these is the fact that, in the absence of physical handicap, intervention services for preventing and/or ameliorating mental retardation are primarily nomedical; they are educational, social, and behavioral. To the extent that their training does not expose them to the nonmedical aspects of child development and the use of these nonmedical services, physicians are less likely to see their need and value. Second, physicians are accustomed to the establishment of firm diagnoses before proceeding to treatment. Early diagnosis of mental retardation is readily made in cases of severe impairment of constitutional origin. For children presenting with mild forms of mental retardation of uncertain etiology, physicians are inclined to await the gradual unfolding of development which establishes a pattern of retarded development before making diagnosis and referral. Third, traditional physician caution expresses itself in concern for the evaluation of new and emerging treatment and intervention programs. In this regard, their professional literature provides but little evaluative evidence demonstrating the proven effectiveness of the different types of nonmedical intervention offerings. Finally, it must be remembered, nonmedical intervention programs for risk infants and young children are a recent development. In their absence, physicians have had little incentive to press for early diagnosis and referral. Aware of the wide intraindividual variations in cognitive development characteristic of infancy and early childhood, they have often held diagnosis in abeyance in the hope of spontaneous improvement and to spare parents the anxiety provoked by a threatening diagnosis without available remediation. Parent anxiety leading to avoidance of diagnosis contributes to this pattern. In these instances, some parents tend to temporize or move away from medical diagnosis with its implications of authority and finality. They seek advice and assistance from nurses, educators, and others whose roles are weighted to service and carry less implication for diagnosis. With this supportive help, some move more readily to diagnosis and assistance.

Substantial as these reasons might be for slowing diagnosis and referral, the strategic position of physicians and their professional relationship with other health professionals requires their full participation in the evolution and use of intervention programs.

Physician orientation is impressed upon the approaches to identification and intervention services of other health professionals. The nurse, medical social worker, physical and occupational therapist, all working under medical direction, are guided, in large measure, by the physician's orientation and decisions governing delivery of their services. The public health nurse, in particular, despite her strategic position for case finding, is guided in her referrals of patients from the private sector by her professional responsibility to refer through the child's physician. In nonmedically organized resources, as those organized under the aegis of education, professional roles and responsibilities for identification and intervention services can, and do, differ. It may be that, as Haynes (this volume) has pointed out, the development and expansion of intervention services beyond those narrowly medical- and physician-oriented call for a redefinition of professional roles, approaches, and responsibilities.

The medical model for diagnosis and intervention is well illustrated by Denhoff and Hyman (this volume). This model, demonstrating medical emphasis on diagnosis, brings forward a representative picture of the traditional working relationships between health professionals and those with the referring medical community. Here, referrals are primarily from physicians and the community's health agencies. The diagnosis and recommendations for treatment and programming resulting from staff evaluation are returned to the referring physician for concurrence before the next steps are taken. Experience and emerging new concepts in the delivery of child health care services are now reshaping its approach.

Evolving from a classic medical model for meeting the needs of young cerebral palsied patients, the model has expanded its intake and services to include all types of children at risk. Sensitive to the problems involved in intake limited to medical referrals and with appreciation for the ability of parents to detect early signs of developmental fault, the project's directorate is now moving toward a policy of self referral. Its outreach activities have been expanded to gain early identification of infants at risk and to effect linkages to other supportive resources in the community. Specialists in education have been added to its comprehensive services as the educational needs of very young risk children have become more apparent. These changes effect a more comprehensive and integrated approach than that provided by the early medical model.

The Portage Project (Shearer and Shearer, this volume), as an educational model of early identification and intervention for mentally retarded infants and young children, stands in sharp contrast to medical models and approaches. Acting independently of medical referral, the Project staff simply announced to the public the Project's readiness to extend educational outreach services to children of preschool age whose parents felt concern for their development. Potential concern for their children's development was the sole criterion for Project acceptance of the child for evaluation. The large numbers of self-referred parents accepting the invitation not only suggests the magnitude of the problem of early developmental delay and the extent of parental concern for the problem, it also communicates the responsiveness of parents when identification is linked to offered services.

In effect, the Portage Project model provides screening, educational diagnosis, and planning and links them directly to a program offering educational services specific to each child's needs. The linkage to services does not end here, for referrals are made to area diagnostic and evaluation clinics of children who, on the basis of education and behavioral assessment, are found to require these services. The procedures employed, then, mobilize a comprehensive array of community resources in direct and continuing service to project children ar.d their families. The simplicity of the model for achieving early screening, identification, and service is apparent. This, and the reported success of its education program in improving the developmental status of programmed children, if substantiated on critical evaluation, commends it as a model for wide application.

It is clear from the foregoing that both health and education have significant contributions to make in advancing procedures that lead to the early identification of children in need of intervention services. For both, identification is oriented to and leads most readily to services linked organizationally with their own professions. Each, acting independently, is less likely to provide full service coverage for children requiring early identification. The involvement and participation of both are indicated to ensure the comprehensive coverage required for early identification leading to intervention services.

Screening, Diagnosis, and Eligibility for Service

Diagnosis as a precondition to treatment is well established in the medical model for services where its effectiveness is amply demonstrated. Extended to include psychological diagnosis, based primarily on tests of intelligence, the medical model of diagnosis has been advanced as a requisite for programs serving mentally retarded persons. Applied as a standard for services to infants and young children with, or suspect for, mental retardation, classical diagnosis presents limitations as well as benefits.

The wide diversity and scope of the literature concerned with screening and diagnosis reviewed by Meier (this volume) reflect long-standing professional preoccupation and concern for diagnosis. To the extent that diagnosis is necessary for the medical treatment of mental retardation and related developmental disabilities of constitutional origin, this emphasis following the medical model is appropriate. But, in infancy and the early years, the vast majority of risk children elude definitive diagnosis, and their condition and its cause remain uncertain. For these children, educational, behavioral, and social interventions are the primary treatment instruments, and, for their application, a definitive diagnosis of mental retardation is regarded by some workers as unnecessary and even potentially harmful in the early years.

The wide intraindividual variations in cognitive development characteristic of infancy and the early years of life have been well demonstrated (Cattell, 1940; Meier, this volume). These variations are a product of differences in individual patterns of maturation in complex interactions with the developing child's early life experiences. Although greater consistency in early measures of cognitive development obtains for established risk children whose retardation is constitutional in origin (Knobloch and Pasamanick, 1960), present understanding of early human development and deficits in the technology of early cognitive assessment sharply limit accurate prediction of developmental outcome in later years. The problems of developing early measures predictive of later cognitive development are such that, in the light of present knowledge and approaches, rapid progress toward this goal appears unlikely (Zeaman, 1975).

Given these uncertainties for the assessment of intelligence during the early years, the diagnosis of mental retardation based upon intelligence measures as the sole criterion is, at best, questionable. Critical of this practice, Doll (1941) advocated use of inclusive criteria for establishing the condition of *mental deficiency*. For Doll, the essential criteria were: 1) social incompetence, 2) due to mental subnormality, 3) which has been developmentally arrested, 4) which obtains at maturity, 5) is of constitutional origin, and 6) is essentially incurable. Doll (1947) advocated use of the term *intellectual (mental) retardation* to effect a distinction from *mental deficiency* when patient evaluation failed to satisfy his inclusive criteria. Doll's distinction between mental deficiency and intellectual (mental) retardation recognizes the uncertainties posed by the presence of early developmental deficits and opens the door to the prospect of positive change for a multitude of young children showing early aberrant development.

Time and semantic usage have dimmed Doll's distinction. Today, the term mental retardation has replaced mental deficiency in common usage, while, at the same time, it has become all embracive as evidenced by the definition promulgated by the American Association on Mental Deficiency: "Mental retardation refers to significantly subaverage general intellectual functioning existing concurrently with deficits in adaptive behavior, and manifested during the developmental period" (Grossman, 1973, p. 5).

The inclusive nature of the term mental retardation gives it particular potency when applied as a diagnostic label. Too often, the distinction to be made between the many disorders and conditions contributing to cognitive deficits are lost to the collective perception of mental retardation with all of its negative implications from the past. Broadly perceived, application of the label establishes attitudes and expectancies in parents, teachers, and others which become determinative of their behavioral transactions with labeled children. Research evidence (Filler et al., 1975) suggests that these transactions may, in turn, shape the child's behavior in the direction of increasing accord with the expectancies determined by the label.

It follows that, during infancy and the first year of life, the screening and diagnostic procedures leading to labeling of children as mentally retarded must be approached with care. In developing and implementing these approaches, it should be observed that retarded cognitive development is but a *sign* of disordered development consequent to an underlying condition. Tests and observations establishing the sign do not constitute diagnosis, they are but a part of diagnostic procedure. The objective of diagnosis, then, is to determine the condition in a given child which leads to his retardation. When this is difficult and nondeterminative, treatment and other intervention need not be deferred until a diagnosis is established. They should proceed on the basis of identified risks and needs.

Alternative approaches to classical diagnosis are possible as a means of identifying the suspect and mentally retarded children for the provision of services. These are approaches that attempt to identify the conditions, both biological and environmental, which contribute to early risk status in children. If successfully developed and implemented, children identified at high risk for becoming mentally retarded or developmentally disabled can be provided intervention services without the necessity of waiting for their retardation and disablement to develop and their condition to be diagnosed. Furthermore, these approaches offer promise for further improving and augmenting diagnosis. Intervention services provided under these approaches move more strongly and effectively toward primary and secondary prevention while maintaining their capability for amelioration.

The Collaborative Perinatal Project of the National Institute of Neurological Diseases and Stroke illustrates the broad conceptual background from which the approaches to determination of risk status are proceeding. This project initiated a longitudinal investigation of the relationships between prenatal and postnatal events and neurological and intellectual outcomes of offspring of mothers enrolled in the project during pregnancy. Both biological and social indicators were studied.

Broman, Nichols, and Kennedy (1975), employing data from the project, studied the relationship between 169 prenatal and postnatal variables and the intellectual performance of 26,760 children at age 4. Although prediction of mental retardation on the basis of the variables examined did not reach clinically useful levels, some antecedent factors having independent association with low levels of intellectual performance were identified. Before birth, the most reliable predictor of mental retardation at age 4 was maternal education. Both social and biological variables from the neonatal period were significantly related with retardation at age 4. These social variables include maternal education and family socioeconomic status, and the biological variables identified were a diagnosis of brain abnormality and neonate size. Delayed motor development and mental test scores along with maternal education emerged during the first year of life among the factors most highly related to retardation. These data suggest the importance of including both biological and social variables in approaches to determination of risk status.

Parmelee (this volume) employs an approach aimed at achieving greater precision for the assessment of infant risk status. The approach recognizes the strong influence exerted by environmental factors in determining developmental outcomes of infants born subject to casualty on a continuum of pregnancy wastage (premature infants). His 9-month critical risk score (CRS), based on scores of pregnancy, perinatal and neonatal biological events, and the infant's early behavioral performance treated additively, provides for the effects of early environmental influences to be expressed. Because this research is in progress, its merits remain to be determined. Preliminary results are promising and supportive of the rationale guiding the approach. Hopefully, it will achieve its objective and lend itself to the development of an effective instrument for the identification of infants at biological high risk.

Advances are also being made to identify the environmental factors associated with high risk. Heber et al. (1972), starting with surveys and studies of children and their parents living in the most poverty stricken slum areas of Milwaukee, moved to identify children at high risk for becoming mentally retarded. A group of children and families meeting the criteria set for environmental high risk were then given a program of total intervention beginning in infancy and continuing to school age.

The investigation began with surveys identifying areas of the city having the strongest attributes of poverty, as: lowest mean family income, greatest population density per living unit, and highest rate of dilapidated housing. Continuing their studies of families from this population, the investigators found that maternal intelligence was the best single indicator of intellectual development in the children. Mothers with IQs of less than 80, though constituting less than one half the total study group, accounted for four fifths of the children with IQs under 80. Furthermore, intelligence levels remained relatively constant over time in the children of brighter mothers, whereas children of the dull mothers showed declining intelligence with increased age. Noteworthy, too, was their finding of congruence of maternal with paternal IQ. On the basis of these findings, the investigators concluded that mental retardation is not randomly distributed among the poor, but is concentrated in the retarded parent rather than the slum environment.

The demographic approach to the determination of infant high risk status employed by Scurletis et al. (this volume) adds support to the notion that effective systems can be developed for the early identification of high risk infants. Scurletis and his colleagues, employing characteristics of pregnant mothers derived from vital statistics, present evidence indicating that certain mothers are at greater risk than others for having babies who expire or are developmentally impaired. As in the studies reported by Broman, Nichols, and Kennedy (1975) and by Heber et al. (1972), low level maternal education was found to be a significant risk indicator, so also were wedlock status and maternal age. These investigators conclude that it is possible to identify pregnancies as high and low risk according to multiple social and biological factors considered simultaneously. The pre-natal risk index complemented by infant risk characteristics determined at birth and postnatally would, according to these investigators, provide a workable index of risk sufficient to warrant movement of an infant identified as high risk into a system of continuing care and service that might safeguard his chances for optimal development.

It is apparent from these and other studies (Braine et al., 1966; Werner et al., 1968) that efforts to develop risk indices must move beyond the child to include events and conditions before birth. Maternal health, broadly conceived, and the capacity of mothers to provide a stimulating social environment for their infants and young children are particular targets for risk identification for two reasons. First, identification of the population of high risk mothers offers opportunitites for health services intervention before birth that are aimed at prevention of abnormal pregnancies resulting in infant mortality and morbidity. Second, identification of maternal antenatal risk factors combined with those derived from study of the infant should produce a more reliable indicator of risk status. Linked to a program of follow up care, as proposed by Scurletis and his colleagues, infants identified early as high risk would receive careful care and observation which would determine their need for continuation in risk status programming or dismissal to ordinary care and treatment. The potential of this proposal for primary prevention on a broad scale gives it special appeal. Continuing efforts to refine and develop its technology are indicated.

Contemporary approaches to screening, diagnosis, and intervention initiated at the federal level invite comparison with approaches aimed at the identification of risk status. The Early Periodic Screening, Diagnosis, and Treatment (EPSDT), Child Find, and Head

Start programs are representative of major contemporary approaches. Implementation of these programs result primarily in the offering of corrective and compensatory services. Identification of infant risk status, on the other hand, provides for services aimed at primary prevention as well as correction and amelioration. Established practice and technology have been determining factors in selecting present approaches to screening, diagnosis, and intervention. Although these approaches have distinct limitations for meeting the early problems of mental retardation, they have been encouraged to serve these purposes because the resources for their implementation are available. Technology for the identification of infant risk status, on the other hand, is formative and not readily available for implementation at this time. The potential for development, application, and contribution to diagnosis and intervention services of approaches to infant risk determination is substantial.

Early Periodic Screening, Diagnosis, and Treatment (EPSDT), detailed by Rojcewicz and Aaronson (this volume), provides screening for the Medicaid eligible population from birth to 21 years of age. Critical evaluation of the EPSDT raises questions regarding the effectiveness of this massive and expensive program for meeting the problem of mental retardation.

Many of the problems implicit in the implementation of the EPSDT program have been anticipated and noted, and recommendations have been made for meeting them in a report prepared by the American Medical Association (AMA) (1975). Notable among these is the problem of parental apathy expressed as a preference to practice crisis medicine through use of emergency services, missed appointments, and less than satisfactory cooperation in following recommendations. These patterns of parent behavior are patently inimical to satisfactory diagnosis and provision of intervention services for children subject to the risk of becoming mentally retarded. The AMA report recommends an integrated and expanded role for health education to increase the sophistication of health care users as a means for meeting this issue. As might be expected, the report does not examine the structure and operation of health provider services as a source contributing to this pattern of parent behavior.

Although the AMA report supports EPSDT screening beginning at birth in the context of a coordinated program of community services and resources, provision of treatment and services for infants with identified problems other than medical pose unique problems requiring solution. In this regard, EPSDT eligibility also carries eligibility for medical treatment; it does not provide eligibility for the extended nonmedical services required for infants and young children at risk for becoming retarded on the basis of other than medically treatable conditions. In view of the recommendation by the American Academy of Pediatrics (1974) that screening should avoid the identification of children with early developmental disabilities in the absence of appropriate programs for treatment, one can reasonably ask concerning the disposition of babies positive for developmental disorder without diagnosable and treatable medical conditions.

Because the services required by these children are most often educational, it is surprising that education was not directly represented in the formulation of AMA policy for EPSDT. At the least, screening to provide a data base for estimating and planning for early educational intervention needs for this group of children would be a distinct service to national and state program development aimed at meeting the needs of the high risk poor. The gap between health providers and education is apparent, and a bridge to span this gap is needed for the effective development of comprehensive intervention programs in the early years. Steps taken by education in the identification of handicapped children further illustrate the problem.

Education's responsibility for identifying handicapped children was clearly established by Congress in the Education Amendments of 1974 (Public Law 93-380). This legislation requires state departments of education to develop plans to identify, evaluate, and diagnose all handicapped children in order to receive federal funds for special education programs. The Education of the Handicapped Act of 1975 (Public Law 94-142) further specifies that state plans shall have a goal: "(that) all handicapped children have available to them . . . a free appropriate public education and related services designed to meet their unique needs." Children in the age range of 3 to 5 years are included under the act's provisions unless inconsistent with state law. This legislation has given impetus to study of child-finding methodologies as each state department of education grapples with the problems of compliance (Child Find, 1975).

It is important to note that the act specifies that identification and education be provided to *all* handicapped children. In this respect it is more comprehensive than other major screening and diagnostic programs as EPSDT and Head Start in which eligibility is determined by family income level. Noteworthy, too, is the recognition of need for identification of handicapped children below school age and the act's provisions linking identification directly to educational services. The period from birth to 3 years remains open to state discretion.

In addition to EPSDT and Child Find, 200 Head Start programs are screening for conditions listed in the EPSDT guidelines (Van Doorninck, 1975). These efforts are augmented by screening programs offered by state departments of health through their Maternal and Child Health and Crippled Children's Divisions and by organizations operating in the private sector. That there is ample opportunity for duplication of efforts, contradiction, and "passing the buck" is evident as Van Doorninck (1975) has noted.

It is evident from the foregoing that the problem of identifying infants and young children suspect for becoming mentally retarded represents a major challenge. The task is compounded for the suspect child under 3 years of age by the absence of well known and organized intervention service programs that press for early identification, by limitations in diagnostic technology, and a confusing complex of divided responsibilities. Too often, for many of these children, the incipient conditions causing or contributing to their pattern of disordered development remain unattended as the children wait upon a firm diagnosis permitting the identification required to gain entry to services. Development of the emerging technology for identifying the risk factors that shape and characterize early disordered development as an alternate strategy to diagnosis is needed. Hopefully, establishment of this technology as a valid means for identifying high risk infants will be accomplished and accepted to permit early intervention efforts to become truly preventive as well as ameliorative.

Parent appreciation for the potential benefits of early childhood education for their special children is evident. This is expressed in their voluntary development and support of infant programs of education and cognitive stimulation and their growing insistence for support of early intervention services. The professional scientific and service leadership have a clear signal from the parents whose initiative, in the past, has set the direction for services requiring the identification of handicapped children (Winkler, 1975). Professional leaders have a choice: they can give impetus to refinement and development of valid technologies and systems for the identification of risk children needing early intervention, or they can wait for this to be mandated.

EARLY EDUCATIONAL INTERVENTION

Early educational intervention programs for risk infants and very young handicapped children present a pattern of delayed but rapidly accelerating development. Parent and professional efforts have, until recently, been more concerned with overcoming traditional views regarding the educability of known retarded children of school age. These views, embodied in state constitutions and statutes governing education, have, until recently, sharply limited or denied education to the mentally retarded (Abeson et al., 1975). It was only in response to pressures from parent groups and concerned educators and other professionals that major changes in educational policies and philosophy have emerged. This effort was crystalized in the Pennsylvania Association for Retarded Citizens vs. State of Pennsylvania litigation, which established the landmark decision on the *right to education* for "ineducable" children (Burt, 1975). Increased legal activities by lawyers have followed and further added to law reform, bringing about new approaches to special education for the handicapped (Kirp, Kuriloff, and Bass, 1975). In the light of this recent history, the fact that we are today considering the provision of educational intervention for children at risk as early as birth and early infancy is paradoxical.

Significant strides have been made toward establishing a basis for justifying early educational intervention, while efforts to secure the right to education have been moving forward. This base exists in several sources. It is found in the rapid growth of publicly and privately supported preschool programs for the handicapped promulgated on the basis of *presumed value* judgments (Ackerman and Moore, this volume). Furthermore, impetus has come from the massive compensatory education programs initiated in the early 1960s for disadvantaged Head Start children, which, more recently, have included handicapped children. These programs were prompted, in large measure, by early research demonstrating dramatic *initial* gains in intelligence effected in deprived children by well designed experimental preschool intervention programs (Gray and Klaus, 1965; Kirk, 1958).

Concurrent with these broad social action programs, an increasing number of experimental projects have been fielded to examine critical dimensions of early educational intervention. The variables examined in this effort toward greater precision and understanding include, among others, age of intervention, parent involvement, site of intervention, and curriculum and instructional methods. The range of developmental outcome variables studied, too, have been expanded as longitudinal studies have permitted study of later noncognitive development and academic achievement. The products of these diverse research efforts, complemented by evaluations from fielded intervention programs, now present a significant body of data subject to synthesis and analysis from which hypotheses to guide future research and program development can be derived.

A continuing flow of research findings from fundamental and applied research on child development undergirds the basis for early educational/developmental intervention. Contributions from both biomedical and behavioral research concerned with specific aspects of development are woven into and reinforce the fabric of some early intervention approaches. Left for discussion in the section of this chapter on research and evaluation, it is sufficient to state here that these research contributions add support for the belief that early education/developmental interventions, guided by precise understanding of developmental processes, can be made effective.

The case for early identification and educational intervention is ultimately contingent upon demonstration of their reciprocal value and effectiveness. It is apparent from the basis provided above that there is far to go to effect this demonstration. Progress toward this goal comes primarily from investigations testing the effectiveness of early educational interventions on environmentally deprived children. Similar studies of biologically handicapped or at risk children are few and the heterogeneity of disorders subsumed under the rubric of mental retardation complicates evaluation of the effectiveness of intervention for retarded children. Because, as noted earlier, the latter experience their own unique patterns of depriving life experiences, the results from studies on the environmentally deprived also have relevance for them. What, then, is the effectiveness of early educational intervention for deprived children?

Deprivation Model

Influenced by the deprivation hypothesis (Hunt, 1961), programs of preschool intervention have been developed as a strategy for counteracting the destructive effects of poverty on the development of young children. Following traditional patterns of educational practice, it was characteristic of most initial programs to use the preschool as the site of intervention, the teacher as the agent of intervention, and to enroll children beginning at age 3. Feedback from this approach has resulted in experimental modifications in which the parent, not the teacher, has primary involvement and responsibility for instruction; the home replaces or is shared with the preschool as the site of intervention; and children under age 3 are enrolled. These new dimensions, added to traditional approaches, have enriched the understanding of and approaches to early educational intervention and have opened new avenues to scientific inquiry. Comprehensive summaries of this literature are given by Bronfenbrenner (1974) and Miller and Dyer (1975).

Early results from evaluation of Head Start and experimental preschool intervention programs for the disadvantaged children were disturbing. As studies were reported, it became apparent that the early initial sharp gains in cognitive development resulting from preschool intervention were not sustained; they were washed out as control children caught up with experimentals when programs were discontinued (a result that might have been anticipated from the twin control studies conducted decades ago by Hilgard (1932) and McGraw (1939). Education's reflex response was to examine more closely its primary instrument for intervention: the preschool and its methods of instruction.

In an examination of preschool methodologies conducted in group settings, Miller and Dyer (1975) studied the effectiveness of four different approaches to preschool instruction. Employing four model preschool programs differentiated by their approaches and methods of instruction, these investigators examined the immediate and long-range effects produced over 4 years on the cognitive, social, motivational, and perceptual development of 4-year-old disadvantaged children. The model programs selected for study were Bereiter-Engelman (Bereiter and Engelman, 1966), DARCEE (Gray et al., 1966), Montessori (1964), and Traditional Head Start (Rainbow Series, 1965).

The four programs studied exhibited different effects on the children. These were expressed in terms of immediate and long-range impact, and, over the 4-year period, the long-range effects were expressed regardless of what programs the children had later. As expected, the didactic programs (Bereiter-Engelman and DARCEE) emphasizing cognitive goals produced higher level immediate increments in IQ and achievement. Although children from all four programs declined in IQ over the 4-year period, the decrements were greater for those children from the programs that had had the greatest initial impact on IQ and achievement. The only preschool effects detectable after a 4-year period were found in the "noncognitive" areas. In effect, the investigation confirms the wash out of early, preschool-induced cognitive gains observed in other studies. Preschool method of instruction, it would appear, is not the agent responsible for this effect.

Much broader dimensions of early life experience emerge as critical change agents producing long-range effects in the comprehensive review and analysis offered by Bronfenbrenner (1974). Initiating this review, Bronfenbrenner selected and studied reports on experimental preschool programs conducted in group settings (Beller, 1972; Gray and Klaus, 1970; Herzog, Newcomb, and Cesen, 1972; Hodges, McCandless, and Specker, 1967; Weikart et al., 1970). The results of his analysis accord with those of Miller and Dyer (1975) noted earlier. All programs, especially those classified as structured cognitive, were effective in establishing substantial initial gains that endured as long as the program was sustained. The initial gains were not followed by continued improvement after 1 year and tended to diminish or wash out when intervention terminated. The analysis of these programs and evidence from other studies suggest to Bronfenbrenner that the reason for these unhappy findings rests beyond the doors of the school. Their source appears more likely to exist in the broad context of early experience, primarily in mother-child interactions in which the mother is both a responsive initiator and sustainer of the child's early experiences.

In support of this assumption, Bronfenbrenner (1974) offers as evidence comparisons made between studies involving direct intervention with infants and those in which interventions are made through the mother. Schaefer's study of direct infant intervention (Schaefer, 1968; Schaefer and Aaronson, 1972) and Levenstein's study (1970) of intervention through the mother are used for comparison.

Schaefer's study provides negative evidence for the effectiveness of direct infant intervention. Direct intervention in the home with disadvantaged infants beginning at 18 months produced no positive effects; in fact, the experimental group showed a drop in measured intelligence at 2 years of age. Schaefer accounts for this drop by observing that studies have shown that the usual decline in mental test scores of infants from low socioeconomic groups does not show up before 18 months of age. Thus, the drop in intellectual level of experimentals might have been anticipated, with the program of direct intervention serving merely to attenuate the decline. For this reason, Schaefer suggests that a program of intervention for disadvantaged infants should begin earlier to counteract the earlier patterns of experience with effect the decline.

The patterns of experience of concern to Schaefer emerged from observations that mothers of the experimental group differed greatly in their interactions with their children. He undertook an analysis of the patterns of mother-child interactions and the IQs of the children at termination of intervention and found the relationship between the mother's acceptance of the child and her educational efforts to parallel the child's competence and adjustment. Here, maternal positive involvement, interest in the child's education, and verbal expressiveness with the child were related to the early intellectual development of the children studied. On this evidence, Schaefer and Aaronson (1972) conclude that the desirable intervention mode is one which supports the development of early relationships, interests, and language. The approach indicated, then, would be family, not child, centered.

Continuing his analysis, Bronfenbrenner finds in Levenstein's (1970) Verbal Interaction Project an independent test of Schaefer and Aaronson's conclusions and recommendation. Focused on the mother-child dyad, verbal interactions, and the mother as the agent for change, Levenstein's project fulfills the requirements for intervention proposed by Schaefer and Aaronson. The approach used by Levenstein sent trained workers (Toy Demonstrators) into the homes of 2- and 3-year-old disadvantaged children for semiweekly half-hour visits over a period of 7 months a year. In the home, the Toy Demonstrators stimulated interaction between mother and child with the aid of toys and books. Their visits were conducted under instruction to recognize that the child's primary and continuing relationship is with the mother and that their efforts should be directed to an enhancement of that relationship.

The results achieved by this approach are encouraging. Substantial gains were achieved by all experimental groups. Children entering the program at age 2 showed gains of about 15 IQ points over controls that they maintained 3 to 4 years after program termination. From his analysis of the program, Bronfenbrenner (1974) concludes:

> Viewed as a whole, the results from Levenstein's five differentially treated experimental groups suggest that the earlier and more intensely mother and child were stimulated to engage in communication around a common activity, the greater and more enduring the gain in IQ achieved by the child (p. 25).

Bronfenbrenner finds additional support for the effectiveness of Levenstein's approach in its conformity to conditions established by research as conducive to early development (Bronfenbrenner, 1974) and its apparent initial success in 18 replications (Levenstein, 1972). He extracts further supportive evidence from a series of experimental studies conducted by Karnes and Badger (1969) for disadvantaged mothers, which are closely similar to Levenstein's with respect to home visits. Karnes' program engaged mothers of disadvantaged infants in weekly group meetings aimed at helping them to establish a working relationship with their 1- to 2-year-old infants and to instruct them in teaching techniques to be used in the home. The group meetings continued for 15 months and were complemented by monthly home visits by staff. Results comparable to Levenstein's were obtained with follow up to 3 years, at which time the experimentals showed a mean IQ 16 points higher than that of a matched comparison group.

When this approach was combined with a preschool program for children, the results were less favorable (Karnes, Hodgins, and Teska, 1969). In this instance, the control children, who received preschool intervention only, actually gained more than did the experimentals receiving the combined program. To account for this reversal, the authors hypothesize that the program changes may have effected a devaluation of mother-child interaction in which the mother's role was less central. Stressing the importance of the mother-child interaction system, Bronfenbrenner addresses this issue by cautioning against the use of approaches that might diminish or disrupt this relationship.

Bronfenbrenner's compelling review indicates that there is, indeed, a case to be made for early intervention with disadvantaged children and their families. It is neither the school nor the teacher, however, that he finds to be most effective in fostering and sustaining the development of the child; it is the family. Considering the intervention evidence as a whole, Bronfenbrenner concludes that the involvement and the active participation of the child's family are critical to the success of any intervention program.

There is evidence from the review that, within the family context, the most effective interventions are those that recognize the importance and power of the mother-child interaction system. From this, Bronfenbrenner (1974) concludes that the primary objective of intervention during the first 3 years is:

> ... the establishment of an enduring emotional relationship between parent and infant involving frequent reciprocal interaction around activities which are challenging to the child. The effect of such interaction is to strengthen the bond between parent and child, enhance motivation, increase the frequency and power of contingent responses, produce mutual adaptation in behavior, and thereby improve the parent's effectiveness as a teacher (p. 56).

Interventions initiated early in life which follow the principles advocated above and which give emphasis to verbal interactions have been shown to be effective and to have cumulative and sustained effects when applied to disadvantaged children and their families. The case for this form of intervention has moved beyond a value judgment to one that rests more firmly on a base of scientific understanding and demonstrated fact. The question now is: Does this approach have relevance and applicability for children at risk for mental retardation resulting from causes other than environmental?

Integration of Handicapped Children in Programs for the Nonhandicapped

The issue of most immediate relevance in the light of the preceding review is that of placement of handicapped children in programs for nonhandicapped children. What is the fate of these children of *double disadvantage* in traditional Head Start programs where their placement is congressionally mandated? The facts are not known, for this aspect of intervention for the disadvantaged trails in federal program evaluation efforts. Also, experimental preschool programs for the disadvantaged shed little light, for here the mentally retarded and handicapped have been systematically excluded for obvious reasons of research design. Answer to this issue, then, must, for now, be sought in the research and evaluation data currently available from preschool intervention programs serving the nonhandicapped. The outlook is not promising.

Evaluation of the immediate and long-term effects produced by early traditional Head Start programs provides little evidence indicating that enduring practical benefits result. Admittedly, benefits may be found on the basis of value judgments, and, indeed, there remains the possibility that extended follow up of participants might still reveal late-appearing positive effects. Placement of handicapped children in these programs, then, remains a value judgment. Because enrollment occurs in a climate of presumed benefit, too little attention has been given to possible adverse effects that might result for some children as a consequence of enrollment. Handicapped children, in particular, are vulnerable to such effects, and they deserve the protection that consideration of possible adverse effects afford.

The early Head Start preschool model, described by Ackerman and Moore (this volume), was developed to counter the destructive effects of poverty on human development. Directed toward this objective, its approach gives emphasis to the provision of experience enrichment offered at the child's natural learning pace. Projected against this background, training objectives and approaches focal to the handicap which characterize and guide intervention programs for handicapped children stand out in sharp contrast. The relative effectiveness of these two different approaches for benefiting handicapped children both generally and for specific handicap has not been established. Differential effects are implied by examination of these approaches as they relate to specific handicapping conditions.

Almost 50 percent of the hanidcapped served by Head Start programs are speech impaired, hearing impaired, or deaf (Ackerman and Moore, this volume). To these handicapping conditions, traditional Head Start provides increased opportunities for incidental learning but little in the way of specific emphasis on and structure for enhancing child verbal interactions, sequenced short-term speech and language goals; nor is there strong provision for parent training in the techniques of speech and language intervention for use in interactions with their child. In view of evidence presented earlier in this chapter (Levenstein, 1970; Schaefer and Aaronson, 1972) indicating the importance of early emphasis on language, particularly verbal interactions of mother and child around a common activity, Head Start provision for facilitating verbal and language activities appears limited relative to other approaches. The implications for the speech and language impaired are great.

The program for hearing-impaired and deaf children presented by Horton (this volume) illustrates the marked differences between programs focal to a handicapping condition with those of traditional preschool-based programs. Horton's model recognizes the importance of home-based training and the involvement and participation of parents. The training facility reflects this recognition; it simulates the natural conditions of a child's home to permit parents to be instructed in the techniques of training their children under natural conditions of home life. The techniques of intervention in which the parents are trained are both general and those specific to deaf and hearing-impaired children. The approach clearly conveys that the parents have primary responsibility for training their child to which objective the program serves as a facilitory agent. This facilitation is aided by the integration into the training facility of the instrumentation necessary for programming the deaf and hearing impaired. Finally, and importantly, this program provides for continuity of programming as the young children move on into public-supported preschool classes.

Horton's evidence supportive of the beneficial effects of the program draws heavily upon the literature concenred with the treatment of the deaf and hearing impaired. Direct evidence drawn from the model program itself offers support for its effectiveness, but the numbers of children followed longitudinally are too small to permit conclusions as to the effectiveness of the program itself. Still, it meets the conditions mentioned earlier by Bronfenbrenner in this chapter as essential for optimal development. In comparison to generic preschool-based programs, most would regard the model as most likely to produce benefit.

The contrasting of focal intervention programs with traditional preschool models could continue to include comparisons of all categories of handicapped children included in Head Start enrollments. In the end, only value judgments would obtain, for the hard data for objective evaluation has not been developed. For the concerned reader in search of a value judgment, contrast reference for physically handicapped children is found in Gordon's (this volume) elegantly structured program; for the mentally retarded, review for contrast might well note the effectiveness of parents as teachers (Baker, this volume; Shearer and Shearer, this volume).

Finally, displacement of parent responsibility and involvement for the child's training onto the preschool is a concern. It is a concern not only as it relates to the retarded and handicapped in Head Start and other preschool based programs; it is a concern because take-over of responsibility by professionals has been characteristic of many serivce activities. The evidence presented here and in the broader literature, while not complete, leaves the clear implication that family involvement is paramount in the success of intervention programs for young children. Acceptance of this principle is well evidenced in most of the demonstration programs presented later in this volume.

Developmental, Behavioral, and Treatment Intervention

Studies concerned with developmental intervention are over-shadowed by the large outpouring of investigations of early educational intervention and experimental programs for the disadvantaged made possible by Head Start. The well developed base for early educational intervention that exists in the system of preschools has facilitated these activities. There is no comparable base for early infant studies. Nevertheless, infant studies are increasing as investigators reach out to hospitals, clinics, and into homes to carry out this important work.

Infant stimulation in the form of handling or other sensory stimulation are prominent intervening variables in the studies of infants. The premature infant has received most attention here, and favorable gains in their early development as a result of handling and sensory stimulation have been reported (Scarr-Salapatek and Williams, 1973; Siqueland, 1969). Again, it is difficult to draw conclusions from these studies because long-range effects were not studied, and the degree of risk for the premature subjects used in these studies was either not established or validated.

The principles of operant conditioning applied by teachers and instructed parents is used successfully in many intervention programs. The effectiveness of the operant approach in aiding retarded children to accomplish mastery of specified developmental tasks that add to their competence and independence is well established. Operant approaches are also an effective means of modifying deviant behaviors that mark a child as different (Baer et al., this volume). The addition of operant procedures to the armamentarium of early intervention programs adds significantly to their power.

Developmental and treatment intervention studies are difficult, time consuming, and expensive. It follows that longitudinal investigations providing tests of the effectiveness of various interventions are few and the results often equivocal. This problem is well illustrated in the efforts made to test the effectiveness of the sensorimotor patterning method of treatment on retarded children.

Sensorimotor patterning as a treatment method emerged in the early 1960s as a treatment method for children with brain damage. A strong advocacy for the method, questioned by members of the scientific community, emerged in the public sector to prompt efforts for a test of this method. Repeatedly, these efforts to develop a research design acceptable to established standards of scientific review failed. Award of federal support for these efforts was, therefore, not provided, and the issue remained unresolved.

Led by the National Association of Retarded Citizens, initiative in the private sector led finally to a test of the method. The results of the study reported by Neman et al. (1975) suggested that some statistically significant benefits resulted from treatment, but none of practical significance were evidenced. The study and its results provoked a strong critique (Zigler and Seitz, 1975), and the method remains open to question. The pace set for this test of the method, the problems faced in fielding it, and the final equivocal results are indicative of the low-level capability for evaluating major treatment and intervention programs.

A New Look

The evidence assembled by this review is not sufficient to support social policy action leading to the development of large-scale efforts promulgating early intervention programs for infants and young children. The review, however, does provide sufficient evidence to warrant efforts to expand the number of experimental demonstration projects and to increase research and evaluation activities related to educational/developmental interventions. This posture, prompted by the review, is conservative in its approach to planning strategies for early intervention. As such, it may be disappointing to many parents whose hopes and aspirations for their struggling children press for new solutions. It should not be disappointing, for the review opens to parents an approach giving direction to immediate steps that can be taken to gain benefits for their children. It is one in which the parents themselves have the power for constructive change.

A Parent Approach

Support *not* intervention for parents of young risk children has emerged from the review as the most promising available approach for producing developmental gains. Findings from the review and the chapters in the volume show that parents are effective teachers of risk children if given appropriate support. Their success in enhancing their child's development rests largely upon their motivation, involvement, and acceptance of responsibility. The early relationship established between mother and infant is given as a fundamental determinant of the child's later course. With acceptance of these principles and the family as the object for support, communities can organize supportive services that enable families to enhance their risk child's development.

Ideally, the approach begins in the newborn nursery. Here, both physicians and nurses are alert to signs of early risk and show concern for the child's developmental well-being as well as health. In their appraisal, signs of risk in the early mother-infant relationship are not ignored (Brazelton, this volume). With evidence of risk and need for support, mother and child are discharged with an accompanying referral to the community health service for nurse support and observations in the home.

In her home visit, the nurse first gives expression of the community's interest and support for the future well-being of the risk infant and family. While observant of total family needs as well as the health of both mother and child, the nurse is supportive of the mother's beneficial child care behaviors. She continues her periodic visits until, after exchanges with the child's physician, determination is made that no risk or continued risk is present. With this determination, she maintains her visits and relationship with the risk child and family and terminates service to the child and family that are doing well.

In the continuing supportive relationship, the nurse extends her knowledge of child care and training to the child through the mother. For family and child requirements beyond her command, she draws upon her knowledge of community or area resources to bring them into family service. In this manner, referral of the family is made to the community's educational resource upon evidence of the risk child's needs for educational assistance in mastering the developmental tasks of childhood.

The transition from nurse and physician to education serivces brings with it a comprehensive understanding of the child's health and developmental status and the family's needs and strengths. Upon educational evaluation and acceptance for service, the child and family enter into the home-based training program offered by the educational resource. The individualized training program is implemented by the parents with the guidance and support of the educator. Continuing, as needed, into the preschool years, the educator monitors the family's and child's needs for adjunctive community services and assists in bringing their support to the family.

The parent approach outlined in the foregoing is but one of many models a community might develop to provide services for risk children. To the extent that other models capture the basic principles involved, they should be effective programs. These principles, restated, are: 1) supportive services are initiated early, 2) are offered on the basis of perceived risk and need, not diagnosis, 3) are family oriented, 4) support and enhance the mother-child interaction system, and 5) are sustained. The requirements of the basic program are modest and can be met. They exist as medical, nursing, and early educational services provided in most communities, or, in their absence, can be developed through existing agency organizations. Needed adjunctive support services may be added to these as available in the community, or they can be developed for area application and utilization. The resources and technology are, or can be, available. The task, now, is to make them work.

Will the parent approach work? The answer is a qualified yes. Its success will depend, in large measure, upon community planning for the organization of serivces necessary to provide the glue that binds together presently divided professional and serivce organization responsibilities. So, too, it depends upon the availability of professionals trained, as in programs of the University-Affiliated Facilities, to be expert not only in their own profession but in the broad principles of child development and family life and with appreciation for the contributions to be made by other disciplines as well. And it will require that parents recognize their own power to advance their child with the support and guidance of community resources provided in the home. The parents have called to their communities for their support, and they have also called upon the research community for the research products and technology to make service support more effective.

RESEARCH AND EVALUATION

Evaluation

The balanced use of research and evaluation is essential to the development of *effective* early intervention programs. Head Start provides ample evidence of the generative and protective functions served by research and evaluation. Here, it was research evidence from experimental preschools that prompted the social action leading to Head Start programs. But the research was not complete. Evaluations soon revealed that the initial congitive benefits produced by preschool intervention were not sustained. Further evaluation of the long-term effects of preschool intervention for the disadvantaged has introduced marked reservations regarding the effectiveness of traditional preschool programs serving the disadvantaged. In doing so, these evaluations have spawned a host of new research studies pointing to new methods of intervention and to the years before preschool as an age for beneficial interventions.

Evaluation of the effectiveness of traditional preschool programs for serving the handicapped has lagged. The congressional mandate for inclusion of handicapped children in Head Start programs carries with it provision for program evaluation. With these children, however, evaluations, providing global measures of program effectiveness will not suffice. To be effective for future program development, these evaluations should, at the least, relate program effects to: 1) indices of graded family risk status; 2) specified patterns of parent and family support behaviors; 3) definitive diagnoses of handicapping conditions; and 4) graded measures of speech and language development of all children on entry and termination of programming. The delay in effecting evaluation of Head Start and other traditional preschool program effects on the handicapped is a major concern. This evaluation demands the highest action priority.

In the same vein, the enthusiasm generated for the demonstration projects reported in this volume must be tempered by evaluation. In view of their high visibility and importance, these programs merit intensive evalution, and, for the most part, this has not been accomplished. Because of the promise of programs employing parents as teachers, these programs, in particular, need replication and presentation in the literature of the hard data necessary to form objective judgments.

The reports provided are not sufficient to give comprehensive understanding of the processes involved in producing program effects (Shearer and Shearer, 1972). Further information is needed to explain why and under what conditions the program benefits some children and not others. The requirements of rigorous evaluation suggested earlier for Head Start programs applies equally to the demonstration projects reported in this volume.

Research

Research progress leading to application in early intervention is evident across a wide range of disciplines and problems. The chapters in the section on research which follow in this volume are illustrative of the wide scope and diversity of these efforts. Spanning the scientific disciplines from neurobiology to the behavioral sciences, both animal and human research, and the age range from birth to school age, these chapters reflect the enormity and complexity of the research efforts. It could not be otherwise, for the studies leading to understanding of the fundamental processes of normal and disordered human development require the contributions of many disciplines throughout the developmental continuum. How these contributions are synthesized and communicated to lend their broader meaning to the understanding of human development for translation to service application is a major task.

Few other areas of research are more vital to the development of early intervention for risk infants than that concerned with the effects produced by the infant's interactions with his stimulus environment. The effects of early experience on behavior and the developing central nervous system are well recognized (Denenberg, 1964; Goldman, 1969; 1972; Kerr, 1975; Newton and Levine, 1968; Rosenzweig, 1971). Given this recognition, how does this knowledge become effective for educational intervention? A study from developmental neurobiology using animals and an educator's home tutoring program for 1- to 2-year-old children suggests an answer.

Using monkeys given orbital lesions in infancy, Goldman (1975) produced evidence indicating that their recovery was facilitated by experience gained as a result of early training. The monkeys operated on were impaired on a number of cognitive tasks when tested between 12 and 18 months of age. When tested again at 24 months, they showed remarkable recovery of function and performed comparably to unoperated on animals of the same age. Comparison was then made with monkeys operated on and raised under identical conditions, with the exception that they had no test training experience at 1 year. Tested at 2 years on the same battery and order of tests given the monkeys with previous test training experience, the untrained monkeys uniformly failed to learn the delayed alternation task. Summing her results, Goldman points out that the intervening training need not be successful at the time of training to express its long-range effects.

Kirk's (1969) experimental home tutoring program for disadvantaged children aged 1 to 2 years has features similar to Goldman's experiment with animals. The children in Kirk's project were given 1 year of home-based tutoring in cognitive skills. At the end of the year, the experimental children showed a small but significant increase in IQ of 5 points as compared with controls. They were then entered in a preschool program for 3-year-olds, where they gained an additional 11 points. From this, Kirk concluded that the early training program was not as effective as later preschool group intervention.

The inferences drawn from their experiments by Goldman and Kirk are of interest. The large gain in IQ shown in the second year, though unusual, did not lead Kirk to infer that the initial training might have contributed to the second year preschool effect. Age and method of educational intervention were his concerns, not a possible neural basis for the effect. Goldman, on the other hand, found in her results implications for special education by concluding that "unsuccessful training would appear to be better than no training at all."

Goldman's studies and those of other investigators in the field of developmental neurobiology have clear implications for their ability to serve special education. The fact that Goldman studied brain-damaged monkeys does not detract from this statement; she could have studied disadvantaged monkeys as well and with greater flexibility and control of independent variables than that possible with human subjects. Studies in developmental neurobiology oriented to the problems of early educational intervention can and should contribute substantially to the design, implementation, and precision of studies of early education using human subjects. Here and elsewhere, the approximation of contributing disciplines is needed to maximize the benefits of developmental studies.

Language development, because of its implications for mental retardation, is still another area attracting investigators from different disciplines. Speech and language disorders rank among the most prominent features of mental retardation. Evidence for the milder forms of mental retardation in the young child is most frequently signalled by delayed speech and language development. The late emergence of readily recognized developmental landmarks for these functions in the second year of life causes parents not to seek help until the child is past 2 years of age. Even then, definitive examination of their auditory acuity is often omitted on medical examination (Lloyd, this volume). The implications of these events for early intervention are recognized.

Butterfield and Cairns (this volume) approach this issue through fundamental research addressed to the determination of effective auditory environments for infants. Their basic investigations clearly demonstrate that infants, even newborns, are attentive to their auditory environment and selectively respond to its varied signals. These studies have obvious implications for early intervention programs. Because of their fundamental research nature, they also open the door to other research opportunities.

Elsewhere, the neural foundations underlying the capacity of infants to respond to their auditory environments is under investigation with animals used as subjects. Buchwald (1975), using kittens, initiated studies of the capacity of the brainstem to encode sensory, especially acoustic, stimuli and to modulate the resultant sensory information so as to produce a learned response.

Buchwald was guided to this research endeavor by other studies showing increased prevalence of partial deafness (Lloyd and Reid, 1967) and the high incidence of premature births, with anoxia as a perinatal complication (Gottfried, 1973), in the mentally retarded population. Clinical and experimental evidence indicating a high degree of vulnerability of the brainstem sensory nuclei, particularly the auditory system, to the damaging effects of anoxia implicated the brainstem as a focal point for study. In these unfinished studies, Buchwald works under the premise that cell damage in the auditory relay nuclei of the brainstem may permit the inflow of sensory stimuli to be garbled into redundant noise instead of encoding specific patterns of information.

An important advance to the understanding of language development will have been made should the results of these fundamental studies with animals substantiate Buchwald's premise. Linked to the approach and technology of Butterfield and Cairns, positive findings could, in the hand of applied researchers, permit clinical study of infants implicated for brainstem pathology and lead to provision of modified auditory environments for involved infants.

The attempt at synthesis here is speculative and involved, and it was purposefully so contrived. The research examples suggest the distance to the research goal within a single discipline (Buchwald, 1975), the gap between fundamental investigators from different disciplines, and the distance between these and applied researchers. These are the realities of research, and they need to be known by parents and consumers.

From Research to Service

Although they have a common goal, the distance that separates researchers from different disciplines diminishes their collective efforts. Similar gaps exert their diminishing effects along the continuum from research to service. They exist between: 1) researchers and providers or professional services; 2) service providers from different professions as medicine and education; 3) service providers and parent consumers; and 4) parent consumers and the community. Collectively, these gaps detract from the expression of a more effective and unified program effort.

Actions have been taken to bring about a more unified and focal program effort. They involve actions to approximate the diverse elements contributing to the total effort at all levels on the research-to-service continuum. The ultimate objective of this action is to enhance communication between all elements and to accomplish thereby a more productive and effective program.

Enactment by Congress, in 1963, of legislation (Public Law 88-164) providing for the construction of Mental Retardation Research Centers and University-Affiliated Facilities represents a major action taken toward the goal of a unified program effort. This legislation provided the base for development of the Mental Retardation Research Centers (MRRC) Program and the University-Affiliated Facilities (U-AF) Program. These companion programs now spearhead the national thrust to combat the problems of mental retardation and related developmental disabilities through their research and service training programs.

Created for the purpose of research on mental retardation and related aspects of human development, the 12 MRRCs forming the Program provide for the research requirements unique to this field of research. Joined administratively and functionally in one center, scientists from the different concerned disciplines foster interdisciplinary research. The need for longitudinal research so well expressed by Gallagher et al. (this volume) is met by the centers with the added benefit made by contributions from not one but several disciplines. Most centers are joined administratively and functionally with a U-AF to permit greater opportunity for applied research and the translation of research findings to service. Collectively, the centers of the MRRC Program join all of the scientific disciplines required for a concerted attack on the many research problems of mental retardation and related developmental disabilities.

Over 40 U-AF are today joined in a concerted effort to provide the trained service personnel required to serve the mentally retarded and developmentally disabled. Cognizant of the total needs of these individuals, the U-AF Program fosters multidisciplinary training to enhance trainee knowledge and understanding of the contributions to be made by all professions. Through U-AF development of satellite training resources, the U-AF Program is expanding its training and service capabilitites to reach and train more workers for the delivery of improved services.

This volume and the conference upon which it is based represents still another effort in the action series directed toward the development of collective efforts and understanding. Here, concerned for the problem of risk infants and young children, all parts of the complex program are gathered together in a common cause. Research scientists from medicine, education, and the behavioral sciences are joined with their counterpart professional service providers to share knowledge, define problems, and serarch for their solution. To their voices still another is added: the voice of parents of risk children as *full partners* in the deliberations. Together, their knowledge, values, and aspirations, though expressed in different languages, provide a comprehensive understanding of the problems, needs, and opportunities that will determine future strategies of intervention services for risk infants and young children.

LITERATURE CITED

Abeson, A., R. L. Burgdorf, Jr., P. J. Casey, and J. W. Kunz. 1975. Access to opportunity. *In* N. Hobbs (ed.), Issues in the Classification of Children, Vol. II, pp. 270–292. Josey-Bass, Inc., San Francisco.

Aldrich, R. A., and A. Holliday. 1971. The Mental Retardation Service Delivery System Project. Research Report No. 3, pp. 1–63. Health Resources Study Center, University of Washington, Seattle; and Department of Social and Health Service, State of Washington, Olympia.

American Academy of Pediatrics. 1974. A Guide to Screening for the Early and Periodic Screening, Diagnosis, and Treatment Program (EPSDT). Department of Health, Education, and Welfare Publication Number (SRS) 74-24516. Washington, D.C.

American Medical Association, Committee on Health Care of the Poor. 1975. Professional Health Provider Participation in Early and Periodic Screening, Diagnosis, and Treatment. Department of Health, Education, and Welfare Publication Number (SRS) 75-24517. Washington, D.C.

Beller, E. K. 1972. Impact of early education in disadvantaged children. *In* S. Ryan (ed.), A Report on Longitudinal Evaluations of Preschool Programs. Office of Child Development, Washington, D.C.

Bereiter, C., and S. Engelman. 1966. Teaching Disadvantaged Children in the Preschool. Prentice-Hall, Englewood Cliffs, New Jersey.

Braine, M. D. S., C. B. Heimer, H. Wortis, and A. M. Freedman. 1966. Factors associated with impairment of the early development of prematures. Monogr. Soc. Res. Child Dev. 31 (Whole No. 106).

Broman, S. H., P. L. Nichols, and W. A. Kennedy. 1975. Preschool IQ: Prenatal and Early Developmental Correlates. Laurence Erlbaum Assoc., Hillsdale, New Jersey.

Bronfenbrenner, U. 1968. Early deprivation: A cross species analysis. *In* S. Levine and G. Newton (eds.), Early Experience in Behavior, pp. 627–764. Charles C Thomas, Springfield, Ill.

Bronfenbrenner, U. 1974. Is Early Intervention Effective? A Report on Longitudinal Evaluations of Preschool Programs, Vol. II. Department of Health, Education, and Welfare, Office of Human Development, Office of Child Development, Children's Bureau. Department of Health, Education, and Welfare Publication Number (OHD) 76-30025. U.S. Government Printing Office, Washington, D.C.

Buchwald, J. S. 1975. Brainstem substrates of sensory information processing and adaptive behavior. *In* N. A. Buchwald and M. A. B. Brazier (eds.), Brain Mechanisms in Mental Retardation, pp. 315–333. Academic Press, New York.

Burt, R. A. 1975. Judicial action to aid the retarded. *In* N. Hobbs (ed.), Issues in the Classification of Children, Vol. II, pp. 293–318. Josey-Bass, San Francisco.

Cattell, P. 1940. The Measurement of Intelligence of Infants and Young Children. Psychological Corporation, New York.

Child Find. 1975. Proceedings from a conference sponsored by the National Coordinating Office for Regional Resource Centers and National Association of State Directors of Special Education, Washington, D.C., March 26–27, 1975. UIS Publication 177.

Denenberg, V. H. 1964. Critical periods, stimulus input, and emotional reactivity: A theory of infantile stimulation. Psych. Rev. 71: 335–351.

Doll, E. A. 1941. The essentials of an inclusive concept of mental deficiency. Amer. J. Ment. Defic. 46: 214–219.

Doll, E. A. 1947. Feeble-mindedness versus intellectual retardation. Amer. J. Ment. Defic. 51: 456–459.

Filler, J. W., Jr., C. C. Robinson, R. A. Smith, L. F. Vincent-Smith, D. D. Bricker, and W. A. Bricker. 1975. Mental retardation. In N. H. Hobbs (ed.), Issues in the Classification of Children, pp. 194–238. Josey-Bass, Inc., San Francisco.

Goldman, P. S. 1969. The relationship between amount of stimulation in infancy and subsequent emotionality. Ann. N.Y. Acad. Sci. 159: 640–650.

Goldman, P. S. 1972. Developmentl determinants of cortical plasticity. Acta Neurobiol. Exper. 32: 495–511.

Goldman, P. S. 1975. Age, sex, and experience as related to the neural basis of cognitive development. In N. A. Buchwald and M. A. B. Brazier (eds.), Brain Mechanisms in Mental Retardation, pp. 379–392. Academic Press, New York.

Gottfried, A. W. 1973. Intellectual consequences of perinatal anoxia. Psych. Bull. 80: 231–242.

Gray, S. W., and R. A. Klaus. 1965. Experimental preschool program for culturally-deprived children. Child Dev. 36: 887–898.

Gray, S. W., and R. A. Klaus. 1970. The early training project: The seventh-year report. Child Dev. 41: 909–924.

Grossman, H. J. 1973. Manual on Terminology and Classification in Mental Retardation. American Association on Mental Deficiency, Washington, D.C.

Heber, R., H. Garber, S. Harrington, and C. Hoffman. 1972. Rehabilitation of Families at Risk for Mental Retardation. Progress Report, SRA, Department of Health, Education, and Welfare, U.S. Government Printing Office, Washington, D.C.

Herzog, E., C. H. Newcomb, and I. H. Cesen. 1972. But some are poorer than others: SES differences in a preschool program. Amer. J. Orthopsych. 42: 4–22.

Hilgard, J. R. 1932. Learning and maturation in preschool children. J. Genet. Psych. 41: 36–56.

Hodges, W. W., B. R. McCandless, and H. H. Specker. 1967. The Development and Evaluation of a Diagnostically Based Curriculum for Preschool Psychosocially Deprived Children. U.S. Office of Education, Washington, D.C.

Hunt, J. McV. 1961. Intelligence and Experience. Ronald Press, New York.

Karnes, M. B., and E. E. Badger. 1969. Training mothers to instruct their infants at home. In M. B. Karnes (ed.), Research and Development Program on Preschool Disadvantaged Children: Final Report, pp. 249–263. U.S. Office of Education. Washington, D.C.

Karnes, M. B., A. S. Hodgins, and J. A. Teska. 1969. The impact of at-home instruction by mothers on performance in the ameliorative preschool. In M. B. Karnes (ed.), Research and Development Program on Preschool Disadvantaged Children: Final Report, pp. 205–212. U.S. Office of Education, Washington, D.C.

Kerr, F. W. L. 1965. Structural and functional evidence of plasticity in the central nervous system. Exper. Neurol. 48: 16–31.

Kirk, S. A. 1958. Early Education of the Mentally Retarded. University of Illinois Press, Urbana.

Kirk, S. A. 1969. The effects of early education with disadvantaged infants. In M. B. Karnes (ed.), Research and Development Program on Preschool Disadvantaged Children: Final Report. U.S. Office of Education, Washington, D.C.

Kirp, D. L., P. F. Kuriloff, and W. G. Bass. 1975. Legal mandates and organizational change. In N. Hobbs (ed.), Issues in the Classification of Children, Vol. II, pp. 319–382. Josey-Bass, Inc., San Francisco.

Knobloch, H., and B. Pasamanick. 1960. Environmental factors affecting human development before and after birth. Pediatrics 26: 210–218.

Levenstein, P. 1970. Cognitive growth in preschoolers through verbal interaction with mothers. Amer. J. Orthopsych. 40: 426–432.

Levenstein, P. 1972. But does it work in homes away from home? Theory into Practice 11: 157–162.

Lloyd, L. L., and M. J. Reid. 1967. The incidence of hearing impairment in an institutionalized mentally retarded population. Amer. J. Ment. Defic. 71: 746–763.

McGraw, M. B. 1939. Later development of children specially trained during infancy. Child Dev. 10: 1–19.

Miller, L. B., and J. L. Dyer. 1975. Four Preschool Programs: Their Dimensions and Effects. Monogr. Soc. Res. Child Dev. 40: Nos. 5 and 6 (Serial No. 162).

Montessori, M. 1964. The Montessori Method. Schocken, New York.

Neman, R., P. Roos, B. M. McCann, F. J. Menolascino, and L. W. Heal. 1975. Experimental evaluation of sensorimotor patterning used with mentally retarded children. Amer. J. Ment. Defic. 79: 372–384.

Newton, G., and S. Levine. 1968. Early Experience and Behavior. C. C. Thomas, Springfield, Ill.

Rainbow Series, Project Head Start. 1965. Office of Economic Opportunity, Washington, D.C.

Rosenzweig, M. R. 1971. Effects of environment in development of brain and behavior. In E. Toback (ed.), Biopsychology of Development, pp. 303–342. Academic Press, New York.

Scarr-Salapatek, S., and M. Williams. 1973. The effects of early stimulation on low-birth-weight infants. Child Dev. 44: 94–101.

Schaefer, E. S. 1968. Progress report: Intellectual stimulation of culturally deprived parents. National Institute of Mental Health, Rockville, Md.

Schaefer, E. S., and M. Aaronson, 1972. Infant Education Research Project: Implementation and implications of the home tutoring program. In R. K. Parker (ed.), The Preschool in Action, pp. 410–436. Allyn and Bacon, Boston.

Shearer, M., and D. Shearer. 1972. The Portage Project: A model for early childhood education. Except. Child. 36: 210–217.

Siqueland, E. 1969. Further developments in infant learning. In Symposium in Learning Processes of Human Infants, XIXth International Congress of Psychology, London.

Van Doorninck, W. 1975. Early and periodic screening, diagnosis, and treatment program. In Child Find. Proceedings from a conference sponsored by the National Coordinating Office for Regional Resource Centers and National Association of State Directors of Special Education, pp. 49–52. Washington, D.C., March 26–27, 1975. UIS Publication 177.

Weikart, D. P., et al. 1970. Longitudinal results of the Ypsilanti Perry Preschool Project, Ypsilanti, Michigan. High/Scope Educational Research Foundation, Ypsilanti.

Werner, E., K. Simonian, J. M. Bierman, and F. E. French. 1968. Cumulative effect of perinatal complications and deprived environment on physical, intellectual, and social development of preschool children. Pediatrics 39: 490–505.

Winkler, P. 1975. Project Child: A special education early childhood identification project. In Child Find. Proceedings from a conference sponsored by the National Coordinating Office for Regional Resource Centers and National Association of State Directors of Special Education, pp. 10–14. Washington, D.C., March 26–27, 1975. UIS Publication 177.

Zeaman, D. 1975. Comments: The strategies of studying early development in relation to intelligence. *In* N. R. Ellis (eds.), Aberrant Development in Infancy: Human and Animal Studies, pp. 263–267. Laurence Erlbaum Assoc., Hillsdale, New Jersey.

Zigler, E., and V. Seitz. 1975. On "An experimental evaluation of sensorimotor patterning": A Critique. Amer. J. Ment. Defic. 79: 483–492.

RESEARCH

Recovery(?) from Early Brain Damage

Robert L. Isaacson, Ph.D.

There can be no doubt that there is "recovery" from brain damage which occurs at any age. The body, and all of its tissues and organs, has the capacity to resist stresses and to minimize the effects of damage. The brain is no exception. In fact, it probably has the greatest insulation from possible dangers both of the external world, because it is encased by thick bone, and from the internal world, by the blood-brain barrier. But what about the brain's restorative powers? In one way, it is more limited than most other organs. Nerve cells are of fixed quantity. They are formed once during development and must last for a life time. If some are destroyed, no new cells can be produced to take their place. Therefore, recovery after brain damage must be explained on some basis other than the generation of new cells to replace those that have been lost. Yet, behavioral, functional recovery is an easily observable phenomenon, occurring in both children and adults. The question here is not whether the brain of the child recovers from damage, but whether the recovery from damage occurring early in life is greater or more complete than that occurring after damage later in life. The answer goes well beyond a simple "yes" or "no," and will lead to quite general issues pertaining to the nature and causes of behavioral changes following brain damage at different ages.

The consequences of brain damage can only be understood in the context of the many changes that follow any insult to the brain. Understanding these changes, and the differences found in them when the damage occurs at various ages, may provide some insight into "recovery."

PHYSIOLOGICAL AND ANATOMICAL CONSEQUENCES OF BRAIN DAMAGE

Any damage to the brain causes a variety of reactions that go far beyond the actual destruction of nerve cells. The precise nature of these reactions depends upon the way in

---

The studies performed in the author's laboratory on the effects of early brain damage have been supported by grant NSF-GB-17354 from the National Science Foundation.

which the lesion is made, the age of the person at the time of the damage, and other constitutional and environmental factors. The reactions include:

1. The actual destruction of cells at the location of the damage

2. The disruption of neural activity in nearby regions as a result of the physical or metabolic disruptions produced by the primary insult

3. Astrocytic reactions at the border of the lesion (and sometimes well beyond)

4. Phagocytosis and invasion by microglia

5. Proliferation of blood vessels in a wide area around the lesion

6. The development of "irritative" reactions at the edge of the lesion

7. Edema

8. The disruption of activity in nearby tissues as a result of the pressure exerted by enclosed areas of bleeding (hematomas)

9. Changes in the cerebrospinal fluid, including pressure, composition, and pollution with blood or infectious agents

10. The creation of hyperexcitable cells in areas to which the damaged regions no longer send nerve impulses (denervation supersensitivity)

11. The creation of neural areas that exhibit a *transient* form of denervation supersensitivity as a result of the decreased input from brain regions whose own activity has been temporarily suppressed because of pressure, the interruption of blood supplies, or other transient factors

12. Retrograde changes in cells whose axons were destroyed by the lesion. Reactions around these degenerating cells include gliosis, phagocytosis, and all of the other responses to degenerating nerve cells

13. Anterograde changes produced upon neurons normally reached by processes from the damaged cells. These indirect effects may result from the loss of neural input or the loss of trophic influences

14. The proliferation of newly formed axon collaterals (sprouts) into cellular regions that had been supplied by fibers from the damaged regions

15. The formation of aberrant fiber tracts (if the damage occurs in infancy)

16. Widespread changes that affect the size and cellular composition of the brain (if the damage occurs in infancy)

Effects of a Transient Nature

Many of the effects of brain damage are of a transient nature. As new blood supplies become established, as hematomas are absorbed, as edema is reduced, areas whose activities had been disrupted may return to near normal acitivities. As a result, the behavioral contributions made by these regions will be restored and a corresponding recovery may be observed. This restoration of activity in temporarily suppressed regions is a natural consequence of changes occurring after brain damage. Different types of changes require different amounts of time. Therefore, progressive changes in behavior after brain damage are to be expected. The restoration of some behavioral capacities that were lost immediately after damage is a natural occurrence; the number and severity of symptoms should decrease over time. This reduction should continue until the transient reactions to the damage have abated or become stabilized. However, some of the reactions may lead to permanent structural and functional changes.

A myriad of changes go on in the brain after damage, and some of them are ephemeral. Some of the physical changes that signal the beginning of physical recovery, or at least the reduction of the original defensive reactions of the brain, include: the reduction of hypertrophied astrocytes, the cessation of the formation of astrocytic processes, the reduction of edema, the restoration of adequate blood supplies by the formation of new blood vessels, and the restoration of normal cerebrospinal fluid pressure and composition. All of these physical changes may produce alterations in the mental and behavioral capacities of the person. At the present time it is not known which of the many physical changes are most important for behavioral changes, but it is likely that all of them play some role in modifying the actions of the person.

Permanent Changes of a Secondary Nature

Many of the changes produced result in permanent alterations in brain structure. These include some portions of the astrocytic response, proliferation of blood vessels, the development of irritative reactions, death of nerve cells resulting from losses of blood supply, supersensitivity, retrograde changes or anterograde changes in other areas, sprouting, the formation of new nerve tracts, and general changes in brain composition. Some of these secondary and permanent alterations of special concern to this author's own research will be considered in detail.

Sprouting Sprouting refers to the proliferation of axon collaterals into areas deprived to some degree of their normal synaptic input. In essence, sprouting refers to the invasion of an area by newly formed axon collaterals that make contact with neurons whose normal input has been reduced. This process begins shortly after the damage and continues for days or weeks.

The result of sprouting is that cells in a particular area come to have a new and abnormal pattern of synaptic input. For example, if the cells of a target region normally receive one third of their input from each of three different sources (call them regions and sources A, B, and C), then immediately after the destruction of region A there will be a 33 percent reduction of total input. In addition, the cells in the target area will be entirely controlled by the remaining sources, i.e., B and C. At this time, each source would contribute equally (one half) to the regulating input to the target area cells. Now suppose axons from source B begin to sprout (and those from C do not) and suppose they occupy all of the synaptic sites formerly used by source A. This would mean that source B has its original 33 percent of the synapses and, in addition, has captured the 33 percent originally belonging to source A. B will have come to control 66 percent of the synapses in the target area.

Therefore, after the lesion there will be a time in which B and C exert equally effective regulatory influences on the target area, but, later, B will come to exert a preponderant influence because of sprouting. At this time the neural systems of the lesioned animal will be abnormal not only because of the loss of input from source A but because of the greater-than-normal influence of source B. This means that as many of the transient effects of the damage are decreasing, new effects of a permanent nature may be developing.

Several empirical questions need to be asked about the effects of sprouting of nerve fibers in response to brain damage. The simplest and most important pertains to whether or not it is "good" or "bad." Does the occurrence of sprouting help to reduce the functional consequences of the brain damage or does it aggravate them? It could help by adding new functional synapses to replace those that have been lost. Perhaps these new synapses could help reduce denervation supersensitivity and/or provide some general trophic influences. However, it could be a hinderance by the creation of abnormal regulatory influences upon the remaining systems. It is possible, of course, that sprouting after some forms of damage would be beneficial but after other forms it could be harmful. At the present time there is insufficient evidence available to resolve the matter. An answer to this question could be of significance to brain damaged people of all ages, because it is not a phenomenon restricted to the young.

In a dissertation recently completed in this author's laboratory, Baisden (1973) undertook a first step toward resolving some of these issues. The idea behind Baisden's work was to compare the effects of surgically induced brain damage in animals in which the normal sprouting reaction occurred and in animals in which it was prevented. Baisden injected a drug into the region of the brain, temporarily destroying the nerve terminals that sprout to form new collaterals after destruction of a second brain region. He then measured the behavior of animals treated in this way with untreated animals after similar damage to the "second brain region." His results indicated that the treatment to prevent sprouting reduced some, but not all, of the usual consequences of the damage.

Abnormal Major Fiber Tracts   Major structural changes that occur after brain damage seem to be confined to animals sustaining damage at early ages. This includes the formation of abnormal, sometimes peculiar, fiber connections of the brain. Some of these malformations of neocortical and limbic system fiber pathways were shown in reports from this author's laboratory (Isaacson, Nonneman, and Schmaltz, 1968; Isaacson and Nonneman, 1973). In some cases fiber pathways of limbic system come to be diverted into neocortical white matter, as shown in Figure 1. The large bundles of fibers seen to turn into the subcortical white matter in this photomicrograph normally would continue inside the neocortex and make connections with other limbic system structures farther forward in the brain. After early damage, these fibers become diverted into regions where they normally would not go. Their normal appearance indicates that these fibers have established effective contacts with cells in brain regions other than those with which contact would be established. The aberrant tracts indicate that it is possible for nerve fibers in the infant brain to accept unusual sites of termination. This greater flexibility in "acceptable terminals" in the infant brain is another source of abnormal neural activity after brain damage. It differs from sprouting in that its effects are more massive (e.g., the course of large fiber systems is diverted).

Some of the aberrant fiber tracts that develop as a consequence of early damage may be useful to the animal. For example, Hicks and D'Amato (1970) found that an

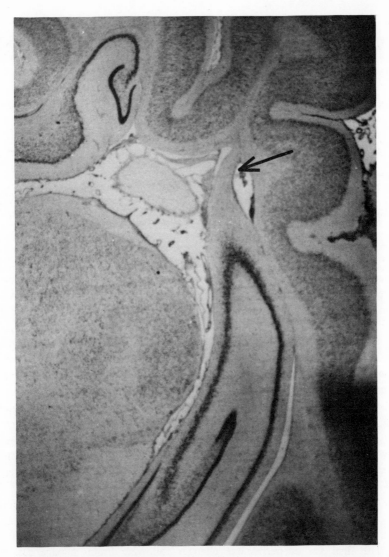

Figure 1. An illustration of abnormal growth of neural fibers from hippocampus into the white matter underneath neocortex in adult cat brain resulting from a neonatal lesion of brain. (Reproduced with permission from Isaacson, Nonneman, and Schmaltz, 1968.)

uncrossed corticospinal pathway develops in the rat after the removal, just after birth, of one hemisphere. This does not develop if the hemisphere is removed a week or two later. This might be related to the somewhat better walking abilities of the animals with damage inflicted just after birth relative to those with later damage.

Studying the visual system, Lund, Cunningham, and Lund (1973) found a similar result. The removal of an eye in newborn rats produced an increased number of fibers from the remaining eye to ipsilateral subcortical structures, in particular the lateral geniculate nucleus and the superior colliculi. The development of these abnormal fibers only occurred in the new born and was not found in animals with eyes removed at 10 days of age or older.

These studies show that the possibility of neuronal growth in the infant is remarkable. They suggest, but do not establish, that the "aberrant" growth of tracts are the bases of some behavioral benefits produced by lesions early in life. It is difficult to see how the abnormal limbic system tracts could improve the capabilities of the person.

Widespread Changes of the Brain Another major change in structure that is only found after brain damage in the neonatal period is a generalized reduction in brain size. This occurs even with relatively small amounts of brain damage restricted to the neocortex. This general hemispheric reduction was first noticed in cats receiving neo-cortical or hippocampal damage as neonates (Isaacson et al., 1968), and Nonneman (1970) made careful measurement of it in rabbits in his thesis.

The general reduction in tissue extends through the entire neocortex above the rhinal fissure, and there are related reductions in neural tissue in the thalamus and brain stem. The reduction amounts to about 20 percent of the volume of the neocortex. In the rabbit it only occurs if the surgical damage is produced in the first 10 days of life. After that only a small volume reduction occurs just at the site of damage.

If the damage occurs on one side of the brain, the reduction of the hemisphere is restricted to that side when it is measured later in adulthood. The reductions of thalamus and brain stem also are only found ipsilateral to the lesion. Illustrations of the reductions in the size of the brain found in adult cats and rabbits after a small amount of unilateral brain damage occurred in infancy are provided in Figures 2, 3, and 4.

The permanent consequences of brain damage must be considered to be the result of all of the permanent changes produced by the lesion. These include the direct effects produced by the destruction of cells at the site of damage *and* all of the permanent secondary changes as well. Because the general reduction of brain size is found only after brain damage in infancy and because it is often accompanied by the formation of abnormal tracts and abnormal configurations of neural cells, it seems that from a structural point of view early damage must be considered to be *more* disastrous than damage occurring later. In the adult, or even the juvenile, results of surgical damage are more localized, aberrant tracts are not formed, and the overall brain volume is not reduced. The final set of permanent changes following brain damage can only be approximated by allowing long recovery periods, although for some lesion-induced changes an infinite amount of time might be needed. This means that it is almost impossible to determine the isolated effect of destruction of one region of the brain; behavior after damage is a result of both direct and indirect changes.

ESTIMATING THE EFFECTS OF BRAIN DAMAGE

The importance of an accurate and consistent estimate of the deficits produced by brain damage is easily demonstrated. Without such an estimate it is impossible to determine if

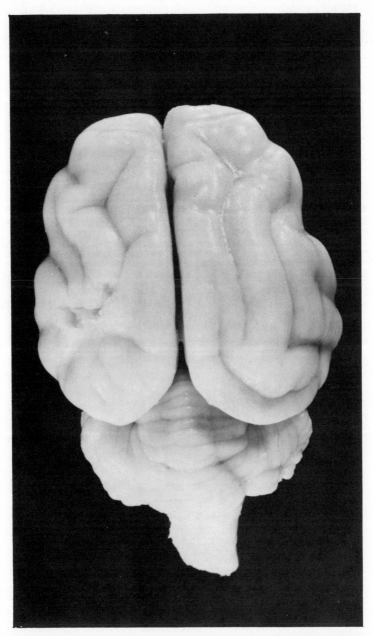

Figure 2. Dorsal view of adult cat brain that had sustained a lesion of the left (right side of brain in figure) hemisphere during the first week of life. Note the marked reduction in the size of the damaged hemisphere. (Reproduced with permission from Isaacson and Nonneman, 1972.)

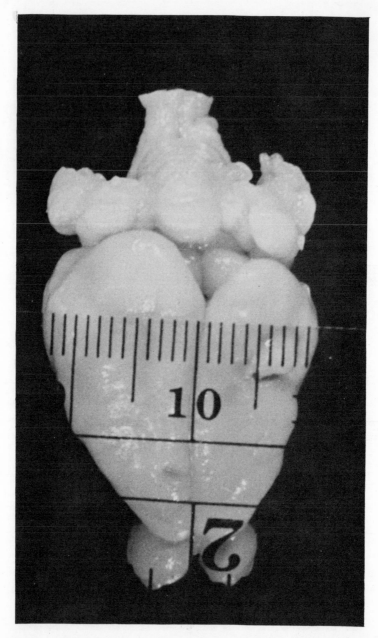

Figure 3. Brain of a month old rabbit that sustained damage to the left hemisphere (left side of figure) during the first week of life. Again note the reduction in the size of the damaged hemisphere. (Reproduced with permission from Nonneman, 1970.)

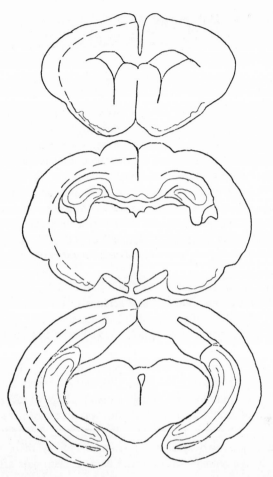

Figure 4. Diagrams of relative differences between the size of damaged and undamaged hemispheres of a 21-day-old rabbit that sustained a small (3 mm in diameter) lesion on the first day after birth. The broken lines indicate the size of the damaged hemisphere. (Reproduced with permission from Nonneman, 1970.)

any "recovery" or "sparing" occurs. If the notion of "recovery of function" after early damage has any meaning beyond those behavioral alterations related to transient second-ary changes, it must refer to a change in the permanent consequences expected to result from a specific type of lesion. If there are procedures or treatments that produce "recovery," such procedures or treatments must be evaluated against the most consistent, long-term consequences of the lesion and not against transitory effects.

The question of "recovery" after lesions early in life must be posed so that the answer is made in terms of behavioral capacities found after similar damage later in life. At this time, therefore, it may be useful to review briefly some of the experimental literature often considered to demonstrate enhanced "recovery" after damage early in life.

Recovery after Damage Made Early in Life

Motor Cortical Lesions About 35 years ago Kennard (1936; 1938) reported that motor cortical lesions occurring early in life produced less impairment of motor abilities and deportment than did lesions sustained at 7 months of age. This report preceded a flurry of other studies that, in general, tended to support the view that lesions made very early in an animal's life were less debilitating than comparable damage later on. These studies by Kennard are somewhat unsettling. There is no doubt but that the animals receiving brain damage at later developmental stages were severely affected and those receiving damage early were far better off. The problem is that the lesions made later in life produced a far greater degree of debilitation than would be expected after destruction of the motor neocortical regions (Bucy, 1966; Lawrence and Kuypers, 1968). It is difficult to believe that the extreme debilitation produced by the brain damage at 7 months of age adequately represents the usual long-term consequences of the neocortical destruction involved. If it does not, the "beneficial" effects of the early lesions may only represent an approximation to the more usual consequences of neocortical destruction made in the mature animal.[1]

Hemispherectomy Hicks and D'Amato (1970) studied the effect of hemispherectomy in infant and mature rats. They found relatively few observable effects of this radical procedure in either the infant- or adult-lesioned animals. One of the few motor effects found after this great amount of damage was a loss of the tactile-placing response on the side opposite to the lesion. This loss occurred regardless of the age of the animal at the time of damage. In the infant-lesioned subjects the placing response was not lost immediately, however. It disappeared about the 17th day after birth. All lesioned animals could perform visual discriminations and gauge jumping distances effectively. About the only change that could be found after adult lesions was an abnormal stride or "gait" of the animals. A correlated observation was that of a structural difference in the brains of the animals lesioned at the two ages. As mentioned before, there was an uncrossed corticospinal system in the animals with surgical damage made just after birth that was usually not found in the rat.

Most important, however, is the demonstration that substantial residual motor and sensory capacities exist after hemispherectomy at both ages. This conclusion is supported by Glassman (1973), who investigated the effects of early (2 to 14 days) and late (5 months) destruction of sensorimotor cortex in cats. The effects of these lesions on placing and hopping reactions were independent of the age of the animal at the time of damage.

Damage to the Visual System Until recently, it was thought that there was some sparing of visual functions in cats after damage to the visual system of kittens that did not occur after similar damage in adults (Doty, 1961). However, according to a more recent report, Doty (1971) now believes that his original results were caused by the fact that certain portions of visual neocortical regions (areas 18 and 19) were not destroyed in the

---

[1] Dr. Karl Pribram has recently informed this author that he looked over the brains of the animals in the Kennard studies and that the animals with lesions made later in life had more damage to subcortical tissues than did those with lesions made in infancy.

kittens. He believes that these areas can subserve visual pattern discriminations in the absence of the primary neocortical projection region (area 17) even with substantial degeneration of the dorsal lateral geniculate nucleus. Relative to "recovery," Doty (1971) now states, ". . . comparison of the effects of removing striate cortex in adult versus neonatal cats does not now encourage the belief that any extensive neural reorganization accrues to the advantage of the neonatal subject."

Recently, Murphy and Stewart (1974) failed to find any beneficial effects of making striate lesions in infancy relative to adulthood on learning a brightness or a pattern discrimination task. This result stands in contrast to the results reported by Steward and Riesen (1972). These latter authors reported that infant-lesioned animals were able to perform well upon a visual cliff, visual placing, and in avoiding obstacles relative to adult-lesioned animals. It is important to note that Stewart and Riesen felt that their adult-lesioned animals could have done these tasks, too. The difference between the infant- and adult-lesioned animals could have been only that the former require no training to do so. This also suggests that the adult-lesioned animals might have been able to perform the task if longer recovery times were allowed even without specific training.

In a series of experiments, Cornwell and his associates (Cornwell, Cornwell, and Overman, 1972; Cornwell and Overman, 1972; Cornwell, Overman, and Nonneman, 1972; Cornwell, Overman, and Ross, 1972; Cornwell et al., 1972) have shown that damage to the visual neocortex in the neonatal period always produces some deficit in visual discrimination performance. Being raised in an enriched environment postoperatively did not improve the performance of the subjects.

Damage to the Subcortical Sites   In a recent study with monkeys, no favorable effect on a delayed response task was observed to follow damage to the caudate nucleus early in life relative to caudate damage made in juvenile monkeys (Goldman and Rosvold, 1972). Kurtz, Rozin, and Teitelbaum (1972) reported that lesions of the ventromedial nuclei of the hypothalamus made at the time of weaning in the rat led to the expected hyper-phagia, even though the onset of the exaggerated eating did not occur for several weeks after the lesion was made. This delayed onset of symptoms is reminiscent of the delayed loss of the placing response found by Hicks and D'Amato (1970) and to the delayed onset of other neurological signs after early brain damage. Lesions in the dorsomedial nucleus of the hypothalamus in the weanling does not protect rats from the usual hypophagia and hypodipsia that normally follow the lesions in adult animals (Bernardis, 1972).

The behavioral consequences of damage to the septal area fail to be reduced by making the lesion early in life. For example, septal lesions made at 7 days after birth in the rat produced enhanced avoidance responding, fixed-ratio responding, and changes in social behavior that were just the same as those following septal area damage in adults (Johnson, 1972). A potential indicator of a benefit derived from the earliness of the lesion, i.e., a greater resistance to extinction after avoidance conditioning, reported previously turned out to be related to the effects of handling the animals (Johnson et al., 1972). In a personal communication, Johnson (1973) has found a similar failure of recovery after early septal lesions on a DRL operant task.

Neocortical Destruction   The vast majority of reports of sparing of recovery of functions after early lesions have come from studies of the effect of neocortical destruction. The conclusions of Tsang (1934; 1936; 1937a; 1937b) to the effect that the earliness of the lesions protects the adult animal from certain consequences of similar damage in adulthood have been accepted, rather uncritically, for many years. However, it now seems that the production of posterior neocortical lesions early in the life of the rat only produces a reduced deficit, relative to lesions made in adulthood, on the acquisition of an 8-cul maze but not upon learning a visual pattern discrimination (Thompson, 1970).

In the past several years there have been a number of studies that seem to indicate that lesions of the prefrontal neocortex of the monkey made early in life produce a greatly reduced behavioral deficit on the delayed response problem (Harlow, Akert, and Schiltz, 1964; Goldman, Rosvold, and Mishkin, 1970; Bowden et al., 1971; Goldman, 1971; Miller, Goldman, and Rosvold, 1973). The evaluation of these studies is made difficult by procedural variables and by the small number of animals used as subjects in most nonhuman primate work. These experiments have been examined in some detail in another report (Isaacson, 1975) and the conclusion is that it is not possible to be sure about any lessened amount of deficit after lesions in infant animals on delayed-response tasks at this time. Regardless of the ultimate resolution of this problem, prefrontal lobe damage early in life does produce its effects on behavior.

Damage to the dorsolateral frontal neocortex of monkeys made at 5 months after birth produces just as great an effect on the learning of an "oddity problem" as lesions made later in life (Thompson et al., 1971). This would indicate that any "recovery" found after early lesions is, at best, "task-dependent" and not a general amelioration of the difficulties.

Franzen and Meyers (1973) found that the effects of early prefrontal lesions on social behavior may not manifest themselves in behavior until the third year of life or later, another example of the delayed onset of the consequences of brain damage.

Recovery of Language Capabilities

The most frequently cited indicator of greater recovery after early versus late brain damage is that of the return of speech. Two types of evidence are involved. The first is of the much greater incidence of "full recovery" from aphasic disturbances after brain damage in children than in adults. The second is the increasing localization of language functions to the left side of the brain with age.

Brain damage can produce language disturbances in both children and in adults. In about one half of the adult patients, recovery takes place with few residual disturbances. The processes underlying recovery take place rather quickly and, if it is to occur, it is often fairly complete about 5 months after the damage. Children with brain damage almost always recover the ability to speak. However, these data do *not* show a greater capacity for greater recovery of a behavioral capacity after early brain damage than after brain damage in maturity, because there is no evidence that the causes of aphasia in childhood and adult life are similar. Furthermore, the differences in symptoms of adult and childhood aphasia are marked. In children the most pronounced language disturbance is an inability to speak. In adults, language disturbances are numerous and varied, but most often are much more than just an inability to speak.

In adults, aphasia most frequently results from occlusion of cerebral blood vessels (stroke), whereas temporary childhood aphasia most frequently follows trauma or seizures. The anatomical areas involved and the secondary processes initiated by these two types of events are probably quite different. In early childhood, damage to either side of the brain can produce temporary disturbances in language. Over the course of development, the situation changes so that damage to the left side of the brain becomes more likely to produce asphasic symptoms and damage to the right side less likely to do so. Where damage to the left side of the brain has occurred early in life, mechanisms of the right side seem to be able to subserve language functions. These observations are compatible with the view that both sides of the brain can subserve language functions early in life. In a few people language does not seem to be localized within the brain's left side, but remains bilaterally represented. In most people, however, language becomes localized to mechanisms of the left hemisphere and this may be due to a suppressive effect of activity in the left hemisphere upon the right (Sperry, 1967). According to this view, the activity in fibers crossing through the corpus callosum prevents the symmetrical representation of language functions in the two hemispheres. This asymmetric storage of information seems to be a characteristic found in some higher primates and in man.

The suppression of language activities in the right hemisphere appears to be a gradual process. The frequency of language related problems after damage to the left hemisphere slowly increases with age. Therefore, if damage occurs to the left hemisphere in childhood before the intercortical suppression is complete, the right hemisphere can exert its own capability to subserve language. Because it has the constitutional capacity to subserve language, this result would not be surprising.

Hebb's Position

In 1942, D. O. Hebb made an important contribution to the study of the effects of brain damage early in the life of the human. He reported data from a variety of sources concerning the intellectual sequelae of brain damage in adults and in children. These conclusions are of far reaching significance.

The first point made by Hebb was that brain damage in the adult most often produces changes in a limited number of characteristics. Many aspects of the person remain unchanged. If the damage to the brain does not involve the left hemisphere speech areas, often no loss of vocabulary or of language capabilities can be detected. Frequently, there is no loss in intelligence as measured by standardized tests. Even extensive removal of neocortical tissues often produces "no obvious mental defects," as was found in a case reported by Rowe (1937) in which a right hemispherectomy was performed. Even extensive bilateral damage can occur without a generalized deterioration of mental abilities. The deficits that are found are of a specific nature. They may be an inability to interpret some aspects of the visual world, difficulties in certain forms of memory, differentiation of abstract phrases and words, disruptions of performance tests demanding speed and accuracy, or other types of specific abilities. The point is that, in the adult, brain damage that does not involve the speech areas often expresses itself in a very limited fashion and many capabilities of the person are not affected at all. Furthermore, scores from tests of general mental abilities may not decline after the brain insult.

When damage to the adult does involve speech areas and produces some form of aphasia, there is again a specialized result. Language abilities are affected but often other forms of behavior are not. Given appropriate conditions of testing, intellectual abilities may also remain unaffected. Unless the speech areas of the brain are damaged, vocabulary is seldom affected and the behavioral deficits are quite limited. If speech areas are involved, the vocabulary may change and there may be other disturbances of language reception or expression, but the overall mental ability of the person may be high and many other skills unaffected.

Brain damage occurring early in life presents quite another picture. Deficits of all sorts of abilities are highly correlated. Performance measures of ability correlate with language abilities, even though the capacity to speak remains. Vocabulary is restricted by brain damage. Furthermore, damage to many portions of the infant brain produce deficiencies in language abilities.

From these observations, Hebb (1942) concluded that an intact and functional cerebrum is of importance for the development of language and other mental abilities but that once language and other cognitive skills have been attained, their retention does not require the intact brain. The greater severity of early brain damage stems from an interference with the ability to develop capabilities dealing with language, problem solving, approaches to problems, and the like. Once these have been established these capacities may function even with damage to a large mass of brain tissue.

The person with early brain damage should be deficient on a wide number of tasks, problems, and abilities because of the need for an intact brain during early learning. It is because of the importance of the integrity of the brain for "early learning" that Hebb (1949) would argue that brain damage early in life is most severe and general.

Task-dependent Recovery

In our work of the past 10 years, recovery after early brain damage has been found on certain behavioral problems. These results have been reported in detail (Isaacson and Nonneman, 1973; Nonneman and Isaacson, 1973).

The notion of task-dependent effects of early brain damage is not new. Teuber and Rudel (1962) pointed out that early brain damage can produce less disabling, equally disabling, or more disabling effects than can later brain damage on different tests of mental function. This would be a test-dependency of early brain damage in humans, comparable to the conclusion that Isaacson and Nonneman have reached at the animal level.

When considering all of the studies that have been considered to demonstrate "sparing" or "recovery" of behavioral abilities after early brain damage, it would seem that the reduced debilitation, if any, is always found in relation to some particular problem, i.e., the behavioral changes are task-specific. Goldstein (1940) had noted a similar phenomenon in testing brain damaged adults: they often failed with some types of tasks under certain conditions, but, under other conditions, they behaved in a normal fashion. Furthermore, not all patients with "similar" brain damage were affected the same way. The question is how this variability in the effects of brain damage can be understood.

Brain Damage Considered to be a Genotypic Change

The consequences of brain damage produced by experimental surgery are not always the same even when comparable damage is inflicted upon similar animals, using identical techniques, in the same laboratory. Often the behavioral differences among lesioned animals cannot be explained on the basis of accidental differences in the size or location of the lesion (Thomas, 1971). The explanation of these different responses to brain damage has to be based upon differences in the animals before surgery.

There can be little doubt that experiences interact with genetic endowments to produce the individual person. They act together to determine the constitution of the individual. From a conceptual view, brain damage can be interpreted as producing a change in this constitution and, in some ways, this change is no different from ones that could have been produced by a different gene structure. Brain damage alters the structure and constitution of the animal or person to produce effects that can gain expression in different ways; both genes and lesions act upon the macro- and micro-structure of the individual. It is upon these structures that behavior is based.

Genes do not govern the development of any structure in any absolute sense. Their effects are always modified by the environment from the time that the egg and sperm are united. In this sense the genes issue invitations for structural development, not commands.

However, even though the interaction of heredity with environment determines structure, the behavior of the individual is not specifiable unless the factors of the immediate environment are also taken into consideration. For convenience it is easier to lapse into less technical language at this point, but it should be remembered that this is only for convenience. It does not indicate that anatomical structures or physiological functions are being neglected.

The reactions of a person in any given situation are determined by 1) a general orientation and 2) specific reactions developed in identical or similar situations in the past. The general orientation and dispositions of a person result over the entire life span. They can be considered as tendencies to be active or passive, aggressive or fearful, optimistic or pessimistic, and include the tendency to approach new situations with certain strategies. They may be considered to include a hierarchy of hypotheses the person has acquired that are used in dealing with the world. Some people treat every new experience with fear and caution, others welcome new experiences and plunge into them with joy. Some mice eagerly explore new environments, others remain immobile in corners of the maze. Some people behave in accordance with the hypothesis that the world is a benevolent place, others think it to be an evil jungle. Some rats approach a new learning problem "believing" that the spatial location of rewards will be important, while others only pay attention to "sign posts" of brightness (Isaacson and Kimble, 1972).

It must also be recognized that each person has many different dispositions. In different people, past experiences in a variety of situations and the conditions of the moment can elicit different general reactions that provide a background for specific reactions. An animal trained in tasks based on the avoidance of pain will approach a new experimental problem more cautiously than one that has not had previous training.

The general dispositions toward behavior are founded in the composition and structure of the brain. At the same time, they are the consequences of a constant interplay among major structural units and systems. There is no "hypothesis center," no "mood region," or any "strategy system." Therefore, because of the ignorance of just how structures interact with each other, one must fall back upon a behavioristic language. In Figures 5 and 6, some of the complexities of the situation are indicated by the contributions of different structures to general behavioral dispositions. The arrows

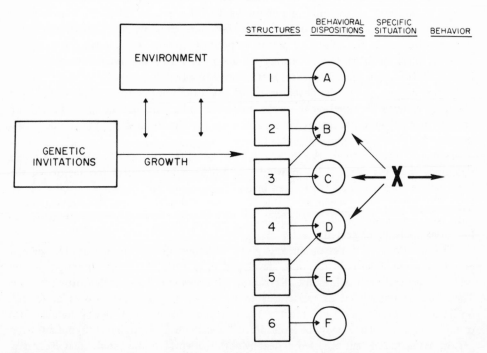

Figure 5. Schematic drawing of the way in which genetic and environmental influences interact to produce a set of structures and "behavioral dispositions" in one individual, designated A. See text for further explanation.

INDIVIDUAL B

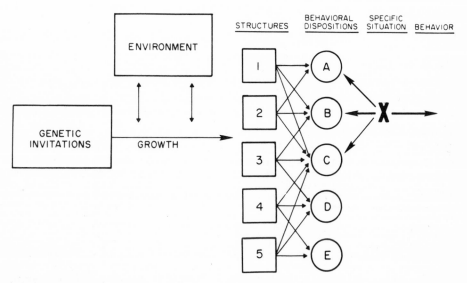

Figure 6. Schematic drawing of developing of structures and "behavioral dispositions" in another individual, designated B.

connecting the squares represent structural units, and the circles represent general behavioral dispositions.

The response of a person in a given situation (represented by the "X" in the drawings) is determined by the relationship of X to the person's past experiences as it affects both the various general dispositions and the specific responses acquired in the same or similar situations in the past. In different persons, the same situation could call out quite different general dispositions and quite different specific responses. A given situation will not have the same relationship to general dispositions in all people. This is shown by the arrows of different thickness connecting the X and the circles.

Note that the two people represented in these figures differ from each other in anatomical systems, behavioral dispositions, and the relationships between them and the specific, immediate environment.

The hypothetical effects of brain damage can bee seen in Figures 7 and 8. Consider blocks three and four to be the damaged regions; also assume that these blocks are more or less similar "major structures" in the two brains. By assuming the completely arbitrary rule that a disposition will be altered if it has a reduction in input from a structural unit and eliminated completely if it has none, the result of the lesion in individual A will eliminate disposition C and alter dispositions B and D. On the other hand, in individual B, elimination of regions three and four will alter dispositions, B, C, D, and E but not

INDIVIDUAL A

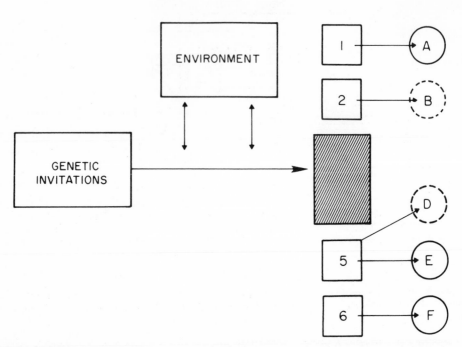

Figure 7. The hypothetical effects of brain damage in individual A. Structural units three and four have been removed, producing a loss of behavioral disposition C and a change in disposition D.

eliminate any. Considering areas three and four in these figures to represent what is commonly called "comparable areas," then the model shows how easily the "same" brain damage can produce such divergent effects in two persons.

This approach can help one to understand the "recovery" seen after brain damage. This is shown in Figure 9. Here, the damage to areas three and four is assumed to have temporarily reduced activity in regions two and five. This results in a much greater effect on the number of behavioral dispositions available to the individual (middle part of figure). As blood supplies are increased, edema is reduced, glia cell reactions change, etc., and regions two and five begin to achieve near normal functions again. As a result, the total effects of the damage are reduced (right hand portion of figure).

The effects of brain damage early in life are also susceptible to analysis along these same lines. The infant has fewer anatomical systems and behavioral dispositions established than does the mature adult. The effect of damage is to produce a loss of some established systems and structures but also to produce abnormal structures that are the special consequences of early brain damage. This is shown in Figure 10. Some of the structures existing in a more or less functional form at the time of the damage can be

INDIVIDUAL B

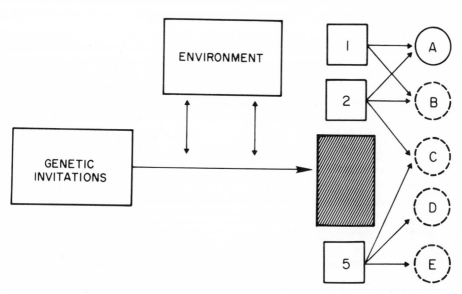

Figure 8. The hypothetical effects of brain damage in individual B. Again, structural units three and four have been destroyed. In this case no behavioral disposition is lost, but all except one have been altered.

influenced, as can some of those that will develop afterward. The structural anomalies induced by the destruction of area two in the infant are shown by the diamond-shaped figures on the right side of the figure. Therefore, the effect of early brain damage is likely to be more complicated and widespread than that found after early brain damage.

The greater variability of behavior found after early brain damage is reflected in a reduction in the likelihood that an animal with a certain type of brain damage will be affected on a particular problem relative to animals with lesions made later in life (Nonneman and Isaacson, 1973). On the other hand, the behavior of an animal with early brain damage is likely to be affected on a larger number of tasks than his adult-lesioned counterpart (Hebb, 1942; 1949).

This type of analysis suggests that the effects produced by brain damage *at any age* should be variable and dependent upon the genetic endowment, developmental history, and the age at which the lesion occurs. Furthermore, it helps one to understand why the effects of brain damage can often only be considered in a probabilistic manner.

Such a description of the behavioral effects of brain damage presents a theoretical problem unless the differences among the animals *before* damage are considered. Individual differences arise from differences in the genetic endowments of the animal as they interact with developmental experiences. For the most part, the animals used in experiments are of a mixed genetic background. The use of inbred strains reduces the variability

INDIVIDUAL A

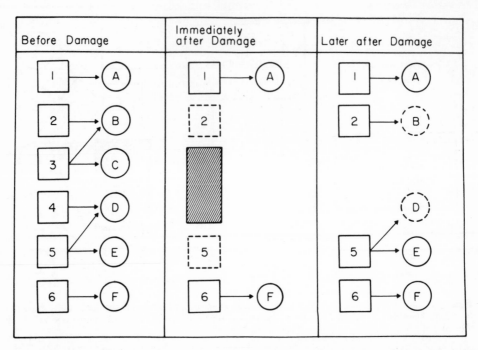

Figure 9. Schematic drawing of the recovery that could be shown after early brain damage. Structural units three and four were lost at the time of damage, units two and five temporarily suppressed because of secondary reactions. This produces a temporary loss of behavioral dispositions B and E. As these secondary reactions subside, activities in units two and five are restored, and behavioral dispositions B and E return.

of behavior in a number of tasks. However, genetic inheritance only involves the events occurring at the time of union of the sperm and the egg. After that, environmental factors make their presence felt. The result is a group of animals with widely different general dispositions toward behavior. Some of these dispositional factors operate so as to make the acquisition of a behavioral task difficult under some conditions but easy under others. It may be that a particular constitutional anomaly might preclude finding a solution to a task at all (Brutkowski, 1959).

The changes in behavioral dispositions in the brain damaged animal will make some tasks easy, others difficult. Yet, the fact is that animals or people with such damage often fail problems that are capable of solution in many different ways and that they should be able to solve. Sometimes they start to solve a problem using an incorrect strategy and fail to change their reactions in order to improve performance. They continue to respond inappropriately while most intact people or animals change to new ways of responding. This perseverative quality of behavior needs to be given additional consideration.

INFANT C

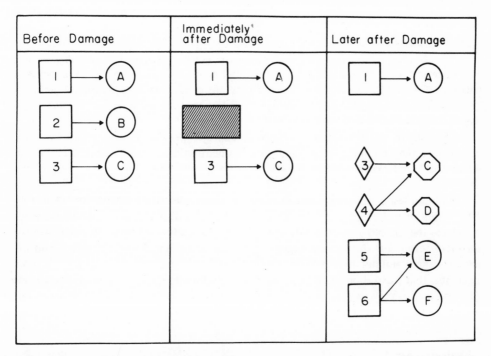

Figure 10. A schematic drawing of the possible effects of brain damage early in life. The smaller number of completed structural units and behavioral dispositions available to the infant are represented in the upper two panels. After damage to structural unit two, the immediate effect is a loss of structural unit B, but this loss also affects the future development of other units, e.g., three and four in the drawing. These abnormal structures are indicated by diamond shaped figures. The abnormal behavioral dispositions that result are indicated by hexagons.

Perseveration after Brain Damage

Part of the constitutional endowments of people and animals include differences in levels of emotionality and the thresholds for frustration. It is a commonplace that both animals and people differ greatly in these reactions. Brain damage may affect these general attributes of behavior as well as any others.

The work of Maier (1949) established that perseverative responding was a hallmark of frustration-instigated behavior. When a problem becomes insoluble, the animal responds in a perseverative manner without regard to the attainment of rewards. According to Maier's work, if a frustration reaction occurs, it does so in all-or-none fashion. It is a "threshold" phenomenon.

If the reactions of an animal to frustration-inducing circumstances are determined by a threshold being exceeded, then behavioral anomalies based upon frustration should be of an all-or-none quality. This all-or-none quality of reactions of brain damaged animals has been found in animals with lesions made in infancy and adulthood. All-or-none effects have also been found in the behavior of retarded people working on a delayed response problem (Isaacson and Perkins, 1973). Very often, there is a complete absence of graded effects. For example, in the report of Nonneman and Isaacson (1973) animals with neonatal destruction of the hippocampus either had starting latencies in a passive avoidance task of less than 1.3 second or beyond 20 seconds. *No* animals had latencies in between. This reinforces the view that the presence or absence of a behavioral deficit is determined by the emotional constitution of the animals, as modified by the brain damage, as it interacts with past and present experiences.

According to this hypothesis, many brain damaged persons perform poorly on tasks, not because they are incapable of doing so, but because they began the problem "on the wrong foot" and experienced non-reward. Frustration-instigated perseverative responding developed.

If a brain lesion alters an animal's ability to tolerate frustrating conditions (Isaacson, 1975), this change could interact with other behavioral dispositions related to the ways in which the animal is motivated, the value of incentives provided, the penalties for incorrect responses, the relative degree of success and failure early in training, and the animal's entire training history. The more intense the circumstances of training, the more likely it is that frustration-based behavior will be exhibited if failure occurs. Because some of these factors may vary from day to day or from moment to moment, whether or not an impairment is found may not be easily predicted.

CONCLUSIONS

When this research was begun in the mid-1960s on the effects of early brain damage, the premise was that it was possible to show recovery or sparing of functions if the brain damage were made early enough in life. Furthermore, it was felt that the behavioral recovery was associated with a decreased amount of structural abnormality (Isaacson, Nonneman, and Schmaltz, 1968). It has taken a long time for these views to change completely. Now, it seems clear that damage to the infant brain produces greater anomalies in structure and behavior than are found after damage to the brain of the mature or juvenile animals.

Whatever recovery does occur after brain damage seems to reflect only those natural processes related to the great number of changes of direct and indirect nature occurring after the damage. These processes are not mysterious. Indeed, many have been well studied by neuropathologists and anatomists. They require no explanation based upon the ability of one area of the brain to take over the functions of another. There is no need to appeal to a concept of vicarious function to understand the consequences of such damage.

The variability of behavior after brain damage in an adult or an infant is understandable once the absurd view is given up that the structure of each and every brain is identical. By accepting the obvious differences among people because of their genetic and environmental backgrounds, it is possible to anticipate and to accept the wide diversities of behavioral alterations found after the damage. The suggestion to consider brain damage effects as if they were genetic effects was made to stress the difference between structural damage (genotypic alteration) and its phenotypic consequences.

Even though this approach stresses the permanent sequelae of brain damage, it is by no means a pessimistic approach. Instead, it should help to focus attention on methods that could limit or decrease secondary, indirect effects of brain damage and to find new ways in which the residual capacities of the person can be utilized.

ACKNOWLEDGMENT

Acknowledgments are due to the following colleagues for their helpful comments on a preliminary version of this manuscript: Dr. Carol Van Hartesveldt, Dr. F. A. King, Dr. S. J. Jourard, and Ms. Linda Lanier, as well as to Dr. Kenneth Heilman for information about language disorders in adults and children.

LITERATURE CITED

Baisden, R. 1973. Behavioral effects of hippocampal lesions after adrenergic depletion of the septal area. Unpublished doctoral dissertation, University of Florida.

Bekoff, M., A. Lockwood, and T. H. Meikle, Jr. 1973. Effects of serial lesions in cat visual cortex on a brightness discrimination. Brain Res. 49: 190–193.

Bernardis, L. L. 1972. Hypophagia, hypodipsia, and hypoactivity following dorso-medial hypothalamic lesions. Physiol. Beh. 8: 1161–1164.

Bowden, D. M., P. S. Goldman, H. E. Rosvold, and R. L. Greenstreet. 1971. Free behavior of rhesus monkeys following lesions of the dorsolateral and orbital prefrontal cortex in infancy. Exper. Brain Res. 12: 265–274.

Bucy, P. C. 1966. The delusion of the obvious. Perspect. Biol. Med. 9: 358–368.

Butters, N., C. Butter, J. Rosen, and D. Stein. 1973. Behavioral effects of sequential and one-stage ablations of orbital prefrontal cortex in the monkey. Exper. Neurol. 39: 204–214.

Butters, N., D. Pandya, D. Stein, and J. Rosen. 1972. A search for the spatial engram within the frontal lobes of monkeys. Acta Biol. Exp. 32: 305–330.

Brutkowski, S. 1959. The solution of a difficult inhibitory task (alternation) by normal and prefrontal dogs. Acta Biol. Exp. 19: 301–312.

Cornwell, P., G. Cornwell, and W. Overman. 1972. Effects of unilateral and bilateral striate lesions in neonatal kittens on visual discrimination. Unpublished manuscript.

Cornwell, P., and W. Overman. 1972. Effects of early rearing conditions and neonatal striate lesions on visually guided behavior in kittens. Unpublished manuscript.

Cornwell, P., W. Overman, and A. Nonneman. 1972. Photically evoked activity in extrastriate cortex after striate lesions. Unpublished manuscript.

Cornwell, P., W. Overman, and C. Ross. 1972. Deficits in visually guided behavior in cats after neonatal lesions. Unpublished manuscript.

Cornwell, P., C. Ross, W. Overman, and K. Levitsky. 1972. Effects of lesions of the visual cortex on performance on the visual cliff. Unpublished manuscript.

Dawson, R. G., L. Conrad, and G. Lynch. 1973. Single and two-stage hippocampal lesions: A similar syndrome. Exper. Neurol. 40: 263–277.

Doty, R. W. 1961. Functional significance of the topographical aspects of the retino-cortical projection. *In* R. Jung and H. Kornhuber (eds.), The Visual System: Neurophysiology and Psychophysics, pp. 228–245. Springer-Verlag, Heidelberg, Germany.

Doty, R. W. 1971. Survival of pattern vision after removal of striate cortex in the adult cat. J. Comp. Neurol. 143: 341–369.

Finger, S., R. A. Marshak, M. Cohen, S. Scheff, R. Trace, and D. Niemand. 1971. Effects of successive and simultaneous lesions of somatosensory cortex on tactile discrimination in the rat. J. Comp. Physiol. Psych. 77: 221–227.

Finger, S., B. Walbran, and D. G. Stein. 1973. Brain damage and behavioral recovery: Serial lesion phenomena. Brain Res. 63: 1–18.

Franzen, E. A., and R. E. Myers. 1973. Age effects on social behavior deficits following prefrontal lesions in monkeys. Brain Res. 54: 277–286.

Glassman, R. B. 1973. Similar effects of infant and adult sensorimotor cortical lesions on cats' posture. Brain Res. 63: 103–110.

Goldman, P. S. 1971. Functional development of the prefrontal cortex in early life and the problem of neuronal plasticity. Exper. Neurol. 32: 366–387.

Goldman, P. S., and H. E. Rosvold. 1972. The effects of selective caudate lesions in infant and juvenile rhesus monkeys. Brain Res. 43: 53–66.

Goldman, P. S., H. E. Rosvold, and M. Mishkin. 1970. Selective sparing of function following prefrontal lobectomy in infant monkeys. Exper. Neurol. 29: 221–226.

Goldstein, K. 1940. Human Nature in the Light of Psychopathology. Harvard University Press, Cambridge, Mass.

Harlow, H. F., K. Akert, and K. A. Schiltz. 1964. The effects of bilateral prefrontal lesions on learned behavior of neonatal, infant, and preadolescent monkeys. *In* J. M. Warren and K. Akert (eds.), The frontal Granular Cortex and Behavior, pp. 126–148. McGraw-Hill, New York.

Hebb, D. O. 1942. The effect of early and late brain injury upon test scores, the nature of normal adult intelligence. Proc. Amer. Phil. Soc. 85: 275–292.

Hebb, D. O. 1949. The Organization of Behavior. Wiley, New York.

Hicks, S. P., and C. J. D'Amato. 1970. Motor-sensory behavior after hemispherectomy in newborn and mature rats. Exper. Neurol. 29: 416–438.

Isaacson, R. L. 1975. The myth of recovery from early brain damage. *In* N. R. Ellis (ed.), Aberrant Development in Infancy: Human and Animal Studies. Lawrence Erlbaum Assoc., Hillsdale, N.J.

Isaacson, R. L. 1974. The Limbic System. Plenum, New York.

Isaacson, R. L., and D. P. Kimble. 1972. Lesions of the limbic system: Their effects upon hypothesis and frustration. Beh. Biol. 7: 767–793.

Isaacson, R. L., and A. J. Nonneman. 1972. Early brain damage and later development. *In* P. Satz and J. J. Ross (eds.), The Disabled Learner. Rotterdam University Press, Rotterdam.

Isaacson, R. L., A. J. Nonneman, and L. W. Schmaltz. 1968. Behavioral and anatomical sequelae of damage to the infant limbic system. *In* R. L. Isaacson (ed.), The Neuropsychology of Development, p. 58. Wiley, New York.

Isaacson, R. L., and M. A. Perkins. 1973. Delayed response performance of mentally retarded patients. Amer. J. Ment. Defic. 77: 737–747.

Johnson, D. A. 1972. Developmental aspects of recovery of function following septal lesions in the infant rat. J. Comp. Physiol. Psych. 78: 331–348.

Johnson, D. A., A. Poplawsky, L. Bieliauskas, and D. Liebert. 1972. Recovery of function on a two-way conditioned avoidance task following septal lesions in infancy: Effects of early handling. Brain Res. 45: 282–287.

Kennard, M. A. 1936. Age and other factors in motor recovery from precentral lesions in monkeys. Amer. J. Physiol. 115: 138–146.

Kennard, M. A. 1938. Reorganization of motor function in the cerebral cortex of monkeys deprived of motor and premotor areas in infancy. J. Neurophys. 1: 477–496.

Kimble, D. P., R. J. Kirkby, and D. G. Stein. 1966. Response perseveration interpretation of passive avoidance deficits in hippocrampectomized rats. J. Comp. Physiol. Psych. 61: 141–143.

Kurtz, R. G., P. Rozin, and P. Teitelbaum. 1972. Ventromedial hypothalamic hyperphagia in the hypophysectomized weaning rat. J. Comp Physiol. Psych. 80: 19–25.

Lawrence, D. G., and H. G. J. M. Kuypers. 1968. The functional organization of the motor system in the monkey. I. The effects of bilateral pyramidal lesions. Brain 91: 1–14.

Lund, R. D., T. J. Cunningham, and J. S. Lund. 1973. Modified optic projections after unilateral eye removal in young rats. Brain Beh. Evol. 8: 51–72.

Maier, N. R. F. 1949. Frustration: The Study of Behavior Without a Goal. McGraw-Hill, New York.

McIntyre, M., and D. G. Stein. 1973. Differential effects of one- vs. two-stage amygdaloid lesions on activity, exploratory, and avoidance behavior in the albino rat. Beh. Biol. 9: 451–465.

Miller, E. A., P. S. Goldman, and H. E. Rosvold. 1973. Delayed recovery of function following orbital prefrontal lesions in infant monkeys. Science 182: 304–306.

Murphy, E. H., and D. L. Stewart. 1974. Effects of neonatal and adult striate lesions on visual discrimination in the rabbit. Exper. Neurol. 42: 89–96.

Nonneman, A. J. 1970. Anatomical and behavioral consequences of early brain damage in the rabbit. Unpublished doctoral dissertation, University of Florida.

Nonneman, A. J., and R. L. Isaacson. 1973. Task dependent recovery after early brain damage. Beh. Biol. 8: 143–172.

Rowe, S. N. 1937. Mental changes following removal of the right cerebral hemisphere for brain tumor. Amer. J. Psych. 94: 605–614.

Schmaltz, L. W., and R. L. Isaacson. 1968. Failure to find savings from spaced two-stage destruction of the hippocampus. Comm. Beh. Biol. 1: 353–359.

Sperry, R. W. 1967. Split-brain approach to learning problems. In G. C. Quarton, T. Melnechuk, and F. O. Schmidt (eds.), The Neurosciences, pp. 714–722. Rockefeller University Press, New York.

Stein, D. G., J. J. Rosen, J. Grasiadei, D. Mishkin, and J. J. Brink. 1969. Central nervous system: Recovery of function. Science 166: 528–530.

Stewart, D. L., and A. H. Riesen. 1972. Adult versus infant brain damage: Behavioral and electrophysiological effects of striatectomy in adult and neonatal rabbits. In G. Newton and A. H. Riesen (eds), Advances in Psychobiology, Vol. 1, pp. 171–211. Wiley, New York.

Teuber, H. L., and R. G. Rudel. 1962. Behavior after cerebral lesions in children and adults. Devel. Med. Child. Neurol. 4: 3.

Thomas, G. J. 1971. Maze retention by rats with hippocampal lesions and with fornicotomies. J. Comp. Physiol. Psych. 75: 41–49.

Thompson, C. I., H. F. Harlow, A. J. Blomquist, and K. A. Schiltz. 1971. Recovery of function following prefrontal lobe damage in rhesus monkeys. Brain Res. 35: 37–48.

Thompson, V. E. 1970. Visual decortication in infancy in rats. J. Comp. Physiol. Psych. 72: 441–451.

Tsang, Y. C. 1934. The functions of the visual areas of the cerebral cortex of the rat in the learning and retention of the maze. I. Comp. Psych. Monogr. 10: 1–56.

Tsang, Y. C. 1936. The functions of the visual areas of the cerebral cortex of the rat in the learning and retention of the maze. II. Comp. Psych. Monogr. 12: 1–41.

Tsang, Y. C. 1937a. Maze learning in rats hemidecorticated in infancy. J. Comp. Psych. 24: 221–254.

Tsang, Y. C. 1937b. Visual sensitivity in rats deprived of visual cortex in infancy. J. Comp. Psych. 24: 225–262.

Early Experience and Plasticity in the Central Nervous System

Morris A. Lipton, M.D.

This conference is devoted to a consideration of the effects of early intervention in both normal and high risk children. For purposes here, high risk children are defined as children who are at risk for normal development as a consequence of genetic, intra-uterine, neonatal, and postnatal hazards. Before birth, interventions are necessarily biological; after birth, they may be psychological and cultural as well. Intervention before birth and during early infancy is usually biological; after that it becomes increasingly psychological and experimental. The classic forms of biological intervention include genetic counseling, ensuring maternal and fetal health during pregnancy and delivery, improving neonatal and postnatal care, and preventing infection and malnutrition during infancy and childhood. Little is known of the "experiences" the fetus encounters, but one may be fairly certain that these are primarily the result of physical and chemical changes in the uterine environment. The psychological experiences of the mother, if they are to have influences on the fetus, must be transduced into physical and chemical terms; and only a little is known about that. Psychological intervention after birth is also a major topic of this conference. It includes the various types of emotional and cognitive stimulation and training that are being used increasingly with infants.

BIOLOGICAL AND PSYCHOLOGICAL INTERVENTION THEORIES

Each type of intervention is based upon its own knowledge and the theories derived from that knowledge. Biological intervention is based upon the information about the normal growth and development of the brain and its vulnerability to vicissitudes. Experimental intervention is based upon those data derived from observation of the behavior of the developing child and from experiments with the effects of psychological and educational interactions with the child.

For the biologist, the anatomy, physiology, and biochemistry of the brain are the primary objects of scrutiny and investigation. On the other hand, many psychologists and educators consider that brain to be a "black box." They can argue quite properly that it is not necessary to know the molecular basis of memory storage and retrieval in order to educate a child. They are concerned with stimuli and responses and with the development and shaping of behavior. They tend to accept the grain as given and biologically immutable, and then work with the child to develop his potential within the limits imposed by his brain. Psychologists and biologists often engage in a type of parallel play. They have different languages, different methods of investigation, and the investigators and practitioners in each discipline require different types of training.

Much useful knowledge has come out of each approach, and this is proper because research in any human problem must go on at several levels of investigation simultaneously. It would be the height of folly to suggest that psychological research stop until the workings of the brain are understood. It is equal folly to state that the contents and function of the "black box" are irrelevant. The demonstration of fundamental metabolic lesions in phenylketonuria, other metabolic illnesses, and their correction by diet, and the discovery and successful treatment of the genetic vitamin dependency illnesses have permitted biologists to offer parents and educators the hope of a child with normal learning potential, even though such a child is genetically defective. It has been learned, in these illnesses, how to prevent the genotype from expressing itself as a phenotype. The development of antipsychotic and antidepressant drugs that work best when combined with simultaneous psychological interventions, and the development of drugs for the minimally brain damaged hyperkinetic child, which renders him more educable, are well known examples of the interactive effects of simultaneous biological and psychological approaches.

NEUROBIOLOGY: A NEW FIELD

It is because of these evident advantages as well as because of the challenges associated with the long standing riddle of the relationship of the brain to the mind and behavior that the new discipline called neurobiology or psychobiology was born. This discipline has an axiom. It is that the brain, as a living organ, is plastic and that it undergoes biological change with experiences that result in learning and memory. The mind-body problem, or the relation of brain to behavior, while the subject of philosophical debate for centuries and of naturalistic experiments since the turn of the century, began to burgeon as an experimental science about a decade ago. Though it is always difficult to pinpoint a definite beginning, this author is inclined to think that it accelerated vastly after another of life's great mysteries, the genetic code, had been solved. Under the flush of this great scientific victory, a large number of the world's best biologists have turned their information, ideas, and technology to the formidable problems of neurobiology.

The field has also attracted those exceptionally bright students who in former days were challenged by subatomic physics or molecular genetics. The scientific literature they have generated is vast, and the field is moving so rapidly that it is impossible to summarize briefly.

What types of problems lie within the province of this new field? They are both basic and applied. The gross and microscopic structure, chemical composition, and function of the many components of the brain is certainly one. The influence of prenatal and postnatal nutrition upon these is an important area of applied research. The structural and functional organization of the neuron and the methods by which neurons communicate with each other is another basic question. The effect of toxic agents and therapeutic drugs on this is the applied corollary. The nature of "plasticity" is a third, and the basic questions here deal with the changes in the nervous system that occur with learning and memory. The applied corollary of this question deals with the mechanisms by which function may be restored after brain tissue injury has occurred. Many more questions may be listed, but a few of these are briefly discussed here.

Oxygen Supply of the Brain

At birth the brain weighs about 350 grams, at maturity its weight has quadrupled to about 1,400 grams. In gross chemical composition it does not differ from most other organs because it contains about the same quantity of protein but more fat and less carbohydrates. The brain is extraordinarily active metabolically. Although the adult brain weighs only 2 percent of the total body, it consumes 20 percent of the oxygen used by the body. The vast majority of this energy seems to be utilized in maintaining itself structurally, for there is no evidence that energy consumption increases with intellectual activity, nor does it drop during sleep. There is also no evidence that oxygen consumption of the brain differs between the bright and the dull person, nor between the sane and the insane person. Diminished oxygen consumption does occur during anesthesia, in some senile dementias, and in some forms of mental retardation associated with genetic errors of metabolic significance.

The previous statements hold true for gross oxygen consumption, which is all that can be measured accurately. It remains possible that measurements of oxygen consumption in local areas might reveal differences in different forms of mental illness or retardation. Furthermore, gross oxygen consumption reveals little of the uses to which the energy is put. It is known that some of it is used in protein synthesis. There is substantial evidence that new protein synthesis is required for the establishment of permanent memory, a prerequisite for learning. It is reasonable to assume that there would be some decrement in those who cannot learn, but this is apparently too small to measure with available techniques. Carbohydrates are the main fuel of the brain. The high energy consumption of the brain and its low carbohydrate content make it especially vulnerable to oxygen deficit or to fluctuations in sugar supplied to it by the blood. Neonatologists monitor these very carefully to avoid irreversible damage.

Microconstituents: Neurotransmitters

Among the macroconstituents there are lipids and proteins that are unique to the brain, but space does not permit discussion of these here. Instead, this discussion will turn to the microconstituents. These include neurotransmitters derived from amino acids in the diet. These are simple compounds chemically, but they are the agents by which neurons communicate with each other. This will be described at greater length when the nature of the neuron is discussed; but at the moment it is sufficient to say that neurons may be classified according to the transmitter that they synthesize and to which they respond. Thus, there are neurons that respond specifically to acetylcholine, noradrenaline, serotonin, and dopamine. Several other putative transmitters, including amino acids and polypeptides, have been suggested, and undoubtedly more will be discovered. Their discovery will not be simple, because the neurotransmitters that are known exist in quantities of the order of a millionth of a gram per gram of brain. The hypothalamic hormones exist in quantities smaller than this by another thousand fold. Hypothalamic hormones are somewhat more chemically complex and consist of three or more amino acids chemically linked in polypeptide chains. Until very recently these hormones were considered to have only one function: to stimulate the pituitary gland. However, new chemical methods sensitive to 10^{-12} grams have revealed that some of them are distributed widely throughout the brain; and psychobiological experiments have shown that in animals they may be directly involved in behaviors such as sex, eating, drinking, and coping. Precisely how these hormones get to different brain regions is not known. They may be synthesized in the hypothalamus and distributed via the circulation, or they may be synthesized by the brain in areas other than the hypothalamus.

Neurons

The basic structure of the brain is the neuron. There are many billions of these cells in the human brain. Intermixed with the neurons are even more small cells called glia. The exact function of these is not known, but in general it is felt that they serve a nutritive role for the specialized and fragile neurons. Recent evidence suggests that they may play an active role in modulating neuronal functions.

Neurons are complete cells with a nucleus and cell body. They are able to perform the many metabolic functions, including protein synthesis, that are necessary for cell survival. They are, however, also highly specialized structurally and functionally for communication with each other and with non-neural tissue. At the cell body end, the cell membrane is not smoothly rounded or squared off as in most cells of the body. Rather, it is vastly branched like a highly complex antenna and, indeed, the branches or dendrites serve to receive signals from other neurons. When such signals are received the highly excitable neuron generates an electrical impulse that passes only in one direction down through the cell body to an axon fiber whose length may vary from a fraction of a millimeter to as much as 15 inches, depending on the nature of the particular neuron. The axon subdivides hundreds or even thousands of times at its terminals. The anatomy of the neuron can perhaps be visualized by considering a single cell that is constructed like a whole tree. The small branches might be considered the dendrites; these coalesce into larger branches, and finally into the trunk (axon). The axon in turn again divides to form the roots and rootlets (terminals). The complexity of the function of a single neuron can be visualized if one considers that it may, through its dendrites, receive signals from a hundred or more other neurons, and can pass them on through its nerve terminals to as many as 5,000 other neurons. Thus, a single neuron is potentially capable of thousands of contacts for communication (synapses) with other neurons. Because there are billions of neurons, the brain has an almost unlimited capacity for receiving and transmitting information. By mechanisms that are also far from being fully understood it has a similar capacity for storing and retrieving information. However it is not established that all visible synapses are necessarily functional. Whether or not they are and under what circumstances they become functional remain important areas for investigation not only because of their intrinsic interest but because of their implications for the restoration of function in the damaged brain.

Neurotransmitter Production and Receptor Sensitivity

Although the passage of a nerve impulse within a nerve is electrical and is the result of a flow of sodium ions, transmission of the impulse across a synapse to a second neuron is largely chemical. When the electrical impulse reaches the nerve terminal it causes the release of quanta of the specialized chemicals called neurotransmitters. These neurotransmitters are made from amino acids by the enzymes of the neuron cell body and are transported down the axon to be stored in tiny vesicles. When a nerve is stimulated and fires electrically they are released through the terminal membrances into the synaptic cleft. At the cleft several things may happen. Some of the molecules may be inactivated and washed away by the blood stream. If some are not used they may be taken up by the neuron that released them and used again. Finally, and most importantly, some molecules traverse the synaptic cleft and react with the dendrite of the second cell. At least five neurotransmitters are known, though likely many more exist. Although not certain, there is evidence that any single neuron reacts with only one specific transmitter. This is because the dendrites of that neuron contain specialized lipoprotein molecules called receptors that appear to act specifically with only one transmitter. There is also reason to believe that the brain also produces chemical modulators which, by altering the sensitivty of the receptor or perhaps the quantity of the transmitter at the receptor site, can affect the threshold at which a neuron fires electrically. Synthetic psychotropic drugs, whether a stimulant such as amphetamine or cocaine, an antidepressant such as the MAO inhibitors or the tricyclics, or an antipsychotic such as the phenothiazines or buyrophenones, all exert their effects through action on the release or inactivation of the neurotransmitters or by alteration of the sensitivity of their receptors. The thyroid hormone increases receptor sensitivity. It is likely that other hormones also act on receptors by either inhibiting or activating them.

It need hardly be necessary to emphasize that both neurons and receptors are not merely components of a complex wiring diagram, but they are living cells capable of metabolic adaptation. Thus, there is an interesting balance between the neuronal capacity to produce neurotransmitters and the sensitivity of the receptors upon which the neurotransmitters act. Through feedback inhibition, if a receptor becomes hypersensitive the neuron will produce less transmitter. Similarly, if receptor sensitivity is diminished by endocrine deficiency or by pharmacological bloackade, the presynaptic neuron will produce more transmitter. Manipulation of the balance between neurotransmitter production and receptor sensitivity is one of the important problems in the development of effective therapeutic agents for neurological and mental illness.

Neurons having a particular transmitter seem to have their cell bodies in fairly localized areas of the primitive evolutionary midbrain, and their axons run in tracts that are not randomly distributed through the brain. Specific neuronal tracts in the phylogenetically old brain are associated with basic vegetative functions like temperature control, sleep, arousal, emotion, and control of heart rate. The neuronal system subserving these functions are immature at birth, and this may account for phenomena like the tremendous ranges of temperature that infants show with illnesss. Recently, central nervous system inadequacy in the control of heart rate has been implicated in the sudden death syndrome of infants. Other neuronal systems found in the neocortex appear to be associated with higher mental functioning, but even these interact with projections of the more primitive systems, so that emotions can influence learning, and thoughts can influence emotion.

Growth and Maturation of the Brain

Growth and maturation of the brain are programmed by genes that coordinate the steps in the brain's development and set limits to its extent and character. Thus, from the embryonic ectodermal neural crest there emerge specialized cells that are destined to become neurons. Simultaneously, the connective tissue and vascular apparatus required for the maintenance of the neurons also emerge. Neurons grow in number by cell division and in size by dendritic proliferation during the embryonic period. Because this is genetically programmed, the rate and extent vary from species to species. The event of birth is merely a step in the continuum of the growth and development of the nervous system. In humans the brain is still quite immature at birth. During gestation, neuroblasts, the precursors of neurons, vigorously increase in number at 15 to 20 weeks. A second burst of proliferation by cell division begins at 25 weeks and continues through the second year after birth. During this period both glia and neurons proliferate. Different portions of the brain complete their capacity to increase cell number at different periods, with the cerebellum being the last. After the number of cells has become fixed the cells change in size by rapidly growing neuronal processes, elaborating dendritic arborizations, forming synapses, and synthesizing the enzymes required for making the chemical neurotransmitters. The maturation process, as well as the process of the laying down of myelin sheaths along the axons of many neurons, accounts for the increase in the mass of the brain from age 2 to 6.

It is evident that neuronal cells are highly specialized for communication and information storage. Inevitably the price of specialization is fragility. Neurons have little capacity for storing energy sources and are highly dependent for fuel upon nutrients supplied via the blood from other organs. When damaged or destroyed, neurons lack the capacity for regeneration characteristic of all other cells in the body. It is know that function may be restored even though the neurons subserving this function are not regenerated. It is possible that there is sufficient redundancy in the number of neurons so that sufficient numbers remain to restore the function. It is also possible that neurons ordinarily having a different function can assume the lost function. It is possible that proliferation of dendrites of existing neurons may permit the establishment of new functional connections. But the mechanisms are only faintly understood.

Nutritional Deprivation and Brain Growth

Studies of the effects of nutritional deprivation on the growth and maturation of the brain have been performed largely in laboratory animals and are relatively sparse in humans. From the animal studies, as well as a few human studies, it appears that nutritional deprivation during the stage of cell division will result in a smaller number of cells, and those which are formed will be small. Nutritional deficiencies later will affect myelinization, arborization, and levels of neuronal transmitter. Experiments with human children cannot ethically be performed, but nutritional deficiencies often occur naturally in underdeveloped and malnourished societies. However, data on psychological consequences of such deprivation, and whether or not they are reversible, are not conclusive. The available data suggest that severe malnutrition during pregnancy and for the first 6 months of life produces irreversible damage. This is manifested behaviorally as a decreased ability to learn. Children malnourished after 2 years of age seem to have damage that is reversible. Workers who have studied this problem in Mexico point out that severe malnutrition is invariably associated with the type of economic and social poverty that results in a simultaneous experiential deprivation. Children are deprived not only of food, but also of smells, sounds, touch, and even visual stimulation. It is difficult, therefore, to attribute the behavioral deficits solely to nutritional deficiencies.

Environmental Pollutants and Brain Growth

The developmental biologist has learned of the susceptibility of the fetal nervous system to environmental pollutants transmitted to it through the mother's placenta. Heavy metals like lead and mercury have been shown to cause serious damage to the nervous system. Chlorinated hydrocarbons can cause prematurity with all of its attendant hazards to the nervous system and elsewhere. The ingestion of certain foods has been shown to lead to an iodine deficiency with associated thyroid deficiency, cretinism, and retarded brain development. Nutritional deficiencies during the period of rapid fetal brain growth can also be damaging. Thus, there is substantial evidence that the fetal brain is especially vulnerable to both environmental toxicity and deficiency. Present technology permits the assessment only of gross damage such as can be seen by neurological examination or by postmortem examination anatomically. There is great need for the development of sophisticated tests for the study of the behavioral effects of intrauterine hazards. Prevention of such damage will, of course, depend not only on the demonstration of danger but also on the appropriate legal and other types of social measures.

Biological Treatment with Drugs

The biological treatment thus far of children with damaged brains is quite limited. Stimulant drugs like ritalin or amphetamine are useful for the treatment of hyperkinetic children with minimal brain damage, but they are subject to side effects, misuse, and abuse. Other drugs that are used were developed for adult illnesses and are used in smaller doses for children. There is reason to suspect that this is not the wisest way to use them. There is much need for additional research with psychotropic drugs on children. Some of this might lead to the development of agents of special utility for children.

Because psychotropic drugs are often used along with psychological techniques such as schooling or special training, it is imperative that more be learned about the effects not only on the undesirable behavior that we hope to eliminate, but also on the alertness, motivation, and learning ability of the child. In adults the available psychotropic drugs, in appropriate dosage, interact favorably with the socialization process; but research on the interaction of biological intervention with psychological intervention in children is badly needed.

EVOLUTIONARY DEVELOPMENT OF THE NERVOUS SYSTEM

If a developing nervous system is not damaged by toxicity or deficiency, it will develop according to a program laid down by the genes for the individual and the species. In primitive organisms, such as snails, the genes permit the development of as few as 50,000 neurons. In man, genes program for many billion neurons. The nervous system of all organisms was developed in evolution to permit the sensing of the inner needs of the organism either for its own survival or for survival of the species through reproduction. The external environment must also be sensed in order to obtain nutrients and to avoid noxious agents. To achieve this, early in evolution a system developed with components that can sense the environment, process the information, and permit appropriate actions like eating, fighting, retreating, or mating. The reflex arc is the simplest nervous system and has only two neurons. The evolutionary advantages of storing information are evident, and learning and memory thus evolved. This involves additional neurons with a capacity to store and retrieve information. At this stage one may speak of the capacity for learning and memory. This capacity is present in the nervous system of the most primitive invertebrates. The unique property of the nervous system that permits this is called plasticity. Individual neurons are plastic because they may elaborate new dendrites and terminals, or they may alter the capacity to synthesize transmitters. Groups of neurons are plastic insofar as new connections may be made.

Plasticity

The term plasticity requires further explanation. In the most primitive animals it may mean only an alteration in the probability of a given response in the interaction of the organism and the environment as a result of experience. In higher species like insects, fish, and birds it allows the inclusion of events responsible for the maturation of a genetically determined species specific fixed action pattern like the pecking behavior of a chick, the mating rituals of fish and birds, and even the complex social behavior of insects. In still higher organisms it permits switching events that allow a given stimulus to produce one or another response depending upon context, as when a dog runs to retrieve a stick that is thrown but cringes when threatened by it. In still higher forms, like humans, it permits the identification of objects through many individual sensory modalities or combinations of them. Thus, a piano may be recognized by sight, sound, touch, or all of them together.

The growth and maturation of the nervous system are regulated by a genetically programmed readout. This readout requires continuous development of the nervous system and provides progressively new potentialities for behavioral response. The environment in which the animal resides after birth determines whether these potentialities will be realized and the exact form it will take. Thus, the genes of the human nervous system create a unique substrate that permits a language repertoire to develop from zero at birth to thousands of words at maturity. But the environment determines how many words will be learned and which of the thousands of known languages the child will actually speak.

Degree and Duration   The degree and duration of plasticity vary with the species and the stage of development. Critical periods for the acquisition or expression of behavior may be very brief or prolonged. They exist whenever the biological substrates of a psychological structure reach an appropriate age and stage of receptivity. At that stage specific environmental experiences are requisites for the development of specific behavioral capacities. If the experiences come too early they are not recognized. If they are not obtained at an appropriate time, that capacity may be lost for life. Thus, a new born chick, if prevented from pecking for 2 days, will starve to death in the midst of a pile of grain. A newly hatched duck exhibits plasticity in his choice of a maternal object and loses it once that object has been found. It will imprint with the first object it encounters and it will follow that object for life, ignoring its own species.

In mammals, critical periods may exist only in the perinatal period or they may be prolonged for many years. Androgens administered perinatally result in permanent differentiation of a male phenotype regardless of the genetic sex specification. When administered a few weeks after birth they have no such effect. The kitten whose eyes are stitched shut from birth for several months remains functionally blind and unable to recognize forms and objects even though it is able to see them.

In many the long duration of plasticity and also the existence of critical periods may be shown in the area of language acquisition. Although language is best learned in early childhood, new language can be learned throughout life. But following puberty it is very difficult to learn the new language without retaining the accent of the original tongue.

Childhood Intervention   These considerations have many implications for childhood intervention. First, the traditional question of how much of a person's behavioral repertoire is determined by the gene and how much by the environment is pointless because during the maturation process genetic expression independent of an environmental context is impossible and environmental elements are assimilated into the central nervous system almost from the moment of conception. That heredity and environment will always interact is assured by the gentically determined plasticity of the nervous system. More pertinent questions deal with the "what" and "when" of the essential environmental ingredients that permit specified behavior to emerge.

Second, it is increasingly clear that learning is not an accumulation of independent habits, but rather it is an integrated elaboration and differentiation of existing behavioral propensities. There is no "tabula rasa" as Locke thought.

Third, critical and optimal periods for learning must exist in man as they do in other species. Much more must be learned about these. Because the relationship between stimulus and response for all types of psychological phenomena follows the shape of an inverted U, care must be taken not to intervene too vigorously or too early. The capacity to cope with an environment that has almost infinite stimuli requires selective attention and the ability to inhibit a response to irrelevant stimuli. It is felt by some that schizophrenia is characterized by an inability to filter out environmental noise appropriately. Care must be used in our enthusiasm not to overdo. On the other hand, we must also learn not to underdo or to do too late. If a genetically determined potential trait is not used as it develops it may be lost.

Finally, the epigentic view of development, held by Piaget, seems to have a sound biological basis. According to this view progression to loftier levels of competence depends upon the child's innate tendency to expand and to differentiate in accordance with environmental contingencies. This occurs by active assimilation of all newly encountered appropriate stimulus-response relationships into the existing cognitive structure. In educational terms the most efficient learning takes place when the material in each lesson is only slightly more complex than can be assimilated into the existing structure. This results in step-wise accommodations known as learning.

Plasticity and Molecular Biology For those who work with high risk children it should be recalled that plasticity has a basis in molecular biology. The plastic properties of the nervous system are not metaphors. Learning involves changes not only in behavior but also in structure, function, and composition of the neuron. It has been shown that sensory input leads to altered electrical activity. This can lead to increased protein biosynthesis and finally to structurally altered brain cells. Although the picture is lacking in detail, changes in electrical activity of areas of the brain associated with responses to specific stimuli have been shown. Changes in the enzyme content of brain cells from animals living in enriched, as contrasted to impoverished, environments have been shown and even changes in the thickness of cortical gray matter and in the structure of individual neurons have been shown to result from experience. A major problem for the neurobiologist in the future will be the development of agents to influence these in a direction that will facilitate learning or recovery from injury.

The solution to this and similar problems mentioned here should permit us to offer sound guidelines for the treatment of the high risk child and to offer to the parent and the educator a person better prepared for education and socialization.

LITERATURE CITED

Nurnberger, J. I. (ed.). 1973. Biological and Environmental Determinants of Early Development. Research Publications of the Association for Research in Nervous and Mental Disease, Vol. 51. Williams and Wilkins Co., Baltimore.

Schmitt, F. O. (ed.). 1970. The Neurosciences Second Study Program. Rockefeller University Press, New York.

Schmitt, F. O., and F. G. Worden (eds.). 1974. The Neurosciences Third Study Program. The MIT Press, Cambridge, Mass.

Discussant's Comments

Dominick P. Purpura, M.D.

Dr. Lipton has summarized the wide range of problems the developmental neurobiologist faces in attempting to specify factors contributing to the normal and abnormal development of brain and behavior in animals. The neurobiologist who strays from the shelter of the experimental laboratory into the clinical problems of human development can be expected to encounter even more complex issues. To begin with, contrary to popular belief there is very little evidence in the literature on human brain development that could permit even the most tentative speculations concerning the relationship between morphophysiological development and the emergence of a particular variety of behavior in the human infant. This should come as no surprise when it is recognized that there has never been a satisfactory study of the morphological development of the human brain from the fifth to sixth month of gestation onwards. Nor for that matter have attempts been made to identify electrophysiological parameters of brain function in the premature infant and to relate these to developmental features of cortical neurons at different developmental stages. Such studies of structure-function relations in the premature infant and full-term neonate must be considered to be of fundamental importance for the understanding of normal developmental processes and the factors capable of significantly altering these in high risk situations.

MORPHOLOGICAL DEVELOPMENT OF NEURONS IN THE CEREBRAL CORTEX

How can the neurobiologist begin to make a contribution to the study of human brain and behavior development? The simplest answer to this question is to begin by studying the morphological development of neurons in the cerebral cortex. Attention to particular features of developmental events of considerable importance from the standpoint of neuronal interaction may provide clues to the nature of aberrant maturational processes associated with behavioral abnormalities. This approach has been followed for a number of years in developmental studies of laboratory animals (Purpura, 1961; 1969; 1972). Application of this approach to studies of the human brain can provide answers to several important questions (Purpura, 1975a).

75

Cortical Dendritic Development

Consider, for example, the question of the time course of dendritic development of cortical neurons (Purpura, 1975a; 1975b). It is now well established that dendrites of cortical neurons provide over 90 percent of the surface area available for synaptic interactions between neurons. However, synapses are not found covering the entire membrane surface of cortical neurons. Rather, there are preferential sites for synaptic interaction. One of the most remarkable observations is that a majority of the synapses concerned with excitatory synaptic events is located on small spine-like protuberances of dendrites. Thus, analysis of the maturational events underlying dendritic differentiation and the appearance of dendritic spines may provide essential information on the probable "synaptic competency" of neurons. Similarly, studies of dendrites and dendritic spine development of cortical neurons in the brains of severely retarded infants and children who succumb for various reasons should permit exploration of the hypothesis that profound developmental and behavioral retardation may have a common pathophysiological substrate at the level of cortical dendrites and dendritic spine synapses (Purpura, 1974).

Influence of Gestational Age

Golgi studies of the brains of mid-gestational fetuses, premature infants, full-term neonates, and infants and children up to 12 years of age have provided a number of tentative answers to questions of cortical dendritic development (Purpura, 1974; 1975a; 1975b). It is evident that different types of cerebral cortex undergo different temporal patterns of dendritic differentiation. In the hippocampus, which has a more primitive cortical organization than the neocortex, pyramidal neurons have acquired well developed apical dendrites by 18 to 20 weeks gestational age (ga) (Figure 1A). Their basilar dendrites are, however, poorly developed until after this period. It is noteworthy that dendritic growth, which is characterized by the appearance of varicosities, filopodia, and dendritic growth cones, is maximal between 18 to 33 weeks ga in the hippocampus. In the motor cortex, dendritic differentiation of pyramidal neurons proceeds somewhat later than 18 to 20 weeks, whereas in the visual cortex dendritic differentiation is later still. In Figure 1 the characteristics of dendritic growth in the largest neurons of the hippocampus are illustrated from 18 to 33 weeks (Figure 1A to D). By the end of this period apical dendrites have acquired most of their spines, but basilar dendrites still exhibit varicosities and growth cones. It is instructive to compare Figure 1D and 1E. Figure 1D is a hippocampal pyramidal neuron from a 33-week-old premature infant who succumbed 1.5 days after delivery. Figure 1E is a pyramidal neuron from the same region of the hippocampus in a 33-week-old infant who was born at 29 weeks ga and survived 4 weeks in an isolet with the usual life support systems. It is evident from the comparison that the neuron from the infant born at 29 weeks ga is more highly differentiated with respect to dendritic branch thickness and dendritic spine characteristics than the neuron from the 33-week-old infant who died after 1.5 days. Examination of another cortical structure in these cases, i.e., the fascia dentata, reveals a similar pattern of relatively advanced

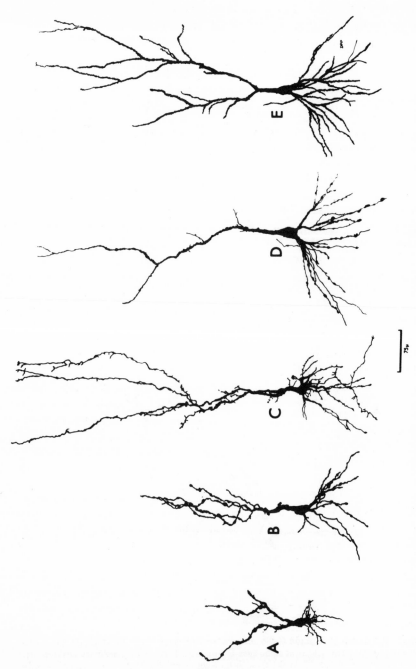

Figure 1. Camera lucida drawings of rapid Golgi preparations of pyramidal neurons of the regio inferior of the hippocampus in the human fetus and premature infant. A, 18 to 20 weeks gestational age (ga); B, 22 weeks ga; C, 24 weeks ga; D, 33 weeks ga; E, 33 weeks ga. Apical and basilar dendrites exhibit characteristic filopodia, growth cones, and varicosities in early phases of dendritic differentiation. Note difference in developmental features of neurons in C and D, in infants of similar ga. Neuron D is from an infant born at 33 weeks ga with a 1.5-day survival. Neuron E is from a 33 weeks ga infant who was born at 29 weeks and survived 4 weeks in an isolet with the usual life support systems. (Reproduced with permission from Purpura, 1975b.)

dendritic development in the premature infant born at the earlier gestational age (Figure 2). It should be pointed out that neurons of the fascia dentata do not simply show increases in dendritic length and spines in the younger premature born, but rather these elements exhibit remarkably different types of dendritic systems of extraordinary expanse as shown in Figure 2F. To this author's knowledge dendritic systems of the type illustrated in Figure 2F have not been observed previously.

One of the obvious questions to be considered in an attempt to define the basis for the markedly different developmental features of cortical neurons in the two infants of similar ga is whether the apparent "accelerated" maturational features of dendrites in the

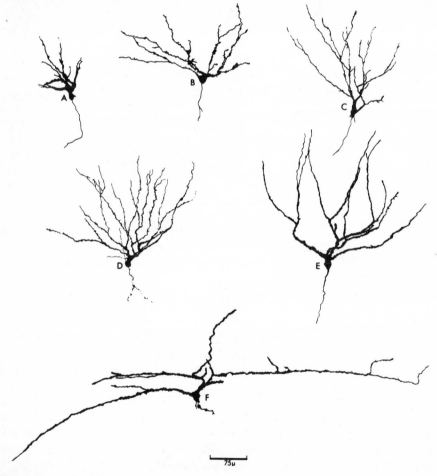

75μ

Figure 2. Camera lucida drawings of rapid Golgi preparations of neurons of the fascia dentata in the human fetus and premature infant. A to E, same ages as in Figure 1. Note extraordinary development of dendrites of the neuron from the 33-week-old ga infant who was born at 29 weeks ga and survived for 4 weeks. (Reproduced with permission from Purpura, 1975b.)

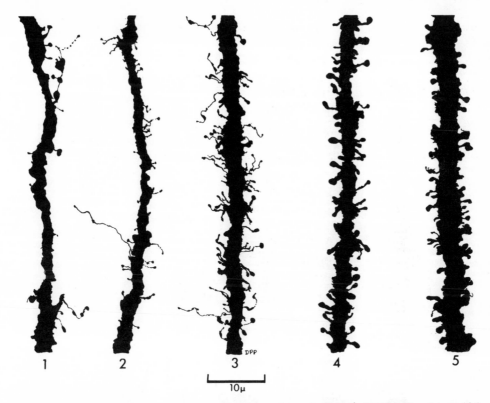

Figure 3. Camera lucida drawings of rapid Golgi preparations of apical dendritic shafts of pyramidal neurons (motor cortex) in the human fetus, premature infant, and normal child. 1, 18 weeks ga; 2, 26 weeks ga; 3, 33 weeks ga; 4, 6 months; 5, 7 years (accident case). Dendritic spine-like processes are thin and long in fetal stages. Increase in stubby and mushroom-shaped spines is evident at 6 months postnatally. Relatively little further change in dendritic spine characteristics is observed at 7 years. (Reproduced with permission from Purpura, 1975b.)

infant born at 29 weeks ga may be attributed to the 4 weeks of extrauterine existence. No answer to this question is possible without an examination of a larger number of cases. Suffice it to say that another age-matched pair of premature infants has been studied with similar but less impressive findings, i.e., slightly more advanced dendritic development in the infant born at an earlier ga. Two inferences may be drawn from these preliminary studies: 1) the differences merely reflect gross errors in calculating gestational ages or, 2) prematurity in some situations may lead to "acceleration" of cortical neuronal development. If the latter possibility is to be seriously entertained, then the burden of proof is placed upon the developmental neurobiologist to define possible consequences of accelerated dendritic development on the premature infant. Evidently electroencephalographic and evoked potential studies do not support the view that prematurity per se accelerates the functional maturation of the brain. However, this may not be surprising, because EEG and evoked potentials provide little information concerning the physiologi-

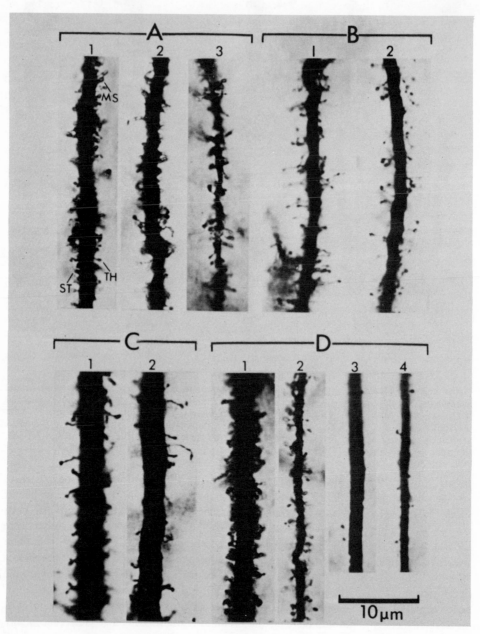

Figure 4.

cal operation of intrinsic synaptic organizations. While the question must be left open as to the impact of prematurity on programs of cortical neuronal differentiation it is also advisable to keep an open mind to the subject as well.

Morphogenesis of Dendritic Spines

There is another area of inquiry amenable to analysis with rapid Golgi preparations of human immature cortex. This is concerned with the morphogenesis of dendritic spines, which are generally recognized as postsynaptic elements of axospinodendritic synapses. The morphogenetic patterns of development of dendritic spines in human immature cerebral cortex are summarized in Figure 3. In the 18- to 22-week old fetus apical dendritic shafts of cortical pyramidal neurons begin to acquire a few long, thin spine-like processes with prominent terminal heads. These processes dominate the shafts of apical dendrites in older fetuses, although by 33 weeks ga a few mushroom-shaped and stubby spines are also observed. It should be pointed out that the classification of dendritic spines into roughly three types, i.e., thin, mushroom-shaped, and stubby, has a firm basis in correlative electron microscope studies (Peters and Kaiserman-Abramof, 1970). It is evident from Figure 3 that a major feature of the normal development of apical dendritic spines of pyramidal neurons of the cerebral cortex consists in the progressive increase in mushroom-shaped and stubby spines.

Attention to the morphological characteristics of dendritic spines in cases of profound mental retardation in which no chromosomal or metabolic disturbances could be defined has disclosed a number of dendritic spine abnormalities (Purpura, 1974b). These are summarized in Figure 4. The normal characteristics of dendritic spines of cortical neurons from a 6-month-old infant are illustrated in Figure 4A. Examples of dendritic shafts of neurons from cortical tissue removed at the time of biopsy from a 10-month-old retarded infant are shown in Figure 4B. Absence of mushroom-shaped and stubby spines are major features of the developmental disturbance observed in the retarded infant. It is of interest that these findings revealed by Golgi staining of cortical tissue removed at the time of biopsy for diagnostic and family counseling purposes were the only positive findings noted in the investigative work-up of this severely retarded infant.

Figure 4. Rapid Golgi preparations of dendrites of motor cortex neurons in normal and profoundly retarded subjects. A, normal 6-month-old infant with negative neurological history, postoperative death. A, 1 and 2, proximal apical dendritic segments of medium sized layer V pyramidal neurons. Three basic types of dendritic spines are identified: thin (TH), stubby (ST), and mushroom-shaped (MS); A, 3, Basilar dendritic segment with a predominance of TH spines. B, 1 and 2, proximal apical dendritic segments of medium sized pyramids in frontal cortex of a 10-month-old retardate. Brain biopsy case. Abnormally long, thin spines predominate; many appear entangled. There is a marked reduction in MS and ST spines. C, 1 and 2, proximal apical dendritic segments of medium pyramidal neurons in motor cortex of a 3-year-old retardate. Note variability in extent of spine loss and distribution of abnormally long, thin spines. D, 1 and 2, proximal and distal segments of apical dendrites, from a normal 7-year-old child, ancient case. D, 3 and 4, examples of apical dendritic segments from a 12-year-old profoundly retarded child. A few TH spines are seen, but otherwise there is almost complete absence of spines. (Reproduced with permission from Purpura, 1974, copyright 1974 by the American Association for the Advancement of Science.)

Somewhat more profound changes in dendritic spine density and characteristics were noted in older pediatric retardates (Figure 4C and D). The impression was gained that the severity of dendritic spine abnormalities was related to the severity and age of the retardate at the time of death. Thus, in the oldest child in this series (12 years old) who was profoundly retarded and functioning at the level of a 1-year-old infant, dendritic shafts of pyramidal neurons were almost totally devoid of spines (Figure 4D, 3 and 4).

CONCLUSION

There is a great temptation to engage in wild speculation concerning these findings in profoundly retarded infants and children who usually pose puzzling diagnostic problems for both the pediatric neurologist and neuropathologist. In agreement with the conclusion of Marin-Padilla (1974), it is likely that abnormalities of dendritic spine morphogenesis that this author has designated dendritic spine "dysgenesis" (Purpura, 1974) are common to a wide range of conditions associated with profound mental retardation. Additionally, abnormalities in dendritic development, including decreased dendritic branching (Huttenlocher, 1974), also appear to be components of the neuromorphological substrate of mental retardation in some cases. The point of emphasis here is that abnormalities of dendritic spines and dendritic branching patterns can be expected to have profound effects on the normal integrative operation of cortical synaptic organizations. If there is a wide spectrum of such changes in cortical synaptic networks in relation to functionally different degrees of mental subnormality, it may be possible to extend such observations as shown in Figure 4 to these cases as well. What is required at this time is a more intensive inquiry into the nature of developmental processes that regulate dendritic differentiation and synaptogenesis in the human immature brain. Such information is essential for a rational approach to the definition of factors that place the infant at risk from the standpoint of neurobehavioral competency.

LITERATURE CITED

Huttenlocher, P. R. 1974. Dendritic development in neocortex of children with mental defect and infantile spasms. Neurology 24: 203–210.

Marin-Padilla, M. 1974. Structural organization of the cerebral cortex (motor area) in human chromosomal aberrations. A Golgi study. I. D_1 (13 to 15) trisomy, Patau syndrome. Brain Res. 66: 375–391.

Peters, A., and I. R. Kaiserman-Abramof. 1970. The small pyramidal neuron of the rat cerebral cortex: The perikaryon, dendrites, and spines. Amer. J. Anat. 127: 321–356.

Purpura, D. P. 1961. Analysis of axodendritic synaptic organizations in immature cerebral cortex. Ann. N. Y. Acad. Sci. 94: 604–654.

Purpura, D. P. 1969. Stability and seizure susceptibility of immature brain. In H. H. Jasper, A. A. Ward, and A. Pope (eds.), Basic Mechanisms of the Epilespsies, pp. 481–505. Little, Brown, Boston, Mass.

Purpura, D. P. 1972. Ontogenetic models in studies of cortical seizure activities. *In* D. P. Purpura, J. K. Penry, D. Tower, D. M. Woodbury, and R. Walter (eds.), Experimental Models of Epilepsy, pp. 531–556. Raven Press, New York.

Purpura, D. P. 1974. Dendritic spine "dysgenesis" and mental retardation. Science 186: 1126–1128.

Purpura, D. P. 1975a. Normal and aberrant development in the cerebral cortex of human fetus and young infant. *In* N. Buchwald and M. A. B. Brazier (eds.), Brain Mechanisms in Mental Retardation. U.C.L.A. Forum in Medical Sciences. Academic Press, New York.

Purpura, D. P. 1975b. Dendritic differentiation in human immature cerebral cortex: Normal and aberrant developmental patterns. *In* G. W. Kreutzberg (ed.), Advances in Neurology. Vol. 12. Raven Press, New York.

From Animal to Infant Research

Victor H. Denenberg, Ph.D., and Evelyn B. Thoman, Ph.D.

Probably the most serious stumbling block in trying to understand the factors underlying high risk conditions with infants and young children is the inability to separate correlational from causal events. For each clinical case there is a vast network of interwoven factors that appear to be associated with the risk state of the infant. How do we know which associations are real and which happenstance? There are two broad approaches to this question: one statistical, the other experimental.

At times it is possible to amass sufficiently large numbers of cases to use statistical procedures to aid in pinpointing potential causal variables; the relationship between thalidimide and birth defects is a powerful example. Even if this approach were successful, there is still the necessity of developing an experimental research program to determine how these particular variables bring about their effects. That is, it is necessary to study the mechanism of action of the potential causal variables. If the variables are acting at a physiological level, then it is necessary to determine things such as hormonal changes, neural development, and biochemical states that are influenced by the event (as, for example, in the study of phenylketonuria (PKU). If the presumed causal factor is operating on a behavioral level, it is necessary to examine the influence of psychological, sociological, and ecological determinants (as, for example, in the study of a ghetto environment).

Clearly, it is often impossible—because of practical, ethical, moral, and legal reasons—to carry out the necessary experiments using human subjects. Thus, one either stays at the level of correlational analysis and clinical treatment, with all the inherent difficulties therein, or one seeks to develop an animal model of the risk condition because this allows one to carry out experimental studies.

The research described in this paper was supported, in part, by research grants from The National Institute of Mental Health (MH-19716) and by the Grant Foundation.

These studies were carried out with the invaluable assistance of Patricia T. Becker.

We firmly believe that knowledge of developmental process will advance most quickly by blending together investigative studies on human infants with experimental studies using animal models. Both the animal laboratory and the human nursery are necessary and integral parts of any major developmental research program and the pathway between these two facilities should be well traveled by students and faculty alike. It is also believed that, as the researcher moves back and forth from one facility to another, fresh insights and new perspectives concerning developmental processes will be gained that would be more difficult to obtain if one were to remain only within one of these research units.

The purpose of this chapter, therefore, is threefold: 1) to discuss the rationale and logical considerations involved in obtaining an animal model; 2) to present an example of research from the animal laboratory; and 3) to describe some human infant research that falls within the same context as the animal model study.

ANIMAL MODELS OF HUMAN DEVELOPMENTAL PROCESSES

The use of animal models is very well established in biology, where homologous structures or physiological processes can be isolated. Thus, there are courses in comparative anatomy, comparative endocrinology, and comparative neurology—just to cite three examples—available in many departments of biology. It is known that when a particular organ system serves the same function in animal and human alike (e.g., the kidney or the thyroid gland) an analysis of the functions and processes involved in the animal preparation will give considerable understanding into the nature of the parallel human organ system.

Moving to the level of behavioral investigation, more difficulty is encountered in developing an animal model because one starts with function and tries to find the underlying structure, while in biology one starts with structure and moves to function. When dealing with functional variables, the validity of any generalizations from one species to another is less certain because one is much less confident that the behaviors observed or the mechanisms underlying them are the same. That is, one is more likely to be dealing with analogous characters, rather than homologous characters, when working with behavioral variables. For a detailed discussion of principles and problems involved in cross-species comparisons, see Denenberg (1972, pp. 2–6).

This section is concerned only with two of the many possible animal models available in developmental research. First to be considered are the logical considerations in choosing and evaluating an animal model of a normal developmental process, and then how one develops an animal model to study an at risk condition will be described.

Animal Models of a Normal Developmental Process

One very common use of animal models is to find a preparation that parallels a normal human event and then to investigate the processes, parameters, and mechanisms underlying this event. The previous examples of the kidney and the thyroid gland fall within this framework. The same approach applies when working with developmental events, and Table 1 presents the logical considerations involved in selecting such an animal model.

Once it has been decided what process one wishes to model, an animal preparation is selected that appears to have an analogous or homologous process. Probably the best example in developmental work is that of physical growth, which has been intensively studied by a number of investigators throughout the world. In our laboratory, we have been interested in the study of sleep-wake behaviors and mother-infant interactions in developing organisms. All three of these processes are present and measurable both in humans and in many animal preparations.

The next step is to devise a measurement procedure with the animal preparation that parallels the one used with humans. Thus, for example, body weight and trunk length can be used with animals and humans alike as measures of physical growth. When studying sleep-wake behaviors, this can be done by means of behavioral descriptions (e.g., REM sleep, non-REM sleep, waking activity) or in conjunction with physiological and neurological measures. When studying mother-infant interactions, one is working at a purely behavioral level for which there is no simple underlying physiological process, and thus the measurement procedures must be restricted to observational recordings of the interactions.

However, having an animal preparation that appears similar to a human condition and having a way of measuring the animal that appears to parallel the way the human is measured is not sufficient to justify the claim that one has an animal model. When working within a developmental framework it is also necessary that the changes in performance of the young animal over its developmental time span parallel those found for the human before it can be concluded that one has a useful animal model. For

Table 1. Logical considerations in choosing and evaluating an animal model of a normal developmental process

---

1. Decide on the human process to be modeled and look for an animal preparation that appears to have an analogous or homologous process. For example:
     Physical growth
     Sleep-wake behaviors
     Mother-infant interactions
2. Apply a measurement procedure to the animal preparation that is similar to the one used with the human. For example:
     Body weight and length as indicators of physical growth
     Behavioral descriptions and/or physiological recordings of sleep-wake behaviors
     Observational recordings of mother-infant interactions

Decision rule: If the animal results parallel those results found with the human over a developmental time span, conclude that it is a useful model. Then set up experiments with the model to study parameters and mechanisms involved in the process under investigation. In doing so, use the findings from the human studies as one major source of hypothesis. Once results from the animal model have been obtained, see how well they fit existing human data, and whether they suggest new directions for research with the human.

example, physical growth in the human follows an incremental function over time, and it is necessary for the animal preparation to show a similar function. With respect to the sleep-wake behaviors, it is known that the amount of REM sleep decreases in the infant as it matures, and it is necessary for an animal preparation to show a similar decrement in the percentage of REM sleep before this can be considered to be a potentially useful animal model. Finally, one characteristic of mother-infant interactions at the human level is that the infant becomes more autonomous and self-sufficient as development occurs, and an animal preparation should show a parallel process.

If these conditions are met, then it may tentatively be concluded that one has an animal model that may be useful for experimental investigations. The usual objective is to study parameters and mechanisms underlying the process being investigated, and findings from human studies will often be used as a major source of generating hypotheses for animal investigations. Once a set of data has been obtained from the animal model, one can see how well they fit existing human data and whether they suggest new directions for research with the human.

Quite often the development of such an animal model is sufficient for one's research needs. However, because the topic of this book is to consider research with high risk infants and young children, the development of an animal model of at-riskness is discussed below.

Development of an Animal Model of At-riskness

An animal model of at-riskness is developed because of an existing dysfunctional human condition. Thus, the reference frame consists of a clinically normal comparison group (commonly called a "control" group) and a naturally occurring dysfunctional group (often called an "experimental" group) that differs from the control groups on some important behavioral or biological measure.

There are two ways of developing such an animal model. First, look for naturally occurring dysfunctional conditions within an animal population that may parallel the human condition. Spontaneous mutations offer one approach, while selecting animals from the extremes of a population is another technique that has been used. Second, create an animal model by experimental intervention using procedures such as surgery, administration of drugs or other chemicals, rearing animals in sensory deprivation, etc.

Once a parallel has been set up at the input, or independent variable, side of the equation, it is necessary to show similarities between the animal model and the human condition at the output, or dependent variable, side as well. Thus, a behavioral or biological measure is used that is analogous or homologous to the measure used with humans. When this measure is applied to the experimental and control animals, it is necessary for the direction of the differences to be the same (and also significant) before it can be concluded that one has a useful animal model. Even if these conditions are met, caution is still necessary in interpreting the results, because of many possibilities of confounding that exist. Table 2 summarizes the logical considerations involved in the development of an animal model of at-riskness.

Table 2. Logical considerations in choosing and evaluating an animal model of at-riskness

Species		Independent variable	Measures
Human	(C)	Clinically normal comparison group ("control" group)	Groups C and E_n are found to differ signi-
	(E_n)	Naturally occurring clinically dysfunctional group ("experi-mental" group)	ficantly on one or more behavioral or biological measures
Subhuman	(C)	Control group	Groups E_n and E_x are
	(E_n)	Naturally occurring dysfunctional group (e.g., via mutant gene or via statistical distribution within a standardized population	compared with Group C on behavioral or biolo-gical measures analogous or homologous to those
	(E_x)	Production of group analogous to human dysfunctional group by experimental techniques	found to discriminate between the human population groups

Decision rule: If the differences between the experimental and control animal groups parallel the differences found in the human population, conclude that it is a useful animal model. Then set up experiments with the animal model to study parameters and mechanisms involved in the processes underlying the independent variables of interest. In doing so use the findings from the human studies as one major source of hypothesis. Once results from the animal model have been obtained, see how well they fit existing human data, and whether they suggest new directions for research with the human.

Control considerations in interpretation of findings: When studying humans, Groups E_n and C are selected from existing populations rather than being created by random assignment. Thus, differences have to be regarded as correlational rather than casual, and serious consideration must be given to other variables that can influence the results. When working with subhuman species, animals are randomly assigned to treatment groups. Thus, differences may be interpreted as being causally determined rather than correlational. However, one must consider possible confounding events within the experimental treatment.

Discussion

Once an animal model has been developed, it can be subjected to a variety of experimental interventions. Various kinds of "therapeutic" procedures can be introduced to determine whether behavior can be modified; and surgical techniques can be used before observing the animal or after behavior has been measured with the objective of changing the behavior. These are techniques that are not usually permissible with the human neonate, and thus the animal model is a valuable source of information that may be applicable, at least in principle, to the human situation. The animal model also offers an important opportunity to the human researcher who, from his observations of neonates, comes up with an hypothesis that he would like to investigate. For many reasons it may not be feasible or possible to test the hypothesis on a human population, but it may be technically possible to make a test of the hypothesis via an animal model. In a similar vein, the animal experimentalist may find some unusually interesting data from his animal preparation that could be taken as a working hypothesis and carried over and studied at the human level. Thus, we envision research involving human neonates and animal models of infant organisms to be a reciprocally facilitating enterprise that will be mutually beneficial both to those primarily concerned with studying neonates and to those whose prime interest is in studying developmental processes via animal preparations. An animal experiment that investigated mother-infant interactions is described below, and it is followed with examples of human research of mother-infant interactions and sleep-wake behaviors.

A RESEARCH EXAMPLE

Animal Model of Mother-Young Interactions in the Rat

Over the past 20 years, research with the rat has shown that the procedure of handling the animal in infancy has wide and profound effects upon its behavior and physiology in adulthood (Denenberg, 1969). Because of the broad range of changes brought about by handling, we became interested, a number of years ago, in determining whether these changes were sufficiently powerful to influence the offspring of handled and nonhandled mothers. Therefore, an experiment was set up in which handled and non-handled females either reared their own young to weaning, or the young were cross-fostered at birth both within and between handled and nonhandled groups (Denenberg and Whimbey, 1963). It was found that the offspring's body weights at weaning and their open-field activity and defecation score at 50 days were affected by their mother's infantile handling experience, and that there were prenatal as well as postnatal influences. Among the several groups in the Denenberg and Whimbey study were two consisting of handled and nonhandled mothers who reared their own pups from birth to weaning. When the offspring of these two groups were compared, the pups from handled mothers were found to weigh more at weaning and to be less active in the open field. Since then, the finding that the offspring of handled mothers are less active in the open-field test has been replicated twice (Denenberg and Rosenberg, 1968; Denenberg and Whimbey, 1968), thus establishing its reliability.

The available evidence strongly pointed to the behavior of the mother between birth and weaning as the probable cause of the performance differences in the open field. Based upon various considerations that are discussed in detail in the original paper (Denenberg and Holloway, 1974), the hypothesis was proposed that the behavior of the handled mother toward her young was sufficiently different from that of the nonhandled mother, so that this was the major cause of the behavioral and physiological changes in the offspring. Furthermore, the prediction was made that the nonhandled mothers stimulated (or handled) their pups more than did handled mothers. To test this hypothesis, a closed circuit television system with video tape recorder was used to time sample the interactive behaviors of handled and nonhandled mothers with their pups between birth and weaning. In addition, the offspring were weighed at weaning and tested in the open-field on days 25 to 28 (Denenberg and Holloway, 1974). The animals were given arbitrary code numbers, and the researcher scoring the video tapes and testing the animals did not know from which group they came.

First of all, the previous findings that offspring of handled mothers weighed more at weaning and were less active in the open field was replicated. In the analysis of the video tapes it was found, during the first 5 days of life, that the nonhandled mothers groomed their pups significantly more at night than did the handled mothers. (Both groups groomed their pups equally often during the daylight hours during the first 5 days.) It was also found, on days 11 to 16, that there was significantly greater mother-pup contant in the nonhandled litters than in the handled litters. Both of these findings are confirmatory of the hypothesis that nonhandled mothers stimulate their pups more than do handled mothers. A finding that had not been predicted, yet one that is consistent with the previous data just described, is that the pups of handled mothers were more quiet than were the pups of nonhandled mothers on days 1 to 5, 11 to 15, and 16 to 20.

Thus, it can be seen that nonhandled mothers stimulate their pups more, and these pups are active in the open field; while handled mothers spend much less time in contact with their pups, their pups are quiet during most of the preweaning period, and they are much less active in the open field. So here, in a relatively simple animal model, one is able to look at some dynamic interactions between a mother and her infants and to follow the course of these interactions throughout the developmental period and into postweaning life. One of the strong suggestions that comes out of this research is that these dynamic interactions begin at birth and that behavioral patterning is being shaped from the moment of the first mother-infant contact.

An examination of some human infant studies investigating similar processes follows.

STUDIES OF SYNCHRONY IN MOTHER-INFANT INTERACTION IN HUMANS

Whether the babies are rats, rabbits, or humans, the general concern is the same: What is the effect of the mother-infant relationship on the development of the young? As a basis for exploring this question, the notion of synchrony is central. The mother and the infant are viewed as a system. Both mother and infant bring to this system characteristics that developed before the infant's birth, and the behavioral interaction thereafter develops as a function of the nature of ongoing changes in each individual's behavior. Ideally, the interaction thrives and develops as a consequence of synchrony, or dovetailing, of behaviors.

Cairns (1968), referring to the interaction of an animal mother and infant, describes response synchrony as "that state of affairs where the behaviors of two animals become mutually dependent, where responses of the one become the cues for the behaviors of the other ... The coordination that is involved in nursing and sucking, maternal stimulation and infant defecation, maternal grooming and infant orientation toward the mammaries all reflect the operation of reciprocal response sequences." A reciprocal response sequence might be depicted as follows: the infant emits a behavior that provides a cue to the mother; the mother responds to the cue, and her response, in turn, affects the infant's behavior.

The mother's response to her infant's cue can be considered appropriate if the effect is facilitative of the infant's behavioral organization. For example, if an infant is crying and the mother picks him up, the baby is likely to stop crying and then to become alert. This is a highly probable sequence. Notably, while the infant is alert, he is more available to environmental stimuli than when he was crying. Therefore, it is meaningful to say that, in such a behavioral sequence, the baby's behavioral organization is facilitated by the mother-infant interaction that occurred.

There may be a sequence of mother and infant behaviors in which the interaction can have a significant but more subtle organizing effect. For example, during feeding, maternal stimulation may have a marked effect on the amount of time the infant spends sucking (Kaye and Brazelton, 1971). The effect of the mother's stimulation is primarily a function of her timing within the infant's ongoing suck-pause pattern. Stimulation early in the pause period is most likely to prolong the pause rather than to induce sucking, whereas stimulation late in the infant's pause period is more likely to elicit sucking. The infant's response to sucking-stimulation can serve as a feedback cue to the mother that she may or may not perceive and respond to appropriately. An appropriate interaction in this case is one that facilitates the infant's sucking process, or at least that does not intrude on the infant's ongoing pattern of feeding.

An illustration of the seriousness of long-term failure of the mother-infant feedback relationship, or the lack of interaction synchrony, is found in research on children who "fail to thrive." Such infants fail to grow and develop normally even though there may be no apparent organic dysfunction. In a study of this problem, Leonard, Rhymes, and Solnit (1966) found marked inadequacy in the mother-infant relationships: the mothers expressed feelings of inadequacy and they appeared incompetent in terms of dealing with the feeding and other activities of their infants. These women were, in fact, failing to thrive in their development as mothers. The authors observed that the developmental characteristics of the infants may have also contributed to the mother-infant difficulties. "Thus, each infant and mother contributed reciprocally to the other's failure to thrive as well as to the faulty relationship between them."

These examples of interactional effects suggest the general rule that the earliest organization of the mother-infant system occurs as a function of the capacities of both the mother and her infant: the infant's capabilities for indicating its states, signaling its needs, and responding to maternal interventions; and the mother's ability to perceive cues provided by her infant and to respond appropriately to these cues. To the extent that the pair is mutually responsive, the relationship should develop in such a way as to facilitate the infant's development. The interactive process may fail to promote the organization and development of the infant when there is a failure of communication between the mother and her infant, and thus a lack of mutual responsiveness. Inadequate or inappropriate stimulation may be at fault, rather than insufficient stimulation per se. This chapter presents a case of mother-infant asynchrony, with a description of the behaviors of both mother and infant that contribute to their difficulties in communication.

Studies of Mother-Infant Synchrony with the Newborn

A major premise for this research is that synchrony in the mother-infant relationship appears and develops from the earliest interactions after birth. Evidence for the importance of these early interactions is found in studies of mothers feeding their newborn infants. Thoman et al. (1970; 1971; 1972) and Kraemer, Korner, and Thoman (1972) found marked differences in both mother and infant behaviors as a function of the parity of the mother. Inexperienced, primiparous mothers take longer to feed their infants, and they change their feeding activities more often; yet they get less formula into their infants. Among breast-feeding mothers, primiparous mothers stimulate their infants more; yet their infants suck less than do infants of multiparous mothers. There may be more than a coincidental relationship between these behavior patterns and those found in studies concerned with birth order (parity) differences in mothering of older children: mothers of first born children are much more persistent, more demanding, more inconsistent, and more attentive than are mothers of second and subsequent children (Hilton, 1968; Lasko, 1954; Stout, 1960; Sutton-Smith, Roberts, and Rosenberg, 1964).

In those studies, the infants were observed first during standardized feedings (at 12 hours of age) before any interaction with the mothers. These feedings revealed differences in the infants' feeding behaviors as a function of medication given the mother during labor, length of labor, and parity of the mother (Kraemer, Korner, and Thoman, 1972). These differences were not apparent when the infants were fed by their mothers, indicating a lack of sensitivity or cue responsiveness on the part of the mothers in contrast to that of the experienced nurses who gave the early feedings.

An additional finding in the feeding studies refers to the influence of the sex of the infant on early interaction: among primiparous mothers, the mother will stimulate a female infant more; she will talk to the infant more; and she will smile at the infant a great deal more than mothers with male infants. These differences do not reflect any apparent differences in the infants' behavior, but they may provide some of the antecedents for differences observed in mother-infant interaction with male and female children at a later stage (Levine, Fischman, and Kagan, 1967; Moss and Robson, 1968).

These studies suggest that lasting patterns of mother-infant interaction may have their inception with the first encounter of mothers and their newborn babies (a suggestion that emerged from our animal model research as well). For this reason, we begin infant studies with early observations of the infant and mother in order to identify threads of behavioral consistency that may be followed as the relationship progresses.

The major objectives of this research with mothers and infants include: 1) identifying unique characteristics of individual infants; 2) identifying the role of both mother and infant in determining the nature of the mother-infant relationship; and 3) determining the effects of the mother-infant relationship on the development of the infant's behavioral characteristics. The feeding interaction studies just described illustrate approaches to the first two objectives: 1) initial characteristics of the infants were determined by the standardized first feedings; and 2) the role of the mothers was apparent in their stimulation of the infants with consequent effect on the infants' feeding behaviors, and mutual influence was found in the effects of the infant's sex on the mother's behaviors during the feeding. In general, there was evidence for more consistent synchrony among multiparous mothers with their infants than among primiparous mother-infant pairs (Thoman et al., 1970; 1971; 1972).

Longitudinal Studies of Mother-Infant Synchrony

In order to include the third research objective listed in the previous paragraph, it is necessary to carry out studies over a long enough period of time to observe developmental changes in the infants' behaviors and in the mother-infant interactive behaviors. A major project now in progress is designed for this purpose. This research is being done in collaboration with Margaret Poindexter, who was then a graduate student at the University of Connecticut. Mothers and infants are observed intensively over the first 5 weeks of the infant's life. Observations begin in the hospital and continue weekly in the home. Each home observation lasts 7 hours, and every 10 seconds during the 7 hours the behaviors that occur are code-recorded. When the infant interacts with the mother, both mother and baby behaviors are recorded; when the infant is alone, observations of infant behaviors are recorded. (This report is concerned only with the infant's states and state-related behaviors, which are listed in Table 3.)

The infant's state is a continuous characteristic, consisting of spontaneous behaviors even when there are no apparent stimuli affecting the baby. The behaviors, therefore, can constitute stimulus cues for the mother, for example crying, visual alertness, sleeping, or even sleep-smiling. The state of an infant determines his response to incoming stimuli, and state behaviors constitute an infant's response to maternal caregiving activities. Thus, there is the possibility for continuous description of the infant, his role in and his response to the interactive process.

Measures of the infant's behavioral states are indicators of his behavioral organization. Infants are considered to show very well organized state behaviors if they have distinct behavioral states, smooth and relatively rapid transitions among states, and relatively regular cycles of states. Infants may be considered to be disorganized with respect to these behaviors if they show mixed or unclear patterns of behavioral states, with frequent and erratic changes in state. It is assumed that the infant's role in the interactive process is largely a function of his behavioral organization. The objective here is to examine the effects of the interactive process on the development of behavioral state organization.

In this chapter, data are presented from state observations of infants that illustrate individual differences among infants over the first weeks of life. We found that apparently normal infants can show marked state disorganization from the first days after birth and that such infants often have developmental difficulties, either behaviorally, physically, or both. Two "disorganized" infants are described below, with a discussion of the implications of their disorganized behaviors for the mother-infant relationship. A third infant is also described, not so much because of lack of organization in the infant's behavior, but because the infant's characteristics and the parents' perceptions of them have led to a lack of synchrony in their interactions.

Table 3. State and state-related behaviors

Infant behavioral states	Infant behaviors
Sleep[a]	Attached to nipple
Regular	(during feeding)
Near regular	Suck
Irregular with REMs	Smile
Irregular with REMs	Vocalize
Irregular with dense REMs	Burp
Wake	Gag
Drowse	Spit up
Daze	Hiccup
Alert	Bowel movement
Waking active	Startle
Fussing	Jerk
Crying	Jitter
Indefinite state	REM (during irregular sleep)
	Grunt
	Frown
	Grimace
	Small movement
	Large movement
	Stretch
	Mouthing
	Rhythmic mouthing
	Yawn
	Sigh sob
	Sigh
	Eyes open
	Hand-mouth

[a]Specific sleep states and REMs are recorded only when the infant is in the crib and is undisturbed.

INDIVIDUAL DIFFERENCES IN STATE BEHAVIORS DURING THE FIRST WEEKS OF LIFE: CONSEQUENCES FOR THE INFANT AND THE MOTHER-INFANT RELATIONSHIP

Procedures for Study

The behavioral patterns that define the infant's behavioral states are as follows:

Quiet Sleep A The infant's eyes are firmly closed and still. There is little or no diffuse motor activity, with the exception of occasional startles or rhythmic mouthing. Respiration is abdominal and relatively slow (average around 36 per minutes), deep, and regular.

Quiet Sleep B All of the characteristics of Quiet Sleep A apply for this category, except respiration, which deviates somewhat from the slow regularity seen in Quiet Sleep

A. In this state, the respiration may be relatively fast, above 46, or show some irregularities. Respiration is primarily abdominal in this state.

Active Sleep without REMs   The infant's eyes are closed, but slow rolling movements may be apparent. Bodily activity can range from minor twitches to writhing and stretching. Respiration is irregular, costal in nature, and generally faster than that seen in Quiet Sleep (average of 46 per minute). Facial movements may include frowns, grimaces, smiles, twitches, mouth movements, and sucking (actually face movements are not very often seen in this category of Active Sleep).

Active Sleep with REMs   The infant's eyes are closed, and REMs occur during the 10-second epoch; other respiration and movement characteristics are the same as those just described for Active Sleep without REMs, except that facial activity is highly likely to accompany REMs or to be interspersed between groups of REMs.

Active Sleep with Dense REMs   Characteristics of this category are the same as those of the other two categories of Active Sleep; however, this one is distinctive for the continuous occurrence of REMs throughout the 10-second observation epoch. REMs in this category are often accompanied by raising of the eyebrows and by eye opening.

Drowsy State   The infant's eyes may either open and close or they may be partially or fully open, but very still and dazed in appearance. There may be some generalized motor activity, and respiration is fairly regular but faster and more shallow than that observed in regular sleep.

Alert Inactivity   The infant's body and face are relatively quiet and inactive, and the eyes are "bright and shining" in appearance (Wolff, 1966).

Waking Activity   The infant's eyes are generally open, but they may be closed. There is generalized motor activity, accompanied by grimacing, grunting, or brief vocalization.

Fussing   The characteristics of this state are the same as those for Waking Activity, but mild, agitated vocalization is continuous, or one cry burst may occur.

Crying   The characteristics of this state are the same as those for Waking Activity, but generalized motor activity is more intense, and cry bursts are continuous.

Indefinite State   The infant's eyes may be closed, or opening and closing. There is generalized motor activity, but there are no sufficient criteria by which the infant's state can be classified as waking or sleeping.

State-related Behaviors   The state-related behaviors that are also recorded are listed in Table 3.

When the infant is interacting with the mother, it is not possible to observe specific categories of sleep. During these times, the observer indicates when the eyes are closed and records the sleep-related behaviors such as Rapid Eye Movements (REMs), smiles, etc. Complete state observations are obtained when the infant is in the crib because only then is it possible to record respiration. For this purpose, a small sensor is placed under the mattress pad, and repiration is recorded on a portable analog chart recorder. Measures of respiration rate during each state occurrence of apnea and periodic respiration are combined with the other behaviors observed to determine the infant's sleep-state, as indicated in the definitions above.

During each weekly observation, 2 to 2.5 hours of state behaviors typically occur in the crib. From preliminary analyses of data from 10 infants, significant individual differences have been found on the following measures: percent of total sleep that is Quiet Sleep; percent of Quiet Sleep that is Quiet Sleep A; percent of Quiet Sleep that is C and D combined. (These two subcategories of Quiet Sleep have been added in later studies.) With respect to respiration measures, babies differ on mean rate of respiration in Quiet and in Active Sleep, and in variability of respiration in these states. Some of these differences will be illustrated in the discussion that follows.

A final measure of individual differences will receive special attention here: the rate of state change per hour. A rate figure is determined because individual state observations vary in length. There is a significant difference among infants on this measure during the first 5 weeks also. Furthermore, there is evidence that this difference persists. Seven of the subjects were observed for a 2-hour state observation at 3 months of age. The rate of state change at 2 days and at 3 months of age for each of these subjects is presented in Figure 1. It is apparent that the behavior at these very disparate ages is very similar. A correlation of 0.81 (p < 0.05) was obtained for this sample size. Clearly, those infants

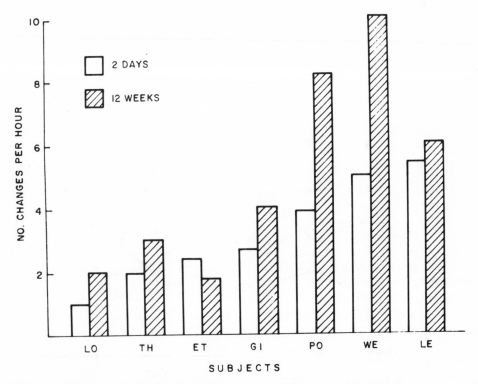

Figure 1. Number of state changes per hour at 2 days and at 12 weeks of age.

that were erratic in their state behaviors during their first days of life continue to be variable for the first months of life.

Case Studies of Two Disorganized Infants

Figure 2 shows the state change rate for five subjects over the first 5 weeks. The four subjects that are very similar represent the normal range of subjects. OB is obviously markedly deviant by 4 weeks of age. It was not possible to obtain the 3-month state observation on this infant because at this age he died of Sudden Infant Death syndrome (SIDS). Retrospective data analyses revealed this infant to be on the disorganized side of each state measure, including the respiration measures.

Figure 3 shows the mean respiration rate and the range of rates for the 5 successive weeks, for four infants, including infant OB. It should be noted that infants WE and EV represent the normal range of infants, whereas OB and PO are markedly deviant by having

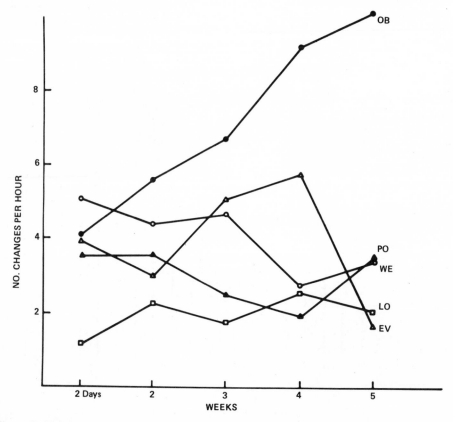

Figure 2. Number of state changes per hour for five subjects during each of the five weekly observations.

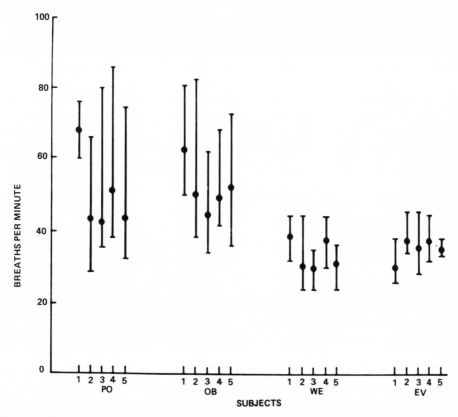

Figure 3. Mean and ranges in respiration rates during regular sleep for four subjects during each of the five weekly observations.

consistently higher mean respiration rates and also by having much more variable respiration rates in all states recorded. In fact, infant PO was very similar to OB in a number of other respects, including erratic state cycles and the occurrence of a cyanotic appearance on occasion during Quiet Sleep. Neither of these infants showed more than an average amount of apnea during their first weeks of life.

The death of infant OB strongly suggested that infant PO, a later subject, could also be at risk for SIDS, although there were no previous guidelines in the literature for such a conclusion. Nevertheless, with the possibility that OB's characteristics provided a new model for SIDS, infant PO was placed on an apnea monitor at 4 weeks of age. Now almost 7 months old, this infant is a healthy and reasonably well adjusted infant, with a very sensitive, responsive mother. The infant's states have continued to be erratic and generally not well organized, but the mother accepts his sporadic awakenings and intermittent fussing with equanimity. The presence of the apnea monitor has not been observed to disrupt the parents' interactions with their infant in any major way.

The outcome for infant PO is yet to be known. However, if the evidence for the role of the mother-infant relationship is correct (Walpole and Hasselmeyer, 1971), this infant's chances of survival should be enhanced by an unusual synchrony in the mother- (and father-) infant relationship. The interactional data are not yet analyzed. This description of the interaction is based on independent clinical reports of two observers.

The mother-infant relationship with infant OB was not such a fortunate one. In the hospital and during the first home observation, the mother was not distinctive from other mothers who are pleased with their newborn infant and eager to get acquainted. However, as the infant remained irritable and unresponsive, her attentions diminished markedly over subsequent weeks. More and more, his erratic behaviors, including vigorous crying and vomiting, went without attention. Table 4 presents data supporting the interpretation that mother OB turned away from her infant as a consequence of his difficult behaviors. This table shows the percent of time during each of the four home observations that mothers spent holding their infants for Mother OB and the mean for six other mothers. The group of mothers held their infants a relatively constant amount of time over the 4 weeks ($\overline{X}$ = 22 percent of the 7-hour observation period). Mother OB held her infant as much as these mothers on the first home observation (22 percent) but during subsequent weeks this amount dropped markedly. The infant's erratic behaviors were consistently present throughout the 4 weeks. It appears that mother OB's reduction in holding time may have been a reaction to her infant's unpredictable behaviors. Thus, the data suggest that the infant's behaviors affected their interaction. Assuming this to be the case, however, one cannot draw definitive conclusions regarding the nature of the effects of this mother-infant interaction on the infant's later aberrant development.

It is clear from the descriptions of these infants how a baby that has erratic, unpredictable behaviors may be a source of frustration and uncertainty for the mother. It is very difficult for a mother to be appropriately responsive with such an infant because his cues may be frequent yet inconsistent. One of the mothers coped by making every effort at consistency despite the infant's mixed communications; another mother coped by withdrawing from the situation (the infant) over the weeks she was observed.

Case Study of a Baby Who Does not Like to Be Held

The next baby to be described was not remarkable in any way with respect to the organization of its state behaviors. However, there was a rather strange form of asynchrony in the mother-infant interactions, which involved the infant's states. The nature of their interactive behaviors is described first, and then this description is supported with data.

The most notable characteristic of the interaction was that the infant became drowsy, and would at times have REMs, within a very short time after being picked up. Drowsiness remained a prevailing state throughout a variety of kinds of stimulation. Even through a feeding of fruit and cereal, the baby continued to be drowsy, except when fussing or crying. The mother was not judged by observers as overstimulating her infant; her stimulation was neither continuous nor vigorous. Nevertheless, there was a consistent sequence of social interaction leading to a state of drowsiness on the part of the infant. It

Table 4. Percent of time during each weekly 7-hour observation that mothers spent holding their infants: mother OB and mean of six other mothers

Week	Mother OB	Average of six other mothers
4	22	20
5	06	23
6	13	20
7	14	18

should be noted that, in most instances, the mother picked the baby up from the crib when he fussed slightly. What was apparent to the observers, and seemingly not apparent to the mother, was that this infant spent a great deal of time being wide eyed and quietly alert, scanning the floral decorations of the sides of the crib. It is not unusual for infants to spend some portion of their time in the crib being awake and alert. If the infant is awake and quiet and the mother is out of the room, she may miss such periods. However, in the case of infant SP this was a very common occurrence, and it was even more remarkable because of the lack of attentiveness during social interaction, which is the time when infants are most likely to be alert.

During the 1-month observation, the mother was observed at one time waving her hand in front of the baby's drowsy face and then she tried showing the baby a rattle. In neither instance could she raise the baby's visual level from a drowse. Only when the baby was put down did he become alert. In talking to her infant, the mother expressed complaints and disappointments about the lack of attentiveness from her infant, and her visual attentiveness to the infant was apparently affected by the infant's behavior. While feeding the infant, she rarely looked directly at the infant's face. She sat with her gaze beyond the infant. While the parents were obviously aware of their infant's inattentive state during social interaction, they did not express concern over this.

Supporting the description of this baby's reaction to social stimulation are data on the distribution of infants' states as a function of their location. Figure 4 shows, for a group of six infants, the mean percent of time spent alert while their mothers were holding them; it also shows the mean percent of time that the babies were alert while awake and in their cribs. Although the absolute time durations differed for these two locations, the percentage figures are very close for each week. Figure 5 shows the same data for baby SP. First of all, it should be noted that the mean percent of time the baby spent alert while being held was generally lower than that for the group of babies. The overall mean for SP over the 4 weeks was 22 percent, whereas the mean for the group of six infants was 33 percent. The more striking difference between this infant and the others is the percent of time the infant spent alert when he was awake and in the crib. The overall mean for the 4 weeks was 67 percent, compared with 31 percent for the

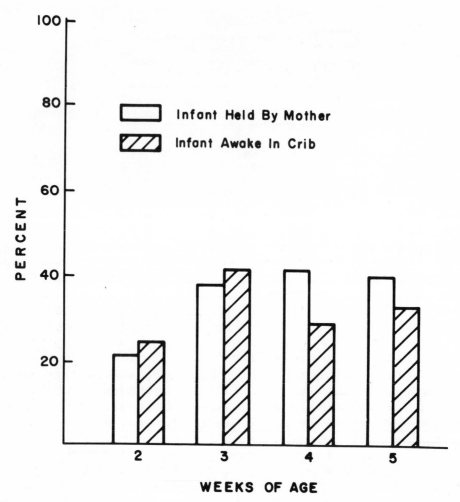

Figure 4. Mean percent of time spent in an alert state by six infants during successive weekly observations: when the infants were being held by their mothers, and when the infants were awake and in the crib.

group of infants. In addition, it should be noted that infant SP did not spend a greater amount of time being awake in his crib than did the other infants. In fact, for the 4 weeks of home observations, infant SP spent a mean of 46 minutes awake and in the crib per week, whereas the mean for the six infants was 61 minutes. The difference is not surprising, because the typical case is for an infant to make waking active noises or to fuss or cry when alone or in the crib, and the mother picks him up very shortly thereafter. Because SP was quiet, the mother apparently failed to observed when the infant was awake and therefore was not aware of the infant's alertness.

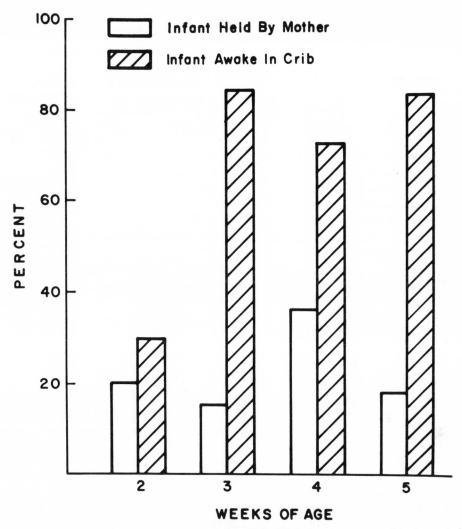

Figure 5. Percent of time spent in an alert state by infant SP during successive weekly observations: when the infant was being held by the mother, and when the infant was awake and in the crib.

The discrepancy in the infant's alertness with the mother and in the crib is evidence for a significant interactional asynchrony. This baby was most alert when the least amount of environmental stimuli were available, and least alert when social and other stimuli were available to be viewed. The mother-infant interaction, then, could not be a source of facilitation for perceptual learning for this infant. In fact, to the contrary, when given social stimulation the infant withdrew from perceptual access to environmental stimuli. Further indications of asynchrony were the expressions of disappointment in the infant's visual behavior by both the father and the mother.

At an interview session following the completion of the home observations, it was suggested that the parents place the infant on a cradle board in the room where they were as a way to help the infant achieve a level of alertness when there were people and activity to be viewed. It was also pointed out that the infant spent a great deal of time awake and alert in the crib as a way of suggesting to the parents to take note of the baby's state when he was in the crib and to provide visual stimulation at these times when he was awake.

Asynchrony as a result of a baby's sensitivity to stimulation is unusual, because most infants are most responsive when they are held and talked to. It is difficult for the parents to perceive the cues given by this kind of infant and to respond to them appropriately because the infant's state responses are atypical. He gives silent cues when the parents are not available, so that extra vigilance would be required on the part of parents to be aware of the infant's states. It would take a great deal of sensitivity by the parents to perceive that their own interaction with their infant could lead to the infant's "withdrawal." This type of behavior resembles descriptions given by parents of autistic children. They often report that, as infants, their children were not cuddly or responsive to being held, so that from the beginning social interaction was not a positive experience for either mother or infant.

Discussion

Our measures of the infant's state provide a basic description of the infant's behaviors. These behaviors are basic because they are equally meaningful at any age. Three infants with deviant state behaviors have been described along with indications of ways in which their behaviors contribute to difficult interactions with their mothers.

Two of these infants were very similar, the one who died and the one with similar state deviations who is currently being observed. It was observed that both of these infants put a strain on the mother-infant relationship. In the case of one mother-infant pair, their lack of communication was apparent in terms of a markedly diminished amount of interaction despite behavioral cues given by the infant for maternal attention. Because of very different personality characteristics of the second mother, the relationship seemed to be a facilitative one for the infant, despite his difficult behaviors. Thus, even though each of these infants played a disruptive role in the mother-infant interaction, the resulting mother-infant relationships differed markedly. One would expect the development of these two infants to be differentially affected by the differing qualities of the mother-infant interaction.

The third baby described also contributes, in a very different way, aberrant behaviors to the mother-infant system by being overly sensitive to the mother's forms of social stimulation. Throughout the 5 weeks of observations, this mother had not learned the aberrant nature of her infant's cues. It would take an extremely sensitive mother, possibly an experienced one, to detect the fact that relatively gentle social stimulation was simply "too much for the baby." In time, the mother of this infant may perceive the baby's need to be undisturbed and may provide the infant with visual stimulation within the crib, or place the infant on a cradle board where he can become alert in locations where social and other environmental visual stimuli are available to him.

The descriptions of three difficult infants illustrate ways in which infants may contribute adversely to the nature of the mother-infant relationship. Because of this, the mother-infant interaction is a less facilitative one for the infant's development.

CONCLUSION

During the interviews with mothers and fathers after the 5 weeks of observation, we encountered parents who are weary, confused, and angry. These are usually parents of "difficult" infants who say they do not understand what "they are doing wrong." All efforts seem so futile with an irritable or erratic infant. Some reassurance is provided by indicating that their baby is still in the process of "getting himself together," and some extra patience, endurance, and attention may help over time. This is far from enough. These observations strongly indicate the need for some form of ongoing support and assistance to be available to the parents during the neonatal period, because this is a time of major adjustment for them. Prenatal instruction and preparation can help, but this is often not completely adequate. It is only after the baby has been born that most parents become aware of the extent and complexity of the demands made on them by the new member of the family. Parents want understanding, and they need to be provided with coping techniques, especially with a difficult infant. Assistance in achieving synchrony in the mother-infant relationship can have lasting consequences for their developing interactive behaviors. We feel this assistance should be available as early as possible before asynchronous patterns develop and interactive problems have to be resolved.

LITERATURE CITED

Cairns, R. B. 1968. Developmental determinants of response synchrony. Presented at the 76th Annual Convention of American Psychological Association, San Francisco, Sept. 2, 1968. Symposium on "Attachment Behaviors in Humans and Animals."

Denenberg, V. H. 1969. The effects of early experience. In E. S. E. Hafez (ed.), The Behaviour of Domestic Animals (2nd ed.). Bailliere, Tindall, and Cox, London.

Denenberg, V. H. 1972. The Development of Behavior. Sinauer Associates, Stamford, Conn.

Denenberg, V. H., and W. Holloway. 1974. Differences in mother-pup interaction as a function of the mother's infantile experiences. Unpublished manuscript.

Denenberg, V. H., and K. M. Rosenberg. 1968. Programming life histories: Effects of maternal and environmental variables upon open-field behavior. Devel. Psychobiol. 1: 93–96.

Denenberg, V. H., and A. E. Whimbey. 1963. Behavior of adult rats is modified by the experiences their mothers had as infants. Science 142: 1192–1193.

Denenberg, V. H., and A. E. Whimbey. 1968. Experimental programming of life histories: Toward an experimental science of individual differences. Devel. Psychobiol. 1: 55–59.

Hilton, I. 1968. The dependent first born and how he grew. Paper presented at the American Psychological Association meeting, San Francisco, Calif.

Kaye, K., and T. B. Brazelton. 1971. Mother-infant interaction in the organization of sucking. Paper presented at the Society for Research in Child Development.

Kraemer, H. C., A. F. Korner, and E. B. Thoman. 1972. Methodological considerations in evaluating the influence of drugs used during labor and delivery on the behavior of the newborn. Devel. Psych. 6: 128–134.

Lasko, J. K. 1954. Parent behavior toward first and second children. Gen. Psych. Monog. 49: 97–137.

Leonard, M. F., J. P. Rhymes, and A. J. Solnit. 1966. Failure to thrive in infants. Amer. J. Dis. Child. 1: 600–612.

Levine, J., C. Fischman, and J. Kagan. 1967. Sex of child and social class as determinants of maternal behavior. Paper presented at the annual meeting of the American Orthopsychiatric Association, Washington, D.C., March 1967.

Moss, H. A., and K. S. Robson. 1968. Maternal influences in early social visual behavior. Child Devel. 39: 401–408.

Stout, A. M. 1960. Parent behavior toward children of differing ordinal position and sibling status. Unpublished doctoral dissertation, University of California.

Sutton-Smith, B., J. M. Roberts, and B. G. Rosenberg. 1964. Sibling associations and role involvement. Merrill-Palmer Quart. 10: 25–38.

Thoman, E. B., C. R. Barnett, and P. H. Leiderman. 1971. Feeding behaviors of newborn infants as a function of parity of the mother. Child Devel. 42: 1471–1483.

Thoman, E. B., P. H. Leiderman, and J. P. Olson. 1972. Neonate-mother interaction during breast feeding. Devel. Psych. 6: 110–118.

Thoman, E. B., A. M. Turner, P. H. Leiderman, and C. R. Barnett. 1970. Neonate-mother interaction: Effects of parity on feeding behavior. Child Devel. 41: 1103–1111.

Walpole, M., and E. B. Hasselmeyer. 1971. Research planning workshop on the Sudden Infant Death Syndrome. August 16, 1971, Bethesda, Maryland. National Institute of Child Health and Human Development, Perinatal Biology and Infant Mortality Branch.

Wolff, P. H. 1966. The causes, controls, and organization of behavior in the neonate. Psych. Issues 5, Monog. 17.

Process Research: Its Use in Prevention and Intervention with High Risk Children

Leonard E. Ross, Ph.D., and Lewis A. Leavitt, M.D.

In 1968, the National Institute of Child Health and Human Development published a book, *Perspective on Human Deprivation: Biological, Psychological, and Sociological*, that presented state-of-the-art papers covering a wide range of behavioral and biomedical research and that developed a number of research policy recommendations. In an overview chapter summarizing the implications of the research reviews, the following statement appears under the heading, "The Interface between Research Policy and Social Action":

> All of this taken together argues persuasively for a new and different kind of cooperation between the pure research scientists and the social practitioner. The research scientist should become more available to the policy maker and the practitioner to identify those variables and processes which have the highest probability of being significant in some particular social problem. The policy maker and the practitioner should make available to the research scientist well designed and well implemented interventions, the study of which would contribute to basic knowledge. Both the scientist and the practitioner should cooperate in the design and implementation of selected intervention programs.

This statement is as true today as it was 6 years ago. There is a clear need for the support of research as a supplement and guide to social action programs. This is particularly true for programs concerned with intellectual deficit. Over the last decade there have been important advances in the understanding of the processes underlying human behavior. New conceptualizations and research methodologies, as well as empirical discoveries concerning learning, attention, cognition, language, parent-child interaction, and the

Preparation of this chapter was supported by NIH research grants HD-05653 and HD-08240 from the National Institute of Child Health and Human Development.

physiological basis of behavior, have important implications for the understanding of intellectual development and intellectual inadequacy.

The support of process oriented research and its integration with assessment and intervention activities is essential at this time. Research that does not have contact with the problems of society can conceptually constrict upon itself and examine less and less important phenomena in greater and greater detail. Similarly, intervention and service programs may never move beyond the demonstration stage and reach acceptable levels of effectiveness and efficiency if they are not evaluated and modified on the basis of the best possible understanding of the fundamental sources and characteristics of intellectual inadequacy.

PROCESS ORIENTED RESEARCH

The goal of process oriented research is to understand the underlying mechanisms or processes of behavior, in which understanding consists in discovering the relationships or laws that hold between the concepts that have reference to the particular behavior of interest. A further stage in understanding involves the development of a conceptual system, theory, or model that accounts for the laws by providing for their derivation.

In general, process oriented research examines some restricted aspect of behavior. Particular cognitive activities, certain learning processes, selected aspects of parent-child relationships, and the development of competence in language are among those that may be selected as the process or processes to be investigated in order to determine the laws governing the processes and their changes with age. The selection of a certain process for investigation does not imply that it operates in isolation. In fact many of the more interesting recent developments in process oriented research have involved the investigation of interrelationships among different processes.

In some cases advances in the understanding of such processes have been characterized by new conceptualizations, as for example the current interest in information-processing approaches to cognitive behavior, while in others the refinement or discovery of useful behavioral measures has led to a better understanding of the factors involved in intellectual performance, as has been the case of psychophysiological research. A few research areas have developed highly quantified theories or models that derive and integrate the behavioral phenomena of interest, while others have remained closely tied to the empirical relationships that have been discovered through research.

Of particular importance for the development of intervention procedures is knowledge regarding developmental changes in the processes underlying intellectual ability. It is a truism that changes do not occur as a function of time per se, but as a function of a complex of maturational and experiential processes that take place over time. The task of the process oriented developmentalist is to specify the process changes that occur as the child develops and, most importantly, to determine the factors responsible for the transitions that occur with time and the rules that describe them.

The availability of detailed information concerning normal process development is of critical importance for the study of the processes underlying intellectual deficit. For example, the study of language processes and memory in children with intellectual deficit is much more meaningful in the context of knowledge concerning language and memory development in normal children. The development of remedial procedures to maximize the capabilities of retarded children depends upon the understanding of how the processes of interest develop under normal circumstances. As Miller and Yoder (1974) point out, programmed development to provide a functional communications system for retarded children must be based on what is known about normal psycholinguistic development. Similarly, the teaching of strategies to aid the retarded child to overcome problems in organizing and rehearsing information so that it is remembered efficiently depends upon knowledge of how these processes develop and are used by normal children. The same is true for virtually all process areas.

Much of the research activity of investigators in a wide variety of behavioral and biomedical disciplines is directed toward the understanding of the processes underlying human behavior. The majority of the articles that appear in many scientific journals, such as the *American Journal of Mental Deficiency* and *Child Development* to name only two, represent such efforts. This information has the highest possible relevance for efforts to predict intellectual deficit or to intervene to reduce its effect.

PROCESS RESEARCH: ITS USE IN PREDICTION AND INTERVENTION

Prematurity and the Problem of Prediction

In the United States several hundred thousand infants a year are born prematurely or of low birth weight. Substantial evidence has been accumulated indicating that infants who are small at birth are at risk for intellectual impairment (Drillien, 1964; Wiener et al., 1968; Wright et al., 1972). Infants born weighing less than 1.5 kg at birth appear to be a particularly high risk group for poor school performance. Specific findings include low intelligence quotients, as well as behavior disorders variously classified as hyperactivity, poor attention span, and difficulties in school adjustment.

Most of the important complications of pregnancy and parturition are associated with prematurity. Asphyxia, hypoglycemia, as well as other conditions potentially injurious to the central nervous sytem, are prominent among the problems of premature infants.

In a study of 72 children weighing 3 lbs or less, Drillien (1964) found that by school age 75 percent have some congenital defect or mental retardation. Lubchenco and others found that 66 percent of infants less than 1.5 kg had visual or central nervous system handicaps. Wright et al. (1972) found that 34 percent of infants less than 1.5 kg at birth had IQs less than 80. These and other investigators provide evidence that there is a continuum of central nervous system injury and risk that, although most profound in the smallest and most premature newborns, is present throughout a wide span of weight and maturation and results in some reduced level of mental functioning even in those who are relatively more mature and not grossly handicapped.

Recent research suggests that gestational age (ga) at birth interacts powerfully with birth weight as a prognostic factor for late development. In particular, the distinction between growth retarded and nongrowth retarded infants in the heterogenous population made up of low birth infants (those under 2,500 gm at birth) appears to be clinically important. One example is the precarious states of glycogen reserves in small-for-gestational-age infants, which places them at great risk for hypoglycemia.

That small-for-gestational-age infants comprise a high risk group is indicated by a report showing 15 percent of 1,300 mentally retarded patients with IQs less than 50 had been small for ga at birth (Collins and Turner, 1971). The use of data on both birth weight and ga for classification of infants into the categories small and appropriate for ga will enable research programs to evaluate more accurately the risk factors for mental retardation and problems of central nervous system development in low birth weight infants.

The last decade has seen major changes in medical care of premature infants. This has been the result of the regionalization of care in special nurseries, the recognition of newborn care as a subspecialty of pediatrics, and the increasing use of respirators and electronic cardiac and respiratory monitoring devices. The influence of these changes has been profound in that increased numbers of infants survive the neonatal period of life. Less obvious has been the impact of these advances on the quality of intellectual functioning of survivors.

The evaluation of the effects of new treatment regimens requires reliable instruments to predict intellectual deficit for the infants involved. To date, reliable prediction of intellectual deficit at school age for subjects tested in infancy has been unrealized for all but severely compromised infants.

Because infant assessment procedures currently in use are generally unreliable in predicting intellectual performance at school age until the child is several years of age (McCall, Hogarty, and Hurlburt, 1972) there is an unfortunate delay in defining which infants have a sustained central nervous system injury that may hamper their social and learning behavior. This delay is disturbing not only to parents and educators who would like to begin remediation programs for brain injured children, but also to physicians who care for newborns. A lag in feedback on the effects of new and changing medical regimens of newborn and premature care on the central nervous system is not only frustrating but also potentially dangerous. New drugs or procedures that appear helpful in treatment during the early days of life may later be shown to have harmful central nervous system sequelae.

Using differing versions of the newborn neurologic examination, workers over the past 2 decades have reported widely varying success in predicting intellectual outcome on follow up longer than 1 year. While these studies hold promise that further refinement of newborn and infant neurologic examinations may provide significant correlative indices to later intellectual function, other approaches to the problem of assessing early substrates of cognitive functioning or intellect are clearly needed.

The neurologists armamentarium of reflexes to be tested has been brought to bear on young infants with less than satisfying results. In 1964, Clark wrote, "It is not difficult to compose lost lists of reflexes which may be elicited from infants, or devise detailed schemata of examination by scratching, thumping, spinning or otherwise invading their privacy. It is a good deal harder to find signs which reliably predict lasting CNS damage."

Although 35 years ago infants born weighing less than 1,500 grams were classed as "previable," recent reports from nurseries in the U.S. and abroad show greater than 50 percent survival of liveborn infants of birth weight less than 1,500 grams. During the last decade alone, survival rate in the 1 to 1.5 kg birth weight group has increased from less than 50 percent to over 70 percent at some newborn centers. Given this change not only in care but also in actual numbers of survivors, there is a clear and present need for reliable means of assessment of this population for the placement of persons in intervention programs, as well as the evaluation of the effectiveness of the programs themselves.

Intervention

Intervention programs have provided impressive evidence that intensive and comprehensive intervention procedures produce dramatic changes in the behavior of children. However, the measures used to assess the change are often sensitive to many nonspecific motivational, social, and stimulus familiarity factors that may or may not continue to facilitate the child's performance in other situations and over extended periods of time. It remains an open question whether the predictive validity of psychometric measures of intellectual functioning is maintained when large changes occur because of intervention procedures. Similarly, it is recognized that improved school performance following intervention may reflect other factors, e.g., student conformity or teacher expectations, rather than changes in basic intellectual capabilities. This is not to say that improvement in intellectual functioning because of changes in general motivational and socialization factors are not important and that such changes are not a legitimate goal of intervention procedures. It is also recognized that a close interaction exists between these factors and learning. However, it would be of great value to determine whether the underlying processes of central importance for intellectual functioning, including motivation and socialization processes, have been changed in any fundamental way by intervention. There is a high probability that the generality and duration of intervention effects will depend upon such process changes.

Evaluative Procedures The necessity to evaluate the component processes of intellectual functioning in a manner beyond that possible by the use of intelligence tests has, of course, been recognized, and many intervention and compensatory education programs have used various tests of cognitive, perceptual, and language development. While these evaluative procedures may be useful in providing a general measure of the overall performance level of the child, thus identifying children with serious developmental delays, those in common use cannot provide the desired analysis of the processes underlying intellectual performance. Often, the tasks have been constructed on the basis of face validity rather than on current research in the process area. It is not enough that such tests differentiate populations, because they may do so for various reasons unrelated to the process presumably evaluated. The paradigms employed often confound a number of factors so that the results are of limited value for accurate prediction, or the more efficient structuring of intervention procedures. For example, tests of discrimination learning performance, attention, memory span, language production, or perceptual motor performance have been demonstrated to be inadequate *in their simple forms* for the investigation of the complexities of cognitive and language processes. Thus, there is little reason to expect performance on such tasks, as part of batteries of tests or screening inventories, to be of greater value in providing information regarding the basic process functioning of the child than are the subtests of conventional intelligence tests.

Recent Developments   Process oriented research must be supported to develop in its own right, and also be brought into much closer contact with the problems of intellectual deficit. There have been encouraging developments in recent years in that the process research that has involved populations with intellectual problems has, to an increasing extent, employed paradigms and conceptual approaches that represent the most recent developments in the experimental and developmental process areas.

Consider a few examples of these developments and the interesting possibilities that they raise for problems of intellectual deficit. A relatively recent development in experimental psychology, which has spread to all areas of behavioral research, is the examination of the processes by which the information contained in sensory input is transformed, elaborated, rehearsed, stored, and retrieved. *Information processing models* have proven tremendously useful as a research tool in helping to understand many of the behavioral phenomena that characterize the areas of perception, learning, memory, and language. In general, cognitive information processing models include: 1) a stage of sensory information store, a high capacity storage system from which information store, a high capacity storage system from which information rapidly decays but from which selected elements are recoded and transferred to the second stage, 2) short-term memory or short-term store, a temporary holding area where information is maintained for immediate use or supported, for example, by rehearsal, and transformed for entry into, 3) long-term store, from which information is retrieved on subsequent occasions.

The possible relation of the information processing approach to problems of intellectual deficit is clear. Are there differences in the way information is initially processed, transformed, rehearsed, stored, and retrieved on the part of the retarded child or a child at risk for mental retardation? Are such differences remediable, or at least can they be minimized by training tailored to the processing difficulties of the individual child? There are other kinds of "spin off" questions that also may prove quite fruitful. Although analysis of the eye-movement-reading relationship has not proven useful in the past in the view of many, it is enjoying a revival of interest because of the demonstration of the close relationship between eye movements and the initial processing characteristics of the organism. New issues concerning the cognitive control of eye movements, rhythmical eye movements, and the perceptual unit processed in reading have profound implications for the understanding of developmental delay.

Also consider the recent developments in the study of *hemispheric specialization*. There has long been speculation about the development of specialization and the possible need for a dominant hemisphere to serve as a coordinator for cognitive processing, especially when considering more complex tasks involving verbal material. Previous observational techniques have been supplanted by dichotic listening tasks and by paradigms that involve accuracy or speed or response after the brief presentation of visual stimuli to the left or right visual field. The accumulation of knowledge concerning hemispheric specialization and its relationship to cognitive processes would be of considerable significance for understanding the development of cognitive competence.

Another major area of development has been that concerned with *psychophysiology* and the relationship between psychophysiological response measures and attentional and cognitive behaviors in children of all ages. The methodological and empirical advances that have characterized this area in recent years have created exciting opportunities, particularly because the procedures may be used with the very young. The concept of the orienting response, new discoveries concerning the evoked potential, and analyses of the multiple components of skin conductance and skin potential responses all will lead to greatly increased knowledge concerning the development of the child.

Currently, one of the most promising areas of research is that concerned with *language acquisition*. Here again analyses of the processes and strategies employed in acquiring language are greatly changing our ideas of language acquisition and are leading to new ways of structuring language intervention programs, for example a change in emphasis from a syntactic to a conceptual-semantic approach to language intervention.

Finally, it should be pointed out that a great deal of effort has been devoted in recent years to *Piaget's system*, particularly his stages of psychological development. Numerous attempts are underway to develop tests involving variations of the Piagetian operations as replacements for conventional sensorimotor and intelligence tests. Similarly, interest has developed in the remediation or acceleration of intellectual development by training the operations that characterize stages of development. Such attempts rest on the assumption that Piaget's observations have identified processes and behaviors that are more basic and important than those examined by the usual psychometric tests, or the specialized tests of cognitive, perceptual, or language performance developed for test batteries. This assumption is quite probably correct, but it remains to be determined whether the Piagetian operations are in themselves of such fundamental importance for general intellectual development that 1) their use in evaluation will provide more useful descriptive and predictive data than other tests, and 2) by training the operations that characterize the stages of development the child's intellectual ability will be so transformed as to have far reaching and long lasting effects. These are empirical questions that must be submitted to rigorous experimental testing.

Certainly, research generated by Piaget's insights is useful in describing intellectual processes, but experimental evidence indicating that memory, attention, and other cognitive processes are themselves components of operations such as transitive inference and conservation must be carefully evaluated before it is concluded that Piaget's system as it is commonly interpreted represents the final level of analysis needed. The excellent analysis by Sullivan (1969) of the issues involved in application of Piaget's system to educational problems should be considered by those interested in the question.

Process Approach and Intervention Goals

The process approach, involving the experimental analysis of the variables affecting a process and the refinement of paradigms to investigate and measure the mechanisms involved, stands in contrast to the current use of test batteries in screening activities and the evaluation of intervention programs. The future holds the promise of process analyses, applied to the individual child, that will identify the problem with much greater accuracy and specificity than are possible at the present time. Similarly, a process analysis will enable the identification of the particular process changes that result from intervention and, eventually, suggest the optimal intervention procedures depending upon the process assessment of the individual child.

While this view of the future may appear to be overly optimistic in view of the usefulness of current screening and assessment procedures, these advances can be achieved, assuming that behavioral and biological process investigators form a working partnership with those involved in intervention programs. Process research has much to gain from closer contact with the immediate problems of the retarded, or those at risk for retardation. Similarly, the long-term success of intervention programs depends upon refining intervention procedures so that they achieve fundamental and long lasting changes in the intellectual functioning of the individual child at a cost society is willing to support. It appears that this is unlikely to occur for significant numbers of those who have a right to such intervention treatment without program development based upon, and evaluated in terms of, process knowledge.

DEVELOPMENTAL PROCESSES IN
CHILDREN AT RISK FOR MENTAL RETARDATION: ONE PROGRAM

The program of research described below is an example of a process oriented program designed to investigate the developmental processes of children at risk for mental retardation. This program, which is supported by the National Institute of Child Health and Human Development, involves the collaborative efforts of four experimental and developmental psychologists and a pediatrician, all affiliated with the Waisman Center for Mental Retardation and Human Development at the University of Wisconsin, Madison. The program has been in the planning stages for almost a year and is currently in its first month of operation. The population of interest is that of the University of Wisconsin Regional Neonatal Care Unit, where the cooperation of the unit offers an opportunity for the comprehensive study of high risk children from birth through school age.

The research program is divided into two parts, the first concerned with the precursors of intellectual development in high risk and normal infants, and the second with the comparison and investigation of cognitive processes in high risk, normal, and retarded children.

Among the overall objectives of the program are the following: 1) the identification and systematic investigation of processes important for the development of intellectual competence; 2) the identification of differences in the functioning of these processes and the specification of their course of development in high risk, retarded, and normal children; and 3) the determination of the value of process difference information obtained early in life in predicting the later intellectual competence of high risk children.

Precursors of Intellectual Development in High Risk and Normal Infants

For the first section of the program, attention, habituation, and the processing of speech stimuli were chosen as examples of cognitive functions that may be indexed during early infancy, as well as throughout later life.

Physiologic recording techniques enable the use of cardiac responses as an index of attending to stimuli in young infants as well as adults. The habituation of these responses on repeated presentation of a given stimulus may be studied as a process that is elicited in early infancy, as well as in childhood and adulthood.

Deficiencies in language development are a general characteristic of children who evidence learning disabilities or mental retardation. Research in infant and adult speech perception in recent years has provided evidence that speech stimuli may be processed differently than other auditory stimuli by the central nervous system.

Because deficiencies in memory capabilities are implicated in retarded and learning disability populations, the investigation of the role of memory factors in infant speech perception should serve to increase the understanding of normal and pathologic development of the perceptual process.

A recently developed technique involving the use of the non-nutritive, high-amplitude sucking response will be used to study the development of speech perception capacities during infancy. The question of categorical discrimination in consonants and vowels, the identification of speech sounds based on phonetic versus acoustic similarity, and the development of discrimination of acoustic cue formation also will be studied.

Many of the proposed programs of early intervention in infancy involve the use of auditory and in particular speech stimuli. Information from the proposed speech perception studies will be of value to developers of auditory environmental stimulation programs.

Cognitive Processes and the
Intellectual Development of High Risk, Normal, and Retarded Children

The three research programs that comprise this division of the project may be considered in relation to current conceptualizations of the stages of information transformation or processing.

One subproject is primarily concerned with the initial part of the processing sequence, i.e., it will utilize conditioning and backward masking paradigms to investigate the sensory information store and the processing of information from this store. Two approaches are represented. In the first, conditioning paradigms (e.g., the comparison of trace and delay conditioning) are used to investigate differences in the stimulus requirements of high risk, retarded, and normal children. The second part of the research program utilizes backward masking paradigms to compare high risk, normal, and retarded populations with respect to the speed of processing information from sensory store. There are indications that processing speed differs as a function of developmental and intellectual level, and this research is planned to provide comprehensive data concerning this processing operation.

A second subproject is planned to investigate the responses used to maintain information in short-term memory. Four problems will be attacked through the utilization of a list retention procedure designed to minimize responding from a decaying trace or from long-term memory. First, alternative operations for measuring rehearsal will be used to validate the list retention procedure. Second, the ability of the three populations to adjust rehearsal strategies to varying task demands will be explored. Third, the generality of the adopted strategies is to be observed in experiments measuring transfer across learning tasks. Finally, the relation of rehearsal to long-term memory and hence learning will be compared across populations. It is the objective of this program to refine the understanding of a response that is developmentally sensitive, to discover how this response relates to other stages in the processing sequence, and to reveal possible new directions for the remediation of cognitive deficiencies.

The third subproject will study the development of organizational and mediational abilities of children from intellectually handicapped, intellectually nonhandicapped, and high risk populations. The experimental tasks include: 1) associative clustering and subjective organization in free recall, and 2) variations of paired associate learning and digit recall. Previous research has revealed that the ability to spontaneously employ efficient information organizing strategies is weak in mentally retarded and young children. This research will gather data bearing on the nature of information organization tendencies in the populations of interest, the degree to which organization may be facilitated via external structuring and/or cueing, and how this organization is retained over time and used in new situations.

SUMMARY

The program's investigation of high risk and normal children is planned to provide information of a kind not available from the usual procedures used in screening for developmental delay. The data obtained will make it possible to evaluate the predictive value of information concerning various processes in infancy and to examine older high risk children in terms of basic cognitive processes. It is believed that such data will be meaningful in assessing the functioning of the individual child, as well as in providing a general characterization and comparison of the process functioning of high risk and normal children.

In the long run, the objective of research of this type are to provide information essential for the prediction of intellectual deficit and to aid in the development of the most effective and efficient intervention procedures to prevent or ameliorate intellectual deficit. It is extremely unlikely that the experimental paradigms employed and the processes investigated in this particular program will be those that will utlimately prove to be the most useful for this purpose. If the history of the contribution of science to human welfare is a guide, progress toward such goals will be gradual indeed, with many changes as research continues in the basic process sciences and as more is learned about how these various processes develop in children at risk for intellectual deficit. The process approach, however, is one that must be vigorously pursued if progress is to be made so that developmental assessment procedures provide predictive as well as normative information, and intervention programs move beyond demonstrations of the effects of intervention to the development of effective and efficient procedures that significantly improve the lives of large numbers of at risk children.

LITERATURE CITED

Clark, D. B. 1964. Abnormal neurological signs in the neonate. *In* Physical Diagnosis of the Newly Born. Report of the Forty-sixth Ross Conference on Pediatric Research, p. 65–71. Ross Laboratories, Columbus, Ohio.

Collins, E., and G. Turner. 1971. The importance of the "small-for-dates" baby to the problem of mental retardation. Med. J. Australia 2: 313–315.

Drillien, D. M. 1964. The Growth and Development of the Prematurely Born Infant. Williams and Wilkins, Baltimore.

Lubchenco, L. O., M. Delivoria-Papadopoulos, and D. Searls. 1972. Long-term follow-up studies of prematurely born infants. J. Ped. 80: 509–512.

McCall, R. B., P. S. Hogarty, and N. Hurlburt. 1972. Transition in infant sensory-motor development in the prediction of childhood IQ. Amer. Psych. 27: 728–748.

Miller, J. F., and D. E. Yoder. 1974. An ontogenetic language teaching strategy for retarded children. *In* R. Schiefelbusch and L. Lloyd (eds.), Language Perspectives—Acquisition, Retardation, and Intervention, pp. 505–528. University Park Press, Baltimore.

National Institute of Child Health and Human Development. 1968. Perspectives on Human Deprivation: Biological, Psychological, and Sociological. National Institutes of Health, Public Health Service, U.S. Department of Health, Education, and Welfare. U.S. Government Printing Office, Washington, D.C.

Sullivan, E. V. 1969. Piagetian theory in the educational milieu: A critical appraisal. Can. J. Beh. Sci. 1: 129–155.

Wiener, G., R. V. Rider, W. C. Oppel, and P. A. Harper. 1968. Correlates of low-birth weight. Pediat. Res. 2: 110–118.

Wright, F. H., R. R. Blough, A. Chamberline, T. Ernest, W. C. Halstead, P. Meier, R. Y. Moore, R. F. Naunton, and F. W. Newell. 1972. A controlled follow-up study of small prematures born from 1952 through 1956. Amer. J. Dis. Child. 124: 506–522.

Caregiver-Infant Interaction and the Development of the High Risk Infant

Leila Beckwith, Ph.D.

It is clearly established that different early rearing conditions associated with levels and kinds of caregiver-infant interaction are capable of significantly influencing a wide range of developing behavior. This fact is consistent with the proposition that most behaviors do not unfold through maturation alone. The effects of early experience have been demonstrated to range from the delay and modification of sequences of development that a priori would appear unrelated to caregiver-infant interaction. Examples are: visually directed reaching (White and Held, 1967) and crawling and walking (Dennis and Najarian, 1957) to the most significant issues in adulthood, such as independent work, marriage, and parenthood (Skeels, 1966). The question is no longer whether early experience with the caregiver can influence the human infant's cognitive, social, and affective development. The questions are: How, in what ways, and with what relative effectiveness for what age infant do specific dimensions of the mother-infant interaction operate; which effects persist, at what later ages, and how are effects modified or attenuated by intervening experience? An excellent recent review of some of these issues in a somewhat different context is found in Horowitz and Paden (1973). The objective in this chapter is to relate selected aspects of the empirical findings and theoretical issues to infants whose cognitive and social development are at risk from prenatal and perinatal causes.

PRENATAL AND PERINATAL FACTORS

Although considerable controversy exists as to which obstetric conditions are hazardous (Parmelee and Haber, 1973) and to what extent (Sameroff and Chandler, 1975), there is

This program has been supported by NIH Contract No. 1-HD-32776, "Diagnostic and Intervention Studies of High Risk Infants"; and by NICHD Grant No. HD-04612, Mental Retardation Research Center, University of California at Los Angeles.

119

widespread recognition that prenatal and perinatal factors may determine not only the probability of survival of the newborn but may also put him at greater statistical risk during his childhood for a variety of handicapping conditions. These include cerebral palsy, sensory deficits, intellectual and attentional deficits, and reading disabilities (Caputo and Mandell, 1970; Drillien, 1964; Kawi and Pasamanick, 1958; Knobloch and Pasamanick, 1959; Pasamanick and Knobloch, 1961; Parmelee and Liverman, 1963; Wiener, 1970; Wiener et al., 1965; Wiener et al., 1968). The effects are not restricted to the cognitive-perceptual-motor domain. They may act to increase incidence of referral for child guidance services (Pasamanick, Rogers, and Lilienfeld, 1956) and, at the extreme, to increase the likelihood of autism (Knobloch and Pasamanick, 1962) and schizophrenia for the child of a schizophrenic parent (Garmezy and Streitman, 1974).

The thesis here is that investigation of behavioral dimensions of caregiver-infant interaction for such babies would be a worthwhile research strategy that has been little used. Increased understanding of the mutual adaptations made by infants and families to each other would make professional intervention more meaningful and would increase the predictive validity of risk designation. Such an approach is emphasized by Sameroff and Chandler (1975) and is consistent with that of other investigators who have stressed the need to combine a neurological approach with a psychosocial one (Drillien, 1964; Wiener, 1962).

Despite evidence of increased risk for an infant who has experienced designated prenatal and perinatal hazards, the infant's development cannot be predicted independently of subsequent caretaking experiences. Prospective studies indicate that the outcome for all babies is more strongly related to environmental hazards than to prenatal and perinatal difficulties (Sameroff and Chandler, 1975; Werner et al., 1968; Wiener et al., 1965). Furthermore, problems arising from prenatal and perinatal difficulties may be attenuated or intensified by the favorableness of the environment (Braine et al., 1966; Drillien, 1964; Wiener, Rider, and Oppel, 1963—but *not* Wiener et al., 1965). In addition, obstetric complications usually expose an infant to specific deviations in early experience that may in themselves be deleterious. Moreover, children characterized as being at risk, from whatever source, such as complications of reproduction or complications of caretaking, are often regarded as passive recipients. Yet, it is probable that the child's characteristics and behaviors elicit and influence his caretaking (Bell, 1971; Korner and Grobstein, 1967; Lewis and Rosenblum, 1974; Sameroff and Chandler, 1975). The child's contribution to his own experience was a neglected research area, as discussed by Caldwell (1964) in her review of "The Effects of Infant Care." It is now recognized as an essential research endeavor, as illustrated by the title of two recent books, *The Effect of the Infant on His Caregiver* (Lewis and Rosenblum, 1974), and *The Competent Infant* (Stone, Smith, and Murphy, 1973). From a previous view of the infant as helpless, infinitely malleable, and needing to be socialized, the recent explosion in research has shown that the human infant at birth possesses well organized behaviors: the ability to discriminate among stimuli and to show a preference for some (Rheingold, 1967), to be biologically programmed to be initiator and responder to human interaction (Ainsworth, 1973; Bowlby, 1958); to actively organize, integrate, and adapt to experience (Bruner,

1969; Piaget, 1952; Rheingold, 1969). Advances in objective techniques for assessing neonate and infant behavior and demonstrable reliable individual differences among neonates now provide the opportunity to examine infant determinants within the caregiver-infant dyad in deviant infants as well as in normal babies.

This review will focus on babies born prematurely without specific severe sensory handicaps. Prematurity is the outcome of a variety of complications of pregnancy; it represents the single most prevalent abnormality associated with birth, and it has been suggested as a modal problem for assessing effects of the continuum of reproductive casualty (Birch and Gussow, 1970). The following is organized into sections describing selected dimensions of caregiving as they affect consequent behavior in the infant, the effects of the infant in evoking and responding to his social experience, and the issues involved in stability of effects. They are illustrated from a selection of pertinent studies and the author's own ongoing research.

SIGNIFICANT DIMENSIONS OF CAREGIVER BEHAVIOR

With the exception of a few studies in which maternal behaviors and attitudes were assessed through self-report (Wiener et al., 1965) or global clinical judgments (Drillien, 1964; Werner, Bierman, and French, 1971), other studies to be discussed later, measures of a caregiver's impact on the development of the risk infant have essentially focused on social status and/or ethnic membership. Because socioeconomic status is one of the few caregiving variables that has been considered in the experience of a risk infant, it merits further analysis.

Socioeconomic Status

As Deutsch (1973) points out, socioeconomic status is not a unitary variable; it is a conglomerate: a shorthand label for a cluster of attributes. The behaviors and attitudes referred to are not specific, homogeneous, or even stable over time. Thus, socioeconomic status is a broad based variable similar in its lack of specificity to the factor labeled "institutionalization." In fact, the model of deprivation arising from the investigation of institutions has been generalized to lower class membership. There is now some question as to whether a difference model rather than a deprivation model may be more accurate, or even whether excessive stimulation rather than deprivation may be more relevant.

An increasing number of studies using naturalistic observations (Kagan, 1969; Kagan and Tulkin, 1971; Lewis and Wilson, 1972; Tulkin and Kagan, 1972; Wachs, Uzgiris, and Hunt, 1971) have indicated that poverty is not analogous to stimulus deprivation nor to the lack of responsiveness often found in orphanage rearing. Neither is it necessarily associated with differences in affective variables.

That is not to say that social status does not powerfully affect a child's development. Regardless of the processes involved, there are no data to contradict the significant correlation between socioeconomic status and IQ scores throughout the entire age range starting from 3 years (Kennedy, Van der Riet, and White, 1963). Furthermore, there appears to be evidence of progressive retardation in children in lower class environments (Klaus and Gray, 1968; Wiener, Rider, and Oppel, 1963). Although there is little doubt that children 3 years of age and older from poverty backgrounds are more likely to show lower scores on intelligence tests, most studies have found no relationship between social class and mental test performance in infants below 2 years of age (Bayley, 1965; Golden and Birns, 1968). But the belief that differences in functioning within the first 2 years of life must exist as precursors to the later IQ differences has generated much research that indicates subtle but significant differences in the rate of attainment of Piagetian developmental landmarks (Wachs, Uzgiris, and Hunt, 1971), selectivity of visual attention (Fantz and Nevis, 1967; Kagan, 1971), auditory attention (Kagan, 1971; Tulkin, 1970), and selectivity in rate of vocalization (Kagan and Tulkin, 1971; Tulkin, 1970).

While social status may be useful for differentiating groups, it cannot be used to understand individual differences within a group. Furthermore, it is such a global variable that, for purposes here, although it may index some significant dimensions of interaction, it does not differentiate others (Tulkin, 1972). There are more specific dimensions of caregiver-infant interaction that have been objectively examined through naturalistic observation and experimental situations. Operating even above a basic minimum threshold (Jensen, 1969), these dimensions have been found to affect a wide variety of cognitive and social behaviors within family-reared infants. The dimensions have been thoughtfully discussed by Ainsworth (1962), Yarrow (1961), and Yarrow and Goodwin (1965), among others, and the relationships to infant behavior recently summarized by Clarke-Stewart (1973).

The "human caregiver," for want of a better term, has been described as the perceptual stimulus within the baby's environment and is the most salient and complex, as well as the most contingent to the baby's behavior (Rheingold, 1961). Moreover, the caregiver not only provides stimulation and reinforcement herself (assuming it is a female), she also mediates stimulation from the inanimate environment.

Amount and Intensity of Stimulation

The amount of contact there is with the infant, regardless of mode, variously labeled as attentiveness (Rubenstein, 1967) or intensity and level of social stimulation (Yarrow et al., 1972), has been shown in some studies to influence IQ scores. This is true whether they are concurrently measured in infancy (Clarke-Stewart, 1973; Yarrow et al., 1972) or later at 10 years of age (Yarrow et al., 1973). The intensity of social stimulation also has been associated with an infant's greater exploration of the novel (Rubenstein, 1967; Yarrow et al., 1972). The variable does not necessarily reflect the overall quantity of time that the mother spends at home with her baby, because time at home may not reflect the number of contacts (Schaffer and Emerson, 1964b). Yet, some influence of the mere availability of the mother in the baby's environment probably does operate; however, to what degree is not sufficiently understood. The issue is particularly relevant to extra home care and substitute caregivers. The evidence is so far equivocal because it appears that those maternal attitudes associated with the decision for extra home care may be also associated with differences in maternal behavior in the baby's presence (Caldwell et al., 1970).

Positions in Space

More specific behaviors subsumed under the rubric of "intensity of stimulation" have also been investigated. Lack of experience in different positions in space, particularly in the prone position, has been implicated in delayed and deviant gross motor development in institutionalized infants (Dennis and Najarian, 1957; Dennis and Sayegh, 1965). Increased, but still minimal, contact stimulation was found to retard the degree of cumulative retardation observed (Casler, 1965). In family infants, also, a high level of physical contact enhances cognitive development as assessed by visual response decrement (Lewis, Goldberg, and Campbell, 1969) and infant IQ tests (Yarrow et al., 1973). As an alternative, several studies (Korner and Thoman, 1970; 1972; White and Castle, 1964) have suggested that proprioceptive-vestibular stimulation associated with picking up and holding a neonate or young infant (more than physical contact per se) may be an important element in mediating changes in arousal level and visual attentiveness. In investigating this dimension, a series of studies by Ainsworth and her associates (Ainsworth, 1973; Ainsworth et al., 1971; Bell and Ainsworth, 1972) indicated that differences in the amount of experience normal family infants have with relatively long pick-up episodes, tender and careful in quality, in the first half year of life, were associated with a reduced amount of crying. It also was associated with active initiation of physical contact as well as readiness to turn to independent activity in the last quarter of the first year. Nevertheless, holding may be clearly beneficial only in the first 6 months of life. Later, it may become confounded with restrictiveness of exploration and activity.

Direct Physical Contact

It has been suggested that handling may be a particularly important dimension in the development of prematurely born babies. First, residence in hospital nurseries in isolettes may deprive the infant of the proprioceptive stimulation (Solkoff et al., 1969) or reciprocal stimulus feedback experiences (Siqueland, 1973) that fetuses or normal term-born babies would have. Second, diminished physical contact that mothers have with their prematurely born infants may diminish the attachment the mother feels toward her infant. In fact, suggestive evidence has been offered (Klaus and Kennell, 1970; Leifer et al., 1972) that the amount of contact a mother has with her newborn may be associated not only with her quality of mothering but also with her satisfaction in other social relationships. Intervention studies that have increased the handling of prematurely born babies in the nursery show significant outcomes in visual conditioning at 4 months of age (Siqueland, 1973) and in gross and fine motor development and activity at 7 to 8 months of age (Solkoff et al., 1969). The effects appear to be mediated by changes in the babies that in turn may evoke differential treatment from their mothers. Thus, for example, handled infants tended to have more toys and greater mother-infant interaction at follow up (Solkoff et al., 1969).

Distant Receptors

In contrast to effects mediated by direct physical contact, the role of distance receptors in social interactions has been emphasized (Walters and Parke, 1965). The amount of mutual gazing that occurs during the first 3 months of life has been found to influence a male infant's later friendliness to a stranger (Robson, Pederson, and Moss, 1969) as well as his visual attentiveness to two-dimensional nonsocial stimuli (Moss and Robson, 1970). As mutual gazing has been shown to be related to specific response classes, so quantity and quality of talking to an infant have been associated with differences in infants' rate of vocalization as well as rate of acquisition of language. Although rate of vocalization is not synonomous with skill, it is highly sensitive to social interaction (Rheingold, 1956; Rheingold and Bayley, 1959) and may index excitement and arousal levels (Jones and Moss, 1971; Kagan, 1969b). Rate of vocalization also shows intriguing sex differences associated with differential treatment by the caregiver (Moss, 1967). The more frequently the caregiver talked to the infant, the greater the rate of infant vocalization was found in one study (Irwin, 1960) but not in others (Kagan, 1969a; Yarrow et al., 1972). When assessed in conjunction with the amount of opportunity given for inanimate environmental exploration, frequency of maternal talking *did* relate to frequency of infant vocalizing (Beckwith, 1971a). More frequent caregiver talking was also associated with more discriminative rate of vocalization, at least in girls (Tulkin, 1971). Not only frequency but also contingency of the caregiver's verbalizations to the infant's vocalizations increased the amount of vocalization (Yarrow et al., 1972) as well as the rate of acquisition of language (Nelson, 1973).

Caregiver Responsiveness

The caregiver's contact with the infant is important not only because it provides exposure to a variety of perceptual stimuli but also because the timing and appropriateness provide reciprocal stimulus feedback experiences and reinforce infant behavior. Although difficult to objectify, variables such as the caregiver's responsiveness to a child's cues (Yarrow et al., 1973), contingency to distress (Yarrow et al., 1972), sensitivity to infant signals (Ainsworth and Bell, 1975), individualization (Yarrow, 1964), the higher the infant's IQ score and the faster the rate of development of both object and person permanence (Bell, 1970). Furthermore, the greater the sensitivity to the infant's signals, the more socially effective a child will be judged to be 10 years later (Yarrow et al., 1973). On the other hand, the more punishing, intrusive, critical, or directing of the child's behavior, the slower the acquisition of language (Nelson, 1973) and the poorer the performance on infant scales (Ainsworth and Bell, 1975) as well as on intelligence tests later in life (Bayley and Schaefer, 1964).

Environment Mediation

The caregiver mediates the infant's interaction with the inanimate environment by providing objects for manipulation and places for exploration. On the other hand, the caregiver may interfere with the infant's goal directed behavior. The variety and kind of objects available to the infant have been found to correlate with Bayley mental development index (Yarrow et al., 1972), exploratory behavior (Rubenstein, 1967; Yarrow et al., 1972), and with some scales of the Uzgiris-Hunt assessment of Piaget stages of sensorimotor development (Wachs, 1973; Wachs, Uzgiris, and Hunt, 1971). There is some suggestion that provision of toys alone may not be significant (Williams and Scarr, 1971). Only when the caregiver highlighted the toys or when the toys became part of social interaction did they relate to infant behavior (Clarke-Stewart, 1973).

Variety and Opportunity of Exploration

The variety of objects available and the opportunity to explore the living space have been pointed to as factors influencing gross motor skill (Williams and Scott, 1953) and infant IQ (Ainsworth and Bell, 1975). Mothers who are insensitive to their babies' signals or have few social contacts with their infants, and who also limit their babies' exploration, have been found to have infants with lower IQ scores (Ainsworth and Bell, 1975; Beckwith, 1971b). Although floor freedom, that is, the amount of time the baby is free to crawl on the floor without restriction (Ainsworth and Bell, 1975), may be too limited in definition, it may represent an important dimension in which the specific behaviors change as the child grows older. White and Watts' (1973) permissiveness and encouragement in exploration, associated with social and cognitive effectiveness in 2-year-olds, may represent the same factor. Not only the range of inanimate experiences available within the home but also the number and kind of trips outside the home contribute to an infant's development in language acquisition (Nelson, 1973), IQ scores (Beckwith, 1971b), and stages of sensorimotor development (Wachs, 1973).

Background Stimuli

While these findings emphasize the importance of varied opportunities for inanimate exploration, the amount of background stimulus bombardment, out of the infant's control, must also be considered. A crowded house, with the TV on most of the time, and without a place for the infant to escape the noise and activity, has been associated with slower language acquisition (Nelson, 1973) and slower sensorimotor development (Wachs, 1973; Wachs, Uzgiris, and Hunt, 1971).

Conclusion

It is most likely that environmental variables interact complexly. Empirical evidence (Ainsworth and Bell, 1975; Beckwith, 1971b) and theoretical formulations (Bowlby,

1958) indicate a redundancy in behavioral development such that reduced experience in one dimension may be adequately compensated by experiences received through another dimension. Clusters, or combined deficits rather than single factors, may be necessary to produce an observable effect. If that is so, professional intervention or family caregiving could be expected to be successful in encouraging a child's competence through a variety of mediating processes.

EFFECTS OF THE INFANT

Infant-initiated Interaction

The preceding discussion and the research on which it is based emphasize the caregiver's influence on the infant but ignore the reciprocal nature of the interaction, as well as the infant's contribution to his own experience (Bell, 1971; Korner, 1971). From the earliest weeks of life, it is the infant who effectively promotes many of the interactions. For example, Moss and Robson (1968) observed the startling phenomenon that 1-month-old infants initiated roughly four out of five interactions. The infant, through his discriminative crying, looking, and smiling, facilitates and maintains interaction (Bell, 1974). His influence is not only immediate but shows long-term effects on the caregiver. As Rheingold (1969) emphasized, the baby more powerfully socializes the adult into parenthood than the parent socializes the infant. At issue is the examination of the manner in which individual differences in infants affect the caregiver and how individual differences among infants modify the effects of the same experience.

Research Strategies

Two research strategies have been used. One assesses differences in the infants, either along a single dimension such as crying or soothability, or in nominal variables such as sex or risk, and observes the effect on the caregiver (Lewis and Rosenblum, 1974). The other strategy examines differential outcomes derived from the match or mismatch between the infant's characteristics and the caregiver's behavior. This view is reflected in Schaffer's (1966) suggestion that a less active baby is the one who will be most handicapped by an unstimulating environment, and Korner's (1974) speculation that the more intensely responsive, more easily aroused infant may experience a highly stimulating environment with some difficulty. On a broader level, Thomas, Chess, and Birch's (1968) longitudinal project has shown that babies who were irritable, intense in their reactions, negative or withdrawing from new situations elicited disharmonious relationships with their families and were referred in the largest proportion for child guidance help. Nevertheless, not all the children had the same outcome. Alternatively, for those parents who maintained sensitivity, emotional support, and promoted new experiences, their infants became competent and effective children.

Individual Differences at Birth

Both strategies are based on the characterization and measurement of individual differences at birth that reflect relatively stable predispositions and that are likely to affect the caregiver. Among the dimensions that have been studied in normal term-born neonates are the following: neonates have been shown to differ in frequency and length of spontaneous crying (Korner, 1971), in crying elicited to interruption of sucking (Bell, Weller, and Waldrop, 1971), and in soothability (Birns, Blank, and Bridger, 1966). Sensory response thresholds show stable individual differences over the neonatal periods (Birns, 1965; Korner, 1974) with visual alertness reliable over the first month of life (Barten and Rouch, 1971). Significant individual as well as sex differences (Moss, 1967) have been found in duration of wakefulness and sleep (Korner, 1974). The greater the wakefulness the more interactions the infant evoked (Moss, 1967).

Babies at risk can be characterized on the same dimensions, and such investigations will show deviances in the infants' behavior that will make the families' adaptations to their babies more difficult. This view is supported by Prechtl's (1963) work in which he described a "hyperexcitability" syndrome that was associated with prenatal and perinatal complications and manifest on neonatal neurologic examination. Longitudinal follow up in the first year of life showed that these infants, when compared to a control group of normal infants, elicited much greater anxiety and rejection from their mothers.

Current Research

The goal of this current research is to describe differential patterns of care associated with risk and to relate those patterns to some of the behavioral characteristics that may differentiate groups of high risk infants from other babies. It is further hoped that differential outcomes as they arise from a more "optimum" match of infant and caregiver interactions will be studied.

This investigation is part of an ongoing project entitled "Diagnostic and Intervention Studies of High-Risk Infants" (Parmelee, 1972). Prematurely born infants were selected for study as a prototype of infants at risk for developmental disabilities from prenatal and perinatal causes. The families of all babies born prematurely at the University of California at Los Angeles nursery during the years 1972 to 1974 were asked to participate in the study, and the babies were then followed prospectively from birth through 2 years of age. The sample covers a wide socioeconomic and ethnic range and includes first and later borns.

As neonates and throughout the first 2 years of life, the infants have been assessed on a variety of laboratory measures, some of which were developed in the larger project and some of which are conventional techniques. Chosen, among others, were assessment measures that were considered most likely to reveal deviances in neurological functioning implicated as sequelae of pre- and perinatal complications (Knobloch and Pasamanick, 1959). Also included were broad based examinations of development: the Gesell Developmental Examination and Piagetian object permanence scale, more specific assessments of visual attention, visual preference, exploratory behavior, and precision of hand manipulation and object use.

Assessment The caregiver-infant interactions were assessed through naturalistic observations in the home at 1, 3, 8, and 24 months (after the expected date of delivery, as reported by the mother in order to make maturational factors comparable for all babies). Naturalistic observations, rather than laboratory or structured situations, were selected because they were thought to have greater ecological validity despite any biases caused by the presence of the observer. This decision allows for a sample of the everyday experience of the infants, whether they are cared for at home by their mothers, fathers, sibs, grandmothers, or a babysitter at the babysitter's house.

Laboratory Measures This report is based on preliminary analyses comparing characterizations of the infants at birth and at term to the observed mother-infant interactions in the home at 1 month past term. For that period, the five laboratory measures of the infant included: 1) an obstetric complications scale, 2) a postnatal complications scale, 3) the Parmelee and Michaelis (1973) newborn neurological examination, 4) neurophysiological sleep measures, and 5) visual attention test. The obstetric complications scale, derived from Prechtl (1968), is assessed at birth and determines the presence or absence of 41 optimal conditions of pregnancy and delivery referring to maternal factors, factors of parturition, and fetal factors. The other measures have been administered at the time the baby reached the date of its expected delivery (as reported by the mother). The postnatal complications scale (Parmelee, 1972) determined the presence or absence of such complications as respiratory distress, infections, and medical procedures such as transfusions and surgery. The Parmelee and Michaelis (1973) newborn neurological examination evaluated infants with respect to muscle tone, reflex patterns of behavior, and states of arousal. The neurophysiological sleep measures assess the concordance among body activity, respiratory patterns, eye movements, and EEG (Parmelee and Stern, 1973). The visual attention measures (Sigman et al., 1973) assessed length of first fixation, total duration of fixation, and average length of fixation to 1-minute presentations of a black and white checkerboard and to flashing lights. In addition to analysing each individual measure, since it has been suggested (Parmelee and Haber, 1973; Sameroff and Chandler, 1975) that prediction of outcome may be enhanced by a consideration of a cluster of factors, the infant's standardized scores on each measure are totalled to make a "neonatal risk" score as described by Parmelee (1972).

Naturalistic Observations The naturalistic observations in the home at 1 month past the expected date of birth is scheduled in the morning. The observation length is based on the infant's sleep-wake cycle rather than on a predetermined length of time. The baby is observed through a cycle that consists of waking from sleep, being fed, and all other activities that occur until again asleep for more than one half of an hour. If a visit happens to begin anywhere but at the beginning of an awake cycle, the observer waits in the home or returns later that day in time to observe that part of the next cycle that had been missed in the first observation. The caregiver is urged to conduct her activities as she normally would. Observations include the activities of bathing, diapering, dressing, putting to sleep, social play, as well as a noninteractional time. All sessions include at least one feeding, whether from the breast, or milk from a bottle held by the caregiver, or propped. The observer is kept uninformed about the baby's test scores and any family background information.

The behaviors of mother and infant are time sampled every 15 seconds using a checklist. The observer wears an automatic timer with an earphone that emits a click every 15 seconds.

Caregiver Behavior   Factors thought to be of particular importance in the caregiver's behavior toward the infant are recorded. These include frequency counts of 15-second time units that note whether the caregiver is in the room with the baby and if so, if the baby is held, rocked, patted, touched, talked to, and/or looked at. The situations in which interactions occur, that is, feeding, burping, diapering, bathing, or social play, are also recorded. In addition, like many other investigators, the interest here is not only in relative variety and intensity of social stimulation but of the contingency and sensitivity of the behavior to the infant's signals. It is apparent that such a dimension involves more human judgment than the former. The difficult problem of making such judgments objective has been dealt with by tagging the caregiver's behavior each time it is seen to occur after the baby's distress, or nondistress vocalization, or smile, if the response matches the baby's signals. "Match" is interpreted loosely. An example of a mismatch to distress would be repeated attempts to feed a baby who would not suck, or repeated attempts to rock to sleep a baby who was not sleepy. So identifying the behaviors allows calculation of the percentage of episodes responded to, as well as of the speed of response.

The Environment   Finally, aspects of the inanimate environment are noted. These include the number and kind of objects within view of the infant and if and how long the televison is on.

Infant Behavior   Categories of infant behavior recorded include frequency counts of 15-second time units of fussing, crying, nondistress vocalizing, and/or looking at the caregiver or the observer.

Observer Reliability   Observer reliability has been assessed at several times before and during the data collection. Reliabilities were determined by computing Pearson correlation coefficients (Edwards, 1946) for the total frequency of a specific behavior each observer had recorded in an observation. The coefficients ranged from 0.70 to 0.97 with a majority above 0.80.

At this point, preliminary analyses have been conducted of some of the frequency data. It is anticipated that characterizations of the caregivers' responsiveness and of the infants' soothability will provide additional necessary information.

Findings   The findings show that individual differences in the infants in laboratory assessments made at term date did correlate with differential amounts in several dimensions of caregiver-infant interaction in the home 1 month later. The newborn neurologic score correlated significantly and negatively with the proportion of time the mother-infant pairs spent in social interaction. The finding supports the importance of early neurologic organization as a characteristic that persists past the neonatal period, influencing response to a wide range of stimuli (Moss and Robson, 1970) and affecting social experiences.

Characterization of the infants on the cluster of "term" assessments, that is, the "term" risk score, related significantly to duration of response holding. Infants, both boys and girls, who scored at greater risk were held more sensitively for a significantly greater proportion of their awake time. Ainsworth and her associates' (1971) investigation with normal infants has suggested that sensitive holding may have important consequences for the infant. Because talking to the babies was correlated with holding the babies, infants of greater risk were then exposed to significantly more language. Sex differences favoring males in the amount of time mothers hold infants has been reported by other investigators (Lewis and Wilson, 1972; Moss, 1967). No previous data exist that compare interactional patterns with boy and girl babies of differing degrees of risk. Why were the high risk babies held for a greater proportion of their awake time? At present only speculations can be offered. The effects were not related to the fussiness of the babies. Neither the high risk boys nor high risk girls fussed or cried more than did the other babies.

At the least, the results are optimistic in that they suggest that the mothers of the more deviant babies have not withdrawn from or rejected their babies. It is not suggested that the finding be generalized beyond this sample because the families participating in this project received extra clinical services from a public health nurse and a social worker. Such support might be a factor in enabling the families to be more nurturant. However, the consequences of increased holding experience are available for study.

Conclusion

The implications for these babies' further development and for their relationships with their mothers await further analysis. Based on the enhancing effects of increased holding in the early months found with normal term infants, examination will be made at 8 months of the greater risk group comparing those babies who continued to receive more holding with those who did not. The supposition is that the poorest cognitive development will be in the group designated at greater risk as neonates who then received the least holding. Furthermore, there is the clearly speculative hypothesis that the inherent homeostasis in the dyad (Bell, 1974) has led to the intensification of one interaction system as a substitute for another. Schaffer and Emerson (1964a) have suggested that babies who receive less holding because they are resistant to the restraints of cuddling may compensate through other kinds of social stimulation. It is possible for speculation that increased holding and increased duration of holding episodes may compensate for lesser mutual gazing.

STABILITY OF EFFECTS

This research strives to describe in detail patterns of caregiver-infant interaction in relationship to babies' development within the first 2 years of life. The significance of such research is intimately tied to the inquiry into the long-term stability of early experience. The questions raised are important ones as well for normal child development. They are no less so for high risk infants, because the determination of who is at risk, as well as the effectiveness of intervention, depends on the stability of effect. Some infant experiences, for some subjects, for some highly significant outcome variables, show dramatic associations with later behavior (Bayley and Schaefer, 1964; Goldfarb, 1943; Kagan and Moss, 1962; Rheingold and Bayley, 1959; Yarrow et al., 1973). On the other hand, many potent associations between the quantity and qualities of infant caregiving and concomitant infant behavior seem to evaporate (Dennis and Najarian, 1957; Kagan and Klein, 1973; Wachs and Cucinotta, 1971). As an example, infant IQ is responsive to several dimensions of mother-infant interaction, but infant intelligence tests have been shown repeatedly to be of little practical value in predicting later intelligence (Stott and Ball, 1965). Prediction of emotional traits may fare little better. Despite this search for trait continuity across time and situations, it sometimes seems as though just as much change as stability has been found (Bell, Weller, and Waldrop, 1971; Kagan, 1971; Macfarlane, 1964). Furthermore, stability of associations may be different for boys and girls (Bayley and Schaefer, 1964; Kagan and Moss, 1962).

Several alternative explanations have been offered. They provide areas for further investigation. First, the ontogeny of cognitive and social behaviors may not yet be well enough known. Thus, cognitive functioning probably depends on a broad band of intellectual and social abilities, each of which develops at a different rate that is dependent on continuous interaction between a person's genetic predispositions and the environmental stimulation he experiences (Bayley and Schaefer, 1964; Hunt, 1961; Hunt and Kirk, 1971; McCall, Hagarty, and Hurlburt, 1972), each of which may assume differential importance, depending on the tasks the person faces. It is apparent that it would be useful to know more about the ontogeny of language acquisition and use (Friedlander, 1970; Nelson, 1973) of prosocial behaviors (Rheingold, 1973), for example, and of social competence (Bronson, 1971; MacFarlane, 1964; White and Watts, 1973).

An alternative point of view is based on a distinction between maturational rate and more permanent qualitative differences in ability (Elkind, 1969; Kagan and Klein, 1973). The point is expressed succinctly in the statement (Kagan and Klein, 1973), that there is no reason to assume that the caterpillar who metamorphoses a bit earlier than his kind is a better adapted or more efficient butterfly.

A third point of view stresses the necessity of later experiences that may act to attenuate or support the effects of early experience. Continuity may then be dependent on periodic reinstatement of early experiences (Wachs and Cucinotta, 1971), or may be directly related to the extent the subsequent environment is reinforcing of given characteristics (Yarrow, 1964). Thus, the effects of early experiences may have been clearer for boys' intellectual performance than for girls', because girls as they become women tended not to be reinforced for achievement (Kagan and Moss, 1962).

The stability of the effects of early experience may be mediated by characteristics of the infant. A finding consistent with that point of view indicates that high intensity of responsiveness in a neonate may lead to low intensity and low responsiveness in a preschooler, (Bell, Weller, and Waldrop, 1971). One factor involved may be the extent to which the infant's characteristics produce reinstating experiences. Intensity of reactiveness may in itself produce painful consequences, or may provoke adverse reinforcement from the caregiver. On the other hand, a more positive cycle is also possible. Siqueland (1973), for example, found that interventions with premature infants in the first few weeks of life changed the babies so that they thereby evoked more responsive interaction from the mother. Similarly, Falender (1973) found that intervention produced more talkative children who asked more questions and made more requests, which in turn provoked more verbal interaction from the mother. This view suggests the possibility that the timing of various accomplishments might be important in so far as it influences the mother's response to her child.

Still another opinion, consistent with animal research (Denenberg, 1969; Levine, 1969) suggests the primacy of early experience to be manifest in motivational factors (Lewis and Goldberg, 1969; Provence and Lipton, 1962) rather than in skills. Differences in cognitive performance would then be demonstrated as related to early experience to the extent to which differences in such variables as risk-taking, persistence, achievement strivings, etc., became significant in the task situation.

Finally, on a broader level, the fact that designated experiences are found to be important for adequate functioning in infancy does not necessarily make them unique to infancy or unnecessary in later life. Sterility and invariance in the inanimate environment and inattention and lack of response from the social environment must be deleterious for all people, regardless of age.

SUMMARY

This chapter emphasizes the point of view that the development of an infant at risk from prenatal and perinatal causes must be understood in terms of the experiences received through transactions with the family to which the infant himself contributes. In support, selected aspects of the research literature are reviewed that demonstrate cognitive and social consequences for normal infants of specific, objective dimensions of interaction with their caregivers. In addition, selected studies of the effects of the normal and deviant infant in evoking and responding to his social experience are reviewed. The design and preliminary findings from this author's own research are presented in the context of further detailed examination of caregiver and infant influences in the prematurely born infant's development.

LITERATURE CITED

Ainsworth, M. D. S. 1962. The effects of maternal deprivation: A review of findings and controversy in the context of research strategy. *In* Deprivation of Maternal Care: A Reassessment of Its Effects. Public Health Paper No. 14, pp. 97–165. World Health Organization, Geneva.

Ainsworth, M. D. S. 1964. Patterns of attachment behavior shown by the infant in interaction with his mother. Merrill-Palmer Quart. 10: 51–58.

Ainsworth, M. D. S. 1973. The development of infant-mother attachment. In B. M. Caldwell and H. N. Riccuiti (eds.), Review of Child Development Research, Vol. 3, pp. 1–94. University of Chicago Press, Chicago.

Ainsworth, M. D. S., and S. M. Bell. 1975. Mother-infant interaction and the development of competence. In K. J. Connolly and J. Bruner (eds.), The Growth of Competence, pp. 97–118. Academic Press, New York.

Ainsworth, M. D. S., S. M. V. Bell, M. P. Blehar, and M. B. Main. 1971. Physical contact: A study of infant responsiveness and its relation to maternal handling. Paper presented at Society for Research in Child Development, April 1–4, Minneapolis, Minn.

Barten, S., and J. Rouch, 1971. Continuity in the development of visual behavior in young infants. Child Devel. 42: 1566–1571.

Bayley, N. 1965. Comparisons of mental and motor test scores for ages 1–15 months by sex, birth order, race, geographical location, and education of parents. Child Devel. 36: 379–411.

Bayley, N., and E. S. Schaefer. 1964. Correlations of maternal and child behaviors with the development of mental abilities. Data from the Berkeley Growth Study. Monogr. Soc. Res. Child Devel. 29: No. 6, 80p.

Beckwith, L. 1971a. Relationships between infants' vocalizations and their mothers' behaviors. Merrill-Palmer Quart. 17: 211–266.

Beckwith, L. 1971b. Relationships between attributes of mothers and their infants' IQ scores. Child Devel. 42: 1083–1097.

Bell, R. Q. 1971. Stimulus control of parent or caretaker behavior by offspring. Devel. Psych. 4: 63–72.

Bell, R. Q. 1974. Contributions of human infants to caregiving and social interaction. In M. Lewis and L. A. Rosenblum (eds.), The Effect of the Infant on its Caregiver, pp. 1–20. Wiley, New York.

Bell, R. Q., G. M. Weller, and M. F. Waldrop. 1971. Newborn and preschooler: Organization of behavior and relations between periods. Monogr. Soc. Res. Child Devel. 36: (Nos. 1–2, Serial No. 142) 145p.

Bell, S. M. 1970. The development of the concept of objects as related to infant-mother attachment. Child Devel. 41: 291–311.

Bell, S. M., and M. D. S. Ainsworth. 1972. Infant crying and maternal responsiveness. Child Devel. 43: 1171–1190.

Birch, H., and C. D. Gussow. 1970. Disadvantaged Children. Grune and Stratton, New York.

Birns, B. 1965. Individual differences in human neonates' responses to stimulation. Child Devel. 36: 249–256.

Birns, B., M. Blank, W. H. Bridger. 1966. The effectiveness of various soothing techniques on human neonates. Psychosom. Med. 28: 316–322.

Bowlby, J. 1958. The nature of the child's tie to his mother. Intern. J. Psychoanal. 39: 350–373.

Braine, M., C. Heimer, H. Wortis, and A. Freedman. 1966. Factors associated with impariment of the early development of prematures. Monogr. Soc. Res. Child Devel. 31: No. 4, 92p.

Bronson, W. C. 1971. The growth of competence: Issues of conceptualization and measurement. In H. R. Schaffer (ed.), The Origins of Human Social Relations, pp. 269–277. Academic Press, New York.

Bruner, J. S. 1969. Process of growth in infancy. In A. Ambrose (ed.), Stimulation in Early Infancy, pp. 205–228. Academic Press, New York.

Caldwell, B. M. 1964. The effects of infant care. *In* M. L. Hoffman and L. W. Hoffman (eds.), Review of Child Development Research, Vol. 1. Russell Sage, New York.

Caldwell, B. M., C. M. Wright, A. S. Honig, and J. Tannenbaum. 1970. Infant day care and attachment. Amer. J. Orthopsych. 40: 397–412.

Caputo, D. V., and W. Mandell. 1970. Consequences of low birth weight. Devel. Psych. 3: 363–384.

Casler, L. 1965. The effects of extratactile stimulation in a group of institutionalized infants. Genet. Psychol. Monogr. 71: 137–175.

Clarke-Stewart, K. A. 1973. Interactions between mothers and their young children: Characteristics and consequences. Mongr. Soc. Res. Child Devel. 38: (6–7, Serial No. 153) 109p.

Denenberg, V. H. 1969. Experimental programming of life histories in the rat. *In* A. Ambrose (ed.), Stimulation in Early Infancy, pp. 21–34. Academic Press, New York.

Dennis, W., and B. Sayegh. 1965. The effect of supplementary experiences upon the behavioral development of infants in institutions. Child Devel. 36: 81–90.

Dennis, W., and P. Najarian. 1957. Infant development under environmental handicap. Psych. Monogr. 71: No. 7, 13p.

Deutsch, C. P. 1973. Social class and child development. *In* B. M. Caldwell and H. N. Ricciuti (eds.), Review of Child Development Research. Vol. 3, pp. 233–282. The University of Chicago Press, Chicago.

Drillien, C. M. 1964. The Growth and Development of the Prematurely Born Infant. Williams and Wilkins, Baltimore.

Edwards, A. L. 1946. Statistical Analysis for Students in Psychology and Education. Rinehart, New York.

Elkind, D. 1969. Piagetian and psychometric conceptions of intelligence. Harvard Educ. Rev. 39: No. 2, 319–337.

Falender, C. 1973. Mother-child interaction and the child's participation in the Milwaukee project: An experiment in the prevention of cultural-familial mental retardation. Paper presented at Society for Research in Child Development Meeting. March 29–April 1, 1973, Philadelphia.

Fantz, R. L., and S. Nevis. 1967. Pattern preferences and perceptual-cognitive development in early infancy. Merrill-Palmer Quart. 13: 77–108.

Friedlander, B. Z. 1970. Receptive language development in infancy: Issues and problems. Merrill-Palmer Quart. 16: 7–51.

Garmezy, N., and S. Streitman. 1974. Children at risk: The search for the antecedents of schizophrenia. Part 1. Conceptual models and research methods. Schiz. Bull. 8: 14–90.

Golden, M., and B. Birns. 1968. Social class and cognitive development in infancy. Merrill-Palmer Quart. 14: 139–149.

Goldfarb, W. 1943. The effects of early institutional care on adolescent personality. J. Exper. Educ. 12: 106–129.

Horowitz, F. D., and L. Y. Paden. 1973. The effectiveness of environmental intervention programs. *In* B. M. Caldwell and H. N. Ricciuti (eds.), Review of Child Development Research, Vol. 3, pp. 331–402. University of Chicago Press, Chicago.

Hunt, J. McV. 1961. Intelligence and Experience. Ronald Press, New York.

Hunt, J. McV., and G. E. Kirk. 1971. Social aspects of intelligence: Evidence and issues. *In* R. Cancro (ed.), Intelligence, Genetics, and Environmental Influences, pp. 262–306. Grune and Stratton, New York.

Irwin, O. C. 1960. Infant speech: Effect of systematic reading of stories. J. Speech Hearing Res. 3: 187–190.

Jensen, A. R. 1969. How much can we boost IQ and scholastic achievement? Harvard Educ. Rev. 39: No. 1, 1–123.

Jones, S. J., and H. A. Moss. 1971. Age, state, and maternal behavior associated with infant vocalizations. Child Devel. 42: 1039–1051.

Kagan, J. 1969a. Continuity in cognitive development during the first year. Merrill-Palmer Quart. 15: 101–119.

Kagan, J. 1969b. Some response measures that show relations between social class and the course of cognitive development in infancy. In A. Ambrose (ed.), Stimulation in Early Infancy, pp. 253–256. Academic Press, New York.

Kagan, J. 1971. Change and Continuity in Infancy. Wiley, New York.

Kagan, J., and R. E. Klein. 1973. Cross-cultural perspectives on early development. Amer. Psych. 28: 947–961.

Kagan, J., and H. Moss. 1962. Birth to Maturity: A Study in Psychological Development. Wiley, New York.

Kagan, J., and S. R. Tulkin. 1971. Social class differences in child rearing during the first year. In H. R. Schaffer (ed.), The Origins of Human Social Relations, pp. 165–183. Academic Press, New York.

Kawi, A., and B. Pasamanick. 1958. Association of factors of pregnancy with reading disorders in childhood. J. Amer. Med. Assoc. 166: 1420–1423.

Kennedy, W., V. Van der Riet, and J. White. 1963. A normative sample of intelligence and achievement of Negro elementary children in the Southeastern United States. Monogr. Soc. Res. Child Devel. 28: No. 90, 112p.

Klaus, R. A., and S. W. Gray. 1968. The early training project for disadvantaged children: A report after five years. Monogr. Soc. Res. Child Devel. 33: No. 4, 66p.

Klaus, M. K., and J. H. Kennell. 1970. Mothers separated from their newborn infants. Pediat. Clin. No. Amer. 17: 1015–1037.

Knobloch, H., and B. Pasamanick. 1959. Syndrome of minimal cerebral damage in infancy. J. Amer. Med. Assoc. 170: 1384–1387.

Knobloch, H., and B. Pasamanick. 1962. Developmental and behavioral approach to neurologic examination in infancy. Child Devel. 33: 181–198.

Korner, A. F. 1971. Individual differences at birth: Implications for early experience and later development. Amer. J. Orthopsych. 41: 608–619.

Korner, A. 1974. The effect of the infant's state, level of arousal, sex, and ontogenetic stage on the caregiver. In M. Lewis and L. A. Rosenblum (eds.), The Effect of the Infant on its Caregiver, pp. 105–122. Wiley, New York.

Korner, A., and R. Grobstein. 1967. Individual differences in irritability and soothability as related to parity in neonates. Unpublished manuscript.

Korner, A., and E. B. Thoman. 1970. Visual alertness in neonates as evoked by maternal care. J. Exper. Child Psych. 10: 67–78.

Korner, A., and E. B. Thoman. 1972. The relative efficacy of contact and vestibular-proprioceptive stimulation in soothing neonates. Child Devel. 43: 443–453.

Leifer, A. D., P. H. Leiderman, C. R. Barnett, and J. A. Williams. 1972. Effects of mother-infant separation on maternal attachment behavior. Child Devel. 43: 1203–1218.

Levine, S. 1969. Infantile stimulation: A perspective. In A. Ambrose (ed.), Stimulation in Early Infancy, pp. 3–8. Academic Press, New York.

Lewis, M. 1972. State as an infant-environment interaction: An analysis of mother-infant behavior as a function of sex. Merrill-Palmer Quart. 18: 95–121.

Lewis, M., and S. Goldberg. 1969. Perceptual-cognitive development in infancy: A generalized expectancy model as a function of the mother-infant interaction. Merrill-Palmer Quart. 15: 81–100.

Lewis, M., and L. A. Rosenblum. 1974. The Effect of the Infant on its Caregiver. Wiley, New York.

Lewis, M., and C. D. Wilson. 1972. Infant development in lower-class American families. Human Devel. 15: 112—127.

Lewis, M., S. Goldberg, and H. Campbell. 1969. A developmental study of information processing within the first three years of life: Response decrement to a redundant signal. Mongr. Child Devel. 34: (9, Serial No. 133), 41p.

Macfarlane, J. 1964. Perspectives on personality consistency and change from the guidance study. Vita Humana 7: 115—126.

McCall, R. B., P. S. Hagarty, and N. Hurlburt. 1972. Transitions in infant sensorimotor development and the prediction of childhood IQ. Amer. Psychol. 27: 728—748.

Moss, H. 1967. Sex, age, and state as determinants of mother-infant interaction. Merrill-Palmer Quart. 13: 19—36.

Moss, H. A., and K. S. Robson. 1968. The role of protest behavior in the development of the mother-infant attachment. Paper presented at American Psychological Association Meeting, Sept. 1—5, San Francisco.

Moss, H. A., and K. S. Robson. 1970. The relation between the amount of time infants spend at various states and the development of visual behavior. Child Devel. 41: 509—517.

Nelson, K. 1973. Structure and strategy in learning to talk. Monogr. Soc. Res. Child Devel. 38: (No. 1—2, Serial No. 149), 135p.

Parmelee, A. H. 1972. Diagnostic and intervention studies of high risk infants. NIH-NICHD 71-2447, USPHS No. HD-3-2776.

Parmelee, A. H., and A. Haber. 1973. Who is the "risk infant"? In H. J. Osofsky (ed.), Clinical Obstetrics and Gynecology, pp. 376—387. Harper and Row, New York.

Parmelee, A. H., and L. Liverman, 1963. Prematurity. In M. Green and R. J. Haggerty (eds.), Ambulatory Pediatrics, pp. 312—324. W. B. Saunders, New York.

Parmelee, A. H., and R. Michaelis. 1973. Parmelee and Michaelis newborn neurological examination. Unpublished manuscript. University of California at Los Angeles.

Parmelee, A. H., M. Sigman, C. B. Kopp, and A. Haber. 1975. The concept of a cumulative risk score for infants. In N. R. Ellis (ed.), Aberrant Development in Infancy: Human and Animal Studies, pp. 113—121. Lawrence Erlbaum, Hillsdale.

Parmelee, A. H., and E. Stern. 1973. Development of states in infants. In C. Clementi, D. Purpura, and F. Mayer (eds.), Sleep and the Maturing Nervous System, pp. 199—228. Academic Press, New York.

Pasamanick, B., and H. Knobloch. 1961. Epidemiological studies on the complications of pregnancy and the birth process. In G. Caplan (ed.), Prevention of Mental Disorder in Children. Basic Books, New York.

Pasamanick, B., M. E. Rogers, and A. M. Lilienfeld. 1956. Pregnancy experience and the development of behavior disorder in children. Amer. J. Psych. 112: 613—618.

Piaget, J. 1952. The Origins of Intelligence in Children. International Universities Press, New York.

Prechtl, H. F. R. 1963. The mother-child interaction in babies with minimal brain damage. In B. M. Foss (eds.), Determinants of Infant Behavior, II, pp. 53—59. Wiley, New York.

Prechtl, H. F. R. 1968. Neurological findings in newborn infants after pre- and paranatal complications. In J. H. P. Jonxis, H. K. A. Visser, and J. A. Troelstra (eds.), Aspects of Prematurity and Dysmaturity, pp. 303—321. Nutricia Symposium, Groningen, May 10—12, 1967. Stenfert, Kroese, Leiden.

Provence, S., and R. C. Lipton. 1962. Infants in Institutions: A comparison of their development with family-reared infants during the first year of life. International Universities Press, New York.

Rheingold, H. L. 1956. The modification of social responsiveness in institutional babies. Monogr. Soc. Res. Child Devel. 21: No. 2, 48p.

Rheingold, H. L. 1961. The effect of environmental stimulation upon social and exploratory behavior in the human infant. *In* B. M. Foss (ed.), Determinants of Infant Behavior, pp. 143–177. Wiley, New York.

Rheingold, H. L. 1967. A comparative psychology of development. *In* H. W. Stevenson, E. H. Hess, and H. L. Rheingold (eds.), Early Behavior: Comparative and Developmental Approaches, pp. 279–293. Wiley, New York.

Rheingold, H. L. 1969. The social and socializing infant. *In* D. A. Goslin (ed.), Handbook of Socialization Theory and Research, pp. 779–790. Rand McNally, Chicago.

Rheingold, H. L. 1973. Independent behavior of the human infant. *In* A. D. Pick (ed.), Minnesota Symposia on Child Psychology, 7: 178–203. University of Minnesota Press, Minneapolis, Minn.

Rheingold, H. L., and N. Bayley. 1959. The later effects of an experimental modification of mothering. Child Devel. 30: 362–372.

Robson, K. S., F. A. Pederson, and H. A. Moss. 1969. Developmental observations of diadic gazing in relation to the fear of strangers and social approach behavior. Child Devel. 40: 619–628.

Rubenstein, J. 1967. Maternal attentiveness and subsequent exploratory behavior in the infant. Child Devel. 38: 1089–1100.

Sameroff, A., and M. Chandler. 1975. Infant casuality and the continuum of infant caretaking. *In* F. D. Horowitz, E. M. Hetherington, M. Siegel, and S. Scarr Salapatek (eds.), Review of Child Development Research, Vol. 4. University of Chicago Press, Chicago.

Schaffer, H. R. 1966. Activity level as a constitutional determinant of infantile reaction to deprivation. Child Devel. 37: 595–602.

Schaffer, H. R., and P. E. Emerson. 1964a. Patterns of response to physical contact in early human development. J. Child Psych. Psychiat. 5: 1–13.

Schaffer, H. R., and P. E. Emerson. 1964b. The development of social attachments in infancy. Monogr. Soc. Res. Child Devel. 29: (3, Serial No. 94), 77p.

Sigman, M., C. B. Kopp, A. H. Parmelee, and W. E. Jeffrey. 1973. Visual attention and neurological organization in neonates. Child Devel. 44: 461–466.

Siqueland, E. R. 1973. Biological and experimental determinants of exploration in infancy. *In* L. J. Stone, H. T. Smith, and L. B. Murphy, (eds.), The Competent Infant, pp. 822–823. Basic Books, New York.

Skeels, H. 1966. Adult status of children with contrasting early life experiences. Monogr. Soc. Res. Child Devel. 31: (3, Serial No. 105), 65p.

Solkoff, N., S. Yaffe, D. Weintraub, and B. Blase. 1969. Effects of handling on the subsequent development of premature infants. Devel. Psych. 1: 765–768.

Stone, L. J., H. T. Smith, and L. B. Murphy. 1973. The Competent Infant. Basic Books, New York.

Stott, L. H., and R. S. Ball. 1965. Infant and preschool mental tests: Review and evaluation. Monogr. Soc. Res. Child Devel. 30: (3, Serial No. 101), 151p.

Thomas, A., S. Chess, and H. Birch. 1968. Temperament and Behavior Disorders in Children. New York University Press, New York.

Tulkin, S. R. 1970. Mother-infant interaction in the first year of life: An inquiry into the influences of social class. Dissertation, Department of Social Relations, Harvard University.

Tulkin, S. R. 1971. Infants reactions to mother's voice and stranger's voice: Social class differences in the first year of life. Presented at Society for Research in Child Development. April 1–4, Minneapolis, Minn.

Tulkin, S. R. 1972. An analysis of the concept of cultural deprivation. Devel. Psych. 6: 326–339.

Tulkin, S. R., and J. Kagan. 1972. Mother-child interaction in the first year of life. Child Devel. 43: 31–41.

Wachs, T. D. 1973. Utilization of a Piagetian approach in investigation of early experience effects: A research strategy and some illustrative data. Paper presented at American Psychological Association Meeting. August 27–31, Montreal, Canada.

Wachs, T., and P. Cucinotta. 1971. The effects of enriched neonatal experiences upon later cognitive functioning. Paper presented at Society for Research in Child Development. April 1–4, Minneapolis, Minn.

Wachs, T. D., I. C. Uzgiris, and J. McV. Hunt. 1971. Cognitive development in infants of different age levels and from different environmental backgrounds: an explanatory investigation. Merrill-Palmer Quart. 17: 283–317.

Walters, R. H., and R. O. Parke. 1965. The role of the distance receptors in the development of social responsiveness. *In* L. P. Lippsitt and C. C. Spiker (eds.), Advances in Child Development and Behavior. Vol. 2, pp. 59–96, Academic Press, New York.

Werner, E. E., J. M. Bierman, and F. E. French. 1971. The Children of Kauai. A Longitudinal Study from the Prenatal Period to Age Ten. University of Hawaii Press, Honolulu.

Werner, E., J. M. Bierman, F. E. French, K. Simonian, A. Connor, R. S. Smith, and M. Campbell. 1968. Reproductive and environmental casualties: A report on the 10-year follow-up of the children of the Kauai pregnancy study. Pediatrics 42: 112–127.

White, B., and P. Castle. 1964. Visual exploratory behavior following postnatal handling of human infants. Percept. Mot. Skills 18: 497–502.

White, B., P. Castle, and R. Held. 1964. Observations in the development of visually directed reaching. Child Devel. 35: 349–364.

White, B., and R. Held. 1967. Plasticity of sensorimotor development in the human infant. *In* J. Hellmuth (ed.), Exceptional Infant, Vol. 1, The Normal Infant, pp. 291–313. Brunner-Mazel, Inc., New York.

White, B. L., and J. C. Watts. 1973. Experience and Environment. Prentice-Hall, Englewood Cliffs, N.J.

Wiener, G. 1962. Psychologic correlates of premature birth: A review. J. Nerv. Ment. Dis. 134: 129–135.

Wiener, G. 1970. The relationship of birth weight and length of gestation to intellectual development at ages 8 to 10 years. J. Pediat. 76: 694–699.

Wiener, G., R. V. Rider, and W. Oppel. 1963. Some correlates of IQ changes in children. Child Devel. 34: 61–67.

Wiener, G., R. V. Rider, W. Oppel, L. K. Fischer, and P. A. Harper. 1965. Correlates of low-birth-weight: Psychological status at 6–7 years of age. Pediatrics 35: 434–444.

Wiener, G., R. V. Rider, W. Oppel, and P. A. Harper. 1968. Correlates of low birth weight. Psychological status at eight to ten years of age. Pediat. Rev. 2: 110–118.

Williams, J., and R. B. Scott. 1953. Growth and development of Negro infants: IV. Motor development and its relationship to child rearing practices in two groups of Negro infants. Child Devel. 24: 103–121.

Williams, M., and S. Scarr. 1971. Effects of short term intervention on performance in low-birth-weight disadvantaged children. Pediatrics 47: 289–298.

Yarrow, L. J. 1961. Maternal deprivation: Toward an empirical and conceptual re-evaluation. Psych. Bull. 58: 459–490.

Yarrow, L. J. 1964. Personality consistency and change: An overview of some conceptual and methodological issues. Vita Humana 7: 67–72.

Yarrow, L. J., and M. S. Goodwin. 1965. Some conceptual issues in the study of mother-infant interaction. Amer. J. Orthopsychiat. 35: 473–481.

Yarrow, L. J., M. S. Goodwin, H. Manheimer, and I. D. Milowe. 1973. Infancy experiences and cognitive and personality development at ten years. *In* L. J. Stone, H. T.

Smith, and L. B. Murphy (eds.), The Competent Infant: Research and Commentary, pp. 1274–1281. Basic Books, New York.

Yarrow, L. J., J. L. Rubenstein, F. A. Pederson, and J. J. Jankowski. 1972. Dimensions of early stimulation and their differential effects on infant development. Merrill-Palmer Quart. 18: 205–218.

Discussant's Comments

Harriet L. Rheingold, Ph.D.

This stellar assemblage bears witness to the thoughtful planning of the conference organizers and no less to the importance of the problem before us. The reports presented here reach a high order of excellence of scholarship and insight, and the research plans document well the most sophisticated thinking of which researchers are now capable. Praise, however well deserved, is nevertheless not the most useful response a discussant can make. Some constructive ideas are expected of one to enhance the possibility of success attending the efforts proposed.

Some of these remarks are very general and apply to much of the research on the topic of the conference, but some are more specific to the papers by Beckwith and by Denenberg and Thoman, the domain I have been assigned.

As has so well been pointed out by Beckwith and Thoman, the earlier view of the consequences of the mother's behavior for the child's development has been corrected, and the consequences of the child's behavior for the mother's is now recognized. It must be clear to all who grapple with this problem that it is not yet well known how to measure the child's input, nor yet how to handle so complex a theoretical construct as an interaction. These chapters, nevertheless, show that the problem is now recognized, and I have faith that a problem once recognized can eventually be solved.

What is still not generally recognized, however, is that because of the consequences of the child's behavior for the caregiver's behavior, the child's behavior cannot be used at any later point of time as a dependent variable. Said another way, neither the child's developmental status nor his performance on subsequent measures—whether intellectual, social, or emotional—can be used as a measure of the parent-child relationship precisely because the child has already contributed to that relationship. When formerly it was thought that only parental behavior was being measured, we were on firmer logical ground in measuring its effect on child behavior; but today we see so clearly that the earlier measures of parental behavior, by themselves, were faulty. Now that we must deal with an interaction between child and parent—itself a great conceptual advance—we know that

---

The preparation of this chapter was supported by NIH Grant 23620 from the National Institute of Child Health and Human Development (CH-23620).

a child's behavior at any time, by any measure, can no longer be attributed solely to parental behavior. As I have said elsewhere, one cannot have the same factor—the child—on both sides of the equation.

I turn now to the main issue of the conference, the high risk child. As a human being and, therefore, as a humane person and a citizen, it goes without saying that I applaud every effort to improve the high risk child's chances to achieve a better life, and admire greatly those who exert such efforts. Still, as a student of child behavior, I must raise a few questions about the contribution these efforts can make to knowledge about normal development—not that knowledge about normal development is the purpose of this conference, but because a chance exists that such a byproduct may seem implicit to some.

I am concerned that the high risk infant may be considered in a theoretical sense as a model that will illuminate the course of development of a normal child. However the high risk infant is identified—as a preterm infant, as a small-for-date infant, or as a child of poor parents—he and his caregivers depart from the normal in important ways. Of consequence for the mother-child relationship is the undoubtedly decreased initiative within the child to contribute, as does a normal child, to that relationship. The parents of that high risk infant, too, will likely depart in some way from the normal, and their behavior is still further modified by the child's.

I am also concerned, as a student of child behavior, about the enormous concentration in these chapters on the very early mother-child interactions. They are of interest in their own right; of this there can be no doubt. But that such interactions in all their minutiae are of consequence for behaviors years hence has not been demonstrated. Of course, what happens today affects what happens tomorrow; but tomorrow brings new variables—illness of parent or child, a new sibling, improved nutrition, and so on—that interact to affect the next day's behavior. No one really proposes that synchrony—or its lack—between mother and infant behaviors during the first weeks and even months of life can account for the child's IQ at 3 years of age, his behavior with peers at 4 years of age, his performance in school, or his choice of vocation or mate, and so on. Yet I fear this belief lives on some place in the minds of all of us. So I say, study such synchrony in its own right, to be sure, for what it can tell about the principles of behavioral interaction, but do not deify the mother-infant relationship to the exclusion of the effects of father, sibling, culture, and so on, on the child's development. Thus, study it in its own right, as similarly we study the infant and mother at risk in their own right.

Now, as an elder statesman, let me have a few final words. All these studies entail ethical matters concerning human research. Let us be watchful that in the process no ethical standard is compromised. Lastly, let me urge you to give your efforts the widest publicity. The public will profit by the information and, in the last analysis, our research does depend on the public's understanding and cooperation, for it is they who supply us with subjects and with funds. Given a chance, they can and should become partners in all our efforts.

The Infant's Auditory Environment

Earl C. Butterfield, Ph.D., and George F. Cairns, Ph.D.

Man is set off from other species chiefly by the complexity and flexibility of his communication skills, and he ranks himself above the other animals because of the power of his language. Men even segregate themselves from one another on the basis of their different languages. Within a tongue, too, classes of men are most accurately discriminated by their mastery of the language, and the sexes mate assortively in fair measure according to the level of their speech skills. In complex societies, at least, men assess their peers by their own use of language, and they designate as incompetent those who use it inadequately, particularly those who fail to speak at all. They judge the development of their young according to the age at which they first speak, ranking this with the age at which they take their first step as the earliest indicator of their children's potential. Significant departures from the norm in either behavior, but particularly in the use of speech, are taken as cardinal signs of mental status. Different kinds of delayed speech or language comprehension can by themselves lead some children to be classed as mentally retarded, deaf, autistic, or aphasic and to be segregated from the normal community and even from family life. The consequent misery and cost to the impaired children, their families, and society are incalculable.

This conference seeks to determine how far we might now go to prevent human suffering and waste by early intervention in the lives of infants who are at risk for significant developmental delay. It is these authors' view that significant developmental delays always involve language and that, in order to succeed, infant intervention programs must prevent language impairments. Unless they do, successful prevention of socially limiting somatic conditions that also afflict developmentally-delayed children will only be viewed as cosmetic achievements. Moreover, striving to reach the goal of preventing language impairment could have the uniquely salutary effect of defusing pseudo issues that distract students of language development (Bricker and Bricker, 1974). The Brickers'

The preparation of this chapter was supported by research grants HD-02528 and H-04756.

have likened the study of language development to an organized sport they call the Language Game. They argue that the players of this game have divided themselves into leagues whose purpose is to defeat one another by inventing more and more compelling answers to foolish questions. Thus, the most overworked non-issue of all, the nature-nurture controversy, has raged most furiously in recent years between students of language development.

It is acknowledged by all that experience plays some role in language development; for if children naturally learn any language, it is the one they hear around them. No one speaks by the rules of a language he has never experienced, even though between them men speak according to thousands of rule systems. It has seemed self-evident to some behaviorally-oriented scholars that because experience determines which language a child speaks, it must also account for how effectively he speaks it (Staats, 1971). But if one simply posits a general purpose, biologically-based, language acquisition capability (Chomsky and Miller, 1963), then it is equally self-evident that the fact of different native languages supports an hereditarian view. Such an inherent capability would allow the child to acquire whatever language he encountered, and performance differences within a language community would be the result of biologically specified differences in language learning competence; which language was learned would be an irrelevant accident of the rearing environment.

These authors stand firmly behind the Brickers' view that arguing issues such as the nature-nurture question is silly and wasteful (Bricker and Bricker, 1974) and are convinced by the Brickers' analyses that a pseudo issue lies at the heart of every major debate between players of the Language Game, and that there is no *theoretical* reason why efforts to prevent language impairment during infancy should fail. If there is any reason to expect the failure of intervention programs like the ones described at this conference, it is that reaching their goals will likely require an understanding of so many complex and varied phenomena. Success will require the translation of diverse and often incomplete understandings into efficient intervention procedures. In view of this, the eclecticism of the designers of intervention efforts can only be taken as a hopeful sign. It is this willingness of theirs to try to build on the findings of others that justifies our presence at this conference.

Because of the importance of auditory experience for the development of language, this chapter reviews evidence that reveals the effective auditory environment of infants. In order to have an impact upon infants, intervention efforts should be based upon knowledge of the environmental manipulations to which they are sensitive; for it is not clear that infants respond to the same aspects of experience to which adults respond (Kessen, 1967). The main purpose of this chapter is cast in terms of environmental variation, because that emphasis simplifies the description and interpretation of research findings. But the question can and, later in this chapter, will be cast in terms of infants' capabilities. Determining the effective environment of infants can amount to answering questions such as: What are their sensory and perceptual capabilities? and What aspects of their environment do infants explore, and to what extent? Answers to questions like these seem to have important implications for how and why infants develop and use language (Freidlander, 1970). Close attention is also given to certain important features of the methods that have generated the findings cited here, because that minimizes interpretative disagreements about the processes underlying them.

In order to put this purpose into perspective, the authors acknowledge at the outset an important new consensus: language depends upon and could not develop without prior cognitive and perceptual growth (Bloom, 1970; 1974; Bowerman, 1973; Brown, 1973; E. Clark, 1973; H. Clark, 1973; Lenneberg, 1971; MacNamara, 1972; Premack and Premack, 1974; Schlesinger, 1971; 1974; Sinclair-de Zwart, 1971; 1973; Slobin, 1973). Thus, Slobin (1973) argued that "the pacesetter in linguistic growth is the child's cognitive growth" (p. 184). MacNamara's (1974) premise is that "when infants begin to learn language, their thought is more developed than their language" (p. 3). Premack and Premack (1974) assert that language can be viewed as a map of existing perceptual and cognitive distinctions and that "if certain perceptual and conceptual abilities are not present, language cannot be acquired at all" (p. 18).

We are tempted, as researchers into mental retardation, to suppose that language deficits of the retarded are all secondary to defects of their cognitive processes. It is hoped that this hypothesis will receive a full and adequate test (Butterfield and Cairns, 1974a), but for the present purpose it must be assumed that language acquisition depends upon more than adequate cognition. MacNamara's (1972) thesis suggests that it does. He argues that children rely in part upon their acquired knowledge of the meaning of words and syntax to infer the phonological rules of their language. He observes that phonological theory distinguishes between variations in speech sounds that convey differences in meaning and those that do not. The child's chore is thus to learn which variations to ignore and which to interpret. Regardless of the role of cognition in this process, the child will likely not solve the puzzle of his language if he does not attend to and discriminate among its spoken features. The distinction between a cognitive basis for language and language itself thus serves to highlight a useful division of experimental labor between examinations of cognition and perception of nonlinguistic events and examinations of more uniquely linguistic and particularly auditory processes that might underlie speech and language defects. This chapter also discusses the infants' auditory processes, particularly as they relate to speech. Thus, this chapter attempts to draw conclusions about the developmental aspects of infants' attention to speech, their segmentation of it, and how they discriminate between its segments. And, because the discrimination of speech is intimately related to how it is categorized (Mattingly et al., 1971), the chapter also considers whether infants differentially classify speech stimuli.

This chapter begins, then, by reviewing evidence about three different aspects of the effective auditory environment of infants. First, data are summarized about infants' responsiveness to qualitative differences among auditory stimuli. Second, findings about infants' responsiveness to boundaries within the speech stream are described. Finally, evidence is reviewed concerning the effects of differences between units of speech. The chapter continues with the organismic or process implications of each of these three bodies of evidence. The implications of all three sets of findings about the effective auditory environment are examined for the question of how infants deploy their attention, and the discriminative processes that might account for how infants respond to differences between speech segments is considered.

THE EFFECTIVE AUDITORY ENVIRONMENT

Qualitative Differences among Auditory Stimuli

First to be considered is whether speech is an effective part of the infant's environment. Two groups of findings show that it is: 1) noncontingent speech changes infants' ongoing behavior (Webster, 1969; Simner, 1971; Condon and Sander, 1974), and 2) contingent speech increases infants' response rates (Rheingold, Gewirtz, and Ross, 1959; Todd and Palmer, 1968; Routh, 1969; Butterfield and Siperstein, 1972; Cairns and Butterfield, 1974).

Behavioral Effects of Noncontingent Speech   Simner (1971) presented newborn cries to some neonates and not to others. Those who received the noncontingent cry cried more often and longer than those who did not. Condon and Sander (1974) performed frame-by-frame analysis of motion pictures of newborn infants to whom they presented recordings of running speech. They observed that the ongoing limb movements of the infants became synchronized with the presented speech. Speech has also been observed to change the ongoing behavior of older infants. Barrett-Goldfarb and Whitehurst (1973) found that 1-year-olds decreased their rate of vocalizing when recordings of their parents' voices were presented. Moreover, 1-year-olds showed preferences between their mother's and father's voices, as judged by the duration of their selections of which voice to listen to. The suppression of their own ongoing vocalizations was greater by the voice they preferred. Turnure (1971) found that the voice of an infant's mother produced motor quieting, even when the voice was distorted, as did the undistorted voice of a stranger. Moreover, 9-month-olds were quieted more than either 3- or 6-month-olds. Webster (1969) performed a finer analysis of the suppressing effect of speech upon infants' vocalizations. He presented either vowel or consonant stimuli and observed infants' vocalic and consonantal productions. Vowels suppressed vocalic behavior, and consonants suppressed consonantal sounds.

In summary, both neonates' and older infants' behavior is changed by noncontingent speech, and the character and degree of the suppression depends upon the age of the infant and the character of the speech presented to him.

Reinforcing Effects of Contingent Speech   Butterfield and Siperstein (1972) showed that neonates would both increase and decrease their non-nutritive suck duration, depending upon which response would increase their access to singing voices. In the same laboratory, Butterfield and Cairns (1974b) failed to increase neonates' rate of high amplitude sucking with contingent presentations of computer-generated speech segments intended to sound like ba and pa. Whether this is because of a lack of reinforcing properties of the synthetic stimuli or to problems with the high amplitude suck procedure remains to be determined.

There have been many demonstrations that speech stimuli act as positive reinforcers for older infants. Todd and Palmer (1968), Haugan and McIntire (1972), Rheingold, Gewirtz, and Ross (1959), and Weisberg (1963) demonstrated that the rate of infants' vocalizations increases when speech sounds are made contingent upon them. This was true despite the fact, cited above, that noncontingent speech decreases the vocalization rate of infants. Sheppard (1969) increased rates of both vocalization and leg kicking with contingent presentations of an infant's mother's voice and blinking lights.

Contingent and noncontingent procedures thus show that both neonates and older infants respond to speech: speech is an effective environmental event for them. How does speech compare to other auditory stimuli?

Comparisons of Speech and other Noncontingent Stimuli Condon and Sander (1974) found that newborn infants synchronized their motor behavior with running samples of spoken English and spoken Chinese, but not with tapping or disconnected English vowel sounds. Simner's (1971) elegant experiments offer additional information about newborns' differential reactions to speech signals. He found that white noise did not elicit as much crying as did another newborn's cry. This was true despite the fact that the moment-to-moment amplitude of the noise was very similar to that of the recorded cry. Thus, the newborns were apparently reacting to something other than the amplitude of the recorded cry. Simner found in another experiment that neither the cry of a 5.5-month infant nor of a synthetically generated cry induced as much crying in newborn infants as did the presentation of another newborn's cry. Thus, newborns respond more to "speech" sounds that are similar to their own.

The only noncontingent comparison of speech stimuli with older infants was reported by Turnure (1972). She observed that both distorted and nondistorted mother's voices reduced the motor activity of children between 3 and 9 months of age. The quieting effect was greater for the older infants; Turnure interpreted this as evidence of increased attention by older infants. Distortion had no observable effect.

Comparisons of Speech and other Contingent Stimuli Butterfield and Siperstein (1972) found that newborns would change their suck durations in order to increase their access to singing and its instrumental accompaniment. When the voices and instruments were presented separately, the voices produced as great an effect as the combined voices and instruments, while the instruments alone produced no differential behavior (Cairns and Butterfield, 1974). When white noise was made contingent upon suck duration, infants responded so as to turn it off rather than to increase it as they did with the voices (Butterfield and Siperstein, 1972). Thus, these investigators showed three points on a neonatal reinforcement continuum: 1) singing voices are positively reinforcing, 2) musical instruments are neutral, and 3) white noise is negatively reinforcing.

Haugan and McIntire (1972) attempted to compare the reinforcer effectiveness of speech, food, and tactile stimulation upon 3- and 6-month-old infants. For speech reinforcers, they employed adults' imitations of the infants' immediately preceding vocalizations. This form of reward was more effective than either food or tactile stimulation but, as the authors point out, the interpretation of the finding is complicated by the possibility that nonimitative speech might not have been as effective as the imitative speech they used. Moreover, there were greater delays in the delivery of food and tactile rewards, and there is no clear way to determine whether the deprivation schedules were the same for the three classes of stimuli.

Friedlander (1968; 1970) has examined the effects of redundancy and meaningfulness of speech samples on preference behavior of infants. His procedure allows the infants to choose between two programs of auditory stimulation, or by leaving a three-position switch in the neutral position to receive no stimulation. He has used this procedure to collect listening preference data from infants in their home environments. Although fine-grained analyses have not been performed on data gathered using this technique, several findings seem clear. First, Friedlander (1968) was able to demonstrate that infants from 11 to 15 months of age would select a recording of the mother's voice with a bright inflection in preference to the mother's voice with a flat inflection. Similarly, he demonstrated that an infant would choose a stranger's voice with a bright inflection in preference to his mother's voice with a flat inflection. Also, a long message that repeated itself every 4 minutes was progressively selected more often in preference to a 20-second sample of the longer message. These results indicate that complex characteristics of the speech stream can control infants' behavior when they are about 1 year of age. Whether this is true for younger infants is unknown.

The Effective Environment of Aberrant Infants   To the best of our knowledge, there have been no adequate tests of whether infants with or who are likely to develop aberrant language respond less or differently to speech than do normal infants. Friedlander, McCarthy, and Soforenko (1967) have used their listening preference techniques with four severely retarded infants whose developmental ages were less than 1 year. They secured usable data from two of these infants, but they did not employ speech stimuli with them. Both infants showed a strong preference for an ascending organ scale over a door chime, and they maintained this preferential behavior over long time spans and despite the fact that doing so required that they accurately track changes in the responses required to produce the two sounds. Thus, for older retarded infants at least, it would be possible to assess responsivity to speech.

Conclusions about Qualitative Differences among Auditory Stimuli   Both contingent and noncontingent procedures show that speech is a more effective part of the newborn infant's environment than other auditory events. It is also clear that the effectiveness of speech as an environmental stimulus is related to how closely it approximates regular connected discourse. Thus, destroying its regular rhythmic characteristics by stringing together normally disconnected vowel sounds results in a marked decrease in the extent to which neonates synchronize their ongoing behavior with speech signals (Condon and Sander, 1974). And contingently presented computer-generated speech segments do not control behavior in the way that running speech in the form of singing does (Butterfield and Cairns, 1974a).

Certain nonspeech stimuli are also effective parts of the infant's auditory environment. But, at least some of these have qualitatively different effects upon infants' behavior than does speech. For example, while neonates respond to contingent white noise, they change their behavior in order to minimize their experience with it, whereas they maximize their experience with speech sounds (Butterfield and Siperstein, 1972). Moreover, other reviewers have shown that the responsivity of infants to noncontingent nonspeech stimuli is directly related to the similarity of those sounds to speech on parameters such as frequency spectrum (Eisenberg, 1969).

The findings on qualitative differences among auditory stimuli say very little about how the infant's effective environment changes with age. This may be because of the very small number of studies employing more than one age level, or it may be that there are only inconsequential developmental changes. A good number of the studies were conducted with neonates, and the degree of differential responsivity to speech shown by them is certainly substantial.

Boundaries within the Speech Stream

The only experiment to examine directly the effects of boundaries within the speech stream upon infants' behavior was conducted by Condon and Sander (1974). Their method was a frame-by-frame analysis of movement patterns of neonates. The authors quantified the degree of synchrony between changes in ongoing movement and the occurrence of boundaries in various auditory stimuli. The degree of synchrony was very high both for boundaries between words and for phone boundaries within words. For example, 94 percent of the movement changes of one newborn infant in a consecutive sequence of 336 frames of film, taken at 30 frames per second, occurred at either a word or a phone boundary of concurrently presented natural discourse. By contrast, only 65 percent of the movement changes during 336 film frames of a control infant, filmed in silence, corresponded to word or phone boundaries when the same sequence of discourse was matched, frame-by-frame, with his behavior. Such differential agreement was observed when the discourse was English and when it was Chinese, even though the neonates were all from English-speaking monolingual families. The synchrony was as high when the discourse was presented by tape recorder as when it was live, thereby ruling out the possibility that the speaker was coordinating his linguistic units with the behavior of the baby. Infants did not synchronize their behavior with normally disconnected vowel sounds, suggesting either that infants key their movement changes on consonants or that some suprasegmental features of speech, such as systematic intonation patterns, organize the synchrony effects. The latter seems more likely, because infants were observed to change their movement patterns at the onset of words beginning with vowels. This thoroughly remarkable experiment demonstrates that phone boundaries are effective environmental stimuli from birth, even when the infant could not have had prenatal experience with the language to which he synchronized his behavior.

Differences between Speech Segments

Given that infants respond to the boundaries between phonetic units, the question is whether they respond differentially to the character of those units. Practically all of the relevant evidence comes from experiments that use some form of the high amplitude suck (HAS) procedure. In each of the several variants of the HAS procedure, young infants are allowed to suck on a non-nutritive pacifier. Following a brief unreinforced baseline period, a speech stimulus is presented each time the infant emits a HAS. When the infant's HAS rate falls below an a priori response decrement criterion, he is either shifted to a different contingent stimulus or left to experience the same one. *Shift* is regarded as the experimental condition and *no shift* as the control. The critical question is whether infants in the *shift* condition show a greater increase in rate of high amplitude sucking immediately following the decrement than do infants in the *no shift* condition. If they do, the conclusion is that the pre and post shift stimuli are effectively different.

Table 1 summarizes the findings of experiments that have compared speech stimuli using the HAS procedure. All of these experiments studied infants in the age range of 2 to 4 months who were born to English-speaking parents. Table 1 describes the contrasted speech segments in terms of how they are classified by native adult speakers of the language from which they are drawn. Except where indicated, the contrasts are phonemic for English. Some of the speech segments were generated by computer, and they are designated synthetic. Others were recordings of native speakers, and they are designated natural. All of the studies compared the results of *shift* and *no shift* conditions. A contrast is called significant when the *shift* group showed a reliably ($p < 0.05$) greater increase in rate of high amplitude sucking from before until after the point of shift than the *no shift* group showed from before until after it met the decrement criterion for which it could have been shifted from one stimulus to another. References to the research reports are included in Table 1.

Table 1 shows 11 significant contrasts between speech segments differing by a single consonant sound. These contrasts included comparisons of both natural and synthetic stimuli, difference in both the first and second of two syllables, and distinctions that do not occur, as well as ones that do, in the language spoken by the children's parents. The fact that there are also five nonsignificant contrasts between consonant sounds does not soften the message of those that are significant. Four of the five nonsignificant contrasts are between synthetic stimuli that adults classify identically and do not discriminate, even though the stimuli are acoustically different from one another. The fifth is of a contrast in the last syllable of natural stimuli with three syllables, and there is a question in the mind of the experimenter whether adults could have discriminated them under conditions of this experiment (Trehub, personal communication). Table 1 also shows five comparisons indicating that infants respond differently to natural vowel stimuli, both when the vowels are presented in isolation and when they follow a consonant, and regardless of the language from which they come. It is concluded here that speech segments are effectively different for infants in the age range of 2 to 4 months. How about younger infants?

In order to explore the role of experience in determining the effectiveness of speech stimuli for infants, Butterfield and Cairns (1974b) conducted an experiment with neonates who averaged in age about 46 hours after birth. They compared two of the synthetic stimuli employed by Eimas (1974a) with older infants. The /pa/ and /ba/ stimuli differed with respect to the presence and absence of a single energy transition. The /pa/ contained the transition, and the /ba/ did not. The neonates who received the

Table 1. Summary of shift/no shift comparisons: the stimuli they contrasted, whether the stimuli were natural of synthetic, whether the shift effect was significant, and the references

Stimuli contrasted	Kind of stimulus	Reference
Consonant contrasts for which the shift effect was significant (p < 0.05)		
1. ba/pa	Synthetic	Eimas et al. (1971)
2. da/ta	Synthetic	Eimas (1974a)
3. dae/gae	Synthetic	Eimas (1974a)
4. dae/gae	Synthetic	Eimas (1974a)
5. ba/pa	Synthetic	Trehub and Rabinovitch (1972)
6. ba/pa	Natural	Trehub and Rabinovitch (1972)
7. da/ta	Natural	Trehub and Rabinovitch (1972)
8. ba/ga	Synthetic	Morse (1972)
9. za/ra	Natural (Czech)	Trehub (1973a)
10. aba/apa	Natural	Trehub (1973a)
11. mapa/pama	Natural	Trehub (1973a)
Consonant contrasts for which the shift effect was not *significant (p < 0.05)*		
12. atapa/ataba	Natural	Trehub (1973a)
13. ba/ba pa/pa	Synthetic	Eimas et al. (1971)
14. da/da ta/ta	Synthetic	Eimas (1974a)
15. dae/gae gae/gae	Synthetic	Eimas (1974a)
16. dae/dae gae/gae	Synthetic	Eimas (1974a)
Vowel contrasts (with significant shift effects)		
17. a/i	Natural	Trehub (1973b)
18. i/u	Natural	Trehub (1973b)
19. pa/pi	Natural	Trehub (1973b)
20. ta/ti	Natural	Trehub (1973b)
21. pa/pa	Natural (French)	Trehub (1973a)

/pa/ first responded significantly more, when shifted to /ba/, than did their *no shift* control. Infants who received /ba/ first did not respond significantly more, when shifted to /pa/, than did their *no shift* control. Because there had been no reports of order effects for older infants, the experiment was replicated, and the /pa/ to /ba/ group again responded significantly to the shift, but the /ba/ to /pa/ group did not. On the hypothesis that experience with the energy transition unique to /pa/ controlled the differential responsivity of neonates, Butterfield and Cairns (1974b) correlated the number of stimulus presentations before shift with the magnitude of the shift effect for both the

/ba/ to /pa/ and the /pa/ to /ba/ groups. This was possible because in the HAS procedure infants differ with respect to how many sucks they emit before the response decrement that provides the occasion to shift. The correlation between the number of pre-shift stimulus presentations and magnitude of change following shift was 0.60 ($p < 0.05$) for the /pa/ to /ba/ infants and -0.07 ($p < 0.25$) for the /ba/ to /pa/ infants. There is thus some evidence that experience with speech stimuli conditions their differential effectiveness, but the requisite experience can easily occur during the first days of life.

IMPLICATIONS FOR THE WAY INFANTS PROCESS AUDITORY EVENTS

Infants respond to qualitative differences between auditory stimuli, to phone boundaries within the speech stream, and to differences between speech segments. What do these facts say about infants' processing mechanisms?

How Infants Deploy Their Attention

In order to interpret the three foregoing groups of studies in terms of infants' attention, it must be assumed that any change in their behavior consequent to either the contingent or noncontingent presentation of an auditory stimulus indicates that they have attended to it. This assumption is not bothersome, but its converse is. Inattention cannot confidently be inferred from no behavioral change. Thus, Butterfield and Cairns (1974b) could not conclude that infants failed to attend to instrumental music, even though they did not change their suck duration for it, but they could conclude from the infants' suck durations that they did attend to singing. Similarly, it cannot be concluded from Friedlander's (1968) findings that infants do not attend to their mothers when they speak with flat inflections, even though they consistently choose recordings of their mothers' talking in bright inflections in preference to their talking in dull ones. Nor is it reasonable to conclude that the infants tested by Haugan and McIntire (1972) failed to notice the food they were offered when they spoke, even though they did not change their rate of speaking for it, while they did change it for contingent imitation of their talking. This is an ubiquitous limit on every method of infant researchers: only a positive response can be interpreted in terms of underlying processes.

There are a number of reasons for allowing only positive behavioral changes to support inferences about underlying processes. For example, they provide conclusive evidence that an experiment's measurement procedures were sensitive and that its infant subjects were in a responsive state. A more interesting reason is that many processes intervene between the presentation of a stimulus and the occurrence of a response, and a failure of any one of those processes could account for the absence of a response. Thus, unless a contingent stimulus has reinforcing properties, it will not provoke a behavioral change. But infants can attend to a stimulus whether or not it is reinforcing. The neonates in our experiments may have attended equally to vocal and instrumental music but found instruments too unrewarding to merit a behavioral change.

The fact that various processes intervene between stimulus and response means that there can be questions about which intervening process is reflected in any particular behavioral change. It seems to these authors that there are no serious questions of this sort about attentive processes. It can be concluded that any behavioral change consequent to either contingent or noncontingent stimulus presentation reflects attention. The argument is simply that a child cannot respond to a stimulus unless he has attended to it. Given this simplifying assumption and the conclusion that nothing can be inferred from a failure to respond, the question of how an infant deploys his attention is equivalent to the question of what his effective environment is.

The evidence about their effective environment indicates that infants attend particularly to speech. They attend to nonspeech auditory events in proportion to how speechlike they are. They attend to boundaries within the speech stream and to differences between speech segments; and they do all of these things from birth. In short, humans attend from birth to the phonological features of the language spoken in their environment. They are, therefore, primed from the very beginning to learn how those features code meaning. They need not first learn to distinguish speech from nonspeech nor how to segment the speech stream. The data on attention are thus consistent with the conclusion that one is forced to by the speed with which most infants acquire language: they must come into the world prepared for that endeavor.

What the data do not reveal is whether weakened attention to speech ever accounts for delays in rate of language acquisition. But the techniques are available for comparative propsective investigations to answer this question. One need only examine a sizable group of infants early in life to determine whether there are individual differences in attention to various speech features. If there are, one need only follow infants longitudinally to see if these differences covary with later indices of language acquisition. If they do, attempts should be made to heighten attention to speech among infants who seem deficient in this regard in order to see whether that will result in greater language achievement later in life.

How Infants Discriminate Speech Segments

Inferring discriminative processes from the findings on infants' effective environments is considerably more complex than inferring how they deploy their attention. The complexity stems in part from the fact that experimental controls, required to rule out conclusively alternative process interpretations, have not been used in studies that have been interpreted in terms of how infants discriminate (Butterfield and Cairns, 1974b). It also stems from the richness of the theoretical account of how adults perceive speech (Liberman, 1970a; 1970b; Liberman et al., 1967; Studdert-Kennedy et al., 1970), and the fact that infant investigators have cast their interpretaions in terms of the adult models (e.g., Eimas, 1974a; 1974b).

Continuous and Categorical Perception The relevant experimental and interpretative issues can most easily be introduced by acknowledging the generalization that adults perceive speech differently from the way they perceive other auditory stimuli. The shorthand for this conclusion is that adults perceive speech in a linguistic mode. This conclusion is based on several lines of evidence, but the most pertinent one is that certain acoustic dimensions are perceived categorically rather than continuously. These include voice-onset-time and place of articulation, which are the dimensions from which investigators of infants' reactions to speech segments have most frequently drawn their stimuli. Other dimensions, like those underlying the perception of vowel sounds, are perceived continuously.

Whether perception is continuous or categorical is determined by comparing how adults categorize stimuli to how they discriminate them. Adults are first asked to categorize a group of stimuli by listening and assigning labels to them. Despite the fact that the stimuli all differ on some acoustic property, adults assign fewer labels than there are stimuli. Those to which they assign different labels are said to vary between categories. Adults are then asked to discriminate between pairs of stimuli that differ equally along the acoustic dimension: for some pairs both members come from the same category, while for other pairs the members come from different categories. If the within-category discriminations are made no better than chance and the between-category discriminations are made essentially perfectly, then perception of the underlying dimension is said to be categorical. The more within-category pairs that are not discriminated, and the more abrupt the increase in rate of successful discrimination around the category boundary, the more convincing the demonstration of categorical perception. Continuous perception is demonstrated when discrimination is as accurate, or nearly as accurate, within categories as it is between categories. By these tests, vowels are perceived continuously, and consonants that differ in voice-onset-time and place of articulation are perceived categorically.

The theoretical explanation for the differences in how consonants and vowels are perceived depends upon the fact that they are produced with qualitatively different articulatory gestures. Stop consonants are articulated in a discontinuous way by constriction at a particular place in the vocal tract, while vowels are produced by continuous changes in the over-all shape of the vocal tract. The hypothesis is that the articulatory movements or their sensory or neural correlates mediate perception. Because the articulatory gestures underlying consonant production are discontinuous, their perception is discontinuous, i.e., categorical. Because vowels are produced by continuous movements, their perception is continuous.

How do the neuromotor correlates of articulatory gestures mediate speech perception? The argument is that the continuously variable auditory stimuli that impinge upon the ear are first subjected to an acoustic feature analysis that yields continuously variable representations of the stimuli's spectral structure, fundamental frequency, intensity, duration, etc. These representations are then subjected to a phonetic feature analysis. This analysis converts some of the outputs of the initial acoustic stage into discrete phoneme-like units or categories. Presumably, this phonetic analysis depends upon some reference to the articulatory system. *Continuous perception* can be thought of as a reflection of the outputs of the first, acoustic, stage of analysis. *Categorical perception* can be thought of as a reflection of the output of the second, phonetic, stage of analysis.

Categorical perception is referred to as perception in the linguistic mode because a phonetic analysis is necessarily a linguistic analysis. Consider now what Eimas (1974a) has to say about the perception of speech by infants:

> Very young infants are certainly sensitive to the segmental sound units of speech. Moreover, they are able to make relatively fine discriminations of both voicing and place cues in a manner that approximates the categorical nature of speech perception found in adult listeners. This processing of speech in a linguistic mode is, we strongly believe, accomplished by means of linguistic feature detectors that are a part of the inherent structure of the human organism. It is the operation or excitation of these detectors that provides in an automatic and relatively simple manner the linguistic information in the form of phonetic features which the infant is capable of utilizing in the perception of speech.

Eimas goes on to describe these linguistic feature detectors as follows:

> There exist detectors that are differentially sensitive to a range of voice-onset-time (VOT) values with greatest sensitivity occurring at the modal production value for a particular voicing distinction. Some VOT values excite both detectors, but, all other things being equal, only the output signal with the greater strength reaches higher centers of processing and integration. The phonetic boundary will lie at the VOT values that excites both detectors equally, all other factors being equal. After adaptation, the sensitivity of the detector is lessened; that is, the output signal is weakened or decreased.

Eimas (1974a) applies these notions directly to the explanation of results obtained from infants with the high amplitude suck procedure:

> Thus, the presentation of a speech signal with voicing information will excite the appropriate detector. The repeated presentation of the same voicing information will result in adaptation of the appropriate detector. The adaptation or lessening of the output signal of the detector may be responsible, either directly or indirectly, for the lessening of the reinforcing properties of the speech signal and the concomitant decrement in response rate to obtain the stimulus. The introduction of a second stimulus that excites the same detector will not be registered as a different or novel stimulus, and hence there will be no recovery of the response to obtain the second stimulus. However, the introduction of a second stimulus that excites a different detector will produce a new or novel experience and result in increased responding to obtain the novel event.

Discriminative Processes Underlying Developmental Delays   Between them, these theoretical accounts of how adults and infants perceive and discriminate speech suggest two classes of discriminative processes that might underlie developmental delays in the acquisition of language. Infants might have insensitive or incomplete sensory analyzers, or they might have incomplete or insensitive linguistic or phonetic analyzers. Their continuous discriminative capabilities might be diminished, or they might not discriminate completely categorically. The models hold that sensory analysis precedes linguistic analysis, and that some but not all of the outputs of the sensory analysis serve as inputs for the linguistic analysis. Those speech signals that receive both sensory and linguistic processing, like the consonants *b* and *p*, are discriminated categorically. Those that receive only sensory analysis, like the vowels, are discriminated continuously. Thus, by analyzing the extent to which infants perceive categorically, one should learn about the intactness of their linguistic processor and the part of their sensory processing system that feeds into it.[1] By assessing infants' continuous discriminative sensitivity, one should learn about the intactness of the remainder of the infant's sensory analyzing system.

Considerations like these explain why this chapter does not review the substantial literature on how infants discriminate nonspeech auditory parameters like the frequency and intensity of pure tones. (A review of this data is available in Kaye, 1970.) Only speech stimuli undergo linguistic analysis, and speech stimuli that do not undergo linguistic analysis could be used to assess speech-relevant sensory processing. The implication is that audiological assessment of infants should rely more on speech stimuli and less on pure tones and noise sources (Cairns and Butterfield, 1974). The availability of synthetic speech segments eliminates the usual objection to this view, that speech stimuli cannot be described objectively and quantitatively. What do the data just presented say about infants' discriminative processes?

Continuous Discrimination in Infants   The pertinent data was summarized in Table 1. They suggest that clinically normal infants discriminate both continuously and categorically, but the findings are not definitive. All of the vowel contrasts (entries 17 through 21 in Table 1) are presumably processed by the sensory analyzer alone, and the fact that all result in significant shift effects suggests that the sensory processing of young infants is intact. But, every one of these contrasts cuts across a phonetic boundary, and one defining characteristic of continuous processing is that discrimination is highly accurate within phonetic categories. Until different /a/, /i/, /u/ or other linguistically identical but acoustically different vowels are contrasted and discrimination of them is demonstrated, it will not be known whether, nor how well, normal infants discriminate continuously. Moreover, these contrasts will need to involve more than one pair of stimuli, because another defining characteristic of continuous discrimination is that it is equally accurate at all points on the discriminated dimension.

Categorical Discrimination in Infants   The evidence seems stronger with respect to whether infants discriminate categorically. Contrasts 1 through 4 and 13 through 16 in Table 1 are the pertinent findings. Contrasts 13 through 16 are between acoustically different consonant sounds, which adults classify as identical. Thus, contrast 13 describes contrasts between two /ba/ sounds that are as different acoustically as are the /ba/ and /pa/ sounds described in contrast 1. Between them, contrasts 1 and 13 represent comparisons of six stimuli, three categorized by adults as /ba/ and three categorized as /pa/. The four stimuli lie at equal intervals along the underlying acoustic dimension of voice-onset-time. The values of the three stimuli can be expressed in milliseconds as −20, 0, +20, +40, +60, and +80, where the first three are classified as /ba/ and the second three

---

[1] It might also be possible to decouple the sensory and linguistic analyzers even for those stimuli that go through both. This could be done by isolating the acoustic cues that are perceived as consonants when they occur in context with a vowel but are not perceived as speech when they are isolated (c.f. Eimas, 1974b).

as /pa/. Contrast 1 compares +20 to +40, and contrast 13 compares −20 to 0, and +60 to +80. Contrast 1 is a between-category shift, and the two contrasts in 13 are within-category shifts. The fact that the two contrasts in 13 resulted in no significant shift effects, while the one in contrast 1 did yield a significant shift effect has been taken as evidence of categorical perception. This is the minimum number of pairs that might be used to determine whether perception is categorical: one pair from each of two phonetic categories and one pair made up of an instance of each of the two categories. This minimum is insufficient to tell how infants perceive categorically.

Consider an experiment on the categorical perception of adults. Pisoni (1971) used 13 stimuli from each of the several dimensions he studied. He compared 12 pairs composed of stimuli that were adjacent on each of his continuua and 11 pairs that were separated by only one intervening stimulus. All of his subjects were required to discriminate all 23 pairs, and when they succeeded with only the four pairs that cut across category boundaries, he inferred that their discrimination was categorical. The importance of using so many pairs is not simply to reduce the probability that only the between-category pairs would result in significant discrimination. It is primarily that the number of contrasted pairs determines the accuracy with which the experimenter can estimate the location and steepness of discrimination gradients. It is the location of the discriminative peaks and the rapidity with which discrimination falls to chance levels around those peaks that defines the extent to which discrimination is categorical (Studdert-Kennedy et al., 1970). In order to assess the possibility that infants differ with respect to how categorically they discriminate, one must be able to examine their discrimination gradients. One must be able to determine whether they discriminate most accurately at those points which specify categories in their language, and be able to tell how well they distinguish between stimuli near those points. The use of only three pairs of stimuli does not allow such determinations, and every relevant experiment with infants uses only three pairs.

There is another fact that complicates the interpretation of the evidence about whether infants discriminate categorically. The importance of interpreting only positive behavioral differences was mentioned above. In the high amplitude suck procedure, a failure to discriminate can only be inferred from no behavioral change. There is a need, therefore, to employ another procedure, one that elicits different responses when the infant judges that two stimuli are identical and when he judges that they are different. An operant discrimination or stimulus control procedure involving two distinct responses is being called for here. Such procedures have yet to be used for the purpose of exploring individual infant's discriminative capacities for auditory events, but there is good reason to believe that they could be applied successfully to young infants (Siqueland and Lipsitt, 1966).

CONCLUSIONS

There remains little doubt that infants attend to speech and that they discriminate among its segments from a very early age. How well they discriminate and the extent to which they discriminate categorically remain to be determined. Whether there are significant individual differences that predict later language status also remains to be determined. If there are such differences, how to remedy them is unclear. It is clear, however, that a new view of young infants has emerged and that the data considered above has contributed importantly to it.

The new view of infants is that they are not merely passive reflexive recipients of environmental stimulation. Rather, they actively process their sensory experiences and act instrumentally to change them. According to the new view, infants are not limited to the perception of simple stimulus dimensions. They can process complex stimulus material and make subtle and sophisticated distinctions between the sensory events in their environments. They may even behave like adults in that the mechanisms they use to process speech are substantially different from those used to process other auditory stimulation.

The implication of this new view is that infants should benefit from early intensive experience with speech. Whether there are differences as to how much individual infants will benefit is now uncertain. An answer to this question should be available as soon as individually reliable, operant discrimination procedures have been developed for the study of infants. The indications are that that will happen soon (Cairns and Butterfield, 1974). Precisely how language experiences should be programmed is also uncertain. One must look to the future findings of the various intervention programs reviewed at this conference for an answer to that question.

LITERATURE CITED

Barrett-Goldfarb, M. D., and G. J. Whitehurst. 1973. Infant vocalizations as a function of parental voice selection. Devel. Psych. 8: 273–276.

Bloom, L. 1970. Language development: Form and Function in Emerging Grammars. MIT Press, Cambridge, Mass.

Bloom, L. 1974. Talking, understanding, and thinking. 1974. In R. L. Schiefelbusch and L. L. Lloyd (eds.), Language Perspective—Acquisition, Retardation, and Intervention, pp. 285–311. University Park Press, Baltimore.

Bowerman, M. 1973. Early Syntactic Development: 1973, A Cross-linguistic Study with Special References to Finnish. Cambridge University Press, Cambridge, England.

Bricker, W., and D. Bricker. 1974. Early language intervention. In R. L. Schiefelbusch and L. L. Lloyd (eds.), Language Perspectives—Acquisition, Retardation and Intervention, pp. 431–468. University Park Press, Baltimore.

Brown, R. 1973. A First Language: The Early Stages. Harvard University Press, Cambridge, Mass.

Butterfield, E. C., and G. F. Cairns. 1974a. Process defects that might underlie aberrant language development. In N. R. Ellis (ed.), Aberrant Development in Infancy, pp. 241–255. Erlbaum Associates, Hillsdale, N.J.

Butterfield, E. C., and G. F. Cairns, Jr. 1974b. Discussion summary—Infant reception research. In R. L. Schiefelbusch and L. L. Lloyd (eds.), Language Perspectives—Acquisition, Retardation, and Intervention, pp. 75–102. University Park Press, Baltimore.

Butterfield, E. C., and G. N. Siperstein. 1972. Influence on contingent auditory stimulation upon non-nutritional suckle. *In* J. Bosma (ed.), Oral Sensation and Perception: The Mouth of the Infant, pp. 313–334. C. C Thomas, Springfield, Ill.

Cairns, G. F., and E. C. Butterfield. 1974. Assessing infants' auditory functioning. *In* B. Z. Friedlander, G. M. Sterritt, and G. E. Kirk (eds.), Exceptional Infant, Vol. III, pp. 84–108. Brunner/Mazel, New York.

Chomsky, N., and G. A. Miller. 1963. Introduction to the formal analysis of natural languages. *In* R. D. Luce, R. R. Bush, and E. Galanter (eds.), Handbook of Mathematical Psychology, Vol. II. Wiley, New York.

Clark, E. V. 1973. What's in a word? On the child's acquisition of semantics in his first language. *In* T. E. Moore (ed.), Cognitive Development and the Acquisition of Language, pp. 65–110. Academic Press, New York.

Clark, H. H. 1973. Space, time, semantics, and the child. *In* T. E. Moore (ed.), Cognitive Development and the Acquisition of Language, pp. 27–64. Academic Press, New York.

Condon, W. S., and L. W. Sander. 1974. Neonate movement is synchronized with adult speech: Interactional participation and language acquisition. Science 183: 99–101.

Eimas, P. D. 1974a. Speech perception in early infancy. *In* L. B. Cohen and P. Salapatek (eds.), Infant Perception. Academic Press, New York.

Eimas, P. D. 1974b. Linguistic processing of speech by young infants. *In* R. L. Schiefelbusch and L. L. Lloyd (eds.), Language Perspectives—Acquisition, Retardation, and Intervention, pp. 55–73. University Park Press, Baltimore.

Eimas, P. D., E. R. Siqueland, P. Jusczyk, and J. Vigorito. 1971. Speech perception in infants. Science 171: 303–306.

Eisenberg, R. B. 1969. Auditory behavior in the human neonate: Functional properties of sound and their ontogenetic implications. Intern. Audiol. 8: 34–45.

Friedlander, B. Z. 1968. The effect of speaker identity, voice, inflection, vocabulary, and message redundancy on infants' selection of vocal reinforcement. J. Exper. Child Psych. 64: 443–459.

Friedlander, B. Z. 1970. Receptive language development in infancy: Issues and problems. Merrill-Palmer Quart. 16: 7–51.

Friedlander, B. Z., J. J. McCarthy, and A. Z. Soforenko. 1967. Automated psychological evaluation with severely retarded institutionalized infants. Amer. J. Ment. Defic. 71: 909–919.

Haugan, G. M., and R. W. McIntire. 1972. Comparisons of vocal imitation, tactile stimulation, and food as reinforcers for infant vocalizations. Devel. Psych. 6: 201–209.

Kaye, H. 1970. Sensory processes. *In* H. W. Reese and L. P. Lipsitt (eds.), Experimental Child Psychology, pp. 33–63. Academic Press, New York.

Kessen, W. 1967. Sucking and looking: Two organized patterns of behavior in the human newborn. *In* H. W. Stevenson, E. H. Hess, and H. L. Rheingold (eds.), Early Behavior: Comparative and Developmental Approaches, pp. 147–179, Wiley, New York.

Lenneberg, E. H. 1971. Of language, knowledge, apes, and brains. J. Psycholing. Res. 1: 1–29.

Liberman, A. M. 1970a. The grammars of speech and language. Cognit. Psych. 1: 301–323.

Liberman, A. M. 1970b. Some characteristics of perception in the speech mode. *In* D. A. Hamburg (ed.), Perception and Its Disorders, Proceedings of A.R.N.M.D., pp. 238–258. Williams and Wilkins, Baltimore.

Liberman, A. M., F. S. Cooper, D. Shankweiler, and M. Studdert-Kennedy. 1967. Perception of the speech code. Psych. Rev. 74: 431–461.

MacNamara, J. 1972. Cognitive basis of language learning in infants. Psych. Rev. 79: 1–13.

Mattingly, I. G., A. M. Liberman, A. K. Syrdal, and T. Halwes. 1971. Discrimination in speech and nonspeech modes. Cognit. Psych. 2: 131–157.

Morse, P. A. 1972. The discrimination of speech and nonspeech stimuli in early infancy. J. Exper. Child Psych. 14: 477–492.

Pisoni, D. B. 1971. On the nature of categorical perception of speech sounds. Unpublished doctoral dissertation, University of Michigan.

Premack, D., and A. J. Premack. 1974. Teaching visual language to apes and language-deficient persons. In R. L. Schiefelbusch and L. L. Lloyd (eds.), Language Perspectives—Acquisition, Retardation, and Intervention, pp. 347–376. University Park Press, Baltimore.

Rheingold, H. L., J. L. Gewirtz, and H. W. Ross. 1959. Social conditioning of vocalizations in the infant. J. Comp. Physiol. Psych. 52: 68–73.

Routh, D. K. 1969. Conditioning of vocal response differentiation in infants. Devel. Psych. 1: 219–226.

Schlesinger, I. M. 1971. Production of utterances and language acquisition. In D. I. Slobin (ed.), The Ontogenesis of Language, pp. 63–102. Academic Press, New York.

Schlesinger, I. M. 1974. Relational concepts underlying language. In R. L. Schiefelbusch and L. L. Lloyd (eds.), Language Perspectives—Acquisition, Retardation, and Intervention, pp. 129–151. University Park Press, Baltimore.

Sheppard, W. C. 1969. Operant control of infant vocal and motor behavior. J. Exper. Child Psych. 7: 36–51.

Simner, M. L. 1971. Newborn's response to the cry of another infant. Devel. Psych. 5: 136–150.

Sinclair-de Zwart, H. 1971. Sensorimotor action patterns as a condition for the acquisition of syntax. In R. Huxley and E. Ingram (eds.), Language Acquisition: Models and Methods, pp. 121–129. Academic Press, New York.

Sinclair-de Zwart, H. 1973. Some remarks on the Genevan point of view on learning with special reference to language learning. In L. L. Hinde and H. C. Hinde (eds.), Constraints on Learning. Academic Press, New York.

Siqueland, E. R., and L. P. Lipsitt. 1966. Conditioned head turning behavior in newborns. J. Exper. Child Psych. 3: 356–376.

Slobin, D. I. 1973. Cognitive prerequisites for the development of grammar. In C. A. Ferguson and D. I. Slobin (eds.), Studies of Child Language Development, pp. 175–276. Holt, Rinehart, and Winston, New York.

Staats, A. W. 1971. Linguistic-mentalistic theory versus an explanatory S-R learning theory of language development. In D. I. Slobin (ed.), The Ontogenesis of Grammar, pp. 103–152. Academic Press, New York.

Studdert-Kennedy, M., A. M. Liberman, K. S. Harris, and F. S. Cooper. 1970. Motor theory of speech perception: A reply to Lane's critical review. Psych. Rev. 77: 234–249.

Todd, B. A., and B. Palmer. 1968. Social reinforcement of infant babbling. Child Devel. 39: 592–596.

Trehub, S. E. 1973a. Auditory-linguistic sensitivity in infants. Unpublished doctoral dissertation, McGill University.

Trehub, S. E. 1973b. Infants' sensitivity to vowel and tonal contrasts. Devel. Psych. 9: 91–96.

Trehub, S. E., and M. S. Rabinovitch. 1972. Auditory-linguistic sensitivity in early infancy. Devel. Psych. 6: 74–77.

Turnure, C. 1971. Response to voice of mother and stranger by babies in the first year. Devel. Psych. 4: 182–190.

Webster, R. L. 1969. Selective suppression of infants vocal response by classes of phonemic stimulation. Devel. Psych. 1: 410–414.

Weisberg, P. 1963. Social and nonsocial conditioning of infant vocalizations. Child Devel. 34: 377–388.

Use of Longitudinal Research in the Study of Child Development

James J. Gallagher, Ph.D., Craig T. Ramey, Ph.D.,
Ron Haskins, Ph.D., and Neal W. Finkelstein, Ph.D.

This chapter offers a particular conception of the longitudinal research design and its place in the study of behavioral development and child psychology. This concept of longitudinal study is intended as a partial antidote to the lack of power that characterizes available behavioral and developmental principles. These authors believe that the longitudinal design is now used infrequently despite the felicitous outcomes that can be expected from its more widespread use. In order to document the potential value of these outcomes, selected examples of previously conducted longitudinal research are presented and discussed.

DEVELOPMENT OF A SCIENTIFIC DISCIPLINE

Most surveys and introductions to the study of scientific method include extensive discussions of observation, experimentation, hypotheses, laws, theory, and validation (Kaplan, 1964; Kemeny, 1959; Kerlinger, 1964). It is possible to arrange these various aspects of the scientific method in a kind of evolutionary order, thereby creating a conceptual model tracing developmental stages in the growth of a scientific discipline. Figure 1 presents one possible model of this type. The thrust of this model is summarized below.

First, a young science begins by observing and classifying the phenomena that constitute its subject matter (Stage 1). From these observations and classifications, the science begins to formulate hypotheses concerning possible relationships between variables (Stage 2). Observed correlations between events are a primary factor suggesting

The preparation of this chapter was supported, in part, by grant HD-03110 from the National Institute of Child Health and Human Development.

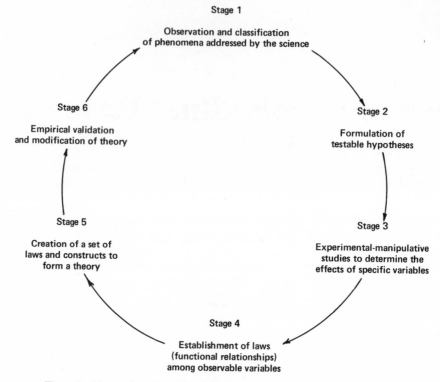

Figure 1. Circumplex schematic of the development of a scientific discipline.

possible functional relationships between variables. On the other hand, the birth of an hypothesis in the mind of an individual scientist cannot be explained by reference to any single factor; for as Kaplan (1964) and Brush (1974) have maintained, hunches, prejudices, philosophical assumptions, and other factors too numerous to name here, have often played a critical role in the creation of hypotheses.

Stage 3 in this model finds scientists testing hypotheses they have framed. The hypothesis is first stated in some precise way, often in mathematical form, and an experiment is designed to test the predicted functional relationship explicitly stated by the hypothesis. After repeated experimental verifications, scientific progress achieves Stage 4, and the hypothesis achieves a status usually implied by the terms "law" or "principle."

As a number of these principles begin to accumulate, it then becomes desirable to see relationships between the sets of variables held to be functionally related by the principles. Such a step is given the name "theory" in the model above (Stage 5). Theories, like principles, can yield deductions that are then subjected to experimental test, although usually not in a direct and straightforward manner, because the level of abstraction characterizing theories is much greater than the level of abstraction with which principles are stated. Stage 6 in the model above, then, is verification and continued modification of theory.

The model presented in Figure 1 is characterized by the logical progression of events in the development of a scientific discipline. The implication is that scientific method, correctly conceived, views scientific progress as the inevitable outcome of a necessary and orderly mode of progression from observation, to hypothesis formation, to experimental test, to establishment of principles, to invention of theory, and to confirmation or modification of theory. Unfortunately, the historical examination of scientific development does not reveal anything like this orderly and neat progression of stages. Skinner's (1956) debunking of the process by which the scientific method proceeds provides numerous examples of the factors impinging upon the scientist as he pursues his investigations, and these factors are neither logical nor orderly. A second example of the problems with orderly models of scientific conduct is provided by Brush (1974), in an article examining the proposition that:

> ... young and impressionable students at the start of a scientific career should be shielded from the writings of contemporary science historians for reasons similar to the one mentioned above—namely, that these writings do violence to the professional ideal and public image of scientists as rational, open-minded investigators, proceeding methodically, grounded incontrovertibly in the outcome of controlled experiments, and seeking objectively for the truth, let the chips fall where they may (p. 1,164).

In short, models such as those presented in Figure 1 should not be taken too literally, although the history of physical sciences has, in general, been similar to that depicted by the model.

VALUE OF OBSERVATION IN BEHAVIORAL SCIENCE

One aspect of the descriptive model presented in Figure 1 seems to be of critical importance; namely, the initial stage of observation and classification. For it is in this initial stage of observation that all subsequent scientific activity is grounded. As Kaplan (1964) has noted, "Observation is ... directed toward ends that lie beyond the act of observation itself: the aim is to secure materials that will play a part in other phases of inquiry, like the formation and validation of hypotheses" (p. 127). One need only consider the examples provided by Darwin, De Toqueville, and Piaget to realize that deliberate observation, characterized by planning and forethought, is of surpassing importance in the initial stages of scientific activity.

But it is precisely this critical first stage of scientific investigation that has least characterized the history of psychology. Wright (1960) makes the point concisely:

> ... psychology in its every branch has done comparatively little watching and recording and examining of events left to happen as they may. Psychological science began with a leap from the armchair to the laboratory and has since generally preferred to do things with its subjects, to give them tasks or problems, to interrogate them, to test them, or at least to draw them into prearranged situations (pp. 71–72).

Nor is Wright the only student of behavior to argue that psychology too quickly became dominated by the experimental approach at the expense of careful observation; for in recent years a number of prestigious and influential developmentalists have echoed this criticism of psychology (Ambrose, 1968; Bateson, 1968; Bronfenbrenner, 1973; Jones, 1972; Schaffer, 1973; Tinbergen, 1972).

Thus, the social sciences in general, and psychology in particular, have failed to ground their science in careful and extensive observations of their respective slices of human behavior. What factors are responsible for this too hasty jump by social sciences to experimental-manipulative methods?

One possible explanation deals with social scientists and their own social status in the hierarchy of scientific disciplines. The social scientists—the anthropologist, the sociologist, the psychologist—are latecomers on the scientific scene. Prestige and resources have been, and still are, controlled by the more respected and secure physical scientists—the physicist and the chemist. Indeed, there are still those in the physical sciences who refuse to accept social science as a truly legitimate member of the scientific community. Such low status in the scientific community often causes the social scientist to respond with "upward striving" behavior, much like the "upward striving" behavior exhibited by lower class family members seeking higher social status. Thus, social scientists tend to emulate those scientists who have a more desired status. These high levels of aspiration have occasionally led social scientists into the premature adoption of techniques and theoretical models characteristic of the physical scientists in order to demonstrate to all concerned that they are as scientific, and as rigorously disciplined, as are their better situated colleagues in the more developed knowledge areas. Social scientists, therefore, have tried to move rapidly beyond the initial stage of observation in the developmental sequence suggested by Figure 1.

RELATIONSHIP BETWEEN METHODS AND PROBLEMS IN BEHAVIORAL SCIENCE

The current objective for the student of behavior, then, is to seek out those methods most appropriate to the problems he faces. This point has been stated succinctly by Broom (1964):

> [The behavioral scientist's] most difficult task is the clarification of method where the precedents and analogies of physical science are inappropriate or obscure. What he needs most is a direct confrontation of methodological problems immediately relevant to his own discipline. He needs to read from the strengths of his own understanding, insights, expertness, and subject matter and not from the insecurity of a limited familiarity with a remote discipline (p. xvii).

If behavioral scientists are to select methods appropriate to the problems at hand, rather than to allow methodological objectives to dictate the selection of problems, they must begin with a careful consideration of the problems they face. If anything is known about behavior development, it is that behavior and its controlling conditions are multivariate both on the side of dependent and independent variables. Behavior is the result of a complex interaction between maturation and experience, between endogenous and exogenous factors. As Schneirla (1966) describes this situation:

> The developmental contributions of the two complexes, maturation and experience, must be viewed as *fused* (i.e., as inseparably coalesced) at all stages in the ontogenesis of any organism. This holistic theory conceptualizes all processes of progressive organization in consecutive early stages of development as fused, coalescing, maturational and experiential functions (pp. 288–289).

If behavior and its controlling conditions are not related in any univariate way, it follows that experimental-manipulative procedures by themselves are not adequate to the untangling of these multivariate relationships. Furthermore, if behavior is the outcome of interactions between endogenous and exogenous factors, between built-in and learned factors, it follows that a proper and necessary perspective for behavioral study is the longitudinal perspective.

Thus, the primary purpose of this chapter is to advocate an approach to the study of behavioral development appropriate to the problems imposed by the multiple relationships between behavior and its controlling conditions. The hallmark of this approach is the longitudinal perspective, but with particular attention to the type of information collected and the circumstances in which it is collected.

APPROPRIATE USE OF THE LONGITUDINAL DESIGN

What are the advantages of the longitudinal method? Bell (1953) has argued that:

> ... it is apparent that the longitudinal approach is not the method par excellence for studying human development. A longitudinal approach should be selected, as any other method, on the basis of its appropriateness to the problem at hand. The problem is when to apply the longitudinal method, rather than how to marshal the courage to face the task (p. 146).

If Bell's point is valid, then it is necessary to specify those problems for which the longitudinal approach is appropriate or necessary and also to state the limitations of longitudinal designs.

Problems Requiring a Longitudinal Design

Cumulative Impact of Independent Variables   As Bell (1953) has noted, "In any study where the cumulative effect of an independent variable on an individual is desired, a longitudinal approach must be used" (p. 146). A pertinent example of this cumulative impact by an independent variable has been discussed by Kagan and Moss (1962). In their analysis of the Fels longitudinal data, they observed that "maternal acceleration of the child's developmental skills showed the highest correlation with adult achievement behavior when the measure of maternal acceleration was obtained during the first three years of life" (p. 3). Such observations, and the implicit suggestion of possible relationships for experimental work, are clearly beyond the reach of cross-sectional data.

Dimensions Underlying Behavioral Change Baltes and Nesselroade (1970) have pointed out that whenever one wants to examine the proposition that the same factor structures or dimensions underlie developmental change, a longitudinal approach is essential. For example, performance on a particular assessment device at time "one" may be the product of a given factor structure underlying the performance at that time; whereas performance on the same assessment device at time "two" may be the product of a new underlying factor or dimension. If this be the case, then the same test may be measuring different abilities at these two times.

Variables Showing Small Changes Kessen (1960) has held that "the longitudinal design is to be favored in the study of those age-functional relationships in which relatively small but individually stable changes over age are expected" (p. 41).

Changes in the Interrelationships between Variables A longitudinal approach is necessary when one wants to examine the interrelationships of environment-organism variables and the way in which these relationships change over time. An excellent example of the misconceptions that result when interrelationships between variables are ignored is provided by the literature on mother-child interaction. As Bell (1968) has argued, the early literature on this topic conceived the direction of effects to be one way, i.e., from mother to child. The model underlying this unidirectional conception has been summarized by Overton and Reese (1973):

> In the mechanistic [S-R] model, not only are efficient causes external to the system under consideration, but also there is an asymmetric relationship between cause and effect. . . . Thus, within this view there is a *unidirectionality* of causal application or a one-way causality, in which effect is strictly dependent upon cause (von Bertalanffy, 1968; Bunge, 1963). This unidirectionality permits the isolation of S-R relationships, and the explanation of changes in terms of efficient stimulus determinants (p. 77).

More recently, however, this unidirectional conception has been replaced by a dyadic conception of mother-infant interaction (see, for example, the volume edited by Lewis and Rosenblum, 1974). Some of the research emerging from this dyadic conception has carefully examined the changing pattern of the interrelationships between maternal and infant behaviors and has relied extensively on the longitudinal design. Thus, for example, Hinde and Spencer-Booth (1968) have analyzed the changes in specific dyadic behaviors by mother and infant rhesus monkeys, and the relationship between these behaviors and the process of infant separation. The upshot of this longitudinal research has been a full appreciation of the contributions by both mother and infant to the changing pattern of dyadic interaction and of the relationship between these dyadic changes and processes such as infant separation.

Patterns of Individual Differences A longitudinal approach is also needed when one seeks to determine patterns of individual differences in behavioral development. The 1965 Colloquium on Longitudinal Studies, convened by the Bethesda Independent National Institute of Child Health and Human Development, stated this point succinctly

(Chipman, 1965): "Only the longitudinal design can show the nature of growth and patterns of change in an individual" (quoted by Wall and Williams, 1970, p. 8). Thus, for example, McCall, Appelbaum, and Hogarty (1973), in a study to be discussed in more detail below, were able to isolate five characteristic patterns of growth in IQ between 2.5 and 17 years. Cross-sectional data, of course, with measurements of different persons at selected ages, would have been inappropriate for inducing such characteristic patterns of IQ change over time. Age-behavior functions emerging from grouped, cross-sectional data, after all, do not necessarily reflect the pattern of growth for any individual subject.

Process Emergence Whenever one wants to study the emergence of a process that presumably underlies the occurrence of specific behavioral acts, detailed and frequent observations of patterns of behavioral change in individual subjects will provide the information from which such processes can be induced. The longitudinal work of Brown and his colleagues (Brown and Fraser, 1964; Brown and Bellugi 1964; Brown, Cazden, and Bellugi, 1968), for example, based on repeated observations of speech in three children between approximately 2 and 4 years of age, allowed the induction of rules expressing changes in the children's linguistic competence. These and similar studies have completely revolutionized the understanding of the speech process in children.

Definitive Test of Stage Theories Whenever one attempts to make a definitive test of any stage theory of development, a longitudinal approach is necessary. For example, if one wanted to test Piaget's stage invariance concept, the only logically conclusive disproof would be the demonstration that a particular child skipped a stage. Such evidence simply cannot be derived from cross-sectional studies because one could never be certain that a given child had not passed through some stage at a very rapid rate or that the investigator had simply not chosen the appropriate ages for investigation.

Limitations of the Longitudinal Design

Just as there are advantages of the longitudinal approach to child development, so, too, are there limitations. Some of these are described below.

Generalization to other Age Cohorts In cases where the sample includes only one age cohort at the beginning of a longitudinal project, the findings may not necessarily generalize to other age cohorts. As Schaie (1965) has pointed out, such cohort differences may be the result of either changes in gene pools across time or of changes in the cultural milieu.

Evaluation of Treatment Effects in Intervention Programs With regard to intervention programs in which successive cohorts of children are enrolled, the limitation of the longitudinal approach mentioned above becomes particularly clear. In some programs, results derived in the early stages may cause alterations in the program administered to subsequently enrolled children. The effects of these program changes may interact with cohort differences, thus limiting the conclusions that may be drawn either from significant or nonsignificant treatment effects.

Artifactual Results from Repeated Measure Designs In any repeated measure design, one must consider the possibility of artifactual results attributable to practice effects.

Because most intervention programs have relied heavily upon repeated administration of standardized measures of intelligence as the primary evaluation tool, careful control of this factor is essential (for a thorough review of the issues inherent in repeated-measures designs, see McCall and Appelbaum, 1973).

Necessity for Limitations on, and Justification of, Types of Data Collected As Sontag (1971) has noted, there was a tendency for earlier longitudinal studies to be non-hypothesis oriented in the attempt to study "the whole child." More frequently than not, this orientation, although noble and bold, led to the massive collection of data for which no clear purpose was specified, and relatively few summarizations of findings found their way into journal or book print. The conclusion to be drawn from this experience is that investigators should carefully plan and justify the particular data they intend to collect.

New and More Sophisticated Measures Developed during the Course of Longitudinal Studies A serious problem with longitudinal designs is that they are conceptually wedded to the particular measures chosen at the outset of data collection. More appropriate or more sophisticated measures developed during the time period covered by the longitudinal study will decrease the study's value. Moreover, changing the measures collected will raise some of the problems discussed above.

Expense of Longitudinal Research Many people have argued that one of the major hindrances to longitudinal research is the substantial amount of money that such projects require. Sontag (1971), on the other hand, has maintained that "longitudinal [research] ... is no more expensive, time consuming, or frustrating than cross-sectional design, and it can provide continuous payoff—payoff which could be obtained in no other way" (p. 1,001).

RELATIVE UNDERUSE OF THE LONGITUDINAL DESIGN

Thus, like any other method, the longitudinal design has its limitations, but it would appear that certain developmental questions can only be answered, while other developmental questions can best be answered, with such a design. This being the case, one would expect to find widespread use of this design in journals of child psychology. Does a review of appropriate journals confirm this expectation? To answer this question, these authors reviewed the last 10 years of *Merrill-Palmer Quarterly*, *Child Development*, and *Journal of Experimental Child Psychology*, and 5 years of *Developmental Psychology* (which began publication in 1969). Any article not reporting information on human subjects (e.g., review articles, theoretical discussions, studies of animals) was discarded from analysis. The remaining articles were classified as longitudinal or cross-sectional, and the number of subjects was noted. In order to receive the classification "longitudinal," a study had to report at least two observations separated by one or more years on a single subject or group of subjects. Retrospective observations were not classified as longitudinal.

Of the 2,561 studies reporting data on human subjects in these journals, only 117, or less than 5 percent, could be classified as longitudinal in accordance with the criteria given above. Figure 2 presents the respective proportions of longitudinal studies for each of the four journals during each year of the 10-year period reviewed. As the functions in Figure 2 indicate quite clearly, the relatively small proportion of longitudinal studies did not vary appreciably across the 10-year period.

A similar picture emerges if the number of subjects involved in longitudinal research is examined. Of the 451,375 subjects for whom information was reported during this period, 45,094, or 10 percent, were studied in longitudinal designs. Even these figures, however, are somewhat misleading because seven of the 117 longitudinal studies accounted for 30,494 of the 45,094 subjects. Thus, 6 percent of all longitudinal studies accounted for 68 percent of the subjects examined longitudinally.

A few impressions concerning these longitudinal studies might be helpful in interpreting the figures given above. First, a number of the reports concerned subjects from the major longitudinal studies begun in the 1920s and 1930s, particularly the Fels study and the Berkeley Growth Study. Thus, some subjects might be included more than once in the data presented above. Second, the dependent measures used in these longitudinal studies were generally of four types: standardized IQ or DQ tests, ratings, questionnaires, or interviews. In short, only a very few of the 117 longitudinal studies reported direct observational data concerning changes in naturally occurring behaviors. Thus, a significant

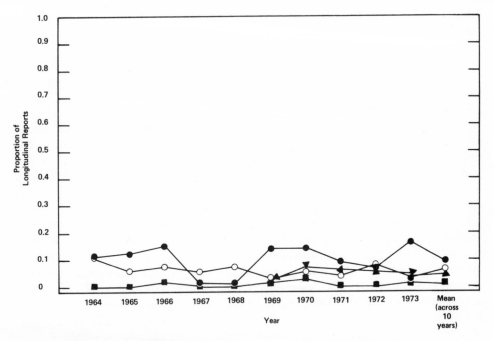

Figure 2. Proportion of longitudinal studies reported in four child psychology journals for each year between 1964 and 1973 and the mean proportion across the 10-year period. Key: Merrill-Palmer Quarterly, ●——●; Child Development, ○——○; Developmental Psychology, ▲——▲; J. of Experimental Child Psychology, ■——■.

proportion of these longitudinal studies seemed to be somewhat *post hoc* in conception; i.e., the investigators gained access to measurements taken on some previous occasion, retested as many of the original subjects as they could locate, and reported their results. In such cases, it would appear that a question for research was suggested by the availability of a particular kind of information, rather than longitudinal data being obtained to provide information pertinent to a previously formulated question.

The conclusion, then, is that the longitudinal design is used infrequently by social scientists interested in behavioral development. Moreover, even when it is used, the dependent measures reported tend to be of relatively constricted types, and almost never include the emergence of, changes in, or relationships between naturally occurring behaviors. Finally, it is used infrequently even to study those problems for which it is particularly and uniquely appropriate. What are the reasons for the relative underuse of this powerful tool?

FORCES IMPEDING LONGITUDINAL RESEARCH

Fluctuating Funds

Longitudinal projects, being large and expensive endeavors, are at the mercy of the forces that influence institutional funding. On the other hand, laboratory or cross-sectional research can usually operate with more limited funds and be reasonably independent of major fluctuations in sources of financial support.

A revealing example of fluctuations in funding sources, and their impact upon longitudinal and programmatic research, was the fate of President Johnson's Great Society legislation. That legislation, of course, was enacted during a period of great enthusiasm for the potential benefits of social science, particularly with regard to the historic problems of poverty and racial discrimination. Enthusiasm generated money, and social scientists were the benefactors of sharp increases in funds for basic and applied research. However, when a general disillusionment set in during the early 1970s about how quickly such problems could be solved, these research funds tended to become scarce once again. Agency managers and their professional advisors, who had the responsibility of allocating the limited sum of available research monies, tended to become quite conservative. Rather than invest in a limited number of major research efforts, as would be typified by longitudinal research, there was a strong tendency to spread limited funds in small amounts to many investigators. Such decisions were easily supported by a generation of social and behavioral scientists brought up in an orthodoxy of good science as best represented by hard-nosed, careful control of independent variables in controlled settings.

Institutional Support

Because longitudinal research generally calls for institutional as opposed to single investigator support, a further complicating dimension is added. Few federal or state agencies that distribute research funds have adopted consistent policies regarding organizational as opposed to single investigator support. Thus, it is hardly surprising that many of the earlier longitudinal efforts were conducted with private foundation funds.

Instrument Use versus Instrument Development

Another force impeding longitudinal study of complex behaviors and their development has been the heavy reliance on standarized measures as the *sine qua non* of respectable social science. This reliance on standardized tests assumes that all behaviors of importance can be produced and measured in the testing situation with the instruments currently available. If this assumption turned out to be false, then it would be necessary either to go through the painful process of instrument building, a task not often viewed with approval in quarters where the availability of methodology is often preferred to significance of problem, or to develop entirely new research strategies that are relatively independent of standardized tests.

LIMITATIONS OF CROSS-SECTIONAL RESEARCH DESIGNS

The alternative to longitudinal research, of course, is the cross-sectional design. Since cross-sectional designs are less bothersome, possibly less expensive, and much quicker than longitudinal designs, if both methods were equally appropriate to the study of developmental problems, one would certainly be wise to emphasize cross-sectional designs in the study of developmental problems (as in fact is currently done). However, consider the following hypothetical statements concerning development, all of which would justify exclusive use of cross-sectional methods:

1. If development were linear in most dimensions, then the developmental stream could be entered after knowing any two points of development and extrapolate forward and backward without fear of distortion.
2. If interactions between variables were unimportant, were constant across individuals, or were constant over time, then charting such interactive changes sequentially over time would be relatively unimportant.
3. If it were historically true that the most important concepts were derived from cross-sectional research and that few innovative concepts came from longitudinal efforts, then it would be safe to scorn long-term efforts.
4. If "representation" in subject populations were more important than "representation" across behavioral dimensions, then cross-sectional approaches would have substantial advantages.

Unfortunately, none of these propositions appears to be true. Instead, development appears to be nonlinear and seems to take a variety of unique twists and turns, particularly in individual cases. Second, the pattern of interaction between variables (between family attitudes and achievement motivation, for example) can change substantially across time. Third, much of what is now known of children and development was the product of intensive observations on a small and select group of children over time, from the work, for example, of Piaget, Brown, Terman, Sears, Gesell, and Bayley. Finally, the atypical population sampling of Freud and Piaget, among others, did not appear to affect drastically transfer of their principles to other children, whereas failure to include a substantial sample of variables can drastically distort the overall developmental portrait of a child or group of children.

SELECTED EXAMPLES OF THE
UNIQUE CONTRIBUTIONS OF LONGITUDINAL RESEARCH

These authors are forced to conclude, then, that information from longitudinal designs is irreplaceable in the attempt to understand the sequential development of behavior. Thus, the objective of this section is to provide selected examples of longitudinal studies that have provided this type of information. Those who are interested in more thorough reviews of longitudinal studies are referred to Kagan (1964), Wall and Williams (1970), and Sontag (1971).

Piaget (1952) has described the epigenesis of specific behavioral and conceptual systems (e.g., permanent object, number, ordinal relations) illustrating, with concrete examples, some of the advantages of longitudinal research listed earlier. For example, Piaget has identified the sequential development of understanding relational concepts such as "larger and smaller than" or "more and less than." Piaget's observations, summarized by Ginsburg and Opper (1969), indicate that the child progresses from 1) an awareness during infancy that the harder he swings his rattle the louder its noise, to 2) the ability to place sticks in size order when he is 5 to 10 years of age, and finally to 3) the capacity, achieved during adolescence, to solve verbally posed problems such as, "If A is larger than B, and A is smaller than C, then which is largest?" All three behaviors reflect understanding of the same concept, albeit at different levels of abstraction and complexity, which suggests that development is cumulative and that new behaviors are modifications of foundations constructed earlier. Thus, Piaget's work demonstrates the unique advantage of longitudinal designs, noted by Kagan (1964), for identifying response systems that are transformed during ontogeny into new and more adaptive behaviors.

Outlining the course of development for a given behavioral dimension and generating hypotheses regarding the factors responsible for this development are also problems for which longitudinal research is most appropriate. With regard specifically to intellectual development, for many years psychologists subscribed to the notions that IQ was constant and that there were no further gains in intelligence past the ages of 18 to 20 years. These conclusions were drawn largely from results of cross-sectional assessments of performance on IQ tests; e.g., the standardization samples of the Stanford-Binet, Wechsler Adult Intelligence Scale (WAIS), and Wechsler Intelligence Scale for Children (WISC) intelligence tests.

Berkeley Growth Study

However, Bayley (1955), drawing upon IQ data from the Berkeley Growth Study (Jones and Bayley, 1941) challenged both of these notions. The Berkeley Growth Study followed 74 infants beginning in the first 2 months of life. Information was collected on the mostly white, middle class subjects every 3 months until 15 months of age, and then every 6 months until 18 years of age. Some subjects were also seen at age 21, and again between ages 25 and 30. The data collected included intelligence test scores, projective tests, inventory and interview assessments of personality, behavioral observations of mother-child interactions, physical growth, and nutritional information.

Using these data, as well as data collected from other longitudinal studies, Bayley (1955) projected that IQ scores of the Berkeley sample would continue to increase up to age 50. This prediction was contradictory to the cross-sectional standardization data of the WAIS (Wechsler, 1958), which indicated a decline in IQ after age 30. However, as Bloom (1964) has noted, Wechsler's growth curves for intelligence could have been biased by differences in educational opportunities in different age or cohort samples.

Bayley (1955) also reported that the Berkeley IQ data indicated frequent and substantial IQ changes for individual children in the first 8 years of life. In fact, these changes in IQ prompted her to suggest that test performance at different ages may have resulted from different organizations of underlying functions or skills. In short, far from being a unitary construct, intelligence seemed to be a developing sequence of hierarchically arranged functions. Recall now the previously stated argument of Baltes and Nesselroade (1970), that longitudinal research is essential for the study of dimensions underlying behavioral change. Bayley's conclusions regarding the development of intelligence, and the factors responsible for such development, provide a clear example of this advantage of the longitudinal method.

Identifying individual differences in patterns of development is another exclusive virtue of longitudinal investigations. The cross-sectional design necessarily compares groups of subjects at different ages, thereby opening the possibility that age-response functions obtained from the means of each age sample may accurately represent few or none of the subjects constituting the sample. When taken together with Bayley's (1955) argument that individuality in patterns of development is the rule rather than the exception, one concludes that this deficiency of cross-sectional designs is a compelling justification for longitudinal research.

McCall, Appelbaum, and Hogarty Study

The recent monograph by McCall, Appelbaum, and Hogarty (1973) illustrates both the prescience of Bayley's argument and the knowledge of patterns in the development of individual differences that can be expected from longitudinal designs. McCall, Appelbaum, and Hogarty (1973) examined data from the Fels longitudinal study with the specific objective of identifying characteristic patterns of IQ change. The Fels longitudinal study (Sontag, Baker, and Nelson, 1958) began in 1929 and has subsequently added six to ten subjects to its sample each year. Currently, there are more than 300 predominantly white, middle class subjects who range from under 1 year to over 40 years of age. A wide variety of information has been collected, e.g., intelligence tests beginning in infancy, projective and inventory personality tests, interviews with the subjects and their mothers, behavioral observations of mother-child interactions at home, and observation of behavior in the Fels nursery school.

Using the Stanford-Binet IQ scores of 80 Fels subjects with relatively complete records, McCall, Appelbaum, and Hogarty (1973) performed a type of cluster analysis that would identify characteristic patterns of individual differences, "Such that the patterns of IQ change over age within a group were relatively homogeneous while the general IQ pattern for one group was different from that for another group" (p. 43). The results of this analysis were the five distinct patterns of IQ growth illustrated in Figure 3. The authors summarized these patterns of individual differences as follows:

> The predominant pattern involving 45% of the subjects was one of relative stability in IQ over age with a slight increase in performance with development [cluster 1]. The remaining patterns were more variable in IQ over age; two were predominantly decreasing and two largely increasing during the preschool period. The decreasing patterns were significantly different from the increasing, and the two patterns within each of these sets were different from each other (pp. 49–50).

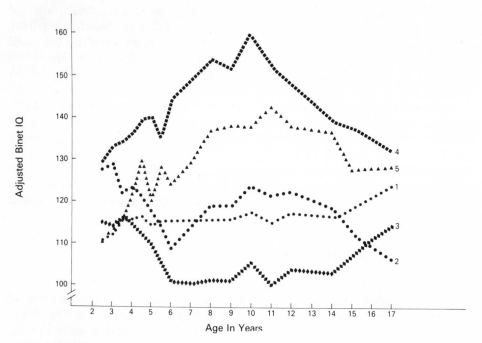

Figure 3. Results of a cluster analysis. (Reprinted by permission from McCall, Appelbaum, and Hogarty, 1973, p. 48.)

Thus, the McCall, Appelbaum, and Hogarty (1973) analysis was successful in uncovering clear patterns of individual differences in IQ development.

A further advantage of longitudinal study illustrated by this monograph was its ability to link the five characteristic patterns of IQ change with parental variables. Using a cluster of 10 parental behavior ratings from the Fels data, the authors were able to discriminate the five patterns of IQ change on the basis of this independent analysis. More specifically, children with declining IQ patterns tended to live in homes that did not attempt to stimulate them and that were characterized by either very severe or very mild punishment routines. On the other hand, children in the groups with IQ increases until approximately 8 years of age tended to live in homes that attempted to accelerate their children by providing encouragement, but also by providing structure and clear patterns of rule enforcement.

Not only were McCall, Appelbaum, and Hogarty (1973) able to isolate characteristic patterns of behavioral change but they were also able to identify environmental factors associated with these changes. Such relationships not only support the value of longitudinal studies as hypothesis-generating mechanisms, but also provide considerable support for the validity of intervention programs—support of the kind that intervention programs have sorely needed since the late 1960s. As the authors themselves concluded in their final paragraph:

> If such specific, individual dynamics characterize a significant portion of the environmental contribution to IQ, then enrichment programs and public schools might attempt to develop curricula and learning processes that are not only sensitive to but capitalize on the individual interest, motivations, and skills of each child. Moreover, although only a few enrichment programs have been successful at raising the IQs of impoverished children substantially past 100 (see Heber, 1969), the present data suggest that considerable change is possible above 100, and the factors that govern the achievement of superior performance may be even more idiosyncratic than those determining shifts at other levels of the scale. At the very least, it is time to permit our theoretical orientations and our practical efforts at providing "stimulating" environments to reflect the complexity of the phenomenon (p. 76).

Kagan and Moss Study

The relationship between parent factors and child behaviors revealed by McCall, Appelbaum, and Hogarty (1973) was consistent with the findings of a previous analysis of the Fels data by Kagan and Moss (1962). However, the 1962 study by Kagan and Moss also illustrates an additional unique advantage of the longitudinal design; namely, the ability to discover the later impact of events that occurred during early development. Such delayed or "sleeper effects" were frequently observed by Kagan and Moss in their analysis of the Fels data.

As part of their study, these authors retested 71 of the Fels subjects enrolled between 1929 and 1939 when they ranged in age from 19 to 29 years. The adults were given tests of intelligence, personality, and autonomic reactivity under conditions of stress. One of the purposes of the study was to identify the causal relations between environmental events in childhood, particularly maternal behavior, and the subjects' behavior later in childhood and adulthood. For example, the mother's behaviors toward the child from birth to 3 years of age were more strongly related to the behavior of the subjects during later childhood or adulthood than contemporaneous measures of maternal behavior.

In particular, a mother's protectiveness toward her child from birth to 3 years of age was a better predictor of her son's passivity at ages 6 to 10 and of her daughter's tendency to withdraw from anxiety-arousing situations in adulthood than were later measures of maternal behavior. Similarly, it was observed that maternal behavior during the child's first 3 years of life was the best predictor of adult intellectual achievement or mastery behavior. For males, maternal protection from birth to 3 years of age was more strongly associated with adult achievement behavior than were measures of the maternal behavior later in childhood. For females, hypercritical maternal evaluations of the child's behavior and maternal acceleration toward the child from birth to 3 years of age were most strongly predictive of adult achievement.

Thus, maternal acceleration between 6 and 10 years of age was strongly related to adult achievement behavior in both boys and girls. Moreover, Kagan and Moss (1962) argued that the pattern and timing of maternal behaviors, as opposed to the influence of specific behaviors at specific times, may have been the critical determinant of the mother's effect on the child's development. Discovering these patterns of causal factors, and particularly those factors whose effects are delayed, can be accomplished only with a longitudinal design.

The Iowa Preschool Laboratory Program

Similarly, longitudinal methods are necessary to evaluate the permanence of the influence of environmental factors on behavior development. An example of such research was the longitudinal evaluation of the Iowa Preschool Laboratory program between 1921 and 1932 (Wellman, 1932; 1934). Children, who entered the preschool at mean age 42 months, were given an IQ test every 6 months while attending the preschool and then yearly until the age of 14.5. During their 18-month average stay in the preschool, these children showed a mean gain of 16 IQ points. Follow up tests indicated that gains made during the 1 to 1.5 years of preschool could be maintained for an average of 12 years, provided the child continued schooling after the preschool program (Wellman, 1934, p. 80).

The Brown Studies

Often the sequential description of a developing behavioral system offers a great deal of information concerning the processes underlying such development. The longitudinal study of language acquisition exemplified by the work of Brown and his colleagues is a case in point (Brown and Fraser, 1964; Brown and Bellugi, 1964; Brown, Cazden, and Bellugi, 1968). Brown and his associates observed three children, two beginning at 18 months of age and the other beginning at 17 months of age. Everything said by the children and to the children during observations was recorded, as well as a description of the nonlinguistic context. Very soon it became clear that the children's early word combinations were not random. Rather, Brown concluded that certain words could be classified on the basis of their positional privileges of occurrence in an utterance. This conclusion, in turn, led Brown and his colleagues to postulate the existence of grammatical classes and to construct rules that expressed the way children combined these grammatical classes.

With further longitudinal investigation, it became clear that the children were acquiring progressively differentiated and hierarchically organized rule systems and not S-R chains, as proposed by the operant analysis of language (Skinner, 1957). To take just one example, a child first correctly used the past tense "ran" but later incorrectly used the form "runned." This incorrect usage had probably never been rewarded by adults, nor was it likely to have been heard in adult speech. In short, the rule for forming past tense verbs had been incorrectly extended. Clearly, then, the process underlying language acquisition was the formation of hierarchically arranged rule systems. Because the emergence of and change in these systems could only have been induced from repeated observations of their behavioral correlates, a unique outcome from longitudinal research can again be seen; namely, the understanding of processes underlying specific behavioral events.

Discussion

The longitudinal research projects discussed here were selected to illustrate not only the potential advantages of the longitudinal design, but also the actual achievements of this research strategy. In general, all the studies discussed above demonstrate the hypothesis-generating function of longitudinal research. And, in fact, nearly all these studies have generated subsequent research by other investigators, either to test the generality of observations in the original study or to explore in more detail the relationships suggested by the original study. However, beyond this hypothesis-generating function of the longitudinal research discussed above, one can point to a particular advantage of the longitudinal design illustrated by each of the studies reviewed; more specifically, longitudinal studies allow one to 1) chart the developmental course of given behaviors, and particularly those behaviors that are transformed into more organized and adaptive behaviors during ontogeny; 2) observe correlational relationships between developing behaviors and the independent variables with which they seem to be related; 3) identify and chart the developmental course of dimensions of individual differences; 4) discover the delayed impact, or permanence of impact, of specific independent variables upon the development of processes underlying behavioral change. In short, longitudinal studies have often succeeded in providing psychologists with the kind of information they are uniquely capable of revealing.

A PROPOSED APPROACH FOR LONGITUDINAL RESEARCH WITH CHILDREN

These authors would like to propose a particular type of longitudinal inquiry which, it is believed, will substantially contribute to the understanding of child development in general, and to the impact of preschool intervention programs in particular. The type of longitudinal inquiry advocated here is characterized by three salient features not sufficiently emphasized in past longitudinal efforts.

Three Features of the Proposed Longitudinal Approach

Types of Data to be Collected   A major criticism of longitudinal research in the past has focused on the types of data collected. Such research tended to collect information concerning physical growth, IQ, and personality composition. In general, the measures were collected primarily in the form of standardized clinical tests, ratings of personality attributes, or retrospective interviews. Relatively few direct observations of typical cognitive and social behaviors were collected.

In fact, there are many studies concerning intellectual development as measured by standardized IQ, but relatively few concerning the development of smiling and fewer still concerning crying. Thus, the measures of behavior selected for longitudinal study have tended to bear little relationship to typical behaviors manifested by typical children in typical settings: running in the park, fighting on the playground, touching in the classroom, playing in the neighborhood. As a consequence, developmentalists are frequently embarrassed when asked to describe what a particular child might be expected to do in a particular, concrete setting.

Clearly, then, future longitudinal research should enlarge the types of information collected. Child development is not particularly in need of another longitudinal study of IQ or physical growth. A science of child development cannot be based exclusively on measurements that are easily obtained, or those for which there is a widely used and reliable instrument. Rather, researchers must begin to record those behaviors typical of the developing child.

These behaviors, although difficult to measure, are readily observable. But they may not be easily observed in a laboratory, particularly those in which responses are specified beforehand by the investigator. Rather, they may be observed in those environments in which children are typically found: classrooms, playgrounds, homes, supermarkets, and neighborhoods. Our subjects are literally crawling, walking, and, more often, running away from us. Why are we not in hot pursuit? Is it our equipment, rating forms, questionnaires, and test manuals that weigh us down? If so, then we should put them aside in favor of pad and pencil.

Specifically, longitudinal studies should collect extensive observational data on the behavior of their subjects in a broad variety of contexts. Examples of these behaviors would include looking, smiling, crying, talking, walking, hitting, and playing. The mother-infant and father-infant interaction systems should also be described by observational data, if possible. Finally, as the child grows older and his social network comes to include peers and adults other than his parents, these should also receive extensive attention.

With specific regard to intervention studies, the collection of observational data should begin to move the researcher away from the relatively limited view of development supplied by measures of intellectual development. The widespread practice must end of evaluating infant programs or preschool programs on the basis of IQ data alone, or of IQ data plus achievement test results once the children reach the public schools. Is it really desirable that the effects of such programs be reduced to a single number?

If there has been an over-reaction by the American public to recent discussions of the relative contributions of genetic and environmental factors to intelligence (Jensen, 1969; Herrnstein, 1971), then we have been hoisted by our own petard. We now find ourselves in a kind of evaluation *cul de sac* created by our propensity to measure the thing for which we have a valid, reliable, and widely respected instrument; namely, IQ.

But surely the effects of intervention programs go beyond IQ. What is the effect of infant programs on mother-child interaction? Are children with preschool experience more capable of following instructions in elementary school? How do they interact with peers? Are they relatively more task oriented than controls without preschool experience?

The answers to these questions, and few infant or preschool programs have collected the observational data requisite to such answers, will serve at least two purposes. First, they will broaden the measures by which populations of children receiving intervention programs are compared to children not receiving such programs and by which the value of these programs are evaluated. Second, and of equal importance, they will be a reminder that the objectives of society and of educational systems are not merely intellectual, and that very important and powerful human development occurs outside the cognitive domain.

Thus, advocacy of more extensive use of observational data would not only provide basic information for comparison of special populations with normative populations, but would also provide a step toward the analysis of factors controlling the development of typical human behaviors. Indeed, it is likely that from extensive observations of actual child behavior in natural situations there will emerge a variety of suggestions for experimental work. An important result of observational data collection, then, would be the generation of hypotheses for experimental testing as suggested by the model of scientific progress proposed earlier in this chapter.

Bidirectionality of Influence between Observational and Experimental-Manipulative Approaches to Child Development It has not been typical in child development research for there to be a dynamic and direct interplay between observational data collection procedures and experimental-manipulative laboratory experiments to explicate the relevant parameters governing behavior. In this respect, child development research lags behind some of the more exciting research currently being generated by the ethological and sociobiological approaches to behavioral development.

Many examples of this progression from careful observation to experimental testing to more enlightened observation may be found in the ethological and sociobiological literatures (Tinbergen, 1952; von Frisch, 1962; Beer, 1973). A single example, however, will both clarify this progression and demonstrate its potential application to the study of human behavioral development.

Rosenblatt's longitudinal observations of kittens in the litter situation (Rosenblatt, Turkewitz, and Schneirla, 1961) led to a variety of experimental tests designed to explore the factors affecting development of maternal-infant interaction, particularly in the feeding situation. An excellent example of these experimental manipulations was Rosenblatt's use of isolation studies. In these studies, he removed groups of kittens from the litter situation for varying periods of time and beginning at various points after parturition. The removed kittens were fed with an "artificial mother" designed to present some of the thermal, tactual, and feeding properties of the biological mother. Upon returning these kittens to the litter situation, Rosenblatt was in a position to observe the importance of learned adjustments between the mother and kittens, as well as learned adjustments by kittens to the general home base situation ("cage orientation"). In general, the results of these experiments showed that although kittens removed from and returned to the artificial brooder could readjust very quickly, readjustment to the mother in the litter situation was substantially more difficult.

The factor of critical importance, then, was the behavioral and functional interchange between the kittens and mother in the home care situation in general, and in the feeding situation in particular. This result, and others beyond the scope of the purpose here, permitted Rosenblatt's (1961) general conclusion that:

> ... developmental accomplishments [depend] upon an intimate fusion of rudimentary learning processes with processes of maturation. The learning postulated is viewed as a maturation-fused elementary pattern of conditioning involving proximal stimuli such as those through tactual, olfactory and thermal experience with female and with the nest situation, and with approach and suckling as nuclear responses (p. 56).

One of the better and relatively few examples of the bidirectionality of influence between careful observations and manipulative-experimental procedures in child development can be found in the work of Piaget (1952) and of those researchers who have been influenced by his ideas.

In describing the style of Piaget's inquiry, Ginsburg and Opper (1969) have noted that Piaget used careful observation to describe the phenomenon under investigation. According to Ginsburg and Opper:

> The intention is to discover and identify the significant processes and problems which at a later stage of investigation may be subject to rigorous statistical test. [Further], Piaget attempts to compensate for the obvious deficincies of the naturalistic procedure by performing informal experiments. If, for example, observation suggests that the child cannot deal with certain kinds of obstacles, Piaget may intervene in the natural course of events by imposing these obstacles on the child and then observe the results. These experiments are, of course, informal, since a very small number of subjects—three at most—is involved, and since the controls are often incomplete (pp. 28–29).

Based upon the results from these informal experiments, Piaget has frequently been led into new areas of observations which, taken as a whole, have resulted in the most widely influential theory of intellectual development in the world today.

Many students of cognitive development in the United States have attempted, with a large degree of success, to formalize carefully both the assessment of children's cognitive abilities in specific situations (e.g., the conservation problems) and the experimental-manipulative studies necessary to isolate the factors controlling the development of these cognitive abilities. However, few of these researchers have been as intent as Piaget on returning to the level of observation after the experimentation to check the ecological validity of their findings.

These authors believe that, in a research strategy, the proper sequence of events to elicit a more profound understanding of human development is as follows:

1. *Observation*: Detailed and sequential analysis of the behavior of children focusing on the interaction of crucial variables over time.

2. *Thinking*: An attempt to integrate knowledge of these sequential actions into existing conceptual models or the inductive addition of new constructs to existing models based on the new data.

3. *Testing*: The generation of specific hypotheses regarding specific types of relationships deduced from the conceptual framework that emerges in Stage 2. Such experiments need to be carefully drawn with extraneous variables controlled as closely as possible.

4. *Observation*: A new set of observations enriched by the preceding steps is now possible. The choice of dimensions to be observed can be based on larger understandings of the crucial variables, and so the sequence continues.

This OTTO sequence, these authors believe, holds the best promise for building a science of child development. On the other hand, it would be wrong to believe or expect that one study or group of studies can embody all of these steps simultaneously.

Interdisciplinary Research   Particular emphasis should be placed on interdisciplinary inquiry within child development. No single discipline can possibly capture the myriad influences that determine the course of a child's development. Nor can any single discipline provide the ultimate truth concerning all basic developmental principles. Thus, a consortium of researchers must be developed that can act together to generate knowledge that transcends the scope any single discipline. Of course, such consortiums have been created from time to time in the past, but they tended to be more multidisciplinary than interdisciplinary in nature. This distinction is illustrated schematically in Figure 4.

Within this model, one would be about, for example, purely psychological research whenever both the independent and the dependent variables were psychological in nature. In contrast, multidisciplinary research would be conducted when different disciplines examined the same subjects but made no attempt to interrelate the various types of data collected within an experimental-manipulative paradigm. In this case the subjects are merely convenient to collect data for each researcher's own discipline.

Finally, truly interdisciplinary research would be conducted only when independent variables were identified within one or more disciplines, while the dependent variables were identified within other disciplines. For example, if one manipulated a psychological variable such as task instructions and measured variables such as GSR, EKG, or some other physiological measure, then one would be involved in psychobiology. Similarly, of one varied some parameter, such as introduction of a nutrition supplement, and measured its psychological consequences, then one would be about the business of biopsychology. It is such studies that create useful linkages between usually discrete bodies of knowledge and that allow a fuller examination of that trite but relevant term "the whole child."

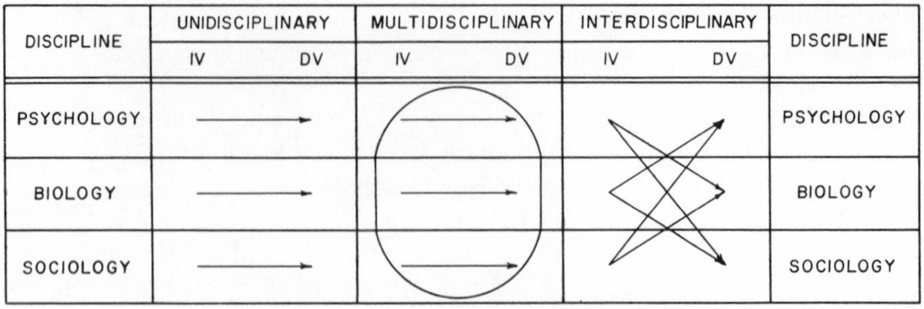

DISCIPLINE	UNIDISCIPLINARY		MULTIDISCIPLINARY		INTERDISCIPLINARY		DISCIPLINE
	IV	DV	IV	DV	IV	DV	
PSYCHOLOGY							PSYCHOLOGY
BIOLOGY							BIOLOGY
SOCIOLOGY							SOCIOLOGY

Figure 4. A model of unidisciplinary, multidisciplinary, and interdisciplinary research. The critical feature of this model is the relationship between independent variables (IV), dependent variables (DV), and the behavioral discipline within whose scope the variables fall.

Expected Benefits of the Proposed Longitudinal Method

Five specific outcomes can be expected from the longitudinal strategy proposed in this chapter.

First, such an approach will create a more comprehensive view of the child's functioning in typical and ecologically valid environments over time.

Second, the discovery of novel relationships among causative factors will be facilitated. These factors may subsequently be brought under rigorous experimental-manipulative test.

Third, the outcome of these experimental-manipulative procedures will be the confirmation of functional relationships between variables. Knowledge of these relationships, in turn, will elevate subsequent observational procedures to higher levels of sophistication.

Fourth, with particular reference to intervention programs, the research approach advocated here would permit a broadening of evaluation techniques. These broader evaluation techniques would both allow and encourage assessment of the fundamental goal of intervention programs in our society, namely, the creation of persons capable of productive participation in the social, leisure, occupational, and service activities that are the hallmarks of our culture.

Fifth, this approach will result in greater returns from research investments because interdisciplinary research encourages the sharing of subjects while it discourages the duplication of samples and the underuse of subjects that have characterized most cross-sectional and many longitudinal studies in the past.

RECOMMENDATIONS

If it is true, as argued here, that longitudinal research is underused and undervalued, then specific steps should be taken to encourage its more widespread use. Five specific recommendations are offered here that will provide such encouragement.

Support to Research Organizations

The policies of major funding agencies, both public and private, need to distinguish between the support of individual project research and organizational programmatic research as illustrated here by longitudinal studies. There are certain research problems that cannot be successfully attacked by a single investigator, no matter how brilliant, perceptive, or energetic that investigator might be. Problem areas needing a longitudinal research approach require an organizational or group effort, not only because of the scope of work, but also because of the need for a diversity of talents, skills, and knowledge that cannot be found in a single investigator.

Data Storage Systems

With the advent of sophisticated computer systems for data storage, retrieval, and analysis, longitudinal projects should be strongly encouraged to make use of such facilities to shorten the data processing time that has been the bane of most large-scale longitudinal efforts. Furthermore, projects using similar instruments should be encouraged to use similar computer formats to facilitate sharing and to allow direct comparison of project results.

Long-term Priority

Public and private funding agencies should provide support for research efforts on major conceptual issues that are longitudinal, ecological, and interdisciplinary in scope; in addition to projects that arise in response to some perceived national crisis, such as the disproportionate failure of disadvantaged children in school.

Population Maintenance in Situ

Funding agencies should allow and even encourage the delivery of support services to the children and families serving as subjects in longitudinal research projects. The recent and justified concern over the rights of human subjects dictates that observations of infants and young children, and particularly of interactions between children and their parents, be conducted in a manner that will not only meet the needs of scientific investigators, but (of equal or greater importance) will promote the development of the child and the integrity of his family. This often means providing services such as day care, health care, nutrition advice or supplements, parent training, or social services. None of these activities has been considered a legitimate part of scientific expenditures in the past.

Long-term Funding Support

Funding agencies should create a substantial financial reserve for the support of long-term research. Such a policy will tend to ensure staff continuity and project stability in these long-term efforts.

These requests are not based on an attempt to substitute the researcher's interests for work based on pressing societal priorities. Rather, they are based on the belief that gains in basic knowledge concerning human development eventually will lead to more wisdom about the developing child, which, when intelligently extrapolated, will provide solutions to these issues of high societal priority.

LITERATURE CITED

Ambrose, A. 1968. The comparative approach to early child development: The data of ethology. *In* E. Miller (ed.), Foundations of Child Psychiatry, pp. 183–232. Pergamon Press, Oxford.

Baltes, P. B., and J. R. Nesselroade. 1970. Multivariate longitudinal and cross-sectional sequences for analyzing ontogenetic and generational change: A methodological note. Devel. Psych. 2: 163–168.

Bateson, P. P. G. 1968. Ethological methods of observing behavior. *In* L. Weiskrantz (ed.), Analysis of Behavioral Change, pp. 389–399. Harper and Row, New York.

Bayley, N. 1955. On the growth of intelligence. Amer. Psych. 10: 805–818.

Beer, C. G. 1973. A view of birds. *In* A. D. Pick (ed.), Minnesota Symposia on Child Psychology, Vol. 7, pp. 47–86. University of Minnesota Press, Minneapolis.

Bell, R. Q. 1953. Convergence: An accelerated longitudinal approach. Child Devel. 24: 145–152.

Bell, R. Q. 1968. A reinterpretation of the direction of effects in studies of socialization. Psych. Rev. 75: 81–95.

Bertalanffy, L. von. 1968. General system theory. George Braziller, New York. Cited in Overton, W. F., and H. W. Reese. 1973. Models of development: Methodological implications. *In* J. R. Nesselroade and H. W. Reese (eds.), Life-span Developmental Psychology: Methodological Issues, pp. 65–86. Academic Press, New York.

Bloom, B. S. 1964. Stability and Change in Human Characteristics. Wiley, New York.

Bronfenbrenner, U. 1973. A theoretical prospective for research on human development. *In* H. P. Dreitzel (ed.), Childhood and Socialization, pp. 337–363. Macmillan, New York.

Broom, L. 1964. Introduction. *In* A. Kaplan (ed.), The Conduct of Inquiry, pp. xvii–xix. Chandler, San Francisco.

Brown, R., and U. Bellugi. 1964. Three processes in the child's acquisition of syntax. Harvard Educ. Rev. 34: 131–151.

Brown, R., C. Cazden, and U. Bellugi. 1968. The child's grammar from I to III. *In* J. P. Hill (ed.), Minnesota Symposia on Child Psychology, Vol. 2, pp. 28–73. University of Minnesota Press, Minneapolis.

Brown, R., and C. Fraser. 1964. The acquisition of syntax. *In* U. Bellugi and R. Brown (eds.), The Acquisition of Language, 29: (No. 92), pp. 43–78. Monogr. Soc. Res. Child Devel.

Brush, S. G. 1974. Should the history of science be rated X? Science 183: 1164–1172.

Bunge, M. 1963. Causality: The Place of the Causal Principle in Modern Science. World Publishing Co., New York. Cited in Overton, W. F., and H. W. Reese. 1973. Models of development: Methodological implications. *In* J. R. Nesseroade and H. W. Reese (eds.), Life-span Developmental Psychology: Methodological Issues, pp. 65–86. Academic Press, New York.

Chipman, S. S. 1965. Bethesda Independent National Institute of Child Health and Human Development. Colloquium on Longitudinal Studies, February 7–10, 1965. Fort Monroe, Va. (preliminary draft). Cited in Wall, W. D., and H. L. Williams. 1970. Longitudinal Studies and the Social Sciences. Heineman, London.

Frisch, K. von. 1962. Dialects in the language of the bees. Sci. Amer. 206: 130–135.

Ginsburg, H., and S. Opper. 1969. Piaget's Theory of Intellectual Development: An Introduction. Prentice-Hall, Englewood Cliffs, N.J.

Heber, R. 1969. Rehabilitation of families at risk for mental retardation. Madison: Regional Rehabilitation Center, University of Wisconsin, Madison.

Herrnstein, R. 1971. I.Q. Atlantic Monthly 228: 43–64.

Hinde, R. A., and Y. Spencer-Booth. 1968. The study of mother-infant interaction in captive group-living rhesus monkeys. Proceed. Royal Soc., Serial B. 169: 177–201.

Jensen, A. R. 1969. How much can we boost I.Q. and scholastic achievement? Harvard Educ. Rev. 39: 1–123.

Jones, H. E., and N. Bayley. 1941. The Berkeley growth study. Child Devel. 12: 167–173.

Jones, N. B. 1972. Characteristics of ethological studies of human behaviour. In N. B. Jones (ed.), Ethological Studies of Child Behaviour. Cambridge University Press, Cambridge, England.

Kagan, J. 1964. American longitudinal research in psychological development. Child Devel. 35: 1–32.

Kagan, J., and H. A. Moss. 1962. Birth to Maturity: A Study in Psychological Development. Wiley, New York.

Kaplan, A. 1964. The Conduct of Inquiry. Chandler, San Francisco.

Kemeny, J. G. 1959. A Philosopher Looks at Science. D. Van Nostrand, New York.

Kerlinger, F. N. 1964. Foundations of Behavioral Research. Holt, Rinehart, and Winston, New York.

Kessen, W. 1960. Research design in the study of developmental problems. In P. Mussen (ed.), Handbook of Research Methods in Child Development. Wiley, New York.

Lewis, M., and L. A. Rosenblum (eds.). 1974. The Effect of the Infant on Its Caregiver. Wiley, New York.

McCall, R. B., and M. I. Appelbaum. 1973. Bias in the analysis of repeated measures designs: Some alternative approaches. Child Devel. 44: 401–415.

McCall, R. B., M. I. Appelbaum, and P. S. Hogarty. 1973. Developmental changes in mental performance. Monogr. Soc. Res. Child Devel. 38: (3, No. 150).

Overton, W. F., and H. W. Reese. 1973. Models of development: Methodological implications. In J. R. Nesselroade and H. W. Reese (eds.), Life-span Developmental Psychology: Methodological Issues, pp. 65–86. Academic Press, New York.

Piaget, J. 1952. The Origins of Intelligence in Children. W. W. Norton, New York.

Rosenblatt, J. S., G. Turkewitz, and T. C. Schneirla. 1961. Early socialization in the domestic cat as based on feeding and other relationships between female and young. In B. M. Foss (ed.), Determinants of Infant Behaviour, Vol. I. pp. 51–74. Methuen, London.

Schaffer, H. R. 1973. Early social behavior and the study of reciprocity. Invited address to the Developmental Psychology Section, British Psychological Society, University of Nottingham, September.

Schaie, K. W. 1965. A general model for the study of developmental problems. Psych. Bull. 64: 92–107.

Schneirla, T. C. 1966. Behavioral development and comparative psychology. Quart. Rev. Biol. 41: 283–302.

Skinner, B. F. 1956. A case history in scientific method. Amer. Psych. 11: 221–233.

Skinner, B. F. 1957. Verbal Behavior. Appleton-Century-Crofts, New York.

Sontag, L. W. 1971. The history of longitudinal research: Implications for the future. Child Devel. 42: 987–1002.

Sontag, L. W., C. T. Baker, and V. L. Nelson. 1958. Mental growth and personality development: A longitudinal study. Monogr. Soc. Res. Child Devel. 23 (No. 68).

Tinbergen, N. 1952. The curious behavior of the stickleback. Sci. Amer. 187: 414–418.

Tinbergen, N. 1972. Foreword. *In* N. B. Jones (ed.), Ethological studies of Child Behaviour, pp. vii–ix. Cambridge University Press, Cambridge, England.

Wall, W. D., and H. L. Williams. 1970. Longitudinal Studies and the Social Sciences. Heinemann, London.

Wechsler, D. 1958. The Measurement and Appraisal of Adult Intelligence. 4th Ed. Williams and Wilkins, Baltimore.

Wellman, B. L. 1932. The effect of preschool attendance upon the I.Q. J. Exper. Ed. 1: 48–69.

Wellman, B. L. 1934. Growth in intelligence under differing school environments. J. Exper. Ed. 3: 59–83.

Wright, H. F. 1960. Observational child study. *In* P. H. Mussen (ed.), Handbook of Research Methods in Child Development, pp. 71–139. Wiley, New York.

Community-based Language Training

Betty Hart, Ph.D., and Todd R. Risley, Ph.D.

Through language, a person interacts with his society, its members, and institutions, and his language determines the immediate response his society returns to him. In entering a new social situation, a person's language ability has a great deal to do with whether he will be tolerated, accepted, or welcomed. In applying for a job, the language behavior of the applicant, his ability to "sell" himself rather than his job record, often determines the reaction of the prospective employer. Working language involves, first, the basic behavioral skills of using language to express needs and to give and ask for information. Second, working language involves the use of language to prompt differential responses from the social environment.

A child's ability to use working language in everyday situations is the most critical determinant of his future success. In particular, his ability to prompt more sophisticated and complex reactions from his social environment is crucial, for the more varied the child's interactions with the environment, the greater his learning will be. Different levels of working language are often highly visible within a group of children entering school for the first time. Some children, those termed by teachers as "unprepared" because they have little working language, are unable even to tell the teacher their names; some children, those with basic language skills, can respond verbally when called on and initiate verbal interactions with teachers when, for instance, they need to use the bathroom. Finally, there are those children with both the basic working language skills and the language ability to prompt more complex interactions with the environment, children termed "inquisitive" or "curious" by teachers; these are the children who volunteer to take a note to the principal's office because they have the language skills to cope with this new and demanding experience.

This chapter is one of a series of articles drafted by the Living Environments Group at the University of Kansas under the direction of Todd R. Risley.

BUILDING A CHILD'S WORKING LANGUAGE

The building of a child's spontaneous, working language begins at birth. With the infant, the focus is on rate, so that the infant learns to employ language with increasing frequency. Then, his parents, or the persons who constitute the child's social environment at that point, begin responding differentially to vocalizations that approximate sounds that are meaningful to them: that is, sounds approximating words in their language, vocalizations that contain content, such as cries of hunger or pain, and the nonverbal language of facial and body position, such as smiles and reaching behavior. As the infant grows into a toddler, the adults who make up his social environment continue to differentiate among the child's language responses: they respond to words and then to sentences from the child. At some point, they begin attending to the goodness of the match between the child's verbalizations and their own, that is, to the child's pronunciation and syntax in terms of the norms of the language of their society. The adults begin to respond to semantics—to require that content be increasingly carried by verbalization rather than by vocalization, and that nonverbal language be appropriately paired with verbal; thus, the toddler's reaching is accompanied by a verbalization containing appropriate content: "cookie." The single words of this holophrastic speech are, for purposes of interaction with the environment, functionally equivalent to the full sentences of adults (McCarthy, 1954). Language structure, whether innate or learned, will continue to develop through telegraphic speech patterns (Brown and Fraser, 1963) into increasingly complex and elaborate grammatical arrangements, perhaps eventually into mathematical notation and other second languages. Nonverbal language will develop into those body cues socially appropriate to verbalization to a variety of persons and in a variety of situations. Given language as communication, these two aspects of language cannot be separated from content, for much of the social interpretation of language content is based on nonverbal cues and syntactic structure. For instance, Tom Bradley communicated far more than a fact when he declared at his inaugural, "I is de Mayor."

Though the teaching processes described below may be effectively employed to build nonverbal cueing behaviors and syntactic structure, for the purposes of this chapter only the language content aspects of communication will be dealt with, and the focus will be on the social imperatives for communication. The child's organization of syntax appears to be essentially complete by the time he is 4 or 5 years old (McNeill, 1966), while semantic development continues well into adulthood. A person's communication with himself, integral and desirable as it is in terms of ordering and expressing his perceptions and experiences, will also not be discussed. Consideration will be limited to the learning of language content as a tool for interaction with other members of society, when the basis of interaction is the need of one person for the help, compliance, cooperation, or friendship of one or more other persons.

GOALS OF LANGUAGE LEARNING

In these limited terms, there are two primary goals of language learning for toddlers: 1) naming: learning the verbal labels for states, actions, and entites in the environment, and 2) requesting: asking for help, information, or compliance. Examples of the behavior are the child's labeling of persons as "mama," of animals, as "doggie," of states, as "No" (meaning, "I don't want to do what you told me to do"), and his requests for help, as "Fall down" (meaning, "I fell down and hurt myself, and I need comfort and a band-aid"), for information, as "Wa dat?" or "Doggie?" and for compliance, as "Go way," or "Cookie" (meaning "May I have—or I want—a cookie").

In the toddler and preschool child, this working language is used for the same basic interactions with the environment, but is elaborated in order to interact on more complex levels with a greater variety of persons and objects in a wider variety and complexity of environments. The child increases his vocabulary of labels for objects, states, and actions, and begins to add general and conceptual terms; he begins to form semantic fields. He adds, for instance, to his store of labels the general term for a category, such as "animal" or "transportation"; he adds terms for concepts of size, number color, time, and distance. He adds terms descriptive of states, such as "thirsty" and "angry," and qualifiers of actions, such as "very," "fast," and "maybe." At the same time, the child increases his ability to request, adding, for instance, terms that signal politeness, such as "please" and "may I," terms that explain reason for request, terms that elicit more complex information, such as "color," "time," and "why," terms that request degrees of compliance, such as "If you don't do that right now . . . ," and terms that return or initiate friendship, such as "Fine, how are you?" The child uses these language tools to increase the precision of his expression and description of his needs and wants, to increase the numbers of friends and acquaintances in his society with whom he can interact, and to increase his ability to enjoy and manipulate his environment by prompting a wider and more complex variety of response from it.

In school, the child's store of language forms the basis for learning to read and write and for his socialization with peers and teachers. More complex and elaborate forms and styles of communication are developed inside and outside of school until, as an adult, a person has the language ability to interact with both friends and strangers, in both familiar and unfamiliar surroundings. He can hold a job, trade in a commercial world, obtain help in the form and to the extent that he needs it, and express his feelings and ideas to his friends and maintain communication with acquaintances. He can respond to the requests and ideas of others, and transmit his skills to his children.

Such language skills, which all adults have, seem natural: learned without effort and/or without direct teaching. In fact, however, they have been learned because someone else—parent, friend, or teacher—has prompted and reacted to a child's language behavior. An adult's command of language now is such that he no longer clearly sees or remembers the process, but process there is. This chapter describes one such process, which may be used by a teacher or parent who wants to maximize a child's learning or remediate a child's working language.

INCIDENTAL TEACHING PROCESS

One process of building spontaneous, working language in the natural environment is called "incidental teaching." Incidental teaching refers to the interactions between an adult and a single child that arise naturally in unstructured situations, and that are used by the adult to transmit information or to give the child practice in building a skill. The incidental teaching situation is child selected: the child himself initiates the interaction by requesting assistance or information from the adult. He uses his working language to prompt an adult response, and his language indicates the focus of his attention, the object that has captivated his interest. The child thus deliberately cues his parent or teacher that the optimum conditions for learning exist: his attention is focused, there is something he wants to know or to have, and the context is that in which the child's working language should continue to occur. In response to the child's prompt, the adult decides whether to use the interaction as a teaching situation and, if so, what he will use the occasion to teach. The process described below refers to language-content teaching; the incidental teaching interaction, however, is applicable to many sorts of learning. For instance, it has been used to teach syntax, the use of compound sentence structure to explain reason for use of play materials (Hart and Risley, 1974a), and to teach letter and word matching and identification (Montes, 1974).

Labeling

A study done with preschool children will serve as an example of the process of incidental teaching. In this study (Hart and Risley, 1974), the incidental teaching process was first applied to labeling, as one would employ it with toddlers. As is frequently the case in the home, many potential play objects in the preschool were out of the reach of children. When the children wanted to use one such object, they asked an adult for it. Frequently, they said, "Can I have that?" Such a request from a child cued a possible incidental teaching situation: the child initiated an interaction by requestiong the aid of an adult, and, at that moment, the child's full attention was focused on a goal, the play object, and on language as a means of obtaining it. The incidental teaching process took place when the adult used this occasion of fully-focused child attention to require a simple additional language response from the child. In the present example, the adult asked the child who said, "Can I have that?" for a single labeling response by asking him, "What is that?" Immediately upon the child's saying, "A car," the adult complied with his request, assisted him in obtaining the car, and praised the child's labeling behavior, which had been the aim of the incidental teaching.

Concept-Language Learning

In the same study, after incidental teaching of labeling, tne process was applied to concept-language learning, as one would with older children. When a child asked for a play material, as by saying, "Can I have that car?" he again initiated, as all such child questions do, a potential incidental teaching situation. His attention was again focused on a goal and on an adult's assistance. In this case, the adult asked, as before, for a single additional language response: a word descriptive of the object, such as color, size, or shape. The child was asked, "What color is that car?" for instance and, as soon as he named a color, such as "blue," the adult complied with his request and assisted him in obtaining the play material.

Further Prompting

The identical incidental teaching process was further used in that study to teach children to use concept terms as modifiers and to identify qualities correctly. This involved requesting a second language response from the child. That is, when the child initiated the incidental teaching situation by asking, "Can I have that car?" the adult asked for a first language response, "What color is that car?" If the child answered, "It's a blue car," and the car was in fact blue, the incidental teaching occasion was complete, and the child was assisted in obtaining the car. If, on the other hand, the child said simply, "Blue," and, if he was correct and if he had thus correctly identified the color blue previously, the adult used the teaching occasion to ask for a second language response by requesting that the child use a complete sentence in which the color word directly qualified the name of the object, as, "It's a blue car." Or, if the child did not identify the color of the car correctly, the adult asked for a second language response from the child in which the color was correctly identified, by saying, "This car is red. What color is this car?" In such instances of asking for a second language response from a child in an incidental teaching situation, a response that is an amplification or a correction of a previous language response, the adult encounters the complexities, the niceties, of the incidental teaching process. The process of prompting is the essence of teaching a new skill. The examples cited of single language responses on the part of a child are instances of the child's practicing working language skills in the process of mastering them; this is an essential component of language learning. However, the complexities of the incidental teaching process lie in the teaching of new and expanded language use. This will be described below.

Using the Incidental Teaching Process

First, it must be reiterated that the incidental teaching process described above is one that occurs naturally and frequently between parents and children in the ordinary course of the child's exploration of his environment. Parents often comment on the frequency with which children initiate incidental teaching interactions: "He's always asking questions." The frequency with which the young child initiates interactions with his parent by asking for assistance, information, or compliance, as opposed to the length of time he plays quietly by himself, as the parent would often like him to do, is indicative of the young child's preference for the incidental teaching situation. Perhaps if the young child had another mode of interaction with the parent, such as making polite conversation about the weather, the child's preference for the incidental teaching interaction that he initiates with his questions and requests would not be so marked; however, it is only through such interactions with his parents and others that the child will eventually learn to make such polite conversation. In addition to parents' subjective estimates, children's preference for an environment in which incidental teaching is available has also been shown empirically by Montes (1974).

Montes used incidental teaching procedures to teach preschool children to identify and match letters of the alphabet. When a child requested teacher assistance in obtaining a play material, the teacher asked the child to match, and then later in the year to identify, either the first letter or the printed name of the play material requested. Incidental teaching not only increased children's ability to recognize letters, but those play materials associated with incidental teaching occasions were systematically preferred by the children. Requests for those materials that initiated incidental teaching increased dramatically when, and only when, the incidental teaching process was paired with the given materials. In fact, when incidental teaching was no longer paired with a certain material, several children "reminded" the teacher to ask them to identify or match a letter to the name of the material (i.e., to respond, as before, with incidental teaching behavior). Others continued to request play materials until they arrived at the name of a material that was associated with incidental teaching.

A similar preference for those play materials associated with incidental teaching was shown in the Hart and Risley (1968; 1974) studies, but in a much less systematic way. Any parent can confirm that the focusing of adult attention is an important factor in such preference. Another factor is that, when correctly done, incidental teaching is brief and pleasant, it does not interfere with the child's play activities, nor does it require him to sit still while an adult demonstrates or asks other members of a group to recite. For this to be true, it is apparent that the adult must have and use the skills that will both teach the child and make the interaction enjoyable. A child who is interrogated, criticized, or repeatedly corrected when he asks for assistance is a child who learns to help himself whenever possible, one who cuts himself off from the socializing processes and influence of his society. Therefore, knowing when to prompt and when to quit are skills highly important to the adult in incidental teaching.

Cues and Prompts

The sequence of cues and prompts in the incidental teaching process has been detailed in Hart and Risley (1974); here, the sequence will be outlined in terms of a single example, the child who asks, "Can I have that?" The cues presented by the adult are two: the most subtle cue, always presented first, is the focus of the adult's attention on the child, eye contact, and a receptive expression. This cue of receptive attention is the cue that must eventually, ideally, control the language behavior of requesting: when a clerk in a store, an employer, or a friend focuses his attention on a person, it is with the expectation that that person will verbalize without an additional cue. For a child in the learning process, however, an additional cue may be necessary; therefore, if the child does not verbalize, the adult presents the second of the cues, the request for verbal behavior: "What do you want?" or the equivalent. A child who does not respond to this cue must be prompted.

Degrees of Prompts

There are three essential degrees of prompts. The fullest degree of prompt asks the child to imitate an adult verbalization; the medium degree of prompt asks the child for partial imitation and partial spontaneous production; while the minimal degree of prompt asks the child for spontaneous production of verbal behavior. In the case of the child who has responded to the cue of the focus of adult attention (or the adult statement, "What do you want?") by saying, "Can I have that?" the fullest degree of adult prompt when using the occasion for incidental teaching of labeling would be, "What is that? That is a car. Can you say 'car'?" The medium degree of prompt in the identical situation would be the adult saying, "What is that? That is a c___." The minimal degree of prompt would be the adult saying only, "What is that?"

The degree of prompt used by the adult will be determined in every case by the response of the child. A child's failure to respond immediately to any level of cue or prompt is signal to the adult to call upon a fuller degree of prompt or cue in order to tell the child more clearly what verbal response will fulfill the incidental teaching interaction. An important aid to the child here is emphasis within the adult's verbal behavior. Risley and Reynolds (1970) showed that children were much more likely to imitate those parts or words in sentences that were stressed by the adult. However, it was noted in this study that the adult's emphasis on certain words in a sentence served to prompt a child concerning crucial components of verbal behavior only when relatively few words were so stressed by the adult. This dimension is applicable to the entire incidental teaching process: when teaching basic language skills, the adult must convey to the child as clearly, briefly, and emphatically as possible the verbal response to be emitted by the child. Only when a child needs no prompts and is responding to cues alone can the adult afford to introduce the sorts of ambiguous and monotonal responses that serve as cues in so much of adult verbal interaction.

After one clear and emphatic prompt to a child, the adult in the incidental teaching situation can afford, in most cases, to prompt only once more; if the child still does not respond, the adult should terminate the teaching interaction by delivering whatever assistance the child needs, then try again, perhaps in a different way, with a different set of prompts, the next time the child initiates an incidental teaching situation. This maintains the pleasant nature of the learning situation for the child, and allows the adult to modify his own prompting behavior without subjecting the child to the adult's exploration of prompting techniques. The adult may be certain that the child will initiate future incidental teaching interactions if the adult has made them pleasant occasions and has arranged the child's environment in ways that will foster their occurrence.

Effect of Environment

The nature and arrangement of living and learning environments for young children have been extensively explicated (Risley and Cataldo, 1974); one study in this series (Doke and Risley, 1972) demonstrated that the quantity of materials available to children in the environment is directly related to the amount of participation by children in preschool activities, regardless of whether children are allowed to choose among activities or required to follow a schedule. In another study, Montes and Risley (1975) arranged an environment in which for successive 3-week periods "free access" to play materials alternated with "limited access" to materials. In "free access" periods, children could select preschool play materials at will, in any quantity and variety desired. In the "limited access" periods, children were required to ask a teacher for permission to check out toys. Under the two conditions, the amount of time the children actually spent playing with materials, selecting materials, and interacting with the teacher did not vary. However, raters' estimates of complexity of sociodramatic play indicated that the "limited access" periods were ones in which children more often engaged in make-believe in regard to actions and situations, and ones in which children talked the most with regard to the play episode. In the "limited access" periods, the children's cooperation and sharing behaviors increased, as they assigned each other "responsibilities" for obtaining a variety of play materials in order to create a common dramatic play episode. The language behaviors involved in creating such dramatic play situations among children, behaviors extremely important and beneficial to the children's growth in socialization, appear to have been the result of simply rearranging the environment.

Staffing Procedures

An important element in environmental arrangement for incidental teaching is the location of adults in terms of their availability to children. LeLaurin and Risley (1972) compared child participation in planned activities when teachers were assigned in terms of "zone" staffing procedures and in terms of "man-to-man" procedures. In the man-to-man procedure, each teacher was responsible for a specified group of children, to whose needs she attended regardless of location of the child. In the zone procedure, on the other hand, a teacher was assigned responsibility for a particular area and for all children who passed through that area. The children's participation in play activities increased under zone staffing. The teacher was immediately available to assist or to conduct incidental teaching with individual children, while the others remained engaged with materials. Zone staffing also facilitates rapid satisfaction of the requests of many children so that they can start on dramatic play or use of materials, as in the "limited access" periods described above.

Importance of Child Initiation of the Incidental Teaching Interaction

In requesting materials from a teacher, some of the children in a group take little of the teacher's time, for they almost anticipate the verbal behavior that will complete the incidental teaching interaction. These children spontaneously and vigorously initiate interaction with the teacher; these children are also those who are "forever asking questions" of their parents at home, of their friends, neighbors, and strangers. These children actively prompt a response from their environment. Their rate of prompting environmental reaction, of asking questions of adults and thus of engaging in incidental teaching interactions, has taught them to recognize and respond to a wide variety of adult cues and prompts. These are the children who, in the study previously cited, could run through the names of many materials until they located that material paired with incidental teaching. These are also the children who spontaneously undertook incidental teaching of other children, prompting them or supplying a response in order to facilitate the other-child-teacher incidental teaching interaction. These are also the children who test high on IQ tests.

The children who test low on IQ tests, on the other hand, are often those children whom a teacher describes as socially inappropriate: as "isolate" or "very quiet" because they rarely initiate or respond to verbal behavior, or as "hyperactive" or "disruptive" because their behavior prompts primarily correction or punishment from the environment. In general, these are children whose approach to other persons in their environment is such that it evokes only low-level interaction: it prompts tolerance, avoidance, or correction, not teaching. Because these children rarely initiate incidental teaching interactions with members of their society, they tend to need repeated prompts when they do enter into such interactions; they lack both language skill and experience in discriminating adult cues. In the terms that the incidental teaching process has been described, a child's need for repeated prompts is a clear indication that he needs more frequent incidental teaching. However, incidental teaching is a child-initiated interaction; and this is a child who has a low rate of initiating interaction with all other persons. In the Montes (1974) study, it was a child such as this who was characterized as a "slow learner"; his ability to recognize letters (initial letters of the names of play materials) was much lower, and his acquisition much more gradual, than that of the median child. For this child, as well as for all others in the group studied, a significant positive correlation was found between the frequency of requests for materials (the initiation of incidental teaching interactions) and correct identification of the initial letter of the names of the materials.

Language Remediation for High Risk Children

What emerges from these observations is the importance of child initiation and the suggestion that the first step in language remediation for high risk children is to increase the frequency with which they initiate incidental teaching. This is done in part by rearranging the environment: using "zone" teacher assignments so that an adult is always available in whatever area the child is in, providing a rich variety of attractive play materials appropriate to the child's skill level and interests and that are arranged and displayed in a fashion that facilitates selection (Montes and Risley, 1975) and presenting play materials designed for social rather than isolate play (Quilitch and Risley, 1973). In the home, such systematic arrangements of the environment should also include moving a variety of play materials into the adult's work area so that the parent can easily and immediately respond to the child, and including materials that encourage or require adult help, explanation, or participation. In remediation, however, the nature of the incidental teaching interaction may be both more important and harder to rearrange in the home; therefore, preschool experience is strongly recommended for the child in need of language skill training.

This factor, the nature of the incidental teaching interaction, requires skill and patience from the adult, especially in remediation. After arranging the environment to ensure that the high risk child will contact play materials and that an adult is immediately available for interaction, the adult begins to work on the child's rate of initiating incidental teaching interactions. To do this, the adult presents the incidental teaching process even though the child has not initiated it. The adult offers the child play materials if the child does not spontaneously select them, and the adult offers attention by frequently focusing on the child and verbalizing to him. Reynolds and Risley (1968) employed such procedures to increase the rate of verbal interaction between teachers and a child who, though socially appropriate, seldom used language. At first, in order to encourage interaction with adults, the incidental teaching process was applied to non-verbal behavior. When the teacher focused her attention on the child, smiled, and offered, "Would you like to play with this car?" if the child looked at the teacher, took the car, and perhaps returned her smile, the incidental teaching occasion was complete. The child was never required or pressed to verbalize at this stage. Only after he began to spon-taneously respond with speech to the teacher's offers of attention and materials did she introduce cues for further verbalization. For instance, when the child accepted the play material offered by the teacher and also said, "Okay," the teacher immediately offered further assistance, saying, "Good. Is there anything else you would like to do with your car and your blocks?" Once the child began to initiate incidental teaching interactions himself, the most important part of the incidental teaching process had been ac-complished. At this point, adults began to work on the child's request behavior. When, as often happened, the child initiated an interaction by speaking very softly with his head bent, the teacher waited until the child looked up before responding with praise and play materials. When the child initiated the interaction by coming to stand near the teacher and watching her silently, the teacher focused her full receptive attention on him but waited until he spoke before speaking herself or offering assistance. Only much later, when the child was not only initiating interactions readily and frequently but also was using his working language to prompt the teacher to interact, did the adult introduce the first prompt for a label.

A number of studies of the incidental teaching process have shown generalized effects on language of high risk children. One group of children to whom incidental teaching was available throughout a year of preschool showed increases in number of words, in vocabulary, and in numbers of sentences used in spontaneous speech that were much greater than those seen in either of two comparison groups. These increases brought the incidentally-taught group of children to levels comparable to a group of university children at the end of the preschool year, while they had begun the preschool year at levels comparable to a matched group of Head Start children (Risley, 1972). This same group of children showed that they could not only generalize an incidentally-taught language behavior to use with other children, but they could conduct incidental teaching situations themselves, including, on occasion, prompting another child (Hart and Risley, 1975). These children also showed spontaneous variety of vocabulary and syntax in language used in incidental teaching situations, indicating that variety of language need not be directly taught or extensively prompted.

CONCLUSION

When the incidental teaching interaction is a rewarding one for the child, the child will not only initiate such interactions but will present obvious cues for adult response. He will use working language to request, to let the adult know, that an opportunity for teaching exists, because his attention is focused and he has some goal that can be mediated by language. These cues presented by the child make it easy for the adult to notice and to take advantage of such opportunities to build the child's working language through incidental teaching in those natural settings where language should occur. It is hoped that this emphasis on working language will not only help children, but also will contribute to the re-orientation of cultural values necessary to focus the goals of education on language use rather than on language form (Cazden, 1970), and lead to general acceptance of the sociolinguistic position that the form of language used by a given speech community is adequate to meet the needs of its users (Shuy, 1970). This emphasis on working language use is particularly critical in the case of high risk children. These children require the creation of especially rich and responsive environments in order to develop the complex working language that will enable them to prompt more sophisticated and elaborated interactions with their society. They need more and better incidental teachers. Such teachers can result only from the focus of more research efforts on these natural teaching processes and a thorough incorporation of them into the culture, so that concepts such as incidental teaching become a ready and familiar resource in family, school, and community life.

LITERATURE CITED

Brown, R., and C. Fraser. 1963. The acquisition of syntax. *In* C. N. Cofer and B. S. Musgrave (eds.), Verbal Behavior and Learning, pp. 158–201. McGraw-Hill, New York.

Cazden, C. B. 1970. The neglected situation in child language research and education. *In* F. Williams (ed.), Language and Poverty, pp. 81–101. Markham, Chicago.

Doke, L. A., and T. R. Risley. 1972. The organization of day care environments: Required versus optional activities. J. Appl. Beh. Anal. 5: 405–420.

Hart, B. M., and T. R. Risley. 1968. Establishing use of descriptive adjectives in the spontaneous speech of disadvantaged preschool children. J. Appl. Beh. Anal. 1: 109–120.

Hart, B. M., and T. R. Risley. 1974. Using preschool materials to modify the language of disadvantaged children. J. Appl. Beh. Anal. 7: 243–256.

Hart, B., and T. R. Risley. 1975. Incidental teaching of language in the preschool. J. Appl. Beh. Anal. 8: 411–420.

LeLaurin, K., and T. R. Risley. 1972. The organization of day care environments: "Zone" versus "man-to-man" staff assignments. J. Appl. Beh. Anal. 5: 225–232.

McCarthy, D. 1954. Language development in children. *In* L. Carmichael (ed.), Manual of Child Psychology, pp. 492–630. Wiley, New York.

McNeill, D. 1966. Developmental psycholinguistics. *In* F. Smith and G. A. Miller (eds.), The Genesis of Language, pp. 15–84. MIT Press, Cambridge, Mass.

Montes, F. 1974. Incidental teaching of beginning reading in a day care center. Doctoral dissertation, University of Kansas, Lawrence.

Montes, F., and T. R. Risley. 1975. Evaluating traditional day care practices: An empirical approach. Child Care Quart. 4: 208–215.

Quilitch, H. R., and T. R. Risley. 1973. The effects of play materials on social play. J. Appl. Beh. Anal. 6: 573–578.

Reynolds, N. J., and T. R. Risley. 1968. The role of social and material reinforcers in increasing talking of a disadvantaged preschool child. J. Appl. Beh. Anal. 1: 253–262.

Risley, T. R. 1972. Spontaneous language and the preschool environment. *In* J. D. Stanley (ed.), Preschool Programs for the Disadvantaged, pp. 92–110. Johns Hopkins University Press, Baltimore.

Risley, T. R., and M. F. Cataldo. 1974. Evaluation of planned activities: The PLA-check measure of classroom participation. Center for Applied Behavior Analysis, Lawrence, Kansas.

Risley, T. R., and N. J. Reynolds. 1970. Emphasis as a prompt for verbal imitation. J. Appl. Beh. Anal. 3: 185–190.

Shuy, R. W. 1970. The sociolinguistic and urban language problems. *In* F. Williams (ed.), Language and Poverty, pp. 335–350. Markham, Chicago.

Discussant's Comments: Language and Communication Aspects

Lyle L. Lloyd, Ph.D.

From the perspective of the audiologist and speech pathologist there are a number of very positive aspects in these chapters, but there are also a few somewhat distressing aspects. It is appropriate that the discussion chapter assigned to focus on language and communication be presented at this point because most of the previous chapters, which dealt with research, also had something to say about communication. This chapter may also serve as a bridge because the comments are based primarily on the research information in the previous chapters, but some of the comments are also based on the program demonstration chapters to follow.

The first and most encouraging aspect of this conference as a whole is the focus on true *early* intervention with a major focus on the *infant* (i.e., from birth to 24 months of age). Frequently, professionals have discussed preschool programs for 3- to 5-year-olds as "early intervention programs" when that is actually "late intervention." Many states think they have taken a major step forward if they have laws or regulations requiring or supporting education of the handicapped as young as 3 years old. The chapters in this volume reflect a trend indicating that such laws or regulations are only a first step and that the focus is now on younger children. The parents and professionals at this conference have a major task ahead of them to further this trend.

FOUNDATIONS FOR LANGUAGE IN EARLY LIFE

In the past, the first 2 years of life have been referred to as the "prelingual years." For example, some writers use 2 years as the arbitrary division between the "prelingual" and "postlingual" onset of deafness. While it is true that before 2 years the child has very limited verbal expression, he is still very *linguistic*. These are actually the most critical years for language learning, and it may even be that the first year is the most critical.

199

This author's personal experiences with the deaf and evidence from recent research on auditory receptive abilities of young infants indicate that the foundation for aural-oral language comprehension is laid in the first year of life. This view is partially based on the Butterfield and Cairns presentation (this volume) and other similar reports (Schiefelbusch and Lloyd, 1974).

Incidental Learning

Much of the language learning during the first year can best be described as *incidental learning*. Although structured teaching does occur (e.g., when a parent reads to a child or points something out to a child), it is more common for the child to hear what is being said by others and how speech is used in various situations. The child overhears what is said about things and happenings and how speech may change what is happening. This information is stored for future reference and use. The developmentally disabled child does not have the same opportunity for incidental language learning. The hearing impaired infant just does not hear speech, while other developmentally disabled infants tend not to encode speech unless it is directed to them. In addition to these limitations in incidental language learning, these children have an even greater problem because many parents tend to provide less direct language stimulation. With the hearing impaired child there is often the false logic that if he cannot hear, why speak to him, and when any developmentally disabled child shows little or no response (or inappropriate responses) to the caregiver's speech stimulation, its frequency tends to be reduced (Denenberg and Thoman, this volume). Although the present use of the term "incidental learning" is not exactly the same as "incidental teaching," as presented by Hart and Risley (this volume), there are some similarities. Hart and Risley's discussion (this volume) of the incidental teaching paradigm is significant for two reasons: 1) involvement of parents in the intervention program, and 2) use of child-initiated, *functional* teaching situations.

Parent Involvement

It is very encouraging to see involvement of the parents as critical change agents and to note the professional recognition of the need for parent involvement. First, in true early intervention the parents are the ones who interact most with the child and who, therefore, have the greatest opportunity to bring about positive change. This suggests that parents are the primary language teachers, and other forms of early intervention not using parents as a primary resource may at best be inefficient and at worst be totally ineffective.

The parents' teaching role may in part involve direct teaching using approaches such as incidental teaching (Hart and Risley, this volume), which emphasizes functional or child relevant situations and topics. But of equal or even greater importance than this direct teaching role is the parents' role in maximizing the child's language learning environment through the provision of increased opportunities for incidental language learning. This aspect of parent involvement has been well emphasized by Horton (this volume). Horton's program for hearing impaired and other language disabled infants involves the parents not as "teachers" but as effective change agents through assisting them to modify: 1) the home environment to maximize auditory input and language, and 2) the parental communicative style in natural parent-infant interactions and activities.

Functional Aspects of Language

The emphasis on relevance and the functional aspects of language presented in this conference is encouraging. In addition to the previously mentioned work by Horton and by Hart and Risley, the functional aspect of language is a major rationale for home-centered programs such as the Portage Project presented by Shearer and Shearer (this volume). This emphasis on relevance and the functional aspects of language is also expressed in several previous chapters. It should be noted that this conference may be an expression of the case where application is equal to or even ahead of the research. The demonstration programs reflect an emphasis on the functional aspects of language. Had this conference been held 10 to 15 years ago, papers reflecting the most current linguistic point of view would have been emphasizing syntax and "generative grammar." However, in recent years there has been a shift from syntax to semantics, or from the form to the function of language. This shift is quite evident in recent books on language and language intervention (e.g., Brown, 1973; Schiefelbusch and Lloyd, 1974).

SERVICE DELIVERY ISSUES

Several other examples of the encouraging aspects of the conference should be highlighted (e.g., communicative aspects of parent-child interactions, parents, and professionals at the same conference, diversity of professions represented, interaction of researchers and practitioners concern for *all* high risk infants and not just the retarded, or just the deaf, or just the cerebral palsied, etc.), but it also seems appropriate to discuss several distressing aspects.

There is very little if anything in the content of these chapters to criticize; therefore, the distressing aspects may best be described as "sins of omission" or things not stressed or not present in the state-of-the-art as reflected by these chapters. These are the lags in detection and assessment and the general lag in the application of the technology currently available.

Early Detection of Developmental Disabilities

At present, there is no comprehensive system for the early detection of all developmental disabilities. Most states screen for phenylketonuria (PKU) in a systematic way. Although Federal legislation (PL 90-248, Title XIX) requires hearing screening of Medicaid children, many communities still do not have routine audiometric screening of children from 3 to 5 years old as part of their well-baby clinics. Only a very few communities have hearing screening programs for children less than 2 or 3 years of age. Very few hospitals or communities have active follow up programs for high risk infants. Health delivery in this country cannot be described as a system. It is highly fragmented. In some cases those using government supported health services get a more comprehensive and in some cases a less comprehensive delivery system than those paying directly for their private health service.

It is easy to criticize the current "non-system," but one should not criticize without offering some possible solutions. One frequent suggestion is a nationalized health system such as that in several Scandinavian countries. They appear to have a much better early detection system for conditions such as hearing impairment. However, there may be some economic, geographic, political, and social differences that preclude the use of those solutions at this time. Therefore, an early detection system should be considered that could be incorporated into the current "non-system" with some people paying for their health services and others receiving such services from government-supported clinics such as well-baby clinics, children and youth clinics, etc.

Screening Tests at Birth and during Preschool Years

One of the few times most children are accessible for screening programs is at the time of birth. Because most children are born in hospitals, this is an ideal time for blood and urine screening tests. It is also an ideal time to enter infants on a high risk registry for follow up screening and assessment procedures. The knowledge and the laboratory procedures exist to implement such a program now. Unfortunately, the tools are lacking for the efficient and effective mass screening of neonates for sensory defects such as hearing impairment. Mass neonate hearing screening has been tried (Downs, 1967) and determined to be unsuccessful (Downs, 1970; Downs and Hemenway, 1972; Goldstein and Tait, 1971).[1] The AAP-AAOO-ASHA Joint Committee on Infant Hearing Screening has recommended the use of a high risk registry rather than neonate screening (AAP, AAOO and ASHA, 1974). The Joint Committee's latest recommendation is as follows:

> In light of the urgent need to detect hearing impairment as early as possible, a 1970 statement of the Joint Committee urged further investigation of screening methods but discouraged routine hearing screening which is not research oriented. In consonance with that statement, and in view of the information that application of high risk data can increase the detectability of congenital hearing impairment perhaps as much as tenfold, the Committee considers it appropriate to make additions to the 1970 statement.
>
> The Committee recommends that, since no satisfactory technique is yet established that will permit hearing screening of all newborns, infants AT RISK for hearing

---

[1] Because several hospitals started neonate hearing screening programs and some professionals may still believe in such an approach, those responsible for making decisions and implementing screening programs should be familiar with all these references. However, for the best single critique of neonate screening the reader is referred to the paper by Goldstein and Tait, 1971.

impairment should be identified by means of history and physical examination. These children should be tested and followed up as hereafter described:

I. The criterion for identifying a newborn as AT RISK for hearing impairment is the presence of one or more of the following:

A. History of hereditary childhood hearing impairment.

B. Rubella or other nonbacterial intrauterine fetal infection (e.g., cytomegalovirus infections, Herpes infection).

C. Defects of ear, nose, or throat. Malformed, low-set or absent pinnae; cleft lip or palate (including submucous cleft); any residual abnormality of the otorhinolaryngeal system.

D. Birthweight less than 1500 grams.

E. Bilirubin level greater than 20 mg/100 ml serum.

II. Infants falling in this category should be referred for an in-depth audiological evaluation of hearing during their first two months of life and, even if hearing appears to be normal, should receive regular hearing evaluations thereafter at office or well-baby clinics. Regular evaluation is important since familial hearing impairment is not necessarily present at birth but may develop at an uncertain period of time later (p. 16).[2]

The widespread use of such a risk registry would be a major step toward the early detection of hearing impairment. Although the shortage of audiologists in some parts of the country may make it impractical for immediate implementation of the recommendation that "an in-depth audiological evalution" of all at risk infants be made during the first 2 months, this is a reasonable goal for the next 5 years. It may be more appropriate to use systematic *early* screening of all at risk infants. One could screen all infants on the registry at 2 to 4 months with follow up screening even for those who pass and an audiologic assessment of those who fail. This would be relatively easy to accomplish with most infants *if* physicians and those in decision-making positions were convinced that early detection is important. That is, if physicians and others in key positions understood the significance of normal hearing to the normal development of language skills and the importance of language and communication to the habilitation of all developmentally disabled persons. If the significance is understood, it is easy to implement hearing screening at a 4-month follow up because: 1) we have the knowledge and technical capability to implement reliable and valid hearing screening with infants between 4 and 12 months of age; and 2) many infants are seen for a series of diphtheria-tetanus-pertussis (DTP) shots at 2, 4, 6, and 18 months. The other frequent immunization point includes the shot for measles, rubella, and mumps, as well as the tuberculin test, at 12 months. These follow up visits suggest a natural system for early hearing screening of all infants. It should become a routine part of the pediatric follow up at 4, 6, and 18 months. After the last of these shots, very few children see a physician or others that could logically be

---

[2] This supplementary statement of the Joint Committee on Infant Hearing Screening was adopted by the Legislative Council of the American Speech and Hearing Association in November 1972, by the Committee on Hearing and Equilibrium of the American Academy of Opthalmology and Otolaryngology in early 1973, and by the Committee on Fetus and Newborn of the American Academy of Pediatrics during the summer of 1973. The original statement appeared in February 1971, Asha.

expected to screen a child's hearing unless the child is very sick or in other major difficulty or until they are 5 or 6 years old, the compulsory school age. Therefore, by building upon existing and recommended practices for immunization one could implement an early detection program based upon: 1) a high risk registry with follow up hearing screening at 2, 4, 6, and 18 months; 2) routine hearing screening of *all* infants at 6 and 18 months using recorded, calibrated, filtered stimuli and behavior observation procedures (e.g., Lloyd and Cox, 1975); 3) pure tone screening of all older children for any disability when they enter organized programs or normal preschool programs; and 4) pure tone screening (or rescreening) of all children when they enter kindergarten (or first grade). The pure tone screening upon entering school would be the first of a series of pure tone screenings as a part of the school program. Naturally, anyone failing these screenings would receive a more complete audiologic assessment (ASHA Committee on Audiometric Evaluation, 1975; Darley, 1961; Lloyd, 1972; Lloyd and Cox, 1975). Screening for visual defects and other problems should be built in at appropriate points. Within a few years the hearing screening aspects of such a system would be further improved through the widespread application of impedance audiometry with infants (Jerger et al., 1974; Keith, 1973; Lamb, 1975; Wilson et al., 1974).[3]

The reasons such programs have not been initiated are: 1) many have not understood the significance of hearing and the early detection and treatment of hearing impairment, and 2) many of those seeing the need did not think it could be done. The person responsible for any program for children should be embarrassed to give either of these two "reasons." The lack of early detection programs can only be blamed on the "professionals"; the parents cannot be blamed for this failure.

Responsibility of Professionals for Early Detection

Parents have tended to be good early detectors. Many parents have sought medical advice before their child was a year old because the infant "did not seem very responsive" and "was not doing things his brothers and sisters did as babies," only to be told by a physician (lacking training and knowledge in the fundamentals of language acquisition) that "it is natural and he will outgrow it," "don't worry if he doesn't outgrow it, we will have him tested, but he is too young to test now," etc. The physician often does this in an attempt to "comfort" or "reassure" the parents and for the two reasons cited in the previous paragraph. Whatever the reason, the well meaning physicians are usually found to be the bottleneck or delay in the system. Two of the chapters in this volume refer to this problem. In one survey, parents were usually the first to suspect a hearing impairment in infants and found that in only 7 percent of the cases was a physician the first to suspect the problem (Horton, this volume). In another survey parents suspected a

---

[3] Some audiologists have been clinically using impedance audiometry for over 15 years. During the past 5 years, it has been recommended for use with infants and young children. These references are some of the more recent ones relative to the use of impedance audiometry with infants.

developmental problem very early, ranging from 25 percent at birth to 72 percent by 6 months, but there was a considerable lag time between when the parents first suspected a problem and when they were referred to a center for help (66 percent, 37 percent, and 10 percent had lag times of over 6 months, 1 year, and 2 years, respectively) (Haynes, this volume).

Unfortunately, many developmentally disabled children such as the retarded will not be screened for hearing for many years. A classic example of this problem (from the author's personal experience) is that of a girl who had the "good fortune" to be institutionalized at 13 years of age. Although her mother sought medical advice when Jane was about 1 year old, her first audiometric screening was at age 13. After a brief "she'll outgrow it" period, Jane's family doctor referred her to a large medical center where she received a "complete pediatric work-up" and a "mental retardation" diagnosis. No one bothered to attempt an audiometric screening test because it was obvious she could hear because she responded to some sounds.[4] Between the time of that first "complete pediatric work-up" and the time she was placed in an institution for the retarded for a 90-day evaluation period, she had additional pediatric examinations, including referrals for psychological examination. No one bothered to refer her for an audiometric screening because she responded to some sounds and could answer some simple questions asked in a normal conversational voice (in a relatively quiet examining room or office). It was obvious that the questions she missed were missed because of her mental retardation and not because of any possible hearing loss. At the age of 13 she received her first pure tone screening test as part of her 90-day evaluation. She failed the screening, and the subsequent audiologic assessment and otologic examination revealed a bilateral sensori-neural hearing impairment that, by the nature of the impairment and the lack of significant etiologic factors in the history, was assumed to be present since birth. She had near normal auditory sensitivity in the low frequencies but a moderately severe loss in the middle and high frequencies. The near normal sensitivity in the low frequencies accounts for the faulty assumptions about her having normal hearing. This hearing loss was not the cause of her retarded development but it was a major compounding factor. Education and habilitation attempts were inefficient when they did not take into account her significant hearing impairment.

Was this girl a form of "professional neglect"? Or was it "professional dyslexia" or "professional inertia" that caused several professionals not to bother giving the girl a simple audiometric screening? It only takes a few minutes to check those who pass a hearing screening and even most of those who fail. Anyone who takes longer than a few minutes needs the screening anyway. No time is wasted in audiometric screening, but years and lives are wasted by not screening.

This discussion of the lag in professional action after parents express concern and of the lack of early detection programs in general places heavy responsibility on the pediatrician and the general practitioner. Unfortunately, too often they practice without

---

[4] It should be noted that most persons with medically and/or communicatively significant hearing impairments will respond to some sounds in at least some situations.

adequate training and preparation in this important area. Most medical schools devote only 1 to 3 hours to everything you wanted to know about hearing and similarly little attention to language and communication, child development, and developmental disabilities such as mental retardation (e.g., de la Cruz, this volume). Many audiologists, educators of the hearing impaired, and speech pathologists who have not taken time to explain early detection and treatment programs to physicians in their communities must also share the blame.

Although there is a need for more research relative to early detection and treatment, a major problem is the application lag. Perhaps many physicians tend not to take early decisive action because many university and community hearing and speech clinics (including some university affiliated facilities) have not been using the clinical procedures that would allow them to make definitive statements about the hearing of infants. Every clinic should be using impedance audiometry (e.g., Jerger et al., 1974; Keith, 1973; Lamb, 1975; Wilson et al., 1974), and the full range of behavioral audiometry including visual and tangible reinforcement (e.g., Fulton, 1974, Fulton and Lloyd, 1969; 1975; Lloyd, 1966; Lloyd and Cox, 1975; Lloyd et al., 1968; Lloyd and Wilson, 1974; Wilson et al., 1974) in testing infants and other difficult-to-test persons.

As an example of professional dyslexia and/or inertia, consider the lag in the widespread adoption of Tangible Reinforcement Operant Conditioning Audiometry (TROCA). By modifying the procedures of others using tangible reinforcement (e.g., Knox, 1960; LaCrosse and Bidlake, 1964; Meyerson and Michael, 1960; 1964), the TROCA procedure was developed in the mid 1960s to test profoundly retarded and other difficult-to-test persons. In 1965 and 1966, the early work with TROCA was reported at three national conventions (Alexander Graham Bell Association for the Deaf, American Association on Mental Deficiency, and American Speech and Hearing Association) plus other state and regional meetings and was subsequently reported in professional journals and books (Fulton and Lloyd, 1969; Lloyd, 1966; Lloyd et al., 1968; Fulton, Spradlin, and Lloyd, 1969). In addition to these rather typical forms of reporting professional developments, a film was made and shown at the American Speech and Hearing Association (1970) and other meetings (Fulton, Spradlin, and Lloyd, 1969). Although TROCA was not originally designed for testing infants, Lloyd et al. (1968) reported its possible application by demonstrating its use with three infants (7, 15, and 18 months old). Unfortunately, 9 years after the first report and 5 years after several professional publications, many clinics still do not include this procedure in their armamentarium. Is it "professional dyslexia," "professional inertia," or is it that $1200 is too much money for the equipment?

In addition to illustrating a specific example of lag in application there may be another lesson in this example. What about the dissemination of information? One would think appropriate means were employed. But were they? All presentations were to limited audiences. Should medical publications have been used? What about lay publications? This may illustrate the need for professionals to start using more than the traditional media to report their findings. An attempt is being made to correct this error by: 1) telling the story to this mixed audience; 2) preparing a publication for physicians

(Lloyd and Cox, 1975) and other professionals; 3) reporting the use with infants to national (Wilson et al., 1974), and international (Lloyd and Wilson, 1974) meetings; and 4) considering other possibilities such as exhibits at a variety of professional meetings.

Early Auditory Stimulation Programs

Along with the discussion of greater application of audiometric procedures to infants, mention should be made of the Butterfield and Cairns report (this volume). This chapter highlights research that has emerged in only 5 years pointing out how infants under 1 year of age are very active language learners. Although these procedures are not ready for immediate clinical application, it is hoped that the laboratory findings are used without the 5- to 10-year or more lag frequently experienced. These early infant reception studies demonstrate that the normal infant is ready for considerable auditory processing. Although there is a need for similar research with at risk infants (e.g., that suggested by Ross and Leavitt, this volume), the present work provides a strong justification for early auditory stimulation programs.

Audiometric Procedures

Early auditory stimulation leads to the topic of the early auditory environment of the high risk infant. However, before discussing that topic, further comments on audiometric procedures and the Butterfield and Cairns chapter seem appropriate. Although the non-nutritive sucking procedures used in infant auditory reception research are not being suggested as routine clinical assessment tools, with further research and development these procedures offer considerable promise as clinical procedures to assess infant's speech discrimination abilities. While there are currently clinical tests to accurately assess the auditory sensitivity of infants as young as 7 months and to estimate auditory sensitivity as young as 5 months (Lloyd, 1975; Lloyd and Cox, 1975; Lloyd et al., 1968; Lloyd and Wilson, 1974; Wilson et al., 1974), reliable procedures are lacking to assess the speech discrimination abilities of children younger than about 2 years. In these comments, there is agreement with the first part of Butterfield and Cairns' statement that "audiological assessment of infants should rely more on speech stimuli and less on pure tones and noise." There is a definite need to develop clinical tools that are more direct measures of the infant's ability to process speech stimuli. However, such a statement should not cause the immediate abandonment of the clinical procedures of impedance and pure tone behavioral audiometry. Although pure tones and bands of noise do not provide direct measures of speech processing ability, they can provide an indirect measure of such ability (including information about the prerequisite abilities) and a direct measure of other auditory abilities.

Lloyd (1972) previously suggested that an audiometric assessment should consider the specific auditory behaviors and aspects of the type of pathology that have major implications for communication programming as follows: 1) auditory sensitivity across the frequency range, 2) stability of the auditory sensitivity, 3) dynamic range and tolerance, 4) recruitment or distortions of loudness, 5) basic auditory discrimination, 6) speech discrimination, 7) habituation and fatigue, and 8) interaural differential of the above measures. He further noted that a wide variety of acoustic stimuli may be used in the audiologic assessment, as is shown in Table 1. These stimuli range over a continuum of degree of specificity of control (listed from easiest to most difficult to specify or control acoustically). The stimuli may also be considered along a continuum of human communicative value representing the frequency of human use in aural-oral communication and a general approximation of the ordering of the stimuli in terms of communicative importance. It will be noted that the two continua run counter to each other or have a negative relationship. Therefore, for some types of auditory abilities, an easily specified stimuli might be quite appropriate, but for other higher level auditory abilities including speech processing, the more difficult to specify stimuli have the highest face validity. Therefore, the audiologist sometimes makes a compromise between reliability and validity. In each case, his choice of stimuli is the one with the highest degree of reliability and validity. It should be noted that at least six of the first seven auditory

Table 1. Continuum of acoustic stimuli relative to specificity and control[a]

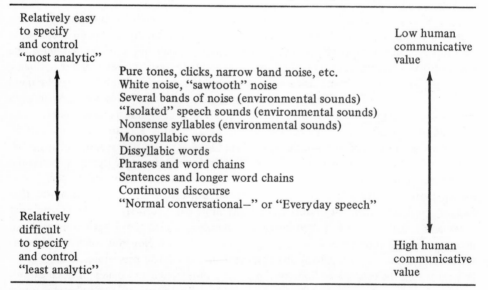

Relatively easy to specify and control "most analytic"

Relatively difficult to specify and control "least analytic"

Low human communicative value

High human communicative value

Pure tones, clicks, narrow band noise, etc.
White noise, "sawtooth" noise
Several bands of noise (environmental sounds)
"Isolated" speech sounds (environmental sounds)
Nonsense syllables (environmental sounds)
Monosyllabic words
Dissyllabic words
Phrases and word chains
Sentences and longer word chains
Continuous discourse
"Normal conversational–" or "Everyday speech"

[a]Because various environmental sounds may fall at a number of points along the continuum, they are shown in parentheses at their three simplest levels. Sounds from noisemakers, toys, musical instruments, and animals have been omitted to simplify the table, but they may be considered along with environmental sounds. It should also be noted that for speech type stimuli, synthetic speech such as that produced by the Bell or Haskins Laboratories for experimental purposes would rank higher in specificity or control than human speech. The stimuli may also be considered along a continuum of human communicative level.

abilities listed above as critical for habilitative planning may be quite reliably and validly assessed with pure tone or noise stimuli. The only one that would definitely require a speech type stimuli for higher face validity is that of "speech discrimination." The interaural differentiation of the seven measures is naturally based upon the measure used to assess the ability. It should also be noted that with pure tone and/or noise band stimuli and currently available behavioral audiometry and impedance audiometry procedures, it is possible to assess the auditory sensitivity across the frequency range, the stability of this auditory sensitivity, and the possible recruitment (or distortions of loudness) and interaural differential of these measures on infants as young as 1 year old. Pure tone and noise band stimuli also provide some useful information about the dynamic range toler- ance and habituation and fatigue aspects of similarly young infants.

Therefore, although there is a need to develop better early assessment procedures involving speech stimuli with the current clinical tools available, the use of pure tone and noise stimuli cannot be abandoned if a relatively comprehensive audiologic assessment is to be obtained.

Early Auditory Environment of the High Risk Infant

In considering language and communication aspects, it seems appropriate to comment on the early auditory environment of the high risk infant. Butterfield and Cairns (this volume) discuss the young infant's auditory abilities, and Horton (this volume) stresses the importance of early auditory input for hearing impaired infants, but little attention has been paid to optimizing the auditory environment of all infants at risk. This lack of specific suggestions may be a result of the paucity of sufficient data for specific programming. The early infant reception research should provide data in this area for future communication programming. Although more data may be needed to provide optimal auditory environments, much more could be done to minimize excessive noise in the early life of the high risk infant. It may be that placing the infant in incubators to save his life may pose major problems in terms of developing auditory abilities and language learning.

De la Cruz (this volume) has called attention to this problem and cited some appropriate references, but there is a need for further research on the effects of incubator noise on the at risk infant. Incubators may affect the developing infant in at least four ways. First, they may result in noise-induced hearing loss. Incubators manufactured today operate at noise levels of 54 to 62 dBA (Falk and Farmer, 1973), which is below the levels considered as allowable for the protection of public health and welfare (e.g. 93 dBA for 4 hours, 90 dBA for 8 hours, and 70 dBA for 24 hours—U.S. Environmental Protection Agency, 1973; 1974). However, some older incubators still in operation exceed these levels. The variation of level with exposure duration is related to recovery time, but infants may be under continuous exposure for days and even weeks with no recovery time. Furthermore, there are no standards set for infants, and such an infant standard may logically be lower than that set for mature ears. There is also the possibility that premature ears may even be more susceptible to noise-induced hearing loss. There may also be interaction effects with other treatment procedures such as drugs.

Second, there may be other physiological effects of incubator noise exposure. Stimulation below 70 dB SPL (linear) has been shown to result in increased ACTH, heart rate, and peripheral vasoconstriction; while 70 to 75 dB SPL (linear) has affected sleep patterns (Broadbent and Burns, 1965; Geber, Anderson, and Van Dyne, 1966; Gädeke et al., 1969; Lehmann and Tamm, 1956; Ward and Fricke, 1969).

Third, even if incubator noise does not produce adverse physiologic change in a given infant, it may be hypothesized that life in an incubator teaches the neonate not to listen. Because the neonate seems to be an active listener and learner, he could soon learn that he has arrived in a world of noise and that the things he hears have no meaning to him and will not help him to organize his world. Therefore, the infant may learn to ignore auditory input.

Fourth, in addition to the possible adverse physiological changes and the learning to ignore auditory input, it seems reasonable that the infant in an incubator may be further handicapped because he tends not to be the target of the same quality and quantity of verbal and other stimulation provided to normal infants. This means the one needing the best verbal stimulation may receive little, if any, stimulation.

The infant in an incubator today is much better off than the infant of 10 years ago, but the above four potential adverse effects of incubator noise clearly indicate a need for both additional research and the immediate clinical application of the best technology and information currently available. Most of the needed research and clinical application are summarized in the report of the American Academy of Pediatrics Committee on Environmental Hazards (Falk, 1974) statement on "Noise Pollution: Neonatal Aspects" as follows:

1. Criteria have not yet been established to protect infants from the effects of noise. In the meanwhile, on the basis of animal experimentation which shows that noise markedly potentiates the ototoxicity of kanamycin, it would be prudent (1) for *manufacturers* of incubators to reduce the noise from motors as much as possible, preferably below 58 dB(A), a level which potentiates the ototoxicity of kanamycin in experimental animals; (2) for *physicians* to limit the use of aminoglycosidic antibiotics and other potential ototoxic drugs in neonates insofar as is consistent with good medical practice; and (3) for *hospital personnel* to eliminate unnecessary noise, including radios played at high volume in the premature nursery.
2. To establish criteria for protecting infants from the effects of noise, additional information is needed on (1) the relation between disorders of hearing, speech or language and a past history of exposure to incubator noise and/or ototoxic drugs (i.e., retrospective studies); and (2) the relation of such exposures to subsequent hearing or speech impairment (i.e., prospective studies).
3. Physicians should be alert for unnecessary noise in nurseries (or use continuous sound level recorders when feasible), and take appropriate action for abatement.

In addition to the AAP Committee statements, research and clinical attention must also be focused on the aspects of learning not to listen and the lack of appropriate stimulation that are the result of placing an infant in an incubator.

SUMMARY

The chapters in this volume provide considerable stimulation for both clinicians and researchers relative to the language and communication aspects of early intervention strategies. The present comments from the perspective of an audiologist-speech patholo-gist have considered the topics of parent involvement, parent-child interactions, the functional aspects of language, incidental learning, incidental teaching, infant auditory receptive abilities, the auditory environment, early hearing screening, and the audiologic assessment of infants.

LITERATURE CITED

AAP, AAOO, and ASHA. 1974. Supplementary statement of joint committee on infant hearing screening. Asha 16: 160.

ASHA Committee on Audiometric Evaluation, Guidelines for Identification Audiometry. 1975. Asha 17: 94–99.

Broadbent, D. E., and W. Burns. 1965. Effects of Noise on Hearing and Performance (Rep. 65–1057). Minist. Def. Med. Res. Council, London.

Brown, R. 1973. A First Language: The Early Stages. MIT Press, Cambridge, Mass.

Butterfield, E. C., and G. F. Cairns. 1974. Summary—Infant reception research. In R. L. Schiefelbusch and L. L. Lloyd (eds.), Language Perspectives—Acquisition, Retardation, and Intervention, pp. 75–84. University Park Press, Baltimore.

Darley, F. L. 1961. Identification audiometry. J. Speech and Hear. Dis. 9: 1–68.

Downs, M. P. 1967. Organization and procedures of a newborn infant screening program. Hearing and Speech News 35: 27–36.

Downs, M. P. 1970. The identification of congential deafness. Trans. Amer. Acad. Ophthal. Otolaryng. 74: 1208–1214.

Downs, M. P., and W. G. Hemenway. 1972. Newborn screening revisited. Hearing and Speech News 40(4): 4–5, 26, 28–29.

Falk, S. A. 1974. Noise pollution: Neonatal aspects. A report of the American Academy of Pediatrics Committee on Environmental Hazards. Pediatrics 54: 476–478.

Falk, S. A., and J. C. Farmer. 1973. Incubator noise and possible deafness. Arch. Otolaryng. 97: 385–387.

Fulton, R. T., and L. L. Lloyd. 1969. Audiometry for the Retarded: With Implications for the Difficult-to-test. Williams and Wilkins, Baltimore.

Fulton, R. T., and L. L. Lloyd. 1975. Auditory Assessment of the Difficult-to-test. Williams and Wilkins, Baltimore.

Fulton, R. T., J. E. Spradlin, and L. L. Lloyd. 1969. Operant Audiometry with Severely Retarded Children (16mm sound, color, 16 min). Produced by the Bureau of Child Research, University of Kansas and Parsons State Hospital and Training Center, Lawrence.

Gädeke, R., B. Döring, F. Keller, and A. Vogel. 1969. The noise level in children's hospital and the wake-up threshold in infants. Acta Paediatr. Scand. 58: 164–170.

Geber, W. F., T. A. Anderson, and V. Van Dyne. 1966. Physiologic responses of the albino rat to chronic noise stress. Arch. Environ. Health 12: 751.

Goldstein, R., and C. Tait. 1971. Critique of neonatal hearing evaluation. J. Speech and Hear. Dis. 36: 3–18.

Jerger, S., J. Jerger, L. Mauldin, and P. Segal. 1974. Studies in impedance audiometry. II. Children less than six years old. Arch. Otolaryng. 99: 1–9.

Keith, R. W. 1973. Impedance audiometry with neonates. Arch. Otolaryng. 97: 465–467

Knox, E. C. 1960. A method of obtaining pure-tone audiograms in young children. J. Laryng. Otolaryng. 74: 475–479.

LaCrosse, E. L., and H. Bidlake. 1964. A method to test the hearing of mentally retarded children. Volta Rev. 66: 27–30.

Lamb, L. E. 1975. Acoustic impedance measurement. *In* R. T. Fulton and L. L. Lloyd (eds.), Auditory Assessment of the Difficult-to-Test. Williams and Wilkins, Baltimore.

Lehmann, G., and J. Tamm. 1956. Uber Verañderungen der Kreislaufdynamik des ruhenden Menschen unter Einwirkung von Geräuschen. Intern Z. Angew Physiol. 16: 217.

Lloyd, L. L. 1966. Behavioral audiometry viewed as an operant procedure. J. Speech and Hear. Dis. 31: 128–136.

Lloyd, L. L. 1972. The audiologic assessment of deaf students. Report of the Proceedings of the 45th Meeting of the Convention of American Instructors of the Deaf, pp. 585–594. Arkansas School for the Deaf, June 1972, Little Rock. U.S. Government Printing Office, Washington, D.C.

Lloyd, L. L. 1975. Pure-tone audiometry. *In* R. T. Fulton and L. L. Lloyd (eds.), Auditory Assessment of the Difficult-to-Test. Williams and Wilkins, Baltimore.

Lloyd, L. L., and B. P. Cox. 1975. Behavioral audiometry with children. *In* M. J. Glasscock (guest ed.), The Otolaryngology Clinics of North America. Symposium on Sensorineural Hearing Loss in Children: Early Detection and Intervention. W. B. Saunders, Philadelphia.

Lloyd, L. L., J. E. Spradlin, and M. J. Reid. 1968. An operant audiometric procedure for difficult-to-test patients. J. Speech and Hear. Dis. 33: 236–245.

Lloyd, L. L., and W. R. Wilson. 1974. Recent developments in the behavioral assessment of the infant's response to auditory stimulation. Presented at the XVI World Congress for Logopedics and Phoniatrics, August 26, Interlaken, Switzerland.

Meyerson, L., and J. L. Michael. 1960. The Measurement of Sensory Thresholds in Exceptional Children: An Experimental Approach to Some Problems of Differential Diagnosis and Education with Special Reference to Hearing. U.S. Office of Education, Cooperative Research Project No. 418. University of Houston, Texas.

Meyerson, L., and J. L. Michael. 1964. Assessment of hearing by operant conditioning procedures. Report of the Proceedings of the International Congress on Education of the Deaf and the 41st Meeting of the Convention of American Instructors of the Deaf, pp. 236–242. Gallaudet College, June 1963. U.S. Government Printing Office, Washington, D.C.

Schiefelbusch, R. L., and L. L. Lloyd. 1974. Language Perspectives–Acquisition, Retardation, and Intervention. University Park Press, Baltimore.

U.S. Environmental Protection Agency. 1973. Public Health and Welfare Criteria for Noise. USEPA Office of Noise Abatement and Control, Washington, D.C.

U.S. Environmental Protection Agency. 1974. Information on Levels of Environmental Noise Requisite to Protect Public Health and Welfare with an Adequate Margin of Safety. USEPA Office of Noise Abatement and Control, Washington, D.C.

Ward, W. D., and J. E. Fricke (eds.). 1969. Proceedings of the Conference: Noise as a Public Health Hazard (ASHA Report No. 4). American Speech and Hearing Association, Washington, D.C.

Wilson, W. R., L. L. Lloyd, T. N. Decker, and J. M. Moore. 1974. The use of behavioral and impedance audiometry in the assessment of hearing of infants. Presented at the National Convention of the Alexander Graham Bell Association for the Deaf, June 21, Atlanta, Ga.

A Programmatic Test of Behavioral Technology: Can It Recover Deviant Children for Normal Public Schooling?

*Donald M. Baer, Ph.D., Trudilee Rowbury, M.A., Ann M. Baer, M.A.,
Emily Herbert, Ph.D., Hewitt B. Clark, Ph.D., and Annabelle Nelson, Ph.D.*

Theories of learning have been around for many years. The necessity to teach has been around considerably longer. Yet it seems that only in recent years has the existence of either had much effect on the conduct of the other. This may have been a paradox. Fortunately, any independence of teaching and learning theories is now departing the scene, and its potential for embarrassment is much reduced. (This embarrassment, after all, may have been acute only for those who taught learning theory with teaching techniques underivable from the theories taught.) Now there may be celebrated a budding behavioral technology whose greatest articulation is seen exactly in the area of teaching: That technology, often called *behavior modification,* certainly is the child of learning theory; but it is a rebellious child, denying the basic values of its parents and occasionally provoking wistful questions about its legitimacy.

LEARNING THEORY

Learning theory, almost without exception throughout its generations, has valued the complete discovery of those variables involved in any aspect of learning processes. Therefore, it valued experimental designs that were sensitive even to weak variables, and these designs were used largely to inform other theorists that there were variables that *their* cosmology had not yet dreamed of. But as nature abhors a vacuum, so learning theories abhor an incomplete theory. Thus, the discovery of every new variable required a new theory that could encompass it together with the old variables. Any number can play that game, and the history of the Nebraska Symposium shows that a considerable number

213

did. It may have seemed in recent years that the main result would be a diversity of theories with which to burden graduate students in psychology and education. Fortunately, something happened as well: a reaction in goals and a derivative reaction in method, attributable primarily to Skinner (1938; 1953), and labeled by its practitioners not as learning theory, but as the *experimental analysis of behavior*.

EXPERIMENTAL ANALYSIS OF BEHAVIOR

The experimental analysis of behavior asked a subtly different question from the one asked by learning theory: not what variables could affect any aspect of learning, but what variables controlled the specific behavior of current interest. If the learning theorist suspected that variable X could sometimes be a factor in learning, he certainly sought whatever combination of setting, subject, and behavior would best allow variable X to display its effects. If X could not be seen to operate in maze-running behavior but did emerge in paired-associate learning, then X-enthusiasts shifted their research to paired-associate formats and to the subjects who could use them, and the shift was applauded as appropriate and ingenious. By contrast, an experimental analysis of maze-running behavior could by no stretch of the imagination be accomplished anywhere but within mazes. If variable X failed to operate there, then variable X was not part of the experimental analysis of maze-running; and rather than being valued because it operated at least somewhere, it was devalued because it did not operate where the researcher's curiosity was currently located. To the extent that experimental analysis restricted its curiosity to a small set of behaviors, it would obviously remain just as precious an enterprise as the learning theories against which it reacted. But just as those theories valued the complete discovery of variables, experimental analysis valued the complete analysis of behaviors—all behaviors, and in every organism practical for study. The question it was asking was about generality; would the experimental analysis of all behaviors be the same, and in all organisms? Or, would behavior prove so diverse that many responses would require different analyses, as would different species? Thus, the primary goal of experimental analysis was superordinate to the analyses themselves: it was the *generality* of these analyses (Sidman, 1960).

Furthermore, the analysis of a behavior had to be done in a single subject at a time and be clear within that subject, or its generality could not be evaluated later. To show that a certain technique controlled the average behavior of a group was unsatisfactory in that it allowed the possibility that only some members of the group were responding to the technique in the way that the average indicated. But generality depended on knowing *how many* subjects responded in the same way and *how many* responded differently or not at all. If all subjects responded alike, then generality was great (and the difference between single-subject design and group design became trivial). But if some appreciable number of subjects responded differently from others, then their experimental analysis was different, and the experimental analysis of a group's mean could not be the experimental analysis of both types of its subjects. Indeed, it might not be the experimental analysis of any subject. Thus, the repetitive analysis of behavior within each single subject and across many single subjects was mandatory. (The fact that a highly general variable would operate similarly in both group and single-subject designs was of slight significance, since that face could be known only after many single-subject analyses had been conducted, at which point their uniformity across subjects would make the group design redundant.) Consequently, group designs disappeared from the methodology of experimental analysis. This had many consequences. It estranged large groups of psychologists, whole divisions of the American Psychological Association, and their subscription to psychological journals (Krantz, 1971). It also robbed experimental analysis of one of the most powerful techniques for the detection of weak or occasional variables: inferential statistics. As a result, experimental analysis restricted itself primarily to powerful, durable variables, the kind that always work clearly. It may be argued that such restriction is automatically a restriction to the truly basic variables that an ultimately sound theory of behavior will emphasize (Risley and Baer, 1973), and is thus a very good thing for a young science. While that point may indeed by argued, a related consequence seems self-evident beyond debate: an analysis that restricts itself to those variables that operate powerfully and repeatedly in changing the behavior of any single subject is thereby a *technology* of behavior change. If there is a technology of behavior change, then it may as well be put to work; for clearly enough, many problems consist mainly of human behaviors. One result can be the bettering of the current world. (However, the value judgment that one behavior is better than another is itself a behavior, and itself subject to modification by the same technology whose consequences are being judged. Thus, behavior modification may ultimately become its own judge, which probably will improve research funding in the area.) Another less problematic result can be the evaluation of the experimental analysis underlying the technology. If technological applications work, as predicted, in the typically uncontrolled and noisy environments where behavioral trouble is found, then the generality of the underlying analyses has indeed been severely tested and still found good.

To a considerable extent, that testing has already begun. In the past 10 years, there have been increasingly numerous applications of the experimental analysis of behavior to social problems. For the most part, so far, these applications have been small in scope, and their targets have more often been the personal troubles of isolated persons than the pervasive problems of large social groups (Ullman and Krasner, 1965; Ulrich, Strachnik, and Mabry, 1966, 1970; Bijou and Baer, 1967). Increasingly, however, application is now being directed toward the systematic solution of group-wide behavioral problems, such as are involved in ghetto education (Wolf, Giles, and Hall, 1968; Hall, Lund, and Jackson, 1968; Risley, Reynolds, and Hart, 1971) or juvenile delinquency (Cohen, Filipczak, and Bis, 1970). This report is aimed at a similar program of application: the recovery of deviant children for normal public schooling.

BEHAVIORAL TECHNOLOGY AND DEVIANT CHILDREN

Even in their preschool years, some children have already been identified as unsuitable for later normal public schooling, perhaps by earning diagnostic labels such as retarded, autistic, or schizophrenic, or through their expulsion from ordinary preschool or kindergarten programs because of unmanageable or dangerous behavior problems, or an apparent inability to learn. Such children have a high probability of being expelled from a primary grade classroom, with consequent assignment either to special education tracks, institutionalization, or home residence without further education (itself a form of institutionalization). If behavioral technology can intervene effectively, it must identify such children, identify the behavior problems that lead to their unsuitability for ordinary classrooms, and then remediate those behavior problems thoroughly enough to allow successful public schooling at the appropriate later age. One mechanism for accomplishing these objectives might be two-fold: 1) a special preschool classroom, populated only by such problem children, within which intensive behavioral techniques of reinforcement and programming are applied; and 2) a parent-training program that complements and extends the classroom program. The major objective of such a research program must be to accomplish *all* the behavioral remediation necessary to success in the primary grades. A subsidiary objective may be at least to demonstrate the extent to which such a program can accomplish *any* of the kinds of behavioral change presumably necessary. Repeated successes in many of these subsidiary objectives implies the possibility of an eventual program containing all the techniques and problems shown to be effective, and thus comprehensive enough to accomplish the major objective.

Behavior Goals: Attending and Instructional Control

Eventually, any such program will require the comprehensive, accurate identification of those behaviors essential or helpful to successful primary grade performance. These will no doubt include many specific cognitive, linguistic, motor, and social skills, a large number of which can be cited at present, but some of which still remain to be identified, even by primary grade educators. However, the first four subjects studied within this program made the identification of some behavioral objectives relatively easy. Although these children displayed a considerable variety of bizarre and disruptive behaviors, they also showed two uniform problems: a large deficit in instructional control and a thorough lack of attending skills. That is, they rarely did what they were asked, no matter how reasonable the request; and they rarely stayed with any activity long enough to approximate its completion, showing instead what is often called hyperactivity or low attention span. Consequently, attending became the first target for remediation, and instructional control the second. However, before either behavioral goal could be approached, some basic tools of behavior modification were required. First among these was a reinforcement system that could be both powerful and practical ("practical" should mean available readily in any preschool classroom). Consequently, a token-mediated system of contingent access to preferred classroom activities was implemented.

Classroom Activities and a Token-mediated Reinforcement System

After a 2-week adaptation period, the preschool room was divided into two areas: a work area and a play, or reinforcer, area. Each day a variety of the children's preferred activities were arranged in the play area. These activities included art materials, house play, water play, taking refreshments, and many others. Some favored activities of each child were included every day.

Tasks to be completed were located in the work area. These tasks consisted of 14 common preschool materials, primarily academic in nature; specifically, they were manipulative, form fitting, building, or visual matching tasks. Seven tasks were available in the work area on Mondays and Wednesdays; the other seven were available on Tuesdays and Thursdays (school met only 4 days each week).

The classroom was staffed by two teachers, one assigned to the work area, the other to the play area. When a child entered the room, he was invited to one of the day's seven tasks in the work area. If he completed any of the seven tasks to a defined criterion, he was given a token that he could trade for 5 minutes in the play area, where he could play freely. When he traded in his token, the play area teacher set a 5-minute timer with the child's name on it. As his timer rang, the child was returned to the work area, and then invited to another task to repeat the cycle. The teachers attended to work behavior with praise, conversation, contact, and help where necessary. The play area teacher talked with the children, played with them if desired, and provided materials.

These conditions were in effect for 90 minutes of each 2.5-hour preschool day: during the first hour and the last half hour. During these times, the behavior of each child was recorded continuously by an observer. Each observer recorded objectively defined task behaviors, continuously time-sampling in intervals of 10 seconds. A criterion for completion was defined for each of the 14 work tasks, and completions were recorded. The reliability of recording completions was sampled at each level of performance throughout the study. The median reliability of each observer ranged from 91 percent to 100 percent agreement.

Figure 1 shows the number of task completions per day for each of the four subjects over a 5-month period. In the first experimental condition each token was delivered contingent on one completion of a work task. For example, a child who placed all pieces of *one* puzzle in their proper places received teacher attention for the work leading to the completion and a token immediately following placement of all the pieces. During this condition, the children's averages ranged between eight and eleven completions per day.

When stability had been reached for all four subjects in the first condition, a reversal condition was initiated (shown as closed black circles). During the reversal condition, differential reinforcement of behavior other than task completion occurred. Throughout this phase, each subject received about the average number of tokens per day that he had earned during the first experimental condition; however, the tokens were delivered contingent on beginning a task, but before completion had occurred. During the reversal, despite the fact that they had dispensed a token merely for approaching a task, the teachers continued to attend to any appropriate work behavior that occurred and to encourage task completions.

Response during the reversal was the same for all subjects: task completions per day decreased. Averages during this condition ranged from five to six completions per day. It is noteworthy that the level was not zero.

For the third experimental condition, the original token contingency was reinstated; a

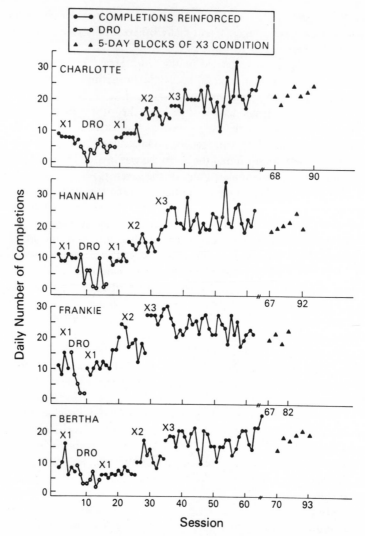

Figure 1. Daily rates of completing academic activities for four children across the experimental conditions of reinforcement.

token was delivered *after* each completion. As always, teacher attention was contingent on work behavior. During this condition the number of completions by each subject returned to the original reinforced level and stabilized. One partial exception should be noted: in Frankie's case there was an increase in the number of completions during the last 3 days of this condition. Thus, contingent access to preferred activities, through token mediation, apparently was effective in controlling the rate of task completions per day for each subject.

With the effectiveness of the procedure verified, a new and typical academic goal was sought: during the condition marked "times 2" the work criterion for reinforcement was doubled. For example, a child working on the several available puzzles had to complete one and then another before a token was delivered. A child working on the one form box available had to complete it, disassemble it, and then re-complete it before a token was given. Thus, the contingency required that each subject perform twice as much work at each task to be reinforced. The double performance was recorded as two completions by the observer.

During the condition marked "times 3," the work criterion for reinforcement was tripled. Otherwise, the rules for token delivery were unchanged.

As Figure 1 shows, all subjects responded alike to the doubling and tripling conditions. In each condition, their average number of completions per day increased in correspondence with the increased criterion. When the rate during the first and last conditions are compared, the number of tasks completed per day is seen to have increased by a multiple of two to three for each subject.

These results show that contingent access to preferred activities, mediated by a token system, can be an effective procedure for establishing and maintaining extended task completions in children who otherwise demonstrate deficits in attending behaviors. If this procedure can be used readily to shape the additional skills necessary to school entrance, if it is known what they are, then an otherwise ineducable population of children can be recaptured for public schooling.

Instructional Control

Still, education does not live by completions alone. Instructional control by a teacher over the activities of her students is also a necessity for a smoothly run classroom. While these children's output was satisfactory in rate, their teachers had little control over the selection of the particular task the child did to earn his token. The teachers systematically invited each child to all the available tasks, one at a time, but the child was free to make his own choice. That is, if the teacher said, "Frankie, how about building with the blocks now?" Frankie might build with the blocks, but he could choose to complete any of the other tasks instead and still earn a token. Indeed, the teachers noted that three children rarely chose the tasks suggested, and even turned away from a task they were approaching if the teacher mentioned it. This degree of negativism was not tolerable if the children were to succeed in a normal preschool or kindergarten class.

Compliance Program Accordingly, formal records were kept for each child of all the teachers' invitations to tasks and of whether or not the child complied. Baseline rates of compliance, defined as the percentage of daily invitations complied with, were collected for all children. These rates were quite low for three of the children, ranging between 14 percent and 38 percent. These three children thus became the subject of a compliance program.

The procedure used was a change in the requirements for earning a token: it was no longer sufficient to complete *any* task; instead, the child was reinforced only for completing the one suggested by the teacher. If he completed the suggested activity he was scored as compliant; if he chose another, he was scored as noncompliant. He received no token if he were noncompliant, and the *same* invitation was then repeated. Indeed, the teacher continued to invite the child to the same task after every noncompliance, until the child complied. When he returned from any token-mediated free play time he was invited to a different task. Except for the compliance requirement, the operation of the token system was unchanged.

The experimental design was a multiple baseline (cf. Baer, Wolf, and Risley, 1968) across the three low-compliance children. That is, baseline records of compliance were collected on all three children. Then the experimental manipulation, i.e., the compliance requirement, was applied to one child at a time. Thus, when compliance was required for the first child, no changes in procedure were made for the second and third. When the first child's rate of compliance had stabilized at a level higher than the baseline, the compliance requirement was added for the second child and later, similarly, for the third.

All relevant behaviors were recorded by observers, one for each child. A continuous time-sampling procedure was used to record the teachers' invitations to specific tasks, whether or not the child complied with the invitation, and all completions of all tasks, whether the child had been invited to them or not. These records were made every 10 seconds, and reliability was computed as a percentage of observer agreement. That is, the two observers' records were matched for the sequence and content of teacher invitations and the child's compliance or noncompliance with each of those invitations (but not for the precise 10-second interval in which each was recorded). Between six and eight half-hour intervals from days scattered throughout the study were double-observed for reliability for each child. There was 100 percent agreement throughout these sessions.

Results The results of the compliance program are shown in Figure 2. The initial compliance rates were quite low. For the first child, Hannah, the mean of baseline compliance was 14 percent. After the introduction of the compliance requirement her compliance rate shifted to a mean of 73 percent. Meanwhile, the second child, Charlotte, had continued in baseline conditions, and her compliance rate had remained low, averaging 23 percent. When the requirement for compliance was added for Charlotte, her compliance rate rose to an average of 52 percent. The third child, Frankie, meanwhile had continued in baseline, showing a fairly steady average of 38 percent compliance. When the compliance requirement was applied to him, his compliance rate rose dramatically to an almost perfect 100 percent.

At this point, the function of the compliance requirement seemed clear. However, neither Charlotte nor Hannah had reached the near-perfect compliance attained by Frankie, and both were judged to be still too noncompliant for comfortable public schooling. For these two girls, a second experimental manipulation was added to the first. A 1-minute time out, sitting in a chair away from the task, was programmed for each noncompliance. This procedure was tried with Charlotte first and, a few days later, with Hannah. For Charlotte, time out was applied when she started to work on a task other than the suggested one. After the time out, she was again invited to the same task the teacher had suggested before. Tokens were given only for compliance, as before. Her

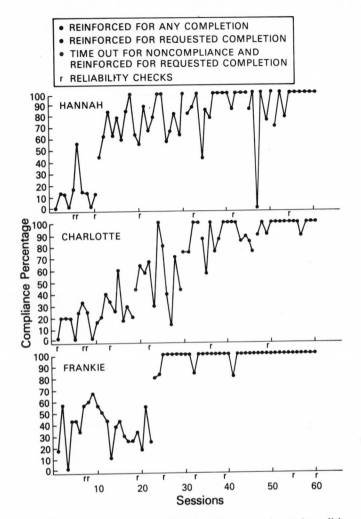

Figure 2. Daily compliance rates of three children across the experimental conditions of reinforcement and time out.

compliance increased from 75 percent to a new average of 87 percent. The time out procedure was then withdrawn, and a downward trend appeared. Time out was reinstated, and a high, steady compliance rate averaging 97 percent was seen.

A similar procedure was applied to Hannah. In her case, time out was imposed not only for choosing a task other than the suggested one but also for getting up and leaving the invited task for a period of more than 30 seconds. Her compliance rate increased to an average of 90 percent. Withdrawal of the time out procedure led to a more variable rate of compliance. With reinstatement of time out, compliance rose to a very steady, high rate. Toward the end of the study, new tasks were introduced, with little effect on compliance rates.

Thus, just as it is possible to increase the work rate of at least some "problem" children by the contingent use of free play time, it is also possible to increase compliance with instructions to work on a particular task, simply by including compliance in the requirements for earning free play time. If the reinforcer is not sufficient in raising compliance to a high level, the addition of a very mild time out procedure may prove effective.

Idiosyncratic Behavior Problems

These programs were applied to all, or nearly all, of the classroom's children because they represented general behavioral skills presumably important to each child. However, each child also presented idiosyncratic behavior problems, as representatives of so thoroughly deviant a population almost invariably will. These were dealt with by correspondingly idiosyncratic programs, which had in common only their basic reliance on the control of behavior through contingencies with consequent stimulation. Two examples will serve as illustrations of the variety necessary: one to deal with excessive violence by one child, another to remediate a very uncosmetic organization of glancing behavior in another child.

Aggressive Behavior   Bertha, 8 years old, had Downs' syndrome and was small for her age but considerably larger than the 4- to 6-year-olds with whom she attended the classroom. Because her behavior contained various examples of extremely aggressive responses, she proved dangerous to the other children, disruptive to the total classroom program, and obviously prejudicial to her own future success in the special education track of a normal public school. Her aggressive responses included choking others, wrapping her arms around them and toppling them to the floor, hitting, kicking, or scratching them, spitting on them, and grabbing things from them. In addition, Bertha displayed a range of attack behavior toward materials: tearing and breaking things, sweeping them off shelves, throwing them forcefully about the classroom, stamping on them, and biting them. In all, 24 separate responses of these kinds were defined and recorded. The occurrence of these behaviors was scored by an observer every 10 seconds; on occasional sessions, a second observer made the same observations. Comparison of these double-session, 10-second by 10-second intervals, yielded reliabilities ranging between 84 percent and 100 percent observer agreement.

For purposes of analysis, Bertha's aggressive responses were categorized into three groups: chokes and armwraps, other attacks toward people, and attacks toward materials. Figure 3 shows her standing rates of each of these categories, expressed as number per hour. Chokes and armwraps averaged 13 per hour; other attacks toward people, 15 per hour; and attacks toward materials, four per hour. These rates appeared stable, despite the teachers' best efforts to attend only to nonaggressive, nondisruptive behavior. However, when Bertha was particularly aggressive toward other children, the teachers were

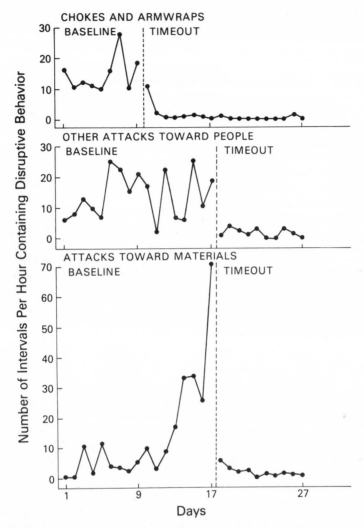

Figure 3. Daily rates of three classes of disruptive behavior by one child across the experimental conditions of time out.

forced to intervene. When such imperfect social contingencies obviously had failed to lower Bertha's baseline rates, a mild punishment procedure was applied as well: isolation for 3 minutes (time out) in a small room adjoining the classroom. Time out was applied as an immediate consequence of chokes and armwraps, signaled by the observer (who was in a better position to see all instances of aggressive or disruptive behavior than were the teachers). On the occasion of each time out, Bertha was escorted to the time out room by one or both teachers, depending on what resistence she might display. After 3 minutes, she was welcomed back to the classroom by a teacher who opened the door of the time out room only if the last 15 seconds of the time out interval had been free of screams, shouts, or other tantrum behaviors.

The effect of time out was examined in a multiple baseline design. First, time out was applied to all incidents of chokes and armwraps but not to other attacks toward people or attacks toward materials. As Figure 3 shows, the effect was prompt, but two-fold: chokes and armwraps quickly declined to a near-zero level, but at the same time, attacks toward materials rocketed to a rate of 71 per hour, in the familiar symptom-substitution format seen when not all members of a response hierarchy are reduced at the same time. (It is noteworthy that other attacks toward people did not increase, perhaps because of generalization of the time out contingency applied to chokes and armwraps, which are two forms of attack toward people.) Consequently, the time out contingency was applied uniformly to all remaining categories of aggressive and disruptive behavior, which quickly dropped to near-zero levels and remained stable at those low levels thereafter.

The outcome of this study was both an increased understanding of punishment, as exemplified by the time out operation, and a child whose behavior allowed the other children and herself to continue in the ongoing classroom programs to their mutual profit. However, it may be important to gain some appreciation of the scheduling parameters involved in the time out procedure, in terms of their ability to maintain tolerably low levels of aggressive and disruptive behavior. Consequently, at a later date, Bertha was exposed to a sequence of variable-ratio schedules of time out. The prevailing continuous schedule set up in this study (fixed ratio 1) was first modified to variable ratio 4 (every fourth aggressive response, on the average, lead to time out); after stability was seen, the schedule was changed to variable ratio 8, and finally to another low ratio: variable ratio 3. Firgure 4 summarizes the average rates of aggressive behavior seen during these conditions. Both determinations of the low variable ratios (variable ratios 3 and 4) resulted in a rate only slightly higher than that maintained under continuous time out (fixed ratio 1). However, the variable ratio 8 schedule produced a rate of disruptive behavior approximately four times higher than the continuous time out schedule. Thus, the threshold of effective control probably lies somewhere in the neighborhood of variable ratio 3. Figure 4 summarizes the average rates of aggressive behavior seen during time would be desirable before any firm assertion is made. Unfortunately, such re-examination, especially when it is aimed at determining the control threshold, is a painful process for the teachers, children, and observers involved.

Uncosmetic Glancing Behavior The second example of idiosyncratic programming concerned a boy with numerous autistic mannerisms. His style of looking at other people might be considered one of these. He glanced at others infrequently and for very brief durations, which left many observers with the impression that he was "nervous," "guilty," or somehow not to be trusted. Consequently, he was seen in individual, 15-minute daily sessions with a female experimenter, who engaged him in a bead-stringing task while she conversed with him, and began analysis of the reinforcement condition that could increase both the frequency and the duration of his glances toward her. Glances were counted on hand counters by both the experimenter and the observer (who

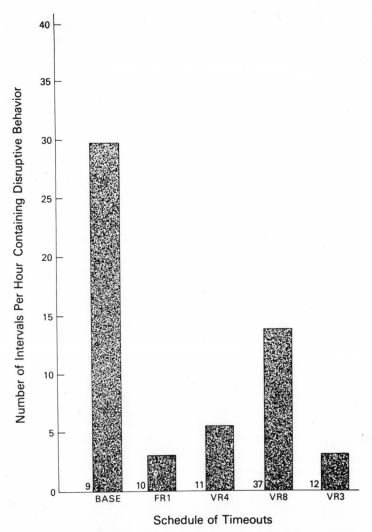

Figure 4. Average rates of disruptive behavior by one child across the experimental schedule of time out.

was behind a one-way mirror). Their mean percentage of agreement for glance frequency was 95 percent. The observer also recorded duration with a stop watch, turning it on as long as Frankie looked at the experimenter. Another observer recorded duration occasionally, and their mean percentage of agreement was 93 percent.

First, the experimenter established a local token system for these brief sessions, in which tokens given by her could be traded at the end of the session for small candies in a suitable ratio. Then baselines of frequency and duration of glancing were gathered, with the token reinforcers being given at moments when the child was not glancing at the experimenter (a differential reinforcement of other-than-glancing, or DRO procedure). Figure 5 shows the results of this baseline (DRO) procedure. Frequency remained low, and duration of these infrequent glances (graphed as Ds) averaged about 1 second. Then, several sessions ensued during which tokens were given for every glance at her seen by the experimenter, and the frequency of these glances immediately climbed, although their duration was unaffected. A brief return to the reinforcement of non-glancing behavior

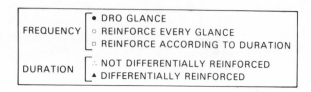

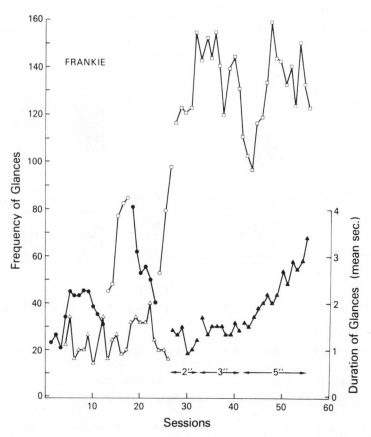

Figure 5. Daily rates and mean durations of glancing by one child across the experimental conditions of reinforcement.

(DRO) promptly showed the role of the token reinforcement in that development, and reinforcement of glancing was resumed. However, after three sessions of reinforcing any glance detected, the experimenter then shifted to a differential pattern of reinforcement: for several sessions, she reinforced only those glances of 2 seconds' duration or longer; and then, for several further sessions, reinforced only glances 3 seconds or more in duration; and finally reinforced only those glances exceeding 5 seconds in duration. The frequency of glancing, now only intermittently reinforced, remained high (although quite variable), but the duration of glancing responded appropriately to the shaping contingencies applied to it, advancing fairly steadily to a final average of 4 seconds per glance. The final rates and durations of glancing were judged attractive, and the special sessions were terminated. The design of the study obviously was hybrid: basically, it was a multiple baseline, in which frequency and duration were reinforced at different times to show that each would respond to the reinforcement operation when it was applied, but not before. In addition, the frequency baseline was subjected to the familiar reversal operations typical of earlier experimental behavior modification (Baer, Wolf, and Risley, 1968).

Home Reinforcement

Throughout the time that these classroom programs were operating, the children's parents were themselves involved in programs of their own, designed to extend the results produced in the classroom to the home environment of each child, as well as to remediate whatever behavior problems might be endemic to the home environment. While the classroom environment had always been constructed for its special purposes, the home environment required *re*structuring of aspects of its previous form, a program which can be considered both an environmental remodeling and an act of love. It is remodeling to require consistent changes in the consequences parents provide for various child behaviors, but it can be a gift of love to provide parents with proven techniques for maintaining valuable behaviors in their children.

It is well documented that behavior consequences may be altered to promote desired behaviors in young children. But it is equally clear that the *maintenance* and *generalization* of these behavioral gains depend on supporting environments that continue to provide appropriate consequences. Thus, this part of the research program focused on the identification and evaluation of economical techniques for remodeling one part of the environment of the children: the behavioral consequences provided by parents. For two mothers, the simple and economical technique of requiring that they count episodes of attention to desired child behavior was effective in modifying both mother and child behavior.

Home Observations of Mother-Child Interactions: Episode Counting

These ladies were the mothers of two children enrolled in a special classroom for preschool children already evaluated as unacceptable for the public education system. Both had successfully completed simple behavior modification exercises in the home, using material consequences to promote desired behaviors. However, in their informal interaction with their children, these mothers were observed to support a variety of undesirable child behaviors with social attention, while failing to attend to many desired child behaviors. It was decided to modify the proportion of parent attention following appropriate and inappropriate child behaviors. Home observations of mother-child interactions were conducted for 1 hour per day, 5 days per week. Child behaviors were recorded in three categories: inappropriate, appropriate, and unoccupied. Maternal attention included any verbal or nonverbal behavior directed toward the child. Child and parent behaviors were recorded as initiations or responses, time sampled in consecutive 10-second intervals. Reliability between observers using this code ranged from 84 percent to 97 percent.

Figure 6 shows the percentage of child behavior recorded as appropriate behavior for one mother-child pair. During baseline, a mean of 53 percent of parent attention followed appropriate child behavior. In the first manipulation, the mother was given a wrist counter and told to count each time she attended to appropriate child behavior. Attention and appropriate child behavior were defined for her, but she was given no further instruction. Figure 6 shows an immediate increase in the percentage of her attention following appropriate child behavior, and a correlated increase in the percentage of appropriate child behavior. The mother's use of the wrist counter was then discontinued,

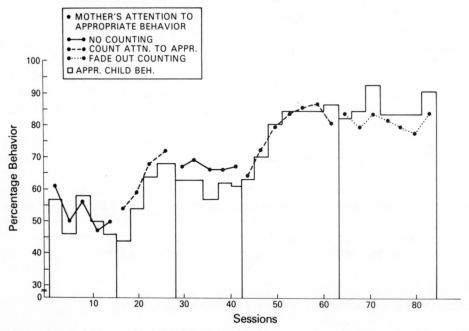

Figure 6. Percentages of appropriate child behavior and of mother's attention to appropriate child behavior across the experimental conditions of mother's counting her attention episodes, for the first mother-child pair.

and her attention to appropriate behavior stabilized near 65 percent. The wrist counter was again prescribed and used, and her attention to appropriate child behavior again increased, this time to about 85 percent. Again, the percentage of appropriate child behavior also increased. Finally, counting was faded out to see if, that way, the changes in parent and child behavior could be better maintained over time. The mother counted on only 3 days of this condition, and she did not count on the last 8 days. Two months after the last data point was collected, follow up observation made in the home showed that 91 percent of the mother's attention followed appropriate behavior, and 92 percent of the child's behavior was appropriate.

For the same mother-child pair, Figure 7 shows changes in parent attention to an important subclass of inappropriate behavior: ritual behavior. For this child, ritualistic verbalizations and body posturing made up most of his inappropriate behaviors. Maternal attention to these ritual behaviors decreased when the mother counted her attention to appropriate behavior, and the child's ritual behavior also decreased.

Similar effectiveness of the counting technique was seen with the second mother-child pair, shown in Figure 8. In baseline, a mean of 73 percent of parent attention followed appropriate child behavior. When the mother was instructed to count her attentions to appropriate behavior, both her attention and appropriate child behavior increased. Termination of counting did not produce a recovery of the original baseline; instead, stability

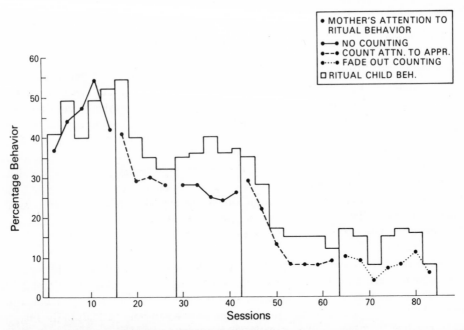

Figure 7. Percentages of ritualistic child behavior and of mother's attention to ritualistic child behavior across the experimental conditions of mother's counting her attention episodes, for the first mother-child pair.

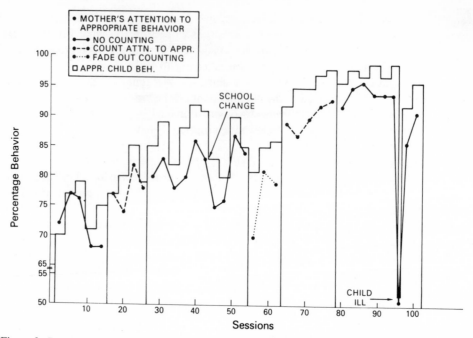

Figure 8. Percentages of appropriate child behavior and of mother's attention to appropriate child behavior across experimental conditions of mother's counting her attention episodes, for the second mother-child pair.

was maintained. Next, it was decided to have the mother count her attentions to inappropriate child behavior. (If counting attention to appropriate behavior increased that behavior, perhaps counting attention to inappropriate behavior would decrease it, too.) However, the mother then increased her attention to inappropriate behavior, thereby decreasing her attention to appropriate behavior. To recover a high level of the terminal behavior, counting attention to appropriate behavior was again introduced, and both parent and child behaviors showed the desired improvement. In the last condition, counting was terminated, and, except for one day when the child was ill, appropriate child behavior and maternal attention were maintained at approximately 90 percent over the next 24 days. (Fading of counting was not used for this parent because her attention to appropriate behavior was maintained at a mean of 81 percent during the first noncounting condition.)

This second mother spent much of the observed time instructing her child in preacademic work activities such as tracing, coloring, and copying. To establish the generality of the desired changes in parent attention to child behaviors, the last condition, in which the parent did not count, was broken into two half-hour periods. In the first, the child was free to engage in play activities. In the second period, the parent spent most of the time instructing her child. Figure 9 shows the percentage of parent attention following appropriate child behavior during work and play activities. As can be seen, there was some difference between the mother's behavior in these conditions, with 93

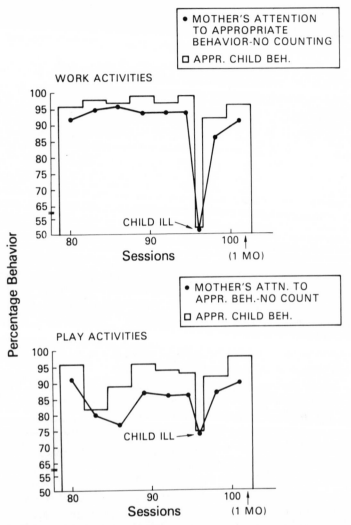

Figure 9. Percentages of appropriate child behavior and of mother's attention to appropriate child behavior in two different activities during the final no-counting condition of the experiment, for the second mother-child pair.

percent of mother attention following appropriate child behavior during work activities and 86 percent during play activities. The last points were obtained 1 month following the termination of the counting manipulation.

Now in progress are long-term follow up observations that will be needed to establish the durability of these changes in parent-child interaction. However, the effectiveness of the counting manipulation, relative to its economy in requiring less than 10 minutes of professional time, is remarkable.

It may be of interest to note that neither mother counted her attention to appropriate behavior accurately. Indeed, agreements between the parents and the observer ranged from 29 percent to 74 percent and showed no improvement over time. It appears that accurate self-recording is not a necessary condition for the modification of parent attention, using this technique. For a third parent, a father, the counting manipulation was not sufficient for modification of his attention, and a more directive cueing technique was used following unsuccessful use of self-recording. Self-recording is not new to behavior modification; however, an experimental analysis of self-recording is just beginning. For two of the three parents with whom the technique was applied, simply counting attention to appropriate child behavior was effective in producing desired changes in both parent and child behavior.

CONCLUSIONS

It appears possible to design well known elements of behavioral technology into a program designed to remediate comprehensive child behavior problems that disqualify children from normal schooling. If the program is adequate, it will allow these children to be schooled in the usual way. To find out if it is adequate, there seems no choice but to let it run for several years and to note its results, not merely in changed baselines of child behavior such as those displayed in this report, but in the actual percentages of its graduates who survive the public school's primary grades, secondary grades, and beyond. However, it is intriguing to note that it will not be enough simply to note that percentage and to applaud this program if it is high. The question will inevitably be: What is the percentage of school success among children similarly thought to be disqualified for normal schooling in their early years, but who get to try it anyhow, and *without* benefit of the program described here? That comparison is an appropriate one, of course; without it, there remains the possibility that all this baseline-changing, experimentally analyzed as it was, nevertheless was so much superstitious behavior, irrelevant to whatever normal school success may follow it. It is an actuarial question posed here, and appropriate to the familiar group designs of traditional psychology. Thus, something of a methodological circle has been completed: the technology necessary to this remedial program was secured largely through a departure from the traditional group design of earlier learning theory research, but the evaluation of the social success of this technology will rest squarely upon just that kind of research design. Perhaps this exercise portends a model of the future roles of these two research modes.

ACKNOWLEDGMENTS

The authors are grateful to many people for the total conduct of this program. Without data, there would have been no program; without an extraordinarily competent and dependable observer staff, there would have been no reliable data. Thus, this report is very much the product of our observers: Linda Wylie, Linda Haskins, Donna Moritz,

Carolyn Knief, Karen Proctor, Katherine Keller, Rebecca Paden, Jan Chance, Steven Franklin, and Susan Young (observer supervisor). Without space, time, and budget, no research could have been conducted. For these, we are indebted to our colleagues, Dr. Barbara Etzel, Director of Preschool Laboratories, Dr. Judith LeBlanc, Coordinator of Preschool Research, and Dr. Frances Horowitz, Chairman of the Department of Human Development; to the United States Office of Education and its National Program in Early Childhood Education, whose funding of the Kansas Center for Research in Early Childhood Education substantially aided this project; and to the National Institute of Child Health and Human Development, whose training grant (HD-00183) provided a postdoctoral Fellowship for Emily Herbert. A report of this research program, essentially identical to this article, was presented to the Second Western Symposium on Learning, at Western Washington State University, Bellingham, Washington, in 1971.

LITERATURE CITED

Baer, D. M., M. M. Wolf, and T. R. Risley. 1968. Some current dimensions of applied behavior analysis. J. Appl. Beh. Anal. 1: 91–97.

Bijou, S. W., and D. M. Baer (eds.). 1967. Child Development: Readings in Experimental Analysis. Appleton-Century-Crofts, New York.

Cohen, H. L., J. Filipczak, and J. Bis. 1970. A study of contingencies applicable to special education: Case I. In R. Ulrich, T. Stachnik, and J. Mabry (eds.), Control of Human Behavior, Vol. II, pp. 51–69. Scott, Foresman, New York.

Hall, R. V., D. Lund, and D. Jackson. 1968. Effects of teacher attention on study behavior. J. Appl. Beh. Anal. 1: 1–12.

Krantz, D. L. 1971. The separate worlds of operant and non-operant psychology. J. Appl. Beh. Anal. 4: 61–70.

Risley, T. R., and D. M. Baer. 1973. Operant behavior modification: The deliberate development of behavior. In B. Caldwell and H. Ricciutti (eds.), Review of Child Development Research, Volume III. Society for Research in Child Development, Chicago.

Risley, T. R., N. Reynolds, and B. Hart. 1971. Behavior modification with disadvantaged preschool children. In R. Bradfield (ed.), Behavior Modification: The Human Effort. Science and Behavior Books, Palo Alto.

Sidman, M. 1960. Tactics of Scientific Research. Basic Books, New York.

Skinner, B. F. 1938. Behaviors of Organisms. Appleton-Century-Crofts, New York.

Skinner, B. F. 1953. Science and Human Behavior, Macmillan, New York.

Ullman, L. P., and L. Krasner. 1965. Case Studies in Behavior Modification. Holt, Rinehart, and Winston, New York.

Ulrich, T., T. Stachnik, and J. Mabry (eds.). 1966, 1970. Control of Human Behavior, Volumes I and II. Scott, Foresman, New York.

Wolf, M. M., D. Giles, and R. V. Hall. 1968. Experiments with token reinforcement in a remedial classroom. Beh. Res. Ther. 6: 51–64.

Some Comments on Trends in Behavioral Research with Children

Sidney W. Bijou, Ph.D.

It is apparent from these chapters that the current trend focuses on specific problems; that is, on problems involving the actions of parents and others. In the past, a great deal of research with children was concerned with global problems and issues (e.g., bottle versus breast feeding) and the findings were less than convincing. If the trend toward specificity continues, this field is on its way to contributing much needed new knowledge on human development in the very early stages.

Another feature of current child research is the increased use of observational techniques in natural settings. It is a movement away from "well established" measurement techniques that have been found wanting, techniques such as the interview, questionnaire, psychometric test, and projective test. Measurement through direct observation has the advantage of encouraging investigators to concentrate on the individual child and to pay more attention to his specific interactions with people and objects both in current and past situations. These are desirable "side effects," but the method may also encourage the naive investigator to be satisfied with simplistic, meaningless conclusions, e.g., a child behaves the way he does because he has been reinforced for doing so, or a child behaves the way he does because of an "unfortunate" family history. The study of child-environment interactions is complicated and, to approach completeness, must take into account at least four functionally-defined classes of variables: 1) the antecedent condition, 2) the response or behavior function, 3) the response consequent, and 4) the general setting condition.

A third feature pertains to longitudinal research alluded to by Dr. Gallagher. At present, longitudinal research is in poor repute mainly because of the expense involved and the limited information produced by such studies in the past. But before totally rejecting longitudinal research, it must be remembered that much of the information about human development can be obtained only through longitudinal research. Hence, longitudinal research must be carried on so that it is no more costly than cross-sectional research and, in order to avoid previous mistakes, it must deal with specific segments of the interactions of a child rather than with all aspects of his development. The chapters by Dr. Risley and Dr. Hart and by Dr. Baer are of this sort, although they have not been presented as longitudinal studies. Both deal with a specific dimension of development: Risley and Hart's with language, and Baer's with academic learning. Segmental longitudinal studies may be experimental with an intervention procedure, or descriptive with only observations of events as they occur.

A few comments are in order on the contents and methods of Risley and Hart's chapter on community-based language training and Baer's chapter on intervention for school entry. The Risley and Hart concept of incidental teaching has provocative implications. The importance of casual learning has been long recognized. It is something that goes on almost all the time, but its greatest rate occurs in the preschool years. During this phase of development, in which the relationship between parent and child is usually intimate, a great deal of the interaction is casual; it is casual in the sense that while the mother carries out her household routines she chats and interacts with her child about all sorts of past, present, and future things and events. Through these interactions, the child learns a great deal about every aspect of his physical and social worlds and his mother's value systems. Risley and Hart have begun to identify the conditions and processes involved and are well on their way toward developing techniques that foster incidental teaching on the part of the mother and incidental learning on the part of the child.

Baer's chapter is of particular interest because it suggests a way of combining individual and group subject experimental designs. His strategy avoids the need for a control group, yet it provides information on the performance of each child in the study. It is, as noted before, a longitudinal study and may be compared with some of the research on follow-through programs. Baer and the rest of us would like to know how well the child maintains the level of achievement he demonstrated in the experimental preschoool. The only way to find out is to go into the public school classrooms and to observe the subsequent behavior of each child. Those who have tried field observational measurement methods know how difficult and how time consuming they are; nevertheless, they are worthwhile because data from these methods will eventually reveal that children succeed or fail after leaving an experimental classroom depending on the specific behaviors of the teacher, the programs assigned, and the characteristics of the classroom in which they are enrolled. It is hoped that some day findings from this kind of research will influence teacher training and school programs, not only for high risk children, but for all children.

Scope and Focus of Research Relevant to Intervention: A Socioecological Perspective

Earl S. Schaefer, Ph.D.

This analysis of the need for a socioecological perspective in research relevant to intervention is motivated by the past findings of intervention research and by a concern for the future of intervention programs. Typically, research and demonstration programs have a limited life span and a limited impact. When funding ends the special programs vanish, whereas the major professions and institutions with more stable support remain. It follows that intervention research will have its greatest continuing impact through influence upon child care, health, and education institutions and professions.

SHIFTS IN INTERVENTION RESEARCH

However, the type of impact that intervention research will have upon the professions and institutions will be determined by the scope and focus of that research. For example, intervention research focused upon the individual, or monad, may encourage the professions to persist in their emphasis on direct care of the individual child. Whether because of the greater accessibility of mothers or of the hypothesis of the greater influence of maternal behavior, research focused upon the mother-child dyad may also contribute to the neglect of fathers in child care, health, and education. Likewise, intervention research that ignores the effect of other family, community, and professional variables upon mother and child may support the current limited focus upon the diagnosis and treatment of the child or of the mother-child dyad. Attention to early intervention without continuing intervention and to short-term rather than long-term evaluation may confirm professional emphasis upon brief, direct care of the child and its immediate effects.

However, findings of early intervention research have contributed to the development of a socioecological perspective that implies a broader scope and a change in focus. Research has moved from a predominant focus on the individual, or monad, to include a focus on the interaction of the mother-child dyad (Beckwith, this volume; Denenberg and Thoman, this volume). Evidence of the need for professional consultation and support during the development of the mother-child relationship (Denenberg and Thoman, this volume) and of the effectiveness of instructions to mothers to attend to the appropriate behavior of their child (Baer et al., this volume) also point to the need to study the interaction of the parent-professional-child triad and its effects upon parental care and child development. Also contributing to a broader scope are other findings that suggest the need to study father-child and husband-wife dyads and the mother-father-child triad as they influence child development. The need for intervention that prevents rather than remediates problems in parent-child relationships is supported by evidence that the parent-child relationship may stabilize in the early days, weeks, or months of life and that the type of hospital care of the mother and infant at the time of delivery may influence maternal attachment to the infant. In addition, evidence that social stresses and supports and professional and institutional policies and practices may influence parental care of the child suggests the importance of studying the ecosystems that influence child care and child development.

Thus, a broadening scope of intervention research is moving from the study of monads and dyads to the study of triads and ecosystems. This research supports a change in focus in a variety of research and service areas. Attention moves from the direct care of the child by the professional to support for family and community care of the child; from the needs of children to those of parents. Furthermore, the focus shifts from the child and parent to the social stresses and supports and the professions and institutions that influence children and parents. Focus also shifts from the need for early care and education of the child to the need for an enduring family and community environment that fosters development. This chapter reviews some of the research that is contributing to a socioecological perspective which may, in turn, lead to a change in emphasis in the professions and institutions that relate to parents and children.

MOTHER-CHILD DYAD

Although study of the individual is necessary to provide a basis for decisions about intervention, Sullivan's (1931) statement concerning psychiatry that, "to isolate its individual subject matter, a personality, from a complex of interpersonal relations . . . is preposterously beside the point" would also apply to research that provides a basis for intervention. The effort to study the family environment of the child has typically led to research on mother-child interaction: initially, the study of the effects of maternal behavior upon the child, but increasingly the study of the child's behavior as a stimulus for parent behavior (Bell, 1971; Denenberg and Thoman, this volume). However, the reciprocal influences of natural mother and child include the possible influence of the intrauterine environment (Sontag, 1941) and of labor and delivery upon characteristics of the child, the influence of the child's characteristics upon maternal behavior (Bell, 1971), and the subsequent influence of stable patterns of maternal behavior upon child behavior.

These circular interactions suggest the need for caution in making interpretations of mother-child correlations as being caused by the child or by the mother. Longitudinal studies of the intercorrelations of behavior of mother and child (Moss, 1967) are needed to determine whether early maternal behavior is more predictive of specific child behavior, as appeared to be true in longitudinal studies (Schaefer and Bayley, 1963; Moore, 1968), or vice versa.

Intervention research designed to change maternal behavior with the child suggests that maternal behavior influences child behavior, but Ramey et al. (this volume) also report that developmental day care for the infant may influence the child's responsiveness, which, in turn, may influence the mother's behavior with the child. The reciprocal influence of parent and child suggests that intervention with either parent or child may begin a sequence of positive interactions. Although interactions are circular, attempts to supplement deficient or distorted parent care of the child in child-centered intervention, as well as attempts to influence parent behavior in parent-centered intervention, still suggest that an efficacious focus of intervention is upon changing adult behavior, which in turn influences child behavior.

FATHER-CHILD DYAD

Despite the fact that in recent years more attention has been given to father-child relationships, the major focus of intervention research and programs, as well as services for children and families, is still upon the mother-child relationship. Yet, correlations between paternal behavior and the child's early intellectual development (Radin, 1973), between the child's perceptions of parent behavior and adolescent alienation (Rode, 1971), and between parent-child relationships and behavior problems of boys (Rutter, 1971), all suggest that the father may have an equal influence on child adjustment and development. Despite the relative inaccessibility of fathers for research and their typically low involvement in child care, health, and education, evidence that positive paternal involvement contributes significantly to child development points to the importance of devoting more effort to working with fathers in both research and service programs.

HUSBAND-WIFE DYAD

In the past, studies of mother-child and father-child dyads have been seen as relevant to intervention, but the husband-wife dyad has been generally ignored by the field of child development. This is shown by the index of the volume on socialization in the *Carmichael's Manual* (Mussen, 1970), which includes no references to marriage or to the husband-wife relationship. Yet Rutter (1971) found that the husband-wife relationship is highly correlated with the antisocial behavior of boys, and Nye (1957) reported that children from unhappy, unbroken homes are more maladjusted than are children from broken homes. Furthermore, failure to establish a stable husband-wife relationship is also related to the high incident of poverty in mother-headed households (U.S. Bureau of Census). Perhaps, through a broadened scope of intervention research that includes father-child and husband-wife dyads, intervention could become more effective by supporting and strengthening the entire network of family relationships.

FAMILY NETWORKS

A focus upon the entire network of family relationships requires more comprehensive conceptualization, quantification, and research, including research on the mother-child, father-child, husband-wife, and sibling dyads (Lowman, 1972; Schaefer, 1974). Research on family networks might test the hypothesis that interventions in one component of the family system may change the previous balance of family relationships. Thus, intervention that focuses the parent's attention upon one child may have an impact upon the parent's relationship to other children. A related area of research would be upon the parent's relationships to two or more children in the same family. Lowman (1972) found, in a family with one child in psychiatric treatment that, while the parents' relationships with that child were more likely to be less positive, relationships with a sibling of that child were more likely to be more positive than were parent-child relationships in families without a child in treatment. Other data suggest that parents have the potentiality for developing very different relationships with the several children in their families. This research finding that a parent may have difficulty only in relating to a particular child suggests the need for further research and service that attempt to support parents in their development of positive relationships with each of their children.

A number of different studies support the hypothesis that current stresses and supports may influence the quality of family care of children. Stresses caused by the presence of a mentally retarded child in the family have been investigated by Schonell and Watt (1956), Kershner (1970), and Stone (1967). Number of children in the family has been related to adequacy of family care by Douglas (1964), Elmer (1967), and Giovannoni and Billingsley (1970), and timing and spacing of births has been related to child abuse by Elmer (1967). Current stresses and lack of social supports have been related to emotional disturbances of mothers during the 4 months after delivery by Gordon and Gordon (1959), to rehospitalization or death of premature infants by Glass, Kolko, and Evans (1971), and to differences between adequate and potentially neglectful or neglectful mothers by Giovannoni and Billingsley (1970). The latter summarize their conclusions as follows: "... The low income neglectful parent is under greater environmental and situational stress and has fewer resources and supports in coping with these stresses than does the adequate mother. It is the current situational strains that predominate among neglectful parents, not those of their past life." Thus, clinical studies suggest that differences in parent-child relationships and child care that are found between socioeconomic groups are also related to the balance of family stresses and supports. Perhaps more attention to the elimination of family stresses and to the development of family support systems rather than to the direct, professional care of children may better serve to foster child development.

PARENTS-PROFESSIONAL-CHILD NETWORK

The need for analysis of family triads and family groups is paralleled by the need to analyse the focus and quality of interaction among the child, the parent or parents, and the professional(s) who offer services to children and families. Chamberlin (1974) reports that parents of 4-year-olds in pediatric care frequently do not discuss their children's definite behavioral or emotional problems with the pediatrician, but that most of those who do discuss such problems report that the professional was helpful. Stine (1962) also found very little discussion of child behavior or development during pediatric visits, and Starfield and Barkowf (1969) report that parents' questions during pediatric visits were often unacknowledged and unanswered. An example of more positive interaction between professional and parent is provided by Baer et al. (this volume), who report that instructing mothers to count the appropriate behaviors of their children led to increases in maternal attention to the child's appropriate behavior and decreases in inappropriate behavior. These studies suggest that research on parent-professional-child interaction may provide a basis for more effective prevention and remediation of children's behavioral and developmental problems through the current professions and institutions.

In Hospital

The hypothesis that policies and practices of the professions and institutions may influence maternal attachment and maternal care is suggested by a study of maternal attachment as influenced by amount of contact between mother and infant in the hospital after delivery (Klaus et al., 1972). Increases in mother-infant contact in the hospital were related to increases in maternal attachment to the infant at 1 month of age, suggesting that separation of mother and infant may interfere with the maternal bonding process. Earlier research on mammals (Hersher, Moore, and Richmond, 1958) and studies of maternal attachment to low birth weight babies in intensive care nurseries (Fanaroff, Kennell, and Klaus, 1972) would support this conclusion. Such research raises the important question of whether our current policies of direct care for children by the health and education professions may be impairing rather than supporting parental care and education of the child. The evidence of the major influence of parents upon children, as well as evaluations of child-centered as contrasted to parent-centered intervention programs (Bronfenbrenner, 1974; Schaefer, 1972), support the conclusion that supplementing the child's care, which may supplant the parent's care, is less cost-effective than strengthening and supporting family care. Perhaps the focus of intervention research should move from the child and from the family to an analysis of the professions and institutions that relate to the child and the family.

Day Care Centers

Research on the effects of group day care for infants and young children as contrasted to home care may have the most immediate application to planning for child care. Although detailed analyses of the child's experiences in the home and in group day care are needed, summative evaluation supports the hypothesis that some types of infant day care may be less effective than home care. Papousek (1970), in summarizing the Czechoslovakian research on the effects of relatively low adult child ratios in group day care, states:

> In comparison with children brought up at home, the children in day-care centers usually show delays in the development of speech, oculomotor coordination, and social behavior, although in somatic and motor development they are equal or slightly better than children in families . . . In a good institution, infants admitted before the fifth month of life crawled and walked sooner than infants admitted from their homes at later ages, but they were slower in speech development. The differences are believed to prove that the positive influence of group rearing in infants is overshadowed by the negative consequences of parental deprivation.

Papousek states that research has contributed to changes in social policy in child care, stressing more home care for infants, but concludes: "Unfortunately, one has to rely more on practical and clinical experiences than on theoretical issues and experimental verification, but this only reflects the actual state of knowledge of such an important process as that of bringing up our future generation."

An American study of children in a university day care center (Schwarz, Strickland, and Krolick, 1974) observed differences in behavior in the center between children who entered during the first year of life and children who entered at 3 and 4 years of age. The authors report that "the infant day-care group was found to be significantly more aggressive, motorically active, and less cooperative with adults." In another study of infant day care, Blehar (1974) reports:

> Findings indicate qualitative disturbances in the mother-child relationship in day-care children, and this was attributed to the disruptive effects of frequent daily separations. The child's age at the time that day care began influenced the kind of disturbance shown. Those who started day care at age two showed avoidant behavior upon reunion with the mother, whereas those who started day care at age three showed anxious, ambivalent behavior.

While infant day care may show immediate negative effects upon the child's relationship with the parent and with other adults, an analysis of its influence on the child's subsequent development is needed. Thus, comprehensive, longitudinal studies of different types of child care are needed to determine short-term and long-term effects upon the child's development.

EFFECT OF A STABLE ENVIRONMENT

The need for longitudinal research is closely associated with the idea of attempting to provide a stable and continuing, growth-promoting environment for the child. The statement that some problems require a longitudinal research design by Gallagher et al. (this volume) is supported by the differences between short-term and long-term evaluations of the effects of child-centered and parent-centered early intervention (Bronfrenbrenner, 1974). Baer et al.'s statement (this volume) that "the maintenance and generalization of these behavioral gains depend on supporting environments that continue to provide appropriate consequence," suggests that the problem of the stability of child behavior is highly related to the problem of the stability of the child's environment, with both problems requiring longitudinal research for their solution.

The highly influential conclusions of Bloom (1964) on the early stabilization of the child's level of intellectual functioning were derived from research on children reared in their own families, probably a relatively stable environment. However, a hypothesis that the stability of the child's level of intellectual functioning may be highly related to the stability of the child's environment is supported by findings of Clarke and Clarke (1959) and Feurerstein (1970) of increases in intellectual level of children who are reared in relatively depriving environments and then moved to more stimulating environments. Further evidence supporting the hypothesis of the need for continuing stimulation are findings that the mean IQ level of children from less advantaged families can be increased by child-centered intervention, but that the level decreases when these interventions are terminated (Bronfrenbrenner, 1974). These research findings indicate the need to shift from the study of early environment and early stimulation to the study of the continuing environment that fosters growth and development throughout the child's life space and life span (Schaefer, 1970).

The fact that the parent, in most cases, provides a continuing and important influence on a child's life suggests that parent-centered intervention might be the logical focus in the attempt to have an enduring impact on the child's environment. The greater cost-effectiveness of parent-centered as contrasted to child-centered intervention is suggested by comparing the results of a child-centered infant education program (Schaefer and Aaronson, 1972) with a parent-centered program (Levenstein, 1970). The child-centered program consisted of more than 300 home visits over a 21-month period, which resulted in an IQ difference of 17 points between tutored and untutored groups, while the parent-centered program consisted of approximately 32 visits over a 7-month period, which resulted in a similar 17 point IQ gain in the tutored subjects. The parent-centered program thus showed equal effectiveness with less cost at the end of the tutoring periods. Follow up on the child-centered program showed no differences between the tutored and the untutored children at the end of first grade, while follow ups on the parent-centered program showed relatively good long-term results (Bronfrenbrenner, 1974). Schaefer and Aaronson (1972) suggest that the child-centered program started too late (the child showed effects of deprivation at the time intervention began at 15 months), ended too early (the child's IQ scores dropped after tutoring was discontinued at 3 years of age), and had the wrong focus (upon the child rather than the parent). Current professions and institutions that provide brief periods of child-centered remediation through supplementing family care also start late, end too early, and have less long-term impact because they are not fostering enduring changes in the child's interaction with his continuing family and community environment.

Several different studies which found that stable patterns of parent behavior may develop during the early weeks, months, and years of life (Schaefer and Bayley, 1960; Moss, 1967; Broussard and Hartner, 1971; Bell and Ainsworth, 1972) and the findings that maternal and infant care in the hospital may influence maternal attachment and maternal care (Klaus et al., 1972) suggest that early infancy may be a promising period for parent-centered intervention. Perhaps enduring patterns of parent-child relationships that have early, continuing, and cumulative effects upon child development (Schaefer and Bayley, 1963) are established during infancy. The hypothesis that such patterns of parent behavior have a cumulative effect upon child behavior, while brief interventions have minimal long-term impact, is supported by Rutter's (1971) conclusion that brief separations from the parent have a minimal, long-term impact on child adjustment, while enduring husband-wife, father-child, and mother-child relationships have a significant relationship to behavior problems in boys. Further longitudinal research on the stability of child behavior and functioning and on the hypothesis that stable patterns of parent behavior have early, continuing, and cumulative effects upon child development is needed as a guide for future intervention.

FUTURE RESEARCH

The findings of intervention research up to the present have many implications both for the scope and focus of future research and for the professions and institutions that provide child care services. Some of the specific areas that have been mentioned as needing research attention are: the whole network of family relationships, including the father-child and husband-wife dyads; patterns of parent-child-professional interaction; and policies and practices of the professions and institutions that provide services to children and families. Longitudinal research on the short- and long-term effects of different types of child care and on the stability of patterns of parental care and of child behavior and functioning is also needed. In addition, new concepts and adequate methods with which to research these areas must be developed.

One important goal for intervention research might be the development of methods for strengthening and supporting family care for the child through the current professions and institutions. The reports of the favorable effects of rooming-in (McBryde, 1951), of increased contact between mother and infant at the time of delivery (Klaus et al., 1972), and of parent-centered interventions (Baer et al. this volume; Levenstein, 1970) suggest that it would be feasible to provide support for parental care through the existing professions and institutions if this were to become a major goal.

Both reviews of the influence of parent behavior upon the child's intellectual development and academic achievement (Hess, 1969; Schaefer, 1972) and reviews of the effects of parent-centered interventions (Lazar and Chapman, 1972; Bronfrenbrenner, 1974) point to the need for a shift from child-centered to parent-centered intervention in the professions and institutions that provide child care services. Yet, the current focus of hospital and pediatric outpatient care on the individual, both mother and child, and the emphasis on providing early schooling and developmental day care indicate that, at present, many professions and institutions are providing direct care and education of the child rather than strengthening and supporting the child's interactions in his family and community environment. More research on the assumptions, policies, practices, and effects of current services for children and families would help to provide a basis for interventions focused upon the professions and institutions, as well as for interventions focused upon families and children.

A broadened focus in research relevant to intervention would be supported by the perspectives of ecology, the science of "the interrelationships of living things to one another and to their environment" (Studdard, 1973). Bronfrenbrenner (1974), from his analysis of the effectiveness of early intervention, has stressed a strategy of ecological intervention. The review of social ecology and of psychological environments by Insel and Moos (1974) has also emphasized the need to conceptualize the "psychological and social dimensions of the environment in a framework of person-milieu interaction." Research on networks of family relationships among father, mother, child, and sibling(s) and research on the influence of social supports, social stresses, and of the professions and institutions upon family care of children and child development move toward the analysis of the ecosystem that influences child development. The possibility that the professions may intentionally supplement, but inadvertently supplant, family care of the child and the growing evidence that strengthening and supporting family care through parent-centered programs is more cost-effective than supplementing through child-centered programs supports the need for research on the professions and institutions as well as on families and children. A broader scope of research suggested by a social ecological analysis of influences on child development and a focus upon the professions and institutions as well as upon families and children would contribute substantially to future intervention and to more effective child care, child health, and education professions and institutions.

ACKNOWLEDGMENT

The author gratefully acknowledges the editorial assistance of Mary Sue Comstock in preparing this chapter.

LITERATURE CITED

Bell, R. Q. 1971. Stimulus control of parent or caretaker behavior by offspring. Devel. Psych. 4: 63–72.

Bell, S. M., and M. D. S. Ainsworth. 1972. Infant crying and maternal responsiveness. Child Devel. 43: 1171–1190.

Blehar, M. C. 1974. Anxious attachment and defensive reactions associated with day care. Child Devel. 45: 683–692.

Bloom, B. S. 1964. Stability and Change in Human Characteristics. Wiley, New York.

Bronfrenbrenner, U. 1974. A report on longitudinal evaluations of preschool programs. Vol. 2. Is early intervention effective? DHEW Publication No. (OHD) 74–25, Washington, D.C.

Broussard, E., and M. S. S. Hartner. 1971. Further considerations regarding maternal perception of the first born. In J. Hellmuth (ed.), Exceptional Infant. Vol. 2. Studies in Abnormalities. Brunner/Mazel, New York.

Chamberlin, R. W. 1974. Management of preschool behavior problems. Ped. Clin. No. Amer. 21: 33–47.

Clarke, A. D. B., and A. M. Clarke. 1959. Recovery from the effects of deprivation. Acta Psych. 16: 137–144.

Douglas, J. W. 1964. The Home and the School: A Study of Ability and Attainment in the Primary School. McGibbon and Kee, London.

Elmer, E. 1967. Children in Jeopardy: A Study of Abused Minors and their Families. University of Pittsburgh Press, Pittsburgh.

Fanaroff, A. A., J. H. Kennell, and M. H. Klaus. 1972. Follow-up of low birth weight infants: The predictive value of maternal visiting patterns. Pediatrics 49: 287–290.

Feuerstein, R. 1970. A dynamic approach to the causation, prevention, and alleviation of retarded performance. In H. C. Haywood (ed.), Social-Cultural Aspects of Mental Retardation, pp. 341–377. Appleton-Century-Crofts, New York.

Giovannoni, J. M., and A. Billingsley. 1970. Child neglect among the poor: A study of parental adequacy in three ethnic groups. Child Welfare 49: 196–204.

Glass, L., N. Kolko, and H. Evans. 1971. Factors influencing predisposition to serious illness in low birth weight infants. Pediatrics 48: 368–371.

Gordon, R. E., and K. Gordon. 1959. Social factors in the prediction and treatment of emotional disorders of pregnancy. Amer. J. Obstet. 77: 1074–1083.

Hersher, L., A. U. Moore, and J. B. Richmond. 1958. Effect of postpartum separation of mother and kid on maternal care in the domestic goat. Science 128: 1343–1348.

Hess, R. D. 1969. Parental behavior and children's school achievement: Implications for Head Start. In E. Grotberg (ed.), Critical Issues in Research Related to Disadvantaged Children. Educational Testing Service, Princeton.

Insel, P. M., and R. H. Moos. 1974. Psychological environments: Expanding the scope of human ecology. Amer. Psych. 29: 179–188.

Kershner, E. 1970. Intelligence and social development in relation to family functioning: Longitudinal comparison of home versus institutional effects. Amer. J. Ment. Defic. 75: 276–278.

Klaus, M. H., R. Jerauld, N. C. Dreger, W. McAlphine, M. Steffa, and J. H. Kennell. 1972. Maternal attachment: Importance of the first postpartum days. New Eng. J. Med. 286: 460–463.

Lazar, J. B., and I. Chapman. 1972. A review of the present status and future needs of programs to develop parenting skills. Prepared for the Interagency Panel on Early Childhood Research and Development. Social Research Group. The George Washington University, April. Washington, D.C.

Levenstein, P. 1970. Cognitive growth in preschoolers through verbal interaction with mothers. Amer. J. Orthopsych. 40: 426–432.

Lowman, J. 1972. The inventory of family feelings: A self-administered measure of family functioning. Paper presented at the Annual Meeting of the Eastern Psychological Association, Boston.

McBryde, A. 1951. Compulsory rooming-in in the ward and private new-born service at Duke Hospital. J. Amer. Med. Assoc. 145: 625–627.

Moore, T. 1968. Language and intelligence: A longitudinal study of the first eight years. Part II: Environmental correlates of mental growth. Human Devel. 11: 1–24.

Moss, H. 1967. Sex, age, and state as determinates of mother-infant interaction. Merrill-Palmer Quart. 13: 19–36.

Mussen, P. H. (ed.). 1970. Carmichael's Manual of Child Psychology. Vol. 2. 3rd Ed. Wiley, New York.

Nye, F. I. 1957. Child adjustment in broken and unbroken homes. Marriage and Family Living 19: 356–361.

Papousek, H. 1970. Effects of group rearing conditions during the preschool years of life. *In* V. H. Denenberg (ed.), Education of the Infant and Young Child, pp. 51–60. Academic Press, New York.

Radin, N. 1973. Observed paternal behaviors as antecedents of intellectual functioning in young boys. Devel. Psych. 8: 369–376.

Rode, A. 1971. Perceptions of parent behavior among alienated adolescents. Adolescence 6: 19–38.

Rutter, M. 1971. Parent-child separation: Psychological effects on the children. J. Child Psych. Psychiat. 12: 233–260.

Schaefer, E. S. 1970. Need for early and continuing education. *In* V. M. Denenberg (ed.), Education of the Infant and Young Child, pp. 61–82. Academic Press, New York.

Schaefer, E. S. 1972. Parents as educators: Evidence from cross-sectional, longitudinal and intervention research. Young Child. 27: 227–239.

Schaefer, E. S. 1974. The network of family relationships: Inventories of perceptions of family members. Paper presented at the Symposium on the Child, the Family, and the Substantive Environment. Southeastern Society for Research in Child Development, March, 1974. Chapel Hill, N.C.

Schaefer, E. S., and M. Aaronson. 1972. Infant education research project: Implementation and implications of a home tutoring program. *In* R. Parker (ed.), The Preschool in Action: Exploring Early Childhood Programs, pp. 410–434. Allyn and Bacon, Boston.

Schaefer, E. S., and N. Bayley. 1960. Consistency of maternal behavior from infancy to preadolescence. J. Abnorm. Soc. Psych. 61: 1–6.

Schaefer, E. S., and N. Bayley. 1963. Maternal behavior, child behavior, and their intercorrelations from infancy through adolescence. Monogr. Soc. Res. Child Devel. 28: (No. 3, Whole No. 87).

Schonell, F., and B. Watts. 1960. A second survey of the effects of a subnormal child on the family unit. Amer. J. Ment. Defic. 64: 862–868.

Schwarz, J. C., R. G. Strickland, and G. Krolick, 1974. Infant day care: Behavioral effects at preschool age. Devel. Psych. 10: 502–506.

Sontag, L. W. 1941. The significance of fetal environmental differences. Amer. J. Obstet. Gyn. 42: 996–1003.

Starfield, B., and S. Barkowf. 1969. Physician's recognition of complaints made by parents about their children's health. Pediatrics 43: 168–172.

Stine, O. 1962. Content and method of health supervision by physicians in child health conferences in Baltimore. Amer. J. Pub. Health 52: 1858–1865.

Stone, N. D. 1967. Family factors in willingness to place the mongoloid child. Amer. J. Ment. Defic. 72: 16–20.

Studdard, G. J. 1973. Common Environmental Terms: A Glossary. Environmental Protection Agency, Washington, D.C.

Sullivan, H. S. 1931. Sociopsychiatric research. Amer. J. Psychiat. 87: 977–991.

U.S. Bureau of Census. 1970. Census of the population: 1970. General social and economic characteristics. Final Report PC(1)-C1. United States Summary. Washington, D.C.

CASE FINDING, SCREENING, DIAGNOSIS, AND TRACKING

Screening, Assessment, and Intervention for Young Children at Developmental Risk

John H. Meier, Ph.D.

The chapters in this section are all concerned with a newly defined and growing national priority for early casefinding, screening, diagnosis, and tracking. The emphasis on *early* has resulted in a focus upon infants and toddlers. At the same time that investigators are seeking the identity of the salient variables for reliably identifying such young children at developmental risk (Parmelee et al., this volume), other pioneers are exploring the ways and means for integrating what is already known into a comprehensive service delivery system (Scurletis and Headrick, this volume). To ensure some national quality control and uniform implementation of efforts to do the most good and the least harm for the greatest number of the nation's children, other national leaders are producing legislation and its attendant guidelines and regulations for early identification and intervention programs (Rojcewicz and Aaronson, this volume). The efficacy of the aforementioned investigations and pragmatic activities rests upon the sophistication of the current state of the art and science about infant growth and development. Unfortunately, because this area of interest is relatively immature, the majority of the literature about it is to be found in obscure and unrefereed journals, unpublished reports, and practically unobtainable papers presented at conferences. The President's Committee on Mental Retardation (PCMR), along with several other federal agencies, sponsored a conference on early screening and assessment that was designed to get together the majority of the known experts on the subject and to pool their knowledge. This conference resulted in a collection of background papers (President's Committee on Mental Retardation, 1973) and a monograph (Meier, 1973b), which organized and presented much of the extant information on the assessment and screening of young children at developmental risk.

METHODS AND MATERIALS FOR
EARLY DEVELOPMENTAL SCREENING AND ASSESSMENT

This chapter addresses the state-of-the-art and science regarding operational or proposed methods and materials for early developmental screening and assessment of young children. It focuses on extant techniques and instruments (Table 1) for the early identification of children who have various developmental disorders or are at considerable risk of later experiencing them. It mentions most and discusses some of the literature reporting sundry related but hitherto isolated efforts at identifying, evaluating, and classifying the developmental status of young children. To prevent a hardening of the categories and, in keeping with the intention to go beyond the paralysis of analysis, a brief section dealing with intervention/prevention is included at the end of this chapter.

To categorize neatly and consistently everything germane to the aforementioned is virtually an impossible task; nevertheless, this chapter attempts to establish at least a point of departure for subsequent, more comprehensive, and sophisticated endeavors and also to prevent any unnecessary duplication of efforts because of ignorance of what has been accomplished. To stay within the scope and focus of this chapter, discussion of the following considerations has been largely omitted and would be conspicuously absent from any complete and balanced presentation: 1) rationale and federal mandates for early and periodic screening, diagnosis, and treatment of developmental disabilities, 2) definition(s) of developmental anomalies, 3) controversial issues regarding at risk registers and populations, 4) some cultural/environmental factors associated with developmental hazards, and 5) some of the broader societal, ethnic, ethical, and legal considerations relative to any massive identification/intervention programs. The focus herein is upon the rudiments necessary for establishing and implementing a massive screening and assessment system to detect, while they are very young and presumably most amenable to treatment and habilitation, infants and children at risk of being or becoming developmentally disabled.

Significant advances have been made beyond both the Procustean notion of making all persons fit a predetermined ideal human mold and the Spartan notion of gross screening by throwing infants into cold water and keeping only those who can save themselves. This chapter is concerned with the reverse side of the coin, that is, with the early identification of those persons who are likely to sink while they can still either be taught to swim in a complex world or properly protected from a fatal total immersion and at least enabled to crawl, walk, or run on land. Such a massive screening program promises to reveal those factors that contribute to developmental risks in varying degrees and thereby to allow them to be weighted in terms of their relative contribution to handicapping conditions. This, in turn, will facilitate the prevention of more serious disabilities that reportedly can be attenuated by early detection and appropriate intervention. Moreover, the appropriateness and efficacy of various intervention/prevention methods and materials can be determined.

Developmental Domain	Page[1]	Test or Procedure	Developer(s) Author(s)	Age Range[2]	Reliability	Validity	Time[5]	Cost per Child[6]	Administration[7]	Recommended Stage[8]
PHYSICAL	30	Automated Multiphasic Health Testing Services	Collen & Cooper	Over 4 yr.	A[3]	A	70	30[5]	Mix	Ter.
	34	Biochemistry & Cytogenetics	Guthrie	5-3 mo.	A	A	U[4]	<1	LT&EE	Sec.
	38	Amniocentesis	O'Brien	C-B	A	A	60	20	P	Sec.
	40	Metabolic	Howell, Holtzman & Thomas	B-3 mo.	A	A	<30	2	LT&EE	Sec.
	41	Ultra-Micro Automated System	Ambrose	B-3 mo.	A	A	60	1	Mix	Sec.
	42	Nutritional Status	Fomen	B-30 mo.	A	U	20	1	PP	Sec.
	44	Gestational Age	Lubchenco	B-1 mo.	A	A	5	2	PP	Sec.
	49	Statistical Mortality Morbidity	MCH	B-12 mo.	A	A	Neg[y]	Neg	P	Pre-Pri
	51	Statistical Epidemiology	Tarjan, et al.	Pre-B	A	A	Neg	Neg	P	Pre-Pri
	55	Data System	Scurletis, et al.	Pre-B	A	A	Neg	Neg	PP	Pri
	57	Prevention	de la Cruz & LaVeck	Pre-C	U[4]	U	U	U	P	Pri & Pre-Pri
	58	Apgar Rating	Apgar	B	A	A	6	1	P	Pri
	59	Vision	Press & Austin	Over 30 mo.	U	U	Neg	1	PP	Pri
	61	Eye Screening	Barker & Hayes	B-5 yr.	U	U	Neg	<1	PP	Pri
	62	Electro-Oculograph	Petre-Quadens	1-6 yr.	A	U	120	10	LT&EE	Ter.
	64	Hearing High-Risk Register	Hardy	C-3 yr.	A	U	Neg	Neg	PP	Pri
	67	Hearing Screening	Young; Downs & Silver	9-12 mo.	A	A	5	2	PP	Pri
	71	Potential Battered Children	Kempe & Helfer; Walworth & Metz; Gil	C-2 yr.	U	U	U	U	P	Sec.
	73	Vocalization Analysis	Filippi & Rousey	B-12 mo.	U	U	40	20	PP	Sec.
	75	Behavioral & Neurological Assessment Scale (I)	Brazelton	B-3 yr.	A	U	40	30	P	Ter.
	75	Neuro-Developmental Observation	Ozer & Richardson	Over 5 yr.	U	U	20	15	PP	Sec.
INTELLECTUAL/ COGNITIVE	80	Attention to Discrepancy	Kagan	B-12 mo.	A	U	30	20	LT,EE	Ter.
	83	Ordinal Scales of Cognitive Dev.	Uzgiris & Hunt	B-3 yr.	U	U	60	30	PP	Sec.
	86	Infant Intelligence Scale (CIIS)	Cattell	B-30 mo.	A	A	25	15	P	Sec.
	86	Bayley Scale of Infant Dev.	Bayley	B-30 mo.	A	A	45	25	P	Sec.
	88	Kuhlmann-Binet Infant Scale	Kuhlmann	B-30 mo.	A	A	30	15	P	Sec.
	88	Griffiths Mental Dev. Scale	Griffiths	B-4 yr.	A	A	30	15	P	Sec.
	89	Gesell Developmental Scale (Revised Scale)	Gesell, et al.	B-5 yr.	A	A	40	30	P	Sec.
	92	Ivanov-Smolensky	Luria	B-24 mo.	A	U	20	15	LT	Ter.
	93	Habituation	Lewis, et al.	B-18 mo.	A	A	30	15	PP	Sec.
	93	Psychophysiological	Crowell	B-3 mo.	A	A	80	50	Mix	Ter.
LAN- GUAGE	98	Playtest	Friedlander	3-12 mo.	A	A	50	25	LT,EE	Ter.
	99	Infant Cry Analysis	Ostwald, et al.	B-3 mo.	A	U	30	15	LT,EE	Ter.
	104	Expressive Language	Reyes, et al.	2-4 yr.	A	A	40	20	PP	Sec.
	108	Receptive Language	Marmor	1-3 yr.	A	U	30	15	PP	Sec.
	108	Early Language Assessment Scale	Honig & Caldwell	3-48 mo.	A	U	30	15	PP	Sec.
SOCIAL/ EMOTIONAL	114	Behavioral & Neurological Assessment Scale (II)	Brazelton, et al.	B-3 yr.	A	U	30	15	PP	Sec.
	114	Behavior Problem Checklist	Quay & Peterson	B-4 yr.	U	U	30	20	P	Sec.
	116	Rimland Diagnostic Check List	Albert & Davis	B-4 yr.	U	U	30	20	P	Sec.
	116	Behavior Checklist	Ogilvie & Shapiro	3-6 yr.	A	U	45	30	P	Sec.
	117	Quantitative Analysis of Tasks	White & Kaban	1-6 yr.	A	A	60	30	PP	Sec.
	118	Behavior Management Observation Scales	Terdal, et al.	B-4 yr.	U	U	60	20	PP	Sec.
	118	Vineland Soc. Maturity Scale	Doll	B-18 yr.	A	A	25	10	PP	Pri/Sec.
	118	Preschool Attainment Record	Doll	B-7 yr.	A	A	30	15	PP	Pri/Sec.
	119	Behavioral Categorical System	DeMyer & Churchill	2-5 yr.	A	U	30	20	P	Sec.
	125	Psychological Assessment: Functional Analysis	Bijou & Peterson	B-Adult	A	A	U	U	P or PP	Ter.
COMPREHENSIVE SYSTEMS	128	First Identification of Neonatal Disabilities (FIND)	Wulkan	B-12 mo.	U	U	U	U	U	All
	128	System of Comprehensive Health Care Screening & Service	Scurletis & Headrick	C-4 yr.	A	U	U	U	Mix	All
	132	Preschool Multiphasic Program	Belleville & Green	B-4 yr.	A	A	U	U	Mix	All
	136	Pluralistic Assessment Project	Mercer	5-11 yr.	U	U	U	U	U	Sec.
	140	Pediatric Multiphasic Program	Allen & Shinefield	Over 4 yr.	A	A	120	30	Mix	All
	143	Rapid Developmental Screening Checklist	Giannini, et al.	B-5 yr.	A	A	5	1	PP,P	Pri
	143	Guide to Normal Milestones of Development	Haynes	B-3 yr.	A	A	15	5	PP,P	Pri
	150	Developmental Screen, Inventory	Knobloch, et al.	5-18 mo.	A	A	20	10	PP,P	Pri
	153	CCD Develop. Progress Scale	Boyd	B-8 yr.	A	A	30	15	PP	Pri
	156	Denver Develop. Screening Test	Frankenburg & Dodds	B-6 yr.	A	A	30	15	PP	Pri
	16	At Risk Register	Alberman & Goldstein, Sheridan; Oppe; Walker	Pre-C	A	A	Neg	Neg	PP,LT	Pre-Pri.
	19	Risk Factors (Kauai Study)	Werner, Bierman & French	Pre-C to 12 yr.	A	A	Neg	Neg	PP	Pre-Pri.

NOTES:
1. Number of first page discussing topic in *Screening and Assessment of Young Children at Developmental Risk* (by Meier, J. H., Wash., D.C., Gov't. Printing Office, 1973).
2. C=Conception; B=Birth.
3. A=Adequate, i.e., >.75, when reported or estimated (only concurrent and face validity — not predictive).
4. U=Unknown — in any category indicates that data are either unavailable, too variable, or sparse.
5. Minutes required for administration and interpretation — estimated average with normally developing child.
6. Estimated total in dollars including time and materials under optimum conditions.
7. P=Professional trained to administer test(s); PP=ParaProfessional, properly trained; LT=Laboratory Technician; EE=Elaborate Equipment (in laboratory and usually not portable); Mix=Combination of preceding. A trained professional is required to interpret test results.
8. Recommended Stage in Screening System — Pri=Primary; Sec.=Secondary; Ter.=Tertiary; Pre-Before.
9. Neg.=Negligible amount of time or cost per child.

PHYSICAL FACTORS

Streamlining Routine Physical Exams and Lab Procedures

To gain some perspective on and appreciation for the multiple factors involved in physical screening, the Automated Multiphasic Health Testing and Services (AMHTS) program (Collen et al., 1970) is exemplary. A Pediatric Multiphasic Program for children 4 years of age and older, which is patterned after the AMHTS, includes behavioral parameters as well. It serves as an example of a comprehensive early screening system, provided that data collection techniques, valid predictive developmental indices, and computer-mediated analytic programs can be extended downward to birth.

Infants and very young children are even more difficult to screen and assess definitively because of the wide range of normal inter- and intra-individual variations as they rapidly grow and develop and also because of their inability to communicate their more subtle sensations and perceptions. Physical screening is often thought to yield the most definitive results among the developmental domains because of the apparent precision of the measuring units and procedures for some parameters. However, as pointed out by Williams (1970), even laboratory reports on measures such as blood sugar level are approximates. Rather than being reported as a single number, say 125, laboratory results should be reported to reflect the range of analytical deviation, thus 125 ± 10.

Automated medical examinations are now becoming fairly well debugged and widespread throughout the United States. Therapy programs are being linked to them in many instances. A modern health maintenance center functions like a luxurious assembly line and, with the assistance of paramedical personnel, analyzes all of the important factors in the adult patient's physical functioning. Such a process has promise for infant and child evaluations but will require considerable modification to use as reports from the relatively nonverbal and unsophisticated infant or from the child's caregivers. It may also require considerable attention to the issues involved in informed consent that fall under the ethical considerations that cannot be dealt with adequately here.

Genetics and Amniocentesis

Guthrie (1972), a pioneer in the development and use of bacterial inhibition tests for phenylketonuria, makes an eloquent case for not only continuing present neonatal screening procedures by also for expanding and further streamlining them. He writes from a knowledgeable and vast experience about several of the cardinal issues in mass screening, including yield, the economics of regional versus local analytic laboratories, automation, simultaneous multiple screening for approximately 40 detectable inherited anomalies, cost/benefit ratios, and the practical application of recent advances.

Another kind of screening automatically occurs when parents give birth to a child with any one of a variety of congenital defects, because both the parents and the physician are then alerted to the possibility of subsequent defective offspring. A Committee Work Group on Research and Prevention issued a report for the President's

Committee on Mental Retardation (1972), the bulk of which is a series of fact sheets organized with a synopsis of the condition, the population at risk, current technology, cost/benefit estimates, current needs, and recommendations for preventive intervention. The various conditions described as contributing to organic mental retardation and amenable to preventive procedures include narcotic addiction in pregnancy, maternal rubella, maternal diabetes, prematurity, lack of prenatal care, maternal iron deficiency, maternal malnutrition and protein deficiency, and adolescent or elderly mothers.

O'Brien (1971) indicates that there are 27 or more neurological diseases involving severe mental retardation that can now be identified and diagnosed during the fourth and fifth months of pregnancy. This is early enough for the safe termination of the pregnancy, if so desired, and it is crucial in order to alleviate the often unwarranted anxiety in a pregnant woman who has some increased likelihood of bearing a genetically defective child. O'Brien also points out that each of the diseases is individually very rare, but taken together they represent a noteworthy proportion of the organic causes of mental retardation and other developmentally disabling conditions. An example is Tay-Sachs disease, and many of the symptoms are described and the manner in which it is inherited is explained. Insofar as screening for this disease is concerned, it is possible to detect adult carriers of the recessive and debilitating genes by a simple blood test or skin test. O'Brien stresses the importance of amniocentesis, a procedure that is still in its early stages of widespread utilization, and, despite rare false positive findings (National Registry for Amniocentesis NICHD, 1975), is nevertheless a reliable and accurate technique for identifying several types of suspected anomalous conditions in the developing fetus.

A helpful booklet (Howell, Holtzman, and Thomas, 1969), excerpted from a thorough laboratory procedures book, is used in the biochemical screening laboratories of the Department of Pediatrics at The Johns Hopkins University School of Medicine in Baltimore and its University Affiliated Facility, the John F. Kennedy Institute for the Habilitation of the Mentally and Physically Handicapped Child. The booklet focuses only on those tests that are simple and practical to perform on large numbers of patients and excludes those tests that are routinely performed in most hospital central laboratories. The tests include: ferric chloride, qualitative dinitrophenylhydrazine, excessive concentration of urinary cystine and homocystine, nitrosonaphthol for increased urinary concentrations of parahydroxyphenyl catabolites, acid mucopolysaccharides, single dimension chromatography for serum amino acids, amino acid electrophoresis-chromatography, thin layer chromatography of sugars in urine, and assays for aryl-sulfatase A activity in urine.

There are some other promising ultramicro automated procedures for quickly and easily identifying newborn infants with a high probability of being or becoming mentally retarded or otherwise developmentally disabled because of organic causes (*Mental Retardation News,* Nov. 1971, p. 3).

The primary difficulty does not lie in administering these selected tests, but rather in coming up with a valid interpretation of their results. Differing levels of sophistication are necessary at different levels of the screening and assessment process. This chapter does not attempt to give a detailed account of the administration and/or interpretation of each test mentioned; rather, it will note its existence as a potentially good candidate for a massive screening system. Moreover, once a high risk or at risk pregnancy is detected or even suspected at various stages of screening, the far more complex and sophisticated assessment (e.g., O'Brien, Ibbott, and Rodgerson, 1968) for confirming the suspicions and differentially diagnosing their nature can be brought in to elaborate the diagnosis.

Nutrition

A report by Fomon (1971) illustrates the importance of knowing not only the child's nutritional status but also the community's nutritional characteristics (e.g., racial and ethnic food preferences, availability of vitamin-fortified bread and milk, iodized salt, and fluoridated water). He identifies routine physical examination and laboratory indicators of nutritional risk, which are spelled out in great detail and constitute little additional investment of time or money when done routinely. In addition, a relatively simple food intake questionnaire and rationale for certain laboratory procedures are presented in terms of massive screening.

Gestational Age

Lubchenco (1970), a pioneer investigator of the effects of prematurity, addresses the difficulties of assessing gestational age and development at birth and expresses hope that a more precise laboratory estimate of gestational age will soon be forthcoming. In spite of the relative imprecision of identifying and describing the small-for-date infant, various developmental charts depict the course of the postnatal growth of premature infants compared to their intrauterine growth. These charts indicate that the notion that these children "grow out" of their retardation, including retarded size and weight, is not supported by the data. In fact, in an earlier article by Lubchenco et al. (1963), many other sequelae to premature birth are identified as developmentally hazardous and manifest in conditions such as social and emotional problems and school learning disabilities. These findings should underscore the importance of identifying premature infants as being at risk for many different developmental disabilities and of following them closely because of the increased probability that they will develop handicaps whose severity is typically inversely proportional to their birth weight.

Statistical Mortality and Morbidity Risk Indicators

To increase the yield of any massive screening system, it is possible to do some preliminary screening by means of various census data. It is suggested that initial screening systems should concentrate on the populations from the highest risk locations that can be identified statistically because they produce the largest percentage of stillborn or defective children per 100,000 pregnancies. References such as the *MCH Exchange* (e.g., Pratt et al., 1972, pp. 37 and 48) and other compilations of national health statistics are very helpful in this determination. Further elaboration on the use of various demographic data to plan a comprehensive screening system for a hypothetical representative United States community of 100,000 is presented in a later section of this chapter.

After a given subset of the entire population is delineated for probable high yield, it is possible to zero in further on other factors that are highly correlated with children at developmental risk. By studying the characteristics of the birth and death population of a previous year, the characteristics of the high risk group can be established by asking each woman of childbearing age the following six critical questions:

1. What is your age?
2. How many years of education have you completed?
3. What is your marital status?
4. How many pregnancies have you had?
5. Have you had a previous fetal death?
6. Have you had a previous child born alive who is now dead?

The responses to these questions will classify each woman with respect to risk of fetal, neonatal, and postneonatal death. To apply such a system effectively, one should have a systematized concept of service that includes an effective outreach and follow up program (Scurletis and Headrick, 1972; Scurletis and Headrick, this volume).

In addition to corroborating some of the socioeconomic and ethnically related findings in the aforementioned statistical approach, de la Cruz and LaVeck (1970) summarize the preconceptual, prenatal, natal, and postnatal causes of developmental disabilities. After discussing these conditions and suggesting some modern management techniques, they proceed to address some challenging and broadening prevention considerations that are germane to the central theme of this chapter. They point out that the advances in medicine and improved health practices in the general population are reducing the demands for crisis treatment and increasing the emphasis on the growth and development of the total person.

Vision

One of the more comprehensive and thorough earlier studies of vision screening is *Vision Screening and the Preschool Child* (Savitz, Reed, and Valadian, 1964). Among many other conclusions and recommendations they, and more recently Lin-Fu (1971), discuss the difficulties inherent in coordinating the several levels and kinds of agencies, personnel, etc., for successfully mounting a massive vision screening program for very young children. One way in which a large group of paraprofessionals might become involved in the early screening of children's vision is suggested in a proposal that parents do the preliminary screening. Although some studies that were conducted using parents who were in middle and upper class socioeconomic strata seemed to work out reasonably well (Lin-Fu, 1971, p. 16 seq.), it is imperative that such studies be conducted in poverty populations, because they are the ones least likely to have other contact with health professionals or paraprofessionals. Nevertheless, the results of some of these preliminary studies are instructive and warrant further consideration and replication.

The chronic quest for physiological indices to intellectual functioning is somewhat encouraged by the correlations reported between eye movements during sleep, recorded by an electro-oculographic instrument, and learning capacities. Of course it is realized that electro-oculographic recording requires some sophisticated apparatus and trained technicians to operate it, thereby ruling it out as a primary or State I screening procedure. Nevertheless, such physiological indices, if proved to have a high predictive value in terms of learning capability (and in this case endocrine activity as well), might be routinely employed as secondary or tertiary screening procedures on children who are being evaluated in controlled situations for other conditions, because it is possible to make these recordings in the home as well as in a clinical setting. The development nature of this phenomenon is clearly illustrated by the large discrepancies shown between various age group clusters.

Data such as the above, along with electroencephalographic indices, promise to yield very early clues to central nervous system integrity, which undoubtedly has a high relationship to higher cortical and presumably cognitive functioning. Along these lines, Crowell (1973) has come up with some highly significant findings relating electro-encephalographic data to visual, auditory, and tactile stimulus-response parameters in infants, which is suggestive of even more sophisticated early estimates of CNS functioning. Such advances might enable secondary and tertiary screening to be accomplished with increased reliability and validity.

Hearing

Perhaps an even more elusive index to developmental disabilities is auditory functioning. In an article on selective hearing loss and some clues for its early identification, Holm and Thompson (1973) describe the difficulties of picking up selective hearing loss in the very young child. They cited one typical case:

> The child in this report was thought at various times to be mentally retarded, emotionally disturbed, and brain damaged before his selective hearing loss was discovered at age 5¼ years. He had developed puzzling behavior secondary to the confusing verbal messages he received and his unpredictability in turn had had a disturbing effect on his environment (p. 451).

In such cases, a high risk register may obviate the pernicious sequelae described above. Some fairly general observations about the benefits of a high risk register plus some specific findings and advantages from the use of such an approach are reported by Bergstrom, Hemenway, and Downs (1971) with reference to hearing loss and deafness that may be affecting as many as 100,000 children of school age in the United States. Along with the familiar litany of developmental red-flag phenomena, they cite some that are peculiar to deafness or hearing loss.

Of course, one of the primary reasons for undertaking early screening is to reduce the time intervening between the onset of a condition and the beginning of some appropriate treatment or prevention of further deterioration. One of the most impressive achievements of the risk register and subsequent screening and assessment is stated by Bergstrom,

Hemenway, and Downs (1971). Diagnosing and fitting children with hearing aids an average of 16 months earlier, as a result of the register, is a magnificent accomplishment.

Abused and Battered Children

Another group of children that should be screened as at risk are those with a high probability of being abused or battered (Helfer and Kemper, 1968). This syndrome has gained enormous visibility lately, and a national center, directed by Dr. C. H. Kempe, was established in 1973 at the University of Colorado Medical Center to investigate further its causes, management, and prevention.

According to a preliminary report (Walworth and Metz, unpublished), it does seem possible to identify children who are likely to suffer psychosocial or medical problems arising from often undetected physical abuse or less flagrant forms of parental mistreatment such as neglect, excessive pressure, cruel ridicule, etc. Using two new parent questionnaires as a part of the procedures for the Pediatric Multiphasic Examination, these investigators checked out parent satisfaction with the behavior of their child and the child's family background as it might relate to his emotional and physical well-being. The preliminary questionnaire findings were such that replication studies with larger numbers of subjects are certainly warranted because they do predict children who are very likely to suffer various kinds of parental mistreatment. Although no actual cases of child battering are reported, an identifiable group of subjects had a much higher incidence of accidental injuries, poisoning or swallowing of foreign objects, poor parental discipline, probable psychosomatic reactions, parent or teacher dissatisfaction, doctors' notations of parental neglect, and indications of the need for counseling. The parents of these children also reflected dissatisfaction with their children's behavior on the behavior questionnaire. If these findings are replicated in a larger and more carefully controlled study, such high-yield questionnaire items would certainly be important to include in the initial interview in a massive screening system.

Using an historical/sociocultural, as opposed to a clinical, approach to physical child abuse, Gil (1971) reveals the pervasiveness of the use of force in childrearing. He contends that the traditional use of violence in childrearing practices in America underlies physical abuse of children. He then places the issue of child abuse in the much larger perspective, which is what makes massive and comprehensive screening so important and at the same time so enormously complex and controversial:

> It is important to keep in mind that physical abuse committed by individual caretakers constitues a relatively small problem within the array of problems affecting the nation's children. Abuse committed by society as a whole against large segments of the next generation through poverty, discrimination, malnutrition, poor housing and neighborhoods, inadequate care for health, education and general wellbeing are far more dangerous problems that merit the highest priority in the development of constructive social policies (p. 394).

On the other side of the coin is an effort to identify children who are prone to violence, which in itself may be a developmental deviation and may precipitate battering or abuse in reaction to the expression of such violent tendencies. For example, the child who is violence-prone and expresses this through uncontrollable temper tantrums at an early age may become the subject of parental abuse and consequent additional handicaps. One novel way of detecting such children is related to deviations from normal speech sounds; these difficulties are reportedly associated with certain aberrant personality characteristics (Filippi and Rousey, 1971). Although such a relatively simple and brief procedure speaks primarily to one particular behavioral pattern of proneness to violence, it does seem to be the sort of painless, unobtrusive, and simple technique suitable for large scale screening, particularly if the yield in terms of other personality and health factors can be determined and reliably and validly elicited. The authors go on to point out that this relatively simple and nonthreatening procedure, using speech sound findings as indicators for potential behavior, should never be a substitute for comprehensive diagnosis but only as one of a series of indications that further evaluation and subsequent intervention be undertaken.

Neurological Screening

The state-of-the-art and science for screening and assessing the integrity of the nervous system in infants and toddlers is itself in need of considerable refinement. The subtle interrelationships between neurological dysfunction and behavior disorders in early child-hood is eloquently presented by Touwen and Prechtl (1970). These same distinctions are equally germane to the contents of all subsequent sections in this chapter, which emphasize the inextricable intersystem and interdisciplinary nature of any comprehensive screening endeavor.

Although Touwen and Prechtl (1970) go into great detail for doing a sophisticated differential diagnosis of hard and soft signs of neurological dysfunction, Brazelton (1973) has systematized and somewhat simplified the heart, or nerve, of the matter. The first page of his Neonatal Behavioral Assessment Scale is largely historical and organic in context, except for the optional "Descriptive Paragraph" section, while the second page is more concerned with the rating of observable behaviors in response to various exogenous and endogenous stimuli, some of which may be construed as being primarily cognitive, linguistic, and/or socioemotional precursors or customary indicators thereof (see following sections). This further emphasizes the importance and perhaps real feasibility of synthesizing a comprehensive multiple-purpose developmental screening system yielding maximum information with a minimum of redundancy. The data required for the completion of even the top of the first page and all of the second page of this Neonatal Behavioral Assessment Scale are germane to several of the preceding and subsequent factors mentioned in this chapter.

Indicative of the neurological/behavioral interface is the Neuro-Developmental Observation (NDO) procedure presented by Ozer et al. (1970) who are taking a highly pragmatic approach to learning problems in school age children. These frequently have their roots in early developmental disabilities. Their experience in using this problem-solving model is leading them to extend it downward for use with younger children. The

15-minute protocol, which in part has grown out of previous efforts to standardize neurological testing, makes use of interdisciplinary health personnel, parents, and teachers in the process of diagnosing and communicating what the child can do.

It is conceivable that the standardized collection of such data on all infants, with the addition of several other heavily weighted prognostic factors described through the chapter, would constitute a primary screening of young children at developmental risk, and could probably be accurately collected by trained paraprofessionals. The addition of these items to existing screening devices, none of which now includes them all, or the creation of supplementary scales, all of which would have to be standardized, is a next logical step in the development of the primary stage of a massive comprehensive screening system. Of course, secondary and tertiary screening and assessment of those children who emerge as borderline or worse would have to be carried out by progressively more sophisticated personnel and procedures. For example, an abnormal rating on several of the items that are highly related to seizure disorders could lead to the critically needed neurological assessment and diagnosis of these conditions at an earlier time. Arangio (1972) states:

> Adequate medical concepts exist in the literature which, if understood by physicians and parents, indicate that neurologic screening can detect, at the least, a suspicion of the presence of a seizure disorder in a child. In short, medical knowledge does exist, but the fact remains that screening doesn't exist . . . (p. 8).

Yet. And that is what this chapter is all about.

INTELLECTUAL/COGNITIVE FACTORS

The study of intellectual and cognitive functioning has been reserved for older children by the majority of investigators. This has had the prophecy-fulfilling result that most studies of intellectual and cognitive functioning have not focused on infants and toddlers because they presumably are preoccupied with simply reacting to sensory stimuli with their motor apparatus without thinking about the relationships between the stimulus and response events. Abstract thought processes cannot be observed, nor can infants and toddlers with minimal language give much verbal hint to the intervening processes that may be mediating their rather predictable responses to a controlled series of stimuli. Historically, Homo sapiens was not thought to be very wise, much less able to reason, until approximately the age of 7 years. Several developmental theories postulate that the early stages of development are exclusively sensorimotor, with essentially no cognitive functioning worthy of investigation occurring until sufficient language capacity has been achieved. In fact, the controversy continues to rage about whether or not an individual can think without having the necessary language to label and represent those events or phenomena about what he is thinking. Of course this chapter cannot treat the numerous subtle nuances of these esoteric debates, but they do serve to point up the inextricable interrelationships among physical, intellectual/cognitive, language, and socioemotional factors.

Despite the many preconceived notions about infant growth and development, several investigators on the cutting edge of this intellectual/cognitive area of inquiry have recently generated some evidence that is contrary to many earlier fatalistic anachronisms. A decade ago a rash of factor analytic studies (Meier, 1965) attempted to ferret out the salient dimensions of intellectual and related functions partly in the parsimonious interest of consolidating and simplifying the assessment of these functions within and across various age and ability subgroups. Another interest was that of creating more accurate assessment instruments and procedures for progressively younger children. Another article of the same vintage acknowledged the agonizingly tedious process of teasing out the factors that would be included in a comprehensive screening system. Meyers and Dingman (1966) state:

> As to next steps, it is believed that the factor content of existing scales has been nearly milked out, that further effort will have to be in the direction of hypothesizing and instrumenting for different groups and different levels, the directions guided by previous studies and adult models. Until it is possible to know what factors exist in continuity, they cannot be placed into age scales designed to reveal them longitudinally. Until more is known about emergence, no comparison of emergence can be accomplished. There is, in short, much to be done (p. 25).

Infant Cognition

More recently, Kagan (1972) reports a series of ingenious experiments, the results of which can be legitimately interpreted to substantiate that infants demonstrate considerable cognitive or hypothesis-forming abilities even before they are 1 year old. After marshalling a great deal of supporting evidence from other laboratories and presenting a compelling synthesis of results from his own investigations, Kagan concluded the article with some implications and suggestions related to early screening. He indicated that, contrary to the prevalent views of child developmentalists during the past 20 years, an infant may be quite thoughtful and able to resolve various discrepancies and even to solve problems:

> For example, the eminent Swiss psychologist Jean Piaget has argued that during the first 18 months of life an infant knows the world only in terms of his sensory impressions and motor activities. Cognitive development, says Piaget, begins after the sensorimotor period ends. These results provide a mild challenge to his view. The infant may be more thoughtful than most psychologists have surmised (p. 81).

Kagan recently promulgated claims about a carefully studied sample of Guatemalan Indian children reared in extreme environmental deprivation who, despite uniform retardation of about 4 months in cognitive and affective development during the first year and a half of life, at 11 years of age performed at levels comparable to American children on some very specific tests of recall and recognition, memory, perceptual and conceptual inference, and analysis. These findings led Kagan (1973) to assert a much greater plasticity in cognitive development than he and most other child developmentalists have acknowledged. They suggest major discontinuities in early cognitive development that interfere with any attempts to predict later ability from early testing.

In contrast is the study reported by Heber et al. (1972), in which more than 20 infants at high risk of becoming functionally retarded, largely because their mother's low intellectual and educational levels, received a thorough-going intervention program. At age 5 the experimental group not only avoided becoming retarded, as their matched controls have become (mean IQ in the 70s), they have achieved a group mean IQ approximating 120. Besides using standard measures of intelligence, this study has employed several additional measures of learning ability and language development that seem to have good predictive validity. When the study is adequately replicated with better controlled and described procedures and measures, there is hope that the better portions can become a part of a comprehensive screening system keyed to appropriate remedial/ preventive methods and materials.

In an article primarily concerned with the many intervention efforts and their results throughout the United States, Starr (1971) reiterates the importance of assessing not only the individual infant but also the context within which he is growing and developing in order to arrive at a contextual and more valid prediction of whether or not he stands some risk of developmental disabilities. Starr (1972) states:

> Historically, developmental psychology has dramatically turned in the last ten years from the maturational viewpoint of development espoused by Gesell and others toward a view which has varied between strict environmentalism and moderate interactionism. In general, psychologists have been most interested in environmental effects given the genetic status of a particular individual with whom they are dealing. Within this context they must assess the effects of environment and, if possible, eliminate deleterious enviroronmental effects while providing appropriate experience (p. 153).

Infant Test Instruments and Procedures

The literature makes increasingly frequent reference to Uzgiris and Hunt's (1966) instrument for assessing psychological development in infants and toddlers. This instrument was originally conceived to study the effects of specific environmental experiences on the rate and course of development in a group of experimental infants. Discussions by Uzgiris and Hunt (1966) illustrate the complexity and partial ordinality-ambiguity of interaction between individual infants and their environments. Some of the semantic nuances become evident when one compares Kagan's notions of representation and his aforementioned challenge to Piaget with Uzgiris and Hunt's interpretation of Piaget's notions of representation. Because a number of the behaviors that must be observed and interpreted are subtle and time-consuming to elicit, this instrument would presumably be a secondary or tertiary stage in the total screening and assessment process and applied only to those children who demonstrated developmental discrepancies on earlier, more gross, screens. Furthermore, the carefully sequenced and detailed approach of Uzgiris and Hunt, in spite of the controversies about semantics and ordinality of developmental unfolding, has lent itself very nicely to the assessment of growth and development during experimental studies on intervention.

Nevertheless, in the interest of equitable treatment and in light of important challenges such as Kagan's, it seems imperative that any studies investigating the salient factors in the cognitive growth and development of infants and toddlers cannot be restricted to the theoretical frame of reference espoused by any one investigator when there is sufficient evidence supporting other equally important factors in the behavioral repertoire of the subjects under study. A theoretically and practically balanced and comprehensive consideration of all intellectual/cognitive factors is needed, regardless of whether the concern is for screening and assessing children at risk of developmental disabilities or for evaluating the results of a carefully designed and implemented intervention and/or prevention program.

There are numerous other instruments that might well serve as the primary, secondary, or tertiary levels of screening for development in this realm (Thomas, 1970). One of the main difficulties with infant tests of intellectual/cognitive functioning is that most of the items for the infant and toddler have traditionally been based on and consequently biased toward sensorimotor functioning (reflecting the aforementioned controversial theories) and are, therefore, more highly related to subsequent sensorimotor development than to intelligence. Because of this, the predictive validity of infant tests has been so low that the results have routinely been regarded with well advised skepticism in terms of their ability to predict the level of intellectual functioning during later childhood, adolescence, and adulthood.

Two infant tests that have been subjected to extensive standardization procedures and have been used in secondary stages of screening and assessment are the Cattell Infant Intelligence Scale (Cattell, 1940) and the Bayley Scales of Infant Development (Bayley, 1969). One study by Erickson, Johnson, and Campbell (1970) investigated the interrelationships among scores on these infant tests when used with children who appeared to be having developmental disabilities. Their study states:

> Results indicated that the scores on the two infant tests were so similar and highly correlated that they might be considered interchangeable in diagnostic settings. Clinically, the Bayley presented advantages of a greater variety of items and separate mental and motor scales, while the Cattell took less time to administer and could be combined with the Stanford-Binet (p. 102).

Erickson, Johnson, and Campbell (1970) concluded that: 1) neither the Cattell Infant Intelligence Scale nor the Bayley Scales of Infant Development have satisfactory predictive validity for normal children or for secondary assessment of children referred through screening tests, 2) 2-year-old children seem to be more easily examined than 3-year-old children, partly because of their increased emotional instability during the third year, and 3) as Wechsler (1966) pointed out in defense of his intelligence scales when they were being challenged and ultimately dismissed in the New York school systems, IQ stability is very probably in large part a function of environmental stability and in no way predicts how a person might behave when the environment is radically modified toward greater enrichment or deprivation. Although frequently mentioned as being of great usefulness for following the impact of intervention efforts with developmentally disabled infants, the Kuhlmann-Binet Infant Scale (Shotwell, 1964) and the Griffiths Mental Development Scale (Lally, 1968) also suffer from a lack of predictive validity.

Prediction of Later Intellectual/Cognitive Functioning

In an article that might legitimately have been included in the later section dealing with socioemotional factors, because it also brings out their importance, Holden (1972) reported a study dealing with the prediction of mental retardation in infancy. His discussion concludes by reiterating the difficulties of using a single predictive factor such as the relatively primitive estimates of intellectual/cognitive functioning available for infants. Holden makes the point and backs it up with several studies, including his own data, that prediction of a group's mean intelligence from infant test results is far better than prediction of an individual's intelligence from his infant performance on intelligence tests. Holden used the Bayley scales in his study, which was part of the Collaborative Study of Cerebral Palsy, Mental Retardation, and Other Neurological and Sensory Disorders of Infancy and Childhood supported by the National Institute of Neurological Diseases and Stroke, although Holden notes that Bayley (1949), before initiating development of the scales bearing her name, found little in the early studies of mental development to indicate a significant positive relationship between *mental* ability in infancy and intelligence at a later age. In fact, Bayley concluded, "It is now well established that we cannot predict later intelligence from the scores of tests made in infancy" (Bayley, 1955, in Holden, 1972, p. 28) (italics by this author).

In contrast to the above, Holden presents some more encouraging findings; similar data must have encouraged Bayley to undertake the development and standardization of the elaborate scales bearing her name: "The problem of accurate prediction of mental development in normal infants has often been controversial. Out of a population 2,875 infants in the Child Development Study at Brown University, 230 subjects were followed to age 4 and 115 to age 7. Each child was 1 month or more below average on the Bayley Scales of Mental or Motor Development at age 8 months. At both ages 4 and 7, mean IQ scores were significantly lower than a control group of 150 children (Holden, 1972, p. 28).

Even the Gesell Developmental Scale (Gesell and Amatruda, 1974) works relatively well for differentiating infants in terms of their neuromotor development, aberrations of which frequently indicate organic causes of mental retardation. Evidence in support of this view has been offered by Dicks-Mireaux (1972) and Knobloch and Pasamanick (1960).

Holden (1972) further complicates the matter by noting that additional factors such as socioeconomic status of family and its members' emotional stability often contribute substantially to the accuracy of predicting developmental disabilities, particularly in borderline cases (see section on Social-Emotional Factors, this chapter).

Using a principal-components factor analysis of infant test scores, McCall, Hogarty, and Hurlburt (1972) continued to trace a path of predominant skills through infancy, suggesting that his path may represent the developmental progression of skills culminating in childhood intellectual skills. A developmental trend is identified as proceeding from "manipulating objects that yield perceptual consequences" to "social imitation of fine motor and verbal behavior" to "verbal labeling and comprehension" to "verbal fluency and grammatical fluency." The authors conclude their thorough-going analysis of the apparent futility of attempting to predict childhood intelligence from scores on extant infant tests by offering several observations that seem germane to the design of screening and assessment procedures for greater predictive validity.

As the child gets older, and the number and complexity of tasks to be mastered become more numerous and more like those that adult intellectual/cognitive functioning involve, it is easier to screen and to assess reliably and validly those who seem to be lagging behind normal intelligence. In a search of the literature dealing with assessment of young children, practically all of the 115 annotated references dealing with preschool tests, screening procedures, and standardized examination methods and materials dealt with children 3 to 6 years old. The listings range from standardized procedures for assessing self-concept to standardized neurologic examinations and numerous related inventories. This is also true of the listings found in Buros (1965 and 1972) but the reader is nevertheless referred to these classic references for further information. The *Head Start Collection* (Educational Testing Service, 1973), *CSE-ECRC Preschool/Kindergarten Test Evaluation* (Hoepfner et al., 1971), and a chapter by Gallagher and Bradley (1972) all provide information about instruments for those engaged in research or the direction of projects involving the same age group.

Changes in Infant State and Response Rate

In an effort to get at sheer intellectual/cognitive functioning in infants, Garber (1971) relates some of his experience with a promising Ivanov-Smolensky technique that simply requires the subject to squeeze a rubber bulb to register his response. He also mentions some of the problems encountered in testing cognitive functioning in very young children with the suggestion that some screening application be made of this technique after it has been further refined. Lewis, Goldberg, and Campbell (1969) have also attempted to obtain a "purer" measure of infant cognitive development, and they have also been influenced by Russian research, primarily that of Sokolov (1963). They argue that the rate of habituation of attention responses to a repeatedly presented signal provides an index of cognitive development. Specifically, more rapid habituation is interpreted to mean that the infant is processing information more effectively, forming a representation of schema of the event more rapidly, and thus is cognitively advanced compared with an infant who habituates more slowly. Lewis, Goldberg, and Campbell (1969) present a variety of evidence in support of this hypothesis, e.g., more rapid habituation among infants with Apgar scores of 10 than among infants with scores less than 10, correlations between rate of habituation at 1 year of age and Stanford-Binet IQ at 44 months (r = 0.46 for girls, 0.50 for boys).

In an effort to analyze the biological substrate that is the precursor and sine qua non of cognitive functioning, Crowell (1973) has been gathering and interpreting heart rate and electroencephalographic data as they are affected by carefully controlled auditory, visual, and tactile stimuli on several hundred newborns during the past decade. He was produced evidence suggesting a relationship between central nervous system integrity and subsequent cognitive functioning. Davis (1971), who has been investigating the same phenomenon with older children, cites the difficulties he has experienced in attempting to measure mental capacity through evoked-potential recordings, but has not abandoned the quest. Although such sophisticated procedures require elaborate and expensive equipment and trained technicians, they would seem quite appropriate for tertiary stage screening and assessment of infants who sensory sensitivities and reflex systems seem below par on other more gross behavioral levels. Thus, there are some promising investigations into psychophysiological measures of intellectual/cognitivie capacity, or at least its precursors, that can be obtained in infancy.

Of course, efforts such as the ones described above in this section require a certain amount of instrumentation and additional studies to streamline the administration for screening and to establish more firmly their validity and reliability. The difficulties in obtaining meaningful behavior of an intellectual/cognitivie kind from infants is attested to by all investigators in the field, and underlies the fact that most infant screening and assessment procedures focus primarily on the more easily elicited, observed, and meas-ured sensorimotor factors. The fact that such sensorimotor development does statistically correlate 0.70 or above with subsequent cognitive functioning, when the data for large groups of normally developing children are reviewed, contributes to a great deal of the confusion in the field, because an illicit conclusion is frequently drawn that a statistical correlation is the same as a cause-effect relationship. Although difficulties in eye-hand coordination or basic reflexes or achievement of gross and fine motor developmental milestones may in some instances reflect disturbance not only of lower brain functions but also of higher cortical functioning, it is quite possible for a person with severe sensorimotor problems to have totally intact higher cortical processes, as demonstrated by an intellectually bright quadriplegic or even a cerebral palsied child; conversely, a given child may be seriously intellectually impaired but be physically well coordinated and up to par in his gross and fine motor milestones. The all-brawn-no-brain syndrome is an exaggerated description of this.

This discussion of screening and assessment of early cognitive development should not close without an additional cautionary note. The state of the infant at the time of testing, that is, the degree of wakefulness and alertness, is an important confounding factor in practically all screening and assessment efforts and frequently has been overlooked. Thus, it is possible that a low score on some screening or assessment procedures may *not* be a function of some deficiency, but rather a function of the infant's being in a state inappropriate for that assessment at the time (Hutt, Lenard, and Prechtl, 1969).

LANGUAGE FACTORS

Receptive Language Development

As stated in the section dealing with intellectual/cognitive factors, in the past a child was not considered to be a thinking person until he had begun to express his thought in a verbal way. Within recent years, however, investigators have developed increasingly accurate and ingenious equipment and procedures for evaluating receptive language in infants and young children. After giving some notions of the state-of-the-art and science regarding the testing of a young child's ability to process auditory stimuli, Friedlander (1971) goes on to explain the value of his automated evaluation techniques for assessing selective listening in infants and young children:

> The principal results show that the two groups of normal children were more and more decisive in their rejection of the degraded sound tracks as the noise interference increased in intensity. However, the language-impaired children listened to both the normal and the increasingly incomprehensible sound tracks with almost identical degrees of attention. Furthermore, these children's total listening response time was just as high as that of the normal children, emphasizing the difference between them (p. 9).

Once again, the utilization of rather sophisticated apparatus is required to assess the selective listening patterns of infants, and even more elaborate instrumentation is required to get at the integration of sound with slight experiences and the interpretation of these normal and abnormal infants. Nevertheless, the screening, at perhaps the tertiary level, of infants in terms of their ability to relate what they see to what they hear would certainly provide a meaningful assessment and prediction of likely learning disabilities in subsequent years.

Butterfield and Cairns (1974) go beyond the assessment of the neonate's ability to discriminate speech and ask how impaired ability affects abnormal language development. They proceed to ask whether infants can be trained in speech discrimination, and they suggest that further experiments are needed to determine whether language intervention programs could be improved by training infants to discriminate speech. If not, why screen for such problems?

Diagnostic Significance of Infant Cry

Ostwald, Phibbs, and Fox (1968) present a review of published infant cry studies along with some of their own laboratory findings, which all tend to indicate that even the crying of infants has diagnostic value when subjected to careful analysis. Indeed, the infant cry is a person's first expressive language and has real meaning and communication value. Of the 24 studies they report from 1938 to 1967, 22 of them have been done since 1927, and over half since 1960. However, more definitive sonographic studies of normal and abnormal vocalization patterns during the first 6 months of life are necessary for predictive screening and assessment.

Expressive Language Development

A technique of assessing expressive language development for 3- to 4-year-old children is that of a sentence repetition task, such as the one developed by Reyes et al. (unpublished). This technique plus several others developed to assess the impact of a thorough intervention program (Heber et al., 1972), has considerable empirical validation in the sense that the experimental groups, which experienced considerable language enrichment, predictably and empirically performed better than did their control counterparts on various and sundry receptive and expressive language assessments. It does seem, from the data reported, that, although there is yet much to learn about factors of length in syntactic complexity, the results of the sentence repetition test may be used as a reasonable estimate of children's language functioning and, because of its straightforward and simple administration, it might actually serve as a part of a screening battery. In addition to the standardized technique of sentence repetition for assessing expressive language development, it is also considered important to determine how well a person can produce speech in a free and open situation. Bernard, Thelen, and Gerber (unpublished) have demonstrated some promising approaches to this on the same population, and their findings corroborate the developmental trends evident in other procedures.

Language Tests and Scales

Marmor (1971) has developed a manual for testing the receptive language ability of 1- to 3-year-old children. The portion of the test for 1- to 2-year-old children measures their ability to understand vocabulary words and to follow verbal instructions by responding to simple object labels and to more difficult labels for classes of objects by identifying their reference object. The instructions require the child to follow simple familiar commands and progress to the more difficult phases of carrying out more complex sequences of behavior. The test items draw upon several established picture vocabulary and language comprehension tests. The manual instructs the examiner in specific procedures in scoring information using the materials to assess receptive language ability. The final score for the 2- to 3-year-olds is expressed as a developmental age equivalent, and the reliability of interobservers in all cases exceeded 0.90, but the instrument still requires additional validation on the basis of longitudinal data before it can be used confidently in a massive screening and assessment project.

Another effort along these lines is found in the early language assessment scale developed by Honig and Caldwell (1966, Part I) and Honig and Brill (1970, Part II). These scales, complete with instructions and scoring or rating sheets, tap both the receptive and the expressive language of infants and toddlers. It is evident from reviewing the reports on the scales that they could be administered and scored rather easily by trained paraprofessionals and might serve as a good secondary stage of language development screening.

Language Screening: An Interdisciplinary Process

It has been repeatedly stated or implied that screening is a multistage procedure, and Grewel (1967) makes a cogent case for both an interdisciplinary and differential diagnosis:

> It is not sufficiently realized that many developmental delays in children must be regarded as belonging to developmental neuropsychology. Speech and language dis-

orders in children confront us with a special aspect of neurology and neuropsychology. The study of these disorders requires thorough knowledge of speech and
its disorders, articulatory as well as verbal. Whereas the neurological symptoms must
be ascertained, phonetic as well as linguistic analysis of the symptoms is necessary,
whereas the relation or correlation with psychological delay or deterioration must be
studied. Differential diagnosis is necessary (p. 864).

From the foregoing very cursory and incomplete review of some language factors, it
should be clear that there is much more to receptive language in infants than their ability
to hear sound and that there is more to their expressive language than the neurophysiological and neuroanatomical integrity of the speech mechanisms (see McNeill,
1970; Berry, 1969; Travis, 1971 for a much more extensive and intensive treatment of
the acquisition of the anomalies in language as explained by various developmental
approaches). Also, implicit throughout all of the comments about screening for developmental disabilities in receptive and expressive language, it must be remembered that
various associative processes are also inferred from the findings on studies of language
input and output. The actual integrity of the central nervous system in processing the
linguistic input properly, i.e., in efficiently categorizing, storing, retrieving, and asso-
ciating data, is still not systematically and scientifically measurable. It is nevertheless
conceivable that certain neurophysiological and electrobiochemical indices to central
nervous system integrity and overall efficiency will be forthcoming in the future. Studies
such as Crowell's (1973), reported in the previous section, are continuing to investigate
these brain behavior relationships, and it is anticipated that they will shed additional light
on the process of language acquisition.

Moreover, the interaction between heredity and environment in terms of language
development and its importance for optimum intellectual/cognitive functioning lead to
the next section dealing with the social and emotional manifestations that are equally
complex and interdependent with the other factors. This makes comprehensive and
massive screening and assessment of children at risk for any of the vast range of
developmental disabilities an extremely complex process.

As in other previously described sophisticated measures of fine phenomena, rather
elaborate instrumentation is required simply in order to analyze properly the characteristics of infant cries. A properly designed combination screening console may very well
allow much of the salient data from the several domains described in this chapter to be
collected and analyzed quite efficiently.

SOCIAL-EMOTIONAL FACTORS

Mother-Infant Attachment Dynamics

At a national conference on early screening and assessment, Starr (1973) summarized his
thorough review of literature and synthesis of current knowledge about the socioemotional developmental factors from birth to 2 years of age. He stated, "At the present

time there are few methods available which are useful in assessing social and emotional development during the first years of life" (p. 45). Starr went on to point out the multiple methodological and ethical difficulties involved in doing basic research on such clinical phenomena in very young children.

Germane to the socioemotional issues of early screening and assessment is a paper presenting a Neonatal Behavioral Assessment Scale by Brazelton (1973). Although this particular paper is addressed primarily to the neurologic "state" of the infant, its intent is to predict his later personality development, which is regarded for purposes of this chapter as largely socioemotional in nature. The first page of the rating scale, entitled: *A Neonatal Behavioral Assessment Scale* (1973), is almost exclusively physically oriented, and the behaviors to be rated on the second page are largely sensorimotor; thus, some discussion of the Scale is in the preceding section regarding Physical Factors. Nevertheless, the scoring sheet also rates things such as cuddliness, consolability, smiles, and general activity level, all of which may be variables contributing to the "sending power" (Murphy, 1968) of the infant and the consequent quality of interaction between him and his caregivers. The reactions that the neonate engenders in his caregivers may be quite predictive of later personality and social development. This example also serves to emphasize the difficulty of separating many of the screening procedures, which overlap several developmental domains.

Structured Parental Observations of Children

An alternative to observing infants and toddlers in order to screen and to assist their socioemotional developmental status is to rely upon the principal mothering adult in the child's life as an informant for completing various questionnaires, checklists, or inventories. One such instrument is a Behavior Problem Checklist (developed by Quay and Peterson, 1967), which has been used with a wide variety of child samples and whose results have been replicated many times in spite of somewhat less than desirable interrater correlations. With regard to the interrater correlations, which are highly variable, and the fairly extensive literature, which implies that parental recall is rather unreliable, Speer (1971) makes a pragmatic observation justifying a wide variability in data for a screening collection system and indicating a circumstantial analysis of any series of data gathering in this fashion. It would, indeed, complicate the process of selecting children at risk, because the degree of their risk estimate would be a function of idiosyncratic perceptions on the part of those reporting about them.

Such an approach might prove enlightening to findings such as those reported by Albert and Davis (1972) regarding the Rimland Diagnostic Checklist on which the discrimination of autistic, normal, and schizophrenic children is quite cloudly and even contradictory at times. It may be that the discrepant results on such checklists are to be expected and are dealt with in a constructive fashion as representing differences in general perceptions of a child, not only by parents of both sexes, but by any other caregiving adults who have primary relations with the child in varying circumstances. They assume that it is more reasonable to ascribe behavioral discrepancies to the reality of qualitative and quantitative differences in interaction patterns because of the phenomenological reporting and perceiving adult than to misperceptions on the part of that adult, because it is readily acknowledged that persons, including children, perform differently in different situations with different people (Gergen, 1972).

Social Adaptation, Maturity, and Achievement Ratings

A somewhat more complex checklist for assessing the social abilities of 1- to 6-year-old children has been developed and is in the process of being refined by Ogilvie and Shapiro (1969). The intent of the checklist is quite appropriate for a screening system. However, it probably would be very difficult to train paraprofessionals to use this checklist reliably and validly in its current form. An overall correlation coefficient of 0.87 was computed on paired one half hour observations of 20 children, ages 3 to 6, in seven preschools. This approach is desirable in that it samples current behavior and does not rely upon recall by parents or other caregivers. However, it does require a structured setting and well trained observers in order to obtain valid and reliable data.

Another approach to analyzing the behavior of 1- to 6-year-old children is in White and Kaban (1971). This systematic approach requires that the observer adopt the child's orientation in order to describe the purpose behind a wide variety of the child's efforts. The manual delineates and exemplifies the highly specific scoring criteria and cites several examples of various kinds of social tasks such as to please, cooperate, gain approval, procure service, achieve social contact, gain attention, and many others.

Some other measures of social adaptation, maturity, and achievement behavior have been organized and annotated by Mercer (1971). Three of these measures seem to offer promise in use at the primary or secondary levels of screening. The first was developed by Terdal (1970):

> Specifically, it relates to behavior management and describes standard observational techniques to be applied in evaluating mother-child interactions that may form a basis for teaching "alternative repertoires" for handling retarded children. Laboratory observations are suggested in addition to interview-based information. Two types of coding sheets are presented which take the form of a matrix coding system. Each employs a time-sampling technique, and taps the child's behavior as well as the parent's response to the child (p. 1).

The other two instruments mentioned by Mercer, which are complementary and obviously extend into several of the preceding developmental domains, are the Vineland Social Maturity Scales (Doll, 1963) and the Preschool Attainment Record (Doll, 1966). Emmerich's (1969) Parent Role Questionnaire also has the potential for being useful in this regard. However, the instrument has not yet been used, let alone validated, with other than middle class parents. The flexibility of being able to rely upon both informant and subject is helpful but would have to be controlled in any standard screening and assessment situation in which comparable data are being collected. Many of the items would be quite appropriate for inclusion in any primary screening questionnaire.

Prediction of Childhood Psychosis

It seems ironic that a conference concerned with high risk factors predictive of childhood schizophrenia was being held at the same time (October, 1972) as the Boston Early Screening and Assessment Conference. The irony lies in the fact that the schedulers for both conferences attempted to avoid as many potential conflicts for likely participants as possible and yet these two certainly competed, especially for some of the behaviorally-oriented members of the community of scholars. It is no great consolation to learn from several who attended the conference on schizophrenia that their collective conclusion was that there really are no valid and reliable predictors of schizophrenia for very young children. Regardless of the rather seductive overly simplistic theories, ranging from sheer organic etiopathology (see the Physical Factors section regarding the quest for a schizo-coccus) to purely environmental causes (such as the schizophrenogenic mothering syndrome), childhood schizophrenia is evidently not yet satisfactorily predictable from early infancy.

Nevertheless, progress is being made in separating young children into at least the more gross categories of psychotic versus nonpsychotic, which is a major task of a screening system. The differential diagnosis of psychotic conditions seems to hinge upon definitions, which in turn influence diagnostic systems and scales as reported by DeMyer et al. (1971).

The pendulum does seem to be swinging back in the direction of biophysiological substrates for many psychotic conditions in early chodhood. Early screening systems will have to make provision for testing and monitoring the infant/child's reactions to challenge in both behavioral and physiological parameters (Alpern, 1967; Small, DeMyer, and Milstein, 1971). Even the schizophrenogenic mother myth may be partially exploded on the basis of the maternal age factors, which appears to be the most salient finding in a study of parents of psychotic, subnormal, and normal children (Allen et al., 1971). Holding all other variables constant, parents of normals were significantly younger at the child's birth, which was an unexpected finding that implied a neurologic and/or genetic link between autism and subnormality.

Functional Analysis for Intervention

In a summary at the end of their paper, Bijou and Peterson (1968) weave together a number of loose ends from the preceding commentaries on various screening and assessment instruments and procedures. Their remarks are not exclusively related to socioemotional factors. Although their emphasis on follow up may not be apropos to screening per se, it is extremely important in the evaluation of whether or not a screening and assessment procedure is leading to accurate identification of children in such a way that description of their problems is sufficient for instituting remediation and/or prevention. This can only be determined on the basis of the efficacy of the treatment program, which is presumably matched to the diagnosis.

COMPREHENSIVE DEVELOPMENTAL SCREENING SYSTEMS

Early Identification and Intervention

This section is primarily concerned with ongoing or proposed endeavors to identify children at developmental risk in a systematic and comprehensive way. The preceding four sections have each, for the most part, included only a limited domain of growth and development and generally excluded the others, so that no one of them addressed the entire range of vicissitudes experienced by the developing human being. It seems appropriate to begin by quoting some notions advanced by Ingram (1969):

> The ways of recognizing congenital handicaps are changing, and the act of diagnosis which depended on the recognition of fully developed clinical syndromes has been increasingly superseded. More and more often handicaps are recognized at routine examinations during infancy or because patients are considered to be "at risk" or suffering from them, and so are followed up (p. 279).

A fairly simple beginning approach to what is being said by Ingram is referred to as the *First Identification of Neonatal Disabilities* (FIND) program described by Wulkan (unpublished) and primarily focused on organically retarded children and their families.

Screening as a Part of Total Service System

A somewhat more advanced conceptualization of the problems involved in a screening system and some suggested solutions are offered by Scurletis and Headrick (1972) and Scurletis and Headrick (this volume). Their System of Comprehensive Health Care Screening and Service for Children employs different levels of screening throughout and is designed to reach out and identify the high risk child and family and to introduce them into the appropriate service system. The use of the system has helped to define many of the characteristics of mothers and families who produce high risk children. These are elaborated by Scurletis and Headrick (this volume).

A preschool multiphasic screening program in rural Kansas is described by Belleville and Green (1971). This system, which is sponsored by the Kansas State Department of Health, was designed to make planned wellness care more accessible to the spread-out rural population. After getting promising results from a preliminary pilot program to identify vision and hearing problems in 3- to 5.5-year-old children and receiving endorsement from the appropriate community agencies, the program has continued to grow. It now serves more counties and has broadened its goals to detect deficiencies of the special senses, mental retardation, emotional and/or behavioral disorders and physical, nutritional, social, and economic deprivation.

Screening in a Pluralistic Society

Although intended for purposes other than the design and development of a screening and assessment system and focused on children 5 to 11 years of age, Mercer (1972) has a number of enlightening findings. The study was fundamentally an epidemiological one to determine the prevalence of mental retardation in Riverside, California. She distinguished between clinical versus social system perspectives and statistical versus pathological models for defining what is normal. Warren (1973) added an engineering model for defining what is normal when discussing normalization and deinstitutionalization. Some of the ethnic implications of screening systems were also pointed out in Mercer's study. In addition to offering some answers to numerous questions about the interaction of ethnic and sociocultural and socioeconomic factors with performance on intelligence tests, this study project is producing several other results relevant to screening and assessment programs in a pluralistic society.

As the pluralistic assessment project generates the products and answers the questions it is designed to tackle, these results will have many applications to earlier screening and assessment efforts as well. The proceedings from a conference sponsored by Educational Testing Service (1973) squarely or at least obliquely faced many of the current social issues in testing. The interpretation of all screening data obtained from minority ethnic groups and lower socioeconomic status populations will have to be weighed in accordance with the relative contributions to the variance that are attributable solely to the environment and that exercise considerable influence on subsequent adaptive behavior. Some of the variables included in fairly interpreting these data number some 520 items in the Adaptive Behavior Inventory for Children (Mercer, 1972). As listed, they would not be appropriate for infants and toddlers, and a downward extension of some of these items would not be feasible; but they do illustrate some other family, neighborhood, and community dimensions that must be taken into consideration.

A Prototype Total System for School-age Children

An exemplary Pediatric Multiphasic Program (Allen and Shinefield, 1969) for children over 4 years of age is designed to administer a series of screening tests in a single visit and has been conducted by the Permanente Medical Group at the Kaiser Foundation Hospital in San Francisco since 1967. The Pediatric Multiphasic examination requires about 1.5 hours and very systematically obtains data in the following parameters: electrocardiogram; blood pressure and blood pulse; bone age by wrist roentgenograms; anthropometry, including various bone diameters, height, and weight; visual acuity; respirometry, including spirometry tests for which adaptations for younger children are now being made; audiometry; intelligence tests, including screens for various learning disabilities; drawing tests, including the Draw-a-Person and the Bender-Gestalt to look for perceptual-motor and conceptual deficiencies; Tuberculin Tine Test; throat and nose cultures for streptococcus; blood tests using an automated blood analyzer; urine tests allowing some prospective studies; neurological maturity scale; and a behavior inventory, which is reponded to be the parent and addresses the areas of sensorimotor development, learning, communication skills, social rapport, interests, creativity, responsibility, and symptomatic behavior. One month after all of the multiphasic testing is completed, the parent returns for interpretation of the results and physical examination of the child by a pediatrician who now has all of the data analyzed by a computer.

When comprehensive screening and assessment systems are planned, there are many helpful considerations contained in the *Provisional Guidelines for Automated Multiphasic Health Testing and Services, Vol. 2, Operational Manual* (Collen et al., 1970), in which several quality control suggestions are contained. For example, the selection of tests for the physical factors (or any other developmental domain) must be in keeping with several clear-cut criteria:

(1) Consideration of reproducibility or precision (consistency of repeated measures); accuracy or validity (true measurment); sensitivity (percent of true positives); and specificity (percent of true negatives)

(2) Yield rate (of previously unknown, or known but uncontrolled conditions) sufficient to provide an acceptable cost per positive case

(3) Minimum physician time for processing

(4) Acceptable to the patient (harmless, reasonable time)

(5) Useful for medical care, or research

(6) Completeness (adequately comprehensive to satisfy users' needs) (Collen, in Collen et al., 1970, pp. 6–7)

A problem commonly raised in most discussions of massive screening is that a standard method for examinee identification is needed that is unambiguous, immutable, and relatively simple. This becomes particularly critical when automation plays an increasingly larger role in the retrieving and processing of data for a large number of relatively mobile infants and toddlers at random intervals.

An example of the use to automation and rather sophisticated instrumentation for screening at the secondary or tertiary level and that is applicable to young children is a technique referred to as phonocardiography, which is actually more accurate than its nonautomated counterpart. Nevertheless, the limitations of automated interpretation of electrocardiographs and vectorcardiographs is acknowledged and cited as an area in which more adequate computer programs must be developed. Other comments relevant to massive screening in general are contained in the aforementioned AMHTS operational manual (Collen et al., 1970) as specifically related to visual acuity, hearing acuity, and anthropometry.

Some of the best developed and empirically validated patient data coding and retrieval forms have also been composed for the Permanente Medical Group's Pediatric Multiphasic Testing Program. These forms are workable data-gathering instruments and enable computer printouts from the correlated storage and retrieval systems to be used and interpreted by a wide variety of appropriate professionals and paraprofessionals. The standardization of data recording across multiple parameters, some of which are digital and others nondigital, is a slow process. Once meaningful and helpful data are at the fingertips of those desiring it, their subsequent cooperation in collecting data in a standard form is markedly improved.

Judging from the efficacy of many early intervention programs (Heber et al., 1972; White et al., 1973), which have the benefit of early differential diagnosis of developmental disabilities, the attendant cost in design and development of such instrumentation would be very small compared to the savings in human functional competence. Cost/

benefit analyses may likely indicate that only a few regional screening centers be established for conducting the tertiary stage screening and assessment and for coordinating the primary and secondary stage screening. Some members of the network of university-affiliated facilities would be eminently well qualified to serve in this capacity.

Multifactorial Developmental Screening Techniques

Because nearly all comprehensive and massive screening programs contain provisions for assessing the developmental progress of children, it is important that some consideration be given to the current status of the multifactorial measuring instruments, methods, and materials now available for doing this. Furthermore, a broad definition of developmental domains is addressed in preceding sections.

The more familiar tests and scales devised by Bayley, Binet, Cattell, Doll, Gesell, Griffiths, Wechsler, and others are briefly described and discussed in previous sections of this chapter. However, each tends to concentrate its indepth assessment on only one or two factors of the developmental domain and requires considerable time and training to administer properly, thereby disqualifying each as a primary screen. At least six new instruments warrant exposition and consideration as primary or secondary level screening instruments. These include the Rapid Developmental Screening Checklist, Guide to Normal Milestones of Development, the Developmental Screening Inventory, the Boyd Developmental Progress Scale, the Denver Developmental Screening Test, and the Progress Assessment Chart.

A very simple and straightforward checklist consisting of 40 items covering the age range from 1 month to 5 years of age was developed by the Committee on Children with Handicaps of the New York Chapter of the American Academy of Pediatrics (Giannini et al., 1972). Called the Rapid Developmental Screening Checklist, this one-page instrument has some brief instructions at the top and is designed to be used by a physician or aide. Once the norms are better established and appropriately adjusted, it might serve as a primary stage screening instrument for a widespread canvasing of a large population in a massive screening and assessment program.

An ingenious device, originally designed by Haynes (1967) for use by nurses dealing with infants and newborn children, serves as a handy reference and perhaps as the basis of a primary screening system:

> The wheel consists of two discs fastened at the center so that they can be rotated one upon the other. A wedge-shaped opening in the top disc permits a view of a section of the bottom disc. On the top disc are listed basic reflex patterns. The bottom disc is divided into 11 wedge sections—one each for the 1st, 2nd, 3rd, 4th, 6th, 9th, 12th, 15th, 18th, 24th, and 36th months of age. As the wheel turns, symbols appear on the bottom disc next to the names of the reflex patterns printed on the top disc; these symbols indicate whether the reflex is present (+), absent (0), evolving or diminishing (±) at that particular stage of development (p. 55).

Also appearing in the wedge-shaped windows are abbreviated statements of some of the major milestones of development for that age.

A more thorough version of a developmental screening instrument, divided into 21 4-week periods spanning approximately 18 months of age, was created by Knobloch, Pasamanick, and Sherard nearly a decade ago and reported by Haynes (1967). The Developmental Screening Inventory breaks each 4-week segment into adaptive, gross motor, fine motor, language, and personal-social categories. Provision is made for recording responses as present, absent, or unknown and whether based upon observation or caregiving adult's report.

The Boyd Developmental Progress Scale (Boyd, 1974) consists of 150 items, some of which are ascertained through parent interview. It is not intended to measure all developmental units, but it is focused on practical and useful developmental skills that are know to emerge at a given age and are related to daily living or are related to subsequent efficiency of adaptive behavior. It is one of several efforts stemming from the early 1960s to describe, pictorially, developmental progress, thus avoiding the errors and misinterpretations involved in age equivalents or quotient scores. As Boyd (1974) describes it:

> The *Boyd Developmental Progress Scale* is a screening device and may be given by any discipline among the helping professions (assuming reasonable care in following the directions). The results are combined in one visual report pictorialized on one page. Follow-up treatment can focus on the *development of desirable "next step"* or *remedial behaviors*. In short, the results should lead to meaningful action—whether more precise diagnosis, more realistic expectations, or more meaningful treatment or training (p. 3).

A review of the literature indicates that validity and reliability studies done on developmental scales have not been widely undertaken or reported and the results are frequently not impressive. An exception to this is the Denver Developmental Screening Test, which has been subjected to relatively extensive and intensive reliability and validity studies. Frankenburg et al. (1971a) state:

> Tester-observer agreement and test-retest stability of the Denver Developmental Screening Test (DDST) were evaluated with 76 and 186 subjects, respectively. The correlation coefficients for mental ages obtained at a 1-week interval were calculated for 13 age groups between 1.5 months and 49 months. Coefficients ranged between .66 and .93 with no age trend displayed (p. 1315).

Of course, regardless of how reliable and easily administered a test is, it is far more crucial to be certain that it is measuring what it claims to be measuring and is, therefore, valid. Frankenburg et al. (1971b) comment:

> In view of the widespread use of the Denver Developmental Screening Test (DDST) for screening the development of preschool aged children, a study was undertaken to evaluate the validity of the DDST. Two hundred thirty-six subjects were evaluated with the DDST and the following criterion tests: Stanford-Binet, Revised Yale Developmental Schedule, Cattell, and the Revised Bayley Infant Scale. Correlations of mental ages obtained with the DDST and the criterion tests varied between .86 and .97. Scoring the DDST as normal, questionable, and abnormal agreed very highly with IQs or DQs obtained on the criterion tests (p. 475).

Most studies conducted that employed the DDST are generally supportive of the instrument in terms of face and concurrent validity. However, in line with some of the preceding remarks in this and earlier sections, concern was expressed about its predictive validity, particularly with minority ethnic groups in poverty settings (Sandler et al., 1970; 1971). One large study (Black, 1971) involved 1,629 preschool children, about equally distributed in age from early infancy through 5 years of age, with a significant swing toward lower SES, as determined by Hollingshead's Two-Factor Index of Social Position (1957), which takes both income and educational level of parents into consideration. This study also partially questions the validity of the DDST as normed and scored for this population. Black (1971) states:

> According to the President's Committee on Mental Retardation (1969), three-fourths of the nation's mental retardation is found in rural and urban low-income, disadvantaged areas. Only 6 percent of the children in the study showed less than normal development as determined by the DDST. This is perhaps less than what one would expect for a population of children having approximately 80 percent in social classes IV and V . . .. (p. 58).

The validation of screening instruments and systems had been undertaken with older preschool and elementary school children (Bakalis, 1972; Denhoff et al., 1969; Hoffman, 1972; Meier, 1971; Sandler, 1972; Wyatt, 1971) and might prove instructive for designing validation studies with infants and younger children. It can be readily determined from Table 1 and the preceding narrative that there are very few, if any, adequate single instruments for primary or subsequent screening and assessment of young children at developmental risk. However, a careful combination of such instruments at appropriate stages and chronological ages promises to compromise a satisfactory comprehensive identification system.

Beyond the Paralysis of Analysis

When a satisfactory comprehensive developmental screening system has been field-tested and thoroughly debugged, it is only useful if it plugs into practical intervention programs. Several successful intervention programs have been reported in the literature. Table 2 presents a matrix of screening, evaluation, and intervention considerations in a composite and essentially self-explanatory format. It is obviously beyond the purview of this chapter to elaborate upon the various procedures, instruments, and model programs indicated at various strategic points in the matrix. Needless to say, it is most desirable for any potential subject in this system to begin and remain normal, thus progressing down the left column. However, for those who yield positive screening results and are subsequently found to have bona fide developmental delays or disabilities, the sooner they are identified and placed in proper matched remediation/prevention programs (examples of which are mentioned in the right column), the better it is for the child, the professional, and the society. Because individual subjects and individual professionals and paraprofessionals bring various requirements to each case, several options are mentioned in the evaluation and intervention columns. This entire chapter, therefore, indicates that considerable additional research must be done regarding optimum matches among and most efficacious approaches to screening, evaluation, and intervention for young children at developmental risk.

TABLE 2
SCREENING, EVALUATION, AND INTERVENTION
FOR YOUNG CHILDREN AT DEVELOPMENTAL RISK*

I Age	II Satisfactory Progress If not →	III Screening and Risk Assessment If screening results or risk factors are positive →	IV Evaluation, Close Observation and Diagnosis to →	V Intervention and Follow-Along →
PRE-CONCEPTUAL	Intent to Conceive Adaptive & Physiological Readiness (Normal Maternal & Family History)	Presence of One or More Maternal Risk Factors: Physical/Medical 1. Malnutrition 2. Age < 16 or > 35 3. Poor Reproductive History 4. Suspect Metabolic and/or Genetic Disease Social/Behavioral 1. Low SES 2. Sixth Grade Education 3. Functionally Illiterate 4. Low Adaptive Behavior Rating	Nutritional/Metabolic Tests Derive Genetic Pedigree Literacy/Educ. Tests Adult Adaptive Behavior Rating (Nihira)	Genetic Counseling (Sterilization) Diet Therapy Contraceptive Counseling (Planned Parenthood) Maternal Training (Jr. & Sr. High School)
PREGNANCY (first 3 mo)	Request for Service (suspected pregnancy confirmed) Regular OB/GYN Checks Normal Progress	Complications During Pregnancy: 1. Infections 2. Rubella 3. Toxemia 4. Drug Overuse 5. Radiation 6. Blood Incompatibility 7. Malnutrition 8. Maternal Psychosis 9. Unwanted Pregnancy	Appropriate Medical Tests to Evaluate Maternal & Embryo Condition Amniocentesis Social/Behavioral Tests of Maternal Ability and Attitudes	Counseling Therapeutic Abortion Psychotherapy
(last 3 mo)	Regular OB/GYN Checks Normal Progress	Above First Request for OB/GYN Services	Evaluation of Maternal and Fetal Condition	Counseling Positive Attitude (Natural Childbirth)
NEWBORN (first month)	Hospital Admission Normal History of Pregnancy and Routine OB/GYN Checks Uneventful Delivery	Complications During Delivery: 1. Hemorrhage 2. Dystocia 3. Excessive Anesthesia 4. Trauma 5. Placental Damage 6. Cesarean 7. Premature (SGA) 8. Postmature 9. Hospital Admission with no Prior OB/GYN Checks	Appropriate Medical Tests to Evaluate Maternal & Infant Condition	Necessary Procedures to Insure Maternal and Infant Viability
INFANCY	Normal Neonatal Growth & Development	Pediatric Physical and Developmental Exam: 1. Apgar (5 min.) 2. Metabolic/Genetic Screens (e.g., PKU) 3. Trauma 4. Infection 5. Malnutrition 6. Head Circumference 7. Guide to Normal Milestones of Development (@ 1 mo.)	Behavioral & Neurological Assessment Scale (Brazelton & Horowitz, @ 1 mo.) Environmental Quality Maternal Attitude & Aptitude (Below for Specifics)	Sensory Stimulation Behavior Modification Environmental Enrichment Maternal Training (Below for Specifics)

		Physical			
INFANCY	Monthly Well-Baby, Physical and Developmental Checks (1st year)	Physical: 1. Trauma 2. Infection 3. Diseases 4. Malnutrition 5. Vision 6. Hearing 7. Maternal Postnatal Depression/ Rejection, Neglect and/or Abuse 8. Prolonged Separation of Infant from Mother	**DQ** — Albert Einstein Scales of Sensori-Motor Development Fantz-Nevis Visual Preference Test White-Held Visually-Directed Prehension Test Gesell Developmental Scale Bayley Scale of Infant Development	Bobath & Ayres (Physical Therapy) Gordon (Home Learning Center — Florida) Gray et al. (DARCEE) Heber & Garber (Milwaukee Project) Keister (North Carolina Infant Day Care) Lally & Honig (Syracuse Infant Project) Levenstein (Mother-Child Home Program) Parent-Child Center Programs (Costello, Holmes) Meier et al. (Education System for High-Risk Infants) Robinson (Frank Porter Graham Infant Project) Weikart & Lambie (Ypsilanti-Carnegie Infant Education Project) White & Kaban (Brookline) Haynes (United Cerebral Palsy Assoc. Infant Stimulation Projects) Bureau of Education for the Handicapped, First Chance Network	
			Cognitive Q — Ordinal Scales of Cognitive Development Griffiths Mental Development Scale Kahn Intelligence Tests Infant Rating Scales (Hoopes) Kuhlman-Binet Infant Scale Infant Intelligence Scale		
	Normal Progress Bi-Monthly Physical and Developmental Checks (2nd year)	Developmental 1. Rapid Developmental Screening Checklist (@ 6 mo and 1 yr) 2. Developmental Screening Inventory (@ 18 mo) 3. Developmental Progress Scale (@ 12, 18, 24 mo) 4. Denver Developmental Screening Test (@ 12, 18, 24 mo) 5. Behavior Problem Checklist (@ 24 mo)	**Environ./ Parent Q** — Caldwell (A Procedure for Patterning Responses of Adults and Children — APPROACH) Parental Attitude Research Instruction Parents' Attitude Scale Wechsler Adult Intelligence Scale (WAIS)		
			Language Q — Irwin Speech Sound Development Test Prelinguistic Infant Vocalization Analysis (Ringwell, et al.) Shield Speech and Language Development Scale Early Language Assessment Scale (Honig) Receptive-Expressive Emergent Language (REEL, Bzoch)		
			Ach. Q — Preschool Attainment Record (Caldwell)		
			P/N Q — Psychophysiological/Neurological Maturity (Brazelton, Crowell)		
			Soc./ Behav. Q — Vineland Social Maturity Scale (Doll) Emotional Maturity Adaptive Behavior Scales (Nihira) Pluralistic Assessment (Mercer)		
TODDLER – EARLY CHILDHOOD	Periodic Physical and Developmental Checks (approximately every 6 mo.) Normal Progress	Pediatric Physical Exams (see above considerations) Developmental Screens (Nos. 4–6 above); Peabody Picture Vocabulary Test; Goodenough-Harris Draw-A-Person	Preschool Inventory (Caldwell) Leiter International Performance Scale Slosson Intelligence Test Raven's Coloured Progressive Matrices Stanford-Binet Intelligence Scale Developmental Articulation Test (Hejna) Illinois Test of Psycholinguistic Abilities (Kirk & McCarthy) Verbal Language Development Scale (Mecham) Developmental Test of Visual-Motor Integration (Beery) Developmental Test of Visual Perception (Frostig) Detroit Tests of Learning Aptitude Minnesota Preschool Scale IPAT Test of G-Culture Fair (Cattell) Arthur Point Scale of Performance Tests California Tests of Mental Maturity and Personality Metropolitan Readiness Test Oseretsky Tests of Motor Proficiency Weoman Auditory Discrimination Test	Model Preschool Programs (by last names of developers — for designation, see sources below). Anderson & Bereiter Blank Hooper Kamii Karnes, Zehrbach, & Teska Meier Miller & Camp Montessori Nedler Nimnicht Palmer Robison Shaeffer & Aaronson Weikart Whitney & Parker	

*Developed by Meier for California Governor's Conference on Prevention of Developmental Disabilities, 1973, pp. 23–24.

SOURCES: Battle and Ackerman (1973); Guthrie and Horne (1971); Hoepfner, Stern, and Nummedal (1971); Meier (1973a and 1973b); Parker (1972); and Williams (1972).

LITERATURE CITED

Albert, R. S., and A. J. Davis. 1971. A reliability study of interparental agreement on the Rimaldn Diagnostic Checklist. J. Clin. Psych. 27: 499–502.

Allen, C. M., and H. R. Shinefield. 1969. Pediatric multiphasic program. Amer. J. Dis. Child. 118: 469–472.

Allen, J., M. K. DeMyer, J. A. Norton, W. Pontius, and E. Young. 1971. Intellectuality of Parents of Psychotic, Subnormal, and Normal Children. J. Autism Child. Schiz. 1(3): 311–326.

Alpern, G. D. 1967. Measurement of "untestable" autistic children. J. Abnormal Psych. 72(6): 478–486.

Arangio, A. 1972. Working paper on adequate neurological examination of all preschool age children. Epilepsy Foundation of America (unpublished). Washington, D.C.

Bakalis, M. J. 1972. Illinois program for screening for learning disabilities. Interim 3: 1–2.

Battle, C. U., and N. C. Ackerman. 1973. Early Identification and Intervention Programs for Infants with Developmental Delay and Their Families: A Summary and Directory. National Easter Seal Society for Crippled Children and Adults, Chicago.

Bayley, N. 1949. Consistency and variability in the growth of intelligence from birth to 18 years. J. Gen. Psych. 75: 165–196.

Bayley, N. 1969. Bayley Scales of Infant Development. Psychological Corp., New York.

Belleville, M., and P. B. Green. 1971. Preschool Mutliphasic Screening Programs in Rural Kansas. Presented at the American Public Health Association, Annual Meeting, School Health Section, October 13, Minneapolis, Minn.

Bergstrom, L., W. G. Hemenway, and M. P. Downs. 1971. A high risk registry to find congenital deafness. Otolaryng. Clin. No. Amer. 4: 369–399.

Bernard, M. E., M. O. Thelen, and H. L. Garber. The Use of Gross Feature Tabulation for the Analysis of Early Language Development (unpublished). University of Wisconsin, Madison.

Berry, M. F. 1969. Language Disorders of Children. Appleton-Century-Crofts, New York.

Bijou, S. W., and R. F. Peterson. 1968. The Psychological Assessment of Children: A Functional Analysis. In Paul McReynolds (ed.), Advances in Psychological Assessment, III, pp. 63–78. Science and Behavior Books, Palo Alto.

Black, R. B. 1971. Final Report: Early Identification of and Intervention for Handicapped Children. Appalachian Regional Commission, Project No. FY–70. Ohio University, Athens.

Boyd, R. D. 1974. The Boyd Developmental Progress Scale. Inland Counties Regional Center, Inc., San Bernadino.

Brazelton, T. B. 1973. Neonatal Behavioral Assessment Scale. Lippincott, Philadelphia.

Buros, O. K. (ed.). 1965 and 1972. The Sixth and Seventh Mental Measurements Yearbook. Gryphon Press, Highland Park.

Butterfield, E. F., and G. F. Cairns. 1974. Discussion summary: Infant reception research. In R. L. Schiefelbusch and L. L. Lloyd (eds.), Language Perspectives–Acquisition, Retardation, and Intervention, pp. 75–102. University Park Press, Baltimore.

Cattell, P. 1940. The measurement of intelligence of infants and young children. Psychological Corp., New York.

Collen, M. F., and G. R. Cooper. 1970. Summary of the Workshop on the Subcommittee Report. In M. F. Collen, R. Feldman, J. Barbaccia, J. Dunn, R. Greenblatt, and A. Mather (eds.), Automated Multiphasic Health Testing and Services, pp. 95–96. U.S. Government Printing Office, Washington, D.C.

Collen, M. F., R. Feldman, J. Barbaccia, J. Dunn, R. Greenblatt, and A. Mather. 1970.

Introductory Statement: Provisional guidelines for Automated Multiphasic Health Testing and Services, pp. 1–3. U.S. Government Printing Office, Washington, D.C.

Crowell, D. H. 1973. Screening and assessment in the cognitive intellectual area. *In* J. H. Meier (ed.), Background Papers of the Boston Conference: Screening and Assessment of Young Children at Developmental Risk, pp. 18–35. U.S. Government Printing Office, Washington, D.C.

Davis, F. B. 1971. The Measurement of Mental Capacity through Evoked Potential Recordings. Educational Records Bureau, Greenwich, Conn.

De la Cruz, F. F., and G. D. LaVeck. 1970. Mental retardation, a challenge to physicians. W. Va. Med. J. 19: 145–153.

DeMyer, M. K., D. W. Churchill, W. Pontius, and K. M. Gilkey. 1971. A comparison of five diagnostic systems for childhood schizophrenia and infantile autism. J. Autism Child. Schiz. 1: 175–189.

Denhoff, E., N. B. D'Wolf, A. Cassidy, A. B. Brindle, E. Danella, A. Gang, T. Maloney, E. Lieberman, and T. Hyman. 1969. Meeting Street School Screening Test. Meeting Street School, Providence, R.I.

Dicks-Mireaux, M. J. 1972. Mental development of infants with Down's syndrome. Amer. J. Ment. Defic. 77: 26–32.

Doll, E. A. 1965. Vineland Social Maturity Scales. American Guidance Services, Circle Pines, Minn.

Doll, E. A. 1966. Preschool Attainment Record. American Guidance Services, Circle Pines, Minn.

Educational Testing Service. 1973. Assessment in a Pluralistic Society. Princeton University Press, Princeton.

Emmerich, W. 1969. The parental role: A functional-cognitive approach. Monogr. Soc. Res. Child Devel. 34 (8, Serial No. 132).

Erickson, M. T., N. M. Johnson, and F. A. Campbell. 1970. Relationships among scores on infant tests for children with developmental problems. Amer. J. Ment. Defic. 75: 102–104.

Filippi, R., and C. L. Rousey. 1971. Positive carriers of violence among children—detection by speech deviations. Ment. Hygiene 55: 157–161.

Fomon, S. J. 1971. Screening children for nutritional status. Report of Maternal and Child Health Services, Department of Health, Education and Welfare. U.S. Government Printing Office, Washington, D.C.

Frankenburg, W., B. Camp, P. A. van Natta, and J. A. Demersseman. 1971a. Reliability and stability of the Denver Developmental Screening Test. Child Devel. 42: 1315–1325.

Frankenburg, W., B. Camp, and P. A. van Natta. 1971b. Validity of the Denver Developmental Screening Test. Child Devel. 42: 475–485.

Friedlander, B. Z. 1971. Automated Evaluation of Selective Listening in Language-impaired and Normal Infants and Young Children. Matern. Child Health Exch. 1(5): 9–12.

Gallagher, J. J., and R. H. Bradley. 1972. Early identification of developmental difficulties. *In* I. Gordon (ed.), Early Childhood Education, pp. 87–121. University of Chicago Press, Chicago.

Garber, H. L. 1971. Measuring differential development in young children. Presented at the American Educational Research Association Meeting, February. New York.

Gergen, K. J. 1972. Multiple identity. Psychology Today, May: 31–35.

Gesell, A. L., and C. S. Amatruda. 1947. Developmental Diagnosis. 2nd Ed. Paul B. Hoeber, New York.

Giannini, M., A. B. Amler, E. Chused, H. J. Cohen, J. H. de Leo, D. Gallerzzo, L. Greenspan, H. Kaessler, M. Haas, H. Michall-Smith, D. O'Hare, K. A. Swallow, L. Taft,

M. Winick, and L. Goodman. 1972. The Rapid Developmental Screening Checklist. American Academy of Pediatrics, New York.

Gil, D. G. 1971. A sociocultural perspective on physical child abuse. Child Welfare 7: 389–395.

Grewel, F. 1967. Differential diagnosis of disorders in the development of language and of speaking. Acta Neurol. Belg. 67: 861–866.

Guthrie, D., and E. V. Horne. 1971. Measures of infant development: An annotated bibliography. Head Start Test Collection. Education Testing Service, Washington, D.C.

Guthrie, R. 1972. Mass screening for genetic disease. Hospital Practice 9: 93–100.

Haynes, U. 1967. A Developmental Approach to Casefinding with Special Reference to Cerebral Palsy, Mental Retardation, and Related Disorders. U.S. Government Printing Office, Washington, D.C.

Heber, R., H. Garber, S. Harrington, C. Hoffman, and C. Falender. 1972. Rehabilitation of Families at Risk of Mental Retardation, A Progress Report. University of Wisconsin, Madison.

Helfer, R., and C. H. Kempe. 1968. The Battered Child. University of Chicago Press, Chicago.

Hoepfner, R., C. Stern, and S. Nummedal. 1971. CSE-ECRC Preschool/Kindergarten Test Evaluations. UCLA Graduate School of Education, Los Angeles.

Hoffman, M. S. 1972. "Slide-Rule" for Catching Potential Learning Disorders Early. Expectations 1: (8) 2.

Holden, R. H. 1972. Prediction of mental retardation in infancy. Ment. Retard. 12: 28–30.

Hollingshead, A. B. 1957. Two-Factor Index of Social Position. (Mimeographed). Chicago.

Holm, V. A., and G. Thompson. 1971a. Selective Hearing Loss: Clues to Early Identification. Dept. of Audiology and Speech, Child Development and Mental Retardation Development Center, University of Washington, Seattle.

Holm, V. A., and G. Thompson. 1971b. Selective hearing loss: Clues to early identification. Unpublished manuscript. Dept. of Audiology and Speech, Child Development and Mental Retardation Center, University of Washington, Seattle.

Honig, A. S., and S. Brill. 1970. A Comparative analysis of the Piagetian development of twelve month old disadvantaged infants in an enrichment center with others not in such a center. Paper presented (enlarged version) at Annual Meeting of American Psychological Association, September, Miami.

Honig, A. S., and B. M. Caldwell. 1966. Early Language Assessment Scale. Parts I and II. Syracuse University Children's Center. Syracuse, New York.

Howell, R. R., N. A. Holtzman, and G. H. Thomas. 1969. Selected Screening Tests for Genetic Metabolic Diseases. The Johns Hopkins University School of Medicine, Baltimore.

Hutt, J. S., H. G. Lenard, and H. F. R. Prechtl. 1969. Psychophysiological studies in newborn infants. In L. Lipsitt and C. Spiker (eds.), Advances in Child Development and Behavior, pp. 127–172. Academic Press, New York.

Illingworth, R. S. 1960. The Development of the Infant and Young Child. Livingstone, Edinburgh.

Ingram, T. T. 1969. The new approach to early diagnosis of handicaps in childhood. Devel. Med. Child Neurol. 11: 279–290.

Kagan, J. 1972. Do infants think? Sci. Amer. March: 74–82.

Kagan, J. 1973. Cross-cultural perspectives on early development. Amer. Psych. 28: 947–961.

Knobloch, H., and B. Pasamanick. 1960. Environmental factors affecting human development before and after birth. Pediatrics 26: 210–218.

Lally, J. R. 1968. A study of the relationships between trained and untrained twelve month old environmentally deprived infants on the "Griffiths Mental Development

Scale." Paper presented at American Educational Research Association Meeting, February. Chicago.

Lewis, M., S. Goldberg, and H. Campbell. 1969. A developmental study of information processing the first year of life: Response decrement to a redundant signal. Monogr. Soc. Res. Child Devel. 34 (9, Serial No. 133).

Lin-Fu, J. S. 1971. Vision screening of children. Maternal and Child Health Service, U.S. Department of Health, Education, and Welfare. U.S. Government Printing Office, Washington, D.C.

Lubchenco, L. O. 1970. Assessment of gestational age and development at birth. Pediatr. Clin. No. Amer. Vol. 17, No. 1.

Lubchenco, L. O., F. A. Horner, L. S. Reed, I. E. Hix, D. Metcalf, R. Cohig, H. C. Elliott, and M. Bourg. 1963. Sequelae of premature birth. Amer. J. Disab. Child. 106: 101–115.

Marmor, J. 1971. Manual for Testing the Language of 1- to 3-year-old Children. Preschool Project, Laboratory of Human Development. Harvard University, Cambridge, Mass.

McCall, R. B., P. S. Hogarty, and N. Hurlburt. 1972. Transitions in infant sensorimotor development and the prediction of childhood IQ. Amer. Psych. 27: 728–748.

McNeill, D. 1970. The Acquisition of Language. Harper and Row, New York.

Meier, J. H. 1965. An Exploratory Factor Analysis of Psychodiagnostic and Case Study Information from Children in Special Education Classes for the Educable Mentally Handicapped. University of Michigan Microfilms, Ann Arbor, Mich.

Meier, J. H. 1971. Prevalence and characteristics of learning disabilities in second grade children. J. Learn. Disab. 4: 1–6.

Meier, J. H. (ed.). 1973a. Background Papers of Boston Conference: Screening and Assessment of Young Children at Developmental Risk. U.S. Government Printing Office, Washington, D.C.

Meier, J. H. 1973b. Screening and Assessment of Young Children at Developmental Risk. U.S. Government Printing Office, Washington, D.C.

Meier, J. H. 1973c. System for Open Learning, Facilitator's Handbook I: SOL Foundations and Rationale. Publisher's Press Inc./Monitor Publications, Denver.

Meier, J. H., and H. P. Martin. 1970. Developmental Retardation. *In* C. H. Kempe, H. Silver, and D. O'Brien (eds.), Current Pediatric Diagnosis and Treatment, pp. 459–464. Lange, Los Altos, Calif.

Meier, J. H., L. L. Segner, and B. B. Grueter. 1970. Early stimulation and education with high risk infants: A preventive approach to mental retardation and learning disabilities. *In* J. Hellmuth (ed.), The Disadvantaged Child, Vol. III, pp. 404–444. Brunner/Mazel, New York.

Mental Retardation News, November, 1971, 3.

Mercer, J. R. 1971. Adaptive Behavior Scales and Bibliography. University of California, Riverside.

Mercer, J. R. 1972. The Origins and Development of the Pluralistic Assessment Project. University of California, Riverside.

Meyers, C. E., and H. F. Dingman. 1966. Factor analytic and structure of intellect models in the study of mental retardation. Amer. J. Ment. Defic. 70: 7–25.

Murphy, L. B. 1968. Child development, then and now. Child. Ed. 44: 302–306.

National Registry for Amniocentesis. 1975. National Institute of Child Health and Human Development, National Institutes of Health. Findings presented at the Annual Meeting of the American Academy of Pediatrics, October 20. Washington, D.C.

O'Brien, D., F. A. Ibbott, and D. D. Rodgerson. 1968. Laboratory Manual of Pediatric Micro Biochemical Techniques (4th Ed.). Harper, New York.

O'Brien, J. S. 1971. How we detect mental retardation before birth. Medical Times 99: 103–108.

Ogilvie, D., and B. Shapiro. 1969. Manual for Assessing Social Abilities of One- to Six-Year-Old Children. Preschool Project. Harvard University, Cambridge, Mass.

Ostwald, P. F., R. Phibbs, and S. Fox. 1968. Diagnostic use of infant cry. Biol. Neonate 13: 68–82.

Ozer, M. N., H. B. Richardson, M. L. Tannhauser, and C. D. Smith. 1970. The diagnostic evaluation of children with learning problems: An interdisciplinary model. Clinical Proceedings, Vol. XXVI, June, No. 6. Children's Hospital, Washington, D.C.

Parker, R. K. (ed.). 1972. The Preschool in Action—Exploring Early Childhood Programs. Allyn and Bacon, Boston.

Pratt, M., L. Giesecke, H. Hogan, M. Konan, and A. Edelin. 1972. Special study: Analysis of U.S. infant mortality by cause of death, color, sex, age at death, and degrees of urbanization of place of residence, 1962–1967. MCH Exchange, 2(3): 15–48.

Prechtl, H., and D. Beintema. 1964. The Neurological Examination of the Full Term Newborn Infant. Little Club Clinics in Developmental Medicine, No. 12. Heinemann Medical Books, London.

President's Committee on Mental Retardation (PCMR). 1972. Report of Work Group on Research and Prevention. Unpublished paper, Washington, D.C.

Quay, H. C., and D. R. Peterson. 1967. Manual for the Behavior Problem Checklist. Children's Research Center, University of Illinois, Champaign.

Reyes, E. V., H. L. Garber, M. O. Thelen, and R. F. Heber. Developmental Differences in Language as Measured by a Sentence Repetition Test. Unpublished paper, University of Wisconsin, Madison.

Sandler, L. 1972. Effectiveness of Screening Instruments in Detection of Developmental Handicaps among Preschool Children. Franklin Institute Research Laboratory, Philadelphia.

Sandler, L., D. Jamison, O. de Liser, L. Cohen, K. Emkey, and H. Keith. 1970. Responses of urban preschol children to a developmental screening test. J. Pediatr. 77: 775–781.

Sandler, L., D. Jamison, O. de Liser, L. Cohen, K. Emkey, and H. Keith. 1972. Developmental test performance of disadvantage children. Except. Child 77: 201–208.

Savitz, R. A., R. B. Reed, and I. Valadian. 1964. Vision Screening of the Preschool Child. Children's Bureau, U.S. Department of Health, Education, and Welfare, Washington, D.C.

Scurletis, T. D., and M. S. Headrick. 1972. A System of Comprehensive Health Care Screening and Service for Children. Paper presented at annual meeting of the American Association of Mental Deficiency, May 15–20, Minneapolis, Minn.

Shotwell, A. 1964. Suitability of the Kohlmann-Binet Infant Scale for assessing intelligence of mental retardates. Amer. J. Ment. Defic. 68: 757–765.

Small, J. G., M. K. DeMyer, and V. Milstein. 1971. CNV responses of autistic and normal children. J. Autism Child. Schiz. 1: 215–231.

Sokolov, Ye. N. 1963. Perception and the conditioned reflex. Trans., S. W. Wayenfeld. Macmillan, New York.

Speer, D. C. 1971. Behavior problem checklist (Peterson-Quay): Baseline data from parents of child guidance and nonclinic children. J. Consult. Clin. Psych. 36: 221–228.

Starr, R. H., Jr. 1971. Cognitive development in infancy: Assessment, acceleration, and actualization. Merrill-Palmer Quart. 17: 153–185.

Starr, R. H., Jr. 1973. Current knowledge: Socioemotional development from birth to two years. In J. H. Meier (ed.), Background Papers of the Boston Conference on Screening and Assessment. U.S. Government Printing Office, Washington, D.C.

Terdal, L. 1970. Behavioral Analysis in Field and Clinic Settings as a Base for Treatment: A Case Study. University of Oregon, Eugene.

Thomas, H. 1970. Psychological assessment instruments for use with human infants. Merrill-Palmer Quart. 16: 179–224.

Touwen, B. C., and H. F. R. Prechtl. 1970. The Neurological Examination of the Child with Minor Nervous Dysfunction. Lippincott, Philadelphia.

Travis, L. E. 1971. Handbook of Speech Pathology and Audiology. Appleton-Century-Crofts, New York.

Uzgiris, I. C., and J. McV. Hunt. 1966. An Instrument for Assessing Infant Psychological Development. (Mimeograph). University of Illinois, Urbana.

Walworth, J., and J. R. Metz. A scale for screening children at risk for abuse: Preliminary findings (unpublished). Permanente Medical Group, San Francisco.

Warren, S. A. 1973. Pros and Cons of Normalization. Paper presented at the New York Medical College Postgraduate Symposium on Mental Retardation, The Sixth Annual International Symposium, March 1973, Vienna, Austria (unpublished).

Wechsler, D. 1966. The I.Q. is an Intelligent Test. New York Times Magazine, June 26, pp. 66, seq.

White, B. L., and B. Kaban. 1971. Manual for Quantitative Analysis of Tasks of One- to Six-Year-Old Children. Preschool Project. Harvard University, Cambridge, Mass.

White, S. H., M. C. Day, P. K. Freeman, S. A. Hantman, and K. P. Messenger. 1973. Federal programs for young children: Review and recommendations. U.S. Government Printing Office, Washington, D.C.

Williams, G. Z. 1970. Critique of the Subcommittee Report. In Collen, M. F., R. Feldman, J. Barbaccia, J. Dunn, R. Greenblatt, and A. Mather (eds.), Automated Multiphasic Health Testing and Services Provisional Guidelines for AMHTS, pp. 84–85. U.S. Government Printing Office, Washington, D.C.

Williams, T. M. 1972. Infant Care: Abstracts of the Literature. Consortium on Early Childbearing and Childrearing, Washington, D.C.

Wulkan, P. D. First Identification of Neonatal Disabilities (FIND). Southern Arizona Training Programs (unpublished).

Wyatt, G. L. 1971. Early Identification of Children with Potential Learning Disabilities. Wellesley Public Schools, Wellesley, Mass.

Diagnosis of the Infant at High Risk for Mental, Motor, and Sensory Handicaps

*Arthur H. Parmelee, M.D., Marian Sigman, Ph.D.,
Claire B. Kopp, Ph.D., and Audrey Haber, Ph.D.*

This chapter presents primarily biological factors that place infants at risk for mental, motor, or sensory handicaps in childhood. The infant should be identified as at risk for such an outcome so that intervention can be made in his environment as early as possible to optimize his development. At the same time, false labeling of infants as at risk must be avoided if the probability of adverse sequelae is low. Furthermore, erroneous diagnosis dilutes the efforts at intervention, because falsely diagnosed infants would develop adequately without assistance.

The concept of a continuum of pregnancy wastage or a continuum of casualty that implies lethal and sublethal outcome for a variety of pregnancy and perinatal factors has been very useful in predicting mortality and illness in the neonatal period and during infancy (Lilienfeld and Parkhurst, 1951). These outcomes can be determined with reasonable accuracy (Drage and Berendes, 1966). The prediction of sublethal outcomes of mental, motor, or sensory handicaps in later childhood has not been as successful. While the concept is undoubtedly valid, the strength of prediction from pregnancy or perinatal events has been very weak, especially for single events. Clusters of pregnancy and perinatal events have been more predictive, but even with these there have been a wide distribution of outcomes ranging from abnormal to superior, regardless of the type of measure used. Thus, even though mean outcome differences for groups of infants considered at risk can be predicted, there is difficulty predicting the outcome of individuals considered at high risk on the basis of pregnancy and perinatal problems (Buck, Gregg, and Stavraky, 1969; Drage, Berendes, and Fisher, 1969; Drillien, 1964;

The program is supported by NICHD/NIH Contract No. 1-HD-3-2776, "Diagnostic and Intervention Studies of High Risk Infants"; and NICHD Grant No. HD-04612, Mental Retardation Research Center, UCLA.

Graham et al., 1962; Heimer, Cutler, and Freedman, 1964; Keith and Gage, 1960; Lubchenco, Delivoria-Papadopoulos, and Searls, 1972; Niswander et al., 1966; Parmelee and Haber, 1973; Rogers, 1968; Sameroff and Chandler, 1974; Schachter and Apgar, 1959; Wiener et al., 1968). The transient nature of some neonatal insults and the recurrent observation that environmental factors can have a stronger influence on the outcome than can the earlier biological events are significant factors in the problem of prediction (Braine et al., 1966; Douglas, 1960; Drage, Berendes, and Fisher, 1969; Drillien, 1964; Knobloch and Pasamanick, 1960; Parmelee and Haber, 1973; Werner et al., 1968).

The present authors' research is concerned with defining the infant at risk, which, it is hoped, may lead to more accurate prediction of developmental outcome. In devising the risk scoring system, it was decided to consider multiple factors as additive in determining degree of risk, as suggested by some recent studies (Smith et al., 1972; Werner et al., 1968). A strategy of multiple short-term predictions is also used; this takes into account the transactional processes between individual and environment that bring about change. This risk score system considers the following clinical observations. 1) Many perinatal problems cause only transient insult, rather than permanent brain injury. Thus, in the newborn period, babies may appear equally ill upon examination, but some will recover completely. 2) Some pregnancy and perinatal problems cause brain injury that is not manifest in obvious ways in the neonatal period, but the deviance becomes more evident as complex behaviors unfold during infancy. 3) Some parents appear intuitively able to provide an optimal environment for an infant with mild neurological deviances, allowing him to compensate.

With these points in mind, it was decided that a useful risk scoring system might be one that: 1) scores pregnancy, perinatal, and neonatal biological events and behavioral performances in an additive fashion; 2) reassesses the infant in the first months of life to sort out those infants with transient brain insult from those with brain injury who remain deviant; and 3) reassesses the infant again primarily on a behavioral basis later in the first year of life, providing time for environments to have an effect on developmental progress.

CUMULATIVE RISK SCORE DESIGN

The cumulative risk score is composed of five items in the neonatal period, four at 3 and 4 months of age, and five at 8 to 9 months of age (Table 1). The following are brief descriptions of each of the risk score items and when they are administered.

Obstetric Complications Scale (First Week after Birth)

The Obstetric Complications Scale (OCS) determines the presence or absence of optimal conditions relating to maternal factors, parturition, and fetal factors. An overall OCS is obtained by summing the number of optimal conditions. The scale is composed of 41 items with optimal conditions defined for each item. The underlying assumption of the

Table 1. Cumulative risk score items and age of administration

Neonatal	3 and 4 months	8 and 9 months
Obstetric complications		
Postnatal events	Pediatric events	Pediatric events
Sleep polygraph	Sleep polygraph	
Newborn neurological	Gesell test	Gesell test
Visual attention	Visual attention	Exploratory behavior
		Hand precision/ sensorimotor schema
		Cognitive test

test is that obstetric complications are usually interrelated; therefore, severe complications are expected to be evident as nonoptimal responses on numerous items, resulting in a lower obstetric score.

Postnatal Factors (Birth to 1 Month)

The Postnatal Factors evaluation is also based on an optimal score concept, and examines the baby's health status during the first postnatal month. Ten assessed items denote the presence or absence of respiratory difficulties, metabolic disturbances, seizures, surgery, etc.

Newborn Neurological Examination (Term)

The Newborn Neurological Examination evaluates muscle tone, reflex patterns of behavior, and states of arousal. The examination can be administered in a short amount of time, with minimal difficulty and stress to a sick infant. The first section of the newborn neurological examination consists of 13 reflex and behavior pattern items, which are assessed for both sides of the body. These items are scored on a one-to-four scale denoting a range from normal tone to absent response. The second section includes evaluation of eye movements, tremor, cry, body movements, and facial weakness. State items are interspersed throughout the examination and receive a separate scoring analysis in terms of change of states.

Visual Attention (Term)

Behaviors to a visual target are analyzed in the newborn period to evaluate the infant's level of visual fixation. His capability to sustain an optimal level of arousal and to inhibit irrelevant responses will affect the type and level of visual responses that are observed. Measures assessed include the length of first fixation to each stimulus, total duration of attention, and average length of time that the infant sustains attention.

Sleep Polygraph (Term and 3 Months)

Polygraphic recordings of 1.5 hours' duration post feeding are used to evaluate sleep state ontogeny and to provide information concerning the development of brain stem and higher center integration. The primary parameters that are assessed include body activity, respiratory patterns, eye movements, and EEG. The first three variables reflect brain stem activity, while the EEG represents emerging cortical activity. The degree of concordance among the variables provides information about the integration of the central nervous system.

Pediatric Evaluation (4 and 9 Months)

A pediatric evaluation is made at 4 and 9 months to identify and to score medical and neurological problems. The format of each evaluation is similar to the obstetric and postnatal events evaluations and is based on the concept of an optimal score.

Developmental Examination (4 and 9 Months)

The Gesell Developmental Examination is used to assess the development level of the infant. Performance is evaluated in the areas of gross-motor, fine-motor, adaptive, language, and personal-social abilities.

Visual Attention (4 Months)

The infant's preferences for particular types of stimuli indicate a developing ability to remember and to differentiate visual stimulus and may be an elementary form of cognition. Parameters used to assess the 4-month-old's visual behaviors consist of the measurement of preferences for complex, novel, and face like stimuli.

Precision of Hand Manipulation and Sensorimotor Schemas (8 Months)

Hand manipulation and the infant's concomitant use of sensorimotor schemas are analyzed to determine how the infant manually approaches an object, and what he does to explore the objects and his surroundings. Of particular interest are the types of visual and manipulative schemas an infant may use as he interacts with objects. The primary parameters that are assessed for precision of hand manipulation include: accuracy, speed and directness of approach, "anticipatory" hand behaviors, and evidence of tremor or extraneous movements. Analyses of sensorimotor schemas are based on the specific behaviors manifested by the infant as he interacts with the test object.

Exploratory Behavior and Preference for Novelty (8 Months)

The infant's exploratory behavior and his preferences for familiar and novel toys and social objects are evaluated using a technique similar to one developed by Rubenstein

(1967). This test measures the infant's ability to explore an object in detail and then to shift his attention to a new object. Behaviors analyzed include the infant's visual and manipulatory responses to familiar and novel objects, as well as his attentive and emotional responses to mother and examiner. The frequency and duration of nondistress vocalization is also noted.

Cognitive Development (9 Months)

The stages of cognitive development are evaluated using an adapted version of the Casati-Lezine Scales of Sensory Motor Development. Assessment focuses on the rate of acquisition of cognitive stages, the range of performance for each stage, and the amount of horizontal decalage manifested by the child. The test consists of seven subscales that reflect the infant's sensorimotor progression in the areas of object permanence, use of intermediaries, exploration, and combination of objects.

Discussion

Pilot studies were conducted on these measures to determine the range and distribution of scores. A range of performance scores from normal to abnormal was established for each test, and the raw scores were converted to standardized scores with means of 100 and standard deviations (SD) of 20. In this way, the scores could be treated as equivalent and all tests summed and averaged to obtain a cumulative risk score at 9 months. It was arbitrarily determined that infants having an average cumulative score of 99 or less at 9 months would be designated as high risk and those with scores equal to or greater than 100 as low risk. The first battery of outcome measures or dependent variables to determine the validity of the risk score will be obtained at 2 years of age. These measures are listed in Table 2.

The flow of patients through the diagnostic procedures and intervention to the outcome measure is indicated in Figure 1. The intervention program will be discussed in detail in another chapter (Kass et al., this volume).

SUBJECTS

The longitudinal sample consists of pre-term infants of 37 weeks' gestation or less with birth weights at 2,500 gms or less, and a control group of full term infants of 39 to 41

Table 2. Evaluative measures (dependent variables): 2 years

Bayley Scales of Infant Development
Cognitive Development Test (Piaget)
Gesell Developmental Examination
Receptive and Expressive Language Test
Exploratory Behavior Measure
Affective Social Assessment

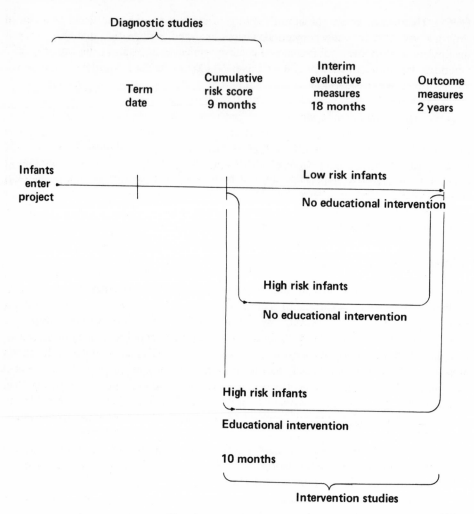

Figure 1. Research flowchart.

weeks' gestation and a birth weight greater than 2,500 grams. All infants are tested at equivalent conceptional ages, defined as gestational age (ga) plus age from birth (Parmelee and Schulte, 1970). Gestational age is calculated from the onset of the mother's last menses. Thus, the newborn tests are administered at 40 weeks' conceptional age, which is the expected date of delivery for the premature infants and the ga of the full-term infants. Date of testing for the later measures is calculated from the expected date of delivery for the pre-terms rather than the actual date of birth.

Subjects include infants from all socioeconomic groups, and attempts are made to equalize the representation of different socioeconomic groups within the risk categories.

At present, socioeconomic status in this study signifies the level of education completed by the infant's mother. Several previous studies have demonstrated a correlation between the level of the mother's education and the intellectual development of the child (Drage, Berendes, and Fisher, 1969; Werner et al., 1968). Data are also being collected on other aspects of family background so that alternative systems of classifying socioeconomic status can be used.

Every infant and family who participates in the longitudinal study receives medical nursing and social work help in an effort to provide support services regardless of risk category. The family is referred to special community resources whenever these are needed for the infant. A subgroup of high risk infants participates in a specialized educational intervention program from 10 to 24 months of age to test the value of such treatment.

DISCUSSION

Preliminary results have been consistent with these authors' original expectation; however, all conclusions are tentative. As of the last data analysis, March 1, 1974, while 76 pre-term infants had complete newborn scores, only 39 were old enough to have completed all of the 9 months tests. Of these 39 infants, 22 would have been considered as high risk on the basis of their newborn score and 17 considered as low risk. However, at 9 months, on the basis of the cumulative risk score on all 14 tests, only 11 were still at high risk and 28 were at low risk. This is consistent with these authors' previous clinical experience and with reported observations of others that infants often improve during the first year of life. However, when the cumulative risk score and its components as independent variables are tested against the dependent outcome measures, there will be a better idea of how much the later measures add to the prediction of outcome. In the final analysis, it may be that the earlier measures in the neonatal period and at 4 months are sufficiently predictive so that a 9 months' cumulative risk score is not warranted.

The correlations of the individual measures with each other and with the 9 months' cumulative risk scores of all 14 items have been reviewed. For most of them there are modest intercorrelations and significant correlations with the total risk score. This gives encouragement, therefore, to continue with all of the tests. On the other hand, there is, so far, no single test that alone would be the predominant predictor. This, then, supports the merits of a cumulative risk score. It is recognized that these findings so far are very preliminary and that there may be some major shifts in correlations as the sample size increases. When the outcome measures have been completed on all babies at 2 years, reassessment can be made of the strength of the individual measures, as well as of the clusters of measures. Ultimately, these authors hope to be able to construct a battery of tests using only the most effective measure with appropriate weighting. One would like to eliminate the more complex measures, such as the sleep polygraph, if this does not weaken the scoring system, in order to make it more generally applicable. In addition, the strength of various components of each measure can be evaluated in relation to the cumulative risk score and later performance so that the individual measures can be improved (Parmelee et al., 1975).

As a separate part of the project, but not included in the present risk score, mother-infant interaction is observed in the home at 1, 3, and 8 months. This aspect of the study is discussed elsewhere in more detail (Beckwith, this volume). A retrospective analysis will attempt to determine those qualities of mother-infant interaction that had an ameliorating effect on infants who were at risk early in infancy and improved by 9 months or 2 years. In addition, an attempt will be made to isolate those factors in mother-infant interaction that correlated with a decline in the infant's development. This information may enable identification of environmental factors that should be included in the risk score. It will also be helpful in the selection of intervention procedures.

The subjects in the longitudinal sample include infants from all socioeconomic groups so that the relationship between socioeconomic status, biological risk, and mother-infant interaction can be examined. These author's current hypothesis is that even though mother-infant interaction is related to social class, mother-infant interaction will have powerful effects on infant development regardless of social class. Analyses will be done to relate mother-child interaction and social class to each other, biological risk factors, and later development.

The need for follow up studies is essential to any research of this nature. However, the general failure of long-term studies to demonstrate a direct relation between early medical events and later outcome suggests that another strategy is needed. Long-term studies fail to take into account the ongoing changes that affect outcome measures. In the past, most studies have attempted to predict development in early childhood from the neonatal period. An alternative strategy is that of repeated predictions over short periods of time. Such a strategy allows for the probable occurrence of changes resulting from transactional processes between the environment and the individual, and it provides the opportunity to identify the nature of these processes. The cumulative risk score was designed with this in mind, and these authors' follow up will continue this strategy.

LITERATURE CITED

Braine, M. D. S., C. B. Heimer, H. Wortis, and A. M. Freedman. 1966. Factors associated with impairment of the early development of prematures. Monogr. Soc. Res. Child Devel. 31: (Whole No. 106).

Buck, C., R. Gregg, K. Stavraky, et al. 1969. The effect of single prenatal and natal complications upon the development of children of mature birthweight. Pediatrics 43: 942–955.

Douglas, J. W. B. 1960. "Premature" children at primary schools. Brit. Med. J. 1: 1008–1013.

Drage, J. S., and H. W. Berendes. 1966. Apgar scores and outcome of the newborn. Pediatr. Clin. No. Amer. 13: 635–643.

Drage, J. S., H. W. Berendes, and P. D. Fisher. 1969. The Apgar scores and four-year psychological examination performance. In Perinatal Factors Affecting Human Development. Pan American Health Organization Scientific Publication No. 185.

Drillien, C. M. 1964. The Growth and Development of the Prematurely Born Infant. Williams and Wilkins, Baltimore.

Graham, F. K., C. B. Ernhard, D. Thurston, and M. Craft. 1962. Development three years after perinatal anoxia and other potentially damaging newborn experiences. Psych. Monogr. 76: (Whole No. 522).

Heimer, C. B., R. Cutler, and A. M. Freedman. 1964. Neurological sequelae of premature birth. Amer. J. Dis. Child. 108: 122–133.

Keith, H. M., and R. P. Gage. 1960. Neurologic lesions in relation to asphyxia of the newborn and factors of pregnancy: long-term follow-up. Pediatrics 26: 616–622.

Knobloch, H., and B. Pasamanick. 1960. Environmental factors affecting human development before and after birth. Pediatrics 26: 210–218.

Lilienfeld, A. M., and E. Parkhurst. 1951. A study of the association of factors of pregnancy and parturition with the development of cerebral palsy. A preliminary report. Amer. J. Hyg. 53: 262–282.

Lubchenco, L. O., M. Delivoria-Papadopoulos, and M. Searls. 1972. Long-term follow-up studies of prematurely born infants. II. Influence of birthweight and gestational age on sequelae. J. Pediatr. 80: 509–512.

Niswander, K. R., E. A. Friedman, D. B. Hoover, et al. 1966. Fetal morbidity following potentially anoxigenic obstetric conditions. I. Abruptio placentae. II. Placenta previa. III. Prolapse of the umbilical cord. Amer. J. Obstetr. Gyn. 95: 838–845.

Parmelee, A. H., and F. J. Schulte. 1970. Developmental testing of preterm and small-for-dates infants. Pediatrics 45: 21–28.

Parmelee, A. H., and A. Haber. 1973. Who is the "Risk Infant"? Clin. Obstetr. Gyn. 16: 376–387.

Parmelee, A. H., M. Sigman, C. B. Kopp, and A. Haber. 1975. The concept of a cumulative risk score for infants. In N. Ellis (ed.), Aberrant Development in Infancy: Human and Animal Studies, pp. 113–121. Laurence Erlbaum Assoc., Hillsdale, N.J.

Rogers, M. G. H. 1968. Risk registers and early detection of handicaps. Devel. Med. Child Neurol. 10: 651–661.

Rubenstein, J. 1967. Maternal attentiveness and subsequent exploratory behavior in the infant. Child Devel. 38: 1089–1100.

Sameroff, A. J., and M. J. Chandler. 1974. Reproductive risk and the continuum of caretaking casualty. In F. D. Horowitz, M. Hetherington, S. Scarr-Salapatek, and G. Siegel (eds.), Review of Child Development Research. University of Chicago Press, Chicago.

Schachter, F. F., and V. Apgar. 1959. Perinatal asphyxia and psychologic signs of brain damage in childhood. Pediatrics 24: 1016–1025.

Smith, A. C., G. L. Flick, G. S. Ferriss, and A. H. Sellmann. 1972. Prediction of developmental outcome at seven years from prenatal perinatal and postnatal events. Child Devel. 43: 495–498.

Werner, E., K. Simonian, J. M. Bierman, and F. E. French. 1968. Cumulative effect of perinatal complications and deprived environment on physical, intellectual, and social development of preschool children. Pediatrics 39: 490–505.

Wiener, G., R. V. Rider, W. C. Oppel, and P. A. Harper. 1968. Correlates of low birthweight. Psychological status at 8 to 10 years of age. Pediat. Res. 2: 110–118.

Mental Health and the Medicaid Screening Program

Stephen Rojcewicz, M.D., and May Aaronson

The Early and Periodic Screening, Diagnosis, and Treatment program (EPSDT) is designed to save the 13 million young people in this country who are eligible for Medicaid from handicapping conditions that lead to chronic and disabling ailments. The implementation of early childhood intervention through EPSDT has enormous potential for impact on the health, mental health, and welfare of the entire country.

The EPSDT effort is part of the federal-state Medicaid program, and it began with Section 1905 (a) (4) (B), Title XIX, of the Social Security Act, as amended in 1967. Signed into law in January 1968 as Public Law 90-248, these amendments require all states participating in the Medicaid program (which now number all but one) to provide early and periodic screening, diagnosis, and treatment services for all persons under 21 who are eligible for Medicaid.

Before this law, Medicaid was purely a financial reimbursement program. It paid bills, period. These amendments require the state welfare agencies to guarantee, or, in many cases to initiate, a comprehensive health services program for children.

The fact that EPSDT is such a fundamental change from Medicaid's earlier operations is responsible for the slow implementation of the program. The issuance of regulations by the Secretary of the Department of Health, Education, and Welfare (HEW), which would have implemented the program in actuality, was delayed for several years and occurred only after the National Welfare Rights Organization had brought suit to implement it. Final regulations were approved on November 4, 1971 and called for full implementation of the program by July 1, 1973. In 1972, Congress passed a penalty provision calling for reduction of Aid for Dependent Children matching funds by 1 percent if a state failed to fully implement the EPSDT program.

Federal leadership for the EPSDT program is vested in the Medical Services Administration (MSA), a component of the Social and Rehabilitation Service (SRS) of HEW. As represented in the Medical Assistance Manual issued by MSA in June 1972, the Social Security Act added a requirement to Medicaid that was intended to direct attention to the importance of preventive health services and early detection and treatment of disease

299

in children eligible for medical assistance. Through this amendment, Congress intended to require states to take aggressive steps to screen, diagnose, and treat children with health problems. Congress was concerned about the variations from state to state in the numbers of children treated for handicapping conditions and health problems that could lead to chronic illness and disability. Senate and House Committee reports had emphasized the need for extending outreach efforts to create awareness of existing health care services. Furthermore, they expressed concern for stimulating the use of these services so that young people can receive medical care before health problems become chronic and irreversible damage occurs.

NATIONAL INSTITUTE OF MENTAL HEALTH AND MEDICAL SERVICE ADMINISTRATION COLLABORATION

The National Institute of Mental Health (NIMH) has become involved in EPSDT because the law calls for screening, diagnosis, and treatment for "physical and mental defects," and because physical and mental health are considered to be inextricably interwoven. The Joint Commission on Mental Health of Children (1969) declares in its final report: "It became increasingly apparent that health, mental health, and environmental influences are interwoven, particularly in the earliest years of life." This same report calls child-rearing our largest "industry" and states that "it will be far more costly in the long run in terms of mental illness, human malfunctioning, and therefore underproductivity, if we do not appropriately support this industry." Continuing with a definition of mental health that considerably broadens the horizons of "mental defects" as used in the law, the report proposed a broader but more meaningful concept of mental health, one which is based on the developmental view with prevention and optimum mental health as the major goal. The report further contends that the mentally healthy life is one in which self-direction and satisfying interdependent relationships prevail, one in which there are meaning, purpose, and opportunity. Finally, the report states: "Lives which are uprooted, thwarted, and denied the growth of their inherent capacities are mentally unhealthy, as are those determined by rigidity, conformity, deprivation, impulsivity, and hostility. Unfulfilled lives cost us twice—once in the loss of human resources, in the apathetic, unhappy, frustrated, and violent souls in our midst, and again in the loss of productivity to our society and the economic costs of dependency."

In keeping with the philosophy expressed above, the NIMH would hope to advance broad, long-range goals for the constituents of the EPSDT program (and eventually for all children) by promoting preventive mental health measures and other optimum conditions that would allow children to mature into purposeful, meaningful adulthood. Short-range, more immediate, goals and objectives would include plans for the developmental assessment of children by adequate techniques at appropriate periodic intervals. Assessment could then be followed by identification and diagnosis of problem areas and, if necessary, by treatment. Keeping in mind a combination of long-range and short-range mental health goals, the MSA and the NIMH are participating in an ongoing collaboration, led and supported by both the Directors of MSA and the NIMH.

An early endeavor emanating from the collaboration between the two agencies was the NIMH/MSA Conference on Developmental Assessment under EPSDT, held in Washington, D.C. on November 14 to 15, 1973. The conference brought together more than 80 national experts from many fields: child psychiatry, psychology, pediatrics, social work, special education, teaching, learning disabilities and communication disorders, neurology, and others. The purpose of the conference was to draw upon the expertise and experience of the participants in order to stimulate a fertile exchange of views related to the complex issues involved in developmental assessment as it would apply to the EPSDT program. This was not an easy task because developmental assessment, especially as applied to young children, is presently more an art than a science.

Although the number of instruments and techniques to serve this purpose are increasing, few, if any, have been sufficiently standardized on the kinds of populations for which they are to be used to make legitimate claims of validity and reliability. This has raised questions about possible cultural bias embedded in screening instruments and diagnostic procedures. Furthermore, identification of mental health problems involves naming or describing them in some fashion and recording the information somewhere to ensure treatment and follow up. What happens if strict confidentiality of records is not maintained and providers of education are informed that a child is educationally handicapped? Could not this information or "labeling" of the child color a teacher's view of his capabilities, making the labels the basis of a self-fulfilling prophesy? Who then would be entitled to see the records? Where would they be maintained? How would they be used? Many emotionally charged issues are involved.

The official conference proceedings, as well as individual position papers stimulated by the conference, are published in *Health Care Screening and Developmental Assessment* (Hersh and Rojcewicz, 1974), and it is available through the National Institute of Mental Health and the Government Printing Office. The following summary is closely based on that document.

Screening does not exist in a vacuum and neither does the child. Screening is not isolated by itself; it must be part of a total system of integrated screening, diagnosis, and treatment. Developmental screening, in particular, requires awareness and utilization of the institutions around a child. These are what Eli Bower calls the Key Integrative Social Systems, or KISS institutions, and they include the health system, the family system, the peer-play system, and the school. Bower believes that screening procedures need to be developed, not to concentrate on pathologies, but to help children make positive passage through those four KISS institutions. The whole process of growing up, he says, should be looked upon as something in which every child has to succeed.

Conference participants felt that there were some advantages to the fact that the state of the art is not sufficiently developed to recommend specific tools for screening and developmental assessment. This limitation was believed to be an advantage in that it negates the possibility of "assembly-line" screening, and requires consideration of the child as an individual and a search for tools that are appropriate to the culture and background of that child. The American Academy of Pediatrics (1974), in cooperation with HEW, has prepared detailed recommendations dealing with these issues.

Earl Schaefer emphasized the vast importance of parents to the EPSDT program. Traditionally, parents have had primary responsibility for the integration of screening, diagnosis, and treatment services for their children, and family relationships are crucial for child adjustment and achievement. The EPSDT Program necessitates major communication and collaboration between health and welfare professionals and parents and thus presents an extraordinary opportunity for upgrading the quality of parenting through parent-oriented education.

Other topics raised were the role of paraprofessionals in screening, the timing and periodicity of screening, and the fact that screening does not equal diagnosis.

Equal evaluation of strengths and weaknesses in social, language, emotional, and motor functioning, with avoidance of labeling in the negative sense, seemed to be universally embraced. The search for culture-fair tools continues. The importance for the screeners, whomever they may be (parent, teacher, paraprofessional, indigenous worker, health professional), to understand the limitations as well as the value of screening was emphasized. Needs for professional association interest and participation were discussed. Finally, citizen advisory boards and councils were recommended as necessary vehicles for maintenance of community interest and to ensure that developmental assessment under EPSDT would be appropriate for the particular community.

Participants were almost unanimous in viewing this federal program as a vehicle for doing a great deal of good for the country's children. It is not often that a federal program evokes such enthusiasm.

IMPLICATIONS OF THE EPSDT PROGRAM

The EPSDT program has potential for making great strides in the area of preventive mental health. Not only will there be the considerable benefit from early intervention among the approximately 13 million children eligible for Medicaid, but the experiences and knowledge gained through such an ambitious program can and should be expanded to the non-Medicaid population. In this way, it could have a major effect on social systems concerned with both populations such as the schools and day care centers.

The potential of the EPSDT program for developing additional knowledge has been pointed out by Hersh and Rojcewicz (1974, p. 15) who recommends that "marker variables," or marker measures, be used nationwide in reporting and evaluating services provided to children. This, he believes, would make it possible to compare parameters of the screening, diagnostic, and treatment programs across the states and localities and, thereby, help to make it possible to define areas of program needs on a more precise basis.

The research base for the screening, diagnostic, and treatment efforts continues to need development and expansion. To this end, the NIMH continues to conduct and support research related to child mental health. It supports innovative demonstration programs, furthers child mental health services through its staffing and training grants to community mental health centers across the nation, and supports the training of certain mental health specialists through colleges and universities. Both its basic and applied research programs continue to provide a knowledge base to which programs such as the EPSDT can turn in search of new tools, methods and techniques, new therapies, and basic understanding of learning behavior processes.

The Early and Periodic Screening, Diagnosis, and Treatment component of the Medicaid program promises to be a giant step in developing and improving our largest "industry": child rearing. The tools and techniques employed in developmental assessment are important to this effort, but these need further study and improvement to reach satisfactory levels of performance. Here, the problem of their use in service to children from the heterogenous cultural groups in America remains a significant problem as does finding the most effective mechanisms for the delivery of knowledge of development in service. The National Institue of Mental Health and the Medical Services Administration are moving to meet these problems through the Medicaid screening program with full recognition of its importance in developing our human resources to their highest potential.

LITERATURE CITED

American Academy of Pediatrics. 1974. A Guide to Screening for the Early and Periodic Screening, Diagnosis, and Treatment Program (EPSDT) under Medicaid. Report prepared for the Department of Health, Education, and Welfare by W. K. Frankenberg and A. F. North. U.S. Government Printing Office, Washington, D.C.

Joint Commission on Mental Health of Children. 1970. Crisis in Child Mental Health: Challenge for the 1970's. Harper and Row, New York.

Hersh, S. P., and S. Rojcewicz. 1974. Health Care Screening and Developmental Assessment. Department of Health, Education, and Welfare Publication ADM 74-115. U.S. Government Printing Office, Washington, D.C.

Comprehensive Developmental Health Services: A Concept and a Plan

Theodore D. Scurletis, M.D., M.P.H., Mary Headrick-Haynes, Ph.D.,
Craig D. Turnbull, Ph.D., and Richard Fallon, M.D.

One of the greatest challenges facing society today is the provision of effective, individualized services to large numbers of people in spite of the many factors in modern life that lead to the depersonalization of such relationships. Nowhere is this challenge greater than in the area of children's services where individualized attention to the child and his family as an ecological unit is essential in order to meet changing developmental needs.

This chapter is concerned, first, with attempts by these authors to face this challenge by conceptualizing a system for providing Comprehensive Developmental Health Services (CDHS) and, second, with their attempts to implement this system in North Carolina. CDHS represents services that focus upon prevention, early detection of health and developmental problems, indepth evaluation and planning for children with special needs, and, finally, access to an adequate array of health intervention alternatives. Above all, CDHS must be available, both geographically and psychologically, to the people who need them; it must be appropriate to their needs insofar as technologically possible; and it must be provided in a way that is acceptable to and maintains the integrity of the consumer.

Two basic premises have influenced the development of this system and its implementation. The first premise is that, while CDHS must be available to all members of the population, some persons will be more likely than others to need health care and specialized services, and/or will be more likely to need assistance in obtaining such services. The second premise is that people must be served primarily in their own communities if services are to be individualized, longitudinal, and accessible. The first of these premises has led to an extensive investigation of the parameters of "risk"; the second has led to the development of a strategy for diversified manpower utilization. Both of these aspects of the problem are dealt with in more detail later in this chapter.

THE CONCEPT

A system is, basically, a method for relating people and technology for the purpose of achieving a goal. Systems have functional parts that are tied together by organizational rules and by a data system that provides guidance and feedback so that the system can be evaluated and altered to meet changing conditions.

Figure 1 is a schematic presentation of the system these authors have developed, indicating the major functional components believed to be necessary to bring the technology of CDHS to the people in need. At the center of the schematic is indicated the target population of high risk persons. While the system is accessible to all members of the population, the main priority is placed upon getting those persons at risk introduced to and maintained in the system. The basis for this will become clear from data to be presented later. The upper pole of the schematic indicates a data system that serves to identify children, particularly those at risk, monitors the services provided for all persons served by the system, and identifies failures in the system. The data system, however, will be only as effective as the people who use the data at the community level. The data system primarily serves to direct the activities of the outreach component of the system. This outreach component encompasses a total Child Health Program which includes casefinding, early and periodic screening for developmental health problems, ongoing personal contact and education in order to maintain people in the system, and follow-through with monitoring of the assistance or treatment provided to children and their families.

Moving to the lower pole of the schematic, it can be seen that outreach is achieved through effective referral and feedback relationships with community services. These services include medical services, preschool and public education programs, generic social services, and the wide range of community-based family support systems provided through local public and private mental health, educational, and other programs.

As previously indicated, communities must provide a wide range of generic services in order to meet the needs of children and families; however, most communities cannot provide or effectively utilize specialized services that are needed by relatively few members of the community or for limited episodes. These services must be provided by a network of regional facilities and a few large, central facilities. Regional services include, for example, interdisciplinary and specialized diagnostic and treatment centers, specialized educational centers, consultative and professional education services, and other program resources. Central services include facilities such as large medical centers, genetic study centers, and training centers for professionals needed to sustain the system.

An essential aspect of the system not adequately depicted by the schematic is that responsibility is fixed with individual health personnel in the local community for

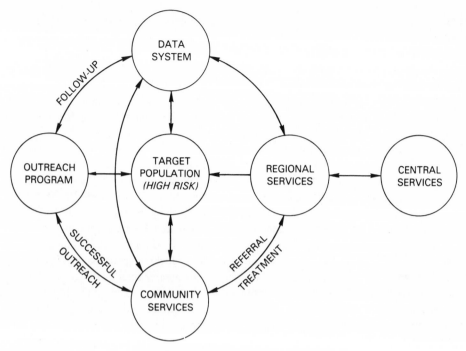

Figure 1. Delivery system model.

introducing people to the system and for obtaining services as needed at the community and regional levels.

As can be seen, all components of the system are tied together by the data system that longitudinally tracks a child and his family throughout the developmental period and cumulatively summarized his needs for services, his utilization of services, and the effectiveness of those services.

THE PLAN

High Risk Target Population

The two most essential components of the system will now be examined in more detail, i.e., the high risk target population and the community outreach component. Earlier, it was mentioned that the concept of risk was basic to the development of the system. If the system is accessible to and utilized at high risk, it will also be utilized, as needed, by persons at low risk. The earlier studies of postneonatal mortaility firmly indicated that preventive health services were less utilized by families with a postneonatal death than by matched survivor groups (Levy et al., 1974). Reports from health departments across the state also indicate that a serious problem in health care is to get the people who most need preventive health services to use the services that are already available.

How then, does one identify quickly and objectively those persons who will be most likely to need health services and least likely to seek and obtain them? These authors began several years ago to approach these questions through the study of fetal, neonatal, and postneonatal mortality (Scurletis et al., 1970; Scurletis, Turnbull, and Corkey, 1973). Two basic questions were asked of the data. First, what characteristics identify those women who produce the highest proportion of mortality and probably morbidity? Second, are there specific characteristics associated with specific types of risk? Mortality studies have consistently identified eight maternal characteristics that are related to fetal and infant death (Scurletis and Headrick-Haynes, 1972). Several of these factors have been implicated less explicitly by other investigators in studies of morbidity (Birch and Gussow, 1971; Heber et al., 1973). These studies are being extended to morbidity, and data from those studies will be included in the model as they become available.

Current data, based upon 1971 vital statistics, focus upon eight characteristics, presented in Table 1, as they relate to mortality. They include: maternal age less than 18 years or more than 34 years (<18, >34); birth order greater than 3 (BO > 3); education less than ninth grade (EDUC < 9); education greater than eight grade but less than completion of high school (EDUC 9 to 11); out of wedlock (OW); previous fetal death (PFD); and previous live births now dead (PLBND). Looking first at the total live birth population, one half of all white births and three fourths of all nonwhite births occurred in the context of some combination of these factors. Following the bottom line across, it can be seen that 57 percent of the women who gave birth in North Carolina account for 71 percent of fetal and neonatal mortality and 80 percent of postneonatal mortality. This population of women produces more than its share of children who die sometime during the first year of life and can be considered at risk. Furthermore, the risk indicators are as highly related to social factors as to biological ones, and the nonwhite population is at relatively greater risk than the white population.

The next three figures show the rates of fetal, neonatal, and postneonatal death associated with each of the eight indicators. These data show that, indeed, different indicators are involved. In the case of fetal mortality, shown in Figure 2 and Tables 2 and 3, maternal age more than 34 years seems to be a primary indicator alone with previous fetal death. In the case of neonatal mortality, shown in Figure 3 and Tables 4 and 5, the PLBND indicator is strongest with approximately equal contribution from each of the others. In the case of postneonatal mortality, shown in Figure 4 and Tables 6 and 7, one begins to see a greater implication of social indicators, including low education, wedlock status, and age. Referring to Table 1, it can be seen that these educational and social factors are associated with a significant number of the live births in North Carolina as well as with a high rate of postneonatal death. The most important feature of these data, however, is that in each case mortality rates were up to four times as high for persons displaying high risk characteristics as for those considered at low risk. When as many as two indicators are considered simultaneously, the mortality rates for high risk children become up to six times as high as those for low risk children. These results are shown in

Table 1. Percentage of live births, fetal, neonatal, and postneonatal deaths by maternal characteristics in North Carolina, 1971

	Live births		Fetal deaths		Neonatal deaths		Postneonatal deaths	
Total events	White 67,220	Nonwhite 28,307	White 837	Nonwhite 670	White 916	Nonwhite 601	White 266	Nonwhite 295
Age < 18	6	16	6	19	11	20	14	20
Age > 34	5	6	10	12	6	7	4	4
BO > 3	15	25	24	28	23	24	23	28
EDUC < 9	7	11	11	14	11	13	16	20
EDUC 9–11	27	41	28	37	34	41	40	53
OW	3	35	7	42	6	38	8	43
PFD	14	12	22	23	23	20	18	11
PLBND	3	6	6	8	10	11	7	10
Any combination of characteristics	50	75	62	83	64	81	71	87

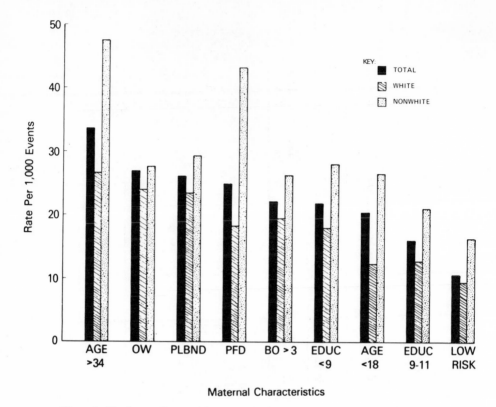

Figure 2. Fetal mortality rates by maternal characteristics in North Carolina, 1971.

Table 8, which is a summary of detailed analysis of the data. These data justify these authors' efforts to reach those persons at risk.

Examining how these data may be put to use, Figure 5 presents a flow diagram that illustrates how these data, as well as other biological indicators of risk, might be used to direct the flow of activities in this system. Initially, the total pregnancy population can be identified as either high or low risk, according to social and biological characteristics. At the time of birth, all persons can be so characterized and become known to the system. As indicated, the premature infant, born to the mother without high social or biological risk, goes into the high risk flow pattern. For ease of selection, the single criteria of low birth weight is used. At the time of term birth, a medical assessment is provided by the delivering physician. The single question, "Was the baby healthy during the nursery period?" can also be used as a single risk indicator. When a specific problem is identified, individualized therapy is begun. If therapy is successful, the child returns to the previous path of either high risk or term normal. Those infants requiring long-range therapy would remain in the individualized treatment path.

Table 2. Fetal mortality rates per 1,000 events, white only, in North Carolina, 1971

	Single characteristic	Rates — Pairs of characteristics						
		OW	PLBND	BO > 3	PFD	EDUC < 9	EDUC 9–11	Age < 18
Total deliveries	12.3							
High risk deliveries:								
Age > 34	26.7	79.4	37.3	26.7	27.9	27.2	25.4	NA[a]
OW	24.0		–[b]	35.9	15.7	33.2	16.8	22.7
PLBND	23.5			28.8	24.2	30.8	20.4	–[b]
BO > 3	19.4				20.4	23.2	19.2	–[b]
PFD	18.3					25.3	19.7	10.6
EDUC < 9	17.9						NA[a]	15.6
EDUC 9–11	12.6							9.4
Age < 18	12.2							
Low risk deliveries	9.3							

[a]NA denotes Not Applicable because characteristics are mutually exclusive.
[b]Rate not given because the denominator for the rate was less than 50.

Table 3. Fetal mortality rates per 1,000 events, nonwhite only, in North Carolina, 1971

	Single characteristic	Rates — Pairs of characteristics						
		PFD	PLBND	EDUC <9	OW	Age <18	BO >3	EDUC 9–11
Total deliveries	23.1							
High risk deliveries:								
Age >34	47.7	63.5	46.5	55.9	49.2	NA[a]	43.1	42.9
PFD	43.3		55.8	52.0	60.6	41.7	40.2	42.9
PLBND	29.4			22.2	36.4	17.9	32.3	25.9
EDUC <9	28.1				22.3	19.4	33.2	NA[a]
OW	27.6					27.7	32.2	25.8
Age <18	26.5						—[b]	23.6
BO >3	26.4							24.0
EDUC 9–11	21.1							
Low risk deliveries	16.4							

[a]NA denotes Not Applicable because characteristics are mutually exclusive.
[b]Rate not given because the denominator for the rate was less than 50.

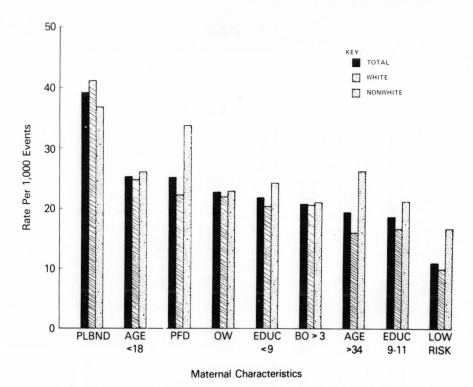

Figure 3. Neonatal mortality rates by maternal characteristics in North Carolina, 1971.

Community Outreach: Child Health Program

Assuming that this data system can identify high risk births on the basis of maternal and infant characteristics, now turn to the problem of focusing services on these persons through the second major facet of the system: the community outreach component. The community outreach component in North Carolina is called the Child Health Program, which consists of three interrelated units and is designed to utilize manpower at the local level in the most effective way.

Family Outreach Worker Unit The first unit of the Child Health Program, which is currently being developed, is the family outreach worker unit. The personnel in this unit are paraprofessionals indigenous to the area or population they serve and are to be trained in developmental health and family advocacy. Their activities are directed and supervised by developmental health professionals. The outreach workers have the primary task of gaining the trust of the people they serve, educating them about preventive health in terms that are meaningful to them, and offering an ongoing link with CDHS. These, then, are the personnel who will seek out those identified as being at risk and will follow through with them as educators and advocates.

Table 4. Neonatal mortality rates per 1,000 events, white only, in North Carolina, 1971

	Single characteristic	Rates — Pairs of characteristics						
		Age < 18	PFD	OW	BO > 3	EDUC < 9	EDUC 9–11	Age > 34
Total live births	13.6							
High risk live births:								
PLBND	41.3	—[b]	62.0	—[b]	38.3	42.4	52.1	31.7
Age < 18	24.7		96.8	15.5	—[b]	24.3	24.3	NA[a]
PFD	22.1			8.0	25.8	28.9	28.9	21.6
OW	22.0				12.4	21.9	18.0	17.2
BO > 3	20.7					30.1	20.6	20.5
EDUC < 9	20.3						NA[a]	27.9
EDUC 9–11	16.8							16.9
Age > 34	15.9							
Low risk live births	9.8							

[a] NA denotes Not Applicable because characteristics are mutually exclusive.

[b] Rate not given because the denominator for the rate was less than 50.

Table 5. Neonatal mortality rates per 1,000 events, nonwhite only, in North Carolina, 1971

	Single characteristic	Rates						
		Pairs of characteristics						
		PFD	Age > 34	Age < 18	EDUC < 9	OW	EDUC 9–11	BO > 3
Total live births	21.2							
High risk live births:								
PLBND	36.9	55.0	30.5	72.7	40.8	31.4	30.2	30.4
PFD	33.8		40.3	43.5	37.8	35.0	26.9	31.6
Age > 34	26.3			NA[a]	29.6	40.2	20.7	26.3
Age < 18	26.1				26.0	26.3	25.3	–[b]
EDUC < 9	24.4					22.8	NA[a]	23.4
OW	23.0						24.5	19.3
EDUC 9–11	21.3							15.3
BO > 3	21.1							
Low risk live births	16.6							

[a]NA denotes Not Applicable because characteristics are mutually exclusive.
[b]Rate not given because the denominator for the rate was less than 50.

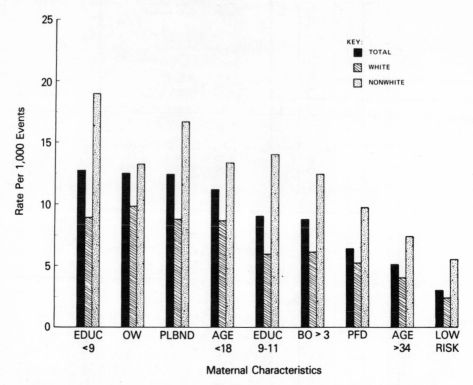

Figure 4. Postneonatal mortality rates by maternal characteristics in North Carolina, 1971.

Nurse Screening Unit The second unit of the Child Health Program is the nurse screening unit, which provides periodic professional physical and developmental assessment and preventive treatment, such as immunizations, to all children served by the system. Personnel in this unit have been and are being specially trained to recognize physical health problems, developmental irregularities, and indications of serious social and emotional difficulties. These professionals in each community have the responsibility of supervising outreach activities involving casefinding, screening, and school health activities. They are also responsible for initiating further action when any developmental health problem is identified or suspected.

Pediatric Clinic The third unit of the Child Health Program is the pediatric clinic. Every child who is identified by the nurse screening unit as having a developmental problem is examined by the pediatrician serving that program, unless the family elects to seek private care. The pediatrician authorizes that a care plan to be developed on the basis of an evaluation that is as extensive as needed. In addition, the pediatric clinic provides backup for the nurse screening unit and periodically provides service to all children in the system.

Table 6. Postneonatal mortality rates per 1,000 events, white only, in North Carolina, 1971

| | | Rates | | | | | | |
| | Single characteristic | Pairs of characteristics | | | | | | |
		EDUC < 9	Age < 18	PLBND	BO > 3	EDUC 9–11	PFD	Age > 34
Total neonatal survivors	4.0							
High risk neonatal survivors:								
OW	9.7	6.4	7.9	_b	31.4	7.7	24.2	17.5
EDUC < 9	8.8		17.5	16.6	7.2	NAa	11.3	7.7
Age < 18	8.8			_b	_b	6.1	11.9	NAa
PLBND	8.7				10.6	8.2	9.9	3.6
BO > 3	6.0					7.4	6.6	5.6
EDUC 9–11	5.8						7.3	1.3
PFD	5.2							3.1
Age > 34	3.9							
Low risk neontal survivors	2.3							

[a]NA denotes Not Applicable because characteristics are mutually exclusive.
[b]Rate not given because the denominator for the rate was less than 50.

Table 7. Postneonatal mortality rates per 1,000 events, nonwhite only, in North Carolina, 1971

| | Single characteristic | Rates | | | | | | |
| | | Pairs of characteristics | | | | | | |
		PLBND	EDUC 9–11	Age < 18	OW	BO > 3	PFD	Age > 34
Total neonatal survivors	10.6							
High risk neonatal survivors:								
EDUC < 9	18.9	23.6	NA[a]	13.9	18.8	20.2	19.6	12.7
PLBND	16.6		22.4	19.6	35.7	19.1	15.1	12.6
EDUC 9–11	13.9			13.8	14.9	13.4	13.1	5.3
Age < 18	13.2				14.1	–[b]	34.1	NA[a]
OW	13.1					19.7	17.2	6.0
BO > 3	12.3						8.7	7.7
PFD	9.6							7.6
Age > 34	7.3							
Low risk neonatal survivors	5.5							

[a]NA denotes Not Applicable because characteristics are mutually exclusive.
[b]Rate not given because the denominator for the rate was less than 50.

Table 8. Mortality rates for high risk pairs of maternal characteristics by time of death and race in North Carolina, 1971

Time of death	White		Nonwhite	
	High risk pair of characteristics	Rate per 1,000 events[a]	High risk pair of characteristics	Rate per 1,000 events[a]
Fetal period	PLBND and age > 34	37.3	PFD and age > 34	63.5
	OW and BO > 3	35.9	PFD and OW	60.6
	OW and EDUC < 9	33.2	EDUC < 9 and age > 34	55.9
	PLBND and EDUC < 9	30.8	PFD and PLBND	55.8
Neonatal period	PLBND and PFD	62.0	PLBND and PFD	55.0
	PLBND and EDUC 9–11	52.1	PLBND and EDUC < 9	40.8
	PLBND and EDUC < 9	42.4	PFD and age > 34	40.3
	PLBND and BO > 3	38.3	PFD and EDUC < 9	37.8
Postneonatal period	OW and BO > 3	31.4	EDUC < 9 and PLBND	23.6
	OW and PFD	24.2	EDUC 9–11 and PLBND	22.4
	Age < 18 and EDUC < 9	17.5	EDUC < 9 and BO > 3	20.2
	EDUC < 9 and PLBND	16.6	OW and BO > 3	19.7

[a]Rates with denominators less than 100 were excluded.

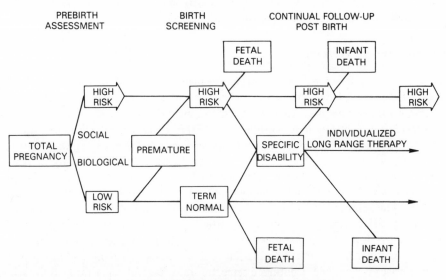

Figure 5. Flow diagram of high risk concept.

Because the primary reason for all casefinding and screening efforts is to provide intervention as soon as possible, the role of special services coordinators is being developed in these community programs. These coordinators will have the skills necessary to "put it all together" for a child and his family, to follow through to see that regional and local services are obtained as needed, and to assist in the direction of outreach acitivites. This will be an additional step toward producing a system in which individual people feel responsible for other individual people and their special needs.

The three units of the Child Health Program are supported by a network of regional and central services throughout the state of North Carolina. At any time that a problem is encountered that cannot be dealt with using community resources, the regional network of services is available. These include, but are not limited to, evaluation in the areas of speech, neurology, orthopedics, physical therapy, special education, psychology, and congenital and genetic disorders. However, the community health professional or co-ordinator maintains responsibility for the patient during and following the utilization of regional and centralized services.

Specifically, this means that when a child is identified by screening as having a health or developmental problem, the process of evaluation is begun, and the child's case and his family situation are reviewed and studied individually. This review may lead to further medical evaluation, social or psychological evaluation, specialized evaluation at the regional level and, certainly, careful attention to parental understanding and attitudes. The primary aim of this evaluation phase is to apprise the parents of the child's condition and to plan with them for intervention and treatment as soon as possible. The family's outreach worker is involved at all stages of this process, when appropriate, and is responsible for following through with the family during treatment. The child will also continue to be screened and/or evaluated as long as they remain in the system, and the effectiveness of treatment can be monitored and changes can be made as needed.

Continued Screening Program

What occurs during screening and following the identification of a developmental health problem is examined here. Extensive casefinding and early and periodic screening are the primary mechanisms used to identify developmental health problems and to implement intervention at the earliest possible point. Every child will be screened at intervals suitable for routine immunizations. As indicated in Figure 6, the screening will occur four times during the first year, three times during the second year, and annually thereafter. Screening will consist of assessing developmental progress using the Denver Developmental Screening Test, preferably administered during a home visit; an extensive array of medical, biochemical, and physical assessments performed at appropriate ages in the clinic; and special screening of vision and hearing. Screening will become more extensive as the child develops. A complete review of previous health status will occur as part of preschool assessment, and this information will be available to the schools, provided parental consent is obtained. Continued screening activities will occur through the school health program and in cooperation with the schools.

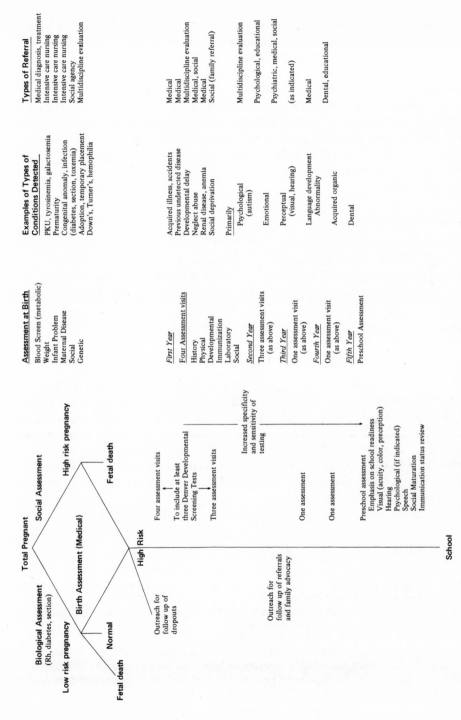

Figure 6. Prevention, early detection, and treatment of disabilities.

As adequate as this screening program may be or appear to be, screening by itself is not the answer to the problem. In fact, screening is only the beginning, because the policy has been adopted that every child who is identified as having a problem or a suspected problem must be given individualized attention and further evaluation as needed. A care plan for every child must be worked out with community professionals and the family. In order to accomplish this result, all units of the system must work in concert to introduce the child and his family into services provided in the community and at regional and central facilities. This transition from identification to evaluation and treatment *must* occur at the site of the screening. In this system, this transition will be mediated by the special services coordinator.

SUMMARY

These authors have presented their conceptualization of a system for the delivery of Comprehensive Developmental Health Services. This system provides for:

1. Preventive services
2. Early detection and screening
3. Diagnosis and evaluation
4. Individualized planning
5. Access to necessary services

This conceptualization is built upon two basic premises: 1) some persons are likely to need more assistance in order to effectively utilize services; and 2) all services should be community related and developed and must be delivered in an individualized, longitudinal, and personalized manner. Finally, a simplified outreach component has been integrated into this system. The outreach has further been related intimately into a community, regional, and central service delivery system. These authors have further emphasized their belief that in the absence of such a system, screening for the early detection of developmental disorders would be futile.

LITERATURE CITED

Birch, H. G., and J. D. Gussow. 1971. Death and Deficit. Disadvantaged Children: Health Nutrition and School Failure. Harcourt, Brace and World, New York.

Heber, R., et al. 1973. Rehabilitation of Families at Risk of Mental Retardation, A Progress Report. University of Wisconsin, Madison.

Levy, M., T. D. Scurletis, E. Siegel, C. D. Turnbull, and J. R. Udry. 1975. The determinants of postneonatal mortality in North Carolina, 1967–1968. Presented at American Public Health Association meeting in New Orleans, October 24, 1974.

Scurletis, T. D., and M. W. Headrick-Haynes. 1972. A system of comprehensive health care screening and service for children. Presented at meeting of American Association on Mental Deficiencies, Minneapolis, Minnesota.

Scurletis, T. D., E. Siegel, J. R. Abernathy, and K. B. Surles. 1970. Maternal and environmental factors in postneonatal mortality. Presented at the Southern Branch, American Public Health Association, May 6.

Scurletis, T. D., C. D. Turnbull, and D. C. Corkey. 1973. High risk indicators of fetal, neonatal, and postneonatal mortality. No. Carol. Med. J. 34: 182–192.

Discussant's Comments

T. Berry Brazelton, M.D.

As the potential for early intervention increases, it becomes more important to be able to evaluate at risk infants as early as possible with an eye to more sophisticated preventive and therapeutic approaches. Early intervention may prevent a compounding of problems that occurs all too easily when the environment cannot adjust appropriately to the infant at risk.

ASSESSING AT RISK INFANTS

Premature and minimally brain damaged infants seem to be less able to compensate in disorganized, depriving environments than do well equipped infants, and their problems of organization in development are compounded early (Greenberg, 1971). Quiet, nondemanding infants do not elicit necessary mothering from already overstressed parents, and they are selected by their neonatal behavior for kwashiorkor and marasmus in poverty-ridden cultures such as those found in Guatemala and Mexico (Cravioto, Delcardie, and Birch, 1966; Klein, Habicht, and Yarbrough, 1971). Hyperkinetic, hypersensitive neonates may press a mother and father into a kind of desperation, producing child-rearing responses from them that reinforce the problems of the child, so that he grows in an overreactive, hostile environment (Heider, 1966).

Parents of children admitted to the wards of the Children's Hospital in Boston for clinical syndromes such as failue to thrive, child abuse, repeated accidents and ingestions, and infantile autism are often successful parents of other children. By history, they associate their failure with the one child to an inability to "understand" him from the neonatal period onward, and they claim a difference from the other children in his earliest reactions to them. If the outcome for such children is to be improved, assessment of the risk in early infancy would mobilize preventive efforts and programs for intervention before the neonate's problems are compounded by an environment that cannot understand him without such help.

ASSESSING AT RISK ENVIRONMENTS

It is also necessary to be able to assess at risk environments, because the impracticality of spreading resources too thin points to the necessity of selecting target populations for efforts at early intervention. With better techniques for assessing strengths and weaknesses in infants and the environments to which they will be exposed, a better understanding may emerge of the mechanisms for failures in development that result in some of the above-mentioned syndromes. Even desperate socioeconomic conditions produce comparable stresses in many families whose children do not have to be salvaged from the clinical syndrome of child abuse, failure to thrive, and kwashiorkor. Minimally brain damaged babies do make remarkable compensatory recoveries in a fostering environment. Understanding the infant and the problems he will present to his parents may enhance our value as supportive figures for them as they adjust to a difficult infant.

EARLY PREDICTION TECHNIQUES

To date, the casefinding techniques in infancy are poor at best. Meier's discussion (this volume) is valuable in that he suggests many new research trends that might lead to new assessment techniques. One exciting trend is reported by Ross and Leavitt (this volume) on attention and habituation as an assessment of cognitive potential and a predictor of fugure CNS function. Parmelee and his group (this volume) are now able to define the necessary neurological studies to diagnose difficulties in early infancy, e.g., EEG sleep studies, organization of state, and attentional behavior. Lubchenco's at risk inventory (Lubchenco et al., 1963) takes into account the perinatal events that predict to morbidity in the neonatal period, and he has been surprisingly accurate in predicting to well-being in the neonatal period.

Nurses and pediatricians have been aware of the value of behavioral assessment as a predictor of well-being. (I recall what started me on my quest to develop my neonatal scale some 20 years ago. It was a nurse of premature infants who was able to say: that baby's going to have 3-day respiratory distress and that one's going to have it for 5 days. The way she could tell this, and she was always right of course, was that the one that was going to have it for 3 days would look at the lights overhead and stop his obligatory breathing, then go on breathing, but the 5-day RDS baby could not do this. She was able to assess this kind of interaction among systems to provide judgments on recovery.) Parmelee (1972) has pointed out that the recovery score in the neonatal period may be one of the best predictors of well-being in the future. We are, I believe, in a position to start collecting cumulative at risk scores in the neonatal period at a time when prevention and crisis intervention are at one of their peak times.

MOTHER-INFANT INTERACTION

These remarks, focused on the neonate, should not obscure concern for their mothers. Klaus and Kennell (1970) have done impressive work in helping create an optimal environment for mother and infant. Their research in pediatric management procedures found that including parents in caregiving procedures in the neonatal period led to an increase in their attachment behaviors. The mothers of ill or at risk premature infants were able to overcome their grief reactions and/or put them to work caring for their sick babies. The energy that had been used in grieving (Lindemann, 1944) seemed to be available to caregiving when the parents were included in an *honest* appraisal of the at risk neonate and were given an active role in his recovery!

Using the Neonatal Behavioral Assessment Scale (Brazelton, 1973), which measures such things as cuddliness and behavioral interactive items, the importance of the mother-infant interaction has been observed repeatedly. The behavioral test items manage to give measures of observer reliability in the range of 0.85 to 90. Hopefully, this is also an indication of the reliability with which one is seeing and measuring the same behavior on which the parents rely as they attach to a new baby.

The Institute of Nutrition of Central America and Panama (INCAP) has been assessing malnourished babies. Here, 3 years ago, it was able to be predicted, with a 0.9 prediction, which neonates would end up with kwashiorkor a year and a half later, or with marasmus in the first year if they tipped over with infection. This is not difficult. These predictions were based on observations of their behavior. They were the babies who were too depleted to elicit mothering and did not call to their mothers for feedings. These overstressed, undernourished mothers with 4 or 5 children already were asked how often they fed the neonate. They would reply "On demand." If, however, 24 hours were spent with them, it was found that the total was three times a day in the neonatal period. So, it is no trick to predict that such babies, when they are hit by an infection in the first year, or weaning in the second year, are going to tip over into a depleted nutritional state. This kind of ability needs to be trusted in order to predict ahead from the neonatal period and to place these interventions in the area of already stressed interactions. One can trust not only the organization and coping capacity of the neonate but also the capacity of the neonate to influence its mother and its surrounding environment. The experience gained in Guatemala with stressed babies suggests a correlation between the neonatal behaviors of cuddliness, habituation, attention, looking at and following the mother's face, and following a red ball, with the mother's nutritional status. At the same time, the babies whose mothers have had less than adequate calories are much more likely to function at a midbrain reflexive level.

The subtle differences that these neonates demonstrated capture the essence of one mother's remark, "He never looks at me. He and I don't quite make it together." Dr. Thoman's discussion (Denenberg and Thoman, this volume) about the discoordination in "state" behaviors seen in babies later found to be at risk is implicit in this kind of mildly disordered neonate. It is often felt that if the pediatrician does not tell a mother he is worried about her baby she will never know it. This is our own kind of medical wishful thinking. Mothers are more concerned than the physician, but they dare not test his concern or admit to themselves that they are worried, for the physician is not offering them help—only labels.

This author is very concerned about the new Early Periodic, Screening, Diagnosis, and

Treatment (EPSDT) program for its potential as a labeling program. The diagnostic potential is increasingly more sophisticated, and EPSDT will undoubtedly mobilize the best of the diagnostic labels. But, so far, there seems to be very little chance that the billions projected for this program are likely to be used for prevention or intervention. Physicians do not know how to reach out for and help poor or alienated subcultures.

The medical model has been steeped in pathology and a kind of missionary approach for too long and is able only to label people who do not understand this model, rather than reach out for and include them in medical thinking. There is need for a kind of approach, which seems best called "advocacy," in which the physician offers himself to concerned parents of at risk children as partners in teamwork to improve the opportunities for their child's outcome. If physicians could approach a program like EPSDT with an attitude to parents of "What do you think you and your baby need?" the physician could then offer his expertise in predicting to the child's future potential and determine with the parents how "*we*" can best work together to help their child realize it. Under these circumstances physicians could, indeed, think of themselves as advocates of children. Identifications of a handicap or a problem can be an *opportunity* for change if physicians make it so.

The most important thing to come of this conference is the approach that focuses on the *interaction* of all concerned. Physicians have been, in the past, focusing on parents; now they are focusing on infants as active participants. It is now time to look at both in an interactive model and to bring fathers into the picture too. The physician should look for their coping strengths and put the labels on these strengths, rather than on the pathology.

PROFESSIONAL INTERACTION WITH MOTHERS

Professional interaction with mothers of at risk infants readily brings the problems of coping into focus. A caring mother feels something she has done has made her relationship to the child go wrong. She is in a grief reaction, according to Lindemann's construct (1944)–grief over the lost perfect child. She feels guilty, helpless, and responsible! In addition to this feeling of inadequacy in herself, when she is faced with an inability to reach the infant, this reinforces the feeling that she is not good for her infant. Most mothers felt that if anybody else could take care of their baby, they would do a better job. The mother's perceived failure of the child becomes a reflection of her own vulnerability. There is a functional overlay that interferes with the mother's and the baby's effectance model which is represented by Kogan and Wimberger's (1966) study of 4-year-olds. Dr. Kogan studied 4-year-old, mildly brain damaged children and compared them to a control group of normal 4-year-olds. She presented each child with a task that was just a little over their heads and told the mothers to help them learn the tasks. She scored the mothers on whether they shaped, shoved, or showed each step of the task, and she also scored them on latency, i.e., to act before the child could complete each step of the task. The mothers of the mildly brain damaged children had little latency, and they all shoved; they did not show or shape. This, at 4 years of age, if agreeing with Erik Erikson's thesis (1950), is really cutting into any opportunity on the part of the 4-year-old child to develop autonomy and a feeling of effectance. Here is represented the dangers of the over-protection with which a grieving mother saddles her slightly damaged child.

These observations reveal that the first task is to effect an understanding *caring* with these mothers. To make such a relationship, the pediatrician must let them know he cares and understands what they are going through: face their grieving with them and support them as important and effective for this child. Also, he must support them in finding out exactly where the child is, not where he or they wish the child were. The easiest way a pediatrician can do this is to use the behavior of the child to let the mother see the child with him and to share with her that he is seeing what she is seeing, and then, with this in mind, begin to give her an image of herself as effective. With this first step accomplished, he can move into the appropriate intervention programs that offer maximum effectiveness.

It seems that, with this transference as a baseline, one can reproduce the results of Chavez, Martinez, and Yaschine (1974) who are working in the area of poverty around Mexico City. Chavez and his colleagues have provided calories to the poverty group they are studying near Mexico City. They have provided nutritional supplementation to the mother while she is carrying her baby, followed by nutritional supplementation of the baby afterward. In order to be sure that mothers really utilized their supplements in the face of the anorexia of chronic malnutrition, it was necessary to give them a good deal of moral support. These mothers, then, had both nutritional supplementation and moral support, while a control group of similar families received neither. There were major differences in the outcome of the mother-child interactional behaviors. The mothers of the supplemented babies talked in longer sentences, and they used adjectives and adverbs as they talked to their children. The babies spoke in complex sentences earlier. The activity levels of the infants, of course, were different, as was their energy. The children explored farther, and they could do more for themselves.

Because these babies were so much more active, the mothers considered this positive. Because food had given them energy, they had to draw in the fathers to help them. They could not take care of these active children by themselves. All of the problems usually associated with poverty and lassitude seemed to be ameliorated by enough calories and support for the mother-child relationship.

As models for intervention are developed, this author would like these models to set as their ultimate goal the *quality of family life*. The target should not be limited to the child, his IQ, and adaptive behavior. Programs are needed that measure success in the child and in the intervention by things such as increased family comfort and decrease in divorce rate, a lower incidence of behavior problems in the siblings, increased opportunities for self expression by mothers, among others. These, perhaps, are pretty soft signs, but they may be a lot more important as measures of the effectiveness of intervention than is a rise in IQ or increased motor capacity on the part of the child. And who can achieve this; can pediatricians—or *must* they rely on parents with their caring and their strengths? This author believes there is no alternative, even if the dreams come true. Why must physicians attempt to put down the values and the strengths in parents and children with whom they could work, if they were ready to look for and acknowledge them? A new model is needed in pediatrics—a nonpathological model. With such a model that identified the *strengths* of parents and children, the pediatrician would present himself as an *advocate* rather than as a *labeler*. The Hawthorn effect would be great—expectation that they would succeed might reinforce their sense of dignity, of their own coping capacities, instead of the kind of expectancy to fail which, too often, they find now.

A NEEDED STUDY OF THE STATE OF PEDIATRIC ART

Those of the Child Development Section of the Academy of Pediatrics have been moving to obtain grant support to conduct a study of the state of "pediatric art" as it is taught in medical schools around the country. The schools where there is any emphasis at all on normal child development, normal parent-child relationships, and healthy physician-patient relationships need to be identified. There are very few, but there is a hunger in most for a new model for health and prevention of disease and psychological problems. The Pediatrics Committee of this group, led by Pearson (this volume), met to establish a plea for just such a study in medical schools and pediatric departments. The proposed study would examine not only the academic and primary care aspects of pediatric training but also the behavioral, social, and economic aspects as well. The proposal calls for a team to visit all departments of pediatrics for an indepth study of programs in developmental processes, mental retardation, developmental disabilities, delivery of care, long-term follow up, continuing education, and the establishment of physician-patient relationships, among other issues of concern. Accompanying this study would be a sampling of practicing pediatricians to determine their involvement and their perceptions of the needs for training in this area.

A second step in this study calls for a follow up planning conference to deal with the results of the study and to recommend steps needed to bring about desired changes. Without the second step conference, the results of the study might gather dust, as happens all too often with such studies.

Step three would involve getting this information before pediatric department chairmen and pediatric organizations, such as the Academy of Pediatrics and the Ambulatory Pediatric Association, as well as the American Board of Pediatrics.

Pediatricians can no longer hide behind the innocence of not having the tools for early diagnosis or the wishful thinking that leads to the postponement of early intervention. Enough is known now to be able to predict which infants and parents need supportive and preventive insights. The expertise and the courage must be developed in young pediatricians to equip them for an approach that will indeed reach out for and include parents and children in an advocacy, a positive approach that will improve the future for children and parents at risk (Brazelton, 1975).

LITERATURE CITED

Brazelton, T. B. 1973. Neonatal Behavioral Assessment Scale: Clinics in Developmental Medicine No. 50. Spastics International Medical Publications in association with: William Heinemann Medical Books. London; Lippincott, Philadelphia.

Brazelton, T. B. 1975. Training Program for Pediatricians in Child Development at the Harvard Medical School. Paper presented at Society for Research in Child Development Meeting, April 17–19, Denver, Col.

Chavez, A., C. Martinez, and T. Yaschine. 1974. Nutrition, Mother-Child Relations, and Behavioral Development in the Young Child from a Rural Community. Instituto Nacional de Nutricion, Mexico City, Mexico.

Cravioto, J., E. Delcardie, and H. B. Birch. 1966. Nutrition, growth and neuro-integrative development. Pediatr. Supp. 38: 319.

Erikson, E. 1950. Childhood and Society. Norton, New York.

Greenberg, N. H. 1971. A comparison of infant-mother interactional behavior in infants with atypical behavior and normal infants. In J. Hellmuth (ed.), Exceptional Infant, Vol. 2, pp. 390. Bruner/Mazel, New York.

Heider, G. M. 1966. Vulnerability in infants and young children. Genet. Psych. Monogr. 73:(1).

Klaus, M., and J. H. Kennell. 1970. Mothers separated from their newborn infants. Ped. Clin. No. Amer. 17: 1015.

Klein, R. E., J. P. Habicht, and C. Yarbrough. 1971. Effect of protein calorie malnutrition on mental development. INCAP Publ. 1: 571.

Kogan, K. L., and H. C. Wimberger. 1966. An approach to defining mother-child interaction styles. Percept. Mot. Skills 23: 1171–1177.

Lindemann, E. 1944. Symptomatology and management of acute grief. Amer. J. Psychiat. 101: 141–148.

Lubchenco, L. O., C. Hansman, M. Dressler, and B. Boyd. 1963. Intrauterine growth estimated from liveborn, birthweight data at 24–42 weeks of gestation. Pediatrics 32: 793.

Parmelee, A. H., and R. Michaelis. 1971. Neurological examination of the newborn exceptional infant. Vol. 2, Exceptional Infant. Bruner/Mazel, New York.

DEMONSTRATION PROJECTS

The Portage Project: A Model for Early Childhood Intervention

David E. Shearer, M.A., and Marsha S. Shearer, M.A.

The Portage Project was originally funded in 1969 by the Education of the Handicapped Act, Public Law 91-230, Title VI, Part C to develop, implement, and demonstrate a model program serving young handicapped children in a rural area.

OVERVIEW

The Portage Project operates administratively through a regional education agency (Cooperative Educational Service Agency No. 12) serving 23 school districts in south-central rural Wisconsin. The Project currently serves 150 children between the ages of birth to 6 years, or up to such time as a child's readiness for a classroom program is demonstrated. The children have been identified as being handicapped in one or more developmental areas. Any preschool child, with any type or degree of handicapping condition residing within the 3,600 square mile area served by the agency, qualifies for the early intervention project.

There is no classroom program. All instruction takes place in each child's home and the teaching is done by the parents. A home teacher is assigned to each child and family. These educators, who may be trained professionals or trained paraprofessionals, visit each one of their 15 families one day per week for 1.5 hours. An individualized curriculum is prescribed weekly based on the assessment of each child's present behaviors in the areas of language, self-help, cognitive, motor, and socialization skills. Utilizing the parents as the teacher, the Portage Project follows the precision teaching model (Lindsley, 1968):

1. At least three *behaviors are targeted* for learning each week. The behaviors and criteria are chosen with the goal that the child (thus the parent) will achieve success in 1 week.
2. *Baseline data are recorded* by the home teacher on each new task before instruction as an additional check on readiness.

3. During the week the parents implement the *actual teaching process itself*, which includes reinforcing desired behaviors and reducing or extinguishing those beahviors that interfere with learning appropriate skills.

4. The home teacher *records post-baseline data* 1 week later to determine if the prescribed behaviors taught by the parents have in fact been learned by the child.

The degree of success with the prescriptions provides weekly feedback to the home teacher. Thus, the home teacher has current objective data on which to plan modifications in weekly curriculum goals. This in turn increases the likelihood of the parent and the child succeeding on the prescriptions for the coming week.

Thus, the Portage Project is a home teaching program attempting to directly involve parents in the education of their children by teaching parents what to teach, how to teach, what to reinforce, and how to observe and record behavior.

RATIONALE FOR THE HOME BASED PROGRAM

As children were being identified, it was clear that classroom programs could not be provided because of the cost and responsibility of transporting very young handicapped children great distances. In addition, even when several children were identified within a smaller geographical area, i.e., one school district, the variance in chronological ages, functioning levels, and handicapping conditions precluded establishing classroom programs. In addition, classroom programs would severely limit parent involvement because of the geographical and psychological distances between home and school. Thus, a major program decision was made: all instruction would take place in the parent and child's natural environment, the home.

Having now experienced this rather unique delivery system, the staff of the Portage Project believes there are inherent *educational* advantages utilizing the home based precision teaching model, in addition to the practical aspect of not having to transport children and provide a center (thus reducing program cost by more than one half). These educational advantages are:

1. *Learning occurs in the parent and child's natural environment;* therefore, the typical problem of transferring back into the home what has been learned in a classroom or clinic does not exist.

2. There is *direct and constant access to behavior as it occurs naturally*. This is more likely to result in curriculum goals that will be functional for the child within his own unique environment. In fact, the differences in cultures, life styles, and value systems held by the parents are incorporated into curriculum planning, because the parents are the final determiners of what and how their child will be taught.

3. It is more likely that *learned behavior will generalize and be maintained* if the behaviors have been learned in the child's home environment and taught by the child's natural reinforcing agent, his parents.

4. If instruction occurs in the home, there is *more opportunity for full family participa-*

tion in the teaching process. Father, sibling, and extended family involvement become a realistic and obtainable goal.

5. There is *access to the full range of behaviors,* many of which could not be targeted for modification within a classroom, such as temper tantrums that only occur in the home.

6. It is hypothesized that the *training of parents,* who already are natural reinforcing agents, *will provide them with the skills necessary to deal with new behaviors when they occur.*

7. Finally, because the home teacher is working on a one-to-one basis with the parents and child, *individualization of instructional goals* for both *is an operational reality.*

REFERRAL SOURCES

Information concerning the availability of the Project is disseminated to community resources throughout the district. The home teachers are responsible for personally contacting professionals within their assigned geographic area for the purpose of continually seeking new referrals.

County health nurses, social workers, physicians, local guidance clinics, and school personnel within the 23 school districts have been major sources of referral. Nearby diagnostic and evaluation centers also refer children to the Project. Public service announcements on local radio stations and newspaper articles describing the project have brought additional referrals, many from parents themselves.

Brochures describing the Project have been left in doctors', dentists', and chiropractors' offices. Many beauty shops and grocery stores have bulletin boards on which are posted a Project brochure. Medical diagnosis is not a prerequisite for child referral, thus referrals are welcome from anyone. Because there was not a complete or accurate listing of preschool handicapped children residing within the area at the time of Project initiation, referrals from every possible source were sought.

IDENTIFICATION AND SCREENING

Each child is screened for Project eligibility by the home teacher who serves the geographic area in which the family resides.

The home teacher contacts the parents and makes an appointment to come to the home to explain the Project and to meet and screen the child. Project eligibility is partially determined by the child's functioning level in five developmental areas: 1) self-help, 2) motor, 3) socialization, 4) cognitive, and 5) language. If there is a significant lag between chronological age and functioning level in any of the areas, the child qualifies for the program. Children with observable disabilities—medical, physical, or behavioral— automatically qualify for service. Additional factors are also considered. A 6-month-old child who is functioning normally will be considered for service if there are siblings attending special education classes, if the parents have attended special education classes, or if there are other reasons for considering the child to be at high risk. Additionally, the Project has never refused service because a child had too many handicaps or had handicaps of too great a degree.

The screening instrument, the Alpern-Boll Developmental Profile (Alpern-Boll, 1972), as well as additional testing, is administered in the home in the presence of the parents utilizing their knowledge of the child. If the child qualifies for service and the parents agree to be in the program, the child's name is then referred to the multidisciplinary team from the school district in which the child resides. If the team agrees that the child has exceptional educational needs and that the Portage Project can best meet these needs, then that school district contracts with the agency to serve the child through the Portage Project. (Local school districts and the Wisconsin Department of Public Instruction, Division for Handicapped Children, have assumed financial responsibility for direct services since 1973.)

ASSESSMENT AND CURRICULUM PLANNING

The Alpern-Boll Developmental Profile is administered to all the children. This is also the screening instrument referred to earlier. This instrument is administered as a parent questionnaire together with direct observation of the child's behavior, when possible. Intelligence tests have also been administered for the purpose of further documenting individual and group gains to assess program effectiveness. It is anticipated that these will no longer be used. The staff believes that the only purpose for testing should be to program curriculum more effectively for children. Thus, tests will be selected and administered solely for this purpose. Stress will continue to be given to informal assessment, which includes observing and recording how a child accomplishes a task, or why he fails to accomplish it. Behavioral checklists will continue to be administered to aid in determining each child's present behavioral skills.

To facilitate planning for individual children, the Project staff has devised the *Portage Guide to Early Education* (Bluma et al., 1976). The guide is in three parts: 1) a Developmental Sequence Checklist, which lists sequential behaviors from birth to 5 years of age in five developmental areas: cognitive, language, self-help, motor, and socialization (Figure 1), 2) a set of Curriculum Cards to match each of the 580 behaviors stated on the Checklist, using behavioral objectives to describe the skill and suggesting materials and curriculum ideas to teach each of these 580 behaviors (Figure 2), and 3) a manual of instructions.

The Checklist (Figure 1) is used to pinpoint the behaviors the child already exhibits in the developmental areas. The behaviors on the Checklist that indicate emerging skills (those unlearned behaviors immediately following learning behaviors) are those that the home teacher may wish to target for learning. The numbered behavior can then be referred to in the deck of cards (Figure 2) that state the goal in behavioral terms and suggest materials and methods for teaching the skill. These materials can only serve as a guide for the home teacher. Fully 50 percent of behaviors actually prescribed for children

Figure 1. Example of one sheet from the Checklist of the Portage Guide to Early Education.

Checklist for Cognition (Sample)

Age level	Card no.	Behavior	Entry behavior	Date achieved
	49	Names 4 common pictures	✓	
	50	Names objects that make sounds	✓	
	51	Copies drawing	✓	
	52	Repeats 2 numbers	✓	
3—4	53	Builds tower of 10 blocks	✓	
	54	Builds a bridge with 3 blocks in imitation	✓	
	55	Builds with blocks in detail, in imitation	✓	
	56	Copies letters M and N		10/73
	57	Adds one part to incomplete man		10/73
	58	Identifies big and little		
	59	Completes 6-piece puzzle	✓	
	60	Draws a square in imitation		11/73
	61	Matches 3 primary colors		
	62	Identifies primary colors		
	63	Counts to 5 in imitation		
	64	Identifies 10 body parts	✓	
	65	Identifies boy and girl	✓	
	66	Identifies heavy and light		
	67	Recognizes stories		

Checklist for Cognition *continued*

Age level	Card no.	Behavior	Entry behavior	Date achieved
	68	Finger plays/words and actions		
	69	Repeats 3—4 numbers		
	70	Names or points to 3 shapes		
	71	Names action pictures		
4—5	72	Counts 10 objects		
	73	Understands number concepts 1—5		
	74	Builds with blocks, complex		
	75	Copies triangle		
	76	Associates activities with night and day		
	77	Weight comparison, less than 1 pound		
	78	Matches related common objects		
	79	Identifies color with object		
	80	Repeats nursery rhymes		
	81	Retells stories		
	82	Sings simple songs		
	83	Adds 3 parts to incomplete man		
	84	Draws a man		
	85	Identifies long and short		
	86	Places object on direction		

Portage Project   CARD NO. 58   COGNITIVE

AGE 3–4

TITLE:
   Identifies big and little

BEHAVIORAL DESCRIPTION:
   The child can tell which ball or book is little, which is big (one-inch difference in size)

SUGGESTED ACTIVITIES AND MATERIALS:
1. Use 5 large blocks and 5 small blocks that are the same color. Begin by having the child sort the blocks into 2 piles according to size. The child should be able to sort without error before going on to pointing to big and little. Praise success so the child knows his response was correct.
2. Use two objects that differ only in size. For example, use two red balls, one big and one little. Begin with very large and very small items. Name the balls or blocks or other objects as big and little. Then ask the child to give you the big ball and then the little one. Change the position of the objects often. When the child can consistently point to big and little without error, begin by having the child name which object is big, which is little.
3. Use small penny size candy bars and the same brand of large candy bars. (Wrappers are the same). Have the child name big, little. Give the candy bars as a reward.
4. Place 6 inch cut out circles and 3 inch cut out circles on the floor. At first have the child step only on the big circles, and then on the little circles. Then have the child tell you which circle to step on (big or little) and he is to tell you if you are correct.
5. Place a treat on one of the circles. The child should correctly tell you if the circle is big or little before getting the treat.
6. Gradually reduce the size of the circles and find other like items which differ in size (1 inch difference) for the child to identify.
7. See Card No. C47, L44.

B58   1972 C.E.S.A. No. 12

Portage Project   CARD NO. 61   COGNITIVE

AGE 3–4

TITLE:
   Matches 3 primary colors

BEHAVIORAL DESCRIPTION:
   The child will match color to color, i.e. red to red, yellow to yellow, blue to blue

SUGGESTED ACTIVITIES AND MATERIALS:
1. Begin using 2 colors–yellow and red. Cut out 6 red and 6 yellow circles. One at a time you place 4 red circles in one pile and 4 yellow circles in another. Hand the child the last 4 circles. He is to place last 4 circles. Guide his hand to help him place the colors correctly if necessary.
2. Leave more circles for him to match and sort and withdraw help. Reward correct matches with praise.
3. Use a peg board and colored pegs. Hold up a red peg and ask the child to find another like this. Repeat with other colors. Instruct child to place pegs in board in rows of colors.
4. Place large colored circles on floor, (red, yellow, and blue). Hand the child one colored circle. Instruct him to step only on the circles which are the same color as the one he is holding.
5. See Card No. C40.

B61   1972 C.E.S.A. No. 12

Figure 2. Two examples from the card deck of the Portage Guide to Early Education.

341

are not to be found on the Checklist; but there may well be a behavior leading to a long-term goal that may be listed on the Checklist. Prescriptions are written with the intention that the parent and child will succeed on each prescribed task within 1 week. Thus, the behaviors listed on the Checklist should often be thought of as long-term goals that need to be divided into smaller behavioral segments. These can be chained together to achieve the long-term goal. Thus, the child, not the Checklist, determines the curriculum.

Following both formal and informal assessment, the home teacher often suggests three or four behaviors that are emerging and could be prescribed. The parents are given the choice as to which behavior they would like to target first.

The chosen goal, stated as a behavioral objective, together with directions, is then written on an activity chart by the home teacher and presented during the next home visit. As parents experience success and gain confidence in their ability to teach their child and to record his behavior, prescriptions are gradually increased to three and four per week. These activities are often in several areas of development. For instance, the parents might be working on reducing tantrums, buttoning, and counting objects, all within the same week.

HOME TEACHING PROCESS

The home teacher writes up an activity chart incorporating the parents' selection of targeted behavior (Figures 3 and 4). Again the most important point is for the home teacher to break down tasks and to prescribe only those that can be achieved within 1 week. This provides the parents with rapid reinforcement, because what is learned by the child is a direct result of parental teaching. The directions are written so that the parents will have no difficulty understanding them, should they need to refer to them during the week. Recording is always uncomplicated and usually involves recording frequency counts, especially in the beginning.

When the activity chart is set up, the home teacher begins modeling teaching techniques for the parents. First, the home teacher introduces the activity to the child and records baseline data: the frequency of correct responses before instruction. This data are recorded on the activity chart. The home teacher then follows the directions that have been written on the chart and begins the teaching process. The home teacher thus is modeling teaching techniques for the parents, showing them what to do and how to do it. After several opportunities, the parents take over and work with the child, modeling for the home teacher. The home teacher then is able to offer suggestions and reinforcement, which increase the likelihood that the parents will record accurately during the week. When materials are necessary, every attempt is made to utilize materials available in the home; however, there are times when materials are brought in and left for the parents to use.

Throughout the visit, the home teacher stresses the importance of working with the child during the week. The home teacher leaves her home and office phone number with the parents and encourages them to call if any question or problem arises during the week. When the home teacher returns the following week, post-baseline data is collected

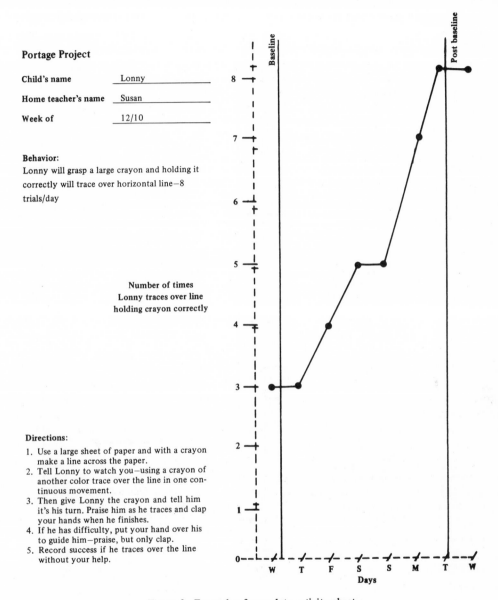

Portage Project

Child's name   Lonny

Home teacher's name   Susan

Week of   12/10

Behavior:
Lonny will grasp a large crayon and holding it
correctly will trace over horizontal line—8
trials/day

**Number of times
Lonny traces over line
holding crayon correctly**

Directions:
1. Use a large sheet of paper and with a crayon
   make a line across the paper.
2. Tell Lonny to watch you—using a crayon of
   another color trace over the line in one continuous movement.
3. Then give Lonny the crayon and tell him
   it's his turn. Praise him as he traces and clap
   your hands when he finishes.
4. If he has difficulty, put your hand over his
   to guide him—praise, but only clap.
5. Record success if he traces over the line
   without your help.

Baseline

Post baseline

Days

Figure 3. Example of complete activity chart.

343

Portage Project

Child's name   Robby

Home teacher's name   Kathy

Week of   3/10

Behavior:
Robby will crawl forward on hands and knees using left-right movement with stomach off the floor (towel for support)

Number of feet crawled forward/trial

Directions:
1. Place a goodie on the floor about 1 ft. in front of Robby. Help position him by putting his hands in front of him.
2. Then take the beach towel and place it under his stomach and pull up holding on to the ends of the towel until he's on his hands and knees.
3. Encourage him to move towards the goodie.
4. Praise each movement forward and as he gains in skill, increase the distance between Robby and the treat.
5. Reward with treat when he reaches it. Practice 6 times each day but just record number of ft. crawled forward on the first 3 trials.

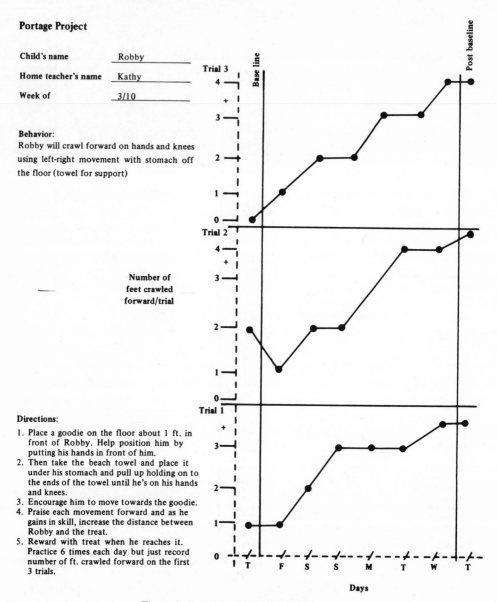

Figure 4. Example of complete activity chart.

344

on the previous week's activities. This helps the home teacher to validate the accuracy of the parent's recording, and it provides the teacher with feedback concerning the degree of success achieved by the child and the child's readiness for the next sequential step. Based on these data, the home teacher alters the previous prescriptions or introduces new activities beginning with taking baseline data. And so the cycle is repeated. At the completion of each home visit, the parents write an evaluation of the week's progress, which often serves as an additional source of information for curriculum planning and modification.

This is the sequence of the home visit process. However, in reality, in the beginning, intermediate and/or additional steps are sometimes necessary to the parent teaching process. Parents are not all the same; therefore, it is as important to individualize the teaching process for them as it is for their child.

Parents who are themselves retarded have also successfully participated in the Project (activity charts are not used; however, the parents still record utilizing adaptations in the charting system).

Babysitters and other caregivers have taught children, and the children's gains have been significant. Parents who, before Project involvement, said they had given up trying to teach their child anything, have, as a result of Project involvement, taught their child a great deal. (Readers are referred to the monograph by Fredericks et al. (1975) for a detailed description of the Project's Parent Training Program.)

STAFF TRAINING

The Project staff consists of special educators, speech clinicians, psychologists, and paraprofessionals. However, *all* staff members are also home teachers. That is their behaviorally defined role, regardless of professional background or additional responsibilities. Professional and paraprofessional home teachers have precisely the same roles and responsibilities, including case finding, assessment, curriculum planning, and data keeping. A study was conducted comparing gains made by children served by paraprofessional and professional home teachers. Interestingly, the data indicate that paraprofessionals did slightly better, though the amount of gain was not statistically significant (Schortinghuis and Frohman, 1974). New staff are provided with indepth preservice training conducted by experienced home teachers (Shearer, 1970). This training usually takes 2 weeks and is individualized for each new staff member depending on their entry knowledge. Approximately half of the training occurs by observing an experienced home teacher in all project components, particularly assessment, the home teaching process, and curriculum planning.

One half day is set aside each week for inservice training. Specific problems encountered during the week are discussed. The entire staff is then able to serve as a valuable resource to each other. The home teacher selects the suggestion that will be carried out the following week, and this is recorded. Two weeks later the home teacher reports back to the group and, if necessary, additional modifications are made until success is achieved. Weekly staff meetings, for the purpose of problem solving, is particularly vital when this delivery system is utilized. The home teachers are "on the road" each day and do not have a teacher down the hall or a principal to provide immediate help as problems arise. Thus, weekly meetings provide the home teachers with suggestions for curriculum modification that can be utilized the following week. As one home teacher said, "Frustration never lasts longer than Friday."

DATA COLLECTION

The *activity charts* that have been left with the parents are collected at the end of each week. These charts together with a *progress report* are turned in weekly. The progress report lists the prescribed behaviors from the previous week, and the home teacher records whether the child has attained criteria needed before success can be recorded. Prescriptions for the coming week are also recorded on the weekly progress report. A *behavioral log* is kept for each child (Figure 5). All activities and the date they were prescribed are written on the log. Each success and the date the prescription was achieved is recorded according to developmental area. This log provides an ongoing record of every behavior prescribed, each success achieved, and the duration of each prescription. Additionally, this log also provides a percentage of success achieved by parent, child, and home teacher. The continual input of data allows supervisory personnel and each home teacher to spot problems quickly, thus providing a continual feedback system for program monitoring and modification (ABT Associates, 1972).

USE OF COMMUNITY RESOURCES

The Portage Project is an educational model. Its only reason for being in the home is to teach the parents to teach the child. Yet, often the parents present other problems to the home teacher for solution. The teachers' expertise is in *teaching,* not social work, counseling, psychology, psychiatry, etc., but it *is* their responsibility to be aware of community resources that can serve these other needs. It then must be the parent's decision whether or not to contact the suggested sources. The option and decision must be left with the parents.

Approximately 60 percent of the children served are seen periodically at outpatient or diagnostic evaluation centers. The home teacher accompanies the parents and child on these clinic visits to elicit suggestions for curriculum from clinic staff and, with the parents, to inform the staff of the progress of the child. Two additional spin-offs of this involvement have included: 1) an increase in referrals from the hospitals and clinics, and 2) perhaps more important, parents and children were no longer waiting for hours to be seen for a few minutes.

The Portage Project staff does not employ a nutritionist, a social worker, an occupational therapist, a nurse, a psychiatrist, or a physical therapist. Although all of these

Portage Project

Behavior Evaluation

Child _____   Period

Teacher _____

Specific goal	Date	Date accomplished					
		Cognitive	Communicative	Motor	Self-help	Socialization	Parent/child
Attends to tasks—10 minutes	9/3						
Places 0 + in formboard with help	9/3	9/10		9/10			
Places 0 + in formboard no trial and error	9/10	9/17		9/17			
Strings 5 beads in 2 minutes—no aid	9/10			9/17			
Stands on 1 ft 5 sec with support	9/10			9/17			
Stands on 1 ft 5 sec no support	9/17			10/2			
Names 7 action pictures in imitation	9/17		9/24				9/24
Names 7 action pictures no model	9/24		10/2				
Names pictures using 3-word phase	9/24						
Put on pants—no aid	10/2				10/9		
Hops on 1 ft in place with support	10/2			10/9			
Unbuttons 4 buttons—through hole pushed ½ way	10/2			10/16	10/16		
Unbuttons 4 buttons—no aid	10/9			10/16	10/16		
Traces letters M and N with finger	10/9	10/16					
Draws letters M and N by connecting dots	10/9	10/16					
Draws square by connecting four dots	10/16	10/23		10/23			
Buttons 4 buttons—through hole pushed ½ way	10/16	10/23		10/23			
Draws in imitation of model	10/16	10/23		10/23			
Total							

Figure 5. Example from behavioral log kept on each enrolled child.

347

people could have been hired while the Project was federally funded, the cost of such personnel would have drastically increased overall cost, thus reducing the likelihood of program continuation with state and local monies. Additionally, model replication in other rural areas would be severely limited because of cost. It is believed that the utilization of existing community resources can best serve the staff, the parents, and the children's needs in a cost-effective manner.

PROJECT EVALUATION RESULTS

The average IQ of the children in the Project was 75, as determined by the Cattell Infant Test and the Stanford-Binet Intelligence Test. The average child in the Project gained 15 months in an 8-month period, as measured by these pre-post assessment tools.

A significant number of the parents have been able to plan curriculum fully and to write up activity charts without teacher assistance. This occurs as parents demonstrate readiness to take more of an active role in planning. Access to the curriculum guide and any other planning aids are made available and any help needed in writing up activity charts is given during the home visit. Gradually, the home teachers visit less frequently as the parents assume responsibilities in the planning as well as the teaching phase of the program.

A significant number of parents have reported that they are using the teaching techniques learned from the home teacher to change behaviors of other family members, in addition to the targeted child.

Children who, because of age, remained in the Project after 1 year were retested in September, and these test results were compared to the scores achieved the previous June. Although it would be expected that some regression would occur, there was no significant difference in the scores. This may indicate that the parents continued to work with and reinforce behaviors even though the home teacher was no longer making visits.

An average of 128 prescriptions were written per child over the program year. The children were successful on 91 percent of the prescriptions written by professional and paraprofessional staff.

An experimental study was conducted involving randomly selected children attending local classroom programs for culturally and economically disadvantaged preschool children. The Stanford-Binet Intelligence Scale, and Cattell Infant Scale, and the Alpern-Boll Developmental Profile were given as pre- and post-tests to both groups. In addition, the Gessell Developmental Schedule was given as a post-test to both groups. Multiple analysis of covariance was used to control for IQ, practice effect, and age. The greater gains made by the Portage Project children in the areas of mental age, IQ, language, academic, and socialization skills were statistically significant, as compared to the group receiving classroom instruction (Peniston, 1972).

Using the children as their own control, test results and behavioral gains were compared and measured. The mean gain in IQ scores on the Stanford-Binet was 18.3 and was statistically significant beyond the 0.01 level (Shearer and Shearer, 1972).

In 1970, 55 children and their families were provided service through federal funding. In 1975, 150 children were served with state and local monies. The Portage Project has been validated by the Joint Dissemination Review Panel for national dissemination and replication.

COST OF PROGRAM SERVICES

School districts contract on a per pupil basis with the Cooperative Educational Service Agency No. 12. Presently, the gross cost charged by the Agency to the school districts is $622 per year per child. The State Department of Public Instruction reimburses each school district 70 percent of teachers' salaries. Thus, local districts pay about 50 percent of total project cost, approximately $300 per year per child. It is anticipated that the cost will continue to be reduced as more children are served by the Project.

THE PORTAGE MODEL

The Portage Model incorporates the major components of the original Portage Project. These include:

1. An educational program that takes place in each enrolled child's home and is implemented by home teachers who visit each family weekly
2. Assessment using the Alpern-Boll Developmental Profile and the Portage Guide to Early Education if appropriate, plus any other assessment instruments necessary to plan curriculum
3. Implementation of the precision teaching model
4. Curriculum planning with the expectation that children will achieve each prescribed goal weekly
5. Weekly staff meetings for the purpose of problem solving and curriculum modification

Portage Project Interaction with Replication Agencies

Funding from the Bureau of Education for the Handicapped (BEH), Office of Education, to the Portage Project has provided training and technical assistance to various additional demonstration sites throughout the nation for replicating the Portage Model. The sites were selected based on a variety of administrative and staffing patterns and funding sources including Head Start, public schools, state institutions, and private facilities. Children served in the replications include the handicapped, the nonhandicapped, and those classified as high risk. Rural and urban sites are included.

A contract between the Portage Project and the replication agency details the commitments of both programs to provide quality service to children. Primarily, the Portage Project provides training to the replication site, which includes a site visit to the agency for 1 week of training in the various components of the Portage Model. Frequently, staff from the replication site visit the Portage Project and go on home visits to see the Project model in operation. At least two additional follow up visits to each replication site are scheduled to observe the program in operation and to help plan for the coming year. The replication site agrees to share pre- and post-data with the Portage Project in order that outreach efforts and their results can be reported to the BEH and disseminated widely. Each contract specifies that after 1 year of training and technical assistance, the replication site will be fully operational and functioning independently of the Portage Project.

These demonstration replications will themselves serve as models in their regional area. It is planned that staff from these replication sites will provide training and technical assistance to additional programs in their region that wish to initiate the Portage Model.

It is hoped that with continued BEH funding for model implementation many children presently not receiving services will receive quality programming to meet their special and exceptional educational needs and, most vitally, to increase training for parents—the child's first and potentially his best teachers.

LITERATURE CITED

ABT Associates Incorporated. 1972. Exemplary Programs for the Handicapped. Vol. III, ERIC Number: ED-079890. Cambridge, Mass.

Alpern, G., and T. Boll. 1972. Developmental Profile. Psychological Development Pub., Indianapolis, Ind.

Bluma, S., M. Shearer, A. Frohman, and J. Hilliard. 1976. Portage Guide to Early Education (Rev. Ed.). Cooperative Educational Service Agency No. 12, Portage, Wis.

Fredricks, H. D., A. Hayden, D. Lillie, M. Shearer, and R. Wiegerink. 1975. Training Parents to Teach: Four Models. Technical Assistance Development Systems, University of North Carolina, Chapel Hill.

Lindsley, O. R. 1968. Training Parents and Teachers to Precisely Manage Children's Behavior. Paper presented at C. S. Mott Foundation-Children's Health Center.

Peniston, E. 1972. An Evaluation of the Portage Project. Unpublished manuscript. The Portage Project, Cooperative Educational Service Agency No. 12, Portage, Wis.

Schortinghuis, N., and A. Frohman. 1974. A comparison of professional and paraprofessional success with preschool children. J. Learn. Disab. 17: 245–247.

Shearer, D. 1970. Staff Training Manual. Unpublished manuscript. The Portage Project, Cooperative Education Service Agency No. 12, Portage, Wis.

Shearer, D., J. Billingsley, A. Frohman, J. Hilliard, F. Johnson, and M. Shearer. 1972. Portage Checklist and Curriculum Guide to Early Education. Cooperative Educational Service Agency No. 12, Portage, Wis.

Shearer, M. 1972. Staff and Parent Training Program of the Portage Project. Unpublished manuscript. The Portage Project, Cooperative Educational Service Agency No. 12, Portage, Wis.

Shearer, M., and D. Shearer. 1972. The Portage Project: A model for early childhood education. Except. Child. 36: 210–217.

The Read Project: Teaching Manuals for Parents of Retarded Children

Bruce L. Baker, Ph.D., and Louis J. Heifetz, Ph.D.

Increasingly voiced is the right of persons who are retarded to remain in the community and to live with dignity and realized competence. This aim presumes not only an accepting and tolerant community, but also a continuum of community-based services to fill the void between solitary home maintenance and total institutional neglect. That such comprehensive services are far from actualized is documented by the observations of select committees (The President's Committee on Mental Retardation) and painfully underscored by the experiences of parents seeking help (Greenfield, 1970).

BACKGROUND

The parent of a retarded child repeatedly confronts two needs: 1) the need for more widespread and equitable distribution of services, and 2) the need for effective services that are more than good intentions. As a variety of community-based programs haphazardly develop to meet the first of these needs, parents themselves have been a suddenly discovered resource. Parents, it appears, are a large, sometimes motivated and certainly inexpensive pool of potential teachers who could, with proper training, take on an expert proactive role in their child's education.

Although parents' associations have long been advocates for better services for retarded children, parents have usually lacked the specific expertise to evaluate the quality of those services or to supplement them in their own daily interactions with their child. Agencies too often have considered the parents to be primarily in need of a

Project supported by Contract No. 72-2016, National Institute of Child Health and Human Development, National Institutes of Health, Bethesda, Maryland. Project officer: Dr. Michael Begab.

therapeutic experience, to "work through" their considerable feelings about their disabled child. While not denying the reality of those feelings, some professionals have recently responded more directly to parents' frequently expressed desire for training in specific management and teaching methods. It seems tenable that many adverse attitudes and feelings are mainly the result of daily frustrations and failures in coping with a retarded child's behavior, and that as parents become more competent as teachers, psychological benefits unobtainable through just talking might ensue.

A promising intervention approach to meet the need for effective services is behavior modification, an application of social learning principles that focuses on observable behaviors and places primary concern on environmental determinants. Looking through this model at "retardation," one is less apt to focus on labels and organic limits as on children who need special help in learning and settings which themselves retard or enhance functioning. In recent years, there have been many encouraging demonstrations of changes in environmental antecedents and consequences leading to changes in a wide range of behaviors such as: self-help skills, speech and language, academic skills, inappropriate, maladaptive, or disruptive behaviors, and social skills (Baker and Ward, 1971; Bensberg, Colwell, and Cassell, 1965; Birnbrauer et al., 1965; Lovaas, 1966; Minge and Ball, 1967).

First reports of behavior modification training for parents usually involved one highly motivated parent, a specific child behavior, and considerable therapist involvement in the training process (Berkowitz and Graziano, 1972; Risley and Wolf, 1967). More recently, there are several simultaneous trends: more complex behaviors are being targeted, parents are being asked for greater involvement in all aspects of programming, and training is being made more cost-effective (Baker, Heifetz, and Brightman, 1974; Hirsch and Walder, 1969).

These recent developments are illustrated in our comprehensive parent training program, operated in conjunction with Camp Freedom, a behavior modification residential camp for retarded children (Baker, 1973a, b; Brightman, 1972). To date, over 200 families have been trained in this program. Training for the entire family is aimed at both the institution of specific training programs with the retarded child and the acquisition of general strategies for observing, recording, and programming.

Parents meet in groups of six to twelve families with primarily preprofessional trainers (siblings of campers participate in separate training institutes at camp). Three precamp sessions generally involve acquiring a theoretical base, assessing the child and beginning a program; a weekend session at camp involves teaching under close supervision; five post camp sessions explore areas of application, obstacles to programming, and future plans. A contract with parents provides for a $50 tuition refund to those attending at least eight of nine sessions, thereby assuring high attendance. The considerable variety of training methods employed includes: lectures, discussions, individual consultation, home visits, hot lines, program exercises, films, video tape feedback of parent teaching, parent-led groups, parent critiques of programs, role-playing, modeling, and live demonstrations.

While the group training format without highly paid professionals decreases costs and the comprehensiveness broadens benefits beyond a single behavior modified, it was still wondered whether more could possibly be done for less. It seemed that many of the training inputs might be further packaged, in written instructional manuals, to both decrease the cost of training and perhaps enhance its effectiveness, because parents would have materials available to review.

The remainder of this chapter will report on the development and initial evaluation of such a series of self-instructional manuals for parents of retarded children.

READ PROJECT SERIES

The Read Project Series (Baker et al., 1973; 1976) currently consists of an Assessment Booklet and 10 instructional manuals in areas where parents expressed the greatest need for guidance: 1) managing behavioral problems, 2) toilet training and other self-help skill training, 3) developing speech and language skills, and 4) teaching constructive play activities. The 10 manuals are: Basic Skills, Early Self-Help Skills, Intermediate Self-Help Skills, Advanced Self-Help Skills, Toilet Training, Beginning Speech, Speech and Language, Early Play Skills, Play Skills, and Behavior Problems (which follows a different format from the 9 skill-teaching manuals).

Each approximately 120-page manual was designed to be self-contained and includes sections on: choosing a target skill, setting the stage, teaching principles (such as guiding and shaping), using rewards, and keeping records of progress. Included also is a section responding to questions most frequently raised by parents. As a result of a pilot survey of parent content preferences, each manual also includes: fictionalized "mini-case studies," which highlight central points in setting up and carrying out a program; many compelling and explanatory illustrations; and a large number of specific program outlines, one of which is to be chosen by the parent for his/her debut as a systematic and intentional behavior modifier (Figure 1A, B, C, and D for sample pages).

The basic notion behind the 10 separate manuals is to provide an approximate custom-tailoring of a parent's training package to the child's current educational needs, while still keeping to a minimum the amount of professional involvement. Separate manuals were written for different skill areas (e.g., self-help, speech, play), but a variety of skills within an area were contained in each manual (e.g., self-help: feeding, grooming, dressing). While the underlying principles of behavior modification remain the same, regardless of the particular area of application, the teaching strategies based upon these fundamentals vary widely. For example, in teaching beginning self-help skills a program relies heavily on physical guidance, backward chaining, shaping, and fading. In teaching higher level self-help skills where teaching can proceed more quickly without the atomistic guidance required by earlier self-help training, more benefit can be derived from verbal instructions. Also, the types of reinforcers and procedures for administering them vary with skill level. The intent was to furnish a parent with only that subset of teaching strategies central to his/her child.

Throughout the manuals, it is also stressed to parents that "no one knows your child as you do" and that the guidelines in the manual are simply that: guidelines, to be

Selections from the READ Project Series

As the world becomes more manageable for your child, it can become more comfortable for you. Your extra patience and effort during the early stages of teaching will be well rewarded by the eventual benefits to you both.

Benefits to You

Tommy eagerly climbed onto the kitchen chair as Mom poured the glass of juice.

"I'll be sitting in the living room, Tommy."

Moments later his older sister, Jill, wandered in to get a cup of coffee and smiled to see Tommy carefully sipping the juice. It hadn't been that long ago that she or Mom needed to be right there every minute helping him but their recent weeks of systematic teaching had now paid off for them all. Tommy was drinking on his own, as Jill called...

"Hey, Mom, you want some more coffee?"

As your child learns to do more for himself he will enjoy his new skills and more learning opportunities will become available to him. And, equally important, you'll be spared a few minutes of routine care-taking-time which has many better uses.

Figure 1A, B, C, and D. Sample pages from the Read Project Series.

A. EXAMINE THE BEHAVIOR

1. Specify the Behavior

Close your eyes for a minute, and picture a little boy who is
HYPERACTIVE. Really. Put this down for a moment and imagine...

"*Imagine a hyper-
active child.*"

...O.K., good. What did you picture the child doing? Was he running
around in circles? Climbing up the bookshelves? Bouncing up and down
on the sofa? Banging his spoon on the plate? Chasing the cat?

b

Figure 1B.

355

INSTRUCTIONS SHOULD SOUND...

<u>LIKE THIS</u>

"Billy, put your foot on the pedal."

<u>NOT LIKE THIS</u>

"O.K., hang on tight so you won't fall off, and swing your leg up over here."

"Good, Susie, now find the picture that looks like this."

"There are sure a lot of pictures here, aren't there? Where's the one that's similar to this one?"

Figure 1C.

PUTTING ON A FRONT BUTTON BLOUSE OR SHIRT (cont.)

When first introducing this program to your child, you put her blouse on with her doing all the steps below in the order presented for 4-5 teaching sessions or until you both feel comfortable with this method. Remember to praise and reward her for her cooperation. Then move on to teach her step by step as outlined in the program.

STEPS INVOLVED

1. Have your child stand facing the collar of the blouse, which lies on the bed as pictured. As you guide her to lean over the blouse, say, "Put your arms in." Guide both of her arms through the armholes and all the way through the sleeves. Have her now stand up straight.

2. Your child's arms are on the back side of the blouse. Place her hands so they grasp the bottom of the blouse (which is now on top!).

3. With your hands on hers, guide her to lift her arms up and over her head, saying, "Put the blouse over your head."

4. Remove both your hands and your child's from the blouse and guide her arms down to her side. The blouse will fall into place.

5. Guide your child's hands to reach back, grasp the blouse, and finish pulling it down, saying, "Pull the back down."

6. Place her hands on each front edge of the blouse and assist her in pulling the blouse front together. Say, "Good, you put your blouse on."

d Now you button the blouse or shirt for your child.

Figure 1D.

flexibly adapted to the particular teaching and learning styles of parent and child and to the home environment in which they interact.

READ PROJECT EVALUATION PROCEDURES

In evaluating the effectiveness of the Read Project Series, several major questions were explored:

1. How effectively can parents (a) learn behavior modification and (b) teach their retarded child, when their only training input is an instructional manual?
2. How much added benefit is there with other training conditions, representing various degrees and types of supplementary professional help?
3. What are the generalized changes in parents and/or child following such an intervention?

Several other questions were investigated, involving dropouts, predictors of successful outcome, and cost-benefit, but because of space limitations these will not be discussed here. For information on these areas, see Baker, Heifetz, and Brightman (1974).

Participants

Families within a 30-mile radius of Boston, each with a retarded child 3 to 14 years of age and appropriate to the skill-levels of the manuals, were solicited through agencies and the media. After a phone interview, 165 families attended one of several "kickoff" meetings, where the Read Project was discussed by staff, with equal emphasis on the service and research components. Following a brief introduction to behavior modification, parents were advised that participants in the project would be randomly assigned to one of four training conditions (varying on amount of input supplementary to the manuals) or a delayed-treatment control group that would later participate in a program incorporating improvements suggested by the experience of the other four conditions. It was stressed, however, that the manuals themselves contained all a parent should need to know to be a more effective teacher and that the manuals alone had been successfully used by parents in the pilot work. At the conclusion of the kickoff meetings, parents who wished to participate completed a card; 160 families chose to participate, and they comprised the sample for the study reported here.

Characteristics of the Parents

The sample was generally a well educated one. The average number of years of schooling was 14.3 for fathers and 13.4 for mothers. Total family income was distributed over a wide range, from under $5,000 to over $50,000; the mean family income was $13,800 (SD = $5,400).

On the Hollingshead Two-Factor Index of Social Position (Hollingshead and Redlich, 1958), which is based on the father's education and occupation, the sample was evenly distributed across social classes, with the exception of under representation of the lowest class (Class V). The percent of families falling in each class was as follows: Class I (15 percent), Class II (21 percent), Class III (21 percent), Class IV (34 percent), and Class V (8 percent).

The mean age of fathers was 42 years, while for mothers it was 39 years. In addition to the retarded child, the average family had 2.7 other children.

As might be expected in a voluntary sample, these families had a history of active involvement in organizations for parents of retarded children: 70 percent had been members of parents groups, and 11 percent had held a formally defined position of leadership in such a group. Thirty-nine percent of parents had been previously exposed in some manner to behavior modification, ranging from a minor exposure through various media (11 percent) to actual use of behavior modification with their own child (4 percent).

Characteristics of the Child

Sixty-two percent of the retarded children were boys and 38 percent were girls. The average age was 7.2 years; 34 percent were between 2 and 5 years old, 34 percent between 6 and 8 years old, and 31 percent were between 9 and 14 years old.

All children in the sample would be classified as organically retarded; none met the usual criteria for cultural-familial retardation (Heber, 1961). Functioning ranged from dull-normal to severely retarded. Regarding educational services, 96 percent of the children were receiving some form of continuous, ongoing schooling, and only 5 percent of the samples were receiving schooling from a private facility.

Training Conditions

The 160 families were arranged into 32 clusters of five, matched on parents' preknowledge of behavior modification (see below) and chronological age of the retarded child; families in each cluster were then randomly assigned to five experimental conditions.

Condition C (Controls Receiving Delayed Training) N = 32 During the 4-month training period of the other four conditions, C parents received no input, either in the form of manuals or professional assistance from Read Project staff. Other ongoing services to the children and parents continued as usual.

Condition MO (Manuals Only, without Professional Assistance) N = 32 All contacts with MO parents during training were by mail, including provision of manuals and provision and return of child skill assessment, and teaching log books (for recording daily activities). At the end of training, parents attended a meeting for completing some post measures and providing feedback on the experience of using the manuals in a self-directed way.

Condition P (Manuals plus Phone Consultation) N = 32 As in the *MO* condition, distribution and receipt of materials for *P* parents was by mail. Their use of the manuals was supplemented by biweekly scheduled phone calls of 20 to 30 minutes' duration, from a given member of the staff. Trainers consulted on current teaching programs and helped formulate plans for upcoming teaching sessions. Condition *P* parents also attended one post-training meeting.

Condition G (Manuals plus Group Training Methods) N = 32 While using the manuals, *G* parents participated in a training program consisting of nine 2-hour meetings. Four such programs operated contemporaneously, with eight families and two trainers in each group. In addition to instructional inputs by the trainers, and the various nonstructured aspects of group support and informal parent talk, there were structured times for parents to consult each other with trainers absent.

Condition GV (Manuals and Group Training and Home Visits) N = 32 The group training component of the *GV* condition followed the same format as the *G* condition. When actual programming began (after the third meeting), trainers carried out scheduled 1-hour in-home consultations between group meetings (six home visits per family). A primary aspect of the visits was the opportunity to observe teaching sessions and to provide immediate feedback to the parents. This was the only condition in which the trainers came into contact with the children.

Trainers

There were two possible "job descriptions" for a trainer: 1) to co-lead an eight-family *G* group and make calls to four *P* families, 2) to co-lead an eight-family *GV* group and visit four of these families.

In addition to a 1-month training program in preparation for consulting with parents, trainers fulfilled three preliminary criteria: 1) previous experience with behavior modification theory and practice, 2) previous work with retarded children, and 3) prior involvement with parents of retarded children. One co-leader in each group had previously run training groups in behavior modification for parents of retarded children and was generally more experienced in behavior modification than the other co-leader. One co-leader in each group was male and one female. Hence, groups were equated for sex and experience of trainers, and phone calls and visits were equally divided between males and females, veteran trainers, and those less experienced.

Sequence of Material

The instructional sequence was the same for all training conditions. The first manual was one of the self-help series, followed mid-way in training by Behavior Problems and, where appropriate, Toilet Training. Speech and Language was covered in a circumscribed way toward the end of training. Hence, the self-help skills manuals were the only ones actively used by all parents in the four training groups and were the ones used longest. For this reason, the consideration of outcome presented here will focus mainly on self-help skills.

RESULTS AND DISCUSSION

Parent Measures: Participation

Of the 128 families assigned to training conditions, six never began and 11 more dropped out during training. Therefore, 111 families (87 percent) maintained participation throughout. An additional 11 families did not return complete post measures, bringing to N = 100 the number of families in most analyses. The number of families with complete data was not significantly different across conditions (MO = 25, P = 23, G = 24, and GV = 28).

Attendance is a relevant measure only for G and GV conditions. Both training conditions showed similarly very high attendance, with families represented at an average of 90 percent of meetings. The modal family had perfect attendance.

Parents in all training conditions were encouraged to fill out teaching logs each day and return the weekly log books. A one-way Analysis of Variance found significant variance among training conditions in percent of days logged (F = 3.19, df = 3.95, and p = 0.035). In MO and P, where logs were mailed, rates were similar and combined to 45 percent; in the G and GV conditions, where the logs were handed in, the combination rate of 59 percent was significantly higher (p < 0.02, two-tailed).

A final participation measure is the number of programs that families carried out with their children. The average number of self-help skills programmed was 4.2. Parents in the G and GV conditions carried out programs in almost twice as many additional areas (i.e., toileting, behavior problems, speech and language) as parents in the MO and P conditions.

Parent Measures: Knowledge of Behavior Modification

Parent knowledge of behavior modification as applied in home settings was assessed by forms A and B of a 20-item multiple choice Behavioral Vignettes Test.[1] The BVT was administered pre- and post-training, to mothers and fathers; it was administered in group meetings with the trainers present, so that no collaboration between parents was possible.

Figure 2 shows the average BVT change score for mothers and fathers in each condition. For mothers, BVT improvement was significant in every condition (p at least

---

[1] A sample BVT item is: Billy is constantly out of his seat in class. A new program is introduced that gives Billy a token every time he stays in his seat for 5 minutes. Which of the following would best suggest that tokens work as a reward for Billy?

a. Billy is allowed to exchange his tokens for a variety of things that he enjoys
b. Billy stays in his seat longer on each of the next 3 days
c. Billy proudly shows his token to teachers and visitors
d. Billy becomes very upset when another child steals his tokens
e. Billy trades his token at the class store for candy, which he likes

Alternate forms of the BVT were used, with half the parents taking A-B and half B-A. Pre- and post data combined from Control parents showed comparable means and standard deviations for the alternative forms ($\bar{X}_A$ = 8.28; SD = 3.36; $\bar{X}_B$ = 9.02; SD = 3.38). Odd-even split half reliabilities yielded the following Spearman Brown corrected r's: Mothers A = 0.83; Fathers A = 0.75; Mothers B = 0.70; Fathers B = 0.82.

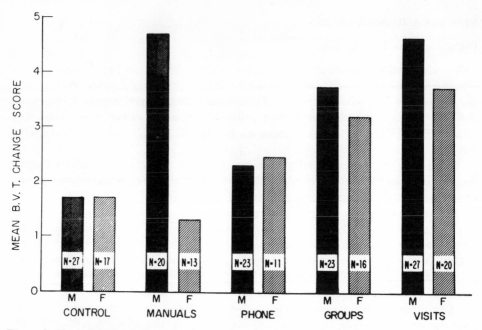

Figure 2. Mean Behavioral Vignettes Test change score for mothers and fathers, by treatment condition.

0.002) and trained mothers showed significantly more improvement than control mothers (p = 0.004). Comparing individual training conditions with Controls, significantly more improvement was shown by mothers in *MO* (p = 0.004), *G* (p = 0.041) and *GV* (p = 0.002); mothers in Condition *P* did not differ significantly from controls.

Among training conditions, an F-test for differences among mean BVT change scores for mothers approached, but did not achieve, significance (p = 0.07). The largest BVT gain was for *MO* mothers, though this differed significantly only from *P* mothers (p = 0.03).

With fathers, BVT improvement increased with the amount of potential trainer contact; the only significant improvement relative to controls was *GV* (p = 0.022), with a trend for *G* (p = 0.10). Most *G* and *GV* fathers did attend the group meetings regularly, though they usually did not become directly involved in teaching; they did, however, help to support their wives' teaching efforts. In the *P* and *MO* conditions, it does not appear that most fathers became involved at all. It seems possible that one long-range benefit of the group training might be sustained teaching by mothers when fathers are available as knowledgeable supporters, if not yet as co-teachers.

In summary, most families remained in the training program, and dropouts were about equal in the four training conditions. As might be expected, the face-to-face conditions resulted in more record keeping and more areas programmed; however, quite unexpectedly, mothers using the manuals without additional consultation showed the largest gain in knowledge of behavior modification principles. Father knowledge, on the other hand, increased with increasing trainer contact.

Child Measures: Self-help

Child skills were assessed by parents pre- and post-training (same time for controls). The 27-page Behavior Assessment Manual (BAM) enables parents to furnish a detailed, comprehensive, and accurate behavioral picture of their child's strengths and deficiencies in the areas covered by the manuals.[2]

The total change in the 42 self-help skills measured by the BAM is shown in Figure 3. The mean aggregate gain in skills was 1.28 for Control children ($p < 0.001$). The gain in each training condition was significant, and significantly (p at least 0.01) greater than for control children, though the differences in gain among the four training conditions did not approach statistical significance, by an analysis of variance.

The average trained parent programmed 4.2 skills, or about 10 percent of the 43 skills measured. Changes in these *programmed skills* accounted for about half the total gain for trained conditions ($\overline{X} = 1.43$ skills), indicating a specific effect of parental teaching efforts on behavioral change in their children.

A complementary question is one of generalization: the extent to which children showed gains in self-help skills that were *not* specifically programmed by parents. Figure 4 shows the mean change in *unprogrammed self-help skills*, those skills which the parent did not program and which were not mastered on the pre-BAM. The greater change in unprogrammed skills for the training conditions pooled over the controls was nearly significant ($p = 0.067$). Taken separately, each training condition showed significant improvement ($p = 0.001$), but only the *MO* condition differed significantly from controls ($p = 0.002$).

Thus, there are both program specific and generalized effects of training, with the *MO* condition displaying the greatest indirect effect.

Similar results are found in the specific area of toilet training. The 85 children who had not completed daytime bowel and/or urine training by the pre-BAM were grouped for analysis into three groups: 1) *control* children, 2) *training condition* children whose parents *did not* program toileting skills during the 15-week training period, 3) and *training condition* children whose parents *did* program toileting skills during the training periods. Programmed children showed the specific effects of programming toilet training, improving more than three times as much in toileting skills as either *controls* ($p = 0.043$) or *unprogrammed* training condition children ($p = 0.013$). While the number of families

---

[2] To estimate the reliability of parent report, independent observers unaware of the child's skill levels visited 33 families pre- (and another 17 post-) training. Observers assessed self-help and speech items that were neither clearly beyond the child's ability to perform at all nor clearly already mastered. Because these middle difficulty items would be the most prone to interobserver disagreement, this was a conservative reliability check; the overall reliability of the BAM would have been higher. Nonetheless, by several methods of estimating reliability, coefficients ranged from $r = 0.87$ to $r = 0.93$, (pre- and post-training), suggesting a high degree of agreement.

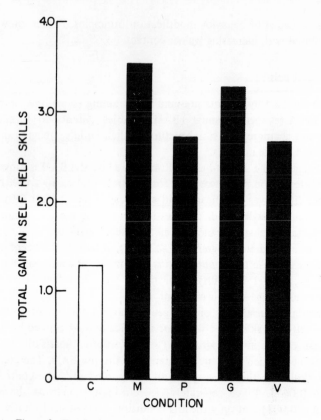

Figure 3. Total gain in self help skills, by treatment condition.

programming toileting in each training condition was small (*MO* = 5, *P* = 3, *G* = 4, and *GV* = 10) it is interesting to note that only in *MO*, where parents used the Toilet Training manual with no additional assistance, was improvement statistically significant (p = 0.02).

The self-help results clearly demonstrate that parents trained in behavior modification can effectively enhance their child's skill repertoire by teaching that usually takes only 10 to 15 minutes a day. The gains relative to controls demonstrate the marginal utility of this training over the child's regular (and much more time consuming) schooling. In considering the gains that did occur in controls, it should be noted that during the experimental period one third of the control mothers had some totally independent efforts at programming, based on the film shown at the kickoff meeting and their experience with the pre-BAM. Their children tended to exhibit greater gains in self-help skills than did the other Control children. Hence, a "purer" control group might have fared even less well, relative to training groups.

The success of the *MO* parents was contrary to the expectancies, which are

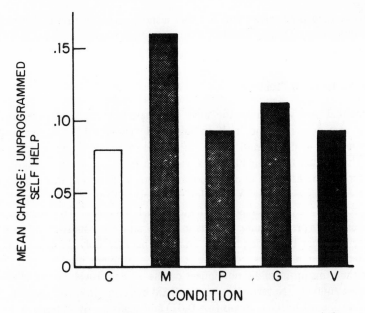

Figure 4. Mean change: unprogrammed self-help by treatment condition.

clearly revealed even in the research design itself: i.e., that the benefits derived from the *P*, *G*, and *GV* conditions would invariably be equal to, and likely greater than, benefits emerging from *MO*. The question was one of cost effectiveness: Would the added benefits of professional support be worth the price? Yet it developed that if one training condition could be said to be superior for self-help, it would be manuals only (*MO*).

It seems understandable, with hindsight, that a mother who is highly motivated to teach her child might read a manual more carefully when it is her only source of information and might teach more consistently without trainers and other parents available to be "understanding" of lapses. The high motivation of the volunteer sample and the strictures of the research context should not, however, be underestimated. It is possible in other (non-research) samples that a smaller proportion of parents would make the commitment to initiate and carry out programs without professional prodding, but the present results suggest that those who *do* make such a commitment will be quite successful.

These results may, of course, be specific to self-help skills. The Self-Help manuals are reported to be quite readable and understandable; they are differentiated enough so that a parent can be given one suited to his/her child. There is enough similarity in the way self-help skills are taught across children that brief program guidelines and suggestions seem rather generally useful. Self-help programming can usually be integrated into daily routine with little extra expenditure of time. Equally good results might obtain in other skill areas, but the present study cannot say conclusively, given that only a proportion of families programmed other areas, and for only a short period of time (a 1-year follow up is currently underway). Despite these shortcomings, the findings with behavior problems should be mentioned.

Child Measures: Behavior Problems

Only one manual was written in the area of behavior problem management, in part because this area does not lend itself to suggested "cookbook" programs but, rather, requires the teacher to understand general principles of behavior and to apply them in a given case. The manual Behavior Problems was given to all parents; it was integrated into the group curriculum, discussed in phone consultations, and accompanied for MO families with a letter encouraging its use. Yet while 79 percent of G and GV parents programmed a behavior problem, only 29 percent of MO and P parents did so. Too, records were kept more consistently by programming parents in the G and GV conditions. The BAM does not adequately reflect behavior problem changes, because only 55 percent of parents programmed behavior problems; for these, only one problem usually was programmed and half the time this problem did not appear on the 32-item BAM. Hence, changes in the total scale were unlikely. Nevertheless, on the BAM behavior problems section, condition GV (only) was superior to the controls ($p = 0.07$) and significantly superior to MO, P, and G combined ($p = 0.025$).

Finally, parents in the P, G, and GV conditions were asked to rate the extra help, in addition to manuals, or calls/meetings/visits. Although differences were not significant for teaching skills, phone calls were less likely to be rated "a great deal of help" with behavior problems than were groups (chi-square = 9.80, $p = 0.002$) or visits (chi-square = 5.71, $p = 0.017$).

Because of the various measurement problems in the area of behavior problems, the group results seem to actually underestimate true changes when behavior problems were programmed. For example, Figure 5 shows two behavior problems, hitting and jumping up from the dinner table, that were reduced quite effectively by condition G families; yet for these children the total BAM improvement was essentially zero.

Conclusion

From the amount of programming and record keeping, from parent evaluations, from the trend in the total BAM change, and in the results of many individual behavior problem charts like those in Figure 5, it is suggested that the face-to-face training conditions are presently superior for behavior problem programming. This is consistent with the experience of other behavior modifiers, that the modeling and feedback of in-home visits are an essential component of teaching autistic children where many of the initial behaviors to be modified fall under the general rubric of behavior problems (Lovaas, personal communication).

Contrary to the teaching of specific skills, which lends itself to suggested program outlines, the management of behavior problems requires applying general principles to the

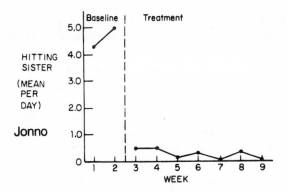

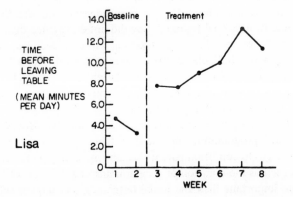

Figure 5. Examples of behavior problems reduced by parents in G condition.

individual, unique case—a more difficult enterprise. While the inferiority of *MO* (and *P*) no doubt relates in part to inadequacies of the Behavior Problem manual itself, it also seems likely that the nature of programming in this area is most apt to require some trainer direction.

FURTHER THOUGHTS

It is important to note that training parents in no way lessens the need for effective community-based services for retarded children. It may certainly reshape somewhat the objectives of those services; for example, if self-help skills are readily taught at home, academic or prevocational skills can receive more attention in school. But a retarded child needs many teachers, and the intent in developing home-based programming is as a supplement, certainly not a substitute, for the community services that are only now beginning to approach adequacy. Indeed, it has been our hope that as families become more able themselves to teach their child, they would look anew at the services he is receiving elsewhere and insist that the community share not only their concern but also their ability.

Several post-training attitude questions are of interest. Training certainly did not instill a "go it alone" attitude, because trained and control parents did not differ post-training in their equally very high *"need for more services for retarded children."* However, trained families (especially *GV*) did rate themselves significantly higher than Control on their *ability to evalute the quality of services (their) child is getting* (p = 0.01). These findings are encouraging, with visions of an increasing body of knowledgeable consumers demanding more effective services. One finding that clouds the issue somewhat, concerns the competence parents felt in teaching. Here, *MO* parents reported *less confidence* in teaching skills or managing behavior problems that did either controls (p = 0.01 skills, p = 0.07 BP) or other training groups combined (p = < 0.01 skills, p = 0.03 BP). Hence, while *MO* parents were at least as knowledgeable and effective in teaching as were parents receiving professional training, they did not experience their effectiveness as much, perhaps, in part because they were teaching without feedback from others. Not only was there no "expert" available to affirm their successful efforts but also there was no one to forgive their occasional lapses. While the latter condition might have driven *MO* parents to more conscientious teaching than in other conditions, the total lack of feedback was not conducive to building confidence.

It remains for the follow up to examine issues as to whether *MO* parents continued with further successful programming or whether their lessened confidence became a liability, and whether group condition parents became increasingly effective evaluators of services. Questions such as the duration of programming or the "spin off" parent benefits are potentially more important than the initial outcomes, and require fuller exploration before a "manuals only" approach is unconditionally embraced. It seems likely that some group training structure with fewer meetings and greater parent reliance on media and each other will be an eventual compromise, maximizing all gains.

LITERATURE CITED

Baker, B. L. 1973a. Camp Freedom: Behavior modification for retarded children in a therapeutic camp setting. Amer. J. Orthopsych. 43: 418–427.

Baker, B. L. 1973b. Parents as teachers: Promise and pitfalls. Paper presented at American Psychological Association Convention, Montreal.

Baker, B. L., A. J. Brightman, L. J. Heifetz, and D. M. Murphy. 1973. Read Project Series: 10 instructional manuals for parents. Behavioral Education Projects, Inc., Cambridge, Mass.

Baker, B. L., A. J. Brightman, L. J. Heifetz, and D. M. Murphy. 1976. Steps to Independence Series. Research Press, Champaign, Ill.

Baker, B. L., L. J. Heifetz, and A. J. Brightman. 1974. Parents as Teachers. Behavioral Education Projects, Inc., Cambridge, Mass.

Baker, B. L., and M. H. Ward. 1971. Reinforcement therapy for behavior problems in severely retarded children. Amer. J. Orthopsych. 41: 124–135.

Bensberg, G. J., C. N. Colwell, and R. H. Cassell. 1965. Teaching the profoundly retarded self-help activities by behavior shaping techniques. Amer. J. Ment. Defic. 69: 674–679.

Berkowitz, B. P., and A. M. Graziano. 1972. Training parents as behavior therapists: A review. Beh. Res. Ther. 10: 297–317.

Birnbrauer, J. S., S. W. Bijou, M. M. Wolf, and J. D. Kidder. 1965. Programmed instruction in the classroom. *In* L. P. Ullmann and L. Krasner (eds.), Case Studies in Behavior Modification, pp. 358–363. Holt, Rinehart, and Winston, New York.

Brightman, A. J. 1972. Toward the non-issues of retardation. Syracuse Law Rev. 23: 1091–1108.

Greenfeld, J. 1970. A Child Called Noah. Holt, Rinehart, and Winston, New York.

Heber, R. 1961. A manual on terminology and classification in mental retardation. Mongraph supplement to Amer. J. Ment. Defic. 2nd Ed.

Hirsch, I., and L. Walder. 1969. Training mothers in groups as reinforcement therapists for their own children. Proceedings of the 77th Annual Convention of the American Psychological Association, 4: 561–562.

Hollingshead, A. B., and R. C. Redlich. 1958. Social Class and Mental Illness: A Community Study. Wiley, New York.

Lovaas, O. I. 1966. Acquisition of imitative speech by schizophrenic children. Science 151: 705–707.

Minge, M. R., and T. S. Ball. 1967. Teaching of self-help skills to profoundly retarded patients. Amer. J. Ment. Defic. 71: 864–868.

President's Panel on Mental Retardation. 1962. A Proposed Program for National Action to Combat Mental Retardation. U.S. Government Printing Office, Washington, D.C.

Risley, T., and M. M. Wolf. 1967. Establishing functional speech in echolalic children. Beh. Res. Ther. 5: 73–88.

Early Intervention for Hearing-impaired Infants and Young Children

Kathryn B. Horton

Early detection and treatment for the hearing-impaired child are widely accepted in the fields of audiology and deaf education as essential to the optimal development of language and speech and ultimate educational achievement. In recent years, techniques to assess definitively the hearing of very young children have been emerging in part from programs of screening for infant hearing established in many hospitals throughout the country. These developments, coupled with the occurrence of the worst rubella epidemic in the United States in 35 years, have led to renewed emphasis on habilitative efforts for the young child with reduced hearing. It has been estimated that between 20,000 and 40,000 babies whose mothers contacted rubella during the early months of pregnancy are damaged in some way (Masland, 1968). At least half of these children have significantly impaired hearing, one of the common complications in rubella babies. This tragic situation has dramatized the importance of and given impetus to their early identification and intervention. These efforts have demonstrated that the goal cannot be limited to the identification of affected children and the measurement of their hearing residual; the goal also must include meaningful and continuing programs of guidance and education both for the children and their parents and for the public at large.

BILL WILKERSON HEARING AND SPEECH PROGRAM

The Bill Wilkerson Hearing and Speech Center program for hearing-impaired children emphasizes the value of detecting hearing impairment in infancy, followed by immediate intervention in the form of an intensive parent teaching program that stresses the maximization of residual hearing to enhance natural language acquisition.

The program for hearing-impaired children from birth to 6 years of age consists of two major components: 1) the Mama Lere Parent Teaching Home for infants and children

371

under age 3 years, and 2) the acoustic preschool for children from ages 3 to 6 years. The first program concentrates on parent instruction involving demonstration teaching in the child's natural environment, intensive audiologic monitoring of the child's hearing, and use of hearing aids. Preschool classes (supported by the Metropolitan Nashville public schools' special education department) are child-oriented, although parent instruction is continued regularly on a less intensive basis. Classes for the younger children include an equal number of normal-hearing children for peer stimulation of language and communication skills, while classes for the older children emphasize individual and small group instruction supplemented by placement for one half day in a regular kindergarten. Emphasis in this chapter is on the early intervention program of the Mama Lere Home because it is considered crucial to the child's later performance in the more formal education system.

EARLY DETECTION

The greatest service one can render a deaf child is to recognize his problem and to secure treatment as soon after birth as possible. While specialized services, including nursery and kindergarten programs for children aged 3 to 6 years, traditionally have been offered for a number of years at speech and hearing centers and at schools with facilities for the deaf, the number of programs providing intensive help for the child less than 3 years, and in particular the infant, has been woefully small. The recognition of the huge increase in the population of hearing-impaired children occasioned by the rubella epidemic has sensitized the professional community to the necessity of encouraging and supporting the establishment of additional programs. But the surface has barely been scratched; in the United States more than 50 percent of the hearing-impaired children less than 6 years still do not have available to them in their communities appropriate diagnostic, therapeutic, and educational services. Some states are devoid of any programs except the traditional residential school usually unavailable until the child is 6 years old. At age 6 years the critical periods for auditory and language learning have long passed, and the child is foreordained to communication that is nonoral. It is the obligation of the diagnosis, treatment, and education of deaf children to respond to the essentially unmet need of the very young deaf child in order to minimize his handicap and to maximize his potential.

Early detection of defective hearing would be markedly facilitated if hearing screening tests were instituted as routine procedures in early pediatric examinations. The growing number of infant hearing screening programs, the introduction of new equipment and procedures to detect hearing loss early in life, and the establishment of services for hearing-impaired children under age 3 years in more communities probably will eventually result in the incorporation of screening tests of hearing into the routine pediatric examination. However, at this point in time, the parents still appear to be the most sensitive parties in first questioning the status of the hearing acuity of their children. In a survey completed in 1969 by the Alexander Graham Bell Association for the Deaf, it was reported that in 70 percent of the participating families, the mother or father was first to suspect hearing loss. In 84 percent of the children surveyed, the hearing loss was suspected before 24 months of age, and in more than half of the cases the parents were concerned before the children were 12 months old. In only 7 percent of the cases was the medical specialist the first to become suspicious of reduced hearing. These findings highlight the necessity of providing for pediatricians and other medical specialists, and for parents and the community at large, a frame of reference regarding the normal development of audition, language, and speech.

At this point, the term "deaf" merits definition and clarification. Of the approximate 3 million children in the United States who are hearing impaired, only a very small number are without any sensitivity to sound. The majority of these have reduced rather than absent sensitivity to sound. Without special help they would encounter major difficulty in language and speech development, many of them failing almost altogether to develop oral communication. In spite of their residual hearing, in an educational sense they are "deaf." However, with appropriately fitted hearing aids, training in the use of their residual hearing, in speechreading, and through special teaching of language and speech beginning at an early age, most of the children will acquire the skills necessary for education and adjustment to the world of hearing people. Children who have had the benefit of very early diagnosis and implementation of intensive programs designed to train their residual hearing have demonstrated vividly the tremendous capacity of the child to learn language in spite of a defective auditory system. The child's acquisition of language and speech occurs so naturally in most instances that most people take the process for granted, and they fail to recognize the critical nature of the first 3 years of life in developing this behavior. The child has acquired most of the verbal skills and structures that serve to undergird his mature use of language and speech by the tender age of 3.5 years. Yet some parents and professionals remain unconcerned with little or no use of meaningful speech. The deaf child and his family participating in an "ideal" program would have been involved actively in treatment for 3 years by the age of 3.5. A yardstick for assessing the course of a child's development of language and hearing is included in a publication prepared by the National Institute of Neurological Diseases and Stroke (NINDS, 1969). This checklist highlights the milestones of communicative development and offers a practical way for medical specialists and parents to evaluate the child's progress.

INFANT INTERVENTION THROUGH PARENT TRAINING

For those familiar with child development principles, it is apparent that the child deprived of hearing in the first 3 years of life is already severely handicapped when compared with his normal-hearing peers; and even though an intensive preschool program is initiated by age 3 years, deficiency in language and communication skills is already a marked problem. Obviously, intervention must be planned much earlier than age 3, by which time the normal-hearing child is fully attuned to his sound environment and indeed is a functionally communicative individual, expressing his wants and exchanging ideas in complete sentences. The years before 3 are thus crucial in effecting change in the course of development that may be anticipated when the sense of hearing is nonfunctional in infancy. The child at this early age is not amenable to a typical child-oriented instruction program even as informal as the nursery-kindergarten class usually is. It is the parents, the child's natural teachers, to whom one must turn. By focusing efforts on the parents and teaching them to capitalize on the innumerable ways in which auditory and language learning can occur on a daily basis in the child's home setting, the child can best be helped.

The Mama Lere Parent Teaching Home was planned, therefore, to give parents of hearing-impaired infants immediate and continuing help in developing their child's ability to understand and to develop spoken language in that period before more formal educational experiences begin. The program emphasizes daily life activities in the home as instruction. The main objectives are: 1) to provide a parent-oriented program appropriate to the needs of the very young child in which skills basic to the attainment of language may be practiced on an extensive basis in the child's home, and 2) through intensive audiologic management to take early advantage of his hearing potential by use of wearable amplification so that all possible assistance is given through the auditory channel.

A basic premise is that the people most important to a young child are his mother and father, and the place most important to him is his home, a setting that offers the most natural learning environment. Because parents normally need help and confidence in knowing what to do to stimulate an awareness and understanding of speech in a deaf child, it seems logical to bring the child and his parents together in a model home where the activities occurring on any day in the life of a young child can easily be simulated. Variations on this type program include the model in which a teacher visits the child's home. The center, however, elected the former plan on the strength of a common setting for all the families enrolled, the simultaneous availability of audiologic services, and the opportunity for use of video tape as an effective demonstration and teaching technique.

CURRICULUM IN THE PARENT TEACHING HOME

The demonstration home began in a rented house one half block from the Bill Wilkerson Center in Nashville. After 5 years there, the present home, a gift of the Justin and Valere Potter Foundation, was occupied. Every effort is made to maintain the relaxed, nonclinical atmosphere of a home; yet, at the same time, the children it serves can conveniently receive ongoing clinical service at the center nearby. The essence of the parent-teacher relationship is informality, for which the staff consciously strives from the first. Parents are urged to dress as they would at home. The teacher spends a great deal of time during each session working in the kitchen as the mother would at home or sitting on the floor with the child, while the parents are led to join in these activities. Parents—both mother and father, if possible—normally come with their deaf child to the home after two audiologic visits during which the child's hearing has been evaluated. Naturally, they are deeply affected by what they have been told and, for many, the audiologic tests confirm their worst fears. For others, the fact that their child has a severe hearing deficit is a new and shocking idea. A strength of the home program is that it allows for counteracting the parents' emotional state by its emphasis on the everyday routines that must be dealt with by everyone in the child's life, despite their state of grief or joy (Knox and McConnell, 1968).

Because the mother is normally the parent who is with the child most of his waking hours, the program focuses on her role in stimulating the child's interest in sound and speech. Thus, the teacher does what the mother of any very young child does: she spends much of her time in the kitchen preparing meals, washing dishes, feeding the child, and performing other chores. She washes windows, sweeps and dusts, folds and sorts clothes, irons, bathes and dresses the child, plays with him, reads to him, and sings to him. But as she carries out these tasks, she demonstrates that every such activity offers a vehicle for communication and the chance to call attention not only to speech but also to other environmental sounds the child must recognize. Though visual stimulation is not excluded, the major effort is to show that most deaf children when wearing hearing aids have sufficient residual hearing to respond to and recognize such sounds.

In this program the key to successful early intervention lies in using parents as agents of change. The premises of the program are very early detection, preferably within the first year of life, and early intervention involving, first, maximizing the child's opportunity to functionally develop his auditory residual through binaural hearing aid use and, second, upgrading his auditory and linguistic environment through intensive parent training. For the last 4 years, the program has been extended to include, in addition to hearing-impaired infants, language delayed infants, including those with general developmental delay.

Program objectives fall into five general categories: 1) to teach parents to optimize the auditory environment for their child, 2) to teach parents how to talk to their child, 3) to familiarize parents with the principles, stages, and sequence of normal language development and to apply this frame of reference in stimulating their child, 4) to teach parents the strategies of behavior management, and 5) to supply affective support to aid the family in coping with their feelings about their child and the stresses that a handicapped child places on the integrity of the family.

Auditory training is given emphasis for both the hearing-impaired and normal-hearing children. In order to teach the parents how to orient their child to sound, they are provided specific instruction on: 1) how to select environment sounds to which to call their child's attention, 2) how to respond visibly and appropriately to the occurrence of sound, thereby stimulating the child's response, 3) to associate consistently all sounds and their sources, and 4) to positively reinforce the child's responses to sound. For hearing-impaired children, the families are given specific assistance by both the audiologists and the teaching staff in helping their children to adjust to full-time binaural hearing aid use.

The focus of the program objectives is on developing receptive language and establishing and/or strengthening the undergirding vocal functions for expressive language. Parents are taught to optimize their linguistic input to their child. The specifics of this teaching are housed in the Rules of Talking (Lillie, 1972). These 27 rules are presented in sequenced clusters and reflect the following parameters: 1) *nonverbal* and 2) *verbal* reinforcement of the child's vocal and/or verbal behaviors, 3) *relevancy* to the immediate situation, interest, and experiential background of the child, 4) *redundancy* in lexical, syntactic, and semantic input, 5) *feedback*, lexical, syntactic, and semantic, 6) *expansion* lexical, syntactic, and semantic, and 7) appropriate use of *intonation* and *stress*.

After a perspective of almost 8 years, there is a "new breed" of deaf child emerging from these efforts—a child whose linguistic characteristics are more like his normal-hearing peers than his deaf peers without early detection and intervention. Similarly exciting results have been witnessed by a number of other programs engaging in similar efforts. Early identification, early amplification, and early parent training for many of these children has meant not only the difference between special education and education in the mainstream but also the difference between inadequate and adequate oral communication.

SOME PRELIMINARY RESULTS

Language Competence

The Parent Teaching Program at the Mama Lere Home has been in existence long enough to enable an assessment of some of the results that may be anticipated from intensive early intervention for hearing-impaired children. Data are accumulating along a number of parameters. Some analyses that have been completed are worthy of mention here to demonstrate the value of carefully planned auditory stimulation for these children in their early formative years. Liff (1973) studied the spoken language of three groups of children, using Lee's (1966) Developmental Sentence Types as a measure of language competence. Lee's premise is that language acquisition involves several steps, each of which is dependent upon success at a lower level. Lee classifies four levels of utterances beginning with one-word sentences and progressing to the subject-predicate model of complete sentence, and five types of sentence utterances beginning with the noun type and continuing through the designative, predicative, verbal, and vocabulary type, each of which may occur at any of the four levels (one-word, two-word, construction, and sentence).

Liff's target experimental group included six children among the first group enrolled at the Mama Lere Home. Each of these children began in the parent program and started wearable hearing aid use before age 3 years (median age, 2 years, 3 months). The second group included five children for whom parent intervention had not been provided and for whom hearing aids had not been fitted until after age 3 years (median age, 4 years). These children were enrolled in a self-contained class for hearing-impaired children, their level of language being inadequate for integration into regular classes. The parents of these subjects had not been involved in the formal parent instruction program at the home because of the age of the child when discovered, although preschool training had been available. A third group included six normal-hearing children enrolled in the same public school second grade classes in which the six early intervention children also participated with the added help of a resource teacher. The teachers of the regular classes were asked to select children for the third group whom they considered average achievers.

When the 50 consecutive utterances produced by the children in each of the above groups were analyzed according to Lee's Developmental Sentence Types, the findings revealed that the language competence of the early intervention children was very similar to that of the normal-hearing group. The statistically significant differences in the study arose only from those comparisons of the late intervention group with either the early intervention or the normal-hearing group. For example, the early intervention group produced on the average 75 percent of their utterances at the sentence level, while the late intervention group produced only 32 percent at that level. The early intervention subjects produced only 8 percent noun type utterances (an immature construction type), while the late intervention group produced 19 percent of such utterances. Verbal type utterances (a more mature construction type) occurred 79 percent of the time in the "early" group compared with only 49 percent for the "late" group. In contrast, the normal-hearing group and the early intervention group were not significantly different from one another in any comparison of type or level of utterance, while significant differences prevailed in almost all comparisons between the late intervention group and either the hearing-impaired children in the early intervention group or the normal-hearing group. It is important to point out here that the severity of the hearing loss for the two hearing-impaired groups was not different, being at a median level of 87 dB for the early group and at 84 dB (actually slightly better) for the late group.

Thus, Liff (1973) concluded that the positive effects of the early intervention program, including the early use of hearing aids before age 3 years, were reflected in the children's ability to express themselves in spoken language which, although not always as morphologically correct as that of their normal-hearing peers nor with as precise articulation, was highly comparable in syntactical structure. This same area of language competence was handled much less adequately by those children whose intervention program occurred as much as about 2 years later.

Educational Achievement

Language competence is assumed to be a primary component denoting a child's readiness to enter school. Thus, it is in the area of later educational achievement that one needs to look in order to evaluate the real influence of infant and preschool efforts. Previous surveys have shown that partially hearing children (with sufficient hearing to develop language through hearing, though at a slower rate) are, on the average, from 0.5 and 2 years educationally retarded, while the deaf child (whose severity of hearing impairment prelingually is great enough to preclude the normal acquisition of language) tends to be about 4 years retarded. While this degree of retardation reflects an indisputable fact that *not to hear* imposes a very serious handicap indeed on the growing child in his attempts to obtain an education, it also reflects in part the inadequacy of our educational approaches that have as yet not broken the barriers permitting full utilization of the intellectual potential that hearing-impaired children have been shown to possess. Early intervention to establish either an auditory or visual language system at the earliest time possible offers some hope for the future in lessening the amount of educational handicap imposed by childhood deafness.

Figure 1 shows the mean percentile ranks for six such children, who had been in the parent-infant program, compared with the 53 normal-hearing second graders enrolled in the same school. It may be noted that the mean percentile ranks on the Metropolitan Achievement Test were virtually equivalent on reading and somewhat lower in mathematics. It is assumed that perhaps the vocabulary used in new math today may have constituted some problem here for the hearing-impaired children, but in any case the fact that their mean total reading percentile was above that of 53 second graders with normal

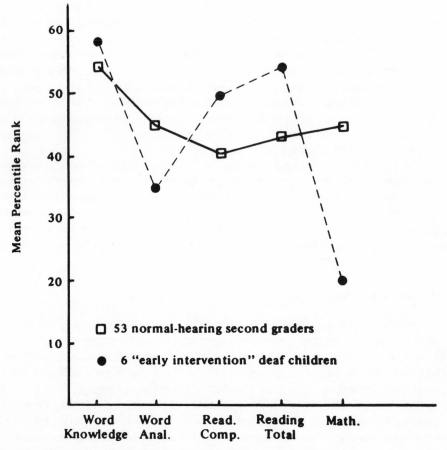

Figure 1. Comparison of 6 hearing-impaired children with 53 normal-hearing second grade peers on standardized Metropolitan Achievement Tests.

hearing is significant in terms of what kind of preparation these children had for competing in regular school. When one considers that the average per capita cost in 1972–1973 at the Tennessee School for the Deaf, the state residential school, was $5,106, the cost efficiency principle is emphasized. For the same year, the average per capita cost for children in the regular classes in the school system in which these children were enrolled was $847. The same cost figure for children enrolled in the program for the hearing-impaired was $1,710, which when compared to a $5,100 institutional rate represents a tremendous saving to the taxpayer. Several of these children could also be expected to enroll full time in regular classes without the resource teacher help within another 3 or 4 years, which increases the cost savings appreciably (McConnell, 1973).

CONCLUSION

Projects like the Wilkerson program demonstrate clearly that early identification and intervention have tremendous pay-offs in habilitation and normalization of hearing-impaired children. However, all such efforts are dependent for their optimal success on early and systematic identification efforts.

Currently, in almost all communities, hearing screening of the juvenile population on a consistent or pervasive basis does not occur until the entry of this population into the public educational system at 5 or 6 years of age, and well after the critical period for the acquisition of language. Detection of hearing impairment during the preschool years occurs on an individual and serendipitous basis. Parents who observe a total lack of response to their child to sound may well seek professional help on their own, but this help-seeking behavior may not occur until the child is 3 or 4 years old, and in cases of moderate hearing impairment, may not occur at all. Systems to reliably detect hearing impairment in infancy and the preschool years have not, as of yet, been implemented on a significant scale. As a result, optimal utilization of intervention strategies cannot be achieved, and demographic statistics on hearing impairment in the preschool age ranges are neither consistently collected nor particularly accurate when they are collected, a situation that makes long-term comprehensive health and educational planning for this population exceedingly difficult. These problems are, in part, the end result of the failure of communities to establish systems for health care that transcend the divisions between public and private health services and between health and education services.

Until systematic screening of sensory and developmentally deficits are added as components of pediatric management, even the most highly developed habilitative efforts will do little more than scratch the surface of the population of children who need and can profit from early intervention efforts.

As medical technology continues its advance toward the prevention, treatment, and ultimate eradication of various organic pathologies, certain areas of sensory deprivation although equally handicapping, remain relatively primitive not only in their detective and rehabilitative techniques but also in the delivery of available methodology. Impairment of hearing is one such area of deprivation. The one most important factor in the management of hearing impairment in young children is, without a doubt, early intervention with some form of amplification. If hearing impairment is not detected at a very early age, and proper intervention steps taken, its handicapping potential is compounded. Without intervention during the critical period for language acquisition, a hearing-impaired child will not develop language normally; without normal language function, intellectual and education growth is retarded. A hearing-impaired child deprived of early detection and intervention is destined to a life of special treatment that will exclude him from the ranks of the normal-hearing, self-sufficient person.

LITERATURE CITED

Fellendorf, G. W., and I. Harrow. 1970. Parent counseling, 1961–1968. Volta Rev. 72: 51–57.

Knox, L., and F. McConnell. 1968. Helping parents to help deaf infants. Children 15: 183–187.

Liff, S. 1973. Early Intervention and Language Development in Hearing Impaired Children. Unpublished master's thesis, Vanderbilt University, Nashville.

Lillie, S. M. 1972. Principles of Parent Teaching for Language Handicapped Children Under Four. Division for Children with Communication Disorders Bulletin IX: 15–19. Council for Exceptional Children, Reston, Va.

Lee, L. 1966. Development Sentence Types: A method for comparing normal and deviant syntactic development. Speech and Hearing Dis. 31: 311–330.

McConnell, F. 1973. The Delivery of Speech and Hearing Services. Unpublished paper presented at the Heuston Woods Conference, Cincinnati, Ohio.

Masland, R. L. 1968. Rubella can rob children of their hearing. Volta Rev. 70: 304–307.

National Institute of Neurological Disease and Stroke. 1969. Learning to Talk. Prepared by the Information Office, National Institute of Neurological Diseases and Stroke. National Institutes of Health, Bethesda, Md.

Parent Programs for Developmental Management

Eric Denhoff, M.D., and Irma Hyman, M.S.W.

The Meeting Street School Parent Programs for Developmental Management (PPDM) has been providing services to handicapped babies for over 15 years. It was designed originally as a home intervention program for cerebral palsied infants, but gradually the program expanded to include all babies with a handicapping or probably handicapping condition (Denhoff and Langdon, 1966). During the past 5 years, infants at risk for later behavioral and learning disabilities have also been provided with services. Opportunities are provided to help all these babies maximize their potential through parent modeling, i.e., by teaching parents how to use supportive developmental techniques properly at home. The number and diversity of the activities are in proportion to the degree and intensity of the disability. However, new knowledge of how babies learn and how the brain works has provided the team with many ideas of how to improve upon interventions.

DESCRIPTION OF PPDM

The PPDM is a service of the Meeting Street School Children's Rehabilitation Center, sponsored by the Rhode Island Easter Seal Society, a voluntary health agency. The service is available to all infants in Rhode Island, nearby Massachusetts, and Connecticut. The PPDM is a comprehensive, therapeutic-educational program designed to meet the total developmental needs of very young children from birth to 3 years of age. The disabilities may vary from the severely disabled multiply handicapped baby to the relatively normal infant with behaviors that concern adults. The program serves about 100 babies a year in 1,000 square feet of space. It has provided service to over 1,000 infants since its inception and has as its goals the following:

1. To provide a community resource to evaluate and help treat atypical and at risk infants

2. To provide a comprehensive developmental management program for infants and their parents through various service models

3. To offer service to the parents of these infants that will enable them to understand their child's disability, and to participate in the program models in an effort to help achieve the child's highest potential

4. Child Advocacy: to involve the agency with various other voluntary and official health, education, and social agencies to plan and provide for a continuity of appropriate services; also to foster the concept of the "rights of infants"

Team Members

The PPDM Team consists of a neurodevelopmentally oriented pediatrician, a physical therapist, an occupational therapist, a speech/language therapist, a social worker, and an early childhood special educator. An adult educator, a psychologist, and a research assistant and the full consultant services of Meeting Street School are available to the team.

Team Evaluation

A parent program for developmental management begins with the referral upon which comprehensive team evaluations are planned on an individual basis. Team evaluations are used to derive as complete a picture as possible of the child and the family, with various team specialties participating in the determination of the child's total functioning and in the adoption of a management plan. Based upon evaluation findings, the child's current status, and the family circumstances, the delivery of services and therapeutic-educational intervention are implemented through one of several alternative service models that have evolved at Meeting Street School. Comprehensive evaluation of the child's functioning and monitoring of the child's progress continue throughout the course of the child's program. The comprehensive assessment procedures and the various service models utilized in PPDM are described in the remarks to follow, as well as the various areas of developmental management in which therapeutic-educational intervention efforts are directed.

COMPREHENSIVE ASSESSMENT

Referral and Assessment

Referrals are from individual physicians, district nurse associations, and other health related agencies. Because experience demonstrates that mothers are the earliest identifiers of baby differences, Meeting Street School is considering accepting direct parent referrals.

Upon referral, pertinent medical and social data are collected. The social worker then meets with the parents (without the baby) for an initial interview to obtain a personalized detailed history and to explain the assessment procedures and program services. The history taking is designed around the problem-oriented record (Appendix 1). An appointment is then made for team assessment, which takes approximately 1 hour. Here the therapeutic team evaluates the baby and identifies levels of developmental functioning.

A neurodevelopmental medical evaluation is then scheduled. After the physician has completed his own evaluation with the full team present, total findings are reviewed, a team impression is arrived at, and a management plan is evolved. Specific recommendations for further medical evaluations are made. A full report is sent to the referring source, and a social worker arranges a parent conference to discuss and interpret the team findings.

The team physician does not directly communicate with the parents unless unusual circumstances warrant. The referring physician or agency is welcome to attend both intake sessions and is given the opportunity to discuss the findings and recommendations with the parents. Most prefer that the team social worker serve as his interpreter.

Developmental Evaluations

Gross Neuromotor/Developmental Evaluation The physical therapist on the team assesses the infant's achievement of the developmental sequences of head control, sitting, modes of locomotion, and advanced movement patterns. In doing so, attention is paid to the child's body awareness, motor planning abilities. and development of motor control at varying age levels. In addition, neuromotor elements of muscle tone, muscle strength, abnormal movement patterns, joint range of motion and postural deviations are assessed and related to functional abilities. Postural reflex status is evaluated and related to the infant's development of appropriate or inappropriate movement patterns and control (Appendix II).

Visual-Perceptual-Motor Evaluation The occupational therapist assesses the infant's functional abilities of efficient visual-perceptual-motor skills. This includes the child's awareness of tactile and kinesthetic stimuli and the visual intake skills of acuity, attention, motility, and discrimination. Fine motor control skills are evaluated in terms of reflex activity, motor planning, and motor control of the head, trunk, and upper extremities. The integration of these skills is observed as the child interacts with his environment in play and develops self-care skills. With the toddler, many play and learning activities are included to assess his perceptual and fine motor skills (Appendix III).

Developmental Language Evaluation The speech and language therapist evaluates the oral mechanism and assesses the ability to suck, swallow, and chew. The ability to hear in a free field is screened. Exploration of expressive language development includes vocal production, nonverbal communication, i.e., gesture and imitative ability, vocabulary development, intelligibility, appropriate use of words and verbal formulation (word order and grammatical development). Receptive ability is determined by assessing comprehension of familiar words, environmental experiences, following age—appropriate directions and concept development (Appendix IV).

Special Educator's Role in Assessment During the evaluation, the special educator is concerned with the behavioral control and adjustment skills and social-emotional maturity that are prerequisite to further concept learning. In addition, the educator may observe and rate parent-child interaction utilizing any one of several parent-child interaction forms (Appendix V). The educator may intervene and request that a specific parent-child interaction situation be set up for observation. Then, the special educator can evaluate the specific parent-child interaction and recommend intervention techniques once the functional team assessment is completed. As skill levels are determined, the educator observes the child's emerging learning style, incorporating strengths and weaknesses, identified by the team into an integrated picture of how the child best learns and what his individual style of dealing with information from his environment is. When indicated, the special educator participates in an "indepth" concept development and prereadiness skills assessment. The educator then coordinates behavioral observations, the functional skill findings, the child's learning style, and his concept levels to form a global picture of the child and his needs as they relate to future educational planning.

The developmental therapists evaluate the baby together with the parents present. They arrive at their assessment of the infant's functional abilities by independent examination, by observing behavior and performance of the baby during a team colleague's interaction with the child and by discussion among team members. In instances where the total team is not utilized for the evaluation procedure, those therapists involved are able to provide a screening in all areas. If further indepth assessment in one of these areas is felt necessary, it is readily available.

Medical Examination

The medical examination combines a neuropediatric assessment with a behavioral examination based upon the best features of a number of neonatal neurological evaluations (Rosenblith, 1956; 1959; 1961; Andre-Thomas, Chesne, and Dargassies, 1960; Prechtl and Beintema, 1964) (Appendix VI A, B, and C). The pediatrician examines the baby on a one-to-one basis, but with the team observing the procedure.

Consolidating Results and Planning Treatment

Following the medical examination, there is an indepth discussion among all members of the PPDM team. The physician tries to place into proper focus the possible medical outcomes and the prognosis. The therapists describe the child's strengths and weaknesses in the various behavioral areas. The social worker provides insights into parental coping, family functioning, and pertinent socioeconomic data. When further medical studies are recommended, every effort is made to assist the family and referring physician with the implementation of these recommendations. A management plan is developed, and the baby and his parents are admitted to a PPDM individual or group model best suited to his needs. No infant is discharged from the program until all features are clarified and appropriate referral is made when the child is around 3 years of age. Supportive help is maintained until placement is completed. Institutionalization is rare.

SERVICE MODELS

Several modes for providing services to the child and his parents are available and will be discussed.

Individual Model

Building an atmosphere of trust, understanding, and care is a very necessary part of any family oriented program. This is initially most easily accomplished by working with an individual child and his parents as a unit. The infant and parents (usually mother) are seen together by any combination of the members of the direct service team (physical therapist, occupational therapist, speech/language therapist, and social worker) on a monthly basis for approximately 1 hour. During this time, the therapists demonstrate to the parents specific intervention techniques geared to enhance the child's functional abilities and cognitive growth. During the session, the parents are given the opportunity to try those activities they will be doing at home, and the therapists are able to give them direct feedback on their interaction with their child, helping them to feel more comfortable in carrying out the suggested activities. Emphasis in the program is placed on dealing with the parents' greatest concerns with their baby and his development and with difficulties arising in the home. Instruction for the specific activities, in addition to being fully discussed with the parents and demonstrated, are written down on a pink sheet delineating objectives, procedures, and expected results for each task (Appendix VII). The parents take a copy home for their use during the months, and the staff retains a copy in the child's record for future reference. If personnel from another community agency are also involved with the child and family, a duplicate pink sheet is shared with them. Time is provided during each monthly session with the parent for discussion of previous recommended activities the rationale for various aspects of programming and the progress of the child. The goal is to allow and to help parents to become more effective in the management of their child. The activities provided can be incorporated into the family's daily routine and can include materials that can be found in the home or made with little expense. Frequently, materials and equipment are loaned or given to families.

Home visits may be made when staff or family feel it would be helpful. These are often related to specific problems arising in the home or to a need to see the child functioning in his more familiar home environment. Home visits have been valuable to both the families and the staff. The parents, when seen in the home setting where they have many reminders of daily routines, often bring up difficulties they would not recall when seen in the center. The staff, after the visit, has a picture of the home surroundings and can make their future suggestions and requests more realistic and workable in relation to the home situation.

Group Models

A variety of group models have been formulated with different staffing patterns devised to meet the specific needs of children and parents. Specific objectives are established for children, mothers, and staff that are involved in each group. Determination of group models and staffing patterns is done yearly on the basis of children's needs and staff availability.

Group Models for Children   Because of the varying therapeutic, educational, medical, social, and cognitive needs of children, a variety of children group models were formed. Specific groups include: 1) two groups of multiply handicapped children who have specific physical needs, 2) one group of children with Down's syndrome, and 3) one group of children ranging in age from 2 to 3 years who exhibit developmental delays in either behavioral organization and control skills, speech and language, visual-perceptual-motor, and/or gross motor delays.

Group Models for Parents   Because of the varying needs of parents, especially mothers, a variety of service models to individualize parent participation were devised. These models include: 1) weekly involvement with their children in the group situation, 2) weekly parent discussion groups with social workers, 3) individual parent counseling provided as an integral part of ongoing total services, and 4) monthly participation in the children's group to receive home programming instructions to become better primary caregivers for their children.

GROUP OBJECTIVES

General Objectives of Groups

Although several types of groups provide services for different kinds of children and their parents, several similar objectives for each of the groups are present in the PPDM program which the team strives to attain. These can be delineated into objectives for parents, for children, and for the staff.

Parents

1. To help parents develop a better understanding of their child's disability in relation to its effect on his functional abilities, his behavior, and other problems and in relation to appropriate ways of dealing with their child and his problems
2. To develop further parent's awareness of the child's individual rate of growth and development so that they may have more realistic expectations for him
3. To provide intensive training in appropriate handling and stimulation techniques for their child through demonstration, observation, implementation, and direct feedback within a group setting
4. To observe and interact with their child and other children in a group of similarly functioning children

5. To participate in parent discussion groups concerning such matters as attitudes, family relationships, and behavior management in connection with being the parent of a handicapped child

Children

1. To be exposed to and learn to interact with other children of similar functional levels in both a therapeutic and play environment
2. To be provided with individualized therapeutic and learning activities appropriate to the child's developmental levels in body awareness and control, visual-perceptual-motor, speech/language, cognitive, and socioemotional areas
3. To learn to interact with a limited number of unfamiliar adults in a therapeutic-educational group program

Staff

1. To determine the most appropriate and effective therapeutic and learning activities for each child through observations and information gathered from the child's performance in the group
2. To act as consultants in one's own specialty to other team members in planning programs for groups of children and for individual children within a group
3. To implement effectively a multidisciplinary model that provides total therapeutic service for the child and his family through regular team conferences and through frequent and efficient use of consultation with appropriate team specialists in achieving program goals
4. To provide immediate informative feedback to parents as they try developmental-therapeutic activities demonstrated by team members so that their effectiveness as their child's primary caregiver may be strengthened and enhanced
5. To establish stronger relationships with parents through frequent contacts over concerns and difficulties they have in managing their child
6. To train students and parents to be assistants to the group leaders within the various therapeutic-educational group settings
7. To better understand the effects of an atypical child on the family, the child's functioning within the family, and the relationship of the family to the community

GROUP MODELS

Multiply Handicapped Group Model

Overview Because parents of a multiply handicapped child have a great deal of frustration in handling their child on a daily basis, it was felt that an intensified weekly program of training in handling, caring for, and understanding their handicapped child and his disability would be most feasible. The group model of parents, children, and staff all working together provides an excellent opportunity for interaction among staff, children, and parents and the development of a strong supportive relationship.

Staffing Pattern   In both multiply handicapped groups, the staff consists of a physical therapist as the group leader and a parent volunteer as an assistant to the physical therapist. A social worker is directly involved with the parents in the group and may work individually with selected parents. In addition, consultants from the various disciplines of speech and language, occupational therapy, education, psychology, and medicine are available for input regarding specific needs of individual children.

Specific Group Features   These two groups of multiply handicapped children meet weekly for a 2-hour period in the morning. Each group consists of approximately five or six children (ages 1 to 3 years) and their mothers. Fathers, grandparents, and other relatives are welcome. (Portions of the sessions are devoted to activities to encourage development of sensorimotor skills, body awareness and control, visual-perceptual-motor, language, and self-care skills.)

Parent Involvement   Initially, mothers and children remain together in the therapy session with the therapist and social worker in attendance. While in the group, the mothers work with their own children carrying out activities supervised by the therapist. When the children become accustomed to the group routine and staff, the mothers, after being involved in the group for the first hour, separate from the children to meet as a group with the social worker for discussion of feelings, attitudes, and concerns. In addition, the mothers write down specific instructions given by the therapists for home programming activities to be carried out during the coming week.

Down's Syndrome Group

Review   Because a number of mothers of children with Down's syndrome were presenting common needs that could best be met by a group situation, a mother's discussion group, which is not only educational but also therapeutic, has as its focus working with the mother's feelings toward her child, toward the father, and toward coping with and managing a child with Down's syndrome. In addition, the mothers often feel isolated with their child's problem and need to share their experiences in order to overcome mutual problems.

Staffing Pattern   Within the Down's syndrome group model, the mothers meet for 2 hours weekly as a group with both the social workers and the speech/language therapist. On occasion, guest lecturers, such as a nutritionist, speak to the group about areas of common concern or interest.

Specific Group Features   The children within this group meet monthly with their mothers for approximately 2.5 hours. This group is led by a physical therapist and a speech/language therapist with the social worker and, on occasion, a public health nurse also in attendance. (Recent studies have shown that children with Down's syndrome need greater emphasis placed upon language development, and, within the framework of this group, concentration on this area is encouraged.) Consultation from other disciplines is available as needed. During the child group session each mother is presented with specific written therapeutic and educational suggestions that are relative to their child's level of development and that are to be carried out within the home environment.

Parent Involvement Because the rationale for establishing this group was specifically geared to meeting mothers' needs in understanding, coping, and handling their child with Down's syndrome, the parents are directly involved on a weekly basis.

Prenursery Group

Overview Because a number of children ranging in age from 2 to 3 years with similar skill inefficiencies needed a group experience specifically to have the opportunities to relate to other children and to ease the separation from mothers, this therapeutic educationally oriented group was formulated.

Staffing Pattern This prenursery group is staffed by a special educator, a parent volunteer, and a high school work-study student. In addition, consultation with personnel from occupational therapy, psychology, and medicine are available in individualing programming.

Specific Group Features The prenursery children's group meets biweekly in the afternoon for a 2.5-hour period. The group consists of six children who exhibit similar developmental delays. The children participate in both free play situations and small group activities to develop further behavioral organization and control and social skills. Individualized activities are incorporated according to a child's emerging learning style to facilitate concept learning. Curricula include field trip activities and the use of audiovisual equipment in the therapy-education program.

Parent Involvement Parents and staff initially meet to discuss the goals of the group. Once a week, while the children are in their group, the mothers meet for 1.5 hours with the social worker to talk about a wide variety of concerns, including their feelings, attitudes, and methods of behavior management. Parents have an opportunity to observe the group once a month and to receive home program recommendations. Evening programs for parents have been planned to allow fathers to participate. Audiovisual equipment has been utilized to allow the fathers to see on tape the children's group.

MANAGEMENT

Within the context of the underlying philosophy of PPDM (the team approach directed toward harmonizing, blending, and integrating input from several disciplines and sources so that total services are provided that are conducive to promoting and maintaining the progress and well-being of the child and his family), major management efforts of PPDM can be seen to proceed along medical, developmental-therapeutic, and parent service lines of intervention. Some of the specific program features of each of these important intervention areas should be described further.

Medical

Recommendations for special medical management are made to the child's pediatrician. This includes medications for seizure control, muscle relaxation, or behavior amelioration. Meeting Street School consultative services in the various medical specialties are made available with the approval of the child's physician.

Developmental-Therapeutic

As previously stated, the fundamental principles of PPDM programming relate to the total child, with all abilities and disabilities considered in providing a comprehensive developmental approach to treatment.

Development of appropriate gross motor skills is encouraged by providing the child with a greater variety of movement experiences. Positioning and guidance to assist and encourage emergence of controlled movement patterns in varying postures is utilized. Tactile and kinesthetic awareness of the body and its position, as well as balance control, are encouraged through various techniques. Parents are given guidance in positioning and handling during daily routines in the home to help break through atypical patterns and reflex influences.

The parents are given guidance in providing appropriate movement and play experiences to stimulate the child's visual-perceptual-motor development. Activities emphasizing tactile stimulation, visual following, and visual recognition develop basic sensory intake skills and self-awareness. Arm and hand control is enhanced through experiences encouraging the exploration and manipulation of objects. Developmental play activities, including simple construction toys, puzzles, hide and seek games, and imaginative play with blocks and crayons focus on the integration of visual skills, play concepts, and fine motor abilities. The stimulation of independence in self-care also integrates these components into functional daily life activities.

In the early months, prelingual stepping stones are developed by concentrating on techniques to reinforce sucking, chewing, and swallowing. Suggestions to encourage receptive-integrative and expressive language skills are included in the repertoire of procedures taught to the parents. Suggestions regarding how the parents can best communicate with their child to promote language development are emphasized.

In addition to skill related techniques, the parents may be counseled in behavior management techniques. Specific goals are set up with procedures defined so that parents may have a plan to follow according to their needs. During program appointments, the parents are given the model to follow, and they may participate directly in carrying out suggestions. If necessary, home visits might be arranged to help carry out behavior management programs. Progress reports on each child participating in the program are sent once a year to the child's physician (Appendix VII A and B). However, communication between staff and physician may be initiated at any time when there is a concern.

Parent Services

It is recognized that parents of handicapped children, who have the burden of care, need emotional support to carry out their daily responsibilities. A well trained social worker is available to provide individual casework and to offer leadership at the weekly parent group discussions. Parents of handicapped children experience various emotional and social reactions to having a handicapped child. Individual casework services are available to assist the parents to cope best with their problems. Group sessions are particularly helpful in providing parents with factual knowledge, self-awareness, and emotional support. They help parents to understand their child's needs at different stages of growth and to examine what they expect of themselves as parents. They have an opportunity to explore the interaction that takes place between parent and child, siblings and the atypical child, and the handicapped child's relationship in general to the total family.

Outcomes

About one half of the babies enter an appropriate Meeting Street School group at 3 years of age. About 20 percent of the infants appear to resolve their difficulties and are referred into regular nursery school programs. About 30 percent of the babies are found to have primary mental deficits and are referred to their local school departments for placement.

A PILOT PROGRAM

The Meeting Street School PPDM participated in a highly interesting pilot project that has contributed greatly to the enrichment and growth of the PPDM Team. As part of a joint collaboration between Meeting Street School, a Community Health Center, and Miriam Hospital of Providence, Rhode Island, a Comprehensive Psychoneuromotor Service Center Clinic was established to identify at risk infants at a young age and to render a comprehensive service through early intervention within the home community of the family. In Rhode Island the incidence of definite neurologically abnormal infants at 1 year of age is 2 percent. Of 129 infants, 3 years of age or less, receiving routine health care at the Community Health Center during 1971–1972, 21 (16 percent) were referred to the PPDM Program because of developmental or behavioral management difficulties. Four of these children moved out of the district, thus making it impossible for long-term follow up to be completed. After final team assessment and follow up of the remaining 17 infants for 1 year, 3 (18 percent) were diagnosed as cerebral palsy, 4 (24 percent) as suspicious but without clear evidence of neurologic abnormality, and 10 (59 percent) were classified as normal.

The cerebral palsy group was continued on at Meeting Street School in an appropriate group while the marginal toddlers were monitored by the Health Center staff. The normal infants were discharged from active surveillance but are reviewed by the Health Center staff from time to time. Regardless of outcome, each parent reported that the guidance and monitoring helped them to understand and to cope with the aberrant manifestations of their baby.

In a previous study, Denhoff, Hainsworth, and Hainsworth (1972) designed a First Year Outcome Index designed to predict those 1-year-old infants who were at risk for school failure 6 years later. An adoption of this index for the selection of at risk infants for the PPDM program is presented in Table 1 (for additional data relating maternal characteristics and pregnancy and birth delivery factors to neurologic impairment at 1 year see Niswander and Gordon (1972) and Table 2). This is being used to explore its merit to help in the better selection of cases.

This pilot study suggests that the incidence of neurologically impaired and at risk infants are perhaps higher than initial statistics have indicated. On the other hand, it also shows that with PPDM programming more than one half of the babies soon adjusted and became manageable for their parents. It is probable that a significant number of the normal children would have developed behavior or developmental problems if interventions had not taken place.

NATIONAL INFANT COLLABORATIVE PROJECT

In July, 1971, the Meeting Street School infant program became involved in the National Infant Collaborative Project of the United Cerebral Palsy Association in joint collaboration with four other centers across the country (Atypical Infant Development Program, Marin County, California; University Hospital School, Iowa City, Iowa; United Cerebral Palsy Association of Greater New Orleans, Inc., New Orleans, Louisiana; UCLA Infant Program, University of California Medical Center, Los Angeles, California). The goals of the project were broad based and aimed at 1) sharing the knowledge, skills, and experiences of the various agencies, 2) developing service models that would best foster infant learning and development, strengthen the family's role as the primary programmer of their child's development, and make maximum and efficient use of personnel, 3) developing curriculum guidelines for atypical children, 4) identifying and assisting in the development of centers that have the potential to provide services for infants, and 5) developing evaluation methods for the goals of the project.

Participation

Participation in the National Infant Collaborative Project during the 3 years of the project (1971–1974) has contributed greatly to the growth of the PPDM and to the evolving of new and more efficient modes of providing services. One major effect of the project has been to broaden considerably the skills and capabilities of PPDM staff such that they possess not only considerable skill in their own area of expertise, but also that they have acquired skills and knowledge from other disciplines to make them more effective as providers of service for the child and his family. In a sense, they have all become child

Table 1. "At risk" infant profile

	Definite	Suspicious
Hyper-reactive		
Cry	4	3
Suck	4	3
Sleep	3	2
Hypertonia	1	0.5
Jittery or tremulous	1	0.5
Hyperactive	1	0.5
Asymmetric reflexes	1	0.5
Hypo-reactive		
Hypotonia	5	3
Hypoactive	4	2
Lethargy	3	1
Delayed development		
Motor	5	2
Mental	5	2
Visual impairment		
Extraocular		
Strabismus		
Esotropia	2	0.5
Exotropia	2	0.5
Alternating	1	0.5
Hearing		
Hearing	3	1

Rating at over 6 months: 0–9 = normal, 10+ = at risk.

"At risk" scores are obtained by noting definite or suspicious features in the child and summing the various weights assigned to each of the characteristics displayed by the child. (Reproduced with permission from Denhoff, Hainsworth, and Hainsworth, 1972.)

developmental specialists with an area of particular expertise rather than only being restricted to the confines of their own discipline with the consequent fractionalization of the child that this approach can engender. Team members have, in addition, become much more aware of the importance not only of a thorough assessment of the child and the development and prescribing of appropriate educational-therapeutic activities designed to hasten child development, but also of the importance of the education and training of adults who must by necessity play a significant role in the child's development. Team members have become more aware of parent-child interactions, parent-parent interactions, and parent-staff interactions as being significant factors that cannot be overlooked if a program is to have maximum long-term effect on the child's development. This has, indeed, been a major benefit of participation in the project. Of course, another benefit of the collaboration with the other agencies has been to broaden and enrich considerably the knowledge base of the team members through opportunities for the

Table 2. Items in history that relate significantly to neurological impairment at 1 year*

	White	Negro
Maternal characteristics		
Age at patient's conception		
40 years	38	27
16 years	35	9
Marital status		
Married	15	16
Unmarried	22	25
Divorced	32	30
Education (years in school)		
0–4	31	55
5–8	20	14
9–12	17	15
13+	12	8
Cigarette smoking (no. cigarettes/day)		
41	33	55
21–30	13	42
None	17	16
Weight previous child		
2000 gms	38	26
2000 gms	18	19
Primipara	13	11
Pregnancy conditions		
Normal (without a "risk" disorder)	17	16
Drug abuse		
Alcoholism	25	—
Hard drugs	45	—
Asthma		
Status		
Asthmaticus	71	125
Acute asthma	55	38
Neurologic		
Mental retardation	82	88
Seizures	60	76
Neurologic disease	27	27
Metabolic		
Hyperthyroidism	—	76
Diabetes	43	48
Hypothyroidism	16	35
Renal		
Nephritis	76	46
Cystitis	33	—
Pyuria	23	23

continued

Table 2.—*Continued*

	White	Negro
Cardiopulmonary		
Organic heart disease	25	57
Rheumatic fever	20	17
Inactive tuberculosis	26	13
Obstetric complications		
None	16	17
Placenta previa	43	13
Hyperemesis gravida	40	18
Abruptio placenta	19	33
Hydramnios	38	18
Cord prolapse	17	15
Vaginal bleeding		
2nd trimester	25	18
Puerperal infection	28	19
Premature rupture		
Membranes 8 hours	16	20
12–13 hours	24	27
24–48 hours	28	33
49 hours	47	44
Cord around neck, 2 loops	26	36
Uterine dysfunction	18	14
Anesthetic shock	—	24

*Numbers refer to changes per 1,000 births (stillbirths and live births) of a mother bearing a neurologically impaired baby when abnormal conditions are present at birth. (Reproduced with permission from Niswander, K. R., and Gordon, M., 1972.)

sharing of experiences and approaches to intervention with professionals from other settings and through input provided by consultants with areas of particular expertise who were made available to the National Infant Collaborative Project and to the individual centers.

Evaluation

The evaluation process of the National Infant Collaborative Project, No. H120391A 0-71-4492(616) was planned initially to evolve during the first year of the project. Staff from Technical Assistance Developmental Systems (TADS), University of North Carolina, housed at the Frank Porter Graham Institute at the University of North Carolina planned to review the "outputs" of the quarterly reports submitted by each of the five participating model centers and to resolve an evaluation model for the subsequent 2 years of the project.

In the second year of the project, 1971–1972, a reordering of the stated goals of the project took place. Data obtained from the Face Sheets for each client served, the Denver Developmental Screening Test Scores, and the Bayley Developmental Test Scores were to be analyzed. This information has more carefully described the different children under age 3 that each center has been servicing.

In addition, the Evaluation Process was to include the products described as planned "Outcomes" by each of the collaborating centers. These products are part of the final report to the nation.

During the second year of the project, an Evaluation Task Force was formed. There is a representative from each one of the centers on this committee as well as a staff member from United Cerebral Palsy Association, Inc. The function of this committee is to review the data collected from the quarterly reports and to monitor the products that each center has agreed to provide for the final report.

PPDM PROGRAM COSTS

Recent cost accounting for this program indicates that the cost per child and his family for 1 year of service is $1,836. The categories utilized in developing the costing include salaries, occupancy, fringe benefits (13.2 percent), supplies and equipment, transportation, consultants, and administration overhead (20 percent). These authors feel that the cost of such a program is quite minimal for the comprehensive medical, developmental-therapeutic, and parent services that are provided. Financial necessity has dictated that programs be developed that are not costly but at the same time do not compromise the committment to attend to the total services needs of the child and his family in promoting long-term welfare. Such costs seem minimal when placed in the context of the importance of effective early intervention with atypical and at risk children for later development.

DISCUSSION

What is unique about the PPDM program? Can it stand up to sharp clinical and scientific appraisal? Can it serve as a model to provide a variety of services to babies whether normal, mildly, or even severely disabled? Are the professional disciplines appropriate or can the services be provided more effectively by other disciplines? Is the model too expensive to have practical application in a variety of settings? Is the model modern and able to withstand rapid social changes during the 20 years ahead? These are all questions that seem appropriate.

Uniqueness

The most unique aspect of the PPDM is that it has been a functioning unit available to the community for over 15 years. At a time when obstetricians and pediatricians were not overly concerned with the outcomes of stressed babies, the PPDM program was meeting the crisis needs of parents who did not wish to institutionalize their babies. While these doctors were waiting for the babies to outgrow their deviant symptoms and signs, PPDM was developing a system of long-term options. Through a combination of trial and error, good judgment, and usage of available scientific knowledge, PPDM is able to offer a practical service program that has withstood the test of time.

Critical Appraisal

The program offers a blend of time proven techniques coupled with methodology adopted from the scientific studies of outstanding child developmental specialists.

Adaptations have been made in the Rosenblith (1961) behavioral assessment, and in the usage of an orderly sequence in early tactile and visual awareness to enhance early learning (Ambrose, 1969).

The PPDM program is trying to identify personality style as suggested by Thomas, Chess, and Birch (1968). It is also incorporating into the program an increasing amount of family supportive counseling. The program is able to identify at a reasonably early time the infant at risk for hyperkinesis and later school failure, and it has learned about the very early use of behavior modifying medication and behavior modification. The program is learning how to assess the infant on an "intake-integration-output" model so that remedial learning techniques can be initiated very early when necessary.

What are the program's weaknesses? Perhaps a persistence in maintaining an individual approach without developing a core curriculum that can apply to a spectrum of disabilities. The failure to develop mini-teams earlier and the failure to use specific professionals to meet specific needs might be considered a weakness. The program should provide more help in nutrition planning, family management, life style assessment, and better management for behavior disorders.

A Model

In an era when pediatricians ask, "What next when medications for behavioral and developmental management become ineffective?" the PPDM program offers several other possibilities and alternatives. With the chronic high demands on the pediatrician's time, utilization of the PPDM model considerably expands the amount and range of services that he can provide in his efforts to achieve optimal long-term outcomes in his patients. The constraints on the pediatrician's time are removed and his services significantly broadened and complemented by the considerably greater time that a well trained team within the PPDM model can devote to working with the child and the family. In addition, important portions of the PPDM model can be readily converted into an office model that can be provided by pediatricians and their aides, especially now that audiovisual and video tape techniques are available. (Because PPDM has not been part of a large institution or agency, the model adopted has not depended on extensive facilities or personnel and can, therefore, be readily adapted to a wide range of situations.)

In the office, the main emphasis should be placed on the infant at risk. These are the small-for-date babies, the infants with respiratory distress in the intensive care unit, and those with hemolytic disorders. In such babies, the earliest focus should be placed upon tactile, visual, and auditory enrichment and an increasing body awareness in space. However, in many such babies stimulation per se may be the improper approach. Many hyperactive children have the origins of their problem in auditory or visual overload, and general stimulation would make them worse.

Team Participants

The type of professional used on a team is not as important as the philosophical attitudes, developmental know-how, and empathy they have with parents and children. The personnel at Meeting Street School are now in a position to train aides or assistants. In so doing, it helps to reduce program costs as well as to expand the caseload.

Is the Model Modern?

The PPDM program is geared to help the handicapped and the marginally impaired, the poverty blighted child, and the normal infant with insecure parents. It is geared to change the focus of the program to the degree that scientific study points out appropriate directions.

The PPDM is ready to meet the challenges provided by the babies who try to survive in an increasingly complex society. Among them are the offsprings of mothers who are fearful of handling their normal babies, or those with post-partum psychoses, or those who are rejecting.

The inclusion of the teacher and the adult programmer on the consultant team helps to translate the needs of the baby to day care personnel and to parents.

Research

The PPDM program provides excellent opportunities for research. The critical areas that require objective documentation are well known. These critical areas include testing the correlative aspects of infancy with later childhood behavior, learning, and cognitive outcomes. The effects of nutrition, mother-infant interactions, infant behavior styles, and early body awareness and perceptual-motor stimulation all require documentation.

An entire schemata of special education has been developed around the body-perceptual-laterality and dominance programs recommended by Kephart, Barsch, and Doman-Delaccato. Are these valid concepts with a permanent impact on learning? Such items lend themselves to research in the PPDM model.

Because the PPDM program has provided services to infants and their families for 15 years to more than 1,000 children and their families, an extensive and varied population is available to study the outcomes of these cases several years after participation in the PPDM program. Comparisons of the outcomes of these children can readily be made with known outcomes of children who did not have the benefit of an early intervention program or for whom early intervention efforts were limited at best. Also, although the PPDM models for providing services have varied and evolved over the years, the elements of providing developmental-therapeutic intervention and stimulation experiences as well as medical and parent services have always been significant aspects of the program. Consequently, although changes in PPDM inspired by changing conditions and new knowledge have been a frequent occurrence, several important types of services have been ever present features of PPDM and provide a solid foundation for investigative studies of the effects of various intervention procedures on later outcomes. Furthermore, through extensive and frequent longitudinal assessment procedures, groups of atypical and at risk children can be identified at a very early age and their progress monitored in an intervention program where effects and outcomes can readily be examined within the context of various research designs.

The PPDM program has its roots in the classical cerebral palsy service model. In diagnosis, the criteria used are tonus, postural reflex status, and developmental level, while in management emphasis is placed upon encouraging movement through stimulation and by using whatever reasonable means necessary to encourage potentially usuable action patterns to become functional. An increasing awareness of individual differences in children, the effects of both individual and family life styles, parental attitudes at different social strata levels, coupled with new knowledge of how the brain processes information and how babies learn have subtly influenced changes in programming. The "cerebral palsy" flavor is now being tempered more and more with behavioral and learning aspects. What are some of the factors that influence changes in curriculum?

Anatomic: It has been found that there are clear differences between the sexes in the histologic (cellular) and architectural (lobe) makeup of the brain. In most, the male right parietal lobe is better designed for motor activities, while the female left temporal is better suited for language (Geschwind, 1972).

Pathologic: It has been found that small-for-date babies especially are prone to have deep venous sludging with consequent damage to the neurons surrounding the ventricles (Towbin, 1969). With cerebral growth and maturation, there is interference in neuronal interconnections between the subcortical tissues resulting in an inability to filter and to select out appropriate stimuli.

Physiologic: It has been found that both the right and the left brain have similar though not identical functions (Geschwind, 1972). A child's unimpaired brain area, in contradistinction to the adult, can often assimilate and take over functions of brain damaged portions, provided the corpus callosum is intact.

If the right parietal brain is better suited to take in sensory information, then why not consistently provide such information just to the left hand and then the right to help in processing and transfer of information?

If cognitive functions depend on an early high protein well balanced diet, because protein intake is related to neuronal development, why not monitor diets more carefully?

Questions such as these arise from the new neurologic information, and as a result these authors often try to explore the validity of the information.

Thus, for instance, establishing a controlled study has been considered to explore whether consistently providing information to the left hand first will, in fact, enhance learning. It should also be explored whether girls should get more "motor" exposure and boys more "language" exposure in view of known early sex differences.

The curriculum, on the basis of previous study, already includes providing early visual-perceptual and tactile-kinesthetic experiences such as showing the baby very early a series of stripes, circles, faces, and geometric forms that have proven of value in early learning (Ambrose, 1969). Auditory and olfactory input follows closely so that all sensory inputs are enriched in an orderly coordinated fashion.

A fascinating issue that needs clarification concerns the effects of perinatal asphyxia or other central nervous system stresses upon the individual temperaments of the baby, as defined by Thomas, Chess, and Birch (1968). They have been able to identify three groupings of infants through clustering of adaptive behavior characteristics: the easy infant, the difficult infant, and the slow-to-warm-up infant. They have found the characteristics of the difficult infant to be present in brain injured children. However, not all children with neurologic impairment have volatile temperaments, and there are some who are easy to rear. This aspect of child rearing will make an interesting study, as will a study in differences between first born and middle born siblings and differences in sex.

THE FUTURE

What about the future? Many new mothers have difficulty in knowing how to rear babies properly. In the past, such mothers depended upon their own parents for guidelines for baby management. Now as young families move about and lose close contact with their close relatives, these authority figures are no longer available. The mothers try to remember how they were reared, but often their remembered experiences no longer seem appropriate in today's world. Now mothers read about the need for very early nuturance, individual behavior characteristics, and the rights of babies. From a stage of bewilderment 10 years ago, they are now seeking help from pediatricians, day care personnel, neighbors, books, and magazines.

In many instances, they turn away from the physician because they feel he is not sufficiently responsive to the behavior needs of the baby, although they are quick to defend his physical care. Some parents have learned about mobiles, music with a beat, and varied lighting to help developmental awareness. Some use these techniques on their own discriminately, but others use them indiscriminately and overtax the developmental capacity of the baby. Naturally, the drives for guidance are affected by many factors such as social class, level of education, and especially poverty and the effects of socioeconomic deprivation on motivation.

It is the feeling of these authors that the PPDM model has a place in dealing with normal babies. There is no need for infant stimulation to help make normal babies brighter or more astute. There is a need, however, to teach parents how to program a baby's life properly so that he will receive the propoer balance of positive and negative reinforcement. Parents must learn that love is not enough, but that child rearing is most effective when structure is mixed in proper portion with permissiveness.

To make such programs effective, these parents need better identification of the individual temperaments of the baby, the relationship of temperament to sex and birth order in the family, and the relationship between maternal attitudes of mothers from different sociologic backgrounds and the child's life style and personality-social development.

When such issues are clarified, perhaps all babies, normal, at risk, or handicapped, will have a better opportunity to grow and to develop in the fashion they were intended.

ACKNOWLEDGMENTS

The authors acknowledge the invaluable assistance of the Meeting Street School Developmental Management Team in the preparation of this paper: A. Beverly Brindle, Physical Therapy; Elaine Lieberman, Feeding, Speech, and Language Therapy; Sharon Mc Dermott, Occupational Therapy; Trude Maloney, Special Education; and Nancy B. D'Wolf and Alice K. Cassidy, Administration.

APPENDIX I

History—PPDM Program

Date:_____

Patient's Name:_____Age:___Sex:___Date of Birth:_____

Father's Name:_____Address:_____

Mother's Name:_____Address:_____

Source of Information:_____Referred by:_____

Major Complaints: (1)_____
                  (2)_____
                  (3)_____
                  (4)_____

Family Background:

	Race	Age	Education	Occupation	Other
Mother					
Father					
Siblings: (1)					
(2)					

Parents:	Yes	No			Yes	No
Natural			married and living together			
Adoptive			unmarried			
			separated			
			divorced			
			widowed			

Family Illnesses/Traits (parents, siblings, first cousins):

	No	Yes	Comment
Hereditary diseases			
Neurologic disorders			
Psychiatric disorders			
Learning disorders			
Seizure disorders			
Alcoholism			
Drug abuse			
Other			

Family Attitudes:

	No	Yes	Comment
Warm and accepting			
Rigid and rejecting			
Over permissive			
Over protective			
Deprivation			
Battering			
Other			
Frequent household moves			

continued

APPENDIX I—*Continued*

Maternal at Risk Features: General characteristics:

	N	AB	Discuss at risk
General health during pregnancy			
Unmarried			
Previous miscarriages			
Age at conception of patient (<18 yrs; 40>at risk)			
Weight gain during pregnancy (>20 lbs at risk)			
Weight loss during pregnancy (at risk)			
Pre-pregnant weight (<100; >160 at risk)			
Maternal height (<58"; >67" at risk)			
Weight previous child (under 5 lbs (2000 gm) at risk)			
Difficulty conceiving (>1 yr at risk)			
Previous miscarriages (at risk)			
Stillbirths (at risk)			
Prematures (at risk)			
Cigarette smoking (30+/day)			
Other			

During Pregnancy Conditions (in order of significance) (circle if present):

	No	Yes
Illness:		
Asthma		
Esp. status		
Seizures		
Mental retardation		
Rheumatic fever		
Diabetes		
Nephritis		
Hard drugs		
Alcohol		
Hyperthyroid/hypothyroid		
Neurological disorders		
Other heart diseases		
Psychiatric/emotional		
Other		

Medicine, Vitamins, Hormones During Pregnancy: _____

Pregnancy Attributed Feelings:

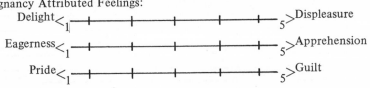

Complications During Pregnancy (circle if present): Placenta previa and separation, severe vomiting, cord prolapse, puerperal sepsis, mid-pregnancy vaginal bleeding with threatened abortion.

continued

APPENDIX I—*Continued*

Obstetrical Factors: Delivery
Hours in Labor _____
Complications during delivery _____
(see current MSS history) _____

Delivery Complications (circle if present): Breech delivery—complicated, breech delivery uncomplicated, complicated or difficult forceps delivery (high, mid.), caesarian section, other _____

Infant:

	Normal	Abnormal		Birth Weight	Birth Length
Apgar Score			Premature		
Resuscitation required			Immature		
Respiratory distress			Dysmature		
RH factor			Postmature		
Jaundice			Mature		
Bilirubin level					
Transfusions					
Other hemolytic disorders					

Activity Level (at 1 year):

Activity	none	constant
Attention	fleeting	sustained
Distractibility	none	intense
Mood quality	calm	irritability
Mood intensity	mild	severe
Rhythmically	regular	irregular
Adaptability	excellent	poor

Behavior Style:
Easy to manage_____Position in family_____
Difficult to manage_____
Slow to warm up_____

Habits:

		No	Yes
Weight gain:	poor		
	excessive		
Cry:	frequent		
	infrequent		
	atypical quality		
Irritability:	with feeding		
	at bedtime		
Sleep:	resistant		
	excessive		
	unusual patterns		
Rhythmic behavior:	thumb sucking		
	rocking		

continued

APPENDIX I—*Continued*

	head banging		
	masturbation		
Contact with adults:	avoids		
Activity:	over friendly		
	over exploratory		
	under exploratory		
	hyperactive		
	hyperkinetic:		
	(hyperactive		
	(short attention		
	(perseveration		
	(mood intensity		
Mood:	passive		
	irritable		
	tantrums		
Bowel habits:	irregular		
	resists training		
	loose		
	constipated		
Urine:	eneuresis		
	resists training		
	less or excessive		
	quantity		

Behavior (at 1 year):

Hyper-reactive	No	Yes	Hypo-reactive	No	Yes
Jumpy			Listless		
Tremors			Lethargic		
Abnormal suck			Floppy		
High pitched cry			Never cries		
Feeding difficulty:			Feeding difficulty:		
Suck			Suck		
Swallow			Swallow		
Chew			Chew		
Strabismus			Strabismus		
Auditory			Auditory		

Developmental Milestones:	Normal	Marginal	Abnormal
Head control (6 wks)			
Smile (8 wks)			
Reach (16 wks)			
Sitting (32 wks)			
Standing (36 wks)			
Walking (18 mos)			
Single words (12 mos)			
2–3 word sentences (30 mos)			
Bowel trained (36 mos)			
Bladder trained (60 mos)			
Handedness ( ) left ( ) right ( ) either			

APPENDIX II

Meeting Street School Gross Motor Developmental Evaluation Battery (Birth to 3 years)

Name: _____ C.A.: _____ D.O.B.: _____ Date: _____

Age Level	A.	Prone Progression	B.	Supine/Sitting	C.	Erect Postures
1 mo.	1.	Prone Suspension—a) head droops, b) head momentarily lifted up	1.	ATNR attitude	1.	"Stepping" if trunk held forward, gone by 1 mo., but persists if head is extended when foot is flat
	2.	Prone placement—head rotates to side	2.	Head kept mainly to one side	2.	Held standing—legs extend briefly, toes flex, resistance to support slight
	3.	Prone-flexor tone, crouched position	3.	Hands tightly fisted	3.	Lifts head when held to shoulder
	4.	Intermittent kicking of legs	4.	Knees resistant to full extension with hips flexed		
	5.	Lifts head momentarily	5.	Turns head through 90°		
			6.	Symmetrical windmill arm movements		
			7.	Kicks legs between flexion and semi-flexion		
			8.	Rolls partway to side		
			9.	Rolls from side to back		
			10.	Pulled to sit—almost complete head lag		
			11.	Held sitting—evenly rounded back, head lifted momentarily, falls forward on chest		
2 mo.	6.	Prone suspension—head maintained in line with	12.	Energetic arm movements	4.	Held standing—holds head up momentarily
			13.	Vigorous head turning		

Note: Solid lines down entire profile represent the chronological age of the child at the time of evaluation, and provides a visual means of comparing the child's level of development in the different skills with the level of development usually associated with children of that age.

	body, momentarily lifted beyond this	14. Vigorous leg thrusting	
7.	Prone—lifts head with plane of face at 45° to mat	15. Pulled to sit—moderate head lag	5. Held standing—takes small fraction of weight briefly
8.	Lifts head repeatedly, not sustained	16. Held sitting—head predominantly erect, bobbing	6. May lift foot
3 mo. 9.	Prone suspension—head maintained well beyond plane of body	17. Head predominantly turned half to side, in mid-position	
10.	Prone—lifts head with plane of face 45°–90° to mat	18. Arms coming toward midline	
		19. Hands open or loosely closed	
11.	Props on forearms, lifts head and shoulders, hips extended, knees flexed	20. Pulled to sit—slight head lag	
12.	Rotates head while extended	21. Held sitting—head erect, unsteady, bobs forward	
13.	On verge of rolling to supine		
4 mo. 14.	Lifts head with plane of face at 90° to mat	22. Head in midline	7. Held standing—sags at hips and limbs
15.	Flops on forearms, one arm flexed, other extended	23. Occasional ATNR posture	8. Attempts to extend legs haphazardly—recurrently
16.	Chest lifted off mat	24. Hands engage	9. Rises to toes
17.	Head held extended	25. Turns head through 180°	10. Downward parachute—legs extend, abduct, and externally rotate
18.	Swimming motions—limbs in extension, weight on abdomen	26. Legs—bilateral flexion with alternate extension	
		27. Lifts legs slightly	
		28. Pulled to sit—slight head lag initially	
		29. Held sitting—head erect, steady, set forward	
		30. Lumbar curve in back	
		31. In sitting, head wobbles if body is swayed	
		32. Sits propped	

continued

APPENDIX II—*Continued*

Age Level	A. Prone Progression	B.	Supine/Sitting	C.	Erect Posture
5 mo.	19. Pivot prone positioning often	33.	Rolls side to side		
	20. Pushes up on hands, arms extended	34.	Begins lifting head and shoulders		
	21. Rolls to supine (5 1/2)	35.	Pulled to sit—no head lag		
	22. Beginning creep on stomach	36.	Held sitting—back straight, head steady		
		37.	No head wobble when body is swayed		
6 mo.	23. Weight on one forearm, reaches with other hand	38.	Toes in mouth, legs extended	11.	Held standing—supports almost all body weight
	24. Pivots in circle on stomach	39.	Pulled to sit—lifts head, assists	12.	Bounces actively on feet (6–7 mos.)
	25. Pushes backward using hands/arms	40.	Rolls to prone		
	26. Draws legs up frog-like kicks out	41.	Sits momentarily learning forward on extended arms		
	27. Rolls over in either direction	42.	Shows same active balance in supported sitting		
		43.	Lateral displacement in sitting—extends arm to support		
7 mo.	28. Pushes high on hands	44.	Pulled to sit—lifts head; pulls self to sitting	13.	Held by hands, supports body weight in standing
	29. Weight on one hand while reaching	45.	Sits alone momentarily,		
	30. Pulls forward on stomach using hands	46.	Rotates trunk to reach object		
8 mo.	31. Progresses on floor, abdomen/back	47.	Sits alone, unsteady, 1 minute or more	14.	Placed standing at rail, holds full weight, wide base
	32. Attains hands and knees position, rocks	48.	Sitting, leans forward, recovers balance		
		49.	Attains sitting with trunk rotation, from prone		

Age			
9 mo.	33. Creeps on hands/knees 34. Suspension bridge— hands/feet 35. Goes from sitting to prone or hands/knees	50. Sits indefinitely with good control 51. Backward displacement in sitting—arms extend to support 52. Pivots in sitting 53. Assumes sitting—no assistance 54. May hitch on buttocks	15. Pulls to stand at rail 16. At rail, lifts and replaces foot 17. "Plops" to sit from rail
10 mo.	36. Creeping—makes near-step with 1 foot		18. Cruises sideways at rail or furniture 19. Walks with 2 hands held
11 mo.	37. Creeping—step with 1 foot	55. Sitting—twists around to pick up object, no difficulty	20. Walks with 1 hand held 21. Cruising, lowers to sit with control
12 mo.	38. Creeping—plantigrade, on hands and feet 39. Assumes kneel—stand		22. Stands alone briefly 23. Walks alone, 2–4 steps, unequal director and length, broad base
13 mo.			24. In walking, arms in "high guard" position
15 mo.			25. Assumes standing position unassisted from back-lying—rolls to stomach, to hands/knees, to standing

continued

APPENDIX II—*Continued*

Age Level	C.	Erect Postures
	26.	Kneels without support
	27.	Walks alone, wide base, whole foot contact, stops and starts again
	28.	In walking, arms at medium guard position (waist high)
	29.	Falls by sitting
18 mo.	30.	Creeps upstairs (hands/knees, hands/feet, hitching)
	31.	Walks alone, fast but wobbly, seldom falls
	32.	In walking, no guard, arms by side
	33.	Walks sideways, backward pulling wheeled toy
	34.	Runs stiffly, fast walk, wobbles, little knee movement
	35.	Walks upstairs one hand held, nonalternating
	36.	Seats self on small chair
	37.	Climbs into adult chair
	38.	Attempts to kick ball, walks into or steps on it
	39.	Hurls ball from standing, without falling
21 mo.	40.	Walks upstairs holding railing
	41.	Walks downstairs, one hand hold
	42.	Squats in play
	43.	Stands on 1 foot with help
	44.	Kicks large ball with demonstration
24 mo.	45.	Walks with heel-toe contact
	46.	Runs fairly well without falling, ankles and knees more flexible
	47.	Walks upstairs, nonalternating, no support
	48.	Walks downstairs, nonalternating, holding railing or alone
	49.	Combines squat and bend to pick up object from floor, returns to standing
	50.	Assumes standing from back—lying by turning to side, pushing up to stand
	51.	Walks backward in imitation
	52.	Tries to stand on walking board
	53.	Kicks large ball without demonstration
	54.	Jumps off step, one foot ahead (step-jump)
	55.	Jumps from 18 inch height with help
30 mo.	56.	Walks upstairs, alternating feet with support
	57.	Walks downstairs, non-alternating, no support

58. Walks on tiptoes with demonstration, few steps
59. Tries to stand on 1 foot alone
60. **Walks on line, general direction**
61. Walks with 1 foot on walking board
62. Stands on walking board with both feet (30–33)
63. Jumps with both feet in place
64. Throws ball (3" or 6" diameter) distance of 5 ft.
65. Walks with rhythmical arm swing
66. Walks upstairs, alternates feet, no support
67. Walks on tiptoes 10 feet
68. Walks on line (1" × 10'), few steps off
69. **Walks backward with demonstration (10 ft.)**
70. Walking board, attempts a step
71. Stands on 1 foot, momentary balance
72. Assumes standing from back, coming forward to sitting, little/no sideways turning, then up
73. **Runs well, turning sharper corners, stopping, dodging**
74. Jumps from bottom step, feet together
75. Jumps from 18 inch height alone, one foot ahead
76. Jumps forward, feet together, 1–3 steps (38)
77. Climbs jungle gym
78. Pedals tricycle
79. **Throws small ball (3 inch diameter) 7 ft. distance**
80. Catches large ball (6" diameter), arms straight

36 mo.

Comments:

continued

411

APPENDIX II—*Continued*

Gross Motor Skills

Head control
1 mo.	lifts (prone)
2 mo.	lifts to 45°
3 mo.	maintains lifted
4 mo.	props on forearms
5 mo.	props on hands
	head steady all positions

Sitting
4 mo.	sits propped
6 mo.	momentary sit with arms forward for support
7 mo.	momentary sit, no support
8 mo.	sits alone, unsteady
9 mo.	attains sit, sits steady

Standing
6 mo.	bounces on feet
8 mo.	stands holding rail
10 mo.	pulls to stand
13 mo.	stands alone
15 mo.	assumes standing, no assist

Locomotion
6 mo.	rolls
7 mo.	belly crawl
9 mo.	creeps hands and knees
11 mo.	cruises
14 mo.	walks alone

Advanced movement patterns
18 mo.	stairs, up; 1 hand held
	beginning run
	climbs on furniture
	walks into ball to kick

VPH Skills

Visual, attention notility/discrimination
2 mo.	horizontal, vertical, circular tracking
4 mo.	inspects hands, objects
5 mo.	focus, any distance
7 mo.	look for object disappeared
19 mo.	matches objects
24 mo.	recognizes pictures
30 mo.	matches pictures, color size

Fine motor control
4 mo.	beginning voluntary grasp
6 mo.	transfers objects
7 mo.	examines by manipulation feels, shakes, bangs
10 mo.	pincer grasp
12 mo.	conscious release
26 mo.	screws keg
36 mo.	adult grasp (crayon)

VPM integration
6 mo.	directed reach
7 mo.	empties
12 mo.	fills
15 mo.	put-together toy, nesting, ringstack, cubes
24 mo.	imitates horizontal and vertical strokes
30 mo.	3 forms in reverse board
36 mo.	copies circle

Communication Skills

Receptive comprehension
6 mo.	movement connected with words (up, come)
	recognizes signs
9 mo.	responds to familiar words
12 mo.	looks for names object, follows simple directions
15 mo.	gives toy on verbal request
	shows items of clothing
18 mo.	points to 1 named picture, 3 body parts
21 mo.	obeys prepositions "in", "on" (in context)
24 mo.	indicates 6–9 named pictures
	understands "more"
30 mo.	identified object by use (3/4)
36 mo.	identified action in pictures
	begins to categorize, differentiates How, Why, When, What
	points to 20–29 named pictures

Vocalization
3 mo.	coos
6 mo.	babbles
	vocalizes feelings
9 mo.	imitates own speech sounds
12 mo.	jargon
30 mo.	disgards jargon

Nonverbal communication

6 mo.   gestures, arms out to be taken,
        closes lips for enough food
9 mo.   understands gestures, plays baby
        game gestures, reaches, rejects
15 mo. points
18 mo. imitates household activities
20 mo. pretends imitatively
36 mo. pretends imaginatively

Vocabulary

11 mo. first word
18 mo. 3–10 words
24 mo. 50–75 words
30 mo. 200–400 words
36 mo. 80% intelligible

Verbal expression

11 mo. says mama meaningfully
14 mo. says and waves bye-bye
16 mo. say ta-ta (thank you)
18 mo. extends word meaning
20 mo. names familiar objects
        names 1 familiar picture
24 mo. connects two words
30 mo. commands others
        grammar emerges
36 mo. 3–4 word sentences
        relates comments in past
        and present
        names 20–29 pictures

21 mo. stairs, up; railing
        down; 1 hand held
        squats to play
24 mo. stairs, up; no support
        down; railing
        runs, more flexible
        kicks ball, no demonstra-
        tion
30 mo. jumps off step (step-jump)
        stairs, up; alternates
        with support
        down; alone
        jumps, feet together
        throws ball 5 feet
36 mo. stairs; up; alternates
        alone
        runs, quick turns, dodges
        jumps from step
        jumps forward
        pedals trike
        climbs jungle gym
        catches large ball

Compiled by A. Beverly Brindle, RPT. Reproduced with permission from the Bureau of Education for the Handicapped, U.S. Office of Education, Washington, D.C.

APPENDIX III
Meeting Street School
Visual Perception Motor Evaluation—Birth to 42 months

Child: _____

D.O.B. _____ D.O.T. _____ C.A. _____

	Understanding		Expression
0–1	Focus 7" from eyes	**0–1**	Opticokinetic nystagmus
	Regards: face, moving red ring, light/dark contrast		Doll's eye
			Nystagmus upon rotation
	Horizontal trackings to midling, beyond midline, 100°		Blink reflex
			Grasp reflex
	Vertical tracking 30°		Fingers pryed open to release
			Supine, retains red ring
			Supine movements are smooth and bilateral
			Startles to light, sound, movement
			Reacts to occlusion of nose and mouth
1–2	Focus 6" from eyes	**1–2**	Hands clenched on contact with involuntary release
	Sustained fixation		Grasp in pronation
	Lateral ocular gaze		Hands pryed open to receive rattle
	Peripheral pursuit at 9" in ATNR		Holds objects 30 seconds or more
	Central pursuit for 90° at 9"		Thumbs idle and useless
	Vertical tracking moving red ring		Beginning hand to mouth
	Circular tracking moving red ring		Gross lateral arm movements
	Beginning to regard ATNR hand		
	Visual preference black and white: Horizontal, vertical, schematic face		
	Free inspection of environment		
	Smiles in response to smile, talk-touch		
	Turns to look for sound		
2–3	Focus 5" from eyes	**2–3**	Hands open 50% of evaluation
	EBR to centrally approaching object		Gross swiping with hands fisted
	Blink on direct visual threat		Overshoots in swiping
	Central pursuit at 5"		Gross symmetrical reaching movements

414

Regards objects in midline with/without
  noise, supine/supported sitting
Horizontal tracking pencil past midline
Attends to ATNR hand
In ATNR, glances from object to hand to
  object
Visually recognizes mother without talking
Smiles in response to smile and nodding
Reacts to face disappearing from sight
Visual preference for novel: red and white
  bullseye, solid/flat objects
Glances from one noisy object to another
Visually recognizes mother

3–4
Focus 3" from eyes
Tracks moving objects in all planes
Tracks ball across table
Prompt regard of toy at midline
Regards raisin
Visual inspection: of hands, of object and
  hand in view
Pursues vanishing horizontal object
Visual preference schematic face and
  irregular orange, red shapes
In midline glances from object to hand to
  object
Visually monitors gross reaching and play

4–5
Focus on object at any distance
Sustained hand regard less common
Glances between object and hand, torso
  turning
Beginning to visually monitor reaching

Retains rattle briefly
Grasp in pronation
Ulnar grasp
Mouthing objects placed in hand
Manipulates red ring
Opening and closing fists repetitiously
Reacts to paper on face

3–4
Fists loosely closed
Retains 1" cube in ulnar-palmer grasp
Simple play with rattle
Manipulates table edge fleetingly/scratches surface
Pulls at dress automatically
Bilateral patterns: hands to midline and clasped
  reaching, contact but no grasp
Supine, reaches for red ring
Side presentation, closes on ring
Mouthing objects
Torso turning

4–5
Arms activate bilaterally on sight of toy/
  in approach to toy
Unilateral reach with open hand contact/
  no contact
Grasp on sight; hand in view/hand not in view

continued

APPENDIX III—*Continued*

Understanding		Expression
Approaches mirror		Beginning voluntary grasp; palmer grasp
Visual Preferences solid/flat		Fingers, clutches body, hair, dress
		Pulls shirt over face
		Explorative paper play
		Retains 2 cubes, 3 or more seconds
		Manipulates table edge actively
		Both hands to mouth
		Beginning to touch bottle with 2 hands
		Hitting in downward motions object on a surface
		production of sound waving motion
		Kicks feet to ring bells
Discriminates stranger	5–6	Grasp with forearm in neutral
Visual preference—form and color		Reaches persistently
Follows falling vertical trajectory		Directed reaching
Begins to look for object disappeared		Rotates wrist freely in manipulation of toys
		Bangs in play (no demonstration)
		Shaking objects
		Plays with strings
		Lifts inverted cup
		Grasps raking/radial
		Attempts to secure pellet
		Reaches for 2nd cube
		Pats Bottle
		Brings feet to mouth
		Transfers objects
Pats mirror image	6–7	Accurate unilateral reaching from shoulder
Regards self in mirror		Examines object by manipulation: shakes, bangs, empties, turns, feels
Looks for object disappeared: horizontally/ vertically		Grasp toy, regards, drops, resecures
Visually inspects bell clapper		Accidental pulling of string to get ring
Attends to scribbling		Retains 2 of 3 cubes

Visual preference: schematic face
  flashing lights
  brightly colored object
  solid objects
Lifts inverted cup by handle

7–8
Playful response to mirror
Partial visible displacement, 1 screen

8–9
Visible displacement, 1 screen
Pulls string adaptively
Rings bell imitatively
Pat-a-cake with assistance
Attempts to secure 3 cubes

Holds 1 object in each hand
Transfers objects
Cracker to mouth
Partial thumb opposition in radial palmar grasp
Grasps in pronation

7–8
Retrieves dropped toy within reach
Differentiated schemas—at least 2
  slides object
  pushes object off
  crumples object
  attempts to tear object
  pats object
  bangs objects together
  shakes objects
Controlled grasp and release for squeeze toys
Cannot release at will
Begins pulling apart activities
Radial raking of pellet to palm
Inferior pincer grasp of pellet
Radial digital grasp with thumb
Beginning grasp in supination
Drinks from cup held by adult
Holds spoon

8–9
Brings 2 objects together at midline
Single arm control
Reaches for toys out of reach
Ring stack apart, random
Systematic dropping
Inferior pincer grasp
Radial raking with wholearm
Feeds self cracker
Holds own bottle
Beginning to hold own cup

continued

APPENDIX III—*Continued*

Understanding	Expression
9–10	**9–10**
Watches things nearby	Throwing
Manipulate string of dangling ring	2 hands perform separately, 1 hand holding, 1 hand manipulating; manipulates 2 objects same time
Pat-a-cake	Bangs objects together
	Wrist extension when rings bell
	Supination
	Beginning to poke
	Pincer grasp for pellet
	Radial digital grasp
	Picks up cup and secures block
	Holds own bottle (h/e)
	Pulls off hat
10–11	**10–11**
Stirs with spoon in imitation	Clasps hands
Looks for bead in box	Bilateral movements: 1 hand assists, 1 hand leads/shifts
	Wrist still slightly flexed on grasp
	Crude deliberate release
	Extended index pokes and prys
	Pincer grasps: attempts to come scribble
	Beginning pulling
	Puts cube in cup/over cup
	Hits or pushes object on table
11–12	**11–12**
Points to missing mouth on picture	Individual finger use
Visible displacement 2 screens	Extension of wrist
Pushes examiner's hand away	Superior pincer grasp
Pulls string to get toy	Difficulty with release
	Offers ball without release
	Empty/fill large containers
	Holds crayon adaptively
	Continues to hit objects together
	Cube and cup: out/in
	Beginning to extend arm or begin dressing
	Attempts ring stack on

Understanding	Expression	Age
	Conscious control supination	12–15
	Precise grasp	
	Holds 2 cubes 1 hand	
	Showing	
	Releases ball with demonstration	
	Releases bead in box hole	
	Large peg in	
	Round form in board	
	Nests 2 boxes	
	3 cubes in cup	
	Attempts 2 block tower	
	Cube tower of 2	
	Exploits paper	
	Unwraps toy	
	Removes cover from box	
	Imitates horizontal scribble/scribbles spontaneously	
	Dangles ring in imitation	
	Turns pages	
	Ring stack together	
	Holds cup/does not put down well	
	With spoon, turns bowl upside down	
	Difficulty getting spoon into mouth	
	Runs spoon across plate	
	Finger feeds	
	Holds arms out at sight of clothes/pushes in	
	Grasps 2 objects with 1 hand	18–20
	Turns pages 2, 3 at a time	
	Pounds peg in pegboard	
	Pops beads apart	
	Pulls a toy	
	Pulls beads off string, puts string in board	
	Nesting 4 cans (T and E)	
	Aware of color	
	Matches familiar objects	

continued

419

APPENDIX III—*Continued*

	Understanding	Expression
21		Horizontal chip can
		Holds crayon with fist
		Scribbles back and forth
		Attempts to imitate vertical
		Looks selectively at pictures
		Imitates simple actions (kiss doll)
		Holds cup with 2 hands, little spilling
		Fills spoon
		Removes hat, socks, shoes, mittens
		Unfastens zipper
		Shrugs off coat
		Attempts to put shoe on
26–30		Recognizes can, upside down and turns over
		Cube tower 5,6
		Circular scribble, few vertical strokes
		Beginning to unscrew jar
		Cube tower of 8
		Screws legs
		Folds paper
		Tears paper
		Clips clothespins on can
		Cuts with scissors
		String small beads
		3 forms reversed board
		Beginning to match 3 dimensional to 2 dimensional
		Matches basic shapes (sorting)
		Beginning to match basic colors
		Imitates OV
		Attempts + with 2 or more strokes
		Copies linear design of page

30—42

Feeds self with fork
Pulls clothing on, off head
Puts arm in pullover
Recognizes self in photo

Closing fist and moving thumb
Imitates most activities with 1 hand
Other hand used as assistor
Adaptive crayon grasp
Localizes to area to be colored
Copies—, 1, 0
Draws man with head
Cube tower of 9, 10
Fills box with cubes
Stereognosis
Matches 3 different sizes
Sequence by size ring stack
Sorts big: little
Imitates simple block designs
Nesting, mostly discriminating
Tower of 4, 5 graduated nesting boxes
Matches familiar pictures
Matches simple black-line pictures
Pictorially aware of upside-down/right side-up
Patience pictures, 2, 3
Sorts pictures of large, small circles
Arranges cut out shapes in line
Constructs bridge/oblique bridge
Finds by matching 1 of several objects in the room
Recall 1 of 4 objects presented
Points to missing nose on the face drawing
Matches 4 sets of colors well
Sorts 2 colors well
Continues simple alternating pattern of 2 color blocks
Puts on pants
Unbuttons, unlaces, unbuckles

Compiled by Sharon McDermott, OTP. Reproduced with permission from the Bureau of Education for the Handicapped, U.S. Office of Education, Washington, D.C.

APPENDIX IV
Meeting Street School—Language Development Scale—Birth to 3 Years

NAME:
NAME:
D.O.E. _____
D.O.B. _____
C.A. _____
NAME: _____

Receptive	Expressive
00–01 Quiets when picked up Response to social approach *Hearing* Response to sound: eye blink startle Activity: decrease cease increase Bell Rattle Light Switch Crumpled Paper Two Blocks Voice (mother/E)	**00–01** Frequent crying: strong weak Saliva babies Non-crying noises: throaty grunt hiccups Random vocalizing: open mouth sounds
01–02 Regards speaker Social smile Inspects surroundings Anticipatory excitement *Hearing* Attends to voice Startle/cry or loud/sudden noises	**01–02** Special crys: hunger pain discomfort Happy noises: gurgles chuckles Coos: musical, vowel-like (an eh oo er)
02–03 Recognizes mother: visually voice Watches speakers face Anticipatory adjustment to lifting Anticipates food by noises/visual signs Recognizes bottle *Hearing* Searches for sound: bell rattle voice	**02–03** Coo sustained (15–20 seconds) Vocalizes 2 different syllables (ah goo) Gutteral sounds (like: K G NG) Vocalizes to social stimuli Imitation: Smile returned

03–04 Aware of strange situations
Aware of many stimuli in environment
  visual auditory
Enjoy frolic play
Hearing
Turns head to source: voice bell rattle
Reacts to quiet voice
	03–04 More noncrying sounds
	Babble: adds sounds like P B D M
	  series of same syllable (ga ga ga)
	Vocalizes when stimulated or playing
	Laughs aloud
	Control of volume (variation)

04–05	Recognizes familiar sounds: his name
	Recognizes attendants
	Discriminates strangers
	Hearing
	Turns head and eyes to speaker (no vision)
		04–05	Cooing stops
			Babble: adds—M NG K G H OO AW OH
			  self initiated
			  stops in response to vocal stimulation
			Vocalizes feelings: pleasure displeasure
			  eagerness satisfaction

05–06	Understands general meanings: friendly, disapproving tones Shows likes/dislikes (toy removal) *Hearing* Plays with noisy toys Listens to own voice Responds to fallen object (sound)	05–06	Babble: Plays at making noises/sounds Socialized vocalizations begin: takes initiative Vocalizes to his image in mirror Vocalizes to music

06–07	Recognizes signs (bib, meal)
	Movement connected with words (up come)
	Particular action associated with effect
	Recognizes familiar people
	Reaction to friendly or angry tones: not automatic
	Hearing
	Turns head and shoulder to familiar sound
		06–07	Babble: continuous chains, marked rhythm
			  adds—B D
			  tries to respond to parent
			  single syllable utterances (ba)
			Tries to establish contact: coughs crys for attention
			Imitates: cough
			Gesture Language: holds out arms to be taken
			  closes lips after enough food

07–08	Appears to recognize familiar words Change of expression (daddy) Anticipates in games (cooperates) Responds to his name (stops activity) Recognizes family: voices names	07–08	Babble: double syllable (gaga dada) adds—T N W—more back vowels Variation of tone/inflection in vocal play Plays speech gesture games (peek-a-boo) Imitates: simple acts (clapping, nodding)

08–09	Adjusts to familiar words: definite action
	  (daddy's coming)
	Understands gestures
	Recognizes people (visual)
	Object dropping game
	Strange anxiety
	Hearing
	Responds to music (bodily movement)
		08–09	Babble: more pitch changes and reduplications
			  4 different double syllables (dada baba
			  mama)
			  combined with gestures
			Calls for attention
			Gesture: Reaching rejecting pushes hand away
			Imitates: begins to duplicate intonations
			  tries to sing melody

continued

423

	Receptive		Expressive

09–10	Baby game (verbal request)
	Offers object (verbal and gesture request)
	Responds to "no" (briefly)
	Responds to children
		09–10	Babble: varies syllables in chain (badada)
			Imitates: own sounds made by others
			   melody patterns of greetings
			Uses exclamation (oh-oh)
			Lip noises ("raspberries")
			First word (mama or dada)
			Gesture: shakes head for "no"
			   pulls clothes for attention

10–11	Looks for 1 names familiar object/person Known daily routine activities *Hearing* Purposeful play with objects for sound	10–11	Word-like syllables Vocalizes in jargon
11–12	Follows simple instruction (Push the car) Inhibit successfully (Don't touch) Anticipates movement in rhyme *Hearing* Responds to whispered speech Responds differently to different sounds	11–12	First word (median age) Jabbers to people and toys Vocalizes to rhyme Imitates: some sound sequences
12–14	Indicates 1–3 named real objects Follows simple commands (baby games, sit down, fetches objects) Offers toy on verbal request Pats named picture (pat doggie) Understands arrival/departure signals Verbal response to some request (Say "bye") Recognizes body part: eyes or nose Behaves according to reaction of others Gives kiss on request Fights with playmate for desired object Likes to listen to words	12–14	Jargon: may contain some true words Says and waves–bye-bye 2–3 word vocabulary (besides mama and dada— One word utterances: multiplicity of meanings Imitates: words pats whistle doll Gesture: indicates wants by pointing and voice
14–16	Recognizes names of same objects Recognizes pictures of a few objects Begins to associate object and its picture	14–16	Jargon: more pauses, greater pitch range Consonant more frequent: F D W N H 4–5 words (names 1 object)

continued

Says "ta-ta" (giving or receiving)
Gesture (with words): expresses wants/needs

16–18
6–7 word vocabulary
Words rather than gestures for needs/wants
Rising inflection for questioning
Imitates: words overheard in conversation

18–20
Words reduplications of syllables (baba gorgie)
Extension of word meaning
Conversational jargon with true words
Joins 2 words as 1 word (allgone)
Names familiar objects
Names 1 or more familiar pictures
Asks for 2 things by name
Imitates: household activities

20–22
Speaking vocabulary 50 words
Imitates: 2–3 syllables sentence
    environmental sounds/motors/animals

22–24
50–75 word vocabulary
Two word utterances (groups of words used with
    infrequently used words: more_____.No_____)
Pronouns (me you)
Asks for more
Creates new words (own meanings)
Names 3–10 pictures
Names 2–5 objects

Interested in pictures in book if named
Gives toys on verbal request (wants back)
May kiss picture of animal
Often negative
Sharp separation reaction
Shows item of clothing

16–18
Turns 1 page at a time
Follows two orders with same object
Indicates 2 out of 4 objects (game request)

18–20
Place behavior to make something happen
Points to 1 or more named pictures
Points to body parts (3/4)
Points to 1 doll part (adds 1 more monthly)
Claims mine
Obeys preposition in/on (in context)
Distinguishes me her (give to me/her)
Knows sequence in dressing process
Indicates wet pants
Knows where things are kept
Pretends (imitative)
Aware of color

20–22
Points to 1 body part/clothes in picture
Follows 3 orders with same object
Indicates 8 named real objects
Indicates 5 named pictures
Tells/runs to sounds (door car bell)
Likes to be read to

22–24
Understands more complex sentences
Understands 2 prepositions: on in

Follows 4 orders with same object
Knows upside down
Indicates 6–9 named pictures
Identifies 5 named objects (group of 6)
Matches familiar objects

	Receptive	Expressive
	Points to 5 named doll parts Points to 4 named body parts in picture Uses familiar objects appropriately Interested in TV commercials, radio Understand more Heeds to: here now	Refers to self by name Imitates: 3–4 syllable sentences (I see you) Attempts to tell about experiences
24–30	Points to 6 named body parts in picture Identifies objects by use (3–4) Understands "big" Gives the object of actions Concept of "one" Identifies self in mirror Asks for help in personal needs (washing) Listens to stories Relays messages (telescoped) Recognizes photos or self/familiar adults Indicates 19–20 named pictures Matches objects to pictures Recognizes 1 named color Space relationship: in on under	Fast increase in vocabulary about 200–400 words Discards jargon 2–3 word phrases Syntax development Grammar emerges: verb plural possessive Acquisition of WH questions (where daddy?) Pronouns: I it this my mine, etc. Refers to self by pronoun Commands others (you do) Initial syllable/word repetitious (nonfluent) Uses some prepositions Names 10 pictures
30–36	Identifies actions in pictures Understands size differences (big-little) Identifies usage of pictured things (4) Memory span lengthening (recalls events)	Imitates: words/word sequences (specific test) Tells use of common objects Announces intentions Tells about experiences Comments on what he is doing Vocabulary 500–1,000 words

Memory of story order	80% intelligible
Counts up to 3	3–4 word sentences
Holds up fingers to show age	Independent development of sentence structure
Matches things by color	Grammatical complexity
Differentiates why how when what	Gives full name
Comprehends cold sleepy hungry	Recites 1–2 nursery rhymes (adds words/gestures)
Words classes in categories	Imitates: Repeats words/phrases compulsively
Protest inaccuracies	Repeats numbers (2 at 30 mo.; 3 at 36 mos.)
Begins to share	Repeats 5–7 syllable sentences
Takes turns	Repeats 2–3 nonsense syllables
Points to 20–29 names pictures	(pah/boo/deee)
Enjoys rhythmic repetitions of others	States action in familiar action pictures
Knows own sex	Names 20–29 pictures
Parallel play	Able to whisper
Pretends (imaginatively)	
Marches pictures of like things	
Listens to stories 5–10 minutes	
Pantomine and object identification	

Compiled by Elaine Lieberman, M.Ed., CCC-SP. Reproduced with permission from the Bureau of Education for the Handicapped, U.S. Office of Education, Washington, D.C.

APPENDIX V

Mother-Child Interaction   Activity:_____
Mother's Name:_____   Date:_____   Observer:_____
		Comments
Initiates talk		
Uses positive physical reinforcement (hugging, smiling, touching, patting)		
Uses negative physical reinforcement (spanking, hitting)		
Uses positive verbal reinforcement (praise, encouragement)		
Uses negative verbal reinforcement		
Ignores		
Mother's talk parallel's child's play		
Initiates activity		
Encourages appropriate play		
Stimulates imaginary play		
Helps with task		
Intervenes when child is frustrated		
Expresses overt annoynace (voice, face)		
Passively watches child		
Restrains physical activity appropr.		
Encourages peer interaction		
Looks to staff for direction		
Looks to other mothers for direction		
Expands and adapts task to developmental level		
Overall Impression: aloof, withdrawing, (passively watching), anxious, indifferent, (actively participating), accepting, insecure		

Child-Mother Interaction   Activity:_____
Child's Name:_____   Date:_____   Recorder:_____
                                                                   M=Mother
		Comments
Responds to M initiating talk		
Looks at M		
Listens to M		
Smiles at M		
Cries		
Follows verbal direction		
Follows with gesture		
Follows without gesture		
Speaks		

continued

APPENDIX V—*Continued*

Echoes M's speech		
Stimulated by M to:		
a. initiate activity		
b. continue activity		
c. complete activity		
d. talk about activity		
e. expand activity		
f. carry through principles on		
subsequent activity		
g. removes self from activity		
Understands M's expectations		
Developmentally lives up to M's		
expectations		
Developmental level lower than		
task level		
Ignores direction		
Performs opposite of M's directions		
Refuses to accept M's direction		
Accepts M's physical contact		
Accepts physical help with task		
Makes appropriate gestures to communicate		
Makes appropriate facial expressions		
Initiates interaction with M		
Persists for interaction with M		
a. with same behaviors		
b. with different behaviors		
Becomes frustrated		
Withdraws from task		
a. remains withdrawn		
b. initiates other activity		
Resists M's physical intervention		
a. screams		
b. throws		
c. kicks		
d. others		
Seeks peer interaction		
Ignores peer interaction		
Passively watches		
Imitates peers		
Actively participates		

APPENDIX VI-A
Neurodevelopmental Evaluation
One year—Three years

Name_____   Age/Months_____Sex_____Race_____
Date of Birth_____   Date of Evaluation_____
Wt._____lbs./ozs./gms   *Neurological Examination*
Body Length_____in./cm.   Gait/posture: N_____Abn_____
Head Circumference_____in./cm.   Describe_____
Chest Circumference_____in./cm.   N_____Abn_____
Blood pressure_____Pulse_____   Describe_____
Head Shape: Normal_____Other_____   Face, symmetry: N_____Abn_____
Fontanelles: Closed (<1cm.) Open_____   Describe_____
  Describe_____   Eyelids/pupils_____
Transillumination: N_____Other_____   Follow/Extraocular mvts._____
Stigmata
Facies_____   Strabismus/Nystagmus_____
Skin Pigmentation_____   Vision_____
Extremities & Spine_____   Prehension: N_____Abn_____
Other_____   Describe
General Physical Examination   Hand Pref. R_____L_____Both
Eyes_____   Phonation (tongue/gag/palate)
Ophthalmoscopic_____   N_____Abn_____Describe_____
Ears_____
Nose, mouth, pharynx_____   Hearing_____
Neck, thorax_____   Sensation, Extremities & Trunk:
Lungs_____   Light Touch: N_____Abn_____
Heart_____   Describe_____
Abdomen_____   Pin Prick: N_____Abn_____
Genitalia_____   Describe_____
Extremities_____   Musculoskeletal: N_____Abn_____
                                                                Describe_____
                                                                Abn. Movements: Describe_____
                                                                        _____

continued

APPENDIX VI-A—*Continued*

Tonus

	Bilat.	Rt.	L
Upper			
Lower			
Neck Flexor			
Neck Extensor			
Trunk			

Reflexes

	Bilat.	Rt.	L
Biceps			
Triceps			
Knee			
Ankle			
Clonus			
Plantar			
Sup. abd.			

Postural Reflexes

	N	Abn
Assym. T-N-R		
Moro		
Reciprocal kick		
Palmar grasp		
Rooting/sucking		
Neck righting		
Placing		
Parachute		
Reciprocal gait		
Landau		

APPENDIX VI–B

Manual for Behavior Examination of the Neonate as modified by Judy F. Rosenblith from pages 6–15 of Frances K. Graham, "Behavioral differences between normal and traumatized newborns: I The test procedures." Psychological Monographs 1956, 70, Whole Number 427. Reproduced by permission of the author and the American Psychological Association

The first page of the examination is concerned with "face sheet" and medical information. Except for the name of the infant and of the examiner, the date, and the condition of the infant (awake-asleep, wet-dry) at the start of the examination, all items on this page should be filled in after completion of the examination. In this way, knowledge about the baby is less likely to influence or bias the examiner's judgment. We record time of testing as the time 15 minutes prior to completion of the examination. Other "face sheet" items are self-explanatory.

Pages 6 and 7 of the examination contain relevant medical information. Parts of them can be filled in from the baby's chart *after* the final examination is *completed*. The remainder will need to be completed from the hospital record at a later time. The information called for on these pages is that in which we are currently interested and which is routinely available to us. Other studies using the Behavioral Examination of the Neonate may well choose different items for inclusion. Note that items on this page are coded for punching on a separate IBM card from that used for the rest of the examination.

GENERAL MATURATION SCALE

This scale, found on page 2 of the examination booklet, consists of 7 items which may be separated into two groups (motor-strength and tactile-adaptive). The items receive varying credits depending upon the level of response. If more than one kind of response occurs to an item, the infant is given credit for the higher-scoring response. The general distinction between low-scoring and high-scoring responses is between generalized, mass movements and more specialized, stimulus-oriented responses. The maximum possible score on the general maturation scale is 18.

Items do not have to be administered in any set order. Some items arouse the infant more completely than do others, and the order of presentation is varied in such a way as to try to achieve or preserve a semi-wakeful state. In general, a second trial, but other items are interspersed. One reason for this is the rapid adaptation to stimuli shown by many infants. When crying occurs, testing is interrupted until the baby is soothed. Rocking, patting, talking to the baby, and pacifiers are used to achieve quieting. If the latter is used, one should try to avoid letting the baby become too dependent on it. A *few, brief* sucks will often quiet the infant without allowing dependence on the pacifier to develop. The pacifier is not permitted during the actual administration of the items. A record is kept of whether the babies' eyes are open or closed on each trial. If the infant is rated as not irritable (see Ratings section of the examination), is only minimally active, and does not open his eyes on some of the trials, conditions for testing are considered unsatisfactory, unless there is strong reason to suppose that this is the characteristic state for this infant. Medical and nurses notes and comments may be helpful in arriving at this decision. The final judgment regarding "examinability" of the infant or validity of various portions of the examination is made at the end of the examination and recorded on page 5. This judgment reflects the examiner's best guess as to whether the same results would be obtained if the infant were examined at a different time.

Item 1. *Prone Head reaction* The infant is placed in the prone position. His arms are extended over the head with palms down, and his head is adjusted so that he is face down with his nose touching the bed. The examiner then lifts her hand from the baby's head being careful not to make this a sudden release of considerable pressure. The baby is then observed for 60 seconds.

No credit is given if the baby neither lifts his head nor turns it sufficiently to the side to free his nose from the mattress.

One credit is given if, *within 20 seconds,* the infant turns his head sufficiently to the side that his nose is no longer buried.

Two credits are given if, *within 60 seconds,* the infant lifts his head so that it *just clears the bed,* regardless of whether he turns it. Credit is not given for clear efforts to raise the head unless the infant succeeds in raising it sufficiently to create, at least momentarily, a space between his face and the bed.

Three credits are given if the infant's head clears the bed one or more times in a very definite manner and for a total period of at least 3 to 4 seconds.

Item 2. *Crawls* This item is observed during administration of item 1. Since the examiner must watch the infant's head intently during the 1st 20 seconds after placing him in a prone position, the time for observing crawling may be extended 20 seconds beyond the minute in which head reaction is observed. Indeed, the infant's hind quarters may be lifted from the bed and lowered again in an effort to restimulate crawling movements. It is important in administering this item that the baby should have a diaper which permits freedom of motion—i.e., a rectangular diaper pinned once at each side. He should not be in a triangular diaper or rectangular diaper with 4 pins holding it. Note that if the baby gets maximum credit on item 1 on the first trial, but not on this item, it is necessary to place the baby in the prone position at least one more time so that item 2 can be properly scored.

No credit is given if the baby does not appear to make definite crawling movements. Repeated RRR (or LLL) movements, or simultaneous movements of both legs do not constitute crawling movements.

No credit is given if the baby appears to be making definite crawling movements, but does not achieve a complete double sequence of such movements. A LR or RLR sequence receives credit at this level.

Two credits are given if there is a complete double sequence of flexions and extensions (i.e. LRLR or RLRL).

On both items 1 and 2 only one trial is given if the infant obtains the maximum score on the first trial. Two trials are given if he does not achieve the maximum of the first trial. Only two are given if he gets the same score on both and appears to be in optimal condition (awake and not crying) on at least one administration. Three trials are given if the first two do not yield the same score, or if they do yield the same score, but the examiner feels that the baby was not in an optimal state. For purposes of final scoring the best performance is used.

Item 3. *Cotton* With the infant lying on his back, a small piece of cotton is lightly placed so that it covers the nostrils and barely touches the upper lip. It is held in position for 20 seconds. (This may require considerable dexterity on the part of the examiner.)

No credit is given in the absence of any definite response to the stimulus.

One credit is given for any change in behavior which is clearly a response to the stimulus. Any easily discriminated movement is credited if it follows the application of the stimulus within 3 seconds. Responses with a longer latency are credited if the examiner feels quite certain that they are not spontaneous movements, but true responses. Long latencies are more likely to be found in relatively inactive infants. Therefore, if a fairly vigorous response occurs at any time during the 20 second presentation period (and there is no other stimulation, e.g. a loud noise outside the door, etc.), it may be credited. If only small movements or twitches occur, they are generally spontaneous and thus not credited.

Two credits are given if the response includes specific movements of *either* the head or mouth. Credit for specific head movements is given for (a) several back and forth movements, or (b) a sustained (i.e. lasting at least 3 or 4 seconds) head retraction. The latter is usually a coordinated body movement of avoidance and involves arching of the back. Specific mouth movement is scored when there is sustained (at least 3–4 seconds) opening of the mouth with movements of one or both lips upward in the direction of the stimulus. Note that crying is not considered a specific response of the mouth. Sucking, yawning, or small lip movements or head movements should be present a majority of the time that any response is present, i.e., the characteristic mode of responding should include specific oriented movements. If the typical response is a generalized mass movement with an occasional specific response, credit is not given at this level. However, an occasional specific response with a background of little other movement is given credit at this level.

Three credits are given if specific head or mouth movements are present more than 50 per cent of the time the stimulus is applied, and they occur simultaneously at least once.

Four credits are given if head, mouth, and coordinated arm movements are all present. Coordinated arm movements are scored if both hands are brought to the midline more than once. The hands customarily are open in a coordinated movement.

However, if the arm movements fulfill the criteria otherwise, and if they definitely do not seem a part of random activity, credit for coordinated arm movements can be given even if the hands are not open. The infant in these cases appears to be "batting at" the stimulus. Credit for coordinated arm movements is also given if the infant uses only one hand, but repeatedly "bats at" the stimulus or at the examiner's hand. A single such coordinated movement is not credited, but there may be some alternation in the kind of specific response, as long as the *characteristic mode* of *responding* is with *specific* oriented *movements*. Coordinated arm movements without head and mouth movements occur only rarely. When they occur, three credits are given. The total time that specific responses occur must be 50 per cent or more of the time that the stimulus is applied.

Item 4. *Paper* With the infant lying on his back, a piece of cellophane, 2" by 3" is lightly held with one hand in such a way that it covers both the nostrils and the mouth. An effort is made to hold the paper far enough out from the mouth to avoid stimulating the sucking reflex. The paper is held in position for 20 seconds.

Zero to four credits are assigned in the same manner as for item 3.

In both items 3 and 4, three trials are always given in order to have the same number of trials on which to base the judgments of persistence and vigor. These judgments constitute the basis of the scores for items 5 and 6.

Item 5. *Persistence* During each of the trials for items 3 and 4, the examiner notes the percentage of time during which the infant is responding to the stimulus. As we found it somewhat difficult to observe the response closely and also follow a stop watch, this judgment is not a precise one. The infant is credited as persistent on a trial if he responds throughout the 20 second period. If there is any one period as long as 3 or 4 seconds during which he does not respond, whether initially, during the mid-period, or near the end of stimulation, persistence is not credited. Persistence is scored as absent on a trial when there is no response to the stimulus.

No credit is given if the baby is not persistent in half of the trials.
One-half credit is given if a persistent response is obtained in 1/2 of the trials, *or* if the examiner is in doubt as to whether the behavior on the majority of the individual trials should or should not be called persistent. Half credits are allowed on this item since it required a more subjective rating than most. Note also that this scoring allows the infant to score 1/2 point even though he is persistent to only one of the stimuli (if he is consistently persistent to it).
One credit is given if a persistent response occurs in two-thirds or more of the trials.

Item 6. *Vigor* The procedure for this item is the same as for item 5. The criterion of vigor is the behavior of the normal, full-term, one-day-old infant. Prematures generally receive half credit on this item. The rate and extent of movement primarily determine the judgment of persistence. Persistent and vigorous behavior tend to occur together, but may occur independently.

No credit is given if the baby is not vigorous on half of the trials.

One-half credit is given if a vigorous response occurs in 1/2 of the trials, or if the examiner is in doubt as to whether the behavior on the majority of the individual trials should or should not be called vigorous.

One credit is given if a vigorous response occurs in at least two-thirds of the trials.

Item 7. *Grasp* With the infant lying on his back, a stirrup, attached to a small spring balance which registers up to 4 pounds is placed in the infant's palm. It is rubbed against the palm until the infant grasps it. His fingers may be arranged by the examiner in eliciting the grasp. A steady gentle pull is then exerted until the infant either releases his grasp or the scale registers a pull greater than 3 pounds (48 oz.). The pull may be at the angle that seems most conducive to the baby maintaining his grasp—i.e., from horizontal (almost straight over the baby's head) to vertical (straight up from the shoulder). The examiner does not attempt to judge the maximum pull to the ounce, but only to the 1/4 pound. Reaching a given 1/4 pound marking is the criterion for recording it (this is done rather than recording to the nearest 1/4 pound). The number of trials is not fixed for this item. The examiner tries to see if a pull of 3 pounds or more can be elicited, and tries to make certain that any discrepancy between the amount pulled by each hand is a real difference in maximum strength of pull. At least 3 trials must be given before accepting a pull or less than 3 pounds or a discrepancy of more than 1/2 pound between the two hands as representative of the baby's strength of grasp. In addition to the amount of credit earned, the amount pulled by each hand is coded. If the baby's pull with both hands is not the same category but in adjacent categories, the lower score is assigned. If the pull of the two hands is more than one category different, the category in between is assigned.

No credit is given if the baby fails to pull 2 1/2 pounds with both hands.

One credit is given if the baby pulls 2 1/2 to 2 3/4 pounds with both hands.

Two credits are given if the baby pulls 3, 3 1/4 or 3 1/2 pounds with both hands.

Three credits are given if the baby pulls 3 3/4 pounds or over with both hands. A motor-strength score which is the sum of the scores on items 1, 2, 6 and 7 is recorded. A tactile-adaptive score which is the sum of the scores on items 3, 4 and 5 is also recorded. These scores are in addition to the general maturation score which is the sum of all the items.

MATURATION SCALE SENSORY FUNCTIONING

Page 3 of neonatal examination contains items which assess sensory functioning of the neonate. The auditory item which Graham had included in her maturation scale, and the visual scale which she had as a separate scale are both found here. Space is also available for other observations relevant to vision and hearing. Codes are provided for recording responses to a small flashlight. It is especially desirable to obtain these responses when the infant's state has not allowed adequate observation of visual following of an object to arrive at a vision score.

Auditory Reaction

With the infant lying on his back, a rattle is shaken gently several times at a distance of about 6 to 8 inches from either side of the head and in line with the ear. The rattle should be one which produces relatively low-pitched sounds. The rattle should not be in the infant's field of vision. The examiner shakes the rattle for approximately 5 seconds. This procedure is repeated for 4 presentations of the rattle. With each presentation the intensity of the shaking is increased *if no* "listening" or reflex type responses have occurred. The range is roughly from a very slight, minimal rattle to as abrupt and sharp a rattle as can be given. Care should be taken not to touch the infant's crib when using the auditory stimuli lest you jiggle the crib. After a pause of 10 to 20 seconds, a bell is sounded. A bicycle bell is used and the intensity with which it is sounded is varied (similarly to rattle). This procedure was adopted because the increasing intensity of stimulation frequently makes it easier to distinguish different kinds of response. However, if one has a good "listening" response at one level of stimulation, increasing the level is apt to lead to the more diffuse (and lower scoring) type of response, thus ruling out the possibility of getting persistent "listening" responses. While more precise control of the stimulus might be desirable, it was felt that the present procedure satisfied the aims set up for the Behavioral Assessment. More precise control of the auditory stimuli would require more elaborate apparatus, and more testing time as well. We have tried to maximize the likelihood of eliciting responses (a) by using both a rattle and a bell and thus varying the quality of the sound, (b) by using both with varied intensities, and (c) by using stimuli which produce noises rather than pure tones.

Although the pacifier was not permitted during actual administration of the maturation items, it is allowed here. Indeed, it may be tried especially for the purpose of providing an indicator response for judging "listening" to the sound. When the pacifier is so used, the sound must not be loud enough to produce a startle which would also be accompanied by a cessation of sucking.

No credit is given in the absence of any clear response to either stimulus.

One credit is given for any change in behavior which is clearly in response to the bell, i.e., which occurs within 4 seconds after the bell is sounded. A Moro or a partial Moro is a common response. Eye blinking or tightening of the eye muscles is a common minimal response and is given credit here.

Two credits are given if the infant responds to the rattle. The same criteria of response are applied as were used for the bell.

Three credits are given if the infant appears to "listen" to the rattle *or* the bell. Opening of the eyes and decreased movement of arms and legs, or, in some (usually older) infants, head turning and eye movement (whether or not in the direction of the stimulus) are credited. Cessation of sucking on a pacifier is also credited as a "listening" response. These should not be scored unless the responses are definitely to the auditory stimulus. Here it is important to note the frequency and type of eye movements when there is quiet in order to be sure that eye movements in the presence of the stimulus represent a departure from this base-line.

Four credits are given if either (a) the "listening" to the rattle or bell is persistent through 3 of the 4 presentations of the rattle or bell, or (b) if the "listening" response occurs only once to one stimulus, but occurs two or more times to the other. This scoring is adhered to even if the "listening" responses are followed by a Moro or startle response.

Five credits are given if persistent "listening" occurs to both the rattle and the bell. This score should be given if "listening" occurs at least 3 times to one stimulus and at least 2 times to the other, with the additional stricture that a total of 6 of the 8 presentations must elicit "listening."

Visual Performance

The general procedure followed, that of observing and categorizing the response to a moving stimulus, is similar to the procedures used by Gesell and other designers of infant tests. It is taken directly from Graham with modification only of the strictness of the criteria for accepting a vision score as valid. This led to a change in the instructions for what constitutes an adequate test and of instructions regarding the amount of effort spent in rousing the infant for the test.

In general, the visual responsiveness of the infant is considered not testable unless it can be assessed when the infant is in a state of alert inactivity. Wolff in his intensive observation of 4 newborns (Psychosomatic Medicine, 1959, 21, 110–118) found visual following in over 60% of trials given in a state of alert inactivity, in only 15% of trials administered when infants were in a state of drowsiness, and in still fewer of the trials given in a state of alert activity or crying.

Observations can be made only when the infant's eyes are open for a sufficient length of time. If a baby does not spontaneously open his eyes, or open them in response to the normal manipulations involved in the examination, only minor efforts to arouse the infant are made (lest an artifically low score be obtained). With many babies this is not a major problem. They are under examination for about half an hour, and during this time may open their eyes on several occasions. Any procedures in progress are interrupted to take advantage of the opportunity, and the observations are repeated if the initial observation period has been too short or was otherwise unsatisfactory.

Administration of the vision scale can be done with the infant in the examiner's arm. This may serve to quiet the infant sufficiently to enable a good test of visual responses. An observation is considered satisfactory if at least 5 trials have been given or the baby has obtained a score of 6 or more in fewer trials. However, an effort to obtain visual responses is not considered a trial, for this purpose, unless the infant is clearly in an alert, quiet state, or can be said to "be paying some attention" to the stimulus.[1] If it is impossible to obtain a satisfactory observation period, the test cannot be included. In this case the responses to the flashlight should be tested.

The stimulus is usually presented with the infant in a supine position. Either the bicycle bell, or the red plastic rattle (about 1 and 3/8 inches in diameter) is used. Either is used in such a way that it makes no sound. However, sound may be made with either to encourage fixation preparatory to following. The sound must cease before following is elicited. Also, fixation cannot be scored at the 3 level if sound is used in obtaining it. In some instances where the infant clearly responds to the examiner's hand it is used. No further effort was made to standardize the stimulus, since we are attempting to determine whether the capacity is present under the most favorable conditions. As some infants seemed to respond more readily to one stimulus than to another, the examiner used whichever one was preferred. Stimuli were changed after one or two trials if they did not elicit a response or if there appeared to be a change in their effectiveness.

The newborn usually does not turn head and eyes toward a stimulus at the periphery. Fixation is limited to a relatively narrow range directly in front of the eyes, an area which is said to be determined by the tonic-neck-reflex. Stimuli are therefore initially presented in this area. The experimenter observes the direction in which one or both eyes appear to be turned and places the stimulus in line with the eyes. He then moves it slowly toward and away from the infant, since the distance from the eyes at which an object can be fixated is also limited, varying from about 3 inches to 12 inches. It may be necessary to shift the stimulus laterally in order to locate the place of regard. If fixation does not occur, the examiner attempts to elicit it by adding an auditory stimulus temporarily (e.g., the bell may be rung softly, the fingers snapped, etc.).

After preliminary efforts to locate the position which is optimal for fixation, there are presented a number of trials in which the stimulus is moved slowly upward from the line of regard or in either horizontal direction for as great a distance as the infant's eyes will follow. Each trial is begun with the stimulus in the place of regard. Visual items are scored both for the type of response which can be elicited and for ease of elicitation. As many trials may be given as are necessary to arrive at these judgments. Undoubtedly this procedure introduces a subjective element. However, it appears to be more adequate than specifying an arbitrary number of trials, since so many difficult-to-define factors may make one trial unsatisfactory—the infant may grow sleepy, may be startled by an extraneous noise, may fixate on something else, may begin to hiccup, etc.

Several aspects of the visual response are considered in making a classification: (a) presence or absence of a kind of response (such as fixation or pursuit); (b) the ease of eliciting the response; (c) the direction of eye movement (horizontal or vertical); (d) the distance the eye moves. These characteristics of the response ordered according to difficulty in such a way that success on one item, such as horizontal pursuit through 30

---

[1] Although an infant sucking a pacifier with eyes open is usually in a state of alert activity (rather than the desire alert inactivity), visual responses may be sought during use of pacifier. The above strictures with regard to when an observation is considered satisfactory must be held to however.

degrees with difficulty, in most cases automatically indicated that the baby had succeeded on lower items. Likewise, failure on one item usually means failure on higher
items. The ordering is partly on an a priori basis—i.e., a baby credited with "easily-elicited
fixation response" is assumed to have passed "Difficult-to-elicit fixation response." Other
items, such as whether "short vertical pursuit" is easier or more difficult than "horizontal
pursuit through 90 degrees" were ordered on the basis of the preliminary findings, *but
credit was given for each only when the response could in fact be elicited*. Each response
(or item), with the exception of the zero point, is given an arbitrary weight of one, so
that the *number of items passed is the baby's score*.

Credit 0 There is no response of fixation or pursuit *and* one of the following abnormal
features is observed: (a) wandering, uncoordinated movements (the eyes move constantly
and generally independently); (b) immobilization or staring; (c) pinpoint pupils, although
the eyes are spontaneously opened and remain open for more than a few seconds. The
zero score is given only when these abnormal features are the *characteristic* response
during observation rather than an isolated episode of nystagmus, etc.

1. No fixation or pursuit but none of the above abnormalities is characteristic.

2. Fixation if brief or obtained with difficulty. The criteria of fixation have been
summarized by Gesell as follows: "Quieting of body activity and of fussing; raising of
upper eyelids and eyebrows; widening of eye slits, wrinkling of forehead, alignment of
eye or eyes with stimulus, and immobilization of one eye or both." The criteria which we
considered essential were those relating to the position of the eye or eyes, i.e., alignment
with the stimulus and immobilization. Various other postural accompaniments, as noted
above, generally occur and probably contribute to the certainty of the subjective
judgment.

3. Fixation is clearly present and easily elicited, i.e., occurs in a majority of the trials.

4. Horizontal pursuit is questionably present. Pursuit is considered to be present when
one or both eyes, having fixated a stimulus, move in the same direction as the moving
stimulus. If the reaction time is short and the infant's eye follows the stimulus relatively
smoothly and moves at about the same rate as the stimulus, there is little difficulty in
identifying this as a pursuit movement. In some cases, however, repeated trials elicit
delayed eye movements in the direction of the stimulus which do not appear to be
random movements but which are not clearly pursuit movement. The present classification includes such cases.

5. Horizontal pursuit movements through an arc of 30 degrees are obtained with
difficulty. This classification does not indicate uncertainty as to whether or not there is a
pursuit movement, but rather whether the movement could be elicited in fewer than 50
per cent of the trials.

6. Horizontal pursuit movements through an arc of 30 degrees are easily obtained, that
is, are present in more than 50 per cent of the trials.

7. Vertical pursuit movements are obtained. These may be very short, but there is
usually little problem in deciding whether they are present. Those movements of the eye

which are upward random deviations generally begin with the eye in a peripheral position from which it rolls slowly upward. They are readily distinguished from the rapid vertical movements which follow fixation and may occur in pursuit of the stimulus.

8. Horizontal pursuit movements through an arc of 90 degrees are obtained.

9. Vertical pursuit is obtained through an arc of more than 30 degrees.

10. Horizontal pursuit movements through an arc of more than 90 degrees are obtained. To accomplish this, the infant must move the head as well as the eyes. The vision score is the total number of the above behaviors which are achieved by the infant.

BEHAVIORAL RATINGS

The next section of the examination (pages 4 and 5) contain the ratings of tension and irritability and many of the items (that are coded rather than scored) which especially contributed to these ratings.

Irritability Rating

Irritability as used here is similar to the concept of physiological irritability—how sensitive the infant is to stimulation, and not how loudly and lustily he cries, or even how much of the time he cries. This means that subjective judgment regarding the state of the infant and/or the cause of crying and fussing is at least as important as the accurate noting of how much crying, fussing, etc. occur. In arriving at this two process type of rating (or judgment), it was felt that the examiner might be aided by having to go through two concrete steps. Therefore one scale has been provided for coding the actual amount of irritable, fussy behavior that occurs. Another scale has been provided for making the final judgment of irritability in the physiological sense used here.

The rating of the amount of irritable or fussy behavior which occurs, like the Irritability Rating itself, has five codes.

One is coded if the baby cries or fusses very rarely.

Two is coded if he cries or fusses up to as much as 1/2 of the examination period, but is easily quieted.

Three is coded if he cries about 1/2 of the time and is difficult to quiet.

Four is coded if he cries or fusses most of the time.

Five is coded if he does not cry or fuss at all during the examination.

Several factors which contribute to the final rating of irritability are:

1. The Intensity of Stimuli which Evoke Crying The normal infant does not usually cry when he is picked up and brought to the examining room and will be disturbed only by the more intense forms of stimulation—loud noises, rough handling, etc. Abnormal infants, on the other hand, may squeal when first picked up and continue to fuss whenever handled or stimulated.

2. The State of the Infant When a normal infant cries, it appears to be because he has become too wide awake, is hungry, or is defecating. Hunger may be suspected in an infant who actively roots if the mouth is brought into contact with any surface and who vigorously sucks the offered pacifier. The normal infant also does not sustain well a too-long wakeful period. If the infant is awake when brought to examination or wakes up almost at once, he generally remains contented only for a brief period and then fairly abruptly bursts into lusty crying. On the other hand, the abnormal infant may fuss almost continuously without opening his eyes and never achieving an alert state.

3. The Cry of the Infant   The normal infant cries loudly and lustily. A weak, high-pitched, "fussy" cry or whimper is characteristic of the abnormal child.

4. Ease of Quieting   The cry of the normal infant may be sustained, and he will not quiet spontaneously—suggesting that internal, not external, stimuli are responsible for the crying. The cry of the abnormal infant, on the other hand is more likely to be intermittent and will usually cease temporarily if the infant is left alone. Occasionally abnormal babies are irritable throughout but are distinguished by the other characteristics noted above.

A scale with 5 intervals or codes is provided for the rating of irritability. A rating of 1 represents the behavior of a normal infant, the most extreme rating (4) represents the extreme and easily identified forms of behavior seen in a grossly abnormal infant. With these points as signposts, babies are actually located anywhere on the continuum. It was felt that an infant who never cried during the examination could not be rated on the same scale. Such an infant might be one with either a normal or abnormal lack of irritability. Therefore these infants are given no irritability rating per se, but coded as not having cried. Other anchors for the scale are as follows:

Normal irritability. Crying is only in response to fairly intense external stimulation or in response to fatigue, hunger, or defecation. The cry itself is loud and sustained.

Just-perceptible irritability. Crying or "fussing" occurs in response to mild stimulation and does not appear to be determined by normal internal states of discomfort, as described under 2 above. Each episode of crying may be brief, but as much as half of the period is so occupied.

Abnormal irritability. Crying occurs in response to many mild stimuli. While the infant appears to be uncomfortable, the discomfort does not seem due to any of the normal internal states described under 2. The cry itself is weak, high-pitched, and almost continuous.

Muscle Tension Rating

The Muscle Tension Rating is designed to measure deviations in the direction of either increased flaccidity (lessened muscle tone) or increased rigidity. Six submeasures are employed in making the rating. Ordinarily, the babies are consistent in the direction of their responses on these submeasures, but some exceptional cases show mild deviations in both directions. In this event the infant is given two ratings. Minor discrepancies between the baby's behavior and these descriptions are solved by using one side or another of the interval for the rating, (i.e., "tense" covers categories 6 and 7). The description of tenseness or just perceptible rigidity is for both of these codes. One chooses the code closer to normal or closer to marked tension according to the direction of the discrepancies.

The six submeasures require rating the following: (1) the nature (flexed or extended) of the supine position which the legs assume spontaneously; (2) the resistance to limb displacement; (3) the response of having the legs pushed back by applying pressure to the soles of the feet; (4) the change in muscle tone in response to being pulled to a sitting position; (5) the amount of spontaneous activity; and (6) the frequency of trembling of body parts and the stimuli which evoke this response. The procedure for obtaining these is as follows:

1. *Leg position* During the examination the examiner observes the leg position which is spontaneously assumed between trials. The record sheet lists five descriptive classifications which describe the position or positions assumed frequently, especially those characteristic of the baby's most alert non-fussy period.

2. *Resistance to limb displacement* a) Legs. The examiner places his hand under the infant's heel, raises the leg through an arc of 45 degrees, and then releases it. The examiner attends both to the change in tone while lifting the leg and to the response of the leg when released. This procedure is repeated several times at intervals during the examination. The response is rated by placing a check after one of the 6 descriptions on the record sheet.

b) Arms. The infant's hand is taken gently and the arm is displaced upward and outward. The exact mixture of these directions depends on the initial position. The final result should be to have the infant's arm approximately 45 degrees up from the bed (from the line that goes along the length of the body) and halfway between horizontal and vertical (from the line that would be formed if both arms were stretched out at right angles from the body). As in the case for legs a check is placed after one of the 6 descriptions given.

3. *Pushes feet* With the infant lying on his back, the examiner places one hand flat against the bottom of both feet in such a way that the infant's knees are flexed. Gentle pressure is exerted against the feet for 20 seconds. The characteristic response is coded according to the four alternatives provided.

4. *Pull-to-sitting* The examiner takes hold of both of the infant's hands and pulls gently two or three times without raising the child from the table. He notes whether the arms respond with increased muscular tonus. The examiner then grasps the infant's forearms and pulls the body forward 45 to 60 degrees, noting the head and shoulder response. This procedure is repeated two or more times before the response is rated. However, the best response is coded. There are six descriptions against which to match the behavior. "Already tense" which occurs as part of two of the descriptions is coded when the child tenses to your touch before you have exerted any pulling on his arms.

5. *Spontaneous movement* This rating is made on the basis of the infant's behavior during the entire examination. A check is placed after one of the five descriptions on the data sheet.

6. *Trembling* Trembling of body parts is observed during the whole period of the

examination. A description of such movements includes the body parts involved, the frequency of occurrence, and whether they occur spontaneously to mild stimuli or only in response to stimuli evoking the Moro reflex. Codes are provided for these behaviors.

At the end of the examination, the overall rating on muscle tension is made. A line with 9 intervals marked off on it is provided for this rating. The middle interval, codes as 5, is twice as long as the others and represents the normal range of tension and flaccidity. The extremes of flaccidity and rigidity, respectively, as seen in a grossly abnormal infant, are represented by the 2 extreme intervals on each end of the line (codes 1, 2, 8, and 9). Just perceptible degrees of abnormality are then represented by the intermediate intervals (or codes 3, 4, 6, and 7). The different intervals on the line are described in terms of the various submeasures as follows:

Abnormal rigidity or marked tension (8 or 9)   1. The characteristic leg position is extended, rigid and elevated. 2. The legs and arms resist displacement and snap back to the initial position when released. 3. It is difficult to push the feet back, and if this is achieved, the baby's legs extend or his body moves backward. 4. The muscles are already tense and do not change tone in response to pull-to-sitting. There is no head lag. 5. There may be any amount of spontaneous activity. 6. Trembling of more than one body part is frequent and may be spontaneous or in response to mild stimuli as well as to startle stimuli.

Just-perceptible rigidity or tenseness (6 or 7) Spontaneous leg position is extended but not rigid or elevated. 2. The legs and arms resist displacement and snap back to the initial position when released. 3. The legs may or may not resist being pushed back, but they do extend (so the baby's body moves back), i.e., the baby may receive a code of 3 or 4, but a 3 would not be considered indicative of tenseness unless it occurs when the baby is in a very quiescent state. 4. The muscles are already tense and do not change tone in response to pull-to-sitting. There is, however, head lag. 5. There may be any amount of spontaneous activity. 6. There is usually some trembling involving more than one body part, which is pronounced in response to startle stimuli and less intense in response to milder stimuli.

Normal muscle tone (5) 1. The spontaneous supine leg position is flexed, or flexed with occasional extension. 2. Muscle tone improves in response to limb displacement, although there may also be slight resistance, especially in the arms. The limbs return relatively slowly to their initial position. 3. There is an increase in muscle tone when the feet are pushed and there may even be an extension of the legs (or pushing back of the body). The latter may be considered to belong here particularly if the infant is in an alert, active state. 4. The muscle tone of the arms and shoulders improves in response to pull-to-sitting. The baby helps to pull his head up and may sit briefly with some head lag. These babies must be distinguished from the tense infant in head erect whom the absence of head lag is not the result of improving muscle tone, but of tension in the whole body so that the baby moves in one piece without the even distribution of tone characteristic of the normal newborn. 5. There may be any amount of spontaneous activity except the condition of minimal activity with eyes open. 6. Trembling, if it occurs, involves only one or two body parts, is not extensive stimuli.

Just-perceptible flaccidity or poor tone (3 or 4) 1. The supine leg position is almost always flexed. 2. There is no change in tone for the arms and none for the legs. The arms and legs fall back to the initial position when released, though, again, the arm may have slightly more tone or control. 3. There is no increase in muscle tone or pushing back of the feet. 4. There is little or no change in tone in response to pull-to-sitting, and there is head lag. 5. Spontaneous activity is minimal. The eyes may be open or closed. 6. There are not more than one or two instances of mild trembling.

Abnormal flaccidity (1 or 2) 1. The supine leg position is always flexed. 2. The initial tone of the legs is poor, they feel "floppy" and weightless. The same is true of the arms but to a slightly lesser extent. There is no change in tone in response to limb displacement, and the limbs fall back to their initial position when released. 3. There is no increase in muscle tone in response to pushing against the feet, even though the baby is apparently awake or alert. 4. The arm and shoulder muscle tone is initially poor and remains so even in response to pull-to-sitting. The head droops markedly. 5. Spontaneous activity is minimal even though the eyes are open. 6. There is no trembling.

OTHER BEHAVIORS

Following the tension rating (which is found on page 5 of the examination) there are three behaviors about which we formerly made notes on our record sheet. They now have had codes established. In addition this page provides an opportunity for calling attention to anything special or unusual about the examination. This is especially for use in the case of behaviors which seemed unusual to the examiner but which will not appear unusual when coded, or for calling attention to behaviors which simply will not fit into the codes. The last allows the examiner to take into account everything he knows about the state of the baby and arrive at a judgment regarding the probable validity or representativeness of the examination. All of the items on this page are to be checked during the examination or *immediately* after its completion.

MEDICAL INFORMATION

Finally, the last pages of the examination booklet (page 6–8) have a number of items of medical information related to mother and baby. These can be filled in, in part, from the medical record of the infant. Some of them have to be obtained from the detailed obstetrical record at a later time. None of these items should be checked or entered until after all of the examination and/or all examinations of that infant have been completed. Only a few items of medical information are currently included. However, there are many unused columns on this card so that as one develops a hypothesis about a relation which one would like to check the pertinent information can be entered.

IBM CODING

The examination booklet is set up to provide codes for punching most of the information from the exam onto IBM cards. The column numbers are indicated at the left of each item and along the extreme right of the examination pages where there is a blank line for entering the appropriate number. Whenever possible the alternatives have been numbered in such a way that when the infant's behavior is decided to fit a given alternative (or score) the number of that alternative is the one to be coded and punched for that column. Where that has not been possible it has sometimes been possible to give the coding instructions directly on the examination sheet. In some instances, however, that also is too difficult and code sheets have to be consulted in order to code the information. These instances are noted on the examination.

Note that the last pages of the examination contain medical information which is coded on a separate IBM card.

Coding: Behavioral Examination

On the general maturation scale O and C stand for eyes open or closed. The appropriate letter or letters are circled for each trial of each item. If the infant's eyes are open during the trial 1 is coded, if they are closed 2 is coded, and if they are both open and closed with neither state clearly predominant a 3 is coded.

1–4 Infant's number

$$
\begin{array}{cc}
& 0 \\
& 0 \\
\text{e.g., 0013 or} & 1 \\
& 3
\end{array}
$$

9–10 Age at examination to nearest hour

col. 9	col. 10
1–1 to 6 hours	1–60 to 66 hours
2–6 to 12 hours	2–66 to 72 hours
3–12 to 18 hours	3–72 to 78 hours
4–18 to 24 hours	4–78 to 84 hours
5–24 to 30 hours	5–84 to 90 hours
6–30 to 36 hours	6–90 to 96 hours
7–36 to 42 hours	7–96 to 108 hours
8–42 to 48 hours	8–108 to 120 hours
9–48 to 54 hours	9–120 to 144 hours
0–54 to 60 hours	0–144+

Note: A punch must be coded in either col. 9 or col. 10 but not in both.

11–14 Date of examination

col. 11–Month

1–January
2–February
3–March
4–April
5–May
6–June
7–July
8–August
9–September
0–October
X–November
Y–December

col. 12–Day

0–if in first ten days of month (1–9)
1–if in second ten days of month (10–19)
2–if in third ten days of month (20–29)
3–if in fourth ten days of month (30–31)

col. 13–Day

code the last digit of date (day of month)

col. 14–Year

code the last digit of year

15–16 Weight

100 grams (g.) = 1 kilogram (kg.)
16 ounces (oz.) = 1 pound (lb.)
1 g. = 0.001 kg.
1 oz. = 0.0625 lb.
1 kg. = 2.2046 lb.

col. 15 Weight at birth

1–1. kg. and under (1 lb. 1 oz. and under)
2–5. kg. to 1. kg. (1 lb. 2 oz. to 2 lb. 4 oz.)
3–1. kg. to 1.5 kg. (2 lb. 4 oz. to 3 lb. 5 oz.)
4–1.5 kg. to 2. kg. (3 lb. 5 oz. to 4 lb. 7 oz.)
5–2. kg. to 2.5 kg. (4 lb. 7 oz. to 5 lb. 9 oz.)
6–2.5 kg. to 3. kg. (5 lb. 9 oz. to 6 lb. 10 oz.)
7–3. kg. to 3.5 kg. (6 lb. 10. oz. to 7 lb. 12 oz.)
8–3.5 kg. to 4. kg. (7 lb. 12 oz. to 8 lb. 14 oz.)
9–4. kg. to 4.5 kg. (8 lb. 14 oz. to 9 lb. 15 oz.)
0–4.5 kg. to 5. kg. (9 lb. 15 oz. to 11 lb. 1 oz.)
X–5. kg. and over (11 lb. 1 oz. and over)
Y–not known

col. 16 Weight at test

1–more than 5 oz. less than at birth
2–3 or 4 oz. less than at birth
3–1 or 2 oz. less than at birth
4–within 1 oz. of birth weight
5–1 or 2 oz. more than at birth
6–3 or 4 oz. more than at birth
7–5 to 8 oz. more than at birth
8–9 to 15 oz. more than at birth
9–over 16 oz. more than at birth

45–46 Weight pulled in categories
col. 45 Right hand and col. 46 Left hand

1—under 1 lb. or no elicitable grasp	Code X in the column of the
2—1, 1 1/4, 1 1/2 lb.	hand that pulls more or Y if that
3—1 3/4, 2, 2 1/4 lb.	hand is 3/4 lb. or more
4—2 1/2, 2 3/4 lb.	greater than the other.
5—3, 3 1/4, 3 1/2 lb.	
6—3 3/4 lb. and over	

62 Tone of cry
col. 62

1—weak and high-pitched	6—med. and low-pitched
2—weak and med-pitched	7—lusty and high-pitched
3—weak and low-pitched	8—lusty and low-pitched
4—med. and high pitched	9—lusty and low-pitched
5—med. and med-pitched	0—does not cry, but whimpers

63 Amount of irritable behavior

col. 63 Code the number under the part of the scale checked.

64 Irritability rating

col. 64 Code as in col. 63

65 Trembling
col. 65

1—mild trembling of chin	9—severe trembling of chin
2—mild trembling of arms	0—severe trembling of arms
3—mild trembling of legs	X—severe trembling of legs
4—mild trembling of two or more	Y—severe trembling of two or more
5—moderate trembling of chin	unpunched if no trembling
6—moderate trembling of arms	
7—moderate trembling of legs	
8—moderate trembling of two or more	

73 Tension rating

col. 73 Code as in col. 63

Coding: Medical Information
1–4 Identification of infant
5—Duration of gestation
Term is computed assuming that EDC is the first day of week 40.

13 Mother's age
col. 13

1—under 13 years	4—19 to 22 years
2—13 to 16 years	5—22 to 26 years

3–16 to 19 years

7–31 to 36 years

8–36 to 40 years

9–40 to 43 years

6–26 to 31 years

0–43 to 46 years

X–over 46 years

Y–not known

14 Mother's weight and height

15 Mother's blood (type and Rh)

col. 15

1–O, neg.	5–B, neg.
2–O, pos.	6–B, post.
3–A, neg.	7–AB, neg.
4–A, pos.	8–AB, pos.
	9–unknown

16 Infant's blood (type and Rh)

col. 16

1–Type and Rh same as mother's

2–Type same, Rh different (mother neg., baby pos.)

3–Rh same, Mother O, baby A

4–Rh same, Mother O baby B

5–Rh different, Mother O baby A

6–Rh different, Mother O baby B

7–Infant's type unknown

8–Mother's type unknown

9–Type different, Rh different—specify

X–Hyperbilirubin noted

Y–Hyperbilirubin not noted

17–21 Infant's Apgar scores

col. 17 In this and the other columns (through col. 21) the infant's score is to be coded using 0 for 10.

There is no provision for coding the times. In our hospital these times are normally set by the standard procedures in use. Use of this information would depend on the practices of individual hospitals.

22 Infant's pain threshold

col. 22 If no score is given in volts, transform to standard scores (mean 50, standard deviation 10).

1–45 to 55	6–30 to 35
2–40 to 45	7–65 to 70
3–55 to 60	8–20 to 30 or under
4–35 to 40	9–70 to 80 or over
5–60 to 65	

23 Resuscitation

24 Oxygen given

27–37 Analgesias
Note the following equivalents:

    1 ss = 1 1/2 grains
    1 grains = 65 mg.
    1 1/2 grains = 100 mg.
    1/150 grain = 0.4 mg.

Amounts indicated on exam form refer to milligrams (mg.) except in the case of Morphine (cols. 37–38) which is shown in grains.

APPENDIX VI-B
Behavioral Examination of the Neonate
Examination Booklet   IBM coding

*1–4*_____# of Examination—see code   1 _____

_____Surname of Neonate   2 _____

_____Given Name of Mother.   3 _____

4 _____

5 Sex of Neonate
  1 Male   2 Female   5 _____

6 Examiner   6 _____

7 Race
  1 White   2 Negro   3 Other   5 Not given   7 _____

8 Religion
  1 Catholic   2 Protestant   3 Jewish   4 Other   5 Not given   8_____

9–10 Age at Examination Hrs._____   9_____
                                      see code sheet   or   10 _____

11–14 Date of Testing ____, ____, ____Time____:____ see code Month   11 _____
                                                              Day   12 _____
          Date of Birth ____ ____ ____Time____:____   Day   13 _____
                                                              Year   14 _____

15 Weight at Birth lbs. ____ oz. ____ kg. ____   see code   15 _____

16 Weight at Test lbs. ____ oz. ____ on ____, ____, ____ kg. ____   see code 16 _____

17 Condition of Infant at start of Examination   17 _____
  1 Dry, Awake   2 Dry, Asleep   3 Wet, Awake
  4 Wet, Asleep   5 Other

	Trials			
	1	2	3	IBM Coding
Maturation: General Scale	OC	OC	OC	

18–23 Head reaction (prone) 60″   HS–18___E–19___
  0—no score   0 ___ ___ ___   MS–20___E–21___
  1—turns head to side within 20″   1 ___ ___ ___   LS–22___E–23___
  2—head barely clears bed in 60″   2 ___ ___ ___
  3—head clears bed very definitely in 60″   3 ___ ___ ___

24–29 Crawls (prone) 60″   OC OC OC   HS–24___E–25___
  0—no score   0 ___ ___ ___   MS–26___E–27___
  1—definite movements in sequence (RL,LRL,etc.)   1 ___ ___ ___   LS–28___E–29___
  2—complete double sequence (LRLR, RLRL)   2 ___ ___ ___

continued

APPENDIX VI-B—*Continued*

30–35 Cotton (supine) 20″   OC OC OC   HS–30___E–31___
  0—no score   0 ___ ___ ___   MS–32___E–33___
  1—any movement (response to S) within 2″   1 ___ ___ ___   LS–34___E–35___
  2—specific movements of head or mouth present   2 ___ ___ ___
  3—specific movements of head or mouth present   3 ___ ___ ___
    more than 50% of response time
  4—head, mouth, and coordinated arm movements   4 ___ ___ ___
    all present, some coordinate R present   PV PV PV
    50% of time

36–41 Paper (supine) 20″   OC OC OC   HS–36___E–37___
  0—no score   0 ___ ___ ___   MS–38___E–39___
  1—same as for cotton   1 ___ ___ ___   LS–40___E–41___
  2—same as for cotton   2 ___ ___ ___
  3—same as for cotton   3 ___ ___ ___
  4—same as for cotton   4 ___ ___ ___
                                                PV PV PV

42 Persistence; percent time infant responds to cotton and paper   42 _____
  score = 1 if persistent response in 2/3 of trials;   code = 1
  score = 1/2 if persistent response in 1/2 of trials;   code = 5
  score = 0 if less;   code = 0

43 Vigor; rate and extent of movements in response to cotton and paper   43 _____
  score = 1 if vigorous response in 2/3 of trials;   code = 1
  score = 1/2 is vigorous response in 1/2 of trials;   code = 5
  score = 0 if less;   code = 0

44–46 Grasp (supine)   RL RL RL
  0—0–2 1/4 lbs.   right hand ___ ___ ___   item score 44 _____
  1—2 1/2 lbs. 2 3/4 lbs.   left hand ___ ___ ___   RH(see code) 45 _____
  2—3, 3 1/4 3 1/2 lbs.   LH(see code) 46 _____
  3—3 3/4 lbs.

47–48 Motor score = sum of scores on items 18, 24, 43, 44.   47 _____
  Code actual score (which can vary from 0 to 8) in 47 and   48 _____
  the 1/2 point if any as 5 in 48.   Score_____

49–50 Tactile adaptive score = sum of scores on items 30, 36, 42.   49 _____
  Code actual score (which can vary from 0 to 9) in 49 and the   50 _____
  1/2 point, if any, as 5 in 50.   Score_____

51–53 Total score on general scale   tens 51 _____
  Tens are coded in 51, digits in 52, and decimals in 53;   digits 52 _____
  if score is a whole number code 0 in 53; but if score   decimals 53 _____
  ends in 1/2 then code 5 in 53.   Score_____

continued

APPENDIX VI-B—*Continued*

Maturation: Sensory Functioning

54–59 Auditory reaction   OC OC OC   HS–54___E–55___
  0—no score   0 ___ ___ ___   MS–56___E–57___
  1—response to bell (startle or blink)   1 ___ ___ ___   LS–58___E–59___
  2—response to rattle (startle or blink)   2 ___ ___ ___
  3—"listening" to rattle or bell   3 ___ ___ ___
  4—persistent "listening" to rattle or bell   4 ___ ___ ___
  5—persistent "listening" to both rattle & bell   5 ___ ___ ___

60 Visual responses—moving object   60 _____
  0 _____No response of fixation or pursuit, and one of the following
               abnormal features is observed: (a) wandering uncoordinated
               movements; (b) immobilization or staring; (c) pinpoint pupils,
               although eyes are spontaneously open and remain open for more
               than a few seconds
  1 _____No fixation or pursuit, but none of above abnormalities
  2 _____Fixation brief, or obtained with difficulty
  3 _____Fixation clearly present and easily elicited, i.e., occurs
               in a majority of trials
  4 _____Horizontal pursuit questionably present
  5 _____Horizontal pursuit movements thru an arch of $30°$ obtained
               in less than 50% of trials
  6 _____Horizontal pursuit thru an arc of more than $30°$ obtained
               in more than 50% of trials
  7 _____Vertical pursuit movements obtained under $30°$
  8 _____Horizontal pursuit thru $90°$ arc obtained
  9 _____Vertical pursuit thru more than $30°$ are obtained
  10 _____Horizontal pursuit thru more than $90°$ obtained; to accomplish
               this the infant must move head as well as eyes
      _____Not testable
 C Code scores 0–9 as such, 10 as X, and not testable as Y

61 Responses to small flashlight   61 _____
  1 No reaction   4 Startle (Moro, etc.)
  2 Following of light   5 Other _____
  3 Blink   6 Not tested
  _____Reaction occurs at distance under 4 inches
  _____Reaction occurs at distance between 4 and 8 inches
  _____Reaction occurs at distance over 8 inches
Other data or notes on vision:
  _____Nystagmus   _____Strabismus
Other data or notes on auditory reaction:

                                                          _____

continued

APPENDIX VI-B—*Continued*

Behavioral Ratings

62 Describe tone of cry: 62 _____

	weak	medium	lusty
see code			
	high-pitched	medium	low-pitched

63 Amount of irritable, fussy behavior that actually occurs   63 _____

· · · · · · · · · ·/· · · · · · · · · ·/· · · · · · · · · ·/· · · · · · · · · ·/· · · · · · · · · ·

1	2	3	4	5
Cries or fusses very rarely	Cries during as much as 1/2 of exam		Cries or fusses most of time	No cry

                    Quiets   Is hard
                    easily   to quiet

64 Irritability rating   64 _____

· · · · · · ·/· · · · · · ·/· · · · · · ·/· · · · · · ·/· · · · · · ·/

  1   2   3   4   5

65 Trembling   65 _____
_____none_____mild_____moderate_____severe

_____arms_____legs_____chin   see code

66 Trembling   66 _____
  1 Spontaneous
  2 To mild stimuli
  3 To startle stimuli

67–68 Displacement of limbs   67 _____
    67–arms   68–legs   68 _____

1_____ _____floppy, fall back
2_____ _____tone improves, slow return position
3_____ _____resist but fall back
4_____ _____resist, but tone improves, slow return to position
5_____ _____resist, snap back to position
6_____ _____mixed
7_____ _____legs already extended, return to position, no
                change in tone

69 Pushes feet   69 _____
  1 No increase in muscle tone or pushing against hand
  2 Definite increase in muscle tone, E can feel increase

_____

continued

APPENDIX VI-B—*Continued*

3 Infant extends legs thus pushing E's hand or pushes against
hand with sufficient force to move himself backward
4 It is difficult to push infant's legs back and they either
extend or his body moves backward
5 Some resistance (or difficult to push legs back) but no
increase in tone

70 Spontaneous movements   70 _____
1 virtually absent (deep sleep)
2 minimal (eyes open, eye movements, etc.)
3 some activity
4 normally active
5 markedly active

71 Supine position   71_____
1 flexed, relaxed
2 flexed, occasional extension
3 extension, not rigid or predominantly elevated
4 extension, rigid *or* elev.
5 extension, rigid and elev.
6 flexed, rigid

72 Pull-to-sitting   72 _____
1 no change in tone, marked droop
2 change in tone, but marked droop
3 slight compensation of head, shoulders tense, not floppy
4 tone improves, slight assistance given; sitting, head erect briefly
5 already tense and no change in tone; head lags
6 already tense and no change in tone; no head lag

73 Comprehensive tension rating   73 _____

. . . . . . / . . . . / . . . . / . . . . / . . . . / . . . . / . . . . / . . . . / . . . . /

  1   2   3   4   5   6   7   8   9

Flaccid   Poor   Normal Tense   Marked
             Tone   Tension

Other Behaviors

74 Ease of startle   74 _____
1 infrequent or rare
2 occasional and to not more than 2 types of stimuli
3 frequent and to several kinds of stimuli
4 other_____specify_____

_____

continued

APPENDIX VI-B—*Continued*

75 Spontaneous hand-mouth activity   75 _____
   1 does not occur
   2 occurs only once or twice and only briefly
   3 is present a number of times briefly
   4 is present a number of times and for sustained periods
   5 is continuous
   6 other_____specify_____

76 Reaction to pacifier   76 _____
   1 Not used
   2 Tried, but infant refuses it
   3 Infant quiets in few sucks
   4 Infant needs considerable help before can suck it,
     but quiets when achieves this
   5 Infant accepts and sucks with moderate efficiency
     and vigor
   6 Infant accepts readily and sucks with good efficiency
     and vigor
   7 Used not as pacifier but to stop hiccups or for testing hearing

77 Special notation   77 _____
   1 see original examination because_____

78 Examiner considers condition of child during examination such that: 78 _____
   1 there is little or no question of validity of exam
   2 there is some question of validity of exam
   3 examiner doubts the exam can be taken as representative of the
     child
   4 the examiner feels certain that the exam is not representative
   5 the examiner feels the maturation score is valid, but
     rest questionable
   7 the examiner feels the maturation and vision scores are valid,
     but rest questionable
   8 the examiner feels the auditory and vision score is valid, but
     rest questionable
   9 the examiner feels the maturation and auditory scores are
     valid, but rest questionable
   Explanation of above _____

Medical Information
1–4 Identification of infant   1 _____
                                       2 _____
                                       3 _____
                                       4 _____

continued

APPENDIX VI-B—*Continued*

5 Duration of gestation   _____weeks
   1—43 weeks or over   5—33 to 37 weeks
   2—41 to 43 weeks   6—29 to 33 weeks
   3—39 to 41 weeks   7—25 to 29 weeks
   4—37 to 39 weeks   8—less than 25 weeks   5 _____

6 Previous pregnancies
   _____Code the actual number, using X or 10 or more   6 _____

7 Born alive_____   7 _____
   1—same number of   4—three less
     previous pregnancies 5—4 or more less
   2—one less   X—no previous
   3—two less   pregnancies
8 Now living_____   8 _____
   1—same as number in 7 4—three less
   2—one less   5—4 or more less
   3—two less   X—no number in 7

9 Delivery type   9 _____
   1 spontaneous   6 breech complicated
   2 low forceps   7 caesarian elective
   3 mid forceps   8 caesarian non-elective
   4 high forceps   9 other, e.g. rotation
   5 breech uncomplicated   Scanzoni, specify_____

10–12 Duration of labor   10 _____
   10—First stage
   1—under 2 hrs.   6—10 to 12 hrs.
   2—2 to 4 hrs.   7—12 to 14 hrs.
   3—4 to 6 hrs.   8—14 to 16 hrs.
   4—6 to 8 hrs.   9—over 16 hrs.
   5—8 to 10 hrs.
   11—Second stage   11 _____
   1—under 1/4 hr.   5—1 1/2 to 2 hrs.
   2—1/4 to 1/2 hr.   6—2 to 2 1/2 hrs.
   3—1/2 to 1 hr.   7—2 1/2 to 3 hrs.
   4—1 to 1 1/2 hrs.   8—3 to 3 1/2 hrs.
                         9—over 3 1/2 hrs.
   12—Total 1st 2 stages   12 _____
   1—under 2 1/4   6—16 1/2 to 20 1/2
   2—2 1/4 to 4 1/2   7—20 1/2 to 24 1/2
   3—4 1/2 to 8 1/2   8—24 1/2 to 30 1/2
   4—8 1/2 to 12 1/2   9—30 1/2 to 36 1/2
   5—12 1/2 to 16 1/2   0—over 36 1/2

continued

APPENDIX VI-B—*Continued*

13 Mother's age_____years   see code   13 _____

14 Mother's weight_____lbs. see code   14 _____
   Mother's height_____

15 Mother's blood   15 _____
   type_____RH_____ see code

16 Infant's blood   16 _____
   type_____RH_____ see code

17—21 Infant's Apgar scores
   17—first score_____time_____ code apgar score   17 _____
   18—second score_____time_____ using 0 for 10   18 _____
   19—third score_____time_____   19 _____
   20—fourth score_____time_____   20 _____
   21—fifth score_____time_____   21 _____

22 Infant's pain threshold   22 _____
   _____ see code

23 Suction   23 _____
   1 Bulb
   2 Gastric
   3 Tracheal

24 Oxygen given   24 _____
   _____None see code
   _____Mask
   _____Postive Pressure
   _____Duration

25 Abnormalities noted in infant's record   25 _____

26 Anaesthesia   26 _____
   1—none   6—cyclopropane
   2—gas (N_2O)   7—other combinations of 2—6
   3—gas and oxygen (N_2O_2) 8—spinal (saddle block)
   4—ether   9—caudal
   5—GOE (gas, O_2 and ether) 0—pudenal
                             X—other combinations, specify_____

27—37 Analgesias   27 _____
        27—28 Nembutal and seconal
   27: administered 2 hours prior to delivery
   1 none   3 200
   2 100   4 over 200

                                                                                    _____
                                                                                    continued

APPENDIX VI-B—*Continued*

28: administered within 48 hours of delivery   28 _____
   1 none   3 300 or 400
   2 100 or 200   4 over 400

29–30 Scopolamine   29 _____
  29: administered within 2 hours of delivery
   1 none   3 .8
   2 .4   4 over .8
  30: administered within 48 hours of delivery   30 _____
   1 none   4 1.2
   2 .4   5 over 1.2
   3 .8

31–32 Demerol   31 _____
  31: administered within 2 hours of delivery
   1 none   4 150
   2 50   5 over 150
   3 100
  32: administered within 48 hours of delivery   32 _____
   1 none   4 250 or 300
   2 50 or 100   5 over 300
   3 150 or 200

33–34 Sparine   33 _____
  33: administered within 2 hours of delivery
   1 none   3 50
   2 25   4 over 50
  34: administered within 48 hours of delivery   34 _____
   1 none   4 125–200
   2 25 or 50   5 over 200
   3 75 to 100

35–36 Phenergan   35 _____
  35: administered within 2 hours of delivery
   1 none   4 50
   2 12 1/2   5 over 50
   3 25
  36: administered within 48 hours of delivery   36 _____
   1 none   3 62 1/2 to 100
   2 12 1/2 to 50 4 112 1/2 and over

37–38 Morphine   37 _____
  37: administered within 2 hours of delivery
   1 none   3 1/2
   2 1/4   4 over 1/2
  38: administered within 48 hours of delivery   38 _____
   1 none   4 3/4
   2 1/4   5 over 3/4
   3 1/2

39 Other analgesias   39 _____

APPENDIX V1-C
Neurodevelopmental Behavior Ratings: Follow up Record

	Year 1 Examinations Age, Date			Year 2 Examinations Age, Date			Year 3 Examinations Age, Date		
	1	2	3	4	5	6	7	8	9
General Maturation:									
Wt.									
L.									
Hd. Size									
Motor Strength—Score									
Head, prone									
Crawling									
Grasp									
Persistence									
Tactile-Adaptive—Score									
Swiping									
Cotton									
Cellophane									
Sensory Maturation—Score									
Auditory									
Visual									
Moving object									
Light									
Irritability—Score									
Cry									
Trembling									
Muscle Tension—Score									
Legs									
Arms									
Feet									
Sitting									
Supine									
Spontaneous movement									
Postural Reflexes									
Moro									
TNR									
Withdrawal									
Placing									
Parachute									
Reciprocal									
Landau									
Deep Reflexes									
B.J.									
K.J.									
A.J.									
Bab.									
Clonus									
Crossed P.									
Sidedness									
Upper Rt.									
L.									
Lower Bil.									

APPENDIX VII

Meeting Street School—75 Charles Field Street, Providence, R.I. 02906   Tele.: 272-3010

Name: Peter   CA: 5 Mos.   Date: March 19, 1973   Next Appointed:

Objective	Program Activity and Materials	Expected Results
To encourage turning head to sound	Hold Peter on your lap facing away from you and have someone else call him or shake a noisemaker 12″ to 18″ from his ear on the same level. Turn his head in the direction of the sound. Also lying on his back	Peter may search for the sound with his eyes and slightly turn his head
To encourage anticipation of being lifted	Before lifting him, hold out your arms and with much excitement in your voice say, "I'm going to pick you up"	When you talk with much expression and use same words with same movement, he'll learn to expect certain actions and get ready to be picked up by moving his shoulders
To get Peter to recognize his bottle	Show him the bottle 3″ from his face in line with mouth before feeding. Say, "See bottle" excitedly	Peter will respond to sounds of your voice and associate pleasure with seeing bottle
To develop more strength in head control	1) Lay him on his back. Hold him around his shoulders and slowly lift him up, getting him to lift his head. When you've pulled him all the way up slowly, lower him down to the point where it becomes difficult for him to keep his head up and hold him there. Use word "up" 2) Lay him on his stomach over rolled up receiving blanket. Place his arms in front to rest on. Use something visually interesting to him to hold and move in front of him. Black and white patterned object or picture is good	He should be able to lift head up better with you holding him around the shoulders and you can help him to hold it up longer He can lift head more when when resting on his arms, hold it up longer and turn to look at the object

continued

461

APPENDIX VII—*Continued*

To develop reaching skills and understand how to use his arms

To help him use his vision more meaningfully

3) Lay him across your lap on stomach, head and shoulders over edge. Encourage head lifting. With mobile in crib, attach large ring with bells tied on and position to either side of him, low enough so with any arm movement he will hit it. Do same when he's seated in your lap at table, positioning roly poly toy or suction toy very close

Present things that Peter is interested in looking at. At this age, either shiny bells or shiny silver material or black and white signs. Hold it in front of him at varying distances, 5"–10". When he is watching it move it slowly to either side

When he swipes the ring, the mobile will move and bells ring and he'll make more of an attempt at reaching to make that happen. Later he'll grab the ring and pull it

He will learn to look at and follow moving things so he uses his vision better

APPENDIX VIII–A
Progress Report–Meeting Street School

	I			II						I Status at last evaluation II Child's progress since last evaluation

Name_____
Date____D.B.____C.A.____
MSS Program
  Group_____Indiv._____
Attendance # Sessionns
  Days Present____Absent____
Therapy received_____
	much difficulty	some difficulty	no difficulty	difficulty worsens	little or no change	some improvement	much improvement	no longer problem	not applicable	Comments

Social-Emotional Behavior										
Social response: (parents, strangers, children)										
Response to environment (apathy vs. involvement)										
Activity level (hyperactive; hypoactive)										
Attention										
Emotional responses (appropriateness)										
Independence										
Frustration tolerance										
Self-stimulation patterns										
Acceptance of limits										
Visual-Perceptual-Motor										
Visual monitoring of fine skills										
Fine motor planning										
Effective use of upper extremities										
Hand preference										
Posturing of fingers/ hands/arms										
Sensory Awareness										
Tactile response: light touch/ pressure/temperature/textures										
Awareness of body in space										
Visual acuity										
Use of vision										
Auditory acuity										
Reaction to sound										
Body Awareness and Control										
Maintaining functional positions										
Attaining functional positions										

continued

APPENDIX VIII-A—*Continued*

										Comments
Movement patterns and their quality										
Planning movements related to environment										
Balance maintenance										
Tolerance of body position changes										
Speech and Language Skills										
Feeding patterns										
Vocal production										
Imitative ability										
Gesture expression										
Development of words										
Appropriate use of words										
Intelligibility										
Puts words together										
Word order and grammatical development										
Understands familiar words										
Follows directions										
Self-Care Skills										
Drinking										
Eating										
Undressing										
Dressing										

APPENDIX VIII—B

MEETING STREET SCHOOL DEVELOPMENTAL PROFILE

NAME: _____

DATE OF BIRTH: _____

DATE OF EVALUATION:

X 1st: _____ age _____ □ 3rd: _____ age

0 2nd: _____ △ 4th:

465

LITERATURE CITED

Ambrose, A. 1969. Stimulation in Early Infancy. Academic Press, New York.

Andre-Thomas, P., P. Chesne, and S. A. Dargassies. 1960. The neurological examination of the infant. Little Club Clinics in Developmental Medicine, No. 1. Spastics Society Medical Education and Information Unit in Association with William Heineman Medical Books, Ltd., London.

Denhoff, D., and M. Langdon. 1966. Cerebral dysfunction: A treatment program for young children. Clin. Pediat. 5: 332–365.

Denhoff, E., P. K. Hainsworth, and M. L. Hainsworth. 1972. The child at risk for learning disorders. Clin. Pediat. 2: 164–170.

Geschwind, N. 1972. Language and the brain. Sci. Amer. 226: 76–83.

Niswander, K. R., and M. Gordon. 1972. The Women and Their Pregnancies. W. B. Saunders, Philadelphia.

Prechtl, H., and D. Beintema. 1964. The neurological examination of the full term newborn infant. Little Club Clinics in Developmental Medicine, No. 12. Spastics Society Medical Education and Information Unit in Association with William Heinemann Medical Book, Ltd., London.

Rosenblith, J. F. 1959. Neonatal assessment. Psych. Repts. 5: 791–792.

Rosenblith, J. F. 1956. Manual for behavioral examination of the neonate. Psych. Monogr. 70: 6–15.

Rosenblith, J. F. 1961. The modified Graham behavior test for neonates: Test-retest reliability, normative data, and hypothesis for future work. Biol. Neonate 3: 174.

Thomas, A., S. Chess, and H. G. Birch. 1968. Temperament and Behavior Disorders in Children. New York University Press, New York.

Towbin, A. 1969. Mental retardation due to germinal matrix infarction. Science 164: 156–161.

Programs Developed in a Rehabilitation Center to Educate and Study Multihandicapped Young Children: State-of-the-Art, 1976

Ronnie Gordon, M.S., and Barbara Schwartz, M.S.

For the past 14.5 years the Institute of Rehabilitation Medicine (IRM) of New York University Medical Center has operated a school for preschool-age children (3 to 6 years old) admitted to the Children's Division as inpatients for differential diagnosis, evaluation, and/or medical, paramedical, and educational therapy.

HISTORY OF THE PROJECTS

Preschool Education

An integral part of the Institute since 1962, this preschool program grew out of a 1-year private grant and experiment to create an appropriate environment for the youngest inpatients.[1] By the end of the third year, the main responsibilities of the preschool program were: 1) to stimulate the intellectual, social, and emotional growth of the young children serviced on the pediatric floor of the rehabilitation center, 2) to provide all medical and paramedical personnel with an opportunity for acquiring more realistic ideas on how the young child's adaptive and cognitive powers grow and function in a naturalistic setting, 3) to compare the intellectual and affective responses of handicapped

---

[1] Continued support for preschool service program from the Evan F. Lilly Memorial Trust.

preschool children with those of normal children as they engage in age-appropriate educational activities, 4) to isolate and to evaluate learning disabilities in youngsters with a variety of handicapping conditions, and 5) to attempt to initiate therapeutic measures to reduce the associated problems during the preschool time period.

When the school was first conceived in 1961, there was concern about the modifications that would have to be made in educational philosophy, classroom procedures, methodology, actual materials, and curricular goals when incorporating a school into an inpatient rehabilitation setting. It was recognized that each child's program would have to fit into a framework of appointments with specific therapy sessions. Therefore, each child's program would have to be noncontinuous and different. The neuromotor and muscular-skeletal disabilities of the children have ranged from minor to severe; their "intelligence" (as measured psychometrically) has varied from superior to grossly defective.

The preschool, which initially was seen as an "adjunct" to the children's medical and training program, is now recognized as an integral part of the rehabilitative services offered to the youngest children in this Medical Center. Educational assessment, based on a developmental criterion, is now routinely mandated and is a salient component of interdisciplinary evaluative procedure. Educational therapy periods are prescribed after assessment by the complete pediatric team and constitute a major portion of the younger children's time on the rehabilitation program.

In 1967 the need for an extension of the preschool project to an outpatient population was dictated by the paucity of services available at that time in the community. Upon discharge from inpatient status, too few of the children could be serviced adequately in programs available in their neighborhoods. In many cases, upon discharge, focus and emphasis were on continued educational stimulation. Concurrently, however, there can exist a continued but less intensified need for ongoing sessions of training with the Physical Therapy Department, Occupational Therapy Department, and/or the Speech Department.

Infant Education

In 1969,[2] an extension of the program to an infant population (below the age of 3) with a wide range of developmental disorders was planned and implemented. The families of these children, as well as the children themselves, were profoundly in need of more supportive services than was estimated to be available to them in the community.

The inpatient Infant School was initiated to provide intensive stimulation for an average duration of 3 months to rotating groups of four children. Each child is admitted and discharged at different time intervals to allow for individual concentration by the staff on each new admission. The transdisciplinary developmental program is coordinated by the educational staff. Parental involvement was and continues to be a critical requirement for admission to this program.

[2] Developed with the support of the U.S. Office of Education, Bureau of Education for the Handicapped, Grant No. OEG-0-9-420325-4603(619).

After 2 years of operating this highly individualized therapeutic program, reports from the parents of discharged "infants" and an examination of the existing facilities in the community revealed that there was a need for another extension of the educational service program. Many of the discharged Infant School multihandicapped children required a follow-through educational situation. The parents of the patients continued to need support and guidance. An outpatient Infant School was designed and put into operation. This project was initiated in 1972, and continues to be one of the components of the comprehensive services for young handicapped children and their families.

Design of Facilities

In the years that the Preschool and Infant Department had been involved with the design, operation, and study of learning environments it had become clear to the educational staff that there was a need to rethink the methods by which the physical space, equipment, and materials would be most facilitating for the very unique population of children serviced. (The first years of experience in a physically inadequate multipurpose dining room provided a wealth of information related to modifications that would be needed to function more effectively.) Historically, the Preschool Learning Laboratory was custom-designed and opened officially in 1968 for the 3- to 6-year-old population; the Infant School was remodeled to house the youngest children in 1970; an outdoor extension of the program, a Therapeutic Playground, engineered and constructed as an extramural learning laboratory and learning environment, was completed and operational in 1972[3]. (Further comment on each of the three environments designed for this multihandicapped population will be presented in the section concerned with Physical Facilities.)

Parallel to the growth of service projects available to children and their families and the design of more functional learning environments was a proportionate growth in interest in the study of the learning patterns of children with different degrees of specific handicapping conditions, as well as children with different medically established diagnostic entities. Teaching strategies of the educational staff were observed, recorded, and examined as the preschool specialists functioned in the naturalistic settings of the developmental programs. A wealth of observational data was available for investigation. Beginning in 1968, a research component was added to the educational department, and an alliance was formed between the two disciplines: education and psychology. (Specific investigations completed and those in process will be described in more detail in the presentation of related research.)

Throughout the years of operation of the service programs, our settings have been the site for internships and field placement for graduate students involved in the study of exceptional children, as well as for those students doing further academic work in the specialties of child development and rehabilitation.

[3] Developed with the support of the U.S. Office of Education, Bureau of Education for the Handicapped, Grant No. OEG-0-9-420325-4603(619).

With the advent of the federal mandate for integration of handicapped children into normal educational settings, it was only logical that this center be involved in the preparation, training, and definition of staff needs of Head Start and day care centers who are either interested in or obligated to integrate into a normal setting a 10 percent proportion of their population to be designated as severely handicapped. This department has assumed a responsibility as one of several resource centers in New York City for guidance and consultation to the staff of the Office of Child Development in its efforts in this direction for the past 2 years. (Details of outreach efforts will be described later in the discussion.)

POPULATION SERVICED

The children who are provided educational evaluation and intervention at this Institute represent the diverse types of physical, mental, and behavioral problems commonly seen in pediatric rehabilitation units. Cerebral palsy, acquired and congenital, with its multiple physical, intellectual, communication, behavioral, and educational problems, is the most prevalent diagnosis.

In recent years the Institute has become frequently involved with children who have minimal motor deficits of neurological origin and also behavioral, perceptual, and communicative problems that are believed to be predictors of future learning dysfunction. Another group of youngsters, the etiology of whose handicap can be traced to maternal rubella, represent an unusual combination of motor, intellectual, and sensory deficits.

This rehabilitation center's intensive clinical program for children with spina bifida associated with myelomeningocele has enabled the department to study the idiosyncratic learning problems of children with hydrocephalus. The outpatient program of the pediatric service refers children with progressive muscular dystrophy, infantile atrophy, and children with a profound variety of limb deformities. In addition to these major categories of handicapping conditions, the program provides developmental services to children with uncommon types of birth defects and diseases of the muscular-skeletal system.

RATIONALE OF THE EDUCATIONAL PHILOSOPHY

The developmental programs offered to the children on the Pediatric Service at IRM and the three facilities that have been specifically contrived and engineered to house the inpatient and outpatient educational programs reflect directly the staff's educational position. Educationally, the program's position has deep roots in a developmental-interaction point of view in which, "Developmental refers to the emphasis on identifiable patterns of growth and modes of experiencing and responding that are associated with increasing chronological age; and interaction refers to the emphasis on the individual child's interaction with the environment" (Biber, 1964). Equal emphasis is placed (in this formulation by Biber) on the "Nature of the environment and on the patterns of the responding child while assuming an environment which provides maximum opportunity for engagement."

Conventional environments do *not* offer opportunity for optimal action or interaction by handicapped children with restricted mobility, reduced stamina, with absence of or abortive limbs, and by those whose neurologic disability interfers with perceptual and spatial organizations.

Conventional ratios of teacher to child do *not* offer opportunity for optimal interaction of handicapped children, either child-to-child or teacher-to-child interaction. Cumulative clinical findings confirm that chronological age as an indicator of stage or level of development needs to be questioned seriously and examined further when dealing with a population of young children whose multiple disabilities often impinge upon both physical and mental growth. In addition, experiential information has indicated repeatedly that one cannot equate a medical diagnosis with an educational diagnosis or prescription. Each child needs to be looked at sensitively and individually in terms of competence, personality, style, and as a composite of strengths and weaknesses. These "exceptional" children are first and foremost children—admittedly, children with an unusual burden of difficulties. It is fully recognized that this handicapped population has needs that are qualitatively very similar to normal children of their mental age but that are quantitatively much greater, and indeed much more difficult to meet.

Knowledge, too, of the medical diagnosis and neuromotor deviations of this very specialized population is necessary if one is to be effective in minimizing the influence of physiological differences as depressors of performance in the learning situation. Familiarity with the many types of cerebral dysfunction that interfere with, restrict, distort, or limit intellectual development as sequelae to an insult to the central nervous system enables a child development specialist to evaluate each child's current cognitive performance and to plan more effectively each young patient's very individualized educational program: one designed to raise this performance to the limits imposed by the child's capacity.

This distinction is being purposefully made between performance and capacity. Extended assessment is always indicated (but not always provided) when working with children with developmental disorders. Performance of the child at one point in time does not necessarily reflect his potential as a learner or his "cognitive capacity," but it often tests his comfort in the situation, his previous exposure to similar tasks, the level of his motivation to work, his interest in the specific material or activity presented, as well as his rapport with the examiner. The findings of Dryman, Birch, and Korn (1970) in studying the performance of normal 6-year-old children are relevant to the work of the preschool with a younger population of children with developmental disorders. Their results "Support the assumption that a meaningful distinction could be made between capacity (representing the potential of the individual) and performance (representing the level at which the individual responds)." Either discrepancy or congruence between performance and capacity can only be established after a very careful extensive investment is made by the educational staff in assessment and intervention by tailoring the curricular goals and the specific learning tasks to each child's current manifest performance in an attempt to gradually maximize the child's ability to respond to more complex problem-solving situations.

Further comment is warranted on the quality and qualification of teachers of exceptional children. The teacher of exceptional children has in common with his or her students an unusual share of problems. She must be able to recognize and identify very readily the developmental profile of each new child in the class, particularly the presence of cognitive dysfunction. In the multihandicapped population there is a wider range of differences than in a normal population. There are obviously more reasons for differences than in normal groups. In addition to the highly publicized mental lags that have been attributed to cultural and social and economic deprivation, we have seen a mosaic of behavioral and cognitive disturbances that are directly related with organic disorders and lack of neurological integrity.

In order to recognize uncommon patterns of learning and behavior, the teacher must be familiar with normal patterns of learning and behavior. After these many years of experience in an educative and evaluative role with this very diversified population of children with their concomittant developmental problems primary to and secondary to their medical diagnosis, the initial conviction that the teaching personnel responsible for preschool developmental programs must be more than just "familiar" with normal children has been confirmed and strengthened. The preschool teacher of multihandicapped children must have had extensive experience in both theoretical and practical work with normal, early childhood populations before assuming the deep responsibility for evaluating and educating exceptional children.

There are considerable discussion, debate, and controversy in the educational community as to what constitutes a sound program for exceptional children. One large group of teacher-therapists involved in "special education" projects focus exclusively on the acquisition of specific skills. Concentration is on discrete abilities. Competence is regarded simplistically as just the addition of new skills.

A deficit approach to education prevails in many "special" educational programs. It is clearly a theoretical preference of many intervention programs as articulated by the agency or sponsor responsible for particular project designs, ones that are often associated with outcome evaluation. There is a tendency, when a specific deficiency is identified in a child, to prescribe a restricted, compensatory program and to define goals that are equivalently specific. At first glance this appears to be a sound rationale for prescriptive teaching for youngsters with developmental problems. The educators in this department question this compartmentalization of functioning and dysfunctioning. It is recognized that there are real limits on the rate and ceilings of overall development of some children, limits imposed by the presence (in degree and in locus) of neurological insult. A disability (whether congential or acquired) that is associated with a disease of, or trauma to, the central nervous system can impinge, and most often does impinge, upon both mental and physical development. It can have a nonspecific, diffuse, and pervading impact on the overall functioning of the child rather than on discrete spheres of development. Delay is rarely unitary in nature.

When these developmental programs were first initiated there was concern for the frequency of marked tendencies toward passivity in the children, as well as a pervading superficiality in their relatedness to people and to objects. These characteristics were found to be as prevalent as the more frequently reported syndrome of hyperactivity. This led to an interest in providing a learning climate that would encourage and allow handicapped children with depressed motivation and fear of failure to interact with more depth and vigor with people and objects, to derive satisfaction and a growing sense of self-worth from successful interactions, as well as to develop new competencies from these encounters. A nurturing environment is one in which the child is free to express his feelings, as well as one which offers him opportunities to experience pleasure. As Hartley, Frank, and Goldenson (1952) stated:

> Definiteness, accomplishment at the end of perseverance with a structured task are gratifying and need a place in any program, but where, one should ask, is there also provision for developing the questioning mode, the interdependent exploring mind, for deepening self-knowledge and utilizing the natural cognitive processes of the preschool child in the service of autonomous mastery of the world of ideas and conflict resolution? It is to fulfill these ends that a supported, guided play program is the essential core of a preschool program for the preschool child.

There is a deep respect for the critical and basic role of play in maturation and development in these programs, and thus the play mode of learning is supported. Cazden (1974) cites Bruner's suggestion that many special skills are practiced and developed in play. She further refers to a study of play in chimpanzees that finds, "Play occurs only in an atmosphere of familiarity, emotional reassurance and lack of tension and danger." A further comment is, "Similar conditions should be important for human children's play as well." These basic conditions are not easily replicated for handicapped children, whose lives are burdened with constant shifts from home to hospital, from the familiar to the unfamiliar, and for children who often elicit a wider range of reaction or absence of reaction from the adults in their mini-environment and whose very dependence and disorganization tend to support feelings of potential and imminent danger and anxiety.

One cannot separate the child's affective state from his mental and physical states. Affective and cognitive processes are not compartmentalized. These programs support the thesis that there is a constant interweaving and interdependence of affective, cognitive, and physical development, and that they are continually and dynamically interactive. Emerging new patterns of responding to people and trusting new people and more complex and differentiated patterns of expressing feelings are very clearly goals of the educational process. They are an integral part of, not separate from, cognitive development. Piaget (1968) claims, "There is constant parallel between affective and intellectual life through childhood . . . affectivity and intelligence are indisassociatable and constitute the two complementary aspects of all human behavior." Clinical impressions and examination after having worked with well over 1,500 multihandicapped young children indicate that changes are most frequently observed in children's emotional status, in the degrees and complexity of their social responsiveness, and in the quality and quantity of self-initiated and independent movement toward people and objects. Experience with the children in the programs further suggests that these changes occur concurrently with positive changes in the child's communication system, reasoning process, and overall cognitive growth. These changes nurture each other; they are dependent upon each other.

As developmentalists, the program subscribes to educational goals that have been clearly articulated for the preschool years (Biber, Wickens, and Shapiro, 1971). These goals are: 1) to serve the child's need to make an impact on the environment with direct physical contact and maneuver, 2) to promote the potential for ordering experience through cognitive strategies, 3) to advance the child's functioning knowledge of his environment, 4) to support the play mode of incorporating experience, 5) to help the child internalize impulse control, 6) to meet the child's need to cope with conflicts intrinsic to his stage of development, 7) to facilitate the development of an image of self as a unique and competent person, and 8) to help the child establish mutually supporting patterns of interaction.

These curricular goals are, in a sense, traditional ones for a preschool program based on a developmental-interaction philosophy. They are as relevant (but more difficult to achieve) in the process of educating handicapped children as they are in the process of educating normal preschool-age children. It is recognized, however, that each deviant child requires a sensitive adjustment and an ongoing and continuous readjustment of these broad long-term goals.

THE SERVICE COMPONENT

Patterns of Operation

Preschool Learning Laboratory   Referrals for inpatient admission for rehabilitation services are traditionally made through medical contacts from clinics, private pediatricians, and other hospitals and agencies concerned with child care. A comprehensive pediatric evaluation begins with a thorough medical examination, which entails the recording and documentation of the medical history of the child and his family, as well as appropriate laboratory and medical examinations. This aids in the definition of those problems that are organically based.

The multidisciplinary team, including the paramedical services—physical therapy, occupational therapy, and the speech and hearing therapies—contribute their evaluation of the functional strengths and deficits that are a consequence of the child's medical problem. Social service reports on the status of the family; the educators and psychologists further define the developmental status of the child and make judgments as to the child's current capacity to benefit from an individualized educational and therapeutic program. This comprehensive pediatric evaluation occurs within the first or second week after the child's admission as an inpatient. The joint findings of the pediatric team are translated into an individualized program for the new admission. The child's progress on this program is reevaluated at intervals of approximately 1 month, with changes in programming implemented when indicated. In addition to these scheduled meetings, informal conferencing is continuous among disciplines and individual therapy areas. The preschool teaching staff records weekly progress notes on specific aspects of the child's development, emerging abilities, and/or problem areas.

One major component of the child's rehabilitation program (for those children younger than 6 years of age) is a prescription of periods of intensive educational therapy in a preschool setting. All children within this age range who are currently inpatients on the 35-bed Children's Division are programmed for periods of education. The number of periods per morning in the education program varies for each child and is dependent upon the child's need for sessions of paramedical therapy within the framework of the five half hour therapy sessions scheduled each morning. (Example: If a child's admission is based on a behavioral disorder and the goal of admission is referral to an appropriate educational setting in the child's family neighborhood, he may well be prescribed all five periods of the morning in the preschool situation. In contrast, a youngster whose development in all aspects of functioning is delayed may have a program that includes two periods of preschool education, one period of physical therapy, one period of occupational therapy, and one period of speech and hearing, daily.)

A maximum of six preschool-age children is scheduled per one half hour session in the preschool facility. This program is staffed by two master child development specialists. They are frequently assisted by either an educational intern or a graduate student who is using this site for field placement. It is believed that this high ratio of staff to child is a critical feature of the program. The findings of a study in this setting confirmed the clinical knowledge and original hypothesis that the number of children in the classroom directly affects the content, the frequency of interactions, and the types of responses of staff and children (Diller et al., 1973).

The curriculum followed and the materials selected each day are influenced by weekly admission changes; the composition of the class at any half hour period is arranged as meticulously as possible to afford each child an optimum working environment with other children at his level. The temporary composition of each session makes flexibility in program imperative, as do the variations in the children's neurological and physical status, chronological ages (3 to 6) and mental ages (1 to 6). When a child needs a one-to-one relationship with the teacher, his need is met. If he cannot benefit from group experience or if he disrupts the group, a tutorial method is used in a corner of the room, free from distraction.

Before the child's discharge, the educators actively initiate referrals (with the collaboration of the Social Service Department) to an appropriate educational facility: to a "neighborhood school" when indicated, or for referral back to the outpatient nursery school program at the Institute. The average stay of a preschool-age child has been statistically approximated at 8 weeks. However, this is only a statistic. It reflects a range of patterns of admission of from 2 weeks for differential diagnosis to extended programs for as long as 6 months for prosthetic training and/or educational intervention before a referral to another situation. In general, however, the program's role is transitory as a "school."

When a referral is made to an outside agency, there is a planned reciprocity of visits of the staff from the referral agency to IRM (usually the director and the teacher to be directly involved in the educational program to which the child is referred). When indicated, IRM staff visit the referred agency, both before and after the child has been admitted to the neighborhood program. Whenver possible and whenever requested, follow up services to external preschool programs, day care centers, Head Start centers, or special programs are provided. Because most of these handicapped youngsters require intermittent and sporadic reassessment and retraining, as well as reevaluation by the Institute's pediatric service, many children are seen by the staff at least once a year following their discharge from the inpatient program. A group of children with specific diagnoses that require more closely spaced and ordered medical supervision are seen with more frequency.

The outpatient preschool program is operated in the afternoons for 2-hour intervals two or three times a week. This form of school referral is made for those children who are not yet ready to be referred to existing programs in their community and/or children who still require, in addition to the continuing preschool education outpatient program, added services of physical therapy and/or the speech department to further enhance their development before discharge from the Institute.

Infant School

Screening Procedures   For those young children (ages 18 months to 3 years) who are being considered for admission as inpatients in the intensive Infant School program,[4] the operational model can be described as follows:

All children referred for this program, geared to four infants at any given time, are screened by the Project Director, the Clinical Director of the children's floor (pediatrician-psychiatrist); and the social service staff. This screening is to determine both the availability of the child to intervention and at the same time the parent's ability to participate actively in their child's program. At this initial contact point, an educational work sample is recorded on video tape, during which the Project Director offers the child a series of activities with educational materials based on initial and ongoing impressions. The objective of this informal "test" situation is to elicit information about the child's current manifest competence, behavior, and responses related to his social, emotional, and intellectual status. Simultaneously, of course, information is gained relating to the interactional patterns of parent and child and parent and examiner.

Implementation of the Program   Parents participate actively one full day a week in the child's educational and therapeutic program and meet with the Project Director weekly to exchange information related to changes in the child in school and at home. These interviews are audio taped and examined for both commonalities of problems and evidence of parents' increased competence to effectively cope with and stimulate their children upon discharge. Each child is evaluated by each discipline represented on the Service in the same pattern required of other pediatric admissions. (The child is seen by the educational staff, the social service staff, and the physical therapy, occupational therapy, speech and hearing, and clinical psychology staffs.)

---

[4] Originally funded under Part C1, Education of the Handicapped Act, 1969 to 1972 U.S. Office of Education, Bureau of Education for the Handicapped, Grant No. OEG-0-9-420325-4603(619).

Within 2 weeks after admission (allowing time for separation and adjustment), a battery of standardized psychological tests is administered, and the child is observed in a naturalistic school setting. The master teacher presents the child with educational tasks appropriate for his estimated developmental level. The child's performance and style of response to these tasks are recorded again on video tape (pretape). Educational goals are individually projected (written) each week for each of the four children in the Infant School; this is a joint effort on the part of the educational staff, the results of which are transmitted to all therapists working with each child.

The teacher-child ratio (2:4) enables each teacher to focus on two children. The staff is often supplemented by teaching interns and parents (each family being assigned a specific parent participation day). The daily program for each child is based on the short-term goals that are established at the weekly meetings of the educational staff. A specific goal may be achieved by the offering of a multiplicity of different learning experiences. For example, if one of the goals for a child is an understanding of containment, he may be involved in placing 1) cubes in a box, and/or 2) sand in a bowl, and/or 3) leaves in a pail, and/or 4) cookie in a pocket, and/or 5) pouring juice in a cup, etc.

All disciplines involved with the infant's program work directly in the infant room in coordination with the educator. They meet at weekly informal Infant School meetings to assess the child's progress and to exchange new information concerning the child's movement in each area of development. Thus, all relevant team members are continually aware of the specific objectives that are outlined for each child and participate in the articulation of strategies planned to achieve the educational and therapeutic goals projected. Throughout the child's stay on program, narrative logs are prepared by the teacher, written to record and to document the changes that have occurred in the child's cognitive, affective, social, and physical development.[5] After a multidisciplinary decision is made that discharge is appropriate (average stay, 3 months) and referral plans have been implemented, a post video tape sample of the child's educational work is recorded. Referral procedures followed are similar to those described for the preschool-age population. During the third month of the infant's participation in the Infant School project, plans are initiated to provide the child and family with continuity of services following discharge.

Follow up   Situations in which there is an absence of an appropriate program in the community or in which the child clearly requires less intensive but still frequent supportive services from the professional staff of the Institute, the child is referred to the Outpatient Infant School. In contrast to the intensive daily program from 9:30 am to 4:00 pm of the inpatient program, the children referred to the outpatient program are brought by their parents to the Institute twice a week in the afternoon for programs of educational intervention and, when indicated, continuing sessions of physical therapy and/or speech and hearing therapy.

---

[5] A research study of the evaluation of the impact of this program resulted from the data generated from this project. U.S. Office of Education, Bureau of Education for the Handicapped, Grant No. OEG-0-72-5386.

The ratio of staff to child, again, is unusually high: two master teachers are assigned to five infants in both the inpatient and the outpatient programs. A clear conviction is held that changes seen in these developmentally delayed younger children could not be effectuated in a setting without the availability of long periods of semi-tutorial sessions with unusually skilled and experienced teachers. An evaluation of the impact of this program on the child, the family, and the change process itself has been rigorously studied.

Physical Facilities

The use of the word "facility" to describe a setting is too limited if it is interpreted as only physical space—a container. The dictionary definition given for the word "facility" is more acceptable: "facility" is, "Something that makes possible the easier performance of any action." The staff is deeply concerned with the action as well as the "something" that makes the action possible. In this area of specialty the action is education. And it is believed that the objectives of an educational program are as clearly reflected in the design and development of behavioral and curricular goals, or in the design and development of research related to the service program. The facilities must be in harmony with the educational point of view that the director of a service program projects and the educational staff implements.

In any developmental-interaction philosophy, the active interaction of the child with his environment is of primary concern. With normal children, it is assumed that a "normal" environment will provide the maximum opportunity for engagement. With deviant children, this is an assumption that cannot be made casually. Modifications and adaptations in both physical space and equipment and materials are clearly needed to support the possibilities for success in the child's encounters with both objects and people.

The Preschool Learning Laboratory   In a school program for normal children blocks of time are allocated to comparatively free play, which, in reality, is self-initiated play based on the interests of the child. The choice of an activity is in turn suggested by both the availability and attractiveness of the materials and accessories on display (on shelves and in storage units) that are readily reached by the smallest student. Normal youngsters, by 3 years of age, have developed sufficient visual and motor competence to examine a room and to walk to an individual area that appears inviting. The selected material can be carried to any appropriate work surface or floor space by the child before he proceeds with his investigation and work. If, at that moment, it is a relationship with a person (peer or teacher) that is important to the youngster, he is free to change his position in the room and to make a decision and move toward the attracting adult or child.

Peer interaction cannot be minimized as a goal of a preschool program. The opportunity to be with other children—to learn the gratification of being part of a group and at the same time to learn the controls required of a group member—contributes directly to the child's development. "Research on development confirms the importance of this peer interaction. Failure to play may contribute to continuing dependence, failure of individuation, and inability to form emotional ties to others" (Freeman, 1967).

These options and this freedom, which are accepted so casually for a normal child, are curtailed, abridged, and often completely removed from the life pattern of a multihandicapped child. If option and freedom of selection and decision making are valued and recognized as implicit and necessary to growth and development, arrangements must be made to provide an engineered environment for the child who cannot readily make the movement, the gesture, the contact, or the choice of an activity.

The overall arrangement and dimensions of the preschool laboratory could only be established after the areas of activities and the range of curricular goals were clearly delineated, with their associated work surfaces defined in both size, shape, and position within the room. A sensitive evaluation had to be made of the movement of children on crutches, using braces, in wheelchairs, in Stryker framers, and on stretcher beds in order to gauge the amount of traffic and space required for movement in and out of the classroom and from one particular activity to another.

In the handicapped population, there is a higher frequency of immature and infantile behavior patterns than is found in normal youngsters of the same chronological age. This is demonstrated in tendencies to make purely physical contact and for impulsive possession of others' materials. For normal children, those who are free to move readily and to readjust positions in space, this conflict situation presents less of a problem. The child can remove himself from an untenable location or relationship and readily establish a new and more favorable work position. However, among the IRM patients with motor dysfunction, many are not free to ambulate or to change position. Commonplace physical relocation requires uncommon effort and change of focus—enough to diminish interest in ongoing acitvity (see Figure 1).

Too often the depth of involvement of the child whose disabilities are related to central nervous system disorders is markedly superficial. In fact, one of the programs' basic objectives is to deepen emotional investment in goal-oriented activities. Creating an effective learning environment—one with enough privacy for each child to be in control of his own materials and yet available to interact with the other children—thus becomes a critical feature of the programs' design. (A monograph has been published with photographs, blueprints, and dimensions of all components of this specialized preschool learning laboratory: Rehabilitation Monograph, No. 39, New York University Medical Center.) It is the staff's considered opinion that the functional design has contributed significantly to the effectiveness in providing educational programs for multihandicapped preschool-age children (see Figure 2).

A propitious setting, if this refers to the plant iself, is not enough. It is but a shell, without content. The content is directly determined by the quality of the personnel who implement the program. Well qualified and experienced preschool child development specialists in a correct ratio of teacher to child *can* be effective and innovative in an unpropitious and disadvantageous setting. However, in an unmodified environment, much time will have to be spent away from the actual education of the child in order to make the necessary continuous adjustments in the physical environment—a constant manipulation of materials, furniture, and accessories. Simultaneously, a contrived and adapted setting with individually designed activity areas and equipment would be attractive but

Figure 1. The easel: available in this lowered position to children without arms who paint with their feet using a paint tray adjusted to the appropriate height.

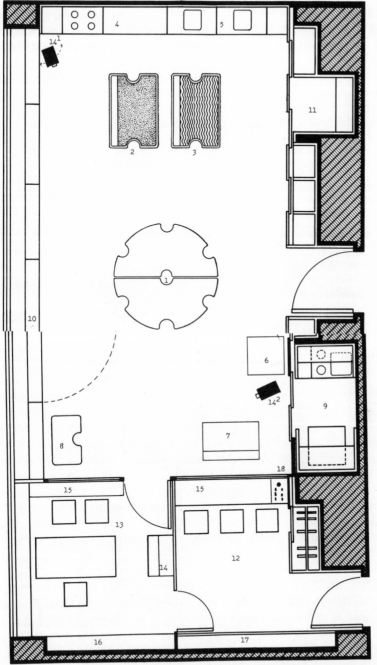

Figure 2. Overview of the Preschool Learning Laboratory. Scale: 1" = 4'. key: 1) group work table, adjustable in height; 2) sand table, adjustable in height; 3) water table, adjustable in height; 4) housekeeping unit; 5) recessed sinks, two wheelchair heights; 6) adjustable easel; 7) carpentry work bench, designed for wheelchair use; 8) tutorial/evaluation area; 9) teachers' kitchen—stove, refrigerator, sink, storage areas; 10) children's low storage area with tambour doors for self-selection of educational materials; 11) staff storage area for educational materals—developmentally sequenced; 12) observation room for staff–tours, professional observations, and extended recordings; 13) parent observation room/office; 14) video tape equipment with remote controls and monitors; 14¹) TV camera; 14²) TV camera; 15) writing shelf, table; 16) reference books; 17) office supplies; 18) audio controls for six ceiling microphones, which can be individually selected.

481

sterile under the guidance of unqualified staff. The effectiveness of the setting increases in direct proportion to the expertise and professional training of the people who translate the purposes for which it was designed. A minimal environment with maximal teaching can result in an effective, valid, and meaningful educational experience for the children. A maximal environment with minimal staff can produce little more than custodial care. Biber (1964) states:

> The "things" alone are not adequate teachers, though unfortunately there are many schools even at more advanced levels where there is a false dependence on materials, equipment and buildings as the carriers of learning. In this young world it is the sensitive teacher who supplies the accents for the child's experience . . . . The teacher's sensitivity can sometimes be measured indirectly; it is almost as if it correlates negatively with the amount of verbalization that accompanies this aspect of her teaching capacity.

A harmonious blending of the best of physical environments and a high quality and ratio of staff is the educational ideal for all children, particularly for those children with a wide range of physically handicapping conditions.

Infant School Many of the features of the core Learning Laboratory were incorporated into the design of the Infant School when a small dormitory was remodeled in 1970 to make it more functional for the new younger population. Of necessity, dimensions were reduced in proportion to the physical size, stamina, and level of motor competence of the younger children. Equipment pieces that had been designed and had proven effective for the preschool classroom were reduced both in height from the floor and in proportion to the reduced number of children to be housed in this setting. Additional designs were added and geared to the very distinctive needs of this group of infants.

Recognizing that their level of motor development was more primitive, with a higher incidence of children rolling, crawling, and not yet in an upright position, carpeting was added to the room, and a specially designed tactile wall was made of Velcro. This adjustable tactile wall allows for placement of a varying and changing group of textures mounted within reach of children not yet standing upright or walking, who are in a prone or supine position (see Figure 3). Wherever possible, handrails were attached along the walls and cabinets to encourage the young child in his efforts to come to a vertical position and to move with comfort, using the handrail for support. Storage cabinets again were designed at floor level with a changing selection of materials appropriate for the changing population of the children in the Infant School. Tambour doors, easily maneuvered by the slightest touch of a child's hand, provide easy access for children who are not yet able to open conventional doors with knobs. A large multipurpose water-play and bath area was designed as part of the bathroom—once again at the appropriate height for the children in the program. There is in this room, as there is in the core Learning Laboratory, a built-in capability for recording with TV cameras and microphones located in the ceiling; these are monitored and remotely controlled from adjacent observation rooms. Figure 4 is a diagram of the Infant School room.

Figure 3. An adjustable tactile wall in the Infant School allows for placement of a varying and changing group of textures mounted within reach of children not yet able to stand upright.

Therapeutic Playground As stated before, the educational position upon which the programs are based is that very young children not only need but are entitled to exposure to all of the learning experiences and peer relationships that are so naturally a part of the daily life of children with developmental integrity. To that end, time and effort were invested in the design of appropriate indoor settings. But that was not enough. Normal children make contact with and explore their outdoor world as well as the indoor spaces that are circumscribed by the classroom. Again, it became clear that the exceptional child is doubly handicapped—handicapped experientially as well as by his primary disability. Parents reported that few of their children who are confined to wheelchairs or restricted by orthopedic devices had access to or could use conventional playground equipment or benefit from play in neighborhood playground facilities. It became evident that, if this program were to assume responsibility for the education of young children at this Institute, the concurrent responsibility for the design and development of a therapeutic playground had to be assumed—an outdoor facility in which the space, equipment, and activity areas were in harmony with the program's educational goals and deepening knowledge of the needs of very young multihandicapped children.

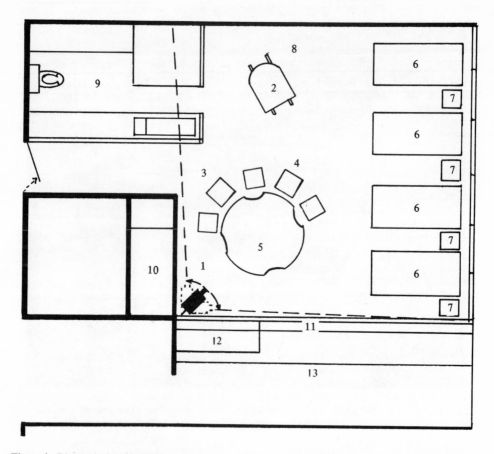

Figure 4. Diagram of Infant Room. Scale 1″ = 3′. Key: 1. Video tape camera; 2. rocking chair; 3. seating for teachers; 4. seating for children; 5. adjustable table with semi-circular cut-outs; 6. cribs; 7. individual cabinets for children's clothes; 8. tactile wall; 9. glass-enclosed bathroom with sliding door; 10. teacher's storage of educational materials; 11. low storage area with handrail for educational material; 12. remote control monitor for video tape; 13. nurse's station.

Keats said, "Nothing ever becomes real until it is experienced." Allowing for opportunities to have real and active experiences outdoors was the primary objective in the design of the therapeutic playground. If a child is to know the difference between an indoor setting and outdoor phenomena, he must be given time to see the sky, to observe a leaf moved by the wind, to feel the texture of grass, dirt, and sand, to see and hear water falling from different levels, to trace a puddle from its source to the point where it vanishes—to understand the mosaic of sound, sight, and textures that are the components of the natural environment.

This does not refer to compensatory situations, but rather to the very core of learning—the foundation of knowledge about their world that is missing or faulty in these children with experiential deprivation and/or developmental dysfunction. In the absence of a sound background in understanding basic relationships and discovering primitive causal associations, the handicapped child is unable to engage efficiently in the most elementary levels of processing of information—information that is needed before more complex and sophisticated functioning can be expected. He is neither able to make judgments about his environment nor to make an impact upon that environment.

Young children who are handicapped, whether in a rehabilitation center or in a community, require similar exposure—in fact, even more intensified exposure to experiences and activities in an outdoor setting that are pedestrian but crucial for young children in general. These experiences should include opportunities for large motor activities, encounters with elements and media that are distinctive to the outdoors, and movement in a prescribed space that is less confining than that of the indoor setting.

Motor skills evolve in a sequential pattern in normal development. They are only momentarily acknowledged as they emerge in a growing child. But for children with developmental disorders of neurophysiological origin, the achievement of each or even one of these motoric milestones can be a monumental accomplishment. The ability to walk from one area to another does not develop in many orthopedically and neurologically impaired youngsters just because it is chronologically appropriate in the schema of normal growth patterns. It is developed as a result of high motivation, intensive effort, training, and practice (see Figure 5). The desire to reach, to grasp, or to crawl, to walk, or to climb has to be instilled and supported by magnifying and continuously reinforcing the satisfaction to be derived from such activities.

In the therapeutic playground a need was seen for clear delineation of activity areas to facilitate the ordering and organization of stimuli for these young patients (see Figure 6). These children too frequently have problems in selecting from a barrage of available coexisting stimuli those that are appropriate for their individual and particular stage of development—information that they could assimilate into their growing body of knowledge. The pleasures and dividends of play outdoors have to be immediately and strongly experienced before many passive youngsters are willing to invest the unusual effort required of them to adapt to the play mode of experiencing objects in their physical world.

In summary, even if one could describe adequately the many variations that exist in nature, the very young child will organize his perceptions of these phenomena only after the stimuli have a real and very personal meaning associated with his own experiences. (The design of specific activity areas and equipment and the educational rationale for their inclusion in this therapeutic playground are included with photographs, blueprints, and measurements in Rehabilitation Monograph No. 47, The Design of a Therapeutic Playground, Institue of Rehabilitation Medicine, New York University Medical Center.)

RELATED RESEARCH

The population of children serviced, the educational philosophy, and the physical environments have been described in the preceding sections. In this section the focus is on

Figure 5. The ability to walk develops as a result of high motivation, intensive effort, training, and practice.

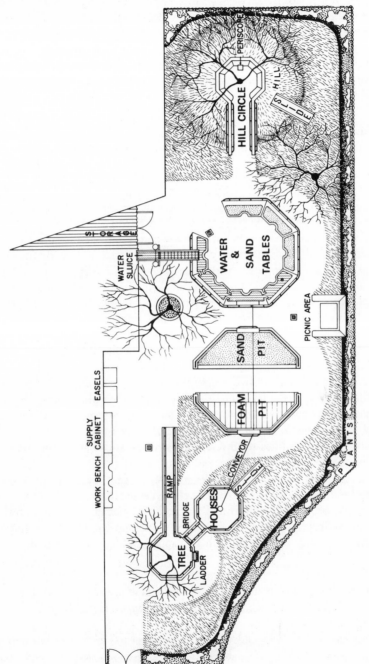

Figure 6. Preschool Therapeutic Playground, an outdoor "Learning Laboratory." Scale: 1" = 15' (approximately).

data generated in this setting that have been of interest to educators and to psychologists. Often there is a gap between the teachers involved with the education of children and the psychologists involved in a systematic study of children in an educational setting. In many ways this program has attempted to bridge that gap. There must be a productive relationship, one based on parity, on respect for each other's competence, and on the awareness of a mutual dependency if knowledge of how children learn and how teachers teach is to increase.

Study of Educational Materials with
Neurologically Impaired and Neurologically Intact Preschool Children

By 1968 it had become evident that the population of children being served in the preschool program represented two distinct groups: the physically handicapped child who was neurologically impaired and the physically handicapped child who was neurologically intact. The differences noted were in the way the children handled educational materials—specifically in their use of tasks with a visual-perceptual component. It was observed that children whose limitations were solely physical (e.g., with a diagnosis of post-poliomyelitis, congenital amputee, skeletal-muscular abnormalities not associated with central nervous system disorders) functioned in their use of materials in a manner similar to a normal population. The disparities observed clinically in these two groups were believed to be significant and quite clearly defined, suggesting that there was developmental divergence in the style and competence with which these two populations coped with goal-oriented materials. Based upon several years of direct involvement and observation, the Project Director hypothesized that this developmental divergence would be reflected in the child's use of two conventional educational materials testing specific target abilities—visual-perceptual skills. One material, the Form Sorting Box, stressed form and shape discrimination and the child's ability to perceive the need for rotation. The second educational material, Montessori Cylinders (graded in diameter but not height) focused on the abilities to differentiate size gradations and error correction in a quasi-seriation problem (Gordon, White, and Diller, 1972).

A psychologist from the Behavioral Science Department joined in this investigation, exemplifying the type of cooperative work between educators and psychologists that can offer results that are both practical and theoretically meaningful. The knowledge the educators derived from extensive experience with normal children at varying levels of maturation could clearly be applied to handicapped children and their educational and developmental status. The educators' concern was not only the achievement (the product of the child's work or the competence with which the child differentiated shape and size) but with the process (the response styles). Additional study of styles of response would yield information about strategies of processing that were obscured by focusing only on achievement (the product).

This study compared 284 children ages 3 to 5.5 years—neurologically impaired and neurologically intact middle class and disadvantaged—in competence and style while working with these two selected educational materials. The children were divided into three groups. Group I was composed of 85 children with specified pathologies related to central nervous system dysfunction. Their diagnoses were either (1) spina bifida with myelomeningocele associated with hydrocephalus or (2) congenital cerebral palsy. All children in this group had medical histories and neurological findings consistent with brain injury. Group II was composed of 75 preschool-age children attending two Head Start programs. Acceptance to both Head Start programs was based on an economic criterion: an annual family income of less than $3,000. Available medical histories revealed no evidence or suggestion of neurological disorder. The inclusion of the Head Start population was of particular interest at that time because the study of acquisition of visual percepts and stylistic qualities in disadvantaged children had been relatively neglected. This was in contrast to the more prevalent emphasis on their language deficits as predictors for later learning problems. Group III consisted of 124 middle class children with no significant medical histories of neurological impairment. This group served as a control group for both Group I and Group II.

The findings of this study, illustrated in Figures 7, 8, and 9, warrant further comment. The results suggested that: 1) simple perceptual recognitions are within the

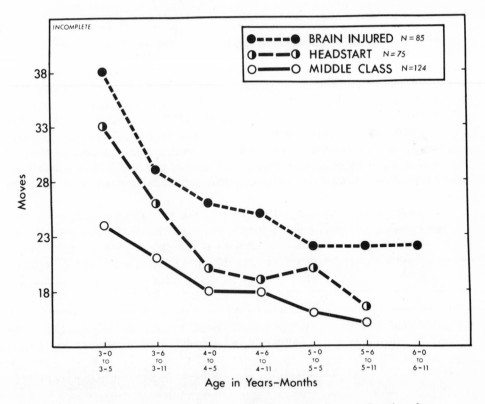

Figure 7. Mean number of moves to complete form sorting box as a function of age.

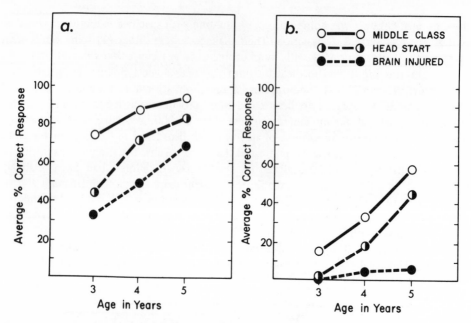

Figure 8. A. Tasks requiring form match only; B, tasks requiring form match and rotation.

capacity of most neurologically impaired children but develop at significantly later chronological ages than they do for Group II and Group III; 2) rotational aspects of the problem require a spatial organization that was not within the competency of Group I during the period of time studied and, based on clinical findings, often does not develop or appear at all for many years; 3) the ability to classify, to look for, and to focus on "sameness" is markedly delayed in children with neurological dysfunction, Group I; and 4) successes are individual rather than cumulative and are more prone to be ignored as references for future action.

Once there is an understanding of the goal of a task, the abilities of both middle class and disadvantaged children (Groups II and III) increase, although at a different rate. This steady rate of progress of organizational skills is not characteristic of neurologically damaged children within the ages studied. In this brain injured (neurologically impaired) group, practice with similar tasks does not consistently enhance future performance. The concepts of sameness and difference appear to be underdeveloped and are easily extinguished in these children by the actual physical effort of manipulation of the forms and/or the time required for completion of one component of the task. Hence, the problem of generalization or transfer of achievement plays a more critical role in neurologically impaired children than in the other groups. Educators, developmental psychologists, and other students of the problem have not given sufficient attention to this issue.

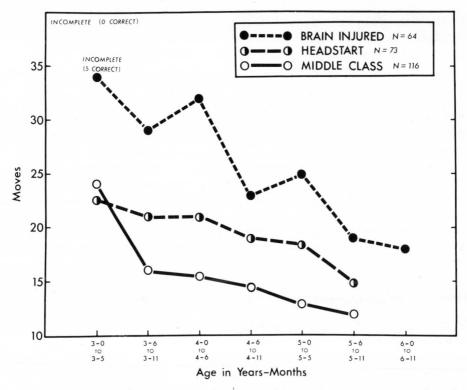

Figure 9. Mean number of moves to complete Montessori Cylinders as a function of age.

It was significant that the neurologically impaired children's performance could be improved by selectively handing a child the individual pieces of the related task, therefore shortening the time interval between each move and eliminating the child's options in deciding on the next move. The lag in the performance of the brain injured child is often related not only to poor discriminatory ability but also to inability to sustain attention and to maintain a focus on a specific task goal. The availability of a teacher is more important in obtaining optimal performance from neurologically impaired children than for either of the two other groups at every level.

Although only two specific pieces of conventional play materials were used in this study involving 284 children, clinical judgment and observational data suggest that comparable results can be anticipated with many materials, many of which are used too casually in preschool programs. A similar sequence of acquired competencies and styles of response would probably emerge at comparable maturation levels in such extended studies. The preschool staff is involved currently in a refinement of hierarchically ordering the task demands of materials and activities offered to the children in our developmental programs.

The study of the Form Box and Montessori Cylinders for evaluating specific abilities that develop in the first 4 to 5 years of life is related to what Bortner and Birch (1970) called, "A child's readiness to respond to different kinds of perceptual demands which are fundamental for future formal learning." The results of this investigation indicate that at each age there appears to be a lawful pattern of competency in visual discrimination and differentiations as well as in relationship thinking. With this frame of reference, marked deviations from these age-specific competencies in a child can suggest to the sensitive and knowledgeable teacher that there is interference of some type in this specific area of cognitive development.

Neurologically impaired children have a different profile of performance from that associated with neurologically intact preschool children. Deviations in overall performance, illogical mistakes, and eccentric styles of response associated with neurological dissonance are easy to detect. These stylistic differences can be contrasted with the logical mistakes and normal response styles that are expected to appear at a particular age and to disappear at a later maturational stage in a normal population—middle class or disadvantaged.

Teaching Styles and Response Patterns in Brain Damaged Children

An investigation which examined the response patterns in brain damaged children who were engaged in visual-motor developmental activities in relation to specific teaching styles was based on data generalized from the same preschool setting at the Institute (Diller et al., 1973).[6] In this investigation the director of the preschool and infant developmental programs acted in the capacity of educational consultant.

The overall purpose of the investigation was to answer the following questions: "Is what is taught related to characteristics of children? Are there aspects of the classroom which are rearranged to take these characteristics into account? Is there something distinctive about a brain injured child that suggests differences in teaching behavior in the classroom?" These questions were to be explored by examining a number of specific issues: 1) Is cognitive functioning in young children unidimensional or multidimensional? 2) Does cognitive functioning differ in the psychological evaluation from other situations? 3) Is there a relationship between differences in cognitive functioning and different medical diagnoses? 4) What are the parameters of teaching behavior in the classroom? 5) Are parameters of a child's cognitive functioning related to parameters of teaching behavior?

Fifty-five physically handicapped brain injured and non-brain injured children from 2.5 to 6.5 years of age were the subjects of the study. The brain injured group of 45 children was diagnosed either as spina bifida (12), cerebral palsy (26), or other types of brain damage (7). The non-brain injured controls (N = 10) were physically handicapped

[6] Supported by a grant from the U.S. Office of Education, Bureau of Education for the Handicapped, Grant No. OEG-0-70-3361(607).

children with a variety of diagnoses (e.g., congenital amputee, rheumatoid arthritis, or myopathy).

Data on each child were generated from classroom observations (five 10-minute samples of classroom behavior), the Stanford Binet Intelligence Test, an evaluation session with two educational toys (the Form Sorting Box and the Montessori Cylinders), and an observational record and report of the master teachers' intent during a 10-minute individual tutorial session. (The examiner/director of educational programs presented the child with six pre-selected educational materials.)

Some of the findings of this investigation were congruent with the initial hypotheses and clinical impressions of the Project Director and educational staff of the preschool developmental programs, specifically that the "relevance of mental age in this sample is heightened by the observation that chronological age appeared to be less important than competence as a determinant of teaching style" (Diller et al., 1973). It had also been hypothesized by the educators and was substantiated by the findings that not only would the mental age or developmental level of the child be reflected in the teacher's style of teaching but that specific handicapping conditions would have direct effects yielding further readjustments of the teacher's pattern of instruction. The teaching and learning situation is interactional with reciprocal changes in the child's responses (related to medical and psychological status) affecting the teacher's response and expectations. Individual patterns of response to cognitive demands, independent of competence, were found for groups of children with diagnoses of cerebral palsy and spina bifida, in contrast to those of the non-brain injured group.

Within the context of individual tutorial sessions, the specific response style of the child, ". . . did not emerge as an important factor." This is not surprising, since good teaching accommodates itself to the child's needs so that task orientation is maintained at a high level. "Individual differences in response style, therefore, are not necessarily synonymous with unsuccessful learning. Under optimal conditions idiosyncratic response styles may be effectively dealt with by the teacher. This points to the need for versatility in teaching style in order to optimize instruction. It also indicates the value of assessing a child's behavior in an on-going learning situation" (Diller et al., 1973). The content of a sample informal protocol of intent, audio taped immediately after the 10-minute tutorial session (see Appendix) illustrates the constant organization and reorganization, shifting of goals, and reassessment of strategies required to make the activities offered successful learning experiences for the individual child.

Evaluation of Behavioral Change in the Infant Program

Research and clinical experience gained during the first 10 years of operation of the preschool and infant programs at IRM were subsequently incorporated into a 3-year indepth study of the impact of the infant program upon the growth and development of young multihandicapped children (Gordon et al., 1975, Part I) and upon their families (Gordon et al., 1975, Part II).

Valid and meaningful educational research must be a direct outgrowth of a program's philosophy of education. Methods of assessing change must be congruent with the teacher's focus and specific goals of the educational program. In this study the criteria by which change was measured were defined through a collaborative effort of the Project Director, the educational staff, the research staff, and when needed, external consultants. A system was developed which allowed researchers to examine individual patterns of growth, investigate the relationship among a variety of patterns, and predict degree and category of change. Growth was defined in terms of emerging competencies and mastery in a number of selected salient areas.

The competencies of prime importance included: 1) the ability to work purposefully with educational materials, 2) the child's responsiveness to the environment, 3) the degree and complexity of social responsiveness, 4) expressive communication with others, 5) the child's expression of affect, and 6) motor development. Of equal importance were the quality and quantity of self-initiated and independent behaviors. These aspects of behavior were viewed as being critical both individually and in their interaction with one another in all situations encountered by the child. Over a period of several years,[7] these criteria were defined and refined into a coding system incorporating seven psycho-educational dimensions (appended) and qualifying behaviors which meet the needs and goals of both the educational and research staff.[8]

In keeping with this interface between research needs and the goals of the educational program, anecdotal records (logs) written by the teacher were selected as the primary source of data (sample appended). This data base was chosen because it reflected the deep concern for the process of change, the emergence over time of individual competencies, and the dynamic interaction of varying aspects of development. These logs were written on three full morning sessions for each child for the duration of the child's stay. A secondary source of data for each child in the study was two (pre and post) video taped evaluation sessions with selected educational materials. Tasks were selected by the director or teacher based upon knowledge of the child and preliminary clinical evaluation of this child's work. Approximately 10 tasks (different for each child) were presented. The specific task, the amount of time, and the teacher's mode of presentation of the material could be varied in a way which permitted the teacher to explore and determine the child's optimal level of functioning within this distinct multihandicapped young population.

The validity of the coding system was substantiated by a rigorous comparison, a substudy, of data from four sources (participating master teacher, intern teacher, non-participating observer, and video taped recordings). Data on one child were collected from the four sources over a 2-week period. Comparative analysis revealed that a similar

---

[7] The initial investigation and guidelines for analysis were developed by Lillian Shapiro with the assistance of Carol Neiditch. The final team of investigators for this study included David Gitler, coordinator, Barbara Schwartz, Ora Ezrachi, and Ronnie Gordon, Project Director.

[8] Copies of the Coding Manual can be obtained from Prof. Ronnie Gordon, Director of Preschool and Infant Developmental Programs, Institute of Rehabilitation Medicine, 400 East 34 Street, New York, N.Y. 10016.

profile of the child was drawn when those episodes reported in all four sources were compared. All of the activities of the day were not recorded, but those behaviors or activities that were selected were truly representative of the child's overall developmental level. Teachers' logs did, in fact, accurately reflect the child's performance.

Some psychologists and educators continue to question the validity of research from "natural settings." The richness of data gained from naturalistic observations has been recognized by others (Wright, 1967) as outweighing many of the deficits. Providing a valid and reliable coding system to study the data generated from the naturalistic setting should make the findings from such an investigation more acceptable to the educational and psychological community. The involvement of the data collector, the master teacher, in the activities need not and did not reduce the validity of the data. Rather, it enhanced the interpretability of the recorded behaviors, adding both the teacher's intent for a specific activity and previous knowledge of the subject.

The 1,540 logs written by teachers were the major source of data and 80 video taped evaluations were the secondary source in this study of the impact of the educational program on the multihandicapped children who ranged in age from 19 to 40 months. When data on the total group (N = 40) of children were analyzed, the child's medical diagnosis, age at admission to the program, socioeconomic status, or ethnicity were *not* found to be predictors of a child's relative status within the group or predictors of change from entry to discharge. The child's mental age, IQ, and the clinically determined developmental status were, however, significantly related to change in various dimensions of functioning. (Within this population the child's IQ and mental age are frequently a composite of clinical impressions and formal psychometric testing.)

The child's mental age (MA) became a substantially weaker indicator of capability and/or competence when the population was regrouped based on clinically determined developmental status into three subgroups: low, middle, and high functioning children. Within the subgroups, MA correlated with the level of functioning in some dimensions and not in others.

It had been hypothesized that change in functioning would be interdependent for children across dimensions; i.e., a child's increased awareness of the environment would be reflected simultaneously in a higher level of social awareness, a greater interest in materials, and usually an accompanying desire to communicate one's needs and feelings more explicitly. This was found to be true. This relationship among dimensions existed regardless of the sample size: total group, subgroups, or an individual child. The division into high (N = 10), middle (N = 11), and low (N = 19) functioning subgroups of children emphasized the fact that distinctive patterns of functioning existed for subgroups of children (Figure 10). The implications of these results for program development were clear:

> The findings suggest that programs should be implemented to work with multiple areas of development rather than on acquisition of segregated skills. Distinct subgroups did emerge, although within-group variability was considerable. In the child who was relatively unimpaired, all of our seven dimensions were necessary in order to describe qualitatively the child's ability and disabilities. The low functioning child,

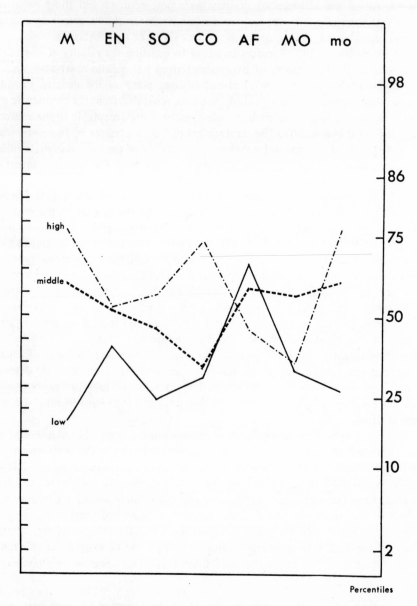

Figure 10. Functioning of subgroups in seven psycho-educational dimensions.

however, could be depicted through the use of groups of two or three dimensions (Gordon et al., 1975, Part I, p. 53).

Ultimately, it became apparent that a more refined analysis of one specific aspect of these children's functioning, their work with materials, might reveal data even more meaningful, both in the evaluation and development of curricular goals. Preliminary scaling of tasks denoting a child's competent work with materials has been piloted. Initial data on the interactions with materials (407 tasks with materials have been clinically scaled) of 40 very young multihandicapped children indicates strongly that this method of assessment may prove to be educationally significant in that the findings relate directly to actual classroom behaviors and activities. This method of educational assessment is being expanded to include a larger number of educational materials and being refined as a system available for use by other educators of deviant and "normal" children for assessment and/or prescription directly within the classroom. Based on these images or profiles of actual levels of performance of children, a teacher can readily develop individualized goals and instructional strategies appropriate and necessary for planning educational intervention for the young child.

Parallel to the individualized developmental therapy programs offered to the children (N = 40) was the program of support, translation of goals, interpretation of developmental status, and guidance offered to their parents through participation in the programs and meetings with the Project Director. Recommendations and expectations for parents were based on our growing knowledge and understanding of their specific concerns and needs. In the discussion section of Analysis of the Interaction between Program and Parents, Jacobson reported:

> The conclusion inevitably follows that counseling of these parents must be finely attuned to their individualized needs and characteristics. . . . Thus, it is possible to say that no interview sequence or the process of counseling can be predicted for any parent. The unfolding of interview sequences is specific to each parent or couple and thus, to some extent, is idiosyncratic. The educational therapeutic team learns much from parents. It was obvious that each and every one of them was as individuated in his or her concerns, anxieties, expectations, participation level, observational ability, capacity to learn to accept interpretations and specific guidance, ability to act upon them and reality orientation as the children were individuated in their syndromes of impairment and their levels of development and functioning (Gordon et al., 1975, Part II, p. 32).

The parents of all children expressed an overwhelming need for support and guidance (Gordon, submitted for publication). The examination of change in parental attitudes revealed ". . . that parents turn to the staff of a program for guidance when they encounter periods of special stress and seem almost incapable of coping with the handicapped children" (Gordon et al., 1975, Part II). It was further suggested that "parents were most suggestible and malleable and more open to change of behavior patterns. It may be that the maximal impact of counseling occurred at such periods when there was a great tendency to depend on the educational therapeutic team for help for themselves and for their children" (Gordon et al., 1975, Part II).

While the needs of each family were handled individually, there were common themes which permeated these interview sessions, such as concerns about the separation of the child from the family and the family from the child. These fears and anxieties were overcome or reduced through on-going discussion with the Project Director and over time by the demonstrated value of the program for their child. The majority of parents also expressed a similar focus of concern related to the child's current manifest ability—that concentration was on potential for improvement in motor ability or communicative skills. At the time of the discharge, it was documented in the analysis of their taped comments that all parents became increasingly cognizant of the multidimensional aspects of their child's functioning. Again, analysis of taped data and quantification of statements related to behaviors and situations observed at home and in school indicated that a majority of the parents had become more sensitive observers of their children's actions and reactions as they (the parents) learned to note specific performance patterns:

> Mrs. C: She was pretty good during the day, not bad with the playing at all. I can see what she has learned since she came here. . . . When she looks at a thing she stays with the toy, she seems to do it in a fashion like she does here.

Another mother revealed how her involvement in the Infant Program had given her a new perspective on the value of appropriate educational materials (toys):

> Mrs. JJ: The toys he used to have are no good. I got him a few new toys—simple little things: You put on a peg. And I got him a little puzzle. It keeps him interested. I could sit there and he doesn't start crying right away. I give him mechanical things: he'll look at it two seconds and start crying. Now you give him something, like his hand. . . . Most of the stuff they have around the Infant Room—that's the kind of toys now that I look for. And they're really simple, little nothings, you know, that really amuse him, which amazes me. I'll go out and get all these rare, rare looking toys that do amazing things and he doesn't like any of them. And pegs and blocks and things like that is what he really likes.

Responses to a questionnaire sent to parents at the conclusion of the study indicated an almost universal satisfaction with the program. One could suggest that there was a higher probability ". . . that parents learned to manage and stimulate their children more effectively as a result of their involvement and active participation in the infant program at IRM" (Gordon et al., 1975, Part II, p. 34).

Both analyses of data related to the handicapped children and their families were in harmony with the developmental-interaction educational goals of this staff. Pre- and post-outcome evaluation methodologies are more amenable to statistical methods but focus too often on isolated aspects of achievement or specific skills or restricted goals rather than on the dynamic process of growth and development. MacDonald (1974) states:

> The goals, in other words, are the crucial and significant aspect of the evaluation process, not the process of measuring. But as is often the case with men, our dreams outreach our means, and what we are witnessing in education today is a wholesale miniaturizing of goals to satisfy the primitiveness of our measurement abilities. . . . We have really gained very little and risked much if we allow our goals for schooling

to be determined by our ability to measure. . . . When we talk technologically about man we *objectify* him. That is, we *abstract* from the total potential of the subject or activities some crucial variable and proceed to act as if this is the entirety of the person or activity. . . .

STAFF EDUCATION—OUTREACH

The Project Director and educational and research staff of the preschool developmental programs at IRM have been and continue to be committed to sharing the experience and knowledge they have gained from working with more than 2,000 multihandicapped children below age 6. Traditional means of dissemination have been found to be of minimal assistance to the teacher with specific needs and many immediate questions. The department has, therefore, undertaken the responsibility for more direct exposure of personnel involved in integrating and/or educating specific groups of multihandicapped children. This approach has been multi-faceted, with roles ranging from: 1) intensive supervision of individuals, teaching interns assigned to the preschool and infant programs for extended periods; 2) provision of field experiences for university graduate students for time periods of several months to a full academic year; 3) interdepartmental orientations related to the subject of child development theory as it relates to planning educational and therapeutic intervention; 4) exposure of medical students, residents, pediatric physiatrists, and rehabilitation specialists to sound practices in delivering services to young children in an institutional setting; 5) mini-placements at IRM of 1 to 2-week duration for the educational staff/educational directors of Head Start and day care centers.

Independent of the duration of the "training" program, all individuals are exposed to the underlying educational philosophy, which, in turn, is reflected in methods chosen to study the child's behavior, assess the educational needs, and prescribe curricular goals. The structure, rationale, and educational position are described through a combination of workshops, seminars, and individual conferences. The comprehensive scope of the program is illustrated in the documentary film produced by this department, "Special Children, Special Needs." This film, projected for a broad audience of educators, rehabilitation specialists, and multidisciplinary personnel, depicts how the philosophy of the program has been translated into the design of three engineered environments, the goals, and the daily activities of the educational staff.

At first our focus was to serve small numbers of graduate students and teaching interns. From 1972–1975, based on the needs assessment of the Agency for Child Development, we had been involved with the in-service education of approximately 100 staff members per year from day care and Head Start centers located in Manhattan.[9]

It was judged then, when these outreach efforts were first initiated, that it would be unrealistic and reflect a cavalier attitude on our part if a plan were proposed that would

---

[9] Partially supported by a grant from the U.S. Office of Education, Bureau of Education for the Handicapped, Grant No. OEG-0-74-0535.

include *all* of the agencies in this large city which required assistance in their efforts to service handicapped children. Our expertise, as well as our commitment, is to the delivery of *sound* developmental programs, sensitive referrals, and effective follow up methods. It would be neither responsible nor feasible to propose that one resource center could provide services for a city the size of New York.

Our staff is even more acutely aware today, with the legal mandate for Head Start to integrate handicapped children, that each of the agencies requires guidance of varying patterns and scope. There are obvious limitations in many centers in the way in which they can cope with the identification and/or the integration of exceptional children into settings conventionally geared to servicing normal children. In addition, our department continues to be sensitive to a resistance to the mandate of integrating handicapped children at varying levels in different centers—a resistance that cannot be instantly ameliorated or handled.

We continue to work with Head Start centers[10] on as individualized a basis as that which we subscribe to for our children/families. This has been accomplished through 15 specialized workshops at the centers and at IRM based on the unique needs of each center, with topics ranging from "Observing the Work and Play of Children" to "Normal and Deviant Speech Patterns." This has supplemented the indepth miniplacements of teachers and administrative staff and large full-day workshops/seminars for the 10 centers to which we are presently committed in a consultation role.

We continue to be concerned with the children/families served in these centers. Children presently enrolled in these centers whose developmental level is questioned by their teachers are observed by members of the IRM staff. Specific recommendations are made to the teacher and, when necessary, additional evaluations by a psychologist, pediatrician, or other specialist may be recommended. On-going support is also offered in those instances when we refer a child from our developmental program.

A conviction was initially expressed that the major thrust of consultative effort and guidance should be individualized, based on an evaluation of each center's readiness and level of professional competence to benefit from specific types of consultative services. Our experience to date has further strengthened that conviction. It would be inconsistent for the program staff, as well as a disservice to the young disabled children and their families represented here, to support or accept a situation where any Head Start agency could respond effectively to the integration mandate without a sound "back-up" system and a clear plan for its implementation and guidance.

DISCUSSION

There has recently been a significant change in attitude toward handicapped children. There is growing recognition among many professionals concerned with deviant development that the very young child needs early and intensive treatment. There is an increased

---

[10] Under contract from the Lower East Side Head Start agencies.

awareness that "the major effect of chronic disease in early childhood is on later motor-linguistic, adaptive, and social behavior. If they are left untreated, handicapped children show increasingly deviant patterns of behavioral development; thus, one firmly established principle is to aim to establish the most normal sequence of development possible" (Ingram, 1973).

A comment by De Hirsch (1974) concerning a patient reflects a similar type of thinking: "But it is a great pity that intensive stimulation was not initiated when Pablo was thirty months old—long before he entered the nursery. I know we had some help there, but by this time the 'critical period', that time when the organism is most sensitive to specific kinds of stimulation, has passed." De Hirsch was speaking particularly about the language of the child and her belief that there is a biological and psychological timetable for its development. She further comments: "At later stages it is far harder to teach children processing in-put and activating in-put. And I am absolutely sure that severe processing difficulties at age three are the precursors of massive learning disabilities."

Judgments as to the appropriateness of an inpatient status for this intensive stimulation before the age of 3, of separation of child from family and the family milieu, have to be made with great sensitivity. In early literature, any separation from family and home was regarded as "noxious" elements of early experience, and always regarded as severely damaging. However, in recent and more sophisticated research, while confirming the importance of institutionalization as an "experience variable," its effects were shown to be less universally severe and modifiable by other coexisting elements of the experiences (Escalona, 1968). The coexisting elements of the experience, the quality and ratio of staff, the overall climate of the learning environment, availability of surrogate mothering, and the capacity to design and to provide an appropriate therapeutic milieu with a multidisciplinary investment for the child, which cannot be satisfied at home, justifies, we believe, our decision to recommend an inpatient program for selected groups of very young children with multiple developmental lags.

Many factors influence our judgment as to the appropriateness of inpatient admission. Among the questions to be weighed carefully for the very youngest population serviced in the Infant School are: 1) To what extent can the infant benefit from an intensive stimulation program based on the initial evaluation of the child's type and extent of physical disability, sensorial deficit, and mental, emotional, and social status? 2) To what extent should the assistance be focused more on the family rather than on the child, specifically when at initial screening we observe a severely involved youngster where a projection of change based on a 3-month inpatient program can be expected to be somewhat limited? Should the program be focused on support for the family in their long-term planning and on their immediate need to understand more fully the severity of the developmental delays of their child? 3) To what extent will separation of family from child allow for a break in the perpetuation of patterns of nonproductive interactional styles of the deviant member and the family? 4) To what extent do the families need relief and distance from the situation of coping psychologically and physically with the handicapped child whose care places unusual demands on both parents and siblings 5) To what extent can we realistically expect the parents to participate actively a full day each week while the child is an inpatient and benefit from his exposure to the prescribed program? 6) To what extent will the families be able to extrapolate and to gain from observation and participation in prescriptive teaching and therapy sessions? Will this participatory relationship result in an increased ability to stimulate the development of their own child once the child is discharged from inpatient status? and 7) To what extent do the gains projected as a result of admission to the inpatient program for a specific child (based on previous clinical experience with similar children) outweigh the possible emotional trauma of separation of the child from the family and/or the family from the child?

We would be less than candid not to express at this time some concurrent concerns related to inpatient admission for young children to *any* setting where they are exposed to a large number of people from different disciplines with distinctive patterns and modes of interacting with children. The educational staff sees itself as an advocate of the child in this setting. Our effort is directed toward minimizing the effect of medical interventions that are necessary, as well as in creating a sound climate for learning. The teaching staff directly and indirectly acts in the role of surrogate family, translating respect for the feelings of the children who, by virtue of their medical needs, may have to be involved in procedures that may cause anxiety and frustration. "A child undergoing surgery, or treatment of injuries, or medical investigation has problems which have to do with the inner meaning of these things for him and the stress he may be experiencing" (MacCarthy, 1974).

Another problem related to inpatient admission warrants discussion. In a hospital or a rehabilitation center, admission as an inpatient is of no financial problem for lower or lower middle class groups of families. Support is available for rehabilitation services needed by their children. It is the middle and upper middle class socioeconomic groups (not eligible for Medicaid or Bureau of Handicapped Children support) that are often deprived of easy access to these comprehensive services. The higher economic group feels that financial stress more strongly and is increasingly penalized by the constant rise of the cost of care. Need and costs for services are ongoing for chronically handicapped children, and too often they must be projected throughout the child's life. Insurance policies and major medical plans cover only a portion of the child's stay in a rehabilitation program. The remainder of the fiscal responsibility reverts to the family. This places the family under financial and psychological strain over and above the unusual initial burden of having a handicapped child as a member of the family.

Our experience suggests strongly that families with infants and young children at risk are families at risk. This is not a judgment made casually. For over 6 years data have been collected relating to the families' needs for intervention in the IRM infant program. Taped weekly interviews with the parent of each infant on program are collected. They focus primarily on educational goals, strategies, and accomplishments. However, in the course of these comparatively open-ended exchanges between the Project Director and the parent, there is a significant amount of information that has been accumulated, which points to the stress, anxiety, and burden of families with handicapped members. Problems directly related to the child's care and also those related to the effect of having a handicapped child on the relationship between husband and wife and on the stability and "normalcy" of other siblings are discussed. A colleague from England states it well: "Every family with a handicapped child or one with a chronic disease has an unenviable task which is on-going and onerous" (Morris, 1974). There is ambivalence expressed in the descriptions of the difficulties encountered in giving up the child even temporarily to someone else's care and the relief in being free from the heavy and lonely burden of providing for a child whose care requires more than the usual amount of mothering and nurturing.

The families we see are those who already have arrived at a point of "accepting" the existence of developmental dissonance or a "special problem" in their young- ster's development. Families often report a history of physicians ignoring their observations that there is something different in their child's development—different either from other children in the family or other children they have observed. They report a pattern of "shopping around" for medical clarification in response to their inability to accept the too frequently reported comment of pediatricians, "Don't worry; just give him time; he'll outgrow it." Many families serviced by the program have had their children assessed and evaluated and reevaluated—and could not find services to follow up an evaluation of developmental dysfunction. On the positive side, a statement can be made that today there are more intervention programs available, that assistance for the child can be sought and received in a multidisciplinary setting where every aspect of the child's development can be monitored and, whenever possible, deficit functioning can be ameliorated by a joint effort of highly professional multidisciplinary teams.

There are, however, still large numbers of young children, whose development is at risk, who are not yet in contact with professionals and resources that are available to assist in a way that can maximize their development. Many of the families of these children are not yet ready to accept the reality of their "differences" (with its associated stigma). Many of the child care agencies involved with providing partial services to these children are not equipped either to make the assessment or to plan a pattern of intervention or referral that is needed. Our own experience in working in an outreach effort with day care and Head Start personnel confirms this impression. Directors, teachers, and social service staff and family counselors report their feelings of inadequacy in providing sound services for the "exceptional child." They report, too, their experience with families who reject any suggestion that their children's behavior and development requires more than the "normal" child care services that are available in the neighborhood. We respect the frustration of agency staffs in their attempt to deal without adequate support services for children and families with prob- lems. We believe that both they and the children they attempt to assist are entitled to more.

The cult of today is to concentrate all efforts on "mainstreaming," "normalizing," and integrating *all* handicapped children in settings geared for a normal population. It is our contention that the people who project these plans indiscriminately do a disservice to both the handicapped child and his family and to the normal child and his family, as well as to the staff of the agencies to which these children are referred. We question how well the writers and program designers who are invested in these new trends really know the needs of the severely multihandicapped children or the functioning of a "normal" classroom situation for young children.

Twenty years of experience in the education of normal and abnormal young children suggests a more conservative approach and a more respectful one, we think, in establishing criteria for the integration of handicapped children in normal settings. We would suggest that there are: 1) some children who can *never* have their educational and medical needs met in other than a specialized setting, 2) another group of children can be integrated into a normal setting but *only after* having had intensive assessment and extended intervention first in a specialized, comprehensive setting with the input of a multidisciplinary staff and only after referral procedures are meticulously and sensitively processed with planned ongoing support, when indicated, from the professionals at the initial agency servicing the child, and 3) a group of children who can be integrated immediately into a normal setting after the child has had a sound comprehensive assessment and the staff of the center (to which the child is referred) has confidence that a supporting team and resources will be available, upon request, in the development of an appropriate program for that child based on those aspects of development identified in the initial assessment that warrant specific attention.

At this time the impact and the actual efficacy of integrating (mainstreaming) on children, families, and staff that service them have not been sensitively documented or studied. The questions of today are: What is the state-of-the-art in 1976? Who, when, where, and how are we to integrate young multi-handicapped children in settings designed for normal children and their families?

In summary, the tremendous investment of professional expertise required to soundly design, operate, and study effective programs for multihandicapped young children cannot be minimized. The range and varieties of disabilities that exist and coexist in the population of exceptional children seen today at the Institute cannot be simplistically treated by "cookbook" approaches and standardized texts supplemented by audiovisual presentations.

If developmental therapy of quality is to be provided that respects the individual differences of these deviant children, it must be recognized that the cost in terms of professional commitment and time is great. Only a mobilization and coordination of effort of all concerned professionals with the backing of city, state, and federal governments can possibly support such an investment. But, as long as there are children who carry the burden of these unusual problems in development, we cannot with dignity do less.

ACKNOWLEDGMENTS

The author would like to thank David Gitler and Ora Ezrachi for their assistance in the preparation of this summary statement.

APPENDIX

Sample Intent of Tutorial Session

I first gave N.D. the Montessori Cylinders. He had just come from a very active session in the playground, and it was my feeling that he might need a very structured, controlled material to bring him down to very directed play. Observing N.D. attempting to remove the cylinders in a chaotic, impulsive way, it was clear that I would have to structure the task even further. I did this simultaneously with an attempt to assess whether N.D. understood the concept of larger, smaller, largest, and smallest, bigger, etc. By controlling the speed at which he removed the cylinders as well as replaced the cylinders, I was able to get a better understanding of his ability to recognize and differentiate sizes. At the same time, it was very clear that the more the teacher provided external controls, the more effective N.D. could be. He is able to discriminate sizes, and he does understand the labels associated with gradations of size.

I next presented matching plaques of faces. This required the kind of investment of attention, visual concentration, that is most difficult for this boy, particularly because many people were entering and leaving the room in his direct line of vision. He had more trouble with this. While he was able to differentiate a face in which one eye was open and the other eye was closed, in contrast to matched plaques in which the face drawing had both eyes open, the task was too complicated for him to do under these environmental circumstances. (I would think that in a quieter atmosphere he would be able to be more effective with this task.) Interestingly, N.D. was not able to close one eye himself—wink— even though I demonstrated this action.

I switched materials and went to the puzzle of the boy and girl, once again verbally assisting him in making choices as to which piece to be approached at a particular time. This structuring of the demands of the puzzle, I felt, improved his performance. Left alone, I had the impression he would have been too disorganized to do it. Yet, with help he was able to complete the task, even the rotations of the bent arms of the girl and boy.

Earlier I offered the form box and structured this already defined material even further by having N.D. group the objects as he took them *out* of the box by their different shapes. This he did well. He labeled them and was reasonably accurate in counting the number of objects of each group (two or three). With this type of initial grouping he was able to insert the pieces in sequence into their correct holes, having difficulty only with the C-shaped form and the triangle. His problems were more of attention, I suspect, than of ability.

Ronnie Gordon, Examiner, and N.D.

Sample Log—Child BB

After others left, I brought over bowl, box of cereal, packets of sugar and small potato masher on a tray. She seemed to recognize the cereal immediately. Tried to open box.

Couldn't. I started to tear and pointed to it. BB finished the tearing independently. When it was opened, she held it up to her face and looked inside. Put hand in, took out a piece, and ate it. I demonstrated mashing cereal. Then I gave her the bowl and the masher. She rejected this physically and by making loud vowel protests. I showed her a sugar packet by shaking it. She took and attempted to open. Could not. I assisted as I had with box. I dumped some and encouraged her to complete the dumping. She showed no interest in dumping. Here I lost the sequence, but somehow I eventually reintroduced the masher. After watching me, she tried to adjust her grasp. At first she vocally protested at my interference, but the noise and the action of the mashing distracted her, and she began to mash independently with well coordinated movement (for her disability). She used her free hand to hold the bowl as she mashed. I gave her a spoon. She used it to eat a little. She was not really enthralled with the taste, so I brought a doll to feed. She had trouble coordinating the reach to the doll's mouth and in keeping the cereal on the spoon as she did. Fed herself a little more. Still not much interest in that. I asked her verbally to feed me. Did not. I demonstrated by taking her hand in mine and placing the spoon in my mouth. She then fed herself one spoonful.

Later she became intrigued with ribbon in doll's hair. Removed it. Held it to her own head in an effort to put it on. I made her a pony tail with it and brought a mirror for her to see. Looked in mirror. I tried to get her to put the doll away in a box. BB took it out again and hugged. Then she began removing all the doll play objects from the box and handing them to me. As she did so, I verbally labeled them for her. When I asked her, "Where does this go?" (about hat), she draped it over the doll's head. Also brought a sock to the foot. She also tried to put the tie-fastened shirt on the doll's head. This seemed reasonable since it had strings like the hat. Together we put everything back into the box. She moved to take out again, so I picked up the box lid and got her focused on putting that on. She could not manage that completely independently, but understood. I helped position it for her.

I pulled out her chair and told her to get down. She wiggled in her seat. Then I discovered that she was strapped in by a strap hidden by her dress. I unfastened. She slid down as I held her hands.

She became interested in the stack of boxes that DD was knocking over. BB had some brief interchange with him (vocal and eye contact). She also attempted to restack the boxes. DD suddenly hit her very hard in the face. She stopped her activity and looked at him with a very strong facial expression that was a mixture of anger and hurt. Clearly showed she did not like that.

At this point I had to phone P.T., speak with BB's mother in hall, etc., and lost the sequence. I do know that Mr. and Mrs. BB joined us for snack and that BB held together much better than she usually does when both parents are present.

At snack she poured her own juice with a little help from me in lifting and positioning.

After snack mother and father took her for a walk. BB walked out of I.R. independently on rollator.

LITERATURE CITED

Biber, B. 1964. Preschool Education. Bank Street Publ.

Biber, B., D. Wickens, and E. Shapiro. 1971. Promoting Cognitive Growth in Young Children. National Association for the Education of Young Children, Washington, D.C.

Bortner, M., and H. G. Birch. 1970. Cognitive capacity and cognitive competence. Amer. J. Ment. Def. 74: 735–744.

Cazden, C. B. 1974. Play and metalinguistic awareness. One dimension of language experience. Urban Rev. 7: 28–39.

De Hirsch, K. 1974. Pablo. Notes toward a therapy. Urban Rev. 7: 40–42.

Diller, L., W. A. Gordon, H. Hanesian, et al. 1973. Response patterns in brain-damaged children and teaching styles. Final Report. United States Office of Education. Project No. 422257. OEG-0-70-3361 (607). Washington, D.C.

Dryman, I., H. G. Birch, and S. J. Korn. 1970. Verbalization and action in the problem-solving of six-year-old children. Yeshiva University (unpublished manuscript).

Escalona, S. K. 1968. The Roots of Individuality. Aldine, Chicago.

Freeman, R. 1967. Emotional reactions of handicapped children. Rehab. Lit. 28: 274–282.

Gordon, R. 1969. The design of a pre-school "learning laboratory" in a rehabilitation center. Rehabilitation Monograph #39. Institute of Rehabilitation Medicine, New York University Medical Center.

Gordon, R. 1972. The design of a pre-school therapeutic playground. An outdoor "learning laboratory." Rehabilitation Monograph #47. Institute of Rehabilitation Medicine, New York University Medical Center.

Gordon, R., D. Gitler, B. Schwartz, O. Ezrachi, and D. C. Brenner. 1975. Evaluation of behavioral change. Part I: Study of multi-handicapped young children. Final Report to the U.S. Department of Health, Education, and Welfare, Office of Education, Bureau of Education for the Handicapped, Project No. H0050SJ, Grant No. OEG-0-72-5386.

Gordon, R., C. Jacobson, D. Gitler, B. Schwartz, O. Ezrachi, and D. C. Brenner. 1975. Evaluation of behavioral change. Part II: Interaction between program and parents. Final Report to the U.S. Department of Health, Education, and Welfare, Office of Education, Bureau of Education for the Handicapped, Project No. H0050SJ, Grant No. OEG-0-72-5386.

Gordon, R., D. White, and L. Diller. 1972. Performance of neurologically impaired preschool children with educational materials. Except. Child. 38: 428–437.

Gordon, R. Special Families of Special Children—Special Needs of Multi-handicapped Children Under Six and their Families—One Opinion. Educ. & Training of the M.R. (submitted for publication).

Hartley, R., L. K. Frank, and R. M. Goldenson. 1952. Understanding Children's Play. Columbia University Press, New York.

Ingram, T. S. 1973. Habilitation and rehabilitation. Devel. Med. Child Neurol. 15: 421–422.

Kohlberg, L., and R. Mayer, 1972. Development as the aim of education. Harvard Ed. Rev. 42: 449–496.

MacCarthy, P. 1974. Communication between children and doctors. Devel. Med. Child Neurol. 16: 279–285.

MacDonald, J. B. 1974. An evaluation of evaluation. Urban Rev. 7: 3–14.

Morris, D. 1974. Coming to terms with social implications. G. P. Magazine, January 18, London.

Piaget, J. 1968. The mental development of the child. *In* J. Piaget (ed.), Six Psychological Studies, p. 15. Vintage Books, New York.

White, B. L., and J. C. Watts. 1973. Experience and Environment: Major Influences on the Development of the Young Child. Prentice-Hall, Englewood Cliffs, N.J.

Wright, H. F. 1967. Recording and Analyzing Child Behavior. Harper and Row, New York.

Film: Special Children, Special Needs. 22 minutes, color, sound, 16 mm. Campus Film Distributors Corp., New York.

The National Collaborative Infant Project

Una B. Haynes, R.N., M.P.H.

The Collaborative Infant Project is directed and coordinated by United Cerebral Palsy Associations, Inc., (UCPA) and is subsidized in part by a grant from the Bureau for Education of the Handicapped (BEH). This project is now in its third year of operation.

OVERVIEW OF THE PROJECT

Collaborating Centers

Initially, the project involved a consortium of five centers at different locations across the United States which were already serving atypical infants under 2 years of age and their families. These centers, which employed a variety of funding, administrative, and staffing patterns, were interested in a collaborative effort to improve their services and make them more comprehensive.

The Meeting Street School, located in Providence, Rhode Island, and described by Denhoff and Hyman in this volume, is a chapter of the National Easter Seal Society for Crippled Children and Adults. The center in New Orleans, Louisiana, is an affiliate of United Cerebral Palsy Associations, Inc. Both of these agencies are supported, in the main, by voluntary funds. The Atypical Infant Nursery (now called the Infant Development Center) in Kentfield, California, is operated under the aegis of the Mental Health and Mental Retardation Program of Marin County, a tax-supported service. The other two centers in the original consortium are affiliated with universities: the University of California at Los Angeles (UCLA) and the University of Iowa at Iowa City. The latter program, located in a rural state, provides periods of residential services (the only one of the original five that incorporates this type of program). Both universities have access to state official tax dollar support. The UCLA-based infant service depends to a larger degree on additional funds from a variety of resources.

The UCPA Project is one of 146 funded by the Office of Education of BEH to identify and to demonstrate exemplary models of services. Referred to collectively as the First Chance Network, each of these projects is also expected to replicate exemplary models of service in whole or in part. UCPA's replication activity is reflected by the addition, since 1971, of 19 other centers, called ripple centers, 14 of which are fully operational and five of which are now in the activation process.

Two of the ripple centers applied for and received BEH grants and are now members of the First Chance Network in their own right. However, they have continued to be very significant contributors to the UCPA project's total body of knowledge and experience. These two are located at the University of Hawaii and at the Suffolk County Rehabilitation Center in Commack, Long Island.

Another pattern of community support and funding for the programs has evolved regarding the other 12 fully operated ripple centers and the five additional centers that are now in the activation process. All of these centers have obtained or have been helped to identify and to mobilize a variety of resources to fund their operations. This is a pattern that will be followed as new centers are added in the future. Attention is drawn to the importance of local funds to support operations for a variety of reasons.

The UCPA Project has focused primary attention on providing comprehensive services for atypical infants from birth to 2 years of age and for their families. Recent legislation, for instance in Massachusetts, suggests that some public schools may begin to turn attention to providing their services for handicapped children from birth. But such services are not yet implemented. A few of the centers in the collaborative project, for example those located in California, are able to transfer many of the children to public school by the age of 3 years because the schools there will accept them at this age. However, most states do not yet provide public school programs until ages 5 or 6.

There are both strong proponents for, and others less favorable to, the principle of providing public school services for handicapped children from birth or as soon thereafter as the handicap is identified. Meanwhile, the collaborative project has faced the reality that other sources of support are needed here and now for atypical infants, and a variety of these resources are being used. These include, but are not restricted to, the fund raising activities of agencies such as United Cerebral Palsy Associations, Inc., the National Easter Seal Society for Crippled Children and Adults, and the National Association for Retarded Citizens. During the past year, it has been possible to mobilize some Revenue Sharing monies and other tax dollars available locally to support operations. These may become a very significant resource until public schools reach down to serve younger children. One publication of the collaborative project (in preparation) addresses these issues, identifies the various resources and the important components involved in obtaining community approval and support alone these lines.

From the onset of this project's activity, there has been a conscious effort not to retain an infant in the specialized centers or expend monies in this way if the child's needs and those of the family can be met by a generic community facility. In order to facilitate this type of transfer, the project centers have been developing a variety of outreach services. For instance, in the past year, workshops, seminars, and other competency building activities were conducted for more than 1,000 persons employed in generic agency settings. These included 736 from public schools, 86 from local day care facilities, 101 from Head Start, and 104 from public and private nursery schools.

During this same period, the collaborative project centers were actively serving 834 infants. From this total, 42 were transferred and integrated into the normal population groups in public and private nursery schools and in Head Start programs. There were 93 additional children who achieved transfer to the public schools.

To gain perspective of the many factors involved, it may be of interest to review briefly some of the characteristics of the target population and the goals, objectives, and activities of this project.

Characteristics of the Population, Casefinding, and Related Activities

A probe of the data pool in March, 1974, based on a sample of 503 infants, provides the data given in Table 1. The frequency of oral-pharyngeal problems in this population,

Table 1. Characteristics of the population from the March 1974 study

Diagnostic characteristics	Percentage of total sample (N=503)	Percentage breakdown
Cerebral palsy	54.4	
Severe		30.7
Moderate		37.4
Mild		27.2
Suspect		4.7
Minimal brain damage	22.5	
Diagnosed		6.6
Suspect		15.9
Visual handicap	37.5	
Blind		15.6
Partial loss		40.8
Suspect loss		43.6
Hearing handicap	12.3	
Deaf		14.5
Partial loss		20.0
Suspect		65.5
Seizure disorders	17.1	
Frequent		7.6
Occasional		9.5
Oral-pharyngeal problems	41.5	
Diagnosed		33.2
Suspect		8.3
Manifest in:		
Speech disorders		83.0
Feeding problems		17.0
Behavior problems	28.4	

composed primarily of patients with cerebral palsy, is not unexpected. The high frequency of speech and feeding disorders associated with early oral-pharyngeal problems indicates the prospective training and service needs associated with these problems. The high frequency of behavior problems among these children (28.4 percent) indicates that these problems represent a significant dimension for management.

The focus of the collaborating centers on very young infants had been expected by some to result in a population with a high proportion of genetically determined conditions. However, this does not seem to be the case, at least as far as this sampling of infants is concerned. Within this group, there are 17.7 percent with some type of known genetically determined condition; 11.1 percent of these are infants with Down's syndrome.

Since the infants in the project are young, (54 percent under 1 year of age at time of application and 15 percent under 6 months), there is understandable caution in arriving at a diagnosis unless the evidence is reasonably clear. But in this sampling, 68 percent have a specific diagnosis.

This project was designed and funded as a demonstration, not a research effort. The data pool is viewed as but one aspect in the total spectrum of evaluation. However, there are some interesting bits of information beginning to surface which appear worthy of some definitive research effort, if monies can be mobilized to pursue investigations.

For instance, in another sampling of the population, 25 percent of parents reported suspecting a problem at birth, 44 percent suspected at 1 month, 55 percent by 3 months, and 72 percent by 6 months. Interestingly, there seems to be no correlation between the mother's education or social class and the time a problem was suspected. Also, if they truly suspect or "know" this early, there is a significant lag time between their first suspicion and the time of their application to the centers for service. In this sampling, 66 percent have a lag time of over 6 months, 37 percent a lag time of over 1 year, and 10 percent a lag time of 2 years or more.

The lag times are about equally long regardless of the mother's education or the family's social class. As expected, there is a suggestion in the data that the higher the mother's education, the more likely she is to have a referral from a private physician, whereas the less educated mothers are more likely to be referred by public health nurses or social workers. Forty-five percent of the referrals come from private physicians, 19 percent from clinic-based physicians, 5.5 percent from public health nurses, and 7.5 percent from some sort of public agency. While the difference is not large, there is some evidence that public health nurses and social workers make referrals at an earlier age than do the physicians. UCPA's medical director is currently activating a consortium including representatives from the American Academy of Pediatrics, the American Academy on Family Practice, and the American Academy of Cerebral Palsy to look at these data and to address some of these factors, among others.

Initially, several of the collaborating centers had a policy whereby only physician referrals would be accepted. However, it appears that certain segments of society are more likely to have contact with public agencies than with physicians. Some of the centers that previously required a physician referral have broadened their policies to accept referrals from other sources including family-initiated applications for service. This is then followed by appropriate contact with the hospital where the infant was born, or with any physician, clinic, or other resource the family might have utilized on the infant's behalf before applying.

One center, located in an area with many low income families, recognized that many of the families at highest risk of having an atypical infant did not have a family physician. However, many of these families received some continuing service from the health department, particularly the public health nurses. As the infant service program was being mounted, the center, in collaboration with the health department, conducted a workshop for the public health nurses on early detection of developmental delay or aberration. Clinical experience in appraisal of the infant was reinforced 1 month later. Since personnel changes occurred during the first year of the infant service operations, the health department requested and cooperated in a second workshop for new personnel 1 year later. It is now planned to continue this program in the near future. This infant center receives 22.7 percent of its referrals from public health nurses, in contrast to the 5.5 percent public health nurse referral rate shown in the pooled data from all the collaborating centers. There may be other variables involved here, but it would be interesting to see if this type of center outreach program would have the same results elsewhere.

At this time, it appears that babies are beginning to be referred at an earlier age. More data are needed before this can be established as a definite trend. Meanwhile, one center changed its name from "The Atypical Infant Nursery" to "Infant Development Center." This happened after this center achieved a working relationship with the physicians and other personnel in the nearby hospital's obstetrical and newborn nursery staff and began to receive referrals directly from the intensive care nursery for newborns at risk.

The Infant Development Center staff has now offered assistance to personnel in the newborn nursery to help with early detection of anomalies and dysfunctions. It is recognized that many families whose infants are transferred to the intensive care nursery soon after birth are already aware that all is not well. If the baby continues to present a challenge to the family's nurturing competencies after hospital discharge and/or if the family feels insecure or anxious about coping, referral can be made directly to the Infant Development Program. The name of the center does not signal that the baby "needs" to be "handicapped."

Some knowledge about the costs of operating the services is already available. At the present time, a group of the collaborating centers have helped to design and carry out a data collection effort detailing the numbers and types of contacts provided to each infant and family over stated periods of time. These data will provide means for looking at the costs of activities in relation to the diagnosis at entry and exit, plus other components. There exists a real need to study cost effectiveness but this demands a significant, specialized effort and funding.

Principles of Service Design

Provision of the support and help required to aid the baby and family during early life is fundamental to the program design even if the suspect baby eventually proves to be normal. Brazelton (1961) called attention to the early interactions of a "difficult" infant noting the strong influence he wields in determining the nature of the mother-child relationship and how the resulting problems in this relationship tend to reinforce the difficulties of the child's psychosocial and physical adaptations to the environment. Such a child can create a significant stress in what might otherwise be a normally nurturing family environment. As a consequence, in developing models of service, consideration must be given to providing services during a stormy or otherwise anxiety producing period of infancy even though it is not assured that the infant will eventually prove to be definitively disabled or handicapped.

Serious consideration has been given to the adverse effects a poor environment can have on an infant by a number of projects that offer appropriate compensatory services to disadvantaged or culturally deprived children. However, attention is called here to the fact that the birth of an infant whose behaviors pose difficulties may adversely effect what might previously have been deemed a "normal" family. Therefore, the infant with early appearing atypical behaviors that present a potentially adverse effect upon the mother and others in his environment deserves attention in the development and implementation of early childhood program. These matters will be referred to again in greater detail in the discussions about normal attachments of infants to parents and caregivers (and particularly to the mother). Fostering and maintaining normal attachments while rendering adequate service to an infant with multiple dysfunctions constitutes another important component in service design and implementation.

In any event, whether or not the infant served early in life later proves to be normal or handicapped, a serious effort has been mounted by all of the collaborating centers to provide as normalizing an environment as possible for all of the infants and their families. Efforts have been made to accomplish this objective in all cases, including the most complex cases that may require several types of professional intervention. When there has been need to integrate medical therapy components with the educational and psychosocial aspects of the program for multiply disabled infants, this has resulted in an approach departing significantly from the traditional approach of rehabilitation service or early education program design.

Goals, Objectives, and the Technical Assistance System

When the UCPA project was initiated in 1971, the primary goal was to identify and distill from the consortium centers the unique aspects of exemplary services that might then be incorporated into an exemplary model or models. Some of the objectives within this overall goal were:

1. To pool knowledge, skills, and experiences for purposes of mutually enriching and expanding services and making them more comprehensive

2. To focus upon the role of the educator in defining what the baby should learn in the first 2 years of life, the learning barriers to be considered in the presence of neurosensory and neuromotor dysfunctions, and what the teacher does in direct contact with the infant and family to overcome them; an additional related objective for the educator is to teach

other team members how to help the baby to learn in the course of their interactions with the infant and family

3. To strengthen the role of the family as the primary teacher and caregiver for children under 2 years of age while, at the same time, avoiding deleterious effects on the life style of the family

4. To develop a model, or models, encompassing those elements that are judged to be the most effective in terms of infant developmental progress with a strong focus upon cognitive development as promoted by the family's nurturing role and the efficient use of personnel

5. To increase team effectiveness in the design and implementation of service programs (this involves a "marriage" between medically related and educationally related parameters of service geared to meet the needs of infants identified as atypical early in life, many of whom tend to evidence multiple dysfunctions)

6. To inform both the scientific and the lay communities about early intervention programs for atypical infants and their families

These goals are being met through various vehicles under the direction and supervision of the project's advisory council. Specialized task forces have been activated to foster staff development and training, evaluation, parent and family involvement, infant curriculum development, and information dissemination.

The presence of multiple dysfunctions among the approximately 1,000 infants now enrolled in this project and the associated special needs of their parents have led to special adaptations in the nature and organization of the service delivery systems. Infants a few months of age cannot tolerate excessive or inconsistent handling by a variety of adult caregivers. The formation of normal attachments between the atypical infant and his parents (and particularly his mother) are at risk in these stressed families. As a consequence, while the collaborating centers are staffed with representatives from a variety of professional disciplines pertinent to the total habilitation of the baby, direct interventions by multiple members of the staff are kept to a minimum consistent with enhancement of the infant's progress. Concerned attention is given to mobilizing the strengths of the parents as the primary teachers and "therapists" during the early months of life. An adaptation of the traditional interdisciplinary team function has been developed. It is identified as the "transdisciplinary approach." This will be discussed later in more detail. A new text on the subject (Haynes and Hutchison, in press) will provide definitive treatment of the transdisciplinary approach.

The project's information dissemination program is moving forward. Two volumes of a bibliography with annotations from approximately 1,500 articles and books from the pertinent literature are now available in limited quantity on short-term loan. Two films are available on loan from UCPA Headquarters in New York. The first is focused upon early detection of anomaly and dysfunction and the second, on a unique environmental design called "The Fun House."

A self-directed learning system for use by agency personnel and parents has been developed. The content of each module focuses upon identified service needs of atypical infants and families. The first module is now being field tested.

Other project components include:

The uniform collection of specified data by all participating centers; these data are computerized, analyzed by the project evaluator, and fed back to the centers on a periodic basis

Staff development workshops for the participating center teams

Provisions for interteam visits

Provisions for specialized, on site, consultations

Provision of an experienced, interdisciplinary "project (site) visit team"

The MIP (Measuring Interaction Project)—by means of a special contract, participating center teams may submit video tapes of staff members teaching parents how to teach and/or otherwise work or play with their child plus a second tape of the parents carrying out the program with the infant. These tapes are critiqued by a panel of experts at the University of Washington in Seattle. Both audio and written feedback is provided for the center participants. This feedback may be used by the participants for self-directed learning or, with their consent, for programs of in-service education. The first module within the proposed self-directed learning system (which will be made available for much wider dissemination) is based upon the experiences derived from this special endeavor. The focus is upon the teaching styles of staff and parents and guidance toward the achievement of exemplary skills.

The information dissemination effort is further implemented by additional materials now under preparation for publication. These include: *Guidelines for the Infant Curriculum; Guidelines for Staff Development; The Project Visit Team: Its Composition, Its Functions, Its Findings;* a report on findings from 100 indepth interviews with parents; a series of technical papers concerned with evaluation, training and treatment techniques, and adapted equipment items plus an analysis of the statistical data from the project as a whole. Appendix A at the end of this chapter contains an outline of the technical assistance system which has been field tested extensively in regard to the centers added to the project during the first 3 years. This system will now be used on behalf of the new centers.

Throughout the years of this project's activity, a major concern and a major influence upon the evolution of the service models stemmed from the characteristics of the target population. One factor of interest is the lack of "segregation by handicap" in the collaborating centers. However, service appropriate to the needs of babies whose primary problems are visual, auditory, neuromotor, behavioral, and disorders of consciousness, acting singly or in combination, must be very carefully planned and carried out. There must be consultants and staff with competency sufficient to see that the very specialized needs receive due attention within the broad context of services needed by all the infants and their families.

The service delivery models and the staff development and technical assistance system have already been field tested in a variety of locations and situations. Thirty-two percent of our families live in middle sized cities. Fifteen percent live in either small cities under 50,000 population or rural areas not near a large or middle size city. The collaborating centers are located in 17 different states (Florida, Georgia, Mississippi, Louisiana, North

Carolina, Delaware, Pennsylvania, New Jersey, New York, Rhode Island, Michigan, Ohio, Iowa, Kansas, California, Oregon, and Hawaii). One agency joined the collaborative effort with an original budget allocation of $3,000 per year of its total funds for the infant service component. It was able to mount this program on a part-time basis by part-time reassignment of its medical therapy staff, strengthening the educational, psychosocial components, and allocating space in its own rehabilitation center. Another agency entered the project with full-time staff and full-time operations, and budgeting in excess of $100,000. Other centers fall between these two examples.

Staff Functions

Until the report on the first 3 years of project collaborative endeavor are completed, it may be of interest to review some of the literature and the experience that led to the evolution of the transdisciplinary approach to staff functions.

The transition to the present approach has been gradual. Elements first began to be delineated, strengthened, and studied more precisely in the course of an earlier project involving collaboration by multiple agencies nationally organized by UCPA and funded in part by the Division of Developmental Disabilities (then called the Mental Retardation Division), Social Rehabilitation Services, Department of Health, Education, and Welfare Grant (56-P-70773-2-01). This project focused upon the improvement of services for individuals with extensive sensory and motor problems in addition to intellectual deficit. A report on this project has been included in the previously mentioned text (Haynes and Hutchison, in press). Very briefly, the term cross-modality was evolved in the course of this first project to call attention to the several modalities within each discipline from which choices could be made to meet the specific needs of each individual in the target population. As the programs were implemented in five cooperating state institutions for the retarded, the term "cross-disciplinary" began to be used to call attention to the fact that specific modalities in the province of a particular discipline could be learned and used by other disciplines in a framework of instruction and team interaction. Team members testing the concept in action found themselves both willing and able to move beyond shared modalities and to share more broadly with each other. As the idea of cross-modality was extended, the phrase "cross-disciplinary" was used to describe the fuller exchange of information, knowledge, and skills across disciplinary lines.

On the advice of lexicographers, the word "transdisciplinary" was invoked by Professor Dorothy Hutchison, the major consultant on staff education in both projects. Transdisciplinary is a more accurate, acceptable, and appropriate term for the following reasons: 1) it lends itself to more consistent interpretation and translation; 2) it suggests a logical and consistent progression via continuing education from the unidisciplinary stance which is the outcome of basic professional education; 3) it connotes the essence of the approach which is, in fact, a transaction among team members who are professional providers of services, and parents or parent surrogates.

Dr. E. Denhoff, the Director of the Meeting Street School Center, has traced, in the year-end report, the transitions that took place in the course of this project. This report highlights the changes from the more traditional interdisciplinary team approach to the transdisciplinary model of staff function. The current model is well illustrated in Dr. Denhoff's chapter reported in this volume. It may be of interest to those who are concerned with infants who have multiple dysfunctions and with their families to review here some of the factors that influenced the use of the transdisciplinary concept. The following discussion reflects the project director's overview.

FACTORS INVOLVED IN THE
TRANSDISCIPLINARY MODEL OF SERVICE DELIVERY

Project Director's Perspective

The body of knowledge now available in each of the areas of professional specialization is now so vast that no one member of a team can be expected to develop the depth of understanding required to differentially appraise all the strengths or all the aspects of dysfunction which are found by definitive study of a child or his family. It seems unreasonable to expect that preparation in any one of the specialty areas might be sufficiently focal or broad enough to consider and determine which of the many available approaches or techniques might be the approach of choice for an atypical infant and its family at any one time. Also, consideration must be given to the many special circumstances arising at various ages and stages of development. It is axiomatic that no child or family should be denied the full depth and breadth of professional competency that might be brought to bear on their behalf. As a consequence, an interdisciplinary team of specialists reflecting all parameters of cognitive, psychosocial, and physical development remains very important to the design, selection, and monitoring of the adequacy of intervention programs for atypical infants.

In addition to the wide range of disabilities mentioned earlier, it was noted during the early months of the infant project that 85 percent of the infant population have multiple dysfunctions. At first glance, the traditional model of interdisciplinary rehabilitation service would appear appropriate. An interdisciplinary team would function as usual for diagnosis and evelution, and the team members would then provide the infants with the medical surveillance, nursing, physical, occupational and speech therapy needed for the alleviation or remediation of the medical problems. However, when dealing with infants in the first months of life, the classical model of interdisciplinary service deliver must be viewed with some caution.

The traditional approach, which is still followed in many centers today, originated during a period in which rehabilitation concern focused on the creation of centers capable of restoring the war injured to the highest possible level of function. Study of the variety of personnel, the types of training they would need, and how they might function together on behalf of the disabled person led to the forging of the "interdisciplinary approach" to rehabilitation. This is an approach whereby a variety of specialists trained for solo practice learned to work together in new ways. Each member of the team shared expertise in the diagnostic and evalution studies required to design a comprehensive program plan. Thereafter, depending upon the type and extent of disability, the physical therapist might, for instance, treat the patient to foster ambulation; the occupational therapist to improve hand function or carry out activities of daily living, while the speech therapist might focus upon the relevant aspects of speech and/or language. Meanwhile, the social worker, psychologist, rehabilitation nurse, or other team members might be assigned, singly or in combination (depending on client needs), to help with other aspects of the total rehabilitation process. Customarily a physician headed the team, arranged for the various consultants involved in the evaluation, listened to the opinions of team colleagues, and then prescribed the nature and extent of the various therapies and other interventions to be carried out.

It was earlier assumed that this traditional approach to rehabilitation using personnel prepared with this orientation was automatically the best possible approach to the management of infants with medically related disabilities which are of developmental origin. Experience has shown that this traditional approach is not necessarily the most appropriate for several reasons.

First, it must be remembered that the working concept of the rehabilitation team employing the interdisciplinary approach involves helping persons who had previously known normalcy and who had a spectrum of normal life experiences before an injury or disease led to disability. There are obviously significantly different requirements for approaches appropriate to persons who have never known normal life experiences. Many of the generic programs of professional preparation and many post graduate courses in rehabilitation for physicians, therapists, nurses, social workers, counselors, and other personnel still focus very heavily upon the "re" in rehabilitation. This body of knowledge and skills is not transferable without modification to the needs of the developmentally disabled. It is of great importance, then, that all concerned with services for infants must have a sound knowledge and understanding of normal growth, plus the impact of dysfunction upon the total spectrum of development. They must also be skillful in developmental approaches to therapeutic interventions.

A second factor to be considered is the amount of handling to which an infant will be subjected. It will be remembered that in the earlier days of the interdisciplinary approach, the sharing of expertise in diagnosis and planning was followed by direct intervention on the part of all team members whose skills were pertinent to the implementation of the program plan. If the infant has multiple disabilities, use of this "classical" approach could subject an infant to handling by as many as three to eight members of a team all actively involved in the implementation of the program plan. For instance, the nurse might be assigned to help with general health needs, maintaining hydration, dealing with constipation, special care of the skin, teaching the mother ways to bathe and comfort the infant, or the other myriad of daily concerns that can arise when a mother has to cope with the needs of an atypical baby. Concomitantly, the physical, occupational, and speech therapists, and others might be directly involved in some segregate aspect of the infant's functioning and/or the environment in which he is nurtured.

During the recent past there has been increasing concern on the part of thoughtful members of interdisciplinary teams, and particularly on the part of specialists in child growth and development, about the impact upon multiply disabled infants who are subjected to so much individualized intervention for such a significant part of their total childhood. Since the infant who is atypical or with some kind of disability is still not sick in the usual sense of the word, other questions might be asked. If he is constantly "treated" by uniformed personnel in a hospital-like milieu, what will this do to his developing concept of self? How will this effect his perception of his parents, the broader family constellation, and the neighbors? Will he not be perceived and treated as a "sick" child?

Before discussing the many adaptations that were made to the traditional ways of providing the medically related services these infants need, attention is first directed to other factors such as the cognitive and psychosocial needs of the infants and their families. Project personnel were aware that research in the area of cognitive development reinforced the importance of providing adjunctive educational and related psychosocial services to supplement medical management and to do so early in life.

Early Infant Learning

A growing body of research evidence supports the view that the young infant, given appropriate experience, is an active learner. Lipsett (1967) has demonstrated the infant's ability to discriminate complex visual patterns as early as the second day of life. Siqueland (1969) presents evidence that there are classes of exteroceptive stimuli, possibly in each of the sensory modalities, which are positive stimuli for the infant and which support motivated approach behaviors. He further suggests that "the elaboration of such diverse behavioral patterns as head movements, visual fixation and tracking, smiling and vocalization may be strongly influenced by their increasing effectiveness in providing the infant with diverse proximal and distal stimuli which function as reinforcers for the infant." Additional support for this view is found in the work of Butterfield (1974) who has demonstrated the infant's responsiveness to variation in frequency of auditory stimuli, and by Papousek (1967) who has shown the infant's selective head turning response to different auditory stimuli. There is evidence, too, that infant development can be improved through training. White and Held (1973) showed that an infant's grasping at objects can be accelerated.

Piaget (1952), Gesell (1947), and others have called attention to the importance of the infant's ability to coordinate and refine sensory input and response output. Kephart (1960), Strauss (1955), and Barsch (1967) have stressed the importance of sensorimotor intactness, its relation to later cognitive development, and the benefits of early physical, sensorimotor activity and movement upon the developing child.

As a consequence of these and other research developments, it appeared desirable to the project planners that the program of management involve the expertise of the early childhood educator, even during the first weeks and months of life. Alerted as soon as it is known or suspected that one or more sensorimotor avenues to learning may be impaired, the educator can help suggest alternate ways of presenting stimuli to foster cognitive development concomitant with the efforts of other specialists to further evaluate, remediate, and/or alleviate the sensorimotor deficits.

Of related interest is the evaluation of the parents' (and particularly the mother's) "teaching style" and the milieu in which the infant is being nurtured. Some mothers are excellent teachers, others are not. Some adapt their basic teaching style to an atypical infant's needs fairly easily, others need sustained help. During this early period there is frequently a high degree of motivation on the part of the parent. The mother can be guided by an expert teacher to achieve skill and reward in the "ping-pong" relationship of fostering attending behaviors by watching for and reinforcing correct responses, and by the appropriate selection and use of stimuli.

Education versus Stimulation

In many reports of programs for atypical infants, the terms "infant stimulation" and "early childhood education" are used synonymously, and there is general acceptance of the view that the infant needs appropriate stimuli to enhance its development. It should be pointed out, however, in dealing with a target population within which there is a significant number of infants with an impaired central nervous system, there must be discrete differentiation of the impaired and non-impaired infants.

The infant who is essentially normal or merely developmentally delayed can most often cope quite effectively in an environment containing apparently "excessive" stimuli. For instance, normal babies in crowded circumstances can frequently "turn off" and "tune out" all high decibel ambient noise, excessive visual and physical stimulation. With intact adaptive mechanisms, they can initiate appropriate self-comforting behaviors and can more readily cope effectively to achieve a reasonable amount of rest. Obviously, a less hectic environment permitting selective attention to a limited variety of stimuli is desirable for normal infants; it is crucial to the infant with multiple impairments.

The infant with an impaired central nervous system can be at special risk in an excessively stimulating milieu. He may not be able to "tune out" and "turn off" in the presence of multiple visual and auditory stimuli. Excess extensor tone, an aberrant tonic neck reflex pattern, an oral-pharyngeal problem, or other sensorimotor dysfunction of central origin can quite likely inhibit the infant's ability to achieve self-comforting behaviors. For instance, the presence of a hyperactive Moro reflex can cause widespread involuntary body motion, sharply awakening the infant when the crib or carriage is jostled, or when he hears a loud noise.

As a consequence, and without drawing too fine a semantic line, project personnel try not to use the term "infant stimulation" when describing their problems. The program goal is a discrete selection of appropriately monitored program elements individually designed to meet the needs of the baby and the family in the environment in which they live.

Attachment Behaviors

An additional factor of importance early in the infant's life is the achievement of normal attachment between the infant and the parents, particularly to the mother. Bowlby (1969) points out that attachment (and attachment behavior) develops as a consequence of proximity and reciprocal interaction. He maintains that the infant has a bias toward attachment to a single figure, usually the mother or parent surrogate, but that attachments can develop to other persons. The nature of other attachments that may develop can both affect the attachment to the mother and the role of the mother in relationship to her child. Rutter (1972), in reassessing maternal deprivation, points particularly to the risk factors in the formation of normal attachments which are present in the stressed family. It is a rare circumstance when the birth of a deviant child does not cause family stress. As a consequence, there are several infant- and family-centered aspects worthy of considerable study in the evolution of appropriate models of service if procedures are to be implemented which do not interfere with formation of normal attachments.

Summarizing briefly, the target population tends to evidence multiple dysfunctions. Assigning many different specialists to work with every area of the infant's dysfunction can result in varied and excessive handling. Using the traditional model of interdisciplinary service, there can be an excessive number of separate adults interacting with the infant "between" the mother and baby. The formation of normal attachments between mother and child is already at risk in a stressed family. How much of this direct, segregate handling is really necessary? How many of these discrete, one-to-one interventions must be provided by a special therapist, nurse, or teacher? Is it not possible to transfer a large part of this knowledge and skill to the parents? In what ways, at what intervals, by whom, and with what continuum of support and assistance can the parent be enabled to meet the infant's need and in a manner most congenial to development and attachment formation?

Toward a New Model of Service

There is little question that parents need and should be given help with daily problems of care and guidance that assist the child to compensate for its deficits. The question is how to provide this assistance most appropriately. The mother-child relationship is central to this issue. Jones et al. (1962) have identified three major factors involved in the overall psychomotor development of the infant: 1) the child himself, 2) the mother and environmental factors, and 3) the interaction between the first two. Jones and her colleagues stressed the work of Call (1969) who states that "what counts most in the learning situation of early infancy and in the mutual adaptation of infant to mother are not only the inborn characteristics of the infant or the mother, but how they each manage to fit together or how they do not fit together." And, Kagan (1966) points out that the mother-child relationship, important as it is for the normal child, may be even more crucial for the infant with a disability. These views provide strong support for programming which avoids multiple handlers and fosters normal attachment behaviors between mother (caregiver) and child. Approaches that move to reduce the number of intervenors are advocated by Jones (1970) who calls attention to the way physical and occupational therapists can be taught by their medical and speech therapy colleagues to help overcome defects in the oral-pharyngeal area. Here, for example, Jones shows how the occupational therapist can supplement her OT program (perhaps aimed at the improvement of self-feeding) by giving the infant with sucking, chewing, or swallowing difficulties the appropriate oral-pharyngeal treatment before the meal by integrating the medical and speech therapy maneuvers with her generic intervention.

This observation suggested that other professionals might similarly be taught. Specifically, the nurse as the one working most closely with the family can be aided by the expert teacher to monitor and guide the educational training of the child. Denhoff et al. (1966) discusses approaches of this type in relation to preschool-age children: how the infant's needs might be met, yet reduce the segregate handling. Denhoff further points out how the home can serve in addition to, or at times as an alternative for, the "clinic" or "center" as the primary base for infant service delivery systems. These concepts of service delivery are further developed and expanded in the work of Gillett (1969) and Finnie (1970) in their discussions of developmental approaches to therapy wherein are shown the many ways achievement of educational and therapeutic goals can be incorporated in the daily handling and interactions of infants by their parents.

The Transdisciplinary Model

When the UCPA collaborative project was initiated, other demonstration projects were providing short periods of training to lay persons who then undertook the major responsibility for carrying out the program in the home. Generally, the populations served in these other demonstration models were older and less severely handicapped children. Emphasis upon enrollment of infants in the collaborative project brought greater attention to the vulnerable infant and a shift to the use of qualified professional personnel but with reduction in the number of involved people and the frequency of "laying on of hands" either at a center or at home. Gradually, from this base and a continuing search for means to bring full team potential to bear through but one or two extendors of service, the transdisciplinary approach evolved.

Experience to date suggests that there are advantages to be gained by adapting the traditional interdisciplinary approach to the transdisciplinary model. Within this model, all aspects of the medical and medically related interventions are closely wedded to the educational and psychosocial components of development. The parents or parent surrogates are viewed in the primary nurturing role of teacher-caregiver. Direct, "one-to-one" interventions by professionals are markedly reduced. One team member is enabled to serve as a team facilitator working in a continuing and close relationship with the infant and family.

Staff Approach and Functions

The transdisciplinary model employs the entire team to provide the full spectrum of its knowledge and expertise to the initial diagnostic work-up and evaluation and the subsequent re-evaluations. The team, however, gives more attention to measures for helping parents or their surrogates to assume a stronger role in this process by teaching them how to observe and record the infant's behavior and, in effect, to assume a true colleague relationship in the team effort.

The integrated transdisciplinary team approach to infant evaluations follows into the planning process for developing and implementing the infant's program of treatment, care, and training. Here, for the first time in some centers, members of the medical team join with educators and colleagues concerned with the cognitive and social aspects of development to specify immediate and long-range goals, stated in quantifiable behavioral as well as medical terms, for the infant and its family.

Following the evaluation and the infant-family program planning phase, most of the centers then choose one or two members of the team (based upon infant and family needs) to serve as team facilitator(s). The facilitator(s) have primary responsibility for supporting and assisting the family to implement the program plan between regularly scheduled re-evaluation sessions conducted by the team as a whole. In particular, the facilitator serves as a continuing and consistent source of assistance and interpretation to the parents who are helped to implement the home program with diminished negative effects on the family's life style. The concentration of responsibility in the hands of the facilitator, it is believed, reduces the parental confusion which results from their attempts to implement advice from several sources.

Other members of the team share their specialized professional skills with, and release their intervention role to, the facilitator(s) during this period while maintaining their professional (or credentialed) accountability on behalf of the infant and his family. This method appears to be proving particularly useful when an infant needs several therapies plus a variety of education measures to foster cognitive as well as other parameters of development but cannot tolerate excessive or inconsistent handling by a variety of adults.

The transdisciplinary approach requires staff members who are both competent and secure in their professional practice. Staff understanding and skill in the principles of adult education are helpful in assessing the readiness of peer team members for learning and in providing them with the instruction necessary for acquisition of the abilities needed to serve as team facilitators. Team unit and confidence are enhanced by facilitator functioning sensitive to factors warranting referral to a team colleague for specialized intervention if and when need arises. Some physicians and other medically related personnel initially may not find it easy to state goals in behavioral terms as they are not accustomed to participating closely in developing and implementing the total infant curriculum. Team members who have had considerable "laying on of hands" as an essential component of their practice do not find it easy to yield this activity to the team facilitator and through the facilitator to the parents. Countering these staff reservations is the satisfaction that comes from knowing that their special skills have been utilized in the evaluations and implementation of the intervention program. The staff knows, too, that their particular expertise is not only "on call" by the team facilitator but also that they may be the one to serve as facilitator when their special skills and qualifications best serve the needs of an infant and the family.

The physician's role within the transdisciplinary approach is a critical one—and one requiring considerable readjustment for the physician. It is through the physician or medicial facility that the atypical infant and the family most often enter into the service system. Physician awareness of the infant's needs in relation to extended services is crucial to early and appropriate delivery of services. And the very nature of infancy warrants continuing medical surveillance even though it may be helped with other than medical parameters of growth and development. While the physician was almost inevitably the "team leader" in the classical rehabilitation center concept, there needs to be flexibility in this team leader role in development centers for atypical infants, where cognitive and psychosocial parameters of growth often surface as the primary concerns. Because of their generic preparation to assume a leadership role that may be truly critical in a crisis situation, some physicians do not find it easy, at first, to slip into the role of a team member rather than that of team leader. However, there are many fine examples of flexibility in team leadership, based upon the primary needs of the infant and family, that are demonstrated in the collaborating centers. This same flexibility is surfacing on the part of educators and behavioral personnel, and it extends to the involvement of parents as major instruments for infant programming.

Parent Role and Contribution

Parent competencies for facilitating the development of the high risk and atypical infant rank as a major untapped resource in most intervention programs. The transdisciplinary model recognizes the parent potential for facilitating the development of the atypical infant and actively seeks to foster and strengthen the parent contribution to the full scope of programming for their infant.

A critical appraisal of infant intervention programs suggests solid reasons for capitalizing on the parent potential for involved parent participation in programming their atypical infant. The advantage of frequency of opportunity for introducing appropriate interventions clearly rests with the parent or caregiver, as opposed to specialized resources and personnel. Added advantage derives to parent programming in terms of consistency of application and continuity of effort. Well informed and adaptively effective parents are, without question, the most effective resource for providing program continuity across the gaps that occur all too frequently in the complex programs for atypical infants as they move to master the developmental tasks required at the different age levels from infancy to school age. A major objective of the transdisciplinary approach, then, is to strengthen parent skills and understanding in the care and training of their infant, to minimize their dependence upon outside intervenors and, by these actions, to maximize the natural advantages inherent in parental care.

Many of the therapeutic goals set by definitive initial evaluations or re-evaluations can be skillfully integrated by the parent caregiver with the usual daily interactions that are a part of home care. Experience has shown that it is a relatively rare occurrence when specialized procedures or materials need to be used beyond that which can be utilized and integrated in the home care program by well motivated and properly instructed parents.

Because intervention programming is based, in large measure, on evaluation information, staff of some collaborating centers believe that it is here where parent involvement and understanding best begin. To this end, parents are involved in the evaluation process. They help in the determination of the baby's needs and strengths, and they take part in the decision-making process of establishing the procedures and materials that will be used in implementing the baby's program and how progress will be evaluated. Fundamental to this approach is the belief that the parents have the "need and right to know" the full nature of the infant's problems and the reasons behind the choice of procedures to be employed in their amelioration or correction.

Parent anxieties and uncertainties which accompany the birth of an atypical infant act to limit parent confidence in their decisions and approach to child care. Turning to the professional community for help during this period of vulnerability, it is easy for the parents to develop an attitude of continuing dependency, too often fostered by professionals, or outside sources. This development can be countered by early service interventions which, from the beginning, act to restore parent confidence through their direct involvement in their infant's evaluation and programming. The extension of this approach to the early developmental years has, as its objective, the development of enduring parent confidence and competencies that give to the parent a sense of accomplishment as they help their child gain greater mastery of its world.

Physical Environment and Equipment

With greater attention now being paid to the milieu in which atypical infants and young children are being nurtured, there is growing awareness that there is little need for most of the equipment found in the traditional rehabilitation centers. This observation also applies to the programs serving developmentally disabled older persons. Many of the traditional equipment items in the average rehabilitation centers are very costly, such as heated pools, large Hubbard tanks, whirlpool baths, paraffin and hot pack equipment, pulleys, weights, and similar devices. Currently, imaginative therapists in the infant programs have been working with team colleagues and parents to create a much more normal environment. When necessary, adaptations are made of tables and chairs of suitable size, toys for indoors and out, and educational materials. Imaginative ways have been found to foster self-motivated movement—balance practice, up and down or in and out experiences, plus generalized exploration in a safe environment. While some braces, crutches, adapted wheelchairs, floor mats, and parallel bars are still seen, the milieu, both indoors and out, can be colorful and normal looking. The path to the playground not only offers challenge and experience, it provides a variety of textures through the aesthetic use of bricks, sand, concrete, grass, and pebbles. Indoor floors may alternate carpeted textures with smooth wood or tile. Clearly, the emphasis is changing from heavy use of specialized equipment to an approach that adapts the natural environment to the accomplishment of therapeutic goals. These changes, under project monitoring, are aimed at reducing the emphasis on medical-like environments and the associated accentuation of the child as different.

Professional use of uniforms is an issue given attention in planning the transdisciplinary approach serving atypical infants. The uniform as a badge of identity and authority has been a matter of important consideration for medical and medically related personnel working in medical settings. However, the close collaboration by members of the transdisciplinary team and the involvement of the parent as a member of the team change these medically oriented considerations on use of uniforms. Colorful, attractive (though easily laundered) clothing is an important component in the creation of the normal environment. There is little need of uniforms for status or authoritarian purposes in the transdisciplinary approach. Here, what one wears is primarily determined by the need to normalize the infant's milieu—not professional needs. Professional need, however, to continue to use the uniform as a symbol of status and responsibility will, no doubt, continue. It can be expected that these attitudes will not disappear overnight in many colleges and universities preparing professional personnel.

Personnel Preparation and Training

During the 1960s, professionals primarily concerned with the cognitive and non-medical aspects of development in the developmentally disabled became increasingly restive with what they deemed a too medically dominated model of service. There resulted an increasing divergence of opinions regarding approaches to service leading to a marked swing toward an educational orientation in many day and residential service programs. There exists, today, a continuing effort to divorce the so-called "medical model" from the "educational model" of service, and many day and 24-hour service programs for the developmentally disabled are now dominated completely by educators and other personnel not related directly to the equally important but medically oriented parameters of the disabled person's total needs. This movement toward separation of services presents significant problems for the development of balanced service programs and for the preparation of personnel to serve in them.

In the exclusively educational setting, careful observation frequently reveals that infants and children are positioned to exacerbate rather than ameliorate neuromotor problems. Also noted are inhibition rather than facilitation of optimum hand function. Inappropriate judgments about "attending behaviors" or "learning potential" are found in regard to persons who are exhibiting unrecognized disorders of consciousness resulting from subtle seizures and, in others, evidence of unrecognized side effects from a medication.

Separation of services presents additional burdens for the atypical child and the family. Travel requirements for the family are increased as they travel to different sites for medical therapies, educational, and day care services. The parents are too frequently confused by apparent inconsistencies in advice, interpretation of problems, and approaches to care and training offered by different and uncoordinated resources. In one facility, the parent or disabled person may be involved very directly in all phases of program planning; in another, they may be left to wait in a hallway while decisions are made for them. These and other problems consequent to separation of services detract significantly from effective programming.

The unfortunate consequences stemming from the marked disparity in the basic orientation and training of "educational" versus "medical" personnel point to a need for reappraisal of our programs of professional preparation. Many campuses lack truly integrated teaching-learning experiences between such personnel as they live and work in the training setting during the years of generic preparation. And, at the postgraduate level, course offerings that purport to stress the "interdisciplinary" approach frequently provide only parallel training with little emphasis on integration of functions. Students have little actual experience with the *role exchange* and *role release* concept while *maintaining accountability which is inherent in the transdisciplinary approach*. This requires considerable depth in understanding of each other's functions, a significant proportion of shared knowledge and shared skills, plus a sincere degree of mutual respect and trust.

Integrated training of professional personnel has been strengthened immeasurably by development of the University-Affiliated Facilities (UAF) program over the past decade. Legislatively mandated to provide training in the full array of professional services required by developmentally disabled persons, the UAF represents a major national effort to meet our needs for an adequate supply of well trained professionals. Approximately 40 UAFs, scattered through the United States, are now operating to provide exemplary training for professionals and workers in the service of the developmental disabilities. In these facilities, and in other major training institutions which give heavy emphasis to interdisciplinary training, the provision of training in transdisciplinary concepts is uneven and achieved only with some difficulty.

There are several deterrents to full acceptance and development of training in the transdisciplinary approach. University organization along school and departmental lines tends to preserve disciplinary identity and to resist subordination of training responsibilities to a training facility or resource which provides a coordinated program of interdisciplinary training. Parallel, rather than truly integrated, training is usually found to be more acceptable to faculty of university schools and departments. This attitude is reinforced by legislative actions and administrative guidelines which segregate and isolate funds for medical care and training from funds for support of educational and social service activities. And, as has been well documented in this conference, there is also the natural tendency of professionals to act to preserve their professional identity by staking out their *territories*. This attitude, often strengthened by economic motives, helps to create a climate resistive to the training of other workers outside the discipline in skills that might be shared.

These limitations should not restrict thoughtful consideration of the potential value of the exchange and sharing of professional skills and knowledge in our training programs. Treatment and care programs developed within insular professional areas of activity may fail to perceive the impact of the treatment program on the person beyond its immediate effect on the specific problem under treatment. Evidence for this is readily found in the medical domain where, in the past, isolation of the newborn infant in the interest of controlling infections failed to consider the impact of this procedure on mother-infant attachment formation. Such oversights are not limited to the medical and medically related disciplines. They occur, too, in the behavioral and educational arenas. The development and implementation of behavior modification (operant conditioning) programs is a case in point.

Highly effective when applied to specific training tasks, behavior modification technology has been utilized increasingly in residential and community care programs serving the multiply disabled. Training of professionals in behavior modification technology commonly proceeds in isolation from interdisciplinary treatment milieus and gives little emphasis to organismic variables. As a consequence, implementation of this technology in the service of persons with multiple disabilities of organic origin can, and often does, ignore the broader context of individual needs and problems beyond the immediate training tasks. A study of the pertinent literature shows that application of the technology often proceeds with limited attention given to the type of evaluation that should precede a program of behavior modification intervention and how the program relates to other parameters of intervention that deserve special attention. Reviews of video tapes and movies demonstrating behavior modification technology frequently show that the analysis of the training task does not include evaluation of sensorimotor limitations and the reflex problems of multiply handicapped subjects. Furthermore, the interventions are shown as proceeding independently of any broad program of intervention that recognizes the needs and problems of the whole person. Added benefits, it is believed, would accrue to behavior modification technolgical applications for multiply handicapped persons if greater use were made of the knowledge and skills available from other disciplines.

SUMMARY

The National Collaborative Infant Project (NCIP) expresses the national concern for high risk infants through its efforts to identify and demonstrate exemplary models of service for these children and their families. Its approach has been shaped, to a large extent, by the population it serves: atypical infants from birth to 2 years of age, many of whom are multiply handicapped. This focus on very young infants has required the adaptation of traditional approaches to habilitation and the development of new models of service.

The project approach recognizes and attaches importance to the great capacity for infants to learn under facilitating conditions. Emphasis, therefore, is placed upon early referrals of infants for service and the early creation within the family care milieu of optimal learning conditions for the infant. To this end, the extension of professional services is viewed as moving primarily through the parent (caregiver) to the infant. Professional assistance is aimed at strengthening and expanding parent understanding and skills in the care and training of the atypical infant and young child.

Establishment of normal infant-mother (caregiver) attachment behaviors is fundamental to the successful application of the project's approach. These behaviors define and set the boundaries for early infant learning experiences, provide the base for effective communication with the external world, and shape the enduring relationship that will guide the child through the early developmental years. The project's approach respects the great vulnerability of the atypical infant and his mother to distortions of normal infant-mother attachment. For this and other reasons, the project has developed a transdisciplinary approach to the delivery of professional services.

Adapted from traditional patterns of care for the handicapped, the transdisciplinary approach is designed to be responsive to the needs and requirements of the *developing* atypical or at risk infant and the family. To the maximum extend consistent with sound and ethical professional practices, it endeavors to pass through to the parents, for their understanding and implementation in a program of infant home care, the professional knowledge and skills commonly reserved for direct professional application. It emphasizes the sharing of knowledge and skills among members of the transdisciplinary team. This sharing has the objective of reducing the number of intervenors needed to meet the many requirements of the multiply handicapped by placing in the hands of a single *facilitator*, selected from the professional team, the maximum complement of interdisciplinary knowledge and skill needed for effective and understanding communication with the parents.

The transdisciplinary approach emphasis upon the contributions from education and other non-medical disciplines effects on approach at variance from traditional medical models of service delivery. Medical contributions are recognized as essential but not dominant within the approach where they are integrated in sustained balance with the contributions from the non-medical disciplines. Professional role visibility is diminished with the sharing of professional knowledge and skills and their application. Parent involvement and participation in evaluation and programming are expanded and given prominence. These modifications accompanied by efforts to provide programming in an attractive and encouraging physical environment strive toward normalization of experiences for the atypical infant and the family.

These changes are not accomplished without difficulty. Resistance to modification of professional roles and the sharing of professional responsibilities occur. Project experience, however, suggests that effective training programs for responsive professionals and students produces workers who function well within the conceptual guidelines of the project's approach. The project, therefore, has developed a broad program of staff development and training involving direct on-site training and audio-visual and printed materials for use in project replication efforts and other training activities.

No belief is held that the transdisciplinary approach represents the optimal approach to the atypical and multiply handicapped infant. Project experience does suggest that it is one approach worthy of continuing consideration as we work toward an improved model of service delivery for risk infants and their families.

APPENDIX

UCPA Collaborative Infant Project: Questions and Answers about Ripple Centers

What is a ripple center?   One important component of this project is replication. This includes the addition of new centers to the original consortium of five collaborating centers. These new centers are called "ripple centers."

Does the project already have ripple centers?   Yes, there are now 15 such centers. They, together with the original five centers, are serving approximately 1,000 atypical infants and their families.

What does the project offer a ripple center?

1. An initial site visit. During or shortly after this visit, a center accepted for inclusion in the project receives two questionnaires. The first is agency-centered. The second is filled out by each member of the "baby team." Data from these form the matrix upon which the project obtains a needs-engendered model for staff development which is used as a basis for future project acitivities.

2. A conference (usually 1 or 2 days at New York headquarters) is then scheduled for the directors of the agencies selected to become ripple centers. If the director is not also serving as a member of the team, the team coordinator is also invited. Travel and per diem costs are paid by the project. The main objectives of this conference are orientation and familiarization to the project as a whole and direct participation by these ripple center personnel in discussions concerned with the staff development workshop to be scheduled for the team, etc.

3. Scheduling of a 3-day in-service training workshop, usually held at the University of Wisconsin in Madison. The project provides travel and per diem for four members of the infant team. When the team is larger, the other members of the team are also warmly welcomed. The project does not have funds sufficient to defray travel or per diem costs for these additional staff members but no tuition fee is charged.

4. With time lines and selection of personnel based upon the center's own needs (and availability of project personnel) a project visit is then scheduled. Two experienced project visitors are sent to the ripple center for 3 days. A special guideline for use by these visitors is shared with the center in advance. The main purposes are to review the program, to serve as catalysts, to share information gleaned from other centers' experience, to supplement and to reinforce or otherwise assist the new center. Sometimes, if a center has a particular need for a consultant with a certain specific area of expertise, this is taken into consideration in the selection of the project visitors. At times, this one member of the team can stay on an extra day to provide this specialized consultation.

Six months after this visit, the ripple center is asked to evaluate the project visit, using a project form as a guideline for this report.

5. Materials, films, and other project resources are shared both before, during, and after these conferences.

6. Following this visit, the project headquarters staff counsels with the center personnel and the project visitors to select an infant center that might prove most helpful. An "interteam" visit is then scheduled with funds provided to pay travel and per diem for 2 days for two people to visit another infant center. The host center is selected with care and prepared for this visit. Following the visit, the ripple center team members are asked to make out a report on this experience, using a special project form as a guideline. (Note: the project's evaluation task force is constantly reviewing reports as outlined under No. 4 and No. 6, as part of the total evaluation of all parameters of this project's activity.)

7. Ripple centers are invited to contribute to, and can receive a continuum of "feedback" from, the data pool of the project as a whole. This is a valuable resource directed by the project evaluator and ultilizes a computer programmer. Special forms are used that will be provided to the participating centers.

8. Dependent upon availability of funds, it is hoped that an evaluation conference will be held in the spring of 1975, involving one member from each center contributing to the total data pool of this project.

9. Ripple centers are invited to participate in the MIP project. Essentially, the project involves the video taping of an infant team member while he or she is working with an infant and teaching the parent(s) to undertake some activity with the child. Thus, the video tape is of the staff member teaching the parent(s) a skill. A second video tape is made with the parent carrying out the teaching activity with their child. These two tapes are sent to MIP staff located at the University of Washington in Seattle. The MIP staff critiques the teaching styles of staff and parent and feeds back information to the center. The feedback is sent in three forms. There are an audio tape, a written commentary, and a checklist. The team member receives the analysis in total confidence. If he or she wishes to share the video tape and various vehicles of feedback with other infant team members, this is encouraged, although not required. These video tape sequences have also been used with parents in an attempt to delineate parent teaching styles as well.

What are the priorities given consideration in selecting agencies for participation as a ripple center? Priority is given to applications from well organized agencies that have basically well prepared staff, a reasonably firm financial base and stability, and are "ready to go" but need the type of assistance this project can give to inaugurate their infant program or expand a limited program to a more comprehensive transdisciplinary approach to programming for handicapped infants and their families. Any center accepted for ripple center service must be willing and able to follow project policy relative to reports of the type and frequency required of the consortium centers. Other factors entering into the selection process are: 1) new and innovative approaches that show promise of improving the entire consortium effort to develop exemplary models of service; 2) agencies in a position to render service to minority groups, inner city or rural populations; 3) agencies with a high potential for fostering replication and, in particular, for extending programs to areas of the United States where there has heretofore been little service available to the handicapped during infancy.

Attention is also paid to the fact that some agencies may need only part of the potential "ripple" service, such as one or two consultation visits and sharing of materials, in order to launch a new or more comprehensive infant program. Others may not need to use project funds due to availability of local monies with which to subsidize a consultation visit, an interteam visit to a consortium center, or participation of their infant team members at the project workshop. (These factors may assist in stretching available project personnel time and project funds to provide more infants and families with quality programming in a relatively short time.)

Also worthy of attention are agencies needing a longer period of time and help with more basic organizational needs, avenues for obtaining funds, staff recruitment, and/or related activities before they are ready to shift current program emphasis to serve handicapped infants or start a new infant program. In these agencies there may be greater need for consultation services in one or more specialty areas, and a period of time may elapse before the center is ready for participation in staff training workshops and all the other parameters of ripple center service.

How does an agency apply to become a ripple center? A letter should be addressed to the project director, Una Haynes, United Cerebral Palsy Associations, Inc., 66 East 34th Street, New York, New York 10016. The letter should outline the agency's interests, give an overview of the current program, and show how the program meets one or more of the criteria detailed above.

When should applications be made? The UCPA Collaborative Project expects to add about 20 centers in 1974–75. Inquiries regarding submission dates for applications should be directed to the Project Director.

Is there anyone available locally to talk about this project? Yes. Every effort will be made to notify a UCPA Program Representative in the District Office nearest your agency site to assist with the application process if any help is desired. This service is not restricted to UCP affiliates. Any agency is eligible for this type of consultation. The only limitations involved are those imposed by distance and/or time constraints of the program representative's total function in the district as a whole.

LITERATURE CITED

Barsch, R. H. 1967. Achieving Perceptual Motor Efficiency. Perceptual-Motor Curriculum, Volume II. Special Child Publication, Seattle.

Bobath, B. 1967. The very early treatment of cerebral palsy. Devel. Med. Child Neurol. 9: 373.

Bowlby, J. 1969. Attachment. Attachment and Loss, Volume II. Hogarthy, London.

Brazelton, T. B. 1961. Psychophysiologic reactions in the neonate: The value of the observation of the neonate. J. Pediat. 38: 508.

Butter, M. 1972. Maternal Deprivation Reassessed. Penguin Books, Baltimore.

Butterfield, E., and G. Saperstein. 1974. Influence of contingent auditory stimulation upon non-nutritive suckle. Paper presented at the Third Symposium on Oral Sensation and Perception: The Mouth of the Infant.

Call, J. D. 1969. Early identification of children with potential learning problems. *In* B. K. Keogh (ed.), Proceedings of a Conference: Early Identification of Children with Potential Learning Problems, pp. 70–83. Mimeographed. University of California at Los Angeles.

Denhoff, E., and M. Langdon (eds.). 1966. Cerebral dysfunction: A treatment program for young children. Clin. Pediat. 6: 332.

Finnie, N. 1970. Handling the Young Cerebral Palsied Child at Home. E. P. Dutton, New York.

Gesell, A. L., and C. S. Armatruda. 1947. Developmental Diagnosis: Normal and Abnormal Child Development, Clinical Methods, and Pediatric Application. Hoeber, New York.

Gillett, H. E. 1969. Systems of Therapy. C. C Thomas, Springfield, Ill.

Haynes, U. H., and D. J. Hutchison. Transdisciplinary: A Team Approach to Service for the Developmentally Disabled. Chas. Slak, New Jersey (in press).

Jones, M. H., W. H. Wenner, A. M. Toezek, and M. L. Barrett. 1962. Prenursery program for children with cerebral palsy. J. Amer. Women's Med. Assoc. 17: 713–719.

Jones, M. H. 1970. A program profile for infants and young children with physical handicaps. *In* G. Hensley and V. W. Patterson (eds.), Interdisciplinary Programming for Infants with Known or Suspected Cerebral Dysfunction, pp. 31–50. Western Interstate Commission for Higher Education, Boulder, Colorado.

Kagan, J. 1966. Psychological development of the child: Part I: Personality, behavior, and temperament. *In* F. Falkner (ed.), Human Development, pp. 326–367. W. B. Saunders, Philadelphia.

Kephart, N. C. 1960. The Slow Learner in the Classroom. C. E. Merrill, Columbus.

Lipsitt, L. 1967. Learning in the human infant. *In* H. W. Stevenson, E. H. Tess, and H. L. Rheingold (eds.), Early Behavior, Comparative and Developmental Approaches, pp. 225–247. Wiley, New York.

Papousek, H. 1967. Conditioning during early postnatal development. *In* Y. Brackbill, and G. S. Thompson (eds.), Behavior in Infancy and Early Childhood, pp. 259–274. Free Press, New York.

Piaget, J. 1952. The Origins of Intelligence in Children. Translated by Margaret Cook. International Universities Press, New York.

Siqueland, E. 1969. Further developments in infant learning. Symposium in learning processes of human infants, 19th International Congress of Psychology, London.

Strauss, A. A., and N. C. Kephart. 1955. Progress in Theory and Clinical Psychopathology and Education of the Brain-injured Child, Volume 2. Grune and Stratton, New York.

White, P. L., and R. Held. 1973. Plasticity of sensory motor development. *In* J. F. Rosenblith and W. Allinsmith (eds.), Causes of Behavior: Readings in Child Development and Educational Psychology, pp. 10–66 (Second Edition), Allyn and Bacon, Boston.

Educational Intervention with High Risk Infants

Ethel R. Kass, M.A., Marian Sigman, Ph.D., Rose F. Bromwich, Ed.D.,
and Arthur H. Parmelee, M.D.

This chapter reviews the philosophy and procedures of the educational intervention program that is part of the Infant Studies Project at the University of California at Los Angeles. This project was organized in July 1971 with the dual aims of developing methods of identification of high risk infants and techniques of intervention with such infants. Before describing the intervention program, the overall project will be discussed.

AN OVERVIEW OF THE INFANT STUDIES PROJECT

For purposes of this discussion, the term "risk" is used to imply an increased probability of handicap in childhood. In the past, infants at risk have been identified on the basis of factors related to infant mortality. However, use of single indicators has not been successful in predicting delayed development in individual infants. Furthermore, deviant behavior tends to unfold and become more definitive during the first year. For this reason, the Infant Studies Project has developed a cumulative risk system that scores the infant's performance on various measures from birth through 9 months of age.

In order to test the validity of this risk score system and the effectiveness of the intervention program, a sample of infants is followed from birth. The longitudinal sample consists of premature infants of 37 weeks' gestational age (ga) or less, with birth weights at 2,500 grams or less, and a control group of full term infants of 39 to 41 weeks' ga, and a birth weight greater than 2,500 grams. A sample of prematurely born infants has been selected because the incidence of impaired functioning in childhood is greater among them than among full term infants. Subjects include infants from all socioeconomic groups, and attempts are made to equalize the representation of sex and socioeconomic groups within the intervention program.

The longitudinal sample of infants is followed from birth to 2 years of age. Each child receives a cumulative risk score at 9 months of age, based on his performance on the 14

535

measures included in the risk score system. Of those infants classified as high risk, 40 infants participate in the educational intervention program from 10 months to 2 years of age. The remaining high risk infants are not offered educational intervention, but they serve as a control group for measuring the effects of intervention. The first series of outcome measures at 2 years of age consists of developmental examinations, a cognitive test of sensorimotor behaviors, measures of receptive and expressive language, and a test of attention and exploration of toys.

Every infant and family who participates in the longitudinal study receives medical, nursing, and social work help in an effort to provide support services regardless of risk category. Outpatient pediatric care includes well-baby clinic visits once a month from birth to 8 months of age, once every 2 months until 15 months of age, and every 3 months until 2 years of age. Acute and emergency care is also provided when needed. Nursing assistance begins at the time of the infant's birth and continues throughout the first 2 years. During the period after birth, when the infant is in the hospital, the nurse provides information to the parents, reassures them, and helps them to interact with the infant. Home visits are made from the time of discharge from the hospital to 4 months of age so that the nurse can support the parents, answer questions about the baby's routine, and observe the baby's milieu. From 4 months to 2 years, home visits are made when necessary. Social worker services consist mainly of consultation with the project staff. The social worker meets with families when this is necessary, and she contacts local agencies so that families with particular problems can receive assistance. All these services are provided for every infant in the longitudinal project. Such services are considered an essential part of good pediatric care and their value does not need testing.

PHILOSOPHY OF EDUCATIONAL INTERVENTION

Clinical support services are often not enough to facilitate optimum development with high risk infants. For such infants and mothers, a concentrated program of educational intervention is required. The goal of educational intervention is to promote optimal development of high risk infants through implementation of special programs of intervention focused on mother-child interactions. Both educational intervention and clinical support services are based on the belief that a strong, positive, and mutually satisfying mother-infant attachment is a primary factor in maximizing infant development. In the case of high risk infants, this mutual relationship between mother and child is often distorted, leading to child care practices that preclude optimal growth. Educational intervention is directed specifically at providing mothers with techniques, practices, and observational skills that enhance maternal ability. Specific content and procedures utilized in educational intervention are developed within this frame of reference.

Educational intervention involves content and process. Content includes the kinds and sequences of mother-child activities to be initiated, elicited, and encouraged; process consists of how this program of activities is to be conveyed or taught to the mother or mother surrogate. In order to meet the wide range of needs presented by different high risk infants and different mother-infant dyads, the educational program planned for each infant and family is highly individualized, and is based on careful assessment of three key areas: 1) developmental characteristics of the infant, 2) the nature of the parent-child interaction, and 3) the environmental resources and limitations of the family and home. The specific goal of this type of assessment is the formulation of an educational plan for each infant and caregiver.

The high risk population includes infants with such diverse characteristics and handicaps that a single standardized intervention procedure cannot be applied to all infants. This is in contrast to intervention with culturally deprived children for whom standardized procedures have been planned and implemented based on the assumption that these children share common deprivations (Gordon and Lally, 1967; Honig and Brill, 1970). Each intervention must follow its own course with a high risk infant, but the organization of intervention as a process and the recording of information can be made standard. Process parameters have been specified and found to be consistent across subjects. Specified content, of course, varies with each mother-child unit. Increased diagnostic and treatment experience with high risk infants will allow the development of definitive categorizations of infant and mother characteristics that will be useful in selecting intervention procedures.

The duration of intervention with each family is 14 months. Educational intervention, then, can be considered a short-term process. The effectiveness of short-term changes in affecting long-term development has been questioned recently from both theoretical and clinical viewpoints (Clarke, 1968; Wachs and Cucinotta, 1971). Approaches to intervention directed at changing only the behavior of the child over a short time period may have limited consequences because the basic environment is unaltered. However, any experience that continued to generate reinforcing environmental events, even if the experience itself is transitory, should produce continuous effects. These authors postulate that the breakdown of interaction between mother and handicapped child is a relatively permanent event in that it creates self-reinforcing consequences. More specifically, the mother's withdrawal from the child aggravates his disturbances and leads, in turn, to further maternal withdrawal. It is believed that this educational intervention program can break this chain of events by creating its own chain with reinforcing feedback of a more positive nature. In other words, successful intervention that strengthens maternal sensitivity and skill creates a mother-child interaction in which the mother experiences success and the infant progresses to his maximum capacity. This mutually satisfying interaction should outlive the duration of the formalized intervention and produce both short-term and long-term results.

The intervention method of this program differs from most previously used practices in that the mother is trained to bring about improvement in her infant's specific area of weakness and to observe and use his strengths in fostering development. The traditional approach to intervention with the handicapped child has frequently focused on the mother's emotional reactions to her child's handicap in an effort to aid her adjustment. When successful, this method has long-term consequences because the child-rearing milieu is modified. However, in many cases, emotional support for the mother is unsuccessful on its own. Unless the mother of a high risk infant knows how to improve her infant's development, her adjustment to his problems will remain incomplete.

In summary, most previous programs have worked either directly with the infant on his developmental problems or with the mother concerning her emotional adjustment to the child. In this program, the focus of concentration is on improving the infant and mother interaction by training the mother to respond to the specific cognitive and developmental strengths and weaknesses of her infant. It takes into account the infant's developmental needs, the mother's characteristics, and her ability to carry out specific intervention plans.

PROCEDURES

Referral

The intervention staff is notified by the project statistician that a baby has been assigned to intervention, and the infant's family is described in general terms by the well-baby clinic team. Two staff members are assigned to the case with selection determined by staff schedules and characteristics. A Spanish-speaking staff member is assigned to the case when the mother speaks only Spanish. A two-member team approach is used for greater objectivity in the observations of the family and for more flexibility in adjusting to the family's needs.

Assessment

The intervention team uses its own independent assessment procedures to augment those employed in the diagnostic study. Such additional assessment is necessary, because the intervention team needs a less formal, more general appraisal of infant and family than that provided by the diagnostic measures. Since intervention is primarily carried out in the home through the family, it is crucial that the infant's milieu be observed.

Assessment is made in three areas: 1) developmental characteristics of the infant, 2) nature of the parent-child interaction, and 3) environmental resources and limitations of family and home. Parent interaction is assessed within a framework of a hierarchy of parental attitudes and behaviors (Bromwich, 1974).

Two home visits are made, each lasting 1 to 1.5 hours, over the first 2 weeks. Besides providing information about daily routines and concerns, these visits serve to introduce the intervention staff to the family. The second home visit is video taped, and the intervener assumes a more active role with the infant, trying out new activities and materials. Special effort is made to arrange this visit at a time when the father can be present. The parents' response to shared observations gives some indication of the family's readiness to accept help and to take initiative. The team is sensitive to the reactions of the parents—procedures that seem to cause discomfort are not utilized.

Following a review of the diagnostic material collected earlier for the risk score, the clinic notes from well-baby visits, and their own observations, the educational intervention team schedules an appointment in the project center. This project center visit provides the opportunity to observe the infant in interaction with his parents with a wide range of materials in varying situations. Furthermore, the mother and infant are observed in a standardized play situation, and their behaviors are video taped. This measure is used throughout intervention as a means of evaluating changes in mother and infant. The project center visit is also used to experiment with materials that are being considred as part of intervention.

Intervention Plan

The team members formulate an initial plan that is shared with the pediatrician, nurse, and social worker who have been responsible for the family. The plan covers the following subjects: 1) goals, 2) special considerations, 3) implementation of goals, and 4) evaluation. It also includes a proposed schedule of visits and preferred methods of communicating techniques. It has been found that the manner in which the team communicates with the parent can be crucial for effective intervention. Different modes include: 1) demonstration, in which specific activities are taught to the mother; 2) modeling, in which the intervener assumes that the mother will imitate her pattern of handling activities; and 3) discussion, in which methods and alternative techniques are explained without demonstration.

Goals The goals that will be the focus of intervention for each family are summarized. In most cases, three or four major objectives are stated in the initial plan. These objectives fall into four main categories:

1. One major objective may be to increase the mother's sensitivity to her child. For this purpose, the intervention team may direct the parent to make specific observations of the child, ask the mother to note what elicits particular behaviors, and help the mother to respond appropriately to particular cues.

2. A second major goal of intervention may be to improve the infant's skills, particularly in specific areas of delayed development. For instance, the intervention team may aim to improve adaptive and language skills, or the infant may be encouraged to develop more advanced social behaviors and a longer attention span. Occasionally, the area of fine motor or gross motor behavior may become the focus of intervention, but there is less emphasis on such skills in this program than has previously been common. It is felt that cognitive development can be advanced despite some handicaps in these areas by emphasizing inputs in areas of strength.

3. A third focus of intervention may be on the overall environment. For instance, the assessment procedure may indicate that the infant would benefit from less intense, less varied, visual and auditory stimulation. On the other hand, a passive infant may need more stimulation than his environment provides for him.

4. A major objective in all intervention cases is to develop a comfortable working relationship with the family. Open communication, an important part of that relationship, is a prerequisite for successful intervention.

Influencing Factors The factors that influence the direction and intensity of the intervention program are considered in the plan. For instance, the number of hours available to a working mother may affect her ability to participate in the program. In some cases, the relationship between the adult caregivers of the child must be taken into account. In pilot work with Spanish-speaking families, it became clear that the relationship of a younger mother to an older woman, such as a baby sitter or grandmother, often would not allow the mother to instruct the older woman. It was necessary for the intervention staff to work directly with the other caregiver. A consideration that might dictate the order of activities offered to an infant would be a parent's particular concern over a specific area of development.

Implementing Goals The program for implementing the more general goals are outlined in the plan. In those cases in which maternal sensitivity is to be sharpened, the mother may be encouraged to spend regular, short periods of time interacting with her child. These play periods can then be reported to the team members and discussed with them. The discussion can give the mother some better methods of responding to her infant. If the major objective is in the area of improvement of skills, alternatives are suggested that allow the infant more opportunity to practice needed skills, perhaps by working around some deficits.

Evaluation Measures Evaluation measures are specified, as well as the timing of evaluation in the plan. The choice of evaluation measures is tied to primary goals. For instance, in those cases in which the primary aim is to increase maternal sensitivity, the evaluation may consist of observations of the mother's choice of play materials and the quality and timing of her responses to her infant's cues. For those cases in which the concentration is on improvement of skills, progress in this area is noted. Expectations of progress may differ, depending on the area of focus. For example, language may not accelerate as rapidly with practice as fine motor skills.

Intervention Visits and Evaluation

Intervention is maintained as a flexible process that deals with new developments as they occur. The focus, frequency, and location of intervention sessions specified in the initial plan may be altered during the course of intervention. For example, a focus of intervention often changes from sharpening the mother's sensitivity to helping her become an active participant in carrying out activities with the infant. The frequency of visits may increase from biweekly to weekly sessions when new stresses occur.

Every 4 months the intervention plan for each infant is reviewed. A project center visit is scheduled in order to evaluate changes in the infant and the relationship between infant and mother. The intervention plan is modified in light of this evaluation.

Intervention visits continue until the infant reaches 2 years of age. At this point, his developmental progress is assessed with the outcome measures mentioned above. Continuing programs are provided for the child until referral to a nursery school is made at 3 years of age.

Recording Information

The intervention team members keep careful records of all stages in the process of intervention. Information provided at time of referral and material collected during assessment is recorded. The initial plan and all subsequent modifications are preserved. After every home visit and project center session, the team members fill out a form describing the appointment in terms of the factors outlined in the initial plan.

The material collected on every infant is subjected to retrospective examination and analysis. From this information, identification is made of those variables that are significantly related to developmental progress as reflected in the 2-year outcome measures. Furthermore, such an examination may permit certain generalizations about the process of intervention, even if the content varies widely from one infant to another. Last, a retrospective examination may uncover generalities in content among infants that may have some relationship to progress during educational intervention. This retrospective analysis follows and supplements the statistical analysis comparing the performance of intervention and control groups with the outcome measures.

REVIEW OF CASES

Although the Infant Studies Project was organized in July 1971, the first year of the project was devoted to pilot studies; therefore, subjects for the longitudinal project were not recruited until July 1972. Thus, the first infants diagnosed as high risk on the basis of the cumulative risk score did not begin intervention until June 1973. Consequently, the intervention staff has had a 2-year pilot period in which to develop procedures and techniques of intervention. At present, four high risk infants from the longitudinal study have entered the intervention program; two of these infants have been in the program for more than 6 months. Two infants suffer from general delays in development, while the other two show significant motor problems as well as developmental lags.

During the pilot project, 27 infants were followed by the intervention staff, and 16 are still in the program. These children were referred by the well-baby clinic staff. While fewer than half of the pilot cases were born prematurely, almost all suffer disabilities like those observed among the high risk prematures in the longitudinal sample. According to Gesell developmental examinations, all the infants in the pilot group were behind age expectations in developmental progress. Eight children also suffered problems in motor coordination, two had impaired hearing, and two had limited vision.

The major goals of the intervention program with pilot cases were those outlined in the previous section under intervention plan. Among the 12 infants followed for more than 1 year, seven had deficits in a specific area that became a focus of intervention, while five mothers were helped to develop greater sensitivity and to provide more appropriate environments for their children. In the majority of those cases with a specific focus, language was the area of concentration in the intervention program. All these infants were in the second year of life. In two pilot cases, the overall level of stimulation, as well as the match between the child's cues and responses to these cues, had to be improved. For one child, this meant encouraging the mother and babysitter to provide more visual stimuli and toys and to interact more frequently with the child. For the other, the aim was to teach the mother to be less intrusive and to provide less overall stimulation. Among the newer cases, the focus in one situation was on fine motor control and in another on social responsiveness. The intervention staff attempted to provide substitute learning experience with objects for a child who had difficulty in holding objects. The approach in the last two cases was more general—aimed at improving the interaction between mother and infant.

CONCLUSIONS

Certain general principles have become clear during this period of pilot work. First, assessment of the strengths of infant and parent is as necessary as assessment of deficits. Intervention is only effective when such strengths can be utilized in working on weaknesses. As Pearson (1972) suggests in a recent chapter on the management of handicapped children, intervention must be based on what the child can do rather than on what he cannot do. As a corollary to this, intervention programs must ensure that disabilities do not mask potentials in other areas. The child's lack of ability in some area may prevent him from practicing other skills. Parental focus on the child's disabilities may also interfere with the parent's recognition of the child's strengths. For these reasons, the intervention staff often focuses on the strengths of the infant and family.

Another generalization is that the initial reception of the intervention team by the family does not predict the family's eventual receptivity to intervention. For this reason, the staff proceeds slowly in making judgments or offering suggestions until the nature of parental concerns and responsiveness is evident. In addition, families do not seem to utilize specific suggestions until they are concerned about the area in which the suggestions are being made. While the intervention staff calls the significance of certain behaviors to the mother's attention, specific suggestions are not made until the parent has expressed some concern about the behavior.

Finally, all intervention programs must attempt to set a balance between a focus on the child's development and responsiveness to the family's needs and style. Family counseling must not replace treatment of the child, although it remains part of intervention. As Pearson (1972) points out, the temptation to emphasize family adjustment instead of the child's training is very strong, particularly with children whose progress is slow. On the other hand, experience in this program has shown that the ability to help the child or to train the parent as therapist is often limited until the family recognizes and accepts the child's problems.

ACKNOWLEDGMENTS

These authors acknowledge the help of their intervention staff members Dorothea Burge, Ronald Fischbach, Margaret Harris, and Armony Share, whose work and words are represented in this chapter and also the consultative assistance of Dr. Barbara Keogh. The program is supported by NIH Contract No. 1-HD-3-2776, "Diagnostic and Intervention Studies of High Risk Infants;" and NICHD Grant No. HD-04612, Mental Retardation Research Center, University of California at Los Angeles.

LITERATURE CITED

Bromwich, R. 1974. A hierarchy of parent interaction with infants. Presented at the annual meeting of the American Orthopsychiatric Association, San Francisco.

Clarke, A. D. B. 1968. Learning and human development. Brit. J. Psychiat. 114: 1061–1077.

Gordon, I., and J. Lally. 1967. Intellectual stimulation of infants and toddlers. Institute for the Development of Human Resources, University of Florida, Gainesville.

Honig, A. S., and S. Brill. 1970. A comparative analysis of the Piagetian development of twelve-month-old disadvantaged infants is an enrichment center with others not in such a center. Presented at the annual meeting of the American Psychological Association, Miami.

Pearson, P. H. 1972. General principles in the management of the developmental disabilities. In P. H. Pearson and C. E. Williams (eds.), Physical Therapy Services in the Developmental Disabilities, pp. 5–15. C. C Thomas, Springfield, Ill.

Wachs, T. D., and P. Cucinotta. 1971. The effects of enriched neonatal experiences upon later cognitive functioning. Devel. Psych. 5: 542–549.

The Infant, Toddler, and Preschool Research and Intervention Project

William A. Bricker, Ph.D., and Diane D. Bricker, Ph.D.

The history of service for the retarded person, although extending across many years, is notable for its lack of success both in terms of teaching the handicapped person complex forms of human behavior or in teaching society to become more tolerant or accepting of deviancy. However, a mandate for change arising from the consumer seems to be pervading the system of governmental support for new programs and new directions as seen in the content of this conference. There are many states in which significant legislation is being enacted to support the local community in providing very early intervention for impaired or high risk children. At this point in history, several important trends are converging to produce what it is believed could be a significant change in educational programs for all handicapped people, regardless of their degree of developmental disability.

THE PROJECT

The rapid development of day care services and early intervention programs for the more severely impaired infant and preschool child poses some exciting prospects for special education as well as for related disciplines. While the increase in such special services is inevitable, the potential problems inherent in the structure of these programs must be anticipated and, hopefully, avoided. This paper describes a program for infants, toddlers, and preschool-age children, many of whom have been classified as moderately to severely retarded or disturbed. The program is noncategorical in all senses of the word: Down's syndrome, hydrocephalic, cerebral palsied, and autistic-like children are enrolled in the same program with an equal number of nonhandicapped children who are developing normally. This program spreads its service base across the preschool developmental range, across the economic continuum from poverty to affluence, and across a broad range

545

of ethnic backgrounds as can be seen from the demographic information presented in Table 1.

The Infant, Toddler, and Preschool Research and Intervention Project (D. Bricker and W. Bricker, 1971; 1972; 1973) has completed its fourth year of operation. During this time, it has developed from a small program covering a limited developmental range with children from middle income families to a project with the potential for helping to produce major changes in the area of educational intervention for young children. The project is based on a system that has been effective with normal children, autistic-like children, those with Down's syndrome or brain damage, as well as with children who have sensory handicaps. This project has been a laboratory for scientists, a sounding board for educational procedures, a mechanism for bringing parents together, and a major training site for students. As the program has evolved during these last 4 years, a number of extremely important issues have surfaced. Resolutions to these issues will provide some of the necessary information to formulate effective educational programs for young at risk or developmentally delayed children.

Critical to the success of early intervention is the need for appropriate assessment instruments or evaluation procedures for gauging the progress of young children. The continued use of standardized intelligence tests is becoming increasingly aversive but, unfortunately, there is a lack of reasonable and useful alternatives. A second issue concerns parental involvement in the child's educational program. Parental participation in their child's training seems highly desirable, but there is little precedent, and only a few general models for obtaining this involvement are being evaluated. The desire, and often the need, for noncategorical education is the third issue. The question of noncategorical education is far from being resolved because teachers continue to be trained in instructing categories of children. Furthermore, the funding for special programs has remained categorically restrictive. Finally, the continuing dissociation of service and research in which researchers do not involve themselves in service projects and service people do not engage in research must be considered an important issue. These four issues capture some of the more important facets of early intervention for the handicapped child. Each of these issues is discussed in the following sections in reference to the problem solving strategy developed in the context of the Infant, Toddler, and Preschool Research and Intervention Project (hereafter referred to as the Toddler Project).

ASSESSMENT AND CLASSIFICATION

The domain of intelligence and intelligence testing is an area of continuing controversy, and only the most naive would propose a total solution to the problems inherent in assessment and subsequent classification of children for evaluation and treatment purposes. The research group of the Toddler Project has analyzed this issue at great length as part of the Project on Classification of Exceptional Children (Hobbs, 1975). This analysis has led to the conclusion that the necessity of providing some means of identifying those individuals who will need special services is undisputable and, further, to the recognition

Table 1. Demographic information on children in the Infant, Toddler, and Preschool Research and Intervention Project

N	Infant Unit 23	Toddler Unit 28	Preschool Unit 27	Total 78
CA (in months)				
Mean	22	36	56	39
Range	5–43	21–50	43–76	5–76
Sex				
Male	9	16	18	43
Female	14	12	9	35
Race				
Black	6	5	9	20
White	16	22	17	55
Other	1	1	1	3
Economic Level[a]				
Upper	1	6	4	11
Middle	8	9	8	25
Lower	14	13	15	42
IQ[b]				
Delayed (N = 33)				
Mean	49 (N = 11)	55 (N = 12)	50 (N = 10)	52
Range	28–64	36–68	32–63	28–68
Nondelayed (N = 41)				
Mean	91 (N = 8)	109 (N = 16)	94 (N = 17)	99
Range	72–119	71–135	70–145	70–145
Etiology[c]				
Down's syndrome	8	8	9	25
Brain injury	3	0	1	4
Suspected genetic disorder	2	1	0	3
General delay	4	2	1	7
Autistic-like	1	1	2	4
Physically handicapped	1	0	0	1
Multiply handicapped	0	0	0	1
Normal–at risk	4	6	5	15
Normal	0	9	9	18

[a]The Upper category refers to families whose income exceeds $12,000 per year. The Middle category refers to families whose income is between $6,000 and $12,000 per year. The Lower category refers to families whose income is less than $6,000 per year.

[b]The Delayed category refers to children who score below 70 on standardized intelligence tests. The Nondelayed category refers to children who score above 70 on a standardized intelligence test. Four infants have not been tested.

[c]Normal–at risk refers to children who score above 70 on a standardized intelligence test but who have additional factors in their environment that would make educational problems a high probability. General delay refers to children who score below 70 on a standardized intelligence test but for whom no specific etiology has been isolated.

that IQ tests have been shown to be efficient predictors of large group differences in academic achievement. However, there must be a questioning of the utility of classification systems that rely upon a *prediction* of academic success as the *criterion* for assigning large numbers of people to gross categories. First, prediction is not really the desired outcome, and second, academic achievement is a relatively poor measure of success in life (McClelland, 1973). As Haywood (1971) has pointed out, "Outside the prediction of academic achievement, intelligence tests probably should not be used at all, especially for the prediction of social adjustment and ultimate success in living in communities." In addition, the categories of mild, moderate, severe, and profound imply that persons within a particular category will exhibit highly similar forms of behavior. Given the present state of knowledge concerning the pervasiveness of individual differences, variation within categories is probably much greater than has been assumed. Finally, categorization and subsequent labeling often proceed on the basis of an enumeration of the qualities a person does not possess. Thus, the absence of behavior defines the nature of the label applied. In this regard, Haywood (1969) has commented, "At the very least, a retarded individual should be diagnosed on the basis of behavior which he does demonstrate, not on the basis of characteristics which we were unable to find" (p. 379).

For all of the above reasons, this program questions the value of classification systems as presently constituted. The ultimate goal of such systems should contribute directly to the optimal adjustment of the person. Obviously, the medical diagnosis of clinical syndromes is a necessary and desirable aspect of those classification systems in mental retardation. Many medical syndromes associated with retardation are treatable (e.g., phenylketonuria, hypothyroidism). However, behavioral classification (measured intelligence and adaptive behavior) as presently assessed does not specify educational treatment and disposition. To classify a child and attach a label cannot be justified unless the child demonstrably benefits from the process (Filler et al., 1975). The alternative to classification that was proposed by Filler et al. (1975) is based primarily on the work of Jean Piaget and his colleagues (Piaget, 1952; 1954; 1970; Piaget and Inhelder, 1969). The present authors have followed the lead of Hunt, who described the relevance of Piaget's theory to intellectual development in *Intelligence and Experience* (1961) and who subsequently reiterated the need for a form of competency-based evaluation (1972). Analysis of the literature on cognitive development leads one to believe that most researchers and practitioners in early intervention do not fully appreciate the thoroughness and complexity of Piaget's position on human development. Furth (1970) among others had defended Piaget in demonstrating that Piaget's theory has avoided the pitfall of both apriority and positivistic empiricism. The present authors have combined several key concepts from the writings of Piaget and now refer to this position as "constructive interaction-adaptation" theory. In this position, behavioral learning theory is not emphasized and, most certainly, any maturational explanations of human development are excluded. The development of human behavior is complex, and intervention approaches must come to grips with this complexity or be doomed to an endless corridor of negative or equivocal results.

The constructive interaction-adaptation position specifies that all forms of behavioral development begin with the exercising of the reflexes. Through the infant's first interactions with objects, the reflexes are elaborated and become coordinated through a series of stages that Piaget has called the sensorimotor period, which lasts from birth to about 2 years of age. During the first three stages of the sensorimotor period, the infant responds involuntarily in a manner consistent with the systems of behavior modification. Actions of the infant produce consequences that are associated with a rapid increase in the rate or intensity of the actions. During the first phases of these primary circular reactions, the infant is under the control of the consequences alone, but, as the action-reaction system continues to operate, the child learns to make discriminations about which objects are suckable, graspable, shakeable, bangable, or throwable. As these action-object relationships increase in number and become coordinated, as in the "eye-hand-grasp-mouth" sequence, the infant's action system moves out of the involuntary mode into one that can be considered voluntary, deliberate, or intentional. That is, the infant begins to discriminate antecedent events and produces action-relevant responses accordingly. Terms like novelty seeking and curiosity become applicable to the infant's behavior. The developmental milestones during this period that are consistent with Piaget's specifications were mapped by Bricker and Chatelanat and can be seen in Figure 1. Within this system, there is *no need for the concept of intelligence* as such, simply adaptations to the various interactions that infants have with people, objects, or events. These interactions form the basis of coordinated schemes from which the infant constructs a practical understanding of his physical and social environment.

Figure 1 can be viewed not only as a representation of the theoretical development of the sensorimotor period but also as a framework to direct training activities. The ascending box structure in Figure 1 represents the increasing complexity of behavior that correlates with increasing chronological age. However, as noted above, the constructive interaction-adaptation position does not include a concept of maturation or a requirement of normative patterns of development. Consistencies among the sequences of development of children are viewed as the result of approximately equivalent interactive experiences occurring at about the same time in life, as well as the result of logical and empirical requirements of a fixed order of structures or schemes in the developmental process. Thus, starting at the bottom of Figure 1 with the exercising of the reflexes, the order of these structures is given in an ascending hierarchy. The right-left dimension of the figure is arbitrary; but the vertical dimension refers to developmental sequence, with schemes of equal distance from the baseline coming into existence at about the same time. The highest point in the figure can be viewed as the terminal state of the sensorimotor period, and it includes the preverbal cognitive prerequisites for semantic, phonological, and syntactic language processes and for understanding space, time, physical causality, seriation, number, and a primitive classification of environmental events including social relationships.

The developmental order and the relationships implied between the various action schemes represented in Figure 1 are an overview of what is thought to be an exciting

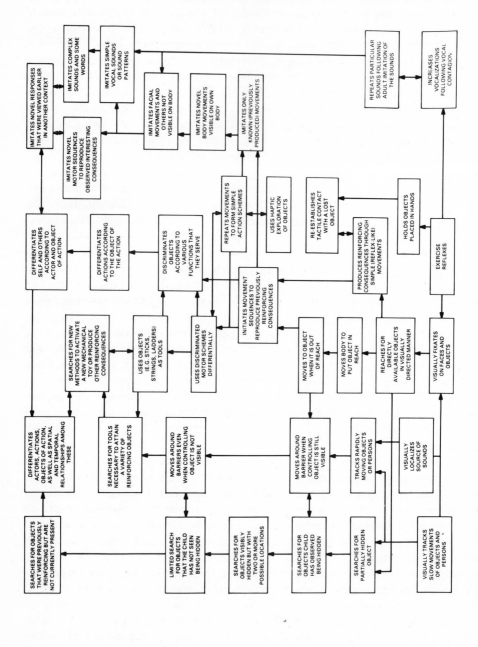

Figure 1. A representation of the theoretical framework for sensorimotor training activities. (Reproduced with permission from Filler et al., 1975.)

merger of theory and data at the procedural level. This merger ultimately may provide the foundation for a functional assessment and classification system. Within this model, procedures must make contact with the abilities of a given child, and then the range, sequence, and nature of instructional events that will provide stimulating mechanisms for moving the child to the next, more complex form of behavior must be specified.

An example of how this system works can be taken from visual tracking and hand-eye coordination represented in Figure 1. These forms of behavior have been described developmentally by Bruner (1969) and White (1969), who have indicated the progression of abilities in these areas and the approximate ages at which each phase occurs. In the conventional classification system, Bruner's and White's procedures could be standardized and then presented to a suitable number of children of various ages to establish the norms of development more precisely. The procedures could then be used to describe the developmental status of a wide range of children (cf. Bayley Scales of Infant Development).

However, in the model proposed here, precise norms are not required because approximate ages of first appearance for each form of behavior could be used, for example, to determine whether a child should be tracking in either the vertical or the horizontal direction. If the child does not track, then subsequent test items might be irrelevant until this form of behavior is acquired. One method for training tracking is to take an object, such as a noise-making toy, that elicits attention responses from the child. The toy is held in front of the infant's eyes until the child is judged to make direct visual contact with the object, then the toy is activated to produce its sound. This is repeated a few times until the child looks at the toy almost immediately upon its presentation. Given visual regard of the object, the next step is to move the toy slowly a few centimeters in a horizontal arc. If the infant tracks the object, the noise maker is again activated; if not, the toy remains in the new position until the child makes visual contact, and then the noise is produced. This cycle can be repeated on a daily basis by the parents or teacher using the noise-making toy as well as other "interesting" objects in order to stimulate generalized visual tracking in the vertical and horizontal planes.

Hand-eye coordination can be established via an overlapping training routine by moving the toy (or other objects) toward the child until the object is within the child's reach. His hands can be physically guided to the object and held in the bimanual grasp position as the object is moved (by the adult during the early phases) to the child's mouth where he can suck for a few moments. As the cycle is repeated (the child's changes in performance determining the number of repetitions), the use of physical guidance can be faded until the child is reaching, grasping, and then moving the object to his mouth without assistance. Before or during the training sessions, various parameters of the task, such as object preferences, are explored because the selection of a nondesired object can mask the extent of the child's repertoire by reducing his motivational state (Filler, 1973). The parent or instructor attempts to shape the target behavior in a variety of functional settings as well as with a variety of objects usually present in the child's environment. Thus, a training goal can be the child's production of a novel form of behavior or the consolidation of a response that may be in the child's repertoire but used inconsistently or with a restricted range of objects.

This training system can be viewed as a process in which the instructor (or experimenter) asks the child a sequence of nonverbal questions through presentation of the materials. In the area of the object permanence concept, the questions could include the following: 1) Does the child reach for objects under any circumstances? 2) If so, will he reach for objects in any position, such as for his bottle when it is lying on its side? 3) Will he reach for the selected objects when they are partially covered? 4) Will he reach for objects that are completely hidden and, in the process, remove the cover? Does he do this only when he views the object being hidden, or will he also search for the object when it is hidden out of his view? 5) Does the child look where the object was last found, or does he look where it was last seen? 6) If the child does not see the object being hidden, and there are several different locations in which the object might be found, does the child search in a sequential and nonredundant manner? The detailed answers to such questions, across repeated testings involving systematic variation in the materials being hidden and in the number and types of locations where they are hidden, provide reasonable data for developing appropriate educational programs.

The above examples of moving directly from testing to instruction demonstrate several important features of this approach. The areas assessed are critical for development and are not simply forms of behavior that predict subsequent development. Second, if the child fails to demonstrate a prerequisite process, the assumption is made that he will probably fail in a more complex area. Consequently, instruction is started when the first failure is detected so that the initial forms of instruction in an area are used to explore the parameters of the child's repertoire in order to determine the extent of his performance and to test various hypotheses about why the child is failing.

Failure could result from motivational variables or from the absence of one or more necessary prerequisite responses. Once the most likely reasons for failure have been isolated, then the information can be used to structure the necessary training. Because operant shaping provides one of the most explicit instructional systems available, it will frequently form the basis of the training program. When criterion performance is reached, the assessment procedure is resumed until another gap or deficiency is detected in the child's repertoire. Ideally, though, assessment and instruction are overlapping procedures in the sense that both aspects should explore the child's abilities not only in the area of particular assessment or instructional program but also in the domains that develop simultaneously and that require similar or related skills common to the particular developmental level.

Simple examples such as hand-eye coordination and training the object permanence concept are only two isolated examples of the many different domains in which retarded infants and preschool children need training. The Toddler Project curriculum includes training routines in walking and other gross motor skills, fine motor skills, self-help skills, as well as in language and sensorimotor development. The constructive interaction-adaptation position has been used to synthesize cognitive, linguistic, and operant approaches to the specifications of educational training routines. Previous research efforts have suggested the efficacy of employing such a linked assessment and training system. (D. Bricker, Vincent-Smith, and W. Bricker, 1973; W. Bricker, 1972; W. Bricker and D. Bricker, 1966; 1970; 1973; Lynch and Bricker, 1972). A future goal is the generation of additional data to support this approach in the assessment, evaluation, and training of young developmentally delayed children.

PARENTAL INVOLVEMENT

A second major issue facing early interventionists is the involvement of parents in ongoing educational programs for their children. A variety of approaches have been conceived and implemented: 1) full day care in which parental contact is minimal (Caldwell and Richmond, 1968), 2) home-based programs in which the parent is either a participant (Schaefer, 1970) or an observer (Rynders and Horrobin, 1972), and 3) educational programs in which variations exist in the amount of parental participation (Horton, 1974; D. Bricker and W. Bricker, 1973). Although the outcome of these varying approaches seems to suggest that no one approach is going to be suitable for all parents and family situations, most early interventionists agree that at least two powerful reasons exist for the inclusion of parents as integral parts of their handicapped child's education and care. First, there are far more handicapped or high risk infants and young children than there are professionally trained staff to provide the necessary care. One obvious solution to this discrepancy is the use of parents to supplement the services provided by professionals. Second, as Tharp and Wetzel (1969) have pointed out, the parent is apt to be more reinforcing to the child than most other adults and, consequently, the parent becomes not only the most available but also the most ideal teacher. Of course, there are parents who, for a variety of reasons, do not learn to work effectively with their child, and alternative approaches must be implemented. If one lesson has been learned during the past 4 years, it has been the need for flexibility in approach toward both children and parents.

The parent training program has not always been flexible, but a variety of experiences have shown that parents require as much individual programming as do children. Treating parents as a homogenous group when they vary from having advanced academic degrees to those who spent their childhood and youth in one of the state residential facilities for the mentally retarded obviously is inappropriate. During the first 2 years of the Toddler Project, parent training and advising was carried out by the research and teaching staff. Although these people were qualified and appropriate for the roles of parent trainers, they were unable to spend adequate time with the parents. During the third year, a parent advisory unit was created. It is composed of three full-time advisors, a social worker, and a part-time coordinator. The primary responsibilities of this component are: 1) to help parents become effective educational change agents with their children, 2) to assist parents in becoming educated consumers of programs and materials offered as services for their children, 3) to offer services for those families with special needs (i.e., help in acquiring food stamps, obtaining proper medical and dental services for a child, special counseling services), and 4) to coordinate educational activities between the home and the classroom.

The majority of parent education has focused on language, motor, sensorimotor, and social areas, which also form the core classroom curriculum. Initially, parents were trained in the use of behavior management skills as prerequisite to working in the curriculum areas. Training was generally conducted in small group sessions; however, when a parent had a special or particularly difficult problem, the parent advisor shifted to individual sessions. Video tapes were made of the parent training her child, which then served as the focal point for helping the parent improve her training skills. The use of video replay appears to be an effective teaching strategy for use with parents (Filler, 1974). Consumer education was carried out by exposing parents to appropriate films, books and other printed matter, informing them about organizations that are concerned with providing education and services for young children, and to arrange meetings with local, state, and national personnel in decision making positions. For example, the director of the special education department in the local public schools has attended two parent meetings expressly to answer questions about what type of services would be available for handicapped children in the future. The parents have also had the opportunity to question representatives of the Joseph P. Kennedy, Jr., Foundation, members of the President's Committee on Mental Retardation, officials of the State Department of Education, as well as persons associated with other early intervention programs. All of these interactions were designed to provide the parent with knowledge about issues that directly concern their child's education. Special services were offered through a variety of mechanisms. These services ranged from holding evening meetings once a month for fathers who could not attend the program during the day to helping a mother learn to read. The primary objective of these special services was to help families move from a crisis existence to more stable and predictable situations by learning to anticipate trouble producing events and developing strategies for meeting these events. For example, the family who repeatedly runs out of food was helped to develop a strategy for spacing food usage across the month, as well as locating other food sources such as government surpluses. The final responsibility of the parent advising component was the coordination of training activities conducted in the classroom and at home. The parent advisors and the teaching staff shared information so that both components could function effectively. The parents should not be working at cross purposes with the classroom program, no more than classroom training should be disrupting parental goals.

The families served primarily within the educational system of the Toddler Project had developmentally delayed children.[1] Generally, mothers (or fathers if possible) of delayed children were requested to spend at least one morning or afternoon a week at the Center. If a child's mother were employed, she could either come to the center on her day off or, if this were not possible, home visits were arranged.

---

[1] This section was taken from a report written by L. Vincent-Smith on the Parent Advising Component of the Infant, Toddler, and Preschool Research and Intervention Project.

Mothers were trained in four major skill areas, which corresponded to the classroom curriculum areas of language, cognitive, motor, and social development. The mothers were generally involved in one or two areas simultaneously. For mothers with children in the toddler and preschool classroom units, the primary emphasis was placed on language. For mothers of children in the infant unit, the emphasis was placed on cognitive development and was focused, more specifically, upon the sensorimotor curriculum and imitation skills. Each of the training groups met once a week.

The social development skills group was divided into two areas: self-help skills and behavior management. The self-help group focused on spoon feeding and cup drinking with the infants, toilet training with the toddlers, and dressing with the preschoolers. Initially, mothers working on these skills would meet in small groups with a parent advisor but, as the mother's skills progressed, supervision was provided by a previously trained mother who assumed responsibility for training new mothers. The group meetings were used to target behavior, discuss training strategies, and evaluate data in the form of weekly probes collected by the mothers. In addition to the group meetings, mothers conducted demonstration sessions for the trainer and themselves. These demonstration sessions were used to evaluate the mother's effectiveness in following program procedures, with emphasis placed on the improvement of shaping skills.

The behavior management group generally was composed of an equal number of mothers of delayed and nondelayed children. Problems in home behavior, such as tantrums and toy throwing, were the general focus. Each mother targeted a problem, collected data, and intervened on one appropriate behavior at a time. The group meeting time was spent evaluating the success of the intervention and discussing "discipline" in general.

The motor development skill group, led by a parent advisor, convened once a week, and the training was divided into two major areas. Mothers in the gross motor group worked primarily on either walking (infants) or more advanced motor skills (toddlers). Group time was used to target behavior and to discuss teaching strategies. Training sessions were conducted by the mothers on each visit to the center and evaluated by the parent advisor. Mothers in the fine motor group worked primarily on skills such as buttoning and lacing. The overall structure of training was the same as for the gross motor group.

The cognitive development group met once a week with two parent advisors and primarily involved mothers of infants. The parent advisors explained the classroom sensorimotor curriculum to the mothers and demonstrated procedures for establishing and maintaining responses. Video tapes of the classroom teachers conducting training sessions were also shown. When possible, mothers conducted training sessions with their infants at least once weekly at the Center, and the parent advisor acted as a supervisor or trainer. Infant mothers' group meetings were also used to discuss other classroom programs and general principles of growth and development. Mothers of infants were involved in classroom activities as often as was feasible.

The language group met once a week and included the majority of the mothers of infant, toddler, and preschool children. The first half hour of the meeting was used as a general forum, and the classroom coordinator discussed general classroom procedures and programs with the mothers. During this time, relevant films, video tapes, and written materials were discussed or presented to the mothers. After the general forum, the mothers were divided into three smaller groups depending on the developmental level of their child. These groups were function/receptive, imitation/expressive, and syntax. These areas corresponded to the target training areas of the classroom language program. The model used to teach the mothers how to conduct home training sessions was a replica of the classroom program. Video tapes of laboratory training sessions were used to demonstrate teaching strategies. Mothers worked with their own children. These sessions were supervised by the parent advisors and, when appropriate, by the speech pathologist.

The number of skill groups in which a mother was involved depended upon the amount of time she was able to spend at the Center and the developmental level of her child. Groups were reconstituted at the beginning of each semester, and a mother remained in a skill group only until her child learned the targeted skill.

Initially, regular home visitations were planned for those families who could not get into the Center. However, because of the size of the population and the complexity of the problems faced by some families coming into the Center, the parent advisors were severely restricted in available time to make home visits for training parents.

Supportive social services were provided to families who required them. Because the majority of families with nondelayed children and some of the families with delayed children met low income guidelines as established by the Department of Public Welfare, social service demands were substantial. Each parent advisor (in addition to being responsible for a skill group) and the social worker carried a caseload of about 20 individual families. They were responsible for providing home visits and social services to these families.

To determine the structure and needs of the family, the parent advisors and the social worker conducted assessments on each family upon entry into the program. These assessments included evaluations on the health, personality, interaction patterns, home environment, employment history and skills, community participation, and attitude toward employment of the parents. The services needed by the families were determined using these assessments. Services have included providing food, clothing, housing, transportation, child care, family planning, vocational or educational training, home management, medical services, and protective services. These services were provided by appropriate community agencies with the parent advisor or social worker serving as a liaison. Periodic reassessment of the family was conducted, and contact was established with new agencies when necessary.

Mothers of nondelayed children were encouraged to come into the Center at least once a month to observe their children in the classrooms and to meet with their parent advisor and teacher. At this time, the child's progress in the classroom and the home was discussed. Information on home stimulation activities was provided to the mother and a demonstration session conducted if necessary. If appropriate, the parent advisor also discussed issues such as hygiene and diet with the mother.

As with other components in the Toddler Project, the parent advising unit is in its embryonic stage, and during the past 4 years many approaches and strategies have been attempted. It is hoped that a useful analysis of training strategies has been developed (Smith et al., 1973), but the job that lies ahead is the validation and refinement of training techniques in order to maximize parental involvement and effectiveness in training their children.

NONCATEGORICAL OR INTEGRATED EDUCATION

As mentioned earlier, the goal of noncategorical education has two major difficulties that will take perseverance and ingenuity to overcome. First, most funds, be they local, state, or federal, are designated on the basis of a child being "officially" labeled as having a specific disability. Some classification and identification is necessary to see that children who need financial assistance receive such aid; however, the current approaches seem antithetical to the desired goal of noncategorical education (Hobbs, 1975). Second, many teacher training programs are based on categorical training, as are the divisions in the Council for Exceptional Children. Consequently, we continue to graduate teachers of the deaf, retarded, or emotionally disturbed who are convinced that their expertise is circumscribed by specific disability areas. No one would argue that special skills are not necessary for a teacher confronted with a partially hearing child or one who is blind, but most of the basic skills or educational approaches transcend these categories. Teachers should first learn how to educate children in specific curriculum areas and then acquire the special procedures needed to structure prosthetic environments required by specific handicapping conditions.

The Infant, Toddler, and Preschool Research and Intervention Project has been engaged in a form of noncategorical education for 4 years, and from this experience it can be argued that noncategorical education should begin in the preschool years through the integration of many types of handicapped children into a single intervention system. In addition, integrated education should be extended to include an equal number of nonhandicapped children to participate in the same program. This is ideal if some of these nonhandicapped children come from homes that are "better than average" in parental understanding of child development principles and that provide exceptionally stimulating environments for their children. Within this model proposed here, a great variety of children can be effectively served under the egis of the same program.

The Toddler Project has been structured to provide educational and counseling services to approximately 80 children and their families. The children ranged in age from 3 months to approximately 6 years. About 33 of the children were classified as developmentally delayed, with a range from those having severe problems to those exhibiting only slight behavioral deviations. The remaining 41 children were considered to be nondelayed; that is, functioning within normal limits in both the social and cognitive domains. The data to date suggest that an arbitrary division between delayed and nondelayed children is not educationally useful; however, the developmental "age" of the child is an adequate basis for determining the level of educational need. Therefore, the children have been placed into various educational units on the basis of developmental age not chronological age. Most of the children in the program received four half days of classroom instruction each week in one of three classroom divisions: infant, toddler, or preschool unit. Each unit had a morning and an afternoon class that served a different group of children, although several children have remained in the project for the entire day. Nine developmentally delayed children and their parents have been served on a once a week or bi-monthly basis in what was called the "Friday Clinic." Members of the staff met with the parents and worked with them in evaluating the child's progress and then demonstrated procedures for further stimulation. This service was offered to families who lived too far from the project to come on a daily basis as well as to young infants or profoundly delayed toddlers who would not currently benefit from being placed in a classroom environment.

During the first year of the program, a morning program was offered for 10 children and an afternoon program for the same number of children. The combined group of children was composed of 11 children with developmental delays and nine children who were from all appearances developing normally. During the inital year of the project, finding parents of normally developing children who were willing to place their child in a program that also included "mentally retarded" children was not easy. Many parents who were eager to have their toddler enrolled in an educational program quickly changed their mind when they learned that handicapped children would be integrated into the same classroom. People often asked during that first year why handicapped and nonhandicapped children were placed in the same program. The answers generally covered three areas, which are discussed below.

Although "mainstreaming" is now a somewhat common term in education and special education, 4 years ago the concept of normalization as described by Wolfensberger (1972) was new. The idea behind normalization is that every child should be entitled to live the most "normal-like" existence possible. That is, any child who can function in a regular public school class should remain there. A child who can be maintained in the regular school program by providing a special support teacher should remain in a regular class rather than be isolated in a self-contained classroom. Only children who cannot function appropriately in a regular education program should be removed to self-contained special classes and, finally, only those few exceptional children who cannot be maintained in the community should be institutionalized. The concept of "mainstreaming," which now has legislative support in many states, provides the maximum opportunity for handicapped children to interact with normally developing peers, thus providing the atypical child with a more normal environment than do programs that only include children with developmental problems. The preschool years would seem to be an ideal time to begin "mainstreaming."

An unexpected outcome of total integration is that not only do the children have the opportunity to explore and learn about each other but, also, the parents of nonhandicapped youngsters have the chance to interact closely with parents of children who have moderate to severe problems. This interaction has the potential of being an enlightening experience for both. An often heard comment by mothers in the project was that they had a real fear of or great uncertainty about mentally retarded children when they entered their child in the program. However, their experiences in the project quickly changed fear to calm with the realization that retarded children are basically much like other children. In a sense, the close interaction between parents has allowed for communication which, we believe, has been important in terms of educating a wide variety of people about developmental difficulties.

Finally, the research by Bandura and others has strongly suggested that children do imitate behavior that produces observable reinforcing environmental events (Bandura, 1967). Perhaps one of the most effective ways for a young delayed child to learn a functional response is to observe the occurrence of that response by another child. For example, by watching a normal youngster drag a chair to the water fountain to get a drink and succeed, the delayed child may be able to imitate the response. This imitation should result in acquiring the desired water plus the independence of not having to ask the teacher or parent for assistance. For these three reasons, the Project became committed to the idea of trying to build a program that could integrate children with a variety of problems and developmental skills without interfering with the developmental progress of any individual child.

INFANT UNIT

The infant unit contained approximately 23 babies ranging in developmental level from 5 to 16 months. This unit has focused on high risk and organically involved children. For example, the current population is composed of eight children with Down's syndrome, three children with documented birth injury, two children with suspected genetic abnormalities, one child with spina bifida, and nine high risk children (e.g., a baby with a fractured skull at 3 months, an autistic-like baby, a baby with general developmental delay for no apparent reason, and a baby from a large family all of whom are educationally retarded). No baby with a normal past history has been included in this unit. This program accommodates babies on either an all day, half day, or once a week basis. The primary emphasis has been the acquisition of sensorimotor skills in order to prepare the baby to move into the toddler unit. If possible, the two teachers that operate this classroom have focused on training the mother or father to work with their baby rather than the teacher working directly with the baby. Unfortunately, this has not always been possible, because many of the children came from low income or middle income backgrounds in which both parents must work. In other families, a mother may have several other preschoolers at home. Finally, a few parents were extremely limited themselves or unable to work effectively with their moderately to severely developmentally delayed child. This variety of needs has mandated a flexible infant program.

The infant program in a classroom setting was the most difficult to bring into a functional existence. Over a year was spent interacting with the infants before a coherent educational program started to emerge. Even the physical setting was difficult to design and arrange in terms of furniture, mats, cribs, parallel bars for walking, diaper changing facilities, and the location and accessibility of toys.

Assessment to determine the developmental level of each baby was done on a relatively informal basis by the teacher with help from graduate students, undergraduate practicum students, and other qualified staff members. These assessments covered motor processes such as visual tracking, visually guided reaching, searching for hidden objects, functional or symbolic use of objects, prehension, self-feeding, walking, and numerous other areas. As often as possible, the ongoing play behavior of the infant was used in the assessments. In other cases, known preferences of the child were used to assess the level of functioning. For example, Filler (1973) demonstrated that the sensorimotor behavior of a young low functioning child was much higher when "spin-able" objects were used in domains such as object permanence, visually directed reaching, and visual tracking. While the term reinforcement is used within the project, every attempt has been made to use functional reinforcers that will naturally maintain behavior once the behavior is acquired. In addition, the preference system of each baby establishes the range of reinforcement that can be used. Thus, the assessment system has been somewhat idiosyncratic and nonstandardized, but the information derived from the assessment leads directly into relevant training tasks. Wide range achievement tests such as the Bayley Scales of Infant Development or the Cattell Infant Intelligence Scale have been used periodically to cross validate the information derived from the more extensive classroom assessment procedures.

The specific goals of the infant classroom have been: 1) the creation of individual programs to develop the child's competencies in the areas of gross motor skills, fine motor skills, sensorimotor, self-help, and social skills; 2) the operationalization and empirical validation of such Piagetian concepts as causality, means-end, object permanence, imitation, and functional usage; 3) the development of a library of video tapes of infant behavior to be used for research, teaching, and parent training; and 4) the provision for each child to develop certain prerequisite forms of behavior necessary for adaptive functioning in the toddler unit.

Because of the nature of the programming and age of children served by the infant unit, the daily schedule has remained purposefully flexible and adaptive. Each child's program generally has included training in sensorimotor, gross and fine motor, social, and self-help skills. Typical intervention periods have run from 3 to 5 minutes followed by rest or free play with a variety of stimulating toys and equipment. The total amount of time spent in direct intervention varies within and across infants, depending on the complexity and difficulty of the daily program and the child's interest and abilities.

TODDLER UNIT

The toddler classroom serves approximately 15 children in the morning and 15 different children in the afternoon classes. Approximately half of these children are developing normally while the others exhibit developmental delays. Children in this unit have ranged in developmental age from approximately 12 to 40 months, while chronological age has ranged from approximately 21 to 50 months. The specific goals for this unit have been to provide each child with: 1) daily group or individual language training, 2) individually programmed gross and fine motor activities, 3) the opportunity to engage in self-directed activities, 4) a consistent environment established and maintained through the application of contingency management techniques, 5) opportunities to develop appropriate cognitive skills such as labeling, problem solving, and concept formation, and 6) adaptive skills necessary for entrance into the preschool unit.

The toddler unit introduces the child to a more structured time schedule that is intended to help provide consistency in the classroom environment. A typical schedule of the daily activities for children in the Toddler unit is presented below.

Opening Group Time   Morning 9:00–9:15 Afternoon 1:00–1:15
    Seat children in chairs.
    Say "Hi" to each child and elicit a response—"Hi," wave, eye contact.
    Sing songs.
    Practice motor imitation, e.g., touch feet, clap hands.
    Have children push their chairs to the tables.

Skill-building Time   Morning 9:15–9:30 Afternoon 1:15–1:30
    During this time, children will be encouraged to work on quiet individual tasks such as puzzles, form boards, etc. Selection of the task will be based on both the child's interest and developmental level.

Programs   Morning 9:30–11:00 Afternoon 1:30–3:00
    Take individual students or small groups to the assigned area and begin work on programs such as language, gross motor, and self-help skills.
    When the first group is finished, tell the children they may play; find the children in the next group, take them to the assigned area, and begin on the program.
    Continue with each group on the schedule until all children have been through their individual programs.

Free Play   Morning 9:30–11:00 Afternoon 1:30–3:00
    (For children when not involved in a program)
    Help a child to find a toy—prompt if he does not or suggest an activity—slide, boat, housekeeping.
    Move around the room giving attention to each child.

Gym Time or Outside   Morning 11:00–11:30 Afternoon 3:00–3:30
    Announce that it is time to put away toys and go to the gym or playground.
    Prompt children to pick up toys and put them away.
    Have children gather at door.
    When leaving the room, have one teacher go first, one teacher help slow-walkers, and one teacher check to make sure that all children get to the gym.
    Activities in the Gym or Outside
    Riding tricycle and any non-pedal toys
    Playing with balls

Jumping and rolling on mats
Running
Games (ring around the roses)

As a general strategy encourage the children to participate in a group game that has as a targeted objective the practice of some gross motor skill, after which free play will be encouraged.

Juice Time   Morning 11:30–11:45 Afternoon 3:30–3:45
Seat children in chairs.
Elicit appropriate responses from each child before giving him juice.
Take the cup when a child is finished.
Snack time will be used to practice self-help feeding and drinking as well as stimu-
lating expressive language.

Closing Time   Morning 11:45–12:00 Afternoon 3:45–4:00
Sing songs.
Practice motor imitations.
Beginning at one end of the group, instruct each child in turn to say good-bye to the
child seated next to him.
Have children say good-bye together.
Tell children to get their coats.

The activities used in the instructional programs are taken from the language, social, sensorimotor, and motor curricula that have been developed in the project during the past 4 years. These curriculum materials currently represent the "best guess" as to the most effective training procedures and content. Undoubtedly, these materials will undergo change as they are used with additional children.

PRESCHOOL UNIT

As in the toddler classroom, the preschool unit has approximately 15 children enrolled in both the morning and afternoon classes. Again, approximately half of these youngsters are functioning within the normal developmental range, while the remaining children are functioning significantly below their expected developmental level in one or several critical skill areas. Children have ranged in developmental age from 36 to 45 months and chronological age from approximately 43 to 76 months. The specific goals for this unit have been to provide each child with opportunities: 1) to develop pre-operational cognitive skills, 2) to develop further and refine more difficult self-help skills, 3) to develop increasingly independent behavior without teacher supervision or continuous reinforcement, 4) to correctly formulate three-word phrases, and 5) to develop certain prerequisite or useful early elementary education skills.

In an effort to assist the child in developing realistic adaptive school skills, the preschool unit has provided an even more supportive time and spatial environment than either the infant or the toddler units. A list of representative daily activities is presented below.

Opening Group Time   Morning 9:00–9:15 Afternoon 1:00–1:15
Children arrive and seat themselves in a semicircle.
Teacher greets child seated next to her and requests that child greet the child next to him by name, continue until everyone is greeted.
Activities for this period may include feltboard, matching games, discrimination exercises, and imitation songs or games.
Direct children to appropriate small group for next activity.

Language and Concept Training Groups   Morning 9:15–10:15 Afternoon 1:15–2:15
Each child attends two small group sessions during this period, a language and a concept training group. Usually, the group composition is the same for both activities.
Activities include: matching, discrimination, naming and imitative tasks, or building of other cognitive and language skills.

Snack Time   Morning 10:15–10:30 Afternoon 2:15–2:30
After each child has put away his materials from small group activity, the snacks are brought to the table.
An appropriate response is elicited from each child before he receives a snack (i.e., labels food correctly).

Story Time or Quiet Games   Morning 10:30–10:50 Afternoon 2:30–2:50
After finishing his snack and helping to clean up, each child is allowed to select a toy for a brief period of free play.
Children are offered opportunity to use the toilet during this period.
Children sit together to hear a story or play a game.

Outdoor Play or Gross Motor Activities   Morning 10:50–11:20 Afternoon 2:50–3:20
Children line up to go to playground or to gym.
Activities outside include: play on equipment such as swings, play in sandbox, or simple group games.
Activities in gym include: trampoline, movement through obstacle course, relay races, simple exercises, and games.

Art or Fine Motor Activities   Morning 11:20–11:45 Afternoon 3:20–3:45
After returning from previous activity, children are directed to chairs.
Children are given various activities designed to develop fine motor coordination.
Activities during this period include: stringing beads, placing pegs in pegboard, painting or drawing, and using scissors.

Closing Group Time   Morning 11:45–12:00 Afternoon 3:45–4:00
Review the day's activities.
Sing songs or play imitation games.
Say good-bye.

The daily schedule provides opportunities for children to participate in a variety of activities and social situations. In each type of activity, the response expected of the child has been based upon the child's competencies. In the large group opening and closing times, when motor imitation and following directions have been emphasized through the use of action songs, the teacher attempts to individualize the commands according to each child's capabilities. The small groups have offered an opportunity for grouping children together on the basis of their level of functioning (i.e., children who need programs in receptive vocabulary on the same level of difficulty have been grouped together). Placements have been flexible however, so that if one child were to make faster progress than another, that child would be moved to a different group. If a particular child needed individual programming in a particular area, he would be given individual work and moved back into a group when his level of performance made that possible.

In all three classroom units, a heavy emphasis has been placed on objective based education. Teachers constructed daily class programs using activities from the four curriculum domains: language, motor, social, and cognitive. Certain validated curriculum objectives were targeted, and activities were pre-planned using a standard program sheet as shown in Table 2. Each programmed objective was evaluated daily using three criteria: 1) appropriateness of target objectives for the developmental level of the child; 2) adequacy of teacher preparation and presentation; and 3) appropriateness of teaching materials. The idea that the responsibility for a child's learning and general developmental progress in the classroom lies with the teacher is a fundamental belief of this project.

All three classroom units have been built on the philosophy of noncategorical or

---

Table 2. Sample completed Teacher Evaluation Form

Infant, Toddler, and Preschool Research and Intervention Project
Evalution Form

Teacher's Name <u>Mrs. Silver</u>   Group <u>Self-help (rotation 3)</u>
Date <u>2/30/74</u>   Members <u>Mike, Karen, James</u>
Objectives of the Activity:
  Each child will demonstrate the ability to tie two laces in a bow
    using a bow card, two consecutive times (or closest approximation
    possible)
  Prerequisite skills: know left, right; fine motor movements
Materials:
  3 student bow tie cards
  1 teacher demonstration bow tie card
  Story of the bow tied rabbit
Programmed Activities:
  Bring out demonstration card and arrange all parts
  Set standards—cards flat on table, tops up, chairs close
  Tell story of bow tied rabbit using demonstration card, end up with bow
  Pass out students' cards
  Tell story again, stop after each part (tying movement) to check
    progress and/or to prompt
  Evaluate progress at end of activity
Evaluation:
Was objective met? James—met criterion level
               Karen—met objective once, but not criterion
               Mike—needed many prompts, did not appear to
               have prerequisite fine motor skills
Teacher behavior—preparation—good; consequation—adequate;
  should have dropped back with Mike
Materials and program—excellent, motivation high
Objective's appropriateness—Mike needs prerequisite fine motor work

---

integrated education with apparent success over the past 4 years. This success can probably be attributed to the careful selection and combining of children into classroom settings, by a dedicated staff that was convinced the idea would work, and by a group of loyal and trusting parents that eventually were able to assure other parents of obtaining quality education for each child participating in the program regardless of his potential or immediate competencies.

RESEARCH AND SERVICE INTERCHANGE

We all have heard that research, especially basic research, and science in general, does not need a goal or a purpose. Science is the mechanism for extending knowledge of the universe. We would not argue with this thesis; in fact, we would like to feel that our own research is within the domain of this scientific effort. The analysis of complex human behavior provides one of the most exciting activities available to scientists today because it not only is an approach to the ontological evolution of human knowledge but also involves an analysis of the processes by which knowledge is extended through theory and research. As Piaget and his colleagues have demonstrated, the development of the sensorimotor processes of young children is no less important or less awe inspiring than the most advanced theoretical propositions tendered by the greatest scientists. Both are constructed out of available experience derived from the unceasing interaction between existing conceptions (structures) and their subsequent operation within a bounded physical environment. The human cycle from zygote to zygote repeats this developmental process of constructive interaction-adaptation, and through each cycle the proverbial "island of ignorance" that sets the parameters of human knowledge may be reduced. The analysis of this complex developmental process involves an important system of investigation concerning the ontology of intellectual behavior and, as a side effect, an examination of the construct of intelligence in its own right. However, the implication of the developmental approach is that no construct concerning an underlying intellective process is necessary since the analysis of the processes involved provides an explanation of the emerging structures and operations of behavior and, thereby, of the complex behavior that was previously explained by the construct of intelligence. By precasting the analysis of the evolution of complex human behavior and discarding the construct of intelligence as a causal force, more rapid progress may be made toward understanding these processes and also finding mechanisms that may influence the course and rate of ontological development of human beings.

The formulation and empirical evaluation of a developmental approach to complex human behavior, especially as expressed in the development of children who are classified as "mentally retarded," has been the underlying theme of our research. In this effort, we have adopted a model based on cartography (W. Bricker, 1970) rather than formulations of behavior that are based on either neurological approaches or on the theory building activities so prevalent in the physical sciences. To us, the development of human behavior (or animal behavior for that matter) is best viewed as a progressive activity that can be mapped from one stage to another with the pattern of individual adaptations that determined the route of this progress represented as pathways along an n-dimensional surface. We have argued that the sequence of progress is determined by the program of training and includes the forms of stimulation (environmental modifications) that are covered by normal child rearing practices existent in a given culture. We have taken the view that these pathways are various theories of development and that the typical mode of progress within a culture is only one of many possible pathways available in reaching a defined destination. Consequently, research in human development within this perspective can be structured around an empirical comparison between two or more pathways from one stage to another which is defined by the culture as being more complex. For example, one of our early investigations compared four methods for establishing auditory stimulus control over the behavior of institutionalized retarded children (W. Bricker and D. Bricker, 1969). The routes were varied as a function of different assumptions about the most efficient pathway from a form of behavior that was not controlled by auditory stimuli to one that was under full control of the various pure tones used in the investigation. Pragmatically, this led to an empirical evaluation of the most efficient means for getting a pure tone audiometric evaluation of the child that was seen as a necessary prerequisite to other facets of language training. We have tried to follow this same approach in the domains of motor and verbal imitation (W. Bricker and D. Bricker, 1972), receptive vocabulary (W. Bricker and D. Bricker, 1970), object naming (W. Bricker and D. Bricker, 1974), and in various attempts at sequenced verbal expression.

Much of our research between 1960 and 1970 was done with institutionalized retarded children. Retrospectively, we could consider this a wasted effort in that much of our time was spent attempting to counter deviant forms of behavior that appeared to result from the institutional care given to the children and to their "tranquilized" state of existence. Our attempts at countering the effects of institutionalization took various forms including aide training, writing a training manual, and developing procedures for the rapid deceleration of unwanted behavior. For each minute of language training research, we seemed to spend 10 minutes contending with behavioral problems seemingly generated by the living conditions of the children. Slowly we came to recognize that we were not studying developmental processes of retarded children but were instead investigating the debilitating and dehumanizing processes of institutional living. Consequently, in 1970, when we started the Toddler Project we were amazed at the differences in the children and delighted at the future prospects for research and intervention. Here we were dealing with potentially retarded children who were living at home and who had not yet developed the deviant forms of behavior that we had previously associated with retarded persons. However, we also learned that the programs of training that has proved efficient and effective with the institutionalized population did not work with our toddlers. In fact, we found that the application of the behaviorally oriented extrinsic reinforcement procedures often tended to restrict rather than enhance the developmental progress of the children. Consequently, we felt compelled to generate new pathways that would prove educationally successful with these young children.

The development of these new pathways has dictated a new relationship to the existing literature on complex human behavior. We have come to appreciate the imprecise but insightful research of Jean Piaget while continuing to value the experimental analyses of behavior as a methodology. For the past few years, we have been working on a synthesis of these two positions. Piaget's writing helps us generate the developmental maps, while Skinner's work along with the substantial contributions of his followers provide detailed procedural alternatives. The domain of early language development provides an extremely interesting example of this synthesis.

In an earlier section, we described some of the interesting developments of the sensorimotor period and have concluded the description with the standard definition of the contingency of reinforcement in which a stimulus is discriminative for a response which has been associated with previous reinforcement. Contingencies of reinforcement are fine for the young infant, but to the toddler we must speak of physical causality, differentiation of means and ends, the development of the object permanence concept, and the knowledge of the spatial and temporal facets of coordinated actions. The analyses of these processes provide us with the basic ingredients out of which we can explore human behavior. Through such analyses we may find the basis for the language development of the 2-year-old, the explanation of his grammatical structuring of words, and the basic relationships between thought and language.

For the infant in a home, the relationships between actions and objects are not few in number. There are spoons, dolls, food in a variety of forms, dishes, breakable brick-a-brack, people, clothes, baths, rubber ducks, tickles on the belly, radios, television, and accidental jabs by the diaper pins followed immediately with cuddling and soothing talk. Such descriptions can be extended endlessly, except that we can fortunately reduce these examples to terms of actions, reaction, and most especially interaction, all of which combine to form a network of functional attribute systems into which the infant weaves the structure of his own behavior. Having no logical or theoretical system for incorporating the organization of these events, the infant constructs a fluid mode of adaptation that is predicated on the range of his own reactions and his momentary affective or motivational states. But these are not vacuous exercises, for out of these constructive-interaction-adaptations the infant establishes a complex attribute system that defines a functional network of people and objects. A spoon is not only an object for transporting food to the mouth but also a hammer, something to throw, a mirror, something to push at one's mother or father in order to provoke them, or a tool for getting rid of the pablum. Using this simple example within the context of Vygotsky's concept formation studies, we see this activity as a chained complex in that no single set of attributes defines the class "spoon" but rather we have a shifting classification depending on the purposes to be served at the moment. Given the lack of a formal logical system, a spoon is not a single event or even a particular conceptual class but rather a bundle of attributes that can be differentially distributed across a wide variety of actions. A spoon may be a spoon to an adult, but we believe to an infant it is a differentially functional tool for all the work there is to be done with objects like a spoon. In one context, a pencil may be in the same class with spoon while in another only other spoons are appropriate.

Starting in 1964, we developed a system of measurement in the domain of receptive vocabulary that still is functional. However, we also developed a series of pathways predicated on a two-choice discrimination paradigm with each supposedly traveling in the direction of discrimination learning set and culminating in conceptual receptive vocabulary. We have published several of these studies, although in each case we have emphasized the measurement aspects and the fact that many of the error responses of the children could be accounted for on the basis of a stimulus control paradigm (W. Bricker and D. Bricker, 1970; D. Bricker, 1972; D. Bricker, Vincent-Smith, and W. Bricker, 1973; Vincent-Smith, D. Bricker, and W. Bricker, 1974). Unfortunately, we have never been able to report success in training conceptual receptive vocabularly in expressively mute children. During the course of these investigations, we tried alternative approaches to mediate the verbal stimulus presented to the child and the object selection made by the child on the basis of that name. In the first procedure (D. Bricker, 1972), an imitative sign was used so that the child learned to make the sign in the presence of the object and then was taught to select that object when the experimenter produced its sign. The extension of the system was for the child to use the sign to mediate the name and the object selection. When this procedure was contrasted with an unmediated control procedure there was a statistically reliable difference in favor of the mediation trained group. The second approach was to train the child to use objects according to their socially appropriate function: a spoon is used to lift soft foods to the mouth; a cup is used for drinking; a ball is used for rolling or throwing. In an investigation of the relationship between functional classification and receptive vocabulary (Vincent-Smith and Chatelanat, 1973) a difference in favor of functional classification was found only for a relatively small group of preverbal toddler age children. In a somewhat more extensive investigation involving children whose mental age was between 19 and 54 months, there were no statistically reliable differences between functional classification and word comprehension. If the child could functionally classify objects according to a socially appropriate system, he could also respond to the name of the object. Consequently, the use of functional classification cannot be considered to be a sufficient causal prerequisite for the development of receptive vocabulary. However, some recent unpublished data (Smith, personal communication) puts this entire issue in a new and interesting perspective.

Smith was asking toddlers to match-to-sample several groups of animals (cows, horses, dogs, cats, and bears) that differed from each other and also differed within each class on variables such as size, color, and posture. Smith also asked the toddlers to name each of the members of the various sets as well as to select the named member of each set. Across a group of 14 children, he found that unless the child could consistently name the members of at least two classes of animals, there was no evidence of either conceptual match-to-sample performance or receptive vocabulary. These data led to a tentative hypothesis that there can be no linguistically valid comprehension of language before some expressive language usage on the part of the child. However, receptive language will occur with greater frequency than expressive language once children have learned to use some class names expressively. Expressive language in this sense could involve the plastic language used by Premack (1974) with Sarah, Peony, and Elizabeth, the sign language used with Washoe by the Gardners (1969), or standard verbal expressions. In any event, such "expressions" may be prerequisite to receptive language that have been previously described as necessary for expressive verbal behavior. However, as indicated earlier, the floating conceptual system of the preverbal child does not abide by the rules of concept formation that typify the performance of the college sophomore (that poor beast of the psychologist's burden). The toddler has no system at all until he attempts to influence the behavior of a listener through expressive language in any of its multiple facets. Here, we seem to agree more with Vygotsky than Piaget in that expressive language brings the attribute system of the denotative aspects of language under the social control of the listener which accidentally shapes the child into understanding that one set of attributes establishes the basis for the concept "spoon," while a somewhat different set operates for the concept "pencil." A more convincing argument might be made for the child's rapid discrimination between the concept "cookie" and the one for "cracker."

This is only one instance in which attempts at teaching children important facets of complex human behavior have led to an interesting theoretical formulation that could alter the course of subsequent training routines with potentially delayed children. This reflects the interaction that must occur between service and research activities. Without the responsibility for making important changes in the behavior of the children being studied, the research can often be lulled into investigations of interesting but relatively trivial processes that may not benefit the children that the research was designed to serve. On the other hand, service programs without a substantial research structure will have no basis in empirical fact for altering the type of activities provided for children. In the Toddler Project, there are several people who serve both research and service roles that help to ensure a reciprocal service–research interchange.

Many of the interesting forms of complex human behavior do not change rapidly. These forms of behavior need to be studied over time and with children who are at the appropriate point in development of the relevant form of behavior. This type of investigation is most feasible when the researcher has longitudinal contact with children who are entering the program in successive waves. If a researcher has contact with 20 babies in the course of 1 year, he will be able to study 60 or more babies in the course of 3 years, and if the service program is serving the family, there will be few problems making successive contacts with the babies. In addition, if the service-research network is strong, there are few problems involved with space, pilot studies, informed consent of parents, absences of the children, or other factors that usually plague researchers when they request entry into other types of service settings. The service setting should be a laboratory from which children can be studied without educational disruption and with the knowledge that service needs are being met so that they need not be the primary concern of the researcher. In such a system, everyone, and most especially that handicapped infant or child, seems to benefit.

CONCLUSION

In this chapter we have presented what we believe to be four important issues in the area of early intervention for high risk infants and children. We have attempted to discuss each of these issues in the context of the approaches we have evolved during our past 4 years with the Infant, Toddler, and Preschool Research and Intervention Project. Let us hasten to add that we are not suggesting that our approaches constitute solutions to these issues. Indeed, we would suspect that a major outcome from this conference may be the recognition of how woefully inadequate our approaches and strategies have been in helping children. Although our population seems to be thriving both affectively and educationally, many of these children are far from being acceptable or capable of fitting the mainstream of community existence. This fact indicates that the major goal of developing appropriate behavior repertoires in these children is not yet a reality.

Most assuredly, the designing and implementing of effective training programs for young handicapped children and their families remains a challenge for many of us from a variety of disciplines. Looking back over our accomplishments as a society dealing with the problems of handicapping conditions, one could easily become dismayed at our lack of viable, productive solutions (Hobbs, 1975). However, we believe the castigation of past failures serves young children less well than proposing future alternatives. We hope this chapter has served this latter function.

ACKNOWLEDGMENTS

The authors wish to express their gratitude to the staff and children of the Infant, Toddler, and Preschool Research and Intervention Project for their many assistances.

The research reported herein was supported in part by the Joseph P. Kennedy, Jr. Foundation, the Institute on Mental Retardation and Intellectual Development (NICHHD Grant No. HD-00973), the Mental Retardation Research Training Program (NICHHD Grant No. HD-00043), the Parental Teaching Style Assessment Program (NICHHD Grant No. HD-07073). Also, we wish to acknowledge the support for the service component of the project from the Tennessee Department of Public Welfare and the Tennessee Department of Mental Health.

LITERATURE CITED

Bandura, A. 1967. The role of modeling processes in personality development. *In* W. Hartup and N. Smothergill (eds.), The Young Child: Review of Research. National Association for the Education of Young Children.

Bricker, D. D. 1972. Imitative sign training as a facilitator of word-object association with low-functioning children. Amer. J. Ment. Defic. 76: 509–516.

Bricker, D. D., and W. A. Bricker. 1971. Toddler Research and Intervention Project Report: Year I. IMRID Behavioral Science Monograph No. 20, Institute on Mental Retardation and Intellectual Development, George Peabody College, Nashville.

Bricker, D. D., and W. A. Bricker. 1972. Toddler Research and Intervention Project Report: Year II. IMRID Behavioral Science Monograph No. 21, Institute on Mental Retardation and Intellectual Development, George Peabody College, Nashville.

Bricker, D. D., and W. A. Bricker. 1973. Infant, Toddler, and Preschool Research and Intervention Project Report: Year III. IMRID, Behavioral Science Monograph No. 23,

Institute on Mental Retardation and Intellectual Development, George Peabody College, Nashville.

Bricker, D. D., L. Vincent-Smith, and W. A. Bricker. 1973. Receptive vocabulary: Performances and selection strategies of delayed and nondelayed toddlers. Amer. J. Ment. Defic. 77: 579–584.

Bricker, W. A. 1970. Identifying and modifying behavioral deficits. Amer. J. Ment. Defic. 75: 16–21.

Bricker, W. A. 1972. A systematic approach to language training. In R. L. Schiefelbusch (ed.), Language of the Mentally Retarded. University Park Press, Baltimore.

Bricker, W. A., and D. D. Bricker. 1966. The use of programmed language training as a means for differential diagnosis and educational remediation among severely retarded children. Peabody Papers in Human Development, Vol. 4, No. 5. George Peabody College, Nashville.

Bricker, W. A., and D. D. Bricker. 1969. Four operant procedures for establishing auditory control with low-functioning children. Amer. J. Ment. Defic. 73: 981–987.

Bricker, W. A., and D. D. Bricker. 1970. Development of receptive vocabulary in severely retarded children. Amer. J. Ment. Defic. 74: 599–607.

Bricker, W. A., and D. D. Bricker. 1972. Assessment and modification of verbal imitation with low-functioning children. J. Speech Hear. Res. 15: 690–698.

Bricker, W. A., and D. D. Bricker. 1973. Behavior modification programmes. In P. Mittler (ed.), Assessment for Learning in the Mentally Handicapped. Churchill Livingstone, London.

Bricker, W. A., and D. D. Bricker. 1974. An early language training strategy. In R. Schiefelbusch and L. Lloyd (eds.), Language Perspectives–Acquisition, Retardation, and Intervention, pp. 431–468. University Park Press, Baltimore.

Bruner, J. S. 1969. Eye, hand, and mind. In D. Elkind and J. H. Flavell (eds.), Studies in Cognitive Development: Essays in Honor of Jean Piaget. Oxford University Press, New York.

Caldwell, B. M., and J. Richmond. 1968. The children's center in Syracuse, New York: In L. Dittman (ed.), Early Child Care–The New Perspective. Atherton Press, New York.

Filler, J. W. 1973. Sensorimotor assessment performance as a function of task materials. In D. Bricker and W. Bricker (eds.), Infant, Toddler, and Preschool Research and Intervention Project Report: Year III. IMRID Behavioral Science Monograph No. 23, Institute on Mental Retardation and Intellectual Development, George Peabody College, Nashville.

Filler, J. W. 1974. Modification of the teaching styles of mothers: The effects of task arrangement on the match-to-sample performance of young retarded children. Doctoral dissertation, George Peabody College, Nashville.

Filler, J. W., Jr., C. C. Robinson, R. A. Smith, L. Vincent-Smith, D. D. Bricker, and W. A. Bricker. 1975. Mental retardation. In N. Hobbs (ed.), Issues in the Classification of Children. Jossey-Bass, San Francisco.

Furth, H. D. 1970. On language and knowing in Piaget's developmental theory. Human Devel. 13: 241–257.

Gardner, R., and B. Gardner. 1969. Teaching sign language to a chimpanzee. Science 165: 664–672.

Haywood, H. C. 1969. Behavioral research in mental retardation: Goals for a new decade. Alabama J. Med. Sci. 6: 378–381.

Haywood, H. C. 1971. Labeling: Efficacy, evils, and caveats. Paper presented at the Joseph P. Kennedy, Jr. Foundation International Symposium on Human Rights, Retardation, and Research, October, 1971, Washington, D.C.

Hobbs, N. 1975. The Futures of Children: Categories, Labels, and Their Consequences. Report of the Project on Classification of Exceptional Children. Jossey-Bass, San Francisco.

Horton, K. B. 1974. Infant intervention and language learning. *In* R. Schiefelbusch and L. Lloyd (eds.), Language Perspectives—Acquisition, Retardation, and Intervention. University Park Press, Baltimore.

Hunt, J. McV. 1961. Intelligence and Experience. Ronald Press, New York.

Hunt, J. McV. 1972. Psychological assessment in education and social class. Paper presented at Conference on the Legal and Educational Consequences of the Intelligence Testing Movement: Handicapped Children and Minority Group Children. University of Missouri, Columbia.

Lynch, J., and W. A. Bricker. 1972. Linguistic theory and operant procedures: Toward an integrated approach to language training for the mentally retarded. Ment. Retard. 10: 12—17.

McClelland, D. C. 1973. Testing for competence rather than for "intelligence." Amer. Psych. 28: 1—14.

Piaget, J. 1952. The Origins of Intelligence in Children. W. W. Norton, New York.

Piaget, J. 1954. The Construction of Reality in the Child. Ballantine Books, New York.

Piaget, J. 1970. Piaget's theory. *In* P. H. Mussen (ed.), Carmichael's Manual of Child Psychology, Vol. 1. (3rd ed.). Wiley, New York.

Piaget, J., and B. Inhelder. 1969. The Psychology of the Child. Basic Books, New York.

Premack, D. 1974. Teaching visual language to apes and language deficient people. *In* R. Schiefelbusch and L. Lloyd (eds.), Language Perspectives—Acquisition, Retardation, and Intervention. University Park Press, Baltimore.

Rynders, J. E., and M. J. Horrobin. 1972. A mobil unit for delivering educational services to Down's syndrome (mongoloid) infants. Research, Development, and Demonstration Center in Education of Handicapped Children. Minneapolis, Minn.

Schaefer, E. S. 1970. Need for early and continuing education. *In* V. H. Denenberg (ed.), Education of the Infant and Young Child. Academic Press, New York.

Smith, R., J. Filler, W. Bricker, C. Robinson, and L. Vincent-Smith. 1973. Evaluation of teaching style: A comparison of teachers and mothers. *In* D. Bricker and W. Bricker (eds.), Infant, Toddler, and Preschool Research and Intervention Project Report: Year III. IMRID Behavioral Science Monograph No. 23, Institute on Mental Retardation and Intellectual Development, George Peabody College, Nashville.

Tharp, R. G., and R. J. Wetzel. 1969. Behavior Modification in the Natural Environment. Academic Press, New York.

Vincent-Smith, L., D. D. Bricker, and W. A. Bricker. 1974. Acquisition of receptive vocabulary in the toddler-age child. Child Devel. 45: 189—193.

Vincent-Smith, L., and G. Chatelanat. 1973. An evaluation of a new assessment procedure: Functional use of objects, receptive vocabulary, and expressive vocabulary. *In* D. Bricker and W. Bricker, (eds.), Infant, Toddler, and Preschool Research and Intervention Project Report: Year III. IMRID Behavioral Science Monograph No. 23, Institute on Mental Retardation and Intellectual Development, George Peabody College, Nashville.

White, B. L. 1969. The initial coordination of sensorimotor schemas in human infants—Piaget's ideas and the role of experience. *In* D. Elkind and J. H. Flavell (eds.), Studies in Cognitive Development. Oxford University Press, New York.

Wolfensberger, W. 1972. The principle of normalization in human services. National Institute on Mental Retardation, Toronto.

Early Intervention for High Risk Infants and Young Children: Programs for Down's Syndrome Children

Alice H. Hayden, Ph.D., and Norris G. Haring, Ed.D.

Mental retardation poses many perplexing problems for all societies. Professionals in different fields have sought to determine its causes; to consider ways in which some of the causes may be prevented; to study factors that contribute to functional retardation; to maximize the potential of this large population; and to help these people become as independent as possible in order to relieve or at least reduce the financial and personal burdens the condition of mental retardation imposes not only for the individual himself but for the society as a whole.

The literature on mental retardation reflects the contributions of professionals from many different disciplines. The following review brings to light possible alternatives to present methods of coping with some of the many problems; it also suggests trends and avenues well worth pursuing through coordinated multidisciplinary research. Perhaps no one discipline has greater vested interest in what can be done for and with retarded persons than the discipline of education, because many educators must eventually inherit all children and youth in the various educational or instructional programs provided and work with them over a longer period of time than do professionals in most other related disciplines.

Educators, then, have great interest in what can be done for these children *before* they enter school—what conditions can be remediated at least in part through various

Down's Syndrome Programs at the Model Preschool Center, Experimental Education Unit, Child Development and Mental Retardation Center, University of Washington, are funded in part through the Handicapped Children's Early Education Assistance Act (Public Law 91-230, Title VI, Part C, Sec. 623) and ESEA Title I 89-313.

types of treatment, and through improved nutrition, environmental conditions, and early intervention. The discipline of education shares with other disciplines the interest in and contribution to early intervention and must accept major responsibility for developing and testing the effectiveness and efficiency of programs designed to maximize the potential of retarded persons.

Representatives of all disciplines working with retarded persons are acutely aware of the many factors that influence the developing human embryo and the child. They recognize that there are some factors over which they can exert control and others for which they do not presently have the knowledge to permit even some control. Educators, however, can exert control over instructional programs. Such control, coupled with on-going assessment of child progress and determined effort to make these programs as effective as possible, at once increases the educators' responsibility and challenge to consider alternative and effective ways of improving instruction for retarded persons in order to prevent or greatly reduce the incidence and prevalence of *functional* retardation. Each discipline concerned with the complex of problems that surround mental retardation has some body of knowledge and expertise to draw upon; if the "war on retardation" is to be won, representatives from the different disciplines must wage it together and recruit the very valuable assistance of parents and informed citizens who see retardation as a common enemy that challenges everyone.

Handicapping conditions are no respectors of race, class, or geography. Their frequency of occurrence is so great that few families can escape having close contact with a handicapped person. Down's syndrome, a genetic anomaly whose most serious behavioral consequence is mental retardation, occurs about once in every 640 births (Smith and Wilson, 1973). It occurs with a higher frequency among women more than 45 years of age—once in every 65 births according to Smith and Wilson, although this may be a cautious estimate (see, for example, Benda, 1969, who places the figure between 20 and 40 per thousand). Furthermore, Down's syndrome is the most prevalent form of severe mental retardation, and its prevalence is increasing because medical technology has found the means to keep alive—and keep alive longer—many more of these children now than in earlier times, when many of them did not survive birth or their first years (Stein and Susser, 1971).

Because of the widespread occurrence of handicapping conditions, there is need for much greater public awareness about them: their causes and progression, and what can be done to prevent or remediate some of them. But there is an equally important need for professionals in many fields to coordinate efforts directed toward early intervention to prevent and remediate those handicapping conditions that *can* be prevented or remediated. There is also a need to explore the most effective means of working with handicapped children and their families. Before describing an educational program for young children with Down's syndrome, this chapter will review some important examples in the literature of very early intervention and some of the emerging social and other trends that may facilitate such critical early programming.

REVIEW OF THE LITERATURE

Young Children

From the educator's standpoint, much of the impetus for identification and intervention with high risk infants, at least in the United States, derived from reports of the efficacy of intervening with the *slightly* older child: the preschooler in a variety of settings.

Some theorists have assumed that development is a function of maturation; certain experiences become available to the organism as a result of the passage of time. However, it is obvious that time alone does not account for all development because those reared in isolation do not develop the same as others. Jeffrey (1958) found that it was possible to teach left-right discrimination to 4-year-old children using appropriately sequenced experiences. Previously, these children had been unable to learn the discrimination as long as only traditional teaching methods were used. Jeffrey's work suggested that rapid development may be promoted with proper programming and sequencing of learning steps.

In 1939, Skeels and Dye reported observations bearing on the effects of differential stimulation on mentally retarded children. Their study grew out of a surprising discovery: they found that two 18-month-old children, both moderately to severely retarded, who were placed (for lack of appropriate space) in an institution for the feeble-minded, rose dramatically in IQ. The children were illegitimate, born of feeble-minded mothers, and originally had IQs of 46 and 35. But after 6 months on a ward for retarded women, 18 to 50 years old, the children had IQs of 77 and 87 on the Kuhlman-Binet test. A year later, they scored 100 and 88, and at ages 40 months and 43 months, they still scored as high as 95 and 93. The investigators were puzzled by this unusual development, and very carefully studied the institutional environment in search of explanations to be found there.

They found that the attendants on the ward and other patients took a great deal of interest in their "babies"; on days off, attendants took the children with them for car rides or shopping trips, brought them toys, books, and playthings. The older female residents played with them and took them for walks.

As a result of this experience, Skeels and Dye persuaded the State Board of Control to approve an informal transfer of 1- and 2-year-old mentally retarded children from the state orphanage to the state school for the retarded. A contrast population remained in the orphanage. Children in the experimental group were placed, singly or in pairs, with brighter and older girls at the state school. Over a 2-year period, the experimental group showed a mean IQ gain of 27.5 points, while the contrast group showed a loss of 26.2 points. Skeels and Dye concluded that a change from retarded to normal intelligence in preschool children may be possible, in the absence of organic pathology, by providing the children with a more adequate psychological environment. Skeels and his other colleagues (Skeels et al., 1938) conducted investigations of the mental development of children from inferior social and intellectual backgrounds who were placed in foster homes during infancy; these further substantiated the findings of the study just discussed. The children consistently attained higher levels of intellectual performance. Kirk and Hunt extended these efforts to focus on the early education of the handicapped child. In the 1950s and early 1960s, both authors provided influential support to the growing belief in the beneficial effects to be realized from early intervention. Kirk (1958) presents evidence suggesting that a child's cultural environment can contribute to the child's retardation and can even cause it to some extent. The work also suggests that education, if presented early enough, can increase the abilities of these children.

On the side of manipulating children's encounters with the environment from birth on to maximize intellectual growth, who knows what might be done? Various bits of evidence " . . . indicate that substantial increases in intelligence as now measured may be possible . . . Such findings indicate that society would not be wasting its time to supply nursery school experience to retarded youngsters of preschool age" (Hunt, 1961).

It was the surge of interest in preschool intervention following reports such as these that helped to produce Head Start. But even as the recommended early childhood programs began to get underway, researchers were realizing that perhaps such efforts ought to begin even earlier: because, as many studies were reconfirming, the infant is learning from the moment of birth, and is even subject to important sources of stimulation before birth.

Neonates

Fantz (1965), using an apparatus that allowed him to measure an infant's visual focusing on either of two presented patterns, established that a neonate less than 2 weeks old can discriminate visual patterns such as stripes, bull's eyes, checkerboards, or simple geometric shapes, and that an infant will focus for longer periods of time on the more complex patterns. He further showed that premature babies have the same visual discrimination capacity as do full-term infants, and that they too "preferred" the patterned stimuli over the plain ones, by focusing for longer periods on the patterns; however, they selected the simpler of the patterned items.

Siqueland and Lipsitt (1966) were among the first researchers to demonstrate that some of the responses in the neonate's repertoire were conditionable and, therefore, that the neonate is actively learning and responding to contingencies present in his environment from birth. The investigators presented infants less than 4 days old with tactile cheek stimulation. Infants often turn their heads laterally in the direction of the source of such stimulation, probably because this response is an adaptive one in a breast feeding situation. The investigators established a baseline rate of head-turning in each direction, then selectively reinforced head-turning to one side only by presenting a primary reinforcer (dextrose-water solution) contingent on head-turning to the right side; turns to the left side were not reinforced. The infants rapidly acquired a high rate of head turns to the right and decreased their rate of head turns to the left. Then the contingencies were reversed, and the infants extinguished rapidly on the right-side turning response, and acquired a high rate of left-side turning.

Rheingold, Gewirtz, and Ross (1959) obtained similar results when they attempted to reinforce infants' vocalizations. Immediately after a spontaneous vocalization by the infant during the experimental phase, the experimenter provided "social" reinforcement in the form of three vocalizations of her own ("tsk, tsk, tsk"), a light touch to the infant's abdomen, and a broad smile. This intervention following vocalization raised the vocalization rate by an average 39 percent the first day and a further 34 percent the second day. In all, conditioning brought about an increase of 86 percent; removal of the reinforcer returned these rates to a level closely approaching baseline within 2 days. The authors suggested, however, that the results produced were quite compatible with the explanation that stimulation alone accounted for the increase.

A more suggestive study of the effects of *socially* significant stimuli was done in 1969 by Simner and Reilly, who showed that not only do infants respond to sounds and discriminate them with considerable accuracy at or shortly after birth, but they also respond to the significance that sounds have for them from a survival standpoint. They respond positively to the sound of a recorded heartbeat simulating the sound heard while in the uterine environment by crying less, sleeping better, and remaining actively alert during the times when they are not sleeping. They respond with obvious distress and crying when hearing the sound of a peer's cry—and show even greater distress when hearing a recording of their own crying!

Smart and Smart (1973) report on many studies that show the infant's considerable learning capacity over all sensory modalities from birth onward. An infant can make discriminations in kinesthetic, olfactory, tactile, and visual/aural dimensions. Friedlander's (1971) reports on infant listening support these findings.

Premature Infants

Children born prematurely and children reared in lower social class environments are especially susceptible to developmental deficits (Willerman, 1972). However, research evidence is accumulating that supports the position that stimulation efforts begun in the premature nursery, even in the isolette, in the first weeks of life have measurable effects on development by the end of the first year.

Kathryn Barnard of the Child Development and Mental Retardation Center, University of Washington, has contrasted the intrauterine environment of the fetus with that of the isolette environment of the premature infant (Barnard, 1973; Barnard and Collar, 1973). The intrauterine environment provides vestibular, auditory, and proprioceptive stimuli; the mother's movement and vital functions provide temporally patterned stimulation. In contrast, the premature infant is deprived of this temporally patterned stimulation. Barnard suggests that "one of the difficulties encountered by the premature infant is that he suffers from stimulus deprivation." It is possible that neurological anomalies resulting from prematurity continue until later ages. Barnard cites Drillien's (1964) findings that 25 percent of the premature population studied had sleep disturbances that continued to 2 years of age. Barnard studied the effects of introducing temporally patterned stimulation (rocking and heartbeat sound) into the environment of premature infants. After 4 weeks of stimulation, the experimental subjects showed a significant increase in quiet sleep and a significant decrease in active sleep when compared to the control group. The change in sleep patterns was accompanied by a greater weight gain and faster neurological development. Barnard interpreted these results to mean that the experimental infants habituated to the stimuli, thus allowing increased sleep. The premature infant who cannot habituate as easily must attend more to stimuli and is less able to sleep. The ability to maintain quiet sleep may correlate with later visual attending ability (Parmelee, 1970) because these processes are controlled by the same area of the brain. Moreoever, the behavioral patterns of the infant who is able to sustain quiet sleep may set up an interaction of a positive character between the infant and his caregiver that could have lasting impact on his development.

Wright (1972) emphasizes that "the vulnerability of prematures is increased significantly if, during infancy, they are reared in an environment providing minimal sensory motor stimulation." The results of the pilot study reported by Wright support his contention. Stimulation (rocking in a crib, music and talk from a radio, visual stimulation from striped sheets, and tactile, kinesthetic, and visual stimulation resulting from handling by a nurse) for 21 days resulted in marked improvements in rooting reflex responding and glucocorticoid chemistries in the experimental group as compared to the control group.

Auditory stimulation alone may produce remarkable effects in premature infants. Katz (1971) introduced a 5-minute tape recording of the voice of the premature infant's mother into the isolette beginning on the fifth day after birth; the tape was played six times a day. At 36 weeks of age, significant gains were found on measures of motor behavior, tactile-adaptive behavior, auditory function, visual function, and muscle tension when these infants were compared to the infants in the control group.

Scarr-Salapatek and Williams (1972) conducted a study with premature infants of impoverished mothers. They found that visual stimulation of the infants in their isolettes, coupled with social stimulation (handling, talking-to, rocking) during eight half-hour feeding sessions, produced significant benefits within a month. In addition, during home visits a social worker provided additional stimulation to the infant and also advice to the mother concerning child care; at the end of 1 year, most of the infants in the experimental group were at normal or nearly normal levels of development with only 21 percent having IQs below 90. In contrast, the control group infants remained one standard deviation below the norm, and 67 percent had IQs below 90. The authors of both studies emphasize that the sterile, non-stimulating environment conventionally provided for premature infants, while protecting the infant from infection, also isolates the infant from the conditions of stimulation needed for development. The sterile environment may, in fact, contribute to sensory deficits and subsequent developmental delays.

Premature children clearly are learning even in the isolette. This learning may have negative consequences: the infant may acquire a habit that must be broken. For example,

Fraiberg, Smith, and Adelson (1969) found that three premature infants in their sample of 10 blind babies resisted cuddling after 3 weeks in the isolette. Because blind infants cannot learn through visual input, tactile stimulation is enormously important for them. Therefore, the investigators urged the mothers to break this learned habit, even though the mothers initially resisted on the grounds that the baby seemed to prefer not to be moved. These 10 blind infants were the subjects of a 3-year home intervention program with emphasis on parent training. By the end of the first year, all 10 children showed exclusive attachment to their parents with differential smiling and vocalizing. Investigators stress the importance of this attachment in order to enhance the effectiveness of the parents as teachers of the blind child.

Down's Syndrome Children: An Overview

Reports concerning the learning capabilities of Down's syndrome children have rarely been as promising as the studies just cited. J. Langdon Down, a British physician, is credited with the first systematic description of this syndrome, although earlier reports had mentioned patients fitting the general description. It is regrettable but likely that his dehumanizing designations for people having the syndrome, "mongolian idiots," (1866)— to say nothing of Séguin's calling them "furfuraceous cretins" (1866)—have over the years lent support to the notion that this population is, first, a homogeneous population, and, more important, a non-educable one. In the century since Down's work was published, writers have speculated about the cause of the configuration of physical and behavioral characteristics that make up Down's syndrome, suggesting agents such as glandular imbalances, trauma, toxins, viruses, parental tuberculosis or alcoholism, or postulating that the syndrome represents cultural "regression" (Penrose and Smith, 1966). Until fairly recently, however, there was all too little speculation about the eventual mental prognosis for children born with Down's syndrome: it was generally assumed to be poor.

Down's syndrome is almost always associated with mental retardation and, in fact, "mongolism is the most common clinically defined type of mental retardation" (Heber, 1970). Writers have disagreed about the exact limits of the children's capabilities. While most Down's syndrome children are categorized as moderately retarded to dull normal (Doris and Sarason, 1969), one study of 13 Down's syndrome children revealed an IQ range of 80 to 120 (Carter, 1966). Despite the broad range of intelligence scores among this population, and obvious examples to the contrary, one source indicated that Down's syndrome children would never achieve an IQ beyond 70 (Heber and Stevens, 1965). Another source states that these children will not grow mentally beyond the age of 6 (Faber, 1968). A pamphlet for parents advises that most Down's syndrome children profit little from instruction and only a few will ever pass the second grade level (French and Scott, 1967). Tizard (1964) suggested that attempts to train these children in school-like situations were ultimately non-productive.

Furthermore, until recently, the prevailing recommendation for these children's care was institutionalization. Physicians, motivated by an understandable wish to spare families the burdens involved in long-term care of retarded children, have very often advised parents to institutionalize the youngsters for their own good and the good of the family (Doris and Sarason, 1969). In a reported exception to this tendency, Melyn and White (1973) comment that in their work in a clinic for mentally handicapped children, their policy is to recommend home rearing for Down's syndrome children unless the child's health or conditions in the home make such an arrangement too difficult. Unfortunately, most studies of Down's syndrome children have been reported on children in institutions becase a population was readily available there.

In 1959, Lejeune, Gautier, and Turpin published their finding that Down's syndrome is the result of a chromosomal anomaly—that all or, in some cases, some cells of people with the syndrome have an extra chromosome. This finding removed at least part of the mystery surrounding Down's syndrome—the "how" if not the "why" of its occurrence. Mysteries have a way of generating a certain amount of folklore. Folklore is almost always based partly on truths, yet it is troublesome in its persistence: it creates and perpetuates fixed ideas. Part of the persistent folklore about people with Down's syndrome is the all too familiar stereotype of the happy-go-lucky "trainable" with a stubborn streak. But increased knowledge of any sort usually helps to thaw out frozen attitudes, to encourage new ways of looking at old topics. The research cited earlier has combined with various social and other trends to encourage investigators to take a new look at the educability of *all* children and to search for the means to enhance their development. And with regard to Down's syndrome children, perhaps it is not entirely coincidental that some of the more innovative reports in the literature in recent years have followed the finding that a genetic anomaly—not unknown, mysterious factors—is responsible for this syndrome.

Some of the folklore persists. Because of the children's distinguishable physical traits—for instance, the transpalmar crease, the neck, ear, eye, and facial characteristics—that can be identified at birth and their developmental lags, there is a prevailing attitude that these children are all alike in their behavior. Such views are often accompanied by a similar perception of Down's syndrome children's capabilities for learning: these children are too often treated as having roughly the same limitations for learning and social involvement.

As educators, we are not inclined to accept without question the results of studies on institutionalized children. Studies such as that of Birch and Cornwell (1969) comparing home-reared and institutionalized Down's syndrome children lend support to the view that environmental differences can greatly affect children's acquisition of motor and speech skills and also their IQ scores. Other studies are discussed in another section of this chapter. The research cited earlier, while not only supporting the view that learning occurs earlier and is affected by more factors than had ever been considered before, also serves to indicate how much is still *not* known about development and about educating intelligence. If anything, this information should promote an open-mindedness about all children's potential and an unwillingness to dismiss as merely trainable any group of children.

SOME RECENT TRENDS THAT
PROMOTE EARLY INTERVENTION WITH YOUNG HANDICAPPED CHILDREN

The "Era of the Child"

In addition to the scientific literature, some of which has been cited, there are other reports indicating that far more attention is being paid to young children, and to increasingly younger children, than before.

First, increased attention to the needs of young children, including young handicapped children, is not the monopoly of a particular region or nation. It is, in fact, world-wide. Reports of groups such as the International Study Group for Early Child Care (Robinson and Robinson, 1973); the avalanche of articles and books about the British Infant Schools; articles in *Soviet Life* (1973) describing the kindergarten in Russia that serves nine million children between the ages of 3 and 6; Bloom's report (1973) on a survey undertaken in 22 countries and the uniform findings concerning the importance of early attention to verbal development; and a recent article concerning Chinese children 56 days to 7 years old, "Child Care in China" (Dollar, 1973) all give ample evidence of acute concerns throughout the world for the education and care of young children, and many of these describe programs that address the needs of young handicapped children.

Here in the United States, the concern for handicapped children has been translated into meaningful action in many states, where either legislation or court decisions in response to the efforts of those concerned with the needs of handicapped children have clearly set out the states' responsibilities to educate *all* children, no matter how severe their handicaps. The Head Start mandate to integrate handicapped with non-handicapped children is a pioneering nationwide effort—that will be replicated in other programs—to extend services to very young handicapped children. Such mandates have forced educators, other professionals and paraprofessionals, and communities to take stock of their enlarged responsibilities and of their needs for assistance in meeting the requirements of the mandates.

Second, in recent years there has been a virtual explosion of programs for children from birth to 6 years of age. Many new programs are being sponsored by community college child centers, private agencies, parent groups, and public schools—the latter in response to their new mandate to educate *all* children. The increase in programs can be considered an outcome of the world-wide interest just discussed, but it must also be seen as a reflection of fundamental changes in social patterns here and abroad. Not the least of these is the changing role of women, including the fact that in America two thirds of them are now working after marriage and motherhood. And, too, there is a considerable increase in the number of one-parent families. These changing patterns indicate that there will be a need for even more day care and preschool services for young children, including young handicapped children, than are now available.

Educators are beginning to reckon now with the implications of extended early childhood programs, because they realize that this increase in services will affect professional and paraprofessional training, parent education, child learning, and curriculum planning not only for educating very young children, but for modifying primary education as these children reach "school age." And, as the public—particularly those families who, in earlier days, could not expect public programs for their handicapped children—becomes more aware of new programs, they, too, through community planning and coordinating committees, are demanding quality and excellence in them (Hayden, 1974b).

Education for Parenting

The general public is not too much influenced by scholarly works that tell about the importance of nutrition, not only in young infants but in prospective mothers. Nor are academic papers about parenting—about parent-child relationships and how they affect a child's development—widely read among adolescents who may be parents within a decade. Yet it is almost impossible to overstate the importance of disseminating whatever information we have about these and other factors if we are to prevent many preventable handicapping conditions. One of the more welcome trends in recent years is that such dissemination is being fostered through programs for junior and senior high school students. MR 72, Islands of Excellence (1972) states:

> Late in 1972, HEW's Office of Education and the Office of Child Development jointly initiated a major program aimed at teaching teenage boys and girls how to become good parents potentially capable of raising children who are mentally, socially, emotionally, and physically healthy. The Education for Parenthood program will begin with a large-scale plan involving several hundred school districts as well as national voluntary organizations serving youth (p. 7).

Other encouraging developments are public school and community college programs in child development, family living, and early childhood education.

Multidisciplinary Approaches to Work with Young Children

In recent years, there has been a trend toward a multidisciplinary approach to working with young children and their families. The need for such an approach has been amply demonstrated in work with handicapped children. Certainly no one discipline has all the expertise needed to cope with the problems of multiply handicapped children. The expertise and the resources developed by personnel in medicine, dentistry, nursing, psychology, education, social work, and speech pathology and audiology, to name but a few disciplines, are essential if prevention, treatment, and possible remediation of certain types of handicapping conditions are to be effected. The establishment of research centers under Public Law 88-164 and the work of University-Affiliated Facilities has demonstrated the effectiveness of such collaborative efforts. These efforts have been extended through child study clinics and day care centers in a variety of field settings. When professionals and paraprofessionals in different disciplines work together, their collaborative research efforts add up to more than the "sum of the parts," and each discipline gains a new respect for the expertise of the others.

Coordinated Efforts among Agencies and Organizations

A trend contributing to the multidisciplinary approach has been the coordinated efforts of different public and private agencies, a trend that has been hastened by legislation at both the federal and state levels. At the federal level, an attempt has been made to bring the efforts of different groups to focus on basic problems and to eliminate or decrease fragmented and isolated efforts. Such a direction also reduces overlapping and separate approaches funded by different agencies of the federal government. Examples of such coordinated efforts and funding are evident in the Office of Human Development/Bureau of Education for the Handicapped experimental projects directed toward effectively integrating handicapped with non-handicapped children in Head Start; by the Head Start Information Project funded by the Office of Human Development/Council for Exceptional Children for disseminating relevant materials and training efforts to assist Head Start in this work; and by the collaboration of the American Academy of Pediatrics with these agencies in promoting their goals.

Other coordinated efforts will require changes in state legislation in order to provide services and instruction for younger children. The admission of handicapped children to school programs when they reach "school age" fails to recognize the special—and documented—needs these children have at a much earlier age. Informed leadership both in the legislatures and in the public sectors can help the public to realize that early identification and intervention with handicapped children can do much to overcome problems of both children and parents in those crucial years between infancy and school age. Effective programs can greatly reduce both the incidence and the severity of later handicapping conditions if signs of high risk are identified at birth or as soon after that as possible and if needed special services and programs are made available. There is no point in compounding the problems of handicapped children and their families through delaying the provision of needed services and programs. Coordinated effort is therefore essential at the state, local, and federal levels if real progress is to be made and if we are to meet some of the goals toward which we strive: 1) providing needed services and programs to all handicapped children by 1980, and 2) reducing by half the number of retarded children and adults in the United States by the turn of the century.

Integration of Handicapped Children

In the past, the public looked to institutions and to professionals in special education to serve handicapped children. There were rarely sufficient funds provided to develop effective programs in either institutional or special education programs, and frequently the staffs lacked expertise and sufficient training to serve these children effectively. Many children received no services. There were long waiting lists for admission to institutions, and the numbers of children recommended for placement in special education programs grew and grew. It has become apparent that such placement for certain children is not the answer to the problems that face society. This is not to say, however, that some people with vision did not early see that these "solutions" could not and would not meet the needs of handicapped children. One has but to review the recommendations of the 1930

White House Conference on Children and Youth (The Story of the White House Conferences on Children and Youth, 1967) to see a blueprint that could have changed all this at a much earlier time. The recommendations were as modern as today and include many of the trends mentioned here, such as the need for education for parenthood and integration of handicapped children into the mainstream.

Today, there is an attempt to reduce the populations in institutions, and many institutions such as those for the retarded have changed markedly in recent years. There are group homes and smaller units designed to meet retarded persons' needs and to move many of them back into the community as rapidly as possible. Special educators recognize that many children such as those who are mildly, and some moderately, handicapped can benefit from an integrated rather than a special education program— provided, of course, that the regular classroom teachers have had training and preparation for meeting the children's special and individual needs. Individualization of instruction is needed for many pupils, not just for the handicapped. Certainly, the regular classroom teacher must be trained to work effectively with children who have learning disabilities if their needs are to be met. Preschools and early intervention programs can do much to prevent some of the learning handicaps of "normal" children.

The mandate to integrate at least 10 percent of handicapped with non-handicapped children in Head Start has done much to remind the public and staff personnel that handicapped children are more similar to than different from the rest of the population. This mandate also shows that there are procedures and teaching techniques that can be taught to professionals and paraprofessionals working in such programs that can eliminate the necessity for placing many of these children in special education instead of regular education programs.

Parent Involvement in School Programs

Many programs now require that parents be involved in activities such as Advisory Councils or career training programs. Parents also volunteer to work in programs to serve as "tutors," providing individual assistance to some children. Such involvement has many benefits to the parents as well as to the programs they serve. There is parent training, including the use of special techniques for handicapped children, that enables the parent to work more effectively with his own child at home. There is the association with other parents, with the staff, and with other children. There is greater consistency in parent behavior, which results in greater consistency in child behavior. Parents are less frustrated in their attempts to deal with their own children when their feelings of inadequacy diminish as they gain competence and confidence. Parents are valuable and helpful partners and they are strong supporters of efforts to provide better and more effective programs for all children.

Dissemination

As stated earlier, there is encouraging evidence that some research findings concerning child development are being transmitted to the general public through educational programs. The many television and radio spot announcements, provided as a public service, that may reach still other people who need special services for handicapped children might also be mentioned. A spin-off benefit of this dissemination is increased participation by members of the community in many efforts to provide more effective programs for all children. Increased participation often leads to a kind of child advocacy— citizens work together to promote necessary programs. A recent example of this activity in the state of Washington, and no doubt elsewhere, is the tremendous effort made by informed citizen groups and individuals to present the case for "Education for All" legislation to the state legislature. The number of man hours spent in the pre-enactment effort is inestimable. Many of the same people are still at work to change the Washington State Attorney General's present interpretation of the law so that it can be extended to cover children from the time of birth.

Another encouraging trend is the requirement by some federal legislation that federally funded projects disseminate information about their programs. Dissemination of this sort, however, cannot begin to be effective without a multidisciplinary audience and without the coordinated efforts of agencies, both mentioned earlier. Finally, disseminated findings are even more effective if they are transmitted to the general public. One rather dramatic example of this occurred not long ago. We and our colleagues have written about our programs for Down's syndrome children in other academic publications and have discussed the programs at meetings and conferences throughout our region and the country. However, when the largest newspaper in Seattle published a Sunday supplement article about the program and included many pictures of the children in their classes (Mills, 1974), for the next 2 weeks the switchboard at the school was jammed with calls about the program, and 12 children whose parents had never heard of it before were enrolled.

PROGRAMS FOR DOWN'S SYNDROME CHILDREN
AT THE EXPERIMENTAL EDUCATION UNIT, CHILD DEVELOPMENT
AND MENTAL RETARDATION CENTER, UNIVERSITY OF WASHINGTON

The Setting

The Experimental Education Unit (EEU) is one of the four component units of the University of Washington's Child Development and Mental Retardation Center (CDMRC), one of the first such multidisciplinary centers whose construction was funded in 1965 through Public Law 88-164. The Center's other Units are: Behavioral Research, Clinical Research (and Diagnosis), and Medical Research. Establishment of the Center brought together professionals from many disciplines in a single facility, the largest and most comprehensive center of its type in the United States.

The Experimental Education Unit's principal purposes are to train undergraduate and graduate students from many disciplines, and professionals and paraprofessionals, in pre-service or inservice programs; to undertake research in instruction and instructional materials; to provide service to handicapped children from birth to 18 years of age who have a wide range of handicaps and to their families; and to disseminate research results. Children receive services in classrooms that provide the setting for practicum training.

Occupancy of the present facilities when they were completed in early 1969 marked the end of a long journey through various temporary quarters for the EEU program, which had its beginnings in 1960 as the Pilot School for Neurologically Impaired Children. The Unit's building was carefully planned and designed to meet certain criteria, including: safety for children; indoor-outdoor relationships and availability of all-weather instructional and recreational areas; separation of adult and child traffic flow; building cost efficiency; ease of maintenance; and flexibility to permit rearrangement of class-rooms and other facilities in order to accommodate change and innovation in programs. Media facilities, including an Instructional Center with closed circuit television cameras for recording classroom activities so that staff and parents can review pupils' progress in videotapes, play a major role in fulfilling the Unit's purposes. One of the most important concerns in planning the facility was that it should have the atmosphere of a school and not of a hospital.

Background

Although the Down's Syndrome Programs are relatively new, having begun in 1971, their antecedents at the University of Washington are not. Over the years, staff members at the CDMRC have served as consultants to state schools for retarded children, including Down's syndrome children; they have also worked directly with the children and staffs in these institutions, helping to develop programs for the children; several of the physicians have provided medical assistance to children with special problems.

The Center's Director, Dr. Irvin Emanuel, has long been interested in several research questions concerning Down's syndrome. Some of these questions include whether young mothers of Down's syndrome children have, in fact, undergone some premature biological aging; and how some of the demographic trends in the United States—the declining birth rate, delayed childbearing—will affect the incidence and prevalence of this anomaly. Scientists in the Medical Research Unit have contributed to the literature on Down's syndrome, and one, Dr. David Smith, has recently co-authored a book for parents and teachers of Down's syndrome children (Smith and Wilson, 1973).

Dr. Vanja Holm of the Center's Clinical Training Unit conducted a short-term project with Down's syndrome infants and their mothers in 1970, training the infants in such skills as standing and walking and working with their mothers to develop feeding and training procedures for the children. In 1968, a Down's Syndrome Infant Stimulation Program was begun at the University's Developmental Psychology Laboratory and then moved to the Child Development and Mental Retardation Center. Mrs. Valentine Dmitriev, who has coordinated the Down's Syndrome Programs in the Model Preschool Center for Handicapped Children at the EEU since their inception, served as Head Teacher in this pilot program and moved with it to the Unit. Her interest in working with Down's syndrome children and her conviction that intervention with these children must begin very early arose, first, from her work in teaching developmental skills to a 7-month-old Down's syndrome infant who was totally unresponsive to his environment and in training the child's mother to work with him at home. She and her co-workers (Dmitriev, Nail, and Harris, 1970) report that, after 5 months of intervention, the child showed achievement in some skills beyond that predicted for a normal child of his age. Mrs. Dmitriev's intensive training of an institutionalized child produced results—including the child's removal from the institution, placement in a foster home, and enrollment in a special education class—that further confirmed her interest (Francis and Dmitriev, 1967).

Several innovative programs in other centers have also contributed to the foundations of our program. Kugel (1970) and Wilson and Parks (1970) report nursery programs used as vehicles for promoting the motor skills development of young institutionalized Down's syndrome children, as a result of which the children showed gains in cognitive skills as well.

One of the most serious criticisms leveled at those who are not altogether pessimistic about Down's syndrome children's educability is that these children's early gains are no cause for jubilation, that such gains will not be maintained. Unfortunately, there are very few reports of long-range studies in which the children's progress through an educational program is followed systematically. Melyn and White (1973), cited earlier, have collected data on 612 Down's syndrome children from birth to age 16, over a period of 20 years, and they report " . . . an overall tendency for the IQ scores of such children to decline with age." But it is not clear from their report whether the children had any training at all after the nursery schools in which they were placed at age 3, nor what sort of program they participated in in these schools. Certainly, one of the most promising long-term studies is that of the group at Sonoma State Hospital in California, and it is somewhat ironic that their results occurred under circumstances that are less than favorable. Their experimental population was institutionalized, and the specific intervention they describe began relatively late, when the children were 5 years old.

As part of a long-term study of institutionalized versus home-reared Down's syndrome children, the Sonoma team of researchers tested the matched control and experimental groups over a period of 8 years, beginning from birth. When the children were 5 years old, the investigators noted that the critical difference between the groups occurred in language development. Moreover, children in the hospital group had suffered an IQ decline. At this point, the investigators began what they describe as the first attempt to use intensive language stimulation training with institutionalized Down's syndrome children. All activities in the children's daily program, including a school program, were exploited for their potential as language stimulators; ward attendants received intensive training in how to increase their own verbal communication with the children and to demand increased communication from them. The authors report that at the 8-year test nine of the ten hospital children were speaking in sentences; the Mental Scale scores of the two groups were almost identical; and, furthermore, the hospital children were maintaining a high rate of mental growth while the home-reared children tended to slow down in their development. By 1967 the children were ready to begin a reading program, and at their 8-year test, nine of the ten children were reading, with comprehension, an average of 250 words each (Rhodes et al., 1969; Bayley et al., 1971). The only appalling note in this narrative is that the program was terminated for budgetary reasons.

Finally, colleagues at the University of Minnesota have been engaged since 1969 in an early intervention program with non-institutionalized Down's syndrome infants. This program emphasizes development of communication skills, particularly receptive skills and concept development. The children are recruited soon after birth and are tested half-yearly until they are 3 years old, then yearly until they are 5. The program also seeks to develop effective curriculum materials and to assess the effects of "early maternal tutoring" on the children's development of communication skills. Preliminary reports (Rynders and Horrobin, 1972; Rynders, personal communication) show that the children "show superior communication and cognitive skills . . . compared to a control group."

Objectives of the Down's Syndrome Programs

To Develop and Use Sequential Programs for Increasing the Children's Rate of Developing Motor, Communication, Social, Cognitive, and Self-help Skills   Our primary program emphasis in the four classes is to bring these children's developmental patterns as close as possible to sequential developmental norms based on normal children's performance. Our goal, as for all EEU pupils, is to prepare these children for placement in regular or special education programs in their home communities.

At this time, there is no way to "cure" Down's syndrome, that is, to reverse the course of this chromosomal accident. Stein and Susser (1971), in discussing the means to reduce the *prevalence* of mental retardation caused by such irreversible anomalies, suggest " . . . limit[ing] the functional disability and social handicap in impaired persons, and cultivat[ing] the maximum intellectual and social potential of those affected." This major objective of our program is, in fact, directed toward both activities. As educators, we would add only that efforts to promote both courses must begin early and must be continued intensively to bring the child's total environment to bear on promoting his development.

In developing sequential programs for the children, our individualized curriculum is based on each child's observed and measured performance so that he is not expected to acquire a new skill until he has mastered its prerequisite skills. But these skills are not developed in a vacuum: they are based on behavioral objectives established for the child by teachers, parents, and consultants. For instance, we may all decide that a child needs to increase his rate of self-feeding and that our immediate objective is to help him learn to lift his cup of milk, drink out of it, and replace the cup on the table. We may add that he will be able to accomplish these tasks with 90 percent success in 4 weeks. The child will not be left to himself to figure out how to meet these objectives that someone else has set for him; he will receive physical prompts as long as he needs them and encouraging reinforcement from those who work with him. Moreover, as observers and data-takers watch and record his performance every day, they will be able to spot any difficulties the child may encounter in his progress. The staff will then examine the program more specifically to determine what components are not working. Such fine-focus monitoring enables the staff to create individualized programs that are based on the child's performance, and not on any preconceived notions about what *should* work. In brief, if he is not learning to drink out of a cup, something is wrong with our program to develop that skill—not with him.

Watching the children's performance over the years has forced our entire staff to raise its expectations about the children's abilities. Probably the most obvious example of this is that it was not our intention, when the program began, to teach these children how to read. Yet, it became clear in observing them systematically and in following their data over the first year and a half of the program that children in the preschool group had acquired the requisite skills to begin a pre-reading and then a reading program. It hardly needs saying that these increased expectations for the children have forced all of us to sharpen our own skills.

Various standardized batteries are used to test the children's progress in all skills at different intervals; they are all based on normal developmental patterns. The children's progress is always measured in the context of normal development. In that sense, they serve as their own controls: their current progress is compared to their earlier progress toward normal sequential development.

To Involve Parents in all Phases of the Programs   Reports in the literature in the last decade have increasingly stressed the important role that parents can play as change agents in the course of their children's development. (For an interesting review of precisely this topic, see Johnson and Katz, 1973.) In the past, however, all too often parents of handicapped children were virtually excluded from any effective participation in remediating their children's handicaps. So often, the "experts" simply did not wish to involve "non-experts" in such matters. As professionals—educators, physicians, nurses— we must share the blame for that exclusion because we not only under-estimated the parents' capabilities, but we also did not know *how* to involve them in such remediation.

Today, such a failure to involve these powerful educators in the educating process would be unthinkable. But meaningful parent involvement does not "happen" automatically. It requires training, encouragement, and acknowledgment of the parents' contribution to their child's development.

Fraiberg and her colleagues (Fraiberg, Smith, and Adelson, 1969) report that in their work with newborn blind infants and their parents, the investigators often pay their first visits to households that are virtually in mourning. Grieving parents have had to cope with the embarrassed silence of friends and relatives in addition to their own turbulent emotions. The investigators report that they are all too often the first people to acknowledge the baby as a human being. Their experience closely parallels that of our staff in their work with parents of newborn Down's syndrome infants. Very often the parents arrive at school holding the baby awkwardly and fearfully and need to be trained to perform this elementary skill. The staff, from the first, encourage the parents to interact with the infant constantly during his waking hours: to cuddle, talk to, hold, and play with the infant. And, at first, parents are often astounded as they watch the staff doing all of those things. But the staff have found that their enthusiasm about the baby is contagious: parents who had earlier been somehow frightened of this infant with his "differences" could begin to react to him as they might have reacted automatically to a normal infant.

Information about parent involvement in the Down's Syndrome Program is voluminous enough to fill several chapters (see, for example, Hayden, 1974a), and must, therefore, be reduced to summary form here. Parents are involved from the moment their child is seen by our staff and then throughout his school program. They are trained to use at home many of the exercises and instructional procedures used at school. When their children reach preschool age, they work in the classrooms: they are trained to be observers, data-takers, and teaching assistants. They use many of the data-taking procedures at home so that they and the staff can determine whether the child's behaviors at home and at school are complementing each other, and can then make informed decisions together about his behavioral objectives and program.

Parents attend staff meetings on the days they have worked in school; they have individual and group conferences with their children's teachers at frequent intervals—if necessary, by telephone. They attend a meeting of all parents in the programs at least once every academic quarter.

So far, we have mentioned only those aspects of their involvement that occur at school. The parents' activities in the larger community are formidable. Some serve as counselors: they are on call at several Seattle hospitals to visit and talk to parents of newborn Down's syndrome infants almost as soon as the new parents have been told about their child's diagnosis. They lecture to students in various University of Washington departments: education, psychology, social work, and in the School of Medicine. Several have written articles for *Sharing Our Caring*, a nationally distributed journal specifically concerned with Down's syndrome. Finally, in what is surely one of the most appropriate testimonials to "parents as partners," several young couples who have moved beyond commuting distance " . . . have been able, on the basis of their training here, to organize and maintain preschool programs for young handicapped children in communities where previously there had been no educational opportunities for this population" (Hayden and Dmitriev, 1975).

To Provide Practicum Training for Students in Undergraduate and Graduate Programs and for Professionals and Paraprofessionals Who Request Further Training Anyone receiving training in the Down's syndrome classes will have a heavy exposure to systematic observation techniques; initial and continuous assessment of performance based on observational data; and setting performance objectives for children that are stated in terms of observable, measurable behaviors. In addition, the trainee will receive supervised practicum experience in working with parents.

Teachers in training must learn how to make accurate assessments of child performance based on systematic observation because they have an excellent vantage point for watching a child over time in a natural setting. They are able to be alert to those handicapping conditions that develop slowly and cumulatively, and they can take steps to remediate them early. Other professionals may see the child in a once-only visit or periodic visits, and in an unfamiliar place like a clinic or office. Richardson (1973) notes, "I don't think you can observe the normal behavior of any child in a clinical situation . . . You have to go where the child lives to see how he really behaves." Friedlander (1971) has also stressed the importance of observing the child's behavior in the natural setting. Others, writing about the urgency of *early* identification of handicapping conditions, stress the teacher's uniquely advantageous position for making the kinds of identification through systematic observation that are often missed by test batteries (Haring and Ridgway, 1967; Allen et al., 1971–72; Haring, Hayden, and Allen, 1971).

Trainees are also expected to become familiar with all aspects of classroom management including instructional and evaluation procedures, materials, activities, and programming. When they have demonstrated competence, they are asked to supervise an area of the classroom—for instance, an activity table where materials and equipment are used for promoting children's fine-motor skills development. Finally, each trainee is assigned an individual program and works with one child. The work involves planning a program for him, including establishing performance objectives; taking baseline data; observing, recording, and assessing his daily performance; modifying the program where necessary; managing the instructional and reinforcement arrangements that the program entails; and conferring frequently with the child's parents in order to share data and to review program decisions together. The trainee's work is supervised by the teaching staff throughout the program.

At the end of every school session, trainees, staff, and participating parents meet to discuss the day's activities, to review children's data and programs, and to plan—on the basis of these data—short- and long-range activities for the class.

To Facilitate Replication and Outreach   The multidisciplinary program for children with Down's syndrome has generated a great deal of interest among teachers of young handicapped children in Washington state, as well as in Idaho and Oregon. As a result, 17 day care centers and three public school programs have requested staff training and technical assistance.

Since 1970, the cumulative figure for attendance by teachers, paraprofessionals, and parents who have attended annual summer workshops given at the Experimental Education Unit, as well as on-site training sessions provided by the coordinator and staff of the Down's Syndrome Programs, has reached 1,000.

Seven day care centers and three public school programs have requested supervision on a regular basis because they are interested in replicating our instructional and staff training procedures. Depending upon the needs of the group, this assistance is being provided at weekly, monthly, or quarterly intervals.

Apart from their work with personnel in other centers, the Down's Syndrome Programs' staff have extensively demonstrated their procedures throughout this region and have given presentations at conferences all over the country. Sometimes the requests for assistance, advice, or training that they receive lead to unusual consultations. Recently, Mrs. Dmitriev was met at the airport in Billings, Montana, where she had attended a Council for Exceptional Children conference, by a mother who wanted advice about her Down's syndrome infant. Someone in Seattle had sent the mother a newspaper article about the program, and she called the Experimental Education Unit to find out if anyone from here would be in her community at any time in the near future.

Finally, staff in the Down's Syndrome Programs have published extensively in a wide variety of monographs and journals, including *Sharing Our Caring*, a journal that is concerned exclusively with Down's syndrome. They have described in quite specific detail the foundations on which certain aspects of the programs are based, and the goals for any particular aspect. For instance, there is a series of articles on exercises to improve motor skills that clearly set out those activities the parent (or other adult) must perform in order to facilitate the child's growth and progress (Dmitriev, 1971a, b).

Population: Pupils and Staff

At this writing, 60 children from birth through 6 years of age are served in the four separate year-round classes. Of the 54 children whose karyotype information was made available to us, all but three have been diagnosed as having a standard trisomy 21 anomaly. Two other children's anomaly is of the mosaic type, and one child's is a chromosomal translocation. Although reports in the literature speculate, and differ, about the learning potential of children with these different varieties of Down's syndrome, (Abelson and Johnson, 1969; Jervis, 1967) we have found no differences in the children's performance that could be attributed to the different diagnoses, nor do the diagnoses pose special problems in developing educational programs for the children.

The children have been admitted to the program at different ages, some of them starting almost immediately after birth, others enrolling whenever their parents learned about the program. They are referred by clinics, physicians, public health nurses, friends, and relatives.

The programs are administered by the authors of this chapter, Dr. Alice H. Hayden and Dr. Norris G. Haring, and coordinated by Mrs. Valentine Dmitriev. Each class is staffed by a head teacher and an assistant teacher, and they are assisted by mothers who work in the classroom—either as observers, data-takers, or as teachers' aides—once a week. Students receiving practicum training serve as aides and observers for varying periods of time.

At present, there are 20 infants in the Infant Learning Class (the children are sometimes first seen at 2 weeks, and intensive training begins when they are 5 weeks old; they stay in this class until they are 18 months old); 11 children in the Early Preschool (18 months to 3 years); 18 children in the Advanced Preschool (3 to 5 years); and 11 children in the Kindergarten class that was begun this year (4.5 to 6 years). While the ages given in parentheses represent the ages of most children in the various classes, there is occasionally some overlapping of age in order to accommodate in the most appropriate class children whose development is either more or less advanced than that of their age-mates, particularly, in the latter case, children who have entered the Programs later than infancy.

Specific Classes in the Down's Syndrome Programs:
Emphases, Developmental Objectives, and Progress Notes

To reiterate, in all classes, our major objective is to promote the children's development of gross and fine motor, social, communication, cognitive, and self-help skills so that their development more nearly approximates the sequential development of normal children. Procedures common to all programs include: identification of target behaviors and sequential skill development, assessment, and intervention. Some activities in the curriculum, of course, serve several functions; for instance, the morning or afternoon snack—during which children in preschool classes sit at a table as though they were having a meal—is an opportunity to practice all skills. But it is also the case that many activities are designed to focus on development of certain kinds of skills and that in each class some skills are emphasized more than others. In general, the progression through the classes is from motor toward more complex cognitive tasks.

The Infant Learning Class Parents and infants come to the Unit once a week for a 30-minute individualized training session in early motor and cognitive development. Parents and staff work together to practice exercises that are designed to promote gross and fine motor development and exercises that enable the infant to be more attuned to his environment, with heavy emphasis on visual and sound stimulation. Parents report that their infants' increasing awareness of the environment, and increased responsiveness to it, facilitate their own increasing responses to the infant—they become much more eager to interact with the baby. Several investigators have stressed the importance of this early establishment of an interactive relationship (Brazelton, 1971; Fraiberg, Smith, and Adelson, 1969). When the baby is about 6 months old, beginning self-help skills that require practice in eye-hand coordination are introduced through the use of finger foods that the infant can grasp.

When parents request additional help at home, a student in training will make home visits. On the whole, parents prefer to have all training sessions at the Unit because they then have an opportunity to meet with other parents whose infants are in the class and to observe the staff working with infants other than their own.

Training goals are based on the Denver Developmental Screening Test (Frankenburg and Dodds, 1967) and on the developmental norms of Gesell and Amatruda (1969). Parents and staff review the child's progress at the weekly sessions, and together they establish weekly developmental goals and the training procedures to be used at home. Some of the goals for the 18-month-old infant are that he will be able, with 80 to 100 percent accuracy, to sit without support and to stand for 5 minutes with support; to make eye contact with people and objects and respond to auditory stimuli; to reach, grasp, hold, and release objects on cue; point to pictures in a book; and perform at least three manipulative tasks, such as placing six rings on a stick, without adult help. Furthermore, these infants will be able to drink from a cup; grasp and hold, bite, and chew crackers (Hayden and Dmitriev, 1975).

Children in the program are assessed twice yearly on Gesell norms; once a month to once every academic quarter on Denver norms; weekly on a Down's Syndrome Assessment Form developed by the staff; and on daily performance data collected in the classroom. Data for the 1972–1973 school year show that all the infants enrolled during that year met and maintained developmental objectives for their various ages and that four of the children were above age level in some skills: one infant in adaptive and language skills, one in personal-social skills, one in motor and adaptive skills, and one in all except motor skills. It is also interesting to note that the one 18-month-old child who had a developmental lag in language of 4 months is a child with a severe heart defect who did not enter the infant program until he was 9 months old. On the Gesell Preliminary Behavior Inventory, the children showed a mean difference of 1 month between their chronological age and their mental age scores.

Preliminary assessments of children presently enrolled in the infant program (some of whom were first enrolled last year) show that they are also meeting developmental objectives.

Early Preschool   Children attend 1.5-hour sessions of the Early Preschool class 4 days a week. Curriculum components for this group emphasize such early self-help skills as dressing and hand-washing, as well as toileting for those children who are ready; work with manipulative materials such as crayons, paste and paper, blocks, puzzles, and pegboards; activities such as playing in a doll corner to promote social *and* motor skills; concept development through work on attending skills and on tasks that require pointing to, placing, or matching objects, and responding to pictures in stories or on flannel boards. The children are helped to develop language skills in all activities, but especially during activities such as snack time, when a child is helped to make vocal requests for what he wants, and in other social activities such as story time, or during "concept development" time, when the child works alone with an adult. Several of the gross motor skills that are given particular emphasis in this group are: sitting to standing, whereby the child learns how to pull himself up from a sitting to a standing position; standing (in order to strengthen leg and back muscles and to help the child develop balance, control, and endurance and, of course, as a requisite skill for walking); and walking. To encourage children to stand for increasingly longer periods, the staff place many of the instructional and play materials on waist-high tables so that the children must stand up to participate. Those who need adult support receive it, and stand only as long as they can without fatigue. While all children who can stand participate in walking exercises, those children who have already begun to walk independently practice more complex exercises such as walking on a rather narrow board—the narrowness forces them to watch their steps and to keep track of where and how they place their feet.

The daily schedule for this class, as well as for the Advanced Preschool Class, is designed to exploit activities that permit all children to participate equally. For instance, arrival at school offers an opportunity to practice an important self-help skill: removing one's coat and hanging it in a locker. Although this task sounds quite simple, breaking it into its component parts gives some idea of the number of complex sub-skills involved. The child must first go to a designated area, the locker area, find his own locker (a picture of the child and his name are posted on the locker), pull off one sleeve after another, remove the coat, and hang it on the hook in the locker. Here, as always, children are given verbal cues and, if necessary, physical prompts until they have mastered the various sub-skills.

The goal for each child is that he will, by about 3 years of age, attain mastery of specific performance objectives within all skill categories with 85 to 100 percent independent competency. The children are assessed on the Denver battery two times a year; on the Down's Syndrome Preschool Performance Inventory daily or weekly; and on daily frequency, duration, and correct and error rates of specific behaviors.

One third of the children in this class had been in the Infant Learning Class. Others joined the class in January and June, 1973. None of the children is 3 years old at this writing; while they have not all reached all of the developmental objectives established, they are all showing increasing skills competence. Some preliminary results are as follows:

In self-help skills, such as handwashing, eating, and coat-removal, the children's mean percent correct responses during Summer Quarter, 1973, were 84 (handwashing); 87 (eating); and 77 (coat removal). These represent gains of from 13 to 28 percent over their Spring Quarter, 1973, performance. Daily data on correct motor and verbal responses of four children, ages 2.6 to 2.9 years, were collected between the third and ninth weeks of school during Autumn Quarter. Three children who attended four sessions a week showed a mean gain of 43 percent. The fourth child, who attended class only 2 days a week during the quarter, showed only a 10 percent increase, suggesting the need for the full-week program. Other data, supporting the need for an *early* program of intervention, are found in the case of one child who had not attended the Infant Class. In January, 1973, he showed developmental lags of 11 months in motor and language behavior and 5 months in personal-social skills, a profile that is more consistent with earlier reports of Down's syndrome children. Moreover, although he is making gains, he is not reaching developmental norms as rapidly as his classmates.

Advanced Preschool Class This class was started in January, 1973, to accommodate those children from the Early Preschool Class who clearly were ready to move to more complex skills development. The children attend 2-hour sessions four times a week. Their daily schedule and categories of activities closely parallel those in the Early Preschool, but special emphasis is placed on language development and on preacademic skills requisite for reading and number concept tasks. Furthermore, their play activities are more complex: block building, dress-up games, and cooperative play. They are also learning to ride tricycles.

A few of the specific developmental objectives for children in this class are that they be able, with 85 to 100 percent independent competency, to: walk up and down stairs unaided; pedal a tricycle 150 feet; climb up and down a 5-foot ladder; match, sort, and select eight pictures at a time; recognize and discriminate seven colors; understand number concepts from one to three; demonstrate an understanding of 10 action verbs and 10 adjectives; approximate all vowel sounds, five consonant sounds, and five combinations of vowels and consonants; name one to ten objects spontaneously; play cooperatively with one to three other children; use a spoon for eating; have clean and dry pants 80 to 100 percent of the time, and use the toilet with minimal assistance.

Assessments follow the Early Preschool Class schedule with the addition, once a year, of the Peabody Picture Vocabulary Test. This test enables children with low verbal skills to demonstrate their receptive and associative capabilities without penalizing them for their verbal deficits.

By the end of Summer Quarter, 1973, 10 children between 4 and 5 years old had reached criterion on their developmental objectives and were ready to move to a kindergarten program. Thirteen children were toilet trained with 90 to 100 percent proficiency. Nine children were riding tricycles independently. All of the 5-year-olds can demonstrate an understanding of 10 prepositions, adjectives, and action verbs. Children who had been in the program for four academic quarters could read at least 30 words, matching and selecting words printed on flash cards. (One child could match and select 103 words during Spring Quarter, 1973).

Data obtained from Peabody Tests administered a year apart show that in the first testing five children who had been in the program between 6 and 12 months showed a mean developmental lag of 5.6 months between their MA and CA scores, while five children newly enrolled in the program showed a mean lag of 21 months. A year later (Autumn, 1973), all of the children tested had maintained or gained in their development. The mean IQ for the children who had been in the program longer went from 84.8 to 88; the gain in the other group was from MIQ 61 to MIQ 74.7 (Hayden and Dmitriev, 1975).

Children presently enrolled in the Advanced Preschool, including some from last year's class and newcomers, are continuing to make gratifying progress. It is still the case that those who have been in the program longer reach developmental criteria sooner than children new to the program, but the newcomers are showing quite steady improvement. We anticipate that those children who will reach age 5 before next autumn and several slightly younger children will have the requisite skills for the kindergarten program.

Kindergarten Class   The Kindergarten Class was added to the Down's Syndrome Programs during Autumn Quarter, 1973. Children attend 2-hour sessions four times a week. While they are still involved in a wide range of activities to continue developing all skills, there is far more emphasis now on cognitive development. The children learn about the calendar: the seasons, months, holidays, and days of the week. They receive individual instruction in reading, math, and speech. Some of the specific developmental objectives for children in this group are: to use appropriately in speech at least half of the nouns, verbs, and adjectives for which they have demonstrated understanding; to relate a flannel board story in sequence; to be able to print their own first names; to understand number concepts from one to five; to discriminate and name all upper and lower case letters of the alphabet; to throw and catch a ball thrown from 5 to 10 feet; to walk up and down stairs alternating feet.

During the most recent academic quarter (Winter, 1974), five children were continuing in a sight reading program; four were in a phonics program (three are using the "Systems 80 Phonics Program"). Both programs continue to be related to the particular child's interests and abilities. The criteria for a child to enter the phonics program are that he have a sight vocabulary of between 75 and 100 words and sufficient attending skills. The children using the "Systems 80" program have successfully completed four to six letters (mean five) and have completed two to twelve primers (mean five). The other children have total sight vocabularies ranging from 36 to 50 (mean 41) words. Children are assessed on the same schedules used in the Advanced Preschool Class.

Projections and Questions for the Future

The most immediate plan to be implemented for children in the programs is to establish a primary class for those who are now approaching 6 years of age and who have the requisite skills to begin more advanced academic work. It is also our intention to phase in a few normal children in the various classes—probably at first the siblings of our pupils—because an integrated class at the Model Preschool Center has demonstrated the usefulness of such an arrangement. The normal children serve as models for the handicapped children; their speech, social behaviors, and attention to tasks very often give the handicapped children useful clues that adults cannot so readily provide. The normal children seem to benefit, too; they have demonstrated no slowing down of their own skills development and they are not bored. Their early experience of going to school with handicapped children should prepare them for the time when more and more handicapped children are accommodated in mainstream education by the public schools as a result of "Education for All" legislation. Parents of the normal children so far enrolled have been enthusiastic about the arrangement—in fact, they sought enrollment for their children.

However, no short-term interventions will have very much impact or value unless they are part of a long-range plan. As we have said earlier, *the* question concerning Down's syndrome children's intellectual prognosis is whether the early gains that so many of them show in response to educational programming can be maintained as the children get older. We do not think the question has been adequately researched. Institutionalized children are, we hope, a dwindling population. However, children living at home but receiving inadequate stimulation and intervention are not a very good test population—after all, normal children receiving inadequate stimulation and intervention might also show declining IQs and capabilities.

In brief, we would like to follow the Down's syndrome children in our classes for as long as possible, providing for them—or working with others to provide—whatever education they are capable of handling.

As part of this long-range plan, we are also interested in finding out precisely how replicable our model is: Will it "travel" to public school special education classes and work without the support system that is found in demonstration centers such as ours? If so, will the children from our own program, transferred to public school, continue to fare well in the transported model? And what about other children who have not had such intensive early intervention? How can they be appropriately placed in the program and assisted in making up for precious time lost in their earlier years?

There are other findings and questions that need examining. For instance, Bayley and her colleagues at Sonoma State Hospital (1971) reported that children in both the hospital and home-reared groups showed variable rates of growth over the 8 years they were studied. In motor skills, for instance, both groups declined between 2 and 5 years, then made gains between 5 and 6 years. Furthermore, in mental growth, while the hospital group began to show some gains at the start of their preschool program, the more dramatic surge followed their exposure to the intensive language program. "There is some indication that, after a slow start, the accelerated growth in competence is at the stage of maturity (that is, a mental age of about 12 to 14 months) at which normal children are starting to use words" (Bayley et al., 1971).

Stein and Susser (1971) cite Down's syndrome as an "excellent epidemiological index" insofar as it is a paradigm for those anomalies resulting in mental retardation in which reduced incidence will not compensate for the increased prevalence caused by the afflicted population's greater longevity. As they point out, those advances that have contributed to increased longevity have not as yet been able to ameliorate or eliminate the mental retardation that results from the anomalies. Substantially reduced incidence of Down's syndrome will depend on a reduced birth rate among older childbearing women. A recent paper from Ireland, where relatively late marriages have been traditional, reports a surprising decline in the number of births to women more than 35 years of age, and a concomitant reduction in the incidence of Down's syndrome, between 1966 and 1971 (O'Brien and Gill, 1972). The authors cite Davis (1971) as stating that "if no women were to conceive over the age of 35, two-thirds of the cases of Down's syndrome would disappear," and report that their own figures support this contention. Stein and Susser estimate a reduction by one third in the number of Down's syndrome births if "the incidence of Down's syndrome at all maternal ages can be kept as low as the incidence among young women . . . " It is impossible to estimate exactly how incidence is or will be affected by genetic counseling because we do not know how widespread such counseling is or what sort of records are kept.

How far in the future we shall see a substantially reduced incidence in Down's syndrome is a question we must leave to demographers and epidemiologists. From our standpoint, the fact remains that there are still large numbers of Down's syndrome children and retarded children with other etiologies who need educational services. If our programs for Down's syndrome children are "transportable," it should be possible to extend their benefits to larger groups of children and also to those whose retardation may be caused by other factors. Replications already in operation augur well for the transportability of the basic model for Down's syndrome children from birth to 6 years of age.

DECISION MAKING AND RESEARCH NEEDS
FOR THE FUTURE FOR ALL HIGH RISK INFANTS

La Veck (1971) has discussed the need for integrating the efforts of the biological, medical, and behavioral sciences in the study of high risk infants. High priority should be given to the study of biological and psychological insult during the early years. For example, much more needs to be learned about the effects of nutrition. The role of neurological and endocrine development in the development of cognition, language, personality, and social role needs to be understood. These are just two of the many areas that need extensive research. It seems that as a little knowledge is gained, questions increase exponentially. Following are a few of the areas that need to be explored. Reliable data for guiding social policy planning for early intervention with high risk infants are urgently needed in addition to answers to specific questions.

Identifying the High Risk Infant

Screening Instruments Gallagher and Bradley (1972), after an exhaustive review of existing early identification measures and child development scales, conclude that they are all far from infallible in detecting potentially handicapping conditions. Follow-up studies have not been done; these are needed so that the number of false-positive and false-negative predictions that occurred using a given screening measure may be identified. Further efforts to improve screening instruments by reducing errors are needed. However, Gallagher and Bradley (1972) point out that, unless society is willing to follow these identifications with programs to remediate deficits, the screening devices "do not really amount to more than an academic interest."

Neurological Examinations Parmelee and Michaelis (1971) also indicate that there are no definitive neurological tests for identifying infants at risk. The difficulty of prediction is compounded by the lack of understanding of nervous system development of the infant. For example, it is difficult to assess muscle tone because of the lack of standards for the normal range of infant muscle tone. Parmelee and Michaelis (1971) state:

> Although at present no completely satisfactory methods for newborn neurological assessment exist, we believe considerable progress has been made in new conceptions of approach and refinement of established techniques . . . It seems that the predominantly behavioral approach may provide the most useful information about the degree of CNS dysfunction during the neonatal period and serve to indicate potential developmental problems (p. 20).

Turkewitz and Birch (1971) emphasize the importance of continued research in this area when they report that infants with low Apgar scores, but still not considered by their pediatricians to be significantly impaired, continued to show evidence of malfunction. Indicators of impairment at birth may fail to identify infants who are at risk either because the indicators are overlooked or considered unimportant, or because the indicator is too insensitive. Infants who appear subnormal at birth but appear normal by the second day may not be identified as high risk even though there is now evidence that such infants may continue to evidence abnormal development.

Ambiguous Indicators The ambiguity of symptoms may result in dramatically inappropriate diagnoses. For example, Kavanagh (1971) reports that a group of children seen at The Johns Hopkins Hospital were inappropriately diagnosed as "hypopituitary dwarfs" because of their small size; however, the apparent endocrine dysfunction vanished, and the children made amazing gains in height when they were placed in foster homes. When the children were returned to their own homes, their growth again stopped; this has been described as the "psychosocial dwarfism" syndrome. Further study is needed in all areas in order that abnormal developmental manifestations can be appropriately diagnosed and treated.

Perinatal Influences of Drugs

Brazelton (1971) cites studies suggesting that there may be critical periods for cellular development that may permanently affect the expression of the genotype. It is important that these critical periods be identified. Smith and Jones (1973) of the Medical

Research Unit, Child Development and Mental Retardation Center at this university, have reported that the infants of chronic alcoholic mothers show significant delays in development. What are the important variables involved in alcoholism that affect the offspring? This area urgently needs further research.

Brazelton also discusses the interaction effects of the child and the mother's reaction to the child in shaping the child's future. The mother's responses are critical, but the child's behavior may reflect his intrauterine and perinatal experiences and, therefore, the child may also shape his mother's response. In addition, Brazelton expresses concern about the use of barbiturates given to the mother before and during delivery; such medication may affect central nervous system reactions for a week, but because there is no apparent permanent damage, the practice is continued. Brazelton suggests that the behavioral effects of such medication during the first week may influence mother-child interaction during its "critical period." The routine use of drugs prenatally and post-natally must be re-evaluated for its effect on subtle subclinical effects on tissue and neural organization and for its effect on early mother-infant interaction that may well have lasting effects on their lives together.

Nutrition

Gross neurologic effects of malnutrition in humans usually disappear with rehabilitation and permanent effects are rare (Winick and Coombs, 1972). However, there has never been a systematic search for more subtle neurologic changes. This is an important area for future research.

It is difficult in studies of human malnutrition to isolate the effects of nourishment from other environmental effects. Yatkin and McLaren (1970) attempted to study the interaction effects of malnutrition and environmental enrichment; children being treated for marasmus were found to have increased developmental quotients when given environmental enrichment as well as improved diet. Winick and Coombs suggested two ways to improve this study in a future replication. First, the developmental quotient measures were closely related to the enrichment procedures employed; using another measure would enhance the validity of the findings. They also suggested that, in addition to the malnourished experimental and control groups, a third group of well-nourished children should be placed in the enriched environment condition. This would help to isolate further the effects of environmental enrichment from nourishment. Warren (1970) also suggests that such studies may be improved by matching children for mental age in order to reveal possible differences between malnourished and well-nourished children of the same mental age.

Willerman (1972) emphasizes the need not only for longitudinal research but specifically for inter-generational research. For example, there is evidence that poor nutrition during a woman's formative years may interfere with her ability to carry a child and consequently increase the risk of prematurity. This factor is probably related to socioeconomic status; the entire area of social, racial, and economic status as predictors of high risk needs to be explored further.

Biological Factors

Willerman (1972) cites data that show a relationship between certain pathologies and high intelligence. For example, retinoblastoma, a rare tumor of childhood that often results in blindness, is associated with "strikingly high intelligence." This suggests that intelligence may be associated with a single major gene (in contrast to the polygenic view) or that some specific secretion of the tumor is associated with high intelligence. Asthma, which may have a genetic component, and high serum uric acid levels associated with gout (which, in turn, has long been considered a "rich man's" disease), are also associated with high intelligence. The biological correlates of intelligence merit further study.

Public Health Considerations

The implication of such trends for public health care is twofold. First, the incidence of mental retardation (and other handicapping conditions) needs to be reduced. Second, maximum intervention is needed to reduce the disabilities of the handicapped. These two directions will require environmental surveillance (including drugs, chemicals, radiation, pollution), improved reporting of incidence and prevalence, better control of infections, reduction of the effects of poverty, family planning, improved and earlier education of the mentally retarded, and research for new ways to reduce incidence (Stein and Susser, 1971).

Robinson and Robinson (1972) reported that other countries, such as the Soviet Union, are more experienced in early childhood education than is the United States. The Robinsons also distinguish between policy planning in socialist countries (which is aimed at preventing problems such as unemployment, child abuse, malnutrition, mental illness, and intellectual inadequacy) and the free-enterprise countries (which is "emergency-induced," making child-related services available only when the family is unable to meet the child's needs). Most countries fall somewhere between these two extremes and, even in the most socialist country, universal early education is not available. High risk infants are given the broadest service in countries such as Sweden and the Soviet Union. However, these programs stress cognitive development very little. For policy making in the United States, it would be invaluable to have available data on early education in other countries; programs successful in reducing the risk of handicaps should be studied for possible adaptation in the United States.

According to Lubovsky (1973), the Soviet Union has the lowest percentage of handicapped children of any country in the world. Progress in decreasing the prevalence of handicapped children has been attributed to the extensive health services offered to pregnant women and infants. These services include 16 obligatory medical examinations of the infant during the first year of life. Moreover, all drugs made available in the Soviet Union are carefully monitored. Lubovsky reports that there have been no rubella epidemics in the Soviet Union for "many years." The social policies of other countries that have been successful in diagnosing, remediating, and preventing handicapping conditions merit serious review in order to determine applications for improving the health and well-being of children in the United States.

Measuring Intelligence

In this controversial matter of measuring intelligence, it is important to realize that there are more than two options: there is no need either to dispense with intelligence measures altogether or to accept standard intelligence measures as if they were perfect. The value of measures of performance and predictions of success cannot be overstated. It is important that such measures focus on the objective observation of performance and to recognize as Dyer (1971) states, that:

> ... too few people realize that intelligence can *be taught* and that the primary business of schools and school teachers is to teach it ... the heart of the process of educational measurement ought to be thought of as the disciplined observation by teachers of the behavior of their pupils, and until we can get this idea across, most of the teaching, not to mention the testing, of little children will continue to be intolerably blind in its operation and dubious in its effects.

Mother-Infant Interaction

Many questions about the nature and consequences of mother-infant interaction remain unanswered. Moreover, techniques for the application of research findings to improve human mother-child interaction need to be developed. At the Primate Center at the University of Washington, Dr. Ruth Bobbit and Dr. Gordon Jensen have developed a coding system for observing behavioral patterns of mother-child interaction. This coding system has been adapted by Dr. Kate Kogan (1974) of the Child Development and Mental Retardation Center, University of Washington, for use with human mothers and children. Because mothers and children become involved in repetitive patterns of behavior, with each member of the dyad influencing the behavior of the other, it has been assumed that by modifying the mother's behavioral input the behavioral patterns of the dyad can be changed. First, Dr. Kogan analyzes two video-taped sessions of interaction. During eight subsequent once-a-week sessions, the mother wears a small earphone. This enables an observer to comment on the interaction and to make suggestions to the mother. After each session there is a discussion of ways to apply the suggestions at home. Follow-up sessions are scheduled 1 year after the tenth session. Follow-up of 30 mothers revealed that 25 reported improved relationships with their children. This example makes clear the potential for application of basic research to improvement of human interaction; more study in this area is needed.

Longitudinal Research

Willerman (1972) emphasized the need for longitudinal studies in relation to nutrition. This need is apparent in other areas as well, especially in the area of early educational intervention with high risk infants. The seminal research projects of Scarr-Salapatek and Williams (1972) and of Wright (1972) with premature infants, and the Sonoma State Hospital study with Down's syndrome children, have been terminated because of funding cuts. Funding on a year-to-year basis is counterproductive; any time spent on long-term planning is wasted, and important beginnings may never reach any conclusion.

One study that has been funded for a long period is the Milwaukee Project (Heber et al., 1972). It has been described as "one of the most important longitudinal studies ever undertaken." Unlike other early intervention projects, the Milwaukee Project began with infants at about 3 months of age. They had been identified as high risk because of a number of factors, especially low maternal intelligence. The study was not designed to raise IQ but "to permit normal intellectual development by mitigating environmentally depressing events" (Garber and Heber, 1973). The objective was to prevent those language, problem-solving, and motivational deficits that are associated with mental retardation and disadvantage. In addition to the educational program for the children, vocational and home management training were provided for the mothers. The preliminary results of the study are promising. The children in the experimental group scored significantly higher on all measures than did the control group children, and the discrepancy has increased with time. The final report of the follow-up of these children in the first grade will be of major significance for those interested in preventing retardation. As Garber and Heber (1973) state: "Indeed, if our country is to seriously challenge the problems of cultural-familial retardation, we must do so at its doorstep and that will require a strategy for prevention, with increased emphasis on early detection and early intervention" (p. 11).

Concluding Statement

The obvious importance of such long-term research cannot be overstated. Future funding considerations must include the need to view the results of early intervention over time.

While educators must contribute to the long-term effort by seeking to improve available programs and to develop new strategies and procedures to maximize retarded children's potential and performance, they must also cope with the "here and now problems"—the many children with varying degrees of retardation in regular and special education classes. These children's progress must be maintained and accelerated if we are to attain the national goal of reducing by half the incidence and prevalence of retardation by the turn of the century.

ACKNOWLEDGMENTS

The authors wish to thank Gael D. McGinness, Constance G. Pious, and Carole Hansen for their help in preparing this manuscript, and Barbara Jacobs, Shirley Huguenin, and Mary Cowger for typing it through several draft stages.

LITERATURE CITED

Abelson, R. D., and R. C. Johnson. 1969. Intellectual, behavioral, and physical characteristics associated with trisomy translocation and mosaic types of Down's syndrome. Amer. J. Ment. Defic. 73: 852–855.

Allen, K. E., J. Rieke, V. Dmitriev, and A. H. Hayden. (Winter) 1971–72. Early warning: Observation as a tool for recognizing potential handicaps in young children. Ed. Horizons 50: 43–55.

Barnard, K. 1973. A Program of Stimulation for Infants Born Prematurely. Presented at the convention of the Society for Research in Child Development, March, Philadelphia.

Barnard, K., and B. S. Collar, 1973. Early diagnosis, interpretation, and intervention. A commentary on the nurse's role. Ann. N.Y. Acad. Sci. 205: 373–382.

Bayley, N., L. Rhodes, B. Gooch, and M. Marcus. 1971. Environmental factors in the development of institutionalized children. In J. Hellmuth (ed.), The Exceptional Infant. Vol. II, pp. 450–472. Brunner/Mazel, New York.

Benda, C. E. 1969. Down's Syndrome. Mongolism and its Management. (Rev. Ed.) Grune and Stratton, New York/London.

Birch, H. G., and A. C. Cornwell. 1969. Psychological and social development in home-reared children with Down's syndrome (mongolism). Amer. J. Ment. Defic. 74: 341–350.

(Bloom, B.) 1973. Verbal education critical before age 10, says Bloom. Report on Preschool Education 5: 8 (November 28).

Brazelton, T. B. 1971. Influence of perinatal drugs on the behavior of the neonate. In J. Hellmuth (ed.), The Exceptional Infant. Vol. II, pp. 419–431. Brunner/Mazel, New York.

Carter, C. H. 1966. Handbook of Mental Retardation Syndromes. C. C Thomas, Springfield, Ill.

Davis, J. 1971. Prevention of brain damage in the newborn. Foundation Day Lectures, Our Lady's Hospital for Sick Children, Crumlin, Dublin.

Dmitriev, V. 1971a. Down's syndrome infant stimulation program. Exercises for the infant, birth to three months. Sharing Our Caring 1: 25–29.

Dmitriev, V. 1971b. Exercises for the infant, birth to three months. Sharing Our Caring 1: 4–7.

Dmitriev, V., G. Nail, and F. R. Harris. 1970. A study in infant treatment of mongolism. Presented at the Tenth Annual Research Meeting of the Department of Institutions, Division of Research, State of Washington, and the University of Washington School of Medicine, Department of Psychiatry, Seattle (February.)

Dollar, B. 1973. Child care in China: "Everything is planned." Sat. Rev. Ed. 1: 29–33.

Doris, J., and S. B. Sarason. 1969. Psychological Problems in Mental Deficiency. Harper and Row, New York.

Down, J. L. 1866. Observations on an ethnic classification of idiots. Clinical Lectures and Reports, London Hospital 3: 259–262.

Drillien, C. M. 1964. The Growth and Development of the Prematurely Born Infant. Williams and Wilkins, Baltimore.

Dyer, H. S. 1971. Testing little children—some old problems in new settings. National Leadership Institute. Teacher Education/Early Childhood. The University of Connecticut Technical Paper, Storrs. (December.)

Faber, N. W. 1968. The Retarded Child. Crown Publishers, New York.

Fantz, R. L. 1965. Visual perception from birth as shown by pattern selectivity. Ann. N.Y. Acad. Sci. 118: 793–814.

Fraiberg, S., M. Smith, and M. A. Adelson. 1969. An educational program for blind infants. J. Spec. Ed. 3: 121–139.

Francis, A., and V. Dmitriev. 1967. Academic Programming for Retarded Children [film]. Fircrest School, Seattle.

Frankenburg, W., and J. Dodds. 1967. Denver Developmental Screening Test. University of Colorado, Denver.

French, E. L., and J. C. Scott. 1967. How You Can Help Your Retarded Child. A Manual for Parents. J. B. Lippincott, Philadelphia.

Friedlander, B. Z. 1971. Listening, language, and the auditory environment. Automated evaluation and intervention. In J. Hellmuth (ed.), The Exceptional Infant. Vol. II, pp. 248–275. Brunner/Mazel, New York.

Gallagher, J. J., and R. H. Bradley. 1972. Early identification of developmental difficulties. In I. J. Gordon (ed.), Early childhood education. The Seventy-first Yearbook of the National Society for Education, pp. 87–122. The University of Chicago Press, Chicago.

Garber, H., and R. Heber. 1973. The Milwaukee Project. Early intervention as a technique to prevent mental retardation. National Leadership Institute. Teacher Education/Early Childhood. The University of Connecticut Technical Paper, Storrs. (March.)

Gesell, A., and C. Amatruda. 1969. Developmental Diagnosis. Harper and Row, New York.

Haring, N. G., A. H. Hayden, and K. E. Allen. 1971. Programs and projects. Intervention in early childhood. Ed. Tech. 11: 52–60.

Haring, N. G., and R. W. Ridgway. 1967. Early identification of children with learning disabilities. Except. Child. 33: 387–395.

Hayden, A. H. 1974a. A center-based parent training model. In J. Crim (ed.), Training Parents to Teach: Four Models. First Chance for Children, Vol. 3, pp. 10–24. Technical Assistance Development Systems, Chapel Hill, North Carolina.

Hayden, A. H. 1974b. Perspectives of early childhood education in special education. In N. G. Haring (ed.), Behavior of Exceptional Children. An Introduction to Special Education, pp. 37–67. Charles E. Merrill, Columbus, Ohio.

Hayden, A. H., and V. Dmitriev. 1975. Multidisciplinary preschool program for Down's syndrome children at the University of Washington Model Preschool Center. In B. Z. Friedlander, G. Kirk, and G. Sterritt (eds.), The Exceptional Infant, Vol. III, pp. 193–221. Brunner/Mazel, New York.

Heber, R. 1970. Epidemiology of Mental Retardation. C. C Thomas, Springfield, Ill.

Heber, R., H. Garber, S. Harrington, C. Hoffman, and C. Falender. 1972. Rehabilitation of Families at Risk for Mental Retardation. Rehabilitation Research and Training Center in Mental Retardation. University of Wisconsin, Madison.

Heber, R., and H. A. Stevens (eds.). 1965. Mental Retardation. University of Chicago Press, Chicago.

Hunt, J. McV. 1961. Intelligence and Experience. The Ronald Press, New York.

Jeffrey, W. E. 1958. Variables in early discrimination learning. 1. Motor responses in the training of a left-right discrimination. Child Devel. 29: 269–275.

Jervis, G. A. (ed.). 1967. Mental Retardation. C. C Thomas, Springfield, Ill.

Johnson, C. A., and R. C. Katz. 1973. Using parents as change agents for their children: A review. J. Child Psych. Psychiat. 14: 181–200.

Katz, V. 1971. Auditory stimulation and developmental behavior of the premature infant. Nursing Res. 20: 196–201.

Kavanagh, J. F. 1971. The genesis and pathogenesis of speech and language. In J. Hellmuth (ed.), The Exceptional Infant, Vol. II, pp. 211–247. Brunner/Mazel, New York.

Kindergarten. 1973. Soviet Life 6: 58–61.

Kirk, S. A. 1958. Early Education of the Mentally Retarded. University of Illinois Press, Urbana.

Kogan, K. 1974. As described by D. Docter in long thread of research stretches for a decade. Health Science Review. University of Washington Health Sciences Center, Seattle. (Spring.)

Kugel, R. B. 1970. Combatting retardation in infants with Down's syndrome. Children 17: 188–192.

La Veck, G. 1971. Introduction. *In* J. Hellmuth (ed.), The Exceptional Infant, Vol. II, pp. vii–ix. Brunner/Mazel, New York.

Lejeune, L., M. Gautier, and R. Turpin. 1959. Les chromosomes humains en culture de tissus. C. R. Acad. Sci. 248: 602.

Lubovsky, V. I. 1973. Special Education. *In* N. P. Kuzin, M. I. Kondakov, P. V. Zimin, M. N. Kolmakova, V. I. Lubovsky, G. V. Berezina, and A. I. Foteya (eds.), Education in the USSR, pp. 93–105. Progress Publishers, Moscow.

Melyn, M. A., and D. T. White. 1973. Mental and developmental milestones of noninstitutionalized Down's syndrome children. Pediatrics 52: 542–545.

MR 72, Islands of Excellence. 1972. Report of the President's Committee on Mental Retardation. Department of Health, Education, and Welfare Pub. No. (OS) 73-7, Washington, D.C.

Mills, D. D. 1974. Things are looking up for Down's syndrome children. The Seattle Times Magazine, Jan. 6: 8–10.

O'Brien, N. G., and D. G. Gill. 1972. Down's syndrome: A dwindling disease? J. Irish Med. Assoc. 65: 465.

Parmelee, A. H. 1970. A panel discussion on sleep cycles in newborn infants. Where might be the gold in these hills? Neuropaediatrie 1(3): 70–77.

Parmelee, A. H., and R. Michaelis. 1971. Neurological examination of the newborn. *In* J. Hellmuth (ed.), The Exceptional Infant, Vol. II, pp. 3–23. Brunner/Mazel, New York.

Penrose, L. S., and G. F. Smith. 1966. Down's Anomaly. J. and A. Churchill, Ltd., London.

Rheingold, H. L., J. L. Gewirtz, and H. W. Ross. 1959. Social conditioning of vocalizations in the infant. J. Comp. Physiol. Psych. 52: 68–73.

Rhodes, L., B. Gooch, E. Y. Siegelman, C. A. Behrns, and R. Metzger. 1969. A Language Stimulation and Reading Program for Severely Retarded Mongoloid Children: A Descriptive Report. California Mental Health Association Research Monograph No. 11. State of California Department of Mental Hygiene, Bureau of Research, Sacramento.

Richardson, S. O. 1973. Neglect of children with language and learning disabilities. Hearing and Speech News 41: 24–27.

Robinson, H. B., and N. M. Robinson. 1972. A cross-cultural view of early education. *In* I. J. Gordon (ed.), Early Childhood Education. The Seventy-first Yearbook of the National Society for Education, pp. 291–315. The University of Chicago Press, Chicago.

Robinson, H. B., and N. M. Robinson (eds.). 1973. International Monograph Series on Early Child Care. Gordon and Breach, New York/London.

Rynders, J., and M. Horrobin. 1972. Enhancement of communication skill development in Downs's syndrome children through early intervention. Annual Report, Research, Development, and Demonstration Center in Education of Handicapped Children. University of Minnesota, Minneapolis.

Scarr-Salapatek, S., and M. L. Williams. 1972. A stimulation program for low birth weight infants. Amer. J. Pub. Health 62: 662–667.

Séguin, E. 1866. Idiocy and Its Treatment by the Physiological Method. William Wood, New York.

Simner, M. L., and B. Reilly. 1969. Response of the newborn infant to the cry of another infant. Presented at the meeting of the Society for Research in Child Development, Santa Monica, Calif. (March.)

Siqueland, E. R., and L. P. Lipsitt. 1966. Conditioned head-turning in human newborns. J. Exper. Child Psych. 3: 356–376.

Skeels, H. M., and H. B. Dye. 1939. A study of the effects of differential stimulation on mentally retarded children. Proc. Amer. Assoc. Ment. Defic. 44: 114–136.

Skeels, H. M., R. Updegraff, B. L. Wellman, and H. M. Williams. 1938. A study of environmental stimulation: An orphanage preschool project. University of Iowa Stud. Child Welfare, Vol. 15.

Smart, M. S., and R. C. Smart (eds.). 1973. Infants: Development and Relationships. Macmillan, New York.

Smith, D. W., and K. Jones. 1973. Fetal alcohol syndrome. Presented at Charles C. Strother Lecture, Child Development and Mental Retardation Center, University of Washington, Seattle. (December.)

Smith, D. W., and A. A. Wilson. 1973. The Child with Down's Syndrome. W. B. Saunders, Philadelphia.

Stein, Z. A., and M. W. Susser. 1971. Changes over time in the incidence and prevalence of mental retardation. In J. Hellmuth (ed.), The Exceptional Infant, Vol. II, pp. 305–340. Brunner/Mazel, New York.

The Story of the White House Conferences on Children and Youth. 1967. Department of Health, Education, and Welfare, Social and Rehabilitation Service, Children's Bureau, Washington, D.C.

Tizard, J. 1964. Residential care of mentally handicapped children. Brit. Med. J. April 2: 1041–1046.

Turkewitz, G., and H. B. Birch. 1971. Neurobehavioral organization of the human newborn. In J. Hellmuth (ed.), The Exceptional Infant, Vol. II, pp. 24–40. Brunner/Mazel, New York.

Warren, N. 1970. Research design for investigation of the lasting behavioral effects of malnutrition. The problem of controls. Soc. Sci. Med. 4: 589–593.

Willerman, L. 1972. Biosocial influences on human development. Amer. J. Orthopsychiat. 42: 452–462.

Wilson, V., and R. Parks. 1970. Promoting ambulation in the severely retarded child. Ment. Retard. 8: 17.

Winick, M., and J. Coombs. 1972. Nutrition, environment, and behavioral development. Ann. Rev. Med. 23: 149–160.

Wright, L. 1971. The theoretical and research base for a program of early stimulation care and training of premature infants. In J. Hellmuth (ed.), The Exceptional Infant, Vol. II, 276–304. Brunner/Mazel, New York.

Yatkin, U. S., and D. S. McLaren. 1970. The behavioral development of infants recovering from severe malnutrition. J. Ment. Defic. Res. 14: 25–32.

Early Intervention with Biologically Handicapped Infants and Young Children: A Preliminary Study with Each Child as His Own Control

Maria E. C. Barrera, M.A., Donald K. Routh, Ph.D., Carol A. Parr, M.S.,
Nancy M. Johnson, Ph.D., Donna S. Arendshorst, B.A.,
Elaine L. Goolsby, M.S.W., and Stephen R. Schroeder, Ph.D.

The purpose of the present study was to evaluate the effectiveness of several types of individually tailored developmental stimulation for infants and young children with biologically based handicaps. Interest in such early intervention strategies dates from the very beginnings of medical, educational, and psychological concern with the retarded child in the United States. In his book on the treatment of the retarded by "the physiological method," Séguin (1971, originally published 1866) described the type of program that was (and is) needed:

> As soon as any function is set down as deficient at its due time of development, the cause must be sought and combatted . . . the mother must often visit with her child the nearest institution, see what is done there to remedy similar cases, and receive the instructions necessary to carry on the same treatment at home. If this proves costly at first . . . it will in the end save the State and families the expense of several years of after-teaching, besides accomplishing more fully the object of treatment [pp. 88–89].

No one doubts that a good day care and home program for handicapped infants and toddlers can enrich the immediate quality of their lives, give the parents a break from the

This research was supported by U.S. Public Health Service, Maternal and Child Health Project No. 916, and by Grant HD-03110 from the National Institute of Child Health and Human Development, Bethesda, Maryland.

609

burden of full time care, and provide training opportunities for students in the relevant professional fields. Like Séguin, however, we would prefer to believe that such a program can also improve the children's later competence in life.

Bloom (1964) has argued that the effect of environmental interventions should be greatest when the most rapid development normally takes place, pointing out that half of the variation in adult intelligence is accounted for (in the sense of being predictable) by the age of 4 years. Like other aspects of development, a child's physical capabilities are also most variable in infancy and early childhood. Solomons, Holden, and Denhoff (1963) found that four out of five cases of spastic hemiplegia seen in the first year of life had resolved when the child was seen 1 to 3 years later, and that four of seven infants with delayed motor development before 1 year of age were normal at age 3. Clearly, intervention in early infancy warrants investigation of the biologically handicapped as well as the socially disadvantaged child.

BACKGROUND OF THE STUDY

The present study took place in the Division for Disorders of Development and Learning, a part of the Biological Sciences Research Center of the Child Development Institute of the University of North Carolina at Chapel Hill. Its basic purpose was to determine whether various types of early intervention would be effective with children who were developmentally handicapped on a biological basis. In contrast to the program at the Frank Porter Graham Child Development Center of the same Child Development Institute, it was basically concerned with competent, non-disadvantaged parents seeking to supplement their skills in dealing with an extraordinarily challenging parental role.

Unfortunately for anyone who seeks a simple solution to his problems, the biologically handicapped child frequently has difficulties of more than one kind, for example in motor development, in perceptual-motor and language areas, in acquiring self-help skills, and in social adaptation. The complexity of the problems involved in dealing with such children has led to the formation of interdisciplinary teams for diagnosis and treatment of the children as well as for training professionals in disciplines such as nursing, physical therapy, speech and hearing, psychology, special education, and social work, in addition to the purely medical specialties involved. The present project had its origin within one such interdisciplinary team.

Since these children's problems are diverse rather than unitary and global, a strategy was called for that permitted the evaluation of a number of different elements of the treatment program. Also, the seriousness of some of the children's problems required immediate attention and precluded the use of a classic experimental group-control group design. The strategy adopted resembles the multiple baseline procedures of Barton, Guess, Garcia, and Baer (1970) except that the dependent measures were developmental levels rather than the frequencies of certain independent response categories. Each child was given continuous treatment and a coordinated home program in the single area of greatest concern, and no attempt was made to evaluate this treatment in a controlled way. Rather, the experimental design applied to the several possible adjunctive areas of treatment and home programming.

Five different types of treatment activity were evaluated: gross motor, fine motor, language, perceptual-cognitive, and personal-social training. It is most convenient to review past research on the effects of these types of training independently.

Treatment programs for children's motor difficulties emphasize either the reduction of pathological patterns of response, i.e., physical therapy, or the stimulation of motor development in general, i.e., physical education. The physical therapist has long been a member of the treatment team for children with cerebral palsy. Unfortunately, the effects of physical therapy have not often been subjected to controlled study. Mead (1968), in a presidential address to the American Academy for Cerebral Palsy, deplored the "palpable lack of any adequate or competent research into the treatment of cerebral palsy" (p. 424). Perhaps the best study up to that time was that of Paine (1962), which, though it was not a controlled study, did include a large series of totally untreated cases in addition to those receiving treatment. Paine concluded that the chief effect of physical therapy was on moderately severe spastics who, with therapy, appeared to develop a better gait and to have fewer contractures. However, many possible confounding variables were noted, for example the fact that untreated patients were more likely to have been mentally retarded than treated ones. Recently, a controlled study of the effects of physical therapy (largely Bobath method) on spastic children has appeared (Wright and Nicholson, 1973), but this was inconclusive because of the relatively small number of children involved.

Physical education, in contrast, has been the subject of several controlled studies with retarded or physically handicapped children, though none of these involved infants and toddlers. Corder (1966), working with teenagers, found significant effects of an intensive physical education program not only upon physical fitness but also upon IQ scores of educable mentally retarded boys. Solomon and Pangle (1967) found similar effects and demonstrated the retention of gains of teenage retarded boys upon follow up 6 weeks later. Edgar et al. (1969) worked with moderately and severely retarded children between the ages of 3 and 8 years, using a Kephart type of sensorimotor training. The trained children had significantly increased scores on Gesell motor items and on language and personal-social items. Morrison and Pothier (1972) similarly demonstrated the effectiveness of individually prescribed sensorimotor activities on the gross motor and language performance of retarded preschoolers as compared to control groups receiving activities with social attention or casually selected (rather than prescribed) gross motor activities.

Fine motor activities have received far less attention in formal research with handicapped children than have gross motor activities. The present authors were unable to locate no controlled studies on the effects of fine motor training on children with biologically based handicaps, though the literature on occupational therapy has many case studies and uncontrolled series of cases. Lillie (1968), in a study of socially deprived educable mentally retarded children of kindergarten age, did find that a 5-month program of motor development lessons led to a significant improvement in the fine motor development of the experimental group as compared to home and regular kindergarten controls. As in the case of many of the treatment programs reviewed, the question of the lasting effects of the intervention remains unanswered.

Controlled studies of language intervention programs have evidently not been carried out with handicapped infants and toddlers, but a number of relevant studies have been done with other populations. Some of the studies have focused rather narrowly on a single procedure or a single dependent measure. Fodor (1967), for example, found that reading stories to 2-year-old children from a low income urban background led to an improvement in their vocabularies, though not their mean length of utterance. Using operant methods, Guess et al. (1968) were able to train a 10-year-old nonverbal retarded girl in imitation and labeling and then in the correct use of singular and plural forms. Experimental control was then demonstrated by reversal of the reinforcement contingencies, leading the girl to label plural displays with singular word forms and vice versa. The pluralization was shown to generalize to new words in "productive" fashion. Nelson, Carskaddon, and Bonvillian (1973) showed, with children 32 to 40 months old, the effectiveness of training in which adults used other sentence forms to recast the children's utterances, as compared to control groups receiving either no treatment or hearing new sentences unrelated to their own. Children in the recast-sentence condition were more advanced linguistically on a number of different post-test measures of syntactic development.

Other language intervention programs have been more ambitious, attempting to teach language similar to the natural adult variety to nonverbal persons. The earliest study of this type was that of Itard with Victor, the Wild Boy of Aveyron (1962, originally published 1801). More recent attempts include the work of Bricker (1972) and Kent (1972) with older retarded children and the Monterey program (Gray and Ryan, 1973) developed with children between 4 and 7 years of age who had delayed language development. A variation of the Monterey program is in use at the Division for Disorders of Development and Learning, and the speech pathologists report an encouraging amount of facilitation of spontaneous language performance in children with various types of language difficulties. These language intervention programs tend to concentrate intensively on a few subjects and to develop flexible experimental procedures adapted to each child's particular needs. They have often included short-term demonstrations of experimental control (e.g., reversal of the contingencies or use of multiple baseline comparisons), but the main logic of these studies depends upon the assumption that the subject (an autistic child or a severely retarded person, for example) would not learn functional language at all if it were not for the intervention. As Bricker (1972) stated, "In many cases of retarded development, we are exploring a wilderness between the child's current repertoire and the defined terminal behavior." Bricker compared a successful language intervention program to a map of such a wilderness. He argued that the validity of the program would be demonstrated "if even a single person reaches the destination" of functional language (p. 84). This logic is probably acceptable when the subjects are older persons with a guarded prognosis for language development. However, when the subjects are young children, one could never know, if functional language developed with the use of a special intervention program, that it would not have developed without the program.

The existing language intervention studies, and indeed developmental psycholinguistics in general, have concentrated on children's development after the 18-month milestone of combining words. A strong argument could be made, however, that important events take place in the first year of the child's life in the system for processing linguistic inputs as well as in vocal expression. Eimas et al. (1971) reported that infants as young as 1 month could distinguish selectively along certain phonemic boundaries. Routh (1969) showed that infants 2 to 7 months old could be conditioned to produce a differential increase in either "vowel" or "consonant" sounds. Friedlander (1970) suggested that young infants get more from listening to language than had previously been thought. Clearly, an intervention program should include language stimulation even when the children are below a 12-month developmental level of functioning.

Attempts at cognitive stimulation of infants have been of greater interest to researchers in the past decade than previously, although similar work with children in the 3- to 6-year age group has been a concern of special educators from Montessori (1965, originally published 1912) to Kirk (1958). The Head Start programs of the 1960s were, of course, directed at remediation of the cognitive difficulties of socially disadvantaged preschoolers. The frequent negative results or failure of long-range carry-over (e.g., Westinghouse Learning Corporation, 1969) were one source of the growing interest in initiating the intervention earlier in the child's life than age 3 and involving the family actively in the intervention process. Among the infant intervention programs for disadvantaged subjects have been those of Heber (cited in Scarr-Salapatek, 1971) and Robinson and Robinson (1971). Robinson and Robinson (1971) found that infants and young preschool children who had been in a day care and stimulation program for 2 years performed better on the Bayley Scales of Infant Development than did home-reared controls. In the Milwaukee Project (Garber, 1973), the subjects were infants born to mentally retarded, black, inner city mothers. These infants were thus demographically at high risk to become progressively more retarded with increasing age. Experimental subjects receiving an intervention program from early infancy showed dramatic gains in IQ, increases that were at last report being translated into good academic progress. In fact, many of these children were reading before they entered first grade. Much of the recent work on intervention with the preschool age group of socially disadvantaged children has stressed the importance of involving the family in the process. Klaus and Gray (1968), for example, not only found evidence for the superiority of the progress of their experimental group to controls but also found evidence of "vertical" diffusion to siblings and "horizontal" diffusion to neighborhood peers of the benefits of intervention.

The only controlled study of cognitive intervention with biologically impaired infants known to the authors is that of Scarr-Salapatek and Williams (1973) with low-birth-weight newborns, who were given extra handling and exposure to human faces and voices as well as patterned visual stimulation in the hospital nursery and then given weekly home visits from a social worker who provided instruction and demonstration to the mothers in developmental stimulation. Of the 30 infants, 15 were assigned to the experimental group and 15 to an untreated control group on a random basis. At 1 year of age, infants in the experimental group had risen significantly, nearly 10 points in terms of Cattell developmental quotients, as compared to controls. Further follow up information on the effects of this early intervention program is not yet available.

The final area of research to be reviewed is that of "personal-social" skills, which, in the age group of concern, refer mostly to feeding and dressing. Feeding skills have been the subject of a number of well controlled studies with older mentally retarded persons, though not with infants. Barton et al. (1970) worked with 16 male retarded persons ranging from 9 to 23 years old. The undesirable mealtime behaviors initially observed were stealing food, using the fingers inappropriately in eating, messy use of eating utensils, and eating food directly from the tray with the mouth or eating spilled food. Time out contingencies (either time out from the meal or a 15-second removal of the food tray) were applied to each of these behaviors in succession over a 6-month period, and in each case the particular objectionable behavior dropped out and was replaced by more appropriate table manners. This was the multiple baseline study to which reference was made in explaining the design of the present research. O'Brien, Bugle, and Azrin (1972), working with a 6-year-old retarded girl, demonstrated that merely teaching correct use of a spoon (by manual guidance, which was gradually faded in the usual reverse chaining fashion) was insufficient to produce continued proper eating behavior. Interruption and extinction of the previous behavior, dipping food directly with the hands, was needed also, though it too was insufficient alone to produce the desired result. O'Brien and Azrin (1972), in the most sophisticated work to date in this area, first worked out a rather complete behavioral description of proper table manners. Then they taught these mealtime behaviors to a group of retarded subjects, who showed great improvement both in comparison to their own baseline and in comparison to an untrained control group. In fact, at follow up, it was shown that the trained subjects had table manners as good as those of non-retarded customers in a public restaurant.

The present intervention program, at its inception, was not a research venture but an attempt to find a workable treatment program for very young retarded children, most of whom had major motor handicaps. It was felt that a group setting might lead to a more coordinated interdisciplinary treatment of the children and to provide an opportunity for the parents to meet together and help one another. In the spring of 1972, a team was organized consisting of a physical therapist, a nurse, a speech pathologist, and a psychologist to work one morning a week with a group of six children while a social worker met with their parents to discuss their concerns.

After the first 6 weeks of operation, a certain degree of frustration had built up among the parents and staff, growing out of the recognition that the program was too limited to make much impact on the slow pace of the child's development. Three of the parents sought out community day care programs for their infants with the support of the staff, because it was felt that these programs could accomplish more for the children. It became apparent that this search for other, more extensive, resources was indeed one appropriate outcome of a parent's participation in the group as it was then constituted.

During the following year, the program was revised in such a way as to make the parents the primary therapeutic agents for their children. During the time the staff spent with the infants each week, programs were developed that could be demonstrated and given to each parent once a month to use at home. At the beginning and the end of the second year of the project, video tapes were made of the interactions between each mother and her child in free play and in a teaching situation to see if these tapes could be reliably scored in terms of the mothers' teaching strategies. During that year, the parents' group continued to meet to discuss mutual concerns and to provide emotional support to each other. It remained evident that the program was still too limited, but in spite of this, the families were enthusiastic about the program, traveling as much as 150 miles each way to participate.

In the fall of 1973, plans were made for the group to provide a better training opportunity for students in the Division for Disorders of Development and Learning. Although the families still came only once a week, the time for staff planning and coordination was expanded. The content of the parents' meetings also shifted to include more emphasis on expected developmental sequences and on behavior modification techniques. The research project described below was formally initiated in February, 1974.

METHOD

Subjects

The 10 infants and toddlers who participated in the project were chosen according to three criteria: 1) age less than 3 years at the time of initial evaluation by the Division for Disorders of Development and Learning, 2) a biological basis for the child's difficulty strongly suspected or confirmed, and 3) a recommendation by the interdisciplinary team that the child be accepted into this treatment program. Although the children were under 3 years when initially accepted, some were older than that when the formal research project began. In one case a child was admitted into the program and subsequently into the research project solely on the recommendation of an outside pediatrician; this was the child with the mildest difficulties in the group. Table 1 provides descriptive information on the children when they were first evaluated by DDDL. The average child in the project was nearly 1.5 years old, was moderately to severely retarded in psychomotor functioning, and had similarly retarded functioning in language and motor areas. There was, as Table 1 indicates, considerable variability from one child to another; there was also considerable variability in the developmental profile of each child. The social class of these families, as indicated by the Hollingshead (1957) two-factor Index of Social Position, was upper middle class in one case, lower middle class in six, and upper lower class in three. Nine families were white and one was black; nine families were Protestant and one was Jewish.

The variety of the difficulties of these children can best be conveyed by quoting the initial diagnostic impression of the team in each case:

Subject 1. Male, 8 months old. Central nervous system maldevelopment, probably of prenatal origin with 1) profound motor and mental retardation, 2) severe hypotonia, 3) probable seizure disorder, and 4) cortical blindness.

Table 1. Information on the families and on the children at initial evaluation

Measure	Mean	Standard deviation	Range	N
Hollingshead Index of Social Position	35.40	10.98	22–51	10
Age of child in months	15.80	4.14	8–20	10
Bayley Scales of Infant Development				
Mental level in months	6.32	3.51	1–9	9
Ratio Developmental Quotient	35.63	16.23	13–73	9
Bzoch-League Receptive-Expressive Emergent Language Scale (REEL)				
Expressive language (months)	5.94	2.40	5–9.5	9
Receptive language (months)	5.83	2.20	2–9.5	9
Gross motor skill level (months) as rated by physical therapist	5.10	1.68	3.5–7	5

Subject 2. Female, 11 months old. Congenital encephalopathy characterized by spastic quadriparesis and severe mental retardation with microcephaly and short stature. Etiology undetermined but possibly related to intrauterine factors not yet determined.

Subject 3. Female, 11 months old. Mild (by the Bayley Scales) to moderate (with respect to language development) mental and motor retardation of unknown etiology, with mild esophoria, symmetrical hyperreflexia, and a history of generalized tonic seizures.

Subject 4. Male, 15 months old. Central nervous system maldevelopment of prenatal origin with 1) incomplete cortical blindness, 2) spastic diplegia, and 3) motor and mental retardation, possibly exaggerated by 1 and 2.

Subject 5. Male, 17 months old. Severe mental and motor retardation with associated spastic quadriparesis, relative microcephaly and bilateral lateral-rectus weakness, secondary to possible prenatal infection, in the first trimester. Also history of placental insufficiency [in a] secondarily small-for-date infant.

Subject 6. Male, 18 months old. 1) Moderate mental retardation and growth retardation, probably resulting from cerebral maldevelopment of prenatal origin. The possibility of a chromosomal disorder still exists in view of the mild physical abnormalities (simian lines, slightly abnormal facies with epicanthal folds). [Chromosomal abnormality was ruled out upon subsequent cytological study.] 2) Chronic constipation secondary to diet.

Subject 7. Female, 18 months old. Presents an unusual looking [appearance] with multiple congenital anomalies and [is] functioning intellectually in the severe range of mental retardation. She probably represents a specific syndrome as yet undescribed. Her multiple abnormalities include 1) microcephaly with skull deformities, 2) multiple bony abnormalities of the ribs and dorsal spine, 3) abnormal facies, 4) multiple skin hemangiomata, and 5) severe mental retardation.

Subject 8. Male, 20 months old. [This was the child who was not evaluated by the complete team. He was referred by a pediatrician with complaints of "low frustration level, behind in motor skills, emotionally immature." He has been tested privately by a psychologist at age 19 months and had received a Bayley Mental Development Index of 63 and a Motor Development Index of 53.]

Subject 9. Female, 20 months old. Moderate mental and severe motor retardation, secondary to central nervous system maldevelopment, probably due to unknown prenatal influence. Severe hypotonia, probably of central origin, [which] exaggerates the development delays.

Subject 10. Male, 20 months old. Severe mental and motor retardation, with associated microcephaly and hypotonic diplegia, probably bordering on early spasticity. Also apparent myoclonus. The etiology is unknown, but [the disorder] may be secondary to perinatal asphyxia. In addition, a bilateral hearing deficit is present, partly secondary to serious otitis media, though possibly in part sensorineural.

By the time the formal research phase of the project began, the age range of the children was 13 to 48 months. At this time, in order to provide a common baseline for treatment planning and evaluation, each child was again evaluated, using the Memphis Comprehensive Developmental Scale. Each child was first observed by a staff member experienced in such evaluations. Parents were interviewed regarding those items which it had not been possible to observe on that particular occasion. The test-retest reliabilities for the different subareas of the Memphis Scale for the children were as follows: Gross Motor, 0.99; Fine Motor, 0.97; Language, 0.92; Perceptual-Cognitive, 0.99; and Personal-Social, 0.98. Table 2 provides descriptive information on the children at beginning of the formal research project. As this table shows, the children were an average of 27 months old at that time, and their average functioning in the areas evaluated ranged from 10 to 14 months.

Treatment Setting

The nursery was a large room, approximately 30 by 40 feet, divided into several different functional areas by pegboard partitions well below the eye level of an adult. On one side of the room there was a caretaking area with a large padded utility table that could be used for changing diapers and a small refrigerator for storage of food and baby bottles. On this side of the room there were also two carpeted activity areas. On the other side of the room was a third carpeted activity area and open space for play. The furniture in the room included two cribs, two play pens, several high chairs, a stroller, five small tables

Table 2. Information on the children at the beginning of the research project

Measure	Mean	Standard deviation	Range	N
Age in months	26.82	13.50	13–48	10
Memphis Comprehensive Developmental Scale scores in months				
Gross Motor	10.72	8.80	1.5–27	10
Fine Motor	10.17	6.55	4.5–22.5	10
Language	10.06	7.30	2–26	10
Perceptual-cognitive	9.89	8.67	1–26	10
Personal-social	14.06	9.44	4.5–31	10

with chairs, four adult chairs, a large physical therapy mat (4 by 8 feet) and six smaller mats, a full-length mirror (2 by 5 feet), portable parallel bars, two wooden combination rocker-stair climbers, a therapeutic infant feeding seat, and two metal cabinets. A large number of commercial and home-made toys designed for young infants and preschool children were available. The nursery directly adjoined a large outdoor play area.

Direct Treatment Program

According to their profiles on the Memphis Comprehensive Developmental Scale at the beginning of the research project, three of the children in the sample had their lowest score in the gross motor area, three in the language area, three in the perceptual-cognitive area, and one in the fine motor area. No child had his greatest impairment in the personal-social area; indeed, as Table 2 shows, this was the area of highest functioning for the overall group. The area of the child's greatest difficulty (usually the lowest area on the Memphis Scale, but other information such as the interdisciplinary team evaluation and the parents' major concerns was also considered) was given continuous treatment. Two of the remaining four areas were also selected at random for treatment, so that each child received treatment in three of the five areas of functioning. Re-evaluation took place after the child completed at least 15 treatment seassions. Of the 10 children in the study, only seven completed this many sessions. The other three children for various reasons were able to attend only infrequently. The experimental hypothesis was that children would make greater developmental progress in the areas of treatment (randomly selected) than in the control areas; that is, that the effects of the formal treatment program would be apparent in addition to the effects of maturation, other life experiences, and any generalization effects of treatment.

Treatment activities were assembled from diverse sources (Furfey, 1972; Karnes, 1973; Quick, Little, and Campbell, 1973; Segner and Patterson, 1970; Sparling, 1973; Valett, 1967). Two independent judges were asked to classify each activity in terms of the area on which it would be presumed to have the greatest impact (gross motor, fine motor, language, etc.) and were able to agree for 82 percent of the time in this judgment. In cases of disagreement, a third judge was asked to decide the classification of the activity. Obviously, the question of the area of maximum impact of an activity is ultimately an empirical one, but some initial classification of this kind was necessary at the outset. New curriculum activities and modifications of old ones were also generated as a byproduct of the present study. Each activity used was described clearly, in writing, so that it could be used by a staff member or a parent previously unfamiliar with the activity.

The nursery operated twice a week from 9:30 a.m. to 12:30 p.m. The usual schedule called for teaching activities within all three intervention areas for each child for the first hour and a half, with nap time from 11:00 to 12:15 and feeding or preparations for going home at 12:15. Approximately 30 minutes were scheduled in the morning for each of the particular intervention activities planned for a particular child on that day, but it seemed more important to fit the activities to the momentary interest, state, and level of boredom of the child than to try to maintain a rigid schedule. Thus, some initial time might be spent making the child comfortable and relaxed, or if he appeared too sleepy or fussy, he was put down for a nap and the activity resumed later. Each activity was carried out by one person with the child, while an observer kept records on the number of trials (if the activity could be so described) and the success or failure of the child to perform the task required of him. Therapists were staff members, graduate students, or trainees in such disciplines as nursing, psychology, speech pathology, special education, and physical and occupational therapy, and university undergraduates.

Before each session, a number of activities were chosen from the child's program, including several in each intervention area, and materials for the activities were prepared in advance. Observers were given information such as the name of the activity, the responses that were to be observed, criteria for success at the activity, and the method of recording appropriate to it. In general, activities that had been mastered in previous sessions were not repeated. Any activity was discontinued on a particular day if the child either showed mastery by five successes or showed by five failures that the task was too difficult in the specified form. Activities found to be too difficult were immediately replaced by simpler ones in the same intervention area. Those on which the child showed partial or incomplete success were usually made a part of the home program, and the descriptive materials on them were given to parents. These were also continued in the nursery proper until the child did show success on them.

Home Treatment Program

Because the children continued to live at home and spent far more time there than in the nursery, it was essential to involve the parents as therapeutic agents if maximum impact of the treatment was to be obtained. The parent program had two components. First, it was concerned with the personal growth of the parents. The parents and a social worker met together on a weekly basis to discuss matters of mutual concern, provide each other emotional support, and learn about topics of interest to them through invited speakers. Personal or marital counseling was available to any parent requesting such a service. Second, the program was concerned with training the parents to carry on an effective treatment program for the child at home. The present research project began with a focus on children and parents separately, in which the children were seen in the nursery and the parents had their separate group meetings. As the project went on, home program materials began to be developed as the staff became familiar with each child, and these were given to the parents in written form so that they could continue the activities at home.

RESULTS

The major results of the study are summarized in Figure 1, which shows the average number of months of progress made by the children on the Memphis Comprehensive

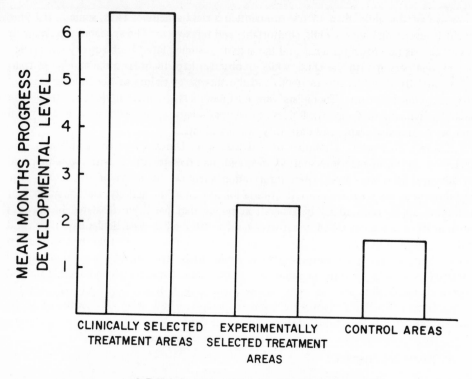

AREAS OF CHILD FUNCTIONING

Figure 1. Months of progress on the Memphis Comprehensive Developmental Scale in the areas of functioning clinically selected for treatment, areas randomly selected for treatment, and control (no treatment) areas for the seven children completing at least 15 sessions in the nursery over a 2- to 3-month period.

Developmental Scale over the 2- to 3-month period of the study. The seven children who completed enough sessions to be meaningfully re-evaluated (at least 15 sessions) made an average of 6.43 months of progress in the area clinically selected for treatment, 2.43 months of progress in the areas selected for treatment on a random or experimental basis, and 1.68 months in the control areas.

When these results were reported at the meeting of the President's Committee on Mental Retardation in Chapel Hill in May 1974, data on only six of the children were available. At that time, the difference between experimental and control treatment areas was reported as statistically significant ($t = 2.39$, $df = 5$, $p < 0.05$). As it happened, the seventh child to complete enough sessions to be re-evaluated made an average of 5 months' progress in the control areas (3 months' progress in gross motor and 7 months' progress in personal-social functioning) and only 1.5 months' progress in the experimentally selected treatment areas. The t test recomputed to include this new information was nonsignificant ($t = 0.64$, $df = 6$, $p > 0.05$).

The difference between the clinically selected treatment areas and experimentally selected treatment areas was significant ($t = 2.16, df = 6, p < 0.05$), as was the difference between clinically selected treatment areas and control areas ($t = 2.36, df = 6, p < 0.05$).

Though the number of cases is too small to make between-subjects comparisons meaningful, it is of interest to look at each area of functioning separately. In the area of Gross Motor skills, it happened that four children were assigned to experimental treatment and three to control. Those receiving experimentally selected treatment had gains of 1.5, 3, 3, and 4.5 months on the Memphis Scale, or a mean gain of 3 months. Those receiving no treatment in this area had gains of 1.5, 1.5, and 3 months, for a mean gain of 2 months. No children received this type of treatment selected on clinical grounds.

In the area of Fine Motor skills, three children were assigned to the control condition. They made 0, 1.5, and 1.5 months' progress in this area, for a mean of 1 month. Three children were experimentally assigned to treatment in this area. They made 1.5, 4.5, and 6 months' progress, or a mean of 4 months. The single child receiving treatment in this area on a clinical basis made 11 months' progress.

In the area of Language, two children were assigned to the control condition, and neither of them made any progress during the time between pre- and post-test. Two children were assigned to language treatment experimentally; one of them made no progress, and the other made 2 months' progress. Three children received language training on a clinical basis, making 2, 10, and 16 months' progress, for a mean of 9.3 months' progress.

In the Perceptual-Cognitive area, two children were assigned to the control condition. They made 3 and 8 months' progress, or a mean of 5.5 months. The two children experimentally assigned to perceptual-cognitive treatment each made 1 month's progress in this area. The three children assigned to perceptual-cognitive training on clinical grounds made 1, 2, and 3 months' progress, for a mean of 2 months.

Finally, in the area of Personal-Social skills, four children were assigned to the control condition. One of them dropped 1 month on retest, and the others made 1, 1.5, and 7 months' progress, for a mean of 2.1 months. The other three children were all experimentally assigned treatment in this area and made 0, 0, and 7.5 months' progress, for a mean of 2.5 months. No child received Personal-Social training on the basis of clinical assignment.

A list of the particular activities used with each child is provided in an appendix to this chapter.

DISCUSSION

From the standpont of methodological rigor, the comparison that can be taken most seriously in the present study is that between the experimentally selected treatment and the control areas of functioning. The difference was in the predicted direction in four cases, with no difference in two and a difference in the opposite direction in one case. The experimentally selected treatment tasks given this last child turned out not to interest her greatly, and she was often distracted by noise or movement elsewhere in the room. Thus, a lot of effort that might have gone into helping her improve her skills was spent in trying to interest her in the task materials. In any case, the small number of children and the relatively short treatment time available in this study suggest caution in interpreting the results as indicating either the efficacy of treatment or its failure. We believe that the present method of using each child as his own control deserves further investigation and can neither be accepted nor discarded on the basis of this study. This novel methodological feature has some promise of making it possible to perform rigorous evaluation of treatment procedures while at the same time not refusing services to any child. This has great appeal from an ethical standpoint; for none of us, as a parent, would like to be offered only untested methods for treating a handicapped child; yet most of us would object if our own child were placed in a no-treatment control group. The method has the disadvantage that the areas of functioning are quite unlikely to be independent of each other. One might thus falsely conclude that a treatment was ineffective when it simply produced generalized effects on all areas of functioning being evaluated. Looking at the different areas treated, the largest differences between experimental and control subjects were in the fine motor area. Given the small number of subjects, this may or may not be a reproducible finding.

The most salient result was the progress of the children in the areas clinically selected for treatment. In the usual uncontrolled study, only such data as these would be presented, and the investigator might be tempted to exult over the fact that these moderately and severely retarded children made progress at a rate that would be accelerated even for normal children. Such an outcome, significantly better than the gains obtained in control areas of functioning, might be interpreted as the result of the efficacy of the treatment given to the children. It must be explained, however, why the children did not do as well in the experimentally selected areas of treatment. After all, the treatments given in the nursery came from the same pool of activities.

One possible interpretation of this spurt in development that must be considered is the possible statistical regression artifact. If one chooses subjects on the basis of low scores on any measure that contains some error (and what measure contains no error?) and then retests the subjects later on the same measure, there will be predictable change toward the mean ("improvement") in the retest scores even with no change in the variable being measured. Luckily, in this case, the children had been retested on the Memphis Scale a week after the initial testing to obtain estimates of retest reliability. If the better scores of the children in clinically selected areas is a regression artifact, it should show up on these immediate retest scores too. On the retest, the children showed a mean of 0.58 month's progress in the control areas, 0.75 month's progress in the experimentally selected areas, and 1.50 months' progress in the clinically selected areas. The t tests comparing these means were all nonsignificant. Thus, a negligible amount of regression artifact, if any, seems to be present.

The most likely explanation for the difference between clinically selected areas of functioning and the others seems to be that the parents spent more time working with their children in their areas of greatest difficulty, using either the home programs or their own ingenuity. Thus, an important implication of this study might be the crucial relevance of the family's concerns about the child in motivating the successful use of home program material.

Early intervention with biologically handicapped infants and young children deserves a thorough trial. Many promising methods of physical therapy, self-help training, language stimulation, cognitive training, and socialization have been devised. In many cases, however, the projects designed to evaluate these intervention procedures have lacked the rigor of method necessary to indicate whether or not the treatments were effective. The preliminary study described here tried to explore a more rigorous method of evaluation that used each child as his own control rather than requiring some of these severely handicapped youngsters to be in an untreated control group. It is felt that the method explored here is promising and deserves a more extensive trial. The expense of research projects such as the present one is quite high, but the expense of using ineffective treatment methods with children is much higher, whether measured in financial or simply in human terms.

ACKNOWLEDGMENTS

The authors would like to thank the following for their assistance. Staff members of the Division for Disorders of Development and Learning who worked with the children and their families included Toby Black, Cathee Huber, Sharon Stangler, and Barbara Stern. University of North Carolina students who took part in the research included Cathy Bailey, Efrat Belkin, Tina Bell, Ann Berry, Tommy Cromer, Debbie Frank, Patricia Griffin, John Haig, Sarah Lockhart, Ann Orr, Christa Peterson, Victoria Shea, Duncan Smith, Cathy Viles, and Charles Woodcock.

APPENDIX

Information on Treatment Programs for Individual Children Who Had at Least 15 Sessions

Subject 1. 16 sessions. Control (untreated) areas: Gross Motor (pretest 1.5 months, post-test 3 months), Language (pretest 2 months, post-test 2 months). Experimental treatment areas: Personal-Social (pretest 4 months, post-test 4 months), Fine Motor (pretest 4.5 months, post-test 6 months). Clinically selected treatment area: Perceptual-Cognitive (pretest 0 months, post-test 2 months). *Personal-Social* activities: Body awareness, peek-a-boo with blanket, self-feeding, pat-a-cake. *Fine Motor* activities: Holding rattle in right and left hand, fisting with small objects, grasping small objects, transferring toys, turning knob to make noise, arm pulling with hanging toys, reaching, feeling texture ball. *Perceptual-Cognitive* activities: Texture stimulation with sponges, finding the bell after it dropped, bell in mid-line, bell in right-left positions, manipulation and transfer with rattle, clap measurement cups, reach for noise maker.

Subject 2. 16 sessions. Control areas: Personal-Social (pretest 6.5 months, post-test 8 months), Fine Motor (pretest 4.5 months, post-test 4.5 months). Experimental treatment areas: Gross Motor (pretest 4.5 months, post-test 7.5 months), Language (pretest 4 months, post-test 4 months). Clinically selected treatment area: Perceptual-Cognitive (pretest 3 months, post-test 4 months). *Gross Motor* activities: Sit unsupported, rolling from stomach to back, rolling prone to side to play, rolling toward toy, rolling from back to stomach, sitting propped to side, pushing up, prone position, crawling position and movements, moving from sitting to lying, tipping from side to side, weight on forearms, side sitting to lying, protective extension sideways, reaching, pulling up from lying position, crouching on knees, bench sitting, creep position, holding hips and head for sitting straight. *Language* activities: Rocking and vocalizing to subject, sound imitation, babbles by therapist as language stimulation, stimulation with many sounds, music box stimulation, spontaneous sound producing, imitation of mouth movement without vocalization, imitation of mouth movement with vocalization, eye contact. *Perceptual-Cognitive* activities: Find music box, attention to voice volume, pat-a-cake, look-and-feel, scarf play with adult, see-feel-hear, reaching for objects, hear-see-do, eye contact, eye contact when called, fisting small objects, hiding and finding objects, peek-a-boo with blanket, pulling jumping jack, holding clacker, bell ringing and manipulating, feeling different textures.

Subject 3. 15 sessions. Control areas: Personal-Social (pretest 10 months, post-test 17 months), Gross Motor (pretest 10 months, post-test 13 months). Experimental treatment areas: Language (pretest 10 months, post-test 12 months), Perceptual-Cognitive (pretest 9 months, post-test 10 months). Clinically selected treatment area: Fine Motor (pretest 7 months, post-test 18 months). *Language* activities: Turn head to sound, pat-a-cake, imitation of vowels, imitation of sounds, look at book, play with toy alone, spontaneous vocalizations, vocalizations (stimulated), tongue clicking, eye contact, imitation of mouth movements, turn to name, syllable imitation, language imitation. *Perceptual-Cognitive* activities: Attention to music box, peek-a-boo, choice with visual display, discrimination of three-colored blocks, finding object under box, see and feel with texture, pull a string with a cookie, imitation of vocalizations, put toy in the box, pulling string with marshmallow, pull lever on toy, take figures out of box and put them in, searching for hidden objects, pulling string with marshmallow II, imitation of mouth movements, find a toy, find a toy under one of two boxes, nesting boxes. *Fine Motor* activities: Pick up small objects, transfer objects, pull toy ring on string, reaching for marshmallows, transfer small objects L-R, putting objects in a box, picking up marshmallows, untying shoe, placing rings on a pole, stack one block, put paper in box, build a tower, put block in box, pull lever on clown toy.

[Subject 4 did not complete enough sessions to be re-tested.]

Subject 5. 16 sessions. Control areas: Gross Motor (pretest 9 months, post-test 10.5 months), Fine Motor (pretest 7.5 months, post-test 9 months). Experimental treatment areas: Personal-Social (pretest 10.5 months, post-test 18 months), Perceptual-Cognitive (pretest 5 months, post-test 6 months). Clinically selected treatment area: Language (pretest 4 months, post-test 6 months). *Personal-Social* activities: Peek-a-boo with blanket, mirror, feet, person, play with mirror, pat-a-cake, response to rhyme, self-feeding, cup drinking, turn to name, game playing, find a toy, rough play, eye contact. *Perceptual-Cognitive* activities: Find music box, play with busy box, stimulus change with toys (texture, visual, auditory), catch a ball, put objects in bottle, find hidden toy. *Language* activities: Eye contact, eye contact when called, blowing: mouth control, imitation of sounds, respond to sound-voice-turn, locate, spontaneous vocalizations, imitation of mouth (lip) movement with prompt.

Subject 6. 18 sessions. Control areas: Personal-Social (pretest 30 months, post-test 31 months), Perceptual-Cognitive (pretest 24 months, post-test 27 months). Experimental treatment areas: Gross Motor (pretest 27 months, post-test 31.5 months), Fine Motor (pretest 21 months, post-test 25.5 months). Clinically selected treatment area: Language (pretest 18 months, post-test 34 months). *Gross Motor* activities: Climbing up and down stairs, jumping, crawling through tunnel, stepping in circles, supporting self on hands, climbing into chair, standing on one foot, walking on strip of paper, throwing small basketball into goal. *Fine Motor* activities: Stringing beads, stacking blocks, working with crayons, putting shapes into shape box, color discrimination (grouping), placing peas in small container, manipulation of play-doh, stacking cylinders on rod, making puzzle, pegboard. *Language* activities: Songs using receptive language, receptive use of color, imitation of single words (objects and body parts), pointing to pictures named by therapist, spontaneous naming of objects and body parts, imitation of two-word phrases, spontaneous two-word combinations, imitation of names of community helpers, identification of community helpers, spontaneous naming of community helpers.

Subject 7. 16 sessions. Control areas: Fine Motor (pretest 6 months, post-test 7.5 months), Language (pretest 9 months, post-test 9 months). Experimental treatment areas: Personal-Social (pretest 7 months, post-test 7 months), Gross Motor (pretest 7 months, post-test 7.5 months). Clinically selected treatment area: Perceptual-Cognitive (pretest 3 months, post-test 6 months). *Personal-Social* activities: eye contact, eye contact when called, hold and drink from cup, pat-a-cake, peek-a-boo (toy, mirror, person), body awareness, tracking moving face, self-feeding. *Gross Motor* activities: Push up to sit from back, bend down and up from knee sit, lie on side, crawl movement, push up, prone, rolls prone supine—supine prone, creep position, roll side to back, standing from sitting, pushing on the swing, walking with support. *Perceptual-Cognitive* activities: Reaching and grasping toys, looking at toy, tracking mirror or toy, see-feel-hear clay texture toys, awareness of environment, manipulation of objects, scarf play, middle line pull toy, pressing toys, playing with play-doh.

Subject 8. 17 sessions. Control areas: Personal-Social (pretest 31 months, post-test 30 months), Perceptual-Cognitive (pretest 26 months, post-test 32 months). Experimental treatment areas: Gross Motor (pretest 27 months, post-test 30 months), Fine Motor (pretest 22.5 months, post-test 28.5 months). Clinically selected treatment area: Language (pretest 26 months, post-test 36 months). *Gross Motor* activities: Climbing up and down stairs, jumping, crawling through tunnel, stepping in circles, throwing basketball into goal, walking on hands, climbing into chair, standing on one foot, jumping on springboard, walking on line, tiptoeing. *Fine Motor* activities: Stringing beads, stacking blocks, putting peas into container, working with crayons, putting shapes in shape box, sorting blocks by color, imitation of block structure, building puzzles, stacking pegs in pegboard. *Language* activities: Imitation and spontaneous naming of objects and body parts, identification of pictures, imitation of two-word phrases, spontaneous two-word combinations, imitation and spontaneous use of carrier phrases ("give me. . ."), receptive use of prepositions, songs with receptive language, naming colors, identification of community workers, spontaneous naming of community workers.

[Subjects 9 and 10 did not complete enough sessions to be re-tested.]

LITERATURE CITED

Barton, E. S., D. Guess, E. Garcia, and D. M. Baer. 1970. Improvement of retardates' mealtime behaviors by timeout procedures using multiple baseline techniques. J. Appl. Beh. Anal. 3: 77–84.

Bloom, B. S. 1964. Stability and Change in Human Characteristics. Wiley, New York.

Bricker, W. A. 1972. A systematic approach to language training. *In* R. L. Schiefelbusch (ed.), Language of the Mentally Retarded, pp. 75–92. University Park Press, Baltimore.

Corder, W. O. 1966. Effects of physical education on the intellectual, physical, and social development of educable mentally retarded boys. Except. Child. 32: 357–364.

Edgar, C. L., T. S. Ball, R. B. McIntyre, and A. M. Shotwell. 1969. Effects of sensory-motor training on adaptive behavior. Amer. J. Ment. Defic. 5: 713–720.

Eimas, P. D., E. R. Siqueland, P. Jusczyk, and J. Vigorito. 1971. Speech perception in infants. Science 171: 303–306.

Fodor, E. M. 1967. The influence of a program of reading on children's language development. J. Comm. Disord. 1: 246–252.

Friedlander, B. Z. 1970. Receptive language development in infancy: Issues and problems. Merrill-Palmer Quart. 16: 7–51.

Furfey, P. (ed.). 1972. Education of Children Aged One to Three: A Curriculum Manual. Catholic University of America, Washington, D.C.

Garber, H. 1973. The Milwaukee project. Invited presentation at the Gatlinburg Conference on Research and Theory in Mental Retardation, Gatlinburg, Tenn. (March 16.)

Gray, B. B., and B. P. Ryan. 1973. A Language Program for the Nonlanguage Child. Research Press, Champaign, Ill.

Guess, D., W. Sailor, G. Rutherford, and D. M. Baer. 1968. An experimental analysis of linguistic development: The productive use of the plural morpheme. J. Appl. Beh. Anal. 1: 225–235.

Hollingshead, A. B. 1957. Two-factor index of social position. Author (mimeo). New Haven, Conn.

Itard, J.-M.-G. 1962. The Wild Boy of Aveyron. (Trans, by G. and M. Humphrey). Appleton-Century-Crofts, New York. (Originally published, 1801.)

Karnes, M. B. 1973. Helping Young Children Develop Language Skills: A Book of Activities. Council for Exceptional Children, Arlington, Va.

Kent, L. R. 1972. A language acquisition program for the retarded. *In* J. E. McLean, D. E. Yoder, and R. L. Schiefelbusch (eds.), Language Intervention with the Retarded: Developing Strategies. University Park Press, Baltimore.

Kirk, S. A. 1958. Early Education of the Mentally Retarded. University of Illinois Press, Chicago.

Klaus, R. A., and S. W. Gray. 1968. The early training project for disadvantaged children: A report after five years. Monogr. Soc. Res. Child Devel. 33 (Whole No. 120): No. 4.

Lillie, D. L. 1968. The effects of motor development lessons on mentally retarded children. Amer. J. Ment. Defic. 72: 803–808.

Mead, S. 1968. The treatment of cerebral palsy. Devel. Med. Child Neurol. 10: 423–426.

Montessori, M. 1965. The Montessori method. (Trans. by A. E. George) Robert Benchley, Cambridge, Mass. (Originally published, 1912.)

Morrison, D., and P. Pothier. 1972. The different remedial motor training programs and the development of mentally-retarded preschoolers. Amer. J. Ment. Defic. 77: 251–258.

Nelson, K. E., G. Carskaddon, and J. D. Bonvillian. 1973. Syntax acquisition: Impact of experimental variation in adult verbal interaction with the child. Child Devel. 44: 497–504.

O'Brien, F., and N. H. Azrin. 1972. Developing proper mealtime behaviors of the institutionalized retarded. J. Appl. Beh. Anal. 5: 389–399.

O'Brien, F., C. Bugle, and N. H. Azrin. 1972. Training and maintaining a retarded child's proper eating. J. Appl. Beh. Anal. 5: 67–72.

Paine, R. S. 1962. On the treatment of cerebral palsy: The outcome of 177 patients, 74 totally untreated. Pediatrics 29: 605–616.

Quick, A. D., T. L. Little, and A. A. Campbell. 1973. Project Memphis. The training of exceptional foster children and their foster parents: Enhancing development progress and parent effectiveness. Memphis State University Park Press, Memphis, Tenn.

Robinson, H. L., and N. M. Robinson. 1971. Longitudinal development of very young children in a comprehensive day care program: The first two years. Child Devel. 42: 1673–1683.

Routh, D. K. 1969. Conditioning of vocal response differentiation in infants. Devel. Psych. 1: 219–226.

Scarr-Salapatek, S. 1971. Unknowns in the IQ equation. Science 174: 1227–1228.

Scarr-Salapatek, S., and M. L. Williams. 1973. The effects of early stimulation on low-birth-weight infants. Child Devel. 44: 94–101.

Segner, L., and C. Patterson. 1970. Ways to help babies grow and learn: Activities for infant education. World Press, Denver.

Séguin, E. 1971. Idiocy and its Treatment by the Physiological Method. Augustus M. Kelley, New York. (Originally published 1866.)

Solomon, A., and R. Pangle. 1967. Demonstrating physical fitness improvement in the EMR. Except. Child. 34: 177–182.

Solomons, G., R. H. Holden, and E. Denhoff. 1963. The changing picture of cerebral dysfunction in early childhood. J. Pediatr. 63: 113–120.

Sparling, J. J. 1973. Carolina infant curriculum project. Unpublished manuscript, University of North Carolina at Chapel Hill.

Valett, R. E. 1967. A Handbook of the Remediation of Learning Disabilities. Fearon, Belmont, Calif.

Westinghouse Learning Corporation. 1969. The Impact of Head Start. Ohio State University, Columbus, Ohio.

Wright, T. and J. Nicholson. 1973. Physiotherapy for the spastic child: An evaluation. Devel. Med. Child Neurol. 15: 146–163.

The Carolina Abecedarian Project: A Longitudinal and Multidisciplinary Approach to the Prevention of Developmental Retardation

Craig T. Ramey, Ph.D., Albert M. Collier, M.D., Joseph J. Sparling, Ph.D., Frank A. Loda, M.D., Frances A. Campbell, M.D., David L. Ingram, M.D., and Neal W. Finkelstein, Ph.D.

To be born poor should not subject a person to a lifetime of intellectual retardation, substandard achievement, and ill health; yet all too often it does.

Children who live in poverty disproportionately show developmental retardation (Deutsch and Brown, 1964; Heber, Dever, and Conry, 1968). Such deficits may have organic causes, but frequently no organic basis can be found for the developmental retardation. Dunn (1963) observed that "there are no known causes for over 90 percent of the mentally retarded individuals in the United States and Canada today and . . . there are no discernible neurological impairments for 99 percent of the IQ 50–75 group." Moreover, the mildly retarded represent an estimated five million persons or 89 percent of all the mentally retarded (Hurley, 1968).

Hunt (1961) and Bloom (1964) have suggested that the low quality of environmental inputs to the poverty level child may be an important factor in the etiology of retardation. Specifically, children from homes of extreme poverty may be deprived of

This research was supported in part by the following agencies: National Institute of Child Health and Human Development, HD-03110; National Heart and Lung Institue, HL-15111-03 and HL-15024-03; Environmental Protection Agency, R-802233; National Institutes of Health, NIAID, 72-2505 and 1-R01-AI 12239-01; and U.S. Army Research and Development Command contracts No. DADA-17-71-C-1095 and DADA-17-73-C-3097. Orange Chatham Comprehensive Health Services, Inc., was supported initially by grant 40405 from the Office of Economic Opportunity and currently by Department of Health, Education, and Welfare contract 04-H-000813-01-0.

various early learning experiences relative to children who are economically more privileged.

The environmentally disadvantaged child is part of a disadvantaged family. These families usually have multiple and interacting social, cultural, economic, and physical problems that prevent them from achieving a satisfactory level of functioning. The new infant in such a family, no matter how much he may be desired by his parents, represents in certain practical ways an added strain on an already stressed family; yet the new infant requires positive family responses if he is to achieve his full potential.

Many types of illness but particularly respiratory illness and its complications interfere with the functioning of children and their families in several ways. The costs of medical care further distress a financially compromised family. These costs include both direct expenses, such as physician fees and drugs, and indirect costs, such as lost wages and transportation to medical facilities. A second effect of the child's illness is the absorption of family energy in nursing care for the sick child, which reduces the time available for other tasks such as employment and child development activities. Another effect of respiratory illness is the limit it places on the ability of the child to respond to environmental stimuli. The acute and chronic effects of otitis media on hearing are the most clearly defined and important of these complications. Meningitis is the most serious of the complications of respiratory illness and can result in death, but more commonly causes permanent central nervous system damage. Respiratory illness and its complications are an important element in the constellation of factors leading to poor developmental outcomes.

The complex and interlocking problems of economic deprivation, increased illness and intellectually stifling, deprived environments present an enormous challenge to those who seek to intervene and to improve the chances of the disadvantaged child.

This chapter describes one such intervention project. The plan of the chapter is as follows: first, a brief overview of previous day care intervention projects, then a description of the Carolina Abecedarian Project and the development of its unique curriculum; results of the curriculum evaluation to date and the results of the psychological studies being carried out; description of the mother-infant interaction studies; a prototypic experiment; and a summary of the medical research findings to date.

PREVIOUS DAY CARE INTERVENTION PROGRAMS

During the 1960s, investigators of child development joined together to press for early intervention programs that had remediation of developmental retardation as their target. Enthusiasm for such endeavors was dashed somewhat in 1969 when the Westinghouse Learning Corporation (1969) published findings which indicated that Project Head Start had achieved far less spectacular results than had been anticipated.

One explanation for the disappointing results may lie in the timing and intensity of the Head Start programs. Perhaps too little program was being applied too late in the child's life to offset the cumulative and pervasive effects of his environmental milieu.

As a response to the Head Start data, two main approaches to early intervention were tried. These were: 1) developmental day care, and 2) home stimulation. Results from these programs have recently received independent review by Stedman et al., (1972) and Bronfenbrenner (1973). Therefore, the literature review will be brief, to set the stage for our project, and only the day care-oriented projects will be discussed.

The criteria used to select the projects to be discussed in this introduction were: 1) that children were admitted to the program as infants, 2) that evaluation data were available, 3) that the children in the program were considered by the investigators to be at high risk for developmental retardation without intervention, and 4) that the program was conducted in the United States. Collectively, these criteria identified projects concerned with remediation as well as prevention of developmental retardation.

A startling finding emerged when these criteria were applied. Contrary to popular and professional opinion, there simply are not many research oriented projects in this country that focus on the eradication of nonorganic developmental retardation. Unfortunately, there are even fewer projects that have taken a preventive approach. Furthermore, most of the "first generation" early intervention projects are effectively over because the children are now of school age, and active intervention has ceased.

Not long ago, reports from institutions that provided residential care for infants and young children indicated that gross developmental retardation was frequently associated with such care. The pioneering work by investigators such as Spitz (1945), Goldfarb (1955), Bowlby (1958), and Dennis and Najarian (1957) indicated that institutionalized rearing was associated with cognitive and affective retardation. However, the exact mechanisms and processes whereby such routine care failed to stimulate normal growth and development were not clearly understood.

Investigations by Brody (1951) and Rheingold (1961) indicated that handling and frequent social contact with infants apparently had a therapeutic effect. With the growing realization that institutional care need not necessarily result in developmental retardation, and in light of the recommendation for intervention earlier in the life span set forth in the Westinghouse Learning Corporation Report (1969) concerning Head Start, a number of therapeutic day care programs were started.

A synopsis of the early research-oriented day care intervention programs was presented by Dittman in 1968. At that time the programs were just barely underway and no systematic data were available on the effects of the programs. Since then, several programs have reported substantial amounts of data, most of which appear quite encouraging, at least with respect to short-term increases in developmental status.

Intervention programs for young children that have reported evaluation results in recent years include programs by Caldwell and Richmond (1968), Weikart and Lambie (1969), Robinson and Robinson (1971), and Heber (1971).

Although social, emotional, and physical development are included among the targeted areas for intervention in each of the mentioned programs, it is cognitive development that has received the most evaluation. Indeed, in several cases, cognitive development apparently is the only area of evaluation. One reason for this unbalanced evaluation is that assessment procedures for cognitive development are more sophisticated at present than are assessment procedures for social and emotional development. Further-more, in many of the programs there simply was no medical component to evaluate or monitor the physical state of the children.

In each of the day care programs the most frequently used means for the evaluation of cognitive development has been periodic administration of standardized tests of early development. The Cattell Infant Intelligence Test, the Bayley Scales of Infant Develop-ment, and the Stanford-Binet Intelligence Test have been the most frequently used assessment instruments.

Caldwell (1967) has reported that enrollment in the infant program at Syracuse University resulted in IQ gains between 10 and 14 points during the first year of life. Furthermore, it appears from her data that those infants who gained most were from the lower socioeconomic groups.

Honig and Brill (1970), also at the Children's Center at Syracuse, have reported that 12-month-old disadvantaged infants who were attending the Center scored significantly higher than non-attending control subjects on Piagetian tasks for object permanence and means-ends relationships.

Similar to Caldwell's findings, Robinson and Robinson (1971) presented data to show that infants who had been in a day care setting for up to 2.5 years evidence increased scores on the Bayley Scales for Infant Development relative to home reared control children. They also found that lower class black children tended to make larger gains than middle class whites.

Weikart (1971) has reported results which demonstrate that early intervention pro-duces an initial spurt in IQ performance for children in a preschool setting; but, after intervention ended, the experimental and control groups' scores tended to converge by third grade. However, the children in the Perry Preschool Project were not admitted to the program until they were 3 years old and had been selected on the basis of low developmental level (IQ 50–85) in the beginning. Thus, the Perry Project is not as directly relevant to the issue of *prevention* of developmental retardation as it is to remediation of low level functioning.

The early intervention project that has generated the most interest recently is Heber's (1971) project in Milwaukee. It is quite understandable why this project has attracted such great attention. Without question, Heber's project is the most relevant project to the issue of preventing mental retardation conducted thus far. It is also the project that has reported the most systematically collected evaluation data.

The basic rationale for Heber's work comes from a survey reported by him in 1968 (Heber et al., 1968). With reference to poverty and retardation, he reported that:

> ... it is not just the "poor" or "lower classes" who contribute the "cultural-familial retardate," it is certain families belonging to a certain group within this population who make the largest contribution. It is a relatively small percentage of families within the deprived economic groups which contributes very heavily to the high prevalence of "cultural-familial" retardation.

Heber substantiated this claim by reporting the results of a survey completed in a slum of Milwaukee. His results showed that mothers with IQs below 80 contributed 78.2 percent of the children with IQs below 80. Furthermore, children whose mothers had IQs above 80 tended themselves to have IQs that remained relatively constant (low 90s) between 13 and 168 months of age. Children whose mothers had IQs below 80 evidenced a progressive decline from about 95 to about 75 over the same time span.

With these results in hand, Heber began an intervention program for a group of 20 infants whose mothers had IQs less than 75. Twenty matched children served as control subjects.

The experimental group children were initially visited in their own homes for several months after birth until a relationship of trust could be established with the mothers. As soon as that was achieved, the infants began attending the Infant Education Center where the experimental infants were provided an intensive social program that began shortly after birth. Support provided for the mother included occupational training in addition to training in homemaking and baby care techniques.

The children were in the Center from morning to late afternoon. Although understandable, it is unfortunate that there does not exist a detailed description of the cirriculum to which the children were exposed. (Heber's project is similar to other intervention programs in this respect.) It is unfortunate in that we are left without a replicable description of one of the most important independent variables in the intervention program.

Heber is not unaware of this limitation. Speaking in a slightly larger, but relevant, context he has noted that:

> We must recognize, of course, that the mass stimulation of both babies and mothers will not permit identification of the specific aspect responsible if the "high risk" experimental babies do show a normal intellectual development. But it is our belief that it is a more efficient research strategy to ask, first of all, whether intellectual development can be influenced by massive intervention into their social environment. If this can be demonstrated, those factors specifically responsible can be brought under subsequent investigation.

Although Heber's results have been criticized on the basis of methodology and treatment specification (Page, 1973), they are nevertheless spectacular. The experimental subjects' mean IQ scores ranged from slightly above 120 at 42 months to more than 125 at 45 months. The difference between the experimental and control group at 45 months was a staggering 33 points, even though both groups had been tested equally frequently. However, in light of the methodological flaws in the Heber project, replication of his results are certainly needed before they are totally accepted as valid.

STRENGTHS AND LIMITATIONS OF THE DAY CARE INTERVENTION DATA

The most encouraging suggestion from these studies is that children need not necessarily be trapped into the cycle of retardation associated with poverty. In fact, as Heber's results most compellingly point out, if they can be replicated, the possibilities for change and growth may be even more dramatic than anyone would have dared hope only a few short years ago.

However, even if Heber's results are valid, not all is settled. Serious questions about center-based intervention that remain unanswered, and which are being addressed in the project currently underway at the Frank Porter Graham Center, include the following:

1. Precisely what services were performed for families in the experimental and control groups? For example, was the day care component of the project the only differentiating factor between the groups or were there differences in the availability of social work services, adequate nutrition, and good medical care as well?

2. What specific curriculum materials were used in the intervention program? How were they selected?

3. Was the child's relationship to his mother and other family members affected by participating in the program?

THE CAROLINA ABECEDARIAN PROJECT

In the fall of 1972, the Carolina Abecedarian Project was begun as an attempt to bring together a multidisciplinary team of researchers that would address itself both to demonstrating that developmental retardation could be prevented and to explaining how various psychological and biological processes were affected by such preventive attempts.

In this section the subject selection process and the major programmatic elements of our project are described.

Selection of Subjects

North Carolina Memorial Hospital, the University of North Carolina's teaching hospital, is the primary referral source for potential subjects for the project. Through its various prenatal clinics pass most of the expectant mothers of Orange County who are likely to meet the criteria for inclusion in our sample. In addition, liaison is maintained with the Orange County Department of Social Services and other community agencies that are likely to have contact with potentially eligible families.

Once a family is identified as being potentially eligible and has had its name referred, the supervisor of the project's infant nursery establishes contact with that family and arranges to see them at their home for an interview to explain the project and to determine if they are interested in participating, if invited to do so. If the supervisor determines that the family potentially meets the criteria for inclusion into the program, the expectant mother is invited to the Frank Porter Graham Child Development Center, where the project is being conducted, for a series of interviews. These interviews are designed to assess her attitudes toward child rearing practices and to gather detailed background and specific demographic information about the family.

One purpose of these interviews is to rate the family on an experimental version "High Risk Index," which is shown in Table 1. This index was constructed before beginning the Abecedarian Project. Weights were assigned to the various factors based upon our "best guess" of their relative importance. Because there was and is little

Table 1. High risk index

Mother's educational level (last grade completed)	Weights	Father's educational level (last grade completed)	Weights	Family income ($)	Weights
6	8	6	8	1,000	8
7	7	7	7	1,001–2,000	7
8	6	8	6	2,001–3,000	6
9	3	9	3	3,001–4,000	5
10	2	10	2	4,001–5,000	4
11	1	11	1	5,001–6,000	0
12	0	12	0		

Other Indications of High Risk and Point Values

Pts.

3   Father absent for reasons other than health or death

3   Absence of maternal relatives in local area (i.e., parents, grandparents, or brothers or sisters of majority age)

3   Siblings of school age who are one or more grades behind age-appropriate grade, or who score equivalently low on school administered achievement tests

3   Payments received from welfare agencies within the past 3 years

3   Record of father's work indicates unstable and unskilled or semi-skilled labor

3   Records of mother's or father's IQ indicates scores of 90 or below

3   Records of each siblings's IQ indicates scores of 90 or below

3   Relevant social agencies in the community indicate that the family is in need of assistance

1   One or more members of the family has sought counseling or professional help in the past 3 years

1   Special circumstances not included in any of the above which are likely contributors to cultural or social disadvantage

Criterion for inclusion in high risk sample is a score ⩾ 11.

epidemiological data concerning the factors linked to developmental retardation it was impossible to assign empirically derived weights to each factor. However, it is hoped that as the sample families are followed it will be possible to derive empirical weights through multiple regression analysis that can be used to predict developmental status more precisely.

After target children are born, qualifying families are pair-matched on sex of the child, maternal IQ, number of siblings, and high risk index scores, and they are randomly assigned to either the experimental or the control group. Table 2 contains a summary of the demographic and psychological characteristics of the first two cohorts of children admitted. To date, 59 families have been offered membership in either the experimental or control groups, and 58 have accepted and all remain in the program except two families, each of whose infant died in the first year of life. One child who died was diagnosed as a "crib death" and the other child died from heart failure secondary to

Table 2. Selected demographic characteristics of the first 2-yearly cohorts admitted to the Abecedarian Program

Group	Mean maternal IQ	Mean family income ($)	Mean maternal education	Mean high risk score	Mean maternal age	Mean number of siblings
Group 1 Center (10 females, 4 males)	80.02	1,964.28	10.14	19.78	19.72	0.72
Group 1 Home (10 females, 4 males)	78.14	1,428.57	10.43	21.2	23.93	1.62
Group 2 Center (7 females, 8 males)	85.78	642.86	10.35	18.93	17.64	0.14
Group 2 Home (8 females, 6 males)	85.57	928.57	10.21	20.78	18.07	0.36

endocardial fibroelastosis. One child had been in the experimental group, and one child had been in the control group.

The Program

Both the experimental and the control subjects receive the following services:

Family Support Social Work Services On a request basis from the parents and from routine visits to all families, the Abecedarian Project seeks to provide all families with goods, services, or guidance in areas such as legal help, family planning, obtaining food, obtaining clothing, or any other services that will help to keep the families intact. However, no advice is given to any of the families concerning how they treat or interact with their children. The only exception to this procedure is that standard well child counseling is provided during routine health checks that are done on a schedule slightly modified from the recommendations of the American Academy of Pediatrics.

Nutritional Supplements Each child in the experimental group receives the bulk of his nutrition at the day care center. Breakfast, lunch, and an afternoon snack are served each day. To control for nutrition as one explanatory variable in observed differences between the experimental and control groups, the control group receives free formula on an unlimited basis for as long as they use it, and plans are underway to provide other nutritional supplements beginning in the second year of life.

Medical Care All medical care for the Center-attending children is provided by the Frank Porter Graham Center medical staff. Free medical care for the control children is provided by the Frank Porter Graham Center staff and two university-affiliated clinics. Thus, all children have available adequate medical care, and the project maintains records on all care delivered.

Transportation   Transportation to and from the Center is provided for all subjects participating in the project.

Payment for Participation   All mothers are paid for participating in any psychological evaluations.

Diapers   Disposable diapers are provided free to the control subjects as an inducement for continuing participation.

The experimental group differs from the control group in that the former receives a planned curriculum administered throughout the day. The day care component of the Center operates from 7:45 a.m. to 5:30 p.m. each weekday.

The Curriculum

The curriculum component of the Abecedarian Project seeks to develop and to evaluate a series of learning activities for children from birth to 36 months of age. Collectively the activities are called the Carolina Infant Curriculum. As the activities are developed and used, they act as the major intervention treatment for the Project. Detailed records of the activities and sequences prescribed for each child are maintained. This concern over specificity is in response to a major problem in most of the previous infant intervention projects: a vague or unspecified treatment.

The curriculum development process for the Carolina Infant Curriculum consists of three steps: 1) objectives are synthesized or selected, 2) curriculum products are developed, and 3) the curriculum products are evaluated. In a fourth step not included in this project, the curriculum will be disseminated with accompanying training packages.

Synthesis of Educational Objectives

The present system for synthesizing curriculum goals has its origins in the theoretical position presented by Ralph Tyler (1950) and later elaborated by others. Within this framework, curriculum objectives are seen as the product of the interaction of a number of sources or factors. The present formulation identifies the interacting sources as 1) consumer opinions, 2) developmental theory, 3) developmental facts, 4) adaptive sets, and 5) high risk indicators.

The five sources from which this system synthesizes curriculum objectives are pictured in Figure 1. The first source of curriculum goals is consumer opinions. Very young children are, of course, the consumers of the infant curriculum. Through interviews, the hopes and aspirations parents have for their children may be determined. Without this knowledge a project might proceed down a blind alley, producing a program that would in the end be rejected by the public it seeks to serve.

The second source for deriving curriculum goals is developmental theory, largely that of Jean Piaget. The theory can be pictured as a ladder. On any rung of a ladder, one can

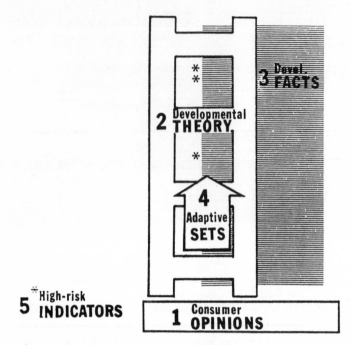

Figure 1. Five sources for synthesizing curriculum objectives.

look backward to see how the current status was arrived at or forward to see which steps are next. The theory helps the curriculum developer do just that.

The third source, developmental facts, acts as a background against which the developmental theory is viewed. Developmental facts provide a great amount of detail with which to supplement the theory. In this project, facts have been gleaned from 30 sources, including Bayley, Buhler, Gesell, Lenneberg, McCarthy, Shirley, and others. The facts are arranged in four broad developmental areas: language, motor, social/emotional, and cognitive/perceptive.

Of all the sources of educational objectives, the most important may be adaptive sets. This is especially true for the Carolina Infant Curriculum because it is created with the implicit purpose of changing or enhancing the adaptive sets of the infant. The child with strong adaptive sets has the tendency to move forward (for example, to explore rather than withdraw, to persist rather than give up easily). Therefore, adaptive sets can be thought of as that class of behaviors which predictably generate age-appropriate success. More simply, adaptive sets are "winning strategies" and are shown as an arrow moving along the ladder. The process of selecting statements of adaptive sets for this project, it should be clear, relies on professionally informed value judgments as well as relying on research findings. Because value judgments exist in *any* process of selection of educational objectives, the Carolina Infant Curriculum Project attempts to identify this bias by making it overt and subject to examination. For example, the following are among the statements of adaptive sets in this project. All of these behaviors can be thought of as being exhibited to an age-appropriate degree with extensive use desired by age 24 months:

1. Uses adults as resources
2. Controls his immediate environment
3. Uses both expressive and receptive language extensively
4. Detaches self from mothering adult and explores independently
5. Exhibits high attention behavior
6. Responds frequently with positive approach to new object or person
7. Easily adapts to changes in environment
8. Executes multi-step activities
9. Anticipates consequences
10. Explores extensively with the distance receptors
11. Uses cooperative behavior
12. Uses basic sharing behavior (showing, giving, pointing)
13. Generates specific instances of a behavior by guidance of a general rule
14. Relates strongly to the family and identifies with the subculture group

The final source of educational objectives is an awareness of high risk indicators coupled with an effort to eliminate these. The indicators are seen as asterisks or "warning signs" along the developmental continuum. To a substantial degree the high risk indicator behaviors are the mirror image of the adaptive set behaviors. That is, the class of behaviors called high risk indicators could be thought of as maladaptive sets, or perhaps "losing strategies." Because this infant curriculum is designed especially for children who are at high risk of developmental retardation and because research is beginning to document some of the behavioral deficits that high risk children consistently develop, it is hoped that these deficits (here called high risk indicators) can be anticipated through educational objectives that are basically preventive.

In using the present system of synthesizing educational objectives, detailed lists of facts and information have been compiled under each of the five "source areas" and arranged on a large wall chart. Because these five areas are thought of as *interacting* sources, all five are utilized in the synthesis of each educational objective. By uniting a piece of information from each of the five areas, a single educational objective is created.

Curriculum Product Development

Once a specific educational objective has been created, the curriculum team moves on to product development. Using their knowledge of children, the team generates ideas for products (sometimes called items or activities) to elicit the behavior specified in the educational objective. The curriculum product is often a game for adult and infant or a toy with special properties. A particular idea for an item is developed further if it meets these criteria: 1) it is a reasonable task that is conceptually related to the five sources of educational objectives; 2) it is capable of being presented by persons of modest education; 3) the child or teacher has observable output behavior, which allows performance to be measured; and 4) the cost associated with the item is minimal. A one-page parent-and-teacher guide sheet, written in simple language and using photographs to illustrate important points, is developed for each product. A sample guide sheet is provided in Figure 2.

The development of parent and teacher training material parallels the curriculum product development. The parent and teacher training materials will consist of slide tapes and pamphlets for a series of training sessions. Parent training will be designed to increase parent skills in 1) use of reinforcement, 2) use of modeling, 3) providing adequate language stimulation, and 4) providing variety of experience. The training sessions will provide the parents with new knowledge in the area of child development and will attempt to influence parent attitudes regarding early education.

Curriculum Use

The curriculum is prescribed on an individual basis. The assignment of activity items to each child is based on the items' age-appropriateness and on staff observations recorded on the child's personal developmental chart. The chart is a chronological listing of developmental facts in four major areas drawn from accepted sources. When a particular behavior of a child such as "inspects own hands" is observed for the first time, the date is noted beside the fact on the child's chart. In addition to providing a written progress record, the chart helps the staff to see whether the child is developing satisfactorily in all areas. It also makes it possible to prescribe activities that are needed by that particular child but that might not ordinarily be assigned to one of his age group.

Staff sessions both formal and informal are held frequently. These provide opportunities for all members to become aware of any special problems concerning an individual child or the group. Meetings are also a vehicle for discussion of appropriateness, purposes, and techniques involved in the use of the curriculum items. These sessions serve as an important part of the informal training for the less experienced members of the staff.

Approximately every 2 weeks for the infants and at longer intervals for the older children, new curriculum item assignments are made. These sometimes include extension of previous items if it is felt necessary. For each child a record is kept of the item assignments and of the dates on which the items are introduced to him. Daily tallies are also kept for each activity done with each child. This ready record enables the staff to be sure that no one child's curriculum activities are neglected or are unevenly administered. These tallies provide data also for determining the effectiveness of separate curriculum items.

Curriculum items for the youngest group are often a part of the general caregiving routine. As the child grows older, the activities become more discrete. Curriculum activities are scheduled typically for the infants during the period after breakfast and bathing and before morning naps. They are scheduled again between lunch and afternoon

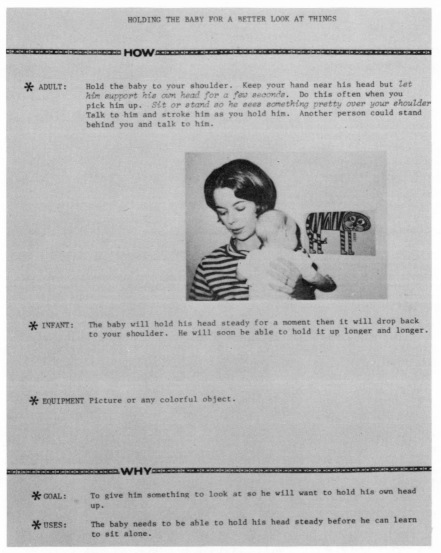

HOLDING THE BABY FOR A BETTER LOOK AT THINGS

HOW

* ADULT: Hold the baby to your shoulder. Keep your hand near his head but *let him support his own head for a few seconds*. Do this often when you pick him up. *Sit or stand so he sees something pretty over your shoulder* Talk to him and stroke him as you hold him. Another person could stand behind you and talk to him.

* INFANT: The baby will hold his head steady for a moment then it will drop back to your shoulder. He will soon be able to hold it up longer and longer.

* EQUIPMENT Picture or any colorful object.

WHY

* GOAL: To give him something to look at so he will want to hold his own head up.

* USES: The baby needs to be able to hold his head steady before he can learn to sit alone.

Figure 2. A sample one-page parent-and-teacher guide sheet.

naps. As individual schedules change, adjustments are made in activity times. The toddlers and older children typically are involved in curriculum activities from mid-morning until lunch and again after naps in the afternoon. In addition to these specified arrangements, the curriculum activities are adjusted to inside or outside, play, dressing, eating, etc., so that when it is functioning properly, the curriculum permeates the whole day.

RESULTS

To evaluate the medical, psychological, and educational consequences of this intervention program, a wide variety of experimental procedures, interviews, standardized tests, attitude assessment measures, controlled naturalistic observations in laboratories, and home observations are repeatedly used. A sampling of the results from each of these procedures is presented in an attempt to represent the style of the inquiry as well as to summarize some of the salient findings to date. However, it must be remembered that the project is still a young and expanding one. Most of the procedures to be discussed are designed to be accomplished within a repeated measures design and only beginning point evaluations exist on some variables. Therefore, these results must be regarded as tentative and preliminary.

Curriculum Evaluation Data

Basic research focuses on the acceptance or denial of various hypotheses, whereas evaluation focuses on the extent to which particular program objectives have been met. The two major objectives for the curriculum component are seen as production and formative evaluation. Summative evaluation, a third objective, will be accomplished through future field testing.

Production Evaluation   The initial task of evaluation is to verify that the system of production is adequate and is in fact working. A review and personal judgment technique by a jury of knowledgeable professionals was chosen for this task. A first step in the evaluation-by-review process was carried out during 1972 to 1973. Several professionals in the area of infancy visited us at our request and reviewed the curriculum system and other aspects of the infant research program. As a result of this review, revisions were made in the curriculum system and several ideas were added to the proposed evaluation plans.

A second, more detailed review, is proposed for 1974 to 1975 when a second group of nationally recognized professionals will be invited as a panel or jury to spend several days together examining the curriculum and the actual materials involved and to prepare a written evaluation report. The panel will be asked to indicate whether the curriculum is consistent with our best knowledge of child development and represents a reasoned program of infant stimulation.

As of March 1974, over 170 curriculum items had been produced and formative evaluation data collected on more than half of these.

Formative Evaluation   An essential task of evaluation is to provide corrective feedback while the curriculum materials are still in a formative stage. It is especially in the formative evaluation of each individual curriculum product or item that the experimental group makes a great contribution to this project. The work described below would be extremely difficult on a field basis.

Data are collected by both the teacher and an observer in the formative evaluation strategy of the Carolina Curriculum. Data forms are filled out when an item is first used with a child and again approximately 2 weeks later. Five areas of information are graphed (as percentages) for each curriculum activitiy and are entered into the decision to accept, modify, or reject the activity. Typically, a 75 percent performance level on four out of the five areas is taken as satisfactory evidence for accepting the objective and activity. Two activities will be used to illustrate the outcomes of this type of evaluation.

The simple activity, "Holding the Baby for a Better Look at Things," was used with 13 infants at an average age of 2.6 months (Figure 3). The objective was "to increase headlifting and looking behavior when the infant is held at the shoulder position." Teachers said that 75 percent of the infants were doing better after approximately 2 weeks' experience with this activity. Indeed, this is verified by the observer's timing of changed behavior. In this case, the target behavior was "a headlift plus visual attention to immediate surroundings." This behavior increased 105 percent over the 2-week period from an average of 53 seconds to an average of 109 seconds. Observations of the teachers' behavior showed that the activity and goal were clear because implementation was rated as successful 97 percent of the time. During only 61 percent of the sessions did the observer rank the teachers' language as adequate (i.e., "Talked to child during most of the activity" or "Talked to child almost constantly"). While the goal is for a 75 percent rating in language on most activities, this lower percent makes sense because the infant and adult are not necessarily facing each other during this activity. Language stimulation is certainly of less importance in this activity than in most others. Finally, 100 percent of the teachers who used this activity expressed a positive opinion of it. Because the

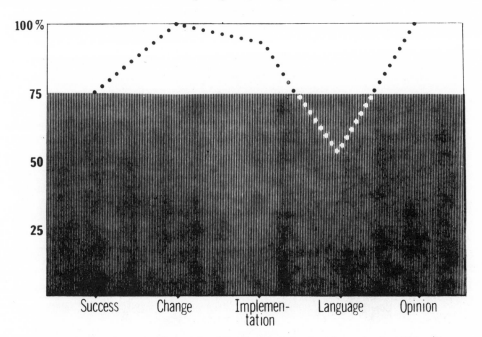

Figure 3. Data evaluation for activity, "Holding the Baby for a Better Look at Things."

guideline of a 75 percent rating in four out of the five data areas was met, the activity and goal were accepted into the curriculum. It should be stressed that the decision-making process depends heavily on informed professional judgment, and that additional observations may justify overriding the guidelines in specific instances. It should also be repeated that the process being described here is formative evaluation (which provides information to help the program developer make decisions) and not research (which tests the validity of hypotheses).

A second activity, "Choosing Between Big and Little," used with eight infants of an average age of 10.8 months, presented a less positive profile. The target behavior observed for change was "to pick up the requested member of a large-small set of two items." Even though teachers again said 75 percent of the infants were doing better after 2 weeks, the teacher judgment was not confirmed by the number of correct choices counted by the observer (Figure 4). In fact, there was no increase in the infants' average number of correct choices of the big and little objects. It would appear from the implementation (79 percent) and language ratings (94 percent) that the teachers were using the activity satisfactorily. The clue is perhaps in the 60 percent positive teacher opinion of this activity. Teachers probably disliked this activity because it was too difficult for many children at this age. As a result, they may have "gone through the motions" of teaching it without that special enthusiasm that is a necessary part of any activity's success. The activity and goal were rejected from the curriculum for this age level. In other instances, an activity may not be rejected but be sent back for revision and retesting.

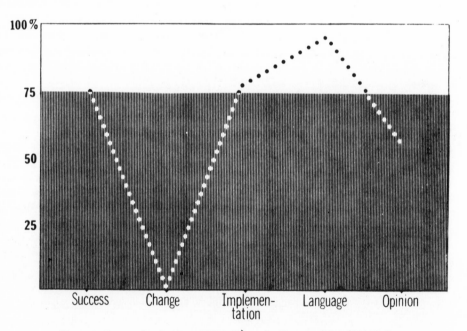

Figure 4. Data evaluation for activity, "Choosing Between Big and Little."

Feedback that aids in the on-going decision-making process is essential to the curriculum developer. By making informed decisions while the goals and activities are in a formative stage, the developer can move the process forward through a series of small corrections with less chance of any large suprises at the end of the road.

Psychological Data

Bayley Scales of Infant Development Results   The Bayley Scales of Infant Development are administered every 3 months, beginning at 3 months of age. Results are available only for the first 28 infants admitted to the program for the full first year's evaluation at present.

Inter-rater reliability on an item-by-item analysis was 91 percent. The mean Mental Developmental Index for the experimental group during the first year was 107.1 versus 100.8 for the controls. This difference is significant by t-test comparison ($p < 0.05$); similar comparisons of the Psychomotor Developmental Index revealed means of 108.3 for the experimentals and 98.7 for the controls. Again, this difference is significant ($p < 0.05$) by t-test comparison.

Attitudinal Results   Relatively little is known about how mothers in the lower socioeconomic groups perceive themselves or how such mothers might differ from other segments of the population in attitudes toward children.

In an attempt to generate data relevant to this issue Emmerich's (1969) adaptation of the Parental Attitudes Research Instrument (PARI) and Rotter's (1966) Internality-Externality Scale (I-E) were administered to 14 experimental and 14 control group mothers in the first year of the program. To aid in understanding the responses of this group to the two instruments, the same instruments were administered to a randomly drawn comparison group of 34 mothers from the same community who had infants born the same year and whose infants were matched for age.

The findings were that mothers in the project, whether in the experimental or the control group, differed significantly from the comparison group on both instruments. On no comparison did the experimental and control mothers differ significantly. The lower class mothers had a mean score on the I-E scale of 11.21 (higher scores indicate more perceived external locus of control). The comparison group had a mean score of 8.55, ($p < 0.02$). The finding that lower class black women describe themselves as more externally controlled is expected; but it is of interest that this female group appears to be more extreme in this regard than are lower class male groups of comparable age (Lefcourt and Ladwig, 1965).

Emmerich's (1969) version of the PARI assesses three factors: Authoritarian Control, Democratic Attitude, and Hostility and Rejection. The lower class mothers described themselves as more authoritarian ($p < 0.001$), less democratic ($p < 0.001$), and less hostile and rejecting ($p < 0.01$), all by t-test comparisons. It has been suggested that Authoritarian Control may be associated with ineffectiveness in the parental role (Emmerich, 1969). That lower class mothers describe themselves as less democratic perhaps goes along with the tendency toward behavioral suppression of children, seen in their more authoritarian orientation. The findings that this group of lower class mothers describe themselves as less hostile and rejecting is interesting considering that many of them face more hardships as parents than do parents in the comparison group. This factor includes scales on marital conflict, rejection of the homemaking role, and irritability. The findings may document a tendency for the more educated women in the comparison group to reject the homemaker-mother role, or perhaps disadvantaged women tend to romanticize the wife-and-mother image.

The Rotter and PARI did not correlate significantly with each other for two of the three factors, but I-E and Democratic Attitude were negatively correlated ($r = -0.37, p < 0.01$). This suggests that parents who feel that they are more in control of their own destinies may wish to foster the same sense of autonomy in their children.

Inventory of Home Stimulation Results   It is assumed that certain environmental experiences are crucial to the social and cognitive development of children. An Inventory for Infants, Home Observation for Measurement of the Environment (HOME), was used to sample certain aspects of the quantity and quality of social, emotional, and cognitive support available to a young child (birth to 3 years) within his home.[1] This Inventory was administered to both experimental and control mothers and to a group of mothers chosen at random from the same community. The random sample was chosen to match the high risk infants on age, sex, and parity. Mean age of the infants, across groups, at the time HOME was administered, was 6.8 months, with a range from 3.5 to 9.5 months. All infants were seen in their own homes with the mother present. Three interviewers collected the data. Mean inter-rater item reliability was 92 percent.

The HOME Inventory consists of six factors, and the items comprising the factors are scored on the basis of direct observation and interview material. The factors include: Emotional and Verbal Responsivity of the Mother, Avoidance of Restriction and Punishment, Organization of the Physical and Temporal Environment, Provision of Appropriate Play Material, Maternal Involvement with the Child, and Opportunities for Variety in Daily Stimulation.

Several demographic variables of the group were also compared along with the HOME factor and total scores; these included maternal age, family income, paternal education, and a Human Density ratio consisting of the number of persons living in the home over the number of rooms.

A multivariate analysis of variance (MANOVA) was computed using the 10 variables mentioned above as separate dependent variables and the three groups as independent variables. The experimental and control families did not differ significantly from one another on any of the 10 variables. However, when the experimental and control groups together were compared to the random sample, each of the 10 comparisons was significant at $p < 0.001$, with the random sample consistently scoring in the higher direction. Table 3 presents a summary of the analysis.

---

[1] The Home Stimulation Inventory (HOME) was developed by Dr. Bettye M. Caldwell and colleagues and was initially reported by B. Caldwell, J. Heider, and B. Kaplan as a paper entitled, "The Inventory of Home Stimulation," presented at the annual meeting of the American Psychological Association, September 1966.

Table 3. MANOVA of home stimulation inventory and selected demographic variables comparing the experimental and control group together with a random sample

Tests of significance using Wilks Lambda Criterion and Canonical Correlations

Tests of Roots	F	DF HYP	DF ERR	p = Less than	R
1 through 2	7.382	22.000	98.000	0.001	0.918
2 through 2	0.543	10.000	49.500	0.851	0.315

Variable	F(2.59)	Mean square	p = Less than	Standardized discriminant function coefficients
Emotional and verbal responsivity of the mother	10.414	31.496	0.001	−0.092
Avoidance of restriction and punishment	8.027	7.024	0.001	0.155
Organization of the physical and temporal environment	13.812	12.663	0.001	0.174
Provision of appropriate play materials	34.188	89.166	0.001	0.142
Maternal involvement with the child	27.393	49.157	0.001	0.278
Opportunities for variety in daily stimulation	17.986	18.694	0.001	−0.033
Maternal age	22.976	383.421	0.001	0.273
Income	41.733	125.437	0.001	0.436
Paternal education	49.674	212.877	0.001	0.848
Density of home populations	9.350	2.567	0.001	0.138

Mother-Infant Interaction Results One of the major issues of very early day care intervention is that the mother-child relationship may be significantly altered by the young child being away from the mother for relatively long periods each day.

This section reports data on 12 experimental dyads and 13 control dyads who were seen in the first year of the program. The experimental subjects and the control subjects were matched on chronological age and sex at the time of taping. The infants ranged in age from 3.5 to 9.5 months of age with a mean of 197 days.

The videotaping took place in an experimental room at the FPG Center, which had a videotape camera with a wide angle lens mounted in one corner. The room was approximately 9 by 11 feet and contained a couch, a chair, a television, and a small table and lamp, as well as a small crib. Toys and magazines were also available.

The mother was instructed that we were examining the activity levels of children when they were near their mother in a new place and that they were to respond to their child just as they would at home. The camera was pointed out to the mother, and the experimenter left the room and videotaping began.

The following frequencies and durations of mother and child behaviors were recorded onto an Esterline-Angus event recorder by two independent observers after the session:

Mother's Behaviors
1. Talks to child
2. Demonstrates toys to child
3. Touches child
4. Holds child
5. Interacts with child without toys
6. Reads to self
7. Reads to child
8. Television on

Infant's Behaviors
1. Vocalizes
2. Fusses/cries
3. Eats and/or sleeps
4. Plays with toys by self
5. Interacts with mother and toy simultaneously
6. Being in the crib
7. Being on the couch with the mother

Mean inter-observer reliability across all categories was 97.6 percent with a range from 91 to 100 percent. Two tailed t-tests were calculated for each of the observed behaviors comparing the experimental and control dyads. Table 4 provides a summary of the significant differences between the experimental and control dyads. It will be noted from this table that Center-attending infants vocalize more and cry less than do control infants. Furthermore, the experimental children interact more with their mothers both with and without toys as props than do the control children. It should also be noted that there seems to be a better "match" in time between the infants' vocalizations and the mothers' vocalizations, which might partially explain the overall superiority of the experimental group's vocal output.

Finally, correlations of each of the 15 variables with age revealed only three significant relationships. These were: 1) that age was negatively correlated with the mother's demonstrating toys ($r = -0.51$, $p < 0.01$), 2) that age was negatively correlated with the

Table 4. Summary of significant differences in mother-infant behaviors comparing experimental and control dyads

Behavior	Experimental group means	Control group means	Level of significance
Child vocalizations (duration in seconds)	137.3	50.3	$p < 0.007$
Fuss/cry (duration in seconds)	43.2	161.4	$p < 0.023$
Child interacts with mother and toys (duration in seconds)	568.9	329.7	$p < 0.060$
Mother interacts with child without toys (duration in seconds)	116.7	11.7	$p < 0.026$
Mother and child vocalize together in same 10-second interval (frequency of intervals)	19.7	5.2	$p < 0.008$

mother's touching the child ($r = -0.56$, $p < 0.004$), and 3) that age was negatively correlated with the mother's interaction with her infant without toys ($r = -0.46$, $p < 0.02$).

Thus, in sum, it appears that participating in the day care program seems to affect the mother-child relationship in an enhancing manner rather than in a detrimental way, at least in the first year of life and with high risk infants as subjects.

Results from Prototypic Experiments A wide variety of naturalistic observations in the nursery and controlled laboratory experiments are conducted to specify naturally occurring conditions or to test basic hypotheses concerning the intervention philosophy.

One example of a controlled naturalistic observation will be presented to give the reader a flavor of this style of observational research.

Finkelstein, O'Brien, and Ramey (1974) have noted that the belief that toys are desirable and should be provided for young children and infants is widely accepted by adults and other adult caregivers. With respect to intellectual development, a great many developmental psychologists, if not all, would support this point of view. For example, Piaget (1970) states that during infancy and early childhood, objective knowledge is acquired through direct actions on objects. However, a theoretical position concerning the influence of toys on social development could not be found in the literature. In addition, the few relevant studies in the literature have not examined the influence of toys on a sufficiently broad set of behaviors in the normal caregiving environment of the infant.

The studies reviewed, including those by Rheingold and her colleagues (Rheingold, 1973; Rheingold and Samuels, 1969; Corter, Rheingold, and Eckerman, 1972) and Maudry and Nekula (1939), led to our conclusion that in the first year of life toys do not facilitate social interactions. Rather, it seems that toys compete with social objects for the infant's attention. When observed in a laboratory setting with his mother and novel toys, the infant spent more time with toys than with his mother. Similarly, when observed with a peer, positive social responses were more likely to be directed toward the toys than the peer.

Beginning in the middle of the second year of life, toys are used to establish and maintain social contact with peers (Maudry and Nekula, 1939) and adults (Rheingold, 1973). Children have been observed giving or showing toys frequently to peers or adults. An important question, to which previous studies have not addressed themselves, concerns the effects of familiar toys on infants' behaviors in familiar environments. This experiment is a study of the influence of toys on the behaviors of infants in their normal rearing environment using methods closely approximating naturalistic observations.

Subjects Six of the 14 infants attending the Frank Porter Graham Child Development Center's Day Nursery who were closest in age were selected to be observed in this study. The sample included four black female infants and two black male infants. The infants ranged in age from 6.5 to 11.5 months and the mean age was 9.5 months.

Setting The observations were made in the nursery, which consists of two bedrooms, two playrooms, and a large central hallway that connects the rooms. The bedrooms contain cribs, and the infants were in these rooms only when they were being put to bed or were asleep. When awake, the infants were usually in one of the playrooms or the hall. Four or five teachers, the other infants, and numerous toys as well as diapering and feeding facilities could be found in these areas.

Procedures The experiment was performed in three phases, each lasting 2 weeks. In each phase, three infants were observed on Monday, Wednesday, and Friday during the first week and on Tuesday and Thursday during the second week. The other three infants were observed on the reverse schedule. Each subject was observed individually for 5 minutes during each of four daily observation periods beginning at 9:30 a.m., 10:30 a.m., 11:30 a.m., and 12:30 p.m. The order in which subjects were observed was determined from a table of random numbers for each hourly period.

During the first two phases, two experimenters observed the infants at a distance of approximately 3 feet from each other. The infants were observed from a distance of approximately 6 feet.

Within the observation period for each subject, 5-second observation intervals alternated with 5-second periods for recording the occurrence of the following behaviors:
1. Vocalization—discrete voiced sounds that were not sounds of distress
2. Crying or Fussing—voiced sounds that were either loud, high-pitched and continuous, or soft, low-pitched, and discrete indications of distress
3. Manipulating Objects—hand contact with inanimate objects that could be moved
4. Sleeping
5. Locomoting by Oneself—crawling or walking with aid and not including being carried
6. Adult-Child Contact—visual regard or tactile contact between an adult and infant initiated by either the infant or the adult. Also included in this category were adult vocal responses directed toward the infant. Those contacts initiated by adults that were necessary to accomplish feeding, diapering, or dressing were not recorded
7. Child-Child Contact—for this measure, any infant other than the subject was considered equivalent to an adult, and the definition of adult contact was used

A subject's score on each dependent variable was the number of 5-second intervals in which the behavior was observed during each phase. In each phase, there were 600 five-second observation intervals.

Observer reliability was computed separately for each behavior of each subject in the second phase of the experiment using product-moment correlations. The median reliability coefficient was 0.96.

Phase I During Phase I, baseline data were collected for each of the seven measures. The observations were made while all the commercially produced or home-made toys normally available were present. No attempt was made to alter the natural situation, and all the infants were free to move about as they pleased. The teachers were not given any instructions by the experimenters, nor were the teachers aware that their behavior was being recorded until after the experiment was completed.

Phase II In the second phase of the experiment, 15 minutes before each hourly observation period, all the toys were removed from the nursery and were not returned until after the three subjects were observed. In all other ways, the procedures for observations were identical to those used in Phase I.

Phase III   The final phase was a repetition of the baseline conditions of Phase I. The toys were again present in the nursery at all times.

Data Analysis and Results   The first step in the data analysis was to randomly assign the subjects to two groups of three each in order to determine which observer's records would be used in the data analysis. One observer's records were used for the subjects in Group 1 in Phase I and for Group 2 in Phase II. The data for the other subjects were obtained from the records of the second observer. In Phase III there was only one observer whose records provided the data for all subjects.

The data for each dependent variable were analyzed in a separate analysis of variance with repeated measures for the effect of phases or conditions. The Box (1954) correction factor was used to adjust the degrees of freedom in order to obtain an estimate of the probability of a Type 1 error that is less affected by violations of the variance-covariance assumptions required for repeated measures (McCall and Appelbaum, 1973).

Results from these analyses indicated significant effects of toy presence on only three of the seven variables. These results are graphically presented in Figure 5. The variables were:

Vocalization	$F_{(1,7)} = 7.806, p < 0.05$
Child-Child Contact	$F_{(1,7)} = 12.162, p < 0.025$
Adult-Child Contact	$F_{(1,6)} = 10.415, p < 0.025$

Post hoc means comparisons using the Newman-Keuls procedures (Winer, 1962) were performed separately for each of the three variables to clarify the effects of the manipulations. The results indicated that toy removal was associated with a significant decrease in the frequency of vocalizations ($p < 0.05$) and a significant increase in the frequency of child-child contacts ($p < 0.05$). Both of these changes continued when the toys were again continuously available in Phase III.

When the toys were removed, adult-child contacts were significantly more frequent than during either baseline phase ($p < 0.05$). The baseline measures of adult-child contact made before and after the toy removal phase were not reliably different.

The influence of toys on the behaviors of infants in the natural caregiving environment as observed in this study is similar to that observed in laboratory settings in earlier studies. Rheingold and Samuels (1969) observed that infants placed in a relatively barren laboratory room with their mothers and toys spent most of the time manipulating the toys. Infants in the same setting without the toys spent as much time manipulating objects in the room, such as their mother, a doorstop, or the drapes. In the present study, when the toys were unavailable the infants found other objects to manipulate, such as tissue boxes or jar caps.

The greater frequency of contacts with the teachers and other infants observed when the toys were not present in Phase II is also consistent with the observations of other investigators who were previously mentioned. It was interesting to find that peer contacts

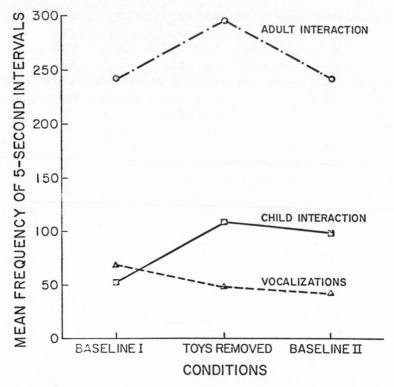

Figure 5. Behaviors as a Function of Presence or Absence of Toys.

continued to occur more frequently in Phase III when the toys were again present during the observation periods. It is possible that peer contacts during Phase II were sufficiently rewarding to maintain their higher frequency of occurrence even when the toys were also available.

In the first year of life, the child does not incorporate toys into social interactions; in the presence of toys the frequency of social contacts is, in fact, *less* than in their absence. If the development of social competence is advanced by frequent interactions with adults and peers, then, at this age, toys may not facilitate social development.

The earlier studies in the literature suggest that the infant uses toys as sources of novel and complex stimulation alternative to that provided by adults and peers. The toys used in this study had been present in the nursery for at least 3 months before the experiment and were not likely to have been novel objects for the infants. Still, novelty could have been an important factor if it were also defined by the new ways the infants were developing to respond toward the toys as time passed. However, in order to understand fully the influence of toys on social development, it is just as important to study how the adult uses those toys. Our informal observations lead to the impression that adults use them as alternatives to providing personal attention. It is likely that adults caring for infants have learned from past experience that an infant left alone with no objects to manipulate will soon begin to cry (e.g., Rheingold and Samuels, 1969) and that an interesting toy will substitute nicely for social stimulation. We observed that the teachers almost always placed a toy before an infant before stepping away. In this study, the behaviors of the adults present during the observations were not restricted in any way by the experimenters. When the toys were not available, it is, therefore, possible that the adults spent more time with the infant in anticipation of their usually annoying cry if left alone. This assumption that the teachers contributed to the observed increase in the frequency of adult-child contacts would also be consistent with the decrease in frequency of adult-child contacts when the toys were again continually present in Phase III.

Whereas toys may facilitate *intellectual* development in the first year of life, it is not clear that this is also true for social development.

Medical Data

Physical illness in any member is an added burden to the disadvantaged family. Respiratory infectious disease is the most common acute illness of man and is the major cause of morbidity in families. The preschool child has approximately eight respiratory illnesses each year and is a frequent source of infection for other family members (Dingle et al., 1964). The burden of respiratory disease is not limited to the disadvantaged family, but these families have fewer resources with which to cope with the consequences of illness. In addition, there is much evidence that serious illness occurs with greater frequency in the socioeconomically deprived. The post neonatal death rate in nonwhite North Carolina infants in 1967 was 15.9/1000 live births compared with only 4.7/1000 live births in white infants. Influenza and pneumonia accounted for 5.2 post neonatal deaths/1000 live births in nonwhite infants in 1967, over four times the mortality rate in white infants (Levy et al., 1974). Studies on the incidence of meningitis (Parke et al., 1972; Fraser et al., 1973) and severe lower respiratory disease in the southeastern United States (Loda et al., 1968) support the view that respiratory infections that cause relatively mild illness in middle class children can lead to serious life-threatening illness in socioeconomically disadvantaged children.

The health research program at the Frank Porter Graham Child Development Center is based on the belief that acute respiratory disease constitutes a major health problem for all children but is a particularly heavy burden on the disadvantaged child. The accumulating evidence that antibiotic therapy is of only limited effectiveness in preventing the severe neurologic sequela of meningitis is a dramatic example of the fact that it is better to prevent disease than to seek to cure it. Preventive medical services require less skilled medical personnel and result in less morbidity than curative medicine. However, to prevent respiratory illness and its complications, it is necessary to increase understanding of the etiology of respiratory disease and the pathophysiology of the complications of these infections. This includes a better understanding of the possible synergistic action of viruses and bacteria in the respiratory tract and a greater understanding of the host response to both natural infection and to vaccine administration, particularly in young children. As a final step, there must be careful clinical trials of potentially effective vaccines.

A review of the role of one respiratory pathogen, *Hemophilus influenzae* type B, may help to illustrate the importance of respiratory disease as a cause of mental retardation, particularly in socioeconomically deprived populations.

H. influenzae type B is the most common cause of bacterial meningitis in children (Smith et al., 1973a). In the antibiotic era, the mortality from this disease has decreased from almost 100 percent to between 5 and 30 percent (Smith et al., 1973c), but even with adequate antimicrobial therapy permanent central nervous system damage occurs in over 50 percent of survivors (Sell et al., 1972a; Sproles et al., 1969). In one study of 86 patients, 14 percent of the patients died, 29 percent had severe or significant central nervous system impairment, 14 percent had possible residual handicaps, and only 43 percent were free of detectable handicaps (Sell et al., 1972a). Even in children apparently free of detectable residual neurological handicaps from meningitis, more detailed psychological testing suggests that these children are functioning intellectually below the level of siblings and classmates matched by age, sex, and social class (Sell et al., 1972b). When extrapolated to the estimated 10,000 cases of *H. influenzae* type B meningitis each year in the United States (Parke et al., 1972; Mortimer, 1973), the magnitude of the problem becomes apparent particularly when the documented incidence of *H. influenzae* type B meningitis currently is rising (Michaels, 1971; Smith and Haynes, 1972).

Epidemiologic studies in Mecklenburg County, North Carolina (Parke et al., 1972) and Charleston County, South Carolina (Fraser et al., 1973) showed the attack rate of *H. influenzae* meningitis in black children was 3.5 to 4 times higher than that in white children. The greatest risk was in low income, black families living in rural areas. An infant in the poorest section of Charleston County has a risk of approximately 1 in 280 of developing *H. influenzae* type B meningitis in the first 5 years of life, the highest risk of any group noted (Fraser et al., 1973; Fraser, Geil, and Feldman, in press). It is known that the highest incidence of *H. influenzae* meningitis occurs in children 7 to 12 months of age and that 89 percent of cases occur between the ages of 3 months and 3 years (Parke et al., 1972; Fraser et al., 1973). In these populations the children at greatest risk have been defined in terms of age and socioeconomic status.

One important area for investigation is the mechanism by which *H. influenzae* type B overcomes the host defense mechanisms in the respiratory tract, invades the bloodstream, and reaches the central nervous system. Carriage of the organism often does not result in disease, but carriage of *H. influenzae* in the respiratory tract is highest in the same age group that has the highest incidence of severe disease due to the organism (Turk, 1967). The studies of microbial interaction in the Frank Porter Graham Center are particualrly relevant to that crucial stage in the pathogenesis of meningitis when *H. influenzae* invades the bloodstream from the respiratory tract.

Because of the failure of antibiotic therapy to prevent permanent central nervous system damage following *H. influenzae* meningitis, emphasis has shifted to the development of an effective vaccine. A vaccine prepared from purified cell wall of *H. influenzae* is now being tested in human clinical trials (Smith et al., 1973c). If the present vaccine, or some modification of it, does prove effective in producing adequate levels of antibody to protect the human infant, the problem will remain of reaching the population at highest risk, the very young, and the poor—the groups most often not reached by existing health services.

The health research program at the Frank Porter Graham Child Development Center (FPG) has focused on the study of respiratory tract infections and their complications, with special emphasis on those microbial agents that produce otitis media and meningitis. The research has been conducted in the FPG longitudinal population that was initiated with the admission of 10 children in 1966. The population has now grown, with the addition of new infants each year, to include 60 children, the present age range being from 6 weeks up to 8 years. Untill September 1972, the children admitted were distributed equally by race, sex, and socioeconomic group; since that time all new infants admitted have been from socioeconomically deprived homes. Medical care has been provided as part of the center services, and only children with varicella and measles are excluded from day care. The children are observed daily, and those children with respiratory symptoms have their respiratory tracts cultured for viruses, mycoplasmas, and bacteria. The stability of the study population has permitted observation of the same children for extended time periods, and longitudinal follow up of the children from early infancy has permitted the documentation of respiratory infections by isolation and serology.

With the increasing numbers of preschool children in group day care, there has been particular concern in the United States about the health hazards that might be created. In order to investigate the validity of this apprehension, studies have been done in the FPG longitudinal population to compare the important etiologic agents and the rates of respiratory illness studies performed on children receiving home care. In 224 child-years of observation of the FPG longitudinal population during the 7-year period (1966 to 1973), there was an average of 6.2 respiratory illnesses per child-year (Table 5). The highest rate occurred in infants 1 year of age, with an average of 8.1 respiratory illnesses per child-year. The rate dropped with increasing age, so that children over 48 months of age had a rate of 5.1 or less respiratory illnesses per child-year. These rates are

Table 5. Frequency of respiratory illnesses by age. Frank Porter Graham Child Development Center, November 1966 to June 1973

Age (years)	Number of respiratory illnesses	Patient years at risk	Respiratory illnesses/ patient year
< 1	330	41	8.0
1	283	35	8.1
2	276	40	6.9
3	220	36	6.1
4	153	30	5.1
5	74	22	3.3
6–8	43	20	2.2
All ages	1,379	224	6.2

quite comparable to the illness rates recorded in the Cleveland, Ohio Family Study, a comprehensive health study that monitored illness in middle class families living at home (Dingle et al., 1964). The only excess in the FPG group occurred in infants under 1 year of age. The Cleveland Family Study noted slightly less than 7 illnesses per child-year in this age group, while the FPG group recorded 8.0 illnesses per child-year.

The effects of sex, race, income, and family size on respiratory illness in the FPG population has been investigated. In 224 child-years of observation, there was more total illness in females than in males (643.7 illnesses per 100 child-years to 584.5 illnesses per 100 child-years); however, females had less severe illnesses than did males (7.9 severe illnesses per 100 child-years to 11.5 severe illnesses per 100 child-years). When race was studied, there was a slight increase in total illness in whites over nonwhites (666.7 illnesses per 100 child-years to 598.4 illnesses per 100 child-years). The effect of family income on total illness and severe illness demonstrated that there was more total illness in the higher income group but more severe illness in the lower income group (Table 6). Family size did not seem to be an important factor on the total number of illnesses of a child in day care (two to three family members, 603.6 illnesses per 100 child-years; four family members, 654.5 illnesses per 100 child-years; five family members, 562.9 illnesses per 100 child-years; six or more familiy members, 651.6 illnesses per 100 child-years).

Not only have the illness rates been similar to that recorded in the observation of children receiving home care, but the types of agents isolated and their age and seasonal incidence have been similar to microbial isolates from children in home care seen in a private pediatric practice in Chapel Hill (Glezen et al., 1971). Table 7 summarizes the respiratory pathogen isolations during the first five years in the FPG study.

The overall isolation data suggest the importance of respiratory syncytial virus and the parainfluenza viruses, particularly type 3. They are even more important because of the frequency with which they are associated with lower respiratory disease. Respiratory syncytial virus and the parainfluenza viruses accounted for over half of the isolates from lower respiratory disease. Illness resulting from respiratory syncytial virus and parainfluenza virus type 3 usually was more severe during the first year of life, which presumably always represented a primary infection. Immunity following these respiratory illnesses was very short, with almost all the infants being reinfected during their second respiratory season, but the symptoms were usually less severe (Loda et al., 1972a). An effective immunoprophylaxis against these agents, administered at an early age, could significantly reduce morbidity in young children in group day care; however, because of

Table 6. Effects of family income on respiratory illness

Income	Severe respiratory illness (illnesses/child-years)	Total respiratory illness (illnesses/child-years)
Low	13.6/100	528.8/100
Middle	10.6/100	593.9/100
Upper	6.1/100	680.8/100

Table 7. Number of isolations of respiratory pathogens from children with respiratory illnesses. Frank Porter Graham Child Development Center, 1966 to 1971[a]

Agents	Number isolates	% of illnesses with isolates
Respiratory syncytial virus	43	4.3
Parainfluenza virus type 1	21	2.1
Parainfluenza virus type 2	28	2.8
Parainfluenza virus type 3	59	5.9
Influenza A2 virus	7	0.7
Influenza B virus	12	1.2
Mumps virus	16	1.6
Adenovirus type 1	16	1.6
Adenovirus type 2	40	4.0
Adenovirus type 5	31	3.1
Adenovirus—not typed	5	0.5
Enteroviruses	65	6.5
Rhinoviruses	41	4.1
Herpesvirus	6	0.6
Group A streptococci	53	5.3
Mycoplasma pneumoniae	6	0.6

[a]Total illnesses studied, 966.

the short duration of immunity produced by these viruses, the vaccine probably would have to be administered annually to provide continuing protection. The adenoviruses, enteroviruses, rhinoviruses, and group A streptococci caused a significant amount of upper respiratory disease, and *Mycoplasma pneumoniae* was isolated from this population on several occasions (Loda et al., 1972b). Despite technologic advances of the past two decades in isolating respiratory pathogens, the etiology of a major segment of acute respiratory tract disease and the mechanism of complications remain undefined.

Certain respiratory disease syndromes in animals and birds have been shown to depend on interacting infectious agents, rather than on single pathogens. Studies were begun in January 1972 to demonstrate the role played by microbial interaction in the pathogenesis of respiratory infections and their complications such as otitis media and meningitis. The children in the longitudinal population were cultured for viruses, bacteria, and mycoplasmas every 2 weeks when well and at the onset of each illness. In preliminary evaluation of the microbial interaction study, computer analysis of microbiological and clinical parameters of 1,187 cultures obtained at the time of acute respiratory illnesses were compared with cultural data from 1,068 specimens obtained from the same children when well (Glezen, Collier, and Loda, 1974). Illnesses were classified according to severity as follows: 1) lower respiratory tract disease accompanied by otitis media, 2) acute otitis media, 3) lower respiratory tract illness alone, 4) febrile uncomplicated upper respiratory illness, and 5) afebrile upper respiratory illness. The results of micro-biologic studies were correlated with the severity of illness observed and the age of the child and compared to the microbiologic data from the "well" cultures. The bacterial isolations included in the analyses were pneumococci, *H. influenzae*, and group A streptococci. Pneumococci were recovered from 719 illness cultures and 513 well cultures; *H. influenzae* from 309 illnesses and 112 well cultures; and group A streptococci from 66 illnesses and 45 well cultures. The frequency of isolation of these bacteria, alone or in combination, with or without a concomitant virus infection was correlated with the age of the subject or the severity of illness and compared with the microbiologic data from well cultures by age of subject. Among the bacterial agents, the isolation of *H. influenza* was best correlated with acute respiratory illness. The frequency of isolation was 26.5 percent from all respiratory illnesses compared with 11.1 percent from well cultures. The isolation rate was slightly higher (32.7 percent) from children with otitis media than from children with other diagnoses. The rate was only 6.0 percent for cultures from well children under 3 years of age, which yielded a ratio of positive cultures of *H. influenzae* of 4.4 to 1 for ill and well children in that age group. The frequency of isolation of pneumococci was 61.6 percent from cultures of children with respiratory illnesses and 52.6 percent from cultures of children when well. When pneumococcus was the only potentially pathogenic bacterium isolated, there was no significant difference in isolation rates between sick and well, by age, or by severity of illness. However, when pneumococci and *H. influenzae* were found in combination there were significant differences (18.9 percent of illness cultures and 7.2 percent of well cultures). When these rates were examined for children under 3 years of age, the ratio of the frequency of cultures positive for both bacteria from ill and well (5.2 to 1) exceeded that for *H. influenzae* alone.

The data obtained to date suggest an interaction between *H. influenzae* and pneumococci and possibly between this combination in the presence of a concomitant virus infection. These associations may come into focus more sharply when enough data have accumulated to look at the relation of specific virus and *H. influenzae* types to specific pneumococcal serotypes (Loda et al., 1973). Studies to date would strenghten the original hypothesis that interactions among diverse microbial agents may be responsible for a segment of respiratory disease, presently of unknown etiology, in children, and it may be responsible for a major proportion of complications of acute respiratory illnesses that may include otitis media, pneumonia, meningitis, and others.

Research has been performed at FPG on the development of virus vaccines for respiratory syncytial, parainfluenza types 1, 2, 3, and influenza viruses. The evaluation of a vaccine in a small population like the Frank Porter Graham Center permits the demonstration of spread and the examination of the interaction of the vaccine virus with other microbial organisms that might also be in any open population. Studies such as these are essential before field trials of such vaccines can be contemplated.

Refinements of the countercurrent immunoelectrophoresis and latex agglutination test are currently being developed in the FPG laboratory. These are rapid methods of detection of *H. influenzae* B antigen in spinal fluid, serum, urine, empyema, and pericardial and subdural fluid (Ingram et al., 1973; Newman et al., 1970; Smith and Ingram, in press). The goal of this research is to provide a test that permits a diagnosis to be made in 5 to 30 minutes of systemic disease caused by *H. influenzae* and specific treatment to be started immediately.

Because respiratory tract infections usually do not result in death, tissue is not available for pathologic examination; therefore, experimental models have been developed in the FPG laboratory to explore the host response and to gain more insight into the pathogenesis of respiratory disease and their complications. The adult Syrian hamster has been used extensively in our laboratory for study of the pathogensis of *Mycoplasma pneumoniae* disease (Denny et al., 1971). This animal model is also being developed for study of respiratory syncytial virus and parainfluenza virus type 3 infections. The Syrian hamster will continue to be employed in the study of respiratory disease to gain information on the mechanisms of disease production, pathology produced, and immunologic response in the animal.

An in vitro tracheal organ culture model has been developed for study of the interaction of individual microbial agents, isolated from children in the FPG population, with ciliated respiratory epithelium (Collier et al., 1969; Collier et al., 1971). Tracheal organ culture permits the maintenance in vitro of viable, differentiated, organized, respiratory epithelium from human fetuses and from hamsters. With this model, tissue from a single human fetus or an animal can be used for control and test groups. Tracheal rings may be infected with a specific number of cloned respiratory pathogens, thus avoiding the effect of secondary invaders seen in in vivo animal models. This system has been demonstrated to be useful for study of bacteria (Denny, 1974), viruses (Hoorn, 1966), mycoplasmas (Collier and Clyde, 1971; Collier, 1972), and combinations of microbial agents (Reed, 1971). The model has permitted study of pathophysiologic alterations resulting from infection of the tissue with respiratory microorganisms by light, immunofluorescence, and electron microscopy, and of metabolic changes through use of radio-labeled precursors of proteins, carbohydrates, and nucleic acids (Collier and Baseman, 1973).

In order to prevent respiratory disease that leads to central nervous system complications, a better understanding must be gained of the interrelationships between microbial agents forming the ecosystem of the respiratory tract and the mechanisms by which microbial agents injure and invade the respiratory epithelium. An understanding of the reciprocal relationships among different respiratory microorganisms may allow development of methods by which these interactions can be altered to benefit the human host.

In addition to studies of the etiology and pathogenesis of respiratory disease, the Frank Porter Graham Child Development Center health program is participating with the Division of Community Pediatrics in programs designed to improve health care delivery, particularly to disadvantaged rural families. The availability of improved health care methods does not mean that they will be used by the families in greatest need of them. There is abundant evidence that disadvantaged families do not benefit fully from existing health care resources (Bergner and Yerby, 1968). The rate of immunization is disappointingly low, particularly with vaccines designed to prevent illness in the very young (United States Immunization Survey, 1973).

The Division of Community Pediatrics provides child care in three community health centers sponsored by Orange Chatham Comprehensive Health Services, Inc., providing care primarily to low income, rural, North Carolina families. The family nurse practitioner is the primary care provider to the young child in these clinics, and these nurse practitioners are effectively supplying high quality care to children in rural areas under physician supervision (Greenberg et al., in press). Recently, the state of North Carolina has launched a program of family nurse practitioner clinics in other rural areas of the state. This program envisions the opening of 10 new rural clinics a year. The family nurse practitioners for these clinics are being trained in a University of North Carolina program that has significant input from the Frank Porter Graham Center staff. This program also has major emphasis on the developmental aspects of child care. Nurse practitioners also have provided child care at the Frank Porter Graham Center for several years in an effort to improve the efficiency of health services to young children in day care (Peters, 1971).

One major need in achieving better health care for disadvantaged children is to enlist the cooperation of families. In the Orange Chatham Comprehensive Health Services, Inc., clinics, the community health workers perform a major role in health education and outreach activities. The community health workers are members of the local community, and they often communicate more effectively with families in the community than do health professionals. An infant stimulation program available to all infants in the Orange Chatham program is now being developed. Community health workers will visit homes to demonstrate and encourage the use of the infant curriculum materials developed in the Frank Porter Graham Center. The merging of health and educational services delivery to infants may have important cost advantages.

In summary, the disadvantaged child is at particular risk of developing major health problems that will contribute significantly to his failure to achieve full physical, cognitive, and social development. Research, therefore, is needed to develop better tools, such as vaccines, to prevent acute illness, particularly respiratory illness. In addition, better methods are needed to deliver these services to families in an efficient and acceptable way. The health care program at the Frank Porter Graham Center is seeking ways that will both reduce the illness burden of these families and provide an efficient system for distributing a wide range of child care services to the consumer including both health and educational services.

SUMMARY AND CONCLUSIONS

The Carolina Abecedarian Project is currently in its second year of operation. At present, a maximum of 2,000 plus pieces of information are collected on each child each year. This information ranges from the identification of specific microbial agents in the child's respiratory tract to the number of social institutions with which the families have contact. It is hoped that such a breadth of information will help the staff to understand the high risk child's development and to ensure the child's normal development.

Because so much data are already available, it is impossible to do more than merely skim the surface in a publication such as this. Also, the availability of this large quantity of data presents some important data management problems. In an attempt not to become swamped in a sea of unrelated data, we are currently establishing a comprehensive, open-ended computer system that will allow access to any portion of the data from a remote terminal. This data system has been fully operational since the fall of 1974. One advantage of such a system is that it facilitates the productive collaboration of investigators from diverse disciplines. Through such collaborative efforts, we hope to grow from a multidisciplinary project into one that is truly interdisciplinary. Through such collaborative efforts, we hope to make a contribution to the knowledge of how to prevent the biological, social, and intellectual stunting that currently is all too frequently the birthright of our most disadvantaged children.

ACKNOWLEDGMENTS

The authors wish to acknowledge gratefully the thoughtful contributions that have been made to this project by the following people: Carrie D. Bynum, Wallace A. Clyde, Floyd W. Denny, Gerald W. Fernald, James J. Gallagher, W. Paul Glezen, Isabelle S. Lewis, Pamela J. Mills, and Carolyn H. O'Brien.

LITERATURE CITED

Bergner, L., and A. S. Yerby. 1968. Low income barriers to use of health services. New Eng. J. Med. 278: 541–546.

Bloom, B. S. 1964. Stability and change in human characteristics. Wiley, New York.

Bowlby, J. 1958. The nature of the child's tie to his mother. Intern. J. Psychoanal. 39: 350–373.

Box, G. E. P. 1954. Some theorems of quadratic forms applied in the study of analysis of variance problems, II: Effects of inequality of variance and correlation between errors in the two-way classification. Ann. Math. Stat. 25: 484–498.

Brody, S. 1951. Patterns of mothering. International Universities Press, New York.

Bronfenbrenner, U. 1973. Is early intervention effective? Paper presented at biennial meeting of the Society for Research in Child Development, Philadelphia. (March.)

Caldwell, B. M., and J. B. Richmond. 1968. The children's center in Syracuse, New York. In L. L. Dirtman (ed.), Early Child Care: The New Perspectives, pp. 326–358. Atherton, New York.

Caldwell, B. M. 1967. What is the optimal learning environment for the young child? Amer. J. Orthopsychiat. 37: 8–21.

Collier, A. M. 1972. Pathogenesis of Mycoplasma pneumoniae infection as studied in the human foetal trachea in organ culture. In J. Birch (ed.), A Ciba Foundation Symposium on Pathogenic Mycoplasmas, pp. 307–327. Elsevoir, Amsterdam.

Collier, A. M., and J. B. Baseman. 1973. Organ culture techniques with mycoplasmas. Ann. N. Y. Acad. Sci. 225: 277–289.

Collier, A. M., and W. A. Clyde. 1971. Relationships between *Mycoplasma pneumoniae* and human respiratory epithelium. Infect. Immun. 3: 694–701.

Collier, A. M., W. A. Clyde, Jr., and F. W. Denny. 1969. Biologic effects of *Mycoplasma pneumoniae* and other mycoplasma from man on hamster tracheal organ culture. Proc. Soc. Exper. Biol. Med. 132: 1153–1158.

Collier, A. M., W. A. Clyde, Jr., and F. W. Denny. 1971. *Mycoplasma penumoniae* in hamster trachael organ culture: Immunofluorescent and electron microscopic studies. Proc. Soc. Exper. Biol. Med. 136: 569–573.

Corter, C. M., H. L. Rheingold, and C. O. Eckerman. 1972. Toys delay the infant's following of his mother. Devel. Psych. 6: 138–145.

Dennis, W., and P. Najarian. 1957. Infant development under environmental handicap. Psych. Monogr. 71: (Whole No. 436).

Denny, F. W. 1974. Effect of a toxin produced by *Haemophilus influenzae* on ciliated respiratory epithelium. J. Infect. Dis. 123: 93–101.

Denny, F. W., W. A. Clyde, Jr., and W. P. Glezen. 1971. *Mycoplasma pneumoniae* disease: Clinical spectrum, pathophysiology, epidemiology, and control. J. Infect. Dis. 123: 74–92.

Deutsch, M., and B. Brown. 1964. Social influence on Negro-White intelligence differences. J. Soc. Issues 20: 24–35.

Dingle, J. H., G. F. Badger, and W. S. Jordan, Jr. 1964. Illness in the Home. Western Reserve University Press, Cleveland.

Dittman, L. L. (ed.) 1968. Early Child Care: The New Perspective. Atherton Press, New York.

Dunn, L. M. (ed.) 1963. Educable mentally retarded children. Exceptional Children in the Schools. Holt, Rinehart, and Winston, New York.

Emmerich, W. 1969. The parental role: A functional-cognitive approach. Monogr. Soc. Res. Child Devel. 34:(8).

Finkelstein, N. W., C. O'Brien, and C. T. Ramey. 1974. The effects of toys on social interaction. Paper presented at biennial meeting of Southeastern Society for Research in Child Development, Chapel Hill, North Carolina. (March.)

Fraser, D. W., C. P. Darby, R. E. Koehler, C. F. Jacobs, and R. A. Feldman. 1973. Risk factors in bacterial meningitis: Charleston County, South Carolina. J. Infect. Dis. 127: 271–277.

Fraser, D. W., C. C. Geil, and R. A. Feldman. Bacterial meningitis in Bernalitto County, New Mexico: A comparison with three other American populations. Amer. J. Epidem. (in press).

Glezen, W. P., A. M. Collier, and F. A. Loda. 1974. Significance of pneumococci and *Hemophilus influenzae* cultured from the nasopharynx of children. Pediat. Res. 8: 425.

Glezen, W. P., F. A. Loda, W. A. Clyde, Jr., R. J. Senior, C. I. Sheaffer, W. G. Conley, and F. W. Denny. 1971. Epidemiologic patterns of acute lower respiratory disease of children in pediatric group practice. J. Pediat. 78: 397–406.

Goldfarb, W. 1955. Emotional and intellectual consequences of psychological depreciation. *In* P. Hock and J. Zubin (eds.), Psychopathology of Childhood, pp. 105–119. Gruen and Stratton, New York.

Greenberg, R. A., F. A. Loda, C. G. Pickard, P. Collins, B. Compton, G. Hargraves, and M. Wilkman. Primary child health care by family nurse practitioners (in press).

Heber, R. 1971. Results of an intervention project. Cited in S. Scarr-Salapatek's Unknowns in the IQ equation. Science 171: 1227–1228.

Heber, R. F., R. B. Dever, and J. Conry. 1968. The influence of environmental and genetic variables on intellectual development. *In* A. J. Pickson, L. A. Hamerlynck, and J. E. Crosson (eds.), Behavioral Research in Mental Retardation. University of Oregon, Eugene.

Honig, A. S., and S. Brill. 1970. A comparative analysis of the Piagetian development of twelve month old disadvantaged infants in an enrichment center with others not in such a center. Paper presented at the meeting of the American Psychological Association, Miami. (September.)

Hoorn, B. 1966. Organ cultures of ciliated epithelium for the study of respiratory viruses. Acta Pathol. Microbiol. Scand. 66 Supp., 183.

Hunt, J. McV. 1961. Intelligence and Experience, pp. 267–288. Ronald Press, New York.

Huntington, D. S., S. Provence, and R. K. Parker (eds.). 1971. Serving Infants. U.S. Government Printing Office, Washington, D.C.

Hurley, R. L. 1968. Poverty and mental retardation: A causal relationship. State of New Jersey, Trenton.

Ingram, D. L., R. O'Reilly, P. Anderson, and D. H. Smith. 1973. Detection of the capsual polysaccharide of *Hemophilus influenzae* B in body fluids. *In* S. H. Sell and D. T. Karzon (eds.), *Hemophilus Influenzae*, pp. 32–43. Vanderbilt University Press, Nashville.

Lefcourt, H. M., and G. W. Ladwig. 1965. The American Negro: A problem in expectancies. J. Personal. Soc. Psych. 1: 377–380.

Levy, M., T. D. Scurletis, E. Siegel, C. Turnbull, and J. R. Udry. 1974. The determinants of post neonatal mortality in North Carolina 1967–1968. Report of the Personal Health Section, Division of Health Services, North Carolina Department of Human Resources, Raleigh, North Carolina. Paper presented at meeting of the American Public Health Association, New Orleans. October 24.

Loda, F. A., W. A. Clyde, W. P. Glezen, R. J. Senior, C. I. Sheaffer, and F. W. Denny, Jr. 1968. Studies on the role of viruses, bacteria, and *M. pneumoniae* as causes of lower respiratory tract infections in children. J. Pediat. 72: 161–176.

Loda, F. A., A. M. Collier, and W. P. Glezen. 1973. Nasal carriage of *Diplococcus pneumoniae* in young children. Clin. Res. 21: 122.

Loda, F. A., W. P. Glezen, A. M. Collier, and F. W. Denny. 1972a. Recurrent respiratory syncytial virus infections. Clin. Res. 20: 103.

Loda, F. A., W. P. Glezen, and W. A. Clyde, Jr. 1972b. Respiratory disease in group day care. Pediat. 49: 428–437.

Maudry, M., and M. Nekula. 1939. Social relations between children of the same age during the first two years of life. J. Genet. Psych. 54: 193–215.

McCall, R. B., and M. I. Appelbaum. 1973. Bias in the analysis of repeated measures designs: Some alternative approaches. Child Devel. 44: 401–415.

Michaels, R. H. 1971. Increase in influenzal meningitis. New Eng. J. Med. 285: 666.

Mortimer, E. A. 1973. Immunization against *Hemophilus influenzae*. Pediat. 52: 633.

Newman, R. B., R. W. Stevens, and H. A. Gaafar. 1970. Latex agglutination test for the diagnosis of *Haemophilus influenzae* meningitis. J. Lab. Clin. Med. 76: 107.

Page, E. B. 1973. Miracle in Milwaukee: Raising the IQ. Ed. Res. 1: 8–16.

Painter, G. 1971. Teach Your Baby. Simon and Schuster, New York.

Parke, J. C., Jr., R. Schneerson, and J. B. Robbins. 1972. The attack rate, age incidence, racial distribution, and case fatality rate of *Hemophilus influenzae* type b meningitis in Meckenburg County, North Carolina. J. Pediat. 81: 765–769.

Peters, A. D. 1971. Health support in day care. *In* E. M. Grotbert (ed.), Day Care: Resources for Decisions. Office of Economic Opportunity, Office of Planning, Research and Evaluation, U.S. Government Printing Office, Washington, D.C.

Piaget, J. 1970. Piaget's theory. *In* P. H. Mussen (ed.), Carmichael's Manual of Child Psychology, pp. 703—732. Wiley, New York.

Reed, S. E. 1971. The interaction of mycoplasmas and influenza viruses in tracheal organ cultures. J. Infect. Dis. 124: 18—25.

Rheingold, H. L. 1961. The effect of environmental stimulation upon social and exploratory behavior in the human infant. *In* B. M. Foss (eds.), Determinants of Infant Behavior, pp. 143—171. Wiley, New York.

Rheingold, H. L. 1973. Independent behavior of the human infant. *In* A. D. Pick (ed.), Minnesota Symposium on Child Psychology, Vol. 7, pp. 175—203. University of Minnesota Press, Minneapolis.

Rheingold, H. L., and H. R. Samuels. 1969. Maintaining the positive behavior of infants by increased stimulation. Devel. Psych. 1: 520—527.

Robinson, H. L., and H. M. Robinson. 1971. Longitudinal development of very young children in a comprehensive day care program: The first two years. Child Devel. 42: 1673—1683.

Rotter, J. B. 1966. Generalized expectancies for internal versus external control of reinforcement. Psych. Monogr. 80: (Whole No. 609).

Segner, L., and C. Patterson. 1970. Ways to Help Babies Grow and Learn: Activities for Infant Education. World Press, Denver.

Sell, S. H. W., R. E. Merrill, E. O. Doyne, and E. P. Zimsky. 1972a. Longterm sequelae of *Hemophilus influenzae* meningitis. Pediat. 49: 206.

Sell, S. H. W., W. W. Webb, J. E. Pate, and E. O. Doyne. 1972b. Psychological sequelae to bacterial meningitis: Two controlled studies. Pediat. 49: 212—217.

Smith, D. H., D. L. Ingram, A. L. Smith, F. Gillis, and M. J. Bresnan. 1973a. Bacterial meningitis, a symposium. Pediat. 52: 586.

Smith, D. H., G. Peter, D. L. Ingram, A. L. Harding, and P. Anderson. 1973b. Children immunized against *Hemophilus influenzae* type B. Pediat. 52: 637.

Smith, D. H., G. Peter, D. L. Ingram, A. L. Harding, and P. Anderson. 1973c. Responses of children immunized with the capsular polysaccharide of *Hemophilus influenzae* type B. Pediat. 52: 637.

Smith, E. W. P., Jr., and R. E. Haynes. 1972. Changing incidence of *Hemophilus influenzae* meningitis. Pediat. 50: 723.

Smith, E. W. P., and D. L. Ingram. Countercurrent immunoelectrophoresis in *Hemophilus influenzae* type B epiglottitis and pericarditis. Pediat. Res. (in press).

Spitz, R. A. 1945. Hospitalism: An inquiry into the genesis of psychiatric conditions in early childhood. Psychoanal. Stud. Child. 1: 53—74.

Sproles, E. T., III., J. Azerrad, C. Williamson, and R. E. Merrill. 1969. Meningitis due to *Hemophilus influenzae*: Long-term sequelae. J. Pediat. 75: 782.

Stedman, D. J., N. J. Anastasiow, P. R. Dokecki, I. J. Gordon, and R. K. Parker. 1972. How can effective early intervention programs be delivered to potentially retarded children? A report for the Office of the Secretary of the Department of Health, Education, and Welfare, Washington, D.C.

Turk, D. C. 1967. Distribution of *Hemophilus influenzae* in healthy human communities. *In* D. C. Turk and J. R. May (eds.), *Hemophilus Influenzae*: Its Clinical Importance. English University Press, London.

Tyler, R. W. 1950. Basic Principles of Curriculum and Instruction. University of Chicago Press, Chicago.

United States Immunization Survey: 1972. U.S. Department of Health, Education, and Welfare, Publication number (HSM) 73-8221, U.S. Government Printing Office, Washington, D.C.

Weikart, D. P. 1971. Early childhood special education for intellectually subnormal and/or culturally different children. High/Scope Educational Research Foundation. Ypsilanti, Michigan. Paper prepared for the National Leadership Institute in Early Childhood Development, Washington, D.C. October.

Weikart, D. P., and D. Z. Lambie. 1969. Early enrichment in infants. Paper presented at the meeting of the American Association for the Advancement of Science, Boston. December.

Westinghouse Learning Coporation. 1969. The Impact of Head Start. Ohio University, Athens.

Winer, B. J. 1962. Statistical principles in experimental design. McGraw-Hill, New York.

STATE-OF-THE-ART

Delivery of Educational Services to Preschool Handicapped Children

Paul R. Ackerman, Jr., Ph.D., and Melvin G. Moore

Any state-of-the-art report dealing with a topic as broad as the education of preschool handicapped children must, of necessity, be based on obsolete data. That is, any data relative to this field must be recognized as only a phase in the evolution of that field. This state-of-the-art report will deal with material and statistics as early as 1971 and as late as 1974 in the United States. It will attempt, by so doing, to show some trends and evolution in this field, but it can make no predictions about the future. The field of preschool education for the handicapped is erratic in growth, and it is presently experiencing a highly accelerated evolutionary spurt. It is a subject that provokes emotion and opinions. It is a field that is not yet based on substantive evaluation of data. No one has yet "proved" the value of various types of preschool educational programming for the handicapped.

But one may *assume* the value of preschool intervention, as have hundreds of thousands of parents and professionals. It is this assumption that is presently seeming to accelerate the growth of such programs. It is this assumption that will, probably, prove true if adequate measures are ever found to evaluate it.

The following information, then, is really a documentation of this assumption. People believe that childhood intervention is good for preschool handicapped children. To what, then, has this assumption led?

STIMULATION OF SERVICES THROUGH FEDERAL LEGISLATION

Handicapped Children's Early Education Program (HCEEP)

The Handicapped Children's Early Education Act (Public Law 91-230, Title VI, Part C, Sec. 623), the stimulus to the federal response to provide services for preschool-age handicapped children, was clearly intended by Congress to demonstrate the feasibility of early education to the American public. The Act provided monies for demonstration

669

programs, insisted that such programs be geographically dispersed, mandated the involvement of parents, and ordered dissemination of the results to the communities that surrounded the preschool programs. Furthermore, the Act insisted that programs be coordinated with other existing programs and that they be evaluated in order to show others their worth. The steadily increasing appropriations for the program were taken to be indicative of Congressional satisfaction with the results of the legislation to date.

The HCEEP presently consists of 117 projects, which are distributed as follows (for fiscal year 1974): 30 projects, designated as Planning/Operational, have been funded to pilot specific demonstration programs for preschool handicapped children and to establish preschool intervention systems. Following a year of planning and operation, 55 projects are in their second and third years of operation, further modifying and validating their curricular systems. In their fourth and fifth year of federal funding are 32 projects, whose federal monies are being utilized for the dissemination and diffusion of their tested and validated models of intervention. In addition to these demonstrations, there is a project funded to provide technical assistance to demonstration projects, a project that seeks to change the attitudes of personnel who may come in contact with handicapped children, and a project designed to prevent the development of serious speech and language problems in preschool handicapped children. A third party evaluation contract has been led to develop cognitive and affective milestones by which to measure the progress of children in early education intervention programs and to determine the efficacy of intervention programs already being funded under the Handicapped Children's Early Education Act. Yearly reports are made summarizing the effects of these projects.

The actual number of children served in the HCEEP projects is shown in Table 1. This table shows that the largest number of children served are those in the age bracket from birth to 5 years. Fourth and Fifth year projects (outreach projects) seek to serve more teachers, administrators, and program planners than children. Hence, outreach projects show a reduction in the numbers of children served. Also, fewer children are served in the first year because of the pilot experimental nature of most first year programs.

Table 1. Handicapped Children's Early Education Program (HCEEP) projects: children served by age group (April 1, 1974)

Project funding year	Number of projects	Children served (years)	
		0-5	6+
1st	30	1,078	349
2nd	30	2,031	222
3rd	25	2,375	35
Outreach	32	1,764	163
Totals	117	7,284	769

Final reports available in the program office of the HCEEP show that in year 1972 to 1973, 91 projects were able to stimulate the replication of themselves, or major components of themselves, to 214 other agencies. These replications accounted for an additional 17,500 children being served by funds other than those paying for services to 4,500 children being served in the HCEEP demonstrations. If this replication activity could be projected, it could be estimated that in 1974 an additional 28,000 children will be served through replication, and in 1975 an estimated 35,000 children would be served. (These projections are based on an estimated replication figure of four children served through replication for every child served through a demonstration project, a seemingly accurate estimate.) Because of manpower constraints, however, it is expected that a geometric progression could not, in fact, occur. It is probably more realistic to base estimates of growth upon the number of projects completing the third year, because such projects will generally be continued on funding other than funds from HCEEP. Such an estimate, based on 30 projects per year completing their third year and serving approximately 2,500 children in each year (and replicating at a ratio of 4:1), would indicate that for every year the HCEEP exists, 10,000 children will be receiving services through replication activities.

In summary, 1974 figures indicate that approximately 8,000 children are being served in HCEEP projects, 10,000 children are being served through replicational activities, and 3,000 children per year are phased out of the program and into facilities for older children. A projection of the numbers of children served each year by the HCEEP would total 13,000 children per year.

Head Start

The legislation and appropriations for Head Start, the Economic Opportunity Amendments of 1972, are provided under Public Law 92-424, Sec. 3(b). This legislation instructs the Secretary of Health, Education, and Welfare to ensure that 10 percent of the enrollment of Head Start populations is handicapped and receiving adequate treatment through the Head Start Program. However, the Act does not authorize additional funds for this effort.

The second annual report to Congress by the Office of Child Development on the integration of handicapped children in Head Start programs indicates that, as of December 1973, a total of 29,000 of the 287,100 children enrolled in full year programs have been referred as handicapped to those programs or had been diagnosed as handicapped by competent professionals after they had been admitted to those programs.

Those 29,000 handicapped children represent 10.1 percent of the total children served in those Head Start programs. It was anticipated that that number may well have reached as high as 13.2 percent by the end of fiscal year 1973. Table 2 represents the number of handicapped children served, by handicapping condition, within those 29,000 children.

The projection of increases in services available to these children, however, is not proportionate to the number of children being served, and it may be inferred that not all

Table 2. Number of handicapped children served through Head Start (December, 1973)

Condition	Total served (no.)	Handicapped (%)
Speech impaired	10,150	35.0
Blind	145	0.5
Deaf	290	1.0
Visually impaired	1,914	6.6
Hearing impaired	2,291	7.9
Physically handicapped	2,726	9.4
Other health or developmental impairment	5,800	20.0
Mentally retarded	2,146	7.4
Emotionally disturbed	3,538	12.2

handicapped children in Head Start are receiving specialized or adequate services. Attempts to evaluate program effort, increase quality, and disseminate information about the program are indicated by expenditures for "special projects" category of the Office of Child Development. Such projects attempt large scale dissemination efforts through the Council for Exceptional Children, third party evaluation efforts through Syracuse University, Technical assistance efforts through the Technical Assistance Development System at the University of North Carolina, and through handbooks produced by the Judge Baker Agency of Boston. In addition, some training of personnel is accomplished through the Training and Technical Assistance funds awarded from the administrative monies given to the regional offices of Child Development. To test effectively models of Head Start intervention with handicapped preschool children, the Office of Child Development funds 14 demonstration projects, of which six are jointly funded with the Bureau of Education of the Handicapped (BEH). These projects are meant to test and validate a series of intervention models, and they are disseminated to other Head Start programs throughout the country. Special monies are awarded for the inclusion of handicapped children in programs of Home Start, Health Start, and Migrant and Indian Services. Head Start regulations require a 10 percent mandate by OCD regions and encourage a 10 percent distribution of handicapped in each local project.

It is expected that unless the appropriations for Head Start does, in the future, contain additional directives, the number of children served by Head Start, and the consequent 10.1 percent figure, will not appreciably change. Thus, the conservative figure of 30,000 handicapped children served per year by Head Start should remain relatively constant.

Public Law 89-313

Legislation for Public Law 89-313, Title 1, as amended by Public Law 91-230, of the Elementary and Secondary Education Act (ESEA), calls for a formula grant distribution of funds to children being treated and educated in state institutions for handicapped children. Such funds, allocated on a per-pupil basis, may be utilized for improvement of intervention programs within the institution, in de-institutionalization efforts, and in efforts for maintenance of children domiciled outside of institutions. As may be seen by Table 3, the number of preschool children served under the auspices of Public Law 89-313 has risen yearly. This may be because of an increased awareness of the service needs of preschool handicapped children in institutions and possibly because of an increase in preschool admissions to state institutions. Although it is expected that the figures for preschool children being served under Public Law 89-313 will show a plateau in growth within the next few years, the figure of 32,000 children per year will probably remain a stable but conservative estimate of the number of preschool handicapped children served under this program.

Part B, Title VI-B, Elementary and Secondary Education Act

Legislation for assistance to states in the education of handicapped children authorizes the Office of Education to award monies to the state education agencies for the purpose of assisting them in initiating programs felt to be useful, as demonstrations, to the rest of the state.

Programs funded under Title VI-B appropriations are generally expended within public school programs. Programs may even be instituted in states that have no supporting legislation for preschool programs for handicapped children. Project funds may also be used to write and to produce materials from these projects in order to affect smooth diffusion of the projects. Reports to the Office of Education indicate that funds expended for preschool handicapped programs from VI-B are often instrumental in affecting attitudes toward increased provision of preschool programs for handicapped children by legislators.

Recent state activities seem to indicate a greater interest in preschool programming for the handicapped. Thus, it is expected that the number of children served through Title VI-B funds will continue to rise on a national level. Only estimated figures are available for the number of handicapped children served under Part B during fiscal year 1972. The actual number served in fiscal year 1973 was 26,300, followed by an increase to 39,903 in fiscal year 1974. Because most of the children served under VI-B are served under downward age extensions of the public school programs, it may be assumed that most of these children are 4 to 6 years old.

Table 3. Preschool children served under Public Law 89-313 (projected estimates)

Year	No.
1972	21,000
1973	25,700
1974	32,059

In summary, the federal effort for education of preschool handicapped children may be described as a strategy of "stimulation." Projects are funded which are useful in demonstrating proven and experimental approaches to preschool educational intervention. Project personnel are charged with documenting and "packaging" their intervention system and disseminating their intervention systems to other agencies interested in establishing programs for the intervention of preschool handicapped children.

In 1974, the estimated total of children served under the four programs mentioned above totaled 120,000 children. This is itemized as: 18,000 children served under HCEEP Programs, 30,000 served under Head Start programs, 32,000 children served under the auspices of Public Law 89-313, and 40,000 children served under Title VI-B. It is expected that unless federal funds are dramatically increased, the number of children served yearly through these authorities will remain relatively constant. A sharp increase in the number of children served would be dependent upon the success of high risk stimulatory efforts in the future and through activities addressing specific target populations for purpose of replication and duplication of existing exemplary projects.

STIMULATION OF SERVICES BY PRIVATE ORGANIZATIONS SERVING PRESCHOOL HANDICAPPED CHILDREN

Many national organizations that target services, research, and training for certain types of handicapped children offer services to preschool handicapped children. In an attempt to determine the number of children being served by a private organization, the largest of these organizations with known service components were surveyed by telephone. It was found that only three agencies, Easter Seal Society, National Association for Retarded Citizens, and United Cerebral Palsy, had figures or estimates of numbers of children served at the preschool level. Table 4 is the result of this survey.

The figures for Easter Seal and United Cerebral Palsy are determined from enrollment data of children served in local chapter service agencies. The figures for the National Association for Retarded Children are estimated figures, based upon the number of units reported serving handicapped children, multiplied by an estimated enrollment figure of 10 preschool handicapped children per unit.

The figure of 143,561 preschool handicapped children served, then, represents an approximation of figures for three large organizations serving preschool handicapped children. It also represents figures that differ from organization to organization in the definition of the term "preschool." Taken with the federal estimate of 120,000 children served, however, it produces a total (presumably non-duplicated) of 263,656 preschool handicapped children counted in special services of 1,000,000 preschool children. This figure represents approximately 26 percent of the total number of children needing services. However, this figure is probably low, because there are unavailable data on the numbers of preschool handicapped children being served from private day care programs, industrial day care programs, other organizations serving handicapped children, private schools, and the like.

Table 4. Preschool Handicapped children receiving services from private organizations at local unit level (FY 1973)

Organization	Estimate of number served	Ages reported serving
National Association for Retarded Children (NARC)	2,800	"Preschool"
National Easter Seal	120,765	0–5
United Cerebral Palsy (UCP)	20,000	0–6
Total	143,565	

TRAINING FOR PERSONNEL WORKING WITH PRESCHOOL HANDICAPPED CHILDREN

Figures released by the Bureau of Education for the Handicapped (BEH), Division of Personnel Preparation, indicate that approximately 500,000 teachers are needed to educate handicapped children in the United States. Approximately 18 percent of handicapped children needing services are preschool-age handicapped children. Thus, 18 percent of 500,000 teachers represent an estimated total of 90,000 teachers needed at this level. If, as was previously estimated, 26 percent of preschool handicapped children are in service programs, then they are being served by 31,500 teachers, which leaves a remaining need of 58,500 teachers to serve preschool handicapped children. The following data intend to delineate the sort of training available to prepare teachers of preschool handicapped children.

Pre-service Training

The major source of federal legislation for training teachers for preschool handicapped children appears to be Title VI, Section D of the Elementary and Secondary Education Act (ESEA). This legislation authorizes payments to universities to train teachers, teacher trainers, and to support personnel for educating handicapped children. In addition to universities, the BEH may make payments to state education agencies to assist them in in-service and pre-service training programs. Title VI-D is administered by the Bureau through "block grants" to universities (through which universities may allocate funds at their discretion, based on targeted activities), grants to assist in developing university programs, grants for projects meeting special needs, and training grants to state education agencies. Many of the universities choose to award fellowships and scholarships in special education and to augment faculty and staff to improve the quality in training of special education personnel. Well over 400 such universities, in all states, receive Title VI-D funds each year.

Because many of the funds administered under this act are awarded to universities on a "block grant" basis, it is difficult to trace the number of students being trained by these funds. Present data from the Division of Personnel (Table 5) indicate that, for fiscal year 1972, a total of 356 students were trained in early childhood education. Of this number, 227 students were full-time, and the remaining 129 were part-time students. The figures indicate that the training patterns are generally directed toward graduate rather than undergraduate studies. These figures do not take into account the number of university students trained to work with young hard-of-hearing/deaf children. Present estimates by Division of Personnel Preparation, BEH, would indicate that current training patterns are not expected to produce many more students per year than was indicated in 1972 to 1973.

Such figures indicate that federal efforts at pre-service training for teachers of preschool handicapped children are totally inadequate to meet the manpower demands within the foreseeable future. At best, the pre-service training by the BEH could expect only to further educate and provide supervision of pre-service and in-service training or personnel working with preschool handicapped children.

In-service Training

The major thrust in the training of teachers to work with preschool handicapped children appears to lie in the area of in-service training, that is, the retraining of personnel to work with preschool handicapped children. It is impossible to define in-service training further than to say that it consists of short-term observations, conducted in practicum settings, and that it is pragmatically oriented. None of the following data include characteristics of academic levels of personnel trained, length of training, content of training, types of handicapped children studied, and the like.

The major in-service federal program for training of personnel to work with preschool handicapped children appears to lie within the Handicapped Children's Early Education Program, in which in-service training is permitted by the demonstration projects. Table 6 indicates that during fiscal year 1972 to 1973, the HCEEP projects trained a total of 19,928 personnel through in-service programs. This training included providing the practica for 2,580 child development students (not necessarily preparing for a career in training preschool *handicapped* children). Such figures clearly indicate that the trend in

Table 5. Total enrollment of full- and part-time trainees in ECE in institutions of higher education receiving training monies from the division of training programs—BEH (academic year 1973)

Training level	Full-time	Part-time	Totals
Undergraduate	59	—	59
Master's degree	137	121	258
Post-master's degree	31	8	39
Totals	227	129	356

Table 6. Persons   receiving   training   through HCEEP projects (FY 1972 to 1973)

Persons	No. trained
HCEEP staff	1,519
HCEEP paraprofessionals	1,907
Head Start staff	2,420
Public school educators	4,369
Day care	2,625
Nursery school	3,061
Volunteers	1,447
Practicum (college and university)	2,580
Total	19,928

the training of personnel to serve preschool handicapped children appears to be in the direction of in-service training. Examination of the above figures, however, cannot give an indication of the numbers of children that will eventually be serviced by this training. Indeed, many teachers trained in in-service education are preparing to work with small numbers of preschool handicapped children integrated with larger numbers of non-handicapped children. The trend toward in-service training in the area of preschool handicapped children seems to reflect a trend toward "mainstreaming" preschool handicapped with preschool non-handicapped children, using in-service training as a facilitator of this administrative pattern. The in-service trend also appears to be in response to the small numbers of trained preschool service personnel. Recognition of the great need for such training has probably resulted in make-shift efforts at mass training. In-service training appears, therefore, the fastest way of producing personnel capable of dealing with the educational problems of preschool handicapped children.

The Head Start program indicated that approximately 39,000 preschool handicapped children are being served in those programs. Because of the integrated nature of these programs, it is perhaps conservative to estimate that at least 3,900 teachers and 3,900 aides are required to serve these children. Head Start has allocated Training and Technical Assistance funds in each region to help influence the training of these personnel. It is difficult to obtain the numbers of personnel trained by Training and Technical Assistance funds to affect adequate staffing of Head Start for preschool handicapped children. It is assumed, however, that since the HCEEP program has trained 2,420 of these personnel, the additional 5,000 personnel needed to adequately train preschool handicapped children in Head Start programs will have to be trained from Training and Technical Assistance funds. Whether or not training of that number of personnel has yet occurred is presently unknown.

Personnel are also trained under the demonstration programs of Title VI, Section B with the monies allocated to state education agencies from Title VI, Section D. At present, however, no figures are available which indicate the number of preschool personnel trained by such programs.

In summary, it would appear that the training programs for personnel to teach preschool handicapped children are woefully lacking in quantity. If approximately 58,000 teachers are needed for educating preschool handicapped children, we are probably a decade away from this target by in-service methods and a millennium away by pre-service methods. What appear to be needed are examinations of in-service programs and standards of teacher competency that may be uniformly taught throughout the country. Because in-service training appears to be the most favored by the field at present, certification standards of great detail would appear helpful and appropriate. The increase in efforts of quality of in-service training through the various federal and private model and demonstration programs would appear to be essential.

STATE LAWS GOVERNING THE
EDUCATION OF PRESCHOOL HANDICAPPED CHILDREN

State laws for preschool handicapped children are contained in Table 7, a product of the state and federal information clearinghouse on handicapped children of the Council for Exceptional Children. An analysis of the laws pertaining to preschool handicapped children by states indicates that, in 1974, 13 states had laws mandating provisions for handicapped children, 30 states had provisions for permissive legislation for preschool handicapped children, and eight states had no provisions for educational services for preschool handicapped children (the District of Columbia is included in these figures).

Table 7. Frequency and lower age limits of mandatory, permissive, and no provisions legislation for educational services to preschool handicapped children (1971 to 1974)

Lower age limits (years)	Number of states by type of legislation[a]					
	Mandatory		Permissive		No provisions	
	1971	1974	1971	1974	1971	1974
0–1	2	4	19	19	In 1971, 12 states had no provi-	
1–2	–	–	–	–	sions under a State Education Agency.	
2–3	1	1	–	1	Three of these states were providing	
3–4	3	6	10	8	educational services under other	
4–5	2	2	2	3	agencies	
5–6	–	–	–	–	In 1974, 8 states had no provisions	
6+	–	–	–	–	under an Educational Agency. Two of these states were providing educational services through other agencies	
Totals	8	13	31	30	1971:12 (3); 1974:8 (2)	

[a]Includes District of Columbia.

These data show that a moderate trend in changing preschool handicapped legislation has been in the area of mandatory legislation. Numerically, this suggests that a total of five states have changed their legislative provisions since 1971.

The quality of preschool education programs in many states may be determined by the day care license procedures in those states. Historically, the licensing of facilities and personnel for child day care services has been under the jurisdiction of state and local governments. However, a 1971 study sponsored jointly by the Office of Child Development and the Office of Economic Opportunity (OCD-OEO) reports that the data from each of the 50 states point to two rather consistent findings: 1) that local and county governments are often the agencies with principle responsibility for processing day care license applications, and 2) that there is an enormous lack of uniformity, not only between states but within states, for almost any facet of day care licensing.

The OCD-OEO report further suggests that the above findings have been a great impediment to efficient functioning of day care programs in general. Because of the fragmented responsibilities between various administrative organizations, there has been confusion in licensing purposes and individual organizational responsibilities that has resulted in unresolved regulation, policy, and procedure discrepancies.

One dimension in which this variability can be seen is a categorical representation across those states that have educational requirements for teacher and director positions in day care programs. Twenty-seven states report the necessity for directors of day care centers to have had some college or equivalent experience; seven states require a minimum of high school graduation, and the remaining 16 states have no explicit educational requirements for the director. Unfortunately, the requirements for teachers in those state day care centers are less vigorous. Only 16 states require those teachers to have had some college or equivalent experience; nine states require a minimum of high school graduation, and the remaining 25 states specify no educational requirements for their day care teachers.

As a result not only of these staff educational requirement differences across states but also of differences in various other program areas dealing with certification for day care centers, task forces involved in the OCD-OEO study have proposed a model day care licensing plan for states to follow. The plan has suggested minimum requirements for: 1) day care licensing, 2) program and staff requirements, 3) health and sanitation requirements, and 4) fire and safety requirements. Although in many instances the suggested regulations and compliance requirements are undoubtedly less than those required by some states, those suggestions for inclusion in a state plan by the OCD-OEO model, if followed, would greatly enhance the state day care provisions in many states. And there would be a direct result of improved services to the children served in those centers.

In summary, progress in providing educational services for preschool handicapped children of all ages through state legislation appears slow. At the present time, the majority of states providing supportive legislation provide it for children above the age of 3. Provisions for children at the infant level occur only in about one third of the states. There appears to be a trend toward mandatory preschool education for the handicapped, but change in this direction is slow. Licensing procedures for day care programs offer little hope for standards of personnel fully equipped to educate preschool handicapped children.

RELEVANT ISSUES

Educational Technology for Preschool Handicapped Children

Because of the unique nature of educating preschool handicapped children, the design of educational technology has been difficult but, when successful, innovative. For purposes of this report, hardware is defined as that type of machinery which assists the child in self-instruction or is stimulating.

The BEH has supported several projects that provide technological hardware in the service of preschool education. At the Lexington School for the Deaf in New York City, research programs are demonstrating the effectiveness of self-stimulating toys in the production of speech and babbling sounds in infants. In Ladsen, South Carolina, an HCEEP project, which involves the use of musical tape cassettes in the homes of severely handicapped children, is being investigated for potential therapeutic value. A project in New Jersey assists parents and teachers, through computer retrieval systems, to assist in the remediation of instructional and developmental problems of their preschool learning disabled youngsters.

Software, or instructional systems to fit hardware, are being designed by many of the demonstration projects in the HCEEP program. Many of these materials are available through a publication entitled, *First Chance Products: A Catalogue of Instructional and Evaluative Materials,* produced by the Technical Assistance Development System at the Unversity of North Carolina, Chapel Hill, North Carolina. The Head Start program is producing resource books that will contain instructional hints and systems for the integration of handicapped with non-handicapped children. The National Center for Educational Media Materials for the Handicapped, Ohio State University, Columbus, Ohio, is developing a library of preschool instructional systems which may, eventually, be usable by administrators or teachers interested in educating preschool handicapped children.

Through research and early childhood education grants from the BEH, new systems of therapeutic play are being developed through the design of innovative playgrounds. At New York University in New York City, the "Mini-Playground," attached to the Rehabilitation Institute, is helping preschool crippled children regain their motor functions. The United Cerebral Palsy school project in New York City is working with inflatable exercise and play equipment that is therapeutically stimulating. The preschool program for Mexican-American children in Las Cruces, New Mexico, is experimenting with newly designed self-stimulating indoor playground equipment. Similar types of experimentation are occurring in almost all of the demonstration projects. As a result, it is expected that generalizations and assumptions on the use of playground equipment to stimulate growth and development will be produced in the future. There appears to be no definitive synthesizing of the use of this equipment at the present time.

In summary, the use of educational technology and systems of hardware, software, and therapeutic environments is in its infancy. When put to informal evaluation, utilization of educational technology for the education of preschool handicapped children has proven promising. Credibility will, however, lie on better programmed research in this area. Because the Division of Research of the BEH will soon be engaging in conferences setting priorities for research in the area of education for preschool handicapped children, perhaps educational technology will assume its rightfully visible place.

Models

To suggest that there is a single "model," or at best even a few "models," in which all programs of early intervention for handicapped children can be neatly categorized is illusory. Frequently, such attempts to do so categorize those "models" on a single program variable. It is far too simplistic to categorize in this fashion without recognition of the complexity of programs across other program variables.

Historically, types of handicapping condition and age of the handicapped child have received major consideration in attempts to define the boundaries on which a given program for handicapped children operates. There are and have been established numerous programs to serve children whose principle diagnosis is mental retardation, learning disabled, emotionally disturbed, speech impaired, deaf, blind, orthopedically handicapped, or developmentally delayed. However, over the past few years there has been a major thrust to forego the strict, categorical classification procedures and, instead, to view the child on the merits of his level of functioning as opposed to his level of dysfunction. The results of this can perhaps be seen in the fact that programs frequently do not restrict the population that they serve to a primary diagnosis, but, rather, are expanding services across multiple handicapping conditions. Most first, second, and third year HCEEP projects are reported to be serving numerous types of handicaps. Very few projects are serving only one categorical handicapping condition, and all handicapping conditions are well represented in terms of the number of projects serving them.

The age of the handicapped child has traditionally been a determinator in the nature and location of services delivered to the handicapped child. In the not too distant past, it was felt that the standard age for entry to public school was also the appropriate time to begin planned intervention in other than the basic health needs of the handicapped child. However, the advent of compensatory education has seen developmental/educational intervention now occurring in infancy.

A third variable by which a program may be identified is that of physical location (or site) for direct child intervention. When considering handicapped children at all ages, it has unquestionably been the center-based program that has been most numerous. As can be seen in Table 8, the center-based program is still most numerous, only slightly more so than the combination of Home/Center program. Within this variable alone are several

Table 8. Number and type of HCEEP projects by location of intervention (1974)

Type	1st Year	2nd Year	3rd Year	Total
Home-based	2	3	1	6
Center-based	18	11	11	40
Home/center-based	10	16	13	39

other considerations as to the site considered most appropriate for a given population. The younger the child, the more frequently the intervention will be in a home-based or combined situation, while the older children (ages 3 to 6 years) are more likely to be housed in a central facility. The distribution of population served also will generally have an effect on the type of program selected by project staff. The more rural the area, the more likely it is that the home will be the site for intervention. Home intervention is frequently administered by parents, with periodic home visits by project staff for planning and demonstration of intervention techniques and lessons. However, staff monitoring need not always be done in the home. It may be done at the center, with the parent observing the child interventionist and then taking home the materials and "techniques" necessary to work with the next series of lessons.

Intervention with older children, as indicated, is typically in a more center-based arrangement. Interventionists here may be project staff, aides, volunteers, etc., with a head teacher generally responsible for the arrangement of the educational environment. Emphasis for parent involvement is also frequently present in center-based programs.

Much of the federal monies for direct services to children specify that each program is to submit specific plans for training of personnel. Determination of those children receiving training is largely a function of the three previously discussed variables (handicapping condition, age of child, location for intervention). Logically, if the principle means for intervention is in a center-based facility, project staff must possess the skill necessary to the particular intervention approach utilized by the project. Therefore, it is usually necessary to give main consideration to the need for professional staff development, because project staff may serve not only as interventionists but as trainers to other on-site paraprofessionals or to parents for home intervention. In either case, the professional staff are the ones who typically make daily environmental decisions as to what type of activities are available to the child. Paraprofessionals and parents are frequently given training in techniques for adult-child interaction that can be applied to activities in the natural home environment.

Of the relatively few variables considered here in established "models" for intervention, none is probably more hotly debated than the design of educational curriculum for the child. While compensatory education has largely been acclaimed for its promotion of learning for later school achievement, there is considerable diversity of opinion as to how those educational experiences should be arranged.

There have been a number of "models" developed for child intervention, but these have largely developed around theoretical orientation, have coined their own terms, and have seldom been considered to exist on a continuum of education intervention techniques. Lillie (1975) suggests that all curricular models exist along a continuous plane of "formality." Although Mayer (1971) does not utilize the term "formality," she would surely agree with Lillie that the basics for considerations along this continuum are in terms of teacher-child, child-material, and child-child interactions.

Four prominent models can be placed sequentially along this continuum by the above interrelationships. However, it must be emphasized that the parameters of the four models are not discrete and that projects purporting to be representative of a particular model may, in fact, be using techniques comparable to those of other models.

A composite of the Lillie and Mayer descriptors applied to well known child-intervention models might result in the following representation of those four models along a left to right continuum of intervention techniques, identified as "informal" to "formal" in nature (Figure 1).

The *Child Development Model* is steeped in "enrichment" with multiple activity areas (art, science, library, housekeeping, etc.) and can easily be recognized as the "model" for many middle class preschool programs and the one model that Head Start adopted in its advent. At each of the activity areas, a teacher or aide is ideally stationed. Their role is to facilitate child involvement and exploration at each station to which a child moves at will. The interactive process is highly child-to-child oriented, with a premium on social and emotional development. Specific learning tasks are not provided because direct instruction is contrary to the concept maintained that, at this developmental stage, the child lacks the readiness to learn from direct instruction, and, therefore, accelerated learning through direct teaching may be harmful to the child's appropriate growth pattern.

Maria Montessori (1964) is the originator of what is here referred to as the *Sensory-Cognitive Model*. The basis for a child's activities here is principally through neatly and orderly arranged manipulative materials in an environment that is constructed with the child in mind. All furniture and wall organizations are appropriate to the size and development of the child and are arranged in systematic order, with classroom space that each child can consider his own.

Each of the manipulative materials are carefully sequenced in size and complexity, reflecting the stage-oriented philosophy. Each child is maximally involved in arranging,

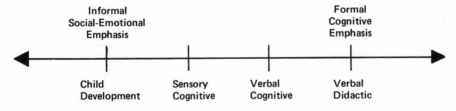

Figure 1. A continuum representation of child-teacher-material interaction.

cleaning, and classifying materials, although he is free to move about the room. Little emphasis is given to language development because Montessori saw small children at a stage insensitive to language development. Intelligence, to Montessori, was the ability to order and to classify objects and concepts as a result of the carefully sequenced materials.

With the classroom arranged into "activity areas," as was the Child Development Model, the *Verbal-Cognitive Model* allows the teacher to take a much more forward approach to directed learning. Weikart's Perry Preschool Model (Weikart et al., 1970) draws heavily on the developmental theory of Piaget, as evidenced by teacher-child interaction, with the teacher eliciting child responses about a particular activity and its generalization to other situations. A child is free to choose the activity he wishes, and he is free to move about or to stay in one area, even after the work for that session is finished. Frequently, each day is begun with a planning period and concluded with a review and evaluation of those previously planned and executed activities.

The most "formal" of the four models considered here is the *Verbal-Didactic Model* championed by Bereiter and Englemann, and is illustrated through their Distar materials. The principle idea of this approach is that there are certain prerequisites a child should have before entering first grade. As a result of this attempt to raise every child to this essential level for success in first grade, each teacher assumes the responsibility for a particular curricular area with all the children. Each teacher then proceeds to group children into groups of similar ability and to lead them through the commercially prepared materials (reading, language, and math) in a highly teacher-oriented verbal sequence of statements, questions, and child responses. The basics of the approach can be viewed as frequent repetition of teacher-child responses accompanied by principles of reinforcement.

The last variable to be considered here with any detail is that of the administrative management and direction. Every project must have some figure or governing body that can be held accountable for the function of that project. Historically, services to handicapped children have been provided primarily through state agencies (i.e., Departments of Mental Health, residential facilities, etc.). However, legislation within the past few years has expanded the scope of services and, as a result, the administrative possibilities for those services. The First Chance Network (HCEEP) is an example of that expansion to many sectors. Table 9 shows that six basic administrative units have been identified as serving current first, second, and third year programs.

Public schools and private agencies presently hold administrative responsibilities for approximately two thirds of the HCEEP projects. Most of the public school projects are direct classroom services, while the private agencies are made up of many of the nationally recognized organizations devoted to upgrading services to handicapped children (National Association of Retarded Citizens, United Cerebral Palsy, Easter Seal Society, etc.). However, other agencies with administrative responsibilities across HCEEP projects include: state agencies, federal agencies, universities, and hospitals.

This section has dealt mainly with five variables that are considered to be of major importance when discussing preschool intervention. Those variables include: 1) handi-

Table 9. Number and type of administrative agencies of first, second, and third year HCEEP projects (1974)

Type	1st Year	2nd Year	3rd Year	Total
Public schools	11	14	6	31
Private agency	8	8	12	28
State agency	6	3	2	11
Federal agency	2	–	–	2
University	3	5	4	12
Hospital	–	–	1	1

capping condition, 2) physical location of project, 3) targets of training, 4) intervention models, and 5) administrative units. However, it must be recognized that there are many variables that could be considered in defining "models" for intervention. Other potential variables that have direct effect on services to children but left unresolved here include: 1) isolative versus integrative populations, 2) levels of funding from funding agent, 3) number of children served by the project, and 4) services delivered by project, to mention only a few. It is the position of these authors that a "model" must take into consideration many more variables than has traditionally been the case if a "model" is to be considered for replication.

Research

A review of the federal agencies' efforts to fund research in the area of preschool education for the handicapped shows an impressive amount of monies being expended in this area, $8,855,536, excluding BEH projects. (A list of those projects may be obtained by writing TADS, University of North Carolina, Chapel Hill, North Carolina.) The general classification of types of research funded by these agencies is listed in Table 10, which shows a scattering of topics among these kinds of research, but a decidedly heavy emphasis on research dealing with effectiveness of direct child intervention systems. (A listing of those projects funded by the Bureau of Education for the Handicapped can be obtained by writing the BEH, Office of Education.)

In recent years, the BEH has attempted to determine further research priorities in the area of preschool handicapped programs, and it commissioned Dr. Thomas Jordan to conduct a needs assessment of those priorities. His conclusions (Jordon, 1971) call for an emphasis in research paradigms that test direct child intervention systems. The BEH is in the process of letting another contract to conduct further research seminars to identify current and updated priorities in early childhood education research. Input from experts in the field, however, indicate that wide-spread dissemination of research findings has not yet been accomplished with efficacy. Furthermore, there seems to be a decided lack of longitudinal research or studies that show the lasting effects of preschool intervention on handicapped children. Many of the demonstration projects are interested in systematic

Table 10. Other types of research funded by federal agencies (excluding BEH) in the area of preschool handicapped children (1974)

Type of research	Number of funded projects
Basic research	6
Causation/prevention (medical)	13
Developmental—effects of handicapping condition (skills)	15
Developmental—parent-child interaction	6
Developmental—social effects of handicapping condition	10
Diagnostic/assessment	4
Direct child intervention	27
Dissemination network development	1
Totals	81

testing of transdisciplinary intervention techniques, a difficult research task at the least. Research, therefore, can best be characterized as spotty and uncoordinated, with need from the field to program, synthesize, and "repackage" it for the practitioner.

STATE-OF-THE-ART SUMMARY

It appears from analysis of interagency data at the federal, state, and local levels, that there is considerable movement in the field of preschool education for handicapped children. The federal government, through its service and training programs, is slowly building a cadre of trained personnel with sufficient expertise to assist others in setting up preschool intervention programs. Private organizations have responded to the need for services that could not be provided in the public sector by establishing private preschool centers. Integration and mainstreaming efforts are occurring in all types of preschool agencies. Despite all of these efforts, however, no more than 26 percent of preschool handicapped children seem to be getting the services they need.

Perhaps this lack of services is caused, in great part, by the lack of trained personnel. A survey of university training programs for the preschool education of teachers equipped to work with preschool handicapped children shows that such programs are small, with little annual yield of trained teachers. Indeed, the largest thrust in the training of personnel seems to be in the in-service area, with major activities occurring because of federal programs. At the rate teachers are being trained both at the pre-service and in-service levels, however, the potential for fulfilling the manpower needs for educating all preschool handicapped children does not seem to be a reality before the targeted date of 1980.

Because the task of educating preschool handicapped children is seen as a state function, the potential of states to support preschool programming was discussed. It was noted that states tend to be changing their laws to mandate services for preschool children, but this change is slow, and preschool children seem to be defined as being more than 3 years of age. Furthermore, state certification and licensing standards do not seem to be any more adequate to ensure trained personnel of high quality to meet the needs of preschool handicapped children than if state laws were more supportive. Indeed, there seems to be a need to increase state support for preschool handicapped programs down to the birth level. Re-examination of certification standards is necessary to ensure excellence of personnel in dealing with such children.

The need for further development in educational technology of preschool handicapped children was noted. Small but significant starts in this area have been made, primarily through programs funded by the BEH, but many additional breakthroughs are needed to simplify and enrich preschool intervention programs for handicapped children.

The labeling of preschool programs as models is a conceptual effort that still needs completion. Although "model" programs have been developed by federal and private sources, there is no common vocabulary to designate what models are, nor evaluation schemes to determine the effectiveness of one model over another. A classification terminology has been suggested in this chapter.

The state of research in early childhood education supported by federal monies appears promising. A relatively large amount of money is being spent on research throughout the various agencies of the government, but there has been no attempt to coordinate, synthesize, and re-package this research for the practitioner, the student, and future researchers. There needs to be, therefore, further emphasis on programming research to answer major research questions, including longitudinal effects of preschool intervention, and a re-prioritizing of research needs.

Because of the major investments of the federal government in preschool education for handicapped children, such education can assume a unique role of leadership in the orchestrated thrust toward the development of the field of education for preschool handicapped children.

LITERATURE CITED

Borinsky, M. E. 1973. Provision of Instruction to Handicapped Pupils in Local Public Schools. Office of Education, Department of Health, Education, and Welfare, Washington, D.C.

Jordon, T., W. Cegelka, E. Gotts, H. Goldstein, F. Kelly, J. Schein, and H. Quay. 1971. Recommendations on priorities for research concerning the education of young handicapped children: A report from the National Program on Early Childhood Education (CEMREL) to the Bureau for Education of the Handicapped. National Program on Early Childhood Education, St. Ann, Missouri.

Lillie, D. L. 1975. Early Childhood Curriculum: An Individualized Approach. Science Research Associates, Chicago.

Mayer, R. S. 1971. A comparative analysis of preschool curriculum models. *In* R. H. Anderson and H. G. Shane (eds.), As the Twig is Bent: Reading in Early Childhood Education. Houghton Mifflin, Boston.

Montessori, M. 1964. The Montessori Method. Schocken, New York.

Office of Child Development. 1971. Day Care Licensing Study Summary Report on Phase 1: State and Local Day Care Licensing Requirements. Department of Health, Education, and Welfare, Washington, D.C.

Office of Child Development. 1973a. Head Start Services to Handicapped Children. Department of Health, Education, and Welfare, Washington, D.C.

Office of Child Development. 1973b. Guides for Day Care Licensing. Department of Health, Education, and Welfare, Washington, D.C.

Office of Child Development. 1974. Guides for Day Care Licensing. Department of Health, Education, and Welfare, Washington, D.C.

Weikart, D. P., et al. 1970. Longitudinal results of the Ypsilanti Perry Preschool Project. High Scope Educational Research Foundation, Ypsilanti, Mich.

Pediatric Care and Training: A Paradox?

Felix F. de la Cruz, M.D., M.P.H., F.A.A.P.

In his address to the members of the Academy of Pediatrics as its first president in 1931, Dr. Isaac Abt told its members that the Academy should "courageously defend ... the rights of the sick and oppressed, promote development of child health, and demand the highest professional standards of morality and education among its members." Over the years, the Academy, with a membership which now exceeds 15,000, has maintained a strong position of advocacy to advance the cause of child health. Its members have tried to uphold the Academy's official goal: "The attainment by all children of the Americas of their full potential for physical, emotional, and social health." In light of the changing pattern of pediatric care, which has resulted in an increasing involvement of pediatricians in the emotional, social, and learning problems of children, are pediatricians properly trained to meet this challenge?

CHANGES IN THE PATTERN OF PEDIATRIC PRACTICE

The pattern of pediatric practice has been evolving for the past several years, particularly since the early 1960s. This period was characterized by the passage of legislative measures that have significant effect on children. These measures include, among others, the establishment of the National Institute of Child Health and Human Development, Project Head Start, Maternal and Infant Care Programs, Medicaid, and Children and Youth Projects.

The changes in the nature of pediatric practice were also affected significantly by improved nutrition, better feeding practices, notably, feeding infants with sterilized milk, wider use of routine immunization against infectious agents, modern sanitation, and the availability of vastly improved chemotherapeutic agents.

In 1934, C. Anderson Aldrich (1934) reported an analysis of the composition of his own private pediatric practice in a fairly well-to-do suburban community. He conducted the study in order to provide a sample of the "relative frequency of the diseases and conditions incurred by the pediatric practitioner . . . as an index to the kind of work for which students are being prepared." Almost 50 percent of his practice was devoted to the care of infectious diseases and 35 percent to the routine care of infants and children, while only 0.5 percent dealt with problems involving the central nervous system and "psychological problems." Aldrich indicated, however, that this 0.5 percent figure was an underestimate and did not reflect the true prevalence of psychological problems, and the time devoted to their prevention in his practice.

Boulware (1958) evaluated the composition of his pediatric practice covering the years 1930 to 1955, using the same analysis of data applied by Aldrich in 1934. The management of infectious diseases and routine care of infants and children took 37 percent each of his time; 2 percent was devoted to the care of disorders involving the central nervous system and psychological problems.

In a more recent study, Rosenbloom (1974) analyzed all 277 million contacts between patients from birth to 15 years of age and private practitioners in 1971 based on information obtained from the National Disease and Therapeutic Index. The Index contains various information about medical practice, such as reasons for and frequency of seeking medical consultation and who provided the medical care. Information is furnished by a sample of physicians from a population that includes all medical doctors and osteopathic physicians in private practice in the United States and excludes only those without primary patient contact. In 1970, pediatricians accounted for 6 percent of all private practicing physicians, but they provided 38 percent of care in 1971 on patients from birth to 15 years of age. Physicians in general practice constituted 31 percent of the total number of physicians in private practice, and they provided 36.6 percent of child-patient contacts. Half the pediatricians' contacts were with patients under 2 years of age, 36 percent with children 2 to 9 years of age, and only 14 percent with those 10 years of age or older. In 1972, 72 percent of the patient contacts were in the office, while 9 percent accounted for hospital contacts. Routine care of infants and children accounted for 36 percent of these contacts, approximately 27 percent for the care of various types of infectious diseases, and almost 10 percent for diseases of the central nervous system, sense organs, and behavioral problems.

A questionnaire survey of 2,000 pediatricians carried out by R. A. Aldrich in 1959 showed that on a typical day (i.e., "yesterday"), a pediatrician sees over 5 percent of children with emotional-behavioral problems (Aldrich, 1960). The contemporary pediatricians' increasing involvement in the care of problems dealing with behavior is apparent when compared to the experience reported by C. A. Aldrich in 1934 and Boulware in 1958.

How are the current pediatricians being trained with sufficient knowledge to enable them to manage efficiently and effectively nonphysical problems that are commonly encountered in pediatric practice?

In 1964, the chairmen of the departments of pediatrics within the medical schools in the United States organized formally into an association so that "they could better meet the national needs for education and research in child health and human development" (Wedgwood, 1972). In 1966 to 1967, an inventory was made of the teaching, service, and research sources of funding and other activities of its members. A follow up inventory was carried out in 1970 to 1971.

The initial inventory showed that nationally there were 2,177 residents in pediatric programs. The 80 departments reporting in the inventory identified responsibility for 1,198 pediatric residents. In addition, there were 741 interns, 53 percent of whom were "straight pediatric interns," while the rest were "mixed" or "rotating interns." (The 1970 to 1971 inventory showed that 80 percent of the interns in the 75 reporting departments of pediatrics were "straight," i.e., care and training dealt exclusively with infants and children.)

The inventory distinguished between two settings—in-patient and ambulatory facilities—and four different categories of patients seen—newborn and premature infants, well child and child development, children with chronic diseases, and "other," which includes the usual acute illnesses of childhood. Interns spend, on the average, nearly 70 percent of their time on the in-patient service. This decreases with each succeeding year of residency to a minimum of about 50 percent for the third year resident. Ambulatory care constituted 25 percent of the interns' assignment, while about one third of the time was spent during each year of residency. It was not until the third year of residency that the trainee spent a significant amount of time (approximately 17 percent) in special settings such as rehabilitation units and special clinics. The intern, first year resident, and second year resident each spent approximately 5 percent of his assignment in these special settings (Figure 1).

Similar changes in emphasis in the type of training were also apparent in the categories of patients seen (Figure 2). Well child and child development problems represented a fairly consistent proportion of the experience throughout internship and residency (approximately 10 to 14 percent). Newborn and premature infants received emphasis in the internship and first year residency (26 and 28 percent) and slightly less emphasis later. As the physician gained experience, there was a marked increase in attention to chronic diseases that consumed almost one third of his time by the third year. There was, therefore, a perceptible shift in training from hospitalized to ambulatory and from acute to chronic disease care during house officer training (Wedgwood, 1967).

Whether or not the type and quality of training that pediatricians receive prepare them to manage the problems that they will often meet in private practice is still open to question. Unfortunately, a large-scale survey to answer this question has not been carried out since the two inventories were completed by the Association of Medical Pediatric Chairmen in 1966 and 1971.

However, in 1964 a study was originated by the Joint Committee on Pediatric Research, Education, and Practice (PREP)[1] to obtain information pertinent to the adequacy of pediatric residency training requirements: "Both content and duration of residency programs were . . . studied as a basis for the American Board of Pediatrics to

---

[1] The committee on PREP is composed of representatives from the American Board of Pediatrics, the American Academy of Pediatrics, the American Pediatric Society, the Pediatric Section of the American Medical Association, and the Society for Pediatric Research.

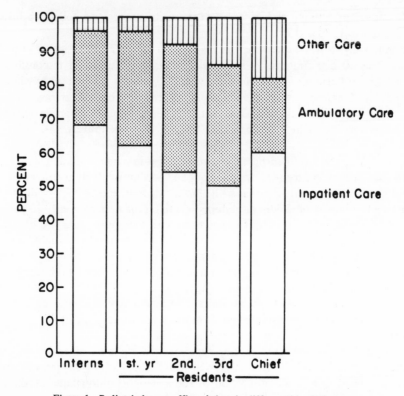

Figure 1. Pediatric house officers' time in different hospital areas.

review need to promulgate modification in programs considered conducive to the Board's general purpose of providing the child population with the highest possible caliber of trained physicians" (Cornely, 1965; Cooke, 1965). To study the adequacy of pediatric residency training, the opinion of every pediatrician in the United States was sought by means of a questionnaire, and a sample of 60 directors of pediatric residency programs were interviewed.

Sixty percent of the pediatricians reported that management of disorders of mental and emotional development were frequently encountered in their practice. Thirty-five percent of these pediatricians felt that they possessed a low level of competence to manage these problems; 38 percent reported a frequent occurrence in their practice of problems dealing with management of sensory and motor developmental disorders; 17 percent of them reported a low level of competence to manage these programs (Table 1).

When asked to rate training opportunities in selected program areas during pediatric residency, 57 percent of practitioners reported insufficient training opportunities were available in continuing care of various manifestations of chronic cerebral dysfunction such as mental retardation and cerebral palsy. Almost three out of every four practitioners rated insufficient training opportunity in the various child care activities in the

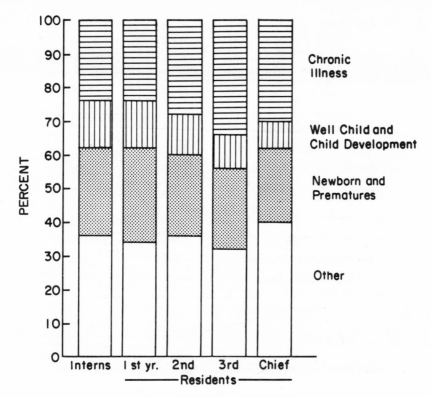

Figure 2. Pediatric house officers' time with different patient categories.

community, schools, and courts (Table 2). The responses of the practitioners, which constituted over 80 percent of the total sample, did not differ significantly from the ratings of the institutional group of pediatricians. The latter group consisted of all pediatricians in full-time salary positions, full-time academic appointments, and full-time administrators.

As shown in Table 3, almost 1,500 respondents indicated a desire to delete areas of out-patient care from their general practice. A significant proportion of pediatricians indicated a desire to delete those portions of their practice dealing with well child care and psychological problems. Only a small proportion (60) suggested deletion of problems dealing with mental retardation from their practice.

Respondents were given the opportunity to identify from a specified list of reasons their choice of areas to delete from general pediatric practice. Because multiple *reasons* were permissible the number of reasons given, as shown in Table 4, exceeded the number of *areas* suggested for deletion. Low level of interest, low level of competence, and "uneconomical" were the predominant reasons given for deletion of mental retardation from their practice, while an overwhelming number of pediatricians gave low level of competence as their reason for deleting "psychological care" from their practice.

Table 1. Percentage distributions of ratings by pediatricians for selected areas of pediatric care, by frequency of occurrence, and feeling of competence

Areas	Frequent Occurrence	Low Competence
Assessment of Normal		
Physical Growth	91%	5%
Mental, Emotional Dev.	83%	19%
Sensory, Motor Dev.	68%	26%
Management of Disorders		
Physical Growth	46%	23%
Mental, Emotional Dev.	60%	35%
Sensory, Motor Dev.	38%	17%

Source: PREP Survey, 1965.

Table 2. Rating of training opportunities in pediatric residency by current position in pediatrics

Training Opportunities	Insufficient Training	
	Practitioner Group (N>6,000)	Institutional Group (N>1100)
Longitudinal care and study of well children	41%	42%
Longitudinal care and study of adolescents	87%	83%
Continuing care of chronic diseases as diabetes, cystic fibrosis	33%	30%
Continuing care of various manifestations of chronic cerebral dysfunction (M.R., C.P.)	57%	49%
Experience in child care as conducted in pediatric practitioner's office	58%	55%
Various child care activities in community, schools, courts	72%	68%
Teaching in hospital by practicing pediatricians	14%	13%

Source: PREP Survey, 1965

Table 3. Areas suggested to be deleted from general pediatrics by 1,457 pediatricians

Areas	Number of Respondents
Well Child Care	261
Psychological Care Problem	245
Practice Management (telephone calls, house calls, etc.)	208
Minor Medical/Surgical Problems	176
Mental Retardation Problems	60
Other	507
	1457

Source: PREP Survey, 1965.

Table 4. Reasons for deletion from pediatric practice for selected patient areas

	Low Clinical Importance	Uneconomical	Low Level Competence	Low Level Interest	Other	Total
Mental Retardation	7	10	16	18	21	72
Psychological Care	13	63	115	55	61	307
Well Child Care	89	29	0	111	62	291

Source: PREP Survey. 1965.

It is significant that not a single pediatrician rated "low level of competence" as the reason for the desire to delete well child care from their practice. A number of them expressed a low level of interest or felt that well child care was of low clinical importance.

Seventy percent of the respondents found their actual experience fairly close to or exactly like expectations; 18 percent gave a "50–50 response"; 8.6 percent rated their experience to be quite different from expectations; and 1.4 percent felt that their experience was nothing like what they expected pediatrics to be.

It is generally accepted that one's level of proficiency and skills is not always reflected on test score performance. Nevertheless, in the absence of a more acceptable device, examinations given by the various specialty boards will probably be with us for years to come. Figure 3 compares the mean scores for five subject categories that were included in the pediatric boards' written examination for the years 1968 to 1970. These are the mean total scores of 3,574 candidates examined from 188 training programs by first and fourth quartiles. The training programs in the top quartile appear to prepare their candidates equally well in each of the categories, while those in the bottom quartile show "singularly weak performances in the growth and development section of the examination" (Burg, 1972).

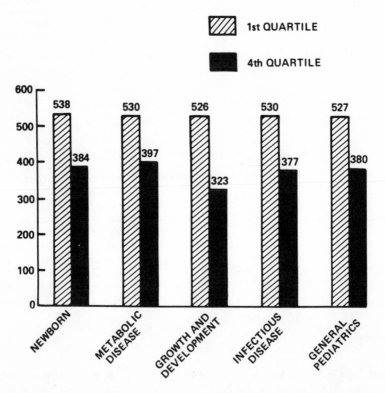

Figure 3. Comparison of mean category scores for all programs in the top and bottom quartile of total scores. (Reproduced with permission from Burg and Wright, 1972.)

One cannot determine the differential contribution of the trainee and the training program to the success or lack of success based on test scores without obtaining comparative scores for each house officer before and after completing his pediatric residency training. Of course, one can easily determine which training program or pediatric department consistently produces or regularly attracts unsuccessful candidates.

Any discussion that attempts to outline or to provide recommendations on training requirements or training models for pediatric house officers must take into account future utilization of its product: the pediatrician. The pediatrician's role must be responsive to community expectations, which are high quality, comprehensive, and continuous pediatric care. This expectation does not vary much from community to community (Aldrich et al., 1971). In addition, a recent survey of staff and families enrolled in a large Children and Youth Project supported the concept that provision of continuity of care in a pediatric setting, compared to a conventional or "multi-station clinic," yielded higher staff and client satisfaction, better patient-practitioner relationship, and greater efficiency (Becker et al., 1974).

Physicians are still responsible for the care of sick people and for preventing people from becoming ill. Substituting intensive work in the behavioral aspects of pediatrics for the medical aspects would be unwise. However, additional experience in pediatrics must be added to the training of pediatricians going into private practice if they are to be responsive to the needs of the community and the children that they serve. With the extension of health care to encompass behavioral, developmental, and cognitive problems, it has become evident that the medical model of care may not only limit but may even prevent professional intervention of these multifactorial problems. We should continue to explore the different roles pediatricians should assume and to plan for the appropriate training that will best prepare them to function within those roles.

PEDIATRIC MODELS

In a recent article, Pless (1974) discusses several models to meet existing demand for pediatric services.

Redistribution of Manpower

Pless (1974) argues that powerful incentives are needed to persuade doctors and their wives to settle in rural or inner city areas with limited educational, social, and cultural resources, or to at least spend more time in areas of greater need while continuing to live in more attractive parts of the country.

Increasing Professionalization: The Consultant Model

Patterned after the British model, the pediatrician will become more specialized and be a consultant to the family physicians and allied health professionals, who will provide primary pediatric care.

This model is in conflict with the concepts of continuous and comprehensive care. Besides, if all pediatricians were to restrict their practices to consultation, most would not be able to survive financially (Moghadam, 1974). Furthermore, Rosenbloom's (1974) analysis of private medical practice in the United States showed that, though the internist sees relatively few children (2 percent), he approaches the ideal of consulting pediatrician much more closely than does the pediatrician in practice. Internists see proportionately more children with complicated medical problems than do pediatricians.

Shifting Professionalization: Pediatricians in Family Medicine

This model provides that the same person who cares for children also provides medical care for older siblings and parents. This ensures continuity of care but runs into the problem of not having enough pediatricians with specialized knowledge and skill about the management of his adult patients. With increasing proportion of straight pediatric internship through the years (20 percent in 1960 to 1964, 22.8 percent before 1930 to 1964, 53 percent in 1966 to 1967, and 80 percent in 1970 to 1971), continuing emphasis in subspecialization, and the overrepresentation of superspecialists in pediatric faculties who provide the guidance and training to the new cadre of pediatricians, and the presence of a very small number of non-pediatricians or non-M.D. members in the pediatric faculty (in 1970 to 1971 there were 5.1 full-time equivalent non-pediatrician or non-M.D. faculty per pediatric department with an average total faculty size of 28 full-time equivalent), this model is doomed to failure. With this kind of an arrangement, the pediatrician's training will be inadequate to practice family medicine.

Decreasing Professionalization: The Expanded Primary Care Model

This model espouses the notion that the physician who accepts responsibility for the treatment of a child's bodily illnesses must also be responsible for the totality of the child's care. This will include management of psychological, social, environmental, behavioral, and cognitive problems as well as practicing preventive pediatrics. With his expanding role, the pediatrician will continue to collaborate and to work with other specialists such as psychologists, educators, public health nurses, speech pathologists, and audiologists, and a growing number of allied health professionals (Silver and Ott, 1973).

EARLY IDENTIFICATION OF CHILDREN AT RISK

Despite the pediatrician's unique opportunity to be the first qualified professional to see the preschool child, to have knowledge about the child's family, including prenatal history, nutrition, history of drug exposure, infections, particularly rubella, cytomegalic inclusion disease, toxoplasmosis, history of genetic disorders, knowledge of socioeconomic status, marital relationship, educational attainment and aspiration, child-rearing practices, family disequilibrium or even the potential for child abuse, the pediatrician often fails to capitalize on these opportunities for early identification and intervention of children at risk for emotional and cognitive disturbances. Led by Dr. Robert Aldrich (Aldrich et al., 1971), investigators at the University of Washington initiated a study in 1969 to investigate a variety of factors related to mental retardation services and the families that use them in selected communities in the state of Washington. They studied, among other variables, the age at which children were first suspected and confirmed as mentally retarded. The average age for suspicion of retardation ranged from 7.8 months for the profoundly retarded to 34.5 months for the mildly retarded. For all sampled children, the average age for suspicion was 25.0 months. The average elapsed time between suspicion and confirmation of mental retardation ranged from 6.2 months for the profoundly retarded to 12.0 months for the mildly retarded, with an average elapsed time of 11.0 months for all sampled children.

In a current national collaborative project administered by the United Cerebral Palsy Associations, Inc. (Figure 4), preliminary analysis of data obtained from about 600 infants showed that health nurses and social workers make more early referrals to the collaborating centers than do physicians (Meisel, personal communication).

There are other occasions when a pediatrician can make a significant contribution to the management of potentially damaging problems. Waldrop has shown that the presence of multiple minor physical anomalies is possibly associated with hyperkinetic, aggressive,

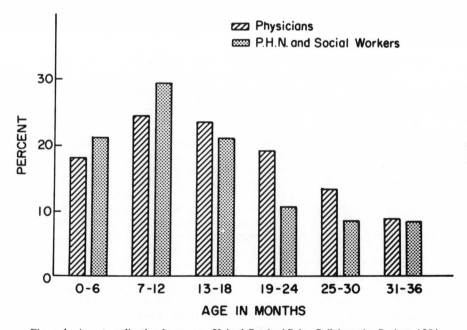

Figure 4. Age at application by source. United Cerebral Palsy Collaborative Project, 1974.

impatient, and intractable behavior (Waldrop et al., 1968; Waldrop and Goering, 1971; Waldrop and Halverson, 1971). Her observations have since been confirmed by Rosenberg and Weller (1973) and Quinn and Rapoport (1974).

Human adults can tolerate about 80 dB sound intensity without producing sensori-neural hearing loss regardless of duration. End-organ tolerance of newborn infants, particularly premature babies, is not known. In experimental animals excessive noise produces deafness by damaging the organ of Corti in the inner ear. Studies on guinea pigs have shown that newborn pups exhibit more pathological changes in the organ of Corti when compared to adult guinea pigs (Falk et al., 1974).

In a recent study, a group of Swedish investigators measured the noise levels inside five different kinds of incubators used for the intensive care of newborn, particularly premature, infants (Blennow et al., 1974). The study revealed 70 to 80 dB sound pressure level at 125 Hz. The recommended standard for an acceptable noise level on a hospital ward in Sweden is 30 dB (A). Since it is known that a noise level of 75 dB disturbs the sleep of infants more than 3 weeks old (Gadeke et al., 1969), and the incubator noise level to which infants, most of whom are prematures, are exposed for weeks or months, exceeds the recommended levels during sleeping hours of adults, it behooves us to examine this aspect of nursery care to determine its long-term sequelae.

There are other areas where pediatricians can play a major role in early identification and intervention. These include prenatal diagnosis of cytogenetic, metabolic, and structural abnormalities through transabdominal amniocentesis, fetoscopy, and amniography; malnutrition before and during pregnancy and its effect on the developing fetus; and early detection and treatment of strabismus, which is essential for visual rehabilitation (Adler and Goldstein, 1974).

Prenatal diagnosis followed, where indicated, by elective abortion is a complex problem because it involves moral, social, legal, ethical, and other issues. Because of its complexity, the positive aspects of prenatal diagnosis, eloquently summarized by Macintyre (1972), is often overlooked:

Incongruous as it may seem to some readers, prenatal genetic evaluation coupled with therapeutic abortion to eliminate a defective conceptus, is both a life-giving and a life-saving procedure. It is life-giving because it provides the means whereby a couple who desire children of their own, but are afraid to initiate pregnancy because of a known genetic risk, may have their desires fulfilled without fear. The procedure can be recognized as life-saving when one considers those cases in which pregnancy is unintentionally initiated by a couple with a known high risk, or in cases in which the risk is ascertained after pregnancy has been achieved. Experience has shown that almost without exception in such cases these couples initially elected to have the pregnancy terminated because of the genetic risk, despite the fact that the fetus might be normal. Prenatal evaluation has been employed in several such cases thus far, and in the majority of instances, abortion has been shown to be unnecessary because the fetus was not genetically unbalanced. There are, in fact, a number of healthy, desired youngsters living today whose lives literally have been saved by this type of genetic engineering, and I think that's great (p. 35).

Finally, the question of what constitutes an ideal training to best prepare pediatricians to cope with his expanding and changing responsibilities in pediatric care, including early assessment and management of high risk infants, is a complex, serious, and important problem that we cannot afford to ignore. If our goal is to help a child achieve his maximum potential as a contributing and happy citizen, we should continue our dialogue on this problem as professionals and concerned citizens dedicated to the welfare of our most important national resource: our children.

LITERATURE CITED

Adler, R., and J. H. Goldstein. 1974. Strabismus screening in pediatrics. J. Pediat. 84: 730–731.

Aldrich, C. A. 1934. The composition of private pediatric practice: A method for keeping adequate clinical records. Amer. J. Dis. Child. 47: 1051–1064.

Aldrich, R. A. 1960. Careers in pediatrics. In R. H. Spitz (ed.), Report of the Thirty-Sixth Ross Conference on Pediatric Research, pp. 57–76. Ross Laboratories, Columbus, Ohio.

Aldrich, R., A. Holliday, D. Colwell, Jr., B. J. Johnson, E. Smith, and R. Sharpley. 1971. The mental retardation services usage and needs among families with retarded children in selected areas of Washington State, Research Report, Vol. 3, No. 17. Department of Social and Health Services, Division of Institutions, State of Washington, Olympia.

Becker, M., R. Drachman, and J. Kirscht. 1974. Continuity of pediatrician: New support for an old shibboleth. J. Pediat. 84: 599–605.

Blennow, G., N. W. Svenningsen, and B. Almquist. 1974. Noise levels in infant incubators (adverse effects?). Pediatrics 53: 29–32.

Boulware, J. R. 1958. The composition of private pediatric practice in a small community in the south of the United States: A twenty-five year survey. Pediatrics 22: 548–558.

Burg, F., and F. H. Wright. 1972. Evaluation of pediatric residents and their training programs. J. Pediat. 80: 183–189.

Cooke, R. E. 1966. Residency training—A summary of findings of the PREP Committee. In H. F. Wright (ed.), Pediatric Residency Training. Proceedings of an Institute sponsored by the American Board of Pediatrics at Atlanta, Georgia, September 17–19, 1965. Pediatrics 38 (4) Part II: 720–725.

Cornely, D. A., M. Bachar, and M. Hankerd. 1965. A study of pediatric residency training and pediatric research projects, prepared for the Joint Committee on Pediatric Research Education and Practice.

Falk, S. A., R. O. Cook, J. K. Haseman, and G. M. Sanders. 1974. Noise-induced inner ear damage in newborn and adult guinea pigs. Laryngoscope 84: 444.

Gadeke, R., B. Doring, F. Keller, and A. Vogel. 1969. The noise level in a children's hospital, and the wake-up threshold in infants. Acta Pediatr. Scand. 58: 164–170.

Macintyre, M. 1972. Professional responsibility in prenatal genetic evaluation, advances in human genetics and their impact on society. Birth Defects Original Article Series, 8 (4): 31–35.

Moghadam, H. 1974. The rare and the plentiful—A dilemma in pediatric manpower. Canad. Med. Assoc. J. 110: 497–498.

Pless, I. B. 1974. The changing face of primary pediatrics. Pediat. Clin. No. Amer. 21: 223–224.

Quinn, P. O., and J. L. Rapoport. 1974. Minor physical anomalies and neurologic status in hyperactive boys. Pediatrics 53: 742–747.

Rosenberg, J., and G. Weller. 1972. Minor physical anomalies and academic performance in young school children. Devel. Med. Child Neurol. 15: 131–135.

Rosenbloom, A. L., and J. P. Ongley. 1974. Who provides what services to children in private medical practice? Amer. J. Dis. Child. 127: 357–361.

Silver, H. K., and J. Ott. 1973. The Child Health Associate: A new health professional to provide comprehensive health care to children. Pediatrics 51: 1–71.

Waldrop, M., F. Pedersen, and R. Q. Bell. 1968. Minor physical anomalies and behavior in preschool children. Child Devel. 39: 391–400.

Waldrop, M., and C. Halverson, Jr. 1971. Minor physical anomalies and hyperactive behavior in young children. In J. Hellmuth (ed.), Exceptional Infant, Vol. 2, pp. 343–380. Brunner/Mazel, New York.

Wedgwood, R. J., C. R. Dean, and J. S. Dydo. 1967. An Inventory of Pediatric Departments: Teaching in Pediatric Departments, Chapter Three (NICHD No. PH 43-68-630). National Institute of Child Health and Human Development, Bethesda, Maryland.

Wedgwood, R. J. 1972. The 1970–1971 Inventory of Pediatric Departments: A Report and a Comparison with the 1966–1967 Inventory (NICHD Order No. PD-135134-3). National Institute of Child Health and Human Development, Bethesda, Maryland.

Nursing: High Risk Infants

Kathryn E. Barnard, R.N., Ph.D.

Description of the knowledge, skills, and practice of the nursing profession in relation to "at risk" infants is the subject of this chapter. For an idealist, this job is difficult because it demands confronting both what *should be* and what *is*. The specific objective is to present the current and potential capability of nursing in providing early interventions designed to achieve optimal cognitive and adaptive behavioral development in the risk infant and young child. The following information is the product both of this author's experience in the past 12 years and that of 17 nursing experts throughout the country. Personal experience has included working with handicapped children and with their parents, teaching courses in the field and, currently, research in early intervention for infants born prematurely and assessment procedures for evaluating the environments of infants during their first years. In December 1973, this author sent out a request to 25 nurses who were known to be active in the field and asked for a "mini state-of-the-art" paper from their own viewpoints, using their specific communities as illustrations. Seventeen responded, all with thoughtful and detailed descriptions. Their names are listed in Appendix A, and they are referred to throughout the text. Their prompt and comprehensive responses meant a more representative statement of the art. This chapter is organized to present a survey of the nursing power, the scope and depth of practice, new frontiers, and recommendations.

During the past few years, there has been an effort through federal legislation and funding to increase the number of nurses in the United States and, more particularly, to increase their level of education. The Interagency Council on Nursing Statistics estimates that an increase of about 3 percent per year of employed registered nurses has occurred from 1966 to 1971; in 1971 there were 723,000 employed registered nurses in the United States. Thus, while the resident population of the United States increased by 5 percent in that same time period (1966 to 1971), the supply of nurses increased by 16 percent. Table 1 gives data from the year 1970[1]: the majority of nurses are employed in hospital

---

[1] The last complete census of nursing manpower was done in 1966. All data after that date have been estimated by the Interagency Conference on Nursing Statistics. This agency is composed of representatives from the National League for Nursing and the Division of Nursing, Public Health Service. Data from *Facts about Nursing, 1970–71*. American Nurses' Association, Kansas City, Missouri. Updated reports of these data have been made for 1972-1973 by the American Nurses' Association in *Facts about Nursing, 1972-73*.

Table 1.[a] Estimated number of employed registered nurses by field of employment and education preparation, 1970

Field of employment	Total	Master's degree or above (%)	Baccalaureate (%)	Associate degree (%)	Diploma (%)
Total	700,000	2.7	11.4	3.2	82.7
Hospital	446,000	0.9	9.0	3.1	87.0
Nursing home	40,000	1.2	8.8	7.8	82.2
Public health (including school)	51,000	6.1	34.3	0.8	58.8
Nursing education	31,000	35.5	41.9	1.0	21.6
Occupational health	20,000	1.0	7.0	2.5	89.5
Private duty, office nurse and other	112,000	0.4	4.1	3.3	92.2

[a]Taken from Facts about Nursing, 1970–1971, with permission of the American Nurses' Association, p. 12.

settings; the next major employment area is private duty and office nursing, and third is in public health. It is in the public health category that the level of nursing education begins to show increasing numbers with education beyond the diploma level. In reality, the majority of practice discussed here is from the approximately 14 percent of the nursing population who have educational preparation at or beyond the baccalaureate level.

Table 2 gives another view of the nursing power source. This table gives an estimate of the number of nurses whose field of interest is maternal and child nursing. This gives a degree of appreciation of the numbers of nurses currently in the manpower system with an actual or potential orientation toward the problem of the handicapped child and his family. Thus, roughly estimated, there are approximately 96,000 nurses whose interest in either maternal and child health or public health make them the focus of our attention in order to see what they are doing and/or potentially can do to optimize the functioning of the infant at risk.

In addition to numbers, certain trends in nursing practice and education are important to note in discussing the current and potential state-of-the-art. These trends are:

1. While the total population of nurses has kept up with population growth, there has always been and continues to be a shortage of nurses in the care of children, poverty groups, rural communities, the aged, and the mentally ill.
2. Although there is a societal demand for an increasing amount of ambulatory and community-based care versus hospital or institution care, the majority of nurses are prepared for *hospital-based* care.
3. Accelerated public education in health and illness has resulted in increased demands for preventive health care services.
4. As expansion of scientific knowledge occurs at an accelerating pace, knowledge becomes obsolete in about 10 to 15 years. Given this present pace, the time span will decrease in the future.

All of these trends imply the necessity of finding ways of decreasing the gap in the generation, acquisition, and practice of knowledge. Continual efforts must be made to update the knowledge of teachers and practitioners of nursing. Toward this goal, many states (for example, California) are in the process of making nursing license renewal

Table 2. Estimation of nursing power with maternal-child interest and area of employment for 1971

Area of employment	Percentage
Hospital	72
Public health	10
Office nursing	10
Nursing education	8
Total number	46,272

dependent upon evidence of continuing education. This places unprecedented demands on colleges and universities to offer relevant courses to the practicing nurse. We need to be keenly aware of the opportunity this presents to orient nursing interest to handicapped children and their families and to increase the skills and knowledge of nurses in our communities.

So much for the background data. What are nurses doing to provide services to the at risk infant and his family? The scope of practice is presented in this chapter in the following manner:

State of practice I: Early identification and follow up from the newborn nursery
State of practice II: Early case-finding (birth to 3 years) in the community
State of practice III: Intervention, birth to 3 years

STATE OF PRACTICE I:
EARLY IDENTIFICATION AND FOLLOW UP FROM THE NEWBORN NURSERY

There are a number of newborn infants, 31 percent, (Denhoff, Hainsworth, and Hainsworth, 1972) who present symptoms of neurological or growth abnormalities that signal potential developmental problems. Infants born before 37 weeks' gestation, small-for-date babies, metabolic disorders, and significant dysmorphology are at risk for development. This risk for later developmental difficulty increases with infants from low socioeconomic groups (Willerman, Broman, and Fiedler, 1970). Table 3 represents the number of nurses who reported an organized system in their communities for identification and follow up of such infants and families. Four programs, each with a somewhat different focus, are described (see Appendix A for the name and address of each responding nurse).

Eunice Kennedy Shriver Center

Mary Scahill, (unpublished data) Eunice Kennedy Shriver Center, University Affiliated Facility at the Walter E. Fernald State School, Waltham, Massachusetts, reports a program that has been in operation since 1970. Here, the nursing department embarked on a program of early intervention with newborns who manifested easily recognizable signs of developmental delays and defects at the time of birth. Since 1970, all newborn referrals

Table 3. Report of organized functional system of hospital-home follow-up of high risk infants from a sample of 18 nursing experts

Yes	10
Sometimes, or in plans	5
None	3

to the Shriver Center have been referred directly to the nursing department. Table 4 presents the referrals beginning as early as 1969. The focus of intervention has been to work through the parents' grief over the immediate crisis of the birth of a child with defects and to help the parents plan for the future of the child and the family. The majority of referrals have been requests for placement. Most of the infants were so severely damaged that continued care at home would have been difficult. In some instances, institutionalization was inappropriate, but it had been recommended by the professional hospital staff without allowing the parents time to cope with and try to resolve the initial crisis of birth. Where institutionalization was appropriate, there was little awareness on the part of the family, and often of the referring professional, of the problem of finding facilities for placement.

Contact with the family is made as soon as possible after the referral. The center nurse visits the family either in the hospital or at home, depending upon the time of the referral. Should the parents be adamant about placement, the nurse provides them with factual information about the lack of state facilities. In the event private placement might be possible, she informs them of the financial difficulties involved. If no such decision has been made, the nurse listens to their concerns and helps them to express their feelings. She gives them factual information regarding home care and her availability on a continuing basis. In either case, the nurse reassures the parents of her continued interest and involvement, in accordance with their wishes, as they plan for the future.

The results of this intervention program indicate that, although the situations may vary, the problems and needs of these parents usually are related to one or more of the following: 1) lack of correct information about their child's condition and prognosis, 2) need for someone to reinterpret events following the initial impact of the birth and diagnosis, 3) the appearance of the infant, rather than the physical care required, 4) willingness of the parents to care for the infant for a short while, provided assistance and emotional support is readily available, and 5) financial status.

Denver General Hospital

In Denver, Colorado, Marilyn Krajicek (unpublished data) from the John F. Kennedy Child Development Center reports a program at the Denver General Hospital where each baby identified as high risk is automatically enrolled in a high risk clinic. In addition, 95 percent of all infants have a referral for at least one visit by a public health nurse from the Denver Visiting Nurses' Association. Priority is given to those children with special problems, mothers with their first baby, or a mother who is breast feeding. Once the referral is made, the nurse is requested to make a visit within 48 hours. If a child is identified as under special care, such as the high risk clinic or private care, the nurse encourages the mother to visit the clinic or the private medical care facility; otherwise, the mother is referred to a neighborhood health center or well baby clinic. In the same city, at Colorado General Hospital, any infant suspected of being at risk and any mother who is at high risk is referred to a public health nurse. In addition, a special well baby

Table 4. Summary of referrals 1967–1973[a]

Date of referral	Age at referral	Diagnosis	Referred by	Request	Present status
5/69	12 days	Lawrence-Moon Bidel syndrome	Mother	Placement	Placed at Fernald
4/70	8 months	Down's syndrome	Mother	Information	Deceased
9/70	4 months	Hydrocephalus	Social worker	Placement	Placed at Fernald
1/71	2 months	Down's syndrome	Neighbor with Down's syndrome child	Home program	At home
7/72	2 months	Hydrocephalus, lissencephaly		Placement	Deceased
9/72	3 days	Down's syndrome	Hospital social worker	Placement	Foster home placement
9/72	9 days	Myelomeningocele, hydrocephalus	Mother	Parent group	At home
10/72	2 days	Severe hydroencephaly	Hospital social worker	Help with home care	Deceased
12/72	6 days	Trisomy 18	Medical center social worker	Placement	Deceased
12/72	2 days	Pierre-Robin syndrome, seizures, mental retardation	Hospital social worker	Placement	Deceased
12/72	4 months	Trisomy 18	Hospital social worker	Placement	Deceased
4/73	6 months	Hydrocephalus, shunted at 3 months, seizures	Father	Placement	Placed at local state hospital

3/73	6 months	Subdural hematoma, blindness, seizures	Social worker	Placement	Unknown, moved out of state
5/73	1 year	Hydrocephalus	Physician	Placement	Deceased
5/73	1 month	Severe brain damage, microcephaly	Medical center social worker	Placement	Deceased
6/73	6 months	Smith-Lemli-Opitz syndrome	Nurse	Home program	Deceased
7/73	6 months	Cornelia de Lange syndrome	Physician	Placement	Nursing home placement
9/73	2 months	Hydrocephalus	Hospital social worker	Placement	Nursing home placement
11/73	1 week	Down's syndrome	Mother	Home program	At home

[a]Mary Scahill (unpublished data), Eunice Kennedy Shriver Center for Mental Retardation, Walter E. Fernald School, Waltham, Massachusetts.

clinic for at risk infants is held at the Colorado General Hospital; it uses staff from the Department of Pediatrics and the John F. Kennedy Child Development Center staff.

Special Children's Center, Inc.

In Ithaca, New York, Mary Ellen Schreher, (unpublished data), clinical coordinator of the Special Children's Center, Inc., reports that at the Thompkins County Hospital, all babies born with a birth weight of 5.5 pounds or less, or with some "aberrant symptoms," are automatically referred to the public health nurse. The babies are followed by her for 6 months. The nurse monitors each child's development with a check list created by the staff at the Special Children's Center, Inc., and she emphasizes sensory stimulation for the infants, as well as routine health care measures. At 6 months of age, the infants showing delayed development or dysfunction are followed by the Home Service Director from the Children's Center, and they are incorporated into the Center's toddler and preschool programs when appropriate.

University of Washington
Child Development and Mental Retardation Center and School of Nursing

In Seattle, a program has been designed to "refocus" the care of the infant born prematurely. The refocus involves more concern for the early development of the infants and for their parents. The work is supported by Maternal Child Health Services, Health Services and Mental Health Administration, grant number MC-R-530348-01-0. The rationale and plan of the program are outlined below.

Refocus: Premature Infants and Parents A review of the state-of-the-art in neonatal intensive care makes it clear that improving the quality of survival depends on several factors. The first requires re-evaluating the meaningful stimulation available for the infant who spends from several weeks to several months in an incubator. Positive gains made by infants given specific stimulation programs (Barnard, 1972, 1973; Hasselmeyer, 1969; Neal, 1967; Segall, 1972; Solkoff et al., 1969) suggest that the modality of stimulation is not the critical issue, but that a systematic plan of stimulation in the changeless incubator is desirable. From this author's point of view, an appropriate program of stimulation would consist of the following:

1. Temporally regulated, low frequency repetitive movements and sounds to improve sleep organization (Barnard, 1972)
2. Visual stimuli of appropriate configurations and colors placed in the incubator to encourage visual orientation during alert states (Scarr and Williams, 1971)
3. Increased tactile stimuli from both nursing staff and the infant's parents at each feeding period (Hasselmeyer, 1969; Solkoff et al., 1969)
4. Visual and auditory stimuli during the infant's alert periods in the form of talking to the infant and guiding him to look at the caregiver's face and to listen to the voice (Segall, 1972)

5. Encouragement of verbal interaction with parent and child during the first year through a home visitor who uses techniques devised by Gordon (1970) and Levenstein (1970)

Likewise, the predictive validity of socioeconomic factors in predicting which high risk infants later have below average developmental achievement (Willerman, Broman, and Fiedler, 1970) suggests that parenting and general environmental support for the infant mediates the outcome of perinatal risk. The families of at risk infants are over-represented by low income and low education families. These families are often in high social stress situations involving conflict between family members and a general disturbance in the financial and emotional support for the family. Recent research indicates that disease outcomes are prevented when people, even with adverse circumstances, have a meaningful support system (Nuckolls, Cassel, and Kaplan, 1972). This notion has been demonstrated repeatedly in parent-initiated groups representing childhood disabilities such as mental retardation, cystic fibrosis, and sudden infant death syndrome. While there have been increased efforts to deal with parents of premature infants, these attempts have been largely restricted to the period of intensive hospital care and, unfortunately, the task of the parents becomes acutely real when they take the infant home; hence, the need for support at this time.

It has been our experience in Seattle that when the infant is discharged from the regional center, the community public health nurse and/or the physician begins to see the family to provide guidance and support. However, many times the community link is never made real because of the difficulty parents have in shifting to a new source of health guidance and support. It appears that parents of premature infants need to develop a relationship with people associated with the intensive care unit which can continue over the baby's first few months at home.

Experience at the University of Washington has demonstrated that "graduate" parents are quite effective in helping new parents during the period of hospitalization and transition from hospital to home. They provide the "living" reassurance that it can be done successfully. A "graduate" parent offers a ready ear for the mother, particularly, to sound off about her reactions, fears, and questions. Seeing parents help other parents has lead us to develop a parent-to-parent approach as the linking agent in helping the parents make the transition from the hospital to community-based support systems.

Parental Care Approach The suggested parental care approach based on previous research is described below.

Efforts to encourage *attachment of parents to the infant* include facilitating frequent visiting of the hospitalized premature infant by the parents and assigning the parents regular aspects of the infant's care which promotes parent-infant interaction such as bathing, feeding, rocking, and handling. A primary care nurse assigned to each set of parents would monitor the reactions of the parents and add support when indicated such as additional counseling with social workers, contacts with other parents, and arranging for brief times away from the hospital unit with the baby before discharge.

Parent-to-parent programs would involve encouraging individual contacts of "graduate" parents with new parents during the hospital period and extending during the first 3 months after discharge. The "graduate" parents would facilitate the parents' movement into a parent group approximately 3 months after the baby is discharged from the hospital.

Parents' groups would be established to provide a network for support and information. Plans are made to incorporate parents into ongoing parents' groups at about 3 months after the infant's hospital discharge. Parents seem both physically and emotionally ready to participate in weekly sessions then, because they have adjusted to the baby and the sleep patterns of all permit more rest. In addition to the weekly daytime session, a monthly evening session to further encourage the fathers' participation is planned. The usual topics of interest are: reactions to having a premature infant, sudden infant death syndrome, developmental expectations, how much stimulation to provide, and the general concerns of parenting.

Summary

As the four programs are reviewed, it becomes clear that when an infant is born with a physical and/or behavioral handicap parents face a tremendous task of adjustment: first, adjustment to their dreams of a normal baby, and second, adaptation to what it is and what to do. While the hospital staff has the opportunity and responsibility to support and to direct the parents initially, they must also assume, at a minimum, an understanding of the adjustments, anxieties, and cares the parents will deal with once the baby goes home. As Scahill and her colleagues (unpublished data, see Table 4) illustrate, support and guidance are equally important for the parents who place or want to place the infant outside of the home. Human beings are able to deal with considerable stress if they have support. The optimal approach should permit health care personnel to manage infants at risk on a longitudinal continuum. The maternal and infant programs funded and reported by the Maternal and Child Health Service (Health Services and Mental Health Administration) have demonstrated the validity of this approach in following the at risk mother during her pregnancy and providing care to the mother both during pregnancy and through the infant's first year. The approach of choice must involve parents in activities that will influence and improve the quality and outcome of their infant's development.

Changes in the infant's behavior depend upon the quality and quantity of support and reinforcement he receives from the responsible caregivers in his life. It is, therefore, critical that an optimal program for a vulnerable infant includes the parents as an integral component of treatment (Gutelius and Kirsch, 1972). Emotional reactions to having an infant at risk, continued survival of the infant, specific techniques of infant stimulation, child rearing techniques, developmental status of the infant, and nutritional practices are illustrations of issues that parents report are of concern to them during the first months and years of the child's life.

The importance of the relationship between early infant developmental factors, parental adaptations, and the subsequent child development has been well defined and described (Bee et al., 1969; Hess and Shipman, 1965; 1967; 1968; Kilgride, Johnson, and Streissguth, 1971; Korner and Grobstein, 1967; Levenstein, 1970; Smith et al., 1972; Streissguth and Bee, 1972; Willerman, Broman, and Fiedler, 1970; Yarrow, 1968; Yarrow et al., 1972). The maternal adaptations that occur early have significant influences on the course of the infant's behavior and his development. In particular, Klaus and Kennell (1970) have indicated the need for the parents of the premature infant to develop healthy affectionate bonds with their infant since these are interfered with because of the premature birth. They need time to realign the anticipation of the parent-child relationship. From the work of Seashore et al. (1973) and Klaus and Kennell (1970) it has been found that parents need to have early contact and caregiving experiences with their infants to increase their self-confidence in parenting. Kaplan (1960) has prescribed that a parent who sees the baby as potentially normal will more often give the infant the realistic care he needs and will take pride and satisfaction in the care they give and in the baby's development.

Continued improvement of an infant's adaptive functioning requires environmental changes. The nurse practitioner is one who can become involved as a primary health care agent responsible and accountable for synthesizing the physiological, psychological, and environmental parameters of human development into preventive models of care that promote improvement of the infant's adaptive abilities (Warrick, 1971; Eyres, 1972).

STATE OF PRACTICE II: CASE IDENTIFICATION

All of the nursing experts reported general case-finding efforts within the local community (Table 5). The use of the Denver Developmental Screening Tool (DDST) as a case-finding method has become widely used in health department programs. One problem frequently mentioned was the amount of time required to train nurses in a generalized health department to do the DDST, coupled with the subsequent high turnover rate in employment of nurses and, therefore, the rapid need for more training.

Nurses' Reports

In Honolulu, Betty Nakaji (unpublished data, see Appendix A), public health nurse with both the Hawaii State Health Department and the Enrichment Program for Handicapped Infants, reports that all of the 60 public health nurses have been trained to do the DDST; 12 of the 60 have completed a pediatric nurse practitioner program offered by the University of Hawaii and have refined their skills in both physical and developmental assessment. Recently, three of the nurses were trained to do the Neonatal Behavioral Assessment Scale (Brazelton, 1973). In home visits, the public health nurses are doing newborn assessments as early as 3 to 5 days after delivery and tagging for closer follow up those babies with suspicious perinatal histories as well as babies in homes with multiple social problems. They have been seeing an increasing number of babies whose parents are "paint sniffing" and/or on "hard" drugs. A number of infants have been identified as

Table 5. Report of case-finding programs within public health programs
from 18 nursing experts

Presence of case-finding program	18
No case-finding program	0

failure-to-thrive with subsequent hospitalization for diagnosis. Of three recent cases, two children were put in foster homes and one child was diagnosed as being an organic growth problem.

Nakaji (unpublished data, see Appendix A) points out that providing these services is difficult because the health department has been faced with budget cuts. Position losses means that services are spread thinner and thinner to cover periodic community crises such as the current rise in the tuberculosis rate and drop in immunity levels in school children. The problem of decreased funding for local health departments is not isolated to Honolulu; many communities are experiencing this. Unfortunately, the pattern that develops is that the case-finding and preventive services to the population with which we are concerned take a low priority in the nurses' case load. Part of this occurs because of the funding base and the fact that fee-for-service cases take priority.

Fay Russell, (unpublished data, see Appendix A), chief nurse of the Child Development Center, University of Tennessee, reports that in Memphis and in Shelby County there is approximately a 15 percent vacancy rate in the available nursing positions. Furthermore, few of the nurses have educational preparation beyond the diploma level. While there is a regular program of referring high risk newborns from the hospital, the follow up is limited by time constraints imposed by the limited staff and lack of preparation to do follow up beyond acute health and medical problems. The support of early and periodic screening programs should help to maintain a constant level of screening in the child-age population. Another reason for the high risk and/or abnormal infant shifting to low priority is that in a generalized public health nursing program, the level of knowledge and skill necessary to deal effectively with cases waxes and wanes with the amount of in-service education or administrative "push." In 1968, a study (Barnard, Sumner, Mahin, 1973) was done in the Seattle-King County Health Department to evaluate the effect on services to handicapped children and their families of having an expert practitioner in mental retardation function in a generalized public health nursing program. The expert practitioner was a generalized staff nurse with additional knowledge and experience in child development and mental retardation. The practitioner role was designed to provide her peers with 1) a role model, 2) consultation on individual cases, and 3) a focal point in the agency for information relating to mental retardation. In addition, she was carrying a general case load. The agency allotted 2 half-days a week to the practitioner role, and the remaining 4 days to her general staff responsibilities.

Several measures were taken of the effect this practitioner had on the practice of the other nurses in the district. Results indicated both an increase in the self-reported perception of competency in the area and an increase in the number of cases and amount of service given. This study is an important one: it provides direction for ways to develop competency of the generalized practitioner through the day-by-day peer contact with an expert practitioner who is also a colleague. The expert practitioner demonstrated a role-model of working with families, provided direct sources of information via her own reading, made available pertinent articles and pamphlets, and channeled new developments from the community that related to mental retardation. An important feature was that the staff viewed this peer to be easier to approach than an "outside" consultant. The informal relationship of the clinical nursing specialist (expert practitioner) provides good opportunities for effective communication and clarification of roles and responsibilities, for sharing information, and for conveying ideas for improving practice (Scully, 1965).

Summary

In the past 10 years, tremendous strides have been made in improving the case-finding techniques of nurses. This has been accomplished by introducing and training them to use the DDST. Additional assessment procedures are needed which are more appropriate to the infancy period and to the adaptational-developmental process. Under a contract[2] with the Division of Nursing of the Health Resources Administration, the University of Washington School of Nursing and Behavioral Research Unit, Child Development and Mental Retardation Center are developing and testing assessment measures that will be used in developing a program of assessment that can fit into the already operational immunization programs for children. At least 85 percent of all children in the United States now receive their infant series of diphtheria-pertussis-tetanus (DPT), polio, and measles vaccines. Hence, an assessment program that adapts to this established health-care mechanism is a reasonable way to go about comprehensive screening. One assessment procedure being tested is a sleep-activity record that the mother completes for a 7-day period. The form is presented in Appendix B. The pretest with both low and high education mothers has demonstrated their willingness and ability to keep such a record. Analysis to date includes assessing whether the infant shows a predictable pattern of sleep-wake-feeding (same times ± 1/2 hour in 5 out of 6 days), average amount of awake happy periods, average amount of crying periods, number of feedings, and the parent's typical response to distress-content infant behavior. This picture of activity demonstrates both characteristics of the infants and the environmental response. It also provides a springboard for intervention. Based on this record, it is possible either to validate the good pattern and parental responses or to talk about the 5 hours of crying per day the mother has recorded.

Case-finding and assessment skills of the public health nurse are considered an important component of public health services. The support of their priority must be continued through federal, state, and local planning. Assessment is the first step and the basis of intervention.

---

[2] This work was funded under Contract No. (NIH) 71-4174 with the Division of Nursing, Bureau of Health Resources and Development, U.S. Public Health Service, Health Resources Administration, Department of Health, Education, and Welfare, Washington, D.C.

STATE OF PRACTICE III: EARLY INTERVENTION

Nurses' Reports

While follow up of high risk infants from the hospital and general case-finding procedures is becoming an expected public health practice, specific and planned intervention to optimize the at risk infant's cognitive and adaptative development is not a function commonly practiced by nurses. Mary Jane Foster (unpublished data, see Appendix A), Director of Nursing at the Mental Retardation Institute, New York Medical College, completed a survey of the nursing activities within eight New York agencies. She reports that in only two of these agencies are nurses involved in specific intervention activities. Table 6 presents the total response from the panel of 18 nursing experts. Thus, there is some basis for saying that in general, nursing involvement in early intervention specifically designed to optimize the child's function is taking place only within specialized infant programs or the University Affiliated Training Centers. This finding would appear to reflect the state-of-the-art. Research does give support in recommending intervention with infants from poor environments (Levenstein, 1970; Streissguth and Bee, 1972); however, there are few systematic studies completed with the biologically at risk infant that permit generalization of the benefit of early intervention or even to say what *does* happen. Projects, such as the ones reported elsewhere in this book, are generating the experience and data needed for deciding how, when, and where to provide intervention.

Raeone Zelle, (unpublished data, see Appendix A), nursing consultant with the Alta California Regional Center in Sacramento, describes how their center became involved in infant intervention:

> Approximately 6 months after our agency opened its door, three infants were referred who had Down's syndrome. The counselors and I acutely sensed the pain which these families were experiencing and the need for intensive support. A counselor and myself conducted an 8-week group counseling session involving these parents. We used a practical, educational-oriented approach versus a therapy-oriented approach because feelings are painful at this stage and can only be expressed over time in a graduated manner. At the end of the 8-week session, we had a potluck group luncheon at one of the parent's home where I assessed the babies and offered individualized management suggestions. Although the luncheon was held on a weekday, all the fathers attended. Regular follow-up luncheons have been held on an ongoing basis. The parents provided positive feedback to their physicians, and we received more referrals. We conducted two more 8-week sessions for parents with

Table 6. Emphasis on nurse follow up of infants with handicaps and their families in reports from 18 nursing experts

Within a public health program	3
Special setting	14
None	1

infants with Down's syndrome. The almost perfect attendance reflected the value of the sessions. The parents became very close and supportive, and they continued to keep in touch after the sessions ended. They evolved into a viable group who realized a need for an intensive interventive program. They elicited my help in finding a funding source and serving as the primary consultant in developing the new program. Our investigation indicated that title VI-B funds were the most promising, and we contacted the most progressive school district in Sacramento County. The Director of Special Education was responsive, but explained that he had a "bare-bones" administrative staff. We would willingly enter into a joint effort with the parents and Alta California Regional Center if someone could write the grant. The parents and I assumed this responsibility, and the grant proposal was approved for funding.

A nurse was written in as the key member of the team because I feel that her educational and field experience best prepares her to intervene with infants and families—more so than a member of any other discipline. However, a Master's Degree in Child Development Nursing was specified because she needs specialized theoretical and practical training to relate to the needs of a developmentally-delayed child. The program was also family-oriented with interventions focused on developing a positive bond between the parents and the child which accentuates the parents' self-esteem in their roles. When the children reach 18 months of age, they participate in a half-day group program twice a week, which provides respite for the mother and parallel contact with other children.

The staff of the Infant Program consists of a psychologist 2/10-time who is responsible for the evaluation process and Title VI administration, a teacher 3/10-time who is primarily responsible for the half-day group program, a physical therapist 1/4-time who intervenes extensively with the infants with cerebral palsy, a full-time nurse who is primarily responsible for the intervention program in the home, and four infant technicians who provide weekly follow-up support in the home and help with the group program.

The approaches are as natural as possible and lend themselves to the daily routine of the home. We have one *cardinal* rule—the approaches are not to elicit crying. I feel that the whole approach has been more family and developmentally oriented because a nurse participated in the developmental stage and is a key member of the team.

One guide providing a developmental framework to intervention is the *Washington Guide to Promoting Development in the Young Child* (Barnard and Powell, 1972). The guide includes the areas of motor, language, play, self-help skills, sleep, and discipline. It is useful for general child-rearing advice and suggestions. The guide is arranged in 3-month age increments through the first year with both the developmental landmarks normally expected. Also given are activities appropriate to support further maturation. A portion of the guide is reproduced in Table 7 for purposes of illustration.

Most nurses are responsive to the idea of early intervention. There were numerous reports of continuing education courses and in-service training in hospitals and public health agencies to introduce the nursing community to early intervention. Imogen Schroder (unpublished data, see Appendix A), Director of Nursing at The John F. Kennedy Institute, The Johns Hopkins University, reported they were providing varying amounts of experience for 350 nursing students per year. She stressed the desirability of developing an internship program for nurses at the bachelor's and master's levels. Doris Julian (unpublished data, see Appendix A), Training Director of Nursing at the Child

Table 7. Language (1 to 3 months)[a]

Expected tasks	Suggested activities
Receptive abilities	
1. Movement of eyes, respiration rate, or body activity changes when bell is rung close to child's head	1. Observe facial expressions, gestures, bodily postures, and movements when vocalization are being produced
2. Smiles when socially stimulated	
3. Has facial, vocal and generalized bodily responses to faces	2. Smile and talk softly in pleasant tone
4. Reacts differentially to adult voice	3. Hold, touch, and interact frequently with infant for pleasure
	4. Refrain from letting infant engage in prolonged and incessant crying
Expressive abilities	
1. Makes prelanguage vocalizations that consist of cooing, throaty sounds, e.g., "gu"	
2. Makes "pleasure" sounds that consists of soft vowels	
3. Makes "sucking" sounds	
4. Crying can be differentiated for discomfort, pain, and hunger as reported by mother	
5. An "A" sound as in the word "cat" is commonly heard in distress crying	

[a]Reproduced with permission from Barnard and Powell, pp. 57–58, 1972.

Development and Rehabilitation Center, University of Oregon, reports that in Multnomah County (Oregon) in 1973, 128 public health nurses, in addition to their generalized caseload, provided services to approximately 3,000 children. She suggests that the answer to providing better services is not more staff but the advanced training of key individuals. All seem to be saying that there is need for further preparation of the nurse if we are to meet our obligation in early intervention.

Summary

While the practice of early intervention with at risk infants cannot be completely defined because of our lack of experience, several key points can and should be made:

For at risk infants less than 1 year of age, the nurse, if not the primary person, should be actively involved in intervention programs with them. The nurse's background in child growth and development and orientation to the family give a valuable perspective from which to plan a program of stimulation with the parents. The nurse's understanding of the medical aspects of the infant's problem enables her to interpret this to the parents and to other staff members. The nurse has knowledge of the physical health and care of the infant. This includes feeding, sleeping, elimination, common illnesses, and treatments.

In addition to nursing, support should be given for the involvement of a variety of disciplines including nutrition, physical therapy, occupational therapy, education, pediatric medicine, and social work. The sharing of knowledge and skills from all of these disciplines is necessary to plan and to implement early intervention programs. Early intervention is more effective when the parents actively participate in the programming for their infant. The programs will be more effective as the staff increase their focus on working with parents. The majority of parents find group participation helpful because of the parent-to-parent communication and support.

NEW FRONTIERS

There are several opporutnities, problems, and issues that are "new frontiers." While they may not be new in content, perhaps with a pioneering spirit we can think "fresh" and develop new solutions. The frontiers are: 1) When, how, and to whom should intervention be offered? 2) How can we disseminate what is now known for public and professional awareness? 3) What strategies can be used to provide the services needed at a cost we can afford?

The first frontier suggests the need for *research*. Here are summarized a few of the questions we need to address immediately. We need to know more about the amount and type of stimulation need for optimal functioning of the central nervous system. There needs to be testing of the approaches now advocated in early intervention. Do our ideas about fostering normal developmental patterns have both short-term and long-term influences? How can we increase our efficiency in predicting who needs intervention? Again and again, we have emphasized the role of the parent: How can we be more effective in supporting this role? Does early intervention serve to strengthen both the child's progress and the integrity of the family unit?

The second frontier implies a focus on *education*. We need to use mass public and professional media to communicate our knowledge and practices. There is no stronger way to engender support than to inform and convince the American public about the needs and the potentials. In the field of nursing, with the national trend of requiring evidence of continuing education for nurse relicensure, we have an unprecedented opportunity to offer courses relevant to the high risk infant and family to the 96,000 nurses in our country now employed in maternal-child and community nursing. This requires support within the university-affiliated centers and schools or colleges of nursing to provide the faculty who will offer the instruction. While continuing education can provide updating and some re-tooling, we also need a sizable group of nurses with advanced preparation in predictive health care, growth and development, counseling, and skills of early intervention.

Every nursing expert providing information for this report emphasized the need for additional nurses in their communities to meet the demand for early intervention.

However, even if there were enough money available to hire additional nurses, there are few prepared to give the type of service needed.

The panel was unanimous in its expression of concern that graduates of baccalaureate and master's degree programs need additional training in child development. There needs to be support of nursing educational efforts within the University-Affiliated Centers to prepare nurse clinicians with specialized knowledge and skills to function in education and practice settings. It seems reasonable to recommend that each community of 250,000 population have at least one nurse with a master's degree whose specialty is the high risk infant and family. This nurse-clinician should be associated with the health department or a major community agency monitoring and providing intervention programs. It appears that there are at least four universities that are now ready to offer graduate level preparation. There is a need for money to provide additional support to these universities. A national goal should be preparation of 100 nurses at the master's degree level over the next 5 years. This means additional faculty within the University-Affiliated Centers, schools of nursing for graduate training programs, and stipends for the students preparing to be specialists in nursing care of the high risk neonate and his family.

One of the strategies in providing the needed *services* is to have people prepared to give the service; this has already been discussed. Providing monitoring and intervention services to at risk infants is not just a concept or idea, it is a reality that involves, nationwide, approximately 1 million new infants per year. We currently do not have screening methods that are sensitive to all parameters (infant, parents, environment) and that are easily and widely used. The screening must be capable of predicting problems, in addition to finding those that already exist. The environment, meaning parent-infant interaction and stimulation, is one of the more powerful determinants of child health outcomes. Presently, the level of maternal education is one marker variable that can be used to select potential at risk interaction-environment conditions. We anticipate having data from a pretest of assessment methods designed to screen for parental-environmental variables by 1976.[3] The most reasonable and comprehensive way to implement screening is within the existing immunization programs. This will require additional monies and, in fact, represent only a small aspect of the approach being suggested. In keeping with current practice, an intervention program for the at risk infant means about 20 home or parent contacts during the first year and enrollment in an infant program during the second and third years. How much would such a program cost for an individual child? Relying on current cost estimates, in the Seattle area[4] this would amount to approximately $1,000 for a home-based program during the first year and $2,500 per year using the center-based intervention program. The multiplication of numbers of infants in need by the cost per individual makes us realize that implementation of our concepts will require refinement of answers to the questions of who, when, how, and for what benefit.

---

[3] Nursing Child Assessment Project, University of Washington Contract No. NIH 71-4174, Division of Nursing, Health Resources Administration.

[4] Costs were determined from estimates furnished by the Seattle-King County Health Department and Spastic Children's Clinic and Preschool, Seattle, Washington, May 1974.

If the past is to be avoided, we have no alternative but to develop effective monitoring and early intervention programs for the infant and family at risk.

RECOMMENDATIONS

We have a huge job to do if we support the idea that at risk infants need to be monitored and offered intervention that maximizes their development. According to the World Almanac and Book of Facts, 1974 edition in the United States there were 3,256,000 births during 1972. (This represented a 15.6 per thousand rate; for the first 6 months of 1973, there was a 5 percent reduction in births, which equaled a 14.8 per thousand rate.) Taking a liberal estimate of suspect or at risk infants (31 percent), this would mean provision within our 50 states for monitoring approximately 1 million infants per year. Even considering 11 percent, the rate of infants that Denhoff, Hainsworth, and Hainsworth (1972) found abnormal or suspect at 12 months, this would mean 356,160 infants per year. In the State of Washington, for example, there were 47,148 births in 1972. Based on this rate, we should be monitoring and providing intervention for 5 to 12 thousand infants per year. With the present resources, it is possible to handle approximately 3 to 4 thousand.

We have all made an assessment of our knowledge and skills. With this measurement, we must chart a new course that will put us ahead of where we now stand.

For nursing involvement to improve, the following recommendations are submitted:

1. Increase public and professional awareness regarding the value of monitoring the at risk infants and providing intervention to optimize their development

2. Support research on longitudinal follow up of at risk infants and families who have had the benefit of intervention programs

3. Encourage sharing of knowledge and skills and practice among disciplines involved

4. Develop and test methods that can effectively screen for at risk status from the standpoint of the infant, his parents, and his immediate environment and incorporate this screening method into existing immunization programs

5. Promote the preparation of master's degree level nursing programs in predictive and preventive health care of neonates and young children. Within the next 5 years, at least 100 nurses should be prepared in high risk infant and family intervention

6. Provide within each regional newborn intensive care facility a nursing position for a person with master's level preparation. The nurse should be responsible for incorporating early development intervention into the hospital care, working with parents, and reinforcing a community follow-through intervention program

7. Provide financial incentive for community agencies to provide services to at risk infants by a fee for service through a third part payment structure

8. Promote the concept of a specialized practitioner in community nursing agencies. This practitioner in care of the at risk infant and his family would provide a role model, a readily available source of peer consultation, and stimulus for services to the target population.

APPENDIX A

Report includes responses from nursing experts in the following regions and states:

Eastern	Middle	Western
Maryland	Michigan	California (2)
Massachusetts (2)	Kansas	Oregon
North Carolina	Ohio (2)	Washington
Florida (2)	Colorado	Hawaii
New York (2)	Tennessee	

Joy Cottrell, Nurse, Infant Development Center, Mission, Kansas, 66202

Marie Cullinane, Director of Nursing, Developmental Evaluation Clinic, The Children's Hospital Medical Center, Boston, Massachusetts 02115

Judith B. Curry, Chief, Nursing, The Nisonger Center, Ohio State University, Columbus, Ohio 43210

Helen Engh, Public Health Nurse, Atypical Infant Program, Department of Health Services, Developmental Disabilities Section, Kentfield, California 94904

Mary Jane Foster, Director, Department of Nursing, Mental Retardation Institute, New York Medical College, Flower and Fifth Avenue Hospital, New York, New York 10029

Catherine Huber, Chief Nursing Specialist, Child Development Institute, Division for Disorders of Development and Learning, The University of North Carolina at Chapel Hill 27514

Doris Julian, Training Director of Nursing, Crippled Children's Division, Child Development and Rehabilitation Center, University of Oregon Medical Schools, Portland, Oregon 97201

Marilyn Krajicek, Chief of Nursing, John F. Kennedy Child Development Center, University of Colorado Medical Center, Denver, Colorado 80220

Betty Nakaji, Nurse, Enrichment Program for Handicapped Infants, School of Public Health, University of Hawaii, Honolulu, Hawaii 96822

Joan Parker, United Cerebral Palsy Infant Program of Polk County, Lakeland, Florida 33803

Ann Pattullo, Program Director for Nursing, Institute for the Study of Mental Retardation and Related Disabilities, Ann Arbor, Michigan 48108

Fay Russell, Chief of Nursing, Child Development Center, University of Tennessee, Memphis, Tennessee 38105

Mary Scahill, Chief Nursing Consultant, Eunice Kennedy Shriver Center, Walter E. Fernald State School, Waverley, Massachusetts 02178

Mary Ellen Schreher, Clinical Coordinator, The Special Children's Center, Inc., Ithaca, New York 14850

Imogen T. Schroder, Director of Nursing, The John F. Kennedy Institute, in affiliation with The Johns Hopkins University, Baltimore, Maryland 21205

Roberta Sherman, The Nisonger Center, Ohio State University, Columbus, Ohio 43210

Theole M. Thomas, Public Health Nurse Consultant, Mailman Center for Child Development, University of Miami, Miami, Florida 33152

Raeone Zelle, Nursing Consultant, Alta California Regional Center, Sacramento, California 95814

APPENDIX B[a]

Sleep Activity Record

Parent's name _____
Last   First

Child's name _____
Last   First

Parent's usual bedtime _____
Mother   Father

Child's place of sleep _____

Parent's usual awakening _____
Mother   Father

Date of Record _____
Beginning   End

Day	a.m. 1	2	3	4	5	6	7	8	9	11	Noon pm. 12	1	2	3	4	5	6	7	8	9	11	M. 12
1																						
2																						
3																						
4																						
5																						
6																						
7																						

Symbols:

Sleep ———————
Awake (crying or unhappy) ∿∿∿
Awake (content, happy) ℓℓℓℓℓ

Feeding (what and how much) □
Parent action (what was done when child awakened) ○
Diaper change ●

[a]Developed by the Nursing Child Assessment Project, University of Washington, Seattle, Kathryn E. Barnard, Principal Investigator, Contract No. NIH-71-4174, Division of Nursing, Health Resources Administration. (Reproduced with permission from Barnard and Powell, 1972.)

723

LITERATURE CITED

American Nurses' Association. 1970–71 Edition. Facts about Nursing: A Statistical Summary. American Nurses' Association, Kansas City, Mo.

Barnard, K. E. 1972. The effect of stimulation on the duration and amount of sleep and wakefulness in the premature infant. Unpublished doctor's dissertation. University of Washington, Seattle.

Barnard, K. E., and M. L. Powell. 1972. Teaching the Mentally Retarded Child: A Family Care Approach. C. V. Mosby, St. Louis.

Barnard, K. E., 1973. A program of stimulation for infants born prematurely. Presented at the Society for Research in Child Development, Philadelphia, Pa. (March 28.)

Barnard, K. E., G. A. Sumner, and M. Mahin. 1973. Study of the expert practitioner in mental retardation with a generalized public health nursing department. In J. Wortis (ed.), Nursing Mental Retardation and Developmental Disability, Vol. V, pp. 72–74. Brunner/Mazel, New York.

Bee, H. L., L. G. Van Egeren, A. P. Streissguth, B. A. Nyman, and M. S. Leckie. 1969. Social Class differences in maternal teaching strategies and speech patterns. Devel. Psych. 1: 726–734.

Brazelton, T. B. 1973. Neonatal Behavioral Assessment Scale. Clinics in Developmental Medicine, No. 50. Spastics Society International Medical Publication, London.

Denhoff, E., P. K. Hainsworth, and M. L. Hainsworth. 1972. The child at risk for learning disorder: Can he be identified during the first year of life? Clin. Pediatr. 11: 164–170.

Eyres, P. J. 1972. The role of the nurse in family-centered nursing care. Nurs. Clin. No. Amer. 7: 27–39.

Gordon, I. J. 1970. Baby Learning Through Baby Play: A Parent's Guide for the First Two Years. St. Martin's Press, New York.

Gutelius, M. F., and A. D. Kirsch. 1972. Factors promoting success in infant education. Presented at the American Public Health Association, Atlantic City, New Jersey. (November.)

Hasselmeyer, E. G. 1969. Behavior patterns of the premature infant. PHS Doc. No. 840., U. S. Department of Health, Education, and Welfare, Public Health Service, Division of Nursing. Washington, D.C.

Hess, R. D., and V. C. Shipman. 1965. Early experience and the socialization of cognitive modes in children. Child Devel. 36: 869–886.

Hess, R. D., and V. C. Shipman. 1967. Cognitive elements in maternal behavior. In J. P. Hill (ed.), Minnesota Symposia on Child Psychology, pp. 58–81. University of Minnesota Press, Minneapolis.

Hess, R. D., and V. C. Shipman. 1968. Maternal influences upon early learning: The cognitive environments of urban preschool children. In R. D. Hess and R. M. Bear (eds.), Early Education: Current Theory, Research, and Action, pp. 91–103. Aldine, Chicago.

Kaplan, D. M., and E. A. Mason. 1960. Maternal reactions to premature birth viewed as an acute emotional disorder. Amer. J. Orthopsych. 30: 539–552.

Kilgride, H., D. Johnson, and A. P. Streissguth. 1971. Early home experiences of newborns as a functions of social class, infant sex, and birth order. Unpublished manuscript, Department of Psychiatry, University of Washington, Seattle.

Klaus, M. H., and J. H. Kennell. 1970. Mothers separated from their newborn infants. Pediatr. Clin. No. Amer. 17: 1015–1037.

Korner, A. F., and R. Grobstein. 1967. Individual differences at birth: Implications for mother-infant relationship and later development. J. Amer. Acad. Child Psych. 6: 676–690.

Levenstein, P. 1970. Cognitive growth in preschoolers through verbal interaction with mothers. Amer. J. Orthopsych. 40: 416–432.

Neal, M. 1967. Relationship between vestibular stimulation and the developmental behavior of the premature infant. Unpublished doctoral dissertation, New York University.

Nuckolls, K. B., J. Cassel, and B. H. Kaplan. 1972. Psychosocial assets, life crisis, and the prognosis of pregnancy. Amer. J. Epidem. 95: 431–441.

Scully, R. N. 1965. The clinical nursing specialist: Practicing nurse. Nursing Outlook 13: 28–30.

Scarr, S., and M. Williams. 1971. The effects of early stimulation on low birth weight. Presented at the Maternal and Child Health Section of the American Public Health Assoc., Minneapolis. (October 14.)

Seashore, M. H., A. D. Leifer, C. R. Barnett, and P. H. Leiderman. 1973. The effects of denial of early mother-infant interaction on maternal self-confidence. J. Pers. Soc. Psych. 26: 369–378.

Segall, M. E. 1972. Cardiac responsivity to auditory stimulation in premature infants. Nursing Res. 21: 15–19.

Smith, A. C., G. L. Ferris, and A. H. Sellman. 1972. Prediction of developmental outcome at seven years from prenatal, perinatal, and postnatal events. Child Devel. 43: 495–507.

Solkoff, N., S. Yaffe, D. Weintrab, and B. Blase. 1969. Effects of handling on the subsequent developments of premature infants. Devel. Psych. 1: 765–768.

Streissguth, A. P., and H. L. Bee. 1972. Mother-child interactions and cognitive development in children. In W. W. Hartup (ed.), The Young Child, pp. 158–183. National Assoc. for the Education of Young Children, Vol. 2. Washington, D.C.

Warrick, L. H. 1971. Family-centered care in the premature nursery. Amer. J. Nurs. 71: 2134–2138.

Willerman, L., S. H. Broman, and M. Fiedler. 1970. Infant development, preschool IQ, and social class. Child Devel. 41: 69–77.

World Almanac and Book of Facts: 1974 Edition. Newspaper Enterprise Association, New York.

Yarrow, L. J. 1968. Conceptualizing the early environment. In Dittman, L. (ed.), Early Child Care: The New Perspectives, pp. 15–26. Atherton Press, New York.

Yarrow, L. J., J. L. Rubenstein, F. A. Pedersen, and J. J. Jankowski. 1972. Dimension of early stimulation and their differential effects on infant development. Merrill-Palmer Quart. 18: 205–218.

Early Intervention with High Risk Infants and Young Children: Implications for Education

Godfrey D. Stevens, Ed.D.

For more than 30 years I have had the privilege of participating in professional and scientific meetings. This meeting with its focus on early intervention with high risk infants is the high point of hundreds of meetings.

At this moment, I am having difficulty with the inevitable information overload and the frustrations related to the difficulties associated with the ever present need to transmute raw, basic, scientific data language into professional practice.

About 200 years ago Jean Marc Gaspard Itard presented a paper to the French Academy on a single clinical case. He tried a variety of intervention strategies, most of which were forms of pedagogy. His work was terminated after 5 years in a fit of angry frustration during which Victor, his young patient, had what may have been a convulsive seizure.

Itard must have experienced a deep sense of personal and scientific frustration. In spite of the Academy's action to honor Itard for the significance of his contribution, he left with a deep sense of failure and with little insight into the significance and implications of his work.

I could not help but wonder about the ultimate significance in the history of human care of current research. This meeting, sponsored by the PCMR and the ACEI, may well one day be viewed as a land mark in the relentless effort to improve the quality of life for everyone. One would hope that this twentieth century event will be remembered vividly.

The nature of my task was spelled out very precisely by Dr. Tjossem and Alberta Meyers. I was feeling a sense of frustration probably not too different from that of Itard's, when the amount of data, some old, but mostly new, began to assume astronomic proportions. However enormous and ambiguous the task, I was asked to monitor the papers for educationally relevant information which might ultimately serve as the basis for new, efficacious educational strategies in the total array of intervention modes.

SOME EMERGING PRINCIPLES

A number of generalizations appear to be emerging from the broad research spectrum of early intervention with high risk infants: 1) the technology and procedures for predicting and identifying high risk neonates is available; 2) the neonate is in his most plastic state, which clearly suggests the viability for intervention from the moment of diagnosis; and 3) behavioral research on animals and humans in the neonatal period is suggestive of the value of early educational intervention.

PARAMETERS OF EDUCATION

First of all, it may be useful to establish the parameters of the educative enterprise. Education is viewed as an interaction between one or more *learners* and one or more *teachers* with an identifiable socially desirable purpose. This interaction is initiated and carried on in an environment designed to enhance the chances of producing agreed upon end product behavior. The final event is an evaluation of the process, which is fed back to the teacher and learner.

The enterprise has attributes of being highly systemized, formalized, standardized, and institutionalized. A unique feature of the educative process in our culture is that it is compulsory. Schooling may well be the most accurate form for this process of education.

SOME UNDERLYING ASSUMPTIONS ABOUT EDUCATION

There are a number of underlying assumptions that will inevitably affect the manner and extent of educational intervention. Some of the more relevant and salient ones are listed below.

1. Everyone has a right to be educated
2. Our society has a two-fold need for developing and maintaining a system of education for the purposes of enhancing the quality of life for each person and to assume the continuation of a government that will serve its constituents
3. Schooling, which is the formalized, institutionalized mode of enculturating the young, is not the only force at work that shapes the day-to-day behavior of the learner
4. The school, as one of the institutions used for educating the young, has a restricted function and is not a social institution that has become "all things to all people"
5. The school is a major institution—perhaps the most significant force in the education of young children—and has shown its capacity to be reformulated in its efforts to fulfill its mission

It would be foolhardy and more than presumptuous on my part to attempt to transmit one set of scientific facts into an orderly and professionally sound set of practices at this meeting. The consequences of this conference can only lead to systematic efforts to generate educationally relevant questions. The search for answers to these questions will lead to improved educational service linked intimately and effectively with other professional practitioners in such a way as to improve the quality of life for children in jeopardy and their families.

SOME QUESTIONS FOR EDUCATORS

Time, and the exhilarating circumstances of this meeting, will not permit the presentation of all of the most insightful questions that might arise from systematic "brain-storming" about the significance of this meeting for educational practices. Some questions that emerge readily are as follows:

1. Will the patrons of the schools be willing to change the traditional character of the schools to better accommodate to a need for systematic educational intervention shortly after birth?

2. Are the services of other educative agencies capable of being articulated with the school?

3. How can groups of concerned, responsible, professionals be brought together to work in groups to help the young high risk learner?

4. Since young parents will need instructions in carrying out their child-caring function, can instructional systems be devised that will enhance their skills?

5. What schemes will need to be devised to provide mechanisms in professional schools for explicit, systematic cross-discipline training that will be designed to facilitate efficient application of current knowledge, processes, and results?

6. Can professional preparation programs for educators be devised that will provide knowledge about orderly human growth and development and, more importantly, knowledge about errors in development and the appropriate educational response to such information?

7. Will it be possible to carry out sophisticated longitudinal research in schools in light of current concern about invasion of privacy, informed consent, and other similar trends in our society?

8. Can we exploit our resources to ensure that every child and his family will have the availability of specialized educational services in every city, town, and hamlet?

9. What kind of, if any, storage-retrieval systems will be needed to accommodate the "knowledge explosion" that will inevitably follow?

10. What changes in legislation at local, state, and federal levels will be necessary to change the present character of the educative enterprise, or to add new features?

11. Can private and public support be developed to assist in planning for the introduction of new services so that social planners, basic researchers, and clinicians alike can probe the feasibility of new procedures and evaluate their effectiveness?

CONCLUSION

It would seem clear that there is a substantial base of knowledge that awaits exploitation to the end that children jeopardized by unfortunate circumstance early in their lives can be helped. One can only be left with a sense of exhilaration and well-being and be led to believe that early workers like Itard, Séguin, and others are somehow enjoying the fruits of their lonely endeavors.

INTERNATIONAL PERSPECTIVE

Canadian Perspective

G. Allan Roeher, Ph.D.

I am impressed with the emphasis placed on child-parent interaction and the importance of the parent in the early childhood services approach at this conference. Historians (and our elders) will be pleased to hear of the re-discovery of an age-old fact—that *children do have parents.* This should give future professions and researchers a whole new lease on future endeavors. I'm being unduly facetious. But, really, we have at times taken ourselves somewhat too seriously in some of our efforts we call research, and sometimes have overlooked what the elders would consider "good common sense." In no way do I intend to reflect negatively on the value and effectiveness of past and current sound research effort. Indeed, the significance and power of the research findings toward a better tomorrow are particularly evident in these chapters—so much so that someone properly referred to this conference as a turning point, as it should help to focus future directions in this field. Those who are professional program planners, though, cannot rest on the laurels of this great event.

CHANGE AGENTS IN SOCIETY

Even during the conference, there appeared to be some signals, often subtle and sometimes perhaps not fully appreciated, suggesting some very major obstacles ahead in achieving the goals that have been so eloquently expressed here by many. One such signal came from the speaker who referred to a special conference called to determine how best to launch early infant nation-wide screening programs, which essentially failed because of the inability of professional people to agree on a common approach. This is not unusual. Unfortunately, it is rather typical of meetings convened to deal with implementation. We get very excited about comparing notes of innovative approaches, but I wonder how often we are prepared truly to agree on the approach in which we might have to subsume or compromise the position that we hold for the common good. Where does this leave the large scale implementer of programs: the legislator, the parent, and the parent organizations or consumer bodies, or the public at large? These, after all, are the major change agents in our society—a point not adequately recognized by many researchers and professionals who would like the change process accelerated.

733

I recall a major study launched some years ago by the large Canadian national organizations on the topic of emotional and learning disorders of children. The first goal was to raise the necessary funds from the federal and provincial governments. The first government we went to provided funds almost without asking, on the grounds that government favor concensus among citizen action and consumer groups about expectations such agencies have regarding the role of government in areas of this kind. Governments are faced with countless approaches—all claiming to have the answers in special education and rehabilitation. Support from society (including governments) will increase when professional people agree among themselves on what there is in common about various theories and approaches and how to get the action underway.

We must learn to communicate with these major societal *change agents* in a much more effective way than we have or probably are doing. Too often, research and professional people view citizen groups as vehicles to supply money but not as change agents.

In order to communicate the technical knowledge to these essential allies—the consumer groups and the public at large—you must make yourselves understood. We must begin to translate the jargon into more understandable language. I think we often cannot really understand each other interprofessionally, let alone attempt to have consumers understand what we are saying. Some professional people do have the facility to speak lucidly and simply and to interpret clearly, and it is they who experience a good response from the consumers or clients.

Referring back to the point about "discovering that children do have parents," we need to listen to parents in order to realize optimal results from research and professional efforts. One of the parent participants said in an earlier chapter that it is as important as diagnosis for professionals to appreciate and to recognize the feelings and emotions of parents. If professionals ignore this matter, parents will, and do, go elsewhere to seek advice; and they will organize on their own. I noted this tendency at the Down's Syndrome Congress in California in 1974 which was attended by some 700 or 800 parents. In asking some parents why they favored some sort of a separation (i.e., a Down's syndrome section or organization within this country) they raised this very point. They felt that when their children were born, they did receive technical information (in fact, some excellent information was sent from the local associations), but they needed and wanted more than technical information. They needed advice and visits from other parents who understood and who genuinely cared.

If we hope to capitalize optimally on the available knowledge, we must again develop the kind of rapport that existed a decade or two ago with the associations that served the handicapped: an equal partnership with clients, parents, and the public, and certainly with the members of our respective professions who (we complain) do not understand us.

FUTURE PROGRESS

This conference constitutes a monumental wealth of essential and relevant knowledge in this growing specialized field. Communications have been good among the delegates.

In order to capitalize on what has been realized here, very pragmatic follow up action might be to clearly ferret out that information about which you can agree upon among yourselves as being important so that organizations and the people who are the *change agents* can become effective implementers on a large scale, on your behalf. In this way, it is possible to develop beyond the current trend to have "islands of excellence" toward more universal coverage with improved services.

In order to realize future significant progress in this area, one can envision two streams of effort moving in parallel. First, an increased continuing emphasis in stimulation of basic research. I stress the word "basic" in contrast to what is often mediocre research or what, in fact, may just be good clinical services under the guise of research. The low yield-high cost of this has disenchanted many legislators and the public and has confused some as to the benefits of research. This backlash can, and is, beginning to hurt some of the basic scientists. Second, as a parallel stream, the mass application of the knowledge around which there is agreement must be advanced.

There is a fundamental and major difference between these two goals and the methods. In basic research, it is appropriate to develop, say, 100 different developmental detection tests or treatment approaches. It is desirable and valuable for a meeting of this kind to discuss them all. But to move from the "isolated islands of excellence" approach to broad programming, it is necessary for professional people to decide and to agree on the use of only a few that can be utilized efficiently on a large scale, even though they may not be perfect. The teacher, the therapist, the parent, and the community agency cannot discriminate between the 100 available tests and cannot cope with the endless bombardment of new jargon, reports of new discoveries, and overwhelming flood of new literature. Too often, each new claim implies to them an improved approach that they may feel compelled to pursue until something new comes along. This kind of phenomenon to which the practitioner is increasingly subjected in recent years becomes self-defeating for all concerned. Ultimately, in order to realize major implementation goals, it will be necessary to strip off the jargon and to reduce the research variables to build a basic approach—curriculum, manpower preparation, and in-service models—which will enable us to realize mass application of sound techniques.

We need to acknowledge that much of the knowledge and technique are not as esoteric as we make them appear. Once we can acknowledge and accept these realities within the professional and research communities, we will find a vast manpower pool to help us do the job—and much of it, paradoxically, is available without the expenditure of new tax dollars. The time may come when we need to accept the fact that the missing ingredient is not always a case of more money. We may have the necessary human and financial resources to do the service job, but only if we learn how to mobilize (or remobilize) the resources of the existing special and generic agencies and the vast human and financial resources that they control. This may even be the case for research support if we separate the quasi research from genuine research effort.

We also have to accept the fact that the public or governments will not significantly support basic research until adequate levels of service have been established at community levels. The analogy of cancer and heart research efforts are clear examples how we can trace through what in fact happened historically. Until good clinical treatment was available, research was of secondary importance. As treatment services began to reach a reasonable level of adequacy, the public and government began to increase support for basic research efforts in order to prevent the problem.

This kind of knowledge and timing is of importance to program and research planners. The primary responsibility for implementation of long-range plans does not necessarily concern you directly, but it is vital that you are cognizant of the need for people to be sophisticated and experienced in organizational systems and dynamics. There is an acute shortage of seasoned people who possess the leadership and skills to translate these kinds of challenges into action using the vast knowledge of organizational systems.

I hope that the organizers of this conference will be able to pursue the implementation phases which logically follow an analysis and consideration of the technical aspects of this vital human services area. Specifically, it calls for a similar type of event, but for those who have the responsibility for planning implementation of long-range nation-wide services.

Latin American Perspective

Eloisa Garcia Etchegoyhen de Lorenzo, M.A.

The comprehensive and integrated coverage of the important facets of research, service, training, and consumer issues provided by this conference promises to have enduring value not only for those of you in the United States but for planners and developers of programs in Latin America as well. I commend the sponsors for developing such a well conceived and designed conference that so adequately addresses one of the most important areas of child development: early intervention.

EARLY INTERVENTION PROGRAMS

Latin America shares with the United States a great interest in and concern for the development of early intervention programs for risk infants. Latin American efforts to strengthen and bring early intervention programs into sharper focus began in the early sixties. Since then, the movement has gained momentum and early intervention programs have been initiated in many Latin American countries. Training programs for professionals, particularly educators, have been established to help further this work. Throughout this period of development, we have been aided by the generous assistance of numerous experts from the United States. Our advances, then, are quite similar to those in the United States. In some ways, I believe, we lead; in other ways we follow. We have encountered many of the same problems as you in the initiation and development of intervention programs; and we have our own special problems. I am pleased, today, to be able to relate to you my impression of our efforts to develop early intervention programs in Latin America and to react to some of the major issues brought forward by the conference.

I had, in 1964 to 1965, the rich opportunity to work with the Secretary's Committee on Mental Retardation, Department of Health, Education, and Welfare, in planning and arranging for the First Interamerican Conference on Mental Retardation, San Juan, Puerto Rico, in October, 1965. Conference planning arrangements called for me to travel to Latin American countries with a team of United States professionals. The purpose of these visitations was to review mental retardation programs and developments in Latin

737

American countries and to establish contacts with professionals working there in the field of mental retardation with the objective of garnering their potential contributions and participation in the conference.

As an educator and principal of School No. 203 for MR children, a special education school in Montevideo, this review afforded me a comprehensive and detailed orientation to Latin American needs and opportunities in the fields of mental retardation and child handicapping conditions that would otherwise have been impossible. Furthermore, this experience brought me into close contact with developments and professionals in the United States. Fortunately, subsequent events made it possible for me to continue these activities.

One of the 10 major recommendations made at the First Interamerican Conference on Mental Retardation called for establishment of a section on mental retardation within the organizational structure of the Interamerican Children's Institue (IACI). This recommendation was successfully implemented, and I was named to head this section. Through this office, it has been possible for the IACI to effect greater coordination of mental retardation planning efforts; disseminate information through conferences, training institutes, and printed information; and to follow program needs and developments throughout Latin America. Early intervention programs for risk infants and their families have had high priority among programs fostered by the Institute.

Our emphasis upon early intervention programs may be questioned by those who are familiar with the general level of development of mental retardation programs in Latin America. True, many of these countries have major problems in meeting the basic educational needs of children at the primary and secondary school levels. Poverty and its associated problems of malnutrition, poor health, and poor living conditions are certainly to be found in a number of countries. Institutional and community facilities providing care and training for the mentally retarded have by no means reached the quantity and quality of those found in the United States. Still, it has seemed to us important that our risk children be reached with constructive programs designed to minimize their early deficiencies and to provide them with greater strengths for adapting to the developmental tasks imposed by their societies. Fully aware of our often limited resources and the tremendous problems faced by many of our risk infants, it has seemed only realistic to move vigorously with corrective programming designed to strengthen not only the child but his family as well. The expected result is that many of these children might move more readily within the mainstream of our social institutions and with less demand for special resources. This effort carries with it a strong emphasis upon family participation in the intervening process.

In 1965, the preschool unit of the special education school for which I was principal envisioned and implemented a cooperative research and service endeavor involving early intervention applications for high risk infants. The Department of Neonatology of the Clinical Hospital (Medical College) cooperated and participated in my project. Criteria established for defining a high risk pregnancy and labor were used as the basis for determining the designation of a high risk infant. High risk infants, so defined, were referred to our school service and the mothers were seen as early as their last month of pregnancy and no later than when their infants were 4 months of age. Upon acceptance of our service, the risk infants were evaluated by a multidisciplinary team consisting of a pediatric neurologist, psychologist, educator, social worker, and physical therapist. Team recommendations for child and family programming were implemented in the home situation by educator home visitors who worked closely with the parents to provide an optimal home program of child care, stimulation, and training. The program of home visitation, augmented by clinic visits for special services and participation in the pre-school program as appropriate to child needs, continued through and into school age or until the child was judged to be free of developmental problems. All children enrolled in the service continued into the public schools either in normal or special education classes.

Unfortunately, our plan to place the project on a research basis faltered for lack of funds to support the research aspects. And, here, I wish to highlight a special problem. It is most difficult to bring into cooperative endeavor the research and service personnel who are ultimately responsible to different administrative organizations and sources of funding. This is particularly so, I believe, when the research problem concerns development, is longitudinal in nature, and continues over an extended period. Adequate funding, particularly unified funding, is necessary to bring the researchers and service personnel from the different disciplines together in a sustained effort. This was not possible for us. Research funds are extremely limited in my country. Although we sought outside support for our project, it proved not to be feasible to gain research support at an international level. The research and evaluation aspects of our program, therefore, lack the scientific rigor that a sound research design customarily provides. We were left with rather crude measures of the program's accomplishments.

Program evaluation, however, was conducted. This consisted of a comparative study of outcomes for children who were fully programmed as contrasted with children who early dropped out of the program after having been referred. A wide variety of disorders were present in both groups of children and, because it was not possible to have matched groups representing the different disorders, the developmental data were treated globally. The comparative developmental data suggested relatively superior developmental attainments by the treated group as compared with the untreated children. The advantage to the treatment group was in the range of 20 to 30 percent, depending upon the developmental modality under measure. Only clinical impressions were available by which to compare the social and emotional adjustment of the children and their families. These clinical impressions support the view that the treated children and their families achieved better adjustment and affected a more optimal integration of the child into the family structure. We regard the results as promising and deserving of more full implementation and evaluation complemented by more adequate research into the processes involved.

Conferences and seminars initiated by the Interamerican Children's Institute beginning in 1967 have been instrumental in advancing Latin American understanding and appreciation for the problem of mental retardation. Among these, a 1969 conference in Montevideo concerned itself primarily with the issue of early intervention. The program, with specialists from the United States, Europe, and Latin America, attracted participants from throughout Latin America. The participants from Venezuela, Panama, Chile, Argentina, and Brazil departed the conference with a strong desire to initiate early intervention programs. The process of intervention program development, as it evolved in Venezuela, is worth mentioning here.

Venezuela has had, for many years, an exceptionally fine program for the care of prematurely born infants. The infants, born in a large maternity clinic operated in Caracas, are returned to their home and mother's care within the usual time interval for discharge for a normal birth. The prematures requiring incubator care are provided an incubator for use in the home. The clinic nurse goes to the home and teaches the mother the proper care of the infants, use of the incubator, and techniques of feeding and hygiene. Although this program is offered to a patient population of low socioeconomic circumstances with limited housing accommodations and physical facilities, the survival rate for these premature infants has been outstandingly good in comparison with those retained in the hospital nursery where the risks of infection are high. This program, as briefly described above, was limited to the provision of health care. It remained for them to extend the concept of early intervention to include enriched developmental care through training the parents in the management of their interactions with these infants at risk because of prematurity.

The expanded concept of intervention had high appeal for many doctors and nurses in Venezuela with responsibilities for the health care programming of the premature infants. Seminars were arranged to permit greater exposure and orientation to the concepts and techniques of intervention. As a result, their programs have been expanded. The nurses now serve as primary home visitors and, in addition to their traditional responsibilities in health care, now train the parents in child development, educational methods, and how to provide optimal stimulation for their infants.

Panama, with enthusiastic support from the government, has one of the most comprehensive early intervention services in Latin America. Services are available in both urban and rural areas. Mobile clinics, staffed by teams of specialists, reach out to provide a wide range of services. Notable among their advances is the development of a detailed curriculum adaptable not only to the so called high risk infant but also to infants living under depriving life circumstances and to children with well defined developmental disorders, such as Down's syndrome and sensorial defects. Panama's programs are looked to with pride and as an exemplary model for Latin America.

Brazil has only recently completed what they call a "Miniplan" project. Miniplan establishes minimum standards for day care centers and for programs offering early intervention. In addition to the intervention programs established in Sao Paulo and Rio de Janeiro, the plan calls for the establishment of four new intervention centers—in the northern Indies and in Southern and Eastern Brazil. We are hopeful that this movement will be successful and that expanded services of high quality will develop in Brazil.

An appreciation for the problems of disadvantaged children living in socially underdeveloped areas of their cities and rural areas has prompted the governments of Peru and Chile to give emphasis to intervention programs in these poor and underdeveloped neighborhoods. In Peru and in Chile, under President Allende, the governments proclaimed intensive day care center development as central to their thrusts to improve the developmental prospects of their children. A look at some of the social conditions that have occurred in Peru, as in other Latin American countries, shows the justification for this approach.

Migration of people from the Sierras and the Peruvian jungles to the vicinity of Lima has led to the buildup of impoverished communities known as "pueblo jovenes." The people came from backward and impoverished areas seeking a better life and a higher standard of living. They have few skills and resources with which to adapt to the social and economic demands of urban life. Upon arrival, they encounter a tremendous scarcity of housing. They are forced to build shacks from paper and whatever construction materials they can find. As the migration continues, these shack communities continue to grow and expand, creating large areas of social blight characterized by poverty, malnutrition, poor health, social maladaptation, and poor educational response by the children. Large families and faulty patterns of child care contribute further to the problem. The majority of infants are turned over for care to an older sibling, often no more than 4 years of age. Children no more than 5 and 6 years of age are often the housekeepers and caregivers for an entire day while the parents are away. It is only too obvious that these children come to school age inadequately prepared to meet the learning and social demands of the school situation.

Doctors and educators, drawing heavily upon the Brazilian experience in meeting the problems of deprivation and cultural adaptation associated with popular migration to urban centers, strongly endorsed and supported the government's efforts to establish a major program of day care centers involving the full participation of the residents of the pueblo joven. Community workers were able to gain the cooperation of the pueblo residents. The fathers and mothers, with their own hands, helped build larger and better shacks to house the day care centers. As in the construction of the day care centers, the broad plan calls for intervention during the early years of childhood, which relies on existing strengths in the family's patterns of life adaptation.

Planning for this program is guided by economic realities and by a philosophy for social change. Limited resources with which to implement these programs dictate that maximum utilization be made of available resources—in this case, the family as a human resource. It is believed that, in the process of effecting social change, reliance should be placed on strengthening individual and family resources through their personal involvement in the process for effecting constructive change. Changes effected by this approach, it is held, promise to be more enduring, self-sustaining and productive of greater independence than an approach that moves directly to supply basic family needs and, thereby, promotes a continuing dependency upon the government and the deliverers of services.

The day care centers program moves, then, to help the families help themselves with better utilization of their existing resources. Under professional guidance, the program calls for training child caregivers to care for their younger siblings in a manner that enriches their lives by providing greater opportunities for social interaction, constructive play involving relevant learning experiences, stimulating play materials, and reinforcement for positive achievements. Parent training provides guidance in wiser expenditures of the family's limited funds for food purchases, home making skills, child development, health and hygiene practices. The process, as you can see, is essentially one of education for constructive change mediated through the day care centers with the cooperation and involvement of the parents and caregivers.

Implementation of these plans calls for the development of a new and appropriate educational curriculum to meet these special problems. The IACI has been asked to assist in this task. I believe that this problem is one of the most important we face in Latin America. The start may seem primitive by United States standards, but it is fundamental to progress for large segments of some Latin American countries. The emphasis attached to the early developing years in this broad program of social change speaks strongly for the underlying faith we hold in the great potential for change inherent in our very young.

PARENT-CHILD INTERACTION

Turning from this brief account of Latin American activities in the area of early intervention, I would like, now, to speak to what I regard as one of the more important issues brought forward by this meeting: the issue of parent-child interaction. Other presentations at this conference have focused on infant-mother (caregiver) interactions including the importance of the attachment between the risk infant and its mother. Implicit, but not sharply stated in these presentations, is the value of *natural* interactions as distinct from the contrived interactions so often associated with infant programming efforts. Infant feeding as a naturally occurring interaction is regarded, from the Latin American perspective, as a key element in the processes leading to the establishment of positive infant-mother interactions and attachment behaviors.

Breast feeding is encouraged in our guidance to all mothers, and particularly for mothers of risk infants. This approach is strongly reinforced by the Latin American culture where breast feeding is deeply ingrained. In this culture it is most difficult for a woman to accept the fact that she cannot breast feed her child and her concept of motherhood rests heavily on her successful accomplishment of breast feeding. Breast feeding, therefore, is virtually attitudinally mandatory for Latin American women and, in Chile, it is supported by law. Disturbances of feeding that can alter the infant-mother relationship attendant to breast feeding, frequent in high risk infants, receive particular attention in our early programming efforts.

Our efforts to ensure the establishment of normal breast feeding begin early. To this end, we seek to identify risk pregnancies in order to ensure early referrals of problem infants. The aim of early referral is to ensure maximum support for the mother who encounters early difficulties in breast feeding her child by offering reasurance, reducing her anxieties, and by providing specific guidance. This guidance involves suggestions for managing such common problems as swallowing difficulties, weak suckling, regurgitation, and those infant reactions to feeding likely to raise the mother's anxieties and, as a result, disturb her lactation. The successful establishment of breast feeding as the basis for a normal infant-mother relationship provides the cornerstone for our continuing programs of early intervention.

I regard the Latin American emphasis on breast feeding for high risk babies as more than a simple expression of difference between Latin and North American cultures. Admittedly, reports of hard research in support of the supposed benefits of breast feeding for atypical infants and their mothers are sparsely reported in the literature. Still, I contend that this is a research problem that investigators in the United States, with their great resources and capacity for research, might well investigate with benefit. The results of the Venezuelan program of early home care for low birth-weight and premature infants, the research on the early attending behaviors of infants, the research on early infant-mother separation as occurs in protracted hospitalization of many infants born at risk, and the studies of mother-infant interaction as it sets the context for the development of communication skills all are closely related to the breast feeding experience. My Latin American experience and logic compel me to believe that our emphasis on breast feeding may be a positive factor in facilitating the development of high risk infants and an important Latin American contribution to our collective efforts on early intervention.

The similarities in Latin American approaches to early intervention with those in the United States far exceed the differences. Our early initiatives to develop programs of early intervention parallel yours in time of onset, growth, and diffusion. Other similarities are found in our joint emphasis upon early detection or risk conditions, mother-infant interaction, the parents and family as the primary mediators of intervention efforts, and an expanded role for the educator in professional team efforts. Approach differences are largely a product of economics and the availability of resources and personnel. Early Latin American emphasis upon available natural resources such as the home, the parents, and family was, no doubt, shaped by necessity as well as professional and scientific philosophy. In this case, our need to do more with less has probably helped us to move ahead of the United States in the program emphasis upon parents and families. It is reassuring to find the viewpoints expressed at this conference those which are not only supportive of this approach but indicative that this is the approach of choice.

From the perspective of developments over the past 10 years, the emergence and growth of programs of early intervention for high risk children in the Americas owes much to cooperative efforts in the sharing of knowledge and technology. These knowledge sharing efforts have involved joint conferences, training institutes, the establishment of mechanisms for information exchange, and the exchange of professional emissaries. Collectively, these activites have revealed our common interests in the broad field of early intervention for high risk infants and young children. They have identified the field as one of major importance and concern across cultures. Innovative efforts of Latin Americans to apply emerging new knowledge and skills in service to their special populations offer insights of value to North American planners who, too, must meet the needs and requirements of their heterogenous population groups. The professional and research knowledge of United States nationals, so freely and generously given, now moves readily into improved services for Latin Americans through Latin American hands. Collectively, these information sharing efforts aimed at a fuller life for children and families at risk have forged new and significant bonds for interamerican understanding and cooperation. In this commerce in basic human values, Latin America senses a full partnership with America and earnestly hopes for its continued development and expansion.

COMMITTEE REPORTS

Report of the Education Committee

Willard W. Hartup, Ed.D.

The issue of professional territories, brought forward in this conference, was solved very neatly by the organizers of the Education Committee because, in selecting me, they selected a representative of what I consider to be a nondiscipline: child development. I want to talk briefly about that issue, but first I want to mention an analogy that will highlight some of the promises and some of the problems of a conference like this. The analogy compares children to pollution. In some ways children and pollution are a great deal alike: there are a lot of each of them, for one thing; they come in various forms, for another; and they both require cleaning up. In addition, the clean-up job, with respect to both children and pollution, is clearly an interdisciplinary task. And therein, I think, lies a major problem.

Interdisciplinary efforts in child development are now several generations old. Such efforts have been very successful when there has been a highly specific research problem to which the rubric of child development can be applied. The issue of high risk infants and young children is an example of this. On other less focal issues, it takes some sort of external coercion to bring about true interdisciplinary cooperation among the various developmental sciences. Institutionalizing those coordinated efforts and maintaining them have been extraordinarily difficult tasks because investigators ordinarily like to remain close to their traditional disciplinary homes.

The great institutes of child development have been co-opted by one or another disciplines because competing disciplines are not strong enough. The five centers founded by the Laura Spelman Rockefeller Memorial some 50 years ago have had various histories. The Institute of Child Development (Minnesota), for example, has been taken over by the psychologists. Similarly, the Institute of Child Behavior and Development (Iowa), originally organized as an interdisciplinary venture, ended its operation solely as the enterprise of psychologists. Neither of these centers, however, was organized to conduct research on a particular problem; both were loose consortia of investigators, each pursuing his own research interests. This history, then, strongly suggests that coordinated interdisciplinary effort in child development is hard to maintain unless it surrounds some particular research or educational problem.

There are good reasons for this, reasons having to do with territoriality, professional status, identity, and recognition and rewards. Nevertheless, these difficulties are critical issues for anyone contemplating new interdisciplinary programs of intervention with high risk infants and young children or with children of any sort. The problems of interdisciplinary programming are not simple, and they are not going to be solved by a lot of rhetoric and exhortation.

When I mentioned earlier that child development is a nondiscipline, I really meant that. Children do not define a discipline; children define a problem. There is absolutely no way that the disciplines relating to developmental processes can all be brought together, organized into a center or institute, and made to function for generation after generation without providing the investigative staff with some substantive problem *about children* to which every person can lend some effort. At the University of Minnesota, outside of the medical school, there are some 19 different departments that have major programs of one sort or another concerned with work on developmental processes. Now, that is appalling in one respect, but in another respect it is life's reality and we have to live with it and deal with it. To me, it represents, to some extent, the pluralism and vigor of the field rather than the overlap and the chaos in it. With this as preamble, I shall now direct my remarks to the issues of concern to the Education Committee.

At the outset, the Education Committee wishes to make one general point: What passes for professionalism in early childhood education is a very different kind of professionalism in many ways from the professionalism that marks the education professions as they relate to the upper schools. This comes about, to some extent, for historical reasons since it has been programs in child development, rather than programs in education, that sheltered and gave rise to the field of early childhood education. The consequences of these historical developments are still with us and will be noticed in many different kinds of projects that utilize the services of early childhood educators. There is a substantive difference between early childhood intervention efforts, including those discussed at the conference, and the strategies of most educational enterprises that involve older children.

Dr. L. Ross (this volume) used a word I use to describe the difference between early childhood education and the other levels of education: "process." The basis for practically all of the great early childhood education efforts has been the processes of child development—these have been the basis for program planning, curricular development, and the training of professionals. Admittedly, it has been the processes underlying behavioral development, rather than somatic development, that have been most heavily emphasized. It has been knowledge about the basic processes of perceptual development, cognitive development, and learning that have provided the content for programs in early education. This contrasts sharply with the emphasis on graded subject matter transference that has been the basis for program development in the upper schools.

There has also been a worthy emphasis on individual differences as a place for beginning work and for organizing educational enterprises for young children. This emphasis passes by different words—baseline, state, status—but the *developmental status* of the individual child has been something that early childhood educators just haven't mouthed as rhetoric. The term is used as their most basic and cardinal principle: assessment and intervention begin and end with a consideration of the status and capabilities of the individual child. Certain other features or characteristics of early childhood programs make them the ones to which more and more educators (including "special" educators) have looked for new ideas. One is the concept of open education which originated in the nursery school; the idea of individual guided instruction (common among early childhood educators for over 50 years) is another.

With these remarks as background, supplemented by the hope that more extended discussions of the scope of early childhood education can occur at future meetings, the Education Committee would like to make the following recommendations.

First, the Committee contends that the capabilities of our society for educational intervention in the lives of young children at risk should be expanded at a rapid rate. Our society in no way has the capability, either in terms of models or in terms of delivery systems, to be able to supply this at the moment.

Second, as a qualification on the first recommendation, we recommend that the expansion of resources for early educational intervention with children at risk be undertaken within the context of theoretical advances and professional efforts directed at all children. There are two reasons for this. First, an enormous supply of lore and fact is currently available to those who would work with handicapped children. These data, which have emanated from more than 50 years of intensive efforts with normal children, should not be wasted. Moreover, its utilization does not require extensive compilation or dissemination effort. Second, the Committee believes most strongly that it is within the context of normal growth and development that the development of children at risk should be viewed. This is not just a question of how one defines development normatively. It is rather a question of how one uses information about growth and development to bring about effective intervention efforts.

Third, the expansion of effort in this area should be multidisciplinary, in spite of the difficulties in achieving that end. This conference has illustrated very well, we believe, the need for greater input from the developmental biological sciences to the education professions, and vice versa, and we know of no way to achieve further rapprochement except by constant pressuring from external sources—from parents, from governmental agencies, and from legislatures.

Fourth, a determined effort should be made to solve the manpower needs of the intervention field. The number of available professionals, as Dr. Ackerman stated (this volume), be they public health nurses, parent trainees, teachers of children, or trainers of developmental scientists, is pitifully small. The training efforts that were spawned by Project Head Start have in no way left us with a cadre of professionals that is sufficient to mount extensive effort in the high risk field. Additionally, models of professional preparation need to be improved. Relatively few educators really know anything about genetic mechanisms and how these relate to development. Very few early childhood educators possess requisite consulting skills for working with community agencies, and too few possess skills for working with parents. There are numerous ways in which the training of educational personnel could be improved.

Finally, the Committee wishes to emphasize the necessity for continuing to support the research underpinnings of educational intervention with high risk infants and children. First of all, the components of educational programs need further work. It is not evident that we need to develop comprehensive, complete models of intervention such as have received the lion's share of support and encouragement during the last 10 years and which were well illustrated by the program demonstrations at this conference. The Committee believes, however, that there is much to be gained from focused, segmented, small-scale component research efforts to develop and to assess the "building blocks" of the intervention program. These "blocks," unlike entire models, can be taken out and installed in other locations, can be disseminated and transferred from location to location and placed into configurations that are determined by the individual teacher or parent trainer. Second, basic developmental research must continue. We know a great deal about how to demonstrate and to make a difference in the lives of individual children, both those at risk and those not at risk. But it is important that we learn more about the processes underlying the acquisition of language, the emergence of the peer attachment system, the development of memory, and the perceptual basis of reading than we presently know. Until advances are made in those areas, our educational technology will be incomplete.

Willard W. Hartup, Ed.D., Chairperson
Madeline Appell, M.A.
Norton L. Beach, Ed.D.
Dallas E. Beyer, M.Ed.
Dorothy H. Cohen, Ed.D.
A. Esther Morgan, M.Ed.
Paul A. Rittmanic, Ph.D.
Will Beth Stephens, Ph.D.

Report of the Pediatrics Committee

Paul H. Pearson, M.D., M.P.H.

The goal of the pediatrician must be to do everything within his professional competence to ensure the optimal physical, cognitive, emotional, and social development of the child. To accomplish this, he must play a vital role in all aspects of child care; in prevention of conditions which place the child at high risk; in early identification of the high risk infant and, more importantly, the infant with a disability; in the assessment and definition of the problems; and, finally, in the development of the management plan. Please note that we said *a* role, for much of this should not occur in professional isolation.

The nature of our social systems, at the present time, provides the pediatrician with the opportunity to carry out these functions in a way not now available to most of our colleague professions who are equally concerned about the development of children. At least this is true for a sizable segment of the infant population. No other profession has a better *opportunity* for such early involvement with the infant and family, for longitudinal observation of development in these earliest months, or for developing an awareness of the interaction between infant and family and the social factors in the infant's environment. With this opportunity goes the chance and the responsibility to initiate the proper intervention at the earliest possible time.

This statement is not an attempt to establish our territorial imperative or to stake out the boundaries of the pediatric domain. We are well aware of the numbers of children for whom these functions are provided for by the family practitioner or the public health nurse, and we also recognize the ever increasing role being played by the eduator and the psychologist through the medium of the increasing numbers of day care and early education programs. Rather, this statement is necessary in order to identify more clearly which steps we now need to take to ensure that pediatricians have requisite skills and the motivation needed to achieve the stated goal. Perhaps equally important would be recommendations for changes in our social system—or nonsystems if we are referring to health care or to comprehensive child care. But these are beyond the scope of this report.

Given the time limitations and the complexity of the problems, the Committee tried to focus on how we could raise the level of competence of pediatricians in the general area of child development, shorten the lag time between first suspicion and confirmation and from confirmation to intervention, increase their ability to deal with the feelings of parents around the problem of having a child with a handicap, and in general reduce the rate of parental dissatisfaction with the physician's management through sensitive and more proper intervention. The answer, of course, lies in the education of pediatricians, as medical students, residents, and practicing specialist. Yet, as brought out in the excellent position chapter by Dr. de la Cruz (this volume), there is little current data on which we can make critical judgments or recommendation on the present pediatric training programs.

We know that the last 10 years have seen an increasing interest in developmental pediatrics in some departments—witness the 30 or more University-Affiliated Facilities and the mental retardation research centers—but there was consensus among the Committee that it was not even approaching an adequate degree. The reasons for this are many, and if there are time and interest this can be brought out in discussion after recommendations. Therefore, the Committee's major recommendation is as follows: as soon as possible, there should be a thorough evaluation of the state of the art of child development programs within departments of pediatrics and medical centers. This study should identify available models of training for students and residents, to determine those factors responsible for the evolution of successful programs as well as the barriers to the development of such programs in other departments.

We suggest this study be carried out by a team of three members—a pediatrician knowledgeable in developmental pediatrics from an academic background, a pediatrician familiar with delivery or primary care, and a social or behavioral scientist from a child development background. This team would visit all departments of pediatrics for an in-depth study of programs in developmental processes, mental retardation, delivery of care, long-term follow up, continuing education, etc. Accompanying this study would be a sampling of practicing pediatricians to determine their involvement and their perceptions of their needs for training in this area.

The second step would be a follow up planning conference to deal with the results of the study and recommend the steps needed to bring about the desired change. Without the second step conference, the results of the study might gather dust as happens all too often with such studies.

Step three would probably involve getting this information before the pediatric power structure, i.e., department chairmen and the executive committees of the major pediatric organizations, for example, the American Academy of Pediatrics and the American Board of Pediatrics.

The benefits and excitement generated by this meeting, with its interchange between educators, behavioral and biological scientists, and physicians, gave rise to the expressed wish that somehow we should do this more often and for more of our respective brethren. It also gave rise to expressions of *optimism* and *concern* regarding the glimpse we were given into some of the intervention programs now under study: optimism at the prospects they suggest of what may be coming available as effective means to optimize the emotional, cognitive, social, and even physical development of children; concern that the multiplicity of intervention curricula now being developed and used in centers around the country may not all be receiving the same rigorous evaluation as those here reported. There needs to be sounded a word of caution, that intervention per se, however well motivated, may have the potential for adverse effects as well as beneficial ones.

We make the plea that even if all too often in the past the medical, behavioral, and educational disciplines have gone their separate ways, we can no longer afford to do so. The findings coming out of the beautifully integrated program we saw at the Frank Porter Graham Center certainly documents this, and we congratulate Dr. Gallagher. The term *interaction* being emphasized at this meeting must also be kept in mind in relation to health and education as well as in the family-infant-professional triad.

Paul H. Pearson, M.D., Chairperson
T. Berry Brazelton, M.D.
Louis Z. Cooper, M.D.
Robert W. Deisher, M.D.
Felix F. de la Cruz, M.D.
Herbert J. Grossman, M.D.
Theodore Scurletis, M.D.
Lawrence T. Taft, M.D.
Miriam G. Wilson, M.D.

Report of the Nursing and Habilitation Committee

Barbara E. Bishop, R.N., M.N.

Committee review has identified major issues in early intervention for high risk infants and young children that can be addressed by answering the following four questions:
1. Why should programs to help the young infant and child at risk be family oriented?
2. What kind of educational opportunities can be offered the public and professional regarding early intervention?
3. How is research essential to intervention programs for high risk infants and their families?
4. What are the major responsibilities of professionals working in the area of early intervention?

First, programs should be family oriented because the problems of the child at risk are the problems of the family. A truly family-oriented approach confers value and concern for all members of the family with a child at risk. Experience indicates that the best results occur when the total family is positively involved in the planning and implementing of the care program. The family-oriented approach means that families and individual family members will have initial and continuing support for their emotional reactions to having and caring for the child family member at risk.

Their potential for care and management of the risk child can grow and mature with the help of professional knowledge that increases their fundamental understanding, specific skills, and confidence in their own capabilities. To this end, parents and other family members, as appropriate, should be involved in the evaluation and program planning processes for themselves and their child; and professional support should be provided primarily in those situations wherein only the professional has the ability to apply the required special skills and knowledge.

The family-oriented programs for the infant at risk need also to include identification of the coping strengths and capabilities of the parents and the family as well as the infant at risk. Special assessment should be made regarding: the father's role in family structure; the father's concerns as they relate to the high risk child; the role of siblings in the family; and the identification of the energy level of the mother.

Another aspect of the family-oriented approach is the identification of the positive support systems available for the family. Parents know that they occasionally need supplementary support to help them cope. This is even more true of families who have members who are at risk. Community health nurses are well aware of family needs for positive support systems beyond those provided by professionals. There frequently comes that time, called the "end of the rope syndrome," when mothers need to be able to say, "I've had it, may I leave my child with you for awhile?" Thus, provision for respite child care, among other supportive services, is a helpful adjunct to conserve maternal energy and to provide for her sense of well-being. Professionals often cannot fill this need, but parents and friends can. In these situations the suitable intervention may be in helping families find for themselves positive support systems within their communities. The programs at the University of Washington described by Barnard and by Hayden and Haring (this volume), capture and illustrate very well the essential elements of the family-oriented approach.

In answer to the second question, the Committee believes that the educational opportunities that need to be offered to public and professionals regarding the child at risk include: 1) public education, which includes family life course from kindergarten through 12th grade with particular emphasis on parenting; 2) public school education for children, which includes learning opportunities about the exceptional child—their strengths, their limitations, and their similarities to other children; and adult education, which should cover the same topics; 3) basic education for professionals, which would include both didactic and clinical learning experiences for all disciplines concerned with infants and children at risk and their families; 4) continuing education available to all professionals and disciplines involved in services for the child at risk with particular attention given to those professionals who did not receive content related to children at risk in their generic training programs; 5) educational activities for professionals, which promote sharing of ideas related to the care of the infants at risk and their families; 6) principles of adult learning for all disciplines including the use of these principles as expressed in interdisciplinary interactions and in interactions with parents.

The educational content recommended for professional training would include: 1) growth and development of children; 2) needs of children at risk and their families; 3) coping skills of families—how to identify and mobilize them; 4) techniques for relating to the family of the child at risk; 5) techniques for including the family in evaluation and treatment of the child at risk; 6) actual procedures and treatments for early intervention with high risk infants.

With respect to the question on research, the Committee believes that research is essential to the establishment of effective early intervention programs. Research is needed to validate existing and newly emerging intervention methods and approaches and to determine their relative effectiveness as applied to different categories of risk children and their families. Beyond these fundamental questions are those concerned with the mechanisms for the delivery of intervention services and their organization. We need answers to the practical questions of who best delivers what needed services and when and where they can be provided most effectively and at least cost. Evaluative research directed toward these questions is needed if we are to be able to demonstrate the cost benefits of these services and to justify their use in our requests for funds to support them. Important, too, are the continually emerging research problems that are determined by practicing clinicians and professionals as these are experienced in practice. Some of these yield to clinical and applied research; others require fundamental research study. It is important, then, that there be a continuous flow of information in both directions along the service-research continuum—from service to clinical research to fundamental research and return to service. There needs to be an ongoing dialogue between researchers and clinicians to ensure ready communication of clinical research problems and the translation of new research findings to service.

Finally, the Committee finds that professionals should have the following other major concerns and responsibilities: 1) professionals, where possible, should effect interdisciplinary efforts to deliver services to the young infant and child at risk and his family; 2) each professional discipline has the responsibility to consider the cost factor of any care delivery system and the potential value of that system; 3) professionals have an ethical responsibility to consider that a care program for a risk child may be detrimental to another family member; therefore, it is essential that there be careful evaluation of programs not only to promote the well-being of infants at risk but also to ensure that they are not detrimental to other family members.

The foregoing recommendations that have emerged from Committee deliberation are felt to require implementation. The Committee considered the problem of implementation and reached the following conclusions.

First, each concerned professional discipline has a major responsibility for communicating to its members the basic concepts undergirding research and the programmatic approaches to early intervention. This knowledge should be incorporated in the literature of each discipline.

Second, the rapidly developing knowledge and activities subsumed under the rubric of early intervention needs to become a part of the working skills of workers already in the field. To this end, each discipline should foster the development of continuing education programs concerned with early intervention issues and approaches at the local, state, and national levels.

Third, the emerging field of early intervention for high risk infants and their families poses new problems for legislative and administrative officials at all levels of government. For this reason, it is imperative that these officials and concerned agency heads be kept well informed of developments in the field of early intervention and that their involvement be secured in fostering its constructive potential for optimizing the development of risk children and the well-being of their families.

The processes for implementation of these recommendations need careful deliberation. Therefore, the Nursing and Habilitation Committee suggests that future conferences be held that are devoted to the problems of program implementation.

Barbara E. Bishop, R.N., M.N., Chairperson
Kathryn E. Barnard, R.N., Ph.D.

Una H. Haynes, R.N., M.P.H.
Catherine Huber, M.S.
Helen Martin, R.N.
Martha Moersch, M.Ed., O.T.R.
Carol Ann Paar, M.S.
Susan Rosen, R.N., M.S.
Mary Scahill, R.N., M.S.
Joyce Stancliffe, B.S.

Report of the Research Committee

Sidney W. Bijou, Ph.D.

To facilitate the quality research on high risk children indicated by the various chapters in this volume, the Research Committee offers the following recommendations.

There is need for a new federal structure, not a new institute, department, or division, but a mechanism designed to review and to support research on early intervention including studies in practical application. At present there is no federal agency concerned with research on delivery systems for this or for any other area. That is to say, research on delivery systems is not considered in the same category as research on basic problems and, hence, they do not ordinarily receive support by committees composed of basic science researchers. Yet delivery systems must be investigated if we are ever going to apply knowledge from basic research. We cannot assume that the publication of research findings will automatically lead to effective application. There is an urgent need, therefore, for a federal reviewing agency that would support applied research on delivery systems, particularly in child health and human development.

The second recommendation pertains to the availability of high risk and normal children for research. To assure investigators that high risk and normal children are available for study, it is necessary that the federal government prepare guidelines on research with children which would protect the health, well-being, and rights of children and their families, and at the same time, not hamper the progress of research. If such guidelines are not established, regulations might be prepared that would restrict, restrain, or terminate research on high risk children because, unfortunately, there are people who believe that research is harmful and is done for self-serving purposes.

The third recommendation refers to the need for a mechanism that would facilitate two-way communication between parents and concerned citizens on one hand and researchers on the other. Researchers have to be more in communication with parents; parents have to be more in touch with researchers. Parents—concerned parents—are the ones who ought to be advocates of basic and applied research on high risk children. Research on both basic and applied research go together. Intervention without a firm basis in empirical knowledge leads nowhere; research without long-range social objectives

can be constrictive and after awhile, trivial. This kind of working relationship between parents and researchers is needed so that parents can become cognizant of the issues involved in setting up research priorities. For example, longitudinal research that requires considerable investment of time and money must be supported even though the results are not immediately apparent. The Research Committee believes that the parent group should be the group that systematically and continuously reviews federal research policy and programming and that the parent group should not accept proposals because it comes from some federal agency. Research proposals ought to be monitored and reviewed by the consumer public—the parents and the groups concerned with parents, that is, the parents themselves should make the researchers aware of research needs.

The fourth recommendation, closely related to the one above, is the need for a mechanism that would foster communication across disciplines when the applied research is multidisciplinary. Some members of the Committee believe that the methods used to date such as conferences, workshops, and publications in professional journals have not been effective in coordinating the efforts of workers in the different disciplines.

The fifth recommendation concerns manpower. The federal government should encourage the university resources to train qualified personnel in the area of high risk research. There is the thought abroad that there are more research personnel than are needed. This may be the case in certain fields of investigation but not in early intervention with high risk infants and young children. There is need in this area for close scrutiny of personnel requirements. Without a sufficient pool of well qualified investigators, the programs discussed at this conference cannot be advanced or established.

The sixth and final recommendation concerns public education on the meaning of a high risk child. The high risk child is not only the mentally retarded child, or the cerebral palsy child; it is any child who has a developmental problem. Diagnosing and labeling offers little help in advancing our knowledge in this area. In dealing with these children the basic questions usually are: What is the deviant behavior? What are the probable conditions? What can be done about it? Parents, and the public in general, should view the task of this area of research and development as that of working with developmental disorders that hold across all children who happen not to be developing normally.

Sidney W. Bijou, Ph.D., Chairperson
Donald M. Baer, Ph.D.
Earl C. Butterfield, Ph.D.
Robert Isaacson, Ph.D.
Cecil B. Jacobson, M.D.
Lewis A. Leavitt, M.D.
Andrew E. Lorincz, M.D.
Dominick P. Purpura, M.D.
Leonard Ross, Ph.D.
Evelyn B. Thoman, Ph.D.
Charlotte Loring White, Ph.D.

can be constrictive and after awhile, trivial. This kind of working relationship between parents and researchers is needed so that parents can become cognizant of the issues involved in setting up research priorities. For example, longitudinal research that requires considerable investment of time and money must be supported even though the results are not immediately apparent. The Research Committee believes that the parent group should be the group that systematically and continuously reviews federal research policy and programming and that the parent group should not accept proposals because it comes from some federal agency. Research proposals ought to be monitored and reviewed by the consumer public—the parents and the groups concerned with parents, that is, the parents themselves should make the researchers aware of research needs.

The fourth recommendation, closely related to the one above, is the need for a mechanism that would foster communication across disciplines when the applied research is multidisciplinary. Some members of the Committee believe that the methods used to date such as conferences, workshops, and publications in professional journals have not been effective in coordinating the efforts of workers in the different disciplines.

The fifth recommendation concerns manpower. The federal government should encourage the university resources to train qualified personnel in the area of high risk research. There is the thought abroad that there are more research personnel than are needed. This may be the case in certain fields of investigation but not in early intervention with high risk infants and young children. There is need in this area for close scrutiny of personnel requirements. Without a sufficient pool of well qualified investigators, the programs discussed at this conference cannot be advanced or established.

The sixth and final recommendation concerns public education on the meaning of a high risk child. The high risk child is not only the mentally retarded child, or the cerebral palsy child; it is any child who has a developmental problem. Diagnosing and labeling offers little help in advancing our knowledge in this area. In dealing with these children the basic questions usually are: What is the deviant behavior? What are the probable conditions? What can be done about it? Parents, and the public in general, should view the task of this area of research and development as that of working with developmental disorders that hold across all children who happen not to be developing normally.

Sidney W. Bijou, Ph.D., Chairperson
Donald M. Baer, Ph.D.
Earl C. Butterfield, Ph.D.
Robert Isaacson, Ph.D.
Cecil B. Jacobson, M.D.
Lewis A. Leavitt, M.D.
Andrew E. Lorincz, M.D.
Dominick P. Purpura, M.D.
Leonard Ross, Ph.D.
Evelyn B. Thoman, Ph.D.
Charlotte Loring White, Ph.D.

Report of the Research Committee

Sidney W. Bijou, Ph.D.

To facilitate the quality research on high risk children indicated by the various chapters in this volume, the Research Committee offers the following recommendations.

There is need for a new federal structure, not a new institute, department, or division, but a mechanism designed to review and to support research on early intervention including studies in practical application. At present there is no federal agency concerned with research on delivery systems for this or for any other area. That is to say, research on delivery systems is not considered in the same category as research on basic problems and, hence, they do not ordinarily receive support by committees composed of basic science researchers. Yet delivery systems must be investigated if we are ever going to apply knowledge from basic research. We cannot assume that the publication of research findings will automatically lead to effective application. There is an urgent need, therefore, for a federal reviewing agency that would support applied research on delivery systems, particularly in child health and human development.

The second recommendation pertains to the availability of high risk and normal children for research. To assure investigators that high risk and normal children are available for study, it is necessary that the federal government prepare guidelines on research with children which would protect the health, well-being, and rights of children and their families, and at the same time, not hamper the progress of research. If such guidelines are not established, regulations might be prepared that would restrict, restrain, or terminate research on high risk children because, unfortunately, there are people who believe that research is harmful and is done for self-serving purposes.

The third recommendation refers to the need for a mechanism that would facilitate two-way communication between parents and concerned citizens on one hand and researchers on the other. Researchers have to be more in communication with parents; parents have to be more in touch with researchers. Parents—concerned parents—are the ones who ought to be advocates of basic and applied research on high risk children. Research on both basic and applied research go together. Intervention without a firm basis in empirical knowledge leads nowhere; research without long-range social objectives

759

can be constrictive and after awhile, trivial. This kind of working relationship between parents and researchers is needed so that parents can become cognizant of the issues involved in setting up research priorities. For example, longitudinal research that requires considerable investment of time and money must be supported even though the results are not immediately apparent. The Research Committee believes that the parent group should be the group that systematically and continuously reviews federal research policy and programming and that the parent group should not accept proposals because it comes from some federal agency. Research proposals ought to be monitored and reviewed by the consumer public—the parents and the groups concerned with parents, that is, the parents themselves should make the researchers aware of research needs.

The fourth recommendation, closely related to the one above, is the need for a mechanism that would foster communication across disciplines when the applied research is multidisciplinary. Some members of the Committee believe that the methods used to date such as conferences, workshops, and publications in professional journals have not been effective in coordinating the efforts of workers in the different disciplines.

The fifth recommendation concerns manpower. The federal government should encourage the university resources to train qualified personnel in the area of high risk research. There is the thought abroad that there are more research personnel than are needed. This may be the case in certain fields of investigation but not in early intervention with high risk infants and young children. There is need in this area for close scrutiny of personnel requirements. Without a sufficient pool of well qualified investigators, the programs discussed at this conference cannot be advanced or established.

The sixth and final recommendation concerns public education on the meaning of a high risk child. The high risk child is not only the mentally retarded child, or the cerebral palsy child; it is any child who has a developmental problem. Diagnosing and labeling offers little help in advancing our knowledge in this area. In dealing with these children the basic questions usually are: What is the deviant behavior? What are the probable conditions? What can be done about it? Parents, and the public in general, should view the task of this area of research and development as that of working with developmental disorders that hold across all children who happen not to be developing normally.

Sidney W. Bijou, Ph.D., Chairperson
Donald M. Baer, Ph.D.
Earl C. Butterfield, Ph.D.
Robert Isaacson, Ph.D.
Cecil B. Jacobson, M.D.
Lewis A. Leavitt, M.D.
Andrew E. Lorincz, M.D.
Dominick P. Purpura, M.D.
Leonard Ross, Ph.D.
Evelyn B. Thoman, Ph.D.
Charlotte Loring White, Ph.D.

Report of the Research Committee

Sidney W. Bijou, Ph.D.

To facilitate the quality research on high risk children indicated by the various chapters in this volume, the Research Committee offers the following recommendations.

There is need for a new federal structure, not a new institute, department, or division, but a mechanism designed to review and to support research on early intervention including studies in practical application. At present there is no federal agency concerned with research on delivery systems for this or for any other area. That is to say, research on delivery systems is not considered in the same category as research on basic problems and, hence, they do not ordinarily receive support by committees composed of basic science researchers. Yet delivery systems must be investigated if we are ever going to apply knowledge from basic research. We cannot assume that the publication of research findings will automatically lead to effective application. There is an urgent need, therefore, for a federal reviewing agency that would support applied research on delivery systems, particularly in child health and human development.

The second recommendation pertains to the availability of high risk and normal children for research. To assure investigators that high risk and normal children are available for study, it is necessary that the federal government prepare guidelines on research with children which would protect the health, well-being, and rights of children and their families, and at the same time, not hamper the progress of research. If such guidelines are not established, regulations might be prepared that would restrict, restrain, or terminate research on high risk children because, unfortunately, there are people who believe that research is harmful and is done for self-serving purposes.

The third recommendation refers to the need for a mechanism that would facilitate two-way communication between parents and concerned citizens on one hand and researchers on the other. Researchers have to be more in communication with parents; parents have to be more in touch with researchers. Parents—concerned parents—are the ones who ought to be advocates of basic and applied research on high risk children. Research on both basic and applied research go together. Intervention without a firm basis in empirical knowledge leads nowhere; research without long-range social objectives

759

Report of the Community Development Committee

Ronald Wiegerink, Ph.D.

Community services emerged as the focal issue in the deliberations of the Community Development Committee. How these services are developed and organized at the community level was viewed as critical to any effective service delivery system, for it is here that the processes of case finding, diagnosis, and intervention for the high risk population begin and end. But the community is not an independent unit that can stand alone in the development and organization of its service programs. The requirements of these comprehensive programs demand that the community relate effectively to supportive efforts offered at regional, state, and national levels. Guided by these considerations, the Committee concluded its deliberations with the development of two general and four specific recommendations.

GENERAL RECOMMENDATIONS

There exists today, a substantial body of scientific knowledge, technology, and professional expertise that can be translated into effective services and delivered to high risk infants, young children, and their families. The offerings presented at this conference offer substantial evidence in support of this view. Unfortunately, this potential capability is concentrated in small, scattered islands of excellence. It needs to be extended to reach greater numbers of high risk children and their families who now receive only mediocre or inadequate services. *Efforts should now be directed toward the development of effective service delivery systems specifically designed to maintain high quality services for much larger populations of high risk children and their families.*

The incidence of high risk infants and young children is highest among the rural and urban poor. These children, developing under depriving life circumstances, are most vulnerable to both biological and environmental insults. Too often, their parents lack the knowledge, skills, and resources to provide them with needed corrective care and training. These children stand most in need of effective case finding, diagnostic, and intervention

761

services. *The developers of community services for high risk infants and their families should give emphasis to the delivery of quality services for families living in rural and urban poor areas.*

SPECIFIC RECOMMENDATIONS

The fundamental concepts undergirding ameliorative and corrective early intervention for high risk infants are poorly understood and recognized by the general public. For many, development of the infant and young child is seen as a rigid, maturational unfolding of development toward the child's biological destiny; and the importance of early infant learning and experience, particularly for the high risk infant, is largely unrecognized. Still, the ultimate development and success of early intervention programs in our communities will depend largely upon the understanding and support of the community members. *A public information program aimed at the development of community understanding of the need for early intervention programs and services for high risk infants and young children should be initiated. It is recommended that the initiative for this action rest with the President's Committee on Mental Retardation and the National Advisory Council on Developmental Disabilities. The information program should involve the coordinated efforts of responsible federal agencies in close cooperation with state, regional, and community agencies and organizations.*

Development of community service programs for high risk young children and their families imposes new demands for the review and establishment of public policy to guide the direction, development, and organization of these community services. The need for review is prompted by the fact that programs of community services for very young risk children and their families is newly and rapidly emerging as a major development. They draw upon a complex array of existing health, education, and human development resources from both the public and private sectors. Within these, the lines of service and budgetary responsibility are not always clear and well defined. Similarly, different concepts of service approaches and responsibility for them exist between the concerned professions where claims of territorial responsibility are, to a large extent, unresolved. In the absence of well conceived and accepted plans for delivery of community services, these conditions predispose to overlap and duplication of services which, in turn, further limits the filling of gaps in needed services. Public policy, based on community consensus, supportive of the development of comprehensive community services for high risk young children and their families is needed. *Interpretive action should be made at all levels of government—national, state, and community—to gain support for the development of comprehensive community services serving the early screening, diagnosis, and intervention needs of high risk infants and young children. The initial step in this effort requires action to achieve professional and user consensus on program requirements and the most effective and efficient approaches to them.*

The wide scope of comprehensive community services utilized in serving high risk infants, young children, and their parents effect unusual demands for service coordination. Among the basic requirements involved in a comprehensive community service program are provision for the medical and health maintenance needs of both the risk child and parent (caregiver), child and parent education, and human development resources including respite care, crisis support, foster care and adoption support services, and family planning, among others. Community provision of these services must recognize and be responsive to the unique nature and needs of each individual child and family situation. And the service delivery system must be responsive to shifts in program requirements as a function of rapid developmental change. *A program of comprehensive community services should provide for central coordination of state, regional, and local services as these might be utilized in serving the risk child and family. Community service coordination should, to the greatest possible extent, provide for assignment and transfers of assignment of responsibility for individual cases.*

Because community service programs for the high risk child less than school age are in early stages of development, careful monitoring of these programs is needed to ensure their effective and orderly growth. A client oriented advocacy system that provides for objective and unbiased review of all aspects of the service delivery program can, the Committee believes, optimize program development. *Provision should be made for a system of advocacy within each community's service program. Ideally, the advocacy system would provide for individual case review in the context of community, regional, and state service response. Community advocates, linked to their counterparts at regional and state levels would have, in addition to individual case advocacy, responsibility for collective advocacy for the development of public policy for community services, and their implementation.*

Ronald Wiegerink, Ph.D., Chairperson
Charles A. Anderson, M.A.
Dr. Mable B. Anderson
Elizabeth M. Boggs, Ph.D.
Alice Kjer, M.A.
William Robertson, M.S.
Doanld J. Stedman, Ph.D.
Evadeen Watts, M.S.W.
William Wilsnack, M.S.W.

Report of the Parents' Committee: Families in Crisis, Families at Risk

H. Rutherford Turnbull, III, LL.M.

This report from the parents of young handicapped children is a report from families in crisis. We would like to emphasize our feelings and our belief, supportable by an avalanche of evidence, that we are families at risk. We have heard much from you about high risk infants, but now we want you to hear from families in crisis and families at risk. That is who we are—who are reporting. To whom are we reporting? I am told, and believe, that we are talking to the Who's Who of early intervention. But more than that, we are reporting to the professionals at large and to society in its entirety. How shall we talk and make this report? We must present it with the most grateful appreciation for this very unusual opportunity to participate in a high watermark of consumerism in the President's Committee on Mental Retardation (PCMR). We must also say that we have great hopes for our further involvement in these conferences, not only by participating in them, but also by planning them and following through on them.

WE LOOK TO SOCIETY

What goals and policies do we parents want society to adopt? We want society to recognize, as you do, that the mentally retarded person has value. One of the parents shared a story with us that poignantly illustrates *our* sense of values. He said that, recently, a fourth grader asked him, "How can you love a dumb kid?" His answer was, "Well, your mother loves you." That story is telling. How do we change attitudes? There's a tremendous cause and effect problem here. What comes first? The programs that create new attitudes, or the attitudes that enable new programs? We do not know. Somewhere the two come together; somewhere they are at one. But the public society must be moved to act; it needs to appreciate what it means to be the parent of whom is asked the question about the ability to love a retarded child. If the public ever is so moved, it—in the governmental and private sectors—must act by underwriting more research and an enormous extension of that research into applied, clinical programs. Our friends, a nation of strangers, and our government must respond; we will insist that they respond. We are dedicated to making them respond by ample funding of research. But we also will demand from you and your colleagues a convincing demonstration of the applied value of that research.

WE LOOK TO THE PARENTS

What goals and policies do we want with respect to parents? We need to train the parents—the parents who are already with us and the parents who will be with us—in the need for early intervention and in how they can have access to the early intervention system and its machinery. Once a disabled child is born, we need to teach parents about the nature and etiology of mental retardation. We do not learn it in school, at the universities, at church, or in the community. We have to learn it from you. We need to teach the parents survival skills, how to cope skills, how just to get along. We need to teach them the value of a positive attitude toward retardation. I recently told an acquaintance, "We're bringing my boy home from school, home from the institution." She said, "What a tremendous challenge." I replied, "No, not at all. What a tremendous opportunity!" We need to eliminate the concept of diad or triad, the narrow focus on parent and child, on parent, child, and professional; we need to expand that limited concept and to replace it with one of the total family. There are fathers, siblings, neighbors, church friends, and interconnecting networks that we call either the real family or the extended family. *That* is the unit that needs to be worked with. When we talk about intervention, we need to emphasize support and not so much intervention.

The family with a mentally retarded child needs support. You need to listen more closely to the family's needs; you need to listen more carefully to us to learn about our problems. A family is not divisible; the retarded child cannot be treated in isolation; the practice of doing so is not as likely to help the child as it is to hurt the whole family. You need to do more than simply intervene; you need to listen to us and then to support us. The issue is: How? We need parent-to-parent referral systems, "listening ears," that provide support and information. And the parents need longitudinal, follow-along services. It is not enough to treat the child from birth to 5 years of age and then to allow him to be lost in the gaps caused by the absence or lack of planning for comprehensive, life-time services.

WE LOOK TO THE PROFESSIONS

What do we want from the professions? Quite clearly, we want more research. We want research because it will help in the prevention of mental retardation and because it will help in the amelioration of mental retardation. That must is self-evident. In hearing the Report of the Pediatricians, the Nurses, and the Community Action Groups, we hear the same message, the same call for research. We endorse it, but we also need to be shown its relevance and application. We believe that you need to train more doctors and other affected professionals in the nature and etiology of mental retardation so that they may make accurate diagnoses and referrals for evaluation and intervention in the early stages of the child's life. How can this be done? We believe it can be accomplished through more and better clinical training and through greater exposure to the retarded child during premedical and medical education. We suggest that the PCMR or an equally prestigious group should make a recommendation to the American Academy of Pediatrics and other pediatric "power groups" (as I heard the phrase used by the Pediatricians' Group) that the medical school curriculum be revised to require further training in retardation. In addition, the medical school curriculum should include a demonstration of the need for and value of an interdisciplinary approach to mental retardation. We do not know how to do it, but we need to make the professionals far more sensitive to the nonmedical needs of the family and attentive to what parents can tell you about their children.

Parents have great powers of observation. They see the child far more frequently and in the child's more usual habitat than the professional ever will. No doubt a layman's diagnosis is simply a layman's diagnosis, but we suggest to you that it has tremendous value. It could be the red flag, the early warning, that professionals need to heed. We ask you not to speak in tongues. Do not use jargon. We do not always understand your professional language. Use language that we, the parents, understand. Bring us into *your* view of *our* children. How would we have you share with us what you know about our children? Do it clearly, frankly, honestly, and humbly.

How do we implement early intervention at the professional level? At the time the diagnosis occurs, we need to have the beginning of a parent-to-parent referral system. We need, at that moment, to begin the listening ear. We also need a referral system into programs. Diagnosis, referral to programs, and referral to survival training must occur nearly simultaneously. The most desirable early intervention system should involve parental participation in the actual training programs for the children, and it should transfer the training from the classroom, the clinic, or the hospital into the home—into the real world of the family. The methods of training the parents can be simple. They can involve, for example, training manuals, a videotape shown at community colleges or over educational TV, and outreach projects directed at consumer groups. Geographic accessibility to early intervention systems can never be equalized, but the lack of it can be minimized by such simple techniques as we have suggested.

WE LOOK TO THE GOVERNMENT

Finally, what goals and policies should our government establish for itself and for our children? By "government" we mean the federal, state, and local governments. We are impressed by some of the demonstrated projects we have learned about, and we recommend that the findings and the methods of those projects be disseminated and replicated throughout the United States with governmental financial sponsorship. We suggest that a model curriculum be developed, and then mandated, on the exceptional child for us in the public school system, beginning at kindergarten or first grade and continuing through the twelfth grade.

How can we ask adults to have positive attitudes about retarded children when they grow up without the ability to have any attitude except negative ones? We need to make known to the parents and to the public information about the available services and resources concerning mental retardation, and that seems to us to be a low-cost, high-yield government function. We need to persuade governments to make available to the public, and especially to the parents, information about the emerging legal rights of the retarded citizen, so that when we go to our school boards or to mental retardation professionals seeking their help, we will know enough to say with confidence, "This is what your representatives, our legislatures, require you to do for our children." And, of course, we need to have our children's constitutional rights established by the legislatures, by administrative rule-making and, if necessary, by the courts.

WHY ARE WE INVOLVED?

So much for our recommendations. We have asked ourselves, "Why are we here? Why have we been invited to this conference?" It is clear that we are *not* here because we are now or perhaps ever will be qualified to speak as professionals on the medical, educational, or technological aspects of mental retardation. But it is also abundantly clear that we are here because we, the parents, are seen to be partners in our—not in your—but in *our* efforts in the field of mental retardation, because we are uniquely qualified to speak about the morality and the ethics of retardation, and because we are uniquely qualified to speak about the ways of combating the inhospitable attitudes of society with respect to the retarded.

We also are invited, we believe, because we are uniquely qualified to draw the attention of some professionals—and we emphasize *some* professionals—to their unintended, but nonetheless injurious, insults to our sensibilities about our children. We are parents at risk. We are as vulnerable as our children. We must live with that fact for the lifetime of our children and frequently thereafter. We recognize, as you do, the intrinsic value of our children. We also gratefully recognize the immediate and ultimate benefits of what you do today and tomorrow in your research and clinical work. But we recognize that you are the exceptional professionals, just as our children are the exceptional children. You are professionals who are human, who are sensitive to our personal and family needs, and who have provided so much to us already. In recognizing your exceptionality and this unusual opportunity to be here, we implicitly recognize that there are many other professionals who may not be like you, who may not be researchers who can carve out new practical applications of their work, who may not be sensitive to our family and personal needs, and who may not be informed, much less competent, to work in the areas of retardation and early intervention.

Our charge to you, then, is this: keep us involved. We can help you immeasurably in seeking the goals and in designing the techniques and strategies of early intervention. We can help in the daily implementation of early intervention. We can help your colleagues. We can influence the private and public sectors of our abundant society to support you and your work.

We ask you to accept our heartfelt gratitude for your generous invitation to participate in this conference. We want to say that we are pleased to join you in what we all affirm, which is the worth of the individual, however retarded, that we want to join hands with you in working on the greatest obstacle of all: the barrier of public acceptance, the notion that because a person is less able, he is less worthy.

Mr. H. Rutherford Turnbull III, Chairperson
Mr. William Bird-Forteza
Mr. and Mrs. William Coolidge
Mrs. Henry Crais
Mr. and Mrs. Heinz L. Horstmeier
Mr. and Mrs. Clifton E. Latta
Mrs. Jay E. Linder
Mrs. Digby Palmer
Mrs. H. Rutherford Turnbull, III

Advisors
Wylda Hammond, M.D.
Mrs. David Pressly
Mrs. Louise Ravenel

CONCLUSION

The Present and the Future

George Tarjan, M.D.

It is, indeed, a great privilege to be the final speaker of this highly important, timely, and successful conference. Before proceeding further, I would like to express our appreciation to the sponsoring agencies, our local hosts, the Conference Planning Executive Commitee, and to all of the speakers. I am confident that in this respect I speak for everyone who attended. I am equally sure that, on the other hand, I speak for all of those who were involved in the organization of the meeting when I express their gratitude to all those who participated; their contributions will add to the outcome and to the likelihood of the implementation of the results. In spite of the risk involved in singling out one person for a special accolade, I want to mention the unique contributions of Dr. Tjossem, without whose leadership there probably would not have been a conference, and certainly not of such outstanding quality as this one.

When I accepted this assignment, I knew that I would have to miss the first days of the meeting. I was sorry about this necessity from the very beginning. After I had a chance to glean the final program, I became even more disappointed. Now that I have observed the enthusiastic responses of all participants, I am further disheartened. The conference collected the most outstanding people in the field of early intervention; in fact, the program booklet could serve as a Who's Who in the field. I envy all of you who were able to attend each session. I, for one, must wait to read the proceedings to catch up with you; I eagerly await doing so.

The Program Committee suggested that my brief speech be entitled "Synthesis and Projection," but I asked for the privilege of changing the title to the current one, primarily because I felt I could not synthesize concepts and reports without being fully acquainted with their content. I am pleased with my decision. It gives me an opportunity to express some of my own ideas and concerns, independent of those presented by other speakers. I will do so in a moment, but first I would like to reflect briefly on a few

Based on the closing comments made at the Conference on Early Intervention, May 8, 1974, Chapel Hill, North Carolina. The work of the author is supported in part by U.S. Department of Health, Education, and Welfare Grant Nos. HD-00345, HD-04612, HD-05540, MH-10473, MCT-927, SRS-54-P-71020/9, SRS-59-P-45192; and the Stanley W. Wright Fund, University of California at Los Angeles.

thoughts that occurred to me as I read the agenda. I am sure that the reports, particularly those about research, must have focused on the complexities of the issues at hand. The state of the art presentations must have clearly emphasized the fact that we are dealing with a problem that requires the contributions of a host of disciplines. The project reports and some of the more technical reports must have called attention to the absence of a single all-purpose solution, mandating us to continued experimentations. In spite of these diversities and complexities, I was impressed that the recommendations presented to us have considerable congruence and can give us a road map for systematic progress.

May I now mention some of my notions as I attempt to synthesize my own thinking about early intervention with high risk infants and children. In this process, I will not try to separate the present from the future; rather, I will intermingle them.

Let me start by commenting on the nature of an "ideal" preventive program. On other occasions I have said, in essence, that such a program should ensure that every child will be born with a healthy central nervous system, that he will have a set of early experiences supportive of intellectual, emotional, and social growth, and that he will be protected from damaging physical and psychological trauma. Since no child can escape all noxae, the program must also strive to maximize the child's ability to cope with unavoidable injurious agents.

Unfortunately, we are far from having reached the level of knowledge and practice that would permit us to claim even an approximation of this Utopian state. For example, in a study conducted not long ago on the Island of Kauai, a follow up of all pregnancies from the fourth week and all resulting children to the age of 10 found rather discouraging results. Out of 1,311 early pregnancies, only 660 10-year olds were found without significant handicaps. The others ended in intrauterine or infant deaths or resulted in children who, by the age of 10 had some type of significant handicap.

Could we improve on this record? The answer, clearly, is yes. Although some solutions must still await additional basic discoveries, the development of better skills in early clinical remediation and the large-scale application of our current knowledge, in themselves, already promise significant advancements. These latter two avenues were the key topics of this conference.

The issues, however, are not simple. Let me single out a few subjects worthy of further considerations. It would be desirable to have the capability to improve, at least at the functional level, the central nervous system of each damaged child. Theoretically, three different avenues are open. First, the discovery of techniques for the growth of new parts or components of the nervous system; second, the development of means of making more effective use of the damaged parts of the nervous system; and third, the improved utilization, along new or different channels, of the remaining healthy parts of the damaged system.

The first approach, at least for the time being, primarily calls for somatically targeted discoveries. Though some advances have already been made, practical solutions are still some time away. The other two avenues lend themselves to an attack through both the somatic as well as the behavioral sciences. We are doing better along these lines, and further advances can be expected in the foreseeable future. To be most effective, our battles in these realms should be fought on an integrated front with interdisciplinary strategies.

The last comment brings me to the important relationships between the somatic and the behavioral aspects of central nervous system function. Though particularly in research there has been a traditional separation between biomedical and behavioral research, with at best occasional collaboration, such separation is no longer desirable or justified. I am not referring to the tactics of individual projects that aim to study highly specific questions from the viewpoint of a single scientific discipline, but rather to major research strategies involving broad attacks on issues.

Placing my views into another context, let me emphasize that in the real world of clinical practice, the somatic and behavioral dimensions are fully interlinked. In general, one cannot observe the somatic matrix of the brain except through its behavioral expressions, and one cannot adequately assess behavioral impairments without taking into proper account the presence and nature of possible organic pathology. Furthermore, interventions, even when conceptually restricted to one domain, unquestionably influence the other; that is to say, drugs modify behavior, and learning in some fashion alters the biochemistry and the physiology of the brain.

Let me continue on this relationship. The somatic matrix of the central nervous system may well determine the maximal level of behavioral performance. But whether this hypothetical level is high or low, i.e., whether the brain is intact and well endowed or whether it is impaired and more poorly endowed, few if any individuals ever reach the zenith of total utilization of their available brain mass. Even without somatically targeted interventions, therefore, behavioral approaches have much to offer toward the improvement of functional performance. In addition, behavioral interventions, particularly during very young ages when the central nervous system is still undergoing development, could positively influence the quality of the brain's somatic organization. Studies that utilize somatic measurements and compare children who respond well to behavioral interventions with those who do not may give us further insights into the nature of the organic limitations.

Let me now turn to a different problem. It is often stated that parsimonious utilization of our resources requires that we concentrate on vulnerable groups. Identification of the members of such a group calls for early screening and assessment. But large scale application of these latter programs raises several questions of its own. Among them are the composition of the target population for screening, the nature of the target manifestations, the specific purposes of screening, its degree of precision, its cost efficiency, and its benefit to risk ratio. I spoke on some of the issues related to screening on a previous occasion; for the moment, let me concentrate only on the benefit to risk ratio and on the question of precision. If the intervention which is to follow positive identification is proven beneficial or at least harmless, and if the benefits outweigh the disadvantages of the concomitant labeling, I would select screening tests that have a minimal chance to yield false negative results even at the cost of a higher proportion of false positives. If, on the other hand, the intervention is apt to produce significant side effects, or labeling itself is apt to carry a substantial risk, I would prefer a test that ensures no false positive findings, even if some false negatives resulted. This problem is so closely linked to any broad scale early screening and intervention program that it should be given careful and continued attention.

My comments to this point might imply that I am looking at the constellation of issues from a rather mechanistic viewpoint. To avoid such implications, let me now focus on a few more individualistic, even idiosyncratic, characteristics of infants and their immediate environments. I will start with the infants or the small children who are to become the beneficiaries of our early intervention programs. First, I want to underscore a common observation of many scientists and clinicians. Though one might be inclined to assume that at an early age, when independence is impossible and when survival hinges on external support, the infants' behavioral repertoire must be limited and their individual variability of a low order, this is not the case. Evidence consistently points to the opposite direction. From the earliest age, infants represent complex personalities with great differences in muscle tone, responsiveness, emotionality, cognition, sociability, and modes of coping with external events.

The addition of infants at risk for developmental abnormalities to the average or intact group further increases variability. In other words, adding "pathological" individuals to the "physiological" group widens the span of the total distribution. My main emphasis, however, is on our limited scientific understanding of the individual differences among high risk children. This fact calls not only for additional research but also for the utilization of our best clinical judgment at the practice level at this time.

Even a clearer insight into the highly unique behavior of each infant is not sufficient. A similar understanding of his immediate environment is equally essential. Early intervention programs are composed of a series of external stimuli to which the infant is expected to respond; his responses in turn evoke modifications in his environment, resulting in new stimuli; and the cycle continues in this fashion. In many respects, this process is very similar to ordinary mother-infant interaction. The importance of this model lies in its capacity to focus our attention on a dyadic relationship in which the behavior of each member is constantly modified by the responses of the other.

Parenthetically, let me give a more concrete example which, by this time, might only be of historical relevance. Nearly 15 years ago, at a time when it was customary to ascribe a crucial etiological role to parental behavior for the deviance of autistic children, I emphasized that the primary abnormality may well lie in the infants' grossly aberrant general muscle tonus, degree of motility or innate perceptual equipment, which in turn may trigger the observed maternal behavior.

To continue on this theme, may I add that as long as infants and young children involved in early stimulation programs spend the major portion of their time with their families, certainly a desirable choice, a clear understanding of that environment is equally important. The role of mothers is well acknowledged in this respect, but infants also spend substantial time with fathers, siblings, and often with other members of an extended family. For adequate individual planning, knowledge about families should encompass information on expectations, capabilities, temperament, and response patterns among other characteristics. For example, parental expectations heavily influence satisfaction or disappointment with the infant's responses and, thereby, the total nature of parent-child interactions.

Turning to parental, particularly maternal, capabilities, may I add the following. Most if not all early intervention programs emphasize the role of the family structure in child rearing. As a consequence, one of their aims is the increased involvement of at least the mothers in the therapeutic or educational process. Some programs limit parental involvement to collateral information about child development, but others go much further. Many use mothers as auxiliary therapists or teachers. At times, the primary emphasis is on teaching the mothers about the techniques of psychological enrichment and then relying primarily on interactions that take place in the home, with the mother being the most critical therapeutic change agent. All this is good, but it emphasizes the need for more understanding of maternal capacities. Mothers are as variable as infants, and until we learn more about them we can only rely on our clinical experience in the intermittent assessment of each mother-infant dyad.

I would now like to discuss, as my last detailed topic, the issues of program evaluation. It is popular as well as essential today to incorporate evaluation into each intervention program. Without it, funding is unlikely, but with it enters a set of major problems. Adequate evaluation in the field of early intervention is not an easy requirement. Let me list a few examples of difficulties one is apt to encounter.

It would be desirable if members of a selected target population could be randomly assigned to the experimental or to the control group. In this way comparisons could be more accurate and meaningful. But such an approach raises ethical questions. Since program initiators are often convinced a priori that their techniques will be beneficial, the random withholding of intervention from the control group may well be construed as unjustified. The use of naturally occurring control groups would be an alternative technique, but this approach poses other problems that derive from the high variability of the infants and mothers. Matching must be based on large numbers of variables resulting in small, if not infinitesimal, cell sizes. Another alternative might be based on the use of "before" and "after" measurements. But this avenue also leads us to a set of hurdles. This time they involve the dependent variables. The trouble lies in the fact that the experimental population is usually composed of infants or young children who change over time, with or without intervention, simply as a consequence of growth and development. Factoring out the impact of treatment is a complex task. The acquisition of a much greater store of data than is available today on natural growth and development might be of greatest help in this respect.

In spite of these difficulties, continued evaluation is essential. I would like to make at least five specific suggestions concerning it. The first involves the continued acquisition of data from natural observations; the second focuses on our need for intensified research in the area of evaluation itself; the third calls for the continued incorporation of evaluation into every project; the fourth emphasizes the preferential use of independent evaluating groups that are not involved in the interventive program itself; and the fifth pleads for the maintenance of diversity in our intervention programs, at least for the time being. Only continued assessment can ultimately lead us toward more effective generalizable solutions.

Let me now briefly mention some additional problems I anticipate. We are living in a period of popular slogans, some of which are proclaimed to be new, as well as the absolute truths or penultimate panaceas. Case managers, program coordinators, mainstreaming, deinstitutionalization, normalization, advocacy, cost efficiency, and class action suits represent but a limited list. Though one can readily raise many pertinent questions about these concepts, it is possible that even the best of programs might become subjects of criticism simply because they do not fit someone's favorite slogan.

Similarly, it is also popular today to attack a concept or a program without much specificity and often under the protective umbrella of individual rights, ethics, or morality. The specter of psychosurgery might soon be followed by that of "psychochemistry," i.e., the use of drugs, or that of "psychomanipulation," i.e., any attempt to alter human behavior. We could reach a point at which it might become almost impossible to do anything that is effective. I consider it also tragic that at times the entire domain of science is subject to suspicion and criticism, suggesting in all scientists a genuine malice at worst and a callous disregard of human rights at best. I find such generalizations unjustified. I have worked with scientists as well as with clinicians and have myself assumed both roles. I have found both groups basically considerate, conscientious, and careful in their pursuit of improved opportunities for their fellow man.

In spite of the pessimistic overtones of my last statements, I remain optimistic. Those of us here today can become the foundation for action tomorrow. We must and we will defend the need for continued research. We must and we will implement our best current clinical concepts. We will strive for increasingly individualized prescriptive interventions and thereafter for more generalizable approaches. We do not have all the answers, but we do know enough to promise progress rather than regress to the next generation of high risk infants. We have the obligation and we have the resources. Our birth rate is declining. This permits and mandates us to concentrate our energies on a smaller number of newborns each year. We can and we must ensure for each child the best opportunities for maximal development and for a better quality of life.

Index

Academy of Pediatrics, 689
American Academy of Pediatrics, 14
American Academy of Pediatrics Com-
    mittee on Environmental Hazards, 210
American Medical Association, 14
Amniocentesis, 254–256
Animal model, of at-riskness, 88
Asynchrony, interactional, 103–104
Attachment behaviors, normal, 521–522
Attention, infant's deployment of,
    152–153
Attitudinal results, 645–646
Audiological assessment, of infants,
    207–209
Auditory environment
    early, of high risk infant, 209–210
    research of effectiveness of, 28
    see also Effective auditory environment
Auditory stimuli
    boundaries in, 149
    differences among, 148–149
    discussed, 146–148
Auditory training, by parents, 375
Autism, 273, 325
Autistic children, 104, 273
Automated Multiphasic Health Testing and
    Services, 276

Behavior
    and brain damage, 57–58
    experimental analysis of, 214–215
    glancing, 224–227
    goals, 216
    problems, management of, 366
Behavioral change, environmental factors
    in, 175
Behavioral states, of infants, defined,
    95–96

Berkeley Growth Study, 173
Biological intervention, theory of, 63–64
Blind infants, parent training with, 579
Boyd Developmental Progress Scale, 278
Brain
    development of, 75–82
    effects of nutritional deprivation on
        growth of, 69
    effects of pollutants on growth of, 69–70
    growth and maturation of, 68–69
    influence of gestational age on
        development of, 76
    microconstituents of, 66
Brain damage
    biological treatment of, 70
    consequences of, 37–42
    and genotypic change, 51–56
    Hebb study of, 49–50
    and language capabilities, 48–49
    permanent changes of, 39–42
    perseveration after, 57
    "recovery" after, 45–48
    and sprouting of nerve fibers, 40
    task-dependent effects of, 50–51
    transient effects of, 38–39
    widespread changes of, 42
Brain damaged children, teaching styles
    for, 492–493
Brazil, early intervention services in, 740
Breast feeding, encouragement of,
    742–743
Brown Studies, 176–177

Cardiac responses, indexing of, in at risk
    infants, 115
Caregiver-infant interactions
    assessment of, 128
    and stability of effects, 130–132

Caregiver responsiveness, effect of, on infant, 124
Casati-Lezine Scales of Sensory Motor Development, 293
Categorical perception, defined, 154–155
Cellular development, critical period of, 599–600
Cerebral palsy, clinical program for, 470
Change agents, in society, 733–734
Check lists
  of behavior, 271–272
  of social ability, 272
Child abuse, screening for risk of, 259–260
Child advocacy, 382
Child Development Model, 683
Child Find, 13
Children at risk, early identification of, 698–701
Chile, intervention programs in, 741
Cognitive development
  evaluation of, 293, 631–632
  and habituation of attention, 266
Cognitive functioning, and CNS integrity, 267
Cognitive processes, and affective processes, 473
Cognitive stimulation, of infants, 613–614
Collaborative Perinatal Project, 12
Community resources, use of, in Portage Project, 347–348
Community services, recommendations for, 761–763
Compliance program, 219–222
Continuous perception, defined, 154
Cortical neurons, dendritic development of, 76
Critical risk score, 12
Cross-sectional design, limitations of, 171–172
Cumulative risk score
  compilation of, 290–293
  merits of, 295
Curriculum evaluation, 642–645

Day care intervention, results of, on mother-infant interaction, 647–649
Day care programs
  for developmental retardation, 630
  evaluation of cognitive development in, 632

Deaf, defined, 373
Deaf children, in preschool program, 21–22
Demographic approach, in determining risk status, 13
Dendritic spine
  morphogenesis of, 81
  related to retardation, 82
Denver Developmental Screening Test, 278
Deprivation hypothesis, 17
Deprivation model, 17–20
Developmental delays, discriminative processes underlying, 155–157
Developmental intervention, 22–23
Developmental level, assessment of, 560
Developmental neurobiologist, issues confronting, 75
Developmental neurobiology, experiment in, 27
Developmental processes, in at-risk children, 114–116
Developmental results, 645
Developmental Screening Inventory, 278
Diagnosis, 10–16
Direct infant intervention, 18–19
Disorganized infants
  case studies of, 98–100
  defined, 94
Down's syndrome
  prevalence, 574
  reducing incidence of, 598
  varieties of, 592
Down's syndrome children
  characteristics of, 579–580
  chromosomal anomaly in, 580
  home-reared vs. institutionalized, 587–588
  home rearing of, 580
  infant learning class for, 593
  intellectual prognosis for, 597
  intelligence of, 579
  parents' contribution to, 589–590
  preschool programs for, 594–596
  programs for, 586–588
  sequential programs for, 588

Early and Periodic Screening, Diagnosis, and Treatment program, 299–302
Early auditory stimulation, programs for, 207

Early educational intervention, 16–17
Early experience, effects of, 26, 130–132
Early identification, of handicapped, 7
Early infant learning, 520–521
Early intervention
  emerging principles of, 728
  "models" of, 681–685
Early Periodic Screening, Diagnosis, and
    Treatment, 13–14
Early prediction, techniques of, 326
Easter Seal Society, 674
Education
  infant, 468–469
  preschool, 467–468
Education Amendments of 1974, 15
Education of the Handicapped Act of
    1975, 15
Educational achievement, early inter-
    vention for, 377–379
Educational intervention, 536–538
  underlying assumptions, 728–729
Educational materials, study of, 488–492
Educational model, for diagnosis and
    intervention, 9–10
Educational objectives, 637–639
Educational practice, questions about, 729
Effective auditory environment
  of aberrant infants, 148
  stimuli available in, 146–152
Elementary and Secondary Education Act,
    672–673
Emotionality, after brain damage, 57–58
Environment
  at risk, assessing, 326
  inanimate, influence of, 125
Environmental factors, associated with
    risk, 5, 12–13, 120, 326
Evaluation, in intervention, 25–26
Evaluation procedures, in Read Project,
    358–360
Expressive language development, 268–269

"Fail to thrive," 92
Family
  at risk, 502, 765
  disadvantaged, 630
  needs of, with multihandicapped child,
    498
  networks, research on, 240
  support of, 513–514, 556, 636

Family-oriented approach, 755–756
Family outreach worker unit, 313
Father-child relationships, in intervention
    research, 239–240
Fine motor training, for biologically
    handicapped, 611–612
First Year Outcome Index, 392
Frustration threshold, after brain damage,
    57–58

Genetic endowment, and brain damage,
    51–56
Gestational age, as risk factor, 256
Gross motor skills, encouraging develop-
    ment of, 390
Gross neuromotor/developmental
    evaluation, 383
Group day care, research on effects of,
    241–242
Group models
  for Down's syndrome, 388–389
  for multiply handicapped, 387–388
  for prenursery children, 389
  of services, 386

Hand-eye coordination, training for,
    551–552
Handicapped children
  integration of, 583–584
  placement of, 20–21
  world-wide interest in, 581
Handicapped Children's Early Education
    Act, 669–671
Handling
  amount of, 519
  of atypical infant, 515
  effect of, 631
  effects of, in rat neonates, 90–91
  importance of, 123–124
  reducing excessive amounts of, 522, 523
Hand manipulation, assessment of, 292
Head Start, 13–14
  centers, 500
  evaluation of, 630–631
  handicapped in, 21, 671–672
  preschool model, 21
  resource books provided by, 680
  work of, 583–584

Health services
  provided by central facilities, 306
  provided by community, 306
  provided by regional facilities, 306
Health Start, 672
Hearing, early screening of, 258–259
Hearing-impaired children
  early detection of, 372–373
  in preschool program, 21–22
Hebb, D. O., study of brain damage done
  by, 49–50
Hemispheric specialization, recent studies
  of, 113
Hemophilus influenzae type B, 654, 658,
  659
High amplitude suck procedure, 150, 152,
  155
High risk index, 634, 635
High risk infant
  early identification of, 598–599
  neurological tests for predicting, 599
High risk mothers, 13
High risk registry, recommendation of,
  202–204
Holding, response, infant reaction to
  duration of, 129–130
Home-based program, 336
Home-based training, for deaf and hearing
  impaired, 22
Home intervention, 682
Home reinforcement, of classroom
  programs, 227
Home Start, 672
Home stimulation results, 646
Home teaching, 335–337, 342–345
Home visits, value of, 385
Husband-wife relationship, in intervention
  research, 239–240

Incidental language learning, 200–201
Incidental teaching
  of alphabet, to preschoolers, 192
  applied to concept-language learning,
    190–191
  applied to labeling, 190
  child-initiated interaction in, 194–195
  cues and prompts in, 192–193
  interactions during, 191–192
  and language remediation, 195–196
  process of, 189–197
  staffing procedures for, 194

Incubator
  noise, 210, 700
  stimulation in, 710
Individual model, of services, 385
Infant
  assessment of, 538–539
  assessment procedures, inadequacy of,
    110
Infant cognition, evidence of, 262–263
Infant cry, diagnostic significance of, 268
Infant learning class, for Down's syndrome
  children, 593
Infant stimulation, 521
Infant-initiated interaction, effects of,
  126–130
Infants
  audiological assessment of, 156
  individual differences of, at birth, 127
  normal, discrimination in, 156
Infants at risk
  assessing, 326
  identifying, 15
Infant School
  follow up after, 477–478
  parent participation in, 476
  teacher-child ratio, 477
Infant tests, of intellectual ability,
  263–265
Infant unit, for high risk and organically
  involved children, 559–560
Infant withdrawal, 104
Information dissemination, 515–516
Information processing, in development,
  112
Institutionalized retarded, research with,
  566
Intellectual/cognitive functioning, in very
  young children, 261–267
Intelligence
  biological correlates of, 601
  measuring, 602
"Intensity of stimulation," and infant
  behaviors, 123
Interamerican Children's Institute, 738
Interdisciplinary efforts, in child
  development, 747–748
Interdisciplinary research, on child
  development, 181
Intervention
  as goal of screening, 320
  biological, 63–64
  developmental, 22–23

direct infant, 18–19
early educational, 16–17
early, program for, 545–546
educational, 536–538
effectiveness of, and stability, 131
evaluation in development of programs
    for, 25–26
goals of, 539–540
preschool, 17, 575–576
in process research, 111–114
psychological, 63
research in development of programs for,
    26–28
Intervention programs, limitations of
    longitudinal design in, 167–168
Intervention research
    into parent-child relationships, 238–239
    and husband-wife relationship, 239–240
    shifts in, 237–238
Intervention studies, observational data in,
    178–179
Iowa Preschool Laboratory Program, 176

Kagan and Moss Study, 175–176

Labeled children, 11
Labeling, effect of, 301
Lag
    in application for services, 512
    in professional action, 205–206
Language
    expressive, 568
    functional aspects of, 201
    receptive, 568
    see also Working language
Language acquisition
    attention in, 153
    cognition in, 145
    recent research in, 113
Language competence, early intervention
    for, 376–377
Language development
    early, 567–568
    expressive, 268–269
    indexing of, in at risk children, 115
    investigation of, 27–28
    receptive, 267–268
    role of experience in, 144
Language evaluation, 383

Language intervention, with biologically
    handicapped, 613
Language learning
    goals of, 188–189
    in early life, 199–200
Language remediation, for high risk
    children, 195–196
Language screening, 269–270
Language tests and scales, 269
Latin America, early intervention efforts
    in, 737–738
Learning, critical periods of, 71–72
Learning environments, 469–470
    effects of, 193–194
Learning theory, 213–214
Longitudinal design
    advantages of, 165
    in determining individual differences,
        166–167
    limitations of, 167–168
    underuse of, 168–170
    unique contributions of, 172
Longitudinal projects, difficulty of
    funding, 170
Longitudinal studies
    necessity for, 602–603
    types of data to be collected in, 178–179

Mainstreaming, of handicapped, 503–504,
    558
Malnutrition, effects of, 600
Maternal attachment, formation of, and
    hospital, 241, 243–244
Maternal-infant interaction, experimental
    manipulations of, 179–180
McCall, Appelbaum, and Hogarty Study,
    173–175
Medicaid, screening required by, 299
Medical model, for diagnosis and
    intervention, 9
Memory capabilities, investigation of, in at
    risk infants, 115
Mental deficiency, criteria for establishing,
    11
Mental retardation
    AAMD definition of, 11
    prediction of, in infancy, 265–266
    preventing, 632–633
    problems posed by, 573
Mental Retardation Research Centers,
    legislation providing for, 29

Mentally retarded, effects of differential stimulation on, 575

Migrant and Indian Services, 672

Molecular biology, and plasticity, 72

Morbidity risk, indicators of, 256–257

Mortality risk factors, 308

Mother, education of, and child development, 295

Mother-child interaction, 536–538
  home observation of, 227–232
  importance of, 20
  intervention research about, 238–239

Mother-child relationship, importance of, 522

Mother-infant attachment, dynamics of, 270–271

Mother-infant interaction
  as a function of infant's sex, 93
  as a function of medication and labor, 93
  as a function of parity, 93
  importance of, 326–328
  laboratory measures of, 128
  longitudinal study of, 94
  research into, 602

Mother-infant relationship, and synchrony, 91–92

Motor skills, development of, in multihandicapped, 485

Multidisciplinary team, in preschool evaluation, 474

Multihandicapped children
  physical facilities for, 478–482
  therapeutic playground for, 483–485

Multiple dysfunctions, occurring in infants, 518

Mutual gazing, influence of, on infant, 124

Mycoplasma pneumoniae, 657, 659

National Association for Retarded Citizens, 674

National Disease and Therapeutic Index, 690

National Infant Collaborative Project, 392–396

Neonatal Behavioral Assessment Scale, 260

Neonate
  at risk for hearing impairment, 203
  learning capacity of, 576–577

Nervous system injury, in premature infants, 108–109

Neurobiology, as new field, 64–65

Neurological screening, 260–261

Neurologically impaired, educational materials for, 488–492

Neuron, as basic brain structure, 66–67

Nervous system, evolutionary development of, 70–72

Neurotransmitters, as microconstituents of brain, 66

Newborn Neurological Examination, 291

Noncategorical education, 557–559

Normal developmental process, animal models of, 86–88

Normalization, 558

Nurses
  in case finding, 713–715
  continuing education for, 719
  in early identification and follow up, 706–707
  involvement of, in early intervention, 716–719
  number of, in maternal and child nursing, 705
  recommendations for improved involvement of, 721

Nurse screening unit, 316

Nutrition, as risk factor, 256, 327

Object permanence concept, testing child for, 552

Observation, value of, in behavioral science, 163–164

Obstetrics Complications Scale, 290–291

Operant conditioning, in intervention program, 23

Outreach efforts, 499–500, 510
  for Down's syndrome children, 591

Panama, early intervention services in, 740

Parental care approach, 711–712

Parent approach, to treating risk children, 24–25

Parenting, education for, 582

Parent-professional-child interaction, analysis of, 241

Parents
  desire for guidance of, 497
  in early intervention, 375
  in EPSDT program, 302

importance of, to professionals, 734
involvement of, in intervention programs,
    553–557
involvement of, in school programs, 584
objectives for, 386
and premature infants, 710–711
role of, in infant intervention programs,
    525–526
teaching role of, 200–201, 351–353
as therapeutic agents, 619
training, programs for, 352, 373–374,
    553–554, 776
use of checklists by, 271–272
Pediatric clinic, 316
Pediatric evaluation, in determining risk,
    292
Pediatric models, 697–698
Pediatric Multiphasic Program, 275
Pediatric practice
    and behavior problems, 690
    changes in pattern of, 689–697
    and management of mental and
        emotional disorders, 692
Pediatrician, opportunity for, in early
    intervention, 751–753
Pediatrics, state of, 330
Perception, continuous and categorical,
    153–155
Personal-social skills, training of, in
    biologically handicapped, 614
Personnel, training of, for rehabilitation
    centers, 527–529
Phonetic units, boundaries between,
    149–152
Physical education, for biologically
    handicapped, 611
Physical environment, for rehabilitation
    programs, 526–527
Physical screening, 254
Physical therapy, for biologically
    handicapped, 611
Physician, referrals by, 512–513
Piaget, use of longitudinal design by, 172
Piaget's system, recent interest in, 113–114
Plasticity
    as concern of neurobiology, 65
    critical periods in development of, 71–72
    defined, 70–71
Play
    role of, in development, 473
    therapeutic, systems of, 680

Postnatal Factors, evaluation of, 291
Poverty
    effects of, 629
    and infant stimulation, 121
Premature infant
    auditory stimulation of, 578
    brain development studies in, need for,
        75
    cortical dendritic development in, 76
    and risk of asphyxia, 109
    and risk of hypoglycemia, 109–110
    stimulus deprivation of, 577–578
    survival rates in, 111
Prematurity
    effects of, 121
Preschool, for Down's syndrome children,
    594–596
Preschool intervention, 17
Preschool unit, for developmentally
    delayed, 562–565
Process-oriented research, 108–109
Professional responsibilities, in care of
    handicapped, 7–10
Profound mental retardation, dendritic
    spines in, 81
Prompts, degrees of, 193
Proprioceptive-vestibular stimulation,
    importance of, 123
Psychological intervention, 63
Psychophysiology, recent study of, 113
Psychosis, in childhood, 273
Psychotropic drugs
    effects of, on neurotransmitter, 67
    necessity of discovering effects of, 70
Public health nurse, 707, 710, 715
    in continuing health service, 513
Public school services, for handicapped,
    510

Rapid Developmental Screening Checklist,
    277
Receptive language development, screening
    for, 267–268
Referrals
    from physician, 512
    from public health nurse, 512
    from social worker, 512
Rehabilitation, traditional approach to,
    518–519
Reinforcement, token-mediated, 216–219

REM sleep, 88, 96
Research
  on delivery systems, 759
  vs. evaluation, 642
  government guidelines needed for, 759
  importance of, to services, 565–569
  in intervention, 26–28
  need for, 735
  on preschool education of handicapped,
    685–686
Respiratory illness
  burden of, in disadvantaged family,
    653–660
  effects of, 630
Right to education, 16
Ripple centers, 510
  detailed description of, 530–533
Risk
  animal model of, 85–86
  biological, 5
  cumulative score of, 290–293
  defined, 535
  demographic approach to determining,
    13
  environmental, 5, 12–13, 120, 326
  established, 5
  mortality factors of, 308
  and prenatal and perinatal factors, 120

Schizophrenia, in childhood, 273
Scientific method, development of,
    161–163
Screening
  goal of, 320
  for hearing, 372–373
  impact of, 301–302
  in Portage Project, 337–338
  programs, neonatal and preschool,
    202–204
Screening systems
  automated, 276
  comprehensive, 274–279
  ethnic implications of, 275
Self-help skills, changes in, 363–366
Sensorimotor patterning, in treating brain
    damage, 23
Sensorimotor schemas, evaluation of, 392
Sensory-Cognitive Model, 683
Service design, 513–514
Services, separation of, burdens of, 527

Sharing Our Caring, 590, 591
Sleep
  in infants, 96–98
  polygraph, 292
Social class, and infant development, 122
Social scientists, status of, in scientific
    disciplines, 164
Social stimulation, infant's reaction to,
    101, 103, 122–123
Socialist countries, early childhood
    education in, 601
Socioecological perspective, in intervention
    research, 237
Socioeconomic status, effects of, on infant,
    121–122
Socioemotional factors, of infant
    development, 270–273
Software, for instructional systems,
    680–681
Special educator, in infant assessment, 384
Speech
  compared to other contingent stimuli,
    147–148
  compared to other noncontingent
    stimuli, 147
  contingent, effects of, 146–147
  noncontingent, effects of, 146
  perception of, by infants, 155
Speech impaired, in Head Start, 21
Speech stream, boundaries within, 149
Spina bifida, clinical program for, 470
Sprouting, 39–40
Stability, of early experience, 130–132
Stable environment, effect of, 242–244
Staff functions, transdisciplinary approach
    to, 517–518
State legislation, for preschool handi-
    capped services, 678–680
Sucking response, in study of speech
    perception, 115
Sudden Infant Death Syndrome, 98, 99
Synchrony
  development of, 93
  in mother-infant relationship, 91–92

Teacher
  importance of, in early identification,
    590
  qualifications of, 472
Teacher training, for preschool programs,
    675–678

Team evaluations, 382
Technical Assistance Developmental
    Systems, 395
Title VI-B appropriations, for preschool
    programming for handicapped,
    673–674
Toddler unit, for developmentally delayed,
    560–562
Token system, in classroom, 216–219
Toys, influence of, on social development,
    649, 651–653
"Transdisciplinary approach," 515
Transdisciplinary model, 523
Treatment setting, for biologically
    handicapped, 617–618

United Cerebral Palsy, 674
University-Affiliated Facilities, 29, 582,
    720

Venezuela, early intervention efforts in,
    740
Verbal-Cognitive Model, 684
Verbal-Didactic Model, 684
Vision, early screening of, 257–258
Visual attention
    assessed at term, 291
    assessed at 4 months, 292
Visual-perceptual-motor evaluation, 383
Visual tracking, test of, 551
Vocalization, rate of, and effect on infant,
    124

Working language
    building of, 188
    importance of, 187
    use of, by child, 189